Apache Server
Commentary

Greg Holden

Nicholas Wells

Matthew Keller

CORIOLIS

President, CEO

Keith Weiskamp

Publisher

Steve Sayre

Acquisitions Editor

Stephanie Wall

Marketing Specialist

Diane Enger

Project Editor

Toni Zuccarini

Technical Reviewer

Thomas Resing

Production Coordinator

Jon Gabriel

Cover Design

Jody Winkler

Layout Design

April Nielsen

CD-ROM Developer

Robert Clarfield

Apache Server Commentary

Limits Of Liability And Disclaimer Of Warranty

Trademarks

The Coriolis Group, LLC
14455 N. Hayden Road, Suite 220
Scottsdale, Arizona 85260

480/483-0192
FAX 480/483-0193
http://www.coriolis.com

Library of Congress Cataloging-in-Publication Data
Holden, Greg
    Apache server commentary/by Greg Holden, Matthew Keller, and Nick Wells
        p.   cm.
    Includes index.
    ISBN 1-57610-468-0
    1. Client/server computing.   2. Apache (Computer file: Apache Group).   I. Keller,
Matthew.   II. Wells, Nicholas.   III. Title.
QA76.9.C55H65   1999
005.7'13769–dc21

99-38874
CIP

Printed in the United States of America
10 9 8 7 6 5 4 3 2 1

CORIOLIS

CORIOLIS

14455 North Hayden Road, Suite 220 • Scottsdale, Arizona 85260

Dear Reader:

The CoriolisOpen™ Press was founded to create a very elite group of books: the ones you keep closest to your machine. Sure, everyone would like to have the Library of Congress at arm's reach, but in the real world, you have to choose the books you rely on every day *very* carefully.

To win a place for our books on that coveted shelf beside your PC, we guarantee several important qualities in every book we publish. These qualities are:

- *Technical accuracy*—It's no good if it doesn't work. Every CoriolisOpen™ Press book is reviewed by technical experts in the topic field, and is sent through several editing and proofreading passes in order to create the piece of work you now hold in your hands.

- *Innovative editorial design*—We've put years of research and refinement into the ways we present information in our books. Our books' editorial approach is uniquely designed to reflect the way people learn new technologies and search for solutions to technology problems.

- *Practical focus*—We put only pertinent information into our books and avoid any fluff. Every fact included between these two covers must serve the mission of the book as a whole.

- *Accessibility*—The information in a book is worthless unless you can find it quickly when you need it. We heavily cross-reference our chapters and the code, to make it easy for you to move right to the information you need.

Here at The Coriolis Group we have been publishing and packaging books, technical journals, and training materials since 1989. We're programmers and authors ourselves, and we take an ongoing active role in defining what we publish and how we publish it. We have put a lot of thought into our books; please write to us at **ctp@coriolis.com** and let us know what you think. We hope that you're happy with the book in your hands, and that in the future, when you reach for Open Source information, you'll turn to one of our books first.

Keith Weiskamp
President and CEO

Jeff Duntemann
VP and Editorial Director

Look For These Other Books From The Coriolis Group:

Perl Black Book

Perl Core Language Little Black Book

Linux Core Kernel Commentary

Linux System Administration White Papers

Linux Programming White Papers

GIMP: The Official Handbook

Once again to my inspiring and delightful daughters, Zosia and Lucy, who lead me into new and more challenging areas of life every day, who teach me how to teach others, and who make everything possible.
—Greg

❧

To Annie, my five pound bundle of joy, who arrived early and made this book late.
—Nicholas

❧

To my family and true friends, who believe in me and support me, no matter how distant I get.
—Matthew

❧

About The Authors

Greg Holden

Greg Holden is the author of ten books about Windows, the Internet, and the World Wide Web. He is president of Stylus Media, a group of editorial, design, and computer professionals who produce both print and electronic publications.

Greg received his M.A. in English from the University of Illinois at Chicago, and then became a reporter for his hometown newspaper. Subsequently, he became assistant director of the publications office at the University of Chicago. It was there that he started to use computers for desktop publishing and, later, to join the community on the World Wide Web.

Greg lives with his two daughters in an old house in Chicago that he will someday finish rehabbing. He is also an active member of Jewel Heart, a Tibetan Buddhist meditation and study group based in Ann Arbor, MI.

Nicholas Wells

Nicholas Wells has written or contributed to numerous books on subjects ranging from Linux and Unix to NetWare and the Web. His work includes authoring the *Linux Web Server Toolkit*, *Teach Yourself KDE*, and *Teach Yourself StarOffice*, as well as several forthcoming Linux-related books and courses. He has also contributed to numerous books including the *Unix System Administrator's Bible* and *Mastering Linux*.

Formerly a programmer and then a technical writer at Novell, Nicholas was a key member of the team documenting NetWare 4 and subsequently created a complete video training series on NetWare security. He is currently featured in a five-tape Linux training video.

Nicholas recently left a Director position at top Linux vendor Caldera Systems, Inc. to write and consult full time. With an MBA and 18 years of experience in the software industry, Nicholas presents regularly at training conferences and user group meetings around the world, often on Linux and the growing Open Source software movement.

Matthew Keller

Matthew Keller is a lead programmer/analyst for the Distributed Computing and Telemedia department at the State University of New York College at Potsdam, as well as a full-time senior at the same college studying computer science and information technology.

In his spare time, Matthew does independent technology consulting through his firm, Digital Logic; teaches computer and technology adult education courses; participates in numerous Open Source projects; writes freeware software such as the Apache Wrapper and SPINdex; and researches Linux and Unix technologies.

Matthew lives in Norwood, NY, while working and pursuing his bachelor's degree.

Acknowledgments

Greg Holden

The driving force behind this book is Stephanie Wall of The Coriolis Group, who provided guidance and encouragement right from the time she suggested the book to me late in 1998. Coriolis publisher Keith Weiskamp deserves credit for making a substantial commitment to the concept of open source software. As if that weren't enough, Coriolis is always a pleasure to work with. It was good to work with project editor Toni Zuccarini once again, and to get the help of technical reviewer Thomas Resing, copyeditor April Eddy, production coordinator Jon Gabriel, and designers April Nielsen and Jody Winkler.

A big tip of the hat goes to my coauthor Nicholas Wells, who gave birth to this book even as his wife gave birth to their first child. My *Apache Server Little Black Book* coauthor Matthew Keller contributed mightily by working on some of the book's most difficult sections.

As always, I need to acknowledge the efforts of David and Sherry Rogelberg and Neil Salkind at Studio B Productions, who have encouraged and supported me as I enlarged my areas of computer expertise and who have found me new challenges to tackle. Thanks again to Ann Lindner, my extraordinary and indispensable assistant, who organizes, edits, proofreads, and helps in other ways too numerous to mention.

Nicholas Wells

A big thank you to Greg Holden for involving me in this project. Having worked with Apache on previous books, I was looking forward to learning a lot of new things by digging into the source code, and I certainly did. Thanks also to my agent Neil Salkind for providing me with an ongoing overabundance of exciting opportunities like this one, and to Toni Zuccarini at Coriolis for her patience and guidance through this project. Finally, thanks to my wife Anne, without whose support nothing worthwhile is accomplished.

Matthew Keller

First and foremost, I'd like to thank Greg Holden for pushing me to get involved in this project and supporting me through the painful process. I have infinitely more respect for "author types" because of it! I'd also like to thank Nick Wells for his part in making this book happen. Many thanks go to the Apache Software Foundation (formerly the Apache Group) for supporting the Apache Server project among others. Big, big thanks go to Dave Brouwer and Justin Sipher for their help, guidance and support through my various professional incarnations at Distributed Computing, and providing a work atmosphere that encourages research and the expansion of knowledge. I'd also like to thank Romeyn Prescott for our many conversations, his friendship, and his assistance in keeping me down here on Earth. I'd also like to thank everyone else at Distributed Computing for their help and support over the years.

Special thanks go to my parents, Mark and Kim, for letting me grow and be who I am, and letting me learn about life the hard way—The Right Way; my loving girlfriend Laurie, who kept her distance (200 miles) while I was working on this project, knowing that I get cranky when deprived of sleep; Professor Michael Nuwer, whose friendship and guidance has continued to help me "Do The Right Thing," and who has made the madness that is my life a little clearer on occasion; Terry Tiernan, whose wisdom and guidance saw me through my most turbulent years; Eric Thern, who has turned himself into one helluva guru in a very short time, and is an asset to me professionally and personally; Heidi D. for listening to my rantings; and Jake M., Jesse C., Amanda H., Judy G., Keith C., and John O. for your various friendships.

Table Of Contents

Introduction

Apache Server Commentary is intended to provide programmers, Web developers, and students with more structured, systematic, and comprehensive comments on the Apache code than have ever been provided before. The authors have examined 38 modules as well as the core code, and provided extensive comments on the most important functions, system calls, and other elements. Each section is explained with descriptive text as well as a flow chart that illustrates its operation.

The inspiration for this and other books in the Commentary series was the vastly popular *Lions' Commentary on UNIX* by John Lions. This book, which has been used and copied by countless computer science students, gives an inside look at the workings of an early version of the Unix operating system.

Apache Server Commentary is also intended to be an "inside" look at the structure and functioning of an extremely popular and powerful program (or, in the case of Apache, a set of interrelated programs). The primary goals of this book are:

- To provide a printed version of the complete source for a recent version of the server. (Version 1.3.6, which is examined in this book, was the most recent release as this was written.)

- To provide a general overview of how each module or core section functions.

- To identify the primary functions in each section.

- To suggest ways in which developers can customize their own versions of Apache by adjusting the code.

The last item in this list—customization—is one of the best reasons to study the Apache code. By understanding how a module works, you can write your own code to make your Web server function the way you want.

The ability to let developers work on the code and gain added functionality is what open source is all about. It's one of the primary reasons why Apache is far and away the most popular server in use on the Web today. Apache is proving to be more popular than servers being sold commercially by Internet powerhouses Microsoft and Netscape. Apache will enable you to serve your own Web site, either on an internal intranet or the wider Internet, with advanced features like scripting, redirection, authentication, and much more.

What You'll Learn In This Book

This book concentrates on explaining how individual lines of code function within Apache modules or the Apache core code. You'll learn how modules are structured

and get suggestions for customizing them to use Apache to organize a Web site, control access to content, and more.

Part I of this book reproduces the Apache source code in a format that is easy to read and cross-reference. The Apache core is presented first, followed by the modules in alphabetical order.

Each of these sections has been numbered consecutively. When a section of commentary later in the book refers to a module, you'll see a little arrow next to that module. The arrow points to the place in the commentary where that module is examined.

After the source code comes Part II, the commentary section that discussed the previous code. The commentary has been divided into individual chapters. Each chapter discusses sections that perform related functions, such as logging or redirection. Line references in the commentary refer to the lines in the source code section of the book.

Following the main body of the book, you'll find an appendix that points you to resources on the Internet where you can find out more about Apache and seek out support. You'll also find an appendix containing the complete GNU General Public License (GPL), which is the distribution license used by Apache. Finally, the book concludes with an index that you can use to search for specific terms or topics, which will make using this book as a reference tool even quicker and more effective.

Observations On The Apache Code

Apache Web server is the supreme Web site developers' tool. Rather than being a self-contained program that uses proprietary code, Apache is open source software that is freely distributed on the Internet. Users evaluate current releases, track down bugs, and suggest improvements in a collaborative fashion via the Apache Web site (**www.apache.org**). Programmers continually add functionality to the server by creating modules that work with the Apache core code via the Apache API. The program grows more powerful and stable as patches are made to it. (The name Apache comes from its nature as "a patchy Web server.")

In order to write modules and patch the Apache code, developers need to understand the structure and primary elements of the Apache core and modules. Traditionally, this has been done by simply reading the code and evaluating the comments that the programmers have included with it. But usually, the authors only comment on sections of particular interest to them, and the level of detail varies depending on the author.

Working with Apache source code can seem like a daunting task, especially for Webmasters who don't consider themselves to be developers *per se*. Once you begin exploring the code, however, you quickly realize that the simplicity of the HTTP protocol and the server/client interaction makes it easy to understand what's going on with just a little research.

Modules pose a different challenge, but reading through several modules, one soon becomes familiar with their structure. The Apache API is used extensively in the modules, making basic operations easy enough. The only challenge at the beginning is understanding the phases of processing to see when Apache uses each of the component functions of a module. After that, virtually every module (with the exception of **mod_perl**, which is not part of the standard Apache release) is fairly straightforward to understand and modify if needed.

Starting with **mod_example** will help you understand how a module is put together, but the lack of comments throughout other modules can be challenging at times. The authors of the code however, are professional about it. They note instances where a feature is weak or untested, or where the implementation is inelegant (this is called a *kludge* in programmer-speak). You can see many of these by searching the source code files for "XXX". The source code is pleasantly free of diatribe and irrelevant commentary.

Unfortunately, because modules are so straightforward and similar (in many respects), once you're familiar with them, the authors of most of the module source code have included very few comments—in many cases, none at all. Hence, the need for this book.

Who This Book Is For

This book assumes that most readers have already set up their own Web sites with Apache and that they want to understand how the server works and how to customize it. Another potential audience is computer programming students, who may not necessarily be running their own Web sites, but who want to understand a practical application of collaborative C programming. Some readers may be programmers who want to contribute their own modules to the Apache Project.

In any case, you are probably attracted to Apache because it's free and it's a proven performer that can handle even the biggest Web sites. This books assumes that you are an experienced C programmer and that you probably already have an Internet connection and have surfed the Web extensively, so you can test Apache and its modules.

How To Use This Book

Feel free to navigate *Apache Server Commentary* in the way that best suits your needs. Because this book is designed to be a reference resource, it isn't necessarily intended to be read from start to finish. Because source code modules point to commentary about them, and lines of commentary point back to the source code, you can approach Apache from either direction. Skip around for the modules that will help with current problems you are encountering and functions you need to perform with Apache.

We welcome your feedback on this book and are available by email for questions or comments. You can reach Greg Holden at **gholden@interaccess.com**, Nicholas Wells at **nwells@xmission.com**, and Matthew Keller at **mgkeller@bigfoot.com**.

Part I

Apache Server Code

Apache Core Code

p 473 **http_core.c**

```
1    #define CORE_PRIVATE
2    #include "httpd.h"
3    #include "http_config.h"
4    #include "http_core.h"
5    #include "http_protocol.h"
6    /* For index_of_response().  Grump. */
7    #include "http_request.h"
8    #include "http_conf_globals.h"
9    #include "http_vhost.h"
10   #include "http_main.h"
11   /* For the default_handler below... */
12   #include "http_log.h"
13   #include "rfc1413.h"
14   #include "util_md5.h"
15   #include "scoreboard.h"
16   #include "fnmatch.h"
17
18   #ifdef USE_MMAP_FILES
19   #include <sys/mman.h>
20
21   /* mmap support for static files based on ideas
22    * from John Heidemann's patch against 1.0.5.  See
23    * <http://www.isi.edu/~johnh/SOFTWARE/APACHE/
24    * index.html>.
25    */
26
27   /* Files have to be at least this big before they're
28    * mmap()d.  This is to deal with systems where the
29    * expense of doing an mmap() and an munmap() outweighs
30    * the benefit for small files.  It shouldn't be set
31    * lower than 1.
32    */
33   #ifndef MMAP_THRESHOLD
34   #ifdef SUNOS4
35   #define MMAP_THRESHOLD          (8*1024)
36   #else
37   #define MMAP_THRESHOLD          1
38   #endif
39   #endif
40   #endif
41
42   /* Server core module... This module provides support
43    * for really basic server operations, including options
44    * and commands which control the operation of other
45    * modules.  Consider this the bureaucracy module.
46    *
47    * The core module also defines handlers, etc., do
48    * handle just enough to allow a server with the core
49    * module ONLY to actually serve documents (though it
50    * slaps DefaultType on all of 'em); this was useful
51    * in testing,but may not be worth preserving.
52    *
53    * This file could almost be mod_core.c, except for
54    * the stuff which affects the http_conf_globals.
55    */
56
57   static void *create_core_dir_config(pool *a, char *dir)
58   {
59       core_dir_config *conf;
60
61       conf = (core_dir_config *)ap_pcalloc(a,
62           sizeof(core_dir_config));
63       if (!dir || dir[strlen(dir) - 1] == '/') {
64           conf->d = dir;
65       }
66       else if (strncmp(dir, "proxy:", 6) == 0) {
67           conf->d = ap_pstrdup(a, dir);
68       }
69       else {
70           conf->d = ap_pstrcat(a, dir, "/", NULL);
71       }
72       conf->d_is_fnmatch = conf->d ?
73           (ap_is_fnmatch(conf->d) != 0) : 0;
74       conf->d_components = conf->d ?
75           ap_count_dirs(conf->d) : 0;
76
77       conf->opts = dir ? OPT_UNSET : OPT_UNSET|OPT_ALL;
78       conf->opts_add = conf->opts_remove = OPT_NONE;
79       conf->override = dir ? OR_UNSET : OR_UNSET|OR_ALL;
80
81       conf->content_md5 = 2;
82
83       conf->use_canonical_name = 1 | 2;
84       /* 2 = unset, default on */
85
86       conf->hostname_lookups = HOSTNAME_LOOKUP_UNSET;
87       conf->do_rfc1413 = DEFAULT_RFC1413 | 2;
88       /* set bit 1 to indicate default */
89       conf->satisfy = SATISFY_NOSPEC;
90
91   #ifdef RLIMIT_CPU
92       conf->limit_cpu = NULL;
```

```
93    #endif
94    #if defined(RLIMIT_DATA) || defined(RLIMIT_VMEM)
95        || defined(RLIMIT_AS)
96        conf->limit_mem = NULL;
97    #endif
98    #ifdef RLIMIT_NPROC
99        conf->limit_nproc = NULL;
100   #endif
101
102       conf->limit_req_body = 0;
103       conf->sec = ap_make_array(a, 2, sizeof(void *));
104   #ifdef WIN32
105       conf->script_interpreter_source =
106           INTERPRETER_SOURCE_UNSET;
107   #endif
108       return (void *)conf;
109   }
110
111   static void *merge_core_dir_configs(pool *a,
112       void *basev, void *newv)
113   {
114       core_dir_config *base = (core_dir_config *)basev;
115       core_dir_config *new = (core_dir_config *)newv;
116       core_dir_config *conf;
117       int i;
118
119       conf = (core_dir_config *)ap_palloc(a,
120           sizeof(core_dir_config));
121       memcpy((char *)conf, (const char *)base,
122           sizeof(core_dir_config));
123       if (base->response_code_strings) {
124        conf->response_code_strings =
125          ap_palloc(a, sizeof(*conf->response_code_strings)
126               * RESPONSE_CODES);
127        memcpy(conf->response_code_strings,
128            base->response_code_strings,
129             sizeof(*conf->response_code_strings)
130                * RESPONSE_CODES);
131       }
132
133       conf->d = new->d;
134       conf->d_is_fnmatch = new->d_is_fnmatch;
135       conf->d_components = new->d_components;
136       conf->r = new->r;
137
138       if (new->opts & OPT_UNSET) {
139        /* there was no explicit setting of new->opts,
140         * so we merge preserve the invariant
141         * (opts_add & opts_remove) == 0
142         */
143        conf->opts_add = (conf->opts_add & ~new->opts_remove)
144            | new->opts_add;
145        conf->opts_remove = (conf->opts_remove &
146            ~new->opts_add)
147                       | new->opts_remove;
148        conf->opts = (conf->opts & ~conf->opts_remove)
149            | conf->opts_add;
150        if ((base->opts & OPT_INCNOEXEC) &&
151             (new->opts & OPT_INCLUDES)) {
152            conf->opts = (conf->opts & ~OPT_INCNOEXEC)
153                 | OPT_INCLUDES;
154        }
155       }
156       else {
157        /* otherwise we just copy, because an explicit
158         * opts setting overrides all earlier +/- modifiers
159         */
160        conf->opts = new->opts;
161        conf->opts_add = new->opts_add;
162        conf->opts_remove = new->opts_remove;
163       }
164
165       if (!(new->override & OR_UNSET)) {
166           conf->override = new->override;
167       }
168       if (new->ap_default_type) {
169           conf->ap_default_type = new->ap_default_type;
170       }
171
172       if (new->ap_auth_type) {
173           conf->ap_auth_type = new->ap_auth_type;
174       }
175       if (new->ap_auth_name) {
176           conf->ap_auth_name = new->ap_auth_name;
177       }
178       if (new->ap_requires) {
179           conf->ap_requires = new->ap_requires;
180       }
181
182       if (new->response_code_strings) {
183        if (conf->response_code_strings == NULL) {
184            conf->response_code_strings = ap_palloc(a,
185            sizeof(*conf->response_code_strings) *
186                RESPONSE_CODES);
187            memcpy(conf->response_code_strings,
188                new->response_code_strings,
```

```
189                 sizeof(*conf->response_code_strings)
190                    * RESPONSE_CODES);
191            }
192         else {
193             for (i = 0; i < RESPONSE_CODES; ++i) {
194                 if (new->response_code_strings[i] != NULL) {
195                     conf->response_code_strings[i]
196                         = new->response_code_strings[i];
197                 }
198             }
199         }
200     }
201     if (new->hostname_lookups != HOSTNAME_LOOKUP_UNSET) {
202         conf->hostname_lookups = new->hostname_lookups;
203     }
204     if ((new->do_rfc1413 & 2) == 0) {
205         conf->do_rfc1413 = new->do_rfc1413;
206     }
207     if ((new->content_md5 & 2) == 0) {
208         conf->content_md5 = new->content_md5;
209     }
210     if ((new->use_canonical_name & 2) == 0) {
211         conf->use_canonical_name = new->use_canonical_name;
212     }
213
214 #ifdef RLIMIT_CPU
215     if (new->limit_cpu) {
216         conf->limit_cpu = new->limit_cpu;
217     }
218 #endif
219 #if defined(RLIMIT_DATA) || defined(RLIMIT_VMEM)
220        || defined(RLIMIT_AS)
221     if (new->limit_mem) {
222         conf->limit_mem = new->limit_mem;
223     }
224 #endif
225 #ifdef RLIMIT_NPROC
226     if (new->limit_nproc) {
227         conf->limit_nproc = new->limit_nproc;
228     }
229 #endif
230
231     if (new->limit_req_body) {
232         conf->limit_req_body = new->limit_req_body;
233     }
234     conf->sec = ap_append_arrays(a, base->sec, new->sec);
235
236     if (new->satisfy != SATISFY_NOSPEC) {
237         conf->satisfy = new->satisfy;
238     }
239
240 #ifdef WIN32
241     if (new->script_interpreter_source !=
242             INTERPRETER_SOURCE_UNSET) {
243         conf->script_interpreter_source =
244             new->script_interpreter_source;
245     }
246 #endif
247
248     return (void*)conf;
249 }
250
251 static void *create_core_server_config(pool *a,
252     server_rec *s)
253 {
254     core_server_config *conf;
255     int is_virtual = s->is_virtual;
256
257     conf = (core_server_config *)ap_pcalloc(a,
258         sizeof(core_server_config));
259 #ifdef GPROF
260     conf->gprof_dir = NULL;
261 #endif
262     conf->access_name = is_virtual ? NULL :
263             DEFAULT_ACCESS_FNAME;
264     conf->ap_document_root = is_virtual ? NULL :
265             DOCUMENT_LOCATION;
266     conf->sec = ap_make_array(a, 40, sizeof(void *));
267     conf->sec_url = ap_make_array(a, 40, sizeof(void *));
268
269     return (void *)conf;
270 }
271
272 static void *merge_core_server_configs(pool *p,
273     void *basev, void *virtv)
274 {
275     core_server_config *base =
276         (core_server_config *)basev;
277     core_server_config *virt =
278         (core_server_config *)virtv;
279     core_server_config *conf;
280
281     conf = (core_server_config *)ap_pcalloc(p,
282         sizeof(core_server_config));
283     *conf = *virt;
284     if (!conf->access_name) {
```

```
285            conf->access_name = base->access_name;
286        }
287        if (!conf->ap_document_root) {
288            conf->ap_document_root = base->ap_document_root;
289        }
290        conf->sec = ap_append_arrays(p, base->sec,
291            virt->sec);
292        conf->sec_url = ap_append_arrays(p, base->sec_url,
293            virt->sec_url);
294
295        return conf;
296    }
297
298    /* Add per-directory configuration entry (for
299     * <directory> section); these are part
300     * of the core server config.
301     */
302
303    CORE_EXPORT(void) ap_add_per_dir_conf(server_rec *s,
304        void *dir_config)
305    {
306        core_server_config *sconf =
307            ap_get_module_config(s->module_config,
308                                    &core_module);
309        void **new_space =
310            (void **)ap_push_array(sconf->sec);
311
312        *new_space = dir_config;
313    }
314
315    CORE_EXPORT(void) ap_add_per_url_conf(server_rec *s,
316        void *url_config)
317    {
318        core_server_config *sconf =
319            ap_get_module_config(s->module_config,
320                                    &core_module);
321        void **new_space =
322            (void **)ap_push_array(sconf->sec_url);
323
324        *new_space = url_config;
325    }
326
327    static void add_file_conf(core_dir_config *conf,
328        void *url_config)
329    {
330        void **new_space =
331            (void **)ap_push_array(conf->sec);
332
333        *new_space = url_config;
334    }
335
336    /* core_reorder_directories reorders the directory
337     * sections such that the 1-component sections come
338     * first, then the 2-component, and so on, finally
339     * followed by the "special" sections.  A section
340     * is "special" if it's a regex, or if it doesn't start
341     * with / -- consider proxy: matching.  All movements
342     * are in-order to preserve the ordering of the
343     * sections from the config files.
344     * See directory_walk().
345     */
346
347    #ifdef HAVE_DRIVE_LETTERS
348    #define IS_SPECIAL(entry_core)      \
349        ((entry_core)->r != NULL \
350         || ((entry_core)->d[0] != '/' &&
351            (entry_core)->d[1] != ':'))
352    #else
353    #define IS_SPECIAL(entry_core)      \
354        ((entry_core)->r != NULL ||
355            (entry_core)->d[0] != '/')
356    #endif
357
358    /* We need to do a stable sort, qsort isn't stable.
359     * So to make it stable we'll be maintaining the
360     * original index into the list, and using it
361     * as the minor key during sorting.  The major
362     * key is the number of components (where a "special"
363     * section has infinite components).
364     */
365    struct reorder_sort_rec {
366        void *elt;
367        int orig_index;
368    };
369
370    static int reorder_sorter(const void *va,
371        const void *vb)
372    {
373        const struct reorder_sort_rec *a = va;
374        const struct reorder_sort_rec *b = vb;
375        core_dir_config *core_a;
376        core_dir_config *core_b;
377
378        core_a = (core_dir_config *)ap_get_module_config
379            (a->elt, &core_module);
380        core_b = (core_dir_config *)ap_get_module_config
```

```
381              (b->elt, &core_module);
382          if (IS_SPECIAL(core_a)) {
383            if (!IS_SPECIAL(core_b)) {
384                return 1;
385            }
386          }
387          else if (IS_SPECIAL(core_b)) {
388            return -1;
389          }
390          else {
391            /* we know they're both not special */
392            if (core_a->d_components < core_b->d_components) {
393                return -1;
394            }
395            else if (core_a->d_components >
396                  core_b->d_components) {
397                return 1;
398            }
399          }
400          /* Either they're both special, or they're both
401           * special and have the same number of components.
402           * In any event, we now have to compare
403           * the minor key. */
404          return a->orig_index - b->orig_index;
405      }
406
407      void ap_core_reorder_directories(pool *p, server_rec *s)
408      {
409          core_server_config *sconf;
410          array_header *sec;
411          struct reorder_sort_rec *sortbin;
412          int nelts;
413          void **elts;
414          int i;
415
416          /* XXX: we are about to waste some ram ...
417           * we will build a new array and we need
418           * some scratch space to do it.  The old array
419           * and the scratch space are never freed.
420           */
421          sconf = ap_get_module_config(s->module_config,
422                  &core_module);
423          sec = sconf->sec;
424          nelts = sec->nelts;
425          elts = (void **)sec->elts;
426
427          /* build our sorting space */
428          sortbin = ap_palloc(p, sec->nelts *
```

```
429              sizeof(*sortbin));
430          for (i = 0; i < nelts; ++i) {
431            sortbin[i].orig_index = i;
432            sortbin[i].elt = elts[i];
433
434          }
435
436          qsort(sortbin, nelts, sizeof(*sortbin),
437              reorder_sorter);
438
439          /* and now build a new array */
440          /* XXX: uh I don't see why we can't reuse
441           * the old array, what
442           * was I thinking? -djg */
443          sec = ap_make_array(p, nelts, sizeof(void *));
444          for (i = 0; i < nelts; ++i) {
445            *(void **)ap_push_array(sec) = sortbin[i].elt;
446          }
447
448          sconf->sec = sec;
449      }
450
451      /******************************************************
452       *
453       * There are some elements of the core config structures
454       * in which other modules have a legitimate interest
455       * (this is ugly, but necessary to preserve NCSA back
456       * -compatibility).  So, we have a bunch of accessors
457       * here...
458       */
459
460      API_EXPORT(int) ap_allow_options(request_rec *r)
461      {
462          core_dir_config *conf =
463            (core_dir_config *)ap_get_module_config
464                (r->per_dir_config, &core_module);
465
466          return conf->opts;
467      }
468
469      API_EXPORT(int) ap_allow_overrides(request_rec *r)
470      {
471          core_dir_config *conf;
472          conf = (core_dir_config *)ap_get_module_config
473                (r->per_dir_config,
474                              &core_module);
475
476          return conf->override;
```

```
477        }
478
479    API_EXPORT(const char *) ap_auth_type(request_rec *r)
480    {
481        core_dir_config *conf;
482
483        conf = (core_dir_config *)ap_get_module_config
484            (r->per_dir_config,
485                                    &core_module);
486        return conf->ap_auth_type;
487    }
488
489    API_EXPORT(const char *) ap_auth_name(request_rec *r)
490    {
491        core_dir_config *conf;
492
493        conf = (core_dir_config *)ap_get_module_config
494            (r->per_dir_config,
495                                    &core_module);
496        return conf->ap_auth_name;
497    }
498
499    API_EXPORT(const char *) ap_default_type(request_rec *r)
500    {
501        core_dir_config *conf;
502
503        conf = (core_dir_config *)ap_get_module_config
504            (r->per_dir_config,
505                                    &core_module);
506        return conf->ap_default_type
507                    ? conf->ap_default_type
508                    : DEFAULT_CONTENT_TYPE;
509    }
510
511    API_EXPORT(const char *) ap_document_root(request_rec *r)
512    /* Don't use this! */
513    {
514        core_server_config *conf;
515
516        conf = (core_server_config *)ap_get_module_config
517            (r->server->module_config,
518                                    &core_module);
519        return conf->ap_document_root;
520    }
521
522    API_EXPORT(const array_header *)
523        ap_requires(request_rec *r)
524    {
525        core_dir_config *conf;
526
527        conf = (core_dir_config *)ap_get_module_config
528            (r->per_dir_config,
529                                    &core_module);
530        return conf->ap_requires;
531    }
532
533    API_EXPORT(int) ap_satisfies(request_rec *r)
534    {
535        core_dir_config *conf;
536
537        conf = (core_dir_config *)ap_get_module_config
538            (r->per_dir_config,
539                                    &core_module);
540
541        return conf->satisfy;
542    }
543
544    /* Should probably just get rid of this... the only
545     * code that cares is part of the core anyway
546     * (and in fact, it isn't publicised to other
547     * modules).
548     */
549
550    char *ap_response_code_string(request_rec *r,
551        int error_index)
552    {
553        core_dir_config *conf;
554
555        conf = (core_dir_config *)ap_get_module_config
556            (r->per_dir_config,
557                                    &core_module);
558
559        if (conf->response_code_strings == NULL) {
560         return NULL;
561        }
562        return conf->response_code_strings[error_index];
563    }
564
565
566    /* Code from Harald Hanche-Olsen <hanche@imf.unit.no> */
567    static ap_inline void do_double_reverse (conn_rec *conn)
568    {
569        struct hostent *hptr;
570
571        if (conn->double_reverse) {
572         /* already done */
```

```
573        return;
574      }
575      if (conn->remote_host == NULL ||
576          conn->remote_host[0] == '\0') {
577      /* single reverse failed, so don't bother */
578      conn->double_reverse = -1;
579      return;
580      }
581      hptr = gethostbyname(conn->remote_host);
582      if (hptr) {
583      char **haddr;
584
585      for (haddr = hptr->h_addr_list; *haddr; haddr++) {
586          if (((struct in_addr *)(*haddr))->s_addr
587          == conn->remote_addr.sin_addr.s_addr) {
588          conn->double_reverse = 1;
589          return;
590          }
591      }
592      }
593      conn->double_reverse = -1;
594    }
595
596    API_EXPORT(const char *) ap_get_remote_host(conn_rec
597        *conn, void *dir_config,
598                              int type)
599    {
600      struct in_addr *iaddr;
601      struct hostent *hptr;
602      int hostname_lookups;
603      int old_stat = SERVER_DEAD;
604      /* we shouldn't ever be in this state */
605
606      /* If we haven't checked the host name, and
607       we want to */
608      if (dir_config) {
609      hostname_lookups =
610          ((core_dir_config *)ap_get_module_config
611              (dir_config, &core_module))
612          ->hostname_lookups;
613      if (hostname_lookups == HOSTNAME_LOOKUP_UNSET) {
614          hostname_lookups = HOSTNAME_LOOKUP_OFF;
615      }
616      }
617      else {
618      /* the default */
619      hostname_lookups = HOSTNAME_LOOKUP_OFF;
620      }
```

```
621
622      if (type != REMOTE_NOLOOKUP
623          && conn->remote_host == NULL
624          && (type == REMOTE_DOUBLE_REV
625              || hostname_lookups != HOSTNAME_LOOKUP_OFF)) {
626      old_stat = ap_update_child_status(conn->child_num,
627          SERVER_BUSY_DNS,
628                          (request_rec*)NULL);
629      iaddr = &(conn->remote_addr.sin_addr);
630      hptr = gethostbyaddr((char *)iaddr,
631          sizeof(struct in_addr), AF_INET);
632      if (hptr != NULL) {
633          conn->remote_host = ap_pstrdup(conn->pool,
634              (void *)hptr->h_name);
635          ap_str_tolower(conn->remote_host);
636
637          if (hostname_lookups ==
638              HOSTNAME_LOOKUP_DOUBLE) {
639          do_double_reverse(conn);
640          if (conn->double_reverse != 1) {
641              conn->remote_host = NULL;
642          }
643          }
644      }
645      /* if failed, set it to the NULL string
646       * to indicate error */
647      if (conn->remote_host == NULL) {
648          conn->remote_host = "";
649      }
650      }
651      if (type == REMOTE_DOUBLE_REV) {
652      do_double_reverse(conn);
653      if (conn->double_reverse == -1) {
654          return NULL;
655      }
656      }
657      if (old_stat != SERVER_DEAD) {
658      (void)ap_update_child_status(conn->child_num,
659          old_stat,
660                          (request_rec*)NULL);
661      }
662
663    /*
664     * Return the desired information; either the remote
665     * DNS name, if found, or either NULL (if the
666     * hostname was requested) or the IP address
667     * (if any identifier was requested).
668     */
```

```
669        if (conn->remote_host != NULL && conn->
670            remote_host[0] != '\0') {
671         return conn->remote_host;
672        }                         ,
673        else {
674         if (type == REMOTE_HOST || type ==
675            REMOTE_DOUBLE_REV) {
676            return NULL;
677         }
678         else {
679            return conn->remote_ip;
680         }
681        }
682    }
683
684    API_EXPORT(const char *)
685        ap_get_remote_logname(request_rec *r)
686    {
687        core_dir_config *dir_conf;
688
689        if (r->connection->remote_logname != NULL) {
690         return r->connection->remote_logname;
691        }
692
693    /* If we haven't checked the identity, and we want to */
694        dir_conf = (core_dir_config *)ap_get_module_config
695            (r->per_dir_config,
696                                &core_module);
697
698        if (dir_conf->do_rfc1413 & 1) {
699         return ap_rfc1413(r->connection, r->server);
700        }
701        else {
702         return NULL;
703        }
704    }
705
706    /* There are two options regarding what the "name" of
707     * a server is.  The"canonical" name as defined
708     * by ServerName and Port, or the "client's name" as
709     * supplied by a possible Host: header or full URI. *
710     * We never trust the port passed in the client's
711     * headers, we always use the port of the actual socket.
712     */
713    API_EXPORT(const char *)
714        ap_get_server_name(const request_rec *r)
715    {
716        core_dir_config *d;
717
718        d = (core_dir_config *)ap_get_module_config
719            (r->per_dir_config,
720                                &core_module);
721        if (d->use_canonical_name & 1) {
722         return r->server->server_hostname;
723        }
724        return r->hostname ? r->hostname :
725            r->server->server_hostname;
726    }
727
728    API_EXPORT(unsigned)
729        ap_get_server_port(const request_rec *r)
730    {
731        unsigned port;
732        core_dir_config *d =
733            (core_dir_config *)ap_get_module_config
734            (r->per_dir_config, &core_module);
735
736        port = r->server->port ? r->server->port :
737            ap_default_port(r);
738
739        if (d->use_canonical_name & 1) {
740         return port;
741        }
742        return r->hostname ? ntohs(r->connection->
743            local_addr.sin_port)
744                : port;
745    }
746
747    API_EXPORT(char *) ap_construct_url(pool *p,
748        const char *uri,
749                        const request_rec *r)
750    {
751        unsigned port;
752        const char *host;
753        core_dir_config *d =
754            (core_dir_config *)ap_get_module_config
755            (r->per_dir_config, &core_module);
756
757        if (d->use_canonical_name & 1) {
758         port = r->server->port ? r->server->port :
759            ap_default_port(r);
760         host = r->server->server_hostname;
761        }
762        else {
763            if (r->hostname) {
764                port = ntohs(r->connection->
```

```
765                local_addr.sin_port);
766          }
767        else if (r->server->port) {
768            port = r->server->port;
769        }
770        else {
771            port = ap_default_port(r);
772        }
773
774        host = r->hostname ? r->hostname : r->server->
775            server_hostname;
776      }
777      if (ap_is_default_port(port, r)) {
778        return ap_pstrcat(p, ap_http_method(r), "://",
779            host, uri, NULL);
780      }
781      return ap_psprintf(p, "%s://%s:%u%s",
782            ap_http_method(r), host, port, uri);
783    }
784
785    API_EXPORT(unsigned long)
786        ap_get_limit_req_body(const request_rec *r)
787    {
788        core_dir_config *d =
789          (core_dir_config *)ap_get_module_config
790            (r->per_dir_config, &core_module);
791
792        return d->limit_req_body;
793    }
794
795    #ifdef WIN32
796    static char* get_interpreter_from_win32_registry(pool
797        *p, const char* ext)
798    {
799        char extension_path[] = "SOFTWARE\\Classes\\";
800        char executable_path[] = "\\SHELL\\OPEN\\COMMAND";
801
802        HKEY hkeyOpen;
803        DWORD type;
804        int size;
805        int result;
806        char *keyName;
807        char *buffer;
808        char *s;
809
810        if (!ext)
811            return NULL;
812        /*
```

```
813     * Future optimization:
814     * When the registry is successfully searched,
815     * store the interpreter string in a table to
816     * make subsequent look-ups faster
817     */
818
819    /* Open the key associated with the script
820     * extension */
821    keyName = ap_pstrcat(p, extension_path, ext, NULL);
822
823    result = RegOpenKeyEx(HKEY_LOCAL_MACHINE, keyName,
824        0, KEY_QUERY_VALUE,
825                    &hkeyOpen);
826
827    if (result != ERROR_SUCCESS)
828        return NULL;
829
830    /* Read to NULL buffer to find value size */
831    size = 0;
832    result = RegQueryValueEx(hkeyOpen, "", NULL,
833        &type, NULL, &size);
834
835    if (result == ERROR_SUCCESS) {
836        buffer = ap_palloc(p, size);
837        result = RegQueryValueEx(hkeyOpen, "", NULL,
838            &type, buffer, &size);
839    }
840
841    RegCloseKey(hkeyOpen);
842
843    if (result != ERROR_SUCCESS)
844        return NULL;
845
846    /* Open the key associated with the interpreter
847     * path */
848    keyName = ap_pstrcat(p, extension_path, buffer,
849        executable_path, NULL);
850
851    result = RegOpenKeyEx(HKEY_LOCAL_MACHINE, keyName,
852        0, KEY_QUERY_VALUE,
853                    &hkeyOpen);
854
855    if (result != ERROR_SUCCESS)
856        return NULL;
857
858    /* Read to NULL buffer to find value size */
859    size = 0;
860    result = RegQueryValueEx(hkeyOpen, "", 0,
```

```
861              &type, NULL, &size);                        909        core_dir_config *d;
862                                                          910        file_type_e fileType = FileTypeUNKNOWN;
863         if (result == ERROR_SUCCESS) {                   911        int i;
864             buffer = ap_palloc(p, size);                 912
865             result = RegQueryValueEx(hkeyOpen, "", 0,    913        d = (core_dir_config *)ap_get_module_config
866                     &type, buffer, &size);               914            (r->per_dir_config,
867         }                                                915                              &core_module);
868                                                          916
869         RegCloseKey(hkeyOpen);                           917        if (d->script_interpreter_source ==
870                                                          918            INTERPRETER_SOURCE_REGISTRY) {
871         if (result != ERROR_SUCCESS)                     919            /*
872             return NULL;                                 920             * Check the registry
873                                                          921             */
874         /*                                               922            *interpreter = get_interpreter_from_win32_registry
875          * The canonical way shell command entries are   923                    (r->pool, ext);
876          * entered in the Win32 registry is as follows:  924            if (*interpreter)
877          *    shell [options] "%1"                       925                return FileTypeSCRIPT;
878          * where                                         926            else {
879          *    shell - full path name to interpreter or   927                ap_log_error(APLOG_MARK,
880          *    shell to run.                              928                    APLOG_NOERRNO|APLOG_INFO, r->server,
881          *      E.g., c:\usr\local\ntreskit\perl\bin\perl.exe   929              "ScriptInterpreterSource config directive
882          *    options - optional switches               930                    set to \"registry\".\n\t"
883          *              E.g., \C                         931                "Registry was searched but interpreter not
884          *    "%1" - Place holder for file to run the    932                    found. Trying the shebang line.");
885          *    shell against.                             933            }
886          *            Typically quoted.                  934        }
887          *                                               935
888          * If we find a %1 or a quoted %1, lop it off.   936        /*
889          */                                              937         * Look for a #! line in the script
890         if (buffer && *buffer) {                         938         */
891             if ((s = strstr(buffer, "\"%1")))            939        hFile = CreateFile(r->filename, GENERIC_READ,
892                 *s = '\0';                                940            FILE_SHARE_READ, NULL,
893             else if ((s = strstr(buffer, "%1")))         941                          OPEN_EXISTING,
894                 *s = '\0';                                942                  FILE_ATTRIBUTE_NORMAL, NULL);
895         }                                                943
896                                                          944        if (hFile == INVALID_HANDLE_VALUE) {
897         return buffer;                                   945            return FileTypeUNKNOWN;
898     }                                                    946        }
899                                                          947
900     API_EXPORT (file_type_e)                             948        bResult = ReadFile(hFile, (void*) &buffer,
901         ap_get_win32_interpreter(const  request_rec *r,  949            sizeof(buffer) - 1,
902                                       char* ext,          950                      &nBytesRead, NULL);
903                               char** interpreter )        951        if (!bResult || (nBytesRead == 0)) {
904     {                                                    952            ap_log_rerror(APLOG_MARK, APLOG_ERR, r,
905         HANDLE hFile;                                    953                      "ReadFile(%s) failed",
906         DWORD nBytesRead;                                954                          r->filename);
907         BOOLEAN bResult;                                 955            CloseHandle(hFile);
908         char buffer[1024];                               956            return (FileTypeUNKNOWN);
```

```
957              }
958          CloseHandle(hFile);
959
960          buffer[nBytesRead] = '\0';
961
962          if ((buffer[0] == '#') && (buffer[1] == '!')) {
963              fileType = FileTypeSCRIPT;
964              for (i = 2; i < sizeof(buffer); i++) {
965                  if ((buffer[i] == '\r')
966                      || (buffer[i] == '\n')) {
967                      break;
968                  }
969              }
970              buffer[i] = '\0';
971              for (i = 2; buffer[i] == ' '; ++i)
972                  ;
973              *interpreter = ap_pstrdup(r->pool, buffer + i );
974          }
975          else {
976              /* Check to see if it's a executable */
977              IMAGE_DOS_HEADER *hdr =
978                  (IMAGE_DOS_HEADER*)buffer;
979              if (hdr->e_magic == IMAGE_DOS_SIGNATURE &&
980                  hdr->e_cblp < 512) {
981                  fileType = FileTypeEXE;
982              }
983          }
984
985          return fileType;
986      }
987      #endif
988
989      /*********************************************************
990       *
991       * Commands... this module handles almost all of the
992       * NCSA httpd.conf commands, but most of the
993       * old srm.conf is in the the modules.
994       */
995
996      static const char end_directory_section[] =
997          "</Directory>";
998      static const char end_directorymatch_section[] =
999          "</DirectoryMatch>";
1000     static const char end_location_section[] =
1001         "</Location>";
1002     static const char end_locationmatch_section[] =
1003         "</LocationMatch>";
1004     static const char end_files_section[] = "</Files>";
1005     static const char end_filesmatch_section[] =
1006         "</FilesMatch>";
1007     static const char end_virtualhost_section[] =
1008         "</VirtualHost>";
1009     static const char end_ifmodule_section[] = "</IfModule>";
1010     static const char end_ifdefine_section[] = "</IfDefine>";
1011
1012
1013     API_EXPORT(const char *) ap_check_cmd_context(cmd_parms
1014         *cmd,
1015                                 unsigned forbidden)
1016     {
1017         const char *gt = (cmd->cmd->name[0] == '<'
1018             && cmd->cmd->name[strlen(cmd->cmd->name)-1] != '>')
1019                     ? ">" : "";
1020
1021         if ((forbidden & NOT_IN_VIRTUALHOST) &&
1022             cmd->server->is_virtual) {
1023             return ap_pstrcat(cmd->pool, cmd->cmd->name, gt,
1024                 " cannot occur within <VirtualHost>
1025                     section", NULL);
1026         }
1027
1028         if ((forbidden & NOT_IN_LIMIT) && cmd->limited !=
1029             -1) {
1030             return ap_pstrcat(cmd->pool, cmd->cmd->name, gt,
1031                 " cannot occur within <Limit> section",
1032                     NULL);
1033         }
1034
1035         if ((forbidden & NOT_IN_DIR_LOC_FILE) ==
1036             NOT_IN_DIR_LOC_FILE
1037         && cmd->path != NULL) {
1038             return ap_pstrcat(cmd->pool, cmd->cmd->name, gt,
1039                 " cannot occur within
1040                     <Directory/Location/Files> "
1041                 "section", NULL);
1042         }
1043
1044         if ((((forbidden & NOT_IN_DIRECTORY)
1045             && (cmd->end_token == end_directory_section
1046             || cmd->end_token ==
1047                 end_directorymatch_section))
1048         || ((forbidden & NOT_IN_LOCATION)
1049             && (cmd->end_token == end_location_section
1050             || cmd->end_token ==
1051                 end_locationmatch_section))
1052         || ((forbidden & NOT_IN_FILES)
```

```
1053            && (cmd->end_token == end_files_section
1054              || cmd->end_token ==
1055                  end_filesmatch_section))) {
1056        return ap_pstrcat(cmd->pool, cmd->cmd->name, gt,
1057                " cannot occur within <",
1058                cmd->end_token+2,
1059                " section", NULL);
1060        }

1062        return NULL;
1063    }

1065    static const char *set_access_name(cmd_parms *cmd,
1066          void *dummy, char *arg)
1067    {
1068        void *sconf = cmd->server->module_config;
1069        core_server_config *conf =
1070            ap_get_module_config(sconf, &core_module);

1072        const char *err = ap_check_cmd_context(cmd,
1073                NOT_IN_DIR_LOC_FILE|NOT_IN_LIMIT);
1074        if (err != NULL) {
1075            return err;
1076        }

1078        conf->access_name = ap_pstrdup(cmd->pool, arg);
1079        return NULL;
1080    }

1082    #ifdef GPROF
1083    static const char *set_gprof_dir(cmd_parms *cmd,
1084          void *dummy, char *arg)
1085    {
1086        void *sconf = cmd->server->module_config;
1087        core_server_config *conf =
1088            ap_get_module_config(sconf, &core_module);

1090        const char *err = ap_check_cmd_context(cmd,
1091                NOT_IN_DIR_LOC_FILE|NOT_IN_LIMIT);
1092        if (err != NULL) {
1093            return err;
1094        }

1096        conf->gprof_dir = ap_pstrdup(cmd->pool, arg);
1097        return NULL;
1098    }
1099    #endif /*GPROF*/
1100
```

```
1101    static const char *set_document_root(cmd_parms *cmd,
1102          void *dummy, char *arg)
1103    {
1104        void *sconf = cmd->server->module_config;
1105        core_server_config *conf =
1106            ap_get_module_config(sconf, &core_module);

1108        const char *err = ap_check_cmd_context(cmd,
1109                NOT_IN_DIR_LOC_FILE|NOT_IN_LIMIT);
1110        if (err != NULL) {
1111            return err;
1112        }

1114        arg = ap_os_canonical_filename(cmd->pool, arg);
1115        if (!ap_is_directory(arg)) {
1116          if (cmd->server->is_virtual) {
1117            fprintf(stderr, "Warning: DocumentRoot
1118                [%s] does not exist\n",
1119                arg);
1120          }
1121          else {
1122            return "DocumentRoot must be a directory";
1123          }
1124        }

1126        conf->ap_document_root = arg;
1127        return NULL;
1128    }

1130    API_EXPORT(void) ap_custom_response(request_rec *r,
1131        int status, char *string)
1132    {
1133        core_dir_config *conf =
1134        ap_get_module_config(r->per_dir_config,
1135            &core_module);
1136        int idx;

1138        if(conf->response_code_strings == NULL) {
1139            conf->response_code_strings =
1140            ap_pcalloc(r->pool,
1141                sizeof(*conf->response_code_strings) *
1142                RESPONSE_CODES);
1143        }

1145        idx = ap_index_of_response(status);

1147        conf->response_code_strings[idx] =
1148            ((ap_is_url(string) || (*string == '/'))
```

```
1149                     && (*string != '"')) ?
1150             ap_pstrdup(r->pool, string) : ap_pstrcat(r->pool,
1151                     "\"", string, NULL);
1152    }
1153
1154    static const char *set_error_document(cmd_parms *cmd,
1155        core_dir_config *conf,
1156                            char *line)
1157    {
1158        int error_number, index_number, idx500;
1159        char *w;
1160
1161        const char *err = ap_check_cmd_context(cmd,
1162            NOT_IN_LIMIT);
1163        if (err != NULL) {
1164            return err;
1165        }
1166
1167        /* 1st parameter should be a 3 digit number,
1168         * which we recognize; convert it into
1169         * an array index
1170         */
1171
1172        w = ap_getword_conf_nc(cmd->pool, &line);
1173        error_number = atoi(w);
1174
1175        idx500 = ap_index_of_response
1176            (HTTP_INTERNAL_SERVER_ERROR);
1177
1178
1179        if (error_number == HTTP_INTERNAL_SERVER_ERROR) {
1180            index_number = idx500;
1181        }
1182        else if ((index_number = ap_index_of_response
1183            (error_number)) == idx500) {
1184            return ap_pstrcat(cmd->pool,
1185                "Unsupported HTTP response code ",
1186                w, NULL);
1187        }
1188
1189        /* The entry should be ignored if it is a
1190         * full URL for a 401 error */
1191
1192        if (error_number == 401 &&
1193            line[0] != '/' && line[0] != '"') {
1194            /* Ignore it... */
1195            ap_log_error(APLOG_MARK,
1196                APLOG_NOERRNO|APLOG_NOTICE, cmd->server,
1197                "cannot use a full URL in a 401
1198                ErrorDocument "
1199                "directive -- ignoring!");
1200        }
1201        else { /* Store it... */
1202            if (conf->response_code_strings == NULL) {
1203                conf->response_code_strings =
1204                    ap_pcalloc(cmd->pool,
1205                        sizeof(*conf->response_code_strings)
1206                        * RESPONSE_CODES);
1207            }
1208            conf->response_code_strings[index_number] =
1209                ap_pstrdup(cmd->pool, line);
1210        }
1211
1212        return NULL;
1213    }
1214
1215    /* access.conf commands...
1216     *
1217     * The *only* thing that can appear in access.conf
1218     * at top level is a<Directory> section.  NB we need
1219     * to have a way to cut the srm_command_loop invoked
1220     * by dirsection (i.e., <Directory>) short when
1221     * </Directory> is seen. We do that by returning an
1222     * error, which dirsection itself recognizes and
1223     * discards as harmless.  Cheesy, but it works.
1224     */
1225
1226    static const char *set_override(cmd_parms *cmd,
1227        core_dir_config *d,
1228                        const char *l)
1229    {
1230        char *w;
1231
1232        const char *err =
1233            ap_check_cmd_context(cmd, NOT_IN_LIMIT);
1234        if (err != NULL) {
1235            return err;
1236        }
1237
1238        d->override = OR_NONE;
1239        while (l[0]) {
1240            w = ap_getword_conf(cmd->pool, &l);
1241            if (!strcasecmp(w, "Limit")) {
1242                d->override |= OR_LIMIT;
1243            }
1244            else if (!strcasecmp(w, "Options")) {
```

```
1245                    d->override |= OR_OPTIONS;
1246           }
1247           else if (!strcasecmp(w, "FileInfo")) {
1248                    d->override |= OR_FILEINFO;
1249           }
1250           else if (!strcasecmp(w, "AuthConfig")) {
1251                    d->override |= OR_AUTHCFG;
1252           }
1253           else if (!strcasecmp(w, "Indexes")) {
1254                    d->override |= OR_INDEXES;
1255           }
1256           else if (!strcasecmp(w, "None")) {
1257                    d->override = OR_NONE;
1258           }
1259           else if (!strcasecmp(w, "All")) {
1260                    d->override = OR_ALL;
1261           }
1262           else {
1263                    return ap_pstrcat(cmd->pool,
1264                        "Illegal override option ", w, NULL);
1265           }
1266           d->override &= ~OR_UNSET;
1267       }
1268
1269       return NULL;
1270   }
1271
1272   static const char *set_options(cmd_parms *cmd,
1273       core_dir_config *d,
1274                       const char *l)
1275   {
1276       allow_options_t opt;
1277       int first = 1;
1278       char action;
1279
1280       while (l[0]) {
1281           char *w = ap_getword_conf(cmd->pool, &l);
1282           action = '\0';
1283
1284           if (*w == '+' || *w == '-') {
1285               action = *(w++);
1286           }
1287           else if (first) {
1288               d->opts = OPT_NONE;
1289               first = 0;
1290           }
1291
1292           if (!strcasecmp(w, "Indexes")) {
```

```
1293               opt = OPT_INDEXES;
1294           }
1295           else if (!strcasecmp(w, "Includes")) {
1296               opt = OPT_INCLUDES;
1297           }
1298           else if (!strcasecmp(w, "IncludesNOEXEC")) {
1299               opt = (OPT_INCLUDES | OPT_INCNOEXEC);
1300           }
1301           else if (!strcasecmp(w, "FollowSymLinks")) {
1302               opt = OPT_SYM_LINKS;
1303           }
1304           else if (!strcasecmp(w, "SymLinksIfOwnerMatch")) {
1305               opt = OPT_SYM_OWNER;
1306           }
1307           else if (!strcasecmp(w, "execCGI")) {
1308               opt = OPT_EXECCGI;
1309           }
1310           else if (!strcasecmp(w, "MultiViews")) {
1311               opt = OPT_MULTI;
1312           }
1313           else if (!strcasecmp(w, "RunScripts")) {
1314   /* AI backcompat. Yuck */
1315               opt = OPT_MULTI|OPT_EXECCGI;
1316           }
1317           else if (!strcasecmp(w, "None")) {
1318               opt = OPT_NONE;
1319           }
1320           else if (!strcasecmp(w, "All")) {
1321               opt = OPT_ALL;
1322           }
1323           else {
1324               return ap_pstrcat(cmd->pool,
1325                   "Illegal option ", w, NULL);
1326           }
1327
1328   /* we ensure the invariant (d->opts_add
1329    * & d->opts_remove) == 0 */
1330           if (action == '-') {
1331               d->opts_remove |= opt;
1332               d->opts_add &= ~opt;
1333               d->opts &= ~opt;
1334           }
1335           else if (action == '+') {
1336               d->opts_add |= opt;
1337               d->opts_remove &= ~opt;
1338               d->opts |= opt;
1339           }
1340           else {
```

```
1341            d->opts |= opt;
1342        }
1343    }
1344
1345    return NULL;
1346 }
1347
1348 static const char *satisfy(cmd_parms *cmd,
1349         core_dir_config *c, char *arg)
1350 {
1351    if (!strcasecmp(arg, "all")) {
1352        c->satisfy = SATISFY_ALL;
1353    }
1354    else if (!strcasecmp(arg, "any")) {
1355        c->satisfy = SATISFY_ANY;
1356    }
1357    else {
1358        return "Satisfy either 'any' or 'all'.";
1359    }
1360    return NULL;
1361 }
1362
1363 static const char *require(cmd_parms *cmd,
1364         core_dir_config *c, char *arg)
1365 {
1366    require_line *r;
1367
1368    if (!c->ap_requires) {
1369        c->ap_requires = ap_make_array(cmd->pool,
1370                2, sizeof(require_line));
1371    }
1372    r = (require_line *)ap_push_array(c->ap_requires);
1373    r->requirement = ap_pstrdup(cmd->pool, arg);
1374    r->method_mask = cmd->limited;
1375    return NULL;
1376 }
1377
1378 CORE_EXPORT_NONSTD(const char *)
1379     ap_limit_section(cmd_parms *cmd, void *dummy,
1380                                const char *arg)
1381 {
1382    const char *limited_methods =
1383            ap_getword(cmd->pool, &arg, '>');
1384    void *tog = cmd->cmd->cmd_data;
1385    int limited = 0;
1386
1387    const char *err = ap_check_cmd_context(cmd,
1388            NOT_IN_LIMIT);
```

```
1389    if (err != NULL) {
1390        return err;
1391    }
1392
1393    /* XXX: NB: Currently, we have no way of checking
1394     * whether <Limit> or <LimitExcept> sections are
1395     * closed properly. (If we would add a
1396     * srm_command_loop() here we might...)
1397     */
1398
1399    while (limited_methods[0]) {
1400        char *method = ap_getword_conf(cmd->pool,
1401                &limited_methods);
1402        int  methnum = ap_method_number_of(method);
1403
1404        if (methnum == M_TRACE && !tog) {
1405            return "TRACE cannot be controlled
1406                by <Limit>";
1407        }
1408        else if (methnum == M_INVALID) {
1409            return ap_pstrcat(cmd->pool,
1410                "unknown method \"", method,
1411                        "\" in <Limit", tog ?
1412                        "Except>" : ">", NULL);
1413        }
1414        else {
1415            limited |= (1 << methnum);
1416        }
1417    }
1418
1419    /* Killing two features with one function,
1420     * if (tog == NULL) <Limit>, else <LimitExcept>
1421     */
1422    cmd->limited = tog ? ~limited : limited;
1423    return NULL;
1424 }
1425
1426 static const char *endlimit_section(cmd_parms *cmd,
1427     void *dummy, void *dummy2)
1428 {
1429    void *tog = cmd->cmd->cmd_data;
1430
1431    if (cmd->limited == -1) {
1432        return tog ? "</LimitExcept> unexpected" :
1433                "</Limit> unexpected";
1434    }
1435
1436    cmd->limited = -1;
```

```
1437              return NULL;
1438      }
1439
1440      /*
1441       * When a section is not closed properly when
1442       * end-of-file is reached, then an error
1443       * message should be printed:
1444       */
1445      static const char *missing_endsection(cmd_parms
1446          *cmd, int nest)
1447      {
1448          if (nest < 2) {
1449              return ap_psprintf(cmd->pool, "Missing %s
1450                  directive at end-of-file",
1451                          cmd->end_token);
1452          }
1453          return ap_psprintf(cmd->pool, "%d missing %s
1454              directives at end-of-file",
1455                      nest, cmd->end_token);
1456      }
1457
1458      /* We use this in <DirectoryMatch> and <FilesMatch>,
1459       * to ensure that people don't get bitten
1460       * by wrong-cased regex matches
1461       */
1462
1463      #ifdef WIN32
1464      #define USE_ICASE REG_ICASE
1465      #else
1466      #define USE_ICASE 0
1467      #endif
1468
1469      static const char *end_nested_section(cmd_parms
1470          *cmd, void *dummy)
1471      {
1472          if (cmd->end_token == NULL) {
1473              return ap_pstrcat(cmd->pool, cmd->cmd->name,
1474                  " without matching <", cmd->cmd->name + 2,
1475                  " section", NULL);
1476          }
1477          /*
1478           * This '!=' may look weird on a string comparison,
1479           * but it's correct -- it's been set up so that
1480           * checking for two pointers to the same datum
1481           * is valid here.  And faster.
1482           */
1483          if (cmd->cmd->name != cmd->end_token) {
1484              return ap_pstrcat(cmd->pool, "Expected ",
1485                  cmd->end_token, " but saw ",
1486                          cmd->cmd->name, NULL);
1487          }
1488          return cmd->end_token;
1489      }
1490
1491      /*
1492       * Report a missing-'>' syntax error.
1493       */
1494      static char *unclosed_directive(cmd_parms *cmd)
1495      {
1496          return ap_pstrcat(cmd->pool, cmd->cmd->name,
1497                  "> directive missing closing '>'",
1498                      NULL);
1499      }
1500
1501      static const char *dirsection(cmd_parms *cmd,
1502          void *dummy, const char *arg)
1503      {
1504          const char *errmsg;
1505          char *endp = strrchr(arg, '>');
1506          int old_overrides = cmd->override;
1507          char *old_path = cmd->path;
1508          core_dir_config *conf;
1509          void *new_dir_conf =
1510              ap_create_per_dir_config(cmd->pool);
1511          regex_t *r = NULL;
1512          const char *old_end_token;
1513          const command_rec *thiscmd = cmd->cmd;
1514
1515          const char *err = ap_check_cmd_context(cmd,
1516                  NOT_IN_DIR_LOC_FILE|NOT_IN_LIMIT);
1517          if (err != NULL) {
1518              return err;
1519          }
1520
1521          if (endp == NULL) {
1522              return unclosed_directive(cmd);
1523          }
1524
1525          *endp = '\0';
1526
1527          cmd->path = ap_getword_conf(cmd->pool, &arg);
1528      #ifdef OS2
1529          /* Fix OS/2 HPFS filename case problem. */
1530          cmd->path = strlwr(cmd->path);
1531      #endif
1532          cmd->override = OR_ALL|ACCESS_CONF;
```

```
1533
1534        if (thiscmd->cmd_data) { /* <DirectoryMatch> */
1535         r = ap_pregcomp(cmd->pool, cmd->path,
1536             REG_EXTENDED|USE_ICASE);
1537        }
1538        else if (!strcmp(cmd->path, "~")) {
1539         cmd->path = ap_getword_conf(cmd->pool, &arg);
1540         r = ap_pregcomp(cmd->pool, cmd->path,
1541             REG_EXTENDED|USE_ICASE);
1542        }
1543        else {
1544         /* Ensure that the pathname is canonical */
1545         cmd->path = ap_os_canonical_filename(cmd->pool,
1546             cmd->path);
1547        }
1548
1549        old_end_token = cmd->end_token;
1550        cmd->end_token = thiscmd->cmd_data ?
1551             end_directorymatch_section :
1552             end_directory_section;
1553        errmsg = ap_srm_command_loop(cmd, new_dir_conf);
1554        if (errmsg == NULL) {
1555         errmsg = missing_endsection(cmd, 1);
1556        }
1557        cmd->end_token = old_end_token;
1558        if (errmsg != (thiscmd->cmd_data
1559                 ? end_directorymatch_section
1560             : end_directory_section)) {
1561         return errmsg;
1562        }
1563
1564        conf = (core_dir_config *)ap_get_module_config
1565             (new_dir_conf, &core_module);
1566        conf->r = r;
1567
1568        ap_add_per_dir_conf(cmd->server, new_dir_conf);
1569
1570        if (*arg != '\0') {
1571         return ap_pstrcat(cmd->pool, "Multiple ",
1572             thiscmd->name,
1573                 "> arguments not (yet) supported.",
1574                     NULL);
1575        }
1576
1577        cmd->path = old_path;
1578        cmd->override = old_overrides;
1579
1580        return NULL;

1581    }
1582
1583    static const char *urlsection(cmd_parms *cmd,
1584        void *dummy, const char *arg)
1585    {
1586        const char *errmsg;
1587        char *endp = strrchr(arg, '>');
1588        int old_overrides = cmd->override;
1589        char *old_path = cmd->path;
1590        core_dir_config *conf;
1591        regex_t *r = NULL;
1592        const char *old_end_token;
1593        const command_rec *thiscmd = cmd->cmd;
1594
1595        void *new_url_conf =
1596             ap_create_per_dir_config(cmd->pool);
1597
1598        const char *err = ap_check_cmd_context(cmd,
1599                 NOT_IN_DIR_LOC_FILE|NOT_IN_LIMIT);
1600        if (err != NULL) {
1601         return err;
1602        }
1603
1604        if (endp == NULL) {
1605         return unclosed_directive(cmd);
1606        }
1607
1608        *endp = '\0';
1609
1610        cmd->path = ap_getword_conf(cmd->pool, &arg);
1611        cmd->override = OR_ALL|ACCESS_CONF;
1612
1613        if (thiscmd->cmd_data) { /* <LocationMatch> */
1614         r = ap_pregcomp(cmd->pool, cmd->path, REG_EXTENDED);
1615        }
1616        else if (!strcmp(cmd->path, "~")) {
1617         cmd->path = ap_getword_conf(cmd->pool, &arg);
1618         r = ap_pregcomp(cmd->pool, cmd->path, REG_EXTENDED);
1619        }
1620
1621        old_end_token = cmd->end_token;
1622        cmd->end_token = thiscmd->cmd_data ?
1623             end_locationmatch_section
1624                     : end_location_section;
1625        errmsg = ap_srm_command_loop(cmd, new_url_conf);
1626        if (errmsg == NULL) {
1627         errmsg = missing_endsection(cmd, 1);
1628        }
```

```
1629        cmd->end_token = old_end_token;
1630        if (errmsg != (thiscmd->cmd_data
1631                        ? end_locationmatch_section
1632                        : end_location_section)) {
1633         return errmsg;
1634        }
1635
1636        conf = (core_dir_config *)ap_get_module_config
1637                (new_url_conf, &core_module);
1638        conf->d = ap_pstrdup(cmd->pool, cmd->path);
1639        /* No mangling, please */
1640        conf->d_is_fnmatch = ap_is_fnmatch(conf->d) != 0;
1641        conf->r = r;
1642
1643        ap_add_per_url_conf(cmd->server, new_url_conf);
1644
1645        if (*arg != '\0') {
1646         return ap_pstrcat(cmd->pool, "Multiple ",
1647                thiscmd->name,
1648                    "> arguments not (yet) supported.",
1649                        NULL);
1650        }
1651
1652        cmd->path = old_path;
1653        cmd->override = old_overrides;
1654
1655        return NULL;
1656    }
1657
1658    static const char *filesection(cmd_parms *cmd,
1659        core_dir_config *c,
1660                        const char *arg)
1661    {
1662        const char *errmsg;
1663        char *endp = strrchr(arg, '>');
1664        int old_overrides = cmd->override;
1665        char *old_path = cmd->path;
1666        core_dir_config *conf;
1667        regex_t *r = NULL;
1668        const char *old_end_token;
1669        const command_rec *thiscmd = cmd->cmd;
1670
1671        void *new_file_conf =
1672                ap_create_per_dir_config(cmd->pool);
1673
1674        const char *err = ap_check_cmd_context(cmd,
1675                NOT_IN_LIMIT|NOT_IN_LOCATION);
1676        if (err != NULL) {
1677         return err;
1678        }
1679
1680        if (endp == NULL) {
1681         return unclosed_directive(cmd);
1682        }
1683
1684        *endp = '\0';
1685
1686        cmd->path = ap_getword_conf(cmd->pool, &arg);
1687        /* Only if not an .htaccess file */
1688        if (!old_path) {
1689         cmd->override = OR_ALL|ACCESS_CONF;
1690        }
1691
1692        if (thiscmd->cmd_data) { /* <FilesMatch> */
1693            r = ap_pregcomp(cmd->pool, cmd->path,
1694                    REG_EXTENDED|USE_ICASE);
1695        }
1696        else if (!strcmp(cmd->path, "~")) {
1697         cmd->path = ap_getword_conf(cmd->pool, &arg);
1698         r = ap_pregcomp(cmd->pool, cmd->path,
1699             REG_EXTENDED|USE_ICASE);
1700        }
1701        else {
1702         /* Ensure that the pathname is canonical */
1703         cmd->path = ap_os_canonical_filename(cmd->pool,
1704             cmd->path);
1705        }
1706
1707        old_end_token = cmd->end_token;
1708        cmd->end_token = thiscmd->cmd_data ?
1709            end_filesmatch_section : end_files_section;
1710        errmsg = ap_srm_command_loop(cmd, new_file_conf);
1711        if (errmsg == NULL) {
1712         errmsg = missing_endsection(cmd, 1);
1713        }
1714        cmd->end_token = old_end_token;
1715        if (errmsg != (thiscmd->cmd_data
1716                    ? end_filesmatch_section
1717                : end_files_section)) {
1718         return errmsg;
1719        }
1720
1721        conf = (core_dir_config *)ap_get_module_config
1722            (new_file_conf,
1723                            &core_module);
1724        conf->d = cmd->path;
```

```
1725        conf->d_is_fnmatch = ap_is_fnmatch(conf->d) != 0;
1726        conf->r = r;
1727
1728        add_file_conf(c, new_file_conf);
1729
1730        if (*arg != '\0') {
1731         return ap_pstrcat(cmd->pool, "Multiple ",
1732             thiscmd->name,
1733                    "> arguments not (yet) supported.",
1734                            NULL);
1735        }
1736
1737        cmd->path = old_path;
1738        cmd->override = old_overrides;
1739
1740        return NULL;
1741    }
1742
1743    /* XXX: NB: Currently, we have no way of checking
1744     * whether <IfModule> sections are closed properly.
1745     * Extra (redundant, unpaired) </IfModule> directives
1746     * are simply silently ignored.
1747     */
1748    static const char *end_ifmod(cmd_parms *cmd,
1749         void *dummy)
1750    {
1751        return NULL;
1752    }
1753
1754    static const char *start_ifmod(cmd_parms *cmd,
1755         void *dummy, char *arg)
1756    {
1757        char *endp = strrchr(arg, '>');
1758        char l[MAX_STRING_LEN];
1759        int not = (arg[0] == '!');
1760        module *found;
1761        int nest = 1;
1762
1763        if (endp == NULL) {
1764         return unclosed_directive(cmd);
1765        }
1766
1767        *endp = '\0';
1768
1769        if (not) {
1770            arg++;
1771        }
1772
1773        found = ap_find_linked_module(arg);
1774
1775        if ((!not && found) || (not && !found)) {
1776            return NULL;
1777        }
1778
1779        while (nest && !(ap_cfg_getline(l, MAX_STRING_LEN,
1780            cmd->config_file))) {
1781         if (!strncasecmp(l, "<IfModule", 9)) {
1782            nest++;
1783         }
1784         if (!strcasecmp(l, "</IfModule>")) {
1785            nest--;
1786         }
1787
1788        }
1789
1790        if (nest) {
1791         cmd->end_token = end_ifmodule_section;
1792         return missing_endsection(cmd, nest);
1793        }
1794        return NULL;
1795    }
1796
1797    API_EXPORT(int) ap_exists_config_define(char *name)
1798    {
1799        char **defines;
1800        int i;
1801
1802        defines = (char **)ap_server_config_defines->elts;
1803        for (i = 0; i < ap_server_config_defines->nelts;
1804             i++) {
1805            if (strcmp(defines[i], name) == 0) {
1806                return 1;
1807         }
1808        }
1809        return 0;
1810    }
1811
1812    static const char *end_ifdefine(cmd_parms *cmd,
1813         void *dummy)
1814    {
1815        return NULL;
1816    }
1817
1818    static const char *start_ifdefine(cmd_parms *cmd,
1819         void *dummy, char *arg)
1820    {
```

```
1821        char *endp;                                    1869        char *endp = strrchr(arg, '>');
1822        char l[MAX_STRING_LEN];                         1870        pool *p = cmd->pool, *ptemp = cmd->temp_pool;
1823        int defined;                                    1871        const char *old_end_token;
1824        int not = 0;                                    1872
1825        int nest = 1;                                   1873        const char *err = ap_check_cmd_context(cmd,
1826                                                         1874            GLOBAL_ONLY);
1827        endp = strrchr(arg, '>');                       1875        if (err != NULL) {
1828        if (endp == NULL) {                             1876            return err;
1829         return unclosed_directive(cmd);                1877        }
1830        }                                               1878
1831                                                         1879        if (endp == NULL) {
1832        *endp = '\0';                                    1880         return unclosed_directive(cmd);
1833                                                         1881        }
1834        if (arg[0] == '!') {                            1882
1835            not = 1;                                     1883        *endp = '\0';
1836         arg++;                                          1884
1837        }                                               1885        /* FIXME: There's another feature waiting to
1838                                                         1886         happen here -- since you can now put multiple
1839        defined = ap_exists_config_define(arg);         1887         addresses/names on a single <VirtualHost>
1840                                                         1888         you might want to use it to group common
1841        if ((!not && defined) || (not && !defined)) {   1889         definitions and then define other "subhosts"
1842         return NULL;                                    1890         with their individual differences.  But
1843        }                                               1891         personally I'd rather just do it with a macro
1844                                                         1892         preprocessor. -djg */
1845        while (nest && !(ap_cfg_getline(l, MAX_STRING_LEN, 1893        if (main_server->is_virtual) {
1846            cmd->config_file))) {                        1894         return "<VirtualHost> doesn't nest!";
1847            if (!strncasecmp(l, "<IfDefine", 9)) {       1895        }
1848                nest++;                                   1896
1849         }                                               1897        errmsg = ap_init_virtual_host(p, arg,
1850         if (!strcasecmp(l, "</IfDefine>")) {            1898            main_server, &s);
1851                nest--;                                   1899        if (errmsg) {
1852         }                                               1900         return errmsg;
1853        }                                               1901        }
1854        if (nest) {                                      1902
1855         cmd->end_token = end_ifdefine_section;          1903        s->next = main_server->next;
1856         return missing_endsection(cmd, nest);           1904        main_server->next = s;
1857        }                                               1905
1858        return NULL;                                     1906        s->defn_name = cmd->config_file->name;
1859    }                                                    1907        s->defn_line_number = cmd->config_file->line_number;
1860                                                         1908
1861    /* httpd.conf commands... beginning with the        1909        old_end_token = cmd->end_token;
1862     * <VirtualHost> business */                        1910        cmd->end_token = end_virtualhost_section;
1863                                                         1911        cmd->server = s;
1864    static const char *virtualhost_section(cmd_parms *cmd, 1912        errmsg = ap_srm_command_loop(cmd,
1865        void *dummy, char *arg)                          1913            s->lookup_defaults);
1866    {                                                    1914        cmd->server = main_server;
1867        server_rec *main_server = cmd->server, *s;       1915        if (errmsg == NULL) {
1868        const char *errmsg;                              1916         errmsg = missing_endsection(cmd, 1);
```

```
1917          }
1918
1919          cmd->end_token = old_end_token;
1920
1921          if (s->srm_confname) {
1922           ap_process_resource_config(s, s->srm_confname,
1923               p, ptemp);
1924          }
1925
1926          if (s->access_confname) {
1927           ap_process_resource_config(s, s->access_confname,
1928               p, ptemp);
1929          }
1930
1931          if (errmsg == end_virtualhost_section) {
1932           return NULL;
1933          }
1934          return errmsg;
1935      }
1936
1937      static const char *set_server_alias(cmd_parms *cmd,
1938          void *dummy,
1939                          const char *arg)
1940      {
1941          if (!cmd->server->names) {
1942           return "ServerAlias only used in <VirtualHost>";
1943          }
1944          while (*arg) {
1945           char **item, *name = ap_getword_conf(cmd->pool,
1946               &arg);
1947           if (ap_is_matchexp(name)) {
1948               item = (char **)ap_push_array(cmd->server->
1949                   wild_names);
1950           }
1951           else {
1952               item = (char **)ap_push_array
1953                   (cmd->server->names);
1954           }
1955           *item = name;
1956          }
1957          return NULL;
1958      }
1959
1960      static const char *add_module_command(cmd_parms *cmd,
1961          void *dummy, char *arg)
1962      {
1963          const char *err = ap_check_cmd_context(cmd,
1964              GLOBAL_ONLY);
1965          if (err != NULL) {
1966              return err;
1967          }
1968
1969          if (!ap_add_named_module(arg)) {
1970           return ap_pstrcat(cmd->pool, "Cannot add module
1971              via name '", arg,
1972                  "': not in list of loaded modules",
1973                      NULL);
1974          }
1975          return NULL;
1976      }
1977
1978      static const char *clear_module_list_command(cmd_parms
1979          *cmd, void *dummy)
1980      {
1981          const char *err = ap_check_cmd_context(cmd,
1982              GLOBAL_ONLY);
1983          if (err != NULL) {
1984              return err;
1985          }
1986
1987          ap_clear_module_list();
1988          return NULL;
1989      }
1990
1991      static const char *set_server_string_slot(cmd_parms
1992          *cmd, void *dummy,
1993                          char *arg)
1994      {
1995          /* This one's pretty generic... */
1996
1997          int offset = (int)(long)cmd->info;
1998          char *struct_ptr = (char *)cmd->server;
1999
2000          const char *err = ap_check_cmd_context(cmd,
2001                  NOT_IN_DIR_LOC_FILE|NOT_IN_LIMIT);
2002          if (err != NULL) {
2003              return err;
2004          }
2005
2006          *(char **)(struct_ptr + offset) = arg;
2007          return NULL;
2008      }
2009
2010      static const char *server_type(cmd_parms *cmd,
2011          void *dummy, char *arg)
2012      {
```

```
2013    const char *err = ap_check_cmd_context(cmd,
2014        GLOBAL_ONLY);
2015    if (err != NULL) {
2016        return err;
2017    }
2018
2019    if (!strcasecmp(arg, "inetd")) {
2020        ap_standalone = 0;
2021    }
2022    else if (!strcasecmp(arg, "standalone")) {
2023        ap_standalone = 1;
2024    }
2025    else {
2026        return "ServerType must be either 'inetd' or
2027            'standalone'";
2028    }
2029
2030    return NULL;
2031 }
2032
2033 static const char *server_port(cmd_parms *cmd,
2034     void *dummy, char *arg)
2035 {
2036    const char *err = ap_check_cmd_context(cmd,
2037        NOT_IN_DIR_LOC_FILE|NOT_IN_LIMIT);
2038    int port;
2039
2040    if (err != NULL) {
2041        return err;
2042    }
2043    port = atoi(arg);
2044    if (port <= 0 || port >= 65536) { /*
2045        65536 == 1<<16 */
2046        return ap_pstrcat(cmd->temp_pool,
2047            "The port number \"", arg,
2048                "\" is outside the appropriate range "
2049                "(i.e., 1..65535).", NULL);
2050    }
2051    cmd->server->port = port;
2052    return NULL;
2053 }
2054
2055 static const char *set_signature_flag(cmd_parms
2056     *cmd, core_dir_config *d,
2057                         char *arg)
2058 {
2059    const char *err = ap_check_cmd_context(cmd,
2060    NOT_IN_LIMIT);
2061    if (err != NULL) {
2062        return err;
2063    }
2064
2065    if (strcasecmp(arg, "On") == 0) {
2066     d->server_signature = srv_sig_on;
2067    }
2068    else if (strcasecmp(arg, "Off") == 0) {
2069        d->server_signature = srv_sig_off;
2070    }
2071    else if (strcasecmp(arg, "EMail") == 0) {
2072     d->server_signature = srv_sig_withmail;
2073    }
2074    else {
2075     return "ServerSignature: use one of: off | on |
2076        email";
2077    }
2078    return NULL;
2079 }
2080
2081 static const char *set_send_buffer_size(cmd_parms *cmd,
2082     void *dummy, char *arg)
2083 {
2084    int s = atoi(arg);
2085    const char *err = ap_check_cmd_context(cmd,
2086        GLOBAL_ONLY);
2087    if (err != NULL) {
2088        return err;
2089    }
2090
2091    if (s < 512 && s != 0) {
2092        return "SendBufferSize must be >= 512 bytes,
2093            or 0 for system default.";
2094    }
2095    cmd->server->send_buffer_size = s;
2096    return NULL;
2097 }
2098
2099 static const char *set_user(cmd_parms *cmd,
2100     void *dummy, char *arg)
2101 {
2102 #ifdef WIN32
2103     ap_log_error(APLOG_MARK,
2104         APLOG_NOERRNO|APLOG_NOTICE, cmd->server,
2105         "User directive has no affect on Win32");
2106     cmd->server->server_uid = ap_user_id = 1;
2107 #else
2108     const char *err = ap_check_cmd_context(cmd,
```

```
2109                NOT_IN_DIR_LOC_FILE|NOT_IN_LIMIT);
2110        if (err != NULL) {
2111            return err;
2112        }
2113
2114        if (!cmd->server->is_virtual) {
2115         ap_user_name = arg;
2116         cmd->server->server_uid = ap_user_id =
2117             ap_uname2id(arg);
2118        }
2119        else {
2120            if (ap_suexec_enabled) {
2121             cmd->server->server_uid = ap_uname2id(arg);
2122            }
2123            else {
2124             cmd->server->server_uid = ap_user_id;
2125             fprintf(stderr,
2126                 "Warning: User directive in <VirtualHost> "
2127                 "requires SUEXEC wrapper.\n");
2128            }
2129        }
2130 #if !defined (BIG_SECURITY_HOLE) && !defined (OS2)
2131        if (cmd->server->server_uid == 0) {
2132         fprintf(stderr,
2133             "Error:\tApache has not been designed to
2134                 serve pages while\n"
2135             "\trunning as root.  There are known race
2136                 conditions that\n"
2137             "\twill allow any local user to read any file
2138                 on the system.\n"
2139             "\tIf you still desire to serve pages as root
2140                 then\n"
2141             "\tadd -DBIG_SECURITY_HOLE to the EXTRA_CFLAGS
2142                 line in your\n"
2143             "\tsrc/Configuration file and rebuild the
2144                 server.  It is\n"
2145             "\tstrongly suggested that you instead
2146                 modify the User\n"
2147             "\tdirective in your httpd.conf file to list
2148                 a non-root\n"
2149             "\tuser.\n");
2150         exit (1);
2151        }
2152 #endif
2153 #endif /* WIN32 */
2154
2155        return NULL;
2156    }
2157
2158 static const char *set_group(cmd_parms *cmd,
2159        void *dummy, char *arg)
2160 {
2161     const char *err = ap_check_cmd_context(cmd,
2162             NOT_IN_DIR_LOC_FILE|NOT_IN_LIMIT);
2163     if (err != NULL) {
2164         return err;
2165     }
2166
2167     if (!cmd->server->is_virtual) {
2168      cmd->server->server_gid = ap_group_id =
2169          ap_gname2id(arg);
2170     }
2171     else {
2172         if (ap_suexec_enabled) {
2173             cmd->server->server_gid = ap_gname2id(arg);
2174         }
2175         else {
2176             cmd->server->server_gid = ap_group_id;
2177             fprintf(stderr,
2178                 "Warning: Group directive in <VirtualHost>
2179                     requires "
2180                 "SUEXEC wrapper.\n");
2181         }
2182     }
2183
2184     return NULL;
2185 }
2186
2187 static const char *set_server_root(cmd_parms *cmd,
2188        void *dummy, char *arg)
2189 {
2190     const char *err = ap_check_cmd_context(cmd,
2191         GLOBAL_ONLY);
2192
2193     if (err != NULL) {
2194         return err;
2195     }
2196
2197     arg = ap_os_canonical_filename(cmd->pool, arg);
2198
2199     if (!ap_is_directory(arg)) {
2200         return "ServerRoot must be a valid directory";
2201     }
2202     ap_cpystrn(ap_server_root, arg,
2203             sizeof(ap_server_root));
2204     return NULL;
```

```
2205      }
2206
2207      static const char *set_timeout(cmd_parms *cmd,
2208          void *dummy, char *arg)
2209      {
2210          const char *err = ap_check_cmd_context(cmd,
2211              NOT_IN_DIR_LOC_FILE|NOT_IN_LIMIT);
2212          if (err != NULL) {
2213              return err;
2214          }
2215
2216          cmd->server->timeout = atoi(arg);
2217          return NULL;
2218      }
2219
2220      static const char *set_keep_alive_timeout(cmd_parms
2221          *cmd, void *dummy,
2222                              char *arg)
2223      {
2224          const char *err = ap_check_cmd_context(cmd,
2225              NOT_IN_DIR_LOC_FILE|NOT_IN_LIMIT);
2226          if (err != NULL) {
2227              return err;
2228          }
2229
2230          cmd->server->keep_alive_timeout = atoi(arg);
2231          return NULL;
2232      }
2233
2234      static const char *set_keep_alive(cmd_parms
2235          *cmd, void *dummy, char *arg)
2236      {
2237          const char *err = ap_check_cmd_context(cmd,
2238              NOT_IN_DIR_LOC_FILE|NOT_IN_LIMIT);
2239          if (err != NULL) {
2240              return err;
2241          }
2242
2243          /* We've changed it to On/Off, but used to
2244           * use numbers so we accept anything
2245           * but "Off" or "0" as "On"
2246           */
2247          if (!strcasecmp(arg, "off") || !strcmp(arg, "0")) {
2248              cmd->server->keep_alive = 0;
2249          }
2250          else {
2251              cmd->server->keep_alive = 1;
2252          }
```

```
2253          return NULL;
2254      }
2255
2256      static const char *set_keep_alive_max(cmd_parms *cmd,
2257          void *dummy, char *arg)
2258      {
2259          const char *err = ap_check_cmd_context(cmd,
2260              NOT_IN_DIR_LOC_FILE|NOT_IN_LIMIT);
2261          if (err != NULL) {
2262              return err;
2263          }
2264
2265          cmd->server->keep_alive_max = atoi(arg);
2266          return NULL;
2267      }
2268
2269      static const char *set_pidfile(cmd_parms *cmd,
2270          void *dummy, char *arg)
2271      {
2272          const char *err = ap_check_cmd_context(cmd,
2273              GLOBAL_ONLY);
2274          if (err != NULL) {
2275              return err;
2276
2277          }
2278
2279          if (cmd->server->is_virtual) {
2280           return "PidFile directive not allowed in
2281              <VirtualHost>";
2282          }
2283          ap_pid_fname = arg;
2284          return NULL;
2285      }
2286
2287      static const char *set_scoreboard(cmd_parms *cmd,
2288          void *dummy, char *arg)
2289
2290      {
2291          const char *err = ap_check_cmd_context(cmd,
2292              GLOBAL_ONLY);
2293          if (err != NULL) {
2294              return err;
2295          }
2296
2297          ap_scoreboard_fname = arg;
2298          return NULL;
2299      }
2300
```

```
2301   static const char *set_lockfile(cmd_parms *cmd,
2302         void *dummy, char *arg)
2303   {
2304       const char *err = ap_check_cmd_context(cmd,
2305             GLOBAL_ONLY);
2306       if (err != NULL) {
2307           return err;
2308       }
2309
2310       ap_lock_fname = arg;
2311       return NULL;
2312   }
2313
2314   static const char *set_idcheck(cmd_parms *cmd,
2315         core_dir_config *d, int arg)
2316   {
2317       const char *err = ap_check_cmd_context(cmd,
2318             NOT_IN_LIMIT);
2319       if (err != NULL) {
2320           return err;
2321       }
2322
2323       d->do_rfc1413 = arg != 0;
2324       return NULL;
2325   }
2326
2327   static const char *set_hostname_lookups(cmd_parms
2328         *cmd, core_dir_config *d,
2329                               char *arg)
2330   {
2331       const char *err = ap_check_cmd_context(cmd,
2332             NOT_IN_LIMIT);
2333       if (err != NULL) {
2334           return err;
2335       }
2336
2337       if (!strcasecmp(arg, "on")) {
2338        d->hostname_lookups = HOSTNAME_LOOKUP_ON;
2339       }
2340       else if (!strcasecmp(arg, "off")) {
2341        d->hostname_lookups = HOSTNAME_LOOKUP_OFF;
2342       }
2343       else if (!strcasecmp(arg, "double")) {
2344        d->hostname_lookups = HOSTNAME_LOOKUP_DOUBLE;
2345       }
2346       else {
2347        return "parameter must be 'on', 'off', or 'double'";
2348       }
2349       return NULL;
2350   }
2351
2352   static const char *set_serverpath(cmd_parms *cmd,
2353         void *dummy, char *arg)
2354   {
2355       const char *err = ap_check_cmd_context(cmd,
2356             NOT_IN_DIR_LOC_FILE|NOT_IN_LIMIT);
2357       if (err != NULL) {
2358           return err;
2359       }
2360
2361       cmd->server->path = arg;
2362       cmd->server->pathlen = strlen(arg);
2363       return NULL;
2364   }
2365
2366   static const char *set_content_md5(cmd_parms *cmd,
2367         core_dir_config *d, int arg)
2368   {
2369       const char *err = ap_check_cmd_context(cmd,
2370             NOT_IN_LIMIT);
2371       if (err != NULL) {
2372           return err;
2373       }
2374
2375       d->content_md5 = arg != 0;
2376       return NULL;
2377   }
2378
2379   static const char *set_use_canonical_name(cmd_parms
2380         *cmd, core_dir_config *d,
2381                               int arg)
2382   {
2383       const char *err = ap_check_cmd_context(cmd,
2384             NOT_IN_LIMIT);
2385
2386       if (err != NULL) {
2387        return err;
2388       }
2389
2390       d->use_canonical_name = arg != 0;
2391       return NULL;
2392   }
2393
2394   static const char *set_daemons_to_start(cmd_parms
2395         *cmd, void *dummy, char *arg)
2396   {
```

```
2397    #ifdef WIN32
2398        fprintf(stderr, "WARNING: StartServers has no
2399                effect on Win32\n");
2400    #else
2401        const char *err = ap_check_cmd_context(cmd,
2402                GLOBAL_ONLY);
2403        if (err != NULL) {
2404            return err;
2405        }
2406
2407        ap_daemons_to_start = atoi(arg);
2408    #endif
2409        return NULL;
2410    }
2411
2412    static const char *set_min_free_servers(cmd_parms
2413        *cmd, void *dummy, char *arg)
2414    {
2415        const char *err = ap_check_cmd_context(cmd,
2416                GLOBAL_ONLY);
2417        if (err != NULL) {
2418            return err;
2419        }
2420
2421        ap_daemons_min_free = atoi(arg);
2422        if (ap_daemons_min_free <= 0) {
2423            fprintf(stderr, "WARNING: detected MinSpareServers
2424                set to non-positive.\n");
2425            fprintf(stderr, "Resetting to 1 to avoid almost
2426                certain Apache failure.\n");
2427            fprintf(stderr, "Please read the
2428                documentation.\n");
2429            ap_daemons_min_free = 1;
2430        }
2431
2432        return NULL;
2433    }
2434
2435    static const char *set_max_free_servers(cmd_parms
2436        *cmd, void *dummy, char *arg)
2437    {
2438        const char *err = ap_check_cmd_context(cmd,
2439                GLOBAL_ONLY);
2440        if (err != NULL) {
2441            return err;
2442        }
2443
2444        ap_daemons_max_free = atoi(arg);
```

```
2445        return NULL;
2446    }
2447
2448    static const char *set_server_limit (cmd_parms
2449        *cmd, void *dummy, char *arg)
2450    {
2451        const char *err = ap_check_cmd_context(cmd,
2452                GLOBAL_ONLY);
2453        if (err != NULL) {
2454            return err;
2455        }
2456
2457        ap_daemons_limit = atoi(arg);
2458        if (ap_daemons_limit > HARD_SERVER_LIMIT) {
2459            fprintf(stderr, "WARNING: MaxClients of %d
2460                exceeds compile time limit "
2461                "of %d servers,\n", ap_daemons_limit,
2462                    HARD_SERVER_LIMIT);
2463            fprintf(stderr, " lowering MaxClients to %d.
2464                To increase, please "
2465                "see the\n", HARD_SERVER_LIMIT);
2466            fprintf(stderr, " HARD_SERVER_LIMIT define in
2467                src/include/httpd.h.\n");
2468            ap_daemons_limit = HARD_SERVER_LIMIT;
2469        }
2470        else if (ap_daemons_limit < 1) {
2471            fprintf(stderr, "WARNING: Require MaxClients >
2472                0, setting to 1\n");
2473            ap_daemons_limit = 1;
2474        }
2475        return NULL;
2476    }
2477
2478    static const char *set_max_requests(cmd_parms
2479        *cmd, void *dummy, char *arg)
2480    {
2481        const char *err = ap_check_cmd_context(cmd,
2482                GLOBAL_ONLY);
2483        if (err != NULL) {
2484            return err;
2485        }
2486
2487        ap_max_requests_per_child = atoi(arg);
2488        return NULL;
2489    }
2490
2491    static const char *set_threads(cmd_parms *cmd,
2492        void *dummy, char *arg) {
```

```
2493        const char *err = ap_check_cmd_context(cmd,
2494            GLOBAL_ONLY);
2495        if (err != NULL) {
2496            return err;
2497        }
2498
2499        ap_threads_per_child = atoi(arg);
2500        if (ap_threads_per_child > HARD_SERVER_LIMIT) {
2501            fprintf(stderr, "WARNING: ThreadsPerChild
2502                of %d exceeds compile time limit "
2503                "of %d threads,\n", ap_threads_per_child,
2504                    HARD_SERVER_LIMIT);
2505            fprintf(stderr, " lowering ThreadsPerChild
2506                to %d.  To increase, please "
2507                "see the\n", HARD_SERVER_LIMIT);
2508            fprintf(stderr, " HARD_SERVER_LIMIT define
2509                in src/include/httpd.h.\n");
2510            ap_threads_per_child = HARD_SERVER_LIMIT;
2511        }
2512        else if (ap_threads_per_child < 1) {
2513            fprintf(stderr, "WARNING: Require ThreadsPerChild >
2514                0, setting to 1\n");
2515            ap_threads_per_child = 1;
2516        }
2517
2518        return NULL;
2519    }
2520
2521    static const char *set_excess_requests(cmd_parms
2522        *cmd, void *dummy, char *arg)
2523    {
2524        const char *err = ap_check_cmd_context(cmd,
2525            GLOBAL_ONLY);
2526        if (err != NULL) {
2527            return err;
2528        }
2529
2530        ap_excess_requests_per_child = atoi(arg);
2531        return NULL;
2532    }
2533
2534
2535    #if defined(RLIMIT_CPU) || defined(RLIMIT_DATA)
2536        || defined(RLIMIT_VMEM) || defined(RLIMIT_NPROC)
2537        || defined(RLIMIT_AS)
2538    static void set_rlimit(cmd_parms *cmd, struct
2539        rlimit **plimit, const char *arg,
2540                        const char * arg2, int type)
2541    {
2542        char *str;
2543        struct rlimit *limit;
2544        /* If your platform doesn't define rlim_t
2545         * then typedef it in ap_config.h */
2546        rlim_t cur = 0;
2547        rlim_t max = 0;
2548
2549        *plimit = (struct rlimit *)ap_pcalloc(cmd->pool,
2550            sizeof(**plimit));
2551        limit = *plimit;
2552        if ((getrlimit(type, limit)) != 0)        {
2553         *plimit = NULL;
2554         ap_log_error(APLOG_MARK, APLOG_ERR, cmd->server,
2555                "%s: getrlimit failed", cmd->cmd->name);
2556         return;
2557        }
2558
2559        if ((str = ap_getword_conf(cmd->pool, &arg))) {
2560         if (!strcasecmp(str, "max")) {
2561            cur = limit->rlim_max;
2562         }
2563         else {
2564            cur = atol(str);
2565         }
2566        }
2567        else {
2568         ap_log_error(APLOG_MARK,
2569            APLOG_NOERRNO|APLOG_ERR, cmd->server,
2570                "Invalid parameters for %s",
2571                    cmd->cmd->name);
2572         return;
2573        }
2574
2575        if (arg2 && (str = ap_getword_conf(cmd->pool,
2576            &arg2))) {
2577         max = atol(str);
2578        }
2579
2580        /* if we aren't running as root, cannot
2581         * increase max */
2582        if (geteuid()) {
2583         limit->rlim_cur = cur;
2584         if (max) {
2585            ap_log_error(APLOG_MARK,
2586                APLOG_NOERRNO|APLOG_ERR, cmd->server,
2587                "Must be uid 0 to raise maximum %s",
2588                    cmd->cmd->name);
```

```
2589             }
2590          }
2591       else {
2592           if (cur) {
2593              limit->rlim_cur = cur;
2594          }
2595           if (max) {
2596              limit->rlim_max = max;
2597          }
2598       }
2599    }
2600    #endif
2601
2602    #if !defined (RLIMIT_CPU) || !(defined (RLIMIT_DATA)
2603          || defined (RLIMIT_VMEM) || defined(RLIMIT_AS))
2604          || !defined (RLIMIT_NPROC)
2605    static const char *no_set_limit(cmd_parms *cmd,
2606       core_dir_config *conf,
2607                      char *arg, char *arg2)
2608    {
2609       ap_log_error(APLOG_MARK, APLOG_NOERRNO|APLOG_ERR,
2610            cmd->server,
2611           "%s not supported on this platform",
2612                cmd->cmd->name);
2613       return NULL;
2614    }
2615    #endif
2616
2617    #ifdef RLIMIT_CPU
2618    static const char *set_limit_cpu(cmd_parms *cmd,
2619       core_dir_config *conf,
2620                      char *arg, char *arg2)
2621    {
2622       set_rlimit(cmd, &conf->limit_cpu, arg,
2623            arg2, RLIMIT_CPU);
2624       return NULL;
2625    }
2626    #endif
2627
2628    #if defined (RLIMIT_DATA) || defined (RLIMIT_VMEM)
2629         || defined(RLIMIT_AS)
2630    static const char *set_limit_mem(cmd_parms *cmd,
2631       core_dir_config *conf,
2632                      char *arg, char * arg2)
2633    {
2634    #if defined(RLIMIT_AS)
2635       set_rlimit(cmd, &conf->limit_mem, arg,
2636            arg2 ,RLIMIT_AS);
2637    #elif defined(RLIMIT_DATA)
2638       set_rlimit(cmd, &conf->limit_mem, arg,
2639            arg2, RLIMIT_DATA);
2640    #elif defined(RLIMIT_VMEM)
2641       set_rlimit(cmd, &conf->limit_mem, arg,
2642            arg2, RLIMIT_VMEM);
2643    #endif
2644       return NULL;
2645    }
2646    #endif
2647
2648    #ifdef RLIMIT_NPROC
2649    static const char *set_limit_nproc(cmd_parms *cmd,
2650       core_dir_config *conf,
2651                      char *arg, char * arg2)
2652    {
2653       set_rlimit(cmd, &conf->limit_nproc, arg,
2654            arg2, RLIMIT_NPROC);
2655       return NULL;
2656    }
2657    #endif
2658
2659    static const char *set_bind_address(cmd_parms
2660       *cmd, void *dummy, char *arg)
2661    {
2662       const char *err = ap_check_cmd_context(cmd,
2663            GLOBAL_ONLY);
2664       if (err != NULL) {
2665          return err;
2666       }
2667
2668       ap_bind_address.s_addr =
2669            ap_get_virthost_addr(arg, NULL);
2670       return NULL;
2671    }
2672
2673    static const char *set_listener(cmd_parms
2674       *cmd, void *dummy, char *ips)
2675    {
2676       listen_rec *new;
2677       char *ports;
2678       unsigned short port;
2679
2680       const char *err = ap_check_cmd_context(cmd,
2681            GLOBAL_ONLY);
2682       if (err != NULL) {
2683          return err;
2684       }
```

```
2685
2686            ports = strchr(ips, ':');
2687            if (ports != NULL) {
2688             if (ports == ips) {
2689                 return "Missing IP address";
2690             }
2691             else if (ports[1] == '\0') {
2692                 return "Address must end in :<port-number>";
2693             }
2694             *(ports++) = '\0';
2695            }
2696            else {
2697             ports = ips;
2698            }
2699
2700            new=ap_pcalloc(cmd->pool, sizeof(listen_rec));
2701            new->local_addr.sin_family = AF_INET;
2702            if (ports == ips) { /* no address */
2703             new->local_addr.sin_addr.s_addr = htonl(INADDR_ANY);
2704            }
2705            else {
2706             new->local_addr.sin_addr.s_addr =
2707                     ap_get_virthost_addr(ips, NULL);
2708            }
2709            port = atoi(ports);
2710            if (!port) {
2711             return "Port must be numeric";
2712            }
2713            new->local_addr.sin_port = htons(port);
2714            new->fd = -1;
2715            new->used = 0;
2716            new->next = ap_listeners;
2717            ap_listeners = new;
2718            return NULL;
2719        }
2720
2721        static const char *set_listenbacklog(cmd_parms
2722            *cmd, void *dummy, char *arg)
2723        {
2724            int b;
2725
2726            const char *err = ap_check_cmd_context(cmd,
2727                    GLOBAL_ONLY);
2728            if (err != NULL) {
2729
2730                return err;
2731            }
2732
2733            b = atoi(arg);
2734            if (b < 1) {
2735                return "ListenBacklog must be > 0";
2736            }
2737            ap_listenbacklog = b;
2738            return NULL;
2739        }
2740
2741        static const char *set_coredumpdir (cmd_parms
2742            *cmd, void *dummy, char *arg)
2743        {
2744            struct stat finfo;
2745            const char *err = ap_check_cmd_context(cmd,
2746                    GLOBAL_ONLY);
2747            if (err != NULL) {
2748                return err;
2749            }
2750
2751            arg = ap_server_root_relative(cmd->pool, arg);
2752            if ((stat(arg, &finfo) == -1) ||
2753                !S_ISDIR(finfo.st_mode)) {
2754             return ap_pstrcat(cmd->pool,
2755                 "CoreDumpDirectory ", arg,
2756                         " does not exist or is not a
2757                                 directory", NULL);
2758            }
2759            ap_cpystrn(ap_coredump_dir, arg,
2760                    sizeof(ap_coredump_dir));
2761            return NULL;
2762        }
2763
2764        static const char *include_config (cmd_parms *cmd,
2765            void *dummy, char *name)
2766        {
2767            name = ap_server_root_relative(cmd->pool, name);
2768
2769            ap_process_resource_config(cmd->server, name,
2770                    cmd->pool, cmd->temp_pool);
2771
2772            return NULL;
2773        }
2774
2775        static const char *set_loglevel(cmd_parms *cmd,
2776            void *dummy, const char *arg)
2777        {
2778            char *str;
2779
2780            const char *err = ap_check_cmd_context(cmd,
```

```
2781                            NOT_IN_DIR_LOC_FILE|NOT_IN_LIMIT);
2782        if (err != NULL) {
2783            return err;
2784        }
2785
2786        if ((str = ap_getword_conf(cmd->pool, &arg))) {
2787            if (!strcasecmp(str, "emerg")) {
2788                cmd->server->loglevel = APLOG_EMERG;
2789            }
2790            else if (!strcasecmp(str, "alert")) {
2791                cmd->server->loglevel = APLOG_ALERT;
2792            }
2793            else if (!strcasecmp(str, "crit")) {
2794                cmd->server->loglevel = APLOG_CRIT;
2795            }
2796            else if (!strcasecmp(str, "error")) {
2797                cmd->server->loglevel = APLOG_ERR;
2798            }
2799            else if (!strcasecmp(str, "warn")) {
2800                cmd->server->loglevel = APLOG_WARNING;
2801            }
2802            else if (!strcasecmp(str, "notice")) {
2803                cmd->server->loglevel = APLOG_NOTICE;
2804            }
2805            else if (!strcasecmp(str, "info")) {
2806                cmd->server->loglevel = APLOG_INFO;
2807            }
2808            else if (!strcasecmp(str, "debug")) {
2809                cmd->server->loglevel = APLOG_DEBUG;
2810            }
2811            else {
2812                return "LogLevel requires level keyword: one of "
2813                    "emerg/alert/crit/error/warn/notice/info/debug";
2814            }
2815        }
2816        else {
2817            return "LogLevel requires level keyword";
2818        }
2819
2820        return NULL;
2821    }
2822
2823    API_EXPORT(const char *) ap_psignature(const
2824        char *prefix, request_rec *r)
2825    {
2826        char sport[20];
2827        core_dir_config *conf;
2828
2829        conf = (core_dir_config *)ap_get_module_config
2830            (r->per_dir_config,
2831                                    &core_module);
2832        if (conf->server_signature == srv_sig_off) {
2833         return "";
2834        }
2835
2836        ap_snprintf(sport, sizeof sport, "%u", (unsigned)
2837            ap_get_server_port(r));
2838
2839        if (conf->server_signature == srv_sig_withmail) {
2840         return ap_pstrcat(r->pool, prefix, "<ADDRESS>"
2841            SERVER_BASEVERSION
2842                " Server at <A HREF=\"mailto:",
2843                r->server->server_admin, "\">",
2844                ap_get_server_name(r), "</A> Port ",
2845                    sport,
2846                "</ADDRESS>\n", NULL);
2847        }
2848        return ap_pstrcat(r->pool, prefix, "<ADDRESS>"
2849            SERVER_BASEVERSION
2850                " Server at ", ap_get_server_name(r),
2851                    " Port ", sport,
2852                "</ADDRESS>\n", NULL);
2853    }
2854
2855    /*
2856     * Load an authorisation realm into our
2857     * location configuration, applying the
2858     * usual rules that apply to realms.
2859     */
2860    static const char *set_authname(cmd_parms *cmd,
2861        void *mconfig, char *word1)
2862    {
2863        core_dir_config *aconfig =
2864            (core_dir_config *)mconfig;
2865
2866        aconfig->ap_auth_name =
2867            ap_escape_quotes(cmd->pool, word1);
2868        return NULL;
2869    }
2870
2871    #ifdef _OSD_POSIX /* BS2000 Logon Passwd file */
2872    static const char *set_bs2000_account(cmd_parms
2873        *cmd, void *dummy, char *name)
2874    {
2875        const char *err = ap_check_cmd_context(cmd,
2876            GLOBAL_ONLY);
```

```
2877        if (err != NULL) {
2878            return err;
2879        }
2880
2881        return os_set_account(cmd->pool, name);
2882    }
2883    #endif /*_OSD_POSIX*/
2884
2885    /*
2886     * Handle a request to include the server's OS platform
2887     * in the Server response header field (the
2888     * ServerTokens directive).  Unfortunately this
2889     * requires a new global in order to communicate
2890     * the setting back to http_main so it can insert the
2891     * information in the right place in the string.
2892     */
2893
2894    static const char *set_serv_tokens(cmd_parms
2895            *cmd, void *dummy, char *arg)
2896    {
2897        const char *err = ap_check_cmd_context(cmd,
2898                GLOBAL_ONLY);
2899        if (err != NULL) {
2900            return err;
2901        }
2902
2903        if (!strcasecmp(arg, "OS")) {
2904            ap_server_tokens = SrvTk_OS;
2905        }
2906        else if (!strcasecmp(arg, "Min") ||
2907             !strcasecmp(arg, "Minimal")) {
2908            ap_server_tokens = SrvTk_MIN;
2909        }
2910        else {
2911            ap_server_tokens = SrvTk_FULL;
2912        }
2913        return NULL;
2914    }
2915
2916    static const char *set_limit_req_line(cmd_parms
2917            *cmd, void *dummy, char *arg)
2918    {
2919        const char *err = ap_check_cmd_context(cmd,
2920                    NOT_IN_DIR_LOC_FILE|NOT_IN_LIMIT);
2921        int lim;
2922
2923        if (err != NULL) {
2924            return err;
2925        }
2926        lim = atoi(arg);
2927        if (lim < 0) {
2928            return ap_pstrcat(cmd->temp_pool,
2929                "LimitRequestLine \"", arg,
2930                        "\" must be a non-negative
2931                            integer", NULL);
2932        }
2933        if (lim > DEFAULT_LIMIT_REQUEST_LINE) {
2934            return ap_psprintf(cmd->temp_pool,
2935                "LimitRequestLine \"%s\" "
2936
2937                "must not exceed the precompiled
2938                    maximum of %d",
2939                    arg, DEFAULT_LIMIT_REQUEST_LINE);
2940        }
2941        cmd->server->limit_req_line = lim;
2942        return NULL;
2943    }
2944
2945    static const char *set_limit_req_fieldsize(cmd_parms
2946        *cmd, void *dummy,
2947                                    char *arg)
2948    {
2949        const char *err = ap_check_cmd_context(cmd,
2950                    NOT_IN_DIR_LOC_FILE|NOT_IN_LIMIT);
2951        int lim;
2952
2953        if (err != NULL) {
2954            return err;
2955        }
2956        lim = atoi(arg);
2957        if (lim < 0) {
2958            return ap_pstrcat(cmd->temp_pool,
2959                "LimitRequestFieldsize \"", arg,
2960                    "\" must be a non-negative
2961                        integer (0 = no limit)",
2962                    NULL);
2963        }
2964        if (lim > DEFAULT_LIMIT_REQUEST_FIELDSIZE) {
2965            return ap_psprintf(cmd->temp_pool,
2966                "LimitRequestFieldsize \"%s\" "
2967                "must not exceed the precompiled
2968                    maximum of %d",
2969                    arg, DEFAULT_LIMIT_REQUEST_FIELDSIZE);
2970        }
2971        cmd->server->limit_req_fieldsize = lim;
2972        return NULL;
```

```
2973    }
2974
2975    static const char *set_limit_req_fields(cmd_parms
2976        *cmd, void *dummy, char *arg)
2977    {
2978        const char *err = ap_check_cmd_context(cmd,
2979                    NOT_IN_DIR_LOC_FILE|NOT_IN_LIMIT);
2980        int lim;
2981
2982        if (err != NULL) {
2983            return err;
2984        }
2985        lim = atoi(arg);
2986        if (lim < 0) {
2987            return ap_pstrcat(cmd->temp_pool,
2988                    "LimitRequestFields \"", arg,
2989                        "\" must be a non-negative
2990                            integer (0 = no limit)",
2991                        NULL);
2992        }
2993        cmd->server->limit_req_fields = lim;
2994        return NULL;
2995    }
2996
2997    static const char *set_limit_req_body(cmd_parms
2998        *cmd, core_dir_config *conf,
2999                                    char *arg)
3000    {
3001        const char *err = ap_check_cmd_context(cmd,
3002            NOT_IN_LIMIT);
3003        if (err != NULL) {
3004            return err;
3005        }
3006
3007        /* WTF: If strtoul is not portable, then write
3008         * a replacement.
3009         *      Instead we have an idiotic define in
3010         *      httpd.h that prevents it from being
3011         *      used even when it is available. Sheesh.
3012         */
3013        conf->limit_req_body = (unsigned long)strtol(arg,
3014            (char **)NULL, 10);
3015        return NULL;
3016    }
3017
3018    #ifdef WIN32
3019    static const char *set_interpreter_source(cmd_parms
3020        *cmd, core_dir_config *d,
3021                                        char *arg)
3022    {
3023        if (!strcasecmp(arg, "registry")) {
3024            d->script_interpreter_source =
3025                    INTERPRETER_SOURCE_REGISTRY;
3026        } else if (!strcasecmp(arg, "script")) {
3027            d->script_interpreter_source =
3028                    INTERPRETER_SOURCE_SHEBANG;
3029        } else {
3030            d->script_interpreter_source =
3031                    INTERPRETER_SOURCE_SHEBANG;
3032        }
3033        return NULL;
3034    }
3035    #endif
3036
3037    /* Note -- ErrorDocument will now work from
3038     * .htaccess files. The AllowOverride of
3039     * Fileinfo allows webmasters to turn it off
3040     */
3041
3042
3043    static const command_rec core_cmds[] = {
3044
3045    /* Old access config file commands */
3046
3047    { "<Directory", dirsection, NULL, RSRC_CONF,
3048        RAW_ARGS,
3049      "Container for directives affecting resources
3050        located in the specified "
3051      "directories" },
3052    { end_directory_section, end_nested_section,
3053        NULL, ACCESS_CONF, NO_ARGS,
3054      "Marks end of <Directory>" },
3055    { "<Location", urlsection, NULL, RSRC_CONF,
3056        RAW_ARGS,
3057      "Container for directives affecting resources
3058        accessed through the "
3059      "specified URL paths" },
3060    { end_location_section, end_nested_section, NULL,
3061        ACCESS_CONF, NO_ARGS,
3062      "Marks end of <Location>" },
3063    { "<VirtualHost", virtualhost_section, NULL,
3064        RSRC_CONF, RAW_ARGS,
3065      "Container to map directives to a particular
3066        virtual host, takes one or "
3067      "more host addresses" },
3068    { end_virtualhost_section, end_nested_section,
```

```
3069        NULL, RSRC_CONF, NO_ARGS,
3070      "Marks end of <VirtualHost>" },
3071    { "<Files", filesection, NULL, OR_ALL, RAW_ARGS,
3072        "Container for directives "
3073      "affecting files matching specified patterns" },
3074    { end_files_section, end_nested_section, NULL,
3075        OR_ALL, NO_ARGS,
3076      "Marks end of <Files>" },
3077    { "<Limit", ap_limit_section, NULL, OR_ALL,
3078        RAW_ARGS, "Container for "
3079      "authentication directives when accessed
3080        using specified HTTP methods" },
3081    { "</Limit>", endlimit_section, NULL, OR_ALL,
3082        NO_ARGS,
3083      "Marks end of <Limit>" },
3084    { "<LimitExcept", ap_limit_section, (void*)1,
3085        OR_ALL, RAW_ARGS,
3086      "Container for authentication directives to
3087        be applied when any HTTP "
3088      "method other than those specified is used to
3089        access the resource" },
3090    { "</LimitExcept>", endlimit_section, (void*)1,
3091        OR_ALL, NO_ARGS,
3092      "Marks end of <LimitExcept>" },
3093    { "<IfModule", start_ifmod, NULL, OR_ALL, TAKE1,
3094      "Container for directives based on existance
3095        of specified modules" },
3096    { end_ifmodule_section, end_ifmod, NULL, OR_ALL, NO_ARGS,
3097      "Marks end of <IfModule>" },
3098    { "<IfDefine", start_ifdefine, NULL, OR_ALL, TAKE1,
3099      "Container for directives based on existance of
3100        command line defines" },
3101    { end_ifdefine_section, end_ifdefine, NULL, OR_ALL,
3102        NO_ARGS,
3103      "Marks end of <IfDefine>" },
3104    { "<DirectoryMatch", dirsection, (void*)1, RSRC_CONF,
3105        RAW_ARGS,
3106      "Container for directives affecting resources
3107        ocated in the "
3108      "specified directories" },
3109    { end_directorymatch_section, end_nested_section,
3110        NULL, ACCESS_CONF, NO_ARGS,
3111      "Marks end of <DirectoryMatch>" },
3112    { "<LocationMatch", urlsection, (void*)1, RSRC_CONF,
3113        RAW_ARGS,
3114      "Container for directives affecting resources
3115        accessed through the "
3116      "specified URL paths" },
3117    { end_locationmatch_section, end_nested_section,
3118        NULL, ACCESS_CONF, NO_ARGS,
3119      "Marks end of <LocationMatch>" },
3120    { "<FilesMatch", filesection, (void*)1, OR_ALL,
3121        RAW_ARGS,
3122      "Container for directives affecting files matching
3123        specified patterns" },
3124    { end_filesmatch_section, end_nested_section, NULL,
3125        OR_ALL, NO_ARGS,
3126      "Marks end of <FilesMatch>" },
3127    { "AuthType", ap_set_string_slot,
3128        (void*)XtOffsetOf(core_dir_config, ap_auth_type),
3129        OR_AUTHCFG, TAKE1,
3130      "An HTTP authorization type (e.g., \"Basic\")" },
3131    { "AuthName", set_authname, NULL, OR_AUTHCFG, TAKE1,
3132      "The authentication realm (e.g. \"Members Only\")" },
3133    { "Require", require, NULL, OR_AUTHCFG, RAW_ARGS,
3134      "Selects which authenticated users or groups may
3135        access a protected space" },
3136    { "Satisfy", satisfy, NULL, OR_AUTHCFG, TAKE1,
3137      "access policy if both allow and require used ('all'
3138        or 'any')" },
3139  #ifdef GPROF
3140    { "GprofDir", set_gprof_dir, NULL, RSRC_CONF, TAKE1,
3141      "Directory to plop gmon.out files" },
3142  #endif
3143
3144  /* Old resource config file commands */
3145
3146    { "AccessFileName", set_access_name, NULL, RSRC_CONF,
3147        RAW_ARGS,
3148      "Name(s) of per-directory config files (default:
3149        .htaccess)" },
3150    { "DocumentRoot", set_document_root, NULL,
3151        RSRC_CONF, TAKE1,
3152      "Root directory of the document tree"  },
3153    { "ErrorDocument", set_error_document, NULL,
3154        OR_FILEINFO, RAW_ARGS,
3155      "Change responses for HTTP errors" },
3156    { "AllowOverride", set_override, NULL, ACCESS_CONF,
3157        RAW_ARGS,
3158      "Controls what groups of directives can be
3159        configured by per-directory "
3160      "config files" },
3161    { "Options", set_options, NULL, OR_OPTIONS, RAW_ARGS,
3162      "Set a number of attributes for a given directory" },
3163    { "DefaultType", ap_set_string_slot,
3164        (void*)XtOffsetOf (core_dir_config, ap_default_type),
```

```
3165      OR_FILEINFO, TAKE1, "the default MIME type for
3166          untypable files" },
3167
3168
3169      /* Old server config file commands */
3170
3171    { "ServerType", server_type, NULL, RSRC_CONF, TAKE1,
3172      "'inetd' or 'standalone'"},
3173    { "Port", server_port, NULL, RSRC_CONF, TAKE1, "A
3174        TCP port number"},
3175    { "HostnameLookups", set_hostname_lookups, NULL,
3176          ACCESS_CONF|RSRC_CONF, TAKE1,
3177      "\"on\" to enable, \"off\" to disable reverse DNS
3178        lookups, or \"double\" to "
3179      "enable double-reverse DNS lookups" },
3180    { "User", set_user, NULL, RSRC_CONF, TAKE1,
3181      "Effective user id for this server"},
3182    { "Group", set_group, NULL, RSRC_CONF, TAKE1,
3183      "Effective group id for this server"},
3184    { "ServerAdmin", set_server_string_slot,
3185      (void *)XtOffsetOf (server_rec, server_admin),
3186          RSRC_CONF, TAKE1,
3187      "The email address of the server administrator" },
3188    { "ServerName", set_server_string_slot,
3189      (void *)XtOffsetOf (server_rec, server_hostname),
3190          RSRC_CONF, TAKE1,
3191      "The hostname of the server" },
3192    { "ServerSignature", set_signature_flag, NULL,
3193          ACCESS_CONF|RSRC_CONF, TAKE1,
3194      "En-/disable server signature (on|off|email)" },
3195    { "ServerRoot", set_server_root, NULL, RSRC_CONF, TAKE1,
3196      "Common directory of server-related files (logs,
3197          confs, etc.)" },
3198    { "ErrorLog", set_server_string_slot,
3199      (void *)XtOffsetOf (server_rec, error_fname),
3200          RSRC_CONF, TAKE1,
3201      "The filename of the error log" },
3202    { "PidFile", set_pidfile, NULL, RSRC_CONF, TAKE1,
3203        "A file for logging the server process ID"},
3204    { "ScoreBoardFile", set_scoreboard, NULL, RSRC_CONF,
3205        TAKE1,
3206        "A file for Apache to maintain runtime process
3207            management information"},
3208    { "LockFile", set_lockfile, NULL, RSRC_CONF, TAKE1,
3209        "The lockfile used when Apache needs to lock
3210            the accept() call"},
3211    { "AccessConfig", set_server_string_slot,
3212      (void *)XtOffsetOf (server_rec, access_confname),
3213          RSRC_CONF, TAKE1,
3214      "The filename of the access config file" },
3215    { "ResourceConfig", set_server_string_slot,
3216      (void *)XtOffsetOf (server_rec, srm_confname),
3217          RSRC_CONF, TAKE1,
3218      "The filename of the resource config file" },
3219    { "ServerAlias", set_server_alias, NULL, RSRC_CONF,
3220        RAW_ARGS,
3221      "A name or names alternately used to access
3222        the server" },
3223    { "ServerPath", set_serverpath, NULL, RSRC_CONF, TAKE1,
3224      "The pathname the server can be reached at" },
3225    { "Timeout", set_timeout, NULL, RSRC_CONF, TAKE1,
3226        "Timeout duration (sec)" },
3227    { "KeepAliveTimeout", set_keep_alive_timeout, NULL,
3228          RSRC_CONF, TAKE1,
3229      "Keep-Alive timeout duration (sec)"},
3230    { "MaxKeepAliveRequests", set_keep_alive_max, NULL,
3231          RSRC_CONF, TAKE1,
3232      "Maximum number of Keep-Alive requests per connection,
3233        or 0 for infinite" },
3234    { "KeepAlive", set_keep_alive, NULL, RSRC_CONF, TAKE1,
3235      "Whether persistent connections should be On or Off" },
3236    { "IdentityCheck", set_idcheck, NULL,
3237          RSRC_CONF|ACCESS_CONF, FLAG,
3238      "Enable identd (RFC 1413) user lookups - SLOW" },
3239    { "ContentDigest", set_content_md5, NULL, OR_OPTIONS,
3240      FLAG, "whether or not to send a Content-MD5 header
3241        with each request" },
3242    { "UseCanonicalName", set_use_canonical_name, NULL,
3243      OR_OPTIONS, FLAG,
3244      "Whether or not to always use the canonical
3245        ServerName : Port when "
3246      "constructing URLs" },
3247    { "StartServers", set_daemons_to_start, NULL,
3248          RSRC_CONF, TAKE1,
3249      "Number of child processes launched at server
3250        startup" },
3251    { "MinSpareServers", set_min_free_servers, NULL,
3252          RSRC_CONF, TAKE1,
3253      "Minimum number of idle children, to handle
3254        request spikes" },
3255    { "MaxSpareServers", set_max_free_servers, NULL,
3256          RSRC_CONF, TAKE1,
3257      "Maximum number of idle children" },
3258    { "MaxServers", set_max_free_servers, NULL,
3259          RSRC_CONF, TAKE1,
3260      "Deprecated equivalent to MaxSpareServers" },
```

```
3261    { "ServersSafetyLimit", set_server_limit, NULL,
3262        RSRC_CONF, TAKE1,
3263      "Deprecated equivalent to MaxClients" },
3264    { "MaxClients", set_server_limit, NULL, RSRC_CONF,
3265        TAKE1,
3266      "Maximum number of children alive at the same time" },
3267    { "MaxRequestsPerChild", set_max_requests, NULL,
3268        RSRC_CONF, TAKE1,
3269      "Maximum number of requests a particular child serves
3270        before dying." },
3271    { "RLimitCPU",
3272 #ifdef RLIMIT_CPU
3273      set_limit_cpu, (void*)XtOffsetOf(core_dir_config,
3274        limit_cpu),
3275 #else
3276      no_set_limit, NULL,
3277 #endif
3278      OR_ALL, TAKE12, "Soft/hard limits for max CPU usage in
3279        seconds" },
3280    { "RLimitMEM",
3281 #if defined (RLIMIT_DATA) || defined (RLIMIT_VMEM) ||
3282        defined (RLIMIT_AS)
3283      set_limit_mem, (void*)XtOffsetOf(core_dir_config,
3284        limit_mem),
3285 #else
3286      no_set_limit, NULL,
3287 #endif
3288      OR_ALL, TAKE12, "Soft/hard limits for max memory
3289        usage per process" },
3290    { "RLimitNPROC",
3291 #ifdef RLIMIT_NPROC
3292      set_limit_nproc, (void*)XtOffsetOf(core_dir_config,
3293        limit_nproc),
3294 #else
3295      no_set_limit, NULL,
3296 #endif
3297      OR_ALL, TAKE12, "soft/hard limits for max number
3298        of processes per uid" },
3299    { "BindAddress", set_bind_address, NULL, RSRC_CONF,
3300        TAKE1,
3301      "'*', a numeric IP address, or the name of a host
3302        with a unique IP address"},
3303    { "Listen", set_listener, NULL, RSRC_CONF, TAKE1,
3304      "A port number or a numeric IP address and a port
3305        number"},
3306    { "SendBufferSize", set_send_buffer_size, NULL,
3307        RSRC_CONF, TAKE1,
3308      "Send buffer size in bytes"},
3309    { "AddModule", add_module_command, NULL, RSRC_CONF,
3310        ITERATE,
3311      "The name of a module" },
3312    { "ClearModuleList", clear_module_list_command, NULL,
3313        RSRC_CONF, NO_ARGS,
3314      NULL },
3315    { "ThreadsPerChild", set_threads, NULL, RSRC_CONF, TAKE1,
3316      "Number of threads a child creates" },
3317    { "ExcessRequestsPerChild", set_excess_requests, NULL,
3318        RSRC_CONF, TAKE1,
3319      "Maximum number of requests a particular child serves
3320        after it is ready "
3321      "to die." },
3322    { "ListenBacklog", set_listenbacklog, NULL, RSRC_CONF,
3323        TAKE1,
3324      "Maximum length of the queue of pending connections,
3325        as used by listen(2)" },
3326    { "CoreDumpDirectory", set_coredumpdir, NULL, RSRC_CONF,
3327        TAKE1,
3328      "The location of the directory Apache changes to
3329        before dumping core" },
3330    { "Include", include_config, NULL, (RSRC_CONF |
3331        ACCESS_CONF), TAKE1,
3332      "Name of the config file to be included" },
3333    { "LogLevel", set_loglevel, NULL, RSRC_CONF, TAKE1,
3334      "Level of verbosity in error logging" },
3335    { "NameVirtualHost", ap_set_name_virtual_host, NULL,
3336        RSRC_CONF, TAKE1,
3337      "A numeric IP address:port, or the name of a host" },
3338 #ifdef _OSD_POSIX
3339    { "BS2000Account", set_bs2000_account, NULL,
3340        RSRC_CONF, TAKE1,
3341      "Name of server User's bs2000 logon account name" },
3342 #endif
3343 #ifdef WIN32
3344    { "ScriptInterpreterSource", set_interpreter_source,
3345        NULL, OR_FILEINFO, TAKE1,
3346      "Where to find interpreter to run Win32 scripts
3347        (Registry or script shebang line)" },
3348 #endif
3349    { "ServerTokens", set_serv_tokens, NULL, RSRC_CONF,
3350        TAKE1,
3351      "Determine tokens displayed in the Server: header -
3352        Min(imal), OS or Full" },
3353    { "LimitRequestLine", set_limit_req_line, NULL,
3354        RSRC_CONF, TAKE1,
3355      "Limit on maximum size of an HTTP request line"},
3356    { "LimitRequestFieldsize", set_limit_req_fieldsize,
```

```
3357            NULL, RSRC_CONF, TAKE1,
3358        "Limit on maximum size of an HTTP request
3359            header field"},
3360    { "LimitRequestFields", set_limit_req_fields, NULL,
3361            RSRC_CONF, TAKE1,
3362        "Limit (0 = unlimited) on max number of header
3363            fields in a request message"},
3364    { "LimitRequestBody", set_limit_req_body,
3365      (void*)XtOffsetOf(core_dir_config, limit_req_body),
3366      OR_ALL, TAKE1,
3367        "Limit (in bytes) on maximum size of request
3368            message body" },
3369    { NULL }
3370    };
3371
3372    /**********************************************************
3373     *
3374     * Core handlers for various phases of server
3375     * operation...
3376     */
3377
3378    static int core_translate(request_rec *r)
3379    {
3380        void *sconf = r->server->module_config;
3381        core_server_config *conf =
3382            ap_get_module_config(sconf, &core_module);
3383
3384        if (r->proxyreq) {
3385            return HTTP_FORBIDDEN;
3386        }
3387        if ((r->uri[0] != '/') && strcmp(r->uri, "*")) {
3388        ap_log_rerror(APLOG_MARK, APLOG_NOERRNO|APLOG_ERR, r,
3389            "Invalid URI in request %s", r->the_request);
3390         return BAD_REQUEST;
3391        }
3392
3393        if (r->server->path
3394         && !strncmp(r->uri, r->server->path,
3395            r->server->pathlen)
3396         && (r->server->path[r->server->pathlen - 1] == '/'
3397          || r->uri[r->server->pathlen] == '/'
3398          || r->uri[r->server->pathlen] == '\0')) {
3399            r->filename = ap_pstrcat(r->pool, conf->
3400                ap_document_root,
3401                    (r->uri + r->server->pathlen), NULL);
3402        }
3403        else {
3404            /*
3405             * Make sure that we do not mess up the
3406             * translation by adding two/'s in a row.
3407             * This happens under windows when the
3408             * document root ends with a /
3409             */
3410            if ((conf->ap_document_root[strlen(conf->
3411                    ap_document_root)-1] == '/')
3412             && (*(r->uri) == '/')) {
3413                r->filename = ap_pstrcat(r->pool, conf->
3414                    ap_document_root, r->uri+1,
3415                        NULL);
3416            }
3417            else {
3418                r->filename = ap_pstrcat(r->pool, conf->
3419                    ap_document_root, r->uri,
3420                        NULL);
3421            }
3422        }
3423
3424        return OK;
3425    }
3426
3427    static int do_nothing(request_rec *r) { return OK; }
3428
3429    #ifdef USE_MMAP_FILES
3430    struct mmap {
3431        void *mm;
3432        size_t length;
3433    };
3434
3435    static void mmap_cleanup(void *mmv)
3436    {
3437        struct mmap *mmd = mmv;
3438
3439        if (munmap(mmd->mm, mmd->length) == -1) {
3440            ap_log_error(APLOG_MARK, APLOG_ERR, NULL,
3441                "Failed to munmap memory of length
3442                    %ld at 0x%lx",
3443                (long) mmd->length, (long) mmd->mm);
3444        }
3445    }
3446    #endif
3447
3448    /*
3449     * Default handler for MIME types without other
3450     * handlers.  Only GET and OPTIONS at this point...
3451     * anyone who wants to write a generic handler for PUT
3452     * or POST is free to do so, but it seems unwise to
```

```
3453      * provide any defaults yet... So, for now,
3454      * we assume that this will always be the last
3455      * handler called and return 405 or 501.
3456      */
3457
3458     static int default_handler(request_rec *r)
3459     {
3460         core_dir_config *d =
3461             (core_dir_config *)ap_get_module_config
3462                 (r->per_dir_config, &core_module);
3463         int rangestatus, errstatus;
3464         FILE *f;
3465     #ifdef USE_MMAP_FILES
3466         caddr_t mm;
3467     #endif
3468
3469         /* This handler has no use for a request body (yet),
3470          * but we still need to read and discard
3471          * it if the client sent one.
3472          */
3473         if ((errstatus = ap_discard_request_body(r)) != OK) {
3474             return errstatus;
3475         }
3476
3477         r->allowed |= (1 << M_GET) | (1 << M_OPTIONS);
3478
3479         if (r->method_number == M_INVALID) {
3480          ap_log_rerror(APLOG_MARK,
3481             APLOG_NOERRNO|APLOG_ERR, r,
3482              "Invalid method in request %s",
3483                  r->the_request);
3484          return NOT_IMPLEMENTED;
3485         }
3486         if (r->method_number == M_OPTIONS) {
3487             return ap_send_http_options(r);
3488         }
3489         if (r->method_number == M_PUT) {
3490             return METHOD_NOT_ALLOWED;
3491         }
3492
3493         if (r->finfo.st_mode == 0 || (r->path_info
3494             && *r->path_info)) {
3495          char *emsg;
3496
3497          emsg = "File does not exist: ";
3498          if (r->path_info == NULL) {
3499             emsg = ap_pstrcat(r->pool, emsg,
3500                 r->filename, NULL);
3501          }
3502          else {
3503             emsg = ap_pstrcat(r->pool, emsg,
3504                 r->filename, r->path_info, NULL);
3505          }
3506          ap_log_rerror(APLOG_MARK,
3507             APLOG_ERR|APLOG_NOERRNO, r, "%s", emsg);
3508          return HTTP_NOT_FOUND;
3509         }
3510         if (r->method_number != M_GET) {
3511             return METHOD_NOT_ALLOWED;
3512         }
3513
3514     #if defined(OS2) || defined(WIN32)
3515         /* Need binary mode for OS/2 */
3516         f = ap_pfopen(r->pool, r->filename, "rb");
3517     #else
3518         f = ap_pfopen(r->pool, r->filename, "r");
3519     #endif
3520
3521         if (f == NULL) {
3522             ap_log_rerror(APLOG_MARK, APLOG_ERR, r,
3523                 "file permissions deny server access:
3524                     %s", r->filename);
3525             return FORBIDDEN;
3526         }
3527
3528         ap_update_mtime(r, r->finfo.st_mtime);
3529         ap_set_last_modified(r);
3530         ap_set_etag(r);
3531         ap_table_setn(r->headers_out, "Accept-Ranges",
3532             "bytes");
3533         if (((errstatus = ap_meets_conditions(r)) != OK)
3534          || (errstatus = ap_set_content_length(r,
3535             r->finfo.st_size))) {
3536             return errstatus;
3537         }
3538
3539     #ifdef USE_MMAP_FILES
3540         ap_block_alarms();
3541         if ((r->finfo.st_size >= MMAP_THRESHOLD)
3542          && (!r->header_only || (d->content_md5 & 1))) {
3543          /* we need to protect ourselves in case we
3544           * die while we've got the
3545           * file mmapped */
3546          mm = mmap(NULL, r->finfo.st_size, PROT_READ,
3547             MAP_PRIVATE,
3548                 fileno(f), 0);
```

```
3549        if (mm == (caddr_t)-1) {
3550            ap_log_rerror(APLOG_MARK, APLOG_CRIT, r,
3551                "default_handler: mmap failed: %s",
3552                    r->filename);
3553        }
3554    }
3555    else {
3556        mm = (caddr_t)-1;
3557    }
3558
3559    if (mm == (caddr_t)-1) {
3560        ap_unblock_alarms();
3561 #endif
3562
3563        if (d->content_md5 & 1) {
3564            ap_table_setn(r->headers_out, "Content-MD5",
3565                ap_md5digest(r->pool, f));
3566        }
3567
3568        rangestatus = ap_set_byterange(r);
3569 #ifdef CHARSET_EBCDIC
3570        /* To make serving of "raw ASCII text" files easy
3571         * (they serve faster since they don't have to be
3572         * converted from EBCDIC), a new"magic" type prefix
3573         * was invented: text/x-ascii-{plain,html,...}
3574         * If we detect one of these content types here,
3575         * we simply correct the type to the real
3576         * text/{plain,html,...} type. Otherwise, we set
3577         * a flag that translation is required later on.
3578         */
3579            ap_checkconv(r);
3580 #endif /*CHARSET_EBCDIC*/
3581
3582        ap_send_http_header(r);
3583
3584        if (!r->header_only) {
3585            if (!rangestatus) {
3586                ap_send_fd(f, r);
3587            }
3588            else {
3589                long offset, length;
3590                while (ap_each_byterange(r, &offset, &length)) {
3591                    /*
3592                     * Non zero returns are more portable than
3593                     * checking for a return of -1.
3594                     */
3595                    if (fseek(f, offset, SEEK_SET)) {
3596                        ap_log_error(APLOG_MARK, APLOG_ERR,
3597                            r->server,
3598                            "Failed to fseek for byterange
3599                                (%ld, %ld)",
3600                            offset, length);
3601                    }
3602                    else {
3603                        ap_send_fd_length(f, r, length);
3604                    }
3605                }
3606            }
3607        }
3608
3609 #ifdef USE_MMAP_FILES
3610    }
3611    else {
3612        struct mmap *mmd;
3613
3614        mmd = ap_palloc(r->pool, sizeof(*mmd));
3615        mmd->mm = mm;
3616        mmd->length = r->finfo.st_size;
3617        ap_register_cleanup(r->pool, (void *)mmd,
3618            mmap_cleanup, mmap_cleanup);
3619        ap_unblock_alarms();
3620
3621        if (d->content_md5 & 1) {
3622            AP_MD5_CTX context;
3623
3624            ap_MD5Init(&context);
3625            ap_MD5Update(&context, (void *)mm,
3626                r->finfo.st_size);
3627            ap_table_setn(r->headers_out, "Content-MD5",
3628                ap_md5contextTo64(r->pool, &context));
3629        }
3630
3631        rangestatus = ap_set_byterange(r);
3632        ap_send_http_header(r);
3633
3634        if (!r->header_only) {
3635            if (!rangestatus) {
3636                ap_send_mmap(mm, r, 0, r->finfo.st_size);
3637            }
3638            else {
3639                long offset, length;
3640                while (ap_each_byterange(r, &offset,
3641                    &length)) {
3642                    ap_send_mmap(mm, r, offset, length);
3643                }
3644            }
```

```
3645        }
3646      }
3647    #endif
3648
3649      ap_pfclose(r->pool, f);
3650      return OK;
3651    }
3652
3653    static const handler_rec core_handlers[] = {
3654    { "*/*", default_handler },
3655    { "default-handler", default_handler },
3656    { NULL, NULL }
3657    };
3658
3659    API_VAR_EXPORT module core_module = {
3660      STANDARD_MODULE_STUFF,
3661      NULL,                 /* initializer */
3662      create_core_dir_config,
3663      /* create per-directory config structure */
3664      merge_core_dir_configs,
3665      /* merge per-directory config structures */
3666      create_core_server_config,
3667      /* create per-server config structure */
3668      merge_core_server_configs,
3669      /* merge per-server config structures */
3670      core_cmds,            /* command table */
3671      core_handlers,        /* handlers */
3672      core_translate,        /* translate_handler */
3673      NULL,              /* check_user_id */
3674      NULL,              /* check auth */
3675      do_nothing,          /* check access */
3676      do_nothing,          /* type_checker */
3677      NULL,              /* pre-run fixups */
3678      NULL,              /* logger */
3679      NULL,              /* header parser */
3680      NULL,              /* child_init */
3681      NULL,              /* child_exit */
3682      NULL              /* post_read_request */
3683    };
```

▶ p 480 **http_main.c**

```
3684    #ifndef SHARED_CORE_BOOTSTRAP
3685    #ifndef SHARED_CORE_TIESTATIC
3686
3687    #ifdef SHARED_CORE
3688    #define REALMAIN ap_main
3689    int ap_main(int argc, char *argv[]);
3690    #else
3691    #define REALMAIN main
3692    #endif
3693
3694    #define CORE_PRIVATE
3695
3696    #include "httpd.h"
3697    #include "http_main.h"
3698    #include "http_log.h"
3699    #include "http_config.h"      /* for read_config */
3700    #include "http_protocol.h"      /* for read_request */
3701    #include "http_request.h"      /* for process_request */
3702    #include "http_conf_globals.h"
3703    #include "http_core.h"
3704    /* for get_remote_host */
3705    #include "http_vhost.h"
3706    #include "util_script.h"
3707    /* to force util_script.c linking */
3708    #include "util_uri.h"
3709    #include "scoreboard.h"
3710    #include "multithread.h"
3711    #include <sys/stat.h>
3712    #ifdef USE_SHMGET_SCOREBOARD
3713    #include <sys/types.h>
3714    #include <sys/ipc.h>
3715    #include <sys/shm.h>
3716    #endif
3717    #ifdef SecureWare
3718    #include <sys/security.h>
3719    #include <sys/audit.h>
3720    #include <prot.h>
3721    #endif
3722    #ifdef WIN32
3723    #include "../os/win32/getopt.h"
3724    #elif !defined(BEOS) && !defined(TPF)
3725    #include <netinet/tcp.h>
3726    #endif
3727
3728    #ifdef HAVE_BSTRING_H
3729    #include <bstring.h>
3730    /* for IRIX, FD_SET calls bzero() */
3731    #endif
3732
3733    #ifdef MULTITHREAD
3734    /* special debug stuff -- PCS */
3735
3736    /* Set this non-zero if you are prepared to put
3737     * up with more than one log entry per second */
```

```
3738   #define SEVERELY_VERBOSE          0
3739
3740      /* APD1() to APD5() are macros to help us debug.
3741       * They can either log to the screen or the error_log
3742       * file. In release builds, these macros do nothing.
3743       * In debug builds, they send messages at priority
3744       * "debug" to the error log file, or if
3745       * DEBUG_TO_CONSOLE is defined,to the console.
3746       */
3747
3748   # ifdef _DEBUG
3749   #  ifndef DEBUG_TO_CONSOLE
3750   #   define APD1(a) ap_log_error(APLOG_MARK,APLOG_DEBUG|
3751           APLOG_NOERRNO,server_conf,a)
3752   #   define APD2(a,b) ap_log_error(APLOG_MARK,APLOG_DEBUG|
3753           APLOG_NOERRNO,server_conf,a,b)
3754   #   define APD3(a,b,c)
3755       ap_log_error(APLOG_MARK,APLOG_DEBUG|
3756       APLOG_NOERRNO,server_conf,a,b,c)
3757   #   define APD4(a,b,c,d)
3758       ap_log_error(APLOG_MARK,APLOG_DEBUG|
3759       APLOG_NOERRNO,server_conf,a,b,c,d)
3760   #   define APD5(a,b,c,d,e)
3761       ap_log_error(APLOG_MARK,APLOG_DEBUG|
3762       APLOG_NOERRNO,server_conf,a,b,c,d,e)
3763   #  else
3764   #   define APD1(a) printf("%s\n",a)
3765   #   define APD2(a,b) do { printf(a,b);
3766           putchar('\n'); } while(0);
3767   #   define APD3(a,b,c) do { printf(a,b,c);
3768           putchar('\n'); } while(0);
3769   #   define APD4(a,b,c,d) do { printf(a,b,c,d);
3770           putchar('\n'); } while(0);
3771   #   define APD5(a,b,c,d,e) do { printf(a,b,c,d,e);
3772           putchar('\n'); } while(0);
3773   #  endif
3774   # else /* !_DEBUG */
3775   #  define APD1(a)
3776   #  define APD2(a,b)
3777   #  define APD3(a,b,c)
3778   #  define APD4(a,b,c,d)
3779   #  define APD5(a,b,c,d,e)
3780   # endif /* _DEBUG */
3781   #endif /* MULTITHREAD */
3782
3783      /* This next function is never used. It is here to
3784       * ensure that if we make all the modules into shared
3785       * libraries that core httpd still includes the full
3786       * Apache API. Without this function the objects in
3787       * main/util_script.c would not be linked into a
3788       * minimal httpd. And the extra prototype is to make
3789       * gcc -Wmissing-prototypes quiet.
3790       */
3791   extern void ap_force_library_loading(void);
3792   void ap_force_library_loading(void) {
3793       ap_add_cgi_vars(NULL);
3794   }
3795
3796   #include "explain.h"
3797
3798   #if !defined(max)
3799   #define max(a,b)          (a > b ? a : b)
3800   #endif
3801
3802   #ifdef WIN32
3803   #include "../os/win32/service.h"
3804   #include "../os/win32/registry.h"
3805   #endif
3806
3807
3808   #ifdef MINT
3809   long _stksize = 32768;
3810   #endif
3811
3812   #ifdef USE_OS2_SCOREBOARD
3813       /* Add MMAP style functionality to OS/2 */
3814   #define INCL_DOSMEMMGR
3815   #define INCL_DOSEXCEPTIONS
3816   #define INCL_DOSSEMAPHORES
3817   #include <os2.h>
3818   #include <umalloc.h>
3819   #include <stdio.h>
3820   caddr_t create_shared_heap(const char *, size_t);
3821   caddr_t get_shared_heap(const char *);
3822   #endif
3823
3824   DEF_Explain
3825
3826   /* Defining GPROF when compiling uses the moncontrol()
3827    * function to disable gprof profiling in the parent,
3828    * and enable it only for request processing in children
3829    * (or in one_process mode).  It's absolutely required
3830    * to get useful gprof results under linux because
3831    * the profile itimers and such are disabled across a
3832    * fork().  It's probably useful elsewhere as well.
3833    */
```

```
3834    #ifdef GPROF
3835    extern void moncontrol(int);
3836    #define MONCONTROL(x) moncontrol(x)
3837    #else
3838    #define MONCONTROL(x)
3839    #endif
3840
3841    #ifndef MULTITHREAD
3842    /* this just need to be anything non-NULL */
3843    void *ap_dummy_mutex = &ap_dummy_mutex;
3844    #endif
3845
3846    /*
3847     * Actual definitions of config globals... here
3848     * because this is for the most part the only
3849     * code that acts on 'em.  (Hmmm... mod_main.c?)
3850     */
3851
3852    int ap_standalone;
3853    uid_t ap_user_id;
3854    char *ap_user_name;
3855    gid_t ap_group_id;
3856    #ifdef MULTIPLE_GROUPS
3857    gid_t group_id_list[NGROUPS_MAX];
3858    #endif
3859    int ap_max_requests_per_child;
3860    int ap_threads_per_child;
3861    int ap_excess_requests_per_child;
3862    char *ap_pid_fname;
3863    char *ap_scoreboard_fname;
3864    char *ap_lock_fname;
3865    char *ap_server_argv0;
3866    struct in_addr ap_bind_address;
3867    int ap_daemons_to_start;
3868    int ap_daemons_min_free;
3869    int ap_daemons_max_free;
3870    int ap_daemons_limit;
3871    time_t ap_restart_time;
3872    int ap_suexec_enabled = 0;
3873    int ap_listenbacklog;
3874    int ap_dump_settings = 0;
3875    API_VAR_EXPORT int ap_extended_status = 0;
3876
3877    /*
3878     * The max child slot ever assigned, preserved across
3879     * restarts.  Necessary to deal with MaxClients changes
3880     * across SIGUSR1 restarts.  We use this value to
3881     * optimize routines that have to scan the entire
3882     * scoreboard.
3883     */
3884    static int max_daemons_limit = -1;
3885
3886    /*
3887     * During config time, listeners is treated as a
3888     * NULL-terminated list. child_main previously
3889     * would start at the beginning of the list each time
3890     * through the loop, so a socket early on in the
3891     * list could easily starve out sockets later on in
3892     * the list.  The solution is to start at the listener
3893     * after the last one processed.  But to do that
3894     * fast/easily in child_main it's way more convenient
3895     * for listeners to be a ring that loops back on itself.
3896     * The routine setup_listeners() is called after
3897     * config time to both open up the sockets and to turn
3898     * the NULL-terminated list into a ring that loops back
3899     * on itself.
3900     *
3901     * head_listener is used by each child to keep track
3902     * of what they consider to be the "start" of the
3903     * ring.  It is also set by make_child to ensure
3904     * that new children also don't starve any sockets.
3905     *
3906     * Note that listeners != NULL is ensured by
3907     * read_config().
3908     */
3909    listen_rec *ap_listeners;
3910    static listen_rec *head_listener;
3911
3912    API_VAR_EXPORT char ap_server_root[MAX_STRING_LEN];
3913    char ap_server_confname[MAX_STRING_LEN];
3914    char ap_coredump_dir[MAX_STRING_LEN];
3915
3916    array_header *ap_server_pre_read_config;
3917    array_header *ap_server_post_read_config;
3918    array_header *ap_server_config_defines;
3919
3920    /* *Non*-shared http_main globals... */
3921
3922    static server_rec *server_conf;
3923    static JMP_BUF APACHE_TLS jmpbuffer;
3924    static int sd;
3925    static fd_set listenfds;
3926    static int listenmaxfd;
3927    static pid_t pgrp;
3928
3929    /* one_process -- debugging mode variable; can be set
```

```
3930    * from the command line with the -X flag.  If set,
3931    * this gets you the child_main loop running in the
3932    * process which originally started up (no detach, no
3933    * make_child), which is a pretty nice debugging
3934    * environment.  (You'll get a SIGHUP early in
3935    * standalone_main; just continue through.  This is
3936    * the server trying to kill off any child
3937    * processes which it might have lying around -- Apache
3938    * doesn't keep track of their pids, it just sends
3939    * SIGHUP to the process group, ignoring it in the root
3940    * process. Continue through and you'll be fine.).
3941    */
3942
3943   static int one_process = 0;
3944
3945   /* set if timeouts are to be handled by the children
3946    * and not by the parent. i.e. child_timeouts =
3947    *!standalone || one_process.
3948    */
3949   static int child_timeouts;
3950
3951   #ifdef DEBUG_SIGSTOP
3952   int raise_sigstop_flags;
3953   #endif
3954
3955   #ifndef NO_OTHER_CHILD
3956   /* used to maintain list of children which aren't
3957    * part of the scoreboard */
3958   typedef struct other_child_rec other_child_rec;
3959   struct other_child_rec {
3960       other_child_rec *next;
3961       int pid;
3962       void (*maintenance) (int, void *, ap_wait_t);
3963       void *data;
3964       int write_fd;
3965   };
3966   static other_child_rec *other_children;
3967   #endif
3968
3969   static pool *pconf;            /* Pool for config stuff */
3970   static pool *ptrans;
3971   /* Pool for per-transaction stuff */
3972   static pool *pchild;
3973   /* Pool for httpd child stuff */
3974   static pool *pcommands;
3975   /* Pool for -C and -c switches */
3976
3977   static int APACHE_TLS my_pid;
```

```
3978   /* it seems silly to call getpid all the time */
3979   #ifndef MULTITHREAD
3980   static int my_child_num;
3981   #endif
3982
3983   scoreboard *ap_scoreboard_image = NULL;
3984
3985   /*
3986    * Pieces for managing the contents of the Server
3987    * response header field.
3988    */
3989   static char *server_version = NULL;
3990   static int version_locked = 0;
3991
3992   /* Global, alas, so http_core can talk to us */
3993   enum server_token_type ap_server_tokens = SrvTk_FULL;
3994
3995   /*
3996    * This routine is called when the pconf pool is
3997    * vacuumed.  It resets the server version string to a
3998    * known value and [re]enables modifications
3999    * (which are disabled by configuration completion).
4000    */
4001
4002   static void reset_version(void *dummy)
4003   {
4004       version_locked = 0;
4005       ap_server_tokens = SrvTk_FULL;
4006       server_version = NULL;
4007   }
4008
4009   API_EXPORT(const char *) ap_get_server_version(void)
4010   {
4011       return (server_version ? server_version :
4012    *  * SERVER_BASEVERSION);
4013   }
4014
4015   API_EXPORT(void) ap_add_version_component(const
4016    *  * char *component)
4017   {
4018       if (! version_locked) {
4019           /*
4020            * If the version string is null, register our
4021            * cleanup to reset the pointer on pool
4022            * destruction. We also know that, if NULL,
4023            * we are adding the original SERVER_BASEVERSION
4024            * string.
4025            */
```

```
4026            if (server_version == NULL) {
4027                ap_register_cleanup(pconf, NULL, (void (*)
4028                    (void *))reset_version,
4029                        ap_null_cleanup);
4030                server_version = ap_pstrdup(pconf,
4031                    component);
4032            }
4033            else {
4034                /*
4035                 * Tack the given component identifier to
4036                 * the end of the existing string.
4037                 */
4038                server_version = ap_pstrcat(pconf,
4039                    server_version, " ",
4040                        component, NULL);
4041            }
4042        }
4043    }
4044
4045    /*
4046     * This routine adds the real server base identity
4047     * to the version string, and then locks out
4048
4049     * changes until the next reconfig.
4050     */
4051    static void ap_set_version(void)
4052    {
4053        if (ap_server_tokens == SrvTk_MIN) {
4054            ap_add_version_component(SERVER_BASEVERSION);
4055        }
4056        else {
4057            ap_add_version_component(SERVER_BASEVERSION "
4058                (" PLATFORM ")");
4059        }
4060        /*
4061         * Lock the server_version string if we're not
4062         * displaying the full set of tokens
4063         */
4064        if (ap_server_tokens != SrvTk_FULL) {
4065            version_locked++;
4066        }
4067    }
4068
4069    static APACHE_TLS int volatile exit_after_unblock = 0;
4070
4071    #ifdef GPROF
4072    /*
4073     * change directory for gprof to plop the gmon.out file
```

```
4074     * configure in httpd.conf:
4075     * GprofDir logs/   -> $ServerRoot/logs/gmon.out
4076     * GprofDir logs/% ->
4077     *   $ServerRoot/logs/gprof.$pid/gmon.out
4078     */
4079    static void chdir_for_gprof(void)
4080    {
4081        core_server_config *sconf =
4082        ap_get_module_config(server_conf->module_config,
4083            &core_module);
4084        char *dir = sconf->gprof_dir;
4085
4086        if(dir) {
4087          char buf[512];
4088          int len = strlen(sconf->gprof_dir) - 1;
4089          if(*(dir + len) == '%') {
4090              dir[len] = '\0';
4091              ap_snprintf(buf, sizeof(buf), "%sgprof.%d",
4092                  dir, (int)getpid());
4093          }
4094          dir = ap_server_root_relative(pconf,
4095              buf[0] ? buf : dir);
4096          if(mkdir(dir, 0755) < 0 && errno != EEXIST) {
4097              ap_log_error(APLOG_MARK, APLOG_ERR,
4098                  server_conf,
4099                    "gprof: error creating
4100                        directory %s", dir);
4101          }
4102        }
4103        else {
4104          dir = ap_server_root_relative(pconf, "logs");
4105        }
4106
4107        chdir(dir);
4108    }
4109    #else
4110    #define chdir_for_gprof()
4111    #endif
4112
4113    /* a clean exit from a child with proper cleanup */
4114    static void clean_child_exit(int code)
4115        __attribute__ ((noreturn));
4116    static void clean_child_exit(int code)
4117    {
4118        if (pchild) {
4119          ap_child_exit_modules(pchild, server_conf);
4120          ap_destroy_pool(pchild);
4121        }
```

```
4122        chdir_for_gprof();
4123        exit(code);
4124    }
4125
4126    #if defined(USE_FCNTL_SERIALIZED_ACCEPT) ||
4127        defined(USE_FLOCK_SERIALIZED_ACCEPT)
4128    static void expand_lock_fname(pool *p)
4129    {
4130        /* XXXX possibly bogus cast */
4131        ap_lock_fname = ap_psprintf(p, "%s.%lu",
4132         ap_server_root_relative(p, ap_lock_fname),
4133            (unsigned long)getpid());
4134    }
4135    #endif
4136
4137    #if defined (USE_USLOCK_SERIALIZED_ACCEPT)
4138
4139    #include <ulocks.h>
4140
4141    static ulock_t uslock = NULL;
4142
4143    #define accept_mutex_child_init(x)
4144
4145    static void accept_mutex_init(pool *p)
4146    {
4147        ptrdiff_t old;
4148        usptr_t *us;
4149
4150        /* default is 8, allocate enough for all the
4151         * children plus the parent */
4152        if ((old = usconfig(CONF_INITUSERS,
4153             HARD_SERVER_LIMIT + 1)) == -1) {
4154          perror("usconfig(CONF_INITUSERS)");
4155          exit(-1);
4156        }
4157
4158        if ((old = usconfig(CONF_LOCKTYPE,
4159             US_NODEBUG)) == -1) {
4160          perror("usconfig(CONF_LOCKTYPE)");
4161          exit(-1);
4162        }
4163        if ((old = usconfig(CONF_ARENATYPE,
4164             US_SHAREDONLY)) == -1) {
4165          perror("usconfig(CONF_ARENATYPE)");
4166          exit(-1);
4167        }
4168        if ((us = usinit("/dev/zero")) == NULL) {
```

```
4170          perror("usinit");
4171          exit(-1);
4172        }
4173
4174        if ((uslock = usnewlock(us)) == NULL) {
4175          perror("usnewlock");
4176          exit(-1);
4177        }
4178    }
4179
4180    static void accept_mutex_on(void)
4181    {
4182        switch (ussetlock(uslock)) {
4183        case 1:
4184          /* got lock */
4185          break;
4186        case 0:
4187          fprintf(stderr, "didn't get lock\n");
4188          clean_child_exit(APEXIT_CHILDFATAL);
4189        case -1:
4190          perror("ussetlock");
4191          clean_child_exit(APEXIT_CHILDFATAL);
4192        }
4193    }
4194
4195    static void accept_mutex_off(void)
4196    {
4197        if (usunsetlock(uslock) == -1) {
4198          perror("usunsetlock");
4199          clean_child_exit(APEXIT_CHILDFATAL);
4200        }
4201    }
4202
4203    #elif defined (USE_PTHREAD_SERIALIZED_ACCEPT)
4204
4205    /* This code probably only works on Solaris ...
4206     * but it works really fast on Solaris.  Note that
4207     * pthread mutexes are *NOT* released when a task
4208     * dies ... the task has to free it itself.  So we
4209     * block signals and try to be nice about
4210     * releasing the mutex.
4211     */
4212
4213    #include <pthread.h>
4214
4215    static pthread_mutex_t *accept_mutex =
4216        (void *)(caddr_t) -1;
4217    static int have_accept_mutex;
```

```
4218   static sigset_t accept_block_mask;
4219   static sigset_t accept_previous_mask;
4220
4221   static void accept_mutex_child_cleanup(void *foo)
4222   {
4223       if (accept_mutex != (void *)(caddr_t)-1
4224         && have_accept_mutex) {
4225         pthread_mutex_unlock(accept_mutex);
4226       }
4227   }
4228
4229   static void accept_mutex_child_init(pool *p)
4230   {
4231       ap_register_cleanup(p, NULL,
4232             accept_mutex_child_cleanup, ap_null_cleanup);
4233   }
4234
4235   static void accept_mutex_cleanup(void *foo)
4236   {
4237       if (accept_mutex != (void *)(caddr_t)-1
4238         && munmap((caddr_t) accept_mutex,
4239             sizeof(*accept_mutex))) {
4240         perror("munmap");
4241       }
4242       accept_mutex = (void *)(caddr_t)-1;
4243   }
4244
4245   static void accept_mutex_init(pool *p)
4246   {
4247       pthread_mutexattr_t mattr;
4248       int fd;
4249
4250       fd = open("/dev/zero", O_RDWR);
4251       if (fd == -1) {
4252         perror("open(/dev/zero)");
4253         exit(APEXIT_INIT);
4254       }
4255       accept_mutex = (pthread_mutex_t *) mmap((caddr_t) 0,
4256             sizeof(*accept_mutex),
4257                     PROT_READ | PROT_WRITE,
4258                     MAP_SHARED, fd, 0);
4259       if (accept_mutex == (void *) (caddr_t) - 1) {
4260         perror("mmap");
4261         exit(APEXIT_INIT);
4262       }
4263       close(fd);
4264       if ((errno = pthread_mutexattr_init(&mattr))) {
4265         perror("pthread_mutexattr_init");
```

```
4266         exit(APEXIT_INIT);
4267       }
4268       if ((errno = pthread_mutexattr_setpshared(&mattr,
4269                         PTHREAD_PROCESS_SHARED))) {
4270         perror("pthread_mutexattr_setpshared");
4271         exit(APEXIT_INIT);
4272       }
4273       if ((errno = pthread_mutex_init(accept_mutex,
4274             &mattr))) {
4275         perror("pthread_mutex_init");
4276         exit(APEXIT_INIT);
4277       }
4278       sigfillset(&accept_block_mask);
4279       sigdelset(&accept_block_mask, SIGHUP);
4280       sigdelset(&accept_block_mask, SIGTERM);
4281       sigdelset(&accept_block_mask, SIGUSR1);
4282       ap_register_cleanup(p, NULL, accept_mutex_cleanup,
4283             ap_null_cleanup);
4284   }
4285
4286   static void accept_mutex_on(void)
4287   {
4288       int err;
4289
4290       if (sigprocmask(SIG_BLOCK, &accept_block_mask,
4291             &accept_previous_mask)) {
4292         perror("sigprocmask(SIG_BLOCK)");
4293         clean_child_exit(APEXIT_CHILDFATAL);
4294       }
4295       if ((err = pthread_mutex_lock(accept_mutex))) {
4296         errno = err;
4297         perror("pthread_mutex_lock");
4298         clean_child_exit(APEXIT_CHILDFATAL);
4299       }
4300       have_accept_mutex = 1;
4301   }
4302
4303   static void accept_mutex_off(void)
4304   {
4305       int err;
4306
4307       if ((err = pthread_mutex_unlock(accept_mutex))) {
4308         errno = err;
4309         perror("pthread_mutex_unlock");
4310         clean_child_exit(APEXIT_CHILDFATAL);
4311       }
4312       /* There is a slight race condition right here...
4313        * if we were to die right now, we'd do another
```

```
4314        * pthread_mutex_unlock.  Now, doing that would let
4315        * another process into the mutex.  pthread mutexes
4316        * are designed to be fast, as such they don't
4317        * have protection for things like testing if the
4318        * thread owning a mutex is actually unlocking it
4319        * (or even any way of testing who owns the mutex).
4320     *
4321        * If we were to unset have_accept_mutex prior to
4322        * releasing the mutex then the race could result
4323        * in the server unable to serve hits.  Doing
4324        * it this way means that the server can continue,
4325        * but an additional child might be in the critical
4326        * section ... at least it's still serving hits.
4327     */
4328        have_accept_mutex = 0;
4329        if (sigprocmask(SIG_SETMASK, &accept_previous_mask,
4330            NULL)) {
4331        perror("sigprocmask(SIG_SETMASK)");
4332        clean_child_exit(1);
4333        }
4334    }
4335
4336    #elif defined (USE_SYSVSEM_SERIALIZED_ACCEPT)
4337
4338    #include <sys/types.h>
4339    #include <sys/ipc.h>
4340    #include <sys/sem.h>
4341
4342    #ifdef NEED_UNION_SEMUN
4343    /* it makes no sense, but this isn't
4344     * defined on solaris */
4345    union semun {
4346        long val;
4347        struct semid_ds *buf;
4348        ushort *array;
4349    };
4350
4351    #endif
4352
4353    static int sem_id = -1;
4354    static struct sembuf op_on;
4355    static struct sembuf op_off;
4356
4357    /* We get a random semaphore ... the lame sysv
4358     * semaphore interface means we have to be sure
4359     * to clean this up or else we'll leak
4360     * semaphores.
4361     */
```

```
4362    static void accept_mutex_cleanup(void *foo)
4363    {
4364        union semun ick;
4365
4366        if (sem_id < 0)
4367        return;
4368        /* this is ignored anyhow */
4369        ick.val = 0;
4370        semctl(sem_id, 0, IPC_RMID, ick);
4371    }
4372
4373    #define accept_mutex_child_init(x)
4374
4375    static void accept_mutex_init(pool *p)
4376    {
4377        union semun ick;
4378        struct semid_ds buf;
4379
4380        /* acquire the semaphore */
4381        sem_id = semget(IPC_PRIVATE, 1, IPC_CREAT
4382            | 0600);
4383        if (sem_id < 0) {
4384        perror("semget");
4385        exit(APEXIT_INIT);
4386        }
4387        ick.val = 1;
4388        if (semctl(sem_id, 0, SETVAL, ick) < 0) {
4389        perror("semctl(SETVAL)");
4390        exit(APEXIT_INIT);
4391        }
4392        if (!getuid()) {
4393        /* restrict it to use only by the appropriate
4394         * user_id ... not that this stops CGIs from
4395         * acquiring it and dinking around with it.
4396         */
4397        buf.sem_perm.uid = ap_user_id;
4398        buf.sem_perm.gid = ap_group_id;
4399        buf.sem_perm.mode = 0600;
4400        ick.buf = &buf;
4401        if (semctl(sem_id, 0, IPC_SET, ick) < 0) {
4402            perror("semctl(IPC_SET)");
4403            exit(APEXIT_INIT);
4404        }
4405        }
4406        ap_register_cleanup(p, NULL, accept_mutex_cleanup,
4407            ap_null_cleanup);
4408
4409        /* pre-initialize these */
```

```
4410        op_on.sem_num = 0;
4411        op_on.sem_op = -1;
4412        op_on.sem_flg = SEM_UNDO;
4413        op_off.sem_num = 0;
4414        op_off.sem_op = 1;
4415        op_off.sem_flg = SEM_UNDO;
4416    }
4417
4418    static void accept_mutex_on(void)
4419    {
4420        if (semop(sem_id, &op_on, 1) < 0) {
4421         perror("accept_mutex_on");
4422         clean_child_exit(APEXIT_CHILDFATAL);
4423        }
4424    }
4425
4426    static void accept_mutex_off(void)
4427    {
4428        if (semop(sem_id, &op_off, 1) < 0) {
4429         perror("accept_mutex_off");
4430         clean_child_exit(APEXIT_CHILDFATAL);
4431        }
4432    }
4433
4434    #elif defined(USE_FCNTL_SERIALIZED_ACCEPT)
4435    static struct flock lock_it;
4436    static struct flock unlock_it;
4437
4438    static int lock_fd = -1;
4439
4440    #define accept_mutex_child_init(x)
4441
4442    /*
4443     * Initialize mutex lock.
4444     * Must be safe to call this on a restart.
4445     */
4446    static void accept_mutex_init(pool *p)
4447    {
4448
4449        lock_it.l_whence = SEEK_SET;
4450        /* from current point */
4451        lock_it.l_start = 0;
4452        /* -"- */
4453        lock_it.l_len = 0;
4454        /* until end of file */
4455        lock_it.l_type = F_WRLCK;
4456        /* set exclusive/write lock */
4457        lock_it.l_pid = 0;
4458        /* pid not actually interesting */
4459        unlock_it.l_whence = SEEK_SET;
4460        /* from current point */
4461        unlock_it.l_start = 0;
4462        /* -"- */
4463        unlock_it.l_len = 0;
4464        /* until end of file */
4465        unlock_it.l_type = F_UNLCK;
4466        /* set exclusive/write lock */
4467        unlock_it.l_pid = 0;
4468        /* pid not actually interesting */
4469
4470        expand_lock_fname(p);
4471        lock_fd = ap_popenf(p, ap_lock_fname,
4472            O_CREAT | O_WRONLY | O_EXCL, 0644);
4473        if (lock_fd == -1) {
4474         perror("open");
4475         fprintf(stderr, "Cannot open lock file:
4476            %s\n", ap_lock_fname);
4477         exit(APEXIT_INIT);
4478        }
4479        unlink(ap_lock_fname);
4480    }
4481
4482    static void accept_mutex_on(void)
4483    {
4484        int ret;
4485
4486        while ((ret = fcntl(lock_fd, F_SETLKW,
4487            &lock_it)) < 0 && errno == EINTR) {
4488         /* nop */
4489        }
4490
4491        if (ret < 0) {
4492         ap_log_error(APLOG_MARK, APLOG_EMERG, server_conf,
4493            "fcntl: F_SETLKW: Error getting accept
4494                lock, exiting!  "
4495            "Perhaps you need to use the LockFile
4496                directive to place "
4497            "your lock file on a local disk!");
4498         clean_child_exit(APEXIT_CHILDFATAL);
4499        }
4500    }
4501
4502    static void accept_mutex_off(void)
4503    {
4504        int ret;
4505
```

```
4506        while ((ret = fcntl(lock_fd, F_SETLKW, &unlock_it))
4507              < 0 && errno == EINTR) {
4508        /* nop */
4509        }
4510        if (ret < 0) {
4511        ap_log_error(APLOG_MARK, APLOG_EMERG, server_conf,
4512                    "fcntl: F_SETLKW: Error freeing accept
4513                            lock, exiting! "
4514                    "Perhaps you need to use the LockFile
4515                            directive to place "
4516                    "your lock file on a local disk!");
4517        clean_child_exit(APEXIT_CHILDFATAL);
4518        }
4519    }
4520
4521    #elif defined(USE_FLOCK_SERIALIZED_ACCEPT)
4522
4523    static int lock_fd = -1;
4524
4525    static void accept_mutex_cleanup(void *foo)
4526    {
4527        unlink(ap_lock_fname);
4528    }
4529
4530    /*
4531     * Initialize mutex lock.
4532     * Done by each child at it's birth
4533     */
4534    static void accept_mutex_child_init(pool *p)
4535    {
4536
4537        lock_fd = ap_popenf(p, ap_lock_fname, O_WRONLY,
4538                0600);
4539        if (lock_fd == -1) {
4540        ap_log_error(APLOG_MARK, APLOG_EMERG, server_conf,
4541                    "Child cannot open lock file: %s",
4542                        ap_lock_fname);
4543        clean_child_exit(APEXIT_CHILDINIT);
4544        }
4545    }
4546
4547    /*
4548     * Initialize mutex lock.
4549     * Must be safe to call this on a restart.
4550     */
4551    static void accept_mutex_init(pool *p)
4552    {
4553        expand_lock_fname(p);
4554        unlink(ap_lock_fname);
4555        lock_fd = ap_popenf(p, ap_lock_fname,
4556                O_CREAT | O_WRONLY | O_EXCL, 0600);
4557        if (lock_fd == -1) {
4558        ap_log_error(APLOG_MARK, APLOG_EMERG, server_conf,
4559                    "Parent cannot open lock file: %s",
4560                        ap_lock_fname);
4561        exit(APEXIT_INIT);
4562        }
4563        ap_register_cleanup(p, NULL, accept_mutex_cleanup,
4564                ap_null_cleanup);
4565    }
4566
4567    static void accept_mutex_on(void)
4568    {
4569        int ret;
4570
4571        while ((ret = flock(lock_fd, LOCK_EX))
4572              < 0 && errno == EINTR)
4573        continue;
4574
4575        if (ret < 0) {
4576        ap_log_error(APLOG_MARK, APLOG_EMERG, server_conf,
4577                    "flock: LOCK_EX: Error getting accept
4578                        lock. Exiting!");
4579        clean_child_exit(APEXIT_CHILDFATAL);
4580        }
4581    }
4582
4583    static void accept_mutex_off(void)
4584    {
4585        if (flock(lock_fd, LOCK_UN) < 0) {
4586        ap_log_error(APLOG_MARK, APLOG_EMERG, server_conf,
4587                    "flock: LOCK_UN: Error freeing accept lock.
4588                        Exiting!");
4589        clean_child_exit(APEXIT_CHILDFATAL);
4590        }
4591    }
4592
4593    #elif defined(USE_OS2SEM_SERIALIZED_ACCEPT)
4594
4595    static HMTX lock_sem = -1;
4596
4597    static void accept_mutex_cleanup(void *foo)
4598    {
4599        DosReleaseMutexSem(lock_sem);
4600        DosCloseMutexSem(lock_sem);
4601    }
```

```
4602    /*
4603     * Initialize mutex lock.
4604     * Done by each child at it's birth
4605     */
4606
4607    static void accept_mutex_child_init(pool *p)
4608    {
4609        int rc = DosOpenMutexSem(NULL, &lock_sem);
4610
4611        if (rc != 0) {
4612        ap_log_error(APLOG_MARK, APLOG_NOERRNO|APLOG_EMERG,
4613            server_conf,
4614                "Child cannot open lock semaphore,
4615                    rc=%d", rc);
4616        clean_child_exit(APEXIT_CHILDINIT);
4617        }
4618    }
4619
4620    /*
4621     * Initialize mutex lock.
4622     * Must be safe to call this on a restart.
4623     */
4624    static void accept_mutex_init(pool *p)
4625    {
4626        int rc = DosCreateMutexSem(NULL, &lock_sem,
4627            DC_SEM_SHARED, FALSE);
4628
4629        if (rc != 0) {
4630        ap_log_error(APLOG_MARK, APLOG_NOERRNO|APLOG_EMERG,
4631            server_conf,
4632                "Parent cannot create lock semaphore,
4633                    rc=%d", rc);
4634        exit(APEXIT_INIT);
4635        }
4636
4637        ap_register_cleanup(p, NULL, accept_mutex_cleanup,
4638            ap_null_cleanup);
4639    }
4640
4641    static void accept_mutex_on(void)
4642    {
4643        int rc = DosRequestMutexSem(lock_sem,
4644            SEM_INDEFINITE_WAIT);
4645
4646        if (rc != 0) {
4647        ap_log_error(APLOG_MARK, APLOG_NOERRNO|APLOG_EMERG,
4648            server_conf,
4649                "OS2SEM: Error %d getting accept lock.
4650                    Exiting!", rc);
4651        clean_child_exit(APEXIT_CHILDFATAL);
4652        }
4653    }
4654
4655    static void accept_mutex_off(void)
4656    {
4657        int rc = DosReleaseMutexSem(lock_sem);
4658
4659        if (rc != 0) {
4660        ap_log_error(APLOG_MARK, APLOG_NOERRNO|APLOG_EMERG,
4661            server_conf,
4662                "OS2SEM: Error %d freeing accept lock.
4663                    Exiting!", rc);
4664        clean_child_exit(APEXIT_CHILDFATAL);
4665        }
4666    }
4667
4668    #else
4669    /* Default -- no serialization.  Other methods *could*
4670     * go here,as #elifs...
4671     */
4672    #if !defined(MULTITHREAD)
4673    /* Multithreaded systems don't complete between
4674     * processes for the sockets. */
4675    #define NO_SERIALIZED_ACCEPT
4676    #define accept_mutex_child_init(x)
4677    #define accept_mutex_init(x)
4678    #define accept_mutex_on()
4679    #define accept_mutex_off()
4680    #endif
4681    #endif
4682
4683    /* On some architectures it's safe to do unserialized
4684     * accept()s in the single Listen case.  But it's
4685     * never safe to do it in the case where there's
4686     * multiple Listen statements.  Define
4687     * SINGLE_LISTEN_UNSERIALIZED_ACCEPT
4688     * when it's safe in the single Listen case.
4689     */
4690    #ifdef SINGLE_LISTEN_UNSERIALIZED_ACCEPT
4691    #define SAFE_ACCEPT(stmt) do {if(ap_listeners->next !=
4692        ap_listeners) {stmt;}} while(0)
4693    #else
4694    #define SAFE_ACCEPT(stmt) do {stmt;} while(0)
4695    #endif
4696
4697    static void usage(char *bin)
```

```
4698   {
4699       char pad[MAX_STRING_LEN];
4700       unsigned i;
4701
4702       for (i = 0; i < strlen(bin); i++)
4703        pad[i] = ' ';
4704       pad[i] = '\0';
4705   #ifdef SHARED_CORE
4706       fprintf(stderr, "Usage: %s [-R directory]
4707            [-d directory] [-f file]\n", bin);
4708   #else
4709       fprintf(stderr, "Usage: %s [-d directory]
4710             [-f file]\n", bin);
4711   #endif
4712       fprintf(stderr, "       %s [-C \"directive\"]
4713            [-c \"directive\"]\n", pad);
4714       fprintf(stderr, "
4715            %s [-v] [-V] [-h] [-l] [-L] [-S] [-t]\n", pad);
4716       fprintf(stderr, "Options:\n");
4717   #ifdef SHARED_CORE
4718       fprintf(stderr, "  -R directory     :
4719            specify an alternate location for shared
4720            object files\n");
4721   #endif
4722       fprintf(stderr, "  -D name          :
4723            define a name for use in <IfDefine name>
4724            directives\n");
4725       fprintf(stderr, "  -d directory     :
4726            specify an alternate initial ServerRoot\n");
4727       fprintf(stderr, "  -f file          :
4728            specify an alternate ServerConfigFile\n");
4729       fprintf(stderr, "  -C \"directive\"   :
4730            process directive before reading config files\n");
4731       fprintf(stderr, "  -c \"directive\"   :
4732            process directive after  reading config files\n");
4733       fprintf(stderr, "  -v               :
4734            show version number\n");
4735       fprintf(stderr, "  -V               :
4736            show compile settings\n");
4737       fprintf(stderr, "  -h               :
4738            list available command line options
4739            (this page)\n");
4740       fprintf(stderr, "  -l               :
4741            list compiled-in modules\n");
4742       fprintf(stderr, "  -L               :
4743            list available configuration directives\n");
4744       fprintf(stderr, "  -S               :
4745            show parsed settings (currently only
4746            vhost settings)\n");
4747       fprintf(stderr, "  -t               :
4748            run syntax test for configuration files
4749            only\n");
4750   #ifdef WIN32
4751       fprintf(stderr, "  -k shutdown      :
4752            tell running Apache to shutdown\n");
4753       fprintf(stderr, "  -k restart       : tell
4754            running Apache to do a graceful restart\n");
4755   #endif
4756       exit(1);
4757   }
4758
4759   /*********************************************************
4760    *
4761    * Timeout handling.  DISTINCTLY not thread-safe, but
4762    * all this stuff has to change for threads
4763    * anyway.  Note that this code allows only
4764    * one timeout in progress at a time...
4765    */
4766
4767   static APACHE_TLS conn_rec *volatile current_conn;
4768   static APACHE_TLS request_rec *volatile timeout_req;
4769   static APACHE_TLS const char
4770        *volatile timeout_name = NULL;
4771   static APACHE_TLS int volatile alarms_blocked = 0;
4772   static APACHE_TLS int volatile alarm_pending = 0;
4773
4774   static void timeout(int sig)
4775   {
4776       void *dirconf;
4777
4778       if (alarms_blocked) {
4779        alarm_pending = 1;
4780        return;
4781       }
4782       if (exit_after_unblock) {
4783        clean_child_exit(0);
4784       }
4785
4786       if (!current_conn) {
4787        ap_longjmp(jmpbuffer, 1);
4788       }
4789
4790       if (timeout_req != NULL)
4791        dirconf = timeout_req->per_dir_config;
4792       else
4793        dirconf = current_conn->server->lookup_defaults;
```

```
4794        if (!current_conn->keptalive) {
4795        ap_log_error(APLOG_MARK, APLOG_NOERRNO|APLOG_INFO,
4796                current_conn->server,
4797                    "[client %s] %s timed out",
4798                current_conn->remote_ip,
4799                timeout_name ? timeout_name : "request");
4800        }
4801
4802        if (timeout_req) {
4803        /* Someone has asked for this transaction to
4804         * just be aborted if it times out...
4805    */
4806
4807        request_rec *log_req = timeout_req;
4808        request_rec *save_req = timeout_req;
4809
4810        /* avoid looping... if ap_log_transaction
4811         * started another timer (say via rfc1413.c)
4812         * we could loop...
4813         */
4814        timeout_req = NULL;
4815
4816        while (log_req->main || log_req->prev) {
4817            /* Get back to original request... */
4818            if (log_req->main)
4819             log_req = log_req->main;
4820            else
4821             log_req = log_req->prev;
4822        }
4823
4824        if (!current_conn->keptalive)
4825            ap_log_transaction(log_req);
4826
4827        ap_bsetflag(save_req->connection->client,
4828            B_EOUT, 1);
4829        ap_bclose(save_req->connection->client);
4830
4831        if (!ap_standalone)
4832            exit(0);
4833
4834        ap_longjmp(jmpbuffer, 1);
4835        }
4836        else {                  /* abort the connection */
4837        ap_bsetflag(current_conn->client, B_EOUT, 1);
4838        ap_bclose(current_conn->client);
4839        current_conn->aborted = 1;
4840        }
4841    }

4842
4843    #ifndef TPF
4844    /*
4845     * These two called from alloc.c to protect its
4846     * critical sections... Note that they can nest (as
4847     * when destroying the sub_pools of a pool which is
4848     * itself being cleared); we have to support that here.
4849     */
4850
4851    API_EXPORT(void) ap_block_alarms(void)
4852    {
4853        ++alarms_blocked;
4854    }
4855
4856    API_EXPORT(void) ap_unblock_alarms(void)
4857    {
4858        --alarms_blocked;
4859        if (alarms_blocked == 0) {
4860         if (exit_after_unblock) {
4861            /* We have a couple race conditions to deal
4862             * with here, we can't allow a timeout that
4863             * comes in this small interval to allow
4864             * the child to jump back to the main loop.
4865             * Instead we block alarms again, and then
4866             * note that exit_after_unblock is being dealt
4867             * with.  We choose this way to solve this
4868             * so that the common path through
4869             * unblock_alarms() is really short.
4870             */
4871            ++alarms_blocked;
4872            exit_after_unblock = 0;
4873            clean_child_exit(0);
4874         }
4875         if (alarm_pending) {
4876            alarm_pending = 0;
4877            timeout(0);
4878         }
4879        }
4880    }
4881    #endif /* TPF */
4882
4883    static APACHE_TLS void (*volatile alarm_fn)
4884        (int) = NULL;
4885    #ifdef WIN32
4886    static APACHE_TLS unsigned int alarm_expiry_time = 0;
4887    #endif /* WIN32 */
4888
4889    #ifndef WIN32
```

```
4890    static void alrm_handler(int sig)
4891    {
4892        if (alarm_fn) {
4893         (*alarm_fn) (sig);
4894        }
4895    }
4896    #endif
4897
4898    unsigned int
4899        ap_set_callback_and_alarm(void (*fn) (int), int x)
4900    {
4901        unsigned int old;
4902
4903    #ifdef WIN32
4904        old = alarm_expiry_time;
4905        if (old)
4906         old -= time(0);
4907        if (x == 0) {
4908         alarm_fn = NULL;
4909         alarm_expiry_time = 0;
4910        }
4911        else {
4912         alarm_fn = fn;
4913         alarm_expiry_time = time(NULL) + x;
4914        }
4915    #else
4916        if (alarm_fn && x && fn != alarm_fn) {
4917         ap_log_error(APLOG_MARK,
4918             APLOG_NOERRNO|APLOG_DEBUG, NULL,
4919             "ap_set_callback_and_alarm:
4920                 possible nested timer!");
4921        }
4922        alarm_fn = fn;
4923    #ifndef OPTIMIZE_TIMEOUTS
4924        old = alarm(x);
4925    #else
4926        if (child_timeouts) {
4927         old = alarm(x);
4928        }
4929        else {
4930         /* Just note the timeout in our scoreboard, no
4931          * need to call the system. We also note that
4932          * the virtual time has gone forward.
4933          */
4934         old = ap_scoreboard_image->
4935             servers[my_child_num].timeout_len;
4936         ap_scoreboard_image->
4937             servers[my_child_num].timeout_len = x;
4938         ++ap_scoreboard_image->
4939             servers[my_child_num].cur_vtime;
4940        }
4941    #endif
4942    #endif
4943        return (old);
4944    }
4945
4946
4947    #ifdef WIN32
4948    API_EXPORT(int) ap_check_alarm(void)
4949    {
4950        if (alarm_expiry_time) {
4951         unsigned int t;
4952
4953         t = time(NULL);
4954         if (t >= alarm_expiry_time) {
4955             alarm_expiry_time = 0;
4956             (*alarm_fn) (0);
4957             return (-1);
4958         }
4959         else {
4960             return (alarm_expiry_time - t);
4961         }
4962        }
4963        else
4964         return (0);
4965    }
4966    #endif /* WIN32 */
4967
4968
4969
4970    /* reset_timeout (request_rec *) resets the timeout
4971     * in effect,as long as it hasn't expired already.
4972     */
4973
4974    API_EXPORT(void) ap_reset_timeout(request_rec *r)
4975    {
4976        int i;
4977
4978        if (timeout_name) {
4979         /* timeout has been set */
4980         i = ap_set_callback_and_alarm(alarm_fn,
4981             r->server->timeout);
4982         if (i == 0)
4983         /* timeout already expired, so set it back to 0 */
4984             ap_set_callback_and_alarm(alarm_fn, 0);
4985
```

```
4986          }
4987      }
4988
4989
4990
4991
4992      void ap_keepalive_timeout(char *name, request_rec *r)
4993      {
4994          unsigned int to;
4995
4996          timeout_req = r;
4997          timeout_name = name;
4998
4999          if (r->connection->keptalive)
5000           to = r->server->keep_alive_timeout;
5001          else
5002           to = r->server->timeout;
5003          ap_set_callback_and_alarm(timeout, to);
5004
5005      }
5006
5007      API_EXPORT(void) ap_hard_timeout(char *name,
5008           request_rec *r)
5009      {
5010          timeout_req = r;
5011          timeout_name = name;
5012
5013          ap_set_callback_and_alarm(timeout,
5014              r->server->timeout);
5015
5016      }
5017
5018      API_EXPORT(void) ap_soft_timeout(char *name,
5019           request_rec *r)
5020      {
5021          timeout_name = name;
5022
5023          ap_set_callback_and_alarm(timeout,
5024              r->server->timeout);
5025
5026      }
5027
5028      API_EXPORT(void) ap_kill_timeout(request_rec *dummy)
5029      {
5030          ap_set_callback_and_alarm(NULL, 0);
5031          timeout_req = NULL;
5032          timeout_name = NULL;
5033      }
```

```
5034
5035
5036      /*
5037       * More machine-dependent networking gooo...
5038       * on some systems, you've got to be *really*
5039       * sure that all the packets are acknowledged
5040       * before closing the connection, since the
5041       * client will not be able to see the last response
5042       * if their TCP buffer is flushed by a RST packet from
5043       * us, which is what the server's TCP stack will send
5044       * if it receives any request data after closing the
5045       * connection.
5046
5047       *
5048       * In an ideal world, this function would be
5049       * accomplished by simply setting the socket option
5050       * SO_LINGER and handling it within the server's TCP
5051       * stack while the process continues on to the next
5052       * request. Unfortunately, it seems that most
5053       * (if not all) operating systems block the server
5054       * process on close() when SO_LINGER is used. For
5055       * those that don't, see USE_SO_LINGER below.  For the
5056       * rest,we have created a home-brew lingering_close.
5057       *
5058       * Many operating systems tend to block, puke, or
5059       * otherwise mishandle calls to shutdown only
5060       * half of the connection.  You should define
5061       * NO_LINGCLOSE in ap_config.h if such is the
5062       * case for your system.
5063       */
5064      #ifndef MAX_SECS_TO_LINGER
5065      #define MAX_SECS_TO_LINGER 30
5066      #endif
5067
5068      #ifdef USE_SO_LINGER
5069      #define NO_LINGCLOSE
5070      /* The two lingering options are exclusive */
5071
5072      static void sock_enable_linger(int s)
5073      {
5074          struct linger li;
5075
5076          li.l_onoff = 1;
5077          li.l_linger = MAX_SECS_TO_LINGER;
5078
5079          if (setsockopt(s, SOL_SOCKET, SO_LINGER,
5080              (char *) &li, sizeof(struct linger)) < 0) {
5081          ap_log_error(APLOG_MARK,
```

```
5082                APLOG_WARNING, server_conf,
5083                    "setsockopt: (SO_LINGER)");
5084        /* not a fatal error */
5085        }
5086    }
5087
5088    #else
5089    #define sock_enable_linger(s)     /* NOOP */
5090    #endif /* USE_SO_LINGER */
5091
5092    #ifndef NO_LINGCLOSE
5093
5094    /* Special version of timeout for lingering_close */
5095
5096    static void lingerout(int sig)
5097    {
5098        if (alarms_blocked) {
5099            alarm_pending = 1;
5100            return;
5101        }
5102
5103        if (!current_conn) {
5104            ap_longjmp(jmpbuffer, 1);
5105        }
5106        ap_bsetflag(current_conn->client, B_EOUT, 1);
5107        current_conn->aborted = 1;
5108    }
5109
5110    static void linger_timeout(void)
5111    {
5112        timeout_name = "lingering close";
5113
5114        ap_set_callback_and_alarm(lingerout,
5115            MAX_SECS_TO_LINGER);
5116    }
5117
5118    /* Since many clients will abort a connection
5119     * instead of closing it, attempting to log an error
5120     * message from this routine will only confuse the
5121     * webmaster. There doesn't seem to be any portable
5122     * way to distinguish between a dropped connection
5123     * and something that might be worth logging
5124     */
5125    static void lingering_close(request_rec *r)
5126    {
5127        char dummybuf[512];
5128        struct timeval tv;
5129        fd_set lfds;

5130        int select_rv;
5131        int lsd;
5132
5133        /* Prevent a slow-drip client from holding us
5134         * here indefinitely */
5135
5136        linger_timeout();
5137
5138        /* Send any leftover data to the client,
5139         * but never try to again */
5140
5141        if (ap_bflush(r->connection->client) == -1) {
5142            ap_kill_timeout(r);
5143            ap_bclose(r->connection->client);
5144            return;
5145        }
5146        ap_bsetflag(r->connection->client, B_EOUT, 1);
5147
5148        /* Close our half of the connection -- send
5149         * the client a FIN */
5150
5151        lsd = r->connection->client->fd;
5152
5153        if ((shutdown(lsd,
5154            1) != 0) || r->connection->aborted) {
5155            ap_kill_timeout(r);
5156            ap_bclose(r->connection->client);
5157            return;
5158        }
5159
5160        /* Set up to wait for readable data on socket... */
5161
5162        FD_ZERO(&lfds);
5163
5164        /* Wait for readable data or error condition
5165         * on socket; slurp up any data that
5166         * arrives...  We exit when we go for an
5167         * interval of tv length without getting any more
5168         * data, get an error from select(), get an error
5169         * or EOF on a read, or the timer expires.
5170         */
5171
5172        do {
5173            /* We use a 2 second timeout because current
5174             * (Feb 97) browsers fail to close a connection
5175             * after the server closes it.  Thus, to avoid
5176             * keeping the child busy, we are only lingering
5177             * long enough for a client that is actively
```

```
5178              * sending data on a connection. This should
5179              * be sufficient unless the connection is massively
5180              * losing packets, in which case we might have
5181              * missed the RST anyway. These parameters are reset
5182              * on each pass, since they might be changed by
5183              * select.
5184              */
5185             FD_SET(lsd, &lfds);
5186             tv.tv_sec = 2;
5187             tv.tv_usec = 0;
5188
5189             select_rv = ap_select(lsd + 1, &lfds, NULL,
5190                 NULL, &tv);
5191
5192         } while ((select_rv > 0) &&
5193                 (read(lsd, dummybuf,
5194                     sizeof dummybuf) > 0));
5195
5196         /* Should now have seen final ack.  Safe to finally
5197          * kill socket */
5198
5199         ap_bclose(r->connection->client);
5200
5201         ap_kill_timeout(r);
5202     }
5203 #endif /* ndef NO_LINGCLOSE */
5204
5205 /*****************************************************
5206  * dealing with other children
5207  */
5208
5209 #ifndef NO_OTHER_CHILD
5210 API_EXPORT(void) ap_register_other_child(int pid,
5211                 void (*maintenance) (int reason,
5212                     void *, ap_wait_t status),
5213                 void *data, int write_fd)
5214 {
5215     other_child_rec *ocr;
5216
5217     ocr = ap_palloc(pconf, sizeof(*ocr));
5218     ocr->pid = pid;
5219     ocr->maintenance = maintenance;
5220     ocr->data = data;
5221     ocr->write_fd = write_fd;
5222     ocr->next = other_children;
5223     other_children = ocr;
5224 }
5225
5226 /* note that since this can be called by a maintenance
5227  * function while we're scanning the other_children
5228  * list, all scanners should protect themself by
5229  * loading ocr->next before calling any maintenance
5230  * function.
5231  */
5232 API_EXPORT(void) ap_unregister_other_child(void *data)
5233 {
5234     other_child_rec **pocr, *nocr;
5235
5236     for (pocr = &other_children; *pocr; pocr =
5237             &(*pocr)->next) {
5238         if ((*pocr)->data == data) {
5239             nocr = (*pocr)->next;
5240             (*(*pocr)->maintenance) (OC_REASON_UNREGISTER,
5241                 (*pocr)->data, -1);
5242             *pocr = nocr;
5243             /* XXX: um, well we've just wasted some space
5244              * in pconf ? */
5245             return;
5246         }
5247     }
5248 }
5249
5250 /* test to ensure that the write_fds are all still
5251  * writable, otherwise
5252  * invoke the maintenance functions as appropriate */
5253 static void probe_writable_fds(void)
5254 {
5255     fd_set writable_fds;
5256     int fd_max;
5257     other_child_rec *ocr, *nocr;
5258     struct timeval tv;
5259     int rc;
5260
5261     if (other_children == NULL)
5262         return;
5263
5264     fd_max = 0;
5265     FD_ZERO(&writable_fds);
5266     do {
5267         for (ocr = other_children; ocr; ocr = ocr->next) {
5268             if (ocr->write_fd == -1)
5269                 continue;
5270             FD_SET(ocr->write_fd, &writable_fds);
5271             if (ocr->write_fd > fd_max) {
5272                 fd_max = ocr->write_fd;
5273             }
```

```
5274          }
5275          if (fd_max == 0)
5276              return;
5277
5278          tv.tv_sec = 0;
5279          tv.tv_usec = 0;
5280          rc = ap_select(fd_max + 1, NULL, &writable_fds,
5281              NULL, &tv);
5282      } while (rc == -1 && errno == EINTR);
5283
5284      if (rc == -1) {
5285          /* XXX: uhh this could be really bad, we could
5286           * have a bad file descriptor due to a bug in
5287           * one of the maintenance routines */
5288          ap_log_unixerr("probe_writable_fds", "select",
5289                  "could not probe writable fds",
5290                      server_conf);
5291          return;
5292      }
5293      if (rc == 0)
5294          return;
5295
5296      for (ocr = other_children; ocr; ocr = nocr) {
5297          nocr = ocr->next;
5298          if (ocr->write_fd == -1)
5299              continue;
5300          if (FD_ISSET(ocr->write_fd, &writable_fds))
5301              continue;
5302          (*ocr->maintenance) (OC_REASON_UNWRITABLE,
5303              ocr->data, -1);
5304      }
5305
5306  }
5307
5308  /* possibly reap an other_child, return 0 if
5309   * yes, -1 if not */
5310  static int reap_other_child(int pid, ap_wait_t status)
5311  {
5312      other_child_rec *ocr, *nocr;
5313
5314      for (ocr = other_children; ocr; ocr = nocr) {
5315          nocr = ocr->next;
5316          if (ocr->pid != pid)
5317              continue;
5318          ocr->pid = -1;
5319          (*ocr->maintenance) (OC_REASON_DEATH, ocr->data,
5320              status);
5321          return 0;
5322      }
5323      return -1;
5324  }
5325  #endif
5326
5327  /**********************************************************
5328   *
5329   * Dealing with the scoreboard... a lot of these
5330   * variables are global only to avoid getting
5331   * clobbered by the longjmp() that happens when
5332   * a hard timeout expires...
5333   *
5334   * We begin with routines which deal with the file
5335   * itself...
5336   */
5337
5338  #ifdef MULTITHREAD
5339  /*
5340   * In the multithreaded mode, have multiple threads -
5341   * not multiple processes that need to talk to each
5342   * other. Just use a simplemalloc. But let the
5343   * routines that follow, think that you have
5344   * shared memory (so they use memcpy etc.)
5345   */
5346
5347  static void reinit_scoreboard(pool *p)
5348  {
5349      ap_assert(!ap_scoreboard_image);
5350      ap_scoreboard_image = (scoreboard *)
5351          malloc(SCOREBOARD_SIZE);
5352      if (ap_scoreboard_image == NULL) {
5353          fprintf(stderr, "Ouch!  Out of memory reiniting
5354              scoreboard!\n");
5355      }
5356      memset(ap_scoreboard_image, 0, SCOREBOARD_SIZE);
5357  }
5358
5359  void cleanup_scoreboard(void)
5360  {
5361      ap_assert(ap_scoreboard_image);
5362      free(ap_scoreboard_image);
5363      ap_scoreboard_image = NULL;
5364  }
5365
5366  API_EXPORT(void) ap_sync_scoreboard_image(void)
5367  {
5368  }
5369
```

```
5370
5371    #else /* MULTITHREAD */
5372    #if defined(USE_OS2_SCOREBOARD)
5373
5374    /* The next two routines are used to access shared
5375     * memory under OS/2.  */
5376    /* This requires EMX v09c to be installed.         */
5377
5378    caddr_t create_shared_heap(const char *name,
5379         size_t size)
5380    {
5381        ULONG rc;
5382        void *mem;
5383        Heap_t h;
5384
5385        rc = DosAllocSharedMem(&mem, name, size,
5386                    PAG_COMMIT | PAG_READ | PAG_WRITE);
5387        if (rc != 0)
5388         return NULL;
5389        h = _ucreate(mem, size, !_BLOCK_CLEAN, _HEAP_REGULAR
5390            | _HEAP_SHARED,
5391             NULL, NULL);
5392        if (h == NULL)
5393         DosFreeMem(mem);
5394        return (caddr_t) h;
5395    }
5396
5397    caddr_t get_shared_heap(const char *Name)
5398    {
5399
5400        PVOID BaseAddress;
5401        /* Pointer to the base address of
5402         *    the shared memory object */
5403        ULONG AttributeFlags;
5404        /* Flags describing characteristics
5405         *    of the shared memory object */
5406        APIRET rc;                /* Return code */
5407
5408        /* Request read and write access to */
5409        /*    the shared memory object       */
5410        AttributeFlags = PAG_WRITE | PAG_READ;
5411
5412        rc = DosGetNamedSharedMem(&BaseAddress, Name,
5413            AttributeFlags);
5414
5415        if (rc != 0) {
5416         printf("DosGetNamedSharedMem error:
5417             return code = %ld", rc);
5418         return 0;
5419        }
5420
5421        return BaseAddress;
5422    }
5423
5424    static void setup_shared_mem(pool *p)
5425    {
5426        caddr_t m;
5427
5428        int rc;
5429
5430        m = (caddr_t)
5431            create_shared_heap("\\SHAREMEM\\SCOREBOARD",
5432            SCOREBOARD_SIZE);
5433        if (m == 0) {
5434         fprintf(stderr, "%s: Could not create OS/2
5435            Shared memory pool.\n",
5436            ap_server_argv0);
5437         exit(APEXIT_INIT);
5438        }
5439
5440        rc = _uopen((Heap_t) m);
5441        if (rc != 0) {
5442         fprintf(stderr,
5443            "%s: Could not uopen() newly created OS/2
5444                    Shared memory pool.\n",
5445            ap_server_argv0);
5446        }
5447        ap_scoreboard_image = (scoreboard *) m;
5448        ap_scoreboard_image->global.running_generation = 0;
5449    }
5450
5451    static void reopen_scoreboard(pool *p)
5452    {
5453        caddr_t m;
5454        int rc;
5455
5456        m = (caddr_t)
5457            get_shared_heap("\\SHAREMEM\\SCOREBOARD");
5458        if (m == 0) {
5459         fprintf(stderr, "%s: Could not find existing
5460            OS/2 Shared memory pool.\n",
5461            ap_server_argv0);
5462         exit(APEXIT_INIT);
5463        }
5464
5465        rc = _uopen((Heap_t) m);
```

```
5466          ap_scoreboard_image = (scoreboard *) m;
5467    }
5468
5469    #elif defined(USE_POSIX_SCOREBOARD)
5470    #include <sys/mman.h>
5471    /*
5472     * POSIX 1003.4 style
5473     *
5474     * Note 1:
5475     * As of version 4.23A, shared memory in QNX must
5476     * reside under /dev/shmem, where no subdirectories
5477     * allowed.
5478     *
5479     * POSIX shm_open() and shm_unlink() will take care
5480     * about this issue, but to avoid confusion, I suggest
5481     * to redefine scoreboard file name in httpd.conf to cut
5482     * "logs/" from it. With default setup actual name will
5483     * be "/dev/shmem/logs.apache_status".
5484     *
5485     * If something went wrong and Apache did not unlinked
5486     * this object upon exit, you can remove it manually,
5487     * using "rm -f" command.
5488     *
5489     * Note 2:
5490     * <sys/mman.h> in QNX defines MAP_ANON, but current
5491     * implementation does NOT support BSD style
5492     * anonymous mapping. So, the order of conditional
5493     * compilation is important: this #ifdef section
5494     * must be ABOVE the next one (BSD style).
5495     *
5496     * I tested this stuff and it works fine for me, but
5497     * if it provides trouble for you, just comment
5498     * out USE_MMAP_SCOREBOARD in QNX section
5499     * of ap_config.h
5500     *
5501     * June 5, 1997,
5502     * Igor N. Kovalenko -- infoh@mail.wplus.net
5503     */
5504
5505    static void cleanup_shared_mem(void *d)
5506    {
5507          shm_unlink(ap_scoreboard_fname);
5508    }
5509
5510    static void setup_shared_mem(pool *p)
5511    {
5512          char buf[512];
5513          caddr_t m;
```

```
5514          int fd;
5515
5516          fd = shm_open(ap_scoreboard_fname, O_RDWR | O_CREAT,
5517                S_IRUSR | S_IWUSR);
5518          if (fd == -1) {
5519          ap_snprintf(buf, sizeof(buf), "%s: could not
5520                open(create) scoreboard",
5521                      ap_server_argv0);
5522          perror(buf);
5523          exit(APEXIT_INIT);
5524          }
5525          if (ltrunc(fd, (off_t) SCOREBOARD_SIZE,
5526                SEEK_SET) == -1) {
5527          ap_snprintf(buf, sizeof(buf), "%s: could not
5528                ltrunc scoreboard",
5529                      ap_server_argv0);
5530          perror(buf);
5531          shm_unlink(ap_scoreboard_fname);
5532          exit(APEXIT_INIT);
5533          }
5534          if ((m = (caddr_t) mmap((caddr_t) 0,
5535
5536                      (size_t) SCOREBOARD_SIZE,
5537                            PROT_READ | PROT_WRITE,
5538                      MAP_SHARED, fd, (off_t) 0)) ==
5539                            (caddr_t) - 1) {
5540          ap_snprintf(buf, sizeof(buf), "%s: cannot mmap
5541                scoreboard",
5542                      ap_server_argv0);
5543          perror(buf);
5544          shm_unlink(ap_scoreboard_fname);
5545          exit(APEXIT_INIT);
5546          }
5547          close(fd);
5548          ap_register_cleanup(p, NULL, cleanup_shared_mem,
5549                ap_null_cleanup);
5550          ap_scoreboard_image = (scoreboard *) m;
5551          ap_scoreboard_image->global.running_generation = 0;
5552    }
5553
5554    static void reopen_scoreboard(pool *p)
5555    {
5556    }
5557
5558    #elif defined(USE_MMAP_SCOREBOARD)
5559
5560    static void setup_shared_mem(pool *p)
5561    {
```

```
5562        caddr_t m;
5563
5564    #if defined(MAP_ANON)
5565    /* BSD style */
5566    #ifdef CONVEXOS11
5567        /*
5568         * 9-Aug-97 - Jeff Venters (venters@convex.hp.com)
5569         * ConvexOS maps address space as follows:
5570         *    0x00000000 - 0x7fffffff : Kernel
5571         *    0x80000000 - 0xffffffff : User
5572         * Start mmapped area 1GB above start of text.
5573         *
5574         * Also, the length requires a pointer as the actual
5575         * length is returned (rounded up to a page
5576         * boundary).
5577         */
5578        {
5579        unsigned len = SCOREBOARD_SIZE;
5580
5581        m = mmap((caddr_t) 0xC0000000, &len,
5582                PROT_READ | PROT_WRITE,
5583                    MAP_ANON | MAP_SHARED, NOFD, 0);
5584        }
5585    #elif defined(MAP_TMPFILE)
5586        {
5587        char mfile[] = "/tmp/apache_shmem_XXXX";
5588        int fd = mkstemp(mfile);
5589        if (fd == -1) {
5590            perror("open");
5591            fprintf(stderr, "%s: Could not open %s\n",
5592                    ap_server_argv0, mfile);
5593            exit(APEXIT_INIT);
5594        }
5595        m = mmap((caddr_t) 0, SCOREBOARD_SIZE,
5596                PROT_READ | PROT_WRITE, MAP_SHARED, fd, 0);
5597        if (m == (caddr_t) - 1) {
5598            perror("mmap");
5599            fprintf(stderr, "%s: Could not mmap %s\n",
5600                    ap_server_argv0, mfile);
5601            exit(APEXIT_INIT);
5602        }
5603        close(fd);
5604        unlink(mfile);
5605        }
5606    #else
5607        m = mmap((caddr_t) 0, SCOREBOARD_SIZE,
5608                PROT_READ | PROT_WRITE,
5609                    MAP_ANON | MAP_SHARED, -1, 0);
5610    #endif
5611        if (m == (caddr_t) - 1) {
5612        perror("mmap");
5613        fprintf(stderr, "%s: Could not mmap memory\n",
5614                ap_server_argv0);
5615        exit(APEXIT_INIT);
5616        }
5617    #else
5618    /* Sun style */
5619        int fd;
5620
5621        fd = open("/dev/zero", O_RDWR);
5622        if (fd == -1) {
5623        perror("open");
5624        fprintf(stderr, "%s: Could not open /dev/zero\n",
5625                ap_server_argv0);
5626        exit(APEXIT_INIT);
5627        }
5628        m = mmap((caddr_t) 0, SCOREBOARD_SIZE,
5629                PROT_READ | PROT_WRITE, MAP_SHARED, fd, 0);
5630        if (m == (caddr_t) - 1) {
5631        perror("mmap");
5632        fprintf(stderr, "%s: Could not mmap /dev/zero\n",
5633                ap_server_argv0);
5634        exit(APEXIT_INIT);
5635        }
5636        close(fd);
5637    #endif
5638        ap_scoreboard_image = (scoreboard *) m;
5639        ap_scoreboard_image->global.running_generation = 0;
5640    }
5641
5642    static void reopen_scoreboard(pool *p)
5643    {
5644    }
5645
5646    #elif defined(USE_SHMGET_SCOREBOARD)
5647    static key_t shmkey = IPC_PRIVATE;
5648    static int shmid = -1;
5649
5650    static void setup_shared_mem(pool *p)
5651    {
5652        struct shmid_ds shmbuf;
5653    #ifdef MOVEBREAK
5654        char *obrk;
5655    #endif
5656
5657        if ((shmid = shmget(shmkey, SCOREBOARD_SIZE,
```

```
5658            IPC_CREAT | SHM_R | SHM_W)) == -1) {
5659  #ifdef LINUX
5660        if (errno == ENOSYS) {
5661            ap_log_error(APLOG_MARK,
5662                APLOG_NOERRNO|APLOG_EMERG, server_conf,
5663                "Your kernel was built without
5664                 CONFIG_SYSVIPC\n"
5665                "%s: Please consult the Apache FAQ for
5666                 details",
5667                ap_server_argv0);
5668        }
5669  #endif
5670        ap_log_error(APLOG_MARK, APLOG_EMERG, server_conf,
5671                "could not call shmget");
5672        exit(APEXIT_INIT);
5673    }
5674    ap_log_error(APLOG_MARK, APLOG_NOERRNO|APLOG_INFO,
5675            server_conf,
5676            "created shared memory segment #%d", shmid);
5677
5678  #ifdef MOVEBREAK
5679    /*
5680     * Some SysV systems place the shared segment WAY
5681     * too close to the dynamic memory break
5682     * point (sbrk(0)). This severely limits the use
5683
5684     * of malloc/sbrk in the program since sbrk will
5685     * refuse to move past that point.
5686     *
5687     * To get around this, we move the break point
5688     * "way up there", attach the segment and
5689     * then move break back down. Ugly
5690     */
5691    if ((obrk = sbrk(MOVEBREAK)) == (char *) -1) {
5692        ap_log_error(APLOG_MARK, APLOG_ERR, server_conf,
5693            "sbrk() could not move break");
5694    }
5695  #endif
5696
5697  #define BADSHMAT    ((scoreboard *)(-1))
5698    if ((ap_scoreboard_image = (scoreboard *)
5699        shmat(shmid, 0, 0)) == BADSHMAT) {
5700        ap_log_error(APLOG_MARK, APLOG_EMERG,
5701            server_conf, "shmat error");
5702        /*
5703         * We exit below, after we try to remove the segment
5704         */
5705        }
```

```
5706    else {              /* only worry about permissions
5707                         * if we attached the segment */
5708        if (shmctl(shmid, IPC_STAT, &shmbuf) != 0) {
5709            ap_log_error(APLOG_MARK, APLOG_ERR, server_conf,
5710            "shmctl() could not stat segment #%d", shmid);
5711        }
5712        else {
5713
5714            shmbuf.shm_perm.uid = ap_user_id;
5715            shmbuf.shm_perm.gid = ap_group_id;
5716            if (shmctl(shmid, IPC_SET, &shmbuf) != 0) {
5717                ap_log_error(APLOG_MARK, APLOG_ERR,
5718                    server_conf,
5719                "shmctl() could not set segment #%d",
5720                    shmid);
5721            }
5722        }
5723    }
5724    /*
5725     * We must avoid leaving segments in the kernel's
5726     * (small) tables.
5727     */
5728    if (shmctl(shmid, IPC_RMID, NULL) != 0) {
5729    ap_log_error(APLOG_MARK, APLOG_WARNING,
5730        server_conf,
5731        "shmctl: IPC_RMID: could not remove
5732            shared memory segment #%d",
5733        shmid);
5734    }
5735    if (ap_scoreboard_image == BADSHMAT)
5736    /* now bailout */
5737    exit(APEXIT_INIT);
5738
5739  #ifdef MOVEBREAK
5740    if (obrk == (char *) -1)
5741    return;                  /* nothing else to do */
5742    if (sbrk(-(MOVEBREAK)) == (char *) -1) {
5743    ap_log_error(APLOG_MARK, APLOG_ERR, server_conf,
5744        "sbrk() could not move break back");
5745    }
5746  #endif
5747    ap_scoreboard_image->global.running_generation = 0;
5748  }
5749
5750  static void reopen_scoreboard(pool *p)
5751  {
5752  }
5753
```

```
5754    #else
5755    #define SCOREBOARD_FILE
5756    static scoreboard _scoreboard_image;
5757    static int scoreboard_fd = -1;
5758
5759    /* XXX: things are seriously screwed if we ever have
5760     * to do a partial read or write ... we could
5761     * get a corrupted scoreboard
5762     */
5763    static int force_write(int fd, void *buffer, int bufsz)
5764    {
5765        int rv, orig_sz = bufsz;
5766
5767        do {
5768         rv = write(fd, buffer, bufsz);
5769         if (rv > 0) {
5770             buffer = (char *) buffer + rv;
5771             bufsz -= rv;
5772         }
5773        } while ((rv > 0 && bufsz > 0) ||
5774             (rv == -1 && errno == EINTR));
5775
5776        return rv < 0 ? rv : orig_sz - bufsz;
5777    }
5778
5779    static int force_read(int fd, void *buffer, int bufsz)
5780    {
5781        int rv, orig_sz = bufsz;
5782
5783        do {
5784         rv = read(fd, buffer, bufsz);
5785         if (rv > 0) {
5786             buffer = (char *) buffer + rv;
5787             bufsz -= rv;
5788         }
5789        } while ((rv > 0 && bufsz > 0) ||
5790             (rv == -1 && errno == EINTR));
5791
5792        return rv < 0 ? rv : orig_sz - bufsz;
5793    }
5794
5795    static void cleanup_scoreboard_file(void *foo)
5796    {
5797        unlink(ap_scoreboard_fname);
5798    }
5799
5800    void reopen_scoreboard(pool *p)
5801    {
5802        if (scoreboard_fd != -1)
5803         ap_pclosef(p, scoreboard_fd);
5804
5805        scoreboard_fd = ap_popenf(p, ap_scoreboard_fname,
5806             O_CREAT | O_BINARY | O_RDWR, 0666);
5807        if (scoreboard_fd == -1) {
5808         perror(ap_scoreboard_fname);
5809         fprintf(stderr, "Cannot open scoreboard file:\n");
5810         clean_child_exit(1);
5811        }
5812    }
5813    #endif
5814
5815    /* Called by parent process */
5816    static void reinit_scoreboard(pool *p)
5817    {
5818        int running_gen = 0;
5819        if (ap_scoreboard_image)
5820         running_gen =
5821             ap_scoreboard_image->global.running_generation;
5822
5823    #ifndef SCOREBOARD_FILE
5824        if (ap_scoreboard_image == NULL) {
5825         setup_shared_mem(p);
5826        }
5827        memset(ap_scoreboard_image, 0, SCOREBOARD_SIZE);
5828        ap_scoreboard_image->global.running_generation =
5829             running_gen;
5830    #else
5831        ap_scoreboard_image = &_scoreboard_image;
5832        ap_scoreboard_fname = ap_server_root_relative(p,
5833             ap_scoreboard_fname);
5834
5835        scoreboard_fd = ap_popenf(p, ap_scoreboard_fname,
5836             O_CREAT | O_BINARY | O_RDWR, 0644);
5837        if (scoreboard_fd == -1) {
5838         perror(ap_scoreboard_fname);
5839         fprintf(stderr, "Cannot open scoreboard file:\n");
5840         exit(APEXIT_INIT);
5841        }
5842        ap_register_cleanup(p, NULL, cleanup_scoreboard_file,
5843             ap_null_cleanup);
5844
5845        memset((char *) ap_scoreboard_image, 0,
5846             sizeof(*ap_scoreboard_image));
5847        ap_scoreboard_image->global.running_generation =
5848             running_gen;
5849        force_write(scoreboard_fd, ap_scoreboard_image,
```

```
5850                sizeof(*ap_scoreboard_image));
5851    #endif
5852    }
5853
5854    /* Routines called to deal with the scoreboard image
5855     * -- note that we do *not* need write locks, since
5856     * update_child_status only updates a *single*
5857     * record in place, and only one process writes to
5858     * a given scoreboard slot at a time (either the child
5859     * process owning that slot, or the parent, noting
5860     * that the child has died).
5861     *
5862     * As a final note -- setting the score entry to getpid()
5863     * is always safe, since when the parent is writing
5864     * an entry, it's only noting SERVER_DEAD
5865     * anyway.
5866     */
5867
5868    ap_inline void ap_sync_scoreboard_image(void)
5869    {
5870    #ifdef SCOREBOARD_FILE
5871        lseek(scoreboard_fd, 0L, 0);
5872        force_read(scoreboard_fd, ap_scoreboard_image,
5873                sizeof(*ap_scoreboard_image));
5874    #endif
5875    }
5876
5877    #endif /* MULTITHREAD */
5878
5879    API_EXPORT(int) ap_exists_scoreboard_image(void)
5880    {
5881        return (ap_scoreboard_image ? 1 : 0);
5882    }
5883
5884    static ap_inline void put_scoreboard_info(int child_num,
5885                            short_score *new_score_rec)
5886    {
5887    #ifdef SCOREBOARD_FILE
5888        lseek(scoreboard_fd,
5889            (long) child_num * sizeof(short_score), 0);
5890        force_write(scoreboard_fd, new_score_rec,
5891            sizeof(short_score));
5892    #endif
5893    }
5894
5895    /* a clean exit from the parent with proper cleanup */
5896    static void clean_parent_exit(int code)
5897        __attribute__((noreturn));
5898    static void clean_parent_exit(int code)
5899    {
5900        /* Clear the pool - including any
5901         * registered cleanups */
5902        ap_destroy_pool(pconf);
5903        exit(code);
5904    }
5905
5906    int ap_update_child_status(int child_num, int status,
5907            request_rec *r)
5908    {
5909        int old_status;
5910        short_score *ss;
5911
5912        if (child_num < 0)
5913         return -1;
5914
5915        ap_sync_scoreboard_image();
5916        ss = &ap_scoreboard_image->servers[child_num];
5917        old_status = ss->status;
5918        ss->status = status;
5919    #ifdef OPTIMIZE_TIMEOUTS
5920        ++ss->cur_vtime;
5921    #endif
5922
5923        if (ap_extended_status) {
5924    #ifndef OPTIMIZE_TIMEOUTS
5925            ss->last_used = time(NULL);
5926    #endif
5927            if (status == SERVER_READY || status ==
5928                SERVER_DEAD) {
5929            /*
5930             * Reset individual counters
5931             */
5932            if (status == SERVER_DEAD) {
5933                ss->my_access_count = 0L;
5934                ss->my_bytes_served = 0L;
5935            }
5936            ss->conn_count = (unsigned short) 0;
5937            ss->conn_bytes = (unsigned long) 0;
5938            }
5939            if (r) {
5940            conn_rec *c = r->connection;
5941            ap_cpystrn(ss->client, ap_get_remote_host(c,
5942                r->per_dir_config,
5943                    REMOTE_NOLOOKUP), sizeof(ss->client));
5944            if (r->the_request == NULL) {
5945                ap_cpystrn(ss->request, "NULL",
```

```
5946                     sizeof(ss->request));
5947             } else if (r->parsed_uri.password == NULL) {
5948                 ap_cpystrn(ss->request, r->the_request,
5949                     sizeof(ss->request));
5950             } else {
5951                 /* Don't reveal the password in the
5952                  * server-status view */
5953                 ap_cpystrn(ss->request, ap_pstrcat(r->pool,
5954                     r->method, " ",
5955                         ap_unparse_uri_components(r->
5956                             pool, &r->parsed_uri,
5957                                 UNP_OMITPASSWORD),
5958
5959                                 r->assbackwards ? NULL :
5960                                     " ", r->protocol, NULL),
5961                         sizeof(ss->request));
5962             }
5963             ss->vhostrec =  r->server;
5964         }
5965     }
5966     if (status == SERVER_STARTING && r == NULL) {
5967         /* clean up the slot's vhostrec pointer
5968          * (maybe re-used) and mark the slot as belonging
5969          * to a new generation.
5970          */
5971         ss->vhostrec = NULL;
5972         ap_scoreboard_image->parent[child_num].generation =
5973             ap_my_generation;
5974 #ifdef SCOREBOARD_FILE
5975         lseek(scoreboard_fd, XtOffsetOf(scoreboard,
5976             parent[child_num]), 0);
5977         force_write(scoreboard_fd, &ap_scoreboard_image->
5978             parent[child_num],
5979             sizeof(parent_score));
5980 #endif
5981     }
5982     put_scoreboard_info(child_num, ss);
5983
5984     return old_status;
5985 }
5986
5987 static void update_scoreboard_global(void)
5988 {
5989 #ifdef SCOREBOARD_FILE
5990     lseek(scoreboard_fd,
5991         (char *) &ap_scoreboard_image->global -(char *)
5992             ap_scoreboard_image, 0);
5993     force_write(scoreboard_fd,
5994         &ap_scoreboard_image->global,
5995         sizeof ap_scoreboard_image->global);
5996 #endif
5997 }
5998
5999 void ap_time_process_request(int child_num, int status)
6000 {
6001     short_score *ss;
6002 #if defined(NO_GETTIMEOFDAY) && !defined(NO_TIMES)
6003     struct tms tms_blk;
6004 #endif
6005
6006     if (child_num < 0)
6007         return;
6008
6009     ap_sync_scoreboard_image();
6010     ss = &ap_scoreboard_image->servers[child_num];
6011
6012     if (status == START_PREQUEST) {
6013 #if defined(NO_GETTIMEOFDAY)
6014 #ifndef NO_TIMES
6015         if ((ss->start_time = times(&tms_blk)) == -1)
6016 #endif /* NO_TIMES */
6017             ss->start_time = (clock_t) 0;
6018 #else
6019         if (gettimeofday(&ss->start_time,
6020             (struct timezone *) 0) < 0)
6021             ss->start_time.tv_sec =
6022                 ss->start_time.tv_usec = 0L;
6023 #endif
6024     }
6025     else if (status == STOP_PREQUEST) {
6026 #if defined(NO_GETTIMEOFDAY)
6027 #ifndef NO_TIMES
6028         if ((ss->stop_time = times(&tms_blk)) == -1)
6029 #endif
6030             ss->stop_time = ss->start_time =
6031                 (clock_t) 0;
6032 #else
6033         if (gettimeofday(&ss->stop_time,
6034             (struct timezone *) 0) < 0)
6035             ss->stop_time.tv_sec =
6036                 ss->stop_time.tv_usec =
6037                 ss->start_time.tv_sec =
6038                 ss->start_time.tv_usec = 0L;
6039 #endif
6040
6041     }
```

```
6042
6043        put_scoreboard_info(child_num, ss);
6044    }
6045
6046    static void increment_counts(int child_num,
6047         request_rec *r)
6048    {
6049        long int bs = 0;
6050        short_score *ss;
6051
6052        ap_sync_scoreboard_image();
6053        ss = &ap_scoreboard_image->servers[child_num];
6054
6055        if (r->sent_bodyct)
6056          ap_bgetopt(r->connection->client, BO_BYTECT, &bs);
6057
6058    #ifndef NO_TIMES
6059        times(&ss->times);
6060    #endif
6061        ss->access_count++;
6062        ss->my_access_count++;
6063        ss->conn_count++;
6064        ss->bytes_served += (unsigned long) bs;
6065        ss->my_bytes_served += (unsigned long) bs;
6066        ss->conn_bytes += (unsigned long) bs;
6067
6068        put_scoreboard_info(child_num, ss);
6069    }
6070
6071    static int find_child_by_pid(int pid)
6072    {
6073        int i;
6074
6075        for (i = 0; i < max_daemons_limit; ++i)
6076          if (ap_scoreboard_image->parent[i].pid == pid)
6077             return i;
6078
6079        return -1;
6080    }
6081
6082    static void reclaim_child_processes(int terminate)
6083    {
6084    #ifndef MULTITHREAD
6085        int i, status;
6086        long int waittime = 1024 * 16;     /* in usecs */
6087        struct timeval tv;
6088        int waitret, tries;
6089        int not_dead_yet;
6090    #ifndef NO_OTHER_CHILD
6091        other_child_rec *ocr, *nocr;
6092    #endif
6093
6094        ap_sync_scoreboard_image();
6095
6096        for (tries = terminate ? 4 : 1; tries
6097             <= 9; ++tries) {
6098         /* don't want to hold up progress any more than
6099          * necessary, but we need to allow children a
6100          * few moments to exit. Set delay with an
6101          * exponential backoff.
6102          */
6103         tv.tv_sec = waittime / 1000000;
6104         tv.tv_usec = waittime % 1000000;
6105         waittime = waittime * 4;
6106         ap_select(0, NULL, NULL, NULL, &tv);
6107
6108         /* now see who is done */
6109         not_dead_yet = 0;
6110         for (i = 0; i < max_daemons_limit; ++i) {
6111             int pid = ap_scoreboard_image->parent[i].pid;
6112
6113             if (pid == my_pid || pid == 0)
6114               continue;
6115
6116             waitret = waitpid(pid, &status, WNOHANG);
6117             if (waitret == pid || waitret == -1) {
6118               ap_scoreboard_image->parent[i].pid = 0;
6119               continue;
6120             }
6121             ++not_dead_yet;
6122             switch (tries) {
6123             case 1:     /*   16ms */
6124             case 2:     /*   82ms */
6125             break;
6126             case 3:     /* 344ms */
6127             /* perhaps it missed the SIGHUP, lets
6128              * try again */
6129             ap_log_error(APLOG_MARK,
6130                 APLOG_NOERRNO|APLOG_WARNING,
6131                     server_conf,
6132                 "child process %d did not exit,
6133                     sending another SIGHUP",
6134                     pid);
6135             kill(pid, SIGHUP);
6136             waittime = 1024 * 16;
6137             break;
```

```
6138            case 4:     /*   16ms */
6139            case 5:     /*   82ms */
6140            case 6:     /*  344ms */
6141             break;
6142            case 7:     /*  1.4sec */
6143             /* ok, now it's being annoying */
6144             ap_log_error(APLOG_MARK,
6145                 APLOG_NOERRNO|APLOG_WARNING,
6146                     server_conf,
6147                 "child process %d still did not exit,
6148                     sending a SIGTERM",
6149                         pid);
6150             kill(pid, SIGTERM);
6151             break;
6152            case 8:     /*   6 sec */
6153             /* die child scum */
6154             ap_log_error(APLOG_MARK,
6155                 APLOG_NOERRNO|APLOG_ERR, server_conf,
6156                 "child process %d still did not exit,
6157                     sending a SIGKILL",
6158                         pid);
6159             kill(pid, SIGKILL);
6160             break;
6161            case 9:     /*  14 sec */
6162             /* gave it our best shot, but alas...  If this
6163              * really is a child we are trying to kill
6164              * and it really hasn't exited, we will likely
6165              * fail to bind to the port after the
6166              * restart.
6167              */
6168             ap_log_error(APLOG_MARK,
6169                 APLOG_NOERRNO|APLOG_ERR, server_conf,
6170                     "could not make child process %d exit, "
6171                     "attempting to continue anyway", pid);
6172             break;
6173            }
6174        }
6175 #ifndef NO_OTHER_CHILD
6176     for (ocr = other_children; ocr; ocr = nocr) {
6177         nocr = ocr->next;
6178         if (ocr->pid == -1)
6179          continue;
6180
6181         waitret = waitpid(ocr->pid, &status, WNOHANG);
6182         if (waitret == ocr->pid) {
6183         ocr->pid = -1;
6184         (*ocr->maintenance) (OC_REASON_DEATH,
6185             ocr->data, status);
6186         }
6187         else if (waitret == 0) {
6188         (*ocr->maintenance) (OC_REASON_RESTART,
6189             ocr->data, -1);
6190         ++not_dead_yet;
6191         }
6192         else if (waitret == -1) {
6193         /* uh what the heck? they didn't call
6194          * unregister? */
6195         ocr->pid = -1;
6196         (*ocr->maintenance) (OC_REASON_LOST,
6197             ocr->data, -1);
6198         }
6199     }
6200 #endif
6201     if (!not_dead_yet) {
6202         /* nothing left to wait for */
6203         break;
6204     }
6205     }
6206 #endif /* ndef MULTITHREAD */
6207 }
6208
6209
6210 #if defined(NEED_WAITPID)
6211 /*
6212    Systems without a real waitpid sometimes lose
6213    a child's exit while waiting for another.  Search
6214    through the scoreboard for missing children.
6215  */
6216 int reap_children(ap_wait_t *status)
6217 {
6218     int n, pid;
6219
6220     for (n = 0; n < max_daemons_limit; ++n) {
6221         ap_sync_scoreboard_image();
6222      if (ap_scoreboard_image->servers[n].status !=
6223         SERVER_DEAD &&
6224         kill((pid =
6225             ap_scoreboard_image->parent[n].pid),
6226             0) == -1) {
6227         ap_update_child_status(n, SERVER_DEAD, NULL);
6228         /* just mark it as having a
6229          * successful exit status */
6230         bzero((char *) status, sizeof(ap_wait_t));
6231         return(pid);
6232     }
6233     }
```

```
6234       return 0;
6235   }
6236   #endif
6237
6238   /* Finally, this routine is used by the caretaker
6239    * process to wait for a while...
6240    */
6241
6242   /* number of calls to wait_or_timeout between writable
6243    * probes */
6244   #ifndef INTERVAL_OF_WRITABLE_PROBES
6245   #define INTERVAL_OF_WRITABLE_PROBES 10
6246   #endif
6247   static int wait_or_timeout_counter;
6248
6249   static int wait_or_timeout(ap_wait_t *status)
6250   {
6251   #ifdef WIN32
6252   #define MAXWAITOBJ MAXIMUM_WAIT_OBJECTS
6253       HANDLE h[MAXWAITOBJ];
6254       int e[MAXWAITOBJ];
6255       int round, pi, hi, rv, err;
6256       for (round = 0; round <= (HARD_SERVER_LIMIT - 1) /
6257           MAXWAITOBJ + 1; round++) {
6258        hi = 0;
6259        for (pi = round * MAXWAITOBJ;
6260            (pi < (round + 1) * MAXWAITOBJ) && (pi <
6261             HARD_SERVER_LIMIT);
6262            pi++) {
6263           if (ap_scoreboard_image->servers[pi].status !=
6264               SERVER_DEAD) {
6265            e[hi] = pi;
6266            h[hi++] = (HANDLE) ap_scoreboard_image->
6267               parent[pi].pid;
6268           }
6269
6270        }
6271        if (hi > 0) {
6272           rv = WaitForMultipleObjects(hi, h, FALSE,
6273               10000);
6274           if (rv == -1)
6275            err = GetLastError();
6276           if ((WAIT_OBJECT_0 <= (unsigned int) rv) &&
6277               ((unsigned int) rv < (WAIT_OBJECT_0 + hi)))
6278            return (ap_scoreboard_image->parent[e[rv -
6279               WAIT_OBJECT_0]].pid);
6280           else if ((WAIT_ABANDONED_0 <=
6281               (unsigned int) rv)
6282               && ((unsigned int) rv <
6283                   (WAIT_ABANDONED_0 + hi)))
6284            return (ap_scoreboard_image->parent
6285               [e[rv - WAIT_ABANDONED_0]].pid);
6286
6287        }
6288       }
6289       return (-1);
6290
6291   #else /* WIN32 */
6292       struct timeval tv;
6293       int ret;
6294
6295       ++wait_or_timeout_counter;
6296       if (wait_or_timeout_counter ==
6297           INTERVAL_OF_WRITABLE_PROBES) {
6298        wait_or_timeout_counter = 0;
6299   #ifndef NO_OTHER_CHILD
6300        probe_writable_fds();
6301   #endif
6302       }
6303       ret = waitpid(-1, status, WNOHANG);
6304       if (ret == -1 && errno == EINTR) {
6305        return -1;
6306       }
6307       if (ret > 0) {
6308        return ret;
6309       }
6310   #ifdef NEED_WAITPID
6311       if ((ret = reap_children(status)) > 0) {
6312        return ret;
6313       }
6314   #endif
6315       tv.tv_sec =
6316           SCOREBOARD_MAINTENANCE_INTERVAL / 1000000;
6317       tv.tv_usec =
6318           SCOREBOARD_MAINTENANCE_INTERVAL % 1000000;
6319       ap_select(0, NULL, NULL, NULL, &tv);
6320       return -1;
6321   #endif /* WIN32 */
6322   }
6323
6324
6325   #if defined(NSIG)
6326   #define NumSIG NSIG
6327   #elif defined(_NSIG)
6328   #define NumSIG _NSIG
6329   #elif defined(__NSIG)
```

```
6330    #define NumSIG __NSIG
6331    #else
6332    #define NumSIG 32    /* for 1998's unixes, this is
6333                           * still a good assumption */
6334    #endif
6335
6336    #ifdef SYS_SIGLIST /* platform has sys_siglist[] */
6337    #define INIT_SIGLIST()  /*nothing*/
6338    #else /* platform has no sys_siglist[], define our own */
6339    #define SYS_SIGLIST ap_sys_siglist
6340    #define INIT_SIGLIST() siglist_init();
6341
6342    const char *ap_sys_siglist[NumSIG];
6343
6344    static void siglist_init(void)
6345    {
6346        int sig;
6347
6348        ap_sys_siglist[0] = "Signal 0";
6349    #ifdef SIGHUP
6350        ap_sys_siglist[SIGHUP] = "Hangup";
6351    #endif
6352    #ifdef SIGINT
6353        ap_sys_siglist[SIGINT] = "Interrupt";
6354    #endif
6355    #ifdef SIGQUIT
6356        ap_sys_siglist[SIGQUIT] = "Quit";
6357    #endif
6358    #ifdef SIGILL
6359        ap_sys_siglist[SIGILL] = "Illegal instruction";
6360    #endif
6361    #ifdef SIGTRAP
6362        ap_sys_siglist[SIGTRAP] = "Trace/BPT trap";
6363    #endif
6364    #ifdef SIGIOT
6365        ap_sys_siglist[SIGIOT] = "IOT instruction";
6366    #endif
6367    #ifdef SIGABRT
6368        ap_sys_siglist[SIGABRT] = "Abort";
6369    #endif
6370    #ifdef SIGEMT
6371        ap_sys_siglist[SIGEMT] = "Emulator trap";
6372    #endif
6373    #ifdef SIGFPE
6374        ap_sys_siglist[SIGFPE] = "Arithmetic exception";
6375    #endif
6376    #ifdef SIGKILL
6377        ap_sys_siglist[SIGKILL] = "Killed";
6378    #endif
6379    #ifdef SIGBUS
6380        ap_sys_siglist[SIGBUS] = "Bus error";
6381    #endif
6382    #ifdef SIGSEGV
6383        ap_sys_siglist[SIGSEGV] = "Segmentation fault";
6384    #endif
6385    #ifdef SIGSYS
6386        ap_sys_siglist[SIGSYS] = "Bad system call";
6387    #endif
6388    #ifdef SIGPIPE
6389        ap_sys_siglist[SIGPIPE] = "Broken pipe";
6390    #endif
6391    #ifdef SIGALRM
6392        ap_sys_siglist[SIGALRM] = "Alarm clock";
6393    #endif
6394    #ifdef SIGTERM
6395        ap_sys_siglist[SIGTERM] = "Terminated";
6396    #endif
6397    #ifdef SIGUSR1
6398        ap_sys_siglist[SIGUSR1] = "User defined signal 1";
6399    #endif
6400    #ifdef SIGUSR2
6401        ap_sys_siglist[SIGUSR2] = "User defined signal 2";
6402    #endif
6403    #ifdef SIGCLD
6404        ap_sys_siglist[SIGCLD] = "Child status change";
6405    #endif
6406    #ifdef SIGCHLD
6407        ap_sys_siglist[SIGCHLD] = "Child status change";
6408    #endif
6409    #ifdef SIGPWR
6410        ap_sys_siglist[SIGPWR] = "Power-fail restart";
6411    #endif
6412    #ifdef SIGWINCH
6413        ap_sys_siglist[SIGWINCH] = "Window changed";
6414    #endif
6415    #ifdef SIGURG
6416        ap_sys_siglist[SIGURG] = "urgent socket condition";
6417    #endif
6418    #ifdef SIGPOLL
6419        ap_sys_siglist[SIGPOLL] = "Pollable event occurred";
6420    #endif
6421    #ifdef SIGIO
6422        ap_sys_siglist[SIGIO] = "socket I/O possible";
6423    #endif
6424    #ifdef SIGSTOP
6425        ap_sys_siglist[SIGSTOP] = "Stopped (signal)";
```

```
6426    #endif
6427    #ifdef SIGTSTP
6428        ap_sys_siglist[SIGTSTP] = "Stopped";
6429    #endif
6430    #ifdef SIGCONT
6431        ap_sys_siglist[SIGCONT] = "Continued";
6432    #endif
6433    #ifdef SIGTTIN
6434        ap_sys_siglist[SIGTTIN] = "Stopped (tty input)";
6435    #endif
6436    #ifdef SIGTTOU
6437        ap_sys_siglist[SIGTTOU] = "Stopped (tty output)";
6438    #endif
6439    #ifdef SIGVTALRM
6440        ap_sys_siglist[SIGVTALRM] = "virtual timer expired";
6441    #endif
6442    #ifdef SIGPROF
6443        ap_sys_siglist[SIGPROF] = "profiling timer expired";
6444    #endif
6445    #ifdef SIGXCPU
6446        ap_sys_siglist[SIGXCPU] = "exceeded cpu limit";
6447    #endif
6448    #ifdef SIGXFSZ
6449        ap_sys_siglist[SIGXFSZ] = "exceeded file size limit";
6450    #endif
6451        for (sig=0; sig < sizeof(ap_sys_siglist)/sizeof
6452             (ap_sys_siglist[0]); ++sig)
6453            if (ap_sys_siglist[sig] == NULL)
6454                ap_sys_siglist[sig] = "";
6455    }
6456    #endif /* platform has sys_siglist[] */
6457
6458
6459    /* handle all varieties of core dumping signals */
6460    static void sig_coredump(int sig)
6461    {
6462        chdir(ap_coredump_dir);
6463        signal(sig, SIG_DFL);
6464    #ifndef WIN32
6465        kill(getpid(), sig);
6466    #else
6467        raise(sig);
6468    #endif
6469        /* At this point we've got sig blocked, because
6470         * we're still inside the signal handler.  When we
6471         * leave the signal handler it will be unblocked,
6472         * and we'll take the signal... and coredump or
6473         * whatever is appropriate for this particular
6474         * Unix.  In addition the parent will see the real
6475         * signal we received -- whereas if we called
6476         * abort() here, the parent would only see SIGABRT.
6477         */
6478    }
6479
6480    /***********************************************************
6481     * Connection structures and accounting...
6482     */
6483
6484    static void just_die(int sig)
6485    {                          /* SIGHUP to child process??? */
6486        /* if alarms are blocked we have to wait to die
6487         * otherwise we might end up with corruption in
6488         * alloc.c's internal structures */
6489        if (alarms_blocked) {
6490            exit_after_unblock = 1;
6491        }
6492        else {
6493            clean_child_exit(0);
6494        }
6495    }
6496
6497    static int volatile usr1_just_die = 1;
6498    static int volatile deferred_die;
6499
6500    static void usr1_handler(int sig)
6501    {
6502        if (usr1_just_die) {
6503            just_die(sig);
6504        }
6505        deferred_die = 1;
6506    }
6507
6508    /* volatile just in case */
6509    static int volatile shutdown_pending;
6510    static int volatile restart_pending;
6511    static int volatile is_graceful;
6512    ap_generation_t volatile ap_my_generation;
6513
6514    #ifdef WIN32
6515    /*
6516     * Signalling Apache on NT.
6517     *
6518     * Under Unix, Apache can be told to shutdown or restart
6519     * by sending various signals (HUP, USR, TERM). On NT we
6520     * don't have easy access to signals, so we use "events"
6521     * instead. The parent apache process goes into a loop
```

```
6522   * where it waits forever for a set of events. Two of
6523   * those events are called
6524   *
6525   *    apPID_shutdown
6526   *    apPID_restart
6527   *
6528   * (where PID is the PID of the apache parent process).
6529   * When one of these is signalled, the Apache parent
6530   * performs the appropriate action. The events can
6531   * become signalled through internal Apache methods
6532   * (e.g. if the child finds a fatal error and needs
6533   * to kill its parent), via the service control
6534   * manager (the control thread will signal the shutdown
6535   * event when requested to stop the Apache service),
6536   * from the -k Apache command line, or from any
6537   * external program which finds the Apache PID from
6538   * the httpd.pid file.
6539   *
6540   * The signal_parent() function, below, is used to
6541   * signal one of these events. It can be called
6542   * by any child or parent process, since it does not
6543   * rely on global variables.
6544   *
6545   * On entry, type gives the event to signal. 0 means
6546   * shutdown, 1 means graceful restart.
6547   */
6548
6549   static void signal_parent(int type)
6550   {
6551       HANDLE e;
6552       char *signal_name;
6553       extern char signal_shutdown_name[];
6554       extern char signal_restart_name[];
6555
6556       /* after updating the shutdown_pending or restart
6557        * flags, we need to wake up the parent process
6558        * so it can see the changes. The parent will
6559        * normally be waiting for either a child process
6560        * to die, or for a signal on the "spache-signal"
6561        * event. So set the"apache-signal" event here.
6562       */
6563
6564       if (one_process) {
6565        return;
6566       }
6567
6568       switch(type) {
6569       case 0: signal_name = signal_shutdown_name; break;
6570       case 1: signal_name = signal_restart_name; break;
6571       default: return;
6572       }
6573
6574       APD2("signal_parent signalling event \"%s\"",
6575           signal_name);
6576
6577       e = OpenEvent(EVENT_ALL_ACCESS, FALSE,
6578           signal_name);
6579       if (!e) {
6580        /* Um, problem, can't signal the parent, which
6581         * means we can't signal ourselves to die.
6582         * Ignore for now...
6583         */
6584        ap_log_error(APLOG_MARK,
6585            APLOG_EMERG|APLOG_WIN32ERROR, server_conf,
6586            "OpenEvent on %s event", signal_name);
6587        return;
6588       }
6589       if (SetEvent(e) == 0) {
6590        /* Same problem as above */
6591        ap_log_error(APLOG_MARK,
6592            APLOG_EMERG|APLOG_WIN32ERROR, server_conf,
6593            "SetEvent on %s event", signal_name);
6594        CloseHandle(e);
6595        return;
6596       }
6597       CloseHandle(e);
6598   }
6599   #endif
6600
6601   /*
6602    * ap_start_shutdown() and ap_start_restart(), below,
6603    * are a first stab at functions to initiate shutdown
6604    * or restart without relying on signals. Previously
6605    * this was initiated in sig_term() and restart()
6606    * signal handlers, but we want to be able to start
6607    * a shutdown/restart from other sources -- e.g. on
6608    * Win32,from the service manager. Now the service
6609    * manager can call ap_start_shutdown() or
6610    * ap_start_restart() as appropiate.  Note that
6611    * these functions can also be called by the child
6612    * processes, since global variables are no longer used
6613    * to pass on the required action to the parent.
6614    */
6615
6616   void ap_start_shutdown(void)
6617   {
```

```
6618   #ifndef WIN32
6619       if (shutdown_pending == 1) {
6620       /* Um, is this _probably_ not an error, if
6621        * the user has tried to do a shutdown twice
6622        * quickly, so we won't worry about reporting it.
6623        */
6624        return;
6625       }
6626       shutdown_pending = 1;
6627   #else
6628       signal_parent(0);
6629       /* get the parent process to wake up */
6630   #endif
6631   }
6632
6633   /* do a graceful restart if graceful == 1 */
6634   void ap_start_restart(int graceful)
6635   {
6636   #ifndef WIN32
6637       if (restart_pending == 1) {
6638       /* Probably not an error - don't bother
6639        * reporting it */
6640        return;
6641       }
6642       restart_pending = 1;
6643       is_graceful = graceful;
6644   #else
6645       signal_parent(1);
6646       /* get the parent process to wake up */
6647   #endif /* WIN32 */
6648   }
6649
6650   static void sig_term(int sig)
6651   {
6652       ap_start_shutdown();
6653   }
6654
6655   static void restart(int sig)
6656   {
6657   #ifndef WIN32
6658       ap_start_restart(sig == SIGUSR1);
6659   #else
6660       ap_start_restart(1);
6661   #endif
6662   }
6663
6664   static void set_signals(void)
6665   {
```

```
6666   #ifndef NO_USE_SIGACTION
6667       struct sigaction sa;
6668
6669       sigemptyset(&sa.sa_mask);
6670       sa.sa_flags = 0;
6671
6672       if (!one_process) {
6673       sa.sa_handler = sig_coredump;
6674   #if defined(SA_ONESHOT)
6675       sa.sa_flags = SA_ONESHOT;
6676   #elif defined(SA_RESETHAND)
6677       sa.sa_flags = SA_RESETHAND;
6678   #endif
6679       if (sigaction(SIGSEGV, &sa, NULL) < 0)
6680           ap_log_error(APLOG_MARK, APLOG_WARNING,
6681               server_conf, "sigaction(SIGSEGV)");
6682   #ifdef SIGBUS
6683       if (sigaction(SIGBUS, &sa, NULL) < 0)
6684           ap_log_error(APLOG_MARK, APLOG_WARNING,
6685               server_conf, "sigaction(SIGBUS)");
6686   #endif
6687   #ifdef SIGABORT
6688       if (sigaction(SIGABORT, &sa, NULL) < 0)
6689           ap_log_error(APLOG_MARK, APLOG_WARNING,
6690               server_conf, "sigaction(SIGABORT)");
6691   #endif
6692   #ifdef SIGABRT
6693
6694       if (sigaction(SIGABRT, &sa, NULL) < 0)
6695           ap_log_error(APLOG_MARK, APLOG_WARNING,
6696               server_conf, "sigaction(SIGABRT)");
6697   #endif
6698   #ifdef SIGILL
6699       if (sigaction(SIGILL, &sa, NULL) < 0)
6700           ap_log_error(APLOG_MARK, APLOG_WARNING,
6701               server_conf, "sigaction(SIGILL)");
6702   #endif
6703       sa.sa_flags = 0;
6704       }
6705       sa.sa_handler = sig_term;
6706       if (sigaction(SIGTERM, &sa, NULL) < 0)
6707       ap_log_error(APLOG_MARK, APLOG_WARNING,
6708           server_conf, "sigaction(SIGTERM)");
6709   #ifdef SIGINT
6710       if (sigaction(SIGINT, &sa, NULL) < 0)
6711           ap_log_error(APLOG_MARK, APLOG_WARNING,
6712               server_conf, "sigaction(SIGINT)");
6713   #endif
```

```
6714    #ifdef SIGXCPU
6715        sa.sa_handler = SIG_DFL;
6716        if (sigaction(SIGXCPU, &sa, NULL) < 0)
6717            ap_log_error(APLOG_MARK, APLOG_WARNING,
6718                server_conf, "sigaction(SIGXCPU)");
6719    #endif
6720    #ifdef SIGXFSZ
6721        sa.sa_handler = SIG_DFL;
6722        if (sigaction(SIGXFSZ, &sa, NULL) < 0)
6723            ap_log_error(APLOG_MARK, APLOG_WARNING,
6724                server_conf, "sigaction(SIGXFSZ)");
6725    #endif
6726    #ifdef SIGPIPE
6727        sa.sa_handler = SIG_IGN;
6728        if (sigaction(SIGPIPE, &sa, NULL) < 0)
6729            ap_log_error(APLOG_MARK, APLOG_WARNING,
6730                server_conf, "sigaction(SIGPIPE)");
6731    #endif
6732
6733        /* we want to ignore HUPs and USR1 while we're
6734         * busy processing one */
6735        sigaddset(&sa.sa_mask, SIGHUP);
6736        sigaddset(&sa.sa_mask, SIGUSR1);
6737        sa.sa_handler = restart;
6738        if (sigaction(SIGHUP, &sa, NULL) < 0)
6739            ap_log_error(APLOG_MARK, APLOG_WARNING,
6740                server_conf, "sigaction(SIGHUP)");
6741        if (sigaction(SIGUSR1, &sa, NULL) < 0)
6742            ap_log_error(APLOG_MARK, APLOG_WARNING,
6743                server_conf, "sigaction(SIGUSR1)");
6744    #else
6745        if (!one_process) {
6746            signal(SIGSEGV, sig_coredump);
6747    #ifdef SIGBUS
6748            signal(SIGBUS, sig_coredump);
6749    #endif /* SIGBUS */
6750    #ifdef SIGABORT
6751            signal(SIGABORT, sig_coredump);
6752    #endif /* SIGABORT */
6753    #ifdef SIGABRT
6754            signal(SIGABRT, sig_coredump);
6755    #endif /* SIGABRT */
6756    #ifdef SIGILL
6757            signal(SIGILL, sig_coredump);
6758    #endif /* SIGILL */
6759    #ifdef SIGXCPU
6760            signal(SIGXCPU, SIG_DFL);
6761    #endif /* SIGXCPU */
6762    #ifdef SIGXFSZ
6763            signal(SIGXFSZ, SIG_DFL);
6764    #endif /* SIGXFSZ */
6765        }
6766
6767        signal(SIGTERM, sig_term);
6768    #ifdef SIGHUP
6769        signal(SIGHUP, restart);
6770    #endif /* SIGHUP */
6771    #ifdef SIGUSR1
6772        signal(SIGUSR1, restart);
6773    #endif /* SIGUSR1 */
6774    #ifdef SIGPIPE
6775        signal(SIGPIPE, SIG_IGN);
6776    #endif /* SIGPIPE */
6777
6778    #endif
6779    }
6780
6781
6782    /********************************************************
6783     * Here follows a long bunch of generic server
6784     * bookkeeping stuff...
6785     */
6786
6787    static void detach(void)
6788    {
6789    #if !defined(WIN32)
6790        int x;
6791
6792        chdir("/");
6793    #if !defined(MPE) && !defined(OS2) && !defined(TPF)
6794    /* Don't detach for MPE because child processes can't
6795     * survive the death of
6796       the parent. */
6797        if ((x = fork()) > 0)
6798            exit(0);
6799        else if (x == -1) {
6800            perror("fork");
6801            fprintf(stderr, "%s: unable to fork new process\n",
6802                ap_server_argv0);
6803            exit(1);
6804        }
6805        RAISE_SIGSTOP(DETACH);
6806    #endif
6807    #ifndef NO_SETSID
6808        if ((pgrp = setsid()) == -1) {
6809            perror("setsid");
```

```
6810        fprintf(stderr, "%s: setsid failed\n",
6811            ap_server_argv0);
6812        exit(1);
6813    }
6814 #elif defined(NEXT) || defined(NEWSOS)
6815    if (setpgrp(0, getpid()) == -1 ||
6816            (pgrp = getpgrp(0)) == -1) {
6817        perror("setpgrp");
6818        fprintf(stderr, "%s: setpgrp or getpgrp failed\n",
6819            ap_server_argv0);
6820        exit(1);
6821    }
6822 #elif defined(OS2) || defined(TPF)
6823    /* OS/2 don't support process group IDs */
6824    pgrp = getpid();
6825 #elif defined(MPE)
6826    /* MPE uses negative pid for process group */
6827    pgrp = -getpid();
6828 #else
6829    if ((pgrp = setpgrp(getpid(), 0)) == -1) {
6830        perror("setpgrp");
6831        fprintf(stderr, "%s: setpgrp failed\n",
6832            ap_server_argv0);
6833        exit(1);
6834    }
6835 #endif
6836
6837    /* close out the standard file descriptors */
6838    if (freopen("/dev/null", "r", stdin) == NULL) {
6839        fprintf(stderr, "%s: unable to replace stdin
6840            with /dev/null: %s\n",
6841            ap_server_argv0, strerror(errno));
6842    /* continue anyhow -- note we can't close out
6843     * descriptor 0 because we have nothing to
6844     * replace it with, and if we didn't have a
6845     * descriptor0 the next file would be created
6846     * with that value ... leading to
6847     * havoc.
6848     */
6849    }
6850    if (freopen("/dev/null", "w", stdout) == NULL) {
6851        fprintf(stderr, "%s: unable to replace stdout
6852            with /dev/null: %s\n",
6853            ap_server_argv0, strerror(errno));
6854    }
6855    /* stderr is a tricky one, we really want it to be
6856     * the error_log, but we haven't opened that yet.
6857     * So leave it alone for now and it'll
6858     * be reopened moments later.
6859     */
6860 #endif /* ndef WIN32 */
6861 }
6862
6863 /* Set group privileges.
6864  *
6865  * Note that we use the username as set in the config
6866  * files, rather than the lookup of to uid -- the
6867  * same uid may have multiple passwd entries,
6868  * with different sets of groups for each.
6869  */
6870
6871 static void set_group_privs(void)
6872 {
6873 #ifndef WIN32
6874    if (!geteuid()) {
6875        char *name;
6876
6877        /* Get username if passed as a uid */
6878
6879        if (ap_user_name[0] == '#') {
6880            struct passwd *ent;
6881            uid_t uid = atoi(&ap_user_name[1]);
6882
6883            if ((ent = getpwuid(uid)) == NULL) {
6884                ap_log_error(APLOG_MARK, APLOG_ALERT,
6885                    server_conf,
6886                    "getpwuid: couldn't determine user
6887                        name from uid %u, "
6888                    "you probably need to modify the
6889                        User directive",
6890                    (unsigned)uid);
6891                clean_child_exit(APEXIT_CHILDFATAL);
6892            }
6893
6894            name = ent->pw_name;
6895        }
6896        else
6897            name = ap_user_name;
6898
6899 #ifndef OS2
6900        /* OS/2 dosen't support groups. */
6901
6902        /* Reset 'groups' attributes. */
6903
6904        if (initgroups(name, ap_group_id) == -1) {
6905            ap_log_error(APLOG_MARK, APLOG_ALERT,
```

```
6906                    server_conf,
6907                    "initgroups: unable to set groups for
6908                        User %s "
6909                    "and Group %u", name,
6910                        (unsigned)ap_group_id);
6911                clean_child_exit(APEXIT_CHILDFATAL);
6912            }
6913    #ifdef MULTIPLE_GROUPS
6914            if (getgroups(NGROUPS_MAX, group_id_list) == -1) {
6915                ap_log_error(APLOG_MARK, APLOG_ALERT,
6916                    server_conf,
6917                    "getgroups: unable to get group list");
6918                clean_child_exit(APEXIT_CHILDFATAL);
6919            }
6920    #endif
6921            if (setgid(ap_group_id) == -1) {
6922                ap_log_error(APLOG_MARK, APLOG_ALERT,
6923                    server_conf,
6924                    "setgid: unable to set group id to
6925                        Group %u",
6926                        (unsigned)ap_group_id);
6927                clean_child_exit(APEXIT_CHILDFATAL);
6928            }
6929    #endif
6930        }
6931    #endif /* ndef WIN32 */
6932    }
6933
6934    /* check to see if we have the 'suexec' setuid wrapper
6935     * installed */
6936    static int init_suexec(void)
6937    {
6938    #ifndef WIN32
6939        struct stat wrapper;
6940
6941        if ((stat(SUEXEC_BIN, &wrapper)) != 0)
6942            return (ap_suexec_enabled);
6943
6944        if ((wrapper.st_mode & S_ISUID) &&
6945                wrapper.st_uid == 0) {
6946            ap_suexec_enabled = 1;
6947        }
6948    #endif /* ndef WIN32 */
6949        return (ap_suexec_enabled);
6950    }
6951
6952    /***********************************************************
6953     * Connection structures and accounting...
6954     */
6955
6956
6957    static conn_rec *new_connection(pool *p,
6958        server_rec *server, BUFF *inout,
6959                    const struct sockaddr_in *remaddr,
6960                    const struct sockaddr_in *saddr,
6961                    int child_num)
6962    {
6963        conn_rec *conn = (conn_rec *) ap_pcalloc(p,
6964            sizeof(conn_rec));
6965
6966        /* Got a connection structure, so initialize
6967         * what fields we can(the rest are zeroed
6968         * out by pcalloc).
6969         */
6970
6971        conn->child_num = child_num;
6972
6973        conn->pool = p;
6974        conn->local_addr = *saddr;
6975        conn->server = server; /* just a guess for now */
6976        ap_update_vhost_given_ip(conn);
6977        conn->base_server = conn->server;
6978        conn->client = inout;
6979
6980        conn->remote_addr = *remaddr;
6981        conn->remote_ip = ap_pstrdup(conn->pool,
6982                    inet_ntoa(conn->remote_addr.sin_addr));
6983
6984        return conn;
6985    }
6986
6987    #if defined(TCP_NODELAY) && !defined(MPE)
6988    static void sock_disable_nagle(int s)
6989    {
6990        /* The Nagle algorithm says that we should delay
6991         * sending partial packets in hopes of getting more
6992         * data.  We don't want to do this; we are not telnet.
6993         * There are bad interactions between persistent
6994         * connections and Nagle's algorithm that have very
6995         * severe performance penalties.  (Failing to
6996         * disable Nagle is not much of a problem with
6997         * simple HTTP.)
6998         *
6999         * In spite of these problems, failure here is
7000         * not a shooting offense.
7001         */
```

```
7002        int just_say_no = 1;
7003
7004        if (setsockopt(s, IPPROTO_TCP, TCP_NODELAY,
7005              (char *) &just_say_no,
7006                  sizeof(int)) < 0) {
7007        ap_log_error(APLOG_MARK, APLOG_WARNING, server_conf,
7008              "setsockopt: (TCP_NODELAY)");
7009        }
7010    }
7011
7012    #else
7013    #define sock_disable_nagle(s)       /* NOOP */
7014    #endif
7015
7016
7017    static int make_sock(pool *p,
7018          const struct sockaddr_in *server)
7019    {
7020        int s;
7021        int one = 1;
7022        char addr[512];
7023
7024        if (server->sin_addr.s_addr != htonl(INADDR_ANY))
7025          ap_snprintf(addr, sizeof(addr),
7026              "address %s port %d",
7027                inet_ntoa(server->sin_addr),
7028                    ntohs(server->sin_port));
7029        else
7030          ap_snprintf(addr, sizeof(addr), "port %d",
7031              ntohs(server->sin_port));
7032
7033        /* note that because we're about to slack
7034         * we don't use psocket */
7035        ap_block_alarms();
7036        if ((s = socket(AF_INET, SOCK_STREAM,
7037              IPPROTO_TCP)) == -1) {
7038          ap_log_error(APLOG_MARK, APLOG_CRIT, server_conf,
7039                "make_sock: failed to get a socket
7040                    for %s", addr);
7041          ap_unblock_alarms();
7042          exit(1);
7043        }
7044
7045        /* Solaris (probably versions 2.4, 2.5, and 2.5.1
7046         * with various levels of tcp patches) has some
7047         * really weird bugs where if you dup the
7048         * socket now it breaks things across SIGHUP
7049         * restarts.  It'll either be unable to bind, or it
7050         * won't respond.
7051         */
7052    #if defined (SOLARIS2) && SOLARIS2 < 260
7053    #define WORKAROUND_SOLARIS_BUG
7054    #endif
7055
7056        /* PR#1282 Unixware 1.x appears to have the same
7057         * problem as solaris */
7058    #if defined (UW) && UW < 200
7059    #define WORKAROUND_SOLARIS_BUG
7060    #endif
7061
7062        /* PR#1973 NCR SVR4 systems appear to have the
7063         * same problem */
7064    #if defined (MPRAS)
7065    #define WORKAROUND_SOLARIS_BUG
7066    #endif
7067
7068    #ifndef WORKAROUND_SOLARIS_BUG
7069        s = ap_slack(s, AP_SLACK_HIGH);
7070
7071        ap_note_cleanups_for_socket(p, s);
7072        /* arrange to close on exec or restart */
7073    #endif
7074
7075    #ifndef MPE
7076    /* MPE does not support SO_REUSEADDR and SO_KEEPALIVE */
7077    #ifndef _OSD_POSIX
7078        if (setsockopt(s, SOL_SOCKET, SO_REUSEADDR,
7079              (char *) &one, sizeof(int)) < 0) {
7080          ap_log_error(APLOG_MARK, APLOG_CRIT, server_conf,
7081                "make_sock: for %s, setsockopt:
7082                    (SO_REUSEADDR)", addr);
7083          close(s);
7084          ap_unblock_alarms();
7085          return -1;
7086        }
7087    #endif /*_OSD_POSIX*/
7088        one = 1;
7089    #ifndef BEOS
7090    /* BeOS does not support SO_KEEPALIVE */
7091        if (setsockopt(s, SOL_SOCKET, SO_KEEPALIVE,
7092              (char *) &one, sizeof(int)) < 0) {
7093          ap_log_error(APLOG_MARK, APLOG_CRIT, server_conf,
7094                "make_sock: for %s, setsockopt:
7095                    (SO_KEEPALIVE)", addr);
7096          close(s);
7097          ap_unblock_alarms();
```

```
7098          return -1;
7099       }
7100  #endif
7101  #endif
7102
7103       sock_disable_nagle(s);
7104       sock_enable_linger(s);
7105
7106       /*
7107        * To send data over high bandwidth-delay
7108        * connections at full speed we must force the TCP
7109        * window to open wide enough to keep the pipe full.
7110        * The default window size on many systems is only
7111        * 4kB.  Cross-country WAN connections of 100ms
7112        * at 1Mb/s are not impossible for well connected
7113        * sites.If we assume 100ms cross-country latency,
7114        * a 4kB buffer limits throughput to 40kB/s.
7115        *
7116        * To avoid this problem I've added the
7117        * SendBufferSize directive to allow the web
7118        * master to configure send buffer size.
7119        *
7120        * The trade-off of larger buffers is that more
7121        * kernel memory is consumed.  YMMV, know your
7122        * customers and your network!
7123        *
7124        * -John Heidemann <johnh@isi.edu> 25-Oct-96
7125        *
7126        * If no size is specified, use the kernel default.
7127        */
7128  #ifndef BEOS
7129  /* BeOS does not support SO_SNDBUF */
7130       if (server_conf->send_buffer_size) {
7131       if (setsockopt(s, SOL_SOCKET, SO_SNDBUF,
7132          (char *) &server_conf->send_buffer_size,
7133              sizeof(int)) < 0) {
7134          ap_log_error(APLOG_MARK, APLOG_WARNING,
7135              server_conf,
7136              "make_sock: failed to set SendBufferSize
7137                  for %s, "
7138              "using default", addr);
7139          /* not a fatal error */
7140       }
7141       }
7142  #endif
7143
7144  #ifdef MPE
7145  /* MPE requires CAP=PM and GETPRIVMODE to bind to ports
```

```
7146   * less than 1024 */
7147       if (ntohs(server->sin_port) < 1024)
7148          GETPRIVMODE();
7149  #endif
7150       if (bind(s, (struct sockaddr *) server,
7151              sizeof(struct sockaddr_in)) == -1) {
7152          ap_log_error(APLOG_MARK, APLOG_CRIT, server_conf,
7153              "make_sock: could not bind to %s", addr);
7154  #ifdef MPE
7155          if (ntohs(server->sin_port) < 1024)
7156             GETUSERMODE();
7157  #endif
7158          close(s);
7159          ap_unblock_alarms();
7160          exit(1);
7161       }
7162  #ifdef MPE
7163       if (ntohs(server->sin_port) < 1024)
7164          GETUSERMODE();
7165  #endif
7166
7167       if (listen(s, ap_listenbacklog) == -1) {
7168          ap_log_error(APLOG_MARK, APLOG_ERR, server_conf,
7169              "make_sock: unable to listen for connections
7170                  on %s", addr);
7171          close(s);
7172          ap_unblock_alarms();
7173          exit(1);
7174       }
7175
7176  #ifdef WORKAROUND_SOLARIS_BUG
7177       s = ap_slack(s, AP_SLACK_HIGH);
7178
7179       ap_note_cleanups_for_socket(p, s);
7180       /* arrange to close on exec or restart */
7181  #endif
7182       ap_unblock_alarms();
7183
7184  #ifndef WIN32
7185       /* protect various fd_sets */
7186       if (s >= FD_SETSIZE) {
7187       ap_log_error(APLOG_MARK,
7188           APLOG_NOERRNO|APLOG_WARNING, NULL,
7189           "make_sock: problem listening on %s,
7190               filedescriptor (%u) "
7191           "larger than FD_SETSIZE (%u) "
7192           "found, you probably need to rebuild Apache
7193               with a "
```

```
7194              "larger FD_SETSIZE", addr, s, FD_SETSIZE);       7242          lr = lr->next;
7195          close(s);                                            7243        } while (lr && lr != ap_listeners);
7196          return -1;                                           7244    }
7197        }                                                      7245
7198    #endif                                                     7246
7199                                                               7247    static int find_listener(listen_rec *lr)
7200        return s;                                              7248    {
7201    }                                                          7249        listen_rec *or;
7202                                                               7250
7203                                                               7251        for (or = old_listeners; or; or = or->next) {
7204    /*                                                         7252          if (!memcmp(&or->local_addr, &lr->local_addr,
7205     * During a restart we keep track of the old listeners     7253              sizeof(or->local_addr))) {
7206     * here, so that we can re-use the sockets.  We            7254              or->used = 1;
7207     * have to do this because we won't be able to             7255              return or->fd;
7208     * re-open the sockets ("Address already in use").         7256          }
7209     *                                                         7257        }
7210     * Unlike the listeners ring, old_listeners is a N         7258        return -1;
7211     * ULL terminated list.                                    7259    }
7212     *                                                         7260
7213     * copy_listeners() makes the copy, find_listener()        7261
7214     * finds an old listener and close_unused_listener()       7262    static void close_unused_listeners(void)
7215     * cleans up whatever wasn't used.                         7263    {
7216     */                                                        7264        listen_rec *or, *next;
7217    static listen_rec *old_listeners;                          7265
7218                                                               7266        for (or = old_listeners; or; or = next) {
7219    /* unfortunately copy_listeners may be called before       7267          next = or->next;
7220     * listeners is a ring */                                  7268          if (!or->used)
7221    static void copy_listeners(pool *p)                        7269              closesocket(or->fd);
7222    {                                                          7270          free(or);
7223        listen_rec *lr;                                        7271        }
7224                                                               7272        old_listeners = NULL;
7225        ap_assert(old_listeners == NULL);                      7273    }
7226        if (ap_listeners == NULL) {                            7274
7227          return;                                              7275
7228        }                                                      7276    /* open sockets, and turn the listeners list into a
7229        lr = ap_listeners;                                     7277     * singly linked ring */
7230        do {                                                   7278    static void setup_listeners(pool *p)
7231          listen_rec *nr = malloc(sizeof *nr);                 7279    {
7232          if (nr == NULL) {                                    7280        listen_rec *lr;
7233              fprintf(stderr, "Ouch!  malloc failed in         7281        int fd;
7234                      copy_listeners()\n");                    7282
7235              exit(1);                                         7283        listenmaxfd = -1;
7236          }                                                    7284        FD_ZERO(&listenfds);
7237          *nr = *lr;                                           7285        lr = ap_listeners;
7238          ap_kill_cleanups_for_socket(p, nr->fd);              7286        for (;;) {
7239          nr->next = old_listeners;                            7287          fd = find_listener(lr);
7240          ap_assert(!nr->used);                                7288          if (fd < 0) {
7241          old_listeners = nr;                                  7289              fd = make_sock(p, &lr->local_addr);
```

```
7290          }
7291          else {
7292              ap_note_cleanups_for_socket(p, fd);
7293          }
7294          if (fd >= 0) {
7295              FD_SET(fd, &listenfds);
7296              if (fd > listenmaxfd)
7297                  listenmaxfd = fd;
7298          }
7299          lr->fd = fd;
7300          if (lr->next == NULL)
7301              break;
7302          lr = lr->next;
7303      }
7304      /* turn the list into a ring */
7305      lr->next = ap_listeners;
7306      head_listener = ap_listeners;
7307      close_unused_listeners();
7308
7309  #ifdef NO_SERIALIZED_ACCEPT
7310      /* warn them about the starvation problem if
7311       * they're using multiple sockets
7312      */
7313      if (ap_listeners->next != ap_listeners) {
7314          ap_log_error(APLOG_MARK,
7315              APLOG_NOERRNO|APLOG_CRIT, NULL,
7316                  "You cannot use multiple Listens safely
7317                      on your system, "
7318                  "proceeding anyway.  See src/PORTING,
7319                      search for "
7320                  "SERIALIZED_ACCEPT.");
7321      }
7322  #endif
7323  }
7324
7325
7326  /*
7327   * Find a listener which is ready for accept().  This
7328   * advances the head_listener global.
7329  */
7330  static ap_inline listen_rec
7331      *find_ready_listener(fd_set * main_fds)
7332  {
7333      listen_rec *lr;
7334
7335      lr = head_listener;
7336      do {
7337          if (FD_ISSET(lr->fd, main_fds)) {
```

```
7338              head_listener = lr->next;
7339              return (lr);
7340          }
7341          lr = lr->next;
7342      } while (lr != head_listener);
7343      return NULL;
7344  }
7345
7346
7347  #ifdef WIN32
7348  static int s_iInitCount = 0;
7349
7350  static int AMCSocketInitialize(void)
7351  {
7352      int iVersionRequested;
7353      WSADATA wsaData;
7354      int err;
7355
7356      if (s_iInitCount > 0) {
7357          s_iInitCount++;
7358          return (0);
7359      }
7360      else if (s_iInitCount < 0)
7361          return (s_iInitCount);
7362
7363      /* s_iInitCount == 0. Do the initailization */
7364      iVersionRequested = MAKEWORD(1, 1);
7365      err = WSAStartup((WORD) iVersionRequested,
7366          &wsaData);
7367      if (err) {
7368          s_iInitCount = -1;
7369          return (s_iInitCount);
7370      }
7371      if (LOBYTE(wsaData.wVersion) != 1 ||
7372          HIBYTE(wsaData.wVersion) != 1) {
7373          s_iInitCount = -2;
7374          WSACleanup();
7375          return (s_iInitCount);
7376      }
7377
7378      s_iInitCount++;
7379      return (s_iInitCount);
7380
7381  }
7382
7383
7384  static void AMCSocketCleanup(void)
7385  {
```

```
7386        if (--s_iInitCount == 0)
7387          WSACleanup();
7388        return;
7389    }
7390    #endif
7391
7392    static void show_compile_settings(void)
7393    {
7394        printf("Server version: %s\n",
7395              ap_get_server_version());
7396        printf("Server built:   %s\n",
7397              ap_get_server_built());
7398        printf("Server's Module Magic Number: %u:%u\n",
7399            MODULE_MAGIC_NUMBER_MAJOR,
7400              MODULE_MAGIC_NUMBER_MINOR);
7401        printf("Server compiled with....\n");
7402    #ifdef BIG_SECURITY_HOLE
7403        printf(" -D BIG_SECURITY_HOLE\n");
7404    #endif
7405    #ifdef SECURITY_HOLE_PASS_AUTHORIZATION
7406        printf(" -D SECURITY_HOLE_PASS_AUTHORIZATION\n");
7407    #endif
7408    #ifdef HAVE_MMAP
7409        printf(" -D HAVE_MMAP\n");
7410    #endif
7411    #ifdef HAVE_SHMGET
7412        printf(" -D HAVE_SHMGET\n");
7413    #endif
7414    #ifdef USE_MMAP_SCOREBOARD
7415        printf(" -D USE_MMAP_SCOREBOARD\n");
7416    #endif
7417    #ifdef USE_SHMGET_SCOREBOARD
7418        printf(" -D USE_SHMGET_SCOREBOARD\n");
7419    #endif
7420    #ifdef USE_OS2_SCOREBOARD
7421        printf(" -D USE_OS2_SCOREBOARD\n");
7422    #endif
7423    #ifdef USE_POSIX_SCOREBOARD
7424        printf(" -D USE_POSIX_SCOREBOARD\n");
7425    #endif
7426    #ifdef USE_MMAP_FILES
7427        printf(" -D USE_MMAP_FILES\n");
7428    #ifdef MMAP_SEGMENT_SIZE
7429        printf(" -D MMAP_SEGMENT_SIZE=%ld\n",
7430              (long)MMAP_SEGMENT_SIZE);
7431    #endif
7432    #endif /*USE_MMAP_FILES*/
7433    #ifdef NO_WRITEV
7434        printf(" -D NO_WRITEV\n");
7435    #endif
7436    #ifdef NO_LINGCLOSE
7437        printf(" -D NO_LINGCLOSE\n");
7438    #endif
7439    #ifdef USE_FCNTL_SERIALIZED_ACCEPT
7440        printf(" -D USE_FCNTL_SERIALIZED_ACCEPT\n");
7441    #endif
7442    #ifdef USE_FLOCK_SERIALIZED_ACCEPT
7443        printf(" -D USE_FLOCK_SERIALIZED_ACCEPT\n");
7444    #endif
7445    #ifdef USE_USLOCK_SERIALIZED_ACCEPT
7446        printf(" -D USE_USLOCK_SERIALIZED_ACCEPT\n");
7447    #endif
7448    #ifdef USE_SYSVSEM_SERIALIZED_ACCEPT
7449        printf(" -D USE_SYSVSEM_SERIALIZED_ACCEPT\n");
7450    #endif
7451    #ifdef USE_PTHREAD_SERIALIZED_ACCEPT
7452        printf(" -D USE_PTHREAD_SERIALIZED_ACCEPT\n");
7453    #endif
7454    #ifdef SINGLE_LISTEN_UNSERIALIZED_ACCEPT
7455        printf(" -D SINGLE_LISTEN_UNSERIALIZED_ACCEPT\n");
7456    #endif
7457    #ifdef NO_OTHER_CHILD
7458        printf(" -D NO_OTHER_CHILD\n");
7459    #endif
7460    #ifdef NO_RELIABLE_PIPED_LOGS
7461        printf(" -D NO_RELIABLE_PIPED_LOGS\n");
7462    #endif
7463    #ifdef BUFFERED_LOGS
7464        printf(" -D BUFFERED_LOGS\n");
7465    #ifdef PIPE_BUF
7466        printf(" -D PIPE_BUF=%ld\n",(long)PIPE_BUF);
7467    #endif
7468    #endif
7469    #ifdef MULTITHREAD
7470        printf(" -D MULTITHREAD\n");
7471    #endif
7472    #ifdef CHARSET_EBCDIC
7473        printf(" -D CHARSET_EBCDIC\n");
7474    #endif
7475    #ifdef NEED_HASHBANG_EMUL
7476        printf(" -D NEED_HASHBANG_EMUL\n");
7477    #endif
7478    #ifdef SHARED_CORE
7479        printf(" -D SHARED_CORE\n");
7480    #endif
7481
```

```
7482    /* This list displays the compiled-in default paths: */
7483    #ifdef HTTPD_ROOT
7484        printf(" -D HTTPD_ROOT=\"" HTTPD_ROOT "\"\n");
7485    #endif
7486    #ifdef SUEXEC_BIN
7487        printf(" -D SUEXEC_BIN=\"" SUEXEC_BIN "\"\n");
7488    #endif
7489    #ifdef SHARED_CORE_DIR
7490        printf(" -D SHARED_CORE_DIR=\""
7491                SHARED_CORE_DIR "\"\n");
7492    #endif
7493    #ifdef DEFAULT_PIDLOG
7494        printf(" -D DEFAULT_PIDLOG=\""
7495                DEFAULT_PIDLOG "\"\n");
7496    #endif
7497    #ifdef DEFAULT_SCOREBOARD
7498        printf(" -D DEFAULT_SCOREBOARD=\""
7499                DEFAULT_SCOREBOARD "\"\n");
7500    #endif
7501    #ifdef DEFAULT_LOCKFILE
7502        printf(" -D DEFAULT_LOCKFILE=\""
7503                DEFAULT_LOCKFILE "\"\n");
7504    #endif
7505    #ifdef DEFAULT_XFERLOG
7506        printf(" -D DEFAULT_XFERLOG=\""
7507                DEFAULT_XFERLOG "\"\n");
7508    #endif
7509    #ifdef DEFAULT_ERRORLOG
7510        printf(" -D DEFAULT_ERRORLOG=\""
7511                DEFAULT_ERRORLOG "\"\n");
7512    #endif
7513    #ifdef TYPES_CONFIG_FILE
7514        printf(" -D TYPES_CONFIG_FILE=\""
7515                TYPES_CONFIG_FILE "\"\n");
7516
7517    #endif
7518    #ifdef SERVER_CONFIG_FILE
7519        printf(" -D SERVER_CONFIG_FILE=\""
7520                SERVER_CONFIG_FILE "\"\n");
7521    #endif
7522    #ifdef ACCESS_CONFIG_FILE
7523        printf(" -D ACCESS_CONFIG_FILE=\""
7524                ACCESS_CONFIG_FILE "\"\n");
7525    #endif
7526    #ifdef RESOURCE_CONFIG_FILE
7527        printf(" -D RESOURCE_CONFIG_FILE=\""
7528                RESOURCE_CONFIG_FILE "\"\n");
7529    #endif

7530    }
7531
7532
7533    /* Some init code that's common between win32 and
7534     * unix... well actually some of it is #ifdef'd
7535     * but was duplicated before anyhow.  This stuff
7536     * is still a mess.
7537     */
7538    static void common_init(void)
7539    {
7540        INIT_SIGLIST()
7541    #ifdef AUX3
7542        (void) set42sig();
7543    #endif
7544
7545    #ifdef WIN32
7546        /* Initialize the stupid sockets */
7547        AMCSocketInitialize();
7548    #endif /* WIN32 */
7549
7550        pconf = ap_init_alloc();
7551        ptrans = ap_make_sub_pool(pconf);
7552
7553        ap_util_init();
7554        ap_util_uri_init();
7555
7556        pcommands = ap_make_sub_pool(NULL);
7557        ap_server_pre_read_config  =
7558            ap_make_array(pcommands, 1, sizeof(char *));
7559        ap_server_post_read_config =
7560            ap_make_array(pcommands, 1, sizeof(char *));
7561        ap_server_config_defines   =
7562            ap_make_array(pcommands, 1, sizeof(char *));
7563    }
7564
7565    #ifndef MULTITHREAD
7566    /*********************************************************
7567     * Child process main loop.
7568     * The following vars are static to avoid getting
7569     * clobbered by longjmp(); they are really
7570     * private to child_main.
7571     */
7572
7573    static int srv;
7574    static int csd;
7575    static int dupped_csd;
7576    static int requests_this_child;
7577    static fd_set main_fds;
```

```
7578
7579    API_EXPORT(void) ap_child_terminate(request_rec *r)
7580    {
7581        r->connection->keepalive = 0;
7582        requests_this_child = ap_max_requests_per_child = 1;
7583    }
7584
7585    static void child_main(int child_num_arg)
7586    {
7587        NET_SIZE_T clen;
7588        struct sockaddr sa_server;
7589        struct sockaddr sa_client;
7590        listen_rec *lr;
7591
7592        /* All of initialization is a critical section,
7593         * we don't care if we're told to HUP or USR1 before
7594         * we're done initializing.  For example, we could
7595         * be half way through child_init_modules() when a
7596         * restart signal arrives, and we'd have no real
7597         * way to recover gracefully and exit properly.
7598         *
7599         * I suppose a module could take forever to
7600         * initialize, but that would be either a broken
7601         * module, or a broken configuration (i.e. network
7602         * problems, file locking problems, whatever). -djg
7603         */
7604        ap_block_alarms();
7605
7606        my_pid = getpid();
7607        csd = -1;
7608        dupped_csd = -1;
7609        my_child_num = child_num_arg;
7610        requests_this_child = 0;
7611
7612        /* Get a sub pool for global allocations in this
7613         * child, so that we can have cleanups occur
7614         * when the child exits.
7615         */
7616        pchild = ap_make_sub_pool(pconf);
7617
7618        /* needs to be done before we switch UIDs so
7619         * we have permissions */
7620        reopen_scoreboard(pchild);
7621        SAFE_ACCEPT(accept_mutex_child_init(pchild));
7622
7623        set_group_privs();
7624    #ifdef MPE
7625        /* Only try to switch if we're running
7626         * as MANAGER.SYS */
7627        if (geteuid() == 1 && ap_user_id > 1) {
7628            GETPRIVMODE();
7629            if (setuid(ap_user_id) == -1) {
7630                GETUSERMODE();
7631                ap_log_error(APLOG_MARK, APLOG_ALERT,
7632                        server_conf,
7633                        "setuid: unable to change uid");
7634                exit(1);
7635            }
7636            GETUSERMODE();
7637        }
7638
7639    #else
7640        /* Only try to switch if we're running as root */
7641        if (!geteuid() && (
7642    #ifdef _OSD_POSIX
7643            os_init_job_environment(server_conf, ap_user_name,
7644                one_process) != 0 ||
7645    #endif
7646            setuid(ap_user_id) == -1)) {
7647            ap_log_error(APLOG_MARK, APLOG_ALERT, server_conf,
7648                    "setuid: unable to change uid");
7649            clean_child_exit(APEXIT_CHILDFATAL);
7650        }
7651    #endif
7652
7653        ap_child_init_modules(pchild, server_conf);
7654
7655        /* done with the initialization critical section */
7656        ap_unblock_alarms();
7657
7658        (void) ap_update_child_status(my_child_num,
7659                SERVER_READY, (request_rec *) NULL);
7660
7661        /*
7662         * Setup the jump buffers so that we can return
7663         * here after a timeout
7664         */
7665        ap_setjmp(jmpbuffer);
7666    #ifndef OS2
7667    #ifdef SIGURG
7668        signal(SIGURG, timeout);
7669    #endif
7670    #endif
7671        signal(SIGALRM, alrm_handler);
7672
7673    #ifdef OS2
```

```
7674    /* Stop Ctrl-C/Ctrl-Break signals going to child
7675     * processes */
7676        {
7677            unsigned long ulTimes;
7678            DosSetSignalExceptionFocus(0, &ulTimes);
7679        }
7680    #endif
7681
7682        while (1) {
7683          BUFF *conn_io;
7684          request_rec *r;
7685
7686          /* Prepare to receive a SIGUSR1 due to graceful
7687           * restart so that we can exit cleanly.  Since
7688           * we're between connections right now it's the
7689           * right time to exit, but we might be blocked in a
7690           * system call when the graceful restart request
7691           * is made. */
7692          usr1_just_die = 1;
7693          signal(SIGUSR1, usr1_handler);
7694
7695          /*
7696           * (Re)initialize this child to a
7697           * pre-connection state.
7698           */
7699
7700          ap_kill_timeout(0);
7701          /* Cancel any outstanding alarms. */
7702          current_conn = NULL;
7703
7704          ap_clear_pool(ptrans);
7705
7706          ap_sync_scoreboard_image();
7707          if (ap_scoreboard_image->global.running_generation
7708              != ap_my_generation) {
7709              clean_child_exit(0);
7710          }
7711
7712    #ifndef WIN32
7713          if ((ap_max_requests_per_child > 0
7714              && requests_this_child++ >=
7715                  ap_max_requests_per_child)) {
7716              clean_child_exit(0);
7717          }
7718    #else
7719          ++requests_this_child;
7720    #endif
7721
7722          (void) ap_update_child_status(my_child_num,
7723              SERVER_READY, (request_rec *) NULL);
7724
7725          /*
7726           * Wait for an acceptable connection to arrive.
7727           */
7728
7729          /* Lock around "accept", if necessary */
7730          SAFE_ACCEPT(accept_mutex_on());
7731
7732          for (;;) {
7733              if (ap_listeners->next != ap_listeners) {
7734                  /* more than one socket */
7735                  memcpy(&main_fds, &listenfds, sizeof(fd_set));
7736                  srv = ap_select(listenmaxfd + 1, &main_fds,
7737                      NULL, NULL, NULL);
7738
7739                  if (srv < 0 && errno != EINTR) {
7740                      /* Single Unix documents select as
7741                       * returning errnos EBADF, EINTR, and
7742                       * EINVAL... and in none of those
7743                       * cases does it make sense to continue.
7744                       * In fact on Linux 2.0.x we seem to end
7745                       * up with EFAULT occasionally, and
7746                       * we'd loop forever due to it.
7747                       */
7748                      ap_log_error(APLOG_MARK, APLOG_ERR,
7749                          server_conf, "select: (listen)");
7750                      clean_child_exit(1);
7751                  }
7752
7753                  if (srv <= 0)
7754                      continue;
7755
7756                  lr = find_ready_listener(&main_fds);
7757                  if (lr == NULL)
7758
7759                      continue;
7760                  sd = lr->fd;
7761              }
7762              else {
7763                  /* only one socket, just pretend we did
7764                   * the other stuff */
7765                  sd = ap_listeners->fd;
7766              }
7767
7768              /* if we accept() something we don't want to
7769               * die, so we have to defer the exit
```

```
7770              */
7771              deferred_die = 0;
7772              usr1_just_die = 0;
7773              for (;;) {
7774               clen = sizeof(sa_client);
7775               csd = accept(sd, &sa_client, &clen);
7776               if (csd >= 0 || errno != EINTR)
7777                    break;
7778               if (deferred_die) {
7779                    /* we didn't get a socket, and we were
7780                     * told to die */
7781                    clean_child_exit(0);
7782               }
7783              }
7784
7785              if (csd >= 0)
7786               break;
7787              /* We have a socket ready for reading */
7788              else {
7789
7790               /* Our old behaviour here was to continue
7791                * after accept()errors.  But this leads
7792                * us into lots of troubles because most of
7793                * the errors are quite fatal.  For example,
7794                * EMFILE can be caused by slow descriptor
7795                * leaks (say in a 3rd party module, or libc).
7796                * It's foolish for us to continue after
7797                * an EMFILE.  We also seem to tickle kernel
7798                * bugs on some platforms which lead to never-
7799                * ending loops here.  So it seems best
7800                * to just exit in most cases.
7801                */
7802                  switch (errno) {
7803      #ifdef EPROTO
7804                  /* EPROTO on certain older kernels really
7805                   * means ECONNABORTED, so we need to
7806                   * ignore it for them. See discussion in
7807                   * new-httpd archives nh.9701 search for
7808                   * EPROTO.
7809                   *
7810                   * Also see nh.9603, search for EPROTO:
7811                   * There is potentially a bug in Solaris
7812                   * 2.x x<6, and other boxes that implement
7813                   * tcp sockets in userland (i.e. on top
7814                   * of STREAMS).  On these systems, EPROTO
7815                   * can actually result in a fatal loop.
7816                   * See PR#981 for example.  It's hard to
7817                   * handle both uses of EPROTO.
7818                   */
7819                  case EPROTO:
7820      #endif
7821      #ifdef ECONNABORTED
7822                  case ECONNABORTED:
7823      #endif
7824                  /* Linux generates the rest of these,
7825                   * other tcp stacks (i.e. bsd) tend to
7826                   * hide them behind getsockopt()
7827                   * interfaces.They occur when the net goes
7828                   * sour or the client disconnects after
7829                   * the three-way handshake has been done
7830                   * in the kernel but before userland has
7831                   * picked up the socket.
7832                   */
7833      #ifdef ECONNRESET
7834                  case ECONNRESET:
7835      #endif
7836      #ifdef ETIMEDOUT
7837                  case ETIMEDOUT:
7838      #endif
7839      #ifdef EHOSTUNREACH
7840                  case EHOSTUNREACH:
7841      #endif
7842      #ifdef ENETUNREACH
7843                  case ENETUNREACH:
7844      #endif
7845                      break;
7846
7847                  default:
7848                      ap_log_error(APLOG_MARK, APLOG_ERR,
7849                          server_conf,
7850                          "accept: (client socket)");
7851                      clean_child_exit(1);
7852                  }
7853              }
7854
7855              /* go around again, safe to die */
7856              usr1_just_die = 1;
7857              if (deferred_die) {
7858               /* ok maybe not, see ya later */
7859               clean_child_exit(0);
7860              }
7861              /* or maybe we missed a signal, you never
7862               * know on systems without reliable signals
7863      */
7864
7865              ap_sync_scoreboard_image();
7866              if (ap_scoreboard_image->
```

```
7866                  global.running_generation !=          7914              conn_io = ap_bcreate(ptrans, B_RDWR | B_SOCKET);
7867                  ap_my_generation) {                    7915
7868              clean_child_exit(0);                       7916      #ifdef B_SFIO
7869          }                                              7917              (void) sfdisc(conn_io->sf_in, SF_POPDISC);
7870      }                                                  7918              sfdisc(conn_io->sf_in, bsfio_new(conn_io->pool,
7871                                                         7919                  conn_io));
7872      SAFE_ACCEPT(accept_mutex_off());                   7920              sfsetbuf(conn_io->sf_in, NULL, 0);
7873      /* unlock after "accept" */                        7921
7874                                                         7922              (void) sfdisc(conn_io->sf_out, SF_POPDISC);
7875      /* We've got a socket, let's at least process      7923              sfdisc(conn_io->sf_out, bsfio_new(conn_io->pool,
7876       * one request off the socket before we accept     7924                  conn_io));
7877       * a graceful restart request.                     7925
7878       */                                                7926              sfsetbuf(conn_io->sf_out, NULL, 0);
7879      signal(SIGUSR1, SIG_IGN);                          7927      #endif
7880                                                         7928
7881      ap_note_cleanups_for_fd(ptrans, csd);              7929              dupped_csd = csd;
7882                                                         7930      #if defined(NEED_DUPPED_CSD)
7883      /* protect various fd_sets */                      7931              if ((dupped_csd = dup(csd)) < 0) {
7884      if (csd >= FD_SETSIZE) {                            7932                  ap_log_error(APLOG_MARK, APLOG_ERR, server_conf,
7885          ap_log_error(APLOG_MARK,                       7933                      "dup: couldn't duplicate csd");
7886              APLOG_NOERRNO|APLOG_WARNING, NULL,         7934                  dupped_csd = csd;      /* Oh well... */
7887          "[csd] filedescriptor (%u) larger than         7935              }
7888              FD_SETSIZE (%u) "                          7936              ap_note_cleanups_for_fd(ptrans, dupped_csd);
7889          "found, you probably need to rebuild Apache    7937
7890              with a "                                   7938              /* protect various fd_sets */
7891          "larger FD_SETSIZE", csd, FD_SETSIZE);         7939              if (dupped_csd >= FD_SETSIZE) {
7892          continue;                                      7940                  ap_log_error(APLOG_MARK,
7893      }                                                  7941                      APLOG_NOERRNO|APLOG_WARNING, NULL,
7894                                                         7942                  "[dupped_csd] filedescriptor (%u) larger
7895      /*                                                 7943                      than FD_SETSIZE (%u) "
7896       * We now have a connection, so set it up with     7944                  "found, you probably need to rebuild
7897       * the appropriate socket options, file            7945                      Apache with a "
7898       * descriptors, and read/write buffers.            7946                  "larger FD_SETSIZE", dupped_csd, FD_SETSIZE);
7899       */                                                7947                  continue;
7900                                                         7948              }
7901      clen = sizeof(sa_server);                          7949      #endif
7902      if (getsockname(csd, &sa_server, &clen) < 0) {     7950              ap_bpushfd(conn_io, csd, dupped_csd);
7903          ap_log_error(APLOG_MARK, APLOG_ERR,            7951
7904              server_conf, "getsockname");               7952              current_conn = new_connection(ptrans, server_conf,
7905          continue;                                      7953                  conn_io,
7906      }                                                  7954                          (struct sockaddr_in *) &sa_client,
7907                                                         7955                          (struct sockaddr_in *) &sa_server,
7908      sock_disable_nagle(csd);                           7956                              my_child_num);
7909                                                         7957
7910      (void) ap_update_child_status(my_child_num,        7958          /*
7911          SERVER_BUSY_READ,                              7959           * Read and process each request found on
7912                      (request_rec *) NULL);             7960           * our connection until no requests are
7913                                                         7961           * left or we decide to close.
```

```
7962        */
7963
7964        while ((r =
7965            ap_read_request(current_conn)) != NULL) {
7966
7967            /* read_request_line has already done a
7968             * signal (SIGUSR1, SIG_IGN);
7969             */
7970
7971            (void) ap_update_child_status(my_child_num,
7972                SERVER_BUSY_WRITE, r);
7973
7974            /* process the request if it was read
7975             * without error */
7976
7977            if (r->status == HTTP_OK)
7978                ap_process_request(r);
7979
7980            if(ap_extended_status)
7981                increment_counts(my_child_num, r);
7982
7983            if (!current_conn->keepalive ||
7984                current_conn->aborted)
7985                break;
7986
7987            ap_destroy_pool(r->pool);
7988            (void) ap_update_child_status(my_child_num,
7989                SERVER_BUSY_KEEPALIVE,
7990                            (request_rec *) NULL);
7991
7992            ap_sync_scoreboard_image();
7993            if (ap_scoreboard_image->global.running_generation
7994                != ap_my_generation) {
7995                ap_bclose(conn_io);
7996                clean_child_exit(0);
7997            }
7998
7999            /* In case we get a graceful restart while
8000             * we're blocked waiting for the request.
8001             *
8002             * XXX: This isn't perfect, we might actually
8003             * read the request and then just die without
8004             * saying anything to the client.  This can
8005             * be fixed by using deferred_die but you have
8006             * to teach buff.c about it so that it can
8007             * handle the EINTR properly.
8008             *
8009             * In practice though browsers (have to)
```

```
8010             * expect keepalive connections to close
8011             * before receiving a response because
8012             * of network latencies and server timeouts.
8013             */
8014            usr1_just_die = 1;
8015            signal(SIGUSR1, usr1_handler);
8016        }
8017
8018        /*
8019         * Close the connection, being careful to send
8020         * out whatever is still in our buffers.  If
8021         * possible, try to avoid a hard close until the
8022         * client has ACKed our FIN and/or has stopped
8023         * sending us data.
8024         */
8025
8026 #ifdef NO_LINGCLOSE
8027        ap_bclose(conn_io);        /* just close it */
8028 #else
8029        if (r && r->connection
8030            && !r->connection->aborted
8031            && r->connection->client
8032            && (r->connection->client->fd >= 0)) {
8033
8034            lingering_close(r);
8035        }
8036        else {
8037            ap_bsetflag(conn_io, B_EOUT, 1);
8038            ap_bclose(conn_io);
8039        }
8040 #endif
8041    }
8042 }
8043
8044 static int make_child(server_rec *s, int slot,
8045     time_t now)
8046 {
8047    int pid;
8048
8049    if (slot + 1 > max_daemons_limit) {
8050        max_daemons_limit = slot + 1;
8051    }
8052
8053    if (one_process) {
8054        signal(SIGHUP, just_die);
8055        signal(SIGINT, just_die);
8056        signal(SIGQUIT, SIG_DFL);
8057        signal(SIGTERM, just_die);
```

```
8058            child_main(slot);
8059        }
8060
8061        /* avoid starvation */
8062        head_listener = head_listener->next;
8063
8064        Explain1("Starting new child in slot %d", slot);
8065        (void) ap_update_child_status(slot, SERVER_STARTING,
8066                (request_rec *) NULL);
8067
8068
8069 #ifndef _OSD_POSIX
8070        if ((pid = fork()) == -1) {
8071 #else /*_OSD_POSIX*/
8072        /* BS2000 requires a "special" version of fork()
8073         * before a setuid() call */
8074        if ((pid = os_fork(ap_user_name)) == -1) {
8075 #endif /*_OSD_POSIX*/
8076            ap_log_error(APLOG_MARK, APLOG_ERR, s, "fork:
8077                Unable to fork new process");
8078
8079            /* fork didn't succeed. Fix the scoreboard or else
8080             * it will say SERVER_STARTING forever and ever
8081             */
8082            (void) ap_update_child_status(slot, SERVER_DEAD,
8083                (request_rec *) NULL);
8084
8085            /* In case system resources are maxxed out, we
8086                don't want Apache running away with the CPU
8087                trying to fork over and over and over again. */
8088            sleep(10);
8089
8090            return -1;
8091        }
8092
8093        if (!pid) {
8094 #ifdef AIX_BIND_PROCESSOR
8095 /* by default AIX binds to a single processor
8096  * this bit unbinds children which will then bind to
8097  * another cpu
8098  */
8099 #include <sys/processor.h>
8100            int status = bindprocessor(BINDPROCESS,
8101                (int)getpid(),
8102                            PROCESSOR_CLASS_ANY);
8103            if (status != OK) {
8104                ap_log_error(APLOG_MARK,
8105                    APLOG_NOERRNO|APLOG_WARNING, server_conf,
8106                        "processor unbind failed %d", status);
8107            }
8108 #endif
8109            RAISE_SIGSTOP(MAKE_CHILD);
8110            MONCONTROL(1);
8111            /* Disable the restart signal handlers and enable
8112             * the just_die stuff. Note that since restart()
8113             * just notes that a restart has been requested
8114             * there's no race condition here.
8115             */
8116            signal(SIGHUP, just_die);
8117            signal(SIGUSR1, just_die);
8118            signal(SIGTERM, just_die);
8119            child_main(slot);
8120        }
8121
8122 #ifdef OPTIMIZE_TIMEOUTS
8123        ap_scoreboard_image->parent[slot].last_rtime = now;
8124 #endif
8125        ap_scoreboard_image->parent[slot].pid = pid;
8126 #ifdef SCOREBOARD_FILE
8127        lseek(scoreboard_fd, XtOffsetOf(scoreboard,
8128            parent[slot]), 0);
8129        force_write(scoreboard_fd,
8130            &ap_scoreboard_image->parent[slot],
8131            sizeof(parent_score));
8132 #endif
8133
8134        return 0;
8135 }
8136
8137
8138 /* start up a bunch of children */
8139 static void startup_children(int number_to_start)
8140 {
8141        int i;
8142        time_t now = time(0);
8143
8144        for (i = 0; number_to_start && i <
8145                ap_daemons_limit; ++i) {
8146            if (ap_scoreboard_image->servers[i].status !=
8147                SERVER_DEAD) {
8148                continue;
8149            }
8150            if (make_child(server_conf, i, now) < 0) {
8151                break;
8152            }
8153            --number_to_start;
```

```
8154          }
8155      }
8156
8157
8158      /*
8159       * idle_spawn_rate is the number of children that will
8160       * be spawned on the next maintenance cycle if
8161       * there aren't enough idle servers.  It is doubled
8162       * up to MAX_SPAWN_RATE, and reset only when a cycle
8163       * goes by without the need to spawn.
8164       */
8165      static int idle_spawn_rate = 1;
8166      #ifndef MAX_SPAWN_RATE
8167      #define MAX_SPAWN_RATE       (32)
8168      #endif
8169      static int hold_off_on_exponential_spawning;
8170
8171      static void perform_idle_server_maintenance(void)
8172      {
8173          int i;
8174          int to_kill;
8175          int idle_count;
8176          short_score *ss;
8177          time_t now = time(0);
8178          int free_length;
8179          int free_slots[MAX_SPAWN_RATE];
8180          int last_non_dead;
8181          int total_non_dead;
8182
8183          /* initialize the free_list */
8184          free_length = 0;
8185
8186          to_kill = -1;
8187          idle_count = 0;
8188          last_non_dead = -1;
8189          total_non_dead = 0;
8190
8191          ap_sync_scoreboard_image();
8192          for (i = 0; i < ap_daemons_limit; ++i) {
8193           int status;
8194
8195           if (i >= max_daemons_limit && free_length ==
8196               idle_spawn_rate)
8197             break;
8198           ss = &ap_scoreboard_image->servers[i];
8199           status = ss->status;
8200           if (status == SERVER_DEAD) {
8201               /* try to keep children numbers as low as
8202               * possible */
8203               if (free_length < idle_spawn_rate) {
8204                   free_slots[free_length] = i;
8205                   ++free_length;
8206               }
8207           }
8208           else {
8209               /* We consider a starting server as idle
8210                * because we started it at least a cycle ago,
8211                * and if it still hasn't finished starting
8212                * then we're just going to swamp things
8213                * worse by forking more. So we hopefully
8214                * won't need to fork more if we count it.
8215                * This depends on the ordering of SERVER_READY
8216                * and SERVER_STARTING.
8217                */
8218               if (status <= SERVER_READY) {
8219                   ++ idle_count;
8220                   /* always kill the highest numbered child if
8221                    * we have to... no really well thought
8222                    * out reason ... other than observing
8223                    * the server behaviour under linux where
8224                    * lower numbered children tend to service
8225                    * more hits (and hence are more likely
8226                    * to have their data in cpu caches).
8227                    */
8228                   to_kill = i;
8229               }
8230
8231               ++total_non_dead;
8232               last_non_dead = i;
8233      #ifdef OPTIMIZE_TIMEOUTS
8234               if (ss->timeout_len) {
8235                   /* if it's a live server, with a live timeout
8236                    * then start checking its timeout */
8237                   parent_score *ps =
8238                       &ap_scoreboard_image->parent[i];
8239                   if (ss->cur_vtime != ps->last_vtime) {
8240                       /* it has made progress, so update its
8241                        * last_rtime,last_vtime */
8242                       ps->last_rtime = now;
8243                       ps->last_vtime = ss->cur_vtime;
8244                   }
8245                   else if (ps->last_rtime + ss->timeout_len <
8246                       now) {
8247                       /* no progress, and the timeout length
8248                        * has been exceeded */
8249                       ss->timeout_len = 0;
```

```
8250                    kill(ps->pid, SIGALRM);
8251
8252               }
8253             }
8254   #endif
8255         }
8256       }
8257       max_daemons_limit = last_non_dead + 1;
8258       if (idle_count > ap_daemons_max_free) {
8259         /* kill off one child... we use SIGUSR1 because
8260          * that'll cause it to shut down gracefully, in
8261          * case it happened to pick up a request
8262          * while we were counting */
8263         kill(ap_scoreboard_image->parent[to_kill].pid,
8264         SIGUSR1);
8265         idle_spawn_rate = 1;
8266       }
8267       else if (idle_count < ap_daemons_min_free) {
8268         /* terminate the free list */
8269         if (free_length == 0) {
8270           /* only report this condition once */
8271           static int reported = 0;
8272
8273           if (!reported) {
8274            ap_log_error(APLOG_MARK,
8275                 APLOG_NOERRNO|APLOG_ERR,
8276                 server_conf,
8277                   "server reached MaxClients setting, "
8278                   "consider"
8279                   " raising the MaxClients setting");
8280            reported = 1;
8281           }
8282           idle_spawn_rate = 1;
8283         }
8284         else {
8285           if (idle_spawn_rate >= 8) {
8286            ap_log_error(APLOG_MARK,
8287                 APLOG_NOERRNO|APLOG_INFO, server_conf,
8288                 "server seems busy, (you may need "
8289                 "to increase StartServers, or "
8290                 "Min/MaxSpareServers), "
8291                 "spawning %d children, there are "
8292                 "%d idle, and "
8293                 "%d total children", idle_spawn_rate,
8294                 idle_count, total_non_dead);
8295           }
8296           for (i = 0; i < free_length; ++i) {
8297   #ifdef TPF
8298             if(make_child(server_conf, free_slots[i],
8299                 now) == -1) {
8300               if(free_length == 1) {
8301                 shutdown_pending = 1;
8302                 ap_log_error(APLOG_MARK,
8303                     APLOG_EMERG, server_conf,
8304                 "No active child processes: shutting down");
8305               }
8306             }
8307   #else
8308             make_child(server_conf, free_slots[i], now);
8309   #endif /* TPF */
8310           }
8311           /* the next time around we want to spawn twice
8312            * as many if this wasn't good enough, but
8313            * not if we've just done a graceful
8314            */
8315           if (hold_off_on_exponential_spawning) {
8316             --hold_off_on_exponential_spawning;
8317           }
8318           else if (idle_spawn_rate < MAX_SPAWN_RATE) {
8319             idle_spawn_rate *= 2;
8320           }
8321         }
8322       }
8323       else {
8324         idle_spawn_rate = 1;
8325       }
8326   }
8327
8328
8329   static void process_child_status(int pid,
8330       ap_wait_t status)
8331   {
8332       /* Child died... if it died due to a fatal error,
8333        * we should simply bail out.
8334        */
8335       if ((WIFEXITED(status)) &&
8336       WEXITSTATUS(status) == APEXIT_CHILDFATAL) {
8337       ap_log_error(APLOG_MARK, APLOG_ALERT|APLOG_NOERRNO,
8338           server_conf,
8339               "Child %d returned a Fatal error... \n"
8340               "Apache is exiting!",
8341               pid);
8342       exit(APEXIT_CHILDFATAL);
8343       }
8344       if (WIFSIGNALED(status)) {
8345       switch (WTERMSIG(status)) {
```

```
8346          case SIGTERM:                          8394
8347          case SIGHUP:                           8395   static void standalone_main(int argc, char **argv)
8348          case SIGUSR1:                          8396   {
8349          case SIGKILL:                          8397       int remaining_children_to_start;
8350              break;                             8398
8351          default:                               8399   #ifdef OS2
8352   #ifdef SYS_SIGLIST                            8400       printf("%s \n", ap_get_server_version());
8353   #ifdef WCOREDUMP                              8401   #endif
8354              if (WCOREDUMP(status)) {           8402
8355               ap_log_error(APLOG_MARK,          8403       ap_standalone = 1;
8356                  APLOG_NOERRNO|APLOG_NOTICE,     8404
8357                      server_conf,               8405       is_graceful = 0;
8358                      "child pid %d exit signal %s (%d), "   8406
8359                      "possible coredump in %s", 8407       if (!one_process) {
8360                      pid, (WTERMSIG(status) >= NumSIG) ? "" :   8408        detach();
8361                      SYS_SIGLIST[WTERMSIG(status)],   8409       }
8362                          WTERMSIG(status),      8410       else {
8363                      ap_coredump_dir);          8411        MONCONTROL(1);
8364              }                                  8412       }
8365          else {                                 8413
8366   #endif                                        8414       my_pid = getpid();
8367              ap_log_error(APLOG_MARK,           8415
8368                  APLOG_NOERRNO|APLOG_NOTICE,     8416       do {
8369                      server_conf,               8417        copy_listeners(pconf);
8370                      "child pid %d exit signal %s (%d)", pid,   8418        if (!is_graceful) {
8371                      SYS_SIGLIST[WTERMSIG(status)],   8419            ap_restart_time = time(NULL);
8372                          WTERMSIG(status));     8420        }
8373   #ifdef WCOREDUMP                              8421   #ifdef SCOREBOARD_FILE
8374              }                                  8422        else if (scoreboard_fd != -1) {
8375   #endif                                        8423            ap_kill_cleanup(pconf, NULL,
8376   #else                                         8424                cleanup_scoreboard_file);
8377              ap_log_error(APLOG_MARK,           8425            ap_kill_cleanups_for_fd(pconf, scoreboard_fd);
8378                  APLOG_NOERRNO|APLOG_NOTICE,     8426        }
8379                      server_conf,               8427   #endif
8380                      "child pid %d exit signal %d",   8428       ap_clear_pool(pconf);
8381                      pid, WTERMSIG(status));    8429       ptrans = ap_make_sub_pool(pconf);
8382   #endif                                        8430
8383          }                                      8431       server_conf = ap_read_config(pconf, ptrans,
8384          }                                      8432           ap_server_confname);
8385   }                                             8433       setup_listeners(pconf);
8386                                                  8434       ap_open_logs(server_conf, pconf);
8387                                                  8435       ap_log_pid(pconf, ap_pid_fname);
8388   /**********************************************   8436       ap_set_version();
8389    * Executive routines.                        8437       /* create our server_version string */
8390    */                                           8438       ap_init_modules(pconf, server_conf);
8391                                                  8439       version_locked++;
8392   #ifndef STANDALONE_MAIN                        8440       /* no more changes to server_version */
8393   #define STANDALONE_MAIN standalone_main        8441       SAFE_ACCEPT(accept_mutex_init(pconf));
```

```
8442        if (!is_graceful) {
8443            reinit_scoreboard(pconf);
8444        }
8445    #ifdef SCOREBOARD_FILE
8446        else {
8447            ap_scoreboard_fname =
8448                    ap_server_root_relative(pconf,
8449                    ap_scoreboard_fname);
8450            ap_note_cleanups_for_fd(pconf, scoreboard_fd);
8451        }
8452    #endif
8453
8454        set_signals();
8455
8456        if (ap_daemons_max_free < ap_daemons_min_free + 1)
8457        /* Don't thrash... */
8458            ap_daemons_max_free = ap_daemons_min_free + 1;
8459
8460        /* If we're doing a graceful_restart then we're
8461         * going to see a lot of children exiting
8462         * immediately when we get into the main loop
8463         * below (because we just sent them SIGUSR1).
8464         * This happens pretty rapidly... and for each
8465         * one that exits we'll start a new one until
8466         * we reach at least daemons_min_free.  But we
8467         * may be permitted to start more than that,
8468         * so we'll just keep track of how many we're
8469         * supposed to start up without the 1 second
8470         * penalty between each fork.
8471         */
8472        remaining_children_to_start = ap_daemons_to_start;
8473        if (remaining_children_to_start >
8474            ap_daemons_limit) {
8475            remaining_children_to_start = ap_daemons_limit;
8476        }
8477        if (!is_graceful) {
8478            startup_children(remaining_children_to_start);
8479            remaining_children_to_start = 0;
8480        }
8481        else {
8482            /* give the system some time to recover
8483             * before kicking into exponential mode */
8484            hold_off_on_exponential_spawning = 10;
8485        }
8486
8487        ap_log_error(APLOG_MARK,
8488                APLOG_NOERRNO|APLOG_NOTICE, server_conf,
8489                "%s configured -
8490                resuming normal operations",
8491                ap_get_server_version());
8492        if (ap_suexec_enabled) {
8493            ap_log_error(APLOG_MARK,
8494                    APLOG_NOERRNO|APLOG_NOTICE, server_conf,
8495                    "suEXEC mechanism enabled
8496                        (wrapper: %s)", SUEXEC_BIN);
8497        }
8498        ap_log_error(APLOG_MARK,
8499                APLOG_NOERRNO|APLOG_INFO, server_conf,
8500                "Server built: %s", ap_get_server_built());
8501        restart_pending = shutdown_pending = 0;
8502
8503        while (!restart_pending && !shutdown_pending) {
8504            int child_slot;
8505            ap_wait_t status;
8506            int pid = wait_or_timeout(&status);
8507
8508            /* XXX: if it takes longer than 1 second for
8509             * all our children to start up and get into
8510             * IDLE state then we may spawn an
8511             * extra child
8512             */
8513            if (pid >= 0) {
8514                process_child_status(pid, status);
8515                /* non-fatal death... note that it's gone
8516                 * in the scoreboard. */
8517                ap_sync_scoreboard_image();
8518                child_slot = find_child_by_pid(pid);
8519                Explain2("Reaping child %d slot %d",
8520                    pid, child_slot);
8521                if (child_slot >= 0) {
8522                    (void) ap_update_child_status(child_slot,
8523                        SERVER_DEAD,
8524                                (request_rec *) NULL);
8525                    if (remaining_children_to_start
8526                        && child_slot < ap_daemons_limit) {
8527                        /* we're still doing a 1-for-1
8528                         * replacement of dead children
8529                         * with new children
8530                         */
8531                        make_child(server_conf, child_slot,
8532                            time(0));
8533                        --remaining_children_to_start;
8534                    }
8535    #ifndef NO_OTHER_CHILD
8536                }
8537                else if (reap_other_child(pid, status) == 0) {
```

```
8538                     /* handled */
8539     #endif
8540             }
8541             else if (is_graceful) {
8542                 /* Great, we've probably just lost a
8543                  * slot in the scoreboard.  Somehow we
8544                  * don't know about this child.
8545                  */
8546                 ap_log_error(APLOG_MARK,
8547                         APLOG_NOERRNO|APLOG_WARNING,
8548                         server_conf,
8549                         "long lost child came home!
8550                             (pid %d)", pid);
8551             }
8552             /* Don't perform idle maintenance when a child
8553              * dies, only do it when there's a timeout.
8554              * Remember only a finite number of children
8555              * can die, and it's pretty pathological
8556              * for a lot to die suddenly.
8557              */
8558             continue;
8559         }
8560         else if (remaining_children_to_start) {
8561             /* we hit a 1 second timeout in which none
8562              * of the previous generation of children
8563              * needed to be reaped... so assume
8564              * they're all done, and pick up the slack
8565              * if any is left.
8566              */
8567             startup_children(remaining_children_to_start);
8568             remaining_children_to_start = 0;
8569             /* In any event we really shouldn't do the
8570              * code below because few of the servers
8571              * we just started are in the IDLE state yet,
8572              * so we'd mistakenly create an extra server.
8573              */
8574             continue;
8575         }
8576
8577         perform_idle_server_maintenance();
8578     }
8579
8580     if (shutdown_pending) {
8581         /* Time to gracefully shut down:
8582          * Kill child processes, tell them to call
8583          * child_exit, etc...
8584          */
8585         if (ap_killpg(pgrp, SIGTERM) < 0) {
8586             ap_log_error(APLOG_MARK, APLOG_WARNING,
8587                     server_conf, "killpg SIGTERM");
8588         }
8589         reclaim_child_processes(1);
8590         /* Start with SIGTERM */
8591
8592         /* cleanup pid file on normal shutdown */
8593         {
8594         const char *pidfile = NULL;
8595         pidfile = ap_server_root_relative (pconf,
8596             ap_pid_fname);
8597         if ( pidfile != NULL && unlink(pidfile) == 0)
8598             ap_log_error(APLOG_MARK,
8599                     APLOG_NOERRNO|APLOG_INFO,
8600                     server_conf,
8601                     "removed PID file %s (pid=%ld)",
8602                     pidfile, (long)getpid());
8603         }
8604
8605         ap_log_error(APLOG_MARK,
8606                 APLOG_NOERRNO|APLOG_NOTICE, server_conf,
8607                 "caught SIGTERM, shutting down");
8608         clean_parent_exit(0);
8609     }
8610
8611     /* we've been told to restart */
8612     signal(SIGHUP, SIG_IGN);
8613     signal(SIGUSR1, SIG_IGN);
8614
8615     if (one_process) {
8616         /* not worth thinking about */
8617         clean_parent_exit(0);
8618     }
8619
8620     /* advance to the next generation */
8621     /* XXX: we really need to make sure this new
8622      * generation number isn't in use by any of the
8623      * children.
8624      */
8625     ++ap_my_generation;
8626     ap_scoreboard_image->global.running_generation =
8627         ap_my_generation;
8628     update_scoreboard_global();
8629
8630     if (is_graceful) {
8631 #ifndef SCOREBOARD_FILE
8632         int i;
8633 #endif
```

```
8634        ap_log_error(APLOG_MARK,
8635            APLOG_NOERRNO|APLOG_NOTICE, server_conf,
8636            "SIGUSR1 received.  Doing graceful restart");
8637
8638        /* kill off the idle ones */
8639        if (ap_killpg(pgrp, SIGUSR1) < 0) {
8640        ap_log_error(APLOG_MARK, APLOG_WARNING,
8641            server_conf, "killpg SIGUSR1");
8642        }
8643 #ifndef SCOREBOARD_FILE
8644        /* This is mostly for debugging... so that we
8645         * know what is still gracefully dealing with
8646         * existing request.  But we can't really
8647         * do it if we're in a SCOREBOARD_FILE because
8648         * it'll cause corruption too easily.
8649         */
8650        ap_sync_scoreboard_image();
8651        for (i = 0; i < ap_daemons_limit; ++i) {
8652        if (ap_scoreboard_image->servers[i].status
8653            != SERVER_DEAD) {
8654            ap_scoreboard_image->servers[i].status =
8655                SERVER_GRACEFUL;
8656        }
8657        }
8658 #endif
8659        }
8660        else {
8661        /* Kill 'em off */
8662        if (ap_killpg(pgrp, SIGHUP) < 0) {
8663            ap_log_error(APLOG_MARK, APLOG_WARNING,
8664                server_conf, "killpg SIGHUP");
8665        }
8666        reclaim_child_processes(0);
8667        /* Not when just starting up */
8668        ap_log_error(APLOG_MARK,
8669            APLOG_NOERRNO|APLOG_NOTICE, server_conf,
8670            "SIGHUP received.  Attempting to restart");
8671        }
8672    } while (restart_pending);
8673
8674    /*add_common_vars(NULL);*/
8675 }                       /* standalone_main */
8676 #else
8677 /* prototype */
8678 void STANDALONE_MAIN(int argc, char **argv);
8679 #endif /* STANDALONE_MAIN */
8680
8681 extern char *optarg;
```

```
8682 extern int optind;
8683
8684 int REALMAIN(int argc, char *argv[])
8685 {
8686    int c;
8687    int configtestonly = 0;
8688    int sock_in;
8689    int sock_out;
8690    char *s;
8691
8692 #ifdef SecureWare
8693    if (set_auth_parameters(argc, argv) < 0)
8694        perror("set_auth_parameters");
8695    if (getluid() < 0)
8696        if (setluid(getuid()) < 0)
8697            perror("setluid");
8698    if (setreuid(0, 0) < 0)
8699        perror("setreuid");
8700 #endif
8701
8702 #ifdef SOCKS
8703    SOCKSinit(argv[0]);
8704 #endif
8705
8706    MONCONTROL(0);
8707
8708    common_init();
8709
8710    if ((s = strrchr(argv[0], '/')) != NULL) {
8711        ap_server_argv0 = ++s;
8712    }
8713    else {
8714        ap_server_argv0 = argv[0];
8715    }
8716
8717    ap_cpystrn(ap_server_root, HTTPD_ROOT,
8718        sizeof(ap_server_root));
8719    ap_cpystrn(ap_server_confname, SERVER_CONFIG_FILE,
8720        sizeof(ap_server_confname));
8721
8722    ap_setup_prelinked_modules();
8723
8724 #ifndef TPF
8725    while ((c = getopt(argc, argv,
8726                "D:C:c:Xd:f:vVlLR:Sth"
8727 #ifdef DEBUG_SIGSTOP
8728                "Z:"
8729 #endif
```

```
8730                )) != -1) {
8731            char **new;
8732            switch (c) {
8733            case 'c':
8734                new = (char **)ap_push_array
8735                        (ap_server_post_read_config);
8736                *new = ap_pstrdup(pcommands, optarg);
8737                break;
8738            case 'C':
8739                new = (char **)ap_push_array
8740                        (ap_server_pre_read_config);
8741                *new = ap_pstrdup(pcommands, optarg);
8742                break;
8743            case 'D':
8744                new = (char **)ap_push_array
8745                        (ap_server_config_defines);
8746                *new = ap_pstrdup(pcommands, optarg);
8747                break;
8748            case 'd':
8749                ap_cpystrn(ap_server_root, optarg,
8750                        sizeof(ap_server_root));
8751                break;
8752            case 'f':
8753                ap_cpystrn(ap_server_confname, optarg,
8754                        sizeof(ap_server_confname));
8755                break;
8756            case 'v':
8757                ap_set_version();
8758                printf("Server version: %s\n",
8759                        ap_get_server_version());
8760                printf("Server built:   %s\n",
8761                        ap_get_server_built());
8762                exit(0);
8763            case 'V':
8764                ap_set_version();
8765                show_compile_settings();
8766                exit(0);
8767            case 'l':
8768                ap_show_modules();
8769                exit(0);
8770            case 'L':
8771                ap_show_directives();
8772                exit(0);
8773            case 'X':
8774                ++one_process;
8775                /* Weird debugging mode. */
8776                break;
8777    #ifdef DEBUG_SIGSTOP
8778            case 'Z':
8779                raise_sigstop_flags = atoi(optarg);
8780                break;
8781    #endif
8782    #ifdef SHARED_CORE
8783            case 'R':
8784                /* just ignore this option here, because it
8785                 * has only effect when SHARED_CORE is used
8786                 * and then it was already handled in the
8787                 * Shared Core Bootstrap program.
8788                 */
8789                break;
8790    #endif
8791            case 'S':
8792                ap_dump_settings = 1;
8793                break;
8794            case 't':
8795                configtestonly = 1;
8796                break;
8797            case 'h':
8798                usage(argv[0]);
8799            case '?':
8800                usage(argv[0]);
8801            }
8802        }
8803    #endif /* TPF */
8804
8805        ap_suexec_enabled = init_suexec();
8806        server_conf = ap_read_config(pconf, ptrans,
8807            ap_server_confname);
8808
8809        if (configtestonly) {
8810            fprintf(stderr, "Syntax OK\n");
8811            exit(0);
8812        }
8813        if (ap_dump_settings) {
8814            exit(0);
8815        }
8816
8817        child_timeouts = !ap_standalone || one_process;
8818
8819        if (ap_standalone) {
8820        ap_open_logs(server_conf, pconf);
8821        ap_set_version();
8822        ap_init_modules(pconf, server_conf);
8823        version_locked++;
8824        STANDALONE_MAIN(argc, argv);
8825        }
```

```
8826        else {
8827            conn_rec *conn;
8828            request_rec *r;
8829            struct sockaddr sa_server, sa_client;
8830            BUFF *cio;
8831            NET_SIZE_T l;
8832
8833            ap_set_version();
8834            /* Yes this is called twice. */
8835            ap_init_modules(pconf, server_conf);
8836            version_locked++;
8837            ap_open_logs(server_conf, pconf);
8838            ap_init_modules(pconf, server_conf);
8839            set_group_privs();
8840
8841    #ifdef MPE
8842            /* Only try to switch if we're running
8843             * as MANAGER.SYS */
8844            if (geteuid() == 1 && ap_user_id > 1) {
8845                GETPRIVMODE();
8846                if (setuid(ap_user_id) == -1) {
8847                    GETUSERMODE();
8848                    ap_log_error(APLOG_MARK, APLOG_ALERT,
8849                        server_conf,
8850                            "setuid: unable to change uid");
8851                    exit(1);
8852                }
8853                GETUSERMODE();
8854            }
8855    #else
8856            /* Only try to switch if we're running as root */
8857            if (!geteuid() && setuid(ap_user_id) == -1) {
8858                ap_log_error(APLOG_MARK, APLOG_ALERT,
8859                    server_conf,
8860                        "setuid: unable to change uid");
8861                exit(1);
8862            }
8863    #endif
8864            if (ap_setjmp(jmpbuffer)) {
8865                exit(0);
8866            }
8867
8868    #ifdef TPF
8869            signal(SIGALRM, alrm_handler);
8870            ecbptr()->ebrout = PRIMECRAS;
8871    #endif /* TPF */
8872
8873    #ifdef TPF
8874    /* TPF only passes the incoming socket number from
8875     * the internet daemon
8876        in ebw000 */
8877        sock_in = * (int*)(&(ecbptr()->ebw000));
8878        sock_out = * (int*)(&(ecbptr()->ebw000));
8879    #elif defined(MPE)
8880    /* HP MPE 5.5 inetd only passes the incoming socket
8881        as stdin (fd 0), whereas HPUX inetd passes the
8882        incoming socket as stdin (fd 0) and stdout (fd 1).
8883        Go figure.  SR 5003355016 has been submitted to
8884        request that the existing functionality be
8885        documented, and then to enhance the functionality
8886        to be like HPUX. */
8887        sock_in = fileno(stdin);
8888        sock_out = fileno(stdin);
8889    #else
8890        sock_in = fileno(stdin);
8891        sock_out = fileno(stdout);
8892    #endif
8893
8894        l = sizeof(sa_client);
8895        if ((getpeername(sock_in, &sa_client, &l)) < 0) {
8896    /* get peername will fail if the input isn't a socket */
8897            perror("getpeername");
8898            memset(&sa_client, '\0', sizeof(sa_client));
8899        }
8900
8901        l = sizeof(sa_server);
8902        if (getsockname(sock_in, &sa_server, &l) < 0) {
8903            perror("getsockname");
8904            fprintf(stderr, "Error getting local address\n");
8905            exit(1);
8906        }
8907        server_conf->port = ntohs(((struct sockaddr_in *)
8908            &sa_server)->sin_port);
8909        cio = ap_bcreate(ptrans, B_RDWR | B_SOCKET);
8910        cio->fd = sock_out;
8911        cio->fd_in = sock_in;
8912        conn = new_connection(ptrans, server_conf, cio,
8913                (struct sockaddr_in *) &sa_client,
8914                (struct sockaddr_in *) &sa_server, -1);
8915
8916        while ((r = ap_read_request(conn)) != NULL) {
8917
8918            if (r->status == HTTP_OK)
8919                ap_process_request(r);
8920
8921            if (!conn->keepalive || conn->aborted)
```

```
8922            break;
8923
8924        ap_destroy_pool(r->pool);
8925      }
8926
8927    ap_bclose(cio);
8928    }
8929    exit(0);
8930  }
8931
8932  #else /* ndef MULTITHREAD */
8933
8934
8935  /*********************************************************
8936   * Multithreaded implementation
8937   *
8938   * This code is fairly specific to Win32.
8939   *
8940   * The model used to handle requests is a set of
8941   * threads.One "main" thread listens for new requests.
8942   * When something becomes available, it does a select
8943   * and places the newly available socket onto a list
8944   * of "jobs" (add_job()). Then any one of a fixed number
8945   * of "worker" threads takes the top job off the job
8946   * list with remove_job() and handles that connection
8947   * to completion. After the connection has finished
8948   * the thread is free to take another job from the
8949   * job list.
8950   *
8951   * In the code, the "main" thread is running within
8952   * the worker_main()function. The first thing this
8953   * function does is create the worker threads, which
8954   * operate in the child_sub_main() function. The
8955   * main thread then goes into a loop within
8956   * worker_main() where they do a select() on the
8957   * listening sockets. The select times out once
8958   * per second so that the thread can check for an
8959   * "exit" signal from the parent process (see
8960   * below). If this signal is set, the thread can exit,
8961   * but only after it has accepted all incoming
8962   * connections already in the listen queue (since
8963   * Win32 appears to through away listened but
8964   * unaccepted connections when a process dies).
8965   *
8966   * Because the main and worker threads exist within a
8967   * single process they are vulnerable to crashes or
8968   * memory leaks (crashes can also be caused within
8969   * modules, of course). There also needs to be a
```

```
8970   * mechanism to perform restarts and shutdowns. This
8971   * is done by creating the main & worker threads
8972   * within a subprocess. A main process (the "parent
8973   * process") creates one (or more) processes to do
8974   * the work, then the parent sits around waiting
8975   * for the working process to die, in which case it
8976   * starts a new one. The parent process also handles
8977   * restarts (by creating a new working process then
8978   * signalling the previous working process exit ) and
8979   * shutdowns (by signalling the working process to
8980   * exit). The parent process operates within the
8981   * master_main() function. This process also handles
8982   * requests from the service manager (NT only).
8983   *
8984   * Signalling between the parent and working process
8985   * uses a Win32 event. Each child has a unique name
8986   * for the event, which is passed to it with the -Z
8987   * argument when the child is spawned. The parent sets
8988   * (signals) this event to tell the child to die. At
8989   * present all children do a graceful die - they finish
8990   * all current jobs _and_ empty the listen queue
8991   * before they exit. A non-graceful die would need
8992   * a second event. The -Z argument in the child is also
8993   * used to create the shutdown and restart events, since
8994   * the prefix (apPID) contains the parent process PID.
8995   *
8996   * The code below starts with functions at the lowest
8997   * level - worker threads, and works up to the top
8998   * level - the main()function of the parent process.
8999   *
9000   *
9001   * The scoreboard (in process memory) contains details
9002   * of the worker threads (within the active working
9003   * process). There is no shared"scoreboard" between
9004   * processes, since only one is ever active at once
9005   * (or at most, two, when one has been told to shutdown
9006   * but is processes outstanding requests, and a new
9007   * one has been started). This is controlled by a
9008   * "start_mutex" which ensures only one working
9009   * process is active at once.
9010   **********************************************************/
9011
9012  /* The code protected by #ifdef
9013   * UNGRACEFUL_RESTARTS/#endif sections
9014   * could implement a sort-of ungraceful restart
9015   * for Win32. instead of
9016   * graceful restarts.
9017   *
```

```
9018        * However it does not work too well because it does
9019        * not intercept a connection already in
9020        * progress (in child_sub_main()). We'd have to
9021        * get that to poll on the exit event.
9022        */
9023
9024       /*
9025        * Definition of jobs, shared by main and worker
9026        * threads.
9027        */
9028
9029       typedef struct joblist_s {
9030           struct joblist_s *next;
9031           int sock;
9032       } joblist;
9033
9034       /*
9035        * Globals common to main and worker threads. This
9036        * structure is not used by the parent process.
9037        */
9038
9039       typedef struct globals_s {
9040       #ifdef UNGRACEFUL_RESTART
9041           HANDLE thread_exit_event;
9042       #else
9043           int exit_now;
9044       #endif
9045           semaphore *jobsemaphore;
9046           joblist *jobhead;
9047           joblist *jobtail;
9048           mutex *jobmutex;
9049           int jobcount;
9050       } globals;
9051
9052       globals allowed_globals =
9053       {0, NULL, NULL, NULL, NULL, 0};
9054
9055       /*
9056        * add_job()/remove_job() - add or remove an accepted
9057        * socket from the list of sockets connected to
9058        * clients. allowed_globals.jobmutex protects
9059        * against multiple concurrent access to the linked
9060        * list of jobs.
9061        */
9062
9063       void add_job(int sock)
9064       {
9065           joblist *new_job;
```

```
9066
9067           ap_assert(allowed_globals.jobmutex);
9068           /* TODO: If too many jobs in queue, sleep, check
9069            * for problems */
9070           ap_acquire_mutex(allowed_globals.jobmutex);
9071           new_job = (joblist *) malloc(sizeof(joblist));
9072           if (new_job == NULL) {
9073             fprintf(stderr, "Ouch!  Out of memory in
9074                 add_job()!\n");
9075           }
9076           new_job->next = NULL;
9077           new_job->sock = sock;
9078           if (allowed_globals.jobtail != NULL)
9079            allowed_globals.jobtail->next = new_job;
9080           allowed_globals.jobtail = new_job;
9081           if (!allowed_globals.jobhead)
9082            allowed_globals.jobhead = new_job;
9083           allowed_globals.jobcount++;
9084           release_semaphore(allowed_globals.jobsemaphore);
9085           ap_release_mutex(allowed_globals.jobmutex);
9086       }
9087
9088       int remove_job(void)
9089       {
9090           joblist *job;
9091           int sock;
9092
9093       #ifdef UNGRACEFUL_RESTART
9094           HANDLE hObjects[2];
9095           int rv;
9096
9097           hObjects[0] = allowed_globals.jobsemaphore;
9098           hObjects[1] = allowed_globals.thread_exit_event;
9099
9100           rv = WaitForMultipleObjects(2, hObjects, FALSE,
9101               INFINITE);
9102           ap_assert(rv != WAIT_FAILED);
9103           if (rv == WAIT_OBJECT_0 + 1) {
9104            /* thread_exit_now */
9105            APD1("thread got exit now event");
9106            return -1;
9107           }
9108           /* must be semaphore */
9109       #else
9110           acquire_semaphore(allowed_globals.jobsemaphore);
9111       #endif
9112           ap_assert(allowed_globals.jobmutex);
9113
```

```
9114    #ifdef UNGRACEFUL_RESTART
9115        if (!allowed_globals.jobhead) {
9116    #else
9117        ap_acquire_mutex(allowed_globals.jobmutex);
9118        if (allowed_globals.exit_now &&
9119                !allowed_globals.jobhead) {
9120    #endif
9121          ap_release_mutex(allowed_globals.jobmutex);
9122          return (-1);
9123        }
9124        job = allowed_globals.jobhead;
9125        ap_assert(job);
9126        allowed_globals.jobhead = job->next;
9127        if (allowed_globals.jobhead == NULL)
9128          allowed_globals.jobtail = NULL;
9129        ap_release_mutex(allowed_globals.jobmutex);
9130        sock = job->sock;
9131        free(job);
9132        return (sock);
9133    }
9134
9135    /*
9136     * child_sub_main() - this is the main loop for the
9137     * worker threads
9138     *
9139     * Each thread runs within this function. They wait within
9140     * remove_job()for a job to become available, then handle
9141     * all the requests on that connection until it is
9142     * closed, then return to remove_job().
9143     *
9144     * The worker thread will exit when it removes a job
9145     * which contains socket number -1. This provides
9146     * a graceful thread exit, since it will never
9147     * exit during a connection.
9148     *
9149     * This code in this function is basically equivalent
9150     * to the child_main()from the multi-process (Unix)
9151     * environment, except that we
9152     *
9153     *  - do not call child_init_modules (child init API
9154     * phase) - block in remove_job, and when unblocked we
9155     * have an already accepted socket, instead of
9156     * blocking on a mutex or select().
9157     */
9158
9159    static void child_sub_main(int child_num)
9160    {
9161        NET_SIZE_T clen;
```

```
9162        struct sockaddr sa_server;
9163        struct sockaddr sa_client;
9164        pool *ptrans;
9165        int requests_this_child = 0;
9166        int csd = -1;
9167        int dupped_csd = -1;
9168        int srv = 0;
9169
9170        ptrans = ap_make_sub_pool(pconf);
9171
9172        (void) ap_update_child_status(child_num,
9173            SERVER_READY, (request_rec *) NULL);
9174
9175        /*
9176         * Setup the jump buffers so that we can return
9177         * here after a timeout.
9178         */
9179    #if defined(USE_LONGJMP)
9180        setjmp(jmpbuffer);
9181    #else
9182        sigsetjmp(jmpbuffer, 1);
9183    #endif
9184    #ifdef SIGURG
9185        signal(SIGURG, timeout);
9186    #endif
9187
9188        while (1) {
9189          BUFF *conn_io;
9190          request_rec *r;
9191
9192          /*
9193           * (Re)initialize this child to a pre-connection
9194           * state.
9195           */
9196
9197          ap_set_callback_and_alarm(NULL, 0);
9198          /* Cancel any outstanding alarms */
9199          timeout_req = NULL;
9200          /* No request in progress */
9201          current_conn = NULL;
9202
9203          ap_clear_pool(ptrans);
9204
9205          (void) ap_update_child_status(child_num,
9206              SERVER_READY,
9207                                (request_rec *) NULL);
9208
9209          /* Get job from the job list. This will block
```

```
9210          * until a job is ready. If -1 is returned then
9211          * the main thread wants us to exit.
9212          */
9213
9214         csd = remove_job();
9215         if (csd == -1)
9216             break;          /* time to exit */
9217         requests_this_child++;
9218
9219         ap_note_cleanups_for_socket(ptrans, csd);
9220
9221         /*
9222          * We now have a connection, so set it up with
9223          * the appropriate socket options, file
9224          * descriptors, and read/write buffers.
9225          */
9226
9227         clen = sizeof(sa_server);
9228         if (getsockname(csd, &sa_server, &clen) < 0) {
9229             ap_log_error(APLOG_MARK, APLOG_WARNING,
9230                 server_conf, "getsockname");
9231             continue;
9232         }
9233         clen = sizeof(sa_client);
9234         if ((getpeername(csd, &sa_client, &clen)) < 0) {
9235             /* get peername will fail if the input
9236              * isn't a socket */
9237             perror("getpeername");
9238             memset(&sa_client, '\0', sizeof(sa_client));
9239         }
9240
9241         sock_disable_nagle(csd);
9242
9243         (void) ap_update_child_status(child_num,
9244                 SERVER_BUSY_READ,
9245                     (request_rec *) NULL);
9246
9247         conn_io = ap_bcreate(ptrans, B_RDWR | B_SOCKET);
9248         dupped_csd = csd;
9249 #if defined(NEED_DUPPED_CSD)
9250         if ((dupped_csd = dup(csd)) < 0) {
9251             ap_log_error(APLOG_MARK, APLOG_ERR, server_conf,
9252                 "dup: couldn't duplicate csd");
9253             dupped_csd = csd;     /* Oh well... */
9254         }
9255         ap_note_cleanups_for_socket(ptrans, dupped_csd);
9256 #endif
9257         ap_bpushfd(conn_io, csd, dupped_csd);
9258
9259         current_conn = new_connection(ptrans, server_conf,
9260             conn_io,
9261                     (struct sockaddr_in *) &sa_client,
9262                     (struct sockaddr_in *) &sa_server,
9263                         child_num);
9264
9265     /*
9266      * Read and process each request found on our
9267      * connection until no requests are left or we
9268      * decide to close.
9269      */
9270
9271     while ((r = ap_read_request(current_conn)) !=
9272         NULL) {
9273         (void) ap_update_child_status(child_num,
9274             SERVER_BUSY_WRITE, r);
9275
9276         if (r->status == HTTP_OK)
9277           ap_process_request(r);
9278
9279         if (ap_extended_status)
9280           increment_counts(child_num, r);
9281
9282         if (!current_conn->keepalive ||
9283             current_conn->aborted)
9284           break;
9285
9286         ap_destroy_pool(r->pool);
9287         (void) ap_update_child_status(child_num,
9288             SERVER_BUSY_KEEPALIVE,
9289                     (request_rec *) NULL);
9290
9291         ap_sync_scoreboard_image();
9292     }
9293
9294     /*
9295      * Close the connection, being careful to send out
9296      * whatever is still in our buffers.  If possible,
9297      * try to avoid a hard close until the client has
9298      * ACKed our FIN and/or has stopped sending us data.
9299      */
9300     ap_kill_cleanups_for_socket(ptrans, csd);
9301
9302 #ifdef NO_LINGCLOSE
9303     ap_bclose(conn_io);      /* just close it */
9304 #else
9305     if (r && r->connection
```

```
9306              && !r->connection->aborted
9307              && r->connection->client
9308              && (r->connection->client->fd >= 0)) {
9309
9310              lingering_close(r);
9311          }
9312          else {
9313              ap_bsetflag(conn_io, B_EOUT, 1);
9314              ap_bclose(conn_io);
9315          }
9316  #endif
9317          }
9318      ap_destroy_pool(ptrans);
9319      (void) ap_update_child_status(child_num,
9320              SERVER_DEAD, NULL);
9321  }
9322
9323
9324  void child_main(int child_num_arg)
9325  {
9326      /*
9327       * Only reason for this function, is to pass in
9328       * arguments to child_sub_main() on its stack so
9329       * that longjump doesn't try to corrupt its local
9330       * variables and I don't need to make those
9331       * damn variables static/global
9332       */
9333      child_sub_main(child_num_arg);
9334  }
9335
9336
9337
9338  void cleanup_thread(thread **handles, int *thread_cnt,
9339          int thread_to_clean)
9340  {
9341      int i;
9342
9343      free_thread(handles[thread_to_clean]);
9344      for (i = thread_to_clean; i <
9345              ((*thread_cnt) - 1); i++)
9346          handles[i] = handles[i + 1];
9347      (*thread_cnt)--;
9348  }
9349  #ifdef WIN32
9350  /*
9351   * The Win32 call WaitForMultipleObjects will only
9352   * allow you to wait for a maximum of
9353   * MAXIMUM_WAIT_OBJECTS (current 64).  Since the
9354   * threading model in the multithreaded
9355   * version of apache wants to use this call,
9356   * we are restricted to a maximum of 64 threads.
9357   * This is a simplistic routine that will
9358   * increase this size.
9359   */
9360  DWORD wait_for_many_objects(DWORD nCount,
9361      CONST HANDLE *lpHandles,
9362                              DWORD dwSeconds)
9363  {
9364      time_t tStopTime;
9365      DWORD dwRet = WAIT_TIMEOUT;
9366      DWORD dwIndex=0;
9367      BOOL bFirst = TRUE;
9368
9369      tStopTime = time(NULL) + dwSeconds;
9370
9371      do {
9372          if (!bFirst)
9373              Sleep(1000);
9374          else
9375              bFirst = FALSE;
9376
9377          for (dwIndex = 0; dwIndex *
9378            MAXIMUM_WAIT_OBJECTS < nCount; dwIndex++) {
9379              dwRet = WaitForMultipleObjects(
9380                      min(MAXIMUM_WAIT_OBJECTS,
9381                      nCount - (dwIndex *
9382                          MAXIMUM_WAIT_OBJECTS)),
9383                      lpHandles + (dwIndex *
9384                          MAXIMUM_WAIT_OBJECTS),
9385                      0, 0);
9386
9387              if (dwRet != WAIT_TIMEOUT) {
9388                  break;
9389              }
9390          }
9391      } while((time(NULL) < tStopTime)
9392          && (dwRet == WAIT_TIMEOUT));
9393
9394      return dwRet;
9395  }
9396  #endif
9397  /*****************************************************
9398   * Executive routines.
9399   */
9400
9401  extern void main_control_server(void *);
```

```
9402    /* in hellop.c */
9403
9404    event *exit_event;
9405    mutex *start_mutex;
9406
9407    #define MAX_SIGNAL_NAME 30   /* Long enough for
9408         apPID_shutdown, where PID is an int */
9409    char signal_name_prefix[MAX_SIGNAL_NAME];
9410    char signal_restart_name[MAX_SIGNAL_NAME];
9411    char signal_shutdown_name[MAX_SIGNAL_NAME];
9412
9413    #define MAX_SELECT_ERRORS 100
9414
9415    /*
9416     * Initialise the signal names, in the global variables
9417     * signal_name_prefix, signal_restart_name and
9418     * signal_shutdown_name.
9419     */
9420
9421    void setup_signal_names(char *prefix)
9422    {
9423        ap_snprintf(signal_name_prefix,
9424             sizeof(signal_name_prefix), prefix);
9425        ap_snprintf(signal_shutdown_name,
9426             sizeof(signal_shutdown_name),
9427         "%s_shutdown", signal_name_prefix);
9428        ap_snprintf(signal_restart_name,
9429             sizeof(signal_restart_name),
9430         "%s_restart", signal_name_prefix);
9431
9432        APD2("signal prefix %s", signal_name_prefix);
9433    }
9434
9435    /*
9436     * worker_main() is main loop for the child process.
9437     * The loop in this function becomes the
9438     * controlling thread for the actually working
9439     * threads (which run in a loop in child_sub_main()).
9440     */
9441
9442    void worker_main(void)
9443    {
9444        int nthreads;
9445        fd_set main_fds;
9446        int srv;
9447        int clen;
9448        int csd;
9449        struct sockaddr_in sa_client;
9450        int total_jobs = 0;
9451        thread **child_handles;
9452        int rv;
9453        time_t end_time;
9454        int i;
9455        struct timeval tv;
9456        int wait_time = 1;
9457        int start_exit = 0;
9458        int start_mutex_released = 0;
9459        int max_jobs_per_exe;
9460        int max_jobs_after_exit_request;
9461        HANDLE hObjects[2];
9462        int count_select_errors = 0;
9463        pool *pchild;
9464
9465        pchild = ap_make_sub_pool(pconf);
9466
9467        ap_standalone = 1;
9468        sd = -1;
9469        nthreads = ap_threads_per_child;
9470        max_jobs_after_exit_request =
9471             ap_excess_requests_per_child;
9472        max_jobs_per_exe = ap_max_requests_per_child;
9473        if (nthreads <= 0)
9474         nthreads = 40;
9475        if (max_jobs_per_exe <= 0)
9476         max_jobs_per_exe = 0;
9477        if (max_jobs_after_exit_request <= 0)
9478         max_jobs_after_exit_request =
9479             max_jobs_per_exe / 10;
9480
9481        if (!one_process)
9482         detach();
9483
9484        my_pid = getpid();
9485
9486        ++ap_my_generation;
9487
9488        copy_listeners(pconf);
9489        ap_restart_time = time(NULL);
9490
9491        reinit_scoreboard(pconf);
9492
9493        /*
9494         * Wait until we have permission to start accepting
9495         * connections. start_mutex is used to ensure
9496         * that only one child ever goes into the
9497         * listen/accept loop at once. Also wait on
```

```
9498          * exit_event,in case we (this child) is told
9499          * to die before we get a chance to serve any
9500          * requests.
9501          */
9502         hObjects[0] = (HANDLE)start_mutex;
9503         hObjects[1] = (HANDLE)exit_event;
9504         rv = WaitForMultipleObjects(2, hObjects, FALSE,
9505              INFINITE);
9506         if (rv == WAIT_FAILED) {
9507          ap_log_error(APLOG_MARK,APLOG_ERR|APLOG_WIN32ERROR,
9508              server_conf,
9509              "Waiting for start_mutex or exit_event -
9510                  process will exit");
9511
9512          ap_destroy_pool(pchild);
9513          cleanup_scoreboard();
9514          exit(0);
9515         }
9516
9517         if (rv == WAIT_OBJECT_0 + 1) {
9518          /* exit event signalled - exit now */
9519          ap_destroy_pool(pchild);
9520          cleanup_scoreboard();
9521          exit(0);
9522         }
9523         /* start_mutex obtained, continue into the select()
9524          * loop */
9525
9526         setup_listeners(pconf);
9527         if (listenmaxfd == -1) {
9528          /* Help, no sockets were made, better log
9529           * something and exit */
9530          ap_log_error(APLOG_MARK,
9531              APLOG_CRIT|APLOG_NOERRNO, NULL,
9532                  "No sockets were created for listening");
9533
9534          signal_parent(0);     /* tell parent to die */
9535
9536          ap_destroy_pool(pchild);
9537          cleanup_scoreboard();
9538          exit(0);
9539         }
9540         set_signals();
9541
9542         /*
9543          * - Initialize allowed_globals
9544          * - Create the thread table
9545          * - Spawn off threads
9546          * - Create listen socket set (done above)
9547          * - loop {
9548          *      wait for request
9549          *      create new job
9550          *   } while (!time to exit)
9551          * - Close all listeners
9552          * - Wait for all threads to complete
9553          * - Exit
9554          */
9555
9556         ap_child_init_modules(pconf, server_conf);
9557
9558         allowed_globals.jobsemaphore = create_semaphore(0);
9559         allowed_globals.jobmutex = ap_create_mutex(NULL);
9560
9561         /* spawn off the threads */
9562         child_handles = (thread *)
9563              alloca(nthreads * sizeof(int));
9564         for (i = 0; i < nthreads; i++) {
9565          child_handles[i] = create_thread((void (*)(void *))
9566              child_main, (void *) i);
9567         }
9568         if (nthreads > max_daemons_limit) {
9569          max_daemons_limit = nthreads;
9570         }
9571
9572         while (1) {
9573 #if SEVERELY_VERBOSE
9574         APD4("child PID %d:
9575              thread_main total_jobs=%d start_exit=%d",
9576              my_pid, total_jobs, start_exit);
9577 #endif
9578         if ((max_jobs_per_exe &&
9579              (total_jobs > max_jobs_per_exe)
9580              && !start_exit)) {
9581          start_exit = 1;
9582          wait_time = 1;
9583          ap_release_mutex(start_mutex);
9584          start_mutex_released = 1;
9585          APD2("process PID %d: start mutex released\n",
9586              my_pid);
9587         }
9588         if (!start_exit) {
9589          rv = WaitForSingleObject(exit_event, 0);
9590          ap_assert((rv == WAIT_TIMEOUT) ||
9591              (rv == WAIT_OBJECT_0));
9592          if (rv == WAIT_OBJECT_0) {
9593           APD1("child: exit event signalled, exiting");
```

```
9594            start_exit = 1;                              9642         */
9595            /* Lets not break yet - we may have threads   9643         ap_log_error(APLOG_MARK, APLOG_ERR,
9596             * to clean up */                             9644             server_conf, "select: (listen)");
9597            /* break;*/                                   9645         count_select_errors++;
9598            }                                             9646         if (count_select_errors > MAX_SELECT_ERRORS) {
9599            rv = wait_for_many_objects(nthreads,          9647             ap_log_error(APLOG_MARK,
9600                child_handles, 0);                        9648                 APLOG_ERR|APLOG_NOERRNO, server_conf,
9601            ap_assert(rv != WAIT_FAILED);                 9649             "Too many errors in select loop.
9602            if (rv != WAIT_TIMEOUT) {                     9650                 Child process exiting.");
9603            rv = rv - WAIT_OBJECT_0;                      9651             break;
9604            ap_assert((rv >= 0) && (rv < nthreads));      9652         }
9605            cleanup_thread(child_handles, &nthreads, rv); 9653         }
9606            break;                                        9654         continue;
9607            }                                             9655     }
9608        }                                                 9656     count_select_errors = 0;
9609                                                          9657     /* reset count of errors */
9610    #if 0                                                 9658     if (srv == 0) {
9611        /* Um, this made us exit before all the          9659         if (start_exit)
9612         * connections in our listen queue were          9660         break;
9613         * dealt with.                                   9661         else
9614         */                                              9662         continue;
9615        if (start_exit && max_jobs_after_exit_request && 9663     }
9616            (count_down-- < 0))                           9664
9617            break;                                        9665     {
9618    #endif                                                9666         listen_rec *lr;
9619        tv.tv_sec = wait_time;                            9667
9620        tv.tv_usec = 0;                                   9668         lr = find_ready_listener(&main_fds);
9621                                                          9669         if (lr != NULL) {
9622        memcpy(&main_fds, &listenfds, sizeof(fd_set));    9670         sd = lr->fd;
9623        srv = ap_select(listenmaxfd + 1, &main_fds,      9671         }
9624            NULL, NULL, &tv);                             9672     }
9625    #ifdef WIN32                                          9673     do {
9626        if (srv == SOCKET_ERROR) {                        9674         clen = sizeof(sa_client);
9627            /* Map the Win32 error into a standard Unix   9675         csd = accept(sd, (struct sockaddr *)
9628             * error condition */                         9676             &sa_client, &clen);
9629            errno = WSAGetLastError();                    9677    #ifdef WIN32
9630            srv = -1;                                     9678         if (csd == INVALID_SOCKET) {
9631        }                                                 9679         csd = -1;
9632    #endif /* WIN32 */                                    9680         errno = WSAGetLastError();
9633                                                          9681         }
9634        if (srv < 0) {                                    9682    #endif /* WIN32 */
9635            /* Error occurred - if EINTR, loop around     9683     } while (csd < 0 && errno == EINTR);
9636             * with problem */                            9684
9637            if (errno != EINTR) {                         9685     if (csd < 0) {
9638            /* A "real" error occurred, log it and        9686    #if defined(EPROTO) && defined(ECONNABORTED)
9639             * increment the count of select errors. This 9687         if ((errno != EPROTO) &&
9640             * count is used to ensure we don't go into   9688             (errno != ECONNABORTED))
9641             * a busy loop of continuour errors.          9689    #elif defined(EPROTO)
```

```
9690            if (errno != EPROTO)
9691    #elif defined(ECONNABORTED)
9692            if (errno != ECONNABORTED)
9693    #endif
9694            ap_log_error(APLOG_MARK, APLOG_ERR, server_conf,
9695                    "accept: (client socket)");
9696        }
9697        else {
9698            add_job(csd);
9699            total_jobs++;
9700        }
9701    }
9702
9703    APD2("process PID %d exiting", my_pid);
9704
9705    /* Get ready to shutdown and exit */
9706    allowed_globals.exit_now = 1;
9707    if (!start_mutex_released) {
9708        ap_release_mutex(start_mutex);
9709    }
9710
9711    #ifdef UNGRACEFUL_RESTART
9712        SetEvent(allowed_globals.thread_exit_event);
9713    #else
9714        for (i = 0; i < nthreads; i++) {
9715            add_job(-1);
9716        }
9717    #endif
9718
9719    APD2("process PID %d waiting for worker
9720            threads to exit", my_pid);
9721    /* Wait for all your children */
9722    end_time = time(NULL) + 180;
9723    while (nthreads) {
9724        rv = wait_for_many_objects(nthreads,
9725                child_handles,
9726                            end_time - time(NULL));
9727        if (rv != WAIT_TIMEOUT) {
9728            rv = rv - WAIT_OBJECT_0;
9729            ap_assert((rv >= 0) && (rv < nthreads));
9730            cleanup_thread(child_handles, &nthreads, rv);
9731            continue;
9732        }
9733        break;
9734    }
9735
9736    APD2("process PID %d killing remaining worker
9737            threads", my_pid);
```

```
9738        for (i = 0; i < nthreads; i++) {
9739            kill_thread(child_handles[i]);
9740
9741            free_thread(child_handles[i]);
9742        }
9743    #ifdef UNGRACEFUL_RESTART
9744        ap_assert(CloseHandle
9745                (allowed_globals.thread_exit_event));
9746    #endif
9747        destroy_semaphore(allowed_globals.jobsemaphore);
9748        ap_destroy_mutex(allowed_globals.jobmutex);
9749
9750        ap_child_exit_modules(pconf, server_conf);
9751        ap_destroy_pool(pchild);
9752
9753        cleanup_scoreboard();
9754
9755        APD2("process PID %d exited", my_pid);
9756        clean_parent_exit(0);
9757    }                       /* standalone_main */
9758
9759    /*
9760     * Spawn a child Apache process. The child process has
9761     * the command line arguments from argc and argv[],
9762     * plus a -Z argument giving the name of an event. The
9763     * child should open and poll or wait on this
9764     * event. When it is signalled, the child should die.
9765     * prefix is a prefix string for the event name.
9766     *
9767     * The child_num argument on entry contains a serial
9768     * number for this child (used to create a unique
9769     * event name). On exit, this number will have been
9770     * incremented by one, ready for the next call.
9771     *
9772
9773     * On exit, the value pointed to be *ev will contain
9774     * the event created to signal the new child process.
9775     *
9776     * The return value is the handle to the child process
9777     * if successful, else -1. If -1 is returned the error
9778     * will already have been logged by ap_log_error().
9779     */
9780
9781    int create_event_and_spawn(int argc, char **argv,
9782        event **ev, int *child_num, char *prefix)
9783    {
9784        char buf[40], mod[200];
9785        int i, rv;
```

```
9786    char **pass_argv = (char **) alloca(sizeof(char *)
9787            * (argc + 3));
9788
9789    /* We need an event to tell the child process to
9790     * kill itself when the parent is doing a
9791     * shutdown/restart. This will be named
9792     * apPID_CN where PID is the parent Apache process
9793     * PID and N is a unique child serial number.
9794     * prefix contains the "apPID" part. The child will
9795     * get the name of this event as its -Z command
9796     * line argument.
9797     */
9798    ap_snprintf(buf, sizeof(buf), "%s_C%d", prefix,
9799            ++(*child_num));
9800    _flushall();
9801    *ev = CreateEvent(NULL, TRUE, FALSE, buf);
9802    if (!*ev) {
9803     ap_log_error(APLOG_MARK,
9804             APLOG_ERR|APLOG_WIN32ERROR, NULL,
9805             "could not create event for child process");
9806     return -1;
9807    }
9808    APD2("create_event_and_spawn(): created process
9809            kill event %s", buf);
9810
9811    pass_argv[0] = argv[0];
9812    pass_argv[1] = "-Z";
9813    pass_argv[2] = buf;
9814    for (i = 1; i < argc; i++) {
9815     pass_argv[i + 2] = argv[i];
9816    }
9817    pass_argv[argc + 2] = NULL;
9818
9819    rv = GetModuleFileName(NULL, mod, sizeof(mod));
9820    if (rv == sizeof(mod)) {
9821     /* mod[] was not big enough for our pathname */
9822     ap_log_error(APLOG_MARK, APLOG_ERR, NULL,
9823             "Internal error: path to Apache process
9824                 too long");
9825     return -1;
9826    }
9827    if (rv == 0) {
9828     ap_log_error(APLOG_MARK,
9829             APLOG_ERR|APLOG_WIN32ERROR, NULL,
9830             "GetModuleFileName() for current process");
9831     return -1;
9832    }
9833    rv = spawnv(_P_NOWAIT, mod, pass_argv);
9834    if (rv == -1) {
9835     ap_log_error(APLOG_MARK,
9836             APLOG_ERR|APLOG_WIN32ERROR, NULL,
9837             "spawn of child process %s failed", mod);
9838     return -1;
9839    }
9840
9841    return rv;
9842    }
9843
9844    /***********************************************************
9845     * master_main - this is the parent (main) process. We
9846     * create a child process to do the work, then sit
9847     * around waiting for either the child to exit, or a
9848     * restart or exit signal. If the child dies, we just
9849     * respawn a new one. If we have a shutdown or graceful
9850     * restart, tell the child to die when it is ready.
9851     * If it is a non-graceful restart, force the child
9852     * to die immediately.
9853     ***********************************************************/
9854
9855    #define MAX_PROCESSES 50
9856    /* must be < MAX_WAIT_OBJECTS-1 */
9857
9858    void cleanup_process(HANDLE *handles, HANDLE *events,
9859        int position, int *processes)
9860    {
9861        int i;
9862        int handle = 0;
9863
9864        CloseHandle(handles[position]);
9865        CloseHandle(events[position]);
9866
9867        handle = (int)handles[position];
9868
9869        for (i = position; i < (*processes)-1; i++) {
9870         handles[i] = handles[i + 1];
9871         events[i] = events[i + 1];
9872        }
9873        (*processes)--;
9874
9875        APD4("cleanup_processes: removed child in slot
9876                %d handle %d, max=%d", position, handle,
9877                *processes);
9878    }
9879
9880    int create_process(HANDLE *handles, HANDLE *events,
9881        int *processes, int *child_num, char
```

```
9882         *kill_event_name, int argc, char **argv)
9883    {
9884        int i = *processes;
9885        HANDLE kill_event;
9886        int child_handle;
9887
9888        child_handle = create_event_and_spawn(argc,
9889            argv, &kill_event, child_num, kill_event_name);
9890        if (child_handle <= 0) {
9891         return -1;
9892        }
9893        handles[i] = (HANDLE)child_handle;
9894        events[i] = kill_event;
9895        (*processes)++;
9896
9897        APD4("create_processes: created child in slot %d
9898            handle %d, max=%d",
9899         (*processes)-1, handles[(*processes)-1],
9900            *processes);
9901
9902        return 0;
9903    }
9904
9905    int master_main(int argc, char **argv)
9906    {
9907        int nchild = ap_daemons_to_start;
9908        event **ev;
9909        int *child;
9910        int child_num = 0;
9911        int rv, cld;
9912        char signal_prefix_string[100];
9913        int i;
9914        time_t tmstart;
9915        HANDLE signal_shutdown_event;
9916        /* used to signal shutdown to parent */
9917        HANDLE signal_restart_event;
9918        /* used to signal a restart to parent */
9919        HANDLE process_handles[MAX_PROCESSES];
9920        HANDLE process_kill_events[MAX_PROCESSES];
9921        int current_live_processes = 0;
9922        /* number of child process we know about */
9923        int processes_to_create = 0;
9924        /* number of child processes to create */
9925        pool *pparent = NULL;
9926        /* pool for the parent process. Cleaned on each
9927         * restart */
9928
9929        nchild = 1;
```

```
9930        /* only allowed one child process for current
9931         * generation */
9932        processes_to_create = nchild;
9933
9934        is_graceful = 0;
9935
9936        ap_snprintf(signal_prefix_string,
9937            sizeof(signal_prefix_string),
9938                "ap%d", getpid());
9939        setup_signal_names(signal_prefix_string);
9940
9941        signal_shutdown_event = CreateEvent(NULL, TRUE,
9942            FALSE, signal_shutdown_name);
9943        if (!signal_shutdown_event) {
9944         ap_log_error(APLOG_MARK,
9945            APLOG_EMERG|APLOG_WIN32ERROR, server_conf,
9946                "Cannot create shutdown event %s",
9947                    signal_shutdown_name);
9948         exit(1);
9949        }
9950        APD2("master_main: created event %s",
9951            signal_shutdown_name);
9952        signal_restart_event = CreateEvent(NULL, TRUE,
9953            FALSE, signal_restart_name);
9954        if (!signal_restart_event) {
9955         CloseHandle(signal_shutdown_event);
9956         ap_log_error(APLOG_MARK,
9957            APLOG_EMERG|APLOG_WIN32ERROR, server_conf,
9958                "Cannot create restart event %s",
9959                    signal_restart_name);
9960         exit(1);
9961        }
9962        APD2("master_main: created event %s",
9963            signal_restart_name);
9964
9965        start_mutex = ap_create_mutex(signal_prefix_string);
9966        ev = (event **) alloca(sizeof(event *) * nchild);
9967        child = (int *) alloca(sizeof(int) * (nchild+1));
9968
9969        while (processes_to_create--) {
9970         service_set_status(SERVICE_START_PENDING);
9971         if (create_process(process_handles,
9972            process_kill_events,
9973            &current_live_processes, &child_num,
9974                signal_prefix_string, argc, argv) < 0) {
9975            goto die_now;
9976         }
9977        }
```

```
9978
9979        service_set_status(SERVICE_RUNNING);
9980
9981        restart_pending = shutdown_pending = 0;
9982
9983        do { /* restart-pending */
9984         if (!is_graceful) {
9985             ap_restart_time = time(NULL);
9986         }
9987         ap_clear_pool(pconf);
9988         pparent = ap_make_sub_pool(pconf);
9989
9990         server_conf = ap_read_config(pconf, pparent,
9991             ap_server_confname);
9992         ap_open_logs(server_conf, pconf);
9993         ap_set_version();
9994         ap_init_modules(pconf, server_conf);
9995         version_locked++;
9996
9997         restart_pending = shutdown_pending = 0;
9998
9999         /* Wait for either a child process to die, or
10000        * for the stop_event to be signalled by the
10001        * service manager or rpc server */
10002        while (1) {
10003            /* Next line will block forever until either a
10004            * child dies, or we get signalled on the
10005            * "apache-signal" event (e.g. if the user is
10006            * requesting a shutdown/restart)
10007            */
10008            if (current_live_processes == 0) {
10009            /* Shouldn't happen, but better safe than
10010             * sorry */
10011            ap_log_error(APLOG_MARK,
10012                APLOG_ERR|APLOG_NOERRNO, server_conf,
10013                    "master_main: no child processes alive!
10014                        creating one");
10015            if (create_process(process_handles,
10016                process_kill_events,
10017                &current_live_processes, &child_num,
10018                    signal_prefix_string,
10019                argc, argv) < 0) {
10020                goto die_now;
10021            }
10022            if (processes_to_create) {
10023                processes_to_create--;
10024            }
10025        }
10026            process_handles[current_live_processes] =
10027                signal_shutdown_event;
10028            process_handles[current_live_processes+1] =
10029                signal_restart_event;
10030            rv = WaitForMultipleObjects
10031                (current_live_processes+2,
10032                (HANDLE *)process_handles,
10033                FALSE, INFINITE);
10034            if (rv == WAIT_FAILED) {
10035            /* Something serious is wrong */
10036            ap_log_error(APLOG_MARK,
10037                APLOG_CRIT|APLOG_WIN32ERROR, server_conf,
10038                "WaitForMultipeObjects on process handles
10039                    and apache-signal -- doing shutdown");
10040            shutdown_pending = 1;
10041            break;
10042            }
10043            if (rv == WAIT_TIMEOUT) {
10044            /* Hey, this cannot happen */
10045            ap_log_error(APLOG_MARK, APLOG_ERR,
10046                server_conf,
10047                "WaitForMultipeObjects with INFINITE
10048                    wait exited with WAIT_TIMEOUT");
10049            shutdown_pending = 1;
10050            }
10051
10052            cld = rv - WAIT_OBJECT_0;
10053            APD4("main process: wait finished, cld=%d
10054                handle %d (max=%d)", cld,
10055                process_handles[cld], current_live_processes);
10056            if (cld == current_live_processes) {
10057            /* shutdown event signalled, we should
10058             * exit now */
10059            if (ResetEvent(signal_shutdown_event) == 0) {
10060                ap_log_error(APLOG_MARK,
10061                    APLOG_ERR|APLOG_WIN32ERROR, server_conf,
10062                "ResetEvent(signal_shutdown_event)");
10063                /* Continue -- since we are doing a
10064                * shutdown anyway */
10065            }
10066            shutdown_pending = 1;
10067            APD3("main process: stop_event signalled:
10068                shutdown_pending=%d, restart_pending=%d",
10069                shutdown_pending, restart_pending);
10070            break;
10071            }
10072            if (cld == current_live_processes+1) {
10073            /* restart event signalled, we should
```

```
10074              * exit now */
10075             if (ResetEvent(signal_restart_event) == 0) {
10076                 ap_log_error(APLOG_MARK,
10077                   APLOG_ERR|APLOG_WIN32ERROR, server_conf,
10078                   "ResetEvent(signal_restart_event)");
10079                 /* Continue -- hopefully the restart will
10080                  * fix the problem */
10081             }
10082             restart_pending = 1;
10083             APD3("main process: stop_event signalled:
10084                   shutdown_pending=%d, restart_pending=%d",
10085                 shutdown_pending, restart_pending);
10086           break;
10087         }
10088         ap_assert(cld < current_live_processes);
10089         cleanup_process(process_handles,
10090             process_kill_events, cld,
10091             &current_live_processes);
10092         APD2("main_process: child in slot %d died", rv);
10093         if (processes_to_create) {
10094           create_process(process_handles,
10095               process_kill_events, &current_live_processes,
10096               &child_num, signal_prefix_string, argc, argv);
10097           processes_to_create--;
10098         }
10099       }
10100       if (!shutdown_pending && !restart_pending) {
10101         ap_log_error(APLOG_MARK,
10102             APLOG_CRIT|APLOG_NOERRNO, server_conf,
10103           "master_main: no shutdown or restart
10104               variables set -- doing shutdown");
10105         shutdown_pending = 1;
10106       }
10107       if (shutdown_pending) {
10108         /* tell all child processes to die */
10109         for (i = 0; i < current_live_processes; i++) {
10110           APD3("main process: signalling child #%d
10111               handle %d to die", i, process_handles[i]);
10112           if (SetEvent(process_kill_events[i]) == 0)
10113             ap_log_error(APLOG_MARK,APLOG_WIN32ERROR,
10114                 server_conf,
10115               "SetEvent for child process in
10116                   slot #%d", i);
10117         }
10118         break;
10119       }
10120       if (restart_pending) {
10121         int children_to_kill = current_live_processes;

10122
10123           APD1("-- Doing graceful restart --");
10124
10125           processes_to_create = nchild;
10126           for (i = 0; i < nchild; ++i) {
10127             if (current_live_processes >= MAX_PROCESSES)
10128               break;
10129             create_process(process_handles,
10130                 process_kill_events,
10131                 &current_live_processes,
10132                 &child_num, signal_prefix_string, argc,
10133                   argv);
10134             processes_to_create--;
10135           }
10136           for (i = 0; i < children_to_kill; i++) {
10137             APD3("main process: signalling child #%d
10138                 handle %d to die", i, process_handles[i]);
10139             if (SetEvent(process_kill_events[i]) == 0)
10140               ap_log_error(APLOG_MARK,APLOG_WIN32ERROR,
10141                   server_conf,
10142                 "SetEvent for child process in
10143                     slot #%d", i);
10144           }
10145         }
10146       ++ap_my_generation;
10147     } while (restart_pending);
10148
10149     /* If we dropped out of the loop we definitly want
10150      * to die completely. We need to make sure we wait
10151      * for all the child process to exit first.
10152      */
10153
10154     APD2("*** main process shutdown, processes=%d ***",
10155         current_live_processes);
10156
10157 die_now:
10158
10159     tmstart = time(NULL);
10160     while (current_live_processes && ((tmstart+60) >
10161         time(NULL))) {
10162       service_set_status(SERVICE_STOP_PENDING);
10163       rv = WaitForMultipleObjects(current_live_processes,
10164           (HANDLE *)process_handles, FALSE, 2000);
10165       if (rv == WAIT_TIMEOUT)
10166         continue;
10167       ap_assert(rv != WAIT_FAILED);
10168       cld = rv - WAIT_OBJECT_0;
10169       ap_assert(rv < current_live_processes);
```

```
10170          APD4("main_process: child in #%d handle %d died,
10171             left=%d",
10172             rv, process_handles[rv], current_live_processes);
10173          cleanup_process(process_handles,
10174             process_kill_events, cld,
10175             &current_live_processes);
10176       }
10177       for (i = 0; i < current_live_processes; i++) {
10178          ap_log_error(APLOG_MARK,
10179             APLOG_ERR|APLOG_NOERRNO, server_conf,
10180             "forcing termination of child #%d
10181                (handle %d)", i, process_handles[i]);
10182          TerminateProcess((HANDLE) process_handles[i], 1);
10183       }
10184
10185       CloseHandle(signal_restart_event);
10186       CloseHandle(signal_shutdown_event);
10187
10188       /* cleanup pid file on normal shutdown */
10189       {
10190          const char *pidfile = NULL;
10191          pidfile = ap_server_root_relative (pparent,
10192             ap_pid_fname);
10193          if ( pidfile != NULL && unlink(pidfile) == 0)
10194             ap_log_error(APLOG_MARK,
10195                APLOG_NOERRNO|APLOG_INFO,
10196                   server_conf,
10197                   "removed PID file %s (pid=%ld)",
10198                   pidfile, (long)getpid());
10199       }
10200
10201       if (pparent) {
10202          ap_destroy_pool(pparent);
10203       }
10204
10205       ap_destroy_mutex(start_mutex);
10206
10207       service_set_status(SERVICE_STOPPED);
10208       return (0);
10209    }
10210
10211    /*
10212     * Send signal to a running Apache. On entry signal
10213     * should contain either "shutdown" or "restart"
10214     */
10215
10216    void send_signal(pool *p, char *signal)
10217    {
10218       char prefix[20];
10219       FILE *fp;
10220       int nread;
10221       char *fname;
10222       int end;
10223
10224       fname = ap_server_root_relative (p, ap_pid_fname);
10225
10226       fp = fopen(fname, "r");
10227       if (!fp) {
10228          printf("Cannot read apache PID file %s\n", fname);
10229          return;
10230       }
10231       prefix[0] = 'a';
10232       prefix[1] = 'p';
10233
10234       nread = fread(prefix+2, 1, sizeof(prefix)-3, fp);
10235       if (nread == 0) {
10236          fclose(fp);
10237          printf("PID file %s was empty\n", fname);
10238          return;
10239       }
10240       fclose(fp);
10241
10242       /* Terminate the prefix string */
10243       end = 2 + nread - 1;
10244       while (end > 0 && (prefix[end] == '\r' ||
10245             prefix[end] == '\n'))
10246          end--;
10247       prefix[end + 1] = '\0';
10248
10249       setup_signal_names(prefix);
10250
10251       if (!strcasecmp(signal, "shutdown"))
10252          ap_start_shutdown();
10253       else if (!strcasecmp(signal, "restart"))
10254          ap_start_restart(1);
10255       else
10256          printf("Unknown signal name \"%s\". Use either
10257             shutdown or restart.\n",
10258             signal);
10259
10260       return;
10261    }
10262
10263    #ifdef WIN32
10264    __declspec(dllexport)
10265       int apache_main(int argc, char *argv[])
```

```
10266   #else
10267   int REALMAIN(int argc, char *argv[])
10268   #endif
10269   {
10270       int c;
10271       int child = 0;
10272       char *cp;
10273       int run_as_service = 1;
10274       int install = 0;
10275       int configtestonly = 0;
10276       char *signal_to_send = NULL;
10277       char *s;
10278
10279       common_init();
10280
10281       if ((s = strrchr(argv[0], '/')) != NULL) {
10282        ap_server_argv0 = ++s;
10283       }
10284       else {
10285        ap_server_argv0 = argv[0];
10286       }
10287
10288       /* Get the serverroot from the registry, if it
10289        * exists. This can be overridden by a command
10290        * line -d argument.
10291        */
10292       if (ap_registry_get_server_root(pconf,
10293             ap_server_root, sizeof(ap_server_root)) < 0) {
10294        /* The error has already been logged. Actually
10295         * it won't have been, because we haven't read
10296         * the config files to find out where our error
10297         * log is. But we can't just ignore the error since
10298         * we might end up using totally the wrong server
10299         * root.
10300         */
10301        exit(1);
10302       }
10303
10304       if (!*ap_server_root) {
10305        ap_cpystrn(ap_server_root, HTTPD_ROOT,
10306             sizeof(ap_server_root));
10307       }
10308       ap_cpystrn(ap_server_confname, SERVER_CONFIG_FILE,
10309             sizeof(ap_server_confname));
10310
10311       ap_setup_prelinked_modules();
10312
10313       while ((c = getopt(argc, argv,
10314             "D:C:c:Xd:f:vVlLZ:iusSthk:")) != -1) {
10315        char **new;
10316       switch (c) {
10317       case 'c':
10318           new = (char **)ap_push_array
10319                 (ap_server_post_read_config);
10320           *new = ap_pstrdup(pcommands, optarg);
10321           break;
10322       case 'C':
10323           new = (char **)ap_push_array
10324                 (ap_server_pre_read_config);
10325           *new = ap_pstrdup(pcommands, optarg);
10326           break;
10327       case 'D':
10328           new = (char **)ap_push_array
10329                 (ap_server_config_defines);
10330           *new = ap_pstrdup(pcommands, optarg);
10331           break;
10332   #ifdef WIN32
10333       case 'Z':
10334           exit_event = open_event(optarg);
10335           APD2("child: opened process event %s", optarg);
10336           cp = strchr(optarg, '_');
10337           ap_assert(cp);
10338           *cp = 0;
10339           setup_signal_names(optarg);
10340           start_mutex = ap_open_mutex(signal_name_prefix);
10341           ap_assert(start_mutex);
10342           child = 1;
10343           break;
10344       case 'i':
10345           install = 1;
10346           break;
10347       case 'u':
10348           install = -1;
10349           break;
10350       case 's':
10351           run_as_service = 0;
10352           break;
10353       case 'S':
10354           ap_dump_settings = 1;
10355           break;
10356       case 'k':
10357           signal_to_send = optarg;
10358           break;
10359   #endif /* WIN32 */
10360       case 'd':
10361           ap_cpystrn(ap_server_root,
```

```
10362            ap_os_canonical_filename(pconf, optarg),
10363            sizeof(ap_server_root));
10364        break;
10365    case 'f':
10366        ap_cpystrn(ap_server_confname,
10367            ap_os_canonical_filename(pconf, optarg),
10368            sizeof(ap_server_confname));
10369        break;
10370    case 'v':
10371        ap_set_version();
10372        printf("Server version: %s\n",
10373            ap_get_server_version());
10374        printf("Server built:   %s\n",
10375            ap_get_server_built());
10376        exit(0);
10377    case 'V':
10378        ap_set_version();
10379        show_compile_settings();
10380        exit(0);
10381    case 'l':
10382        ap_show_modules();
10383        exit(0);
10384    case 'L':
10385        ap_show_directives();
10386        exit(0);
10387    case 'X':
10388        ++one_process;     /* Weird debugging mode. */
10389        break;
10390    case 't':
10391        configtestonly = 1;
10392        break;
10393    case 'h':
10394        usage(argv[0]);
10395    case '?':
10396        usage(argv[0]);
10397    }
10398    }
10399
10400    if (!child && run_as_service) {
10401     service_cd();
10402    }
10403
10404    server_conf = ap_read_config(pconf, ptrans,
10405        ap_server_confname);
10406
10407    if (configtestonly) {
10408        fprintf(stderr, "Syntax OK\n");
10409        exit(0);
10410    }
10411
10412    if (signal_to_send) {
10413     send_signal(pconf, signal_to_send);
10414     exit(0);
10415    }
10416
10417    if (!child && !ap_dump_settings && !install) {
10418     ap_log_pid(pconf, ap_pid_fname);
10419    }
10420    ap_set_version();
10421    ap_init_modules(pconf, server_conf);
10422    ap_suexec_enabled = init_suexec();
10423    version_locked++;
10424    if (!install) {
10425     ap_open_logs(server_conf, pconf);
10426    }
10427    set_group_privs();
10428
10429 #ifdef OS2
10430     printf("%s running...\n", ap_get_server_version());
10431 #endif
10432 #ifdef WIN32
10433     if (!child && !install) {
10434        printf("%s running...\n", ap_get_server_version());
10435     }
10436 #endif
10437
10438     if (one_process && !exit_event)
10439      exit_event = create_event(0, 0, NULL);
10440     if (one_process && !start_mutex)
10441      start_mutex = ap_create_mutex(NULL);
10442     /*
10443      * In the future, the main will spawn off a couple
10444      * of children and monitor them. As soon as a child
10445      * exits, it spawns off a new one
10446      */
10447     if (child || one_process) {
10448      if (!exit_event || !start_mutex)
10449         exit(-1);
10450      worker_main();
10451      ap_destroy_mutex(start_mutex);
10452      destroy_event(exit_event);
10453     }
10454     else {
10455      service_main(master_main, argc, argv,
10456            "Apache", install, run_as_service);
10457     }
```

```
10458
10459        clean_parent_exit(0);
10460        return 0;      /* purely to avoid a warning */
10461    }
10462
10463    #endif /* ndef MULTITHREAD */
10464
10465    #else  /* ndef SHARED_CORE_TIESTATIC */
10466
10467    /*
10468    **   Standalone Tie Program for Shared Core support
10469    **
10470    **   It's purpose is to tie the static libraries and
10471    **   the shared core library under link-time and
10472    **   passing execution control to the real main function
10473    **   in the shared core library under run-time.
10474    */
10475
10476    extern int ap_main(int argc, char *argv[]);
10477
10478    int main(int argc, char *argv[])
10479    {
10480        return ap_main(argc, argv);
10481    }
10482
10483    #endif /* ndef SHARED_CORE_TIESTATIC */
10484    #else  /* ndef SHARED_CORE_BOOTSTRAP */
10485
10486    /*
10487    **   Standalone Bootstrap Program for Shared Core support
10488    **
10489    **   It's purpose is to initialise the LD_LIBRARY_PATH
10490    **   environment variable therewith the Unix loader is
10491    **   able to start the Standalone Tie Program (see above)
10492    **   and then replacing itself with this program by
10493    **   immediately passing execution to it.
10494    */
10495
10496    #include <stdio.h>
10497    #include <stdlib.h>
10498    #include <string.h>
10499
10500    #include "ap_config.h"
10501    #include "httpd.h"
10502
10503    #if defined(HPUX) || defined(HPUX10) || defined(HPUX11)
10504    #define VARNAME "SHLIB_PATH"
10505    #else
10506    #define VARNAME "LD_LIBRARY_PATH"
10507    #endif
10508
10509    #ifndef SHARED_CORE_DIR
10510    #define SHARED_CORE_DIR HTTPD_ROOT "/libexec"
10511    #endif
10512
10513    #ifndef SHARED_CORE_EXECUTABLE_PROGRAM
10514    #define SHARED_CORE_EXECUTABLE_PROGRAM "lib" \
10515        TARGET ".ep"
10516    #endif
10517
10518    extern char *optarg;
10519    extern int   optind;
10520
10521    int main(int argc, char *argv[], char *envp[])
10522    {
10523        char prog[MAX_STRING_LEN];
10524        char llp_buf[MAX_STRING_LEN];
10525        char **llp_slot;
10526        char *llp_existing;
10527        char *llp_dir;
10528        char **envpnew;
10529        int c, i, l;
10530
10531        /*
10532         * parse argument line,
10533         * but only handle the -L option
10534         */
10535        llp_dir = SHARED_CORE_DIR;
10536        while ((c = getopt(argc, argv,
10537            "D:C:c:Xd:f:vVlLR:SZ:th")) != -1) {
10538        switch (c) {
10539        case 'D':
10540        case 'C':
10541        case 'c':
10542        case 'X':
10543        case 'd':
10544        case 'f':
10545        case 'v':
10546        case 'V':
10547        case 'l':
10548        case 'L':
10549        case 'S':
10550        case 'Z':
10551        case 't':
10552        case 'h':
10553        case '?':
```

```
10554          break;
10555       case 'R':
10556          llp_dir = strdup(optarg);
10557          break;
10558       }
10559    }
10560
10561    /*
10562     * create path to SHARED_CORE_EXECUTABLE_PROGRAM
10563     */
10564    ap_snprintf(prog, sizeof(prog), "%s/%s", llp_dir,
10565          SHARED_CORE_EXECUTABLE_PROGRAM);
10566
10567    /*
10568     * adjust process environment therewith
10569     * the Unix loader is able to start the
10570     * SHARED_CORE_EXECUTABLE_PROGRAM.
10571     */
10572    llp_slot = NULL;
10573    llp_existing = NULL;
10574    l = strlen(VARNAME);
10575    for (i = 0; envp[i] != NULL; i++) {
10576       if (strncmp(envp[i], VARNAME "=", l+1) == 0) {
10577          llp_slot = &envp[i];
10578          llp_existing = strchr(envp[i], '=') + 1;
10579       }
10580    }
10581    if (llp_slot == NULL) {
10582       envpnew = (char **)malloc(sizeof(char *)*(i + 2));
10583       if (envpnew == NULL) {
10584          fprintf(stderr, "Ouch!  Out of memory
10585             generating envpnew!\n");
10586       }
10587       memcpy(envpnew, envp, sizeof(char *)*i);
10588       envp = envpnew;
10589       llp_slot = &envp[i++];
10590       envp[i] = NULL;
10591    }
10592    if (llp_existing != NULL)
10593       ap_snprintf(llp_buf, sizeof(llp_buf), "%s=%s:%s",
10594          VARNAME, llp_dir, llp_existing);
10595    else
10596       ap_snprintf(llp_buf, sizeof(llp_buf), "%s=%s",
10597          VARNAME, llp_dir);
10598    *llp_slot = strdup(llp_buf);
10599
10600    /*
10601     * finally replace our process with
```

```
10602     * the SHARED_CORE_EXECUTABLE_PROGRAM
10603     */
10604    if (execve(prog, argv, envp) == -1) {
10605       fprintf(stderr,
10606          "%s: Unable to exec Shared Core Executable
10607             Program '%s'\n",
10608          argv[0], prog);
10609       return 1;
10610    }
10611    else
10612       return 0;
10613 }
10614
10615 #endif /* ndef SHARED_CORE_BOOTSTRAP */
10616
```

p 490 ## http_log.c

```
10617 #define CORE_PRIVATE
10618 #include "httpd.h"
10619 #include "http_conf_globals.h"
10620 #include "http_config.h"
10621 #include "http_core.h"
10622 #include "http_log.h"
10623 #include "http_main.h"
10624
10625 #include <stdarg.h>
10626
10627 typedef struct {
10628       char    *t_name;
10629       int     t_val;
10630 } TRANS;
10631
10632 #ifdef HAVE_SYSLOG
10633
10634 static const TRANS facilities[] = {
10635    {"auth",    LOG_AUTH},
10636 #ifdef LOG_AUTHPRIV
10637    {"authpriv",LOG_AUTHPRIV},
10638 #endif
10639 #ifdef LOG_CRON
10640    {"cron",    LOG_CRON},
10641 #endif
10642 #ifdef LOG_DAEMON
10643    {"daemon",  LOG_DAEMON},
10644 #endif
10645 #ifdef LOG_FTP
10646    {"ftp",     LOG_FTP},
```

```
10647  #endif
10648  #ifdef LOG_KERN
10649      {"kern",      LOG_KERN},
10650  #endif
10651  #ifdef LOG_LPR
10652      {"lpr",       LOG_LPR},
10653  #endif
10654  #ifdef LOG_MAIL
10655      {"mail",      LOG_MAIL},
10656  #endif
10657  #ifdef LOG_NEWS
10658      {"news",      LOG_NEWS},
10659  #endif
10660  #ifdef LOG_SYSLOG
10661      {"syslog",     LOG_SYSLOG},
10662  #endif
10663  #ifdef LOG_USER
10664      {"user",      LOG_USER},
10665  #endif
10666  #ifdef LOG_UUCP
10667      {"uucp",      LOG_UUCP},
10668  #endif
10669  #ifdef LOG_LOCAL0
10670      {"local0",     LOG_LOCAL0},
10671  #endif
10672  #ifdef LOG_LOCAL1
10673      {"local1",     LOG_LOCAL1},
10674  #endif
10675  #ifdef LOG_LOCAL2
10676      {"local2",     LOG_LOCAL2},
10677  #endif
10678  #ifdef LOG_LOCAL3
10679      {"local3",     LOG_LOCAL3},
10680  #endif
10681  #ifdef LOG_LOCAL4
10682      {"local4",     LOG_LOCAL4},
10683  #endif
10684  #ifdef LOG_LOCAL5
10685      {"local5",     LOG_LOCAL5},
10686  #endif
10687  #ifdef LOG_LOCAL6
10688      {"local6",     LOG_LOCAL6},
10689  #endif
10690  #ifdef LOG_LOCAL7
10691      {"local7",     LOG_LOCAL7},
10692  #endif
10693      {NULL,         -1},
10694  };
```

```
10695  #endif
10696
10697  static const TRANS priorities[] = {
10698      {"emerg",     APLOG_EMERG},
10699      {"alert",     APLOG_ALERT},
10700      {"crit",      APLOG_CRIT},
10701      {"error",     APLOG_ERR},
10702      {"warn",      APLOG_WARNING},
10703      {"notice",     APLOG_NOTICE},
10704      {"info",      APLOG_INFO},
10705      {"debug",     APLOG_DEBUG},
10706      {NULL,        -1},
10707  };
10708
10709  static int error_log_child(void *cmd,
10710      child_info *pinfo)
10711  {
10712      /* Child process code for 'ErrorLog "|..."';
10713       * may want a common framework for this,
10714       * since I expect it will be common for other
10715       * foo-loggers to want this sort of thing...
10716       */
10717      int child_pid = 0;
10718
10719      ap_cleanup_for_exec();
10720  #ifdef SIGHUP
10721      /* No concept of a child process on Win32 */
10722      signal(SIGHUP, SIG_IGN);
10723  #endif /* ndef SIGHUP */
10724  #if defined(WIN32)
10725      child_pid = spawnl(_P_NOWAIT, SHELL_PATH,
10726          SHELL_PATH, "/c", (char *)cmd, NULL);
10727      return(child_pid);
10728  #elif defined(OS2)
10729      /* For OS/2 we need to use a '/' */
10730      execl(SHELL_PATH, SHELL_PATH, "/c", (char *)cmd,
10731          NULL);
10732  #else
10733      execl(SHELL_PATH, SHELL_PATH, "-c", (char *)cmd,
10734          NULL);
10735  #endif
10736      exit(1);
10737      /* NOT REACHED */
10738      return(child_pid);
10739  }
10740
10741  static void open_error_log(server_rec *s, pool *p)
10742  {
```

```
10743        char *fname;
10744
10745        if (*s->error_fname == '|') {
10746         FILE *dummy;
10747
10748         if (!ap_spawn_child(p, error_log_child,
10749            (void *)(s->error_fname+1),
10750                    kill_after_timeout, &dummy,
10751                       NULL, NULL)) {
10752             perror("ap_spawn_child");
10753             fprintf(stderr, "Couldn't fork child for
10754                    ErrorLog process\n");
10755             exit(1);
10756         }
10757
10758         s->error_log = dummy;
10759        }
10760
10761 #ifdef HAVE_SYSLOG
10762        else if (!strncasecmp(s->error_fname, "syslog", 6)) {
10763         if ((fname = strchr(s->error_fname, ':'))) {
10764            const TRANS *fac;
10765
10766            fname++;
10767            for (fac = facilities; fac->t_name; fac++) {
10768             if (!strcasecmp(fname, fac->t_name)) {
10769                 openlog(ap_server_argv0,
10770                       LOG_NDELAY|LOG_CONS|LOG_PID,
10771                        fac->t_val);
10772                 s->error_log = NULL;
10773                 return;
10774             }
10775            }
10776         }
10777         else
10778            openlog(ap_server_argv0,
10779                 LOG_NDELAY|LOG_CONS|LOG_PID, LOG_LOCAL7);
10780
10781         s->error_log = NULL;
10782        }
10783 #endif
10784        else {
10785         fname = ap_server_root_relative(p, s->error_fname);
10786         if (!(s->error_log = ap_pfopen(p, fname, "a"))) {
10787             perror("fopen");
10788             fprintf(stderr, "%s: could not open error
10789                 log file %s.\n",
10790                 ap_server_argv0, fname);
10791             exit(1);
10792         }
10793        }
10794 }
10795
10796 void ap_open_logs(server_rec *s_main, pool *p)
10797 {
10798     server_rec *virt, *q;
10799     int replace_stderr;
10800
10801     open_error_log(s_main, p);
10802
10803     replace_stderr = 1;
10804     if (s_main->error_log) {
10805      /* replace stderr with this new log */
10806      fflush(stderr);
10807      if (dup2(fileno(s_main->error_log),
10808            STDERR_FILENO) == -1) {
10808         ap_log_error(APLOG_MARK, APLOG_CRIT, s_main,
10810         "unable to replace stderr with error_log");
10811      } else {
10812         replace_stderr = 0;
10813      }
10814     }
10815     /* note that stderr may still need to be replaced
10816      * with something because it points to the old
10817      * error log, or back to the tty of the
10818      * submitter.
10819      */
10820     if (replace_stderr && freopen("/dev/null", "w",
10821          stderr) == NULL) {
10822      ap_log_error(APLOG_MARK, APLOG_CRIT, s_main,
10823         "unable to replace stderr with /dev/null");
10824     }
10825
10826     for (virt = s_main->next; virt; virt = virt->next) {
10827      if (virt->error_fname)
10828      {
10829         for (q=s_main; q != virt; q = q->next)
10830          if (q->error_fname != NULL &&
10831             strcmp(q->error_fname,
10832                  virt->error_fname) == 0)
10833             break;
10834         if (q == virt)
10835          open_error_log(virt, p);
10836         else
10837          virt->error_log = q->error_log;
10838      }
```

```
10839        else
10840            virt->error_log = s_main->error_log;
10841      }
10842  }
10843
10844  API_EXPORT(void) ap_error_log2stderr(server_rec *s) {
10845      if (   s->error_log != NULL
10846          && fileno(s->error_log) != STDERR_FILENO)
10847          dup2(fileno(s->error_log), STDERR_FILENO);
10848  }
10849
10850  static void log_error_core(const char *file, int line,
10851      int level,
10852              const server_rec *s, const request_rec *r,
10853              const char *fmt, va_list args)
10854  {
10855      char errstr[MAX_STRING_LEN];
10856      size_t len;
10857      int save_errno = errno;
10858      FILE *logf;
10859
10860      if (s == NULL) {
10861          /*
10862           * If we are doing stderr logging (startup),
10863           * don't log messages that are above the default
10864           * server log level unless it is a startup/shutdown
10865           * notice
10866           */
10867          if (((level & APLOG_LEVELMASK) != APLOG_NOTICE) &&
10868              ((level & APLOG_LEVELMASK) > DEFAULT_LOGLEVEL))
10869              return;
10870          logf = stderr;
10871      }
10872      else if (s->error_log) {
10873          /*
10874           * If we are doing normal logging, don't log
10875           * messages that are above the server log level
10876           * unless it is a startup/shutdown notice
10877           */
10878          if (((level & APLOG_LEVELMASK) != APLOG_NOTICE) &&
10879              ((level & APLOG_LEVELMASK) > s->loglevel))
10880              return;
10881          logf = s->error_log;
10882      }
10883      else {
10884          /*
10885           * If we are doing syslog logging, don't log
10886           * messages that are above the server log level
10887           * (including a startup/shutdown notice)
10888           */
10889          if ((level & APLOG_LEVELMASK) > s->loglevel)
10890              return;
10891          logf = NULL;
10892      }
10893
10894      if (logf) {
10895          len = ap_snprintf(errstr, sizeof(errstr), "[%s] ",
10896              ap_get_time());
10897      } else {
10898          len = 0;
10899      }
10900
10901      len += ap_snprintf(errstr + len,
10902          sizeof(errstr) - len,
10903          "[%s] ", priorities[level &
10904              APLOG_LEVELMASK].t_name);
10905
10906      if (file && (level & APLOG_LEVELMASK) ==
10907          APLOG_DEBUG) {
10908  #ifdef _OSD_POSIX
10909      char tmp[256];
10910      char *e = strrchr(file, '/');
10911
10912      /* In OSD/POSIX, the compiler returns
10913       * for __FILE__ a string like:
10914       * __FILE__="*POSIX(/usr/include/stdio.h)"
10915       * (it even returns an absolute path for
10916       * sources in the current directory).
10917       * Here we try to strip this down to
10918       * the basename.
10919       */
10920      if (e != NULL && e[1] != '\0') {
10921          ap_snprintf(tmp, sizeof(tmp), "%s", &e[1]);
10922          e = &tmp[strlen(tmp)-1];
10923          if (*e == ')')
10924              *e = '\0';
10925          file = tmp;
10926      }
10927  #endif /*_OSD_POSIX*/
10928      len += ap_snprintf(errstr + len,
10929          sizeof(errstr) - len,
10930          "%s(%d): ", file, line);
10931      }
10932      if (r) {
10933          /* XXX: TODO: add a method of selecting whether
10934           * logged client addresses are in dotted quad
```

```
10935        * or resolved form... dotted quad is the
10936        * most secure, which is why I'm implementing it
10937        * first. -djg
10938        */
10939       len += ap_snprintf(errstr + len,
10940            sizeof(errstr) - len,
10941            "[client %s] ", r->connection->remote_ip);
10942       }
10943    if (!(level & APLOG_NOERRNO)
10944        && (save_errno != 0)
10945 #ifdef WIN32
10946        && !(level & APLOG_WIN32ERROR)
10947 #endif
10948        ) {
10949       len += ap_snprintf(errstr + len,
10950            sizeof(errstr) - len,
10951            "(%d)%s: ", save_errno, strerror(save_errno));
10952       }
10953 #ifdef WIN32
10954    if (level & APLOG_WIN32ERROR) {
10955       int nChars;
10956       int nErrorCode;
10957
10958       nErrorCode = GetLastError();
10959       len += ap_snprintf(errstr + len,
10960            sizeof(errstr) - len,
10961            "(%d)", nErrorCode);
10962
10963       nChars = FormatMessage(
10964            FORMAT_MESSAGE_FROM_SYSTEM,
10965            NULL,
10966            nErrorCode,
10967            MAKELANGID(LANG_NEUTRAL, SUBLANG_DEFAULT),
10968                // Default language
10969            (LPTSTR) errstr + len,
10970            sizeof(errstr) - len,
10971            NULL
10972       );
10973       len += nChars;
10974       if (nChars == 0) {
10975            /* Um, error occurred, but we can't recurse
10976             * to log it again (and it would probably
10977             * only fail anyway), so lets just log
10978             * the numeric value.
10979             */
10980            nErrorCode = GetLastError();
10981            len += ap_snprintf(errstr + len,
10982                sizeof(errstr) - len,
10983                "(FormatMessage failed with code %d): ",
10984                nErrorCode);
10985       }
10986       else {
10987            /* FormatMessage put the message in the buffer,
10988             * but it may have appended a newline (\r\n).
10989             * So remove it and use ": " instead like the
10990             * Unix errors. The error may also end with
10991             * a . before the return - if so, trash it.
10992             */
10993            if (len > 1 && errstr[len-2] == '\r'
10994                && errstr[len-1] == '\n') {
10995                if (len > 2 && errstr[len-3] == '.')
10996                    len--;
10997                errstr[len-2] = ':';
10998                errstr[len-1] = ' ';
10999            }
11000       }
11001    }
11002 #endif
11003
11004    len += ap_vsnprintf(errstr + len,
11005            sizeof(errstr) - len, fmt, args);
11006
11007    /* NULL if we are logging to syslog */
11008    if (logf) {
11009       fputs(errstr, logf);
11010       fputc('\n', logf);
11011       fflush(logf);
11012    }
11013 #ifdef HAVE_SYSLOG
11014    else {
11015       syslog(level & APLOG_LEVELMASK, "%s", errstr);
11016    }
11017 #endif
11018 }
11019
11020 API_EXPORT(void) ap_log_error(const char *file,
11021    int line, int level,
11022            const server_rec *s, const char *fmt, ...)
11023 {
11024    va_list args;
11025
11026    va_start(args, fmt);
11027    log_error_core(file, line, level, s, NULL, fmt, args);
11028    va_end(args);
11029 }
11030
```

```
11031   API_EXPORT(void) ap_log_rerror(const char *file,
11032       int line, int level,
11033               const request_rec *r, const char *fmt, ...)
11034   {
11035       va_list args;
11036
11037       va_start(args, fmt);
11038       log_error_core(file, line, level, r->server, r,
11039           fmt, args);
11040       /*
11041        * IF the error level is 'warning' or more severe,
11042        * AND there isn't already error text associated
11043        * with this request, THEN make the message text
11044        * available to ErrorDocument and other error
11045        * processors.  This can be disabled by stuffing
11046        * something, even an empty string, into the
11047        * "error-notes" cell before calling this routine.
11048       */
11049       if (((level & APLOG_LEVELMASK) <= APLOG_WARNING)
11050       && (ap_table_get(r->notes, "error-notes") == NULL)) {
11051       ap_table_setn(r->notes, "error-notes",
11052               ap_pvsprintf(r->pool, fmt, args));
11053       }
11054       va_end(args);
11055   }
11056
11057   void ap_log_pid(pool *p, char *fname)
11058   {
11059       FILE *pid_file;
11060       struct stat finfo;
11061       static pid_t saved_pid = -1;
11062       pid_t mypid;
11063
11064       if (!fname)
11065        return;
11066
11067       fname = ap_server_root_relative(p, fname);
11068       mypid = getpid();
11069       if (mypid != saved_pid && stat(fname, &finfo) == 0) {
11070           /* USR1 and HUP call this on each restart.
11071            * Only warn on first time through for this pid.
11072            *
11073            * XXX: Could just write first time through too,
11074            * although that may screw up scripts
11075            * written to do something based on the last
11076            * modification time of the pid file.
11077           */
11078           ap_log_error(APLOG_MARK,
11079                   APLOG_NOERRNO|APLOG_WARNING, NULL,
11080               ap_psprintf(p,
11081                   "pid file %s overwritten -- Unclean
11082                       shutdown of previous Apache run?",
11083                       fname)
11084               );
11085       }
11086
11087       if(!(pid_file = fopen(fname, "w"))) {
11088        perror("fopen");
11089           fprintf(stderr, "%s: could not log pid
11090                   to file %s\n",
11091               ap_server_argv0, fname);
11092           exit(1);
11093       }
11094       fprintf(pid_file, "%ld\n", (long)mypid);
11095       fclose(pid_file);
11096       saved_pid = mypid;
11097   }
11098
11099   API_EXPORT(void) ap_log_error_old(const char *err,
11100       server_rec *s)
11101   {
11102       ap_log_error(APLOG_MARK, APLOG_ERR, s, "%s", err);
11103   }
11104
11105   API_EXPORT(void) ap_log_unixerr(const char *routine,
11106       const char *file,
11107                   const char *msg, server_rec *s)
11108   {
11109       ap_log_error(file, 0, APLOG_ERR, s, "%s", msg);
11110   }
11111
11112   API_EXPORT(void) ap_log_printf(const server_rec *s,
11113       const char *fmt, ...)
11114   {
11115       va_list args;
11116
11117       va_start(args, fmt);
11118       log_error_core(APLOG_MARK, APLOG_ERR, s, NULL,
11119           fmt, args);
11120       va_end(args);
11121   }
11122
11123   API_EXPORT(void) ap_log_reason(const char *reason,
11124       const char *file, request_rec *r)
11125   {
11126       ap_log_error(APLOG_MARK, APLOG_ERR, r->server,
```

```
11127              "access to %s failed for %s, reason: %s",
11128              file,
11129              ap_get_remote_host(r->connection,
11130                  r->per_dir_config, REMOTE_NAME),
11131              reason);
11132  }
11133
11134  API_EXPORT(void) ap_log_assert(const char *szExp,
11135      const char *szFile, int nLine)
11136  {
11137      fprintf(stderr, "[%s] file %s, line %d,
11138              assertion \"%s\" failed\n",
11139          ap_get_time(), szFile, nLine, szExp);
11140  #ifndef WIN32
11141      /* unix assert does an abort leading to a core
11142       * dump */
11143      abort();
11144  #else
11145      exit(1);
11146  #endif
11147  }
11148
11149  /* piped log support */
11150
11151  #ifndef NO_RELIABLE_PIPED_LOGS
11152  /* forward declaration */
11153  static void piped_log_maintenance(int reason,
11154      void *data, ap_wait_t status);
11155
11156  static int piped_log_spawn(piped_log *pl)
11157  {
11158      int pid;
11159
11160      ap_block_alarms();
11161      pid = fork();
11162      if (pid == 0) {
11163      /* XXX: this needs porting to OS2 and WIN32 */
11164      /* XXX: need to check what open fds the logger is
11165       * actually passed, XXX: and CGIs for that
11166       * matter ... cleanup_for_exec *should*
11167       * XXX: close all the relevant stuff, but hey,
11168       * it could be broken. */
11169      RAISE_SIGSTOP(PIPED_LOG_SPAWN);
11170      /* we're now in the child */
11171      close(STDIN_FILENO);
11172      dup2(pl->fds[0], STDIN_FILENO);
11173
11174      ap_cleanup_for_exec();
```

```
11175          signal(SIGCHLD, SIG_DFL);      /* for HPUX */
11176          signal(SIGHUP, SIG_IGN);
11177          execl(SHELL_PATH, SHELL_PATH, "-c",
11178              pl->program, NULL);
11179          fprintf(stderr,
11180              "piped_log_spawn: unable to
11181                  exec %s -c '%s': %s\n",
11182              SHELL_PATH, pl->program, strerror (errno));
11183          exit(1);
11184      }
11185      if (pid == -1) {
11186          fprintf(stderr,
11187              "piped_log_spawn: unable to fork(): %s\n",
11188                  strerror (errno));
11189          ap_unblock_alarms();
11190          return -1;
11191      }
11192      ap_unblock_alarms();
11193      pl->pid = pid;
11194      ap_register_other_child(pid, piped_log_maintenance,
11195          pl, pl->fds[1]);
11196      return 0;
11197  }
11198
11199
11200  static void piped_log_maintenance(int reason,
11201      void *data, ap_wait_t status)
11202  {
11203      piped_log *pl = data;
11204
11205      switch (reason) {
11206      case OC_REASON_DEATH:
11207      case OC_REASON_LOST:
11208          pl->pid = -1;
11209          ap_unregister_other_child(pl);
11210          if (pl->program == NULL) {
11211              /* during a restart */
11212              break;
11213          }
11214          if (piped_log_spawn(pl) == -1) {
11215              /* what can we do?  This could be the error log
11216               * we're having problems opening up... */
11217              fprintf(stderr,
11218                  "piped_log_maintenance: unable to
11219                      respawn '%s': %s\n",
11220                  pl->program, strerror(errno));
11221          }
11222          break;
```

```
11223
11224        case OC_REASON_UNWRITABLE:
11225         if (pl->pid != -1) {
11226             kill(pl->pid, SIGTERM);
11227         }
11228         break;
11229
11230        case OC_REASON_RESTART:
11231         pl->program = NULL;
11232         if (pl->pid != -1) {
11233             kill(pl->pid, SIGTERM);
11234         }
11235         break;
11236
11237        case OC_REASON_UNREGISTER:
11238         break;
11239        }
11240    }
11241
11242
11243    static void piped_log_cleanup(void *data)
11244    {
11245        piped_log *pl = data;
11246
11247        if (pl->pid != -1) {
11248         kill(pl->pid, SIGTERM);
11249        }
11250        ap_unregister_other_child(pl);
11251        close(pl->fds[0]);
11252        close(pl->fds[1]);
11253    }
11254
11255
11256    static void piped_log_cleanup_for_exec(void *data)
11257    {
11258        piped_log *pl = data;
11259
11260        close(pl->fds[0]);
11261        close(pl->fds[1]);
11262    }
11263
11264
11265    API_EXPORT(piped_log *) ap_open_piped_log(pool *p,
11266         const char *program)
11267    {
11268        piped_log *pl;
11269
11270        pl = ap_palloc(p, sizeof (*pl));
```

```
11271        pl->p = p;
11272        pl->program = ap_pstrdup(p, program);
11273        pl->pid = -1;
11274        ap_block_alarms ();
11275        if (pipe(pl->fds) == -1) {
11276         int save_errno = errno;
11277         ap_unblock_alarms();
11278         errno = save_errno;
11279         return NULL;
11280        }
11281        ap_register_cleanup(p, pl, piped_log_cleanup,
11282             piped_log_cleanup_for_exec);
11283        if (piped_log_spawn(pl) == -1) {
11284         int save_errno = errno;
11285         ap_kill_cleanup(p, pl, piped_log_cleanup);
11286         close(pl->fds[0]);
11287         close(pl->fds[1]);
11288         ap_unblock_alarms();
11289         errno = save_errno;
11290         return NULL;
11291        }
11292        ap_unblock_alarms();
11293        return pl;
11294    }
11295
11296    API_EXPORT(void) ap_close_piped_log(piped_log *pl)
11297    {
11298        ap_block_alarms();
11299        piped_log_cleanup(pl);
11300        ap_kill_cleanup(pl->p, pl, piped_log_cleanup);
11301        ap_unblock_alarms();
11302    }
11303
11304    #else
11305    static int piped_log_child(void *cmd, child_info *pinfo)
11306    {
11307        /* Child process code for 'TransferLog "|..."';
11308         * may want a common framework for this, since I
11309         * expect it will be common for other foo-loggers
11310         * to want this sort of thing...
11311         */
11312        int child_pid = 1;
11313
11314        ap_cleanup_for_exec();
11315    #ifdef SIGHUP
11316        signal(SIGHUP, SIG_IGN);
11317    #endif
11318    #if defined(WIN32)
```

```
11319        child_pid = spawnl(_P_NOWAIT, SHELL_PATH,
11320            SHELL_PATH, "/c", (char *)cmd, NULL);
11321        return(child_pid);
11322  #elif defined(OS2)
11323        /* For OS/2 we need to use a '/' */
11324        execl (SHELL_PATH, SHELL_PATH, "/c",
11325            (char *)cmd, NULL);
11326  #else
11327        execl (SHELL_PATH, SHELL_PATH, "-c",
11328            (char *)cmd, NULL);
11329  #endif
11330        perror("exec");
11331        fprintf(stderr, "Exec of shell for logging
11332            failed!!!\n");
11333        return(child_pid);
11334  }
11335
11336
11337  API_EXPORT(piped_log *) ap_open_piped_log(pool *p,
11338        const char *program)
11339  {
11340        piped_log *pl;
11341        FILE *dummy;
11342
11343        if (!ap_spawn_child(p, piped_log_child,
11344            (void *)program,
11345                kill_after_timeout, &dummy, NULL, NULL)) {
11346        perror("ap_spawn_child");
11347        fprintf(stderr, "Couldn't fork child for piped
11348            log process\n");
11349        exit (1);
11350        }
11351        pl = ap_palloc(p, sizeof (*pl));
11352        pl->p = p;
11353        pl->write_f = dummy;
11354
11355        return pl;
11356  }
11357
11358
11359  API_EXPORT(void) ap_close_piped_log(piped_log *pl)
11360  {
11361        ap_pfclose(pl->p, pl->write_f);
11362  }
11363  #endif
11364
```

mod_access.c

`p 441`

```
11365  #include "httpd.h"
11366  #include "http_core.h"
11367  #include "http_config.h"
11368  #include "http_log.h"
11369  #include "http_request.h"
11370
11371  enum allowdeny_type {
11372        T_ENV,
11373        T_ALL,
11374        T_IP,
11375        T_HOST,
11376        T_FAIL
11377  };
11378
11379  typedef struct {
11380        int limited;
11381        union {
11382          char *from;
11383          struct {
11384              unsigned long net;
11385              unsigned long mask;
11386          } ip;
11387        } x;
11388        enum allowdeny_type type;
11389  } allowdeny;
11390
11391  /* things in the 'order' array */
11392  #define DENY_THEN_ALLOW 0
11393  #define ALLOW_THEN_DENY 1
11394  #define MUTUAL_FAILURE 2
11395
11396  typedef struct {
11397        int order[METHODS];
11398        array_header *allows;
11399        array_header *denys;
11400  } access_dir_conf;
11401
11402  module MODULE_VAR_EXPORT access_module;
11403
11404  static void *create_access_dir_config(pool *p,
11405        char *dummy)
11406  {
11407        access_dir_conf *conf =
11408        (access_dir_conf *) ap_pcalloc(p,
11409            sizeof(access_dir_conf));
11410        int i;
```

```
11411          for (i = 0; i < METHODS; ++i)
11412           conf->order[i] = DENY_THEN_ALLOW;
11413        conf->allows = ap_make_array(p, 1,
11414              sizeof(allowdeny));
11415        conf->denys = ap_make_array(p, 1,
11416              sizeof(allowdeny));
11417
11418
11419        return (void *) conf;
11420    }
11421
11422    static const char *order(cmd_parms *cmd, void *dv,
11423        char *arg)
11424    {
11425        access_dir_conf *d = (access_dir_conf *) dv;
11426        int i, o;
11427
11428        if (!strcasecmp(arg, "allow,deny"))
11429          o = ALLOW_THEN_DENY;
11430        else if (!strcasecmp(arg, "deny,allow"))
11431          o = DENY_THEN_ALLOW;
11432        else if (!strcasecmp(arg, "mutual-failure"))
11433          o = MUTUAL_FAILURE;
11434        else
11435          return "unknown order";
11436
11437        for (i = 0; i < METHODS; ++i)
11438          if (cmd->limited & (1 << i))
11439              d->order[i] = o;
11440
11441        return NULL;
11442    }
11443
11444    static int is_ip(const char *host)
11445    {
11446        while ((*host == '.') || ap_isdigit(*host))
11447          host++;
11448        return (*host == '\0');
11449    }
11450
11451    static const char *allow_cmd(cmd_parms *cmd, void *dv,
11452        char *from, char *where)
11453    {
11454        access_dir_conf *d = (access_dir_conf *) dv;
11455        allowdeny *a;
11456        char *s;
11457
11458        if (strcasecmp(from, "from"))
11459          return "allow and deny must be followed by 'from'";
11460
11461        a = (allowdeny *) ap_push_array(cmd->info ?
11462            d->allows : d->denys);
11463        a->x.from = where;
11464        a->limited = cmd->limited;
11465
11466        if (!strncasecmp(where, "env=", 4)) {
11467          a->type = T_ENV;
11468          a->x.from += 4;
11469
11470        }
11471        else if (!strcasecmp(where, "all")) {
11472          a->type = T_ALL;
11473
11474        }
11475        else if ((s = strchr(where, '/'))) {
11476          unsigned long mask;
11477
11478          a->type = T_IP;
11479          /* trample on where, we won't be using it
11480           * any more */
11481          *s++ = '\0';
11482
11483          if (!is_ip(where)
11484            || (a->x.ip.net = ap_inet_addr(where))
11485                == INADDR_NONE) {
11486              a->type = T_FAIL;
11487              return "syntax error in network portion of
11488                  network/netmask";
11489          }
11490
11491          /* is_ip just tests if it matches [\d.]+ */
11492          if (!is_ip(s)) {
11493              a->type = T_FAIL;
11494              return "syntax error in mask portion of
11495                  network/netmask";
11496          }
11497          /* is it in /a.b.c.d form? */
11498          if (strchr(s, '.')) {
11499              mask = ap_inet_addr(s);
11500              if (mask == INADDR_NONE) {
11501                a->type = T_FAIL;
11502                return "syntax error in mask portion of
11503                    network/netmask";
11504              }
11505          }
11506          else {
```

```
11507          /* assume it's in /nnn form */
11508          mask = atoi(s);
11509          if (mask > 32 || mask <= 0) {
11510           a->type = T_FAIL;
11511           return "invalid mask in network/netmask";
11512          }
11513          mask = 0xFFFFFFFFUL << (32 - mask);
11514          mask = htonl(mask);
11515        }
11516       a->x.ip.mask = mask;
11517
11518      }
11519      else if (ap_isdigit(*where) && is_ip(where)) {
11520       /* legacy syntax for ip addrs: a.b.c. ==>
11521            a.b.c.0/24 for example */
11522       int shift;
11523       char *t;
11524       int octet;
11525
11526       a->type = T_IP;
11527       /* parse components */
11528       s = where;
11529       a->x.ip.net = 0;
11530       a->x.ip.mask = 0;
11531       shift = 24;
11532       while (*s) {
11533          t = s;
11534          if (!ap_isdigit(*t)) {
11535           a->type = T_FAIL;
11536           return "invalid ip address";
11537          }
11538          while (ap_isdigit(*t)) {
11539           ++t;
11540          }
11541          if (*t == '.') {
11542           *t++ = 0;
11543          }
11544          else if (*t) {
11545           a->type = T_FAIL;
11546           return "invalid ip address";
11547          }
11548          if (shift < 0) {
11549           return "invalid ip address, only 4
11550                octets allowed";
11551          }
11552          octet = atoi(s);
11553          if (octet < 0 || octet > 255) {
11554           a->type = T_FAIL;
11555           return "each octet must be between 0
11556                and 255 inclusive";
11557          }
11558          a->x.ip.net |= octet << shift;
11559          a->x.ip.mask |= 0xFFUL << shift;
11560          s = t;
11561          shift -= 8;
11562       }
11563       a->x.ip.net = ntohl(a->x.ip.net);
11564       a->x.ip.mask = ntohl(a->x.ip.mask);
11565      }
11566      else {
11567       a->type = T_HOST;
11568      }
11569
11570      return NULL;
11571  }
11572
11573  static char its_an_allow;
11574
11575  static const command_rec access_cmds[] =
11576  {
11577      {"order", order, NULL, OR_LIMIT, TAKE1,
11578       "'allow,deny', 'deny,allow', or
11579            'mutual-failure'"},
11580      {"allow", allow_cmd, &its_an_allow,
11581            OR_LIMIT, ITERATE2,
11582       "'from' followed by hostnames or
11583            IP-address wildcards"},
11584      {"deny", allow_cmd, NULL, OR_LIMIT, ITERATE2,
11585       "'from' followed by hostnames or IP-address
11586            wildcards"},
11587      {NULL}
11588  };
11589
11590  static int in_domain(const char *domain, const
11591      char *what)
11592  {
11593      int dl = strlen(domain);
11594      int wl = strlen(what);
11595
11596      if ((wl - dl) >= 0) {
11597       if (strcasecmp(domain, &what[wl - dl]) != 0)
11598          return 0;
11599
11600       /* Make sure we matched an *entire* subdomain --
11601        * if the user said 'allow from good.com', we
11602        * don't want people from nogood.com
```

```
11603        * to be able to get in.
11604        */
11605
11606       if (wl == dl)
11607           return 1;          /* matched whole thing */
11608       else
11609           return (domain[0] == '.' ||
11610               what[wl - dl - 1] == '.');
11611       }
11612       else
11613        return 0;
11614   }
11615
11616   static int find_allowdeny(request_rec *r,
11617       array_header *a, int method)
11618   {
11619       allowdeny *ap = (allowdeny *) a->elts;
11620       int mmask = (1 << method);
11621       int i;
11622       int gothost = 0;
11623       const char *remotehost = NULL;
11624
11625       for (i = 0; i < a->nelts; ++i) {
11626        if (!(mmask & ap[i].limited))
11627           continue;
11628
11629        switch (ap[i].type) {
11630        case T_ENV:
11631            if (ap_table_get(r->subprocess_env,
11632                ap[i].x.from)) {
11633             return 1;
11634            }
11635            break;
11636
11637        case T_ALL:
11638            return 1;
11639
11640        case T_IP:
11641            if (ap[i].x.ip.net != INADDR_NONE
11642             && (r->connection->remote_addr.sin_addr.s_addr
11643                & ap[i].x.ip.mask) == ap[i].x.ip.net) {
11644             return 1;
11645            }
11646            break;
11647
11648        case T_HOST:
11649            if (!gothost) {
```

```
11650            remotehost = ap_get_remote_host(r->connection,
11651                r->per_dir_config,
11652                        REMOTE_DOUBLE_REV);
11653
11654            if ((remotehost == NULL) || is_ip(remotehost))
11655                gothost = 1;
11656            else
11657                gothost = 2;
11658            }
11659
11660            if ((gothost == 2) && in_domain(ap[i].x.from,
11661                remotehost))
11662             return 1;
11663            break;
11664
11665        case T_FAIL:
11666            /* do nothing? */
11667            break;
11668        }
11669        }
11670
11671       return 0;
11672   }
11673
11674   static int check_dir_access(request_rec *r)
11675   {
11676       int method = r->method_number;
11677       access_dir_conf *a =
11678       (access_dir_conf *)
11679       ap_get_module_config(r->per_dir_config,
11680           &access_module);
11681       int ret = OK;
11682
11683       if (a->order[method] == ALLOW_THEN_DENY) {
11684        ret = FORBIDDEN;
11685        if (find_allowdeny(r, a->allows, method))
11686           ret = OK;
11687        if (find_allowdeny(r, a->denys, method))
11688           ret = FORBIDDEN;
11689       }
11690       else if (a->order[method] == DENY_THEN_ALLOW) {
11691        if (find_allowdeny(r, a->denys, method))
11692           ret = FORBIDDEN;
11693        if (find_allowdeny(r, a->allows, method))
11694           ret = OK;
11695       }
11696       else {
```

```
11697        if (find_allowdeny(r, a->allows, method)
11698            && !find_allowdeny(r, a->denys, method))
11699            ret = OK;
11700        else
11701            ret = FORBIDDEN;
11702        }
11703
11704        if (ret == FORBIDDEN
11705        && (ap_satisfies(r) != SATISFY_ANY ||
11706            !ap_some_auth_required(r))) {
11707        ap_log_rerror(APLOG_MARK,
11708            APLOG_NOERRNO|APLOG_ERR, r,
11709                "client denied by server configuration: %s",
11710                r->filename);
11711        }
11712
11713        return ret;
11714    }
11715
11716
11717
11718    module MODULE_VAR_EXPORT access_module =
11719    {
11720        STANDARD_MODULE_STUFF,
11721        NULL,                  /* initializer */
11722        create_access_dir_config,
11723        /* dir config creater */
11724        NULL,
11725        /* dir merger -- default is to override */
11726        NULL,                  /* server config */
11727        NULL,                  /* merge server config */
11728        access_cmds,
11729        NULL,                  /* handlers */
11730        NULL,                  /* filename translation */
11731        NULL,                  /* check_user_id */
11732        NULL,                  /* check auth */
11733        check_dir_access,         /* check access */
11734        NULL,                  /* type_checker */
11735        NULL,                  /* fixups */
11736        NULL,                  /* logger */
11737        NULL,                  /* header parser */
11738        NULL,                  /* child_init */
11739        NULL,                  /* child_exit */
11740        NULL                   /* post read-request */
11741    };
11742    mod_actions.c
```

▶ mod_actions.c

p 459

```
11743    #include "httpd.h"
11744    #include "http_config.h"
11745    #include "http_request.h"
11746    #include "http_core.h"
11747    #include "http_protocol.h"
11748    #include "http_main.h"
11749    #include "http_log.h"
11750    #include "util_script.h"
11751
11752    typedef struct {
11753        table *action_types;       /* Added with Action... */
11754        char *scripted[METHODS];   /* Added with Script... */
11755    } action_dir_config;
11756
11757    module action_module;
11758
11759    static void *create_action_dir_config(pool *p,
11760        char *dummy)
11761    {
11762        action_dir_config *new =
11763        (action_dir_config *) ap_palloc(p,
11764            sizeof(action_dir_config));
11765
11766        new->action_types = ap_make_table(p, 4);
11767        memset(new->scripted, 0, sizeof(new->scripted));
11768
11769        return new;
11770    }
11771
11772    static void *merge_action_dir_configs(pool *p,
11773        void *basev, void *addv)
11774    {
11775        action_dir_config *base =
11776            (action_dir_config *) basev;
11777        action_dir_config *add =
11778            (action_dir_config *) addv;
11779        action_dir_config *new =
11780            (action_dir_config *) ap_palloc(p,
11781                        sizeof(action_dir_config));
11782        int i;
11783
11784        new->action_types = ap_overlay_tables(p,
11785            add->action_types,
11786                        base->action_types);
11787
```

```
11788          for (i = 0; i < METHODS; ++i) {
11789              new->scripted[i] =
11790                      add->scripted[i] ? add->scripted[i]
11791                                       : base->scripted[i];
11792          }
11793          return new;
11794      }
11795
11796      static const char *add_action(cmd_parms *cmd,
11797          action_dir_config * m, char *type,
11798                          char *script)
11799      {
11800          ap_table_setn(m->action_types, type, script);
11801          return NULL;
11802      }
11803
11804      static const char *set_script(cmd_parms *cmd,
11805          action_dir_config * m,
11806                          char *method, char *script)
11807      {
11808          int methnum;
11809
11810          methnum = ap_method_number_of(method);
11811          if (methnum == M_TRACE)
11812              return "TRACE not allowed for Script";
11813          else if (methnum == M_INVALID)
11814              return "Unknown method type for Script";
11815          else
11816              m->scripted[methnum] = script;
11817
11818          return NULL;
11819      }
11820
11821      static const command_rec action_cmds[] =
11822      {
11823          {"Action", add_action, NULL, OR_FILEINFO, TAKE2,
11824           "a media type followed by a script name"},
11825          {"Script", set_script, NULL, ACCESS_CONF |
11826              RSRC_CONF, TAKE2,
11827           "a method followed by a script name"},
11828          {NULL}
11829      };
11830
11831      static int action_handler(request_rec *r)
11832      {
11833          action_dir_config *conf = (action_dir_config *)
11834              ap_get_module_config(r->per_dir_config,
11835                  &action_module);
11836          const char *t, *action = r->handler ? r->handler :
11837                  r->content_type;
11838          const char *script;
11839          int i;
11840
11841          /* Set allowed stuff */
11842          for (i = 0; i < METHODS; ++i) {
11843              if (conf->scripted[i])
11844                  r->allowed |= (1 << i);
11845          }
11846
11847          /* First, check for the method-handling scripts */
11848          if (r->method_number == M_GET) {
11849              if (r->args)
11850                  script = conf->scripted[M_GET];
11851              else
11852                  script = NULL;
11853          }
11854          else {
11855              script = conf->scripted[r->method_number];
11856          }
11857
11858          /* Check for looping, which can happen if the
11859           * CGI script isn't */
11860          if (script && r->prev && r->prev->prev)
11861              return DECLINED;
11862
11863          /* Second, check for actions (which override the
11864           * method scripts) */
11865          if ((t = ap_table_get(conf->action_types,
11866                  action ? action :
11867                      ap_default_type(r)))) {
11868              script = t;
11869              if (r->finfo.st_mode == 0) {
11870                  ap_log_rerror(APLOG_MARK,
11871                      APLOG_NOERRNO|APLOG_ERR, r,
11872                      "File does not exist: %s", r->filename);
11873                  return NOT_FOUND;
11874              }
11875          }
11876
11877          if (script == NULL)
11878              return DECLINED;
11879
11880          ap_internal_redirect_handler(ap_pstrcat(r->pool,
11881              script, ap_escape_uri(r->pool,
11882                  r->uri), r->args ? "?" : NULL,
11883                      r->args, NULL), r);
11884          return OK;
11885      }
```

```
11886
11887   static const handler_rec action_handlers[] =
11888   {
11889       {"*/*", action_handler},
11890       {NULL}
11891   };
11892
11893   module action_module =
11894   {
11895       STANDARD_MODULE_STUFF,
11896       NULL,                   /* initializer */
11897       create_action_dir_config,
11898       /* dir config creater */
11899       merge_action_dir_configs,
11900       /* dir merger -- default is to override */
11901       NULL,                   /* server config */
11902       NULL,                   /* merge server config */
11903       action_cmds,            /* command table */
11904       action_handlers,        /* handlers */
11905       NULL,                   /* filename translation */
11906       NULL,                   /* check_user_id */
11907       NULL,                   /* check auth */
11908       NULL,                   /* check access */
11909       NULL,                   /* type_checker */
11910       NULL,                   /* fixups */
11911       NULL,                   /* logger */
11912       NULL,                   /* header parser */
11913       NULL,                   /* child_init */
11914       NULL,                   /* child_exit */
11915       NULL                    /* post read-request */
11916   };
11917   #include "httpd.h"
```

p 449 ▶ mod_alias.c

```
11918   #include "http_config.h"
11919
11920   typedef struct {
11921       char *real;
11922       char *fake;
11923       char *handler;
11924       regex_t *regexp;
11925       int redir_status;
11926       /* 301, 302, 303, 410, etc */
11927   } alias_entry;
11928
11929   typedef struct {
11930       array_header *aliases;
11931       array_header *redirects;
```

```
11932   } alias_server_conf;
11933
11934   typedef struct {
11935       array_header *redirects;
11936   } alias_dir_conf;
11937
11938   module MODULE_VAR_EXPORT alias_module;
11939
11940   static void *create_alias_config(pool *p,
11941       server_rec *s)
11942   {
11943       alias_server_conf *a =
11944       (alias_server_conf *) ap_pcalloc(p,
11945           sizeof(alias_server_conf));
11946
11947       a->aliases = ap_make_array(p, 20,
11948           sizeof(alias_entry));
11949       a->redirects = ap_make_array(p, 20,
11950           sizeof(alias_entry));
11951       return a;
11952   }
11953
11954   static void *create_alias_dir_config(pool *p, char *d)
11955   {
11956       alias_dir_conf *a =
11957       (alias_dir_conf *) ap_pcalloc(p,
11958           sizeof(alias_dir_conf));
11959       a->redirects = ap_make_array(p, 2,
11960           sizeof(alias_entry));
11961       return a;
11962   }
11963
11964   static void *merge_alias_config(pool *p,
11965       void *basev, void *overridesv)
11966   {
11967       alias_server_conf *a =
11968       (alias_server_conf *) ap_pcalloc(p,
11969           sizeof(alias_server_conf));
11970       alias_server_conf *base = (alias_server_conf *)
11971           basev, *overrides = (alias_server_conf *)
11972               overridesv;
11973       a->aliases = ap_append_arrays(p,
11974           overrides->aliases, base->aliases);
11975       a->redirects = ap_append_arrays(p,
11976           overrides->redirects, base->redirects);
11977       return a;
11978   }
11979
11980   static void *merge_alias_dir_config(pool *p,
```

```
11981        void *basev, void *overridesv)
11982    {
11983        alias_dir_conf *a =
11984        (alias_dir_conf *) ap_pcalloc(p,
11985            sizeof(alias_dir_conf));
11986        alias_dir_conf *base = (alias_dir_conf *) basev,
11987            *overrides = (alias_dir_conf *) overridesv;
11988        a->redirects = ap_append_arrays(p,
11989            overrides->redirects, base->redirects);
11990        return a;
11991    }
11992
11993    static const char *add_alias_internal(cmd_parms *cmd,
11994        void *dummy, char *f, char *r,
11995                            int use_regex)
11996    {
11997        server_rec *s = cmd->server;
11998        alias_server_conf *conf =
11999        (alias_server_conf *)
12000            ap_get_module_config(s->module_config,
12001            &alias_module);
12002        alias_entry *new = ap_push_array(conf->aliases);
12003
12004        /* XX r can NOT be relative to DocumentRoot
12005         * here... compat bug. */
12006
12007        if (use_regex) {
12008         new->regexp = ap_pregcomp(cmd->pool, f,
12009            REG_EXTENDED);
12010         if (new->regexp == NULL)
12011            return "Regular expression could not be
12012                compiled.";
12013        }
12014
12015        new->fake = f;
12016        new->real = r;
12017        new->handler = cmd->info;
12018
12019        return NULL;
12020    }
12021
12022    static const char *add_alias(cmd_parms *cmd,
12023        void *dummy, char *f, char *r)
12024    {
12025        return add_alias_internal(cmd, dummy, f, r, 0);
12026    }
12027
12028    static const char *add_alias_regex(cmd_parms *cmd,
```

```
12029        void *dummy, char *f, char *r)
12030    {
12031        return add_alias_internal(cmd, dummy, f, r, 1);
12032    }
12033
12034    static const char *add_redirect_internal(cmd_parms
12035        *cmd, alias_dir_conf * dirconf,
12036                        char *arg1, char *arg2,
12037                            char *arg3,
12038                            int use_regex)
12039    {
12040        alias_entry *new;
12041        server_rec *s = cmd->server;
12042        alias_server_conf *serverconf =
12043        (alias_server_conf *)
12044            ap_get_module_config(s->module_config,
12045            &alias_module);
12046        int status = (int) (long) cmd->info;
12047        regex_t *r = NULL;
12048        char *f = arg2;
12049        char *url = arg3;
12050
12051        if (!strcasecmp(arg1, "gone"))
12052         status = HTTP_GONE;
12053        else if (!strcasecmp(arg1, "permanent"))
12054         status = HTTP_MOVED_PERMANENTLY;
12055        else if (!strcasecmp(arg1, "temp"))
12056         status = HTTP_MOVED_TEMPORARILY;
12057        else if (!strcasecmp(arg1, "seeother"))
12058         status = HTTP_SEE_OTHER;
12059        else if (ap_isdigit(*arg1))
12060         status = atoi(arg1);
12061        else {
12062         f = arg1;
12063         url = arg2;
12064        }
12065
12066        if (use_regex) {
12067         r = ap_pregcomp(cmd->pool, f, REG_EXTENDED);
12068         if (r == NULL)
12069            return "Regular expression could not
12070                be compiled.";
12071        }
12072
12073        if (ap_is_HTTP_REDIRECT(status)) {
12074         if (!url)
12075            return "URL to redirect to is missing";
12076         if (!use_regex && !ap_is_url(url))
```

```
12077            return "Redirect to non-URL";
12078        }
12079    else {
12080     if (url)
12081        return "Redirect URL not valid for this status";
12082     }
12083
12084     if (cmd->path)
12085      new = ap_push_array(dirconf->redirects);
12086     else
12087      new = ap_push_array(serverconf->redirects);
12088
12089     new->fake = f;
12090     new->real = url;
12091     new->regexp = r;
12092     new->redir_status = status;
12093     return NULL;
12094 }
12095
12096 static const char *add_redirect(cmd_parms *cmd,
12097        alias_dir_conf * dirconf, char *arg1,
12098                  char *arg2, char *arg3)
12099 {
12100     return add_redirect_internal(cmd, dirconf,
12101         arg1, arg2, arg3, 0);
12102 }
12103
12104 static const char *add_redirect_regex(cmd_parms *cmd,
12105        alias_dir_conf * dirconf,
12106          char *arg1, char *arg2, char *arg3)
12107 {
12108     return add_redirect_internal(cmd, dirconf, arg1,
12109         arg2, arg3, 1);
12110 }
12111
12112 static const command_rec alias_cmds[] =
12113 {
12114    {"Alias", add_alias, NULL, RSRC_CONF, TAKE2,
12115     "a fakename and a realname"},
12116    {"ScriptAlias", add_alias, "cgi-script",
12117        RSRC_CONF, TAKE2,
12118     "a fakename and a realname"},
12119    {"Redirect", add_redirect, (void *)
12120        HTTP_MOVED_TEMPORARILY,
12121     OR_FILEINFO, TAKE23,
12122    "an optional status, then document to be redirected
12123            and destination URL"},
```

```
12124    {"AliasMatch", add_alias_regex, NULL, RSRC_CONF,
12125        TAKE2,
12126     "a regular expression and a filename"},
12127    {"ScriptAliasMatch", add_alias_regex, "cgi-script",
12128        RSRC_CONF, TAKE2,
12129     "a regular expression and a filename"},
12130    {"RedirectMatch", add_redirect_regex, (void *)
12131        HTTP_MOVED_TEMPORARILY,
12132     OR_FILEINFO, TAKE23,
12133     "an optional status, then a regular expression
12134        and destination URL"},
12135    {"RedirectTemp", add_redirect, (void *)
12136        HTTP_MOVED_TEMPORARILY,
12137     OR_FILEINFO, TAKE2,
12138     "a document to be redirected, then the destination
12139        URL"},
12140    {"RedirectPermanent", add_redirect, (void *)
12141        HTTP_MOVED_PERMANENTLY,
12142     OR_FILEINFO, TAKE2,
12143     "a document to be redirected, then the
12144        destination URL"},
12145    {NULL}
12146 };
12147
12148 static int alias_matches(const char *uri, const
12149     char *alias_fakename)
12150 {
12151     const char *end_fakename = alias_fakename +
12152         strlen(alias_fakename);
12153     const char *aliasp = alias_fakename, *urip = uri;
12154
12155     while (aliasp < end_fakename) {
12156      if (*aliasp == '/') {
12157        /* any number of '/' in the alias matches
12158         * any number in the supplied URI, but there
12159         * must be at least one... */
12160         */
12161         if (*urip != '/')
12162         return 0;
12163
12164         while (*aliasp == '/')
12165         ++aliasp;
12166         while (*urip == '/')
12167         ++urip;
12168      }
12169      else {
12170        /* Other characters are compared literally */
12171        if (*urip++ != *aliasp++)
```

```
12172              return 0;
12173          }
12174      }
12175
12176      /* Check last alias path component matched
12177       * all the way */
12178
12179      if (aliasp[-1] != '/' && *urip != '\0' &&
12180          *urip != '/')
12181      return 0;
12182
12183      /* Return number of characters from URI which
12184       * matched (may be greater than length of alias,
12185       * since we may have matched doubled slashes)
12186       */
12187
12188      return urip - uri;
12189  }
12190
12191  static char *try_alias_list(request_rec *r,
12192      array_header *aliases, int doesc, int *status)
12193  {
12194      alias_entry *entries = (alias_entry *) aliases->elts;
12195      regmatch_t regm[10];
12196      char *found = NULL;
12197      int i;
12198
12199      for (i = 0; i < aliases->nelts; ++i) {
12200          alias_entry *p = &entries[i];
12201          int l;
12202
12203          if (p->regexp) {
12204              if (!regexec(p->regexp, r->uri,
12205                  p->regexp->re_nsub + 1, regm, 0)) {
12206              if (p->real) {
12207                  found = ap_pregsub(r->pool, p->real, r->uri,
12208                      p->regexp->re_nsub + 1, regm);
12209                  if (found && doesc) {
12210                      found = ap_escape_uri(r->pool, found);
12211                  }
12212              }
12213              else {
12214                  /* need something non-null */
12215                  found = ap_pstrdup(r->pool, "");
12216              }
12217          }
12218      }
12219      else {
```

```
12220              l = alias_matches(r->uri, p->fake);
12221
12222              if (l > 0) {
12223                  if (doesc) {
12224                      char *escurl;
12225                      escurl = ap_os_escape_path(r->pool,
12226                          r->uri + l, 1);
12227
12228                      found = ap_pstrcat(r->pool, p->real,
12229                          escurl, NULL);
12230                  }
12231                  else
12232                      found = ap_pstrcat(r->pool, p->real,
12233                          r->uri + l, NULL);
12234              }
12235          }
12236
12237          if (found) {
12238              if (p->handler) {
12239              /* Set handler, and leave a note for mod_cgi */
12240                  r->handler = p->handler;
12241                  ap_table_setn(r->notes, "alias-forced-type",
12242                      r->handler);
12243              }
12244
12245              *status = p->redir_status;
12246
12247              return found;
12248          }
12249
12250      }
12251
12252      return NULL;
12253  }
12254
12255  static int translate_alias_redir(request_rec *r)
12256  {
12257      void *sconf = r->server->module_config;
12258      alias_server_conf *serverconf =
12259      (alias_server_conf *) ap_get_module_config(sconf,
12260          &alias_module);
12261      char *ret;
12262      int status;
12263
12264      if (r->uri[0] != '/' && r->uri[0] != '\0')
12265      return DECLINED;
12266
12267      if ((ret = try_alias_list(r, serverconf->redirects,
```

```
12268              1, &status)) != NULL) {
12269          if (ap_is_HTTP_REDIRECT(status)) {
12270              /* include QUERY_STRING if any */
12271              if (r->args) {
12272                  ret = ap_pstrcat(r->pool, ret, "?",
12273                      r->args, NULL);
12274              }
12275              ap_table_setn(r->headers_out, "Location", ret);
12276          }
12277          return status;
12278      }
12279
12280      if ((ret = try_alias_list(r, serverconf->aliases, 0,
12281          &status)) != NULL) {
12282          r->filename = ret;
12283          return OK;
12284      }
12285
12286      return DECLINED;
12287  }
12288
12289  static int fixup_redir(request_rec *r)
12290  {
12291      void *dconf = r->per_dir_config;
12292      alias_dir_conf *dirconf =
12293      (alias_dir_conf *) ap_get_module_config(dconf,
12294          &alias_module);
12295      char *ret;
12296      int status;
12297
12298      /* It may have changed since last time,
12299       * so try again */
12300
12301      if ((ret = try_alias_list(r, dirconf->redirects,
12302          1, &status)) != NULL) {
12303          if (ap_is_HTTP_REDIRECT(status))
12304              ap_table_setn(r->headers_out, "Location", ret);
12305          return status;
12306      }
12307
12308      return DECLINED;
12309  }
12310
12311  module MODULE_VAR_EXPORT alias_module =
12312  {
12313      STANDARD_MODULE_STUFF,
12314      NULL,                    /* initializer */
12315      create_alias_dir_config,
```

```
12316      /* dir config creater */
12317      merge_alias_dir_config,
12318      /* dir merger -- default is to override */
12319      create_alias_config,      /* server config */
12320      merge_alias_config,       /* merge server configs */
12321      alias_cmds,               /* command table */
12322      NULL,            /* handlers */
12323      translate_alias_redir,
12324      /* filename translation */
12325      NULL,               /* check_user_id */
12326      NULL,               /* check auth */
12327      NULL,               /* check access */
12328      NULL,               /* type_checker */
12329      fixup_redir,         /* fixups */
12330      NULL,               /* logger */
12331      NULL,               /* header parser */
12332      NULL,               /* child_init */
12333      NULL,               /* child_exit */
12334      NULL               /* post read-request */
12335  };
```

▶ p 499 **mod_asis.c**

```
12336  #include "httpd.h"
12337  #include "http_config.h"
12338  #include "http_protocol.h"
12339  #include "http_log.h"
12340  #include "util_script.h"
12341  #include "http_main.h"
12342  #include "http_request.h"
12343
12344  static int asis_handler(request_rec *r)
12345  {
12346      FILE *f;
12347      const char *location;
12348
12349      r->allowed |= (1 << M_GET);
12350      if (r->method_number != M_GET)
12351          return DECLINED;
12352      if (r->finfo.st_mode == 0) {
12353          ap_log_rerror(APLOG_MARK,
12354              APLOG_NOERRNO|APLOG_ERR, r,
12355                  "File does not exist: %s", r->filename);
12356          return NOT_FOUND;
12357      }
12358
12359      f = ap_pfopen(r->pool, r->filename, "r");
12360
12361      if (f == NULL) {
```

```
12362         ap_log_rerror(APLOG_MARK, APLOG_ERR, r,
12363                   "file permissions deny server access:
12364                   %s", r->filename);
12365         return FORBIDDEN;
12366     }
12367
12368     ap_scan_script_header_err(r, f, NULL);
12369     location = ap_table_get(r->headers_out, "Location");
12370
12371     if (location && location[0] == '/' &&
12372     ((r->status == HTTP_OK) ||
12373         ap_is_HTTP_REDIRECT(r->status))) {
12374
12375         ap_pfclose(r->pool, f);
12376
12377         /* Internal redirect -- fake-up a pseudo-request */
12378         r->status = HTTP_OK;
12379
12380         /* This redirect needs to be a GET no matter
12381          * what the original
12382          * method was.
12383          */
12384         r->method = ap_pstrdup(r->pool, "GET");
12385         r->method_number = M_GET;
12386
12387         ap_internal_redirect_handler(location, r);
12388         return OK;
12389     }
12390
12391     ap_send_http_header(r);
12392     if (!r->header_only)
12393         ap_send_fd(f, r);
12394
12395     ap_pfclose(r->pool, f);
12396     return OK;
12397 }
12398
12399 static const handler_rec asis_handlers[] =
12400 {
12401     {ASIS_MAGIC_TYPE, asis_handler},
12402     {"send-as-is", asis_handler},
12403     {NULL}
12404 };
12405
12406 module MODULE_VAR_EXPORT asis_module =
12407 {
12408     STANDARD_MODULE_STUFF,
12409     NULL,             /* initializer */
```

```
12410     NULL,
12411     /* create per-directory config structure */
12412     NULL,
12413     /* merge per-directory config structures */
12414     NULL,
12415     /* create per-server config structure */
12416     NULL,
12417     /* merge per-server config structures */
12418     NULL,             /* command table */
12419     asis_handlers, /* handlers */
12420     NULL,             /* translate_handler */
12421     NULL,             /* check_user_id */
12422     NULL,             /* check auth */
12423     NULL,             /* check access */
12424     NULL,             /* type_checker */
12425     NULL,             /* pre-run fixups */
12426     NULL,             /* logger */
12427     NULL,             /* header parser */
12428     NULL,             /* child_init */
12429     NULL,             /* child_exit */
12430     NULL              /* post read-request */
12431 };
```

▶ p 443 mod_auth.c

```
12432 #include "httpd.h"
12433 #include "http_config.h"
12434 #include "http_core.h"
12435 #include "http_log.h"
12436 #include "http_protocol.h"
12437 #include "ap_md5.h"
12438
12439 typedef struct auth_config_struct {
12440     char *auth_pwfile;
12441     char *auth_grpfile;
12442     int auth_authoritative;
12443 } auth_config_rec;
12444
12445 static void *create_auth_dir_config(pool *p,
12446     char *d)
12447 {
12448     auth_config_rec *sec =
12449     (auth_config_rec *) ap_pcalloc(p,
12450         sizeof(auth_config_rec));
12451     sec->auth_pwfile = NULL;
12452     /* just to illustrate the default really */
12453     sec->auth_grpfile = NULL;
12454     /* unless you have a broken HP cc */
12455     sec->auth_authoritative = 1;
```

```
12456          /* keep the fortress secure by default */
12457          return sec;
12458      }
12459
12460      static const char *set_auth_slot(cmd_parms *cmd,
12461          void *offset, char *f, char *t)
12462      {
12463          if (t && strcmp(t, "standard"))
12464            return ap_pstrcat(cmd->pool, "Invalid auth file
12465               type: ", t, NULL);
12466
12467          return ap_set_file_slot(cmd, offset, f);
12468      }
12469
12470      static const command_rec auth_cmds[] =
12471      {
12472          {"AuthUserFile", set_auth_slot,
12473           (void *) XtOffsetOf(auth_config_rec, auth_pwfile),
12474               OR_AUTHCFG, TAKE12,
12475           "text file containing user IDs and passwords"},
12476          {"AuthGroupFile", set_auth_slot,
12477           (void *) XtOffsetOf(auth_config_rec,
12478               auth_grpfile), OR_AUTHCFG, TAKE12,
12479           "text file containing group names and
12480               member user IDs"},
12481          {"AuthAuthoritative", ap_set_flag_slot,
12482           (void *) XtOffsetOf(auth_config_rec,
12483               auth_authoritative),
12484           OR_AUTHCFG, FLAG,
12485           "Set to 'no' to allow access control to be passed
12486               along to lower modules if the UserID is not
12487               known to this module"},
12488          {NULL}
12489      };
12490
12491      module MODULE_VAR_EXPORT auth_module;
12492
12493      static char *get_pw(request_rec *r, char *user,
12494          char *auth_pwfile)
12495      {
12496          configfile_t *f;
12497          char l[MAX_STRING_LEN];
12498          const char *rpw, *w;
12499
12500          if (!(f = ap_pcfg_openfile(r->pool, auth_pwfile))) {
12501            ap_log_rerror(APLOG_MARK, APLOG_ERR, r,
12502                   "Could not open password file: %s",
12503                       auth_pwfile);
```

```
12504          return NULL;
12505          }
12506          while (!(ap_cfg_getline(l, MAX_STRING_LEN, f))) {
12507            if ((l[0] == '#') || (!l[0]))
12508                continue;
12509            rpw = l;
12510            w = ap_getword(r->pool, &rpw, ':');
12511
12512            if (!strcmp(user, w)) {
12513                ap_cfg_closefile(f);
12514                return ap_getword(r->pool, &rpw, ':');
12515            }
12516          }
12517          ap_cfg_closefile(f);
12518          return NULL;
12519      }
12520
12521      static table *groups_for_user(pool *p, char *user,
12522          char *grpfile)
12523      {
12524          configfile_t *f;
12525          table *grps = ap_make_table(p, 15);
12526          pool *sp;
12527          char l[MAX_STRING_LEN];
12528          const char *group_name, *ll, *w;
12529
12530          if (!(f = ap_pcfg_openfile(p, grpfile))) {
12531 /*add?     aplog_error(APLOG_MARK, APLOG_ERR, NULL,
12532               "Could not open group file: %s",
12533                       grpfile);*/
12534          return NULL;
12535          }
12536
12537          sp = ap_make_sub_pool(p);
12538
12539          while (!(ap_cfg_getline(l, MAX_STRING_LEN, f))) {
12540            if ((l[0] == '#') || (!l[0]))
12541                continue;
12542            ll = l;
12543            ap_clear_pool(sp);
12544
12545            group_name = ap_getword(sp, &ll, ':');
12546
12547            while (ll[0]) {
12548                w = ap_getword_conf(sp, &ll);
12549                if (!strcmp(w, user)) {
12550                  ap_table_setn(grps, ap_pstrdup(p,
12551                       group_name), "in");
```

```
12552              break;
12553
12554          }
12555        }
12556      }
12557      ap_cfg_closefile(f);
12558      ap_destroy_pool(sp);
12559      return grps;
12560  }
12561
12562  /* These functions return 0 if client is OK, and
12563   * proper error status if not... either AUTH_REQUIRED,
12564   * if we made a check, and it failed, or SERVER_ERROR,
12565   * if things are so totally confused that we couldn't
12566   * figure out how to tell if the client is authorized
12567   * or not.
12568   *
12569   * If they return DECLINED, and all other modules also
12570   * decline, that's treated by the server core
12571   * as a configuration error, logged and
12572   * reported as such.
12573   */
12574
12575  /* Determine user ID, and check if it really is that
12576   * user, for HTTP
12577   * basic authentication...
12578   */
12579
12580  static int authenticate_basic_user(request_rec *r)
12581  {
12582      auth_config_rec *sec =
12583      (auth_config_rec *) ap_get_module_config(r->
12584          per_dir_config, &auth_module);
12585      conn_rec *c = r->connection;
12586      const char *sent_pw;
12587      char *real_pw;
12588      char *invalid_pw;
12589      int res;
12590
12591      if ((res = ap_get_basic_auth_pw(r, &sent_pw)))
12592       return res;
12593
12594      if (!sec->auth_pwfile)
12595       return DECLINED;
12596
12597      if (!(real_pw = get_pw(r, c->user,
12598          sec->auth_pwfile))) {
12599        if (!(sec->auth_authoritative))
```

```
12600          return DECLINED;
12601        ap_log_rerror(APLOG_MARK,
12602            APLOG_NOERRNO|APLOG_ERR, r,
12603              "user %s not found: %s", c->user,
12604                  r->uri);
12605        ap_note_basic_auth_failure(r);
12606        return AUTH_REQUIRED;
12607      }
12608      invalid_pw = ap_validate_password(sent_pw, real_pw);
12609      if (invalid_pw != NULL) {
12610        ap_log_rerror(APLOG_MARK,
12611            APLOG_NOERRNO|APLOG_ERR, r,
12612              "user %s: authentication failure
12613                for \"%s\": %s",
12614                c->user, r->uri, invalid_pw);
12615        ap_note_basic_auth_failure(r);
12616        return AUTH_REQUIRED;
12617      }
12618      return OK;
12619  }
12620
12621  /* Checking ID */
12622
12623  static int check_user_access(request_rec *r)
12624  {
12625      auth_config_rec *sec =
12626      (auth_config_rec *) ap_get_module_config(r->
12627          per_dir_config, &auth_module);
12628      char *user = r->connection->user;
12629      int m = r->method_number;
12630      int method_restricted = 0;
12631      register int x;
12632      const char *t, *w;
12633      table *grpstatus;
12634      const array_header *reqs_arr = ap_requires(r);
12635      require_line *reqs;
12636
12637      /* BUG FIX: tadc, 11-Nov-1995.  If there is no
12638       * "requires" directive,
12639       * then any user will do.
12640       */
12641      if (!reqs_arr)
12642       return (OK);
12643      reqs = (require_line *) reqs_arr->elts;
12644
12645      if (sec->auth_grpfile)
12646       grpstatus = groups_for_user(r->pool, user,
12647          sec->auth_grpfile);
```

```
12648        else
12649         grpstatus = NULL;
12650
12651        for (x = 0; x < reqs_arr->nelts; x++) {
12652
12653          if (!(reqs[x].method_mask & (1 << m)))
12654              continue;
12655
12656          method_restricted = 1;
12657
12658          t = reqs[x].requirement;
12659          w = ap_getword_white(r->pool, &t);
12660          if (!strcmp(w, "valid-user"))
12661              return OK;
12662          if (!strcmp(w, "user")) {
12663              while (t[0]) {
12664                w = ap_getword_conf(r->pool, &t);
12665                if (!strcmp(user, w))
12666                    return OK;
12667              }
12668          }
12669          else if (!strcmp(w, "group")) {
12670              if (!grpstatus)
12671                return DECLINED;
12672                /* DBM group?  Something else? */
12673
12674              while (t[0]) {
12675                w = ap_getword_conf(r->pool, &t);
12676                if (ap_table_get(grpstatus, w))
12677                    return OK;
12678              }
12679          } else if (sec->auth_authoritative) {
12680              /* if we aren't authoritative, any require
12681               * directive could be valid even if we don't
12682               * grok it.  However, if we are authoritative,
12683               * we can warn the user they did something
12684               * wrong. That something could be a missing
12685               * "AuthAuthoritative off", but more likely
12686               * is a typo in the require directive.
12687               */
12688              ap_log_rerror(APLOG_MARK,
12689                    APLOG_NOERRNO|APLOG_ERR, r,
12690              "access to %s failed, reason: unknown require
12691                    directive:"
12692              "\"%s\"", r->uri, reqs[x].requirement);
12693          }
12694        }
12695
12696        if (!method_restricted)
12697          return OK;
12698
12699        if (!(sec->auth_authoritative))
12700          return DECLINED;
12701
12702        ap_log_rerror(APLOG_MARK,
12703              APLOG_NOERRNO|APLOG_ERR, r,
12704        "access to %s failed, reason: user %s
12705              not allowed access",
12706          r->uri, user);
12707
12708        ap_note_basic_auth_failure(r);
12709        return AUTH_REQUIRED;
12710    }
12711
12712    module MODULE_VAR_EXPORT auth_module =
12713    {
12714        STANDARD_MODULE_STUFF,
12715        NULL,                  /* initializer */
12716        create_auth_dir_config,
12717        /* dir config creater */
12718        NULL,
12719        /* dir merger -- default is to override */
12720        NULL,                  /* server config */
12721        NULL,                  /* merge server config */
12722        auth_cmds,             /* command table */
12723        NULL,                  /* handlers */
12724        NULL,                  /* filename translation */
12725        authenticate_basic_user,   /* check_user_id */
12726        check_user_access,         /* check auth */
12727        NULL,                  /* check access */
12728        NULL,                  /* type_checker */
12729        NULL,                  /* fixups */
12730        NULL,                  /* logger */
12731        NULL,                  /* header parser */
12732        NULL,                  /* child_init */
12733        NULL,                  /* child_exit */
12734        NULL                   /* post read-request */
12735    };
```

▶ p. 444 mod_auth_anon.c

```
12736    #include "httpd.h"
12737    #include "http_config.h"
12738    #include "http_core.h"
12739    #include "http_log.h"
12740    #include "http_protocol.h"
12741    #include "http_request.h"
```

```
12742
12743    typedef struct auth_anon {
12744        char *password;
12745        struct auth_anon *next;
12746    } auth_anon;
12747
12748    typedef struct {
12749
12750        auth_anon *auth_anon_passwords;
12751        int auth_anon_nouserid;
12752        int auth_anon_logemail;
12753        int auth_anon_verifyemail;
12754        int auth_anon_mustemail;
12755        int auth_anon_authoritative;
12756
12757    } anon_auth_config_rec;
12758
12759    static void *create_anon_auth_dir_config(pool *p,
12760         char *d)
12761    {
12762        anon_auth_config_rec *sec =
12763            (anon_auth_config_rec *)
12764        ap_pcalloc(p, sizeof(anon_auth_config_rec));
12765
12766        if (!sec)
12767         return NULL;           /* no memory... */
12768
12769        /* just to illustrate the defaults really. */
12770        sec->auth_anon_passwords = NULL;
12771
12772        sec->auth_anon_nouserid = 0;
12773        sec->auth_anon_logemail = 1;
12774        sec->auth_anon_verifyemail = 0;
12775        sec->auth_anon_mustemail = 1;
12776        sec->auth_anon_authoritative = 0;
12777        return sec;
12778    }
12779
12780    static const char *anon_set_passwd_flag(cmd_parms *cmd,
12781                        anon_auth_config_rec * sec, int arg)
12782    {
12783        sec->auth_anon_mustemail = arg;
12784        return NULL;
12785    }
12786
12787    static const char *anon_set_userid_flag(cmd_parms *cmd,
12788                        anon_auth_config_rec * sec, int arg)
12789    {
12790        sec->auth_anon_nouserid = arg;
12791        return NULL;
12792    }
12793    static const char *anon_set_logemail_flag(cmd_parms *cmd,
12794                        anon_auth_config_rec * sec, int arg)
12795    {
12796        sec->auth_anon_logemail = arg;
12797        return NULL;
12798    }
12799    static const char *anon_set_verifyemail_flag(cmd_parms *cmd,
12800                        anon_auth_config_rec * sec, int arg)
12801    {
12802        sec->auth_anon_verifyemail = arg;
12803        return NULL;
12804    }
12805    static const char
12806        *anon_set_authoritative_flag(cmd_parms *cmd,
12807                        anon_auth_config_rec * sec, int arg)
12808    {
12809        sec->auth_anon_authoritative = arg;
12810        return NULL;
12811    }
12812
12813    static const char
12814        *anon_set_string_slots(cmd_parms *cmd,
12815                    anon_auth_config_rec * sec, char *arg)
12816    {
12817
12818        auth_anon *first;
12819
12820        if (!(*arg))
12821         return "Anonymous string cannot be empty, use
12822             Anonymous_NoUserId instead";
12823
12824        /* squeeze in a record */
12825        first = sec->auth_anon_passwords;
12826
12827        if (
12828            (!(sec->auth_anon_passwords = (auth_anon *)
12829                ap_palloc(cmd->pool, sizeof(auth_anon)))) ||
12830            (!(sec->auth_anon_passwords->password = arg))
12831        )
12832            return "Failed to claim memory for an
12833                anonymous password...";
12834
12835        /* and repair the next */
12836        sec->auth_anon_passwords->next = first;
12837
```

```
12838      return NULL;
12839  }
12840
12841  static const command_rec anon_auth_cmds[] =
12842  {
12843      {"Anonymous", anon_set_string_slots, NULL,
12844          OR_AUTHCFG, ITERATE,
12845       "a space-separated list of user IDs"},
12846      {"Anonymous_MustGiveEmail", anon_set_passwd_flag,
12847          NULL, OR_AUTHCFG, FLAG,
12848       "Limited to 'on' or 'off'"},
12849      {"Anonymous_NoUserId", anon_set_userid_flag,
12850          NULL, OR_AUTHCFG, FLAG,
12851       "Limited to 'on' or 'off'"},
12852  {"Anonymous_VerifyEmail", anon_set_verifyemail_flag,
12853          NULL, OR_AUTHCFG, FLAG,
12854   "Limited to 'on' or 'off'"},
12855      {"Anonymous_LogEmail", anon_set_logemail_flag,
12856          NULL, OR_AUTHCFG, FLAG,
12857       "Limited to 'on' or 'off'"},
12858      {"Anonymous_Authoritative",
12859          anon_set_authoritative_flag, NULL,
12860          OR_AUTHCFG, FLAG,
12861       "Limited to 'on' or 'off'"},
12862
12863      {NULL}
12864  };
12865
12866  module MODULE_VAR_EXPORT anon_auth_module;
12867
12868  static int anon_authenticate_basic_user(request_rec *r)
12869  {
12870      anon_auth_config_rec *sec =
12871      (anon_auth_config_rec *)
12872          ap_get_module_config(r->per_dir_config,
12873                              &anon_auth_module);
12874      conn_rec *c = r->connection;
12875      const char *sent_pw;
12876      int res = DECLINED;
12877
12878      if ((res = ap_get_basic_auth_pw(r, &sent_pw)))
12879       return res;
12880
12881      /* Ignore if we are not configured */
12882      if (!sec->auth_anon_passwords)
12883       return DECLINED;
12884
12885      /* Do we allow an empty userID and/or
```

```
12886       * is it the magic one
12887       */
12888
12889      if (((!(c->user[0])) && (sec->auth_anon_nouserid)) {
12890       res = OK;
12890      }
12891      }
12892      else {
12893       auth_anon *p = sec->auth_anon_passwords;
12894       res = DECLINED;
12895       while ((res == DECLINED) && (p != NULL)) {
12896          if (!(strcasecmp(c->user, p->password)))
12897           res = OK;
12898          p = p->next;
12899       }
12900      }
12901      if (
12902      /* username is OK */
12903          (res == OK)
12904      /* password been filled out ? */
12905          && ((!sec->auth_anon_mustemail) ||
12906              strlen(sent_pw))
12907      /* does the password look like an
12908       * email address ? */
12909          && ((!sec->auth_anon_verifyemail)
12910          || ((strpbrk("@", sent_pw) != NULL)
12911          && (strpbrk(".", sent_pw) != NULL)))) {
12912      if (sec->auth_anon_logemail &&
12913          ap_is_initial_req(r)) {
12914          ap_log_rerror(APLOG_MARK,
12915              APLOG_NOERRNO|APLOG_INFO, r,
12916              "Anonymous: Passwd <%s> Accepted",
12917              sent_pw ? sent_pw : "\'none\'");
12918      }
12919      return OK;
12920      }
12921      else {
12922       if (sec->auth_anon_authoritative) {
12923          ap_log_rerror(APLOG_MARK,
12924              APLOG_NOERRNO|APLOG_ERR, r,
12925              "Anonymous: Authoritative,
12926                  Passwd <%s> not accepted",
12927              sent_pw ? sent_pw : "\'none\'");
12928          return AUTH_REQUIRED;
12929       }
12930      /* Drop out the bottom to return DECLINED */
12931      }
12932
12933      return DECLINED;
```

```
12934    }
12935
12936    static int check_anon_access(request_rec *r)
12937    {
12938    #ifdef NOTYET
12939        conn_rec *c = r->connection;
12940        anon_auth_config_rec *sec =
12941        (anon_auth_config_rec *)
12942            ap_get_module_config(r->per_dir_config,
12943                                 &anon_auth_module);
12944
12945        if (!sec->auth_anon)
12946         return DECLINED;
12947
12948        if (strcasecmp(r->connection->user, sec->auth_anon))
12949         return DECLINED;
12950
12951        return OK;
12952    #endif
12953        return DECLINED;
12954    }
12955
12956
12957    module MODULE_VAR_EXPORT anon_auth_module =
12958    {
12959        STANDARD_MODULE_STUFF,
12960        NULL,                /* initializer */
12961        create_anon_auth_dir_config,
12962        /* dir config creater */
12963        NULL,            /* dir merger ensure strictness */
12964        NULL,            /* server config */
12965        NULL,            /* merge server config */
12966        anon_auth_cmds,     /* command table */
12967        NULL,            /* handlers */
12968        NULL,            /* filename translation */
12969        anon_authenticate_basic_user,
12970        /* check_user_id */
12971        check_anon_access,        /* check auth */
12972        NULL,            /* check access */
12973        NULL,            /* type_checker */
12974        NULL,            /* fixups */
12975        NULL,            /* logger */
12976        NULL,            /* header parser */
12977        NULL,            /* child_init */
12978        NULL,            /* child_exit */
12979        NULL            /* post read-request */
12980    };
```

▶ p 445 mod_auth_db.c

```
12981    #include "httpd.h"
12982    #include "http_config.h"
12983    #include "http_core.h"
12984    #include "http_log.h"
12985    #include "http_protocol.h"
12986    #include <db.h>
12987    #include "ap_md5.h"
12988
12989    #if defined(DB_VERSION_MAJOR) && (DB_VERSION_MAJOR == 2)
12990    #define DB2
12991    #endif
12992
12993    typedef struct {
12994
12995        char *auth_dbpwfile;
12996        char *auth_dbgrpfile;
12997        int auth_dbauthoritative;
12998    } db_auth_config_rec;
12999
13000    static void *create_db_auth_dir_config(pool *p, char *d)
13001    {
13002        db_auth_config_rec *sec
13003        = (db_auth_config_rec *) ap_pcalloc(p,
13004         sizeof(db_auth_config_rec));
13005        sec->auth_dbpwfile = NULL;
13006        sec->auth_dbgrpfile = NULL;
13007        sec->auth_dbauthoritative = 1;
13008         /* fortress is secure by default */
13009        return sec;
13010    }
13011
13012    static const char *set_db_slot(cmd_parms *cmd,
13013        void *offset, char *f, char *t)
13014    {
13015        if (!t || strcmp(t, "db"))
13016         return DECLINE_CMD;
13017
13018        return ap_set_file_slot(cmd, offset, f);
13019    }
13020
13021    static const command_rec db_auth_cmds[] =
13022    {
13023        {"AuthDBUserFile", ap_set_file_slot,
13024         (void *) XtOffsetOf(db_auth_config_rec,
13025            auth_dbpwfile),
13026         OR_AUTHCFG, TAKE1, NULL},
```

```
13027        {"AuthDBGroupFile", ap_set_file_slot,
13028         (void *) XtOffsetOf(db_auth_config_rec,
13029             auth_dbgrpfile),
13030         OR_AUTHCFG, TAKE1, NULL},
13031        {"AuthUserFile", set_db_slot,
13032         (void *) XtOffsetOf(db_auth_config_rec,
13033             auth_dbpwfile),
13034         OR_AUTHCFG, TAKE12, NULL},
13035        {"AuthGroupFile", set_db_slot,
13036         (void *) XtOffsetOf(db_auth_config_rec,
13037             auth_dbgrpfile),
13038         OR_AUTHCFG, TAKE12, NULL},
13039        {"AuthDBAuthoritative", ap_set_flag_slot,
13040         (void *) XtOffsetOf(db_auth_config_rec,
13041             auth_dbauthoritative),
13042         OR_AUTHCFG, FLAG,
13043         "Set to 'no' to allow access control to be
13044             passed along to lower modules if the userID
13045             is not known to this module"},
13046        {NULL}
13047    };
13048
13049    module db_auth_module;
13050
13051    static char *get_db_pw(request_rec *r, char *user,
13052        const char *auth_dbpwfile)
13053    {
13054        DB *f;
13055        DBT d, q;
13056        char *pw = NULL;
13057
13058        memset(&d, 0, sizeof(d));
13059        memset(&q, 0, sizeof(q));
13060
13061        q.data = user;
13062        q.size = strlen(q.data);
13063
13064    #ifdef DB2
13065        if (db_open(auth_dbpwfile, DB_HASH, DB_RDONLY, 0664,
13066             NULL, NULL, &f) != 0) {
13067    #else
13068        if (!(f = dbopen(auth_dbpwfile, O_RDONLY, 0664,
13069             DB_HASH, NULL))) {
13070    #endif
13071            ap_log_rerror(APLOG_MARK, APLOG_ERR, r,
13072                    "could not open db auth file: %s",
13073                        auth_dbpwfile);
13074            return NULL;
13075        }
13076
13077    #ifdef DB2
13078        if (!((f->get) (f, NULL, &q, &d, 0))) {
13079    #else
13080        if (!((f->get) (f, &q, &d, 0))) {
13081    #endif
13082            pw = ap_palloc(r->pool, d.size + 1);
13083            strncpy(pw, d.data, d.size);
13084            pw[d.size] = '\0';      /* Terminate the string */
13085        }
13086
13087    #ifdef DB2
13088        (f->close) (f, 0);
13089    #else
13090        (f->close) (f);
13091    #endif
13092        return pw;
13093    }
13094
13095    /* We do something strange with the group file.  If
13096     * the group file contains any : we assume the
13097     * format is
13098     *     key=username value=":"groupname [":"anything
13099     *     here is ignored]
13100     * otherwise we now (0.8.14+) assume that the format is
13101     *     key=username value=groupname
13102     * The first allows the password and group files to
13103     * be the same physical DB file;   key=username
13104     * value=password":"groupname[":"anything]
13105     *
13106     * mark@telescope.org, 22Sep95
13107     */
13108
13109    static char *get_db_grp(request_rec *r, char *user,
13110        const char *auth_dbgrpfile)
13111    {
13112        char *grp_data = get_db_pw(r, user, auth_dbgrpfile);
13113        char *grp_colon;
13114        char *grp_colon2;
13115
13116        if (grp_data == NULL)
13117         return NULL;
13118
13119        if ((grp_colon = strchr(grp_data, ':')) != NULL) {
13120         grp_colon2 = strchr(++grp_colon, ':');
13121         if (grp_colon2)
13122             *grp_colon2 = '\0';
```

```
13123        return grp_colon;
13124      }
13125      return grp_data;
13126    }
13127
13128    static int db_authenticate_basic_user(request_rec *r)
13129    {
13130        db_auth_config_rec *sec =
13131        (db_auth_config_rec *)
13132            ap_get_module_config(r->per_dir_config,
13133                            &db_auth_module);
13134        conn_rec *c = r->connection;
13135        const char *sent_pw;
13136        char *real_pw, *colon_pw;
13137        char *invalid_pw;
13138        int res;
13139
13140        if ((res = ap_get_basic_auth_pw(r, &sent_pw)))
13141         return res;
13142
13143        if (!sec->auth_dbpwfile)
13144         return DECLINED;
13145
13146        if (!(real_pw = get_db_pw(r, c->user,
13147            sec->auth_dbpwfile))) {
13148         if (!(sec->auth_dbauthoritative))
13149            return DECLINED;
13150         ap_log_rerror(APLOG_MARK,
13151             APLOG_NOERRNO|APLOG_ERR, r,
13152                 "DB user %s not found: %s",
13153                     c->user, r->filename);
13154         ap_note_basic_auth_failure(r);
13155         return AUTH_REQUIRED;
13156        }
13157        /* Password is up to first : if exists */
13158        colon_pw = strchr(real_pw, ':');
13159        if (colon_pw) {
13160         *colon_pw = '\0';
13161        }
13162        invalid_pw = ap_validate_password(sent_pw, real_pw);
13163        if (invalid_pw != NULL) {
13164         ap_log_rerror(APLOG_MARK,
13165             APLOG_NOERRNO|APLOG_ERR, r,
13166                 "DB user %s: authentication failure
13167                     for \"%s\": %s",
13168                     c->user, r->uri, invalid_pw);
13169         ap_note_basic_auth_failure(r);
13170         return AUTH_REQUIRED;
13171        }
13172        return OK;
13173    }
13174
13175    /* Checking ID */
13176
13177    static int db_check_auth(request_rec *r)
13178    {
13179        db_auth_config_rec *sec =
13180        (db_auth_config_rec *)
13181            ap_get_module_config(r->per_dir_config,
13182                            &db_auth_module);
13183        char *user = r->connection->user;
13184        int m = r->method_number;
13185
13186        const array_header *reqs_arr = ap_requires(r);
13187        require_line *reqs = reqs_arr ? (require_line *)
13188            reqs_arr->elts : NULL;
13189
13190        register int x;
13191        const char *t;
13192        char *w;
13193
13194        if (!sec->auth_dbgrpfile)
13195         return DECLINED;
13196        if (!reqs_arr)
13197         return DECLINED;
13198
13199        for (x = 0; x < reqs_arr->nelts; x++) {
13200
13201         if (!(reqs[x].method_mask & (1 << m)))
13202            continue;
13203
13204         t = reqs[x].requirement;
13205         w = ap_getword_white(r->pool, &t);
13206
13207         if (!strcmp(w, "group") && sec->auth_dbgrpfile) {
13208            const char *orig_groups, *groups;
13209            char *v;
13210
13211            if (!(groups = get_db_grp(r, user,
13212                sec->auth_dbgrpfile))) {
13213             if (!(sec->auth_dbauthoritative))
13214                return DECLINED;
13215             ap_log_rerror(APLOG_MARK,
13216                 APLOG_NOERRNO|APLOG_ERR, r,
13217                     "user %s not in DB group file %s: %s",
13218                     user, sec->auth_dbgrpfile, r->filename);
```

```
13219              ap_note_basic_auth_failure(r);
13220              return AUTH_REQUIRED;
13221          }
13222          orig_groups = groups;
13223          while (t[0]) {
13224              w = ap_getword_white(r->pool, &t);
13225              groups = orig_groups;
13226              while (groups[0]) {
13227                  v = ap_getword(r->pool, &groups, ',');
13228                  if (!strcmp(v, w))
13229                      return OK;
13230              }
13231          }
13232          ap_log_rerror(APLOG_MARK,
13233                  APLOG_NOERRNO|APLOG_ERR, r,
13234                  "user %s not in right group: %s",
13235                      user, r->filename);
13236          ap_note_basic_auth_failure(r);
13237          return AUTH_REQUIRED;
13238      }
13239  }
13240
13241      return DECLINED;
13242  }
13243
13244
13245  module db_auth_module =
13246  {
13247      STANDARD_MODULE_STUFF,
13248      NULL,                   /* initializer */
13249      create_db_auth_dir_config,
13250      /* dir config creater */
13251      NULL,
13252      /* dir merger -- default is to override */
13253      NULL,                   /* server config */
13254      NULL,                   /* merge server config */
13255      db_auth_cmds,           /* command table */
13256      NULL,                   /* handlers */
13257      NULL,                   /* filename translation */
13258      db_authenticate_basic_user,    /* check_user_id */
13259      db_check_auth,              /* check auth */
13260      NULL,                   /* check access */
13261      NULL,                   /* type_checker */
13262      NULL,                   /* fixups */
13263      NULL,                   /* logger */
13264      NULL,                   /* header parser */
13265      NULL,                   /* child_init */
13266      NULL,                   /* child_exit */
13267      NULL                    /* post read-request */
13268  };
```

mod_auth_db.module

```
13269  Name: db_auth_module
13270  ConfigStart
13271      DB_VERSION=''
13272      DB_LIB=''
13273      if ./helpers/TestCompile func db_open; then
13274          DB_VERSION='Berkeley-DB/2.x'
13275      else
13276          if ./helpers/TestCompile lib db db_open; then
13277              DB_VERSION='Berkeley-DB/2.x'
13278              DB_LIB='-ldb'
13279          else
13280              if ./helpers/TestCompile func dbopen; then
13281                  DB_VERSION='Berkeley-DB/1.x'
13282              else
13283                  if ./helpers/TestCompile lib
13284                      db dbopen; then
13285                      DB_VERSION='Berkeley-DB/1.x'
13286                      DB_LIB='-ldb'
13287                  fi
13288              fi
13289          fi
13290      fi
13291      if [ ".$DB_VERSION" != . ]; then
13292          if [ ".$DB_LIB" != . ]; then
13293              LIBS="$LIBS $DB_LIB"
13294              echo "    using $DB_VERSION for
13295                  mod_auth_db ($DB_LIB)"
13296          else
13297              echo "    using $DB_VERSION for
13298                  mod_auth_db (-lc)"
13299          fi
13300      else
13301          echo "Error: Neither Berkeley-DB/1.x nor
13302              Berkeley-DB/2.x library found."
13303          echo "    Either disable mod_auth_db or
13304              provide us with the paths"
13305          echo "    to the Berkeley-DB include and
13306              library files."
13307          echo "    (Hint: INCLUDES, LDFLAGS, LIBS)"
13308          exit 1
13309      fi
13310  ConfigEnd
```

p 446 **mod_auth_dbm.c**

```
13311    #include "httpd.h"
13312    #include "http_config.h"
13313    #include "http_core.h"
13314    #include "http_log.h"
13315    #include "http_protocol.h"
13316    #include <ndbm.h>
13317    #include "ap_md5.h"
13318
13319    /*
13320     * Module definition information - the part between
13321     * the -START and -END lines below is used by
13322     * Configure. This could be stored in a separate
13323     * instead.
13324     *
13325     * MODULE-DEFINITION-START
13326     * Name: dbm_auth_module
13327     * ConfigStart
13328         . ./helpers/find-dbm-lib
13329     * ConfigEnd
13330     * MODULE-DEFINITION-END
13331     */
13332
13333    typedef struct {
13334
13335        char *auth_dbmpwfile;
13336        char *auth_dbmgrpfile;
13337        int auth_dbmauthoritative;
13338
13339    } dbm_auth_config_rec;
13340
13341    static void *create_dbm_auth_dir_config(pool *p,
13342        char *d)
13343    {
13344        dbm_auth_config_rec *sec
13345        = (dbm_auth_config_rec *) ap_pcalloc(p,
13346            sizeof(dbm_auth_config_rec));
13347
13348        sec->auth_dbmpwfile = NULL;
13349        sec->auth_dbmgrpfile = NULL;
13350        sec->auth_dbmauthoritative = 1;
13351        /* fortress is secure by default */
13352
13353        return sec;
13354    }
13355
13356    static const char *set_dbm_slot(cmd_parms *cmd,
13357        void *offset, char *f, char *t)
13358    {
13359        if (!t || strcmp(t, "dbm"))
13360         return DECLINE_CMD;
13361
13362        return ap_set_file_slot(cmd, offset, f);
13363    }
13364
13365    static const command_rec dbm_auth_cmds[] =
13366    {
13367        {"AuthDBMUserFile", ap_set_file_slot,
13368        (void *) XtOffsetOf(dbm_auth_config_rec,
13369            auth_dbmpwfile),
13370        OR_AUTHCFG, TAKE1, NULL},
13371        {"AuthDBMGroupFile", ap_set_file_slot,
13372        (void *) XtOffsetOf(dbm_auth_config_rec,
13373            auth_dbmgrpfile),
13374        OR_AUTHCFG, TAKE1, NULL},
13375        {"AuthUserFile", set_dbm_slot,
13376        (void *) XtOffsetOf(dbm_auth_config_rec,
13377            auth_dbmpwfile),
13378        OR_AUTHCFG, TAKE12, NULL},
13379        {"AuthGroupFile", set_dbm_slot,
13380        (void *) XtOffsetOf(dbm_auth_config_rec,
13381            auth_dbmgrpfile),
13382        OR_AUTHCFG, TAKE12, NULL},
13383        {"AuthDBMAuthoritative", ap_set_flag_slot,
13384        (void *) XtOffsetOf(dbm_auth_config_rec,
13385            auth_dbmauthoritative),
13386        OR_AUTHCFG, FLAG, "Set to 'no' to allow access
13387            control to be passed along to lower modules,
13388             if the UserID is not known in this module"},
13389        {NULL}
13390    };
13391
13392    module dbm_auth_module;
13393
13394    static char *get_dbm_pw(request_rec *r, char *user,
13395        char *auth_dbmpwfile)
13396    {
13397        DBM *f;
13398        datum d, q;
13399        char *pw = NULL;
13400
13401        q.dptr = user;
13402    #ifndef NETSCAPE_DBM_COMPAT
13403        q.dsize = strlen(q.dptr);
13404    #else
13405        q.dsize = strlen(q.dptr) + 1;
```

```
13406    #endif
13407
13408
13409        if (!(f = dbm_open(auth_dbmpwfile, O_RDONLY,
13410               0664))) {
13411         ap_log_rerror(APLOG_MARK, APLOG_ERR, r,
13412                  "could not open dbm auth file: %s",
13413                     auth_dbmpwfile);
13414         return NULL;
13415        }
13416
13417        d = dbm_fetch(f, q);
13418
13419        if (d.dptr) {
13420         pw = ap_palloc(r->pool, d.dsize + 1);
13421         strncpy(pw, d.dptr, d.dsize);
13422         pw[d.dsize] = '\0';       /* Terminate the string */
13423        }
13424
13425        dbm_close(f);
13426        return pw;
13427    }
13428
13429    /* We do something strange with the group file.
13430     * If the group file contains any : we
13431     * assume the format is
13432     *      key=username value=":"groupname
13433     *      [":"anything here is ignored]
13434     * otherwise we now (0.8.14+) assume that the format is
13435     *      key=username value=groupname
13436     * The first allows the password and group files
13437     * to be the same physical DBM file;
13438     * key=username value=password":"groupname[":"anything]
13439     *
13440     * mark@telescope.org, 22Sep95
13441     */
13442
13443    static char *get_dbm_grp(request_rec *r, char *user,
13444         char *auth_dbmgrpfile)
13445    {
13446        char *grp_data = get_dbm_pw(r, user,
13447             auth_dbmgrpfile);
13448        char *grp_colon;
13449        char *grp_colon2;
13450
13451        if (grp_data == NULL)
13452         return NULL;
13453
13454        if ((grp_colon = strchr(grp_data, ':')) !=
13455             NULL) {
13456         grp_colon2 = strchr(++grp_colon, ':');
13457         if (grp_colon2)
13458             *grp_colon2 = '\0';
13459         return grp_colon;
13460        }
13461        return grp_data;
13462    }
13463
13464    static int dbm_authenticate_basic_user(request_rec *r)
13465    {
13466        dbm_auth_config_rec *sec =
13467        (dbm_auth_config_rec *)
13468             ap_get_module_config(r->per_dir_config,
13469                       &dbm_auth_module);
13470        conn_rec *c = r->connection;
13471        const char *sent_pw;
13472        char *real_pw, *colon_pw;
13473        char *invalid_pw;
13474        int res;
13475
13476        if ((res = ap_get_basic_auth_pw(r, &sent_pw)))
13477         return res;
13478
13479        if (!sec->auth_dbmpwfile)
13480         return DECLINED;
13481
13482        if (!(real_pw = get_dbm_pw(r, c->user,
13483             sec->auth_dbmpwfile))) {
13484         if (!(sec->auth_dbmauthoritative))
13485             return DECLINED;
13486         ap_log_rerror(APLOG_MARK,
13487             APLOG_NOERRNO|APLOG_ERR, r,
13488                "DBM user %s not found: %s",
13489                    c->user, r->filename);
13490         ap_note_basic_auth_failure(r);
13491         return AUTH_REQUIRED;
13492        }
13493        /* Password is up to first : if exists */
13494        colon_pw = strchr(real_pw, ':');
13495        if (colon_pw) {
13496         *colon_pw = '\0';
13497        }
13498        invalid_pw = ap_validate_password(sent_pw, real_pw);
13499        if (invalid_pw != NULL) {
13500         ap_log_rerror(APLOG_MARK,
13501             APLOG_NOERRNO|APLOG_ERR, r,
```

```
13502                 "DBM user %s: authentication failure
13503                     for \"%s\": %s",
13504                 c->user, r->uri, invalid_pw);
13505         ap_note_basic_auth_failure(r);
13506         return AUTH_REQUIRED;
13507     }
13508     return OK;
13509 }
13510
13511 /* Checking ID */
13512
13513 static int dbm_check_auth(request_rec *r)
13514 {
13515     dbm_auth_config_rec *sec =
13516     (dbm_auth_config_rec *)
13517         ap_get_module_config(r->per_dir_config,
13518                             &dbm_auth_module);
13519     char *user = r->connection->user;
13520     int m = r->method_number;
13521
13522     const array_header *reqs_arr = ap_requires(r);
13523     require_line *reqs = reqs_arr ? (require_line *)
13524         reqs_arr->elts : NULL;
13525
13526     register int x;
13527     const char *t;
13528     char *w;
13529
13530     if (!sec->auth_dbmgrpfile)
13531      return DECLINED;
13532     if (!reqs_arr)
13533      return DECLINED;
13534
13535     for (x = 0; x < reqs_arr->nelts; x++) {
13536
13537      if (!(reqs[x].method_mask & (1 << m)))
13538         continue;
13539
13540      t = reqs[x].requirement;
13541      w = ap_getword_white(r->pool, &t);
13542
13543      if (!strcmp(w, "group") && sec->auth_dbmgrpfile) {
13544         const char *orig_groups, *groups;
13545         char *v;
13546
13547         if (!(groups = get_dbm_grp(r, user,
13548             sec->auth_dbmgrpfile))) {
13549          if (!(sec->auth_dbmauthoritative))
```

```
13550             return DECLINED;
13551          ap_log_rerror(APLOG_MARK,
13552             APLOG_NOERRNO|APLOG_ERR, r,
13553             "user %s not in DBM group file %s: %s",
13554                 user, sec->auth_dbmgrpfile,
13555                     r->filename);
13556          ap_note_basic_auth_failure(r);
13557          return AUTH_REQUIRED;
13558         }
13559         orig_groups = groups;
13560         while (t[0]) {
13561          w = ap_getword_white(r->pool, &t);
13562          groups = orig_groups;
13563          while (groups[0]) {
13564             v = ap_getword(r->pool, &groups, ',');
13565             if (!strcmp(v, w))
13566                 return OK;
13567          }
13568         }
13569         ap_log_rerror(APLOG_MARK,
13570             APLOG_NOERRNO|APLOG_ERR, r,
13571             "user %s not in right group: %s",
13572                 user, r->filename);
13573         ap_note_basic_auth_failure(r);
13574         return AUTH_REQUIRED;
13575      }
13576     }
13577
13578     return DECLINED;
13579 }
13580
13581
13582 module dbm_auth_module =
13583 {
13584     STANDARD_MODULE_STUFF,
13585     NULL,               /* initializer */
13586     create_dbm_auth_dir_config,
13587     /* dir config creater */
13588     NULL,
13589     /* dir merger -- default is to override */
13590     NULL,               /* server config */
13591     NULL,               /* merge server config */
13592     dbm_auth_cmds,       /* command table */
13593     NULL,               /* handlers */
13594     NULL,               /* filename translation */
13595     dbm_authenticate_basic_user,    /* check_user_id */
13596     dbm_check_auth,         /* check auth */
13597     NULL,               /* check access */
```

```
13598        NULL,                    /* type_checker */
13599        NULL,                    /* fixups */
13600        NULL,                    /* logger */
13601        NULL,                    /* header parser */
13602        NULL,                    /* child_init */
13603        NULL,                    /* child_exit */
13604        NULL                     /* post read-request */
13605    };
```

mod_autoindex.c

```
13606    mod_autoindex.c
13607    #include "httpd.h"
13608    #include "http_config.h"
13609    #include "http_core.h"
13610    #include "http_request.h"
13611    #include "http_protocol.h"
13612    #include "http_log.h"
13613    #include "http_main.h"
13614    #include "util_script.h"
13615
13616    module MODULE_VAR_EXPORT autoindex_module;
13617
13618    /*************************************************
13619     *
13620     * Handling configuration directives...
13621     */
13622
13623    #define HRULE 1
13624    #define NO_HRULE 0
13625    #define FRONT_MATTER 1
13626    #define END_MATTER 0
13627
13628    #define FANCY_INDEXING 1       /* Indexing options */
13629    #define ICONS_ARE_LINKS 2
13630    #define SCAN_HTML_TITLES 4
13631    #define SUPPRESS_LAST_MOD 8
13632    #define SUPPRESS_SIZE 16
13633    #define SUPPRESS_DESC 32
13634    #define SUPPRESS_PREAMBLE 64
13635    #define SUPPRESS_COLSORT 128
13636    #define NO_OPTIONS 256
13637
13638    #define K_PAD 1
13639    #define K_NOPAD 0
13640
13641    #define K_NOADJUST 0
13642    #define K_ADJUST 1
13643    #define K_UNSET 2
```

```
13644
13645    /*
13646     * Define keys for sorting.
13647     */
13648    #define K_NAME 'N'
13649    /* Sort by file name (default) */
13650    #define K_LAST_MOD 'M'  /* Last modification date */
13651    #define K_SIZE 'S'
13652    /* Size (absolute, not as displayed) */
13653    #define K_DESC 'D'        /* Description */
13654
13655    #define D_ASCENDING 'A'
13656    #define D_DESCENDING 'D'
13657
13658    /*
13659     * These are the dimensions of the default icons
13660    supplied with Apache.
13661     */
13662
13663    #define DEFAULT_ICON_WIDTH 20
13664    #define DEFAULT_ICON_HEIGHT 22
13665
13666    /*
13667     * Other default dimensions.
13668     */
13669    #define DEFAULT_NAME_WIDTH 23
13670
13671    struct item {
13672        char *type;
13673        char *apply_to;
13674        char *apply_path;
13675        char *data;
13676    };
13677
13678    typedef struct autoindex_config_struct {
13679
13680        char *default_icon;
13681        int opts;
13682        int incremented_opts;
13683        int decremented_opts;
13684        int name_width;
13685        int name_adjust;
13686        int icon_width;
13687        int icon_height;
13688        char *default_order;
13689
13690        array_header *icon_list, *alt_list,
13691            *desc_list, *ign_list;
```

```
13692      array_header *hdr_list, *rdme_list;
13693
13694   } autoindex_config_rec;
13695
13696   static char c_by_encoding, c_by_type, c_by_path;
13697
13698   #define BY_ENCODING &c_by_encoding
13699   #define BY_TYPE &c_by_type
13700   #define BY_PATH &c_by_path
13701
13702   /*
13703   Return true if the specified string refers to
13704   the parent directory (i.e., * matches ".."
13705   or "../"). Hopefully this one call is significantly
13706   less * expensive than multiple strcmp() calls.
13707   */
13708   static ap_inline int is_parent(const char *name)
13709   {
13710   /*
13711   * Now, IFF the first two bytes are dots, and
13712   the third byte is either * EOS (\0) or a slash
13713   followed by EOS, we have a match.
13714   */
13715      if (((name[0] == '.') && (name[1] == '.'))
13716       && ((name[2] == '\0')
13717        || ((name[2] == '/') && (name[3] == '\0')))) {
13718       return 1;
13719      }
13720      return 0;
13721   }
13722
13723   /*
13724   This routine puts the standard HTML header at
13725   the top of the index page. We include the DOCTYPE
13726   because we may be using features therefrom (i.e.,
13727   HEIGHT and WIDTH attributes on the icons if
13728   we're FancyIndexing).
13729   */
13730
13731   static void emit_preamble
13732        (request_rec *r, char *title)
13733   {
13734      ap_rvputs(r, "<!DOCTYPE HTML
13735         PUBLIC \"-//W3C//DTD HTML 3.2 Final//EN\">\n",
13736         "<HTML>\n <HEAD>\n  <TITLE>Index of ", title,
13737         "</TITLE>\n </HEAD>\n <BODY>\n", NULL);
13738   }
13739
13740   static void push_item(array_header *arr, char
13741      *type, char *to, char *path, char *data)
13742   {
13743      struct item *p = (struct item *)
13744         ap_push_array(arr);
13745
13746      if (!to) {
13747         to = "";
13748      }
13749      if (!path) {
13750         path = "";
13751      }
13752
13753      p->type = type;
13754      p->data = data ? ap_pstrdup
13755         (arr->pool, data) : NULL;
13756      p->apply_path = ap_pstrcat
13757         (arr->pool, path, "*", NULL);
13758
13759      if ((type == BY_PATH) && (!ap_is_matchexp(to))) {
13760         p->apply_to =
13761            ap_pstrcat(arr->pool, "*", to, NULL);
13762      }
13763      else if (to) {
13764         p->apply_to = ap_pstrdup(arr->pool, to);
13765      }
13766      else {
13767         p->apply_to = NULL;
13768      }
13769   }
13770
13771   static const char *add_alt(cmd_parms *cmd,
13772      void *d, char *alt, char *to)
13773   {
13774      if (cmd->info == BY_PATH) {
13775
13776         if (!strcmp(to, "**DIRECTORY**")) {
13777            to = "^^DIRECTORY^^";
13778         }
13779      }
13780      if (cmd->info == BY_ENCODING) {
13781         ap_str_tolower(to);
13782      }
13783
13784      push_item(((autoindex_config_rec *)
13785         d)->alt_list, cmd->info, to,
13786            cmd->path, alt);
13787      return NULL;
```

```
13788    }
13789
13790    static const char *add_icon(cmd_parms *cmd,
13791        void *d, char *icon, char *to)
13792    {
13793        char *iconbak = ap_pstrdup(cmd->pool, icon);
13794
13795        if (icon[0] == '(') {
13796            char *alt;
13797            char *cl = strchr(iconbak, ')');
13798
13799            if (cl == NULL) {
13800                return "missing closing paren";
13801            }
13802            alt = ap_getword_nc(cmd->pool,
13803                &iconbak, ',');
13804            *cl = '\0';   /* Lose closing paren */
13805            add_alt(cmd, d, &alt[1], to);
13806        }
13807        if (cmd->info == BY_PATH) {
13808            if (!strcmp(to, "**DIRECTORY**")) {
13809                to = "^^DIRECTORY^^";
13810            }
13811        }
13812        if (cmd->info == BY_ENCODING) {
13813            ap_str_tolower(to);
13814        }
13815
13816        push_item(((autoindex_config_rec *)
13817            d)->icon_list, cmd->info, to,
13818                cmd->path, iconbak);
13819        return NULL;
13820    }
13821
13822    static const char *add_desc(cmd_parms *cmd,
13823        void *d, char *desc, char *to)
13824    {
13825        push_item(((autoindex_config_rec *)
13826            d)->desc_list, cmd->info, to,
13827                cmd->path, desc);
13828        return NULL;
13829    }
13830
13831    static const char *add_ignore(cmd_parms *cmd,
13832        void *d, char *ext)
13833    {
13834        push_item(((autoindex_config_rec *)
13835            d)->ign_list, 0, ext, cmd->path, NULL);
```

```
13836            return NULL;
13837    }
13838
13839    static const char *add_header(cmd_parms *cmd,
13840        void *d, char *name)
13841    {
13842        if (strchr(name, '/')) {
13843            return "HeaderName cannot contain a /";
13844        }
13845        push_item(((autoindex_config_rec *)
13846         d)->hdr_list, 0, NULL, cmd->path,
13847                name);
13848        return NULL;
13849    }
13850
13851    static const char *add_readme(cmd_parms *cmd,
13852        void *d, char *name)
13853    {
13854        if (strchr(name, '/')) {
13855            return "ReadmeName cannot contain a /";
13856        }
13857        push_item(((autoindex_config_rec *)
13858            d)->rdme_list, 0, NULL, cmd->path,
13859                name);
13860        return NULL;
13861    }
13862
13863    /* A legacy directive, FancyIndexing is superseded
13864    by the IndexOptions keyword. But for compatibility..
13865    */
13866
13867    static const char *fancy_indexing(cmd_parms *cmd,
13868        void *d, int arg)
13869    {
13870        int curopts;
13871        int newopts;
13872        autoindex_config_rec *cfg;
13873
13874        cfg = (autoindex_config_rec *) d;
13875        curopts = cfg->opts;
13876        if (curopts & NO_OPTIONS) {
13877            return "FancyIndexing directive conflicts
13878                with existing "
13879                    "IndexOptions None";
13880        }
13881        newopts = (arg ? (curopts | FANCY_INDEXING) :
13882            (curopts & ~FANCY_INDEXING));
13883        cfg->opts = newopts;
```

```
13884        return NULL;
13885    }
13886
13887    static const char *add_opts(cmd_parms *cmd,
13888          void *d, const char *optstr)
13889    {
13890        char *w;
13891        int opts;
13892        int opts_add;
13893        int opts_remove;
13894        char action;
13895        autoindex_config_rec *d_cfg =
13896              (autoindex_config_rec *) d;
13897
13898        opts = d_cfg->opts;
13899
13900        opts_add = d_cfg->incremented_opts;
13901        opts_remove = d_cfg->decremented_opts;
13902        while (optstr[0]) {
13903            int option = 0;
13904
13905            w = ap_getword_conf(cmd->pool, &optstr);
13906            if ((*w == '+') || (*w == '-')) {
13907                action = *(w++);
13908            }
13909            else {
13910                action = '\0';
13911            }
13912            if (!strcasecmp(w, "FancyIndexing")) {
13913                option = FANCY_INDEXING;
13914            }
13915            else if (!strcasecmp(w, "IconsAreLinks")) {
13916                option = ICONS_ARE_LINKS;
13917            }
13918            else if (!strcasecmp(w, "ScanHTMLTitles")) {
13919                option = SCAN_HTML_TITLES;
13920            }
13921            else if (!strcasecmp(w,
13922                "SuppressLastModified")) {
13923                    option = SUPPRESS_LAST_MOD;
13924            }
13925            else if (!strcasecmp(w, "SuppressSize")) {
13926                option = SUPPRESS_SIZE;
13927            }
13928            else if (!strcasecmp(w,
13929                "SuppressDescription")) {
13930                    option = SUPPRESS_DESC;
13931            }
13932            else if (!strcasecmp(w,
13933                "SuppressHTMLPreamble")) {
13934                    option = SUPPRESS_PREAMBLE;
13935            }
13936            else if (!strcasecmp(w,
13937                "SuppressColumnSorting")) {
13938                    option = SUPPRESS_COLSORT;
13939            }
13940            else if (!strcasecmp(w, "None")) {
13941                if (action != '\0') {
13942                    return "Cannot combine '+' or
13943                        '-' with 'None' keyword";
13944                }
13945                opts = NO_OPTIONS;
13946                opts_add = 0;
13947                opts_remove = 0;
13948            }
13949            else if (!strcasecmp(w, "IconWidth")) {
13950                if (action != '-') {
13951                    d_cfg->icon_width = DEFAULT_ICON_WIDTH;
13952                }
13953                else {
13954                    d_cfg->icon_width = 0;
13955                }
13956            }
13957            else if (!strncasecmp(w, "IconWidth=", 10)) {
13958                if (action == '-') {
13959                    return "Cannot combine '-'
13960                        with IconWidth=n";
13961                }
13962                d_cfg->icon_width = atoi(&w[10]);
13963            }
13964            else if (!strcasecmp(w, "IconHeight")) {
13965                if (action != '-') {
13966                    d_cfg->icon_height = DEFAULT_ICON_HEIGHT;
13967                }
13968                else {
13969                    d_cfg->icon_height = 0;
13970                }
13971            }
13972            else if (!strncasecmp(w, "IconHeight=", 11)) {
13973                if (action == '-') {
13974                    return "Cannot combine '-' with
13975                        IconHeight=n";
13976                }
13977                d_cfg->icon_height = atoi(&w[11]);
13978            }
13979            else if (!strcasecmp(w, "NameWidth")) {
```

```
13980          if (action != '-') {
13981           return "NameWidth with no value may
13982                    only appear as "
13983                    "'-NameWidth'";
13984          }
13985          d_cfg->name_width = DEFAULT_NAME_WIDTH;
13986          d_cfg->name_adjust = K_NOADJUST;
13987      }
13988      else if (!strncasecmp(w, "NameWidth=", 10)) {
13989          if (action == '-') {
13990           return "Cannot combine '-'
13991                    with NameWidth=n";
13992          }
13993          if (w[10] == '*') {
13994           d_cfg->name_adjust = K_ADJUST;
13995          }
13996          else {
13997           int width = atoi(&w[10]);
13998
13999           if (width < 1) {
14000                return "NameWidth value must be
14001                        greater than 1";
14002           }
14003           d_cfg->name_width = width;
14004           d_cfg->name_adjust = K_NOADJUST;
14005          }
14006      }
14007      else {
14008          return "Invalid directory indexing option";
14009      }
14010      if (action == '\0') {
14011          opts |= option;
14012          opts_add = 0;
14013          opts_remove = 0;
14014      }
14015      else if (action == '+') {
14016          opts_add |= option;
14017          opts_remove &= ~option;
14018      }
14019      else {
14020          opts_remove |= option;
14021          opts_add &= ~option;
14022      }
14023      }
14024      if ((opts & NO_OPTIONS) &&
14025          (opts & ~NO_OPTIONS)) {
14026      return "Cannot combine other IndexOptions
14027              keywords with 'None'";
14028      }
14029      d_cfg->incremented_opts = opts_add;
14030      d_cfg->decremented_opts = opts_remove;
14031      d_cfg->opts = opts;
14032      return NULL;
14033  }
14034
14035  static const char *set_default_order(cmd_parms *cmd,
14036          void *m, char *direction,
14037                          char *key)
14038  {
14039      char temp[4];
14040      autoindex_config_rec *d_cfg =
14041          (autoindex_config_rec *) m;
14042
14043      ap_cpystrn(temp, "k=d", sizeof(temp));
14044      if (!strcasecmp(direction, "Ascending")) {
14045       temp[2] = D_ASCENDING;
14046      }
14047      else if (!strcasecmp(direction, "Descending")) {
14048       temp[2] = D_DESCENDING;
14049      }
14050      else {
14051       return "First keyword must be 'Ascending'
14052            or 'Descending'";
14053      }
14054
14055      if (!strcasecmp(key, "Name")) {
14056       temp[0] = K_NAME;
14057      }
14058      else if (!strcasecmp(key, "Date")) {
14059       temp[0] = K_LAST_MOD;
14060      }
14061      else if (!strcasecmp(key, "Size")) {
14062       temp[0] = K_SIZE;
14063      }
14064      else if (!strcasecmp(key, "Description")) {
14065       temp[0] = K_DESC;
14066      }
14067      else {
14068       return "Second keyword must be 'Name',
14069            'Date', 'Size', or "
14070            "'Description'";
14071      }
14072
14073      if (d_cfg->default_order == NULL) {
14074       d_cfg->default_order = ap_palloc(cmd->pool, 4);
14075       d_cfg->default_order[3] = '\0';
```

```
14076          }
14077          ap_cpystrn(d_cfg->default_order, temp,
14078               sizeof(temp));
14079          return NULL;
14080      }
14081
14082      #define DIR_CMD_PERMS OR_INDEXES
14083
14084      static const command_rec autoindex_cmds[] =
14085      {
14086          {"AddIcon", add_icon,
14087               BY_PATH, DIR_CMD_PERMS, ITERATE2,
14088           "an icon URL followed by one or
14089               more filenames"},
14090          {"AddIconByType", add_icon, BY_TYPE,
14091               DIR_CMD_PERMS, ITERATE2,
14092           "an icon URL followed by one or
14093               more MIME types"},
14094          {"AddIconByEncoding", add_icon,
14095               BY_ENCODING, DIR_CMD_PERMS, ITERATE2,
14096           "an icon URL followed by one or more
14097               content encodings"},
14098          {"AddAlt", add_alt, BY_PATH, DIR_CMD_PERMS,
14099               ITERATE2,
14100           "alternate descriptive text followed
14101               by one or more filenames"},
14102          {"AddAltByType", add_alt, BY_TYPE,
14103               DIR_CMD_PERMS, ITERATE2,
14104           "alternate descriptive text followed by
14105               one or more MIME types"},
14106          {"AddAltByEncoding", add_alt, BY_ENCODING,
14107               DIR_CMD_PERMS, ITERATE2,
14108           "alternate descriptive text followed by one
14109               or more content encodings"},
14110          {"IndexOptions", add_opts, NULL,
14111               DIR_CMD_PERMS, RAW_ARGS,
14112           "one or more index options"},
14113          {"IndexOrderDefault", set_default_order,
14114               NULL, DIR_CMD_PERMS, TAKE2,
14115           "{Ascending,Descending}
14116               {Name,Size,Description,Date}"},
14117          {"IndexIgnore", add_ignore, NULL,
14118               DIR_CMD_PERMS, ITERATE,
14119           "one or more file extensions"},
14120          {"AddDescription", add_desc, BY_PATH,
14121               DIR_CMD_PERMS, ITERATE2,
14122           "Descriptive text followed by one or
14123               more filenames"},
14124          {"HeaderName", add_header, NULL,
14125               DIR_CMD_PERMS, TAKE1, "a filename"},
14126          {"ReadmeName", add_readme, NULL,
14127               DIR_CMD_PERMS, TAKE1, "a filename"},
14128          {"FancyIndexing", fancy_indexing, NULL,
14129               DIR_CMD_PERMS, FLAG,
14130           "Limited to 'on' or 'off' (superseded by
14131               IndexOptions FancyIndexing)"},
14132          {"DefaultIcon", ap_set_string_slot,
14133           (void *) XtOffsetOf(autoindex_config_rec,
14134               default_icon),
14135           DIR_CMD_PERMS, TAKE1, "an icon URL"},
14136          {NULL}
14137      };
14138
14139      static void *create_autoindex_config(pool *p,
14140          char *dummy)
14141      {
14142          autoindex_config_rec *new =
14143          (autoindex_config_rec *) ap_pcalloc(p,
14144               sizeof(autoindex_config_rec));
14145
14146          new->icon_width = 0;
14147          new->icon_height = 0;
14148          new->name_width = DEFAULT_NAME_WIDTH;
14149          new->name_adjust = K_UNSET;
14150          new->icon_list = ap_make_array(p, 4,
14151               sizeof(struct item));
14152          new->alt_list = ap_make_array(p, 4,
14153               sizeof(struct item));
14154          new->desc_list = ap_make_array(p, 4,
14155               sizeof(struct item));
14156          new->ign_list = ap_make_array(p, 4,
14157               sizeof(struct item));
14158          new->hdr_list = ap_make_array(p, 4,
14159               sizeof(struct item));
14160          new->rdme_list = ap_make_array(p, 4,
14161               sizeof(struct item));
14162          new->opts = 0;
14163          new->incremented_opts = 0;
14164          new->decremented_opts = 0;
14165          new->default_order = NULL;
14166
14167          return (void *) new;
14168      }
14169
14170      static void *merge_autoindex_configs(pool *p,
14171          void *basev, void *addv)
```

```
14172   {
14173       autoindex_config_rec *new;
14174       autoindex_config_rec *base =
14175           (autoindex_config_rec *) basev;
14176       autoindex_config_rec *add =
14177           (autoindex_config_rec *) addv;
14178
14179       new = (autoindex_config_rec *) ap_pcalloc(p,
14180           sizeof(autoindex_config_rec));
14181       new->default_icon = add->default_icon ?
14182           add->default_icon
14183                           : base->default_icon
14184       new->icon_height = add->icon_height ?
14185           add->icon_height : base->icon_height;
14186       new->icon_width = add->icon_width ?
14187           add->icon_width : base->icon_width;
14188
14189       new->alt_list = ap_append_arrays
14190           (p, add->alt_list, base->alt_list);
14191       new->ign_list = ap_append_arrays
14192           (p, add->ign_list, base->ign_list);
14193       new->hdr_list = ap_append_arrays
14194           (p, add->hdr_list, base->hdr_list);
14195       new->desc_list = ap_append_arrays
14196           (p, add->desc_list, base->desc_list);
14197       new->icon_list = ap_append_arrays
14198           (p, add->icon_list, base->icon_list);
14199       new->rdme_list = ap_append_arrays
14200           (p, add->rdme_list, base->rdme_list);
14201       if (add->opts & NO_OPTIONS) {
14202         /*
14203          * If the current directory says 'no options'
14204          * then we also clear any incremental mods from
14205          * being inheritable further down.
14206          */
14207         new->opts = NO_OPTIONS;
14208         new->incremented_opts = 0;
14209         new->decremented_opts = 0;
14210       }
14211       else {
14212         /*
14213          * If there were any non-incremental options
14214          * selected for this directory, they dominate
14215          * and we don't inherit *anything.*
14216          * Contrariwise, we *do* inherit if the only
14217          * settings here are incremental ones.
14218          */
14219         if (add->opts == 0) {
14220           new->incremented_opts =
14221             (base->incremented_opts
14222                       | add->incremented_opts)
14223                           & ~add->decremented_opts;
14224           new->decremented_opts =
14225             (base->decremented_opts
14226                       | add->decremented_opts);
14227           /*
14228            * We may have incremental settings, so
14229            * make sure we don't inadvertently
14230            * inherit an IndexOptions None from above.
14231            */
14232           new->opts = (base->opts & ~NO_OPTIONS);
14233         }
14234         else {
14235           /*
14236            * There are local non-incremental
14237            * settings, which clear all inheritance
14238            * from above.  They *are* the new
14239            * base settings.
14240            */
14241           new->opts = add->opts;;
14242         }
14243         /*
14244          * We're guaranteed that there'll be no
14245          * overlap between the add-options and the
14246          * remove-options.
14247          */
14248         new->opts |= new->incremented_opts;
14249         new->opts &= ~new->decremented_opts;
14250       }
14251       /*
14252        * Inherit the NameWidth settings if there
14253        * aren't any specific to the new location;
14254        * otherwise we'll end up using the defaults
14255        * set in the config-rec creation routine.
14256        */
14257       if (add->name_adjust == K_UNSET) {
14258         new->name_width = base->name_width;
14259         new->name_adjust = base->name_adjust;
14260       }
14261       else {
14262         new->name_width = add->name_width;
14263         new->name_adjust = add->name_adjust;
14264       }
14265
14266       new->default_order = (add->default_order != NULL)
14267         ? add->default_order : base->default_order;
```

```
14268        return new;
14269    }
14270
14271    /***************************************************
14272     *
14273     * Looking things up in config entries...
14274     */
14275
14276    /* Structure used to hold entries when we're
14277    actually building an index */
14278
14279    struct ent {
14280        char *name;
14281        char *icon;
14282        char *alt;
14283        char *desc;
14284        off_t size;
14285        time_t lm;
14286        struct ent *next;
14287        int ascending;
14288        char key;
14289    };
14290
14291    static char *find_item(request_rec *r,
14292        array_header *list, int path_only)
14293    {
14294        const char *content_type = r->content_type;
14295        const char *content_encoding =
14296            r->content_encoding;
14297        char *path = r->filename;
14298
14299        struct item *items = (struct item *)
14300            list->elts;
14301        int i;
14302
14303        for (i = 0; i < list->nelts; ++i) {
14304          struct item *p = &items[i];
14305
14306        /* Special cased for ^^DIRECTORY^^ and
14307           ^^BLANKICON^^ */
14308         if ((path[0] == '^') ||
14309            (!ap_strcmp_match(path, p->apply_path))) {
14310            if (!*(p->apply_to)) {
14311             return p->data;
14312            }
14313            else if (p->type == BY_PATH ||
14314                path[0] == '^') {
14315               if (!ap_strcmp_match(path,
```

```
14316                p->apply_to)) {
14317                return p->data;
14318             }
14319          }
14320          else if (!path_only) {
14321           if (!content_encoding) {
14322                if (p->type == BY_TYPE) {
14323                 if (content_type
14324                        && !ap_strcasecmp_match(content_
14325                                    p->apply_to)) {
14326                    return p->data;
14327                }
14328               }
14329            }
14330            else {
14331               if (p->type == BY_ENCODING) {
14332                if (!ap_strcasecmp_match(content_encoding,
14333                                p->apply_to)) {
14334                    return p->data;
14335                }
14336               }
14337            }
14338          }
14339         }
14340        }
14341      return NULL;
14342    }
14343
14344    #define find_icon(d,p,t) find_item(p,d->icon_list,t)
14345    #define find_alt(d,p,t) find_item(p,d->alt_list,t)
14346    #define find_desc(d,p) find_item(p,d->desc_list,0)
14347    #define find_header(d,p) find_item(p,d->hdr_list,0)
14348    #define find_readme(d,p) find_item(p,d->rdme_list,0)
14349
14350    static char *find_default_icon
14351        (autoindex_config_rec *d, char *bogus_name)
14352    {
14353        request_rec r;
14354
14355        /* Bleah.  I tried to clean up find_item, and
14356         * it lead to this bit of ugliness.   Note
14357         * that the fields initialized are precisely
14358         * those that find_item looks at...
14359         */
14360
14361        r.filename = bogus_name;
14362        r.content_type = r.content_encoding = NULL;
14363
```

```
14364        return find_item(&r, d->icon_list, 1);
14365    }
14366
14367    static int ignore_entry(autoindex_config_rec *d,
14368         char *path)
14369    {
14370        array_header *list = d->ign_list;
14371        struct item *items = (struct item *) list->elts;
14372        char *tt;
14373        int i;
14374
14375        if ((tt = strrchr(path, '/')) == NULL) {
14376         tt = path;
14377        }
14378        else {
14379         tt++;
14380        }
14381
14382        for (i = 0; i < list->nelts; ++i) {
14383         struct item *p = &items[i];
14384         char *ap;
14385
14386         if ((ap = strrchr(p->apply_to, '/')) == NULL) {
14387             ap = p->apply_to;
14388         }
14389         else {
14390             ap++;
14391         }
14392
14393    #ifndef CASE_BLIND_FILESYSTEM
14394         if (!ap_strcmp_match(path, p->apply_path)
14395             && !ap_strcmp_match(tt, ap)) {
14396             return 1;
14397         }
14398    #else  /* !CASE_BLIND_FILESYSTEM */
14399         /*
14400          * On some platforms, the match must be
14401          * case-blind.  This is really a factor of the
14402          * filesystem involved, but we can't detect
14403          * that reliably - so we have to granularise
14404          * at the OS level.
14405          */
14406         if (!ap_strcasecmp_match(path, p->apply_path)
14407             && !ap_strcasecmp_match(tt, ap)) {
14408             return 1;
14409         }
14410    #endif /* !CASE_BLIND_FILESYSTEM */
14411        }
14412        return 0;
14413    }
14414
14415    /***************************************************
14416     *
14417     * Actually generating output
14418     */
14419
14420    /*
14421     * Look for the specified file, and pump it into
14422     * the response stream if we find it.
14423     */
14424    static int insert_readme(char *name,
14425         char *readme_fname, char *title,
14426                int hrule, int whichend, request_rec *r)
14427    {
14428        char *fn;
14429        FILE *f;
14430        struct stat finfo;
14431        int plaintext = 0;
14432        request_rec *rr;
14433        autoindex_config_rec *cfg;
14434        int autoindex_opts;
14435
14436        cfg = (autoindex_config_rec *)
14437             ap_get_module_config(r->per_dir_config,
14438             &autoindex_module);
14439        autoindex_opts = cfg->opts;
14440        /* XXX: this is a load of crap, it needs to
14441         * do a full sub_req_lookup_uri */
14442        fn = ap_make_full_path(r->pool, name,
14443             readme_fname);
14444        fn = ap_pstrcat(r->pool, fn, ".html", NULL);
14445        if (stat(fn, &finfo) == -1) {
14446         /* A brief fake multiviews search
14447          * for README.html */
14448         fn[strlen(fn) - 5] = '\0';
14449         if (stat(fn, &finfo) == -1) {
14450             return 0;
14451         }
14452         plaintext = 1;
14453         if (hrule) {
14454             ap_rputs("<HR>\n", r);
14455         }
14456        }
14457        else if (hrule) {
14458         ap_rputs("<HR>\n", r);
14459        }
```

```
14460        /* XXX: when the above is rewritten properly,
14461         * this necessary security
14462         * check will be redundant. -djg */
14463        rr = ap_sub_req_lookup_file(fn, r);
14464        if (rr->status != HTTP_OK) {
14465         ap_destroy_sub_req(rr);
14466         return 0;
14467        }
14468        ap_destroy_sub_req(rr);
14469        if (!(f = ap_pfopen(r->pool, fn, "r"))) {
14470            return 0;
14471        }
14472        if ((whichend == FRONT_MATTER)
14473         && (!(autoindex_opts & SUPPRESS_PREAMBLE))) {
14474         emit_preamble(r, title);
14475        }
14476        if (!plaintext) {
14477         ap_send_fd(f, r);
14478        }
14479        else {
14480         char buf[IOBUFSIZE + 1];
14481         int i, n, c, ch;
14482         ap_rputs("<PRE>\n", r);
14483         while (!feof(f)) {
14484            do {
14485             n = fread(buf, sizeof(char), IOBUFSIZE, f);
14486            }
14487            while (n == -1 && ferror(f) &&
14488                    errno == EINTR);
14489            if (n == -1 || n == 0) {
14490             break;
14491            }
14492            buf[n] = '\0';
14493            c = 0;
14494            while (c < n) {
14495                for (i = c; i < n; i++) {
14496                 if (buf[i] == '<' || buf[i] ==
14497                        '>' || buf[i] == '&') {
14498                  break;
14499                 }
14500                }
14501                ch = buf[i];
14502                buf[i] = '\0';
14503                ap_rputs(&buf[c], r);
14504                if (ch == '<') {
14505                    ap_rputs("&lt;", r);
14506                }
14507                else if (ch == '>') {
14508                    ap_rputs("&gt;", r);
14509                }
14510                else if (ch == '&') {
14511                    ap_rputs("&amp;", r);
14512                }
14513                c = i + 1;
14514            }
14515         }
14516        }
14517        ap_pfclose(r->pool, f);
14518        if (plaintext) {
14519         ap_rputs("</PRE>\n", r);
14520        }
14521        return 1;
14522    }
14523
14524
14525    static char *find_title(request_rec *r)
14526    {
14527        char titlebuf[MAX_STRING_LEN], *find = "<TITLE>";
14528        FILE *thefile = NULL;
14529        int x, y, n, p;
14530
14531        if (r->status != HTTP_OK) {
14532         return NULL;
14533        }
14534        if (r->content_type
14535         && (!strcmp(r->content_type, "text/html")
14536            || !strcmp(r->content_type,
14537             INCLUDES_MAGIC_TYPE))
14538         && !r->content_encoding) {
14539            if (!(thefile = ap_pfopen(r->pool,
14540                    r->filename, "r"))) {
14541             return NULL;
14542            }
14543         n = fread(titlebuf, sizeof(char),
14544            MAX_STRING_LEN - 1, thefile);
14545         if (n <= 0) {
14546            ap_pfclose(r->pool, thefile);
14547            return NULL;
14548         }
14549         titlebuf[n] = '\0';
14550         for (x = 0, p = 0; titlebuf[x]; x++) {
14551            if (ap_toupper(titlebuf[x]) == find[p]) {
14552             if (!find[++p]) {
14553                if ((p = ap_ind(&titlebuf[++x],
14554                    '<')) != -1) {
14555                 titlebuf[x + p] = '\0';
```

```
14556                    }
14557                    /* Scan for line breaks for
14558                     * Tanmoy's secretary */
14559                    for (y = x; titlebuf[y]; y++) {
14560                        if ((titlebuf[y] == CR) ||
14561                            (titlebuf[y] == LF)) {
14562                            if (y == x) {
14563                                x++;
14564                            }
14565                            else {
14566                                titlebuf[y] = ' ';
14567                            }
14568                        }
14569                    }
14570                    ap_pfclose(r->pool, thefile);
14571                    return ap_pstrdup(r->pool,
14572                        &titlebuf[x]);
14573                }
14574            }
14575            else {
14576                p = 0;
14577            }
14578        }
14579        ap_pfclose(r->pool, thefile);
14580    }
14581    return NULL;
14582 }
14583
14584 static struct ent *make_autoindex_entry(char
14585     *name, int autoindex_opts,
14586                         autoindex_config_rec *d,
14587                         request_rec *r, char keyid,
14588                         char direction)
14589 {
14590     struct ent *p;
14591
14592     if ((name[0] == '.') && (!name[1])) {
14593      return (NULL);
14594     }
14595
14596     if (ignore_entry(d, ap_make_full_path(r->pool,
14597         r->filename, name))) {
14598             return (NULL);
14599     }
14600
14601     p = (struct ent *) ap_pcalloc(r->pool,
14602         sizeof(struct ent));
14603     p->name = ap_pstrdup(r->pool, name);
```

```
14604     p->size = -1;
14605     p->icon = NULL;
14606     p->alt = NULL;
14607     p->desc = NULL;
14608     p->lm = -1;
14609     p->key = ap_toupper(keyid);
14610     p->ascending = (ap_toupper(direction)
14611         == D_ASCENDING);
14612
14613     if (autoindex_opts & FANCY_INDEXING) {
14614      request_rec *rr =
14615             ap_sub_req_lookup_file(name, r);
14616
14617      if (rr->finfo.st_mode != 0) {
14618          p->lm = rr->finfo.st_mtime;
14619          if (S_ISDIR(rr->finfo.st_mode)) {
14620              if (!(p->icon =
14621                    find_icon(d, rr, 1))) {
14622                  p->icon = find_default_icon(d,
14623                      "^^DIRECTORY^^");
14624              }
14625              if (!(p->alt = find_alt(d, rr, 1))) {
14626                  p->alt = "DIR";
14627              }
14628              p->size = -1;
14629              p->name = ap_pstrcat(r->pool,
14630                  name, "/", NULL);
14631          }
14632          else {
14633              p->icon = find_icon(d, rr, 0);
14634              p->alt = find_alt(d, rr, 0);
14635              p->size = rr->finfo.st_size;
14636          }
14637      }
14638
14639      p->desc = find_desc(d, rr);
14640
14641      if ((!p->desc) && (autoindex_opts &
14642          SCAN_HTML_TITLES)) {
14643          p->desc = ap_pstrdup(r->pool, find_title(rr));
14644      }
14645
14646      ap_destroy_sub_req(rr);
14647     }
14648     /*
14649      * We don't need to take any special action
14650      * for the file size key.  If
14651      * we did, it would go here.
```

```
14652         */
14653         if (keyid == K_LAST_MOD) {
14654             if (p->lm < 0) {
14655                 p->lm = 0;
14656             }
14657         }
14658         return (p);
14659     }
14660
14661     static char *terminate_description
14662             (autoindex_config_rec *d, char *desc,
14663                         int autoindex_opts)
14664     {
14665         int maxsize = 23;
14666         register int x;
14667
14668         if (autoindex_opts & SUPPRESS_LAST_MOD) {
14669          maxsize += 19;
14670         }
14671         if (autoindex_opts & SUPPRESS_SIZE) {
14672          maxsize += 7;
14673         }
14674
14675         for (x = 0; desc[x] && (maxsize > 0 ||
14676             desc[x]=='<'); x++) {
14677          if (desc[x] == '<') {
14678             while (desc[x] != '>') {
14679             if (!desc[x]) {
14680                 maxsize = 0;
14681                 break;
14682             }
14683             ++x;
14684             }
14685          }
14686          else if (desc[x] == '&') {
14687             /* entities like &auml; count as
14688              * one character */
14689             --maxsize;
14690             for ( ; desc[x] != ';'; ++x) {
14691              if (desc[x] == '\0') {
14692                     maxsize = 0;
14693                     break;
14694              }
14695             }
14696          }
14697          else {
14698             --maxsize;
14699          }
14700         }
14701         if (!maxsize && desc[x] != '\0') {
14702          desc[x - 1] = '>';       /* Grump. */
14703          desc[x] = '\0';             /* Double Grump! */
14704         }
14705         return desc;
14706     }
14707
14708     /*
14709      * Emit the anchor for the specified field.  If a
14710      * field is the key for the current request, the
14711      * link changes its meaning to reverse the order
14712      * when selected again.  Non-active fields always
14713      * start in ascending order.
14714      */
14715     static void emit_link(request_rec *r, char *anchor,
14716         char fname, char curkey,
14717                     char curdirection, int nosort)
14718     {
14719         char qvalue[5];
14720         int reverse;
14721
14722         if (!nosort) {
14723          qvalue[0] = '?';
14724          qvalue[1] = fname;
14725          qvalue[2] = '=';
14726          qvalue[4] = '\0';
14727          reverse = ((curkey == fname) &&
14728              (curdirection == D_ASCENDING));
14729          qvalue[3] = reverse ? D_DESCENDING : D_ASCENDING;
14730          ap_rvputs(r, "<A HREF=\"", qvalue, "\">",
14731              anchor, "</A>", NULL);
14732         }
14733         else {
14734             ap_rputs(anchor, r);
14735         }
14736     }
14737
14738     /*
14739      * Fit a string into a specified buffer width,
14740      * marking any truncation.  The size argument is
14741      * the actual buffer size, including the \0
14742      * termination byte.  The buffer will be prefilled
14743      * with blanks.If the pad argument is false, any
14744      * extra spaces at the end of the buffer are
14745      * omitted.  (Used when constructing anchors.)
14746      */
14747     static ap_inline char *widthify(const char *s,
```

```
14748          char *buff, int size, int pad)
14749    {
14750        int s_len;
14751
14752        memset(buff, ' ', size);
14753        buff[size - 1] = '\0';
14754        s_len = strlen(s);
14755        if (s_len > (size - 1)) {
14756         ap_cpystrn(buff, s, size);
14757         if (size > 1) {
14758             buff[size - 2] = '>';
14759         }
14760         if (size > 2) {
14761             buff[size - 3] = '.';
14762         }
14763         if (size > 3) {
14764             buff[size - 4] = '.';
14765         }
14766        }
14767        else {
14768         ap_cpystrn(buff, s, s_len + 1);
14769         if (pad) {
14770             buff[s_len] = ' ';
14771         }
14772        }
14773        return buff;
14774    }
14775
14776    static void output_directories
14777        (struct ent **ar, int n,
14778                        autoindex_config_rec *d,
14779                        request_rec *r,
14780                        int autoindex_opts, char
14781                        keyid, char direction)
14782    {
14783        int x;
14784        char *name = r->uri;
14785        char *tp;
14786        int static_columns = (autoindex_opts &
14787            SUPPRESS_COLSORT);
14788
14789        pool *scratch = ap_make_sub_pool(r->pool);
14790        int name_width;
14791        char *name_scratch;
14792
14793        if (name[0] == '\0') {
14794         name = "/";
14795        }
```

```
14796
14797        name_width = d->name_width;
14798        if (d->name_adjust == K_ADJUST) {
14799         for (x = 0; x < n; x++) {
14800             int t = strlen(ar[x]->name);
14801             if (t > name_width) {
14802              name_width = t;
14803             }
14804         }
14805        }
14806        ++name_width;
14807        name_scratch = ap_palloc(r->pool,
14808            name_width + 1);
14809        memset(name_scratch, ' ', name_width);
14810        name_scratch[name_width] = '\0';
14811
14812        if (autoindex_opts & FANCY_INDEXING) {
14813         ap_rputs("<PRE>", r);
14814         if ((tp = find_default_icon(d,
14815             "^^BLANKICON^^"))) {
14816             ap_rvputs(r, "<IMG SRC=\"",
14817                 ap_escape_html(scratch, tp),
14818                 "\" ALT=\"      \"", NULL);
14819             if (d->icon_width && d->icon_height) {
14820              ap_rprintf
14821                 (
14822                  r,
14823                  " HEIGHT=\"%d\" WIDTH=\"%d\"",
14824                  d->icon_height,
14825                  d->icon_width
14826                 );
14827             }
14828             ap_rputs("> ", r);
14829         }
14830         emit_link(r, widthify("Name", name_scratch,
14831                 (name_width > 5) ? 5 :
14832                     name_width, K_NOPAD),
14833             K_NAME, keyid, direction, static_columns);
14834         if (name_width > 5) {
14835             memset(name_scratch, ' ', name_width);
14836             name_scratch[name_width] = '\0';
14837             ap_rputs(&name_scratch[5], r);
14838         }
14839         /*
14840          * Emit the guaranteed-at-least-one-space-
14841          * between-columns byte.
14842          */
14843         ap_rputs(" ", r);
```

```
14844        if (!(autoindex_opts & SUPPRESS_LAST_MOD)) {
14845            emit_link(r, "Last modified",
14846                    K_LAST_MOD, keyid, direction,
14847                    static_columns);
14848            ap_rputs("    ", r);
14849        }
14850        if (!(autoindex_opts & SUPPRESS_SIZE)) {
14851            emit_link(r, "Size", K_SIZE, keyid,
14852                    direction, static_columns);
14853            ap_rputs(" ", r);
14854        }
14855        if (!(autoindex_opts & SUPPRESS_DESC)) {
14856            emit_link(r, "Description", K_DESC,
14857                    keyid, direction,
14858                    static_columns);
14859        }
14860        ap_rputs("\n<HR>\n", r);
14861    }
14862    else {
14863        ap_rputs("<UL>", r);
14864    }
14865
14866    for (x = 0; x < n; x++) {
14867
14868        char *anchor, *t, *t2;
14869        char *pad;
14870        int nwidth;
14871
14872        ap_clear_pool(scratch);
14873
14874        if (is_parent(ar[x]->name)) {
14875            t = ap_make_full_path(scratch, name, "../");
14876            ap_getparents(t);
14877            if (t[0] == '\0') {
14878                t = "/";
14879            }
14880            /* 1234567890123456 */
14881            t2 = "Parent Directory";
14882            pad = name_scratch + 16;
14883            anchor = ap_escape_html(scratch,
14884                ap_os_escape_path(scratch, t, 0));
14885        }
14886        else {
14887            t = ar[x]->name;
14888            pad = name_scratch + strlen(t);
14889            t2 = ap_escape_html(scratch, t);
14890            anchor = ap_escape_html(scratch,
14891                ap_os_escape_path(scratch, t, 0));
14892        }
14893
14894        if (autoindex_opts & FANCY_INDEXING) {
14895            if (autoindex_opts & ICONS_ARE_LINKS) {
14896                ap_rvputs(r, "<A HREF=\"",
14897                    anchor, "\">", NULL);
14898            }
14899            if ((ar[x]->icon) || d->default_icon) {
14900                ap_rvputs(r, "<IMG SRC=\"",
14901                    ap_escape_html(scratch,
14902                        ar[x]->icon ? ar[x]->icon
14903                            : d->default_icon),
14904                    "\" ALT=\"[", (ar[x]->alt ?
14905                        ar[x]->alt : "   "),
14906                    "]\"", NULL);
14907                if (d->icon_width && d->icon_height) {
14908                    ap_rprintf(r, " HEIGHT=\"%d\"
14909                        WIDTH=\"%d\"",
14910                            d->icon_height, d->icon_width);
14911                }
14912                ap_rputs(">", r);
14913            }
14914            if (autoindex_opts & ICONS_ARE_LINKS) {
14915                ap_rputs("</A>", r);
14916            }
14917
14918            ap_rvputs(r, " <A HREF=\"", anchor, "\">",
14919                widthify(t2, name_scratch,
14920                    name_width, K_NOPAD),
14921                "</A>", NULL);
14922            /*
14923             * We know that widthify() prefilled the
14924             * buffer with spaces before
14925             * doing its thing, so use them.
14926             */
14927            nwidth = strlen(t2);
14928            if (nwidth < (name_width - 1)) {
14929                name_scratch[nwidth] = ' ';
14930                ap_rputs(&name_scratch[nwidth], r);
14931            }
14932            /*
14933             * The blank before the storm.. er, before
14934             * the next field.
14935             */
14936            ap_rputs(" ", r);
14937            if (!(autoindex_opts & SUPPRESS_LAST_MOD))
14938                if (ar[x]->lm != -1) {
14939                    char time_str[MAX_STRING_LEN];
```

```
14940                    struct tm *ts = localtime(&ar[x]->lm);
14941                    strftime(time_str, MAX_STRING_LEN,
14942                        "%d-%b-%Y %H:%M  ", ts);
14943                    ap_rputs(time_str, r);
14944                }
14945                else {
14946                    /*Length="22-Feb-1998 23:42  "
14947                     * (see 4 lines above) */
14948                    ap_rputs("                   ", r);
14949                }
14950            }
14951            if (!(autoindex_opts & SUPPRESS_SIZE)) {
14952                ap_send_size(ar[x]->size, r);
14953                ap_rputs("  ", r);
14954            }
14955            if (!(autoindex_opts & SUPPRESS_DESC)) {
14956                if (ar[x]->desc) {
14957                    ap_rputs(terminate_description
14958                        (d, ar[x]->desc,
14959                            autoindex_opts), r);
14960                }
14961            }
14962        }
14963        else {
14964            ap_rvputs(r, "<LI><A HREF=\"",
14965                anchor, "\"> ", t2,
14966                "</A>", pad, NULL);
14967        }
14968        ap_rputc('\n', r);
14969    }
14970    if (autoindex_opts & FANCY_INDEXING) {
14971        ap_rputs("</PRE>", r);
14972    }
14973    else {
14974        ap_rputs("</UL>", r);
14975    }
14976 }
14977
14978 /*
14979  * Compare two file entries according to the sort
14980  * criteria.  The return is essentially
14981  * a signum function value.
14982  */
14983
14984 static int dsortf(struct ent **e1, struct ent **e2)
14985 {
14986     struct ent *c1;
14987     struct ent *c2;
14988     int result = 0;
14989
14990     /*
14991      * First, see if either of the entries is for
14992      * the parent directory. If so, that
14993      * *always* sorts lower than anything else.
14994      */
14995     if (is_parent((*e1)->name)) {
14996         return -1;
14997     }
14998     if (is_parent((*e2)->name)) {
14999         return 1;
15000     }
15001     /*
15002      * All of our comparisons will be of the c1
15003      * entry against the c2 one, so assign them
15004      * appropriately to take care of the ordering.
15005      */
15006     if ((*e1)->ascending) {
15007         c1 = *e1;
15008         c2 = *e2;
15009     }
15010     else {
15011         c1 = *e2;
15012         c2 = *e1;
15013     }
15014     switch (c1->key) {
15015     case K_LAST_MOD:
15016         if (c1->lm > c2->lm) {
15017             return 1;
15018         }
15019         else if (c1->lm < c2->lm) {
15020             return -1;
15021         }
15022         break;
15023     case K_SIZE:
15024         if (c1->size > c2->size) {
15025             return 1;
15026         }
15027         else if (c1->size < c2->size) {
15028             return -1;
15029         }
15030         break;
15031     case K_DESC:
15032         result = strcmp(c1->desc ? c1->desc : "",
15033             c2->desc ? c2->desc : "");
15034         if (result) {
15035             return result;
```

```
15036              }
15037           break;
15038         }
15039       return strcmp(c1->name, c2->name);
15040  }
15041
15042
15043  static int index_directory(request_rec *r,
15044                 autoindex_config_rec *autoindex_conf)
15045  {
15046      char *title_name =
15047             ap_escape_html(r->pool, r->uri);
15048      char *title_endp;
15049      char *name = r->filename;
15050
15051      DIR *d;
15052      struct DIR_TYPE *dstruct;
15053      int num_ent = 0, x;
15054      struct ent *head, *p;
15055      struct ent **ar = NULL;
15056      char *tmp;
15057      const char *qstring;
15058      int autoindex_opts = autoindex_conf->opts;
15059      char keyid;
15060      char direction;
15061
15062      if (!(d = ap_popendir(r->pool, name))) {
15063       ap_log_rerror(APLOG_MARK, APLOG_ERR, r,
15064             "Can't open directory for index:
15065                  %s", r->filename);
15066       return HTTP_FORBIDDEN;
15067      }
15068
15069      r->content_type = "text/html";
15070
15071      ap_send_http_header(r);
15072
15073      if (r->header_only) {
15074       ap_pclosedir(r->pool, d);
15075       return 0;
15076      }
15077      ap_hard_timeout("send directory", r);
15078
15079      /* Spew HTML preamble */
15080
15081      title_endp = title_name + strlen(title_name) - 1;
15082
15083      while (title_endp > title_name &&
15084            *title_endp == '/') {
15085       *title_endp-- = '\0';
15086      }
15087
15088      if ((!(tmp = find_header(autoindex_conf, r)))
15089       || (!(insert_readme(name, tmp, title_name,
15090          NO_HRULE, FRONT_MATTER, r)))
15091      ) {
15092       emit_preamble(r, title_name);
15093       ap_rvputs(r, "<H1>Index of ", title_name,
15094          "</H1>\n", NULL);
15095      }
15096
15097      /*
15098       * Figure out what sort of indexing (if any)
15099       * we're supposed to use.
15100       *
15101       * If no QUERY_STRING was specified or column
15102       * sorting has been explicitly disabled, we
15103       * use the default specified by the
15104       * IndexOrderDefault directive (if there is one);
15105       * otherwise, we fall back to ascending by name.
15106       */
15107      qstring = r->args;
15108      if ((autoindex_opts & SUPPRESS_COLSORT)
15109       || ((qstring == NULL) || (*qstring == '\0'))) {
15110       qstring = autoindex_conf->default_order;
15111      }
15112      /*
15113       * If there is no specific ordering defined for
15114       * this directory,default to ascending by
15115       * filename.
15116       */
15117      if ((qstring == NULL) || (*qstring == '\0')) {
15118       keyid = K_NAME;
15119       direction = D_ASCENDING;
15120      }
15121      else {
15122       keyid = *qstring;
15123       ap_getword(r->pool, &qstring, '=');
15124       if (qstring != '\0') {
15125           direction = *qstring;
15126       }
15127       else {
15128           direction = D_ASCENDING;
15129       }
```

```
15130        }
15131
15132        /*
15133         * Since we don't know how many dir. entries
15134         * there are, put them into a linked list and
15135         * then arrayificate them so qsort can use them.
15136         */
15137        head = NULL;
15138        while ((dstruct = readdir(d))) {
15139            p = make_autoindex_entry(dstruct->d_name,
15140                autoindex_opts,
15141                    autoindex_conf, r, keyid, direction);
15142            if (p != NULL) {
15143                p->next = head;
15144                head = p;
15145                num_ent++;
15146            }
15147        }
15148        if (num_ent > 0) {
15149            ar = (struct ent **) ap_palloc(r->pool,
15150                        num_ent * sizeof(struct ent *));
15151            p = head;
15152            x = 0;
15153            while (p) {
15154                ar[x++] = p;
15155                p = p->next;
15156            }
15157
15158            qsort((void *) ar, num_ent,
15159                sizeof(struct ent *),
15160                (int (*)(const void *,
15161                const void *)) dsortf);
15162        }
15163        output_directories(ar, num_ent, autoindex_conf,
15164            r, autoindex_opts, keyid,
15165                direction);
15166        ap_pclosedir(r->pool, d);
15167
15168        if ((tmp = find_readme(autoindex_conf, r))) {
15169            if (!insert_readme(name, tmp, "",
15170                    ((autoindex_opts &
15171                        FANCY_INDEXING) ? HRULE
15172                                        : NO_HRULE),
15173                    END_MATTER, r)) {
15174                ap_rputs(ap_psignature("<HR>\n", r), r);
15175            }
15176        }
```

```
15177        ap_rputs("</BODY></HTML>\n", r);
15178
15179        ap_kill_timeout(r);
15180        return 0;
15181    }
15182
15183    /* The formal handler... */
15184
15185    static int handle_autoindex(request_rec *r)
15186    {
15187        autoindex_config_rec *d;
15188        int allow_opts = ap_allow_options(r);
15189
15190        d = (autoindex_config_rec *)
15191            ap_get_module_config(r->per_dir_config,
15192                            &autoindex_module);
15193
15194        r->allowed |= (1 << M_GET);
15195        if (r->method_number != M_GET) {
15196            return DECLINED;
15197        }
15198
15199        /* OK, nothing easy.  Trot out the
15200         * heavy artillery... */
15201
15202        if (allow_opts & OPT_INDEXES) {
15203            /* KLUDGE -- make the sub_req lookups happen
15204             * in the right directory. Fixing this in
15205             * the sub_req_lookup functions themselves is
15206             * difficult, and would probably break
15207             * virtual includes...
15208             */
15209
15210            if (r->filename[strlen(r->filename) - 1]
15211                != '/') {
15212                r->filename = ap_pstrcat(r->pool,
15213                    r->filename, "/", NULL);
15214            }
15215            return index_directory(r, d);
15216        }
15217        else {
15218            ap_log_rerror(APLOG_MARK,
15219                APLOG_NOERRNO|APLOG_ERR, r,
15220                    "Directory index forbidden by
15221                        rule: %s", r->filename);
15222            return HTTP_FORBIDDEN;
15223        }
```

```
15224    }
15225
15226
15227    static const handler_rec autoindex_handlers[] =
15228    {
15229        {DIR_MAGIC_TYPE, handle_autoindex},
15230        {NULL}
15231    };
15232
15233    module MODULE_VAR_EXPORT autoindex_module =
15234    {
15235        STANDARD_MODULE_STUFF,
15236        NULL,             /* initializer */
15237        create_autoindex_config,
15238        /* dir config creater */
15239        merge_autoindex_configs,
15240        /* dir merger -- default is to override */
15241        NULL,             /* server config */
15242        NULL,             /* merge server config */
15243        autoindex_cmds,       /* command table */
15244        autoindex_handlers,     /* handlers */
15245        NULL,
15246        /* filename translation */
15247        NULL,             /* check_user_id */
15248        NULL,             /* check auth */
15249        NULL,             /* check access */
15250        NULL,             /* type_checker */
15251        NULL,             /* fixups */
15252        NULL,             /* logger */
15253        NULL,             /* header parser */
15254        NULL,             /* child_init */
15255        NULL,             /* child_exit */
15256        NULL              /* post read-request */
15257    };
```

p 500 mod_cern_meta.c

```
15258    #include "httpd.h"
15259    #include "http_config.h"
15260    #include <sys/types.h>
15261    #include <sys/stat.h>
15262    #include "util_script.h"
15263    #include "http_log.h"
15264    #include "http_request.h"
15265
15266    #define DIR_CMD_PERMS OR_INDEXES
15267
15268    #define DEFAULT_METADIR        ".web"
```

```
15269    #define DEFAULT_METASUFFIX     ".meta"
15270    #define DEFAULT_METAFILES     0
15271
15272    module MODULE_VAR_EXPORT cern_meta_module;
15273
15274    typedef struct {
15275        char *metadir;
15276        char *metasuffix;
15277        char *metafiles;
15278    } cern_meta_dir_config;
15279
15280    static void *create_cern_meta_dir_config(pool *p,
15281        char *dummy)
15282    {
15283        cern_meta_dir_config *new =
15284        (cern_meta_dir_config *) ap_palloc(p,
15285            sizeof(cern_meta_dir_config));
15286
15287        new->metadir = NULL;
15288        new->metasuffix = NULL;
15289        new->metafiles = DEFAULT_METAFILES;
15290
15291        return new;
15292    }
15293
15294    static void *merge_cern_meta_dir_configs(pool *p,
15295        void *basev, void *addv)
15296    {
15297        cern_meta_dir_config *base =
15298            (cern_meta_dir_config *) basev;
15299        cern_meta_dir_config *add =
15300            (cern_meta_dir_config *) addv;
15301        cern_meta_dir_config *new =
15302        (cern_meta_dir_config *) ap_palloc(p,
15303            sizeof(cern_meta_dir_config));
15304
15305        new->metadir = add->metadir ? add->metadir :
15306            base->metadir;
15307        new->metasuffix = add->metasuffix ?
15308            add->metasuffix : base->metasuffix;
15309        new->metafiles = add->metafiles;
15310
15311        return new;
15312    }
15313
15314    static const char *set_metadir(cmd_parms *parms,
15315        cern_meta_dir_config * dconf, char *arg)
```

```
15316   {
15317       dconf->metadir = arg;
15318       return NULL;
15319   }
15320
15321   static const char *set_metasuffix(cmd_parms *parms,
15322       cern_meta_dir_config * dconf, char *arg)
15323   {
15324       dconf->metasuffix = arg;
15325       return NULL;
15326   }
15327
15328   static const char *set_metafiles(cmd_parms *parms,
15329       cern_meta_dir_config * dconf, char *arg)
15330   {
15331       dconf->metafiles = arg;
15332       return NULL;
15333   }
15334
15335
15336   static const command_rec cern_meta_cmds[] =
15337   {
15338       {"MetaFiles", set_metafiles, NULL,
15339           DIR_CMD_PERMS, FLAG,
15340       "Limited to 'on' or 'off'"},
15341       {"MetaDir", set_metadir, NULL, DIR_CMD_PERMS, TAKE1,
15342        "the name of the directory containing meta files"},
15343       {"MetaSuffix", set_metasuffix, NULL,
15344           DIR_CMD_PERMS, TAKE1,
15345        "the filename suffix for meta files"},
15346       {NULL}
15347   };
15348
15349   /* XXX: this is very similar to ap_scan_script_header_
15350    * err_core... are the differences deliberate, or
15351    * just a result of bit rot?
15352    */
15353   static int scan_meta_file(request_rec *r, FILE *f)
15354   {
15355       char w[MAX_STRING_LEN];
15356       char *l;
15357       int p;
15358       table *tmp_headers;
15359
15360       tmp_headers = ap_make_table(r->pool, 5);
15361       while (fgets(w, MAX_STRING_LEN - 1, f) != NULL) {
15362
15363           /* Delete terminal (CR?)LF */
15364
15365           p = strlen(w);
15366           if (p > 0 && w[p - 1] == '\n') {
15367               if (p > 1 && w[p - 2] == '\015')
15368                   w[p - 2] = '\0';
15369               else
15370                   w[p - 1] = '\0';
15371           }
15372
15373           if (w[0] == '\0') {
15374               return OK;
15375           }
15376
15377           /* if we see a bogus header don't ignore it.
15378            * Shout and scream */
15379
15380           if (!(l = strchr(w, ':'))) {
15381               ap_log_rerror(APLOG_MARK,
15382                       APLOG_NOERRNO|APLOG_ERR, r,
15383                       "malformed header in meta file: %s",
15384                           r->filename);
15385               return SERVER_ERROR;
15386           }
15387
15388           *l++ = '\0';
15389           while (*l && ap_isspace(*l))
15390               ++l;
15391
15392           if (!strcasecmp(w, "Content-type")) {
15393               char *tmp;
15394               /* Nuke trailing whitespace */
15395
15396               char *endp = l + strlen(l) - 1;
15397               while (endp > l && ap_isspace(*endp))
15398                *endp-- = '\0';
15399
15400               tmp = ap_pstrdup(r->pool, l);
15401               ap_content_type_tolower(tmp);
15402               r->content_type = tmp;
15403           }
15404           else if (!strcasecmp(w, "Status")) {
15405               sscanf(l, "%d", &r->status);
15406               r->status_line = ap_pstrdup(r->pool, l);
15407           }
15408           else {
15409               ap_table_set(tmp_headers, w, l);
```

```
15410            }
15411        }
15412        ap_overlap_tables(r->headers_out, tmp_headers,
15413                AP_OVERLAP_TABLES_SET);
15414        return OK;
15415    }
15416
15417    static int add_cern_meta_data(request_rec *r)
15418    {
15419        char *metafilename;
15420        char *last_slash;
15421        char *real_file;
15422        char *scrap_book;
15423        FILE *f;
15424        cern_meta_dir_config *dconf;
15425        int rv;
15426        request_rec *rr;
15427
15428        dconf = ap_get_module_config(r->per_dir_config,
15429                &cern_meta_module);
15430
15431        if (!dconf->metafiles) {
15432         return DECLINED;
15433        };
15434
15435        /* if ./.web/$1.meta exists then output 'asis' */
15436
15437        if (r->finfo.st_mode == 0) {
15438         return DECLINED;
15439        };
15440
15441        /* is this a directory? */
15442        if (S_ISDIR(r->finfo.st_mode) ||
15443                r->uri[strlen(r->uri) - 1] == '/') {
15444         return DECLINED;
15445        };
15446
15447        /* what directory is this file in? */
15448        scrap_book = ap_pstrdup(r->pool, r->filename);
15449        /* skip leading slash, recovered in
15450         * later processing */
15451        scrap_book++;
15452        last_slash = strrchr(scrap_book, '/');
15453        if (last_slash != NULL) {
15454         /* skip over last slash */
15455         real_file = last_slash;
15456            real_file++;
15457            *last_slash = '\0';
15458        }
15459        else {
15460         /* no last slash, buh?! */
15461         ap_log_rerror(APLOG_MARK,
15462                APLOG_NOERRNO|APLOG_ERR, r,
15463                 "internal error in mod_cern_meta: %s",
15464                 r->filename);
15465         /* should really barf, but hey, let's
15466          * be friends... */
15467         return DECLINED;
15468        };
15469
15470        metafilename = ap_pstrcat(r->pool, "/",
15471                    scrap_book, "/",
15472                    dconf->metadir ? dconf->metadir :
15473                    DEFAULT_METADIR,
15474                    "/", real_file,
15475                dconf->metasuffix ? dconf->metasuffix :
15476                    DEFAULT_METASUFFIX,
15477                    NULL);
15478
15479        /* XXX: it sucks to require this subrequest to
15480         * complete, because this means people must leave
15481         * their meta files accessible to the world.
15482         * A better solution might be a "safe open"
15483         * feature of pfopen to avoid pipes,
15484         * symlinks, and crap like that.
15485         */
15486        rr = ap_sub_req_lookup_file(metafilename, r);
15487        if (rr->status != HTTP_OK) {
15488         ap_destroy_sub_req(rr);
15489         return DECLINED;
15490        }
15491        ap_destroy_sub_req(rr);
15492
15493        f = ap_pfopen(r->pool, metafilename, "r");
15494        if (f == NULL) {
15495         if (errno == ENOENT) {
15496            return DECLINED;
15497         }
15498         ap_log_rerror(APLOG_MARK, APLOG_ERR, r,
15499             "meta file permissions deny server
15500                access: %s", metafilename);
15501        return FORBIDDEN;
```

```
15502        };
15503
15504        /* read the headers in */
15505        rv = scan_meta_file(r, f);
15506        ap_pfclose(r->pool, f);
15507
15508        return rv;
15509    }
15510
15511    module MODULE_VAR_EXPORT cern_meta_module =
15512    {
15513        STANDARD_MODULE_STUFF,
15514        NULL,                  /* initializer */
15515        create_cern_meta_dir_config,
15516        /* dir config creater */
15517        merge_cern_meta_dir_configs,
15518        /* dir merger -- default is to override */
15519        NULL,                  /* server config */
15520        NULL,                  /* merge server configs */
15521        cern_meta_cmds,        /* command table */
15522        NULL,                  /* handlers */
15523        NULL,                  /* filename translation */
15524        NULL,                  /* check_user_id */
15525        NULL,                  /* check auth */
15526        NULL,                  /* check access */
15527        NULL,                  /* type_checker */
15528        add_cern_meta_data,    /* fixups */
15529        NULL,                  /* logger */
15530        NULL,                  /* header parser */
15531        NULL,                  /* child_init */
15532        NULL,                  /* child_exit */
15533        NULL                   /* post read-request */
15534    };
```

▶ mod_cgi.c
`p 460`

```
15535    #include "httpd.h"
15536    #include "http_config.h"
15537    #include "http_request.h"
15538    #include "http_core.h"
15539    #include "http_protocol.h"
15540    #include "http_main.h"
15541    #include "http_log.h"
15542    #include "util_script.h"
15543    #include "http_conf_globals.h"
15544
15545    module MODULE_VAR_EXPORT cgi_module;
```

```
15546
15547    /* KLUDGE -- for back-combatibility, we don't have
15548     * to check ExecCGI in ScriptAliased directories,
15549     * which means we need to know if this request
15550     * came through ScriptAlias or not... so the Alias
15551     * module leaves a note for us.
15552     */
15553
15554    static int is_scriptaliased(request_rec *r)
15555    {
15556        const char *t = ap_table_get(r->notes,
15557            "alias-forced-type");
15558        return t && (!strcasecmp(t, "cgi-script"));
15559    }
15560
15561    /* Configuration stuff */
15562
15563    #define DEFAULT_LOGBYTES 10385760
15564    #define DEFAULT_BUFBYTES 1024
15565
15566    typedef struct {
15567        char *logname;
15568        long logbytes;
15569        int bufbytes;
15570    } cgi_server_conf;
15571
15572    static void *create_cgi_config(pool *p,
15573        server_rec *s)
15574    {
15575        cgi_server_conf *c =
15576        (cgi_server_conf *) ap_pcalloc(p,
15577            sizeof(cgi_server_conf));
15578
15579        c->logname = NULL;
15580        c->logbytes = DEFAULT_LOGBYTES;
15581        c->bufbytes = DEFAULT_BUFBYTES;
15582
15583        return c;
15584    }
15585
15586    static void *merge_cgi_config(pool *p, void *basev,
15587        void *overridesv)
15588    {
15589        cgi_server_conf *base = (cgi_server_conf *) basev,
15590            *overrides = (cgi_server_conf *) overridesv;
15591
```

```
15592        return overrides->logname ? overrides : base;
15593    }
15594
15595    static const char *set_scriptlog(cmd_parms *cmd,
15596        void *dummy, char *arg)
15597    {
15598        server_rec *s = cmd->server;
15599        cgi_server_conf *conf =
15600        (cgi_server_conf *)
15601            ap_get_module_config(s->module_config,
15602            &cgi_module);
15603
15604        conf->logname = arg;
15605        return NULL;
15606    }
15607
15608    static const char *set_scriptlog_length(cmd_parms *cmd,
15609        void *dummy, char *arg)
15610    {
15611        server_rec *s = cmd->server;
15612        cgi_server_conf *conf =
15613        (cgi_server_conf *)
15614            ap_get_module_config(s->module_config,
15615            &cgi_module);
15616
15617        conf->logbytes = atol(arg);
15618        return NULL;
15619    }
15620
15621    static const char *set_scriptlog_buffer(cmd_parms *cmd,
15622        void *dummy, char *arg)
15623    {
15624        server_rec *s = cmd->server;
15625        cgi_server_conf *conf =
15626        (cgi_server_conf *)
15627            ap_get_module_config(s->module_config,
15628            &cgi_module);
15629
15630        conf->bufbytes = atoi(arg);
15631        return NULL;
15632    }
15633
15634    static const command_rec cgi_cmds[] =
15635    {
15636        {"ScriptLog", set_scriptlog, NULL, RSRC_CONF, TAKE1,
15637        "the name of a log for script debugging info"},
```

```
15638        {"ScriptLogLength", set_scriptlog_length, NULL,
15639            RSRC_CONF, TAKE1,
15640        "the maximum length (in bytes) of the script
15641            debug log"},
15642        {"ScriptLogBuffer", set_scriptlog_buffer, NULL,
15643            RSRC_CONF, TAKE1,
15644        "the maximum size (in bytes) to record of a POST
15645            request"},
15646        {NULL}
15647    };
15648
15649    static int log_scripterror(request_rec *r,
15650        cgi_server_conf * conf, int ret,
15651                    int show_errno, char *error)
15652    {
15653        FILE *f;
15654        struct stat finfo;
15655
15656        ap_log_rerror(APLOG_MARK, show_errno|APLOG_ERR, r,
15657            "%s: %s", error, r->filename);
15658
15659        if (!conf->logname ||
15660        ((stat(ap_server_root_relative(r->pool,
15661            conf->logname), &finfo) == 0)
15662        &&   (finfo.st_size > conf->logbytes)) ||
15663            ((f = ap_pfopen(r->pool,
15664                ap_server_root_relative(r->pool,
15665                conf->logname),
15666                "a")) == NULL)) {
15667        return ret;
15668        }
15669
15670        /* "%% [Wed Jun 19 10:53:21 1996]
15671         * GET /cgi-bin/printenv HTTP/1.0" */
15672        fprintf(f, "%%%% [%s] %s %s%s%s %s\n",
15673            ap_get_time(), r->method, r->uri,
15674            r->args ? "?" : "", r->args ? r->args : "",
15675                r->protocol);
15676        /* "%% 500 /usr/local/apache/cgi-bin */
15677        fprintf(f, "%%%% %d %s\n", ret, r->filename);
15678
15679        fprintf(f, "%%error\n%s\n", error);
15680
15681        ap_pfclose(r->pool, f);
15682        return ret;
15683    }
```

```
15684
15685   static int log_script(request_rec *r,
15686       cgi_server_conf * conf, int ret,
15687           char *dbuf, const char *sbuf,
15688               BUFF *script_in, BUFF *script_err)
15689   {
15690       array_header *hdrs_arr =
15691               ap_table_elts(r->headers_in);
15692       table_entry *hdrs = (table_entry *) hdrs_arr->elts;
15693       char argsbuffer[HUGE_STRING_LEN];
15694       FILE *f;
15695       int i;
15696       struct stat finfo;
15697
15698       if (!conf->logname ||
15699         ((stat(ap_server_root_relative(r->pool,
15700             conf->logname), &finfo) == 0)
15701         &&   (finfo.st_size > conf->logbytes)) ||
15702           ((f = ap_pfopen(r->pool,
15703               ap_server_root_relative(r->pool,
15704                   conf->logname),
15705                   "a")) == NULL)) {
15706
15707       /* Soak up script output */
15708       while (ap_bgets(argsbuffer, HUGE_STRING_LEN,
15709           script_in) > 0)
15710           continue;
15711       while (ap_bgets(argsbuffer, HUGE_STRING_LEN,
15712           script_err) > 0)
15713           continue;
15714       return ret;
15715       }
15716
15717       /* "%% [Wed Jun 19 10:53:21 1996]
15718        * GET /cgi-bin/printenv HTTP/1.0" */
15719       fprintf(f, "%%%% [%s] %s %s%s%s %s\n",
15720           ap_get_time(), r->method, r->uri,
15721           r->args ? "?" : "", r->args ? r->args :
15722               "", r->protocol);
15723       /* "%% 500 /usr/local/apache/cgi-bin" */
15724       fprintf(f, "%%%% %d %s\n", ret, r->filename);
15725
15726       fputs("%request\n", f);
15727       for (i = 0; i < hdrs_arr->nelts; ++i) {
15728         if (!hdrs[i].key)
15729             continue;
```

```
15730       fprintf(f, "%s: %s\n", hdrs[i].key, hdrs[i].val);
15731       }
15732       if ((r->method_number == M_POST ||
15733           r->method_number == M_PUT)
15734       && *dbuf) {
15735       fprintf(f, "\n%s\n", dbuf);
15736       }
15737
15738       fputs("%response\n", f);
15739       hdrs_arr = ap_table_elts(r->err_headers_out);
15740       hdrs = (table_entry *) hdrs_arr->elts;
15741
15742       for (i = 0; i < hdrs_arr->nelts; ++i) {
15743         if (!hdrs[i].key)
15744             continue;
15745         fprintf(f, "%s: %s\n", hdrs[i].key, hdrs[i].val);
15746       }
15747
15748       if (sbuf && *sbuf)
15749         fprintf(f, "%s\n", sbuf);
15750
15751       if (ap_bgets(argsbuffer, HUGE_STRING_LEN,
15752           script_in) > 0) {
15753         fputs("%stdout\n", f);
15754         fputs(argsbuffer, f);
15755         while (ap_bgets(argsbuffer, HUGE_STRING_LEN,
15756             script_in) > 0)
15757             fputs(argsbuffer, f);
15758         fputs("\n", f);
15759       }
15760
15761       if (ap_bgets(argsbuffer, HUGE_STRING_LEN,
15762           script_err) > 0) {
15763         fputs("%stderr\n", f);
15764         fputs(argsbuffer, f);
15765         while (ap_bgets(argsbuffer, HUGE_STRING_LEN,
15766             script_err) > 0)
15767             fputs(argsbuffer, f);
15768         fputs("\n", f);
15769       }
15770
15771       ap_bclose(script_in);
15772       ap_bclose(script_err);
15773
15774       ap_pfclose(r->pool, f);
15775       return ret;
```

```
15776    }
15777
15778    /********************************************************
15779     *
15780     * Actual CGI handling...
15781     */
15782
15783
15784    struct cgi_child_stuff {
15785        request_rec *r;
15786        int nph;
15787        int debug;
15788        char *argv0;
15789    };
15790
15791    static int cgi_child(void *child_stuff,
15792        child_info *pinfo)
15793    {
15794        struct cgi_child_stuff *cld = (struct
15795            cgi_child_stuff *) child_stuff;
15796        request_rec *r = cld->r;
15797        char *argv0 = cld->argv0;
15798        int child_pid;
15799
15800    #ifdef DEBUG_CGI
15801    #ifdef OS2
15802        /* Under OS/2 need to use device con. */
15803        FILE *dbg = fopen("con", "w");
15804    #else
15805        FILE *dbg = fopen("/dev/tty", "w");
15806    #endif
15807        int i;
15808    #endif
15809
15810        char **env;
15811
15812        RAISE_SIGSTOP(CGI_CHILD);
15813    #ifdef DEBUG_CGI
15814        fprintf(dbg, "Attempting to exec %s as %sCGI child
15815            (argv0 = %s)\n",
15816            r->filename, cld->nph ? "NPH " : "", argv0);
15817    #endif
15818
15819        ap_add_cgi_vars(r);
15820        env = ap_create_environment(r->pool,
```

```
15821            r->subprocess_env);
15822
15823    #ifdef DEBUG_CGI
15824        fprintf(dbg, "Environment: \n");
15825        for (i = 0; env[i]; ++i)
15826            fprintf(dbg, "'%s'\n", env[i]);
15827    #endif
15828
15829    #ifndef WIN32
15830        ap_chdir_file(r->filename);
15831    #endif
15832        if (!cld->debug)
15833            ap_error_log2stderr(r->server);
15834
15835        /* Transumute outselves into the script.
15836         * NB only ISINDEX scripts get decoded arguments.
15837         */
15838
15839        ap_cleanup_for_exec();
15840
15841        child_pid = ap_call_exec(r, pinfo, argv0, env, 0);
15842    #ifdef WIN32
15843        return (child_pid);
15844    #else
15845
15846        /* Uh oh.  Still here.  Where's the kaboom?
15847         * There was supposed to be an
15848         * EARTH-shattering kaboom!
15849         *
15850         * Oh, well.  Muddle through as best we can...
15851         *
15852         * Note that only stderr is available at this
15853         * point, so don't pass in
15854         * a server to aplog_error.
15855         */
15856
15857        ap_log_error(APLOG_MARK, APLOG_ERR, NULL,
15858            "exec of %s failed", r->filename);
15859        exit(0);
15860        /* NOT REACHED */
15861        return (0);
15862    #endif
15863    }
15864
15865    static int cgi_handler(request_rec *r)
```

```
15866   {
15867       int retval, nph, dbpos = 0;
15868       char *argv0, *dbuf = NULL;
15869       BUFF *script_out, *script_in, *script_err;
15870       char argsbuffer[HUGE_STRING_LEN];
15871       int is_included = !strcmp(r->protocol, "INCLUDED");
15872       void *sconf = r->server->module_config;
15873       cgi_server_conf *conf =
15874       (cgi_server_conf *) ap_get_module_config(sconf,
15875           &cgi_module);
15876
15877       struct cgi_child_stuff cld;
15878
15879       if (r->method_number == M_OPTIONS) {
15880       /* 99 out of 100 CGI scripts, this is all
15881        * they support */
15882       r->allowed |= (1 << M_GET);
15883       r->allowed |= (1 << M_POST);
15884       return DECLINED;
15885       }
15886
15887       if ((argv0 = strrchr(r->filename, '/')) != NULL)
15888       argv0++;
15889       else
15890       argv0 = r->filename;
15891
15892       nph = !(strncmp(argv0, "nph-", 4));
15893
15894       if (!(ap_allow_options(r) & OPT_EXECCGI) &&
15895           !is_scriptaliased(r))
15896       return log_scripterror(r, conf, FORBIDDEN,
15897           APLOG_NOERRNO,
15898                   "Options ExecCGI is off in
15899                       this directory");
15900       if (nph && is_included)
15901       return log_scripterror(r, conf, FORBIDDEN,
15902           APLOG_NOERRNO,
15903                   "attempt to include NPH CGI
15904                       script");
15905
15906  #if defined(OS2) || defined(WIN32)
15907       /* Allow for cgi files without the .EXE extension
15908        * on them under OS/2 */
15909       if (r->finfo.st_mode == 0) {
15910       struct stat statbuf;
15911       char *newfile;
15912
15913       newfile = ap_pstrcat(r->pool, r->filename,
15914           ".EXE", NULL);
15915
15916
15917       if ((stat(newfile, &statbuf) != 0) ||
15918           (!S_ISREG(statbuf.st_mode))) {
15919       return log_scripterror(r, conf, NOT_FOUND, 0,
15920               "script not found or unable to stat");
15921       } else {
15922           r->filename = newfile;
15923       }
15924       }
15925  #else
15926       if (r->finfo.st_mode == 0)
15927       return log_scripterror(r, conf, NOT_FOUND,
15928           APLOG_NOERRNO,
15929                   "script not found or unable to stat");
15930  #endif
15931       if (S_ISDIR(r->finfo.st_mode))
15932       return log_scripterror(r, conf, FORBIDDEN,
15933           APLOG_NOERRNO,
15934                   "attempt to invoke directory
15935                       as script");
15936       if (!ap_suexec_enabled) {
15937       if (!ap_can_exec(&r->finfo))
15938           return log_scripterror(r, conf, FORBIDDEN,
15939               APLOG_NOERRNO,
15940                   "file permissions deny server
15941                       execution");
15942       }
15943
15944       if ((retval = ap_setup_client_block(r,
15945           REQUEST_CHUNKED_ERROR)))
15946       return retval;
15947
15948       ap_add_common_vars(r);
15949       cld.argv0 = argv0;
15950       cld.r = r;
15951       cld.nph = nph;
15952       cld.debug = conf->logname ? 1 : 0;
15953
15954  #ifdef CHARSET_EBCDIC
15955       /* XXX:@@@ Is the generated/included output ALWAYS
```

```
15956              * in text/ebcdic format?
15957             /* Or must we check the Content-Type first? */
15958             ap_bsetflag(r->connection->client, B_EBCDIC2ASCII, 1);
15959    #endif /*CHARSET_EBCDIC*/
15960
15961             /*
15962              * we spawn out of r->main if it's there so that
15963              * we can avoid waiting for free_proc_chain to
15964              * cleanup in the middle of an SSI request -djg
15965              */
15966             if (!ap_bspawn_child(r->main ? r->main->pool :
15967                     r->pool, cgi_child,
15968                     (void *) &cld, kill_after_timeout,
15969                     &script_out, &script_in, &script_err)) {
15970             ap_log_rerror(APLOG_MARK, APLOG_ERR, r,
15971                     "couldn't spawn child process: %s",
15972                         r->filename);
15973             return HTTP_INTERNAL_SERVER_ERROR;
15974             }
15975
15976             /* Transfer any put/post args, CERN style... */
15977              * Note that we already ignore SIGPIPE in the
15978              * core server.
15979              */
15980
15981             if (ap_should_client_block(r)) {
15982             int dbsize, len_read;
15983
15984             if (conf->logname) {
15985                 dbuf = ap_pcalloc(r->pool, conf->bufbytes + 1);
15986                 dbpos = 0;
15987             }
15988
15989             ap_hard_timeout("copy script args", r);
15990
15991             while ((len_read =
15992                 ap_get_client_block(r, argsbuffer,
15993                     HUGE_STRING_LEN)) > 0) {
15994                 if (conf->logname) {
15995                 if ((dbpos + len_read) > conf->bufbytes) {
15996                     dbsize = conf->bufbytes - dbpos;
15997                 }
15998                 else {
15999                     dbsize = len_read;
16000                 }
```

```
16001                 memcpy(dbuf + dbpos, argsbuffer, dbsize);
16002                 dbpos += dbsize;
16003                 }
16004                 ap_reset_timeout(r);
16005                 if (ap_bwrite(script_out, argsbuffer, len_read)
16006                     < len_read) {
16007                 /* silly script stopped reading, soak up
16008                  * remaining message */
16009                 while (ap_get_client_block(r, argsbuffer,
16010                     HUGE_STRING_LEN) > 0) {
16011                     /* dump it */
16012                 }
16013                 break;
16014                 }
16015             }
16016
16017             ap_bflush(script_out);
16018
16019             ap_kill_timeout(r);
16020             }
16021
16022             ap_bclose(script_out);
16023
16024             /* Handle script return... */
16025             if (script_in && !nph) {
16026             const char *location;
16027             char sbuf[MAX_STRING_LEN];
16028             int ret;
16029
16030             if ((ret = ap_scan_script_header_err_buff(r,
16031                 script_in, sbuf))) {
16032                 return log_script(r, conf, ret, dbuf, sbuf,
16033                     script_in, script_err);
16034             }
16035
16036    #ifdef CHARSET_EBCDIC
16037             /* Now check the Content-Type to decide if
16038              conversion is needed */
16039             ap_checkconv(r);
16040    #endif /*CHARSET_EBCDIC*/
16041
16042             location = ap_table_get(r->headers_out,
16043                 "Location");
16044
16045             if (location && location[0] == '/' &&
```

```
16046            r->status == 200) {
16047
16048            /* Soak up all the script output */
16049            ap_hard_timeout("read from script", r);
16050            while (ap_bgets(argsbuffer, HUGE_STRING_LEN,
16051                script_in) > 0) {
16052             continue;
16053            }
16054            while (ap_bgets(argsbuffer, HUGE_STRING_LEN,
16055                script_err) > 0) {
16056             continue;
16057            }
16058            ap_kill_timeout(r);
16059
16060
16061            /* This redirect needs to be a GET no matter
16062             * what the original method was.
16063             */
16064            r->method = ap_pstrdup(r->pool, "GET");
16065            r->method_number = M_GET;
16066
16067            /* We already read the message body (if any),
16068             * so don't allow the redirected request
16069             * to think it has one.  We can ignore
16070             * Transfer-Encoding, since we used
16071             * REQUEST_CHUNKED_ERROR.
16072             */
16073            ap_table_unset(r->headers_in,
16074                 "Content-Length");
16075
16076            ap_internal_redirect_handler(location, r);
16077            return OK;
16078        }
16079        else if (location && r->status == 200) {
16080            /* XX Note that if a script wants to
16081             * produce its own Redirect body, it
16082             * now has to explicitly *say* "Status: 302"
16083             */
16084            return REDIRECT;
16085        }
16086
16087        ap_send_http_header(r);
16088        if (!r->header_only) {
16089            ap_send_fb(script_in, r);
16090        }
```

```
16091        ap_bclose(script_in);
16092
16093        ap_soft_timeout("soaking script stderr", r);
16094        while (ap_bgets(argsbuffer, HUGE_STRING_LEN,
16095            script_err) > 0) {
16096            continue;
16097        }
16098        ap_kill_timeout(r);
16099        ap_bclose(script_err);
16100    }
16101
16102    if (script_in && nph) {
16103        ap_send_fb(script_in, r);
16104    }
16105
16106    return OK;
16107 /* NOT r->status, even if it has changed. */
16108 }
16109
16110 static const handler_rec cgi_handlers[] =
16111 {
16112    {CGI_MAGIC_TYPE, cgi_handler},
16113    {"cgi-script", cgi_handler},
16114    {NULL}
16115 };
16116
16117 module MODULE_VAR_EXPORT cgi_module =
16118 {
16119    STANDARD_MODULE_STUFF,
16120    NULL,                /* initializer */
16121    NULL,                /* dir config creater */
16122    NULL,
16123    /* dir merger -- default is to override */
16124    create_cgi_config,      /* server config */
16125    merge_cgi_config,       /* merge server config */
16126    cgi_cmds,               /* command table */
16127    cgi_handlers,           /* handlers */
16128    NULL,                /* filename translation */
16129    NULL,                /* check_user_id */
16130    NULL,                /* check auth */
16131    NULL,                /* check access */
16132    NULL,                /* type_checker */
16133    NULL,                /* fixups */
16134    NULL,                /* logger */
16135    NULL,                /* header parser */
16136    NULL,                /* child_init */
```

```
16137        NULL,              /* child_exit */
16138        NULL               /* post read-request */
16139    };
```

p 447 **mod_digest.c**

```
16140   #include "httpd.h"
16141   #include "http_config.h"
16142   #include "http_core.h"
16143   #include "http_log.h"
16144   #include "http_protocol.h"
16145   #include "util_md5.h"
16146
16147   typedef struct digest_config_struct {
16148       char *pwfile;
16149   } digest_config_rec;
16150
16151   typedef struct digest_header_struct {
16152       char *username;
16153       char *realm;
16154       char *nonce;
16155       char *requested_uri;
16156       char *digest;
16157   } digest_header_rec;
16158
16159   static void *create_digest_dir_config(pool *p,
16160        char *d)
16161   {
16162       return ap_pcalloc(p, sizeof(digest_config_rec));
16163   }
16164
16165   static const char *set_digest_slot(cmd_parms *cmd,
16166        void *offset, char *f, char *t)
16167   {
16168       if (t && strcmp(t, "standard"))
16169        return ap_pstrcat(cmd->pool, "Invalid auth file
16170            type: ", t, NULL);
16171
16172       return ap_set_string_slot(cmd, offset, f);
16173   }
16174
16175   static const command_rec digest_cmds[] =
16176   {
16177       {"AuthDigestFile", set_digest_slot,
16178     (void *) XtOffsetOf(digest_config_rec, pwfile),
```

```
16179            OR_AUTHCFG, TAKE12, NULL},
16180       {NULL}
16181   };
16182
16183   module MODULE_VAR_EXPORT digest_module;
16184
16185   static char *get_hash(request_rec *r, char *user,
16186       char *auth_pwfile)
16187   {
16188       configfile_t *f;
16189       char l[MAX_STRING_LEN];
16190       const char *rpw;
16191       char *w, *x;
16192
16193       if (!(f = ap_pcfg_openfile(r->pool, auth_pwfile))) {
16194        ap_log_rerror(APLOG_MARK, APLOG_ERR, r,
16195                "Could not open password file: %s",
16196                    auth_pwfile);
16197        return NULL;
16198       }
16199       while (!(ap_cfg_getline(l, MAX_STRING_LEN, f))) {
16200        if ((l[0] == '#') || (!l[0]))
16201            continue;
16202        rpw = l;
16203        w = ap_getword(r->pool, &rpw, ':');
16204        x = ap_getword(r->pool, &rpw, ':');
16205
16206        if (x && w && !strcmp(user, w) &&
16207            !strcmp(ap_auth_name(r), x)) {
16208            ap_cfg_closefile(f);
16209            return ap_pstrdup(r->pool, rpw);
16210        }
16211       }
16212       ap_cfg_closefile(f);
16213       return NULL;
16214   }
16215
16216   /* Parse the Authorization header, if it exists */
16217
16218   static int get_digest_rec(request_rec *r,
16219       digest_header_rec * response)
16220   {
16221       const char *auth_line = ap_table_get(r->headers_in,
16222                    r->proxyreq ? "Proxy-Authorization"
16223                            : "Authorization");
```

```
16224      int l;
16225      int s, vk = 0, vv = 0;
16226      const char *t;
16227      char *key, *value;
16228      const char *scheme;
16229
16230      if (!(t = ap_auth_type(r)) || strcasecmp(t,
16231          "Digest"))
16232        return DECLINED;
16233
16234      if (!ap_auth_name(r)) {
16235        ap_log_rerror(APLOG_MARK,
16236            APLOG_NOERRNO|APLOG_ERR, r,
16237              "need AuthName: %s", r->uri);
16238        return SERVER_ERROR;
16239      }
16240
16241      if (!auth_line) {
16242        ap_note_digest_auth_failure(r);
16243        return AUTH_REQUIRED;
16244      }
16245
16246      if (strcasecmp(scheme = ap_getword_white(r->pool,
16247          &auth_line), "Digest")) {
16248        /* Client tried to authenticate using wrong
16249         * auth scheme */
16250        ap_log_error(APLOG_MARK,
16251            APLOG_NOERRNO|APLOG_ERR, r->server,
16252              "client used wrong authentication
16253                    scheme: %s for %s",
16254              scheme, r->uri);
16255        ap_note_digest_auth_failure(r);
16256        return AUTH_REQUIRED;
16257      }
16258
16259      l = strlen(auth_line);
16260
16261      /* Note we don't allocate l + 1 bytes for these
16262       * deliberately, because there has to be at least
16263       * one '=' character for either of these two
16264       * new strings to be terminated.  That takes care
16265       * of the need for +1.
16266       */
16267      key = ap_palloc(r->pool, l);
16268      value = ap_palloc(r->pool, l);
16269
16270      /* There's probably a better way to do this, but
16271       * for the time being... */
16272
16273 #define D_KEY 0
16274 #define D_VALUE 1
16275 #define D_STRING 2
16276 #define D_EXIT -1
16277
16278      s = D_KEY;
16279      while (s != D_EXIT) {
16280        switch (s) {
16281        case D_STRING:
16282          if (auth_line[0] == '\"') {
16283            s = D_VALUE;
16284          }
16285          else {
16286            value[vv] = auth_line[0];
16287            vv++;
16288          }
16289          auth_line++;
16290          break;
16291
16292        case D_VALUE:
16293          if (ap_isalnum(auth_line[0])) {
16294            value[vv] = auth_line[0];
16295            vv++;
16296          }
16297          else if (auth_line[0] == '\"') {
16298            s = D_STRING;
16299          }
16300          else {
16301            value[vv] = '\0';
16302
16303            if (!strcasecmp(key, "username"))
16304                response->username = ap_pstrdup(r->pool,
16305                    value);
16306            else if (!strcasecmp(key, "realm"))
16307                response->realm = ap_pstrdup(r->pool,
16308                    value);
16309            else if (!strcasecmp(key, "nonce"))
16310                response->nonce = ap_pstrdup(r->pool,
16311                    value);
16312            else if (!strcasecmp(key, "uri"))
16313                response->requested_uri =
```

```
16314                ap_pstrdup(r->pool, value);
16315            else if (!strcasecmp(key, "response"))
16316                response->digest = ap_pstrdup(r->pool,
16317                    value);
16318
16319            vv = 0;
16320            s = D_KEY;
16321        }
16322        auth_line++;
16323        break;
16324
16325    case D_KEY:
16326        if (ap_isalnum(auth_line[0])) {
16327            key[vk] = auth_line[0];
16328            vk++;
16329        }
16330        else if (auth_line[0] == '=') {
16331            key[vk] = '\0';
16332            vk = 0;
16333            s = D_VALUE;
16334        }
16335        auth_line++;
16336        break;
16337    }
16338
16339    if (auth_line[-1] == '\0')
16340        s = D_EXIT;
16341    }
16342
16343    if (!response->username || !response->realm ||
16344        !response->nonce ||
16345    !response->requested_uri || !response->digest) {
16346    ap_note_digest_auth_failure(r);
16347    return AUTH_REQUIRED;
16348    }
16349
16350    r->connection->user = response->username;
16351    r->connection->ap_auth_type = "Digest";
16352
16353    return OK;
16354 }
16355
16356 /* The actual MD5 code... whee */
16357
16358 static char *find_digest(request_rec *r,
16359                digest_header_rec * h, char *a1)
16360 {
16361    return ap_md5(r->pool,
16362            (unsigned char *)ap_pstrcat(r->pool, a1,
16363                ":", h->nonce, ":",
16364                    ap_md5(r->pool,
16365                (unsigned char *)ap_pstrcat(r->pool,
16366                    r->method, ":",
16367                    h->requested_uri, NULL)),
16368                    NULL));
16369 }
16370
16371 /* These functions return 0 if client is OK, and
16372  * proper error status if not... either AUTH_REQUIRED,
16373  * if we made a check, and it failed, or
16374  * SERVER_ERROR, if things are so totally confused
16375  * that we couldn't figure out how to tell if
16376  * the client is authorized or not.
16377  *
16378  * If they return DECLINED, and all other modules
16379  * also decline, that's treated by the server
16380  * core as a configuration error, logged and
16381  * reported as such.
16382  */
16383
16384 /* Determine user ID, and check if it really is
16385  * that user, for HTTP basic authentication...
16386  */
16387
16388 static int authenticate_digest_user(request_rec *r)
16389 {
16390    digest_config_rec *sec =
16391    (digest_config_rec *)
16392        ap_get_module_config(r->per_dir_config,
16393                    &digest_module);
16394    digest_header_rec *response =
16395        ap_pcalloc(r->pool, sizeof(digest_header_rec));
16396    conn_rec *c = r->connection;
16397    char *a1;
16398    int res;
16399
16400    if ((res = get_digest_rec(r, response)))
16401    return res;
16402
16403    if (!sec->pwfile)
```

```
16404        return DECLINED;
16405
16406        if (!(a1 = get_hash(r, c->user, sec->pwfile))) {
16407         ap_log_rerror(APLOG_MARK,
16408            APLOG_NOERRNO|APLOG_ERR, r,
16409              "user %s not found: %s", c->user, r->uri);
16410         ap_note_digest_auth_failure(r);
16411         return AUTH_REQUIRED;
16412        }
16413        if (strcmp(response->digest, find_digest(r,
16414            response, a1))) {
16415         ap_log_rerror(APLOG_MARK,
16416            APLOG_NOERRNO|APLOG_ERR, r,
16417              "user %s: password mismatch: %s",
16418                 c->user, r->uri);
16419         ap_note_digest_auth_failure(r);
16420         return AUTH_REQUIRED;
16421        }
16422        return OK;
16423    }
16424
16425    /* Checking ID */
16426
16427    static int digest_check_auth(request_rec *r)
16428    {
16429        char *user = r->connection->user;
16430        int m = r->method_number;
16431        int method_restricted = 0;
16432        register int x;
16433        const char *t;
16434        char *w;
16435        const array_header *reqs_arr;
16436        require_line *reqs;
16437
16438        if (!(t = ap_auth_type(r)) ||
16439            strcasecmp(t, "Digest"))
16440         return DECLINED;
16441
16442        reqs_arr = ap_requires(r);
16443        /* If there is no "requires" directive,
16444         * then any user will do.
16445         */
16446        if (!reqs_arr)
16447         return OK;
16448        reqs = (require_line *) reqs_arr->elts;
```

```
16449
16450        for (x = 0; x < reqs_arr->nelts; x++) {
16451
16452         if (!(reqs[x].method_mask & (1 << m)))
16453             continue;
16454
16455         method_restricted = 1;
16456
16457         t = reqs[x].requirement;
16458         w = ap_getword_white(r->pool, &t);
16459         if (!strcmp(w, "valid-user"))
16460             return OK;
16461         else if (!strcmp(w, "user")) {
16462             while (t[0]) {
16463              w = ap_getword_conf(r->pool, &t);
16464              if (!strcmp(user, w))
16465                 return OK;
16466             }
16467         }
16468         else
16469             return DECLINED;
16470        }
16471
16472        if (!method_restricted)
16473         return OK;
16474
16475        ap_note_digest_auth_failure(r);
16476        return AUTH_REQUIRED;
16477    }
16478
16479    module MODULE_VAR_EXPORT digest_module =
16480    {
16481        STANDARD_MODULE_STUFF,
16482        NULL,                /* initializer */
16483        create_digest_dir_config,
16484        /* dir config creater */
16485        NULL,
16486        /* dir merger -- default is to override */
16487        NULL,                /* server config */
16488        NULL,                /* merge server config */
16489        digest_cmds,          /* command table */
16490        NULL,            /* handlers */
16491        NULL,            /* filename translation */
16492        authenticate_digest_user,     /* check_user_id */
16493        digest_check_auth,          /* check auth */
```

```
16494        NULL,              /* check access */
16495        NULL,              /* type_checker */
16496        NULL,              /* fixups */
16497        NULL,              /* logger */
16498        NULL,              /* header parser */
16499        NULL,              /* child_init */
16500        NULL,              /* child_exit */
16501        NULL               /* post read-request */
16502    };
```

p 507 mod_dir.c

```
16503    #include "httpd.h"
16504    #include "http_config.h"
16505    #include "http_core.h"
16506    #include "http_request.h"
16507    #include "http_protocol.h"
16508    #include "http_log.h"
16509    #include "http_main.h"
16510    #include "util_script.h"
16511
16512    module MODULE_VAR_EXPORT dir_module;
16513
16514    typedef struct dir_config_struct {
16515    array_header *index_names;
16516    } dir_config_rec;
16517
16518    #define DIR_CMD_PERMS OR_INDEXES
16519
16520    static const char *add_index(cmd_parms *cmd,
16521         void *dummy, char *arg)
16522    {
16523    dir_config_rec *d = dummy;
16524
16525    if (!d->index_names) {
16526    d->index_names = ap_make_array(cmd->pool, 2,
16527     sizeof(char *));
16528    }
16529    *(char **)ap_push_array(d->index_names) = arg;
16530    return NULL;
16531    }
16532
16533    static const command_rec dir_cmds[] =
16534    {
16535    {"DirectoryIndex", add_index, NULL,
16536    DIR_CMD_PERMS, ITERATE,
```

```
16537    "a list of file names"},
16538    {NULL}
16539    };
16540
16541    static void *create_dir_config(pool *p, char *dummy)
16542    {
16543    dir_config_rec *new =
16544    (dir_config_rec *) ap_pcalloc(p,
16545        sizeof(dir_config_rec));
16546
16547    new->index_names = NULL;
16548    return (void *) new;
16549    }
16550
16551    static void *merge_dir_configs(pool *p,
16552        void *basev, void *addv)
16553    {
16554    dir_config_rec *new = (dir_config_rec *)
16555        ap_pcalloc(p, sizeof(dir_config_rec));
16556    dir_config_rec *base = (dir_config_rec *) basev;
16557    dir_config_rec *add = (dir_config_rec *) addv;
16558
16559    new->index_names = add->index_names ? add->index_names
16560        : base->index_names;
16561    return new;
16562    }
16563
16564    static int handle_dir(request_rec *r)
16565    {
16566    dir_config_rec *d =
16567     (dir_config_rec *)
16568        ap_get_module_config(r->per_dir_config,
16569    &dir_module);
16570    char *dummy_ptr[1];
16571    char **names_ptr;
16572    int num_names;
16573    int error_notfound = 0;
16574
16575    if (r->uri[0] == '\0' || r->uri[strlen(r->uri) - 1]
16576        != '/') {
16577    char *ifile;
16578    if (r->args != NULL)
16579    ifile = ap_pstrcat(r->pool, ap_escape_uri(r->pool,
16580        r->uri),
16581    "/", "?", r->args, NULL);
```

```
16582   else
16583   ifile = ap_pstrcat(r->pool, ap_escape_uri(r->pool,
16584       r->uri),
16585   "/", NULL);
16586
16587   ap_table_setn(r->headers_out, "Location",
16588   ap_construct_url(r->pool, ifile, r));
16589   return HTTP_MOVED_PERMANENTLY;
16590   }
16591
16592   /* KLUDGE -- make the sub_req lookups happen in
16593       the right directory. Fixing this in the sub_req_lookup
16594   functions themselves is difficult, and would
16595   probably break virtual includes...
16596   */
16597
16598   if (r->filename[strlen(r->filename) - 1] != '/') {
16599   r->filename = ap_pstrcat(r->pool, r->filename, "/",
16600       NULL);
16601   }
16602
16603   if (d->index_names) {
16604   names_ptr = (char **)d->index_names->elts;
16605   num_names = d->index_names->nelts;
16606   }
16607   else {
16608   dummy_ptr[0] = DEFAULT_INDEX;
16609   names_ptr = dummy_ptr;
16610   num_names = 1;
16611   }
16612
16613   for (; num_names; ++names_ptr, --num_names) {
16614   char *name_ptr = *names_ptr;
16615   request_rec *rr = ap_sub_req_lookup_uri(name_ptr, r);
16616
16617   if (rr->status == HTTP_OK && rr->finfo.st_mode != 0) {
16618   char *new_uri = ap_escape_uri(r->pool, rr->uri);
16619
16620   if (rr->args != NULL)
16621   new_uri = ap_pstrcat(r->pool, new_uri, "?", rr->args,
16622       NULL);
16623   else if (r->args != NULL)
16624   new_uri = ap_pstrcat(r->pool, new_uri, "?", r->args,
16625       NULL);
16626
16627   ap_destroy_sub_req(rr);
16628   ap_internal_redirect(new_uri, r);
16629   return OK;
16630   }
16631
16632   /* If the request returned a redirect, propagate it
16633    * to the client */
16634
16635   if (ap_is_HTTP_REDIRECT(rr->status) ||
16636   (rr->status == HTTP_NOT_ACCEPTABLE
16637       && num_names == 1)) {
16638
16639   ap_pool_join(r->pool, rr->pool);
16640   error_notfound = rr->status;
16641   r->notes = ap_overlay_tables(r->pool, r->notes,
16642       rr->notes);
16643   r->headers_out = ap_overlay_tables(r->pool,
16644       r->headers_out,
16645   rr->headers_out);
16646   r->err_headers_out = ap_overlay_tables(r->pool,
16647       r->err_headers_out,
16648   rr->err_headers_out);
16649   return error_notfound;
16650   }
16651
16652   /* If the request returned something other than 404
16653   (or 200), it means the module encountered some sort of
16654   problem. To be secure, we should return the error,
16655   rather than create along a (possibly unsafe)
16656   directory index.
16657   *
16658   So we store the error, and if none of the listed
16659   files exist, we return the last error response we
16660   got, instead of a directory listing.
16661   */
16662   if (rr->status && rr->status != HTTP_NOT_FOUND
16663       && rr->status != HTTP_OK)
16664   error_notfound = rr->status;
16665
16666   ap_destroy_sub_req(rr);
16667   }
16668
16669   if (error_notfound)
16670   return error_notfound;
16671
```

```
16672   if (r->method_number != M_GET)
16673   return DECLINED;
16674
16675   /* nothing for us to do, pass on through */
16676
16677   return DECLINED;
16678   }
16679
16680
16681   static const handler_rec dir_handlers[] =
16682   {
16683   {DIR_MAGIC_TYPE, handle_dir},
16684   {NULL}
16685   };
16686
16687   module MODULE_VAR_EXPORT dir_module =
16688   {
16689   STANDARD_MODULE_STUFF,
16690   NULL,                    /* initializer */
16691   create_dir_config,       /* dir config creater */
16692   merge_dir_configs,
16693   /* dir merger -- default is to override */
16694   NULL,                    /* server config */
16695   NULL,                    /* merge server config */
16696   dir_cmds,                /* command table */
16697   dir_handlers,            /* handlers */
16698   NULL,                    /* filename translation */
16699   NULL,                    /* check_user_id */
16700   NULL,                    /* check auth */
16701   NULL,                    /* check access */
16702   NULL,                    /* type_checker */
16703   NULL,                    /* fixups */
16704   NULL,                    /* logger */
16705   NULL,                    /* header parser */
16706   NULL,                    /* child_init */
16707   NULL,                    /* child_exit */
16708   NULL                     /* post read-request */
16709   };
```

▶ mod_env.c
p 493

```
16710   #include "httpd.h"
16711   #include "http_config.h"
16712
16713   typedef struct {
16714   table *vars;
16715   char *unsetenv;
16716   int vars_present;
16717   } env_server_config_rec;
16718
16719   module MODULE_VAR_EXPORT env_module;
16720
16721   static void *create_env_server_config
16722        (pool *p, server_rec *dummy)
16723   {
16724   env_server_config_rec *new =
16725   (env_server_config_rec *) ap_palloc(p, sizeof
16726        (env_server_config_rec));
16727   new->vars = ap_make_table(p, 50);
16728   new->unsetenv = "";
16729   new->vars_present = 0;
16730   return (void *) new;
16731   }
16732
16733   static void *merge_env_server_configs
16734        (pool *p, void *basev, void *addv)
16735   {
16736   env_server_config_rec *base =
16737        (env_server_config_rec *) basev;
16738   env_server_config_rec *add =
16739        (env_server_config_rec *) addv;
16740   env_server_config_rec *new =
16741   (env_server_config_rec *) ap_palloc
16742        (p, sizeof(env_server_config_rec));
16743
16744   table *new_table;
16745   table_entry *elts;
16746   array_header *arr;
16747
16748   int i;
16749   const char *uenv, *unset;
16750
16751   /*
16752   new_table = copy_table( p, base->vars );
16753   foreach $element ( @add->vars ) {
16754   table_set( new_table, $element.key, $element.val );
16755   };
16756   foreach $unsetenv ( @UNSETENV ) {
16757   table_unset( new_table, $unsetenv );
16758   }
16759   */
```

```
16760
16761    new_table = ap_copy_table(p, base->vars);
16762
16763    arr = ap_table_elts(add->vars);
16764    elts = (table_entry *)arr->elts;
16765
16766    for (i = 0; i < arr->nelts; ++i) {
16767    ap_table_setn(new_table, elts[i].key, elts[i].val);
16768    }
16769
16770    unset = add->unsetenv;
16771    uenv = ap_getword_conf(p, &unset);
16772    while (uenv[0] != '\0') {
16773    ap_table_unset(new_table, uenv);
16774    uenv = ap_getword_conf(p, &unset);
16775    }
16776
16777    new->vars = new_table;
16778
16779    new->vars_present = base->vars_present ||
16780        add->vars_present;
16781
16782    return new;
16783    }
16784
16785    static const char *add_env_module_vars_passed
16786        (cmd_parms *cmd, char *struct_ptr,
16787    const char *arg)
16788    {
16789    env_server_config_rec *sconf =
16790    ap_get_module_config(cmd->server->module_config,
16791        &env_module);
16792    table *vars = sconf->vars;
16793    char *env_var;
16794    char *name_ptr;
16795
16796    while (*arg) {
16797    name_ptr = ap_getword_conf(cmd->pool, &arg);
16798    env_var = getenv(name_ptr);
16799    if (env_var != NULL) {
16800    sconf->vars_present = 1;
16801    ap_table_setn(vars, name_ptr, ap_pstrdup
16802        (cmd->pool, env_var));
16803    }
16804    }
```

```
16805    return NULL;
16806    }
16807
16808    static const char *add_env_module_vars_set
16809        (cmd_parms *cmd, char *struct_ptr,
16810    const char *arg)
16811    {
16812    env_server_config_rec *sconf =
16813    ap_get_module_config(cmd->server->module_config,
16814        &env_module);
16815    table *vars = sconf->vars;
16816    char *name, *value;
16817
16818    name = ap_getword_conf(cmd->pool, &arg);
16819    value = ap_getword_conf(cmd->pool, &arg);
16820
16821    /* name is mandatory, value is optional.
16822        no value means
16823    set the variable to an empty string
16824    */
16825
16826
16827    if ((*name == '\0') || (*arg != '\0')) {
16828    return "SetEnv takes one or two arguments.
16829        An environment variable name and an
16830        optional value to pass to CGI.";
16831    }
16832
16833    sconf->vars_present = 1;
16834    ap_table_setn(vars, name, value);
16835
16836    return NULL;
16837    }
16838
16839    static const char *add_env_module_vars_unset
16840        (cmd_parms *cmd, char *struct_ptr,
16841    char *arg)
16842    {
16843    env_server_config_rec *sconf =
16844    ap_get_module_config(cmd->server->
16845        module_config, &env_module);
16846    sconf->unsetenv = sconf->unsetenv ?
16847    ap_pstrcat(cmd->pool, sconf->
16848        unsetenv, " ", arg, NULL) :
16849    arg;
```

```
16850   return NULL;
16851   }
16852
16853   static const command_rec env_module_cmds[] =
16854   {
16855   {"PassEnv", add_env_module_vars_passed, NULL,
16856   RSRC_CONF, RAW_ARGS, "a list of environment
16857        variables to pass to CGI."},
16858   {"SetEnv", add_env_module_vars_set, NULL,
16859   RSRC_CONF, RAW_ARGS, "an environment variable
16860        name and a value to pass to CGI."},
16861   {"UnsetEnv", add_env_module_vars_unset, NULL,
16862   RSRC_CONF, RAW_ARGS, "a list of variables to
16863        remove from the CGI environment."},
16864   {NULL},
16865   };
16866
16867   static int fixup_env_module(request_rec *r)
16868   {
16869   table *e = r->subprocess_env;
16870   server_rec *s = r->server;
16871   env_server_config_rec *sconf =
16872        ap_get_module_config(s->module_config,
16873   &env_module);
16874   table *vars = sconf->vars;
16875
16876   if (!sconf->vars_present)
16877   return DECLINED;
16878
16879   r->subprocess_env =
16880        ap_overlay_tables(r->pool, e, vars);
16881
16882   return OK;
16883   }
16884
16885   module MODULE_VAR_EXPORT env_module =
16886   {
16887   STANDARD_MODULE_STUFF,
16888   NULL,                     /* initializer */
16889   NULL,                     /* dir config creater */
16890   NULL,
16891   /* dir merger -- default is to override */
16892   create_env_server_config, /* server config */
16893   merge_env_server_configs,
16894   /* merge server configs */
16895   env_module_cmds,          /* command table */
16896   NULL,                     /* handlers */
16897   NULL,                     /* filename translation */
16898   NULL,                     /* check_user_id */
16899   NULL,                     /* check auth */
16900   NULL,                     /* check access */
16901   NULL,                     /* type_checker */
16902   fixup_env_module,         /* fixups */
16903   NULL,                     /* logger */
16904   NULL,                     /* header parser */
16905   NULL,                     /* child_init */
16906   NULL,                     /* child_exit */
16907   NULL                      /* post read-request */
16908   };
```

▶ p 502 mod_expires.c

```
16909   #include <ctype.h>
16910   #include "httpd.h"
16911   #include "http_config.h"
16912   #include "http_log.h"
16913
16914   typedef struct {
16915       int active;
16916       char *expiresdefault;
16917       table *expiresbytype;
16918   } expires_dir_config;
16919
16920   /* from mod_dir, why is this alias used?
16921    */
16922   #define DIR_CMD_PERMS OR_INDEXES
16923
16924   #define ACTIVE_ON       1
16925   #define ACTIVE_OFF      0
16926   #define ACTIVE_DONTCARE 2
16927
16928   module MODULE_VAR_EXPORT expires_module;
16929
16930   static void *create_dir_expires_config(pool *p,
16931       char *dummy)
16932   {
16933       expires_dir_config *new =
16934       (expires_dir_config *) ap_pcalloc(p,
16935           sizeof(expires_dir_config));
16936       new->active = ACTIVE_DONTCARE;
16937       new->expiresdefault = "";
16938       new->expiresbytype = ap_make_table(p, 4);
```

```
16939        return (void *) new;
16940    }
16941
16942    static const char *set_expiresactive(cmd_parms *cmd,
16943        expires_dir_config * dir_config, int arg)
16944    {
16945        /* if we're here at all it's because someone
16946         * explicitly set the active flag
16947         */
16948        dir_config->active = ACTIVE_ON;
16949        if (arg == 0) {
16950            dir_config->active = ACTIVE_OFF;
16951        };
16952        return NULL;
16953    }
16954
16955    /* check_code() parse 'code' and return NULL or an error
16956     * response string.  If we return NULL then real_code
16957     * contains code converted to the cnnnn format.
16958     */
16959    static char *check_code(pool *p, const char *code,
16960        char **real_code)
16961    {
16962        char *word;
16963        char base = 'X';
16964        int modifier = 0;
16965        int num = 0;
16966        int factor = 0;
16967
16968        /* 0.0.4 compatibility? 
16969         */
16970        if ((code[0] == 'A') || (code[0] == 'M')) {
16971            *real_code = (char *)code;
16972            return NULL;
16973        };
16974
16975        /* <base> [plus] {<num> <type>}*
16976         */
16977
16978        /* <base>
16979         */
16980        word = ap_getword_conf(p, &code);
16981        if (!strncasecmp(word, "now", 1) ||
16982            !strncasecmp(word, "access", 1)) {
16983            base = 'A';
16984        }
16985        else if (!strncasecmp(word, "modification", 1)) {
16986            base = 'M';
16987        }
16988        else {
16989            return ap_pstrcat(p, "bad expires code,
16990                unrecognised <base> '",
16991                            word, "'", NULL);
16992        };
16993
16994        /* [plus]
16995         */
16996        word = ap_getword_conf(p, &code);
16997        if (!strncasecmp(word, "plus", 1)) {
16998            word = ap_getword_conf(p, &code);
16999        };
17000
17001        /* {<num> <type>}*
17002         */
17003        while (word[0]) {
17004            /* <num>
17005             */
17006            if (ap_isdigit(word[0])) {
17007                num = atoi(word);
17008            }
17009            else {
17010                return ap_pstrcat(p, "bad expires code,
17011                    numeric value expected <num> '",
17012                                word, "'", NULL);
17013            };
17014
17015            /* <type>
17016             */
17017            word = ap_getword_conf(p, &code);
17018            if (word[0]) {
17019                /* do nothing */
17020            }
17021            else {
17022                return ap_pstrcat(p, "bad expires code,
17023                    missing <type>", NULL);
17024            };
17025
17026            factor = 0;
17027            if (!strncasecmp(word, "years", 1)) {
17028                factor = 60 * 60 * 24 * 365;
```

```
17029                }
17030            else if (!strncasecmp(word, "months", 2)) {
17031                factor = 60 * 60 * 24 * 30;
17032            }
17033            else if (!strncasecmp(word, "weeks", 1)) {
17034                factor = 60 * 60 * 24 * 7;
17035            }
17036            else if (!strncasecmp(word, "days", 1)) {
17037                factor = 60 * 60 * 24;
17038            }
17039            else if (!strncasecmp(word, "hours", 1)) {
17040                factor = 60 * 60;
17041            }
17042            else if (!strncasecmp(word, "minutes", 2)) {
17043                factor = 60;
17044            }
17045            else if (!strncasecmp(word, "seconds", 1)) {
17046                factor = 1;
17047            }
17048            else {
17049                return ap_pstrcat(p, "bad expires code,
17050                    unrecognised <type>",
17051                        "'", word, "'", NULL);
17052            };
17053
17054            modifier = modifier + factor * num;
17055
17056            /* next <num>
17057             */
17058            word = ap_getword_conf(p, &code);
17059        };
17060
17061        *real_code = ap_psprintf(p, "%c%d", base, modifier);
17062
17063        return NULL;
17064    }
17065
17066    static const char *set_expiresbytype(cmd_parms *cmd,
17067        expires_dir_config * dir_config, char *mime,
17068        char *code)
17069    {
17070        char *response, *real_code;
17071
17072        if ((response = check_code(cmd->pool, code,
17073            &real_code)) == NULL) {
17074            ap_table_setn(dir_config->expiresbytype,
17075                mime, real_code);
17076            return NULL;
17077        };
17078        return ap_pstrcat(cmd->pool,
17079                    "'ExpiresByType ", mime, " ", code,
17080                    "': ", response, NULL);
17081    }
17082
17083    static const char *set_expiresdefault(cmd_parms *cmd,
17084        expires_dir_config * dir_config, char *code)
17085    {
17086        char *response, *real_code;
17087
17088        if ((response = check_code(cmd->pool, code,
17089            &real_code)) == NULL) {
17090            dir_config->expiresdefault = real_code;
17091            return NULL;
17092        };
17093        return ap_pstrcat(cmd->pool,
17094                    "'ExpiresDefault ", code, "': ",
17095                    response, NULL);
17096    }
17097
17098    static const command_rec expires_cmds[] =
17099    {
17100        {"ExpiresActive", set_expiresactive, NULL,
17101            DIR_CMD_PERMS, FLAG,
17102        "Limited to 'on' or 'off'"},
17103        {"ExpiresBytype", set_expiresbytype, NULL,
17104            DIR_CMD_PERMS, TAKE2,
17105        "a MIME type followed by an expiry date code"},
17106        {"ExpiresDefault", set_expiresdefault, NULL,
17107            DIR_CMD_PERMS, TAKE1,
17108        "an expiry date code"},
17109        {NULL}
17110    };
17111
17112    static void *merge_expires_dir_configs(pool *p,
17113        void *basev, void *addv)
17114    {
17115        expires_dir_config *new = (expires_dir_config *)
17116                ap_pcalloc(p, sizeof(expires_dir_config));
17117        expires_dir_config *base =
17118                (expires_dir_config *) basev;
```

```
17119        expires_dir_config *add =
17120            (expires_dir_config *) addv;
17121
17122        if (add->active == ACTIVE_DONTCARE) {
17123            new->active = base->active;
17124        }
17125        else {
17126            new->active = add->active;
17127        };
17128
17129        if (add->expiresdefault != '\0') {
17130            new->expiresdefault = add->expiresdefault;
17131        };
17132
17133        new->expiresbytype = ap_overlay_tables(p,
17134            add->expiresbytype,
17135                              base->expiresbytype);
17136        return new;
17137    }
17138
17139    static int add_expires(request_rec *r)
17140    {
17141        expires_dir_config *conf;
17142        char *code;
17143        time_t base;
17144        time_t additional;
17145        time_t expires;
17146        char age[20];
17147
17148        if (ap_is_HTTP_ERROR(r->status))
17149        /* Don't add Expires headers to errors */
17150            return DECLINED;
17151
17152        if (r->main != NULL)    /* Say no to subrequests */
17153            return DECLINED;
17154
17155        conf = (expires_dir_config *)
17156            ap_get_module_config(r->per_dir_config,
17157            &expires_module);
17158        if (conf == NULL) {
17159        ap_log_rerror(APLOG_MARK,
17160                APLOG_NOERRNO|APLOG_ERR, r,
17161                    "internal error: %s", r->filename);
17162            return SERVER_ERROR;
17163        };
```

```
17164
17165        if (conf->active != ACTIVE_ON)
17166            return DECLINED;
17167
17168        /* we perhaps could use the default_type(r) in
17169         * its place but that may be 2nd guesing the
17170         * desired configuration... calling table_get
17171         * with a NULL key will SEGV us
17172         *
17173         * I still don't know *why* r->content_type would
17174         * ever be NULL, this is possibly a result of
17175         * fixups being called in many different
17176         * places.  Fixups is probably the wrong place
17177         * to be doing all this work...  Bah.
17178         *
17179         * Changed as of 08.Jun.96 don't DECLINE, look
17180         * for an ExpiresDefault.
17181         */
17182        if (r->content_type == NULL)
17183            code = NULL;
17184        else
17185            code = (char *) ap_table_get(conf->expiresbytype,
17186                r->content_type);
17187
17188        if (code == NULL) {
17189            /* no expires defined for that type, is
17190             * there a default? */
17191            code = conf->expiresdefault;
17192
17193            if (code[0] == '\0')
17194                return OK;
17195        };
17196
17197        /* we have our code */
17198
17199        switch (code[0]) {
17200        case 'M':
17201        if (r->finfo.st_mode == 0) {
17202                /* file doesn't exist on disk, so we can't
17203                 * do anything based on modification time.
17204                 * Note that this does _not_ log an error.
17205                 */
17206            return DECLINED;
17207        }
17208            base = r->finfo.st_mtime;
```

```
17209            additional = atoi(&code[1]);
17210            break;
17211        case 'A':
17212            /* there's been some discussion and it's
17213             * possible that 'access time' will be
17214             * stored in request structure
17215             */
17216            base = r->request_time;
17217            additional = atoi(&code[1]);
17218            break;
17219        default:
17220            /* expecting the add_* routines to be
17221             * case-hardened this is just a
17222             * reminder that module is beta
17223             */
17224            ap_log_rerror(APLOG_MARK,
17225              APLOG_NOERRNO|APLOG_ERR, r,
17226                       "internal error: bad expires
17227                          code: %s", r->filename);
17228            return SERVER_ERROR;
17229        };
17230
17231        expires = base + additional;
17232        ap_snprintf(age, sizeof(age), "max-age=%d",
17233             (int) expires - (int) r->request_time);
17234        ap_table_setn(r->headers_out, "Cache-Control",
17235             ap_pstrdup(r->pool, age));
17236        tzset();
17237        /* redundant? called implicitly by localtime,
17238                               * at least under FreeBSD
17239                               */
17240        ap_table_setn(r->headers_out, "Expires",
17241             ap_gm_timestr_822(r->pool, expires));
17242        return OK;
17243    }
17244
17245    module MODULE_VAR_EXPORT expires_module =
17246    {
17247        STANDARD_MODULE_STUFF,
17248        NULL,                        /* initializer */
17249        create_dir_expires_config,   /* dir config creater */
17250        merge_expires_dir_configs,
17251        /* dir merger -- default is to override */
17252        NULL,                        /* server config */
17253        NULL,
17254        /* merge server configs */
17255        expires_cmds,                /* command table */
17256        NULL,                        /* handlers */
17257        NULL,
17258        /* filename translation */
17259        NULL,                        /* check_user_id */
17260        NULL,                        /* check auth */
17261        NULL,                        /* check access */
17262        NULL,                        /* type_checker */
17263        add_expires,                 /* fixups */
17264        NULL,                        /* logger */
17265        NULL,                        /* header parser */
17266        NULL,                        /* child_init */
17267        NULL,                        /* child_exit */
17268        NULL                         /* post read-request */
17269    };
```

▶ p 504 **mod_headers.c**

```
17270    #include "httpd.h"
17271    #include "http_config.h"
17272
17273    typedef enum {
17274        hdr_add = 'a',
17275        /* add header (could mean multiple hdrs) */
17276        hdr_set = 's',
17277        /* set (replace old value) */
17278        hdr_append = 'm',
17279        /* append (merge into any old value) */
17280        hdr_unset = 'u'
17281        /* unset header */
17282    } hdr_actions;
17283
17284    typedef struct {
17285        hdr_actions action;
17286        char *header;
17287        char *value;
17288    } header_entry;
17289
17290    /*
17291     * headers_conf is our per-module configuration. This
17292     * is used as both a per-dir and per-server config
17293     */
17294    typedef struct {
17295        array_header *headers;
```

```
17296  } headers_conf;
17297
17298  module MODULE_VAR_EXPORT headers_module;
17299
17300  static void *create_headers_config(pool *p,
17301      server_rec *s)
17302  {
17303      headers_conf *a =
17304      (headers_conf *) ap_pcalloc(p,
17305          sizeof(headers_conf));
17306
17307      a->headers = ap_make_array(p, 2,
17308          sizeof(header_entry));
17309      return a;
17310  }
17311
17312  static void *create_headers_dir_config(pool *p,
17313      char *d)
17314  {
17315      return (headers_conf *) create_headers_config(p,
17316          NULL);
17317  }
17318
17319  static void *merge_headers_config(pool *p, void *basev,
17320      void *overridesv)
17321  {
17322      headers_conf *a =
17323      (headers_conf *) ap_pcalloc(p,
17324          sizeof(headers_conf));
17325      headers_conf *base = (headers_conf *) basev,
17326          *overrides = (headers_conf *) overridesv;
17327
17328      a->headers = ap_append_arrays(p, base->headers,
17329          overrides->headers);
17330
17331      return a;
17332  }
17333
17334
17335  static const char *header_cmd(cmd_parms *cmd,
17336      headers_conf * dirconf, char *action,
17337      char *hdr, char *value)
17338  {
17339      header_entry *new;
17340      server_rec *s = cmd->server;
```

```
17341      headers_conf *serverconf =
17342      (headers_conf *)
17343          ap_get_module_config(s->module_config,
17344          &headers_module);
17345      char *colon;
17346
17347      if (cmd->path) {
17348          new = (header_entry *)
17349              ap_push_array(dirconf->headers);
17350      }
17351      else {
17352          new = (header_entry *)
17353              ap_push_array(serverconf->headers);
17354      }
17355
17356      if (!strcasecmp(action, "set"))
17357          new->action = hdr_set;
17358      else if (!strcasecmp(action, "add"))
17359          new->action = hdr_add;
17360      else if (!strcasecmp(action, "append"))
17361          new->action = hdr_append;
17362      else if (!strcasecmp(action, "unset"))
17363          new->action = hdr_unset;
17364      else
17365          return "first argument must be add, set,
17366              append or unset.";
17367
17368      if (new->action == hdr_unset) {
17369          if (value)
17370              return "Header unset takes two arguments";
17371      }
17372      else if (!value)
17373          return "Header requires three arguments";
17374
17375      if ((colon = strchr(hdr, ':')))
17376          *colon = '\0';
17377
17378      new->header = hdr;
17379      new->value = value;
17380
17381      return NULL;
17382  }
17383
17384  static const command_rec headers_cmds[] =
17385  {
```

```
17386      {"Header", header_cmd, NULL, OR_FILEINFO, TAKE23,
17387       "an action, header and value"},
17388      {NULL}
17389  };
17390
17391  static void do_headers_fixup(request_rec *r,
17392         array_header *headers)
17393  {
17394      int i;
17395
17396      for (i = 0; i < headers->nelts; ++i) {
17397          header_entry *hdr = &((header_entry *)
17398                  (headers->elts))[i];
17399          switch (hdr->action) {
17400          case hdr_add:
17401              ap_table_addn(r->headers_out,
17402                  hdr->header, hdr->value);
17403              break;
17404          case hdr_append:
17405              ap_table_mergen(r->headers_out,
17406                  hdr->header, hdr->value);
17407              break;
17408          case hdr_set:
17409              ap_table_setn(r->headers_out,
17410                  hdr->header, hdr->value);
17411              break;
17412          case hdr_unset:
17413              ap_table_unset(r->headers_out, hdr->header);
17414              break;
17415          }
17416      }
17417
17418  }
17419
17420  static int fixup_headers(request_rec *r)
17421  {
17422      void *sconf = r->server->module_config;
17423      headers_conf *serverconf =
17424      (headers_conf *) ap_get_module_config(sconf,
17425          &headers_module);
17426      void *dconf = r->per_dir_config;
17427      headers_conf *dirconf =
17428      (headers_conf *) ap_get_module_config(dconf,
17429          &headers_module);
17430
17431      do_headers_fixup(r, serverconf->headers);
17432      do_headers_fixup(r, dirconf->headers);
17433
17434      return DECLINED;
17435  }
17436
17437  module MODULE_VAR_EXPORT headers_module =
17438  {
17439      STANDARD_MODULE_STUFF,
17440      NULL,                       /* initializer */
17441      create_headers_dir_config, /* dir config creater */
17442      merge_headers_config,
17443      /* dir merger -- default is to override */
17444      create_headers_config,     /* server config */
17445      merge_headers_config,      /* merge server configs */
17446      headers_cmds,              /* command table */
17447      NULL,                      /* handlers */
17448      NULL,                      /* filename translation */
17449      NULL,                      /* check_user_id */
17450      NULL,                      /* check auth */
17451      NULL,                      /* check access */
17452      NULL,                      /* type_checker */
17453      fixup_headers,             /* fixups */
17454      NULL,                      /* logger */
17455      NULL,                      /* header parser */
17456      NULL,                      /* child_init */
17457      NULL,                      /* child_exit */
17458      NULL                       /* post read-request */
17459  };
```

▶ mod_imap.c

```
17460  #include "httpd.h"
17461  #include "http_config.h"
17462  #include "http_request.h"
17463  #include "http_core.h"
17464  #include "http_protocol.h"
17465  #include "http_main.h"
17466  #include "http_log.h"
17467  #include "util_script.h"
17468
17469  #define IMAP_MAGIC_TYPE "application/x-httpd-imap"
17470  #define MAXVERTS 100
17471  #define X 0
17472  #define Y 1
```

```
17473
17474   #define IMAP_MENU_DEFAULT "formatted"
17475   #define IMAP_DEFAULT_DEFAULT "nocontent"
17476   #define IMAP_BASE_DEFAULT "map"
17477
17478   #ifdef SUNOS4
17479   double strtod();                /* SunOS needed this */
17480   #endif
17481
17482   module MODULE_VAR_EXPORT imap_module;
17483
17484   typedef struct {
17485       char *imap_menu;
17486       char *imap_default;
17487       char *imap_base;
17488   } imap_conf_rec;
17489
17490   static void *create_imap_dir_config(pool *p,
17491       char *dummy)
17492   {
17493       imap_conf_rec *icr =
17494       (imap_conf_rec *) ap_palloc(p,
17495           sizeof(imap_conf_rec));
17496
17497       icr->imap_menu = NULL;
17498       icr->imap_default = NULL;
17499       icr->imap_base = NULL;
17500
17501       return icr;
17502   }
17503
17504   static void *merge_imap_dir_configs(pool *p,
17505       void *basev, void *addv)
17506   {
17507       imap_conf_rec *new = (imap_conf_rec *)
17508           ap_pcalloc(p, sizeof(imap_conf_rec));
17509       imap_conf_rec *base = (imap_conf_rec *) basev;
17510       imap_conf_rec *add = (imap_conf_rec *) addv;
17511
17512       new->imap_menu = add->imap_menu ?
17513           add->imap_menu : base->imap_menu;
17514       new->imap_default = add->imap_default ?
17515           add->imap_default
17516                                   : base->imap_default;
17517       new->imap_base = add->imap_base ?
17518           add->imap_base : base->imap_base;
17519
17520       return new;
17521   }
17522
17523
17524   static const command_rec imap_cmds[] =
17525   {
17526       {"ImapMenu", ap_set_string_slot,
17527       (void *) XtOffsetOf(imap_conf_rec, imap_menu),
17528           OR_INDEXES, TAKE1,
17529    "the type of menu generated: none, formatted,
17530           semiformatted, unformatted"},
17531       {"ImapDefault", ap_set_string_slot,
17532       (void *) XtOffsetOf(imap_conf_rec, imap_default),
17533           OR_INDEXES, TAKE1,
17534       "the action taken if no match: error, nocontent,
17535           referer, menu, URL"},
17536       {"ImapBase", ap_set_string_slot,
17537       (void *) XtOffsetOf(imap_conf_rec, imap_base),
17538           OR_INDEXES, TAKE1,
17539       "the base for all URL's: map, referer, URL
17540           (or start of)"},
17541       {NULL}
17542   };
17543
17544   static int pointinrect(const double point[2],
17545       double coords[MAXVERTS][2])
17546   {
17547       double max[2], min[2];
17548       if (coords[0][X] > coords[1][X]) {
17549           max[0] = coords[0][X];
17550           min[0] = coords[1][X];
17551       }
17552       else {
17553           max[0] = coords[1][X];
17554           min[0] = coords[0][X];
17555       }
17556
17557       if (coords[0][Y] > coords[1][Y]) {
17558           max[1] = coords[0][Y];
17559           min[1] = coords[1][Y];
17560       }
17561       else {
17562           max[1] = coords[1][Y];
```

```
17563              min[1] = coords[0][Y];
17564          }
17565
17566          return ((point[X] >= min[0] &&
17567                  point[X] <= max[0]) &&
17568                   (point[Y] >= min[1] &&
17569                  point[Y] <= max[1]));
17570      }
17571
17572      static int pointincircle(const double point[2],
17573          double coords[MAXVERTS][2])
17574      {
17575          double radius1, radius2;
17576
17577          radius1 = ((coords[0][Y] - coords[1][Y]) *
17578                  (coords[0][Y] - coords[1][Y]))
17579              + ((coords[0][X] - coords[1][X]) *
17580                  (coords[0][X] - coords[1][X]));
17581
17582          radius2 = ((coords[0][Y] - point[Y]) *
17583                  (coords[0][Y] - point[Y]))
17584              + ((coords[0][X] - point[X]) *
17585                  (coords[0][X] - point[X]));
17586
17587
17588          return (radius2 <= radius1);
17589      }
17590
17591      #define fmin(a,b) (((a)>(b))?(b):(a))
17592      #define fmax(a,b) (((a)>(b))?(a):(b))
17593
17594      static int pointinpoly(const double point[2],
17595          double pgon[MAXVERTS][2])
17596      {
17597          int i, numverts, crossings = 0;
17598          double x = point[X], y = point[Y];
17599
17600          for (numverts = 0; pgon[numverts][X] != -1
17601                  && numverts < MAXVERTS;
17602           numverts++) {
17603          /* just counting the vertexes */
17604          }
17605
17606          for (i = 0; i < numverts; i++) {
17607              double x1=pgon[i][X];
```

```
17608              double y1=pgon[i][Y];
17609              double x2=pgon[(i + 1) % numverts][X];
17610              double y2=pgon[(i + 1) % numverts][Y];
17611              double d=(y - y1) * (x2 - x1) - (x - x1) *
17612                  (y2 - y1);
17613
17614              if ((y1 >= y) != (y2 >= y)) {
17615                  crossings +=y2 - y1 >= 0 ? d >= 0 : d <= 0;
17616              }
17617              if (!d && fmin(x1,x2) <= x && x <= fmax(x1,x2)
17618                  && fmin(y1,y2) <= y && y <= fmax(y1,y2)) {
17619                  return 1;
17620              }
17621          }
17622          return crossings & 0x01;
17623      }
17624
17625
17626      static int is_closer(const double point[2],
17627          double coords[MAXVERTS][2],
17628                      double *closest)
17629      {
17630          double dist_squared = ((point[X] - coords[0][X])
17631                      * (point[X] - coords[0][X]))
17632                      + ((point[Y] - coords[0][Y])
17633                      * (point[Y] - coords[0][Y]));
17634
17635          if (point[X] < 0 || point[Y] < 0) {
17636              return (0);
17637              /* don't mess around with negative coordinates */
17638          }
17639
17640          if (*closest < 0 || dist_squared < *closest) {
17641              *closest = dist_squared;
17642              return (1);
17643              /* if this is the first point or
17644               * is the closest yet
17645                  set 'closest' equal to this distance^2 */
17646          }
17647
17648          return (0);
17649          /* if it's not the first or closest */
17650
17651      }
17652
```

```
17653   static double get_x_coord(const char *args)
17654   {
17655       char *endptr;              /* we want it non-null */
17656       double x_coord = -1;
17657       /* -1 is returned if no coordinate is given */
17658
17659       if (args == NULL) {
17660           return (-1);
17661       /* in case we aren't passed anything */
17662       }
17663
17664       while (*args && !ap_isdigit(*args) && *args != ',') {
17665           args++;
17666           /* jump to the first digit, but not past
17667                                   a comma or end */
17668       }
17669
17670       x_coord = strtod(args, &endptr);
17671
17672       if (endptr > args) {
17673       /* if a conversion was made */
17674           return (x_coord);
17675       }
17676
17677       return (-1);
17678       /* else if no conversion was made,
17679                             or if no args was given */
17680   }
17681
17682   static double get_y_coord(const char *args)
17683   {
17684       char *endptr;              /* we want it non-null */
17685       char *start_of_y = NULL;
17686       double y_coord = -1;   /* -1 is returned on error */
17687
17688       if (args == NULL) {
17689           return (-1);
17690           /* in case we aren't passed anything */
17691       }
17692
17693       start_of_y = strchr(args, ',');      /* the comma */
17694
17695       if (start_of_y) {
17696
17697           start_of_y++;
17698           /* start looking at the character after
17699                                   the comma */
17700
17701           while (*start_of_y && !ap_isdigit(*start_of_y)) {
17702               start_of_y++;
17703               /* jump to the first digit, but not
17704                                   past the end */
17705           }
17706
17707           y_coord = strtod(start_of_y, &endptr);
17708
17709           if (endptr > start_of_y) {
17710               return (y_coord);
17711           }
17712       }
17713
17714       return (-1);
17715       /* if no conversion was made, or
17716                           no comma was found in args */
17717   }
17718
17719
17720   /* See if string has a "quoted part", and if so set
17721    * *quoted_part to the first character of the
17722    * quoted part, then hammer a \0 onto the trailing
17723    * quote, and set *string to point at the first
17724    * character past the second quote.
17725    *
17726    * Otherwise set *quoted_part to NULL, and leave
17727    * *string alone.
17728    */
17729   static void read_quoted(char **string,
17730        char **quoted_part)
17731   {
17732       char *strp = *string;
17733
17734       /* assume there's no quoted part */
17735       *quoted_part = NULL;
17736
17737       while (ap_isspace(*strp)) {
17738           strp++;
17739           /* go along string until non-whitespace */
17740       }
17741
17742       if (*strp == '"') {
```

```
17743        /* if that character is a double quote */
17744           strp++;                    /* step over it */
17745         *quoted_part = strp;
17746        /* note where the quoted part begins */
17747
17748           while (*strp && *strp != '"') {
17749             ++strp;         /* skip the quoted portion */
17750           }
17751
17752           *strp = '\0';    /* end the string with a NUL */
17753
17754           strp++;
17755          /* step over the last double quote */
17756         *string = strp;
17757        }
17758    }
17759
17760    /*
17761     * returns the mapped URL or NULL.
17762     */
17763    static char *imap_url(request_rec *r, const char *base,
17764         const char *value)
17765    {
17766    /* translates a value into a URL. */
17767        int slen, clen;
17768        char *string_pos = NULL;
17769        const char *string_pos_const = NULL;
17770        char *directory = NULL;
17771        const char *referer = NULL;
17772        char *my_base;
17773
17774        if (!strcasecmp(value, "map") || !strcasecmp(value,
17775            "menu")) {
17776         return ap_construct_url(r->pool, r->uri, r);
17777        }
17778
17779        if (!strcasecmp(value, "nocontent") ||
17780            !strcasecmp(value, "error")) {
17781          return ap_pstrdup(r->pool, value);
17782          /* these are handled elsewhere,
17783                              so just copy them */
17784        }
17785
17786        if (!strcasecmp(value, "referer")) {
17787          referer = ap_table_get(r->headers_in, "Referer");
17788          if (referer && *referer) {
17789            return ap_pstrdup(r->pool, referer);
17790          }
17791          else {
17792            /* XXX:  This used to do *value = '\0'; ...
17793             * which is totally bogus because it hammers
17794             * the passed in value, which can be a string
17795               * constant, or part of a config, or
17796               * whatever.  Total garbage.
17797               * This works around that without
17798               * changing the rest of this code much
17799               */
17800            value = "";
17801            /* if 'referer' but no referring page,
17802                                null the value */
17803          }
17804        }
17805
17806    string_pos_const = value;
17807    while (ap_isalpha(*string_pos_const)) {
17808      string_pos_const++;
17809      /* go along the URL from the map
17810                              until a non-letter */
17811    }
17812    if (*string_pos_const == ':') {
17813      /* if letters and then a colon (like http:) */
17814      /* it's an absolute URL, so use it! */
17815      return ap_pstrdup(r->pool, value);
17816    }
17817
17818    if (!base || !*base) {
17819        if (value && *value) {
17820          return ap_pstrdup(r->pool, value);
17821          /* no base: use what is given */
17822        }
17823      /* no base, no value: pick a simple default */
17824      return ap_construct_url(r->pool, "/", r);
17825    }
17826
17827    /* must be a relative URL to be combined with
17828     * base */
17829    if (strchr(base, '/') == NULL &&
17830        (!strncmp(value, "../", 3)
17831        || !strcmp(value, ".."))) {
17832      ap_log_rerror(APLOG_MARK,
```

```
17833                APLOG_NOERRNO|APLOG_ERR, r,
17834                    "invalid base directive in map
17835                        file: %s", r->uri);
17836            return NULL;
17837        }
17838    my_base = ap_pstrdup(r->pool, base);
17839    string_pos = my_base;
17840    while (*string_pos) {
17841        if (*string_pos == '/' && *(string_pos + 1)
17842            == '/') {
17843            string_pos += 2;
17844          /* if there are two slashes, jump over them */
17845            continue;
17846        }
17847        if (*string_pos == '/') {
17848        /* the first single slash */
17849            if (value[0] == '/') {
17850                *string_pos = '\0';
17851            }                /* if the URL from the
17852                             * map starts from root,
17853                               end the base URL string
17854                               at the first single
17855                                   slash */
17856            else {
17857                directory = string_pos;
17858                /* save the start of
17859                            the directory portion */
17860
17861                string_pos = strrchr(string_pos, '/');
17862                        /* now reuse string_pos */
17863                string_pos++;
17864                /* step over that last slash */
17865                *string_pos = '\0';
17866            }                /* but if the map url is
17867                               relative, leave the
17868                               slash on the base (if
17869                               there is one) */
17870            break;
17871        }
17872        string_pos++;      /* until we get to the
17873                            end of my_base without
17874                            finding a slash by itself */
17875    }
17876
17877    while (!strncmp(value, "../", 3) ||
```

```
17878        !strcmp(value, "..")) {
17879
17880        if (directory && (slen = strlen(directory))) {
17881
17882            /* for each '..',  knock a directory off
17883               the end by ending the string right
17884               at the last slash. But only consider
17885               the directory portion: don't eat
17886               into the server name.  And only try if
17887               a directory portion was found */
17888
17889            clen = slen - 1;
17890
17891            while ((slen - clen) == 1) {
17892
17893                if ((string_pos = strrchr(directory,
17894                    '/'))) {
17895                    *string_pos = '\0';
17896                }
17897                clen = strlen(directory);
17898                if (clen == 0) {
17899                    break;
17900                }
17901            }
17902
17903            value += 2;        /* jump over the '..'
17904                                that we found in the
17905                                value */
17906        }
17907        else if (directory) {
17908            ap_log_rerror(APLOG_MARK,
17909                APLOG_NOERRNO|APLOG_ERR, r,
17910                    "invalid directory name in map
17911                        file: %s", r->uri);
17912            return NULL;
17913        }
17914
17915    if (!strncmp(value, "/../", 4) || !strcmp(value,
17916        "/..")) {
17917        value++;       /* step over the '/' if there
17918                        are more '..' to do.  This
17919                        way, we leave the starting
17920                        '/' on value after the last
17921                        '..', but get rid of it
17922                        otherwise */
```

```
17923        }
17924
17925     }                         /* by this point, value does
17926                                 not start with '..' */
17927
17928     if (value && *value) {
17929      return ap_pstrcat(r->pool, my_base, value, NULL);
17930     }
17931     return my_base;
17932 }
17933
17934 static int imap_reply(request_rec *r, char *redirect)
17935 {
17936     if (!strcasecmp(redirect, "error")) {
17937         return SERVER_ERROR;    /* they actually
17938                                 requested an error! */
17939     }
17940     if (!strcasecmp(redirect, "nocontent")) {
17941         return HTTP_NO_CONTENT; /* tell the client to
17942             keep the page it has */
17943     }
17944     if (redirect && *redirect) {
17945         ap_table_setn(r->headers_out, "Location",
17946             redirect);
17947         return REDIRECT;         /* must be a URL, so
17948                                 redirect to it */
17949     }
17950     return SERVER_ERROR;
17951 }
17952
17953 static void menu_header(request_rec *r, char *menu)
17954 {
17955     r->content_type = "text/html";
17956     ap_send_http_header(r);
17957     ap_hard_timeout("send menu", r);
17958     /* killed in menu_footer */
17959
17960     ap_rvputs(r, "<html><head>\n<title>Menu for ",
17961         r->uri,
17962         "</title>\n</head><body>\n", NULL);
17963
17964     if (!strcasecmp(menu, "formatted")) {
17965         ap_rvputs(r, "<h1>Menu for ", r->uri,
17966             "</h1>\n<hr>\n\n", NULL);
17967     }
```

```
17968
17969     return;
17970 }
17971
17972 static void menu_blank(request_rec *r, char *menu)
17973 {
17974     if (!strcasecmp(menu, "formatted")) {
17975         ap_rputs("\n", r);
17976     }
17977     if (!strcasecmp(menu, "semiformatted")) {
17978         ap_rputs("<br>\n", r);
17979     }
17980     if (!strcasecmp(menu, "unformatted")) {
17981         ap_rputs("\n", r);
17982     }
17983     return;
17984 }
17985
17986 static void menu_comment(request_rec *r, char *menu,
17987     char *comment)
17988 {
17989     if (!strcasecmp(menu, "formatted")) {
17990         ap_rputs("\n", r);
17991         /* print just a newline if 'formatted' */
17992     }
17993     if (!strcasecmp(menu, "semiformatted") && *comment) {
17994         ap_rvputs(r, comment, "\n", NULL);
17995     }
17996     if (!strcasecmp(menu, "unformatted") && *comment) {
17997         ap_rvputs(r, comment, "\n", NULL);
17998     }
17999     return;                /* comments are ignored in the
18000                             'formatted' form */
18001 }
18002
18003 static void menu_default(request_rec *r, char *menu,
18004     char *href, char *text)
18005 {
18006     if (!strcasecmp(href, "error") || !strcasecmp(href,
18007         "nocontent")) {
18008         return;            /* don't print such lines,
18009                             these aren't really href's */
18010     }
18011     if (!strcasecmp(menu, "formatted")) {
18012         ap_rvputs(r, "<pre>(Default) <a href=\"", href,
```

```
18013                    "\">", text,
18014                    "</a></pre>\n", NULL);
18015        }
18016        if (!strcasecmp(menu, "semiformatted")) {
18017            ap_rvputs(r, "<pre>(Default) <a href=\"", href,
18018                    "\">", text,
18019                    "</a></pre>\n", NULL);
18020        }
18021        if (!strcasecmp(menu, "unformatted")) {
18022            ap_rvputs(r, "<a href=\"", href, "\">", text,
18023                    "</a>", NULL);
18024        }
18025        return;
18026    }
18027
18028    static void menu_directive(request_rec *r, char *menu,
18029         char *href, char *text)
18030    {
18031        if (!strcasecmp(href, "error") || !strcasecmp(href,
18032            "nocontent")) {
18033            return;            /* don't print such lines, as
18034                                this isn't really an href */
18035        }
18036        if (!strcasecmp(menu, "formatted")) {
18037            ap_rvputs(r, "<pre>         <a href=\"", href,
18038                    "\">", text,
18039                    "</a></pre>\n", NULL);
18040        }
18041        if (!strcasecmp(menu, "semiformatted")) {
18042            ap_rvputs(r, "<pre>         <a href=\"", href,
18043                    "\">", text,
18044                    "</a></pre>\n", NULL);
18045        }
18046        if (!strcasecmp(menu, "unformatted")) {
18047            ap_rvputs(r, "<a href=\"", href, "\">", text,
18048                    "</a>", NULL);
18049        }
18050        return;
18051    }
18052
18053    static void menu_footer(request_rec *r)
18054    {
18055        ap_rputs("\n\n</body>\n</html>\n", r);
18056        /* finish the menu */
18057        ap_kill_timeout(r);
18058    }
18059
18060    static int imap_handler(request_rec *r)
18061    {
18062        char input[MAX_STRING_LEN];
18063        char *directive;
18064        char *value;
18065        char *href_text;
18066        char *base;
18067        char *redirect;
18068        char *mapdflt;
18069        char *closest = NULL;
18070        double closest_yet = -1;
18071
18072        double testpoint[2];
18073        double pointarray[MAXVERTS + 1][2];
18074        int vertex;
18075
18076        char *string_pos;
18077        int showmenu = 0;
18078
18079        imap_conf_rec *icr =
18080            ap_get_module_config(r->per_dir_config,
18081            &imap_module);
18082
18083        char *imap_menu = icr->imap_menu ? icr->imap_menu :
18084            IMAP_MENU_DEFAULT;
18085        char *imap_default = icr->imap_default
18086                    ? icr->imap_default :
18087                        IMAP_DEFAULT_DEFAULT;
18088        char *imap_base = icr->imap_base ? icr->imap_base :
18089            IMAP_BASE_DEFAULT;
18090
18091        configfile_t *imap;
18092
18093        if (r->method_number != M_GET) {
18094         return DECLINED;
18095        }
18096
18097        imap = ap_pcfg_openfile(r->pool, r->filename);
18098
18099        if (!imap) {
18100            return NOT_FOUND;
18101        }
18102
```

```
18103      base = imap_url(r, NULL, imap_base);
18104      /* set base according
18105                                            to default */
18106      if (!base) {
18107       return HTTP_INTERNAL_SERVER_ERROR;
18108      }
18109      mapdflt = imap_url(r, NULL, imap_default);
18110      /* and default to
18111                                            global default */
18112      if (!mapdflt) {
18113       return HTTP_INTERNAL_SERVER_ERROR;
18114      }
18115
18116      testpoint[X] = get_x_coord(r->args);
18117      testpoint[Y] = get_y_coord(r->args);
18118
18119      if ((testpoint[X] == -1 || testpoint[Y] == -1) ||
18120          (testpoint[X] == 0 && testpoint[Y] == 0)) {
18121          /* if either is -1 or if both are zero
18122          (new Lynx) */
18123          /* we don't have valid coordinates */
18124          testpoint[X] = -1;
18125          testpoint[Y] = -1;
18126          if (strncasecmp(imap_menu, "none", 2)) {
18127              showmenu = 1;
18128              /* show the menu _unless_ ImapMenu is
18129                                            'none' or 'no' */
18130          }
18131      }
18132
18133      if (showmenu) {    /* send start of imagemap menu if
18134                                    we're going to */
18135          menu_header(r, imap_menu);
18136      }
18137
18138      while (!ap_cfg_getline(input, sizeof(input), imap)) {
18139          if (!input[0]) {
18140              if (showmenu) {
18141                  menu_blank(r, imap_menu);
18142              }
18143              continue;
18144          }
18145
18146          if (input[0] == '#') {
18147              if (showmenu) {
18148                  menu_comment(r, imap_menu, input + 1);
18149              }
18150              continue;
18151          }                   /* blank lines and comments are
18152                              ignored if we aren't printing a menu */
18153
18154      /* find the first two space delimited fields,
18155       * recall that ap_cfg_getline has removed
18156       * leading/trailing whitespace.
18157       *
18158       * note that we're tokenizing as we go... if we
18159       * were to use the ap_getword() class of functions
18160       * we would end up allocating extra memory for
18161       * every line of the map file
18162       */
18163          string_pos = input;
18164      if (!*string_pos) {
18165      /* need at least two fields */
18166          goto need_2_fields;
18167      }
18168
18169      directive = string_pos;
18170      while (*string_pos && !ap_isspace(*string_pos))
18171          {      /* past directive */
18172          ++string_pos;
18173      }
18174      if (!*string_pos) {
18175      /* need at least two fields */
18176          goto need_2_fields;
18177      }
18178      *string_pos++ = '\0';
18179
18180      if (!*string_pos) {
18181      /* need at least two fields */
18182          goto need_2_fields;
18183      }
18184      while(*string_pos && ap_isspace(*string_pos))
18185          { /* past whitespace */
18186          ++string_pos;
18187      }
18188
18189      value = string_pos;
18190      while (*string_pos && !ap_isspace(*string_pos))
18191          {      /* past value */
18192          ++string_pos;
18193      }
18194      if (ap_isspace(*string_pos)) {
```

```
18195            *string_pos++ = '\0';
18196        }
18197        else {
18198            /* end of input, don't advance past it */
18199            *string_pos = '\0';
18200        }
18201
18202        if (!strncasecmp(directive, "base", 4)) {
18203        /* base, base_uri */
18204            base = imap_url(r, NULL, value);
18205        if (!base) {
18206          goto menu_bail;
18207        }
18208            continue;
18209            /* base is never printed to a menu */
18210        }
18211
18212        read_quoted(&string_pos, &href_text);
18213
18214        if (!strcasecmp(directive, "default")) {
18215            /* default */
18216            mapdflt = imap_url(r, NULL, value);
18217        if (!mapdflt) {
18218          goto menu_bail;
18219        }
18220            if (showmenu) {     /* print the default if
18221                                   there's a menu */
18222                redirect = imap_url(r, base, mapdflt);
18223            if (!redirect) {
18224                goto menu_bail;
18225            }
18226                menu_default(r, imap_menu, redirect,
18227                    href_text ? href_text : mapdflt);
18228            }
18229            continue;
18230        }
18231
18232        vertex = 0;
18233        while (vertex < MAXVERTS &&
18234                sscanf(string_pos, "%lf%*[, ]%lf",
18235                    &pointarray[vertex][X],
18236                    &pointarray[vertex][Y]) == 2) {
18237            /* Now skip what we just read... we can't
18238            use ANSIism %n */
18239            while (ap_isspace(*string_pos)) {
18240                /* past whitespace */
```

```
18241                string_pos++;
18242            }
18243            while (ap_isdigit(*string_pos)) {
18244            /* and the 1st number */
18245                string_pos++;
18246            }
18247            string_pos++;        /* skip the ',' */
18248            while (ap_isspace(*string_pos)) {
18249            /* past any more whitespace */
18250                string_pos++;
18251            }
18252            while (ap_isdigit(*string_pos)) {
18253            /* 2nd number */
18254                string_pos++;
18255            }
18256            vertex++;
18257        }                  /* so long as there are more
18258                                vertices to read, and we
18259                                have room, read them in. We
18260                                start where we left off of
18261                                the last sscanf, not at the
18262                                beginning. */
18263
18264        pointarray[vertex][X] = -1;
18265        /* signals the end of vertices */
18266
18267        if (showmenu) {
18268          if (!href_text) {
18269            read_quoted(&string_pos, &href_text);
18270            /* href text could
18271                                be here instead */
18272          }
18273            redirect = imap_url(r, base, value);
18274          if (!redirect) {
18275            goto menu_bail;
18276          }
18277            menu_directive(r, imap_menu, redirect,
18278                    href_text ? href_text : value);
18279            continue;
18280        }
18281        /* note that we don't make it past here if we
18282        are making a menu */
18283
18284        if (testpoint[X] == -1 || pointarray[0][X] == -1) {
18285            continue;        /* don't try the following
18286                                tests if testpoints are
```

```
18287                         invalid, or if there are no
18288                         coordinates */
18289        }
18290
18291        if (!strcasecmp(directive, "poly")) {   /* poly */
18292
18293            if (pointinpoly(testpoint, pointarray)) {
18294            ap_cfg_closefile(imap);
18295                redirect = imap_url(r, base, value);
18296            if (!redirect) {
18297                return HTTP_INTERNAL_SERVER_ERROR;
18298            }
18299                return (imap_reply(r, redirect));
18300            }
18301            continue;
18302        }
18303
18304        if (!strcasecmp(directive, "circle")) {
18305            /* circle */
18306
18307            if (pointincircle(testpoint, pointarray)) {
18308            ap_cfg_closefile(imap);
18309                redirect = imap_url(r, base, value);
18310            if (!redirect) {
18311                return HTTP_INTERNAL_SERVER_ERROR;
18312            }
18313                return (imap_reply(r, redirect));
18314            }
18315            continue;
18316        }
18317
18318        if (!strcasecmp(directive, "rect")) {
18319            /* rect */
18320
18321            if (pointinrect(testpoint, pointarray)) {
18322            ap_cfg_closefile(imap);
18323                redirect = imap_url(r, base, value);
18324            if (!redirect) {
18325                return HTTP_INTERNAL_SERVER_ERROR;
18326            }
18327                return (imap_reply(r, redirect));
18328            }
18329            continue;
18330        }
18331
18332        if (!strcasecmp(directive, "point")) {
18333                /* point */
18334
18335            if (is_closer(testpoint, pointarray,
18336                &closest_yet)) {
18337                closest = ap_pstrdup(r->pool, value);
18338            }
18339
18340            continue;
18341        }                   /* move on to next line
18342                            whether it's closest or not */
18343
18344        }                   /* nothing matched, so we get
18345                            another line! */
18346
18347    ap_cfg_closefile(imap);      /* we are done with the
18348                            map file; close it */
18349
18350    if (showmenu) {
18351        menu_footer(r);       /* finish the menu and we
18352                            are done */
18353        return OK;
18354    }
18355
18356    if (closest) {              /* if a 'point' directive
18357                            has been seen */
18358        redirect = imap_url(r, base, closest);
18359    if (!redirect) {
18360        return HTTP_INTERNAL_SERVER_ERROR;
18361    }
18362        return (imap_reply(r, redirect));
18363    }
18364
18365    if (mapdflt) {        /* a default should be defined,
18366                            even if only 'nocontent' */
18367        redirect = imap_url(r, base, mapdflt);
18368    if (!redirect) {
18369        return HTTP_INTERNAL_SERVER_ERROR;
18370    }
18371        return (imap_reply(r, redirect));
18372    }
18373
18374    return HTTP_INTERNAL_SERVER_ERROR;
18375    /* If we make it this far, we failed.
18376     * They lose! */
18377
18378 need_2_fields:
```

```
18379        ap_log_rerror(APLOG_MARK, APLOG_NOERRNO|APLOG_ERR, r,
18380            "map file %s, line %d syntax error: requires at "
18381                 "least two fields", r->uri,
18382                 imap->line_number);
18383        /* fall through */
18384 menu_bail:
18385        ap_cfg_closefile(imap);
18386        if (showmenu) {
18387         /* There's not much else we can do ... we've
18388          * already sent the headers to the client.
18389          */
18390         ap_rputs("\n\n[an internal server error
18391             occured]\n", r);
18392         menu_footer(r);
18393         return OK;
18394        }
18395        return HTTP_INTERNAL_SERVER_ERROR;
18396 }
18397
18398
18399 static const handler_rec imap_handlers[] =
18400 {
18401        {IMAP_MAGIC_TYPE, imap_handler},
18402        {"imap-file", imap_handler},
18403        {NULL}
18404 };
18405
18406 module MODULE_VAR_EXPORT imap_module =
18407 {
18408        STANDARD_MODULE_STUFF,
18409        NULL,                  /* initializer */
18410        create_imap_dir_config,  /* dir config creater */
18411        merge_imap_dir_configs,
18412        /* dir merger -- default is to override */
18413        NULL,                  /* server config */
18414        NULL,                  /* merge server config */
18415        imap_cmds,             /* command table */
18416        imap_handlers,         /* handlers */
18417        NULL,                  /* filename translation */
18418        NULL,                  /* check_user_id */
18419        NULL,                  /* check auth */
18420        NULL,                  /* check access */
18421        NULL,                  /* type_checker */
18422        NULL,                  /* fixups */
18423        NULL,                  /* logger */
18424        NULL,                  /* header parser */
18425        NULL,                  /* child_init */
18426        NULL,                  /* child_exit */
18427        NULL                   /* post read-request */
18428 };
```

▶ p 553 mod_include.c

```
18429 #ifdef USE_PERL_SSI
18430 #include "config.h"
18431 #undef VOIDUSED
18432 #ifdef USE_SFIO
18433 #undef USE_SFIO
18434 #define USE_STDIO
18435 #endif
18436 #include "modules/perl/mod_perl.h"
18437 #else
18438 #include "httpd.h"
18439 #include "http_config.h"
18440 #include "http_request.h"
18441 #include "http_core.h"
18442 #include "http_protocol.h"
18443 #include "http_log.h"
18444 #include "http_main.h"
18445 #include "util_script.h"
18446 #endif
18447
18448 #define STARTING_SEQUENCE "<!--#"
18449 #define ENDING_SEQUENCE "-->"
18450 #define DEFAULT_ERROR_MSG "[an error occurred while
18451         processing this directive]"
18452 #define DEFAULT_TIME_FORMAT "%A, %d-%b-%Y %H:%M:%S %Z"
18453 #define SIZEFMT_BYTES 0
18454 #define SIZEFMT_KMG 1
18455 #ifdef CHARSET_EBCDIC
18456 #define RAW_ASCII_CHAR(ch)
18457         os_toebcdic[(unsigned char)ch]
18458 #else /*CHARSET_EBCDIC*/
18459 #define RAW_ASCII_CHAR(ch)  (ch)
18460 #endif /*CHARSET_EBCDIC*/
18461
18462 module MODULE_VAR_EXPORT includes_module;
18463
18464 /* just need some arbitrary non-NULL pointer
18465 which can't also be a request_rec */
18466 #define NESTED_INCLUDE_MAGIC    (&includes_module)
18467
18468 /* ------------- Environment function ----------- */
```

```
18469
18470   /* XXX: could use ap_table_overlap here */
18471   static void add_include_vars(request_rec *r,
18472       char *timefmt)
18473   {
18474   #ifndef WIN32
18475       struct passwd *pw;
18476   #endif /* ndef WIN32 */
18477       table *e = r->subprocess_env;
18478       char *t;
18479       time_t date = r->request_time;
18480
18481       ap_table_setn(e, "DATE_LOCAL", ap_ht_time(r->pool,
18482           date, timefmt, 0));
18483       ap_table_setn(e, "DATE_GMT", ap_ht_time(r->pool,
18484           date, timefmt, 1));
18485       ap_table_setn(e, "LAST_MODIFIED",
18486               ap_ht_time(r->pool, r->finfo.st_mtime,
18487                   timefmt, 0));
18488       ap_table_setn(e, "DOCUMENT_URI", r->uri);
18489       ap_table_setn(e, "DOCUMENT_PATH_INFO",
18490           r->path_info);
18491   #ifndef WIN32
18492       pw = getpwuid(r->finfo.st_uid);
18493       if (pw) {
18494           ap_table_setn(e, "USER_NAME",
18495               ap_pstrdup(r->pool, pw->pw_name));
18496       }
18497       else {
18498           ap_table_setn(e, "USER_NAME",
18499               ap_psprintf(r->pool, "user#%lu",
18500                   (unsigned long) r->finfo.st_uid));
18501       }
18502   #endif /* ndef WIN32 */
18503
18504       if ((t = strrchr(r->filename, '/'))) {
18505           ap_table_setn(e, "DOCUMENT_NAME", ++t);
18506       }
18507       else {
18508           ap_table_setn(e, "DOCUMENT_NAME", r->uri);
18509       }
18510       if (r->args) {
18511           char *arg_copy = ap_pstrdup(r->pool, r->args);
18512
18513           ap_unescape_url(arg_copy);
18514           ap_table_setn(e, "QUERY_STRING_UNESCAPED",
18515               ap_escape_shell_cmd(r->pool, arg_copy));
18516       }
18517   }
18518
18519
18520
18521   /* --------------- Parser functions ------------- */
18522
18523   #define OUTBUFSIZE 4096
18524   /* PUT_CHAR and FLUSH_BUF currently only work within
18525    * the scope of find_string(); they are hacks to
18526    * avoid calling rputc for each and every character
18527    * output.  A common set of buffering calls for this
18528    * type of output SHOULD be implemented.
18529    */
18530   #define PUT_CHAR(c,r) \
18531   { \
18532       outbuf[outind++] = c; \
18533       if (outind == OUTBUFSIZE) { \
18534           FLUSH_BUF(r) \
18535       }; \
18536   }
18537
18538   /* there SHOULD be some error checking on the return
18539    * value of rwrite, however it is unclear what
18540    * the API for rwrite returning errors is and
18541    * little can really be done to help the error in
18542    * any case.
18543    */
18544   #define FLUSH_BUF(r) \
18545   { \
18546       ap_rwrite(outbuf, outind, r); \
18547       outind = 0; \
18548   }
18549
18550   /*
18551    * f: file handle being read from
18552    * c: character to read into
18553    * ret: return value to use if input fails
18554    * r: current request_rec
18555    *
18556    * This macro is redefined after find_string()
18557    * for historical reasons to avoid too many code
18558    * changes.  This is one of the many things
18559    * that should be fixed.
18560    */
18561   #define GET_CHAR(f,c,ret,r) \
```

```
18562    { \
18563      int i = getc(f); \
18564      if (i == EOF) { /* either EOF or error -- needs
18565              error handling if latter */ \
18566          if (ferror(f)) { \
18567              fprintf(stderr, "encountered error in
18568                  GET_CHAR macro, " \
18569                      "mod_include.\n"); \
18570          } \
18571          FLUSH_BUF(r); \
18572          ap_pfclose(r->pool, f); \
18573          return ret; \
18574      } \
18575      c = (char)i; \
18576    }
18577
18578    static int find_string(FILE *in, const char *str,
18579        request_rec *r, int printing)
18580    {
18581        int x, l = strlen(str), p;
18582        char outbuf[OUTBUFSIZE];
18583        int outind = 0;
18584        char c;
18585
18586        p = 0;
18587        while (1) {
18588            GET_CHAR(in, c, 1, r);
18589            if (c == str[p]) {
18590                if ((++p) == l) {
18591                    FLUSH_BUF(r);
18592                    return 0;
18593                }
18594            }
18595            else {
18596                if (printing) {
18597                    for (x = 0; x < p; x++) {
18598                        PUT_CHAR(str[x], r);
18599                    }
18600                    PUT_CHAR(c, r);
18601                }
18602                p = 0;
18603            }
18604        }
18605    }
18606
18607    #undef FLUSH_BUF
18608    #undef PUT_CHAR
18609    #undef GET_CHAR
18610    #define GET_CHAR(f,c,r,p) \
18611      { \
18612        int i = getc(f); \
18613        if (i == EOF) { /* either EOF or error -- needs
18614                    error handling if latter */ \
18615            if (ferror(f)) { \
18616                fprintf(stderr, "encountered error in
18617                    GET_CHAR macro, " \
18618                        "mod_include.\n"); \
18619            } \
18620            ap_pfclose(p, f); \
18621            return r; \
18622        } \
18623        c = (char)i; \
18624    }


18627    /*
18628     * decodes a string containing html entities or numeric
18629     * character references. 's' is overwritten with
18630     * the decoded string. If 's' is syntatically
18631     * incorrect, then the followed fixups will be made:
18632     * unknown entities will be left undecoded; references
18633     * to unused numeric characters will be deleted.
18634     * In particular, &#00; will not be decoded, but
18635     * will be deleted.
18636     *
18637     * drtr
18638     */
18639
18640    /* maximum length of any ISO-LATIN-1 HTML
18641     * entity name. */
18642    #define MAXENTLEN (6)
18643
18644    /* The following is a shrinking transformation,
18645    therefore safe. */
18646
18647    static void decodehtml(char *s)
18648    {
18649        int val, i, j;
18650        char *p = s;
18651        const char *ents;
18652        static const char * const entlist[MAXENTLEN + 1] =
18653        {
18654            NULL,                    /* 0 */
```

```
18655            NULL,                  /* 1 */
18656            "lt\074gt\076",        /* 2 */
18657            "amp\046ETH\320eth\360",       /* 3 */
18658            "quot\042Auml\304Euml\313Iuml\317Ouml\326Uuml\
18659              334auml\344euml\353\
18660    iuml\357ouml\366uuml\374yuml\377",      /* 4 */
18661            "Acirc\302Aring\305AElig\306Ecirc\312Icirc\
18662              316Ocirc\324Ucirc\333\
18663    THORN\336szlig\337acirc\342aring\345aelig\346ecirc\
18664              352icirc\356ocirc\364\
18665    ucirc\373thorn\376",           /* 5 */
18666            "Agrave\300Aacute\301Atilde\303Ccedil\
18667              307Egrave\310Eacute\311\
18668    Igrave\314Iacute\315Ntilde\321Ograve\322Oacute\
18669              323Otilde\325Oslash\330\
18670    Ugrave\331Uacute\332Yacute\335agrave\340aacute\
18671              341atilde\343ccedil\347\
18672    egrave\350eacute\351igrave\354iacute\355ntilde\
18673              361ograve\362oacute\363\
18674    otilde\365oslash\370ugrave\371uacute\372yacute\
18675              375"    /* 6 */
18676            };
18677
18678        for (; *s != '\0'; s++, p++) {
18679            if (*s != '&') {
18680                *p = *s;
18681                continue;
18682            }
18683            /* find end of entity */
18684            for (i = 1; s[i] != ';' && s[i] != '\0'; i++) {
18685                continue;
18686            }
18687
18688            if (s[i] == '\0') {  /* treat as normal data */
18689                *p = *s;
18690                continue;
18691            }
18692
18693            /* is it numeric ? */
18694            if (s[1] == '#') {
18695                for (j = 2, val = 0; j < i &&
18696                    ap_isdigit(s[j]); j++) {
18697                    val = val * 10 + s[j] - '0';
18698                }
18699                s += i;
18700                if (j < i || val <= 8 || (val >=
18701                    11 && val <= 31) ||
18702                    (val >= 127 && val <= 160) || val >= 256) {
18703                    p--;             /* no data to output */
18704                }
18705                else {
18706                    *p = RAW_ASCII_CHAR(val);
18707                }
18708            }
18709            else {
18710                j = i - 1;
18711                if (j > MAXENTLEN || entlist[j] == NULL) {
18712                    /* wrong length */
18713                    *p = '&';
18714                    continue;        /* skip it */
18715                }
18716                for (ents = entlist[j]; *ents !=
18717                        '\0'; ents += i) {
18718                    if (strncmp(s + 1, ents, j) == 0) {
18719                        break;
18720                    }
18721                }
18722
18723                if (*ents == '\0') {
18724                    *p = '&';          /* unknown */
18725                }
18726                else {
18727                    *p = RAW_ASCII_CHAR(((const unsigned
18728                        char *) ents)[j]);
18729                    s += i;
18730                }
18731            }
18732        }
18733
18734        *p = '\0';
18735    }
18736
18737    /*
18738     * extract the next tag name and value.
18739     * if there are no more tags, set the tag name to 'done'
18740     * the tag value is html decoded if dodecode is non-zero
18741     */
18742
18743    static char *get_tag(pool *p, FILE *in, char *tag,
18744        int tagbuf_len, int dodecode)
18745    {
18746        char *t = tag, *tag_val, c, term;
18747
18748        /* makes code below a little less cluttered */
18749        --tagbuf_len;
18750
```

```
18751        do {                              /* skip whitespace */
18752            GET_CHAR(in, c, NULL, p);
18753        } while (ap_isspace(c));
18754
18755        /* tags can't start with - */
18756        if (c == '-') {
18757            GET_CHAR(in, c, NULL, p);
18758            if (c == '-') {
18759                do {
18760                    GET_CHAR(in, c, NULL, p);
18761                } while (ap_isspace(c));
18762                if (c == '>') {
18763                    ap_cpystrn(tag, "done", tagbuf_len);
18764                    return tag;
18765                }
18766            }
18767            return NULL;                /* failed */
18768        }
18769
18770        /* find end of tag name */
18771        while (1) {
18772            if (t - tag == tagbuf_len) {
18773                *t = '\0';
18774                return NULL;
18775            }
18776            if (c == '=' || ap_isspace(c)) {
18777                break;
18778            }
18779            *(t++) = ap_tolower(c);
18780            GET_CHAR(in, c, NULL, p);
18781        }
18782
18783        *t++ = '\0';
18784        tag_val = t;
18785
18786        while (ap_isspace(c)) {
18787            GET_CHAR(in, c, NULL, p);   /* space before = */
18788        }
18789        if (c != '=') {
18790            ungetc(c, in);
18791            return NULL;
18792        }
18793
18794        do {
18795            GET_CHAR(in, c, NULL, p);    /* space after = */
18796        } while (ap_isspace(c));
18797
18798        /* we should allow a 'name' as a value */
18799
18800        if (c != '"' && c != '\'') {
18801            return NULL;
18802        }
18803        term = c;
18804        while (1) {
18805            GET_CHAR(in, c, NULL, p);
18806            if (t - tag == tagbuf_len) {
18807                *t = '\0';
18808                return NULL;
18809            }
18810    /* Want to accept \" as a valid character
18811     * within a string. */
18812            if (c == '\\') {
18813                *(t++) = c;             /* Add backslash */
18814                GET_CHAR(in, c, NULL, p);
18815                if (c == term) {    /* Only if */
18816                    *(--t) = c;
18817                /* Replace backslash ONLY for terminator */
18818                }
18819            }
18820            else if (c == term) {
18821                break;
18822            }
18823            *(t++) = c;
18824        }
18825        *t = '\0';
18826        if (dodecode) {
18827            decodehtml(tag_val);
18828        }
18829        return ap_pstrdup(p, tag_val);
18830    }
18831
18832    static int get_directive(FILE *in, char *dest,
18833        size_t len, pool *p)
18834    {
18835        char *d = dest;
18836        char c;
18837
18838        /* make room for nul terminator */
18839        --len;
18840
18841        /* skip initial whitespace */
18842        while (1) {
18843            GET_CHAR(in, c, 1, p);
18844            if (!ap_isspace(c)) {
18845                break;
18846            }
```

```
18847          }
18848          /* now get directive */
18849          while (1) {
18850           if (d - dest == len) {
18851              return 1;
18852           }
18853              *d++ = ap_tolower(c);
18854              GET_CHAR(in, c, 1, p);
18855              if (ap_isspace(c)) {
18856                  break;
18857              }
18858          }
18859          *d = '\0';
18860          return 0;
18861      }
18862
18863      /*
18864       * Do variable substitution on strings
18865       */
18866      static void parse_string(request_rec *r, const
18867          char *in, char *out,
18868                      size_t length, int leave_name)
18869      {
18870          char ch;
18871          char *next = out;
18872          char *end_out;
18873
18874          /* leave room for nul terminator */
18875          end_out = out + length - 1;
18876
18877          while ((ch = *in++) != '\0') {
18878              switch (ch) {
18879              case '\\':
18880               if (next == end_out) {
18881                /* truncated */
18882                *next = '\0';
18883                return;
18884               }
18885                  if (*in == '$') {
18886                      *next++ = *in++;
18887                  }
18888                  else {
18889                      *next++ = ch;
18890                  }
18891                  break;
18892              case '$':
18893                  {
18894                  char var[MAX_STRING_LEN];
```

```
18895          const char *start_of_var_name;
18896          const char *end_of_var_name;
18897          /* end of var name + 1 */
18898          const char *expansion;
18899          const char *val;
18900          size_t l;
18901
18902          /* guess that the expansion won't happen */
18903          expansion = in - 1;
18904          if (*in == '{') {
18905              ++in;
18906              start_of_var_name = in;
18907              in = strchr(in, '}');
18908              if (in == NULL) {
18909                      ap_log_rerror(APLOG_MARK,
18910                          APLOG_NOERRNO|APLOG_ERR,
18911                      r, "Missing '}'
18912                          on variable \"%s\"",
18913                      expansion);
18914                      *next = '\0';
18915                      return;
18916                  }
18917              end_of_var_name = in;
18918              ++in;
18919          }
18920          else {
18921              start_of_var_name = in;
18922              while (ap_isalnum(*in) || *in == '_') {
18923                ++in;
18924              }
18925              end_of_var_name = in;
18926          }
18927          /* what a pain, too bad there's no
18928           * table_getn where you can
18929           * pass a non-nul terminated string */
18930          l = end_of_var_name - start_of_var_name;
18931          if (l != 0) {
18932              l = (l > sizeof(var) - 1) ?
18933                  (sizeof(var) - 1) : l;
18934              memcpy(var, start_of_var_name, l);
18935              var[l] = '\0';
18936
18937              val = ap_table_get(r->subprocess_env, var);
18938              if (val) {
18939               expansion = val;
18940               l = strlen(expansion);
18941              }
18942              else if (leave_name) {
```

```
18943            l = in - expansion;
18944            }
18945            else {
18946            break;      /* no expansion to be done */
18947            }
18948        }
18949        else {
18950            /* zero-length variable name causes just
18951             * the $ to be copied */
18952            l = 1;
18953        }
18954        l = (l > end_out - next) ? (end_out - next) : l;
18955        memcpy(next, expansion, l);
18956        next += l;
18957            break;
18958        }
18959    default:
18960        if (next == end_out) {
18961        /* truncated */
18962        *next = '\0';
18963        return;
18964        }
18965        *next++ = ch;
18966        break;
18967    }
18968    }
18969    *next = '\0';
18970    return;
18971 }
18972
18973 /* --------------- Action handlers --------------- */
18974
18975 static int include_cgi(char *s, request_rec *r)
18976 {
18977    request_rec *rr = ap_sub_req_lookup_uri(s, r);
18978    int rr_status;
18979
18980    if (rr->status != HTTP_OK) {
18981        return -1;
18982    }
18983
18984    /* No hardwired path info or query allowed */
18985
18986    if ((rr->path_info && rr->path_info[0]) ||
18987        rr->args) {
18988        return -1;
18989    }
18990    if (rr->finfo.st_mode == 0) {
```

```
18991        return -1;
18992    }
18993
18994    /* Script gets parameters of the *document*,
18995     * for back compatibility */
18996
18997    rr->path_info = r->path_info;
18998    /* hard to get right; see mod_cgi.c */
18999    rr->args = r->args;
19000
19001    /* Force sub_req to be treated as a CGI request,
19002     * even if ordinary typing rules would
19003     * have called it something else.
19004     */
19005
19006    rr->content_type = CGI_MAGIC_TYPE;
19007
19008    /* Run it. */
19009
19010    rr_status = ap_run_sub_req(rr);
19011    if (ap_is_HTTP_REDIRECT(rr_status)) {
19012        const char *location =
19013            ap_table_get(rr->headers_out, "Location");
19014        location = ap_escape_html(rr->pool, location);
19015        ap_rvputs(r, "<A HREF=\"", location, "\">",
19016            location, "</A>", NULL);
19017    }
19018
19019    ap_destroy_sub_req(rr);
19020 #ifndef WIN32
19021    ap_chdir_file(r->filename);
19022 #endif
19023
19024    return 0;
19025 }
19026
19027 /* ensure that path is relative, and does not contain
19028  * ".." elements essentially ensure that it does
19029  * not match the regex: (^/|(^|/)\.\.(/|$))
19030  * XXX: this needs os abstraction... consider c:..\foo
19031  * in win32
19032  */
19033 static int is_only_below(const char *path)
19034 {
19035 #ifdef HAVE_DRIVE_LETTERS
19036    if (path[1] == ':')
19037    return 0;
19038 #endif
```

```
19039        if (path[0] == '/') {
19040          return 0;
19041        }
19042        if (path[0] == '.' && path[1] == '.'
19043            && (path[2] == '\0' || path[2] == '/')) {
19044          return 0;
19045        }
19046        while (*path) {
19047          if (*path == '/' && path[1] == '.' && path[2] == '.'
19048              && (path[3] == '\0' || path[3] == '/')) {
19049            return 0;
19050          }
19051          ++path;
19052        }
19053        return 1;
19054    }
19055
19056    static int handle_include(FILE *in, request_rec *r,
19057          const char *error, int noexec)
19058    {
19059        char tag[MAX_STRING_LEN];
19060        char parsed_string[MAX_STRING_LEN];
19061        char *tag_val;
19062
19063        while (1) {
19064            if (!(tag_val = get_tag(r->pool, in, tag,
19065              sizeof(tag), 1))) {
19066                return 1;
19067            }
19068            if (!strcmp(tag, "file") || !strcmp(tag,
19069                "virtual")) {
19070                request_rec *rr = NULL;
19071                char *error_fmt = NULL;
19072
19073                parse_string(r, tag_val, parsed_string,
19074                    sizeof(parsed_string), 0);
19075                if (tag[0] == 'f') {
19076                    /* be safe; only files in this
19077                            directory
19078                     * or below allowed */
19079                  if (!is_only_below(parsed_string)) {
19080                        error_fmt = "unable to include
19081                            file \"%s\" "
19082                            "in parsed file %s";
19083                    }
19084                    else {
19085                        rr = ap_sub_req_lookup_file
19086                            (parsed_string, r);
```

```
19087                    }
19088                }
19089                else {
19090                    rr = ap_sub_req_lookup_uri
19091                        (parsed_string, r);
19092                }
19093
19094                if (!error_fmt && rr->status != HTTP_OK) {
19095                    error_fmt = "unable to include \"%s\"
19096                        in parsed file %s";
19097                }
19098
19099                if (!error_fmt && noexec && rr->content_type
19100                    && (strncmp(rr->content_type,
19101                        "text/", 5))) {
19102                    error_fmt = "unable to include potential
19103                        exec \"%s\" "
19104                        "in parsed file %s";
19105                }
19106                if (error_fmt == NULL) {
19107    /* try to avoid recursive includes.  We do this
19108     * by walking up the r->main list of
19109     * subrequests, and at each level walking back
19110     * through any internal redirects.  At each
19111     * step, we compare the filenames and the URIs.
19112     *
19113     * The filename comparison catches a recursive
19114     * include with an ever-changing URL, eg.
19115     * <!--#include virtual="$REQUEST_URI/$
19116     *    QUERY_STRING?$QUERY_STRING/x"-->
19117     * which, although they would eventually be
19118     * caught because we have a limit on the length
19119     * of files, etc., can recurse for a while.
19120     *
19121     * The URI comparison catches the case where the
19122     * filename is changed while processing the
19123     * request, so the current name is never the
19124     * same as any previous one. This can happen
19125     * with "DocumentRoot /foo" when you request "/"
19126     * on the server and it includes "/". This only
19127     * applies to modules such as mod_dir that
19128     * (somewhat improperly) mess with r->filename
19129     * outside of a filename translation phase.
19130     */
19131                    int founddupe = 0;
19132                    request_rec *p;
19133                    for (p = r; p != NULL && !founddupe;
19134                        p = p->main) {
```

```
19135              request_rec *q;
19136              for (q = p; q != NULL; q = q->prev) {
19137               if ( (strcmp(q->filename,
19138                     rr->filename) == 0) ||
19139                   (strcmp(q->uri, rr->uri) == 0) ){
19140                  founddupe = 1;
19141                  break;
19142               }
19143              }
19144            }

19146            if (p != NULL) {
19147               error_fmt = "Recursive include
19148                     of \"%s\" "
19149                     "in parsed file %s";
19150            }
19151          }

19153          /* see the Kludge in send_parsed_file for why */
19154          if (rr)
19155           ap_set_module_config(rr->request_config,
19156               &includes_module, r);

19158          if (!error_fmt && ap_run_sub_req(rr)) {
19159             error_fmt = "unable to include \"%s\"
19160                   in parsed file %s";
19161          }
19162 #ifndef WIN32
19163            ap_chdir_file(r->filename);
19164 #endif
19165          if (error_fmt) {
19166             ap_log_rerror(APLOG_MARK,
19167                APLOG_NOERRNO|APLOG_ERR,
19168                r, error_fmt, tag_val, r->filename);
19169             ap_rputs(error, r);
19170          }

19172        /* destroy the sub request if it's not
19173         * a nested include */
19174        if (rr != NULL
19175       && ap_get_module_config(rr->request_config,
19176          &includes_module)
19177          != NESTED_INCLUDE_MAGIC) {
19178       ap_destroy_sub_req(rr);
19179        }
19180      }
19181      else if (!strcmp(tag, "done")) {
19182         return 0;
```

```
19183          }
19184        else {
19185          ap_log_rerror(APLOG_MARK,
19186             APLOG_NOERRNO|APLOG_ERR, r,
19187                "unknown parameter \"%s\"
19188                    to tag include in %s",
19189                tag, r->filename);
19190          ap_rputs(error, r);
19191        }
19192      }
19193 }

19195 typedef struct {
19196     request_rec *r;
19197     char *s;
19198 } include_cmd_arg;

19200 static int include_cmd_child(void *arg,
19201     child_info *pinfo)
19202 {
19203     request_rec *r = ((include_cmd_arg *) arg)->r;
19204     char *s = ((include_cmd_arg *) arg)->s;
19205     table *env = r->subprocess_env;
19206     int child_pid = 0;
19207 #ifdef DEBUG_INCLUDE_CMD
19208 #ifdef OS2
19209     /* under OS/2 /dev/tty is referenced as con */
19210     FILE *dbg = fopen("con", "w");
19211 #else
19212     FILE *dbg = fopen("/dev/tty", "w");
19213 #endif
19214 #endif
19215 #ifndef WIN32
19216     char err_string[MAX_STRING_LEN];
19217 #endif

19219 #ifdef DEBUG_INCLUDE_CMD
19220     fprintf(dbg, "Attempting to include
19221         command '%s'\n", s);
19222 #endif

19224     if (r->path_info && r->path_info[0] != '\0') {
19225        request_rec *pa_req;

19227        ap_table_setn(env, "PATH_INFO",
19228          ap_escape_shell_cmd(r->pool, r->path_info));

19230        pa_req = ap_sub_req_lookup_uri(ap_escape_uri
```

```
19231                 (r->pool, r->path_info), r);
19232             if (pa_req->filename) {
19233                 ap_table_setn(env, "PATH_TRANSLATED",
19234                     ap_pstrcat(r->pool, pa_req->filename,
19235                         pa_req->path_info,
19236                             NULL));
19237             }
19238         }
19239
19240         if (r->args) {
19241             char *arg_copy = ap_pstrdup(r->pool, r->args);
19242
19243             ap_table_setn(env, "QUERY_STRING", r->args);
19244             ap_unescape_url(arg_copy);
19245             ap_table_setn(env, "QUERY_STRING_UNESCAPED",
19246                 ap_escape_shell_cmd(r->pool, arg_copy));
19247         }
19248
19249         ap_error_log2stderr(r->server);
19250
19251 #ifdef DEBUG_INCLUDE_CMD
19252         fprintf(dbg, "Attempting to exec '%s'\n", s);
19253 #endif
19254         ap_cleanup_for_exec();
19255         /* set shellcmd flag to pass arg to SHELL_PATH */
19256         child_pid = ap_call_exec(r, pinfo, s,
19257             ap_create_environment(r->pool, env),
19258                 1);
19259 #ifdef WIN32
19260         return (child_pid);
19261 #else
19262         /* Oh, drat.  We're still here.  The log file
19263          * descriptors are closed, so we have to
19264          * whimper a complaint onto stderr...
19265          */
19266
19267 #ifdef DEBUG_INCLUDE_CMD
19268         fprintf(dbg, "Exec failed\n");
19269
19270 #endif
19271         ap_snprintf(err_string, sizeof(err_string),
19272             "exec of %s failed, reason: %s
19273                 (errno = %d)\n",
19274                 SHELL_PATH, strerror(errno), errno);
19275         write(STDERR_FILENO, err_string,
19276             strlen(err_string));
19277         exit(0);
19278         /* NOT REACHED */
19279         return (child_pid);
19280 #endif /* WIN32 */
19281 }
19282
19283 static int include_cmd(char *s, request_rec *r)
19284 {
19285     include_cmd_arg arg;
19286     BUFF *script_in;
19287
19288     arg.r = r;
19289     arg.s = s;
19290
19291     if (!ap_bspawn_child(r->pool,
19292             include_cmd_child, &arg,
19293                 kill_after_timeout, NULL, &script_in,
19294                     NULL)) {
19295         ap_log_rerror(APLOG_MARK, APLOG_ERR, r,
19296             "couldn't spawn include command");
19297         return -1;
19298     }
19299
19300     ap_send_fb(script_in, r);
19301     ap_bclose(script_in);
19302     return 0;
19303 }
19304
19305 static int handle_exec(FILE *in, request_rec *r,
19306     const char *error)
19307 {
19308     char tag[MAX_STRING_LEN];
19309     char *tag_val;
19310     char *file = r->filename;
19311     char parsed_string[MAX_STRING_LEN];
19312
19313     while (1) {
19314         if (!(tag_val = get_tag(r->pool, in, tag,
19315                 sizeof(tag), 1))) {
19316             return 1;
19317         }
19318         if (!strcmp(tag, "cmd")) {
19319             parse_string(r, tag_val, parsed_string,
19320                 sizeof(parsed_string), 1);
19321             if (include_cmd(parsed_string, r) == -1) {
19322                 ap_log_rerror(APLOG_MARK,
19323                     APLOG_NOERRNO|APLOG_ERR, r,
19324                         "execution failure for
19325                             parameter \"%s\" "
19326                         "to tag exec in file %s",
```

```
19327                          tag, r->filename);
19328                  ap_rputs(error, r);
19329              }
19330              /* just in case some stooge
19331               * changed directories */
19332  #ifndef WIN32
19333              ap_chdir_file(r->filename);
19334  #endif
19335          }
19336          else if (!strcmp(tag, "cgi")) {
19337              parse_string(r, tag_val, parsed_string,
19338                  sizeof(parsed_string), 0);
19339              if (include_cgi(parsed_string, r) == -1) {
19340                  ap_log_rerror(APLOG_MARK,
19341                      APLOG_NOERRNO|APLOG_ERR, r,
19342                          "invalid CGI ref \"%s\"
19343                              in %s", tag_val, file);
19344                  ap_rputs(error, r);
19345              }
19346              /* grumble groan */
19347  #ifndef WIN32
19348              ap_chdir_file(r->filename);
19349  #endif
19350          }
19351          else if (!strcmp(tag, "done")) {
19352              return 0;
19353          }
19354          else {
19355              ap_log_rerror(APLOG_MARK,
19356                  APLOG_NOERRNO|APLOG_ERR, r,
19357                      "unknown parameter \"%s\"
19358                          to tag exec in %s",
19359                          tag, file);
19360              ap_rputs(error, r);
19361          }
19362      }
19363
19364  }
19365
19366  static int handle_echo(FILE *in, request_rec *r,
19367      const char *error)
19368  {
19369      char tag[MAX_STRING_LEN];
19370      char *tag_val;
19371
19372      while (1) {
19373          if (!(tag_val = get_tag(r->pool, in, tag,
19374              sizeof(tag), 1))) {
19375              return 1;
19376          }
19377          if (!strcmp(tag, "var")) {
19378              const char *val =
19379                  ap_table_get(r->subprocess_env, tag_val);
19380
19381              if (val) {
19382                  ap_rputs(val, r);
19383              }
19384              else {
19385                  ap_rputs("(none)", r);
19386              }
19387          }
19388          else if (!strcmp(tag, "done")) {
19389              return 0;
19390          }
19391          else {
19392              ap_log_rerror(APLOG_MARK,
19393                  APLOG_NOERRNO|APLOG_ERR, r,
19394                      "unknown parameter \"%s\"
19395                          to tag echo in %s",
19396                          tag, r->filename);
19397              ap_rputs(error, r);
19398          }
19399      }
19400  }
19401
19402  #ifdef USE_PERL_SSI
19403  static int handle_perl(FILE *in, request_rec *r,
19404      const char *error)
19405  {
19406      char tag[MAX_STRING_LEN];
19407      char parsed_string[MAX_STRING_LEN];
19408      char *tag_val;
19409      SV *sub = Nullsv;
19410      AV *av = newAV();
19411
19412      if (ap_allow_options(r) & OPT_INCNOEXEC) {
19413          ap_log_rerror(APLOG_MARK,
19414              APLOG_NOERRNO|APLOG_ERR, r,
19415                  "#perl SSI disallowed by
19416                      IncludesNoExec in %s",
19417                      r->filename);
19418          return DECLINED;
19419      }
19420      while (1) {
19421          if (!(tag_val = get_tag(r->pool, in, tag,
19422              sizeof(tag), 1))) {
```

```
19423              break;
19424          }
19425          if (strnEQ(tag, "sub", 3)) {
19426              sub = newSVpv(tag_val, 0);
19427          }
19428          else if (strnEQ(tag, "arg", 3)) {
19429              parse_string(r, tag_val, parsed_string,
19430                  sizeof(parsed_string), 0);
19431              av_push(av, newSVpv(parsed_string, 0));
19432          }
19433          else if (strnEQ(tag, "done", 4)) {
19434              break;
19435          }
19436      }
19437      perl_stdout2client(r);
19438      perl_setup_env(r);
19439      perl_call_handler(sub, r, av);
19440      return OK;
19441  }
19442  #endif
19443
19444  /* error and tf must point to a string with room for at
19445   * least MAX_STRING_LEN characters
19446   */
19447  static int handle_config(FILE *in, request_rec *r,
19448      char *error, char *tf,
19449                          int *sizefmt)
19450  {
19451      char tag[MAX_STRING_LEN];
19452      char *tag_val;
19453      char parsed_string[MAX_STRING_LEN];
19454      table *env = r->subprocess_env;
19455
19456      while (1) {
19457          if (!(tag_val = get_tag(r->pool, in, tag,
19458            sizeof(tag), 0))) {
19459              return 1;
19460          }
19461          if (!strcmp(tag, "errmsg")) {
19462              parse_string(r, tag_val, error,
19463                  MAX_STRING_LEN, 0);
19464          }
19465          else if (!strcmp(tag, "timefmt")) {
19466              time_t date = r->request_time;
19467
19468              parse_string(r, tag_val, tf,
19469                  MAX_STRING_LEN, 0);
19470              ap_table_setn(env, "DATE_LOCAL",
19471                  ap_ht_time(r->pool, date, tf, 0));
19472              ap_table_setn(env, "DATE_GMT",
19473                  ap_ht_time(r->pool, date, tf, 1));
19474              ap_table_setn(env, "LAST_MODIFIED",
19475                      ap_ht_time(r->pool,
19476                          r->finfo.st_mtime, tf, 0));
19477          }
19478          else if (!strcmp(tag, "sizefmt")) {
19479              parse_string(r, tag_val, parsed_string,
19480                  sizeof(parsed_string), 0);
19481              decodehtml(parsed_string);
19482              if (!strcmp(parsed_string, "bytes")) {
19483                  *sizefmt = SIZEFMT_BYTES;
19484              }
19485              else if (!strcmp(parsed_string, "abbrev")) {
19486                  *sizefmt = SIZEFMT_KMG;
19487              }
19488          }
19489          else if (!strcmp(tag, "done")) {
19490              return 0;
19491          }
19492          else {
19493              ap_log_rerror(APLOG_MARK,
19494                  APLOG_NOERRNO|APLOG_ERR, r,
19495                      "unknown parameter \"%s\"
19496                          to tag config in %s",
19497                      tag, r->filename);
19498              ap_rputs(error, r);
19499          }
19500      }
19501  }
19502
19503
19504  static int find_file(request_rec *r, const
19505      char *directive, const char *tag,
19506                  char *tag_val, struct stat *finfo,
19507                      const char *error)
19508  {
19509      char *to_send;
19510      request_rec *rr;
19511      int ret=0;
19512
19513      if (!strcmp(tag, "file")) {
19514          ap_getparents(tag_val);
19515          /* get rid of any nasties */
19516
19517          rr = ap_sub_req_lookup_file(tag_val, r);
19518
```

```
19519        if (rr->status ==
19520          HTTP_OK && rr->finfo.st_mode != 0) {
19521            to_send = rr->filename;
19522            if ((ret = stat(to_send, finfo)) == -1) {
19523                ap_log_rerror(APLOG_MARK, APLOG_ERR, r,
19524                        "unable to get information
19525                            about \"%s\" "
19526                        "in parsed file %s",
19527                        to_send, r->filename);
19528                ap_rputs(error, r);
19529            }
19530        }
19531        else {
19532            ret = -1;
19533            ap_log_rerror(APLOG_MARK, APLOG_ERR, r,
19534                    "unable to lookup information
19535                        about \"%s\" "
19536                    "in parsed file %s",
19537                    tag_val, r->filename);
19538            ap_rputs(error, r);
19539        }
19540
19541        ap_destroy_sub_req(rr);
19542
19543        return ret;
19544    }
19545    else if (!strcmp(tag, "virtual")) {
19546        rr = ap_sub_req_lookup_uri(tag_val, r);
19547
19548        if (rr->status ==
19549          HTTP_OK && rr->finfo.st_mode != 0) {
19550            memcpy((char *) finfo, (const char *)
19551                &rr->finfo,
19552                    sizeof(struct stat));
19553            ap_destroy_sub_req(rr);
19554            return 0;
19555        }
19556        else {
19557            ap_log_rerror(APLOG_MARK,
19558                APLOG_NOERRNO|APLOG_ERR, r,
19559                    "unable to get information
19560                        about \"%s\" "
19561                    "in parsed file %s",
19562                    tag_val, r->filename);
19563            ap_rputs(error, r);
19564            ap_destroy_sub_req(rr);
19565            return -1;
19566        }
19567        }
19568        else {
19569            ap_log_rerror(APLOG_MARK,
19570                    APLOG_NOERRNO|APLOG_ERR, r,
19571                    "unknown parameter \"%s\" to
19572                        tag %s in %s",
19573                    tag, directive, r->filename);
19574            ap_rputs(error, r);
19575            return -1;
19576        }
19577 }
19578
19579
19580 static int handle_fsize(FILE *in, request_rec *r,
19581    const char *error, int sizefmt)
19582 {
19583    char tag[MAX_STRING_LEN];
19584    char *tag_val;
19585    struct stat finfo;
19586    char parsed_string[MAX_STRING_LEN];
19587
19588    while (1) {
19589        if (!(tag_val = get_tag(r->pool, in, tag,
19590          sizeof(tag), 1))) {
19591            return 1;
19592        }
19593        else if (!strcmp(tag, "done")) {
19594            return 0;
19595        }
19596        else {
19597            parse_string(r, tag_val, parsed_string,
19598                sizeof(parsed_string), 0);
19599            if (!find_file(r, "fsize", tag, parsed_string,
19600                &finfo, error)) {
19601                if (sizefmt == SIZEFMT_KMG) {
19602                    ap_send_size(finfo.st_size, r);
19603                }
19604                else {
19605                    int l, x;
19606 #if defined(BSD) && BSD > 199305
19607                    /* ap_snprintf can't handle %qd */
19608                    sprintf(tag, "%qd", finfo.st_size);
19609 #else
19610                    ap_snprintf(tag, sizeof(tag), "%ld",
19611                        finfo.st_size);
19612 #endif
19613                    l = strlen(tag);    /* grrr */
19614                    for (x = 0; x < l; x++) {
```

```
19615                        if (x && (!((l - x) % 3))) {
19616                            ap_rputc(',', r);
19617                        }
19618                        ap_rputc(tag[x], r);
19619                    }
19620                }
19621            }
19622        }
19623    }
19624 }
19625
19626 static int handle_flastmod(FILE *in, request_rec *r,
19627        const char *error, const char *tf)
19628 {
19629     char tag[MAX_STRING_LEN];
19630     char *tag_val;
19631     struct stat finfo;
19632     char parsed_string[MAX_STRING_LEN];
19633
19634     while (1) {
19635         if (!(tag_val = get_tag(r->pool, in, tag,
19636           sizeof(tag), 1))) {
19637             return 1;
19638         }
19639         else if (!strcmp(tag, "done")) {
19640             return 0;
19641         }
19642         else {
19643             parse_string(r, tag_val, parsed_string,
19644                 sizeof(parsed_string), 0);
19645             if (!find_file(r, "flastmod", tag,
19646                 parsed_string, &finfo, error)) {
19647                 ap_rputs(ap_ht_time(r->pool,
19648                     finfo.st_mtime, tf, 0), r);
19649             }
19650         }
19651     }
19652 }
19653
19654 static int re_check(request_rec *r, char *string,
19655        char *rexp)
19656 {
19657     regex_t *compiled;
19658     int regex_error;
19659
19660     compiled = ap_pregcomp(r->pool, rexp,
19661         REG_EXTENDED | REG_NOSUB);
19662     if (compiled == NULL) {
```

```
19663         ap_log_rerror(APLOG_MARK,
19664           APLOG_NOERRNO|APLOG_ERR, r,
19665                 "unable to compile pattern
19666                     \"%s\"", rexp);
19667         return -1;
19668     }
19669     regex_error = regexec(compiled, string, 0,
19670         (regmatch_t *) NULL, 0);
19671     ap_pregfree(r->pool, compiled);
19672     return (!regex_error);
19673 }
19674
19675 enum token_type {
19676     token_string,
19677     token_and, token_or, token_not, token_eq, token_ne,
19678     token_rbrace, token_lbrace, token_group,
19679     token_ge, token_le, token_gt, token_lt
19680 };
19681 struct token {
19682     enum token_type type;
19683     char value[MAX_STRING_LEN];
19684 };
19685
19686 /* there is an implicit assumption here that string
19687  * is at most MAX_STRING_LEN-1
19688  * characters long...
19689  */
19690 static const char *get_ptoken(request_rec *r,
19691     const char *string, struct token *token)
19692 {
19693     char ch;
19694     int next = 0;
19695     int qs = 0;
19696
19697     /* Skip leading white space */
19698     if (string == (char *) NULL) {
19699         return (char *) NULL;
19700     }
19701     while ((ch = *string++)) {
19702         if (!ap_isspace(ch)) {
19703             break;
19704         }
19705     }
19706     if (ch == '\0') {
19707         return (char *) NULL;
19708     }
19709
19710     token->type = token_string; /* the default type */
```

```
19711      switch (ch) {
19712      case '(':
19713          token->type = token_lbrace;
19714          return (string);
19715      case ')':
19716          token->type = token_rbrace;
19717          return (string);
19718      case '=':
19719          token->type = token_eq;
19720          return (string);
19721      case '!':
19722          if (*string == '=') {
19723              token->type = token_ne;
19724              return (string + 1);
19725          }
19726          else {
19727              token->type = token_not;
19728              return (string);
19729          }
19730      case '\'':
19731          token->type = token_string;
19732          qs = 1;
19733          break;
19734      case '|':
19735          if (*string == '|') {
19736              token->type = token_or;
19737              return (string + 1);
19738          }
19739          break;
19740      case '&':
19741          if (*string == '&') {
19742              token->type = token_and;
19743              return (string + 1);
19744          }
19745          break;
19746      case '>':
19747          if (*string == '=') {
19748              token->type = token_ge;
19749              return (string + 1);
19750          }
19751          else {
19752              token->type = token_gt;
19753              return (string);
19754          }
19755      case '<':
19756          if (*string == '=') {
19757              token->type = token_le;
19758              return (string + 1);
```

```
19759          }
19760          else {
19761              token->type = token_lt;
19762              return (string);
19763          }
19764      default:
19765          token->type = token_string;
19766          break;
19767      }
19768      /* We should only be here if we are in a string */
19769      if (!qs) {
19770          token->value[next++] = ch;
19771      }
19772
19773      /*
19774       * Yes I know that goto's are BAD.  But, c doesn't
19775       * allow me to exit a loop from a switch
19776       * statement.  Yes, I could use a flag,
19777       * but that is (IMHO) even less readable/maintainable
19778       * than the goto.
19779       */
19780      /*
19781       * I used the ++string throughout this section so
19782       * that string ends up pointing to the next
19783       * token and I can just return it
19784       */
19785      for (ch = *string; ch != '\0'; ch = *++string) {
19786          if (ch == '\\') {
19787              if ((ch = *++string) == '\0') {
19788                  goto TOKEN_DONE;
19789              }
19790              token->value[next++] = ch;
19791              continue;
19792          }
19793          if (!qs) {
19794              if (ap_isspace(ch)) {
19795                  goto TOKEN_DONE;
19796              }
19797              switch (ch) {
19798              case '(':
19799                  goto TOKEN_DONE;
19800              case ')':
19801                  goto TOKEN_DONE;
19802              case '=':
19803                  goto TOKEN_DONE;
19804              case '!':
19805                  goto TOKEN_DONE;
19806              case '|':
```

```
19807                    if (*(string + 1) == '|') {
19808                        goto TOKEN_DONE;
19809                    }
19810                    break;
19811                case '&':
19812                    if (*(string + 1) == '&') {
19813                        goto TOKEN_DONE;
19814                    }
19815                    break;
19816                case '<':
19817                    goto TOKEN_DONE;
19818                case '>':
19819                    goto TOKEN_DONE;
19820                }
19821                token->value[next++] = ch;
19822            }
19823            else {
19824                if (ch == '\'') {
19825                    qs = 0;
19826                    ++string;
19827                    goto TOKEN_DONE;
19828                }
19829                token->value[next++] = ch;
19830            }
19831        }
19832    TOKEN_DONE:
19833        /* If qs is still set, I have an unmatched ' */
19834        if (qs) {
19835            ap_rputs("\nUnmatched '\n", r);
19836            next = 0;
19837        }
19838        token->value[next] = '\0';
19839        return (string);
19840    }
19841
19842
19843    /*
19844     * Hey I still know that goto's are BAD.  I don't
19845     * think that I've ever used two in the same project,
19846     * let alone the same file before.  But, I absolutely
19847     * want to make sure that I clean up the memory in all
19848     * cases.  And, without rewriting this completely, the
19849     * easiest way is to just branch to the return code
19850     * which cleans it up.
19851     */
19852    /* there is an implicit assumption here that expr is
19853     * at most MAX_STRING_LEN-1
19854     * characters long...
19855     */
19856    static int parse_expr(request_rec *r, const char *expr,
19857        const char *error)
19858    {
19859        struct parse_node {
19860            struct parse_node *left, *right, *parent;
19861            struct token token;
19862            int value, done;
19863        }        *root, *current, *new;
19864        const char *parse;
19865        char buffer[MAX_STRING_LEN];
19866        pool *expr_pool;
19867        int retval = 0;
19868
19869        if ((parse = expr) == (char *) NULL) {
19870            return (0);
19871        }
19872        root = current = (struct parse_node *) NULL;
19873        expr_pool = ap_make_sub_pool(r->pool);
19874
19875        /* Create Parse Tree */
19876        while (1) {
19877            new = (struct parse_node *) ap_palloc(expr_pool,
19878                            sizeof(struct parse_node));
19879            new->parent = new->left = new->right =
19880                (struct parse_node *) NULL;
19881            new->done = 0;
19882            if ((parse = get_ptoken(r, parse, &new->token))
19883                == (char *) NULL) {
19884                break;
19885            }
19886            switch (new->token.type) {
19887
19888            case token_string:
19889    #ifdef DEBUG_INCLUDE
19890                ap_rvputs(r, "      Token: string (",
19891                    new->token.value, ")\n", NULL);
19892    #endif
19893                if (current == (struct parse_node *) NULL) {
19894                    root = current = new;
19895                    break;
19896                }
19897                switch (current->token.type) {
19898                case token_string:
19899                    if (current->token.value[0] != '\0') {
19900                        strncat(current->token.value, " ",
19901                            sizeof(current->token.value)
19902                            - strlen(current->token.value) - 1);
```

```
19903                    }
19904                    strncat(current->token.value,
19905                       new->token.value,
19906                            sizeof(current->token.value)
19907                       - strlen(current->token.value) - 1);
19908                current->token.value[sizeof
19909                    (current->token.value) - 1] = '\0';
19910                    break;
19911            case token_eq:
19912            case token_ne:
19913            case token_and:
19914            case token_or:
19915            case token_lbrace:
19916            case token_not:
19917            case token_ge:
19918            case token_gt:
19919            case token_le:
19920            case token_lt:
19921                new->parent = current;
19922                current = current->right = new;
19923                break;
19924            default:
19925                ap_log_rerror(APLOG_MARK,
19926                    APLOG_NOERRNO|APLOG_ERR, r,
19927                        "Invalid expression
19928                            \"%s\" in file %s",
19929                        expr, r->filename);
19930                ap_rputs(error, r);
19931                goto RETURN;
19932            }
19933            break;
19934
19935        case token_and:
19936        case token_or:
19937    #ifdef DEBUG_INCLUDE
19938            ap_rputs("      Token: and/or\n", r);
19939    #endif
19940            if (current == (struct parse_node *) NULL) {
19941                ap_log_rerror(APLOG_MARK,
19942                    APLOG_NOERRNO|APLOG_ERR, r,
19943                        "Invalid expression
19944                            \"%s\" in file %s",
19945                        expr, r->filename);
19946                ap_rputs(error, r);
19947                goto RETURN;
19948            }
19949            /* Percolate upwards */
19950            while (current != (struct parse_node *)
19951                NULL) {
19952                switch (current->token.type) {
19953                case token_string:
19954                case token_group:
19955                case token_not:
19956                case token_eq:
19957                case token_ne:
19958                case token_and:
19959                case token_or:
19960                case token_ge:
19961                case token_gt:
19962                case token_le:
19963                case token_lt:
19964                    current = current->parent;
19965                    continue;
19966                case token_lbrace:
19967                    break;
19968                default:
19969                    ap_log_rerror(APLOG_MARK,
19970                        APLOG_NOERRNO|APLOG_ERR, r,
19971                            "Invalid expression
19972                                \"%s\" in file %s",
19973                            expr, r->filename);
19974                    ap_rputs(error, r);
19975                    goto RETURN;
19976                }
19977                break;
19978            }
19979            if (current == (struct parse_node *) NULL) {
19980                new->left = root;
19981                new->left->parent = new;
19982                new->parent = (struct parse_node *) NULL;
19983                root = new;
19984            }
19985            else {
19986                new->left = current->right;
19987                current->right = new;
19988                new->parent = current;
19989            }
19990            current = new;
19991            break;
19992
19993        case token_not:
19994    #ifdef DEBUG_INCLUDE
19995            ap_rputs("      Token: not\n", r);
19996    #endif
19997            if (current == (struct parse_node *) NULL) {
19998                root = current = new;
```

```
19999              break;
20000            }
20001          /* Percolate upwards */
20002          while (current != (struct parse_node *)
20003            NULL) {
20004            switch (current->token.type) {
20005            case token_not:
20006            case token_eq:
20007            case token_ne:
20008            case token_and:
20009            case token_or:
20010            case token_lbrace:
20011            case token_ge:
20012            case token_gt:
20013            case token_le:
20014            case token_lt:
20015                break;
20016            default:
20017                ap_log_rerror(APLOG_MARK,
20018                  APLOG_NOERRNO|APLOG_ERR, r,
20019                      "Invalid expression
20020                        \"%s\" in file %s",
20021                      expr, r->filename);
20022                ap_rputs(error, r);
20023                goto RETURN;
20024            }
20025            break;
20026          }
20027          if (current == (struct parse_node *) NULL) {
20028            new->left = root;
20029            new->left->parent = new;
20030            new->parent = (struct parse_node *) NULL;
20031            root = new;
20032          }
20033          else {
20034            new->left = current->right;
20035            current->right = new;
20036            new->parent = current;
20037          }
20038          current = new;
20039          break;

20040
20041        case token_eq:
20042        case token_ne:
20043        case token_ge:
20044        case token_gt:
20045        case token_le:
20046        case token_lt:
```

```
20047 #ifdef DEBUG_INCLUDE
20048          ap_rputs("     Token: eq/ne/ge/gt/le/lt\n", r);
20049 #endif
20050          if (current == (struct parse_node *) NULL) {
20051            ap_log_rerror(APLOG_MARK,
20052              APLOG_NOERRNO|APLOG_ERR, r,
20053                  "Invalid expression \"%s\"
20054                        in file %s",
20055                  expr, r->filename);
20056            ap_rputs(error, r);
20057            goto RETURN;
20058          }
20059          /* Percolate upwards */
20060          while (current != (struct parse_node *)
20061            NULL) {
20062            switch (current->token.type) {
20063            case token_string:
20064            case token_group:
20065                current = current->parent;
20066                continue;
20067            case token_lbrace:
20068            case token_and:
20069            case token_or:
20070                break;
20071            case token_not:
20072            case token_eq:
20073            case token_ne:
20074            case token_ge:
20075            case token_gt:
20076            case token_le:
20077            case token_lt:
20078            default:
20079                ap_log_rerror(APLOG_MARK,
20080                  APLOG_NOERRNO|APLOG_ERR, r,
20081                      "Invalid expression
20082                        \"%s\" in file %s",
20083                      expr, r->filename);
20084                ap_rputs(error, r);
20085                goto RETURN;
20086            }
20087            break;
20088          }
20089          if (current == (struct parse_node *) NULL) {
20090            new->left = root;
20091            new->left->parent = new;
20092            new->parent = (struct parse_node *) NULL;
20093            root = new;
20094          }
```

```
20095            else {
20096                new->left = current->right;
20097                current->right = new;
20098                new->parent = current;
20099            }
20100            current = new;
20101            break;
20102
20103        case token_rbrace:
20104 #ifdef DEBUG_INCLUDE
20105            ap_rputs("      Token: rbrace\n", r);
20106 #endif
20107            while (current != (struct parse_node *)
20108                NULL) {
20109              if (current->token.type ==
20110                token_lbrace) {
20111                current->token.type = token_group;
20112                break;
20113              }
20114              current = current->parent;
20115            }
20116            if (current == (struct parse_node *) NULL) {
20117                ap_log_rerror(APLOG_MARK,
20118                    APLOG_NOERRNO|APLOG_ERR, r,
20119                        "Unmatched ')' in \"%s\"
20120                            in file %s",
20121                    expr, r->filename);
20122                ap_rputs(error, r);
20123                goto RETURN;
20124            }
20125            break;
20126
20127        case token_lbrace:
20128 #ifdef DEBUG_INCLUDE
20129            ap_rputs("      Token: lbrace\n", r);
20130 #endif
20131            if (current == (struct parse_node *) NULL) {
20132                root = current = new;
20133                break;
20134            }
20135            /* Percolate upwards */
20136            while (current != (struct parse_node *)
20137                NULL) {
20138              switch (current->token.type) {
20139              case token_not:
20140              case token_eq:
20141              case token_ne:
20142              case token_and:
20143              case token_or:
20144              case token_lbrace:
20145              case token_ge:
20146              case token_gt:
20147              case token_le:
20148              case token_lt:
20149                break;
20150              case token_string:
20151              case token_group:
20152              default:
20153                ap_log_rerror(APLOG_MARK,
20154                    APLOG_NOERRNO|APLOG_ERR, r,
20155                        "Invalid expression \"%s\"
20156                            in file %s",
20157                        expr, r->filename);
20158                ap_rputs(error, r);
20159                goto RETURN;
20160              }
20161              break;
20162            }
20163            if (current == (struct parse_node *) NULL) {
20164              new->left = root;
20165              new->left->parent = new;
20166              new->parent = (struct parse_node *) NULL;
20167              root = new;
20168            }
20169            else {
20170              new->left = current->right;
20171              current->right = new;
20172              new->parent = current;
20173            }
20174            current = new;
20175            break;
20176        default:
20177            break;
20178        }
20179    }
20180
20181    /* Evaluate Parse Tree */
20182    current = root;
20183    while (current != (struct parse_node *) NULL) {
20184        switch (current->token.type) {
20185        case token_string:
20186 #ifdef DEBUG_INCLUDE
20187            ap_rputs("      Evaluate string\n", r);
20188 #endif
20189            parse_string(r, current->token.value, buffer,
20190                sizeof(buffer), 0);
```

```
20191            ap_cpystrn(current->token.value, buffer,
20192                sizeof(current->token.value));
20193            current->value = (current->token.value[0]
20194                != '\0');
20195            current->done = 1;
20196            current = current->parent;
20197            break;
20198
20199        case token_and:
20200        case token_or:
20201 #ifdef DEBUG_INCLUDE
20202            ap_rputs("      Evaluate and/or\n", r);
20203 #endif
20204            if (current->left == (struct parse_node *)
20205                NULL ||
20206                current->right == (struct parse_node *)
20207                    NULL) {
20208                ap_log_rerror(APLOG_MARK,
20209                    APLOG_NOERRNO|APLOG_ERR, r,
20210                        "Invalid expression \"%s\"
20211                            in file %s",
20212                        expr, r->filename);
20213                ap_rputs(error, r);
20214                goto RETURN;
20215            }
20216            if (!current->left->done) {
20217                switch (current->left->token.type) {
20218                case token_string:
20219                    parse_string(r,
20220                        current->left->token.value,
20221                            buffer, sizeof(buffer), 0);
20222                    ap_cpystrn(current->left->
20223                        token.value, buffer,
20224                            sizeof(current->left->
20225                                token.value));
20226                current->left->value = (current->left->
20227                    token.value[0] != '\0');
20228                    current->left->done = 1;
20229                    break;
20230                default:
20231                    current = current->left;
20232                    continue;
20233
20234                }
20235            }
20236            if (!current->right->done) {
20237                switch (current->right->token.type) {
20238                case token_string:
20239                    parse_string(r,
20240                        current->right->token.value,
20241                            buffer, sizeof(buffer), 0);
20242                    ap_cpystrn(current->right->
20243                        token.value, buffer,
20244                            sizeof(current->right->
20245                                token.value));
20246                current->right->value = (current->right->
20247                    token.value[0] != '\0');
20248                    current->right->done = 1;
20249                    break;
20250                default:
20251                    current = current->right;
20252                    continue;
20253                }
20254            }
20255 #ifdef DEBUG_INCLUDE
20256            ap_rvputs(r, "      Left: ",
20257                current->left->value ? "1" : "0",
20258                    "\n", NULL);
20259            ap_rvputs(r, "      Right: ",
20260                current->right->value ? "1" : "0",
20261                    "\n", NULL);
20262 #endif
20263            if (current->token.type == token_and) {
20264                current->value = current->left->value
20265                    && current->right->value;
20266            }
20267            else {
20268                current->value = current->left->value
20269                    || current->right->value;
20270            }
20271 #ifdef DEBUG_INCLUDE
20272            ap_rvputs(r, "      Returning ",
20273                current->value ? "1" : "0",
20274                    "\n", NULL);
20275 #endif
20276            current->done = 1;
20277            current = current->parent;
20278            break;
20279
20280        case token_eq:
20281        case token_ne:
20282 #ifdef DEBUG_INCLUDE
20283            ap_rputs("      Evaluate eq/ne\n", r);
20284 #endif
20285            if ((current->left ==
20286                (struct parse_node *) NULL ||
```

```
20287                    (current->right ==
20288                        (struct parse_node *) NULL) ||
20289                    (current->left->token.type !=
20290                        token_string) ||
20291                    (current->right->token.type !=
20292                        token_string)) {
20293                    ap_log_rerror(APLOG_MARK,
20294                        APLOG_NOERRNO|APLOG_ERR, r,
20295                            "Invalid expression \"%s\"
20296                                in file %s",
20297                            expr, r->filename);
20298                    ap_rputs(error, r);
20299                    goto RETURN;
20300                }
20301                parse_string(r, current->left->token.value,
20302                        buffer, sizeof(buffer), 0);
20303                ap_cpystrn(current->left->token.value,
20304                    buffer,
20305                    sizeof(current->left->token.value));
20306                parse_string(r, current->right->
20307                    token.value,
20308                        buffer, sizeof(buffer), 0);
20309                ap_cpystrn(current->right->token.value,
20310                    buffer,
20311                    sizeof(current->right->token.value));
20312                if (current->right->token.value[0] == '/') {
20313                    int len;
20314                    len = strlen(current->right->
20315                        token.value);
20316                    if (current->right->token.value
20317                        [len - 1] == '/') {
20318                        current->right->token.value
20319                        [len - 1] = '\0';
20320                    }
20321                    else {
20322                        ap_log_rerror(APLOG_MARK,
20323                            APLOG_NOERRNO|APLOG_ERR, r,
20324                                "Invalid rexp \"%s\"
20325                                    in file %s",
20326                                current->right->
20327                                    token.value, r->filename);
20328                        ap_rputs(error, r);
20329                        goto RETURN;
20330                    }
20331    #ifdef DEBUG_INCLUDE
20332                    ap_rvputs(r, "    Re Compare (",
20333                        current->left->token.value,
20334                        ") with /", &current->right->
20335                        token.value[1], "/\n", NULL);
20336    #endif
20337                    current->value =
20338                        re_check(r, current->left->
20339                            token.value,
20340                                &current->right->
20341                                    token.value[1]);
20342                }
20343                else {
20344    #ifdef DEBUG_INCLUDE
20345                    ap_rvputs(r, "    Compare (",
20346                        current->left->token.value,
20347                        ") with (", current->right->
20348                            token.value, ")\n", NULL);
20349    #endif
20350                    current->value =
20351                        (strcmp(current->left->token.value,
20352                            current->right->
20353                                token.value) == 0);
20354                }
20355                if (current->token.type == token_ne) {
20356                    current->value = !current->value;
20357                }
20358    #ifdef DEBUG_INCLUDE
20359                ap_rvputs(r, "    Returning ",
20360                    current->value ? "1" : "0",
20361                    "\n", NULL);
20362    #endif
20363                current->done = 1;
20364                current = current->parent;
20365                break;
20366            case token_ge:
20367            case token_gt:
20368            case token_le:
20369            case token_lt:
20370    #ifdef DEBUG_INCLUDE
20371                ap_rputs("    Evaluate ge/gt/le/lt\n", r);
20372    #endif
20373                if ((current->left == (struct parse_node *)
20374                    NULL) ||
20375                    (current->right == (struct parse_node *)
20376                        NULL) ||
20377                    (current->left->token.type !=
20378                        token_string) ||
20379                    (current->right->token.type !=
20380                        token_string)) {
20381                    ap_log_rerror(APLOG_MARK,
20382                        APLOG_NOERRNO|APLOG_ERR, r,
```

```
20383                         "Invalid expression \"%s\"
20384                             in file %s",
20385                         expr, r->filename);
20386                ap_rputs(error, r);
20387                goto RETURN;
20388            }
20389            parse_string(r, current->left->token.value,
20390                    buffer, sizeof(buffer), 0);
20391            ap_cpystrn(current->left->token.value,
20392                buffer,
20393                sizeof(current->left->token.value));
20394            parse_string(r, current->right->token.value,
20395                    buffer, sizeof(buffer), 0);
20396            ap_cpystrn(current->right->token.value,
20397                buffer,
20398                sizeof(current->right->token.value));
20399 #ifdef DEBUG_INCLUDE
20400            ap_rvputs(r, "        Compare (",
20401                current->left->token.value,
20402                  ") with (", current->right->
20403 token.value, ")\n", NULL);
20404 #endif
20405            current->value =
20406                strcmp(current->left->token.value,
20407                    current->right->token.value);
20408            if (current->token.type == token_ge) {
20409                current->value = current->value >= 0;
20410            }
20411            else if (current->token.type == token_gt) {
20412                current->value = current->value > 0;
20413            }
20414            else if (current->token.type == token_le) {
20415                current->value = current->value <= 0;
20416            }
20417            else if (current->token.type == token_lt) {
20418                current->value = current->value < 0;
20419            }
20420            else {
20421                current->value = 0;     /* Don't return
20422                    -1 if unknown token */
20423            }
20424 #ifdef DEBUG_INCLUDE
20425            ap_rvputs(r, "        Returning ",
20426                current->value ? "1" : "0",
20427                  "\n", NULL);
20428 #endif
20429            current->done = 1;
20430            current = current->parent;
20431            break;
20432
20433        case token_not:
20434            if (current->right != (struct parse_node *)
20435                NULL) {
20436                if (!current->right->done) {
20437                    current = current->right;
20438                    continue;
20439                }
20440                current->value = !current->right->value;
20441            }
20442            else {
20443                current->value = 0;
20444            }
20445 #ifdef DEBUG_INCLUDE
20446            ap_rvputs(r, "        Evaluate !: ",
20447                current->value ? "1" : "0",
20448                  "\n", NULL);
20449 #endif
20450            current->done = 1;
20451            current = current->parent;
20452            break;
20453
20454        case token_group:
20455            if (current->right != (struct parse_
20456                node *) NULL) {
20457                if (!current->right->done) {
20458                    current = current->right;
20459                    continue;
20460                }
20461                current->value = current->right->value;
20462            }
20463            else {
20464                current->value = 1;
20465            }
20466 #ifdef DEBUG_INCLUDE
20467            ap_rvputs(r, "        Evaluate (): ",
20468                current->value ? "1" : "0",
20469                  "\n", NULL);
20470 #endif
20471            current->done = 1;
20472            current = current->parent;
20473            break;
20474
20475        case token_lbrace:
20476            ap_log_rerror(APLOG_MARK,
20477                APLOG_NOERRNO|APLOG_ERR, r,
20478                    "Unmatched '(' in \"%s\"
```

```
20479                        in file %s",
20480                     expr, r->filename);
20481            ap_rputs(error, r);
20482            goto RETURN;
20483
20484        case token_rbrace:
20485            ap_log_rerror(APLOG_MARK,
20486                APLOG_NOERRNO|APLOG_ERR, r,
20487                    "Unmatched ')' in \"%s\""
20488                        in file %s",
20489                     expr, r->filename);
20490            ap_rputs(error, r);
20491            goto RETURN;
20492
20493        default:
20494            ap_log_rerror(APLOG_MARK,
20495                APLOG_NOERRNO|APLOG_ERR, r,
20496                "bad token type");
20497            ap_rputs(error, r);
20498            goto RETURN;
20499        }
20500    }
20501
20502    retval = (root == (struct parse_node *) NULL) ?
20503        0 : root->value;
20504  RETURN:
20505    ap_destroy_pool(expr_pool);
20506    return (retval);
20507 }
20508
20509 static int handle_if(FILE *in, request_rec *r,
20510     const char *error,
20511             int *conditional_status, int *printing)
20512 {
20513    char tag[MAX_STRING_LEN];
20514    char *tag_val;
20515    char *expr;
20516
20517    expr = NULL;
20518    while (1) {
20519        tag_val = get_tag(r->pool, in, tag,
20520            sizeof(tag), 0);
20521        if (*tag == '\0') {
20522            return 1;
20523        }
20524        else if (!strcmp(tag, "done")) {
20525            if (expr == NULL) {
20526            ap_log_rerror(APLOG_MARK,
```

```
20527                APLOG_NOERRNO|APLOG_ERR, r,
20528                "missing expr in if statement: %s",
20529                r->filename);
20530            ap_rputs(error, r);
20531            return 1;
20532        }
20533        *printing = *conditional_status =
20534            parse_expr(r, expr, error);
20535 #ifdef DEBUG_INCLUDE
20536        ap_rvputs(r, "**** if conditional_status=\"",
20537            *conditional_status ? "1" : "0", "\"\n",
20538                NULL);
20539 #endif
20540        return 0;
20541        }
20542        else if (!strcmp(tag, "expr")) {
20543            expr = tag_val;
20544 #ifdef DEBUG_INCLUDE
20545            ap_rvputs(r, "**** if expr=\"",
20546                expr, "\"\n", NULL);
20547 #endif
20548        }
20549        else {
20550            ap_log_rerror(APLOG_MARK,
20551                APLOG_NOERRNO|APLOG_ERR, r,
20552                    "unknown parameter \"%s\" to
20553                        tag if in %s",
20554                    tag, r->filename);
20555            ap_rputs(error, r);
20556        }
20557    }
20558 }
20559
20560 static int handle_elif(FILE *in, request_rec *r,
20561     const char *error,
20562                int *conditional_status,
20563                    int *printing)
20564 {
20565    char tag[MAX_STRING_LEN];
20566    char *tag_val;
20567    char *expr;
20568
20569    expr = NULL;
20570    while (1) {
20571        tag_val = get_tag(r->pool, in, tag,
20572            sizeof(tag), 0);
20573        if (*tag == '\0') {
20574            return 1;
```

```
20575                }
20576            else if (!strcmp(tag, "done")) {
20577  #ifdef DEBUG_INCLUDE
20578            ap_rvputs(r, "**** elif
20579                conditional_status=\"",
20580                    *conditional_status ? "1" : "0",
20581                        "\"\n", NULL);
20582  #endif
20583            if (*conditional_status) {
20584                *printing = 0;
20585                return (0);
20586            }
20587          if (expr == NULL) {
20588            ap_log_rerror(APLOG_MARK,
20589                APLOG_NOERRNO|APLOG_ERR, r,
20590                    "missing expr in elif statement: %s",
20591                    r->filename);
20592            ap_rputs(error, r);
20593            return 1;
20594          }
20595            *printing = *conditional_status =
20596                    parse_expr(r, expr, error);
20597  #ifdef DEBUG_INCLUDE
20598            ap_rvputs(r, "**** elif
20599                conditional_status=\"",
20600                    *conditional_status ? "1" : "0",
20601                        "\"\n", NULL);
20602  #endif
20603            return 0;
20604        }
20605        else if (!strcmp(tag, "expr")) {
20606            expr = tag_val;
20607  #ifdef DEBUG_INCLUDE
20608            ap_rvputs(r, "**** if expr=\"", expr,
20609                "\"\n", NULL);
20610  #endif
20611        }
20612        else {
20613            ap_log_rerror(APLOG_MARK,
20614                APLOG_NOERRNO|APLOG_ERR, r,
20615                    "unknown parameter \"%s\" to
20616                        tag if in %s",
20617                    tag, r->filename);
20618            ap_rputs(error, r);
20619        }
20620    }
20621  }
20622
```

```
20623  static int handle_else(FILE *in, request_rec *r,
20624      const char *error,
20625                      int *conditional_status,
20626                          int *printing)
20627  {
20628      char tag[MAX_STRING_LEN];
20629
20630      if (!get_tag(r->pool, in, tag, sizeof(tag), 1)) {
20631          return 1;
20632      }
20633      else if (!strcmp(tag, "done")) {
20634  #ifdef DEBUG_INCLUDE
20635          ap_rvputs(r, "**** else conditional_status=\"",
20636                  *conditional_status ? "1" : "0", "\"\n",
20637                      NULL);
20638  #endif
20639          *printing = !(*conditional_status);
20640          *conditional_status = 1;
20641          return 0;
20642      }
20643      else {
20644          ap_log_rerror(APLOG_MARK,
20645                  APLOG_NOERRNO|APLOG_ERR, r,
20646                  "else directive does not take
20647                      tags in %s",
20648                  r->filename);
20649          if (*printing) {
20650              ap_rputs(error, r);
20651          }
20652          return -1;
20653      }
20654  }
20655
20656  static int handle_endif(FILE *in, request_rec *r,
20657      const char *error,
20658                      int *conditional_status,
20659                          int *printing)
20660  {
20661      char tag[MAX_STRING_LEN];
20662
20663      if (!get_tag(r->pool, in, tag, sizeof(tag), 1)) {
20664          return 1;
20665      }
20666      else if (!strcmp(tag, "done")) {
20667  #ifdef DEBUG_INCLUDE
20668          ap_rvputs(r, "**** endif conditional_status=\"",
20669                  *conditional_status ? "1" : "0", "\"\n",
20670                      NULL);
```

```
20671   #endif
20672           *printing = 1;
20673           *conditional_status = 1;
20674           return 0;
20675       }
20676       else {
20677           ap_log_rerror(APLOG_MARK,
20678                   APLOG_NOERRNO|APLOG_ERR, r,
20679                       "endif directive does not take
20680                               tags in %s",
20681               r->filename);
20682           ap_rputs(error, r);
20683           return -1;
20684       }
20685   }
20686
20687   static int handle_set(FILE *in, request_rec *r,
20688       const char *error)
20689   {
20690       char tag[MAX_STRING_LEN];
20691       char parsed_string[MAX_STRING_LEN];
20692       char *tag_val;
20693       char *var;
20694
20695       var = (char *) NULL;
20696       while (1) {
20697           if (!(tag_val = get_tag(r->pool, in, tag,
20698                   sizeof(tag), 1))) {
20699               return 1;
20700           }
20701           else if (!strcmp(tag, "done")) {
20702               return 0;
20703           }
20704           else if (!strcmp(tag, "var")) {
20705               var = tag_val;
20706           }
20707           else if (!strcmp(tag, "value")) {
20708               if (var == (char *) NULL) {
20709                   ap_log_rerror(APLOG_MARK,
20710                       APLOG_NOERRNO|APLOG_ERR, r,
20711                           "variable must precede value
20712                                   in set directive in %s",
20713                       r->filename);
20714                   ap_rputs(error, r);
20715                   return -1;
20716               }
20717               parse_string(r, tag_val, parsed_string,
20718                   sizeof(parsed_string), 0);
```

```
20719                   ap_table_setn(r->subprocess_env, var,
20720                       ap_pstrdup(r->pool, parsed_string));
20721               }
20722               else {
20723                   ap_log_rerror(APLOG_MARK,
20724                       APLOG_NOERRNO|APLOG_ERR, r,
20725                           "Invalid tag for set directive in
20726                                   %s", r->filename);
20727                   ap_rputs(error, r);
20728                   return -1;
20729               }
20730       }
20731   }
20732
20733   static int handle_printenv(FILE *in, request_rec *r,
20734       const char *error)
20735   {
20736       char tag[MAX_STRING_LEN];
20737       char *tag_val;
20738       array_header *arr =
20739               ap_table_elts(r->subprocess_env);
20740       table_entry *elts = (table_entry *) arr->elts;
20741       int i;
20742
20743       if (!(tag_val = get_tag(r->pool, in, tag,
20744               sizeof(tag), 1))) {
20745           return 1;
20746       }
20747       else if (!strcmp(tag, "done")) {
20748           for (i = 0; i < arr->nelts; ++i) {
20749               ap_rvputs(r, elts[i].key, "=", elts[i].val,
20750                   "\n", NULL);
20751           }
20752           return 0;
20753       }
20754       else {
20755           ap_log_rerror(APLOG_MARK,
20756                   APLOG_NOERRNO|APLOG_ERR, r,
20757                       "printenv directive does not take
20758                               tags in %s",
20759               r->filename);
20760           ap_rputs(error, r);
20761           return -1;
20762       }
20763   }
20764
20765
20766
```

```
20767   /* ---------------- The main function ------------ */
20768
20769   /* This is a stub which parses a file descriptor. */
20770
20771   static void send_parsed_content(FILE *f, request_rec *r)
20772   {
20773       char directive[MAX_STRING_LEN],
20774            error[MAX_STRING_LEN];
20775       char timefmt[MAX_STRING_LEN];
20776       int noexec = ap_allow_options(r) & OPT_INCNOEXEC;
20777       int ret, sizefmt;
20778       int if_nesting;
20779       int printing;
20780       int conditional_status;
20781
20782       ap_cpystrn(error, DEFAULT_ERROR_MSG, sizeof(error));
20783       ap_cpystrn(timefmt, DEFAULT_TIME_FORMAT,
20784            sizeof(timefmt));
20785       sizefmt = SIZEFMT_KMG;
20786
20787   /*  Turn printing on */
20788       printing = conditional_status = 1;
20789       if_nesting = 0;
20790
20791   #ifndef WIN32
20792       ap_chdir_file(r->filename);
20793   #endif
20794       if (r->args) {              /* add QUERY stuff to env
20795                                    * cause it ain't yet */
20796           char *arg_copy = ap_pstrdup(r->pool, r->args);
20797
20798           ap_table_setn(r->subprocess_env,
20799               "QUERY_STRING", r->args);
20800           ap_unescape_url(arg_copy);
20801           ap_table_setn(r->subprocess_env,
20802               "QUERY_STRING_UNESCAPED",
20803                   ap_escape_shell_cmd(r->pool,
20804                       arg_copy));
20805       }
20806
20807       while (1) {
20808           if (!find_string(f, STARTING_SEQUENCE, r,
20809             printing)) {
20810               if (get_directive(f, directive,
20811                 sizeof(directive), r->pool)) {
20812               ap_log_rerror(APLOG_MARK,
20813                   APLOG_NOERRNO|APLOG_ERR, r,
20814                       "mod_include: error reading
20815                           directive in %s",
20816                       r->filename);
20817               ap_rputs(error, r);
20818                   return;
20819               }
20820           if (!strcmp(directive, "if")) {
20821               if (!printing) {
20822                   if_nesting++;
20823               }
20824               else {
20825                   ret = handle_if(f, r, error,
20826                       &conditional_status,
20827                           &printing);
20828                   if_nesting = 0;
20829               }
20830               continue;
20831           }
20832           else if (!strcmp(directive, "else")) {
20833               if (!if_nesting) {
20834                   ret = handle_else(f, r, error,
20835                       &conditional_status,
20836                           &printing);
20837               }
20838               continue;
20839           }
20840           else if (!strcmp(directive, "elif")) {
20841               if (!if_nesting) {
20842                   ret = handle_elif(f, r, error,
20843                       &conditional_status,
20844                           &printing);
20845               }
20846               continue;
20847           }
20848           else if (!strcmp(directive, "endif")) {
20849               if (!if_nesting) {
20850                   ret = handle_endif(f, r, error,
20851                       &conditional_status,
20852                           &printing);
20853               }
20854               else {
20855                   if_nesting--;
20856               }
20857               continue;
20858           }
20859           if (!printing) {
20860               continue;
20861           }
20862           if (!strcmp(directive, "exec")) {
```

```
20863                    if (noexec) {
20864                        ap_log_rerror(APLOG_MARK,
20865                            APLOG_NOERRNO|APLOG_ERR, r,
20866                        "exec used but not allowed in %s",
20867                        r->filename);
20868                        if (printing) {
20869                            ap_rputs(error, r);
20870                        }
20871                        ret = find_string(f,
20872                            ENDING_SEQUENCE, r, 0);
20873                    }
20874                    else {
20875                        ret = handle_exec(f, r, error);
20876                    }
20877                }
20878                else if (!strcmp(directive, "config")) {
20879                    ret = handle_config(f, r, error,
20880                        timefmt, &sizefmt);
20881                }
20882                else if (!strcmp(directive, "set")) {
20883                    ret = handle_set(f, r, error);
20884                }
20885                else if (!strcmp(directive, "include")) {
20886                    ret = handle_include(f, r, error, noexec);
20887                }
20888                else if (!strcmp(directive, "echo")) {
20889                    ret = handle_echo(f, r, error);
20890                }
20891                else if (!strcmp(directive, "fsize")) {
20892                    ret = handle_fsize(f, r, error, sizefmt);
20893                }
20894                else if (!strcmp(directive, "flastmod")) {
20895                    ret = handle_flastmod(f, r, error,
20896                            timefmt);
20897                }
20898                else if (!strcmp(directive, "printenv")) {
20899                    ret = handle_printenv(f, r, error);
20900                }
20901    #ifdef USE_PERL_SSI
20902                else if (!strcmp(directive, "perl")) {
20903                    ret = handle_perl(f, r, error);
20904                }
20905    #endif
20906                else {
20907                    ap_log_rerror(APLOG_MARK,
20908                        APLOG_NOERRNO|APLOG_ERR, r,
20909                        "unknown directive \"%s\" "
20910                        "in parsed doc %s",
20911                        directive, r->filename);
20912                    if (printing) {
20913                        ap_rputs(error, r);
20914                    }
20915                    ret = find_string(f, ENDING_SEQUENCE,
20916                        r, 0);
20917                }
20918                if (ret) {
20919                    ap_log_rerror(APLOG_MARK,
20920                        APLOG_NOERRNO|APLOG_ERR, r,
20921                        "premature EOF in parsed file %s",
20922                        r->filename);
20923                    return;
20924                }
20925            }
20926            else {
20927                return;
20928            }
20929        }
20930 }
20931
20932 /********************************************************
20933  *
20934  * XBITHACK.  Sigh...  NB it's configurable
20935  * per-directory; the compile-time
20936  * option only changes the default.
20937  */
20938
20939 module includes_module;
20940 enum xbithack {
20941     xbithack_off, xbithack_on, xbithack_full
20942 };
20943
20944 #ifdef XBITHACK
20945 #define DEFAULT_XBITHACK xbithack_full
20946 #else
20947 #define DEFAULT_XBITHACK xbithack_off
20948 #endif
20949
20950 static void *create_includes_dir_config(pool *p,
20951     char *dummy)
20952 {
20953     enum xbithack *result = (enum xbithack *)
20954         ap_palloc(p, sizeof(enum xbithack));
20955     *result = DEFAULT_XBITHACK;
20956     return result;
20957 }
20958
```

```
20959   static const char *set_xbithack(cmd_parms *cmd,
20960         void *xbp, char *arg)
20961   {
20962       enum xbithack *state = (enum xbithack *) xbp;
20963
20964       if (!strcasecmp(arg, "off")) {
20965           *state = xbithack_off;
20966       }
20967       else if (!strcasecmp(arg, "on")) {
20968           *state = xbithack_on;
20969       }
20970       else if (!strcasecmp(arg, "full")) {
20971           *state = xbithack_full;
20972       }
20973       else {
20974           return "XBitHack must be set to Off, On,
20975               or Full";
20976       }
20977
20978       return NULL;
20979   }
20980
20981   static int send_parsed_file(request_rec *r)
20982   {
20983       FILE *f;
20984       enum xbithack *state =
20985       (enum xbithack *) ap_get_module_config(r->
20986           per_dir_config, &includes_module);
20987       int errstatus;
20988       request_rec *parent;
20989
20990       if (!(ap_allow_options(r) & OPT_INCLUDES)) {
20991           return DECLINED;
20992       }
20993       r->allowed |= (1 << M_GET);
20994       if (r->method_number != M_GET) {
20995           return DECLINED;
20996       }
20997       if (r->finfo.st_mode == 0) {
20998           ap_log_rerror(APLOG_MARK,
20999               APLOG_NOERRNO|APLOG_ERR, r,
21000               "File does not exist: %s",
21001                   (r->path_info
21002                   ? ap_pstrcat(r->pool, r->filename,
21003                       r->path_info, NULL)
21004                   : r->filename));
21005           return HTTP_NOT_FOUND;
21006       }
21007
21008       if (!(f = ap_pfopen(r->pool, r->filename, "r"))) {
21009           ap_log_rerror(APLOG_MARK, APLOG_ERR, r,
21010               "file permissions deny server
21011                   access: %s", r->filename);
21012           return HTTP_FORBIDDEN;
21013       }
21014
21015       if ((*state == xbithack_full)
21016   #if !defined(OS2) && !defined(WIN32)
21017       /*  OS/2 dosen't support Groups. */
21018           && (r->finfo.st_mode & S_IXGRP)
21019   #endif
21020           ) {
21021           ap_update_mtime(r, r->finfo.st_mtime);
21022           ap_set_last_modified(r);
21023       }
21024       if ((errstatus = ap_meets_conditions(r)) != OK) {
21025           return errstatus;
21026       }
21027
21028       ap_send_http_header(r);
21029
21030       if (r->header_only) {
21031           ap_pfclose(r->pool, f);
21032           return OK;
21033       }
21034
21035       if ((parent = ap_get_module_config(r->request_config,
21036       &includes_module))) {
21037       /* Kludge -- for nested includes, we want to keep
21038        * the subprocess environment of the base document
21039        * (for compatibility); that means torquing our
21040        * own last_modified date as well so that the
21041        * LAST_MODIFIED variable gets reset to the proper
21042        * value if the nested document resets
21043        * <!--#config timefmt-->. We also insist that the
21044        * memory for this subrequest not be destroyed,
21045        * that's dealt with in handle_include().
21046        */
21047       r->subprocess_env = parent->subprocess_env;
21048       ap_pool_join(parent->pool, r->pool);
21049       r->finfo.st_mtime = parent->finfo.st_mtime;
21050       }
21051       else {
21052       /* we're not a nested include, so we create an
21053        * initial environment */
21054           ap_add_common_vars(r);
```

```
21055          ap_add_cgi_vars(r);
21056          add_include_vars(r, DEFAULT_TIME_FORMAT);
21057      }
21058      /* XXX: this is bogus, at some point we're going
21059       * to do a subrequest, and when we do it we're
21060       * going to be subjecting code that doesn't
21061       * expect to be signal-ready to SIGALRM.  There
21062       * is no clean way to fix this, except to put
21063       * alarm support into BUFF. -djg
21064       */
21065      ap_hard_timeout("send SSI", r);
21066
21067  #ifdef CHARSET_EBCDIC
21068      /* XXX:@@@ Is the generated/included output
21069       * ALWAYS in text/ebcdic format? */
21070      ap_bsetflag(r->connection->client,
21071              B_EBCDIC2ASCII, 1);
21072  #endif
21073
21074      send_parsed_content(f, r);
21075
21076      if (parent) {
21077       /* signify that the sub request should
21078        *not be killed */
21079       ap_set_module_config(r->request_config,
21080           &includes_module,
21081           NESTED_INCLUDE_MAGIC);
21082      }
21083
21084      ap_kill_timeout(r);
21085      return OK;
21086  }
21087
21088  static int send_shtml_file(request_rec *r)
21089  {
21090      r->content_type = "text/html";
21091      return send_parsed_file(r);
21092  }
21093
21094  static int xbithack_handler(request_rec *r)
21095  {
21096  #if defined(OS2) || defined(WIN32)
21097      /* OS/2 dosen't currently support the xbithack.
21098       * This is being worked on. */
21099      return DECLINED;
21100  #else
21101      enum xbithack *state;
21102
21103      if (!(r->finfo.st_mode & S_IXUSR)) {
21104          return DECLINED;
21105      }
21106
21107      state = (enum xbithack *)
21108          ap_get_module_config(r->per_dir_config,
21109                               &includes_module);
21110
21111      if (*state == xbithack_off) {
21112          return DECLINED;
21113      }
21114      return send_parsed_file(r);
21115  #endif
21116  }
21117
21118  static const command_rec includes_cmds[] =
21119  {
21120      {"XBitHack", set_xbithack, NULL, OR_OPTIONS,
21121          TAKE1, "Off, On, or Full"},
21122      {NULL}
21123  };
21124
21125  static const handler_rec includes_handlers[] =
21126  {
21127      {INCLUDES_MAGIC_TYPE, send_shtml_file},
21128      {INCLUDES_MAGIC_TYPE3, send_shtml_file},
21129      {"server-parsed", send_parsed_file},
21130      {"text/html", xbithack_handler},
21131      {NULL}
21132  };
21133
21134  module MODULE_VAR_EXPORT includes_module =
21135  {
21136      STANDARD_MODULE_STUFF,
21137      NULL,                       /* initializer */
21138      create_includes_dir_config, /* dir config creater */
21139      NULL,
21140      /* dir merger -- default is to override */
21141      NULL,                       /* server config */
21142      NULL,
21143      /* merge server config */
21144      includes_cmds,              /* command table */
21145      includes_handlers,          /* handlers */
21146      NULL,
21147      /* filename translation */
21148      NULL,                       /* check_user_id */
21149      NULL,                       /* check auth */
21150      NULL,                       /* check access */
```

```
21151      NULL,                        /* type_checker */
21152      NULL,                        /* fixups */
21153      NULL,                        /* logger */
21154      NULL,                        /* header parser */
21155      NULL,                        /* child_init */
21156      NULL,                        /* child_exit */
21157      NULL                         /* post read-request */
21158   };
```

p 545 **mod_info.c**

```
21159   #include "httpd.h"
21160   #include "http_config.h"
21161   #include "http_core.h"
21162   #include "http_log.h"
21163   #include "http_main.h"
21164   #include "http_protocol.h"
21165   #include "util_script.h"
21166   #include "http_conf_globals.h"
21167
21168   typedef struct {
21169   char *name;                  /* matching module name */
21170   char *info;                  /* additional info */
21171   } info_entry;
21172
21173   typedef struct {
21174   array_header *more_info;
21175   } info_svr_conf;
21176
21177   typedef struct info_cfg_lines {
21178   char *cmd;
21179   char *line;
21180   struct info_cfg_lines *next;
21181   } info_cfg_lines;
21182
21183   module MODULE_VAR_EXPORT info_module;
21184   extern module *top_module;
21185
21186   static void *create_info_config
21187        (pool *p, server_rec *s)
21188   {
21189   info_svr_conf *conf = (info_svr_conf *)
21190        ap_pcalloc(p, sizeof(info_svr_conf));
21191
21192   conf->more_info =
21193        ap_make_array(p, 20, sizeof(info_entry));
21194   return conf;
21195   }
```

```
21196
21197   static void *merge_info_config(pool *p,
21198        void *basev, void *overridesv)
21199   {
21200   info_svr_conf *new = (info_svr_conf *)
21201        ap_pcalloc(p, sizeof(info_svr_conf));
21202   info_svr_conf *base = (info_svr_conf *) basev;
21203   info_svr_conf *overrides =
21204        (info_svr_conf *) overridesv;
21205
21206   new->more_info = ap_append_arrays(p,
21207        overrides->more_info, base->more_info);
21208   return new;
21209   }
21210
21211   static char *mod_info_html_cmd_string(const
21212        char *string, char *buf, size_t buf_len)
21213   {
21214   const char *s;
21215   char *t;
21216   char *end_buf;
21217
21218   s = string;
21219   t = buf;
21220   /* keep space for \0 byte */
21221   end_buf = buf + buf_len - 1;
21222   while ((*s) && (t < end_buf)) {
21223   if (*s == '<') {
21224   strncpy(t, "&lt;", end_buf - t);
21225   t += 4;
21226   }
21227   else if (*s == '>') {
21228   strncpy(t, "&gt;", end_buf - t);
21229   t += 4;
21230   }
21231   else if (*s == '&') {
21232   strncpy(t, "&amp;", end_buf - t);
21233   t += 5;
21234   }
21235   else {
21236   *t++ = *s;
21237   }
21238   s++;
21239   }
21240   /* oops, overflowed... don't overwrite */
21241   if (t > end_buf) {
21242   *end_buf = '\0';
21243   }
```

```
21244   else {
21245   *t = '\0';
21246   }
21247   return (buf);
21248   }
21249
21250   static info_cfg_lines *mod_info_load_config
21251        (pool *p, const char *filename,
21252   request_rec *r)
21253   {
21254   char s[MAX_STRING_LEN];
21255   configfile_t *fp;
21256   info_cfg_lines *new, *ret, *prev;
21257   const char *t;
21258
21259   fp = ap_pcfg_openfile(p, filename);
21260   if (!fp) {
21261   ap_log_rerror(APLOG_MARK, APLOG_WARNING, r,
21262   "mod_info: couldn't open config file %s",
21263   filename);
21264   return NULL;
21265   }
21266   ret = NULL;
21267   prev = NULL;
21268   while (!ap_cfg_getline(s, MAX_STRING_LEN, fp)) {
21269   if (*s == '#') {
21270   continue;            /* skip comments */
21271   }
21272   new = ap_palloc(p, sizeof(struct info_cfg_lines));
21273   new->next = NULL;
21274   if (!ret) {
21275   ret = new;
21276   }
21277   if (prev) {
21278   prev->next = new;
21279   }
21280   t = s;
21281   new->cmd = ap_getword_conf(p, &t);
21282   if (*t) {
21283   new->line = ap_pstrdup(p, t);
21284   }
21285   else {
21286   new->line = NULL;
21287   }
21288   prev = new;
21289   }
21290   ap_cfg_closefile(fp);
21291   return (ret);
21292   }
21293
21294   static void mod_info_module_cmds
21295        (request_rec *r, info_cfg_lines *cfg,
21296   const command_rec *cmds, char *label)
21297   {
21298   const command_rec *cmd = cmds;
21299   info_cfg_lines *li = cfg, *li_st =
21300        NULL, *li_se = NULL;
21301   info_cfg_lines *block_start = NULL;
21302   int lab = 0, nest = 0;
21303   char buf[MAX_STRING_LEN];
21304
21305   while (li) {
21306   if (!strncasecmp(li->cmd, "<directory", 10) ||
21307   !strncasecmp(li->cmd, "<location", 9) ||
21308   !strncasecmp(li->cmd, "<limit", 6) ||
21309   !strncasecmp(li->cmd, "<files", 6)) {
21310   if (nest) {
21311   li_se = li;
21312   }
21313   else {
21314   li_st = li;
21315   }
21316   li = li->next;
21317   nest++;
21318   continue;
21319   }
21320   else if (nest && (!strncasecmp(li->cmd,
21321        "</limit", 7) ||
21322   !strncasecmp(li->cmd, "</location", 10) ||
21323   !strncasecmp(li->cmd, "</directory", 11) ||
21324   !strncasecmp(li->cmd, "</files", 7))) {
21325   if (block_start) {
21326   if ((nest == 1 && block_start == li_st) ||
21327   (nest == 2 && block_start == li_se)) {
21328   ap_rputs("<dd><tt>", r);
21329   if (nest == 2) {
21330   ap_rputs("  ", r);
21331   }
21332   ap_rputs(mod_info_html_cmd_string
21333        (li->cmd, buf, sizeof(buf)), r);
21334   ap_rputs(" ", r);
21335   if (li->line) {
21336   ap_rputs(mod_info_html_cmd_string
21337        (li->line, buf, sizeof(buf)), r);
21338   }
21339   ap_rputs("</tt>\n", r);
```

```
21340    nest--;
21341    if (!nest) {
21342    block_start = NULL;
21343    li_st = NULL;
21344    }
21345    else {
21346    block_start = li_st;
21347    }
21348    li_se = NULL;
21349    }
21350    else {
21351    nest--;
21352    if (!nest) {
21353    li_st = NULL;
21354    }
21355    li_se = NULL;
21356    }
21357    }
21358    else {
21359    nest--;
21360    if (!nest) {
21361    li_st = NULL;
21362    }
21363    li_se = NULL;
21364    }
21365    li = li->next;
21366    continue;
21367    }
21368    cmd = cmds;
21369    while (cmd) {
21370    if (cmd->name) {
21371    if (!strcasecmp(cmd->name, li->cmd)) {
21372    if (!lab) {
21373    ap_rputs("<dt><strong>", r);
21374    ap_rputs(label, r);
21375    ap_rputs("</strong>\n", r);
21376    lab = 1;
21377    }
21378    if (((nest && block_start == NULL) ||
21379    (nest == 2 && block_start == li_st)) &&
21380    (strncasecmp(li->cmd, "<directory", 10) &&
21381    strncasecmp(li->cmd, "<location", 9) &&
21382    strncasecmp(li->cmd, "<limit", 6) &&
21383    strncasecmp(li->cmd, "</limit", 7) &&
21384    strncasecmp(li->cmd, "</location", 10) &&
21385    strncasecmp(li->cmd, "</directory", 11) &&
21386    strncasecmp(li->cmd, "</files", 7))) {
21387    ap_rputs("<dd><tt>", r);
21388    ap_rputs(mod_info_html_cmd_string
21389        (li_st->cmd, buf, sizeof(buf)), r);
21390    ap_rputs(" ", r);
21391    if (li_st->line) {
21392    ap_rputs(mod_info_html_cmd_string
21393        (li_st->line, buf, sizeof(buf)), r);
21394    }
21395    ap_rputs("</tt>\n", r);
21396    block_start = li_st;
21397    if (li_se) {
21398    ap_rputs("<dd><tt>  ", r);
21399    ap_rputs(mod_info_html_cmd_string
21400        (li_se->cmd, buf, sizeof(buf)), r);
21401    ap_rputs(" ", r);
21402    if (li_se->line) {
21403    ap_rputs(mod_info_html_cmd_string
21404        (li_se->line, buf, sizeof(buf)), r);
21405    }
21406    ap_rputs("</tt>\n", r);
21407    block_start = li_se;
21408    }
21409    }
21410    ap_rputs("<dd><tt>", r);
21411    if (nest) {
21412    ap_rputs("  ", r);
21413    }
21414    if (nest == 2) {
21415    ap_rputs("  ", r);
21416    }
21417    ap_rputs(mod_info_html_cmd_string
21418        (li->cmd, buf, sizeof(buf)), r);
21419    if (li->line) {
21420    ap_rputs(" <i>", r);
21421    ap_rputs(mod_info_html_cmd_string
21422        (li->line, buf, sizeof(buf)), r);
21423    ap_rputs("</i>", r);
21424    }
21425    ap_rputs("</tt>", r);
21426    }
21427    }
21428    else
21429    break;
21430    cmd++;
21431    }
21432    li = li->next;
21433    }
21434    }
21435
```

```
21436    static char *find_more_info(server_rec *s,
21437        const char *module_name)
21438    {
21439    int i;
21440    info_svr_conf *conf = (info_svr_conf *)
21441        ap_get_module_config(s->module_config,
21442    &info_module);
21443    info_entry *entry = (info_entry *)
21444        conf->more_info->elts;
21445
21446    if (!module_name) {
21447    return 0;
21448    }
21449    for (i = 0; i < conf->more_info->nelts; i++) {
21450    if (!strcmp(module_name, entry->name)) {
21451    return entry->info;
21452    }
21453    entry++;
21454    }
21455    return 0;
21456    }
21457
21458    static int display_info(request_rec *r)
21459    {
21460    module *modp = NULL;
21461    char buf[MAX_STRING_LEN], *cfname;
21462    char *more_info;
21463    const command_rec *cmd = NULL;
21464    const handler_rec *hand = NULL;
21465    server_rec *serv = r->server;
21466    int comma = 0;
21467    info_cfg_lines *mod_info_cfg_httpd = NULL;
21468    info_cfg_lines *mod_info_cfg_srm = NULL;
21469    info_cfg_lines *mod_info_cfg_access = NULL;
21470
21471    r->allowed |= (1 << M_GET);
21472    if (r->method_number != M_GET)
21473    return DECLINED;
21474
21475    r->content_type = "text/html";
21476    ap_send_http_header(r);
21477    if (r->header_only) {
21478    return 0;
21479    }
21480    ap_hard_timeout("send server info", r);
21481
21482    ap_rputs("<html><head><title>Server
21483        Information</title></head>\n", r);
21484    ap_rputs("<body><h1 align=center>
21485        Apache Server Information</h1>\n", r);
21486    if (!r->args || strcasecmp(r->args, "list")) {
21487    cfname = ap_server_root_relative
21488        (r->pool, ap_server_confname);
21489    mod_info_cfg_httpd =
21490        mod_info_load_config(r->pool, cfname, r);
21491    cfname = ap_server_root_relative
21492        (r->pool, serv->srm_confname);
21493    mod_info_cfg_srm = mod_info_load_config
21494        (r->pool, cfname, r);
21495    cfname = ap_server_root_relative
21496        (r->pool, serv->access_confname);
21497    mod_info_cfg_access = mod_info_load_config
21498        (r->pool, cfname, r);
21499    if (!r->args) {
21500    ap_rputs("<tt><a href=\"#server\">Server
21501        Settings</a>, ", r);
21502    for (modp = top_module; modp;
21503        modp = modp->next) {
21504    ap_rprintf(r, "<a href=\"#%s\">%s</a>",
21505        modp->name, modp->name);
21506    if (modp->next) {
21507    ap_rputs(", ", r);
21508    }
21509    }
21510    ap_rputs("</tt><hr>", r);
21511
21512    }
21513    if (!r->args || !strcasecmp(r->args,
21514        "server")) {
21515    ap_rprintf(r, "<a name=\"server\">
21516        <strong>Server Version:</strong> "
21517    "<font size=+1><tt>%s</tt></a></font><br>\n",
21518    ap_get_server_version());
21519    ap_rprintf(r, "<strong>Server Built:</strong> "
21520    "<font size=+1><tt>%s</tt></a></font><br>\n",
21521    ap_get_server_built());
21522    ap_rprintf(r, "<strong>API Version:</strong> "
21523    "<tt>%d:%d</tt><br>\n",
21524    MODULE_MAGIC_NUMBER_MAJOR,
21525        MODULE_MAGIC_NUMBER_MINOR);
21526    ap_rprintf(r, "<strong>Run Mode:
21527        </strong> <tt>%s</tt><br>\n",
21528    (ap_standalone ? "standalone" : "inetd"));
21529    ap_rprintf(r, "<strong>User/Group:</strong> "
21530    "<tt>%s(%d)/%d</tt><br>\n",
21531    ap_user_name, (int) ap_user_id,
```

```
21532        (int) ap_group_id);
21533  ap_rprintf(r, "<strong>Hostname/port:</strong> "
21534  "<tt>%s:%u</tt><br>\n",
21535  serv->server_hostname, serv->port);
21536  ap_rprintf(r, "<strong>Daemons:</strong> "
21537  "<tt>start: %d    "
21538  "min idle: %d    "
21539  "max idle: %d    "
21540  "max: %d</tt><br>\n",
21541  ap_daemons_to_start, ap_daemons_min_free,
21542  ap_daemons_max_free, ap_daemons_limit);
21543  ap_rprintf(r, "<strong>Max Requests:</strong> "
21544  "<tt>per child: %d    "
21545  "keep alive: %s    "
21546  "max per connection: %d</tt><br>\n",
21547  ap_max_requests_per_child,
21548  (serv->keep_alive ? "on" : "off"),
21549  serv->keep_alive_max);
21550  ap_rprintf(r, "<strong>Threads:</strong> "
21551  "<tt>per child: %d    </tt><br>\n",
21552  ap_threads_per_child);
21553  ap_rprintf(r, "<strong>Excess requests:</strong> "
21554  "<tt>per child: %d    </tt><br>\n",
21555  ap_excess_requests_per_child);
21556  ap_rprintf(r, "<strong>Timeouts:</strong> "
21557  "<tt>connection: %d    "
21558  "keep-alive: %d</tt><br>",
21559  serv->timeout, serv->keep_alive_timeout);
21560  ap_rprintf(r, "<strong>Server Root:</strong> "
21561  "<tt>%s</tt><br>\n", ap_server_root);
21562  ap_rprintf(r, "<strong>Config File:</strong> "
21563  "<tt>%s</tt><br>\n", ap_server_confname);
21564  ap_rprintf(r, "<strong>PID File:</strong> "
21565  "<tt>%s</tt><br>\n", ap_pid_fname);
21566  ap_rprintf(r, "<strong>Scoreboard File:</strong> "
21567  "<tt>%s</tt><br>\n", ap_scoreboard_fname);
21568  }
21569  ap_rputs("<hr><dl>", r);
21570  for (modp = top_module; modp; modp = modp->next) {
21571  if (!r->args || !strcasecmp(modp->name, r->args)) {
21572  ap_rprintf(r, "<dt><a name=\"%s\">"
21573      "<strong>Module Name:</strong> "
21574  "<font size=+1><tt>%s</tt></a></font>\n",
21575  modp->name, modp->name);
21576  ap_rputs("<dt><strong>Content handlers:"
21577  "</strong>", r);
21578  hand = modp->handlers;
21579  if (hand) {
21580  while (hand) {
21581  if (hand->content_type) {
21582  ap_rprintf(r, " <tt>%s</tt>\n",
21583      hand->content_type);
21584  }
21585  else {
21586  break;
21587  }
21588  hand++;
21589  if (hand && hand->content_type) {
21590  ap_rputs(",", r);
21591  }
21592  }
21593  }
21594  else {
21595  ap_rputs("<tt> <EM>none</EM></tt>", r);
21596  }
21597  ap_rputs("<dt><strong>Configuration Phase
21598      Participation:</strong> \n",
21599  r);
21600  if (modp->child_init) {
21601  ap_rputs("<tt>Child Init</tt>", r);
21602  comma = 1;
21603  }
21604  if (modp->create_dir_config) {
21605  if (comma) {
21606  ap_rputs(", ", r);
21607  }
21608  ap_rputs("<tt>Create Directory Config</tt>", r);
21609  comma = 1;
21610  }
21611  if (modp->merge_dir_config) {
21612  if (comma) {
21613  ap_rputs(", ", r);
21614  }
21615  ap_rputs("<tt>Merge Directory Configs</tt>", r);
21616  comma = 1;
21617  }
21618  if (modp->create_server_config) {
21619  if (comma) {
21620  ap_rputs(", ", r);
21621  }
21622  ap_rputs("<tt>Create Server Config</tt>", r);
21623  comma = 1;
21624  }
21625  if (modp->merge_server_config) {
21626  if (comma) {
21627  ap_rputs(", ", r);
```

```
21628   }
21629   ap_rputs("<tt>Merge Server Configs</tt>", r);
21630   comma = 1;
21631   }
21632   if (modp->child_exit) {
21633   if (comma) {
21634   ap_rputs(", ", r);
21635   }
21636   ap_rputs("<tt>Child Exit</tt>", r);
21637   comma = 1;
21638   }
21639   if (!comma)
21640   ap_rputs("<tt> <EM>none</EM></tt>", r);
21641   comma = 0;
21642   ap_rputs("<dt><strong>Request Phase
21643       Participation:</strong> \n",
21644   r);
21645   if (modp->post_read_request) {
21646   ap_rputs("<tt>Post-Read Request</tt>", r);
21647   comma = 1;
21648   }
21649   if (modp->header_parser) {
21650   if (comma) {
21651   ap_rputs(", ", r);
21652   }
21653   ap_rputs("<tt>Header Parse</tt>", r);
21654   comma = 1;
21655   }
21656   if (modp->translate_handler) {
21657   if (comma) {
21658   ap_rputs(", ", r);
21659   }
21660   ap_rputs("<tt>Translate Path</tt>", r);
21661   comma = 1;
21662   }
21663   if (modp->access_checker) {
21664   if (comma) {
21665   ap_rputs(", ", r);
21666   }
21667   ap_rputs("<tt>Check Access</tt>", r);
21668   comma = 1;
21669   }
21670   if (modp->ap_check_user_id) {
21671   if (comma) {
21672   ap_rputs(", ", r);
21673   }
21674   ap_rputs("<tt>Verify User ID</tt>", r);
21675   comma = 1;
21676   }
21677   if (modp->auth_checker) {
21678   if (comma) {
21679   ap_rputs(", ", r);
21680   }
21681   ap_rputs("<tt>Verify User Access</tt>", r);
21682   comma = 1;
21683   }
21684   if (modp->type_checker) {
21685   if (comma) {
21686   ap_rputs(", ", r);
21687   }
21688   ap_rputs("<tt>Check Type</tt>", r);
21689   comma = 1;
21690   }
21691   if (modp->fixer_upper) {
21692   if (comma) {
21693   ap_rputs(", ", r);
21694   }
21695   ap_rputs("<tt>Fixups</tt>", r);
21696   comma = 1;
21697   }
21698   if (modp->logger) {
21699   if (comma) {
21700   ap_rputs(", ", r);
21701   }
21702   ap_rputs("<tt>Logging</tt>", r);
21703   comma = 1;
21704   }
21705   if (!comma)
21706   ap_rputs("<tt> <EM>none</EM></tt>", r);
21707   comma = 0;
21708   ap_rputs("<dt><strong>Module Directives:
21709       </strong> ", r);
21710   cmd = modp->cmds;
21711   if (cmd) {
21712   while (cmd) {
21713   if (cmd->name) {
21714   ap_rprintf(r, "<dd><tt>%s - <i>",
21715   mod_info_html_cmd_string(cmd->name,
21716   buf, sizeof(buf)));
21717   if (cmd->errmsg) {
21718   ap_rputs(cmd->errmsg, r);
21719   }
21720   ap_rputs("</i></tt>\n", r);
21721   }
21722   else {
21723   break;
```

```
21724    }
21725    cmd++;
21726    }
21727    ap_rputs("<dt><strong>Current Configuration:
21728        </strong>\n", r);
21729    mod_info_module_cmds(r,
21730        mod_info_cfg_httpd, modp->cmds,
21731    "httpd.conf");
21732    mod_info_module_cmds(r,
21733        mod_info_cfg_srm, modp->cmds,
21734    "srm.conf");
21735    mod_info_module_cmds(r,
21736        mod_info_cfg_access, modp->cmds,
21737    "access.conf");
21738    }
21739    else {
21740    ap_rputs("<tt> none</tt>\n", r);
21741    }
21742    more_info = find_more_info
21743        (serv, modp->name);
21744    if (more_info) {
21745    ap_rputs("<dt><strong>Additional Information:
21746        </strong>\n<dd>",
21747    r);
21748    ap_rputs(more_info, r);
21749    }
21750    ap_rputs("<dt><hr>\n", r);
21751    if (r->args) {
21752    break;
21753    }
21754    }
21755    }
21756    if (!modp && r->args && strcasecmp
21757        (r->args, "server")) {
21758    ap_rputs("<b>No such module</b>\n", r);
21759    }
21760    }
21761    else {
21762    for (modp = top_module; modp;
21763        modp = modp->next) {
21764    ap_rputs(modp->name, r);
21765    if (modp->next) {
21766    ap_rputs("<br>", r);
21767    }
21768    }
21769    }
21770    ap_rputs("</dl>\n", r);
21771    ap_rputs(ap_psignature("",r), r);
```

```
21772    ap_rputs("</body></html>\n", r);
21773    /* Done, turn off timeout,
21774        close file and return */
21775    ap_kill_timeout(r);
21776    return 0;
21777    }
21778
21779    static const char *add_module_info
21780        (cmd_parms *cmd, void *dummy, char *name,
21781    char *info)
21782    {
21783    server_rec *s = cmd->server;
21784    info_svr_conf *conf = (info_svr_conf *)
21785        ap_get_module_config(s->module_config,
21786    &info_module);
21787    info_entry *new = ap_push_array(conf->more_info);
21788
21789    new->name = name;
21790    new->info = info;
21791    return NULL;
21792    }
21793
21794    static const command_rec info_cmds[] =
21795    {
21796    {"AddModuleInfo", add_module_info,
21797        NULL, RSRC_CONF, TAKE2,
21798    "a module name and additional information
21799        on that module"},
21800    {NULL}
21801    };
21802
21803    static const handler_rec info_handlers[] =
21804    {
21805    {"server-info", display_info},
21806    {NULL}
21807    };
21808
21809    module MODULE_VAR_EXPORT info_module =
21810    {
21811    STANDARD_MODULE_STUFF,
21812    NULL,                    /* initializer */
21813    NULL,                    /* dir config creater */
21814    NULL,
21815    /* dir merger -- default is to override */
21816    create_info_config,      /* server config */
21817    merge_info_config,       /* merge server config */
21818    info_cmds,               /* command table */
21819    info_handlers,           /* handlers */
```

```
21820    NULL,                   /* filename translation */
21821    NULL,                   /* check_user_id */
21822    NULL,                   /* check auth */
21823    NULL,                   /* check access */
21824    NULL,                   /* type_checker */
21825    NULL,                   /* fixups */
21826    NULL,                   /* logger */
21827    NULL,                   /* header parser */
21828    NULL,                   /* child_init */
21829    NULL,                   /* child_exit */
21830    NULL                    /* post read-request */
21831    };
```

▶ p 519 mod_log_agent.c

```
21832    #include "httpd.h"
21833    #include "http_config.h"
21834    #include "http_log.h"
21835
21836    module agent_log_module;
21837
21838    static int xfer_flags = (O_WRONLY | O_APPEND |
21839         O_CREAT);
21840    #ifdef OS2
21841    /* OS/2 dosen't support users and groups */
21842    static mode_t xfer_mode = (S_IREAD | S_IWRITE);
21843    #else
21844    static mode_t xfer_mode = (S_IRUSR | S_IWUSR |
21845         S_IRGRP | S_IROTH);
21846    #endif
21847
21848    typedef struct {
21849        char *fname;
21850        int agent_fd;
21851    } agent_log_state;
21852
21853    static void *make_agent_log_state(pool *p,
21854        server_rec *s)
21855    {
21856        agent_log_state *cls =
21857        (agent_log_state *) ap_palloc(p,
21858         sizeof(agent_log_state));
21859
21860        cls->fname = "";
21861        cls->agent_fd = -1;
21862
21863        return (void *) cls;
21864    }
21865
21866    static const char *set_agent_log(cmd_parms *parms,
21867        void *dummy, char *arg)
21868    {
21869        agent_log_state *cls =
21870        ap_get_module_config(parms->server->module_config,
21871                             &agent_log_module);
21872
21873        cls->fname = arg;
21874        return NULL;
21875    }
21876
21877    static const command_rec agent_log_cmds[] =
21878    {
21879        {"AgentLog", set_agent_log, NULL,
21880             RSRC_CONF, TAKE1,
21881         "the filename of the agent log"},
21882        {NULL}
21883    };
21884
21885    static void open_agent_log(server_rec *s, pool *p)
21886    {
21887        agent_log_state *cls =
21888             ap_get_module_config(s->module_config,
21889                               &agent_log_module);
21890
21891        char *fname = ap_server_root_relative(p,
21892             cls->fname);
21893
21894        if (cls->agent_fd > 0)
21895            return;
21896
21897    /* virtual log shared w/main server */
21898
21899        if (*cls->fname == '|') {
21900            piped_log *pl;
21901
21902            pl = ap_open_piped_log(p, cls->fname + 1);
21903            if (pl == NULL) {
21904             ap_log_error(APLOG_MARK, APLOG_ERR, s,
21905                    "couldn't spawn agent log pipe");
21906             exit(1);
21907            }
21908            cls->agent_fd = ap_piped_log_write_fd(pl);
21909        }
21910        else if (*cls->fname != '\0') {
21911            if ((cls->agent_fd = ap_popenf(p, fname,
21912                 xfer_flags, xfer_mode)) < 0) {
21913                ap_log_error(APLOG_MARK, APLOG_ERR, s,
```

```
21914                      "could not open agent log file
21915                       %s.", fname);
21916            exit(1);
21917        }
21918     }
21919 }
21920
21921 static void init_agent_log(server_rec *s, pool *p)
21922 {
21923     for (; s; s = s->next)
21924         open_agent_log(s, p);
21925 }
21926
21927 static int agent_log_transaction(request_rec *orig)
21928 {
21929     agent_log_state *cls =
21930       ap_get_module_config(orig->server->module_config,
21931                            &agent_log_module);
21932
21933     char str[HUGE_STRING_LEN];
21934     const char *agent;
21935     request_rec *r;
21936
21937     if (cls->agent_fd < 0)
21938         return OK;
21939
21940     for (r = orig; r->next; r = r->next)
21941         continue;
21942     if (*cls->fname == '\0')
21943
21944     /* Don't log agent */
21945
21946         return DECLINED;
21947
21948     agent = ap_table_get(orig->headers_in,
21949         "User-Agent");
21950     if (agent != NULL) {
21951         ap_snprintf(str, sizeof(str), "%s\n", agent);
21952         write(cls->agent_fd, str, strlen(str));
21953     }
21954
21955     return OK;
21956 }
21957
21958 module agent_log_module =
21959 {
21960     STANDARD_MODULE_STUFF,
21961     init_agent_log,        /* initializer */
```

```
21962     NULL,                 /* create per-dir config */
21963     NULL,                 /* merge per-dir config */
21964     make_agent_log_state, /* server config */
21965     NULL,                 /* merge server config */
21966     agent_log_cmds,       /* command table */
21967     NULL,                 /* handlers */
21968     NULL,                 /* filename translation */
21969     NULL,                 /* check_user_id */
21970     NULL,                 /* check auth */
21971     NULL,                 /* check access */
21972     NULL,                 /* type_checker */
21973     NULL,                 /* fixups */
21974     agent_log_transaction, /* logger */
21975     NULL,                 /* header parser */
21976     NULL,                 /* child_init */
21977     NULL,                 /* child_exit */
21978     NULL                  /* post read-request */
21979 };
```

p 522 **mod_log_config.c**

```
21980 #define DEFAULT_LOG_FORMAT "%h %l %u %t \"%r\" %>s %b"
21981
21982 #include "httpd.h"
21983 #include "http_config.h"
21984 #include "http_core.h"          /* For REMOTE_NAME */
21985 #include "http_log.h"
21986 #include <limits.h>
21987
21988 module MODULE_VAR_EXPORT config_log_module;
21989
21990 static int xfer_flags = (O_WRONLY | O_APPEND | O_CREAT);
21991 #if defined(OS2) || defined(WIN32)
21992 /* OS/2 dosen't support users and groups */
21993 static mode_t xfer_mode = (S_IREAD | S_IWRITE);
21994 #else
21995 static mode_t xfer_mode = (S_IRUSR | S_IWUSR |
21996     S_IRGRP | S_IROTH);
21997 #endif
21998
21999 /* POSIX.1 defines PIPE_BUF as the maximum number of
22000  * bytes that is guaranteed to be atomic when writing
22001  * a pipe.  And PIPE_BUF >= 512 is guaranteed.  So
22002  * we'll just guess 512 in the event the system
22003  * doesn't have this.  Now, for file writes there
22004  * is actually no limit,the entire write is atomic.
22005  * Whether all systems implement this correctly is
22006  * another question entirely ... so we'll just use
22007  * PIPE_BUF because it's probably a good guess as to
```

```
22008    * what is implemented correctly everywhere.
22009    */
22010
22011   #ifdef PIPE_BUF
22012   #define LOG_BUFSIZE     PIPE_BUF
22013   #else
22014   #define LOG_BUFSIZE     (512)
22015   #endif
22016
22017   /*
22018    * multi_log_state is our per-(virtual)-server
22019    * configuration. We store an array of the logs
22020    * we are going to use, each of type config_log_state.
22021    * If a default log format is given by LogFormat,
22022    * store in default_format(backward compat. with
22023    * mod_log_config).  We also store for each virtual
22024    * server a pointer to the logs specified for the
22025    * main server, so that if this vhost has no logs
22026    * defined, we can use the main server's logs instead.
22027    *
22028    * So, for the main server, config_logs contains a
22029    * list of the log files and server_config_logs in
22030    * empty. For a vhost, server_config_logs points to
22031    * the same array as config_logs in the main server,
22032    * and config_logs points to the array of logs defined,
22033    * inside this vhost which might be empty.
22034    */
22035
22036   typedef struct {
22037       char *default_format_string;
22038       array_header *default_format;
22039       array_header *config_logs;
22040       array_header *server_config_logs;
22041       table *formats;
22042   } multi_log_state;
22043
22044   /*
22045    * config_log_state holds the status of a single log
22046    * file. fname might be NULL, which means this module
22047    * does no logging for this request. format might be
22048    * NULL, in which case the default_format from the
22049    * multi_log_state should be used, or if that is NULL as
22050    * well, use the CLF. log_fd is -1 before the log file
22051    * is opened and set to a valid fd after it is opened.
22052    */
22053
22054   typedef struct {
22055       char *fname;
22056       char *format_string;
22057       array_header *format;
22058       int log_fd;
22059       char *condition_var;
22060   #ifdef BUFFERED_LOGS
22061       int outcnt;
22062       char outbuf[LOG_BUFSIZE];
22063   #endif
22064   } config_log_state;
22065
22066   /*
22067    * Format items...
22068    * Note that many of these could have ap_sprintfs
22069    * replaced with static buffers.
22070    */
22071
22072   typedef const char *(*item_key_func) (request_rec *,
22073       char *);
22074
22075   typedef struct {
22076       item_key_func func;
22077       char *arg;
22078       int condition_sense;
22079       int want_orig;
22080       array_header *conditions;
22081   } log_format_item;
22082
22083   static char *format_integer(pool *p, int i)
22084   {
22085       return ap_psprintf(p, "%d", i);
22086   }
22087
22088   static char *pfmt(pool *p, int i)
22089   {
22090       if (i <= 0) {
22091           return "-";
22092       }
22093       else {
22094           return format_integer(p, i);
22095       }
22096   }
22097
22098   static const char *constant_item(request_rec *dummy,
22099       char *stuff)
22100   {
22101       return stuff;
22102   }
22103
```

```
22104   static const char *log_remote_host(request_rec *r,
22105       char *a)
22106   {
22107       return ap_get_remote_host(r->connection,
22108       r->per_dir_config,
22109                                       REMOTE_NAME);
22110   }
22111
22112   static const char *log_remote_address(request_rec *r,
22113       char *a)
22114   {
22115       return r->connection->remote_ip;
22116   }
22117
22118   static const char *log_remote_logname(request_rec *r,
22119       char *a)
22120   {
22121       return ap_get_remote_logname(r);
22122   }
22123
22124   static const char *log_remote_user(request_rec *r,
22125       char *a)
22126   {
22127       char *rvalue = r->connection->user;
22128
22129       if (rvalue == NULL) {
22130           rvalue = "-";
22131       }
22132       else if (strlen(rvalue) == 0) {
22133           rvalue = "\"\"";
22134       }
22135       return rvalue;
22136   }
22137
22138   static const char *log_request_line(request_rec *r,
22139       char *a)
22140   {
22141       /* NOTE: If the original request contained a
22142        * password, we re-write the request line here
22143        * to contain XXXXXX instead: (note the truncation
22144        * before the protocol string for HTTP/0.9 requests)
22145        * (note also that r->the_request contains the
22146        * unmodified request)
22147        */
22148       return (r->parsed_uri.password) ?
22149               ap_pstrcat(r->pool, r->method, " ",
22150                       ap_unparse_uri_components(r->pool,
22151                           &r->parsed_uri, 0),
```

```
22152                           r->assbackwards ? NULL : " ",
22153                               r->protocol, NULL)
22154                           : r->the_request;
22155
22156   }
22157
22158   static const char *log_request_file(request_rec *r,
22159       char *a)
22160   {
22161       return r->filename;
22162   }
22163   static const char *log_request_uri(request_rec *r,
22164       char *a)
22165   {
22166       return r->uri;
22167   }
22168   static const char *log_status(request_rec *r, char *a)
22169   {
22170
22171       return pfmt(r->pool, r->status);
22172   }
22173
22174   static const char *log_bytes_sent(request_rec *r,
22175       char *a)
22176   {
22177       if (!r->sent_bodyct) {
22178           return "-";
22179       }
22180       else {
22181           long int bs;
22182           ap_bgetopt(r->connection->client,
22183                   BO_BYTECT, &bs);
22184       return ap_psprintf(r->pool, "%ld", bs);
22185       }
22186   }
22187
22188   static const char *log_header_in(request_rec *r,
22189       char *a)
22190   {
22191       return ap_table_get(r->headers_in, a);
22192   }
22193
22194   static const char *log_header_out(request_rec *r,
22195       char *a)
22196   {
22197       const char *cp = ap_table_get(r->headers_out, a);
22198       if (!strcasecmp(a, "Content-type")
22199               && r->content_type) {
```

```
22200                cp = r->content_type;
22201        }
22202        if (cp) {
22203            return cp;
22204        }
22205        return ap_table_get(r->err_headers_out, a);
22206    }
22207
22208    static const char *log_note(request_rec *r, char *a)
22209    {
22210        return ap_table_get(r->notes, a);
22211    }
22212    static const char *log_env_var(request_rec *r, char *a)
22213    {
22214        return ap_table_get(r->subprocess_env, a);
22215    }
22216
22217    static const char *log_request_time(request_rec *r,
22218         char *a)
22219    {
22220        int timz;
22221        struct tm *t;
22222        char tstr[MAX_STRING_LEN];
22223
22224        t = ap_get_gmtoff(&timz);
22225
22226        if (a && *a) {                  /* Custom format */
22227            strftime(tstr, MAX_STRING_LEN, a, t);
22228        }
22229        else {                          /* CLF format */
22230            char sign = (timz < 0 ? '-' : '+');
22231            size_t l;
22232
22233            if (timz < 0) {
22234                timz = -timz;
22235            }
22236
22237            strftime(tstr, MAX_STRING_LEN,
22238              "[%d/%b/%Y:%H:%M:%S ", t);
22239         l = strlen(tstr);
22240            ap_snprintf(tstr + l, sizeof(tstr) - l,
22241                     "%c%.2d%.2d]", sign, timz / 60,
22242                         timz % 60);
22243        }
22244
22245        return ap_pstrdup(r->pool, tstr);
22246    }
22247
22248    static const char *log_request_duration(request_rec *r,
22249         char *a)
22250    {
22251        return ap_psprintf(r->pool, "%ld",
22252                time(NULL) - r->request_time);
22253    }
22254
22255    /* These next two routines use the canonical
22256     * name:port so that log parsers don't need to
22257     * duplicate all the vhost parsing crud.
22258     */
22259    static const char *log_virtual_host(request_rec *r,
22260         char *a)
22261    {
22262        return r->server->server_hostname;
22263    }
22264
22265    static const char *log_server_port(request_rec *r,
22266         char *a)
22267    {
22268        return ap_psprintf(r->pool, "%u",
22269           r->server->port ? r->server->port :
22270           ap_default_port(r));
22271    }
22272
22273    /* This respects the setting of UseCanonicalName
22274     * so that the dynamic mass virtual hosting
22275     * trick works better.
22276     */
22277
22278    static const char *log_server_name(request_rec *r,
22279         char *a)
22280    {
22281        return ap_get_server_name(r);
22282    }
22283
22284    static const char *log_child_pid(request_rec *r,
22285         char *a)
22286    {
22287        return ap_psprintf(r->pool, "%ld",
22288        (long) getpid());
22289    }
22290
22291    /*****************************************************
22292     *
22293     * Parsing the log format string
22294     */
22295
```

```
22296
22297    static struct log_item_list {
22298        char ch;
22299        item_key_func func;
22300        int want_orig_default;
22301    } log_item_keys[] = {
22302
22303        {
22304            'h', log_remote_host, 0
22305        },
22306        {
22307            'a', log_remote_address, 0
22308        },
22309        {
22310            'l', log_remote_logname, 0
22311        },
22312        {
22313            'u', log_remote_user, 0
22314        },
22315        {
22316            't', log_request_time, 0
22317        },
22318        {
22319            'T', log_request_duration, 1
22320        },
22321        {
22322            'r', log_request_line, 1
22323        },
22324        {
22325            'f', log_request_file, 0
22326        },
22327        {
22328            'U', log_request_uri, 1
22329        },
22330        {
22331            's', log_status, 1
22332        },
22333        {
22334            'b', log_bytes_sent, 0
22335        },
22336        {
22337            'i', log_header_in, 0
22338        },
22339        {
22340            'o', log_header_out, 0
22341        },
22342        {
22343            'n', log_note, 0
22344        },
22345        {
22346            'e', log_env_var, 0
22347        },
22348        {
22349            'V', log_server_name, 0
22350        },
22351        {
22352            'v', log_virtual_host, 0
22353        },
22354        {
22355            'p', log_server_port, 0
22356        },
22357        {
22358            'P', log_child_pid, 0
22359        },
22360        {
22361            '\0'
22362        }
22363    };
22364
22365    static struct log_item_list *find_log_func(char k)
22366    {
22367        int i;
22368
22369        for (i = 0; log_item_keys[i].ch; ++i)
22370            if (k == log_item_keys[i].ch) {
22371                return &log_item_keys[i];
22372            }
22373
22374        return NULL;
22375    }
22376
22377    static char *parse_log_misc_string(pool *p,
22378        log_format_item *it,
22379                                       const char **sa)
22380    {
22381        const char *s;
22382        char *d;
22383
22384        it->func = constant_item;
22385        it->conditions = NULL;
22386
22387        s = *sa;
22388        while (*s && *s != '%') {
22389            s++;
22390        }
22391        /*
```

```
22392          * This might allocate a few chars extra if
22393          * there's a backslash escape in the
22394          * format string.
22395          */
22396         it->arg = ap_palloc(p, s - *sa + 1);
22397
22398         d = it->arg;
22399         s = *sa;
22400         while (*s && *s != '%') {
22401          if (*s != '\\') {
22402              *d++ = *s++;
22403          }
22404          else {
22405              s++;
22406              switch (*s) {
22407              case '\\':
22408               *d++ = '\\';
22409               s++;
22410               break;
22411              case 'n':
22412               *d++ = '\n';
22413               s++;
22414               break;
22415              case 't':
22416               *d++ = '\t';
22417               s++;
22418               break;
22419              default:
22420               /* copy verbatim */
22421               *d++ = '\\';
22422               /*
22423                * Allow the loop to deal with this *s in the
22424                * normal fashion so that it handles end of string
22425                * etc. properly.
22426                */
22427               break;
22428              }
22429          }
22430         }
22431         *d = '\0';
22432
22433         *sa = s;
22434         return NULL;
22435     }
22436
22437     static char *parse_log_item(pool *p,
22438         log_format_item *it, const char **sa)
22439     {
22440         const char *s = *sa;
22441
22442         if (*s != '%') {
22443             return parse_log_misc_string(p, it, sa);
22444         }
22445
22446         ++s;
22447         it->condition_sense = 0;
22448         it->conditions = NULL;
22449         it->want_orig = -1;
22450         it->arg = "";          /* For safety's sake... */
22451
22452         while (*s) {
22453             int i;
22454             struct log_item_list *l;
22455
22456             switch (*s) {
22457             case '!':
22458                 ++s;
22459                 it->condition_sense = !it->condition_sense;
22460                 break;
22461
22462             case '<':
22463                 ++s;
22464                 it->want_orig = 1;
22465                 break;
22466
22467             case '>':
22468                 ++s;
22469                 it->want_orig = 0;
22470                 break;
22471
22472             case ',':
22473                 ++s;
22474                 break;
22475
22476             case '{':
22477                 ++s;
22478                 it->arg = ap_getword(p, &s, '}');
22479                 break;
22480
22481             case '0':
22482             case '1':
22483             case '2':
22484             case '3':
22485             case '4':
22486             case '5':
22487             case '6':
```

```
22488          case '7':
22489          case '8':
22490          case '9':
22491              i = *s - '0';
22492              while (ap_isdigit(*++s)) {
22493                  i = i * 10 + (*s) - '0';
22494              }
22495              if (!it->conditions) {
22496                  it->conditions = ap_make_array(p,
22497                      4, sizeof(int));
22498              }
22499              *(int *) ap_push_array(it->conditions) = i;
22500              break;
22501
22502          default:
22503              l = find_log_func(*s++);
22504              if (!l) {
22505                  char dummy[2];
22506
22507                  dummy[0] = s[-1];
22508                  dummy[1] = '\0';
22509                  return ap_pstrcat(p,
22510                   "Unrecognized LogFormat directive %",
22511                              dummy, NULL);
22512              }
22513              it->func = l->func;
22514              if (it->want_orig == -1) {
22515                  it->want_orig = l->want_orig_default;
22516              }
22517              *sa = s;
22518              return NULL;
22519          }
22520      }
22521
22522      return "Ran off end of LogFormat parsing args
22523          to some directive";
22524  }
22525
22526  static array_header *parse_log_string(pool *p,
22527      const char *s, const char **err)
22528  {
22529      array_header *a = ap_make_array(p, 30,
22530          sizeof(log_format_item));
22531      char *res;
22532
22533      while (*s) {
22534          if ((res = parse_log_item(p,
22535          (log_format_item *) ap_push_array(a), &s))) {
22536              *err = res;
22537              return NULL;
22538          }
22539      }
22540
22541      s = "\n";
22542      parse_log_item(p, (log_format_item *)
22543          ap_push_array(a), &s);
22544      return a;
22545  }
22546
22547  /***************************************************
22548   *
22549   * Actually logging.
22550   */
22551
22552  static const char *process_item(request_rec *r,
22553      request_rec *orig,
22554                      log_format_item *item)
22555  {
22556      const char *cp;
22557
22558      /* First, see if we need to process this
22559       * thing at all... */
22560
22561      if (item->conditions &&
22562          item->conditions->nelts != 0) {
22563          int i;
22564          int *conds = (int *) item->conditions->elts;
22565          int in_list = 0;
22566
22567          for (i = 0; i < item->conditions->nelts; ++i) {
22568              if (r->status == conds[i]) {
22569                  in_list = 1;
22570                  break;
22571              }
22572          }
22573
22574          if ((item->condition_sense && in_list)
22575              || (!item->condition_sense && !in_list)) {
22576              return "-";
22577          }
22578      }
22579
22580      /* We do.  Do it... */
22581
22582      cp = (*item->func) (item->want_orig ? orig : r,
22583          item->arg);
```

```
22584          return cp ? cp : "-";
22585   }
22586
22587   #ifdef BUFFERED_LOGS
22588   static void flush_log(config_log_state *cls)
22589   {
22590       if (cls->outcnt && cls->log_fd != -1) {
22591           write(cls->log_fd, cls->outbuf, cls->outcnt);
22592           cls->outcnt = 0;
22593       }
22594   }
22595   #endif
22596
22597   static int config_log_transaction(request_rec *r,
22598        config_log_state *cls,
22599                         array_header *default_format)
22600   {
22601       log_format_item *items;
22602       char *str, *s;
22603       const char **strs;
22604       int *strl;
22605       request_rec *orig;
22606       int i;
22607       int len = 0;
22608       array_header *format;
22609       char *envar;
22610
22611       if (cls->fname == NULL) {
22612           return DECLINED;
22613       }
22614
22615       /*
22616        * See if we've got any conditional
22617            envariable-controlled logging decisions
22618        * to make.
22619        */
22620       if (cls->condition_var != NULL) {
22621        envar = cls->condition_var;
22622        if (*envar != '!') {
22623            if (ap_table_get(r->subprocess_env,
22624            envar) == NULL) {
22625            return DECLINED;
22626            }
22627        }
22628        else {
22629            if (ap_table_get(r->subprocess_env,
22630                &envar[1]) != NULL) {
22631            return DECLINED;
22632            }
22633        }
22634       }
22635
22636       format = cls->format ? cls->format : default_format;
22637
22638       strs = ap_palloc(r->pool, sizeof(char *) *
22639           (format->nelts));
22640       strl = ap_palloc(r->pool, sizeof(int) *
22641           (format->nelts));
22642       items = (log_format_item *) format->elts;
22643
22644       orig = r;
22645       while (orig->prev) {
22646
22647           orig = orig->prev;
22648       }
22649       while (r->next) {
22650           r = r->next;
22651       }
22652
22653       for (i = 0; i < format->nelts; ++i) {
22654           strs[i] = process_item(r, orig, &items[i]);
22655       }
22656
22657       for (i = 0; i < format->nelts; ++i) {
22658           len += strl[i] = strlen(strs[i]);
22659       }
22660
22661   #ifdef BUFFERED_LOGS
22662       if (len + cls->outcnt > LOG_BUFSIZE) {
22663           flush_log(cls);
22664       }
22665       if (len >= LOG_BUFSIZE) {
22666           str = ap_palloc(r->pool, len + 1);
22667           for (i = 0, s = str; i < format->nelts; ++i) {
22668               memcpy(s, strs[i], strl[i]);
22669               s += strl[i];
22670           }
22671           write(cls->log_fd, str, len);
22672       }
22673       else {
22674           for (i = 0, s = &cls->outbuf[cls->outcnt];
22675                   i < format->nelts; ++i) {
22676               memcpy(s, strs[i], strl[i]);
22677               s += strl[i];
22678           }
22679           cls->outcnt += len;
```

```
22680        }
22681  #else
22682      str = ap_palloc(r->pool, len + 1);
22683
22684      for (i = 0, s = str; i < format->nelts; ++i) {
22685          memcpy(s, strs[i], strl[i]);
22686          s += strl[i];
22687      }
22688
22689      write(cls->log_fd, str, len);
22690  #endif
22691
22692      return OK;
22693  }
22694
22695  static int multi_log_transaction(request_rec *r)
22696  {
22697      multi_log_state *mls =
22698              ap_get_module_config(r->server->module_config,
22699                                   &config_log_module);
22700      config_log_state *clsarray;
22701      int i;
22702
22703      /*
22704       * Log this transaction..
22705       */
22706
22707      if (mls->config_logs->nelts) {
22708          clsarray = (config_log_state *)
22709                  mls->config_logs->elts;
22710          for (i = 0; i < mls->config_logs->nelts; ++i) {
22711              config_log_state *cls = &clsarray[i];
22712
22713              config_log_transaction(r, cls,
22714                  mls->default_format);
22715          }
22716      }
22717      else if (mls->server_config_logs) {
22718          clsarray = (config_log_state *)
22719                  mls->server_config_logs->elts;
22720          for (i = 0; i <
22721                  mls->server_config_logs->nelts; ++i) {
22722              config_log_state *cls = &clsarray[i];
22723
22724              config_log_transaction(r, cls,
22725                  mls->default_format);
22726          }
22727      }
```

```
22728
22729      return OK;
22730  }
22731
22732  /*****************************************************
22733   *
22734   * Module glue...
22735   */
22736
22737  static void *make_config_log_state(pool *p,
22738      server_rec *s)
22739  {
22740      multi_log_state *mls;
22741
22742      mls = (multi_log_state *) ap_palloc(p,
22743          sizeof(multi_log_state));
22744      mls->config_logs = ap_make_array(p, 1,
22745          sizeof(config_log_state));
22746      mls->default_format_string = NULL;
22747      mls->default_format = NULL;
22748      mls->server_config_logs = NULL;
22749      mls->formats = ap_make_table(p, 4);
22750      ap_table_setn(mls->formats, "CLF",
22751          DEFAULT_LOG_FORMAT);
22752
22753      return mls;
22754  }
22755
22756  /*
22757   * Use the merger to simply add a pointer from the
22758   * vhost log state to the log of logs specified
22759   * for the non-vhost configuration.  Make sure
22760   * vhosts inherit any globally-defined format names.
22761   */
22762
22763  static void *merge_config_log_state(pool *p,
22764      void *basev, void *addv)
22765  {
22766      multi_log_state *base = (multi_log_state *) basev;
22767      multi_log_state *add = (multi_log_state *) addv;
22768
22769      add->server_config_logs = base->config_logs;
22770      if (!add->default_format) {
22771          add->default_format_string =
22772              base->default_format_string;
22773          add->default_format = base->default_format;
22774      }
22775      add->formats = ap_overlay_tables(p,
```

```
22776                    base->formats,
22777                    add->formats);
22778
22779        return add;
22780  }
22781
22782  /*
22783   * Set the default logfile format, or define a nickname
22784   * for a format string.
22785   */
22786  static const char *log_format(cmd_parms *cmd,
22787          void *dummy, char *fmt,
22788                                     char *name)
22789  {
22790      const char *err_string = NULL;
22791      multi_log_state *mls =
22792          ap_get_module_config(cmd->server->module_config,
22793                               &config_log_module);
22794
22795      /*
22796       * If we were given two arguments, the second is
22797       * a name to be given to the format.  This syntax
22798       * just defines the nickname - it doesn't actually
22799       * make the format the default.
22800       */
22801
22802      if (name != NULL) {
22803          parse_log_string(cmd->pool, fmt, &err_string);
22804          if (err_string == NULL) {
22805              ap_table_setn(mls->formats, name, fmt);
22806          }
22807      }
22808      else {
22809          mls->default_format_string = fmt;
22810          mls->default_format =
22811              parse_log_string(cmd->pool, fmt, &err_string);
22812      }
22813      return err_string;
22814  }
22815
22816
22817  static const char *add_custom_log(cmd_parms *cmd,
22818          void *dummy, char *fn,
22819                                     char *fmt, char *envclause)
22820  {
22821      const char *err_string = NULL;
22822      multi_log_state *mls =
22823          ap_get_module_config(cmd->server->module_config,
```

```
22824                               &config_log_module);
22825      config_log_state *cls;
22826
22827      cls = (config_log_state *)
22828          ap_push_array(mls->config_logs);
22829      cls->condition_var = NULL;
22830      if (envclause != NULL) {
22831        if (strncasecmp(envclause, "env=", 4) != 0) {
22832            return "error in condition clause";
22833        }
22834        if ((envclause[4] == '\0')
22835            || ((envclause[4] == '!')
22836                && (envclause[5] == '\0'))) {
22837            return "missing environment variable name";
22838        }
22839        cls->condition_var = ap_pstrdup(cmd->pool,
22840            &envclause[4]);
22841      }
22842
22843      cls->fname = fn;
22844      cls->format_string = fmt;
22845      if (fmt == NULL) {
22846          cls->format = NULL;
22847      }
22848      else {
22849          cls->format = parse_log_string(cmd->pool,
22850              fmt, &err_string);
22851      }
22852      cls->log_fd = -1;
22853
22854      return err_string;
22855  }
22856
22857  static const char *set_transfer_log(cmd_parms *cmd,
22858      void *dummy, char *fn)
22859  {
22860      return add_custom_log(cmd, dummy, fn, NULL, NULL);
22861  }
22862
22863  static const char *set_cookie_log(cmd_parms *cmd,
22864      void *dummy, char *fn)
22865  {
22866      return add_custom_log(cmd, dummy, fn,
22867        "%{Cookie}n \"%r\" %t", NULL);
22868  }
22869
22870  static const command_rec config_log_cmds[] =
22871  {
```

```
22872      {"CustomLog", add_custom_log, NULL, RSRC_CONF,
22873           TAKE23,
22874       "a file name, a custom log format string or
22875           format name, "
22876       "and an optional \"env=\" clause (see docs)"},
22877      {"TransferLog", set_transfer_log, NULL,
22878           RSRC_CONF, TAKE1,
22879       "the filename of the access log"},
22880      {"LogFormat", log_format, NULL, RSRC_CONF,
22881           TAKE12,
22882       "a log format string (see docs) and an optional
22883           format name"},
22884      {"CookieLog", set_cookie_log, NULL, RSRC_CONF,
22885           TAKE1,
22886       "the filename of the cookie log"},
22887      {NULL}
22888 };
22889
22890 static config_log_state *open_config_log(server_rec *s,
22891     pool *p,
22892                                 config_log_state *cls,
22893                      array_header *default_format)
22894 {
22895     if (cls->log_fd > 0) {
22896         return cls;
22897     /* virtual config shared w/main server */
22898     }
22899
22900     if (cls->fname == NULL) {
22901         return cls;
22902     /* Leave it NULL to decline.  */
22903     }
22904
22905     if (*cls->fname == '|') {
22906         piped_log *pl;
22907
22908         pl = ap_open_piped_log(p, cls->fname + 1);
22909         if (pl == NULL) {
22910             exit(1);
22911         }
22912         cls->log_fd = ap_piped_log_write_fd(pl);
22913     }
22914     else {
22915         char *fname = ap_server_root_relative(p,
22916                 cls->fname);
22917         if ((cls->log_fd = ap_popenf(p, fname,
22918                 xfer_flags, xfer_mode)) < 0) {
22919             ap_log_error(APLOG_MARK, APLOG_ERR, s,
22920                                 "could not open transfer
22921                                     log file %s.", fname);
22922             exit(1);
22923         }
22924     }
22925 #ifdef BUFFERED_LOGS
22926     cls->outcnt = 0;
22927 #endif
22928
22929     return cls;
22930 }
22931
22932 static config_log_state *open_multi_logs(server_rec *s,
22933     pool *p)
22934 {
22935     int i;
22936     multi_log_state *mls =
22937             ap_get_module_config(s->module_config,
22938                                 &config_log_module);
22939     config_log_state *clsarray;
22940     const char *dummy;
22941     const char *format;
22942
22943     if (mls->default_format_string) {
22944       format = ap_table_get(mls->formats,
22945           mls->default_format_string);
22946       if (format) {
22947         mls->default_format = parse_log_string(p,
22948           format, &dummy);
22949       }
22950     }
22951
22952     if (!mls->default_format) {
22953         mls->default_format = parse_log_string(p,
22954             DEFAULT_LOG_FORMAT, &dummy);
22955     }
22956
22957     if (mls->config_logs->nelts) {
22958       clsarray = (config_log_state *)
22959         mls->config_logs->elts;
22960       for (i = 0; i < mls->config_logs->nelts; ++i) {
22961         config_log_state *cls = &clsarray[i];
22962
22963         if (cls->format_string) {
22964         format = ap_table_get(mls->formats,
22965             cls->format_string);
22966         if (format) {
22967             cls->format = parse_log_string(p,
```

```
22968              format, &dummy);
22969          }
22970        }
22971
22972          cls = open_config_log(s, p, cls,
22973            mls->default_format);
22974      }
22975    }
22976    else if (mls->server_config_logs) {
22977      clsarray = (config_log_state *)
22978          mls->server_config_logs->elts;
22979      for (i = 0; i < mls->server_config_logs->
22980          nelts; ++i) {
22981        config_log_state *cls = &clsarray[i];
22982
22983        if (cls->format_string) {
22984          format = ap_table_get(mls->formats,
22985            cls->format_string);
22986          if (format) {
22987            cls->format = parse_log_string(p,
22988              format, &dummy);
22989          }
22990        }
22991
22992          cls = open_config_log(s, p, cls,
22993            mls->default_format);
22994      }
22995    }
22996
22997    return NULL;
22998 }
22999
23000 static void init_config_log(server_rec *s, pool *p)
23001 {
23002    /* First, do "physical" server, which gets
23003     * default log fd and format for the virtual
23004     * servers, if they don't override...
23005     */
23006
23007    open_multi_logs(s, p);
23008
23009    /* Then, virtual servers */
23010
23011    for (s = s->next; s; s = s->next) {
23012        open_multi_logs(s, p);
23013    }
23014 }
23015
23016 #ifdef BUFFERED_LOGS
23017 static void flush_all_logs(server_rec *s, pool *p)
23018 {
23019    multi_log_state *mls;
23020    array_header *log_list;
23021    config_log_state *clsarray;
23022    int i;
23023
23024    for (; s; s = s->next) {
23025      mls = ap_get_module_config(s->module_config,
23026        &config_log_module);
23027      log_list = NULL;
23028      if (mls->config_logs->nelts) {
23029          log_list = mls->config_logs;
23030      }
23031      else if (mls->server_config_logs) {
23032          log_list = mls->server_config_logs;
23033      }
23034      if (log_list) {
23035        clsarray = (config_log_state *) log_list->elts;
23036        for (i = 0; i < log_list->nelts; ++i) {
23037            flush_log(&clsarray[i]);
23038        }
23039      }
23040    }
23041 }
23042 #endif
23043
23044 module MODULE_VAR_EXPORT config_log_module =
23045 {
23046    STANDARD_MODULE_STUFF,
23047    init_config_log,       /* initializer */
23048    NULL,                  /* create per-dir config */
23049    NULL,                  /* merge per-dir config */
23050    make_config_log_state, /* server config */
23051    merge_config_log_state, /* merge server config */
23052    config_log_cmds,       /* command table */
23053    NULL,                  /* handlers */
23054    NULL,                  /* filename translation */
23055    NULL,                  /* check_user_id */
23056    NULL,                  /* check auth */
23057    NULL,                  /* check access */
23058    NULL,                  /* type_checker */
23059    NULL,                  /* fixups */
23060    multi_log_transaction, /* logger */
23061    NULL,                  /* header parser */
23062    NULL,                  /* child_init */
23063 #ifdef BUFFERED_LOGS
```

```
23064        flush_all_logs,              /* child_exit */
23065   #else
23066        NULL,
23067   #endif
23068        NULL                    /* post read-request */
23069   };
```

mod_log_referer.c
p 520

```
23070   #include "httpd.h"
23071   #include "http_config.h"
23072   #include "http_log.h"
23073
23074   module referer_log_module;
23075
23076   static int xfer_flags = (O_WRONLY | O_APPEND | O_CREAT);
23077
23078   #ifdef OS2
23079   /* OS/2 lacks support for users and groups */
23080   static mode_t xfer_mode = (S_IREAD | S_IWRITE);
23081   #else
23082   static mode_t xfer_mode = (S_IRUSR | S_IWUSR |
23083        S_IRGRP | S_IROTH);
23084   #endif
23085
23086   typedef struct {
23087        char *fname;
23088        int referer_fd;
23089        array_header *referer_ignore_list;
23090   } referer_log_state;
23091
23092   static void *make_referer_log_state(pool *p,
23093        server_rec *s)
23094   {
23095        referer_log_state *cls =
23096        (referer_log_state *) ap_palloc(p,
23097         sizeof(referer_log_state));
23098
23099        cls->fname = "";
23100        cls->referer_fd = -1;
23101        cls->referer_ignore_list = ap_make_array(p,
23102             1, sizeof(char *));
23103        return (void *) cls;
23104   }
23105
23106   static const char *set_referer_log(cmd_parms *parms,
23107        void *dummy, char *arg)
23108   {
```

```
23109        referer_log_state *cls =
23110        ap_get_module_config(parms->server->module_config,
23111                             &referer_log_module);
23112
23113        cls->fname = arg;
23114        return NULL;
23115   }
23116
23117   static const char *add_referer_ignore(cmd_parms *parms,
23118        void *dummy, char *arg)
23119   {
23120        char **addme;
23121        referer_log_state *cls =
23122        ap_get_module_config(parms->server->module_config,
23123                             &referer_log_module);
23124
23125        addme = ap_push_array(cls->referer_ignore_list);
23126        ap_str_tolower(arg);
23127        *addme = arg;
23128        return NULL;
23129   }
23130
23131   static const command_rec referer_log_cmds[] =
23132   {
23133        {"RefererLog", set_referer_log, NULL, RSRC_CONF,
23134             TAKE1,
23135        "the filename of the referer log"},
23136        {"RefererIgnore", add_referer_ignore, NULL,
23137             RSRC_CONF, ITERATE,
23138        "referer hostnames to ignore"},
23139        {NULL}
23140   };
23141
23142   static void open_referer_log(server_rec *s, pool *p)
23143   {
23144        referer_log_state *cls =
23145             ap_get_module_config(s->module_config,
23146                             &referer_log_module);
23147
23148        char *fname = ap_server_root_relative(p,
23149             cls->fname);
23150
23151        if (cls->referer_fd > 0)
23152             return;
23153   /* virtual log shared w/main server */
23154
23155        if (*cls->fname == '|') {
23156             piped_log *pl;
```

```
23157
23158          pl = ap_open_piped_log(p, cls->fname + 1);
23159          if (pl == NULL) {
23160              ap_log_error(APLOG_MARK, APLOG_ERR, s,
23161                  "couldn't spawn referer log pipe");
23162                  exit(1);
23163              }
23164
23165          cls->referer_fd = ap_piped_log_write_fd(pl);
23166          }
23167          else if (*cls->fname != '\0') {
23168              if ((cls->referer_fd = ap_popenf(p, fname,
23169              xfer_flags, xfer_mode)) < 0) {
23170              ap_log_error(APLOG_MARK, APLOG_ERR, s,
23171                "could not open referer log file %s.", fname);
23172              exit(1);
23173          }
23174          }
23175  }
23176
23177  static void init_referer_log(server_rec *s, pool *p)
23178  {
23179      for (; s; s = s->next)
23180          open_referer_log(s, p);
23181  }
23182
23183  static int referer_log_transaction(request_rec *orig)
23184  {
23185      char **ptrptr, **ptrptr2;
23186      referer_log_state *cls =
23187        ap_get_module_config(orig->server->module_config,
23188                                  &referer_log_module);
23189
23190      char *str;
23191      const char *referer;
23192      char *referertest;
23193      request_rec *r;
23194
23195      if (cls->referer_fd < 0)
23196          return OK;
23197
23198      for (r = orig; r->next; r = r->next)
23199          continue;
23200      if (*cls->fname == '\0')     /* Don't log referer */
23201          return DECLINED;
23202
23203      referer = ap_table_get(orig->headers_in, "Referer");
23204      if (referer != NULL) {
```

```
23205
23206          referertest = ap_pstrdup(orig->pool, referer);
23207          ap_str_tolower(referertest);
23208          /* The following is an upsetting mess of
23209              pointers. I'm sorry  Anyone with the motiviation
23210              and/or the time should feel free to
23211              make this cleaner... */
23212
23213          ptrptr2 = (char **)
23214            (cls->referer_ignore_list->elts +
23215                  (cls->referer_ignore_list->nelts *
23216                  cls->referer_ignore_list->elt_size));
23217
23218          /* Go through each element of the ignore list
23219              and compare it to the referer_host.  If we
23220              get a match, return without logging */
23221
23222          for (ptrptr = (char **)
23223                cls->referer_ignore_list->elts;
23224              ptrptr < ptrptr2;
23225              ptrptr = (char **) ((char *) ptrptr +
23226              cls->referer_ignore_list->elt_size)) {
23227              if (strstr(referertest, *ptrptr))
23228                  return OK;
23229          }
23230
23231
23232          str = ap_pstrcat(orig->pool, referer, " -> ",
23233                  r->uri, "\n", NULL);
23234          write(cls->referer_fd, str, strlen(str));
23235      }
23236
23237      return OK;
23238  }
23239
23240  module referer_log_module =
23241  {
23242      STANDARD_MODULE_STUFF,
23243      init_referer_log,       /* initializer */
23244      NULL,                   /* create per-dir config */
23245      NULL,                   /* merge per-dir config */
23246      make_referer_log_state, /* server config */
23247      NULL,                   /* merge server config */
23248      referer_log_cmds,       /* command table */
23249      NULL,                   /* handlers */
23250      NULL,                   /* filename translation */
23251      NULL,                   /* check_user_id */
23252      NULL,                   /* check auth */
```

```
23253        NULL,                    /* check access */
23254        NULL,                    /* type_checker */
23255        NULL,                    /* fixups */
23256        referer_log_transaction, /* logger */
23257        NULL,                    /* header parser */
23258        NULL,                    /* child_init */
23259        NULL,                    /* child_exit */
23260        NULL                     /* post read-request */
23261    };
```

p 462 **mod_mime.c**

```
23262    #define MIME_PRIVATE
23263
23264    #include "httpd.h"
23265    #include "http_config.h"
23266    #include "http_log.h"
23267
23268    typedef struct handlers_info {
23269        char *name;
23270    } handlers_info;
23271
23272    typedef struct {
23273        table *forced_types;
23274        /* Additional AddTyped stuff */
23275        table *encoding_types;
23276        /* Added with AddEncoding... */
23277        table *language_types;
23278        /* Added with AddLanguage... */
23279        table *handlers;
23280        /* Added with AddHandler...  */
23281        array_header *handlers_remove;
23282        /* List of handlers to remove */
23283
23284        char *type;
23285        /* Type forced with ForceType  */
23286        char *handler;
23287        /* Handler forced with SetHandler */
23288        char *default_language;
23289        /* Language if no AddLanguage ext found */
23290    } mime_dir_config;
23291
23292    module MODULE_VAR_EXPORT mime_module;
23293
23294    static void *create_mime_dir_config(pool *p,
23295         char *dummy)
23296    {
23297        mime_dir_config *new =
```

```
23298        (mime_dir_config *) ap_palloc(p,
23299            sizeof(mime_dir_config));
23300
23301    new->forced_types = ap_make_table(p, 4);
23302    new->encoding_types = ap_make_table(p, 4);
23303    new->language_types = ap_make_table(p, 4);
23304    new->handlers = ap_make_table(p, 4);
23305    new->handlers_remove = ap_make_array(p, 4,
23306            sizeof(handlers_info));
23307
23308    new->type = NULL;
23309    new->handler = NULL;
23310    new->default_language = NULL;
23311
23312    return new;
23313    }
23314
23315    static void *merge_mime_dir_configs(pool *p,
23316        void *basev, void *addv)
23317    {
23318        mime_dir_config *base = (mime_dir_config *) basev;
23319        mime_dir_config *add = (mime_dir_config *) addv;
23320        mime_dir_config *new =
23321            (mime_dir_config *) ap_palloc(p,
23322                sizeof(mime_dir_config));
23323        int i;
23324        handlers_info *hand;
23325
23326        hand = (handlers_info *) add->handlers_remove->elts;
23327        for (i = 0; i < add->handlers_remove->nelts; i++) {
23328            ap_table_unset(base->handlers, hand[i].name);
23329        }
23330
23331        new->forced_types = ap_overlay_tables(p,
23332            add->forced_types,
23333                                    base->forced_types);
23334        new->encoding_types = ap_overlay_tables(p,
23335            add->encoding_types,
23336                                    base->encoding_types);
23337        new->language_types = ap_overlay_tables(p,
23338            add->language_types,
23339                                    base->language_types);
23340        new->handlers = ap_overlay_tables(p, add->handlers,
23341                                    base->handlers);
23342
23343        new->type = add->type ? add->type : base->type;
23344        new->handler = add->handler ? add->handler : b
23345            ase->handler;
```

```
23346        new->default_language = add->default_language ?
23347             add->default_language : base->default_language;
23348
23349        return new;
23350    }
23351
23352    static const char *add_type(cmd_parms *cmd,
23353          mime_dir_config * m, char *ct,
23354                                        char *ext)
23355    {
23356        if (*ext == '.')
23357            ++ext;
23358
23359        ap_str_tolower(ct);
23360        ap_table_setn(m->forced_types, ext, ct);
23361        return NULL;
23362    }
23363
23364    static const char *add_encoding(cmd_parms *cmd,
23365          mime_dir_config * m, char *enc,
23366                                        char *ext)
23367    {
23368        if (*ext == '.')
23369            ++ext;
23370        ap_str_tolower(enc);
23371        ap_table_setn(m->encoding_types, ext, enc);
23372        return NULL;
23373    }
23374
23375    static const char *add_language(cmd_parms *cmd,
23376          mime_dir_config * m, char *lang,
23377                                        char *ext)
23378    {
23379        if (*ext == '.')
23380            ++ext;
23381        ap_str_tolower(lang);
23382        ap_table_setn(m->language_types, ext, lang);
23383        return NULL;
23384    }
23385
23386    static const char *add_handler(cmd_parms *cmd,
23387          mime_dir_config * m, char *hdlr,
23388                                        char *ext)
23389    {
23390        if (*ext == '.')
23391            ++ext;
23392        ap_str_tolower(hdlr);
23393        ap_table_setn(m->handlers, ext, hdlr);
```

```
23394        return NULL;
23395    }
23396
23397    /*
23398     * Note handler names that should be un-added for
23399     * this location.  This will keep the association
23400     * from being inherited, as well, but not
23401     * from being re-added at a subordinate level.
23402     */
23403    static const char *remove_handler(cmd_parms *cmd,
23404          void *m, char *ext)
23405    {
23406        mime_dir_config *mcfg = (mime_dir_config *) m;
23407        handlers_info *hand;
23408
23409        if (*ext == '.') {
23410            ++ext;
23411        }
23412        hand = (handlers_info *)
23413                ap_push_array(mcfg->handlers_remove);
23414        hand->name = ap_pstrdup(cmd->pool, ext);
23415        return NULL;
23416    }
23417
23418    /* The sole bit of server configuration that the
23419     * MIME module has is the name of
23420     * its config file, so...
23421     */
23422
23423    static const char *set_types_config(cmd_parms *cmd,
23424          void *dummy, char *arg)
23425    {
23426        ap_set_module_config(cmd->server->module_config,
23427              &mime_module, arg);
23428        return NULL;
23429    }
23430
23431    static const command_rec mime_cmds[] =
23432    {
23433        {"AddType", add_type, NULL, OR_FILEINFO, ITERATE2,
23434         "a mime type followed by one or more file
23435              extensions"},
23436        {"AddEncoding", add_encoding, NULL, OR_FILEINFO,
23437              ITERATE2,
23438         "an encoding (e.g., gzip), followed by one or more
23439              file extensions"},
23440        {"AddLanguage", add_language, NULL, OR_FILEINFO,
23441              ITERATE2,
```

```
23442        "a language (e.g., fr), followed by one or more
23443            file extensions"},
23444    {"AddHandler", add_handler, NULL, OR_FILEINFO,
23445            ITERATE2,
23446      "a handler name followed by one or more file
23447            extensions"},
23448    {"ForceType", ap_set_string_slot_lower,
23449     (void *)XtOffsetOf(mime_dir_config, type),
23450            OR_FILEINFO, TAKE1,
23451      "a media type"},
23452    {"RemoveHandler", remove_handler, NULL,
23453            OR_FILEINFO, ITERATE,
23454      "one or more file extensions"},
23455    {"SetHandler", ap_set_string_slot_lower,
23456     (void *)XtOffsetOf(mime_dir_config, handler),
23457            OR_FILEINFO, TAKE1,
23458      "a handler name"},
23459    {"TypesConfig", set_types_config, NULL,
23460            RSRC_CONF, TAKE1,
23461      "the MIME types config file"},
23462    {"DefaultLanguage", ap_set_string_slot,
23463     (void*)XtOffsetOf(mime_dir_config,
23464            default_language), OR_FILEINFO, TAKE1,
23465      "language to use for documents with no other
23466            language file extension" },
23467    {NULL}
23468 };
23469
23470 /* Hash table  -- only one of these per daemon;
23471  * virtual hosts can get private versions
23472  * through AddType...
23473  */
23474
23475 /* MIME_HASHSIZE used to be 27 (26 chars and one
23476  * "non-alpha" slot), but with character sets
23477  * like EBCDIC, this is insufficient because the
23478  * range 'a'...'z' is not contigous. Defining it
23479  * as ('z'-'a'+2) is equivalent to 27 in ASCII,
23480  * and makes it work in EBCDIC.
23481  */
23482 #define MIME_HASHSIZE ('z'-'a'+2)
23483 #define hash(i) (ap_isalpha(i) ? (ap_tolower(i)) -
23484        'a' : (MIME_HASHSIZE-1))
23485
23486 static table *hash_buckets[MIME_HASHSIZE];
23487
23488 static void init_mime(server_rec *s, pool *p)
23489 {
23490    configfile_t *f;
23491    char l[MAX_STRING_LEN];
23492    int x;
23493    char *types_confname =
23494        ap_get_module_config(s->module_config,
23495        &mime_module);
23496
23497    if (!types_confname)
23498        types_confname = TYPES_CONFIG_FILE;
23499
23500    types_confname = ap_server_root_relative(p,
23501        types_confname);
23502
23503    if (!(f = ap_pcfg_openfile(p, types_confname))) {
23504        ap_log_error(APLOG_MARK, APLOG_ERR, s,
23505            "could not open mime types log
23506                file %s.", types_confname);
23507        exit(1);
23508    }
23509
23510    for (x = 0; x < MIME_HASHSIZE; x++)
23511        hash_buckets[x] = ap_make_table(p, 10);
23512
23513    while (!(ap_cfg_getline(l, MAX_STRING_LEN, f))) {
23514        const char *ll = l, *ct;
23515
23516        if (l[0] == '#')
23517            continue;
23518        ct = ap_getword_conf(p, &ll);
23519
23520        while (ll[0]) {
23521            char *ext = ap_getword_conf(p, &ll);
23522            ap_str_tolower(ext);   /* ??? */
23523            ap_table_setn(hash_buckets[hash(ext[0])],
23524                ext, ct);
23525        }
23526    }
23527    ap_cfg_closefile(f);
23528 }
23529
23530 static int find_ct(request_rec *r)
23531 {
23532    const char *fn = strrchr(r->filename, '/');
23533    mime_dir_config *conf =
23534    (mime_dir_config *)
23535        ap_get_module_config(r->per_dir_config,
23536        &mime_module);
23537    char *ext;
```

```
23538        const char *orighandler = r->handler;
23539        const char *type;
23540
23541        if (S_ISDIR(r->finfo.st_mode)) {
23542            r->content_type = DIR_MAGIC_TYPE;
23543            return OK;
23544        }
23545
23546        /* TM -- FIXME
23547         * if r->filename does not contain a '/', the
23548         * following passes a null pointer
23549         * to getword, causing a SEGV ..
23550         */
23551
23552        if (fn == NULL)
23553            fn = r->filename;
23554
23555        /* Parse filename extensions, which can
23556         * be in any order */
23557        while ((ext = ap_getword(r->pool, &fn, '.'))
23558               && *ext) {
23559            int found = 0;
23560
23561            /* Check for Content-Type */
23562            if ((type = ap_table_get(conf->forced_types,
23563                    ext))
23564              || (type =
23565                ap_table_get(hash_buckets[hash(*ext)],
23566                    ext))) {
23567                r->content_type = type;
23568                found = 1;
23569            }
23570
23571            /* Check for Content-Language */
23572            if ((type = ap_table_get(conf->language_types,
23573                    ext))) {
23574                const char **new;
23575
23576                r->content_language = type;
23577                /* back compat. only */
23578                if (!r->content_languages)
23579                    r->content_languages =
23580                        ap_make_array(r->pool, 2,
23581                        sizeof(char *));
23582                new = (const char **)
23583                    ap_push_array(r->content_languages);
23584                *new = type;
23585                found = 1;
```

```
23586            }
23587
23588            /* Check for Content-Encoding */
23589            if ((type = ap_table_get(conf->encoding_types,
23590                    ext))) {
23591                if (!r->content_encoding)
23592                    r->content_encoding = type;
23593                else
23594                    r->content_encoding =
23595                        ap_pstrcat(r->pool,
23596                            r->content_encoding,
23597                                ", ", type, NULL);
23598                found = 1;
23599            }
23600
23601            /* Check for a special handler, but not
23602             * for proxy request */
23603            if ((type = ap_table_get(conf->handlers,
23604                    ext)) && !r->proxyreq) {
23605                r->handler = type;
23606                found = 1;
23607            }
23608
23609            /* This is to deal with cases such as
23610             * foo.gif.bak, which we want to not have
23611             * a type. So if we find an unknown extension,
23612             * we zap the type/language/encoding and
23613             * reset the handler
23614             */
23615
23616            if (!found) {
23617                r->content_type = NULL;
23618                r->content_language = NULL;
23619                r->content_languages = NULL;
23620                r->content_encoding = NULL;
23621                r->handler = orighandler;
23622            }
23623
23624        }
23625
23626    /* Set default language, if none was specified by
23627     * the extensions and we have a
23628     * DefaultLanguage setting in force
23629     */
23630
23631    if (!r->content_languages &&
23632        conf->default_language) {
23633        const char **new;
```

```
23634
23635          r->content_language = conf->default_language;
23636          /* back compat. only */
23637          if (!r->content_languages)
23638              r->content_languages =
23639                  ap_make_array(r->pool, 2, sizeof(char *));
23640          new = (const char **)
23641                  ap_push_array(r->content_languages);
23642          *new = conf->default_language;
23643      }
23644
23645      /* Check for overrides with ForceType/SetHandler */
23646
23647      if (conf->type && strcmp(conf->type, "none"))
23648          r->content_type = conf->type;
23649      if (conf->handler && strcmp(conf->handler, "none"))
23650          r->handler = conf->handler;
23651
23652      if (!r->content_type)
23653          return DECLINED;
23654
23655      return OK;
23656  }
23657
23658  module MODULE_VAR_EXPORT mime_module =
23659  {
23660      STANDARD_MODULE_STUFF,
23661      init_mime,                  /* initializer */
23662      create_mime_dir_config,     /* dir config creator */
23663      merge_mime_dir_configs,     /* dir config merger */
23664      NULL,                       /* server config */
23665      NULL,                       /* merge server config */
23666      mime_cmds,                  /* command table */
23667      NULL,                       /* handlers */
23668      NULL,                       /* filename translation */
23669      NULL,                       /* check_user_id */
23670      NULL,                       /* check auth */
23671      NULL,                       /* check access */
23672      find_ct,                    /* type_checker */
23673      NULL,                       /* fixups */
23674      NULL,                       /* logger */
23675      NULL,                       /* header parser */
23676      NULL,                       /* child_init */
23677      NULL,                       /* child_exit */
23678      NULL                        /* post read-request */
23679  };
```

mod_mime_magic.c

p. 465

```
23680  #include "httpd.h"
23681  #include "http_config.h"
23682  #include "http_request.h"
23683  #include "http_core.h"
23684  #include "http_log.h"
23685  #include "http_protocol.h"
23686
23687  #include <utime.h>
23688
23689
23690  /*
23691   * data structures and related constants
23692   */
23693
23694  #define MODNAME         "mod_mime_magic"
23695  #define MIME_MAGIC_DEBUG         0
23696
23697  #define MIME_BINARY_UNKNOWN
23698      "application/octet-stream"
23699  #define MIME_TEXT_UNKNOWN     "text/plain"
23700
23701  #define MAXMIMESTRING        256
23702
23703  /* HOWMANY must be at least 4096 to
23704   * make gzip -dcq work */
23705  #define HOWMANY      4096
23706  /* SMALL_HOWMANY limits how much work we do to
23707   * figure out text files */
23708  #define SMALL_HOWMANY 1024
23709  #define MAXDESC      50
23710  /* max leng of text description */
23711  #define MAXstring 64
23712  /* max leng of "string" types */
23713
23714  struct magic {
23715      struct magic *next;
23716      /* link to next entry */
23717      int lineno;
23718      /* line number from magic file */
23719
23720      short flag;
23721  #define INDIR    1          /* if '>(...)' appears,  */
23722  #define   UNSIGNED 2        /* comparison is unsigned */
23723      short cont_level;          /* level of ">" */
23724      struct {
23725       char type;             /* byte short long */
```

```
23726        long offset;            /* offset from indirection */
23727    } in;
23728    long offset;                /* offset to magic number */
23729    unsigned char reln;
23730    /* relation (0=eq, '>'=gt, etc) */
23731    char type;
23732    /* int, short, long or string. */
23733    char vallen;
23734    /* length of string value, if any */
23735 #define BYTE     1
23736 #define SHORT    2
23737 #define LONG     4
23738 #define STRING   5
23739 #define DATE     6
23740 #define BESHORT    7
23741 #define BELONG     8
23742 #define BEDATE     9
23743 #define LESHORT    10
23744 #define LELONG     11
23745 #define LEDATE     12
23746    union VALUETYPE {
23747      unsigned char b;
23748      unsigned short h;
23749      unsigned long l;
23750      char s[MAXstring];
23751      unsigned char hs[2];
23752    /* 2 bytes of a fixed-endian "short" */
23753      unsigned char hl[4];
23754    /* 2 bytes of a fixed-endian "long" */
23755    } value;
23756    /* either number or string */
23757    unsigned long mask;
23758    /* mask before comparison with value */
23759    char nospflag;
23760    /* supress space character */
23761
23762    /* NOTE: this string is suspected of
23763     * overrunning - find it! */
23764    char desc[MAXDESC];          /* description */
23765 };
23766
23767 /*
23768  * data structures for tar file recognition
23769  * -------------------------------------------------
23770  * Header file for public domain tar (tape archive)
23771  * program.
23772  *
23773  * @(#)tar.h 1.20 86/10/29    Public Domain. Created
23774  * 25 August 1985 by John
23775  * Gilmore, ihnp4!hoptoad!gnu.
23776  *
23777  * Header block on tape.
23778  *
23779  * I'm going to use traditional DP naming conventions
23780  * here. A "block" is a big chunk of stuff that we
23781  * do I/O on. A "record" is a piece of info that we
23782  * care about. Typically many "record"s fit into a
23783  * "block".
23784  */
23785 #define RECORDSIZE    512
23786 #define NAMSIZ      100
23787 #define TUNMLEN      32
23788 #define TGNMLEN      32
23789
23790 union record {
23791    char charptr[RECORDSIZE];
23792    struct header {
23793      char name[NAMSIZ];
23794      char mode[8];
23795      char uid[8];
23796      char gid[8];
23797      char size[12];
23798      char mtime[12];
23799      char chksum[8];
23800      char linkflag;
23801      char linkname[NAMSIZ];
23802      char magic[8];
23803      char uname[TUNMLEN];
23804      char gname[TGNMLEN];
23805      char devmajor[8];
23806      char devminor[8];
23807    } header;
23808 };
23809
23810 /* The magic field is filled with this if uname
23811  * and gname are valid. */
23812 #define   TMAGIC        "ustar  "
23813 /* 7 chars and a null */
23814
23815 /*
23816  * file-function prototypes
23817  */
23818 static int ascmagic(request_rec *,
23819      unsigned char *, int);
23820 static int is_tar(unsigned char *, int);
23821 static int softmagic(request_rec *,
```

```
23822        unsigned char *, int);
23823    static void tryit(request_rec *,
23824        unsigned char *, int);
23825    static int zmagic(request_rec *,
23826        unsigned char *, int);
23827
23828    static int getvalue(server_rec *,
23829        struct magic *, char **);
23830    static int hextoint(int);
23831    static char *getstr(server_rec *, char *,
23832        char *, int, int *);
23833    static int parse(server_rec *, pool *p, char *, int);
23834
23835    static int match(request_rec *, unsigned char *, int);
23836    static int mget(request_rec *, union VALUETYPE *,
23837        unsigned char *,
23838            struct magic *, int);
23839    static int mcheck(request_rec *, union VALUETYPE *,
23840        struct magic *);
23841    static void mprint(request_rec *, union VALUETYPE *,
23842        struct magic *);
23843
23844    static int uncompress(request_rec *, int, const
23845        unsigned char *,
23846                unsigned char **, int);
23847    static long from_oct(int, char *);
23848    static int fsmagic(request_rec *r, const char *fn);
23849
23850    /*
23851
23852     * includes for ASCII substring recognition
23853     * formerly "names.h" in file command
23854     *
23855     * Original notes: names and types used by ascmagic in
23856     * file(1). These tokens are here because they can
23857     * appear anywhere in the first HOWMANY bytes, while
23858     * tokens in /etc/magic must appear at fixed offsets
23859     * into the file. Don't make HOWMANY too high
23860     * unless you have a very fast CPU.
23861     */
23862
23863    /* these types are used to index the table 'types':
23864     * keep em in sync! */
23865    /* HTML inserted in first because this is a web
23866     * server module now */
23867    #define L_HTML    0    /* HTML */
23868    #define L_C       1    /* first and foremost on UNIX */
23869    #define L_FORT    2    /* the oldest one */
23870    #define L_MAKE    3    /* Makefiles */
23871    #define L_PLI     4    /* PL/1 */
23872    #define L_MACH    5    /* some kinda assembler */
23873    #define L_ENG     6    /* English */
23874    #define L_PAS     7    /* Pascal */
23875    #define L_MAIL    8    /* Electronic mail */
23876    #define L_NEWS    9    /* Usenet Netnews */
23877
23878    static char *types[] =
23879    {
23880        "text/html",        /* HTML */
23881        "text/plain",        /* "c program text", */
23882        "text/plain",        /* "fortran program text", */
23883        "text/plain",        /* "make commands text", */
23884        "text/plain",        /* "pl/1 program text", */
23885        "text/plain",        /* "assembler program text", */
23886        "text/plain",        /* "English text", */
23887        "text/plain",        /* "pascal program text", */
23888        "message/rfc822",    /* "mail text", */
23889        "message/news",      /* "news text", */
23890        "application/binary",
23891        /* "can't happen error on names.h/types", */
23892        0
23893    };
23894
23895    static struct names {
23896        char *name;
23897        short type;
23898    } names[] = {
23899
23900        /* These must be sorted by eye for optimal
23901         * hit rate Add to this list only
23902        /* after substantial meditation */
23903        {
23904        "<html>", L_HTML
23905        },
23906        {
23907        "<HTML>", L_HTML
23908        },
23909        {
23910        "<head>", L_HTML
23911        },
23912        {
23913        "<HEAD>", L_HTML
23914        },
23915        {
23916        "<title>", L_HTML
23917        },
```

```
23918        {
23919          "<TITLE>", L_HTML
23920        },
23921        {
23922          "<h1>", L_HTML
23923        },
23924        {
23925          "<H1>", L_HTML
23926        },
23927        {
23928          "<!--", L_HTML
23929        },
23930        {
23931          "<!DOCTYPE HTML", L_HTML
23932        },
23933        {
23934          "/*", L_C
23935        },
23936        /* must precede "The", "the", etc. */
23937        {
23938          "#include", L_C
23939        },
23940        {
23941          "char", L_C
23942        },
23943        {
23944          "The", L_ENG
23945        },
23946        {
23947          "the", L_ENG
23948        },
23949        {
23950          "double", L_C
23951        },
23952        {
23953          "extern", L_C
23954        },
23955        {
23956          "float", L_C
23957        },
23958        {
23959          "real", L_C
23960        },
23961        {
23962          "struct", L_C
23963        },
23964        {
23965          "union", L_C
```

```
23966        },
23967        {
23968          "CFLAGS", L_MAKE
23969        },
23970        {
23971          "LDFLAGS", L_MAKE
23972        },
23973        {
23974          "all:", L_MAKE
23975        },
23976        {
23977          ".PRECIOUS", L_MAKE
23978        },
23979        /*
23980         * Too many files of text have these words
23981         * in them.  Find another way to
23982         * recognize Fortrash.
23983         */
23984 #ifdef    NOTDEF
23985        {
23986          "subroutine", L_FORT
23987        },
23988        {
23989          "function", L_FORT
23990        },
23991        {
23992          "block", L_FORT
23993        },
23994        {
23995          "common", L_FORT
23996        },
23997        {
23998          "dimension", L_FORT
23999        },
24000        {
24001          "integer", L_FORT
24002        },
24003        {
24004          "data", L_FORT
24005        },
24006 #endif /* NOTDEF */
24007        {
24008          ".ascii", L_MACH
24009        },
24010        {
24011          ".asciiz", L_MACH
24012        },
24013        {
```

```
24014        ".byte", L_MACH
24015      },
24016      {
24017        ".even", L_MACH
24018      },
24019      {
24020        ".globl", L_MACH
24021      },
24022      {
24023        "clr", L_MACH
24024      },
24025      {
24026        "(input,", L_PAS
24027      },
24028      {
24029        "dcl", L_PLI
24030      },
24031      {
24032        "Received:", L_MAIL
24033      },
24034      {
24035        ">From", L_MAIL
24036      },
24037      {
24038        "Return-Path:", L_MAIL
24039      },
24040      {
24041        "Cc:", L_MAIL
24042      },
24043      {
24044        "Newsgroups:", L_NEWS
24045      },
24046      {
24047        "Path:", L_NEWS
24048      },
24049      {
24050        "Organization:", L_NEWS
24051      },
24052      {
24053        NULL, 0
24054      }
24055    };
24056
24057    #define NNAMES
24058        ((sizeof(names)/sizeof(struct names)) - 1)
24059
24060    /*
24061     * Result String List (RSL)
```

```
24062     *
24063     * The file(1) command prints its output.  Instead,
24064     * we store the various"printed" strings in a list
24065     * (allocating memory as we go) and concatenate
24066     * them at the end when we finally know how much
24067     * space they'll need.
24068     */
24069
24070    typedef struct magic_rsl_s {
24071        char *str;
24072        /* string, possibly a fragment */
24073        struct magic_rsl_s *next;
24074        /* pointer to next fragment */
24075    } magic_rsl;
24076
24077    /*
24078     * Apache module configuration structures
24079     */
24080
24081    /* per-server info */
24082    typedef struct {
24083        char *magicfile;     /* where magic be found */
24084        struct magic *magic; /* head of magic config list */
24085        struct magic *last;
24086    } magic_server_config_rec;
24087
24088    /* per-request info */
24089    typedef struct {
24090        magic_rsl *head;          /* result string list */
24091        magic_rsl *tail;
24092        unsigned suf_recursion;
24093        /* recursion depth in suffix check */
24094    } magic_req_rec;
24095
24096    /*
24097     * configuration functions - called by Apache
24098     * API routines
24099     */
24100
24101    module mime_magic_module;
24102
24103    static void *create_magic_server_config(pool *p,
24104        server_rec *d)
24105    {
24106        /* allocate the config - use pcalloc because it
24107         * needs to be zeroed */
24108        return ap_pcalloc(p,
24109            sizeof(magic_server_config_rec));
```

```
24110    }
24111
24112    static void *merge_magic_server_config(pool *p,
24113        void *basev, void *addv)
24114    {
24115        magic_server_config_rec *base =
24116            (magic_server_config_rec *) basev;
24117        magic_server_config_rec *add =
24118            (magic_server_config_rec *) addv;
24119        magic_server_config_rec *new =
24120            (magic_server_config_rec *)
24121                    ap_palloc(p,
24122                        sizeof(magic_server_config_rec));
24123
24124        new->magicfile = add->magicfile ? add->magicfile :
24125            base->magicfile;
24126        new->magic = NULL;
24127        new->last = NULL;
24128        return new;
24129    }
24130
24131    static const char *set_magicfile(cmd_parms *cmd,
24132        char *d, char *arg)
24133    {
24134        magic_server_config_rec *conf =
24135            (magic_server_config_rec *)
24136        ap_get_module_config(cmd->server->module_config,
24137                &mime_magic_module);
24138
24139        if (!conf) {
24140         return MODNAME ": server structure not allocated";
24141        }
24142        conf->magicfile = arg;
24143        return NULL;
24144    }
24145
24146    /*
24147     * configuration file commands - exported to Apache API
24148     */
24149
24150    static const command_rec mime_magic_cmds[] =
24151    {
24152        {"MimeMagicFile", set_magicfile, NULL,
24153            RSRC_CONF, TAKE1,
24154         "Path to MIME Magic file (in file(1) format)"},
24155        {NULL}
24156    };
24157
24158    /*
24159     * RSL (result string list) processing routines
24160     *
24161     * These collect strings that would have been printed
24162     * in fragments by file(1) into a list of magic_rsl
24163     * structures with the strings. When complete,
24164     * they're concatenated together to become the
24165     * MIME content and encoding
24166     * types.
24167     *
24168     * return value conventions for these functions:
24169     * functions which return int: failure = -1,
24170     * other = result functions which return pointers:
24171     * failure = 0, other = result
24172     */
24173
24174    /* allocate a per-request structure and put it
24175     * in the request record */
24176    static magic_req_rec *magic_set_config(request_rec *r)
24177    {
24178        magic_req_rec *req_dat = (magic_req_rec *)
24179            ap_palloc(r->pool,
24180                        sizeof(magic_req_rec));
24181
24182        req_dat->head = req_dat->tail = (magic_rsl *) NULL;
24183        ap_set_module_config(r->request_config,
24184            &mime_magic_module, req_dat);
24185        return req_dat;
24186    }
24187
24188    /* add a string to the result string list for
24189     * this request */
24190    /* it is the responsibility of the caller to
24191     * allocate "str" */
24192    static int magic_rsl_add(request_rec *r, char *str)
24193    {
24194        magic_req_rec *req_dat = (magic_req_rec *)
24195                ap_get_module_config(r->request_config,
24196                    &mime_magic_module);
24197        magic_rsl *rsl;
24198
24199        /* make sure we have a list to put it in */
24200        if (!req_dat) {
24201         ap_log_rerror(APLOG_MARK,
24202            APLOG_NOERRNO | APLOG_ERR, r,
24203                MODNAME ": request config should
24204                    not be NULL");
24205         if (!(req_dat = magic_set_config(r))) {
```

```
24206              /* failure */
24207              return -1;
24208          }
24209      }
24210
24211      /* allocate the list entry */
24212      rsl = (magic_rsl *) ap_palloc(r->pool,
24213          sizeof(magic_rsl));
24214
24215      /* fill it */
24216      rsl->str = str;
24217      rsl->next = (magic_rsl *) NULL;
24218
24219      /* append to the list */
24220      if (req_dat->head && req_dat->tail) {
24221       req_dat->tail->next = rsl;
24222       req_dat->tail = rsl;
24223      }
24224      else {
24225       req_dat->head = req_dat->tail = rsl;
24226      }
24227
24228      /* success */
24229      return 0;
24230  }
24231
24232  /* RSL hook for puts-type functions */
24233  static int magic_rsl_puts(request_rec *r, char *str)
24234  {
24235      return magic_rsl_add(r, str);
24236  }
24237
24238  /* RSL hook for printf-type functions */
24239  static int magic_rsl_printf(request_rec *r,
24240      char *str,...)
24241  {
24242      va_list ap;
24243
24244      char buf[MAXMIMESTRING];
24245
24246      /* assemble the string into the buffer */
24247      va_start(ap, str);
24248      ap_vsnprintf(buf, sizeof(buf), str, ap);
24249      va_end(ap);
24250
24251      /* add the buffer to the list */
24252      return magic_rsl_add(r, strdup(buf));
24253  }
```

```
24254
24255  /* RSL hook for putchar-type functions */
24256  static int magic_rsl_putchar(request_rec *r, char c)
24257  {
24258      char str[2];
24259
24260      /* high overhead for 1 char - just hope they
24261          don't do this much */
24262      str[0] = c;
24263      str[1] = '\0';
24264      return magic_rsl_add(r, str);
24265  }
24266
24267  /* allocate and copy a contiguous string from a result
24268   * string list */
24269  static char *rsl_strdup(request_rec *r, int start_frag,
24270      int start_pos, int len)
24271  {
24272      char *result;           /* return value */
24273      int cur_frag,
24274      /* current fragment number/counter */
24275          cur_pos,
24276      /* current position within fragment */
24277          res_pos;          /* position in result string */
24278      magic_rsl *frag;        /* list-traversal pointer */
24279      magic_req_rec *req_dat = (magic_req_rec *)
24280              ap_get_module_config(r->request_config,
24281                  &mime_magic_module);
24282
24283      /* allocate the result string */
24284      result = (char *) ap_palloc(r->pool, len + 1);
24285
24286      /* loop through and collect the string */
24287      res_pos = 0;
24288      for (frag = req_dat->head, cur_frag = 0;
24289        frag->next;
24290        frag = frag->next, cur_frag++) {
24291       /* loop to the first fragment */
24292       if (cur_frag < start_frag)
24293          continue;
24294
24295       /* loop through and collect chars */
24296       for (cur_pos = (cur_frag == start_frag) ?
24297          start_pos : 0;
24298          frag->str[cur_pos];
24299          cur_pos++) {
24300          if (cur_frag >= start_frag
24301              && cur_pos >= start_pos
```

```
24302          && res_pos <= len) {
24303              result[res_pos++] = frag->str[cur_pos];
24304              if (res_pos > len) {
24305                  break;
24306              }
24307          }
24308      }
24309  }
24310
24311      /* clean up and return */
24312      result[res_pos] = 0;
24313  #if MIME_MAGIC_DEBUG
24314      ap_log_rerror(APLOG_MARK,
24315              APLOG_NOERRNO | APLOG_DEBUG, r,
24316              MODNAME ": rsl_strdup() %d chars: %s",
24317                  res_pos - 1, result);
24318  #endif
24319      return result;
24320  }
24321
24322  /* states for the state-machine algorithm in
24323   * magic_rsl_to_request() */
24324  typedef enum {
24325      rsl_leading_space, rsl_type, rsl_subtype,
24326          rsl_separator, rsl_encoding
24327  } rsl_states;
24328
24329  /* process the RSL and set the MIME info in the
24330   * request record */
24331  static int magic_rsl_to_request(request_rec *r)
24332  {
24333      int cur_frag,
24334      /* current fragment number/counter */
24335
24336          cur_pos,
24337      /* current position within fragment */
24338          type_frag,
24339      /* content type starting point: fragment */
24340          type_pos,
24341      /* content type starting point: position */
24342          type_len,
24343      /* content type length */
24344          encoding_frag,
24345      /* content encoding starting point: fragment */
24346          encoding_pos,
24347      /* content encoding starting point: position */
24348          encoding_len;
24349      /* content encoding length */
```

```
24350
24351      magic_rsl *frag;        /* list-traversal pointer */
24352      rsl_states state;
24353
24354      magic_req_rec *req_dat = (magic_req_rec *)
24355              ap_get_module_config(r->request_config,
24356                  &mime_magic_module);
24357
24358      /* check if we have a result */
24359      if (!req_dat || !req_dat->head) {
24360       /* empty - no match, we defer to other
24361        * Apache modules */
24362       return DECLINED;
24363      }
24364
24365      /* start searching for the type and encoding */
24366      state = rsl_leading_space;
24367      type_frag = type_pos = type_len = 0;
24368      encoding_frag = encoding_pos = encoding_len = 0;
24369      for (frag = req_dat->head, cur_frag = 0;
24370        frag && frag->next;
24371        frag = frag->next, cur_frag++) {
24372       /* loop through the characters in the fragment */
24373       for (cur_pos = 0; frag->str[cur_pos]; cur_pos++) {
24374           if (ap_isspace(frag->str[cur_pos])) {
24375           /* process whitespace actions for each state */
24376           if (state == rsl_leading_space) {
24377               /* eat whitespace in this state */
24378               continue;
24379           }
24380           else if (state == rsl_type) {
24381               /* whitespace: type has no slash! */
24382               return DECLINED;
24383           }
24384           else if (state == rsl_subtype) {
24385               /* whitespace: end of MIME type */
24386               state++;
24387               continue;
24388           }
24389           else if (state == rsl_separator) {
24390               /* eat whitespace in this state */
24391               continue;
24392           }
24393           else if (state == rsl_encoding) {
24394               /* whitespace: end of MIME encoding */
24395               /* we're done */
24396               frag = req_dat->tail;
24397               break;
```

```
24398            }
24399        else {
24400            /* should not be possible */
24401            /* abandon malfunctioning module */
24402            ap_log_rerror(APLOG_MARK,
24403                APLOG_NOERRNO | APLOG_ERR, r,
24404                MODNAME ": bad state %d (ws)", state);
24405            return DECLINED;
24406        }
24407        /* NOTREACHED */
24408        }
24409        else if (state == rsl_type &&
24410                frag->str[cur_pos] == '/') {
24411        /* copy the char and go to rsl_subtype state */
24412        type_len++;
24413        state++;
24414        }
24415        else {
24416        /* process non-space actions for each state */
24417        if (state == rsl_leading_space) {
24418            /* non-space: begin MIME type */
24419            state++;
24420            type_frag = cur_frag;
24421            type_pos = cur_pos;
24422            type_len = 1;
24423            continue;
24424        }
24425        else if (state == rsl_type ||
24426                state == rsl_subtype) {
24427            /* non-space: adds to type */
24428            type_len++;
24429            continue;
24430        }
24431        else if (state == rsl_separator) {
24432            /* non-space: begin MIME encoding */
24433            state++;
24434            encoding_frag = cur_frag;
24435            encoding_pos = cur_pos;
24436            encoding_len = 1;
24437            continue;
24438        }
24439        else if (state == rsl_encoding) {
24440            /* non-space: adds to encoding */
24441            encoding_len++;
24442            continue;
24443        }
24444        else {
24445            /* should not be possible */
24446            /* abandon malfunctioning module */
24447            ap_log_rerror(APLOG_MARK,
24448                APLOG_NOERRNO | APLOG_ERR, r,
24449                MODNAME ": bad state %d (ns)", state);
24450            return DECLINED;
24451            }
24452        /* NOTREACHED */
24453        }
24454        /* NOTREACHED */
24455    }
24456    }
24457
24458    /* if we ended prior to state rsl_subtype,
24459     * we had incomplete info */
24460    if (state != rsl_subtype && state !=
24461            rsl_separator &&
24462        state != rsl_encoding) {
24463        /* defer to other modules */
24464        return DECLINED;
24465    }
24466
24467    /* save the info in the request record */
24468    if (state == rsl_subtype || state == rsl_encoding ||
24469        state == rsl_encoding) {
24470        char *tmp;
24471        tmp = rsl_strdup(r, type_frag, type_pos, type_len);
24472        /* XXX: this could be done at config time
24473         * I'm sure... but I'm confused by
24474         * all this magic_rsl stuff. -djg */
24475        ap_content_type_tolower(tmp);
24476        r->content_type = tmp;
24477    }
24478    if (state == rsl_encoding) {
24479        char *tmp;
24480        tmp = rsl_strdup(r, encoding_frag,
24481                        encoding_pos, encoding_len);
24482        /* XXX: this could be done at config time
24483         * I'm sure... but I'm confused by
24484         * all this magic_rsl stuff. -djg */
24485        ap_str_tolower(tmp);
24486        r->content_encoding = tmp;
24487    }
24488
24489    /* detect memory allocation errors */
24490    if (!r->content_type ||
24491        (state == rsl_encoding && !r->content_encoding)) {
24492        return HTTP_INTERNAL_SERVER_ERROR;
24493    }
```

```
24494
24495      /* success! */
24496      return OK;
24497  }
24498
24499  /*
24500   * magic_process - process input file r
24501   * Apache API request record(formerly called "process"
24502   * in file command, prefix added for clarity) Opens
24503   * the file and reads a fixed-size buffer to begin
24504   * processing the contents.
24505   */
24506  static int magic_process(request_rec *r)
24507  {
24508      int fd = 0;
24509      unsigned char buf[HOWMANY + 1];
24510      /* one extra for terminating '\0' */
24511      int nbytes = 0;
24512      /* number of bytes read from a datafile */
24513      int result;
24514
24515      /*
24516       * first try judging the file based on its
24517       * filesystem status
24518       */
24519      switch ((result = fsmagic(r, r->filename))) {
24520      case DONE:
24521       magic_rsl_putchar(r, '\n');
24522       return OK;
24523      case OK:
24524       break;
24525      default:
24526       /* fatal error, bail out */
24527       return result;
24528      }
24529
24530      if ((fd = ap_popenf(r->pool, r->filename,
24531           O_RDONLY, 0)) < 0) {
24532       /* We can't open it, but we were able to stat it. */
24533       ap_log_rerror(APLOG_MARK, APLOG_ERR, r,
24534               MODNAME ": can't read `%s'", r->filename);
24535       /* let some other handler decide what the
24536        * problem is */
24537       return DECLINED;
24538      }
24539
24540      /*
24541       * try looking at the first HOWMANY bytes
```

```
24542       */
24543      if ((nbytes = read(fd, (char *) buf,
24544           sizeof(buf) - 1)) == -1) {
24545       ap_log_rerror(APLOG_MARK, APLOG_ERR, r,
24546               MODNAME ": read failed: %s", r->filename);
24547       return HTTP_INTERNAL_SERVER_ERROR;
24548      }
24549
24550      if (nbytes == 0)
24551       magic_rsl_puts(r, MIME_TEXT_UNKNOWN);
24552      else {
24553       buf[nbytes++] = '\0';      /* null-terminate it */
24554       tryit(r, buf, nbytes);
24555      }
24556
24557      (void) ap_pclosef(r->pool, fd);
24558      (void) magic_rsl_putchar(r, '\n');
24559
24560      return OK;
24561  }
24562
24563
24564  static void tryit(request_rec *r,
24565      unsigned char *buf, int nb)
24566  {
24567      /*
24568       * Try compression stuff
24569       */
24570      if (zmagic(r, buf, nb) == 1)
24571       return;
24572
24573      /*
24574       * try tests in /etc/magic (or surrogate magic file)
24575       */
24576      if (softmagic(r, buf, nb) == 1)
24577       return;
24578
24579      /*
24580       * try known keywords, check for ascii-ness too.
24581       */
24582      if (ascmagic(r, buf, nb) == 1)
24583       return;
24584
24585      /*
24586       * abandon hope, all ye who remain here
24587       */
24588      magic_rsl_puts(r, MIME_BINARY_UNKNOWN);
24589  }
```

```
24590
24591   #define    EATAB {while (ap_isspace((unsigned char)
24592       *1)) ++1;}
24593
24594   /*
24595    * apprentice - load configuration from the magic file r
24596    * API request record
24597    */
24598   static int apprentice(server_rec *s, pool *p)
24599   {
24600       FILE *f;
24601       char line[BUFSIZ + 1];
24602       int errs = 0;
24603       int lineno;
24604   #if MIME_MAGIC_DEBUG
24605       int rule = 0;
24606       struct magic *m, *prevm;
24607   #endif
24608       char *fname;
24609
24610       magic_server_config_rec *conf =
24611           (magic_server_config_rec *)
24612               ap_get_module_config(s->module_config,
24613                   &mime_magic_module);
24614
24615       fname = ap_server_root_relative(p, conf->magicfile);
24616       f = ap_pfopen(p, fname, "r");
24617       if (f == NULL) {
24618        ap_log_error(APLOG_MARK, APLOG_ERR, s,
24619               MODNAME ": can't read magic file %s",
24620                   fname);
24621        return -1;
24622       }
24623
24624       /* set up the magic list (empty) */
24625       conf->magic = conf->last = NULL;
24626
24627       /* parse it */
24628       for (lineno = 1; fgets(line, BUFSIZ, f) != NULL;
24629           lineno++) {
24630        int ws_offset;
24631
24632        /* delete newline */
24633        if (line[0]) {
24634            line[strlen(line) - 1] = '\0';
24635        }
24636
24637        /* skip leading whitespace */
24638        ws_offset = 0;
24639        while (line[ws_offset] &&
24640            ap_isspace(line[ws_offset])) {
24641            ws_offset++;
24642        }
24643
24644        /* skip blank lines */
24645        if (line[ws_offset] == 0) {
24646            continue;
24647        }
24648
24649        /* comment, do not parse */
24650        if (line[ws_offset] == '#')
24651            continue;
24652
24653   #if MIME_MAGIC_DEBUG
24654        /* if we get here, we're going to use it
24655         * so count it */
24656        rule++;
24657   #endif
24658
24659        /* parse it */
24660        if (parse(s, p, line + ws_offset, lineno) != 0)
24661            ++errs;
24662       }
24663
24664       (void) ap_pfclose(p, f);
24665
24666   #if MIME_MAGIC_DEBUG
24667       ap_log_error(APLOG_MARK,
24668           APLOG_NOERRNO | APLOG_DEBUG, s,
24669           MODNAME ": apprentice
24670               conf=%x file=%s m=%s m->next=%s last=%s",
24671           conf,
24672           conf->magicfile ? conf->magicfile : "NULL",
24673           conf->magic ? "set" : "NULL",
24674           (conf->magic && conf->magic->next) ?
24675               "set" : "NULL",
24676           conf->last ? "set" : "NULL");
24677       ap_log_error(APLOG_MARK, APLOG_NOERRNO |
24678           APLOG_DEBUG, s,
24679           MODNAME ": apprentice read %d lines,
24680               %d rules, %d errors",
24681           lineno, rule, errs);
24682   #endif
24683
24684   #if MIME_MAGIC_DEBUG
24685       prevm = 0;
```

```
24686        ap_log_error(APLOG_MARK, APLOG_NOERRNO |
24687               APLOG_DEBUG, s,
24688               MODNAME ": apprentice test");
24689       for (m = conf->magic; m; m = m->next) {
24690         if (ap_isprint((((unsigned long) m) >> 24) & 255) &&
24691             ap_isprint((((unsigned long) m) >> 16) & 255) &&
24692             ap_isprint((((unsigned long) m) >> 8) & 255) &&
24693             ap_isprint(((unsigned long) m) & 255)) {
24694           ap_log_error(APLOG_MARK, APLOG_NOERRNO |
24695               APLOG_DEBUG, s,
24696               MODNAME ": apprentice: POINTER CLOBBERED! "
24697               "m=\"%c%c%c%c\" line=%d",
24698               (((unsigned long) m) >> 24) & 255,
24699               (((unsigned long) m) >> 16) & 255,
24700               (((unsigned long) m) >> 8) & 255,
24701                 ((unsigned long) m) & 255,
24702                 prevm ? prevm->lineno : -1);
24703           break;
24704         }
24705         prevm = m;
24706       }
24707  #endif
24708
24709       return (errs ? -1 : 0);
24710  }
24711
24712  /*
24713   * extend the sign bit if the comparison is
24714   * to be signed
24715   */
24716  static unsigned long signextend(server_rec *s,
24717       struct magic *m, unsigned long v)
24718  {
24719       if (!(m->flag & UNSIGNED))
24720       switch (m->type) {
24721           /*
24722            * Do not remove the casts below.  They are
24723            * vital. When later compared with the data,
24724            * the sign extension must have happened.
24725            */
24726       case BYTE:
24727           v = (char) v;
24728           break;
24729       case SHORT:
24730       case BESHORT:
24731       case LESHORT:
24732           v = (short) v;
24733           break;
```

```
24734       case DATE:
24735       case BEDATE:
24736       case LEDATE:
24737       case LONG:
24738       case BELONG:
24739       case LELONG:
24740           v = (long) v;
24741           break;
24742       case STRING:
24743           break;
24744       default:
24745           ap_log_error(APLOG_MARK, APLOG_NOERRNO |
24746               APLOG_ERR, s,
24747               MODNAME ": can't happen: m->type=%d",
24748                   m->type);
24749           return -1;
24750       }
24751       return v;
24752  }
24753
24754  /*
24755   * parse one line from magic file, put into
24756   * magic[index++] if valid
24757   */
24758  static int parse(server_rec *serv, pool *p, char *l,
24759       int lineno)
24760  {
24761       struct magic *m;
24762       char *t, *s;
24763       magic_server_config_rec *conf =
24764           (magic_server_config_rec *)
24765               ap_get_module_config(serv->module_config,
24766                   &mime_magic_module);
24767
24768       /* allocate magic structure entry */
24769       m = (struct magic *) ap_pcalloc(p,
24770           sizeof(struct magic));
24771
24772       /* append to linked list */
24773       m->next = NULL;
24774       if (!conf->magic || !conf->last) {
24775        conf->magic = conf->last = m;
24776       }
24777       else {
24778        conf->last->next = m;
24779        conf->last = m;
24780       }
24781
```

```
24782        /* set values in magic structure */
24783        m->flag = 0;
24784        m->cont_level = 0;
24785        m->lineno = lineno;
24786
24787        while (*l == '>') {
24788         ++l;                    /* step over */
24789         m->cont_level++;
24790        }
24791
24792        if (m->cont_level != 0 && *l == '(') {
24793         ++l;                    /* step over */
24794         m->flag |= INDIR;
24795        }
24796
24797        /* get offset, then skip over it */
24798        m->offset = (int) strtol(l, &t, 0);
24799        if (l == t) {
24800         ap_log_error(APLOG_MARK, APLOG_NOERRNO |
24801             APLOG_ERR, serv,
24802                 MODNAME ": offset %s invalid", l);
24803        }
24804        l = t;
24805
24806        if (m->flag & INDIR) {
24807         m->in.type = LONG;
24808         m->in.offset = 0;
24809         /*
24810          * read [.lbs][+-]nnnnn)
24811          */
24812         if (*l == '.') {
24813             switch (*++l) {
24814             case 'l':
24815              m->in.type = LONG;
24816              break;
24817             case 's':
24818              m->in.type = SHORT;
24819              break;
24820             case 'b':
24821              m->in.type = BYTE;
24822              break;
24823             default:
24824              ap_log_error(APLOG_MARK, APLOG_NOERRNO |
24825                  APLOG_ERR, serv,
24826                  MODNAME ": indirect offset type
24827                      %c invalid", *l);
24828             break;
24829            }
```

```
24830             l++;
24831            }
24832            s = l;
24833            if (*l == '+' || *l == '-')
24834             l++;
24835            if (ap_isdigit((unsigned char) *l)) {
24836
24837                m->in.offset = strtol(l, &t, 0);
24838                if (*s == '-')
24839                 m->in.offset = -m->in.offset;
24840            }
24841            else
24842                t = l;
24843            if (*t++ != ')') {
24844                ap_log_error(APLOG_MARK, APLOG_NOERRNO |
24845                    APLOG_ERR, serv,
24846                    MODNAME ": missing ')' in indirect
24847                        offset");
24848            }
24849            l = t;
24850        }
24851
24852
24853        while (ap_isdigit((unsigned char) *l))
24854         ++l;
24855        EATAB;
24856
24857 #define NBYTE           4
24858 #define NSHORT          5
24859 #define NLONG           4
24860 #define NSTRING         6
24861 #define NDATE           4
24862 #define NBESHORT        7
24863 #define NBELONG         6
24864 #define NBEDATE         6
24865 #define NLESHORT        7
24866 #define NLELONG         6
24867 #define NLEDATE         6
24868
24869     if (*l == 'u') {
24870      ++l;
24871      m->flag |= UNSIGNED;
24872     }
24873
24874     /* get type, skip it */
24875     if (strncmp(l, "byte", NBYTE) == 0) {
24876      m->type = BYTE;
24877      l += NBYTE;
```

```
24878          }
24879          else if (strncmp(l, "short", NSHORT) == 0) {
24880              m->type = SHORT;
24881              l += NSHORT;
24882          }
24883          else if (strncmp(l, "long", NLONG) == 0) {
24884              m->type = LONG;
24885              l += NLONG;
24886          }
24887          else if (strncmp(l, "string", NSTRING) == 0) {
24888              m->type = STRING;
24889              l += NSTRING;
24890          }
24891          else if (strncmp(l, "date", NDATE) == 0) {
24892              m->type = DATE;
24893              l += NDATE;
24894          }
24895          else if (strncmp(l, "beshort", NBESHORT) == 0) {
24896              m->type = BESHORT;
24897              l += NBESHORT;
24898          }
24899          else if (strncmp(l, "belong", NBELONG) == 0) {
24900              m->type = BELONG;
24901              l += NBELONG;
24902          }
24903          else if (strncmp(l, "bedate", NBEDATE) == 0) {
24904              m->type = BEDATE;
24905              l += NBEDATE;
24906          }
24907          else if (strncmp(l, "leshort", NLESHORT) == 0) {
24908              m->type = LESHORT;
24909              l += NLESHORT;
24910          }
24911          else if (strncmp(l, "lelong", NLELONG) == 0) {
24912              m->type = LELONG;
24913              l += NLELONG;
24914          }
24915          else if (strncmp(l, "ledate", NLEDATE) == 0) {
24916              m->type = LEDATE;
24917              l += NLEDATE;
24918          }
24919          else {
24920              ap_log_error(APLOG_MARK, APLOG_NOERRNO |
24921                  APLOG_ERR, serv,
24922                      MODNAME ": type %s invalid", l);
24923              return -1;
24924          }
24925          /* New-style anding: "0 byte&0x80 =0x80

24926           * dynamically linked" */
24927          if (*l == '&') {
24928              ++l;
24929              m->mask = signextend(serv, m, strtol(l, &l, 0));
24930          }
24931          else
24932              m->mask = ~0L;
24933          EATAB;
24934
24935          switch (*l) {
24936          case '>':
24937          case '<':
24938              /* Old-style anding: "0 byte &0x80
24939               * dynamically linked" */
24940          case '&':
24941          case '^':
24942          case '=':
24943              m->reln = *l;
24944              ++l;
24945              break;
24946          case '!':
24947              if (m->type != STRING) {
24948                  m->reln = *l;
24949                  ++l;
24950                  break;
24951              }
24952              /* FALL THROUGH */
24953          default:
24954              if (*l == 'x' && ap_isspace((unsigned char) l[1])) {
24955                  m->reln = *l;
24956                  ++l;
24957                  goto GetDesc;       /* Bill The Cat */
24958              }
24959              m->reln = '=';
24960              break;
24961          }
24962          EATAB;
24963
24964          if (getvalue(serv, m, &l))
24965              return -1;
24966          /*
24967           * now get last part - the description
24968           */
24969      GetDesc:
24970          EATAB;
24971          if (l[0] == '\b') {
24972              ++l;
24973              m->nospflag = 1;
```

```
24974          }
24975      else if ((l[0] == '\\') && (l[1] == 'b')) {
24976          ++l;
24977          ++l;
24978          m->nospflag = 1;
24979      }
24980      else
24981          m->nospflag = 0;
24982      strncpy(m->desc, l, sizeof(m->desc) - 1);
24983      m->desc[sizeof(m->desc) - 1] = '\0';
24984
24985  #if MIME_MAGIC_DEBUG
24986      ap_log_error(APLOG_MARK, APLOG_NOERRNO |
24987              APLOG_DEBUG, serv,
24988              MODNAME ": parse line=%d m=%x next=%x
24989                  cont=%d desc=%s",
24990              lineno, m, m->next, m->cont_level, m->desc);
24991  #endif /* MIME_MAGIC_DEBUG */
24992
24993      return 0;
24994  }
24995
24996  /*
24997   * Read a numeric value from a pointer, into the value
24998   * union of a magic pointer, according to the
24999   * magic type.  Update the string pointer to point
25000   * just after the number read.  Return 0 for success,
25001   * non-zero for failure.
25002   */
25003  static int getvalue(server_rec *s, struct magic *m,
25004      char **p)
25005  {
25006      int slen;
25007
25008      if (m->type == STRING) {
25009          *p = getstr(s, *p, m->value.s, sizeof(m->value.s),
25010              &slen);
25011          m->vallen = slen;
25012      }
25013      else if (m->reln != 'x')
25014          m->value.l = signextend(s, m, strtol(*p, p, 0));
25015      return 0;
25016  }
25017
25018  /*
25019   * Convert a string containing C character escapes.
25020   * Stop at an unescaped space or tab. Copy the
25021   * converted version to "p", returning its length in
```

```
25022   * *slen. Return updated scan pointer as function
25023   * result.
25024   */
25025  static char *getstr(server_rec *serv, register char *s,
25026      register char *p,
25027              int plen, int *slen)
25028  {
25029      char *origs = s, *origp = p;
25030      char *pmax = p + plen - 1;
25031      register int c;
25032      register int val;
25033
25034      while ((c = *s++) != '\0') {
25035          if (ap_isspace((unsigned char) c))
25036              break;
25037          if (p >= pmax) {
25038              ap_log_error(APLOG_MARK, APLOG_NOERRNO |
25039                  APLOG_ERR, serv,
25040                  MODNAME ": string too long: %s", origs);
25041              break;
25042          }
25043          if (c == '\\') {
25044              switch (c = *s++) {
25045
25046              case '\0':
25047                  goto out;
25048
25049              default:
25050                  *p++ = (char) c;
25051                  break;
25052
25053              case 'n':
25054                  *p++ = '\n';
25055                  break;
25056
25057              case 'r':
25058                  *p++ = '\r';
25059                  break;
25060
25061              case 'b':
25062                  *p++ = '\b';
25063                  break;
25064
25065              case 't':
25066                  *p++ = '\t';
25067                  break;
25068
25069              case 'f':
```

```
25070            *p++ = '\f';
25071            break;
25072
25073        case 'v':
25074            *p++ = '\v';
25075            break;
25076
25077            /* \ and up to 3 octal digits */
25078        case '0':
25079        case '1':
25080        case '2':
25081        case '3':
25082        case '4':
25083        case '5':
25084        case '6':
25085        case '7':
25086            val = c - '0';
25087            c = *s++;        /* try for 2 */
25088            if (c >= '0' && c <= '7') {
25089                val = (val << 3) | (c - '0');
25090                c = *s++;        /* try for 3 */
25091                if (c >= '0' && c <= '7')
25092                    val = (val << 3) | (c - '0');
25093                else
25094                    --s;
25095            }
25096            else
25097                --s;
25098            *p++ = (char) val;
25099            break;
25100
25101            /* \x and up to 3 hex digits */
25102        case 'x':
25103            val = 'x';        /* Default if no digits */
25104            c = hextoint(*s++);        /* Get next char */
25105            if (c >= 0) {
25106                val = c;
25107                c = hextoint(*s++);
25108                if (c >= 0) {
25109                    val = (val << 4) + c;
25110                    c = hextoint(*s++);
25111                    if (c >= 0) {
25112                        val = (val << 4) + c;
25113                    }
25114                    else
25115                        --s;
25116                }
25117                else

25118                    --s;
25119            }
25120            else
25121                --s;
25122            *p++ = (char) val;
25123            break;
25124        }
25125    }
25126    else
25127        *p++ = (char) c;
25128    }
25129 out:
25130    *p = '\0';
25131    *slen = p - origp;
25132    return s;
25133 }
25134
25135
25136 /* Single hex char to int; -1 if not a hex char. */
25137 static int hextoint(int c)
25138 {
25139    if (ap_isdigit((unsigned char) c))
25140        return c - '0';
25141    if ((c >= 'a') && (c <= 'f'))
25142        return c + 10 - 'a';
25143    if ((c >= 'A') && (c <= 'F'))
25144        return c + 10 - 'A';
25145    return -1;
25146 }
25147
25148
25149 /*
25150  * return DONE to indicate it's been handled
25151  * return OK to indicate it's a regular file still
25152  * needing handling other returns indicate
25153  * a failure of some sort
25154  */
25155 static int fsmagic(request_rec *r, const char *fn)
25156 {
25157    switch (r->finfo.st_mode & S_IFMT) {
25158    case S_IFDIR:
25159        magic_rsl_puts(r, DIR_MAGIC_TYPE);
25160        return DONE;
25161    case S_IFCHR:
25162        /*
25163         * (void) magic_rsl_printf(r,"character special
25164         * (%d/%d)", major(sb->st_rdev),
25165         * minor(sb->st_rdev));
```

```
25166        */
25167        (void) magic_rsl_puts(r, MIME_BINARY_UNKNOWN);
25168        return DONE;
25169   #ifdef S_IFBLK
25170      case S_IFBLK:
25171        /*
25172         * (void) magic_rsl_printf(r,"block special
25173         * (%d/%d)", major(sb->st_rdev),
25174         * minor(sb->st_rdev));
25175         */
25176        (void) magic_rsl_puts(r, MIME_BINARY_UNKNOWN);
25177        return DONE;
25178        /* TODO add code to handle V7 MUX and
25179         * Blit MUX files */
25180   #endif
25181   #ifdef    S_IFIFO
25182      case S_IFIFO:
25183        /*
25184         * magic_rsl_puts(r,"fifo (named pipe)");
25185         */
25186        (void) magic_rsl_puts(r, MIME_BINARY_UNKNOWN);
25187        return DONE;
25188   #endif
25189   #ifdef    S_IFLNK
25190      case S_IFLNK:
25191        /* We used stat(), the only possible reason for
25192         * this is that the symlink is broken.
25193         */
25194        ap_log_rerror(APLOG_MARK, APLOG_NOERRNO |
25195             APLOG_ERR, r,
25196                MODNAME ": broken symlink (%s)", fn);
25197        return HTTP_INTERNAL_SERVER_ERROR;
25198   #endif
25199   #ifdef    S_IFSOCK
25200   #ifndef __COHERENT__
25201      case S_IFSOCK:
25202        magic_rsl_puts(r, MIME_BINARY_UNKNOWN);
25203        return DONE;
25204   #endif
25205   #endif
25206      case S_IFREG:
25207        break;
25208      default:
25209        ap_log_rerror(APLOG_MARK, APLOG_NOERRNO |
25210             APLOG_ERR, r,
25211                MODNAME ": invalid mode 0%o.", (unsigned
25212                     int)r->finfo.st_mode);
25213        return HTTP_INTERNAL_SERVER_ERROR;
```

```
25214        }
25215
25216        /*
25217         * regular file, check next possibility
25218         */
25219        if (r->finfo.st_size == 0) {
25220          magic_rsl_puts(r, MIME_TEXT_UNKNOWN);
25221          return DONE;
25222        }
25223        return OK;
25224   }
25225
25226   /*
25227    * softmagic - lookup one file in database (already
25228    * read from /etc/magic by apprentice.c). Passed
25229    * the name and FILE * of one file to be typed.
25230    */
25231         /* ARGSUSED1 *//* nbytes passed for
25232              * regularity, maybe need later */
25233   static int softmagic(request_rec *r, unsigned char
25234        *buf, int nbytes)
25235   {
25236        if (match(r, buf, nbytes))
25237          return 1;
25238
25239        return 0;
25240   }
25241
25242   /*
25243    * Go through the whole list, stopping if you find a
25244    * match.  Process all the continuations of
25245    * that match before returning.
25246    *
25247    * We support multi-level continuations:
25248    *
25249    * At any time when processing a successful top-level
25250    * match, there is a current continuation level; it
25251    * represents the level of the last successfully
25252    * matched continuation.
25253    *
25254    * Continuations above that level are skipped as, if
25255    * we see one, it means that the continuation that
25256    * controls them - i.e. the lower-level continuation
25257    * preceding them - failed to match.
25258    *
25259    * Continuations below that level are processed as, if
25260    * we see one, it means we've finished processing
25261    * or skipping higher-level continuations under the
```

```
25262       * control of a successful or unsuccessful lower-level
25263       * continuation, and are now seeing the next
25264       * lower-level continuation and should process it.  The
25265       * current continuation level reverts to the level of
25266       * the one we're seeing.
25267       *
25268       * Continuations at the current level are processed as,
25269       * if we see one, there's no lower-level continuation
25270       * that may have failed.
25271       *
25272       * If a continuation matches, we bump the current
25273       * continuation level so that higher-level
25274       * continuations are processed.
25275       */
25276      static int match(request_rec *r, unsigned char *s,
25277          int nbytes)
25278      {
25279      #if MIME_MAGIC_DEBUG
25280          int rule_counter = 0;
25281      #endif
25282          int cont_level = 0;
25283          int need_separator = 0;
25284          union VALUETYPE p;
25285          magic_server_config_rec *conf =
25286              (magic_server_config_rec *)
25287              ap_get_module_config(r->server->module_config,
25288                  &mime_magic_module);
25289          struct magic *m;
25290
25291      #if MIME_MAGIC_DEBUG
25292          ap_log_rerror(APLOG_MARK, APLOG_NOERRNO |
25293              APLOG_DEBUG, r,
25294              MODNAME ": match conf=%x file=%s m=%s
25295                  m->next=%s last=%s",
25296              conf,
25297              conf->magicfile ? conf->magicfile : "NULL",
25298              conf->magic ? "set" : "NULL",
25299              (conf->magic && conf->magic->next) ? "set" :
25300                  "NULL",
25301              conf->last ? "set" : "NULL");
25302      #endif
25303
25304      #if MIME_MAGIC_DEBUG
25305          for (m = conf->magic; m; m = m->next) {
25306          if (ap_isprint(((((unsigned long) m) >> 24) & 255) &&
25307              ap_isprint(((((unsigned long) m) >> 16) & 255) &&
25308              ap_isprint(((((unsigned long) m) >> 8) & 255) &&
25309              ap_isprint((((unsigned long) m) & 255)) {
25310              ap_log_rerror(APLOG_MARK, APLOG_NOERRNO |
25311                  APLOG_DEBUG, r,
25312                  MODNAME ": match: POINTER CLOBBERED! "
25313                  "m=\"%c%c%c%c\"",
25314                  (((unsigned long) m) >> 24) & 255,
25315                  (((unsigned long) m) >> 16) & 255,
25316                  (((unsigned long) m) >> 8) & 255,
25317                  ((unsigned long) m) & 255);
25318              break;
25319          }
25320          }
25321      #endif
25322
25323          for (m = conf->magic; m; m = m->next) {
25324      #if MIME_MAGIC_DEBUG
25325          rule_counter++;
25326          ap_log_rerror(APLOG_MARK, APLOG_NOERRNO |
25327              APLOG_DEBUG, r,
25328              MODNAME ": line=%d desc=%s", m->lineno,
25329                  m->desc);
25330      #endif
25331
25332          /* check if main entry matches */
25333          if (!mget(r, &p, s, m, nbytes) ||
25334              !mcheck(r, &p, m)) {
25335          struct magic *m_cont;
25336
25337          /*
25338           * main entry didn't match, flush its
25339           * continuations
25340           */
25341          if (!m->next || (m->next->cont_level == 0)) {
25342              continue;
25343          }
25344
25345          m_cont = m->next;
25346          while (m_cont && (m_cont->cont_level != 0)) {
25347      #if MIME_MAGIC_DEBUG
25348          rule_counter++;
25349          ap_log_rerror(APLOG_MARK, APLOG_NOERRNO |
25350              APLOG_DEBUG, r,
25351              MODNAME ": line=%d mc=%x mc->next=%x
25352                  cont=%d desc=%s",
25353              m_cont->lineno, m_cont,
25354              m_cont->next, m_cont->cont_level,
25355              m_cont->desc);
25356      #endif
25357          /*
```

```
25358                  * this trick allows us to keep *m in sync
25359                  * when the continue advances the pointer
25360                  */
25361                 m = m_cont;
25362                 m_cont = m_cont->next;
25363             }
25364             continue;
25365         }
25366
25367         /* if we get here, the main entry
25368          * rule was a match */
25369         /* this will be the last run through the loop */
25370 #if MIME_MAGIC_DEBUG
25371         ap_log_rerror(APLOG_MARK, APLOG_NOERRNO |
25372             APLOG_DEBUG, r,
25373             MODNAME ": rule matched, line=%d type=%d %s",
25374             m->lineno, m->type,
25375             (m->type == STRING) ? m->value.s : "");
25376 #endif
25377
25378         /* print the match */
25379         mprint(r, &p, m);
25380
25381         /*
25382          * If we printed something, we'll need to print a
25383          * blank before we print something else.
25384          */
25385         if (m->desc[0])
25386             need_separator = 1;
25387         /* and any continuations that match */
25388         cont_level++;
25389         /*
25390          * while (m && m->next && m->next->cont_level
25391          * != 0 && ( m = m->next))
25392          */
25393         m = m->next;
25394         while (m && (m->cont_level != 0)) {
25395 #if MIME_MAGIC_DEBUG
25396             ap_log_rerror(APLOG_MARK, APLOG_NOERRNO |
25397                 APLOG_DEBUG, r,
25398                 MODNAME ": match line=%d cont=%d
25399                     type=%d %s",
25400                 m->lineno, m->cont_level, m->type,
25401                 (m->type == STRING) ? m->value.s : "");
25402 #endif
25403             if (cont_level >= m->cont_level) {
25404                 if (cont_level > m->cont_level) {
25405                     /*
```

```
25406                      * We're at the end of the level
25407                      * "cont_level" continuations.
25408                      */
25409                     cont_level = m->cont_level;
25410                 }
25411                 if (mget(r, &p, s, m, nbytes) &&
25412                     mcheck(r, &p, m)) {
25412                     /*
25414                      * This continuation matched. Print its
25415                      * message, with a blank before it if
25416                      * the previous item printed and
25417                      * this item isn't empty.
25418                      */
25419                     /* space if previous printed */
25420                     if (need_separator
25421                         && (m->nospflag == 0)
25422                         && (m->desc[0] != '\0')
25423                         ) {
25424                         (void) magic_rsl_putchar(r, ' ');
25425                         need_separator = 0;
25426                     }
25427                     mprint(r, &p, m);
25428                     if (m->desc[0])
25429                         need_separator = 1;
25430
25431                     /*
25432                      * If we see any continuations at a
25433                      * higher level, process them.
25434                      */
25435                     cont_level++;
25436                 }
25437             }
25438
25439             /* move to next continuation record */
25440             m = m->next;
25441         }
25442 #if MIME_MAGIC_DEBUG
25443     ap_log_rerror(APLOG_MARK, APLOG_NOERRNO |
25444         APLOG_DEBUG, r,
25445             MODNAME ": matched after %d rules",
25446                 rule_counter);
25447 #endif
25448     return 1;            /* all through */
25449     }
25450 #if MIME_MAGIC_DEBUG
25451     ap_log_rerror(APLOG_MARK, APLOG_NOERRNO |
25452         APLOG_DEBUG, r,
25453             MODNAME ": failed after %d rules",
```

```
25454              rule_counter);
25455 #endif
25456     return 0;                /* no match at all */
25457 }
25458
25459 static void mprint(request_rec *r, union VALUETYPE *p,
25460     struct magic *m)
25461 {
25462     char *pp, *rt;
25463     unsigned long v;
25464
25465     switch (m->type) {
25466     case BYTE:
25467     v = p->b;
25468     break;
25469
25470     case SHORT:
25471     case BESHORT:
25472     case LESHORT:
25473     v = p->h;
25474     break;
25475
25476     case LONG:
25477     case BELONG:
25478     case LELONG:
25479     v = p->l;
25480     break;
25481
25482     case STRING:
25483     if (m->reln == '=') {
25484         (void) magic_rsl_printf(r, m->desc, m->value.s);
25485     }
25486     else {
25487         (void) magic_rsl_printf(r, m->desc, p->s);
25488     }
25489     return;
25490
25491     case DATE:
25492     case BEDATE:
25493     case LEDATE:
25494     /* XXX: not multithread safe */
25495     pp = ctime((time_t *) & p->l);
25496     if ((rt = strchr(pp, '\n')) != NULL)
25497         *rt = '\0';
25498     (void) magic_rsl_printf(r, m->desc, pp);
25499     return;
25500     default:
25501     ap_log_rerror(APLOG_MARK, APLOG_NOERRNO |
```

```
25502              APLOG_ERR, r,
25503              MODNAME ": invalid m->type (%d)
25504                  in mprint().",
25505              m->type);
25506     return;
25507     }
25508
25509     v = signextend(r->server, m, v) & m->mask;
25510     (void) magic_rsl_printf(r, m->desc,
25511         (unsigned long) v);
25512 }
25513
25514 /*
25515  * Convert the byte order of the data we are looking at
25516  */
25517 static int mconvert(request_rec *r, union VALUETYPE *p,
25518     struct magic *m)
25519 {
25520     char *rt;
25521
25522     switch (m->type) {
25523     case BYTE:
25524     case SHORT:
25525     case LONG:
25526     case DATE:
25527     return 1;
25528     case STRING:
25529     /* Null terminate and eat the return */
25530     p->s[sizeof(p->s) - 1] = '\0';
25531     if ((rt = strchr(p->s, '\n')) != NULL)
25532         *rt = '\0';
25533     return 1;
25534     case BESHORT:
25535     p->h = (short) ((p->hs[0] << 8) | (p->hs[1]));
25536     return 1;
25537     case BELONG:
25538     case BEDATE:
25539     p->l = (long)
25540         ((p->hl[0] << 24) | (p->hl[1] << 16) |
25541             (p->hl[2] << 8) | (p->hl[3]));
25542     return 1;
25543     case LESHORT:
25544     p->h = (short) ((p->hs[1] << 8) | (p->hs[0]));
25545     return 1;
25546     case LELONG:
25547     case LEDATE:
25548     p->l = (long)
25549         ((p->hl[3] << 24) | (p->hl[2] << 16) |
```

```
25550                 (p->hl[1] << 8) | (p->hl[0]));
25551       return 1;
25552     default:
25553       ap_log_rerror(APLOG_MARK, APLOG_NOERRNO |
25554             APLOG_ERR, r,
25555                 MODNAME ": invalid type %d in
25556                     mconvert().", m->type);
25557       return 0;
25558     }
25559  }
25560
25561
25562  static int mget(request_rec *r, union VALUETYPE *p,
25563       unsigned char *s,
25564
25565          struct magic *m, int nbytes)
25566  {
25567      long offset = m->offset;
25568
25569      if (offset + sizeof(union VALUETYPE) > nbytes)
25570              return 0;
25571
25572      memcpy(p, s + offset, sizeof(union VALUETYPE));
25573
25574      if (!mconvert(r, p, m))
25575       return 0;
25576
25577      if (m->flag & INDIR) {
25578
25579        switch (m->in.type) {
25580        case BYTE:
25581            offset = p->b + m->in.offset;
25582            break;
25583        case SHORT:
25584            offset = p->h + m->in.offset;
25585            break;
25586        case LONG:
25587            offset = p->l + m->in.offset;
25588            break;
25589        }
25590
25591        if (offset + sizeof(union VALUETYPE) > nbytes)
25592                return 0;
25593
25594        memcpy(p, s + offset, sizeof(union VALUETYPE));
25595
25596        if (!mconvert(r, p, m))
25597            return 0;
```

```
25598       }
25599       return 1;
25600  }
25601
25602  static int mcheck(request_rec *r, union VALUETYPE *p,
25603      struct magic *m)
25604  {
25605      register unsigned long l = m->value.l;
25606      register unsigned long v;
25607      int matched;
25608
25609      if ((m->value.s[0] == 'x') && (m->value.s[1] ==
25610          '\0')) {
25611       ap_log_rerror(APLOG_MARK, APLOG_NOERRNO |
25612          APLOG_ERR, r,
25613              MODNAME ": BOINK");
25614       return 1;
25615      }
25616
25617      switch (m->type) {
25618      case BYTE:
25619       v = p->b;
25620       break;
25621
25622      case SHORT:
25623      case BESHORT:
25624      case LESHORT:
25625       v = p->h;
25626       break;
25627
25628      case LONG:
25629      case BELONG:
25630      case LELONG:
25631      case DATE:
25632      case BEDATE:
25633      case LEDATE:
25634       v = p->l;
25635       break;
25636
25637      case STRING:
25638       l = 0;
25639       /*
25640        * What we want here is: v = strncmp(m->value.s,
25641              p->s, m->vallen);
25642        * but ignoring any nulls.  bcmp doesn't give
25643        * -/+/0 and isn't universally available anyway.
25644        */
25645       v = 0;
```

```
25646        {
25647            register unsigned char *a = (unsigned char *)
25648                m->value.s;
25649
25650            register unsigned char *b = (unsigned char *)
25651                p->s;
25652            register int len = m->vallen;
25653
25654            while (--len >= 0)
25655                if ((v = *b++ - *a++) != 0)
25656                    break;
25657        }
25658        break;
25659    default:
25660        /*  bogosity, pretend that it just wasn't a match */
25661        ap_log_rerror(APLOG_MARK, APLOG_NOERRNO |
25662            APLOG_ERR, r,
25663                MODNAME ": invalid type %d in
25664                    mcheck().", m->type);
25665        return 0;
25666    }
25667
25668    v = signextend(r->server, m, v) & m->mask;
25669
25670    switch (m->reln) {
25671    case 'x':
25672 #if MIME_MAGIC_DEBUG
25673        ap_log_rerror(APLOG_MARK, APLOG_NOERRNO |
25674            APLOG_DEBUG, r,
25675                "%lu == *any* = 1", v);
25676 #endif
25677        matched = 1;
25678        break;
25679
25680    case '!':
25681        matched = v != 1;
25682 #if MIME_MAGIC_DEBUG
25683        ap_log_rerror(APLOG_MARK, APLOG_NOERRNO |
25684            APLOG_DEBUG, r,
25685                "%lu != %lu = %d", v, 1, matched);
25686 #endif
25687        break;
25688
25689    case '=':
25690        matched = v == 1;
25691 #if MIME_MAGIC_DEBUG
25692
25693        ap_log_rerror(APLOG_MARK, APLOG_NOERRNO |
25694            APLOG_DEBUG, r,
25695                "%lu == %lu = %d", v, 1, matched);
25696 #endif
25697        break;
25698
25699    case '>':
25700        if (m->flag & UNSIGNED) {
25701            matched = v > 1;
25702 #if MIME_MAGIC_DEBUG
25703            ap_log_rerror(APLOG_MARK, APLOG_NOERRNO |
25704                APLOG_DEBUG, r,
25705                    "%lu > %lu = %d", v, 1, matched);
25706 #endif
25707        }
25708        else {
25709            matched = (long) v > (long) 1;
25710 #if MIME_MAGIC_DEBUG
25711            ap_log_rerror(APLOG_MARK, APLOG_NOERRNO |
25712                APLOG_DEBUG, r,
25713                    "%ld > %ld = %d", v, 1, matched);
25714 #endif
25715        }
25716        break;
25717
25718    case '<':
25719        if (m->flag & UNSIGNED) {
25720            matched = v < 1;
25721 #if MIME_MAGIC_DEBUG
25722            ap_log_rerror(APLOG_MARK, APLOG_NOERRNO |
25723                APLOG_DEBUG, r,
25724                    "%lu < %lu = %d", v, 1, matched);
25725 #endif
25726        }
25727        else {
25728            matched = (long) v < (long) 1;
25729 #if MIME_MAGIC_DEBUG
25730            ap_log_rerror(APLOG_MARK, APLOG_NOERRNO |
25731                APLOG_DEBUG, r,
25732                    "%ld < %ld = %d", v, 1, matched);
25733 #endif
25734        }
25735        break;
25736
25737    case '&':
25738        matched = (v & 1) == 1;
25739 #if MIME_MAGIC_DEBUG
25740        ap_log_rerror(APLOG_MARK, APLOG_NOERRNO |
25741            APLOG_DEBUG, r,
```

```
25742                "((%lx & %lx) == %lx) = %d", v, 1, 1,
25743                    matched);
25744 #endif
25745        break;
25746
25747     case '^':
25748        matched = (v & 1) != 1;
25749 #if MIME_MAGIC_DEBUG
25750        ap_log_rerror(APLOG_MARK, APLOG_NOERRNO |
25751            APLOG_DEBUG, r,
25752                "((%lx & %lx) != %lx) = %d", v, 1, 1,
25753                    matched);
25754 #endif
25755        break;
25756
25757     default:
25758        /* bogosity, pretend it didn't match */
25759        matched = 0;
25760        ap_log_rerror(APLOG_MARK, APLOG_NOERRNO |
25761            APLOG_ERR, r,
25762                MODNAME ": mcheck: can't happen: invalid
25763                    relation %d.",
25764                m->reln);
25765        break;
25766     }
25767
25768     return matched;
25769 }
25770
25771 /* an optimization over plain strcmp() */
25772 #define    STREQ(a, b)    (*(a) == *(b) && strcmp((a),
25773     (b)) == 0)
25774
25775 static int ascmagic(request_rec *r, unsigned char *buf,
25776     int nbytes)
25777 {
25778     int has_escapes = 0;
25779     unsigned char *s;
25780     char nbuf[HOWMANY + 1];        /* one extra for
25781         terminating '\0' */
25782     char *token;
25783     register struct names *p;
25784     int small_nbytes;
25785
25786     /* these are easy, do them first */
25787
25788     /*
25789      * for troff, look for . + letter + letter
```

```
25790      * or .\"; this must be done to
25791      * disambiguate tar archives' ./file and
25792      * other trash from real troff input.
25793      */
25794     if (*buf == '.') {
25795        unsigned char *tp = buf + 1;
25796
25797        while (ap_isspace(*tp))
25798            ++tp;              /* skip leading whitespace */
25799        if ((ap_isalnum(*tp) || *tp == '\\') &&
25800            (ap_isalnum(*(tp + 1)) || *tp == '"')) {
25801            magic_rsl_puts(r, "application/x-troff");
25802            return 1;
25803        }
25804     }
25805     if ((*buf == 'c' || *buf == 'C') &&
25806            ap_isspace(*(buf + 1))) {
25807        /* Fortran */
25808        magic_rsl_puts(r, "text/plain");
25809        return 1;
25810     }
25811
25812     /* look for tokens from names.h - this is
25813      * expensive!, so we'll limit
25814      * ourselves to only SMALL_HOWMANY bytes */
25815     small_nbytes = (nbytes > SMALL_HOWMANY) ?
25816        SMALL_HOWMANY : nbytes;
25817     /* make a copy of the buffer here because strtok()
25818        will destroy it */
25819     s = (unsigned char *) memcpy(nbuf, buf,
25820        small_nbytes);
25821     s[small_nbytes] = '\0';
25822     has_escapes = (memchr(s, '\033',
25823        small_nbytes) != NULL);
25824     /* XXX: not multithread safe */
25825     while ((token = strtok((char *) s,
25826        " \t\n\r\f")) != NULL) {
25827     s = NULL;          /* make strtok()
25828        keep on tokin' */
25829     for (p = names; p < names + NNAMES; p++) {
25830         if (STREQ(p->name, token)) {
25831         magic_rsl_puts(r, types[p->type]);
25832         if (has_escapes)
25833             magic_rsl_puts(r, " (with escape
25834                 sequences)");
25835         return 1;
25836         }
25837     }
```

```
25838        }
25839
25840        switch (is_tar(buf, nbytes)) {
25841        case 1:
25842         /* V7 tar archive */
25843         magic_rsl_puts(r, "application/x-tar");
25844         return 1;
25845        case 2:
25846         /* POSIX tar archive */
25847         magic_rsl_puts(r, "application/x-tar");
25848         return 1;
25849        }
25850
25851        /* all else fails, but it is ascii... */
25852        if (has_escapes) {
25853         /* text with escape sequences */
25854         /* we leave this open for further
25855          * differentiation later */
25856         magic_rsl_puts(r, "text/plain");
25857        }
25858        else {
25859         /* plain text */
25860         magic_rsl_puts(r, "text/plain");
25861        }
25862        return 1;
25863    }
25864
25865
25866    /*
25867     * compress routines: zmagic() - returns 0 if not
25868     * recognized, uncompresses and prints information
25869     * if recognized uncompress(s, method, old, n, newch)
25870     * - uncompress old into new, using method, return
25871     * sizeof new
25872     */
25873
25874    static struct {
25875        char *magic;
25876        int maglen;
25877        char *argv[3];
25878        int silent;
25879        char *encoding;     /* MUST be lowercase */
25880    } compr[] = {
25881
25882        {
25883        "\037\235", 2, {
25884            "uncompress", "-c", NULL
25885        }, 0, "x-compress"
25886        },
25887        {
25888        "\037\213", 2, {
25889            "gzip", "-dcq", NULL
25890        }, 1, "x-gzip"
25891        },
25892        /*
25893         * XXX pcat does not work, cause I don't know how
25894         * to make it read stdin,so we use gzip
25895         */
25896        {
25897        "\037\036", 2, {
25898            "gzip", "-dcq", NULL
25899        }, 0, "x-gzip"
25900        },
25901    };
25902
25903    static int ncompr = sizeof(compr) / sizeof(compr[0]);
25904
25905    static int zmagic(request_rec *r, unsigned char *buf,
25906        int nbytes)
25907    {
25908        unsigned char *newbuf;
25909        int newsize;
25910        int i;
25911
25912        for (i = 0; i < ncompr; i++) {
25913         if (nbytes < compr[i].maglen)
25914             continue;
25915         if (memcmp(buf, compr[i].magic,
25916             compr[i].maglen) == 0)
25917             break;
25918        }
25919
25920        if (i == ncompr)
25921         return 0;
25922
25923        if ((newsize = uncompress(r, i, buf,
25924             &newbuf, nbytes)) > 0) {
25925         tryit(r, newbuf, newsize);
25926
25927         /* set encoding type in the request record */
25928         r->content_encoding = compr[i].encoding;
25929        }
25930        return 1;
25931    }
25932
25933
```

```
25934  struct uncompress_parms {
25935      request_rec *r;
25936      int method;
25937  };
25938
25939  static int uncompress_child(void *data,
25940      child_info *pinfo)
25941  {
25942      struct uncompress_parms *parm = data;
25943  #if defined(WIN32)
25944      int child_pid;
25945  #endif
25946
25947      if (compr[parm->method].silent) {
25948        close(STDERR_FILENO);
25949      }
25950
25951  #if defined(WIN32)
25952      child_pid = spawnvp(compr[parm->method].argv[0],
25953            compr[parm->method].argv);
25954      return (child_pid);
25955  #else
25956      execvp(compr[parm->method].argv[0],
25957          compr[parm->method].argv);
25958      ap_log_rerror(APLOG_MARK, APLOG_ERR, parm->r,
25959          MODNAME ": could not execute `%s'.",
25960          compr[parm->method].argv[0]);
25961      return -1;
25962  #endif
25963  }
25964
25965
25966  static int uncompress(request_rec *r, int method,
25967      const unsigned char *old,
25968            unsigned char **newch, int n)
25969  {
25970      struct uncompress_parms parm;
25971      BUFF *bin, *bout;
25972      pool *sub_pool;
25973
25974      parm.r = r;
25975      parm.method = method;
25976
25977      /* We make a sub_pool so that we can collect our
25978       * child early, otherwise there are cases (i.e.
25979       * generating directory indicies with mod_autoindex)
25980       * where we would end up with LOTS of zombies.
25981       */
```

```
25982      sub_pool = ap_make_sub_pool(r->pool);
25983
25984      if (!ap_bspawn_child(sub_pool, uncompress_child,
25985          &parm, kill_always,
25986              &bin, &bout, NULL)) {
25987        ap_log_rerror(APLOG_MARK, APLOG_ERR, r,
25988            MODNAME ": couldn't spawn uncompress
25989                process: %s", r->uri);
25990      return -1;
25991      }
25992
25993      if (ap_bwrite(bin, old, n) != n) {
25994        ap_destroy_pool(sub_pool);
25995        ap_log_rerror(APLOG_MARK, APLOG_ERR, r,
25996            MODNAME ": write failed.");
25997      return -1;
25998      }
25999      ap_bclose(bin);
26000      *newch = (unsigned char *) ap_palloc(r->pool, n);
26001      if ((n = ap_bread(bout, *newch, n)) <= 0) {
26002        ap_destroy_pool(sub_pool);
26003        ap_log_rerror(APLOG_MARK, APLOG_ERR, r,
26004            MODNAME ": read failed %s", r->filename);
26005      return -1;
26006      }
26007      ap_destroy_pool(sub_pool);
26008      return n;
26009  }
26010
26011  /*
26012   * is_tar() -- figure out whether file is a tar archive.
26013   *
26014   * Stolen (by author of file utility) from the public
26015   * domain tar program: Public Domain version written
26016   * 26 Aug 1985 John Gilmore (ihnp4!hoptoad!gnu).
26017   *
26018   * @(#)list.c 1.18 9/23/86 Public Domain -
26019   * gnu $Id: mod_mime_magic.c,v 1.7
26020   * 1997/06/24 00:41:02 ikluft Exp ikluft $
26021   *
26022   * Comments changed and some code/comments
26023   * reformatted for file command by Ian Darwin.
26024   */
26025
26026  #define    isodigit(c)    ( ((c) >= '0')
26027        && ((c) <= '7') )
26028
26029  /*
```

```
26030    * Return 0 if the checksum is bad (i.e., probably
26031    * not a tar archive), 1 for old UNIX tar file,
26032    * 2 for Unix Std (POSIX) tar file.
26033    */
26034
26035    static int is_tar(unsigned char *buf, int nbytes)
26036    {
26037        register union record *header =
26038                (union record *) buf;
26039        register int i;
26040        register long sum, recsum;
26041        register char *p;
26042
26043        if (nbytes < sizeof(union record))
26044                return 0;
26045
26046        recsum = from_oct(8, header->header.chksum);
26047
26048        sum = 0;
26049        p = header->charptr;
26050        for (i = sizeof(union record); --i >= 0;) {
26051          /*
26052           * We can't use unsigned char here because of
26053           * old compilers, e.g. V7.
26054           */
26055          sum += 0xFF & *p++;
26056        }
26057
26058        /* Adjust checksum to count the "chksum"
26059         * field as blanks. */
26060        for (i = sizeof(header->header.chksum); --i >= 0;)
26061          sum -= 0xFF & header->header.chksum[i];
26062        sum += ' ' * sizeof header->header.chksum;
26063
26064        if (sum != recsum)
26065          return 0;              /* Not a tar archive */
26066
26067        if (0 == strcmp(header->header.magic, TMAGIC))
26068          return 2;             /* Unix Standard tar archive */
26069
26070        return 1;               /* Old fashioned tar archive */
26071    }
26072
26073
26074    /*
26075     * Quick and dirty octal conversion.
26076     *
26077     * Result is -1 if the field is invalid
26078     * (all blank, or nonoctal).
26079     */
26080    static long from_oct(int digs, char *where)
26081    {
26082        register long value;
26083
26084        while (ap_isspace(*where)) {        /* Skip spaces */
26085          where++;
26086          if (--digs <= 0)
26087                return -1;            /* All blank field */
26088        }
26089        value = 0;
26090        while (digs > 0 && isodigit(*where)) {
26091          /* Scan til nonoctal */
26092          value = (value << 3) | (*where++ - '0');
26093          --digs;
26094        }
26095
26096        if (digs > 0 && *where && !ap_isspace(*where))
26097          return -1;            /* Ended on non-space/nul */
26098
26099        return value;
26100    }
26101
26102    /*
26103     * Check for file-revision suffix
26104     *
26105     * This is for an obscure document control system used
26106     * on an intranet. The web representation of each
26107     * file's revision has an @1, @2, etc appended with
26108     * the revision number.  This needs to be stripped off
26109     * to find the file suffix, which can be recognized
26110     * by sending the name back through a sub-request.
26111     * The base file name (without the @num suffix) must
26112     * exist because its type will be used as the result.
26113     */
26114    static int revision_suffix(request_rec *r)
26115    {
26116        int suffix_pos, result;
26117        char *sub_filename;
26118        request_rec *sub;
26119
26120    #if MIME_MAGIC_DEBUG
26121        ap_log_rerror(APLOG_MARK, APLOG_NOERRNO |
26122                APLOG_DEBUG, r,
26123                MODNAME ": revision_suffix checking %s",
26124                    r->filename);
26125    #endif /* MIME_MAGIC_DEBUG */
```

```
26126
26127        /* check for recognized revision suffix */
26128        suffix_pos = strlen(r->filename) - 1;
26129        if (!ap_isdigit(r->filename[suffix_pos])) {
26130         return 0;
26131        }
26132        while (suffix_pos >= 0 &&
26133                ap_isdigit(r->filename[suffix_pos]))
26134         suffix_pos--;
26135        if (suffix_pos < 0 ||
26136             r->filename[suffix_pos] != '@') {
26137         return 0;
26138        }
26139
26140        /* perform sub-request for the file name
26141         * without the suffix */
26142        result = 0;
26143        sub_filename = ap_pstrndup(r->pool, r->filename,
26144             suffix_pos);
26145 #if MIME_MAGIC_DEBUG
26146        ap_log_rerror(APLOG_MARK, APLOG_NOERRNO |
26147             APLOG_DEBUG, r,
26148             MODNAME ": subrequest lookup for %s",
26149                sub_filename);
26150 #endif /* MIME_MAGIC_DEBUG */
26151        sub = ap_sub_req_lookup_file(sub_filename, r);
26152
26153        /* extract content type/encoding/language
26154         * from sub-request */
26155        if (sub->content_type) {
26156         r->content_type = ap_pstrdup(r->pool,
26157             sub->content_type);
26158 #if MIME_MAGIC_DEBUG
26159         ap_log_rerror(APLOG_MARK, APLOG_NOERRNO |
26160             APLOG_DEBUG, r,
26161                MODNAME ": subrequest %s got %s",
26162                sub_filename, r->content_type);
26163 #endif /* MIME_MAGIC_DEBUG */
26164         if (sub->content_encoding)
26165          r->content_encoding =
26166          ap_pstrdup(r->pool, sub->content_encoding);
26167         if (sub->content_language)
26168          r->content_language =
26169          ap_pstrdup(r->pool, sub->content_language);
26170         result = 1;
26171        }
26172
26173        /* clean up */
26174        ap_destroy_sub_req(sub);
26175
26176        return result;
26177 }
26178
26179 /*
26180  * initialize the module
26181  */
26182
26183 static void magic_init(server_rec *main_server, pool *p)
26184 {
26185     int result;
26186     magic_server_config_rec *conf;
26187     magic_server_config_rec *main_conf;
26188     server_rec *s;
26189 #if MIME_MAGIC_DEBUG
26190     struct magic *m, *prevm;
26191 #endif /* MIME_MAGIC_DEBUG */
26192
26193     main_conf = ap_get_module_config(main_server->
26194         module_config, &mime_magic_module);
26195     for (s = main_server; s; s = s->next) {
26196      conf = ap_get_module_config(s->module_config,
26197         &mime_magic_module);
26198      if (conf->magicfile == NULL && s != main_server) {
26199         /* inherits from the parent */
26200         *conf = *main_conf;
26201      }
26202      else if (conf->magicfile) {
26203         result = apprentice(s, p);
26204         if (result == -1)
26205         return;
26206 #if MIME_MAGIC_DEBUG
26207         prevm = 0;
26208         ap_log_error(APLOG_MARK, APLOG_NOERRNO |
26209             APLOG_DEBUG, s,
26210             MODNAME ": magic_init 1 test");
26211         for (m = conf->magic; m; m = m->next) {
26212          if (ap_isprint((((unsigned long) m) >>
26213             24) & 255) &&
26214             ap_isprint((((unsigned long) m) >> 16)
26215             & 255) &&
26216             ap_isprint((((unsigned long) m) >> 8)
26217             & 255) &&
26218             ap_isprint(((unsigned long) m) & 255)) {
26219          ap_log_error(APLOG_MARK, APLOG_NOERRNO |
26220             APLOG_DEBUG, s,
26221             MODNAME ": magic_init 1: POINTER
```

```
26222                    CLOBBERED! "
26223                    "m=\"%c%c%c%c\" line=%d",
26224                    (((unsigned long) m) >> 24) & 255,
26225                    (((unsigned long) m) >> 16) & 255,
26226                    (((unsigned long) m) >> 8) & 255,
26227                    ((unsigned long) m) & 255,
26228                    prevm ? prevm->lineno : -1);
26229                break;
26230            }
26231            prevm = m;
26232        }
26233 #endif
26234        }
26235      }
26236 }
26237
26238 /*
26239  * Find the Content-Type from any resource
26240  * this module has available
26241  */
26242
26243 static int magic_find_ct(request_rec *r)
26244 {
26245     int result;
26246     magic_server_config_rec *conf;
26247
26248     /* the file has to exist */
26249     if (r->finfo.st_mode == 0 || !r->filename) {
26250      return DECLINED;
26251     }
26252
26253     /* was someone else already here? */
26254     if (r->content_type) {
26255      return DECLINED;
26256     }
26257
26258     conf = ap_get_module_config(r->server->
26259         module_config, &mime_magic_module);
26260     if (!conf || !conf->magic) {
26261      return DECLINED;
26262     }
26263
26264     /* initialize per-request info */
26265     if (!magic_set_config(r)) {
26266      return HTTP_INTERNAL_SERVER_ERROR;
26267     }
26268
26269     /* try excluding file-revision suffixes */
```

```
26270     if (revision_suffix(r) != 1) {
26271      /* process it based on the file contents */
26272      if ((result = magic_process(r)) != OK) {
26273          return result;
26274      }
26275     }
26276
26277     /* if we have any results, put them in
26278      * the request structure */
26279     return magic_rsl_to_request(r);
26280 }
26281
26282 /*
26283  * Apache API module interface
26284  */
26285
26286 module mime_magic_module =
26287 {
26288     STANDARD_MODULE_STUFF,
26289     magic_init,               /* initializer */
26290     NULL,               /* dir config creator */
26291     NULL,
26292     /* dir merger -- default is to override */
26293     create_magic_server_config,     /* server config */
26294     merge_magic_server_config,
26295     /* merge server config */
26296     mime_magic_cmds,          /* command table */
26297     NULL,               /* handlers */
26298     NULL,               /* filename translation */
26299     NULL,               /* check_user_id */
26300     NULL,               /* check auth */
26301     NULL,               /* check access */
26302     magic_find_ct,          /* type_checker */
26303     NULL,               /* fixups */
26304     NULL,               /* logger */
26305     NULL,               /* header parser */
26306     NULL,               /* child_init */
26307     NULL,               /* child_exit */
26308     NULL               /* post read-request */
26309 };
```

p 452 ▶ mod_negotiation.c

```
26310 #include "httpd.h"
26311 #include "http_config.h"
26312 #include "http_request.h"
26313 #include "http_protocol.h"
26314 #include "http_core.h"
```

```
26315   #include "http_log.h"
26316   #include "util_script.h"
26317
26318   /* Commands -- configuring document caching on a
26319    * per (virtual?)server basis...
26320    */
26321
26322   typedef struct {
26323       array_header *language_priority;
26324   } neg_dir_config;
26325
26326   module MODULE_VAR_EXPORT negotiation_module;
26327
26328   static void *create_neg_dir_config(pool *p, char *dummy)
26329   {
26330       neg_dir_config *new = (neg_dir_config *)
26331           ap_palloc(p, sizeof(neg_dir_config));
26332
26333       new->language_priority = ap_make_array(p, 4,
26334           sizeof(char *));
26335       return new;
26336   }
26337
26338   static void *merge_neg_dir_configs(pool *p,
26339       void *basev, void *addv)
26340   {
26341       neg_dir_config *base = (neg_dir_config *) basev;
26342       neg_dir_config *add = (neg_dir_config *) addv;
26343       neg_dir_config *new = (neg_dir_config *)
26344           ap_palloc(p, sizeof(neg_dir_config));
26345
26346       /* give priority to the config in the subdirectory */
26347       new->language_priority = ap_append_arrays(p,
26348           add->language_priority,
26349                           base->language_priority);
26350       return new;
26351   }
26352
26353   static const char *set_language_priority(cmd_parms
26354       *cmd, void *n, char *lang)
26355   {
26356       array_header *arr = ((neg_dir_config *)
26357           n)->language_priority;
26358       char **langp = (char **) ap_push_array(arr);
26359
26360       *langp = lang;
26361       return NULL;
26362   }
```

```
26363
26364   static const char *cache_negotiated_docs(cmd_parms
26365       *cmd, void *dummy,
26366                                       char *dummy2)
26367   {
26368       void *server_conf = cmd->server->module_config;
26369
26370       ap_set_module_config(server_conf,
26371           &negotiation_module, "Cache");
26372       return NULL;
26373   }
26374
26375   static int do_cache_negotiated_docs(server_rec *s)
26376   {
26377       return (ap_get_module_config(s->module_config,
26378           &negotiation_module) != NULL);
26379   }
26380
26381   static const command_rec negotiation_cmds[] =
26382   {
26383       {"CacheNegotiatedDocs", cache_negotiated_docs,
26384           NULL, RSRC_CONF, NO_ARGS,
26385        "no arguments (either present or absent)"},
26386       {"LanguagePriority", set_language_priority, NULL,
26387           OR_FILEINFO, ITERATE,
26388        "space-delimited list of MIME language
26389           abbreviations"},
26390       {NULL}
26391   };
26392
26393   /*
26394    * Record of available info on a media type specified
26395    * by the client(we also use 'em for encodings
26396    * and languages)
26397    */
26398
26399   typedef struct accept_rec {
26400       char *name;                 /* MUST be lowercase */
26401       float quality;
26402       float max_bytes;
26403       float level;
26404       char *charset;              /* for content-type only */
26405   } accept_rec;
26406
26407   /*
26408    * Record of available info on a particular variant
26409    *
26410    * Note that a few of these fields are updated by the
```

```
26411    * actual negotiation code.  These are:
26412    *
26413    * level_matched -- initialized to zero.  Set to the
26414    *              value of level if the client actually
26415    *              accepts this media type at that level
26416    *              (and *not* if it got in on a wildcard).
26417    *              See level_cmp below.
26418    * mime_stars -- initialized to zero. Set to the number
26419    *              of stars present in the best matching
26420    *              Accept header element.1 for star/star,
26421    *              2 for type/star and 3 for type/subtype.
26422    *
26423    * definite -- initialized to 1.  Set to 0 if there is a
26424    *              match which makes the variant non-definite
26425    *              according to the rules in rfc2296.
26426    */
26427
26428    typedef struct var_rec {
26429        request_rec *sub_req;
26430        /* May be NULL (is, for map files) */
26431        char *mime_type;            /* MUST be lowercase */
26432        char *file_name;
26433        const char *content_encoding;
26434        array_header *content_languages;
26435        /* list of languages for this variant */
26436        char *content_charset;
26437        char *description;
26438
26439        /* The next five items give the quality values for
26440         * the dimensions of negotiation for this variant.
26441         * They are obtained from the appropriate header
26442         * lines, except for source_quality, which is
26443         * obtained from the variant itself (the 'qs'
26444         * parameter value from the variant's mime-type).
26445         * Apart from source_quality, these values are set
26446         * when we find the quality for each variant(see
26447         * best_match()). source_quality is set from the
26448         * 'qs' parameter of the variant description or
26449         * mime type: see set_mime_fields().
26450         */
26451        float lang_quality;
26452        /* quality of this variant's language */
26453        float encoding_quality;     /* ditto encoding */
26454        float charset_quality;      /* ditto charset */
26455        float mime_type_quality;    /* ditto media type */
26456
26457        float source_quality;
26458        /* source quality for this variant */
26459
26460        /* Now some special values */
26461        float level;
26462        /* Auxiliary to content-type... */
26463        float bytes;
26464        /* content length, if known */
26465        int lang_index;
26466        /* pre HTTP/1.1 language priority stuff */
26467        int is_pseudo_html;
26468        /* text/html, *or* the INCLUDES_MAGIC_TYPEs */
26469
26470        /* Above are all written-once properties of the
26471         * variant.  The three fields below are changed
26472         * during negotiation:
26473         */
26474
26475        float level_matched;
26476        int mime_stars;
26477        int definite;
26478    } var_rec;
26479
26480    /* Something to carry around the state of negotiation
26481     * (and to keep all of this thread-safe)...
26482     */
26483
26484    typedef struct {
26485        pool *pool;
26486        request_rec *r;
26487        char *dir_name;
26488        int accept_q;
26489        /* 1 if an Accept item has a q= param */
26490        float default_lang_quality;
26491        /* fiddle lang q for variants with no lang */
26492
26493        /* the array pointers below are NULL if the
26494         * corresponding accept headers are not present
26495         */
26496        array_header *accepts;            /* accept_recs */
26497        array_header *accept_encodings;   /* accept_recs */
26498        array_header *accept_charsets;    /* accept_recs */
26499        array_header *accept_langs;       /* accept_recs */
26500
26501        array_header *avail_vars;    /* available variants */
26502
26503        int count_multiviews_variants;
26504        /* number of variants found on disk */
26505
26506        int is_transparent;
```

```
26507        /* 1 if this resource is trans. negotiable */
26508
26509
26510        int dont_fiddle_headers;
26511        /* 1 if we may not fiddle with accept hdrs */
26512        int ua_supports_trans;
26513        /* 1 if ua supports trans negotiation */
26514        int send_alternates;
26515        /* 1 if we want to send an Alternates header */
26516        int may_choose;
26517        /* 1 if we may choose a variant for the client */
26518        int use_rvsa;
26519        /* 1 if we must use RVSA/1.0 negotiation algo */
26520 } negotiation_state;
26521
26522 /* A few functions to manipulate var_recs.
26523  * Cleaning out the fields...
26524  */
26525
26526 static void clean_var_rec(var_rec *mime_info)
26527 {
26528     mime_info->sub_req = NULL;
26529     mime_info->mime_type = "";
26530     mime_info->file_name = "";
26531     mime_info->content_encoding = NULL;
26532     mime_info->content_languages = NULL;
26533     mime_info->content_charset = "";
26534     mime_info->description = "";
26535
26536     mime_info->is_pseudo_html = 0;
26537     mime_info->level = 0.0f;
26538     mime_info->level_matched = 0.0f;
26539     mime_info->bytes = 0.0f;
26540     mime_info->lang_index = -1;
26541     mime_info->mime_stars = 0;
26542     mime_info->definite = 1;
26543
26544     mime_info->charset_quality = 1.0f;
26545     mime_info->encoding_quality = 1.0f;
26546     mime_info->lang_quality = 1.0f;
26547     mime_info->mime_type_quality = 1.0f;
26548     mime_info->source_quality = 0.0f;
26549 }
26550
26551 /* Initializing the relevant fields of a variant
26552  * record from the accept_info read out of its
26553  * content-type, one way or another.
26554  */
```

```
26555
26556 static void set_mime_fields(var_rec *var,
26557        accept_rec *mime_info)
26558 {
26559     var->mime_type = mime_info->name;
26560     var->source_quality = mime_info->quality;
26561     var->level = mime_info->level;
26562     var->content_charset = mime_info->charset;
26563
26564     var->is_pseudo_html = (!strcmp(var->mime_type,
26565            "text/html")
26566      || !strcmp(var->mime_type, INCLUDES_MAGIC_TYPE)
26567      || !strcmp(var->mime_type, INCLUDES_MAGIC_TYPE3));
26568 }
26569
26570 /* Create a variant list validator in r using info
26571  * from vlistr. */
26572
26573 static void set_vlist_validator(request_rec *r,
26574        request_rec *vlistr)
26575 {
26576     /* Calculating the variant list validator is
26577      * similar to calculating an etag for the
26578      * source of the variant list information, so
26579      * we use ap_make_etag().  Note that this
26580      * validator can be 'weak' in extreme case.
26581      */
26582
26583     ap_update_mtime (vlistr, vlistr->finfo.st_mtime);
26584     r->vlist_validator = ap_make_etag(vlistr, 0);
26585
26586     /* ap_set_etag will later take r->vlist_validator
26587      * into account when creating the etag header
26588      */
26589 }
26590
26591
26592 /**********************************************************
26593  *
26594  * Parsing (lists of) media types and their parameters,
26595  * as seen in HTTPD header lines and elsewhere.
26596  */
26597
26598 /*
26599  * Get a single mime type entry -- one media type and
26600  * parameters; enter the values we recognize into
26601  * the argument accept_rec
26602  */
```

```
26603
26604   static const char *get_entry(pool *p,
26605       accept_rec *result,
26606                               const char *accept_line)
26607   {
26608       result->quality = 1.0f;
26609       result->max_bytes = 0.0f;
26610       result->level = 0.0f;
26611       result->charset = "";
26612
26613       /*
26614        * Note that this handles what I gather is
26615        * the "old format",
26616        *
26617        *    Accept: text/html text/plain moo/zot
26618        *
26619        * without any compatibility kludges -- if the
26620        * token after the MIME type begins with a
26621        * semicolon, we know we're looking at parms,
26622        * otherwise, we know we aren't.  (So why all
26623        * the pissing and moaning in the CERN server
26624        * code?  I must be missing something).
26625        */
26626
26627       result->name = ap_get_token(p, &accept_line, 0);
26628       ap_str_tolower(result->name);
26629       /* You want case-insensitive,
26630                               * you'll *get* case-insensitive.
26631                                                       */
26632
26633       /* KLUDGE!!! Default HTML to level 2.0 unless the
26634        * browser *explicitly* says something else.
26635        */
26636
26637       if (!strcmp(result->name, "text/html") &&
26638           (result->level == 0.0)) {
26639           result->level = 2.0f;
26640       }
26641       else if (!strcmp(result->name,
26642           INCLUDES_MAGIC_TYPE)) {
26643           result->level = 2.0f;
26644       }
26645       else if (!strcmp(result->name,
26646           INCLUDES_MAGIC_TYPE3)) {
26647           result->level = 3.0f;
26648       }
26649
26650       while (*accept_line == ';') {
26651           /* Parameters ... */
26652
26653       char *parm;
26654       char *cp;
26655       char *end;
26656
26657       ++accept_line;
26658       parm = ap_get_token(p, &accept_line, 1);
26659
26660       /* Look for 'var = value' -- and make sure
26661        * the var is in lcase. */
26662
26663       for (cp = parm; (*cp && !ap_isspace(*cp) &&
26664               *cp != '='); ++cp) {
26665           *cp = ap_tolower(*cp);
26666       }
26667
26668       if (!*cp) {
26669           continue;        /* No '='; just ignore it. */
26670       }
26671
26672       *cp++ = '\0';            /* Delimit var */
26673       while (*cp && (ap_isspace(*cp) || *cp == '=')) {
26674           ++cp;
26675       }
26676
26677       if (*cp == '"') {
26678           ++cp;
26679           for (end = cp;
26680               (*end && *end != '\n' && *end != '\r'
26681                       && *end != '\"');
26682               end++);
26683       }
26684       else {
26685           for (end = cp; (*end && !ap_isspace(*end));
26686               end++);
26687       }
26688       if (*end) {
26689           *end = '\0';
26690                   /* strip ending quote or return */
26691       }
26692       ap_str_tolower(cp);
26693
26694       if (parm[0] == 'q'
26695           && (parm[1] == '\0' || (parm[1] == 's'
26696           && parm[2] == '\0'))) {
26697           result->quality = atof(cp);
26698       }
```

```
26699            else if (parm[0] == 'm' && parm[1] == 'x' &&
26700                    parm[2] == 'b' && parm[3] == '\0') {
26701                result->max_bytes = atof(cp);
26702
26703            }
26704            else if (parm[0] == 'l' && !strcmp(&parm[1],
26705                "evel")) {
26706                result->level = atof(cp);
26707            }
26708            else if (!strcmp(parm, "charset")) {
26709                result->charset = cp;
26710            }
26711        }
26712
26713        if (*accept_line == ',') {
26714            ++accept_line;
26715        }
26716
26717        return accept_line;
26718    }
26719
26720    /**********************************************************
26721     *
26722     * Dealing with header lines ...
26723     *
26724     * Accept, Accept-Charset, Accept-Language and Accept-
26725     * Encoding are handled by do_header_line() - they
26726     * all have the same basic structure of a list of
26727     * items of the format    name; q=N; charset=TEXT
26728     *
26729     * where charset is only valid in Accept.
26730     */
26731
26732    static array_header *do_header_line(pool *p, const
26733        char *accept_line)
26734    {
26735        array_header *accept_recs;
26736
26737        if (!accept_line) {
26738            return NULL;
26739        }
26740
26741        accept_recs = ap_make_array(p, 40,
26742            sizeof(accept_rec));
26743
26744        while (*accept_line) {
26745            accept_rec *new = (accept_rec *)
26746                    ap_push_array(accept_recs);
```

```
26747            accept_line = get_entry(p, new, accept_line);
26748        }
26749
26750        return accept_recs;
26751    }
26752
26753    /* Given the text of the Content-Languages: line from
26754     * the var map file, return an array containing the
26755     * languages of this variant
26756     */
26757
26758    static array_header *do_languages_line(pool *p,
26759        const char **lang_line)
26760    {
26761        array_header *lang_recs = ap_make_array(p, 2,
26762            sizeof(char *));
26763
26764        if (!lang_line) {
26765            return lang_recs;
26766        }
26767
26768        while (**lang_line) {
26769            char **new = (char **) ap_push_array(lang_recs);
26770            *new = ap_get_token(p, lang_line, 0);
26771            ap_str_tolower(*new);
26772            if (**lang_line == ',' || **lang_line == ';') {
26773                ++(*lang_line);
26774            }
26775        }
26776
26777        return lang_recs;
26778    }
26779
26780    /**********************************************************
26781     *
26782     * Handling header lines from clients...
26783     */
26784
26785    static negotiation_state
26786        *parse_accept_headers(request_rec *r)
26787    {
26788        negotiation_state *new =
26789            (negotiation_state *) ap_pcalloc(r->pool,
26790                    sizeof(negotiation_state));
26791        accept_rec *elts;
26792        table *hdrs = r->headers_in;
26793        int i;
26794
```

```
26795        new->pool = r->pool;
26796        new->r = r;
26797        new->dir_name = ap_make_dirstr_parent(r->pool,
26798            r->filename);
26799
26800        new->accepts = do_header_line(r->pool,
26801            ap_table_get(hdrs, "Accept"));
26802
26803        /* calculate new->accept_q value */
26804        if (new->accepts) {
26805            elts = (accept_rec *) new->accepts->elts;
26806
26807            for (i = 0; i < new->accepts->nelts; ++i) {
26808                if (elts[i].quality < 1.0) {
26809                    new->accept_q = 1;
26810                }
26811            }
26812        }
26813
26814        new->accept_encodings =
26815            do_header_line(r->pool, ap_table_get(hdrs,
26816                "Accept-Encoding"));
26817        new->accept_langs =
26818            do_header_line(r->pool, ap_table_get(hdrs,
26819                "Accept-Language"));
26820        new->accept_charsets =
26821            do_header_line(r->pool, ap_table_get(hdrs,
26822                "Accept-Charset"));
26823
26824        new->avail_vars = ap_make_array(r->pool, 40,
26825            sizeof(var_rec));
26826
26827        return new;
26828    }
26829
26830
26831    static void parse_negotiate_header(request_rec *r,
26832        negotiation_state *neg)
26833    {
26834        const char *negotiate = ap_table_get(r->headers_in,
26835            "Negotiate");
26836        char *tok;
26837
26838        /* First, default to no TCN, no Alternates, and the
26839         * original Apache negotiation algorithm with
26840         * fiddles for broken browser configs.
26841         *
26842         * To save network bandwidth, we do not configure
26843         * to send an Alternates header to the user agent
26844         * by default.  User agents that want an Alternates
26845         * header for agent-driven negotiation will have
26846         * to request it by sending an appropriate Negotiate
26847         * header.
26848         */
26849        neg->ua_supports_trans   = 0;
26850        neg->send_alternates     = 0;
26851        neg->may_choose          = 1;
26852        neg->use_rvsa            = 0;
26853        neg->dont_fiddle_headers = 0;
26854
26855        if (!negotiate)
26856            return;
26857
26858        if (strcmp(negotiate, "trans") == 0) {
26859            /* Lynx 2.7 and 2.8 send 'negotiate: trans' even
26860             * though they do not support transparent
26861             * content negotiation, so for Lynx we ignore
26862             * the negotiate header when its contents are
26863             * exactly "trans". If future versions of Lynx
26864             * ever need to say 'negotiate: trans', they can
26865             * send the equivalent 'negotiate: trans, trans'
26866             * instead to avoid triggering the workaround
26867             * below.
26868             */
26869            const char *ua = ap_table_get(r->headers_in,
26870                "User-Agent");
26871
26872            if (ua && (strncmp(ua, "Lynx", 4) == 0))
26873                return;
26874        }
26875
26876        neg->may_choose = 0;
26877        /* An empty Negotiate would require 300 response */
26878
26879        while ((tok = ap_get_list_item(neg->pool,
26880            &negotiate)) != NULL) {
26881
26882            if (strcmp(tok, "trans") == 0 ||
26883                strcmp(tok, "vlist") == 0 ||
26884                strcmp(tok, "guess-small") == 0 ||
26885                ap_isdigit(tok[0]) ||
26886                strcmp(tok, "*") == 0) {
26887
26888                /* The user agent supports transparent
26889                 * negotiation */
26890                neg->ua_supports_trans = 1;
```

```
26891
26892                    /* Send-alternates could be configurable,
26893                     * but note that it must be 1 if we have
26894                     * 'vlist' in the negotiate header.
26895                     */
26896                    neg->send_alternates = 1;
26897
26898                    if (strcmp(tok, "1.0") == 0) {
26899                        /* we may use the RVSA/1.0 algorithm,
26900                         * configure for it */
26901                        neg->may_choose = 1;
26902                        neg->use_rvsa = 1;
26903                        neg->dont_fiddle_headers = 1;
26904                    }
26905                    else if (tok[0] == '*') {
26906                        /* we may use any variant selection
26907                         * algorithm, configure
26908                         * to use the Apache algorithm
26909                         */
26910                        neg->may_choose = 1;
26911
26912                        /* We disable header fiddles on the
26913                         * assumption that a client sending
26914                         * Negotiate knows how to send correct
26915                         * headers which don't need fiddling.
26916                         */
26917                        neg->dont_fiddle_headers = 1;
26918                    }
26919                }
26920            }
26921
26922    #ifdef NEG_DEBUG
26923        fprintf(stderr, "dont_fiddle_headers=%d"
26924                " use_rvsa=%d ua_supports_trans=%d "
26925                "send_alternates=%d, may_choose=%d\n",
26926                neg->dont_fiddle_headers, neg->use_rvsa,
26927                neg->ua_supports_trans,
26928                    neg->send_alternates, neg->may_choose);
26929    #endif
26930
26931    }
26932
26933    /* Sometimes clients will give us no Accept info at
26934     * all; this routine sets up the standard default for
26935     * that case, and also arranges for us to be willing to
26936     * run a CGI script if we find one.  (In fact, we set up
26937     * to dramatically prefer CGI scripts in cases where
26938     * that's appropriate, e.g., POST or when URI includes
26939     * query args or extra path info).
26940     */
26941    static void maybe_add_default_accepts(negotiation_state
26942        *neg,
26943                                          int prefer_scripts)
26944    {
26945        accept_rec *new_accept;
26946
26947        if (!neg->accepts) {
26948            neg->accepts = ap_make_array(neg->pool, 4,
26949                    sizeof(accept_rec));
26950
26951            new_accept = (accept_rec *)
26952                ap_push_array(neg->accepts);
26953
26954            new_accept->name = "*/*";
26955            new_accept->quality = 1.0f;
26956            new_accept->level = 0.0f;
26957            new_accept->max_bytes = 0.0f;
26958        }
26959
26960        new_accept = (accept_rec *)
26961                ap_push_array(neg->accepts);
26962
26963        new_accept->name = CGI_MAGIC_TYPE;
26964        if (neg->use_rvsa) {
26965            new_accept->quality = 0;
26966        }
26967        else {
26968            new_accept->quality = prefer_scripts ?
26969                    2.0f : 0.001f;
26970        }
26971        new_accept->level = 0.0f;
26972        new_accept->max_bytes = 0.0f;
26973    }
26974
26975    /***********************************************************
26976     *
26977     * Parsing type-map files, in Roy's meta/http format
26978     * augmented with #-comments.
26979     */
26980
26981    /* Reading RFC822-style header lines, ignoring
26982     * #-comments and handling continuations.
26983     */
26984
26985    enum header_state {
26986        header_eof, header_seen, header_sep
```

```
26987    };
26988
26989    static enum header_state get_header_line(char *buffer,
26990         int len, FILE *map)
26991    {
26992        char *buf_end = buffer + len;
26993        char *cp;
26994        int c;
26995
26996        /* Get a noncommented line */
26997
26998        do {
26999            if (fgets(buffer, MAX_STRING_LEN, map) == NULL) {
27000                return header_eof;
27001            }
27002        } while (buffer[0] == '#');
27003
27004        /* If blank, just return it -- this ends
27005         * information on this variant */
27006
27007        for (cp = buffer; (*cp && ap_isspace(*cp)); ++cp) {
27008            continue;
27009        }
27010
27011        if (*cp == '\0') {
27012            return header_sep;
27013        }
27014
27015        /* If non-blank, go looking for header lines, but
27016         * note that we still have to treat comments
27017         * specially...
27018         */
27019
27020        cp += strlen(cp);
27021
27022        while ((c = getc(map)) != EOF) {
27023            if (c == '#') {
27024                /* Comment line */
27025                while ((c = getc(map)) != EOF && c != '\n') {
27026                    continue;
27027                }
27028            }
27029            else if (ap_isspace(c)) {
27030                /* Leading whitespace.  POSSIBLE continuation
27031                 * line Also, possibly blank -- if so, we
27032                 * ungetc() the final newline so that we will
27033                 * pick up the blank line the next time 'round.
27034                 */
27035
27036                while (c != EOF && c != '\n' &&
27037                    ap_isspace(c)) {
27038
27039                    c = getc(map);
27040                }
27041
27042                ungetc(c, map);
27043
27044                if (c == '\n') {
27045                    return header_seen;     /* Blank line */
27046                }
27047
27048                /* Continuation */
27049
27050                while (cp < buf_end - 2 && (c = getc(map))
27051                    != EOF && c != '\n') {
27052                    *cp++ = c;
27053                }
27054
27055                *cp++ = '\n';
27056                *cp = '\0';
27057            }
27058            else {
27059
27060                /* Line beginning with something other than
27061                 * whitespace */
27062
27063                ungetc(c, map);
27064                return header_seen;
27065            }
27066        }
27067
27068        return header_seen;
27069    }
27070
27071    /* Stripping out RFC822 comments */
27072
27073    static void strip_paren_comments(char *hdr)
27074    {
27075        /* Hmmm... is this correct?  In Roy's latest draft,
27076         * (comments) can nest! */
27077        /* Nope, it isn't correct.  Fails to handle
27078         * backslash escape as well.    */
27079
27080        while (*hdr) {
27081            if (*hdr == '"') {
27082                hdr = strchr(hdr, '"');
```

```
27083            if (hdr == NULL) {
27084                return;
27085            }
27086            ++hdr;
27087        }
27088        else if (*hdr == '(') {
27089            while (*hdr && *hdr != ')') {
27090                *hdr++ = ' ';
27091            }
27092
27093            if (*hdr) {
27094                *hdr++ = ' ';
27095            }
27096        }
27097        else {
27098            ++hdr;
27099        }
27100    }
27101 }
27102
27103 /* Getting to a header body from the header */
27104
27105 static char *lcase_header_name_return_body(char
27106        *header, request_rec *r)
27107 {
27108    char *cp = header;
27109
27110    for ( ; *cp && *cp != ':' ; ++cp) {
27111        *cp = ap_tolower(*cp);
27112    }
27113
27114    if (!*cp) {
27115        ap_log_rerror(APLOG_MARK,
27116                APLOG_NOERRNO|APLOG_ERR, r,
27117                    "Syntax error in type map --
27118                        no ':': %s", r->filename);
27119        return NULL;
27120    }
27121
27122    do {
27123        ++cp;
27124    } while (*cp && ap_isspace(*cp));
27125
27126    if (!*cp) {
27127        ap_log_rerror(APLOG_MARK,
27128                APLOG_NOERRNO|APLOG_ERR, r,
27129                    "Syntax error in type map --
27130                        no header body: %s",
```

```
27131                        r->filename);
27132        return NULL;
27133    }
27134
27135    return cp;
27136 }
27137
27138 static int read_type_map(negotiation_state *neg,
27139        request_rec *rr)
27140 {
27141    request_rec *r = neg->r;
27142    FILE *map;
27143    char buffer[MAX_STRING_LEN];
27144    enum header_state hstate;
27145    struct var_rec mime_info;
27146    int has_content;
27147
27148    /* We are not using multiviews */
27149    neg->count_multiviews_variants = 0;
27150
27151    map = ap_pfopen(neg->pool, rr->filename, "r");
27152    if (map == NULL) {
27153        ap_log_rerror(APLOG_MARK, APLOG_ERR, r,
27154                "cannot access type map file: %s",
27155                    rr->filename);
27156        return HTTP_FORBIDDEN;
27157    }
27158
27159    clean_var_rec(&mime_info);
27160    has_content = 0;
27161
27162    do {
27163        hstate = get_header_line(buffer,
27164            MAX_STRING_LEN, map);
27165
27166        if (hstate == header_seen) {
27167            char *body1 =
27168                lcase_header_name_return_body(buffer,
27169                    neg->r);
27170            const char *body;
27171
27172            if (body1 == NULL) {
27173                return SERVER_ERROR;
27174            }
27175
27176            strip_paren_comments(body1);
27177            body = body1;
27178
```

```
27179            if (!strncmp(buffer, "uri:", 4)) {
27180                mime_info.file_name =
27181                    ap_get_token(neg->pool, &body, 0);
27182            }
27183            else if (!strncmp(buffer, "content-type:",
27184                13)) {
27185                struct accept_rec accept_info;
27186
27187                get_entry(neg->pool, &accept_info, body);
27188                set_mime_fields(&mime_info, &accept_info);
27189                has_content = 1;
27190            }
27191            else if (!strncmp(buffer,
27192                "content-length:", 15)) {
27193                mime_info.bytes = atof(body);
27194                has_content = 1;
27195            }
27196            else if (!strncmp(buffer,
27197                "content-language:", 17)) {
27198                mime_info.content_languages =
27199                    do_languages_line(neg->pool,
27200                                        &body);
27201                has_content = 1;
27202            }
27203            else if (!strncmp(buffer,
27204                "content-encoding:", 17)) {
27205                mime_info.content_encoding =
27206                    ap_get_token(neg->pool, &body, 0);
27207                has_content = 1;
27208            }
27209            else if (!strncmp(buffer,
27210                "description:", 12)) {
27211                char *desc = ap_pstrdup(neg->pool, body);
27212                char *cp;
27213
27214                for (cp = desc; *cp; ++cp) {
27215                    if (*cp=='\n') *cp=' ';
27216                }
27217                if (cp>desc) *(cp-1)=0;
27218                mime_info.description = desc;
27219            }
27220        }
27221        else {
27222            if (*mime_info.file_name && has_content) {
27223                void *new_var =
27224                    ap_push_array(neg->avail_vars);
27225
27226                memcpy(new_var, (void *) &mime_info,
27227                    sizeof(var_rec));
27228            }
27229
27230            clean_var_rec(&mime_info);
27231            has_content = 0;
27232        }
27233    } while (hstate != header_eof);
27234
27235    ap_pfclose(neg->pool, map);
27236
27237    set_vlist_validator(r, rr);
27238
27239    return OK;
27240 }
27241
27242
27243 /* Sort function used by read_types_multi. */
27244 static int variantsortf(var_rec *a, var_rec *b) {
27245
27246     /* First key is the source quality, sort in
27247      * descending order. */
27248
27249     /* XXX: note that we currently implement no method
27250      * of setting the source quality for multiviews
27251      * variants, so we are always comparing
27252      * 1.0 to 1.0 for now
27253      */
27254     if (a->source_quality < b->source_quality)
27255         return 1;
27256     if (a->source_quality > b->source_quality)
27257         return -1;
27258
27259     /* Second key is the variant name */
27260     return strcmp(a->file_name, b->file_name);
27261 }
27262
27263 /*********************************************************
27264  *
27265  * Same as read_type_map, except we use a filtered
27266  * directory listing as the map...
27267  *
27268  */
27269
27270 static int read_types_multi(negotiation_state *neg)
27271 {
27272     request_rec *r = neg->r;
27273
27274     char *filp;
```

```
27275        int prefix_len;
27276        DIR *dirp;
27277        struct DIR_TYPE *dir_entry;
27278        struct var_rec mime_info;
27279        struct accept_rec accept_info;
27280        void *new_var;
27281
27282        clean_var_rec(&mime_info);
27283
27284        if (!(filp = strrchr(r->filename, '/'))) {
27285            return DECLINED;        /* Weird... */
27286        }
27287
27288        if (strncmp(r->filename, "proxy:", 6) == 0) {
27289            return DECLINED;
27290        }
27291
27292        ++filp;
27293        prefix_len = strlen(filp);
27294
27295        dirp = ap_popendir(neg->pool, neg->dir_name);
27296
27297        if (dirp == NULL) {
27298            ap_log_rerror(APLOG_MARK, APLOG_ERR, r,
27299                        "cannot read directory for multi:
27300                            %s", neg->dir_name);
27301            return HTTP_FORBIDDEN;
27302        }
27303
27304        while ((dir_entry = readdir(dirp))) {
27305            request_rec *sub_req;
27306
27307            /* Do we have a match? */
27308
27309            if (strncmp(dir_entry->d_name, filp,
27310                    prefix_len)) {
27311                continue;
27312            }
27313            if (dir_entry->d_name[prefix_len] != '.') {
27314                continue;
27315            }
27316
27317            /* Yep.  See if it's something which we have
27318             * access to, and which has a known type and
27319             * encoding (as opposed to something which we'll
27320             * be slapping default_type on later).
27321             */
27322
27323            sub_req =
27324                ap_sub_req_lookup_file(dir_entry->d_name, r);
27325
27326            /* If it has a handler, we'll pretend it's a CGI
27327             * script,since that's a good indication of
27328             * the sort of thing it might be doing.
27329             */
27330            if (sub_req->handler && !sub_req->content_type) {
27331                sub_req->content_type = CGI_MAGIC_TYPE;
27332            }
27333
27334            if (sub_req->status != HTTP_OK ||
27335                    !sub_req->content_type) {
27336                ap_destroy_sub_req(sub_req);
27337                continue;
27338            }
27339
27340            /* If it's a map file, we use that instead
27341             * of the map we're building...
27342             */
27343
27344            if ((((sub_req->content_type) &&
27345                !strcmp(sub_req->content_type,
27346                    MAP_FILE_MAGIC_TYPE)) ||
27347                ((sub_req->handler) &&
27348                !strcmp(sub_req->handler, "type-map")))) {
27349
27350                ap_pclosedir(neg->pool, dirp);
27351                neg->avail_vars->nelts = 0;
27352                if (sub_req->status != HTTP_OK) {
27353                    return sub_req->status;
27354                }
27355                return read_type_map(neg, sub_req);
27356            }
27357
27358            /* Have reasonable variant --
27359             * gather notes. */
27360
27361            mime_info.sub_req = sub_req;
27362            mime_info.file_name = ap_pstrdup(neg->pool,
27363                dir_entry->d_name);
27364            if (sub_req->content_encoding) {
27365                mime_info.content_encoding =
27366                    sub_req->content_encoding;
27367            }
27368            if (sub_req->content_languages) {
27369                mime_info.content_languages =
27370                    sub_req->content_languages;
```

```
27371              }                                         27419     * Using strcmp()is legit, because everything has
27372                                                        27420     * already been smashed to lowercase.
27373          get_entry(neg->pool, &accept_info,           27421     *
27374                sub_req->content_type);                 27422     * Note also that if we get an exact match on the media
27375          set_mime_fields(&mime_info, &accept_info);    27423     * type, we update level_matched for use in level_cmp
27376                                                        27424     * below...
27377          new_var = ap_push_array(neg->avail_vars);     27425     *
27378          memcpy(new_var, (void *) &mime_info,          27426     * We also give a value for mime_stars, which is used
27379            sizeof(var_rec));                            27427     * later. It should be 1 for star/star, 2 for type/star
27380                                                        27428     * and 3 for type/subtype.
27381          neg->count_multiviews_variants++;             27429     */
27382                                                        27430
27383          clean_var_rec(&mime_info);                    27431    static int mime_match(accept_rec *accept_r,
27384      }                                                 27432         var_rec *avail)
27385                                                        27433    {
27386      ap_pclosedir(neg->pool, dirp);                    27434        char *accept_type = accept_r->name;
27387                                                        27435        char *avail_type = avail->mime_type;
27388      set_vlist_validator(r, r);                         27436        int len = strlen(accept_type);
27389                                                        27437
27390      /* Sort the variants into a canonical order.  The  27438        if (accept_type[0] == '*') {
27391       * negotiation result sometimes depends on the order 27439        /* Anything matches star/star */
27392       * of the variants.  By sorting the variants into a 27440            if (avail->mime_stars < 1) {
27393       * canonical order, rather than using the order in   27441                avail->mime_stars = 1;
27394       * which readdir() happens to return them, we ensure 27442            }
27395       * that the negotiation result will be consistent   27443            return 1;
27396       * over filesystem backup/restores and over         27444        }
27397       * all mirror sites.                               27445        else if ((accept_type[len - 1] == '*') &&
27398       */                                                27446                !strncmp(accept_type, avail_type,
27399                                                        27447                 len - 2)) {
27400      qsort((void *) neg->avail_vars->elts,             27448            if (avail->mime_stars < 2) {
27401            neg->avail_vars->nelts,                     27449                avail->mime_stars = 2;
27402            sizeof(var_rec), (int (*)(const void *,      27450            }
27403                const void *)) variantsortf);           27451            return 1;
27404                                                        27452        }
27405      return OK;                                        27453        else if (!strcmp(accept_type, avail_type)
27406    }                                                  27454                || (!strcmp(accept_type, "text/html")
27407                                                        27455                    && (!strcmp(avail_type,
27408                                                        27456                        INCLUDES_MAGIC_TYPE)
27409    /*****************************************************  27457                        || !strcmp(avail_type,
27410     * And now for the code you've been waiting for...  27458                            INCLUDES_MAGIC_TYPE3)))) {
27411     * actually finding a match to the client's         27459            if (accept_r->level >= avail->level) {
27412     * requirements.                                    27460                avail->level_matched = avail->level;
27413     */                                                27461                avail->mime_stars = 3;
27414                                                        27462                return 1;
27415    /* Matching MIME types ... the star/star and foo/star 27463            }
27416     * commenting conventions are implemented here.  (You 27464        }
27417     * know what I mean by star/star, but just try       27465
27418     * mentioning those three characters in a C comment). 27466        return OK;
```

```
27467    }
27468
27469    /* This code implements a piece of the tie-breaking
27470     * algorithm between variants of equal quality.  This
27471     * piece is the treatment of variants of the same base
27472     * media type, but different levels.  What we want to
27473     * return is the variant at the highest level that the
27474     * client explicitly claimed to accept.
27475     *
27476     * If all the variants available are at a higher level
27477     * than that, or if the client didn't say anything
27478     * specific about this media type at all and these
27479     * variants just got in on a wildcard, we prefer the
27480     * lowest level, on grounds that that's the one that
27481     * the client is least likely to choke on.
27482     *
27483     * (This is all motivated by treatment of levels in
27484     * HTML -- we only want to give level 3 to browsers
27485     * that explicitly ask for it; browsers that don't,
27486     * including HTTP/0.9 browsers that only get the
27487     * implicit"Accept: * / *" [space added to avoid
27488     * confusing cpp -- no, that syntax doesn't really
27489     * work] should get HTML2 if available).
27490     *
27491     * (Note that this code only comes into play when we
27492     * are choosing among variants of equal quality, where
27493     * the draft standard gives us a fair bit of leeway
27494     * about what to do.  It ain't specified by the
27495     * standard; rather, it is a choice made by this
27496     * server about what to do in cases where the standard
27497     * does not specify a unique course of action).
27498     */
27499
27500    static int level_cmp(var_rec *var1, var_rec *var2)
27501    {
27502        /* Levels are only comparable between matching
27503         * media types */
27504
27505        if (var1->is_pseudo_html && !var2->is_pseudo_html) {
27506            return 0;
27507        }
27508
27509        if (!var1->is_pseudo_html && strcmp(var1->mime_type,
27510                var2->mime_type)) {
27511            return 0;
27512        }
27513        /* The result of the above if statements is that, if
27514         * we get to here, both variants have the same
```

```
27515     * mime_type or both are pseudo-html.
27516     */
27517
27518        /* Take highest level that matched, if either
27519         * did match. */
27520
27521        if (var1->level_matched > var2->level_matched) {
27522            return 1;
27523        }
27524        if (var1->level_matched < var2->level_matched) {
27525            return -1;
27526        }
27527
27528        /* Neither matched.  Take lowest level, if there's
27529         * a difference. */
27530
27531        if (var1->level < var2->level) {
27532            return 1;
27533        }
27534        if (var1->level > var2->level) {
27535            return -1;
27536        }
27537
27538        /* Tied */
27539
27540        return 0;
27541    }
27542
27543    /* Finding languages.  The main entry point is
27544     * set_language_quality() which is called for
27545     * each variant. It sets two elements in the
27546     * variant record:
27547     *   language_quality  - the 'q' value of the 'best'
27548     *                       matching language from
27549     *                       Accept-Language: header
27550     *                       (HTTP/1.1)
27551     *   lang_index    -   Pre HTTP/1.1 language priority,
27552     *                       using position of language on
27553     *                       the Accept-Language: header,
27554     *                       if present, else
27555     *                       LanguagePriority
27556     *                       directive order.
27557     *
27558     * When we do the variant checking for best variant,
27559     * we use language quality first, and if a tie,
27560     * language_index next (this only applies
27561     * when _not_ using the RVSA/1.0 algorithm). If
27562     * using the RVSA/1.0 algorithm, lang_index
```

```
27563    * is never used.
27564    *
27565    * set_language_quality() calls find_lang_index()
27566    * and find_default_index()to set lang_index.
27567    */
27568
27569    static int find_lang_index(array_header *accept_langs,
27570        char *lang)
27571    {
27572        accept_rec *accs;
27573        int i;
27574
27575        if (!lang || !accept_langs) {
27576            return -1;
27577        }
27578
27579        accs = (accept_rec *) accept_langs->elts;
27580
27581        for (i = 0; i < accept_langs->nelts; ++i) {
27582            if (!strncmp(lang, accs[i].name,
27583                    strlen(accs[i].name))) {
27584                return i;
27585            }
27586        }
27587
27588        return -1;
27589    }
27590
27591    /* This function returns the priority of a given
27592     * language according to LanguagePriority.  It is used
27593     * in case of a tie between several languages.
27594     */
27595
27596    static int find_default_index(neg_dir_config *conf,
27597        char *lang)
27598    {
27599        array_header *arr;
27600        int nelts;
27601        char **elts;
27602        int i;
27603
27604        if (!lang) {
27605            return -1;
27606        }
27607
27608        arr = conf->language_priority;
27609        nelts = arr->nelts;
27610        elts = (char **) arr->elts;
27611
27612        for (i = 0; i < nelts; ++i) {
27613            if (!strcasecmp(elts[i], lang)) {
27614                return i;
27615            }
27616        }
27617
27618        return -1;
27619    }
27620
27621    /* set_default_lang_quality() sets the quality we apply
27622     * to variants which have no language assigned to
27623     * them. If none of the variants have a language, we are
27624     * not negotiating on language, so all are acceptable,
27625     * and we set the default q value to 1.0. However if
27626     * some of the variants have languages, we set this
27627     * default to 0.001. The value of this default will
27628     * be applied to all variants with no explicit
27629     * language -- which will have the effect of making them
27630     * acceptable, but only if no variants with an explicit
27631     * language are acceptable. The default q value
27632     * set here is assigned to variants with no language
27633     * type in set_language_quality().
27634     *
27635     * Note that if using the RVSA/1.0 algorithm, we don't
27636     * use this fiddle.
27637     */
27638
27639    static void set_default_lang_quality(negotiation_state
27640        *neg)
27641    {
27642        var_rec *avail_recs = (var_rec *)
27643            neg->avail_vars->elts;
27644        int j;
27645
27646        if (!neg->dont_fiddle_headers) {
27647            for (j = 0; j < neg->avail_vars->nelts; ++j) {
27648                var_rec *variant = &avail_recs[j];
27649                if (variant->content_languages &&
27650                    variant->content_languages->nelts) {
27651                    neg->default_lang_quality = 0.001f;
27652                    return;
27653                }
27654            }
27655        }
27656
27657        neg->default_lang_quality = 1.0f;
27658    }
```

```
27659
27660    /* Set the language_quality value in the variant record.
27661     * Also assigns lang_index for back-compat.
27662     *
27663     * To find the language_quality value, we look for the
27664     * 'q' value of the 'best' matching language on the
27665     * Accept-Language header. The 'best' match is the
27666     * language on Accept-Language header which matches the
27667     * language of this variant either fully, or as far
27668     * as the prefix marker (-). If two or more languages
27669     * match, use the longest string from the Accept-
27670     * Language header (see HTTP/1.1 [14.4])
27671     *
27672     * When a variant has multiple languages, we find the
27673     * 'best' match for each variant language tag as above,
27674     * then select the one with the highest q value. Because
27675     * both the accept-header and variant can have multiple
27676     * languages, we now have a hairy loop-within-a-loop
27677     * here.
27678     *
27679     * If the variant has no language and we have no Accept-
27680     * Language items, leave the quality at 1.0 and return.
27681     *
27682     * If the variant has no language, we use the default as
27683     * set by set_default_lang_quality() (1.0 if we are not
27684     * negotiating on language, 0.001 if we are).
27685     *
27686     * Following the setting of the language quality, we
27687     * drop through to set the old 'lang_index'. This
27688     * is set based on either the order of the languages on
27689     * the Accept-Language header, or the order on the
27690     * LanguagePriority directive. This is only used
27691     * in the negotiation if the language qualities tie.
27692     */
27693
27694    static void set_language_quality(negotiation_state *neg,
27695        var_rec *variant)
27696    {
27697        char *firstlang;
27698        int idx;
27699
27700        if (!variant->content_languages ||
27701            !variant->content_languages->nelts) {
27702            /* This variant has no content-language, so use
27703             * the default quality factor for variants
27704             * with no content-language(previously set by
27705             * set_default_lang_quality()).Leave the factor
27706             * alone (it remains at 1.0) when we may not
27707             * fiddle with the headers.
27708             */
27709            if (!neg->dont_fiddle_headers) {
27710                variant->lang_quality =
27711                    neg->default_lang_quality;
27712            }
27713            if (!neg->accept_langs) {
27714                return;      /* no accept-language header */
27715            }
27716
27717        }
27718        else {
27719            /* Variant has one (or more) languages.  Look for
27720             * the best match. We do this by going through
27721             * each language on the variant description
27722             * looking for a match on the Accept-Language
27723             * header. The best match is the longest matching
27724             * language on the header. The final result is
27725             * the best q value from all the languages on the
27726             * variant description.
27727             */
27728
27729            if (!neg->accept_langs) {
27730                /* no accept-language header makes the
27731                 * variant indefinite */
27732                variant->definite = 0;
27733            }
27734            else {     /* There is an accept-language with 0
27735                        * or more items */
27736                accept_rec *accs = (accept_rec *)
27737                    neg->accept_langs->elts;
27738                accept_rec *best = NULL, *star = NULL;
27739                accept_rec *bestthistag;
27740                char *lang, *p;
27741                float fiddle_q = 0.0f;
27742                int any_match_on_star = 0;
27743                int i, j, alen, longest_lang_range_len;
27744
27745                for (j = 0; j
27746                  < variant->content_languages->nelts; ++j) {
27747                    p = NULL;
27748                    bestthistag = NULL;
27749                    longest_lang_range_len = 0;
27750                    alen = 0;
27751
27752                    /* lang is the variant's language-tag,
27753                     * which is the one we are allowed to
27754                     * use the prefix of in HTTP/1.1
```

```
27755        */
27756        lang = ((char **)
27757        (variant->content_languages->elts))[j];
27758
27759        /* now find the best (i.e. longest)
27760         * matching Accept-Language header
27761         * language. We put the best match
27762         * for this tag in bestthistag. We
27763         * cannot update the overall best (based
27764         * on q value) because the best match
27765         * for this tag is the longest language
27766         * item on the accept header, not
27767         * necessarily the highest q.
27768         */
27769        for (i = 0; i
27770            < neg->accept_langs->nelts; ++i) {
27771            if (!strcmp(accs[i].name, "*")) {
27772                if (!star) {
27773                    star = &accs[i];
27774                }
27775                continue;
27776            }
27777            /* Find language. We match if either
27778             * the variant language tag exactly
27779             * matches the language range from
27780             * the accept header, or a prefix of
27781             * the variant language tag up to
27782             * a '-' character matches the whole
27783             * of the language range in the
27784             * Accept-Language header.  Note
27785             * that HTTP/1.x allows any number
27786             * of '-' characters in a tag or
27787             * range, currently only tags with
27788             * zero or one '-' characters are
27789             * definedfor general use (see
27790             * rfc1766).
27791             *
27792             * We only use language range in the
27793             * Accept-Language header the best
27794             * match for the variant language
27795             * tag if it is longer than the
27796             * previous best match.
27797             */
27798
27799            alen = strlen(accs[i].name);
27800
27801            if ((strlen(lang) >= alen) &&
27802                !strncmp(lang, accs[i].name,
27803                alen) &&
27804                ((lang[alen] == 0) || (lang[alen]
27805                == '-')) ) {
27806
27807                if (alen >
27808                    longest_lang_range_len) {
27809                    longest_lang_range_len = alen;
27810                    bestthistag = &accs[i];
27811                }
27812            }
27813
27814            if (!bestthistag &&
27815                !neg->dont_fiddle_headers) {
27816                /* The next bit is a fiddle. Some
27817                 * browsers might be configured to
27818                 * send more specific language
27819                 * ranges than desirable. For
27820                 * example, an Accept-Language of
27821                 * en-US should never match
27822                 * variants with languages en or
27823                 * en-GB. But US English speakers
27824                 * might pick en-US as their
27825                 * language choice.  So this
27826                 * fiddle checks if the language
27827                 * range has a prefix, and if so,
27828                 * it matches variants which
27829                 * match that prefix with a
27830                 * priority of 0.001. So a request
27831                 * for en-US would match variants
27832                 * of types en and en-GB, but at
27833                 * much lower priority than matches
27834                 * of en-US directly, or of any
27835                 * other language listed on
27836                 * the Accept-Language header.
27837                 * Note that this fiddle does not
27838                 * handle multi-level prefixes.
27839                 */
27840                if ((p = strchr(accs[i].name,
27841                    '-'))) {
27842                    int plen = p - accs[i].name;
27843
27844                    if (!strncmp(lang,
27845                        accs[i].name, plen)) {
27846                        fiddle_q = 0.001f;
27847                    }
27848                }
27849            }
27850        }
```

```
27851              /* Finished looking at Accept-Language
27852               * headers, the best(longest) match is
27853               * in bestthistag, or NULL if no match
27854               */
27855              if (!best ||
27856                  (bestthistag && bestthistag->
27857                      quality > best->quality)) {
27858                  best = bestthistag;
27859              }
27860
27861              /* See if the tag matches on a * in
27862               * the Accept-Language header. If so,
27863               * record this fact for later use
27864               */
27865              if (!bestthistag && star) {
27866                  any_match_on_star = 1;
27867              }
27868          }
27869
27870          /* If one of the language tags of the
27871           * variant matched on *, we need to see
27872           * if its q is better than that of any
27873           * non-* match on any other tag of the
27874           * variant.  If so the * match takes
27875           * precedence and the overall match is not
27876           * definite.
27877           */
27878          if ( any_match_on_star &&
27879              ((best && star->quality > best->quality) ||
27880              (!best)) ) {
27881              best = star;
27882              variant->definite = 0;
27883          }
27884
27885          variant->lang_quality = best ?
27886              best->quality : fiddle_q;
27887      }
27888  }
27889
27890    /* Now set the old lang_index field. Since this is
27891     * old stuff anyway, don't bother with handling
27892     * multiple languages per variant, just use the
27893     * first one assigned to it
27894     */
27895    idx = 0;
27896    if (variant->content_languages
27897        && variant->content_languages->nelts) {
27898        firstlang = ((char **)
```

```
27899              variant->content_languages->elts)[0];
27900      }
27901      else {
27902          firstlang = "";
27903      }
27904      if (!neg->accept_langs) {   /* Client doesn't care */
27905          idx = find_default_index((neg_dir_config *)
27906              ap_get_module_config(
27907                  neg->r->per_dir_config, &negotiation_module),
27908                                    firstlang);
27909      }
27910      else {                        /* Client has Accept-Language */
27911          idx = find_lang_index(neg->accept_langs,
27912              firstlang);
27913      }
27914      variant->lang_index = idx;
27915
27916      return;
27917  }
27918
27919  /* Determining the content length -- if the map didn't
27920   * tell us, we have to do a stat() and remember
27921   * for next time.
27922   *
27923   * Grump.  For Apache, even the first stat here may
27924   * well be redundant (for multiviews) with a
27925   * stat() done by the sub_req machinery.  At
27926   * some point, that ought to be fixed.
27927   */
27928
27929  static float find_content_length(negotiation_state
27930      *neg, var_rec *variant)
27931  {
27932      struct stat statb;
27933
27934      if (variant->bytes == 0) {
27935          char *fullname = ap_make_full_path(neg->pool,
27936              neg->dir_name,
27937                                    variant->file_name);
27938
27939          if (stat(fullname, &statb) >= 0) {
27940              /* Note, precision may be lost */
27941              variant->bytes = (float) statb.st_size;
27942          }
27943      }
27944
27945      return variant->bytes;
27946  }
```

```
27947
27948   /* For a given variant, find the best matching
27949    * Accept: header and assign the Accept: header's
27950    * quality value to the mime_type_quality field of the
27951    * variant, for later use in determining the
27952    * best matching variant.
27953    */
27954
27955   static void set_accept_quality(negotiation_state
27956       *neg, var_rec *variant)
27957   {
27958       int i;
27959       accept_rec *accept_recs;
27960       float q = 0.0f;
27961       int q_definite = 1;
27962
27963       /* if no Accept: header, leave quality alone (will
27964        * remain at the default value of 1)
27965        *
27966        * XXX: This if is currently never true because
27967        * of the effect of maybe_add_default_accepts().
27968        */
27969       if (!neg->accepts) {
27970           if (variant->mime_type && *variant->mime_type)
27971               variant->definite = 0;
27972           return;
27973       }
27974
27975       accept_recs = (accept_rec *) neg->accepts->elts;
27976
27977       /*
27978        * Go through each of the ranges on the Accept:
27979        * header,looking for the 'best' match with this
27980        * variant's content-type. We use the best match's
27981        * quality value (from the Accept: header) for this
27982        * variant's mime_type_quality field.
27983        *
27984        * The best match is determined like this:
27985        *    type/type is better
27986        *         than type/ * is better than * / *
27987        *    if match is type/type, use the level
27988        *    mime param if available
27989        */
27990       for (i = 0; i < neg->accepts->nelts; ++i) {
27991
27992           accept_rec *type = &accept_recs[i];
27993           int prev_mime_stars;
27994
27995           prev_mime_stars = variant->mime_stars;
27996
27997           if (!mime_match(type, variant)) {
27998               continue;
27999               /* didn't match the content type at all */
28000           }
28001           else {
28002               /* did match - see if there were less or
28003                * more stars than in previous match
28004                */
28005               if (prev_mime_stars == variant->mime_stars) {
28006                   continue;
28007                   /* more stars => not as good a match */
28008               }
28009           }
28010
28011           /* Check maxbytes -- not in HTTP/1.1 or TCN */
28012
28013           if (type->max_bytes > 0
28014               && (find_content_length(neg, variant) >
28015                       type->max_bytes)) {
28016               continue;
28017           }
28018
28019           /* If we are allowed to mess with the q-values
28020            * and have no explicit q= parameters in the
28021            * accept header, make wildcards very low, so
28022            * we have a low chance of ending up with them
28023            * if there's something better.
28024            */
28025
28026           if (!neg->dont_fiddle_headers && !neg->accept_q &&
28027               variant->mime_stars == 1) {
28028               q = 0.01f;
28029           }
28030           else if (!neg->dont_fiddle_headers &&
28031                   !neg->accept_q &&
28032                   variant->mime_stars == 2) {
28033               q = 0.02f;
28034           }
28035           else {
28036               q = type->quality;
28037           }
28038
28039
28040           q_definite = (variant->mime_stars == 3);
28041       }
28042   variant->mime_type_quality = q;
```

```
28043        variant->definite = variant->definite
28044            && q_definite;
28045
28046    }
28047
28048    /* For a given variant, find the 'q' value of the
28049     * charset given on the Accept-Charset line. If
28050     * no charsets are listed, assume value of '1'.
28051     */
28052    static void set_charset_quality(negotiation_state
28053        *neg, var_rec *variant)
28054    {
28055        int i;
28056        accept_rec *accept_recs;
28057        char *charset = variant->content_charset;
28058        accept_rec *star = NULL;
28059
28060        /* if no Accept-Charset: header, leave quality
28061         * alone (will remain at the default value of 1)
28062         */
28063        if (!neg->accept_charsets) {
28064            if (charset && *charset)
28065                variant->definite = 0;
28066            return;
28067        }
28068
28069        accept_recs = (accept_rec *)
28070            neg->accept_charsets->elts;
28071
28072        if (charset == NULL || !*charset) {
28073            /* Charset of variant not known */
28074
28075            /* if not a text / * type, leave
28076             * quality alone */
28077            if (!(!strncmp(variant->mime_type, "text/", 5)
28078                || !strcmp(variant->mime_type,
28079                    INCLUDES_MAGIC_TYPE)
28080                || !strcmp(variant->mime_type,
28081                    INCLUDES_MAGIC_TYPE3)
28082                ))
28083                return;
28084
28085            /* Don't go guessing if we are in strict header
28086             * mode, e.g. when running the rvsa, as any
28087             * guess won't be reflected in the variant
28088             * list or content-location headers.
28089             */
28090            if (neg->dont_fiddle_headers)
28091                return;
28092
28093            charset = "iso-8859-1";
28094            /* The default charset for HTTP text types */
28095        }
28096
28097        /*
28098         * Go through each of the items on the
28099         * Accept-Charset header, looking for a match with
28100         * this variant's charset. If none match,
28101         * charset is unacceptable, so set quality to 0.
28102         */
28103        for (i = 0; i < neg->accept_charsets->nelts; ++i) {
28104
28105            accept_rec *type = &accept_recs[i];
28106
28107            if (!strcmp(type->name, charset)) {
28108                variant->charset_quality = type->quality;
28109                return;
28110            }
28111            else if (strcmp(type->name, "*") == 0) {
28112                star = type;
28113            }
28114        }
28115        /* No explicit match */
28116        if (star) {
28117            variant->charset_quality = star->quality;
28118            variant->definite = 0;
28119            return;
28120        }
28121        /* If this variant is in charset iso-8859-1,
28122         * the default is 1.0 */
28123        if (strcmp(charset, "iso-8859-1") == 0) {
28124            variant->charset_quality = 1.0f;
28125        }
28126        else {
28127            variant->charset_quality = 0.0f;
28128        }
28129    }
28130
28131
28132    /* is_identity_encoding is included for back-compat,
28133     * but does anyone use 7bit, 8bin or binary
28134     * in their var files??
28135     */
28136
28137    static int is_identity_encoding(const char *enc)
28138    {
```

```
28139        return (!enc || !enc[0] || !strcmp(enc, "7bit")
28140              || !strcmp(enc, "8bit")
28141                || !strcmp(enc, "binary"));
28142    }
28143
28144    /*
28145     * set_encoding_quality determines whether the encoding
28146     * for a particular variant is acceptable
28147     * for the user-agent.
28148     *
28149     * The rules for encoding are that if the user-agent
28150     * does not supply any Accept-Encoding header, then
28151     * all encodings are allowed but a variant with no
28152     * encoding should be preferred. If there is an
28153     * empty Accept-Encoding header, then no encodings are
28154     * acceptable. If there is a non-empty Accept-Encoding
28155     * header, then any of the listed encodings are
28156     * acceptable, as well as no encoding unless the
28157     * "identity" encoding is specifically excluded.
28158     */
28159    static void set_encoding_quality(negotiation_state
28160        *neg, var_rec *variant)
28161    {
28162        accept_rec *accept_recs;
28163        const char *enc = variant->content_encoding;
28164        accept_rec *star = NULL;
28165        float value_if_not_found = 0.0f;
28166        int i;
28167
28168        if (!neg->accept_encodings) {
28169            /* We had no Accept-Encoding header, assume that
28170             * all encodings are acceptable with a low
28171             * quality, but we prefer no encoding if
28172             * available.
28173             */
28174            if (!enc || is_identity_encoding(enc))
28175                variant->encoding_quality = 1.0f;
28176            else
28177                variant->encoding_quality = 0.5f;
28178
28179            return;
28180        }
28181
28182        if (!enc || is_identity_encoding(enc)) {
28183            enc = "identity";
28184            value_if_not_found = 0.0001f;
28185        }
28186
28187        accept_recs = (accept_rec *)
28188            neg->accept_encodings->elts;
28189
28190        /* Go through each of the encodings on the
28191         * Accept-Encoding: header, looking for a match
28192         * with our encoding. x- prefixes are ignored.
28193         */
28194        if (enc[0] == 'x' && enc[1] == '-') {
28195            enc += 2;
28196        }
28197        for (i = 0; i < neg->accept_encodings->nelts; ++i) {
28198
28199            char *name = accept_recs[i].name;
28200
28201            if (name[0] == 'x' && name[1] == '-') {
28202                name += 2;
28203            }
28204
28205            if (!strcmp(name, enc)) {
28206                variant->encoding_quality =
28207                    accept_recs[i].quality;
28208                return;
28209            }
28210
28211            if (strcmp(name, "*") == 0) {
28212                star = &accept_recs[i];
28213            }
28214
28215        }
28216        /* No explicit match */
28217        if (star) {
28218            variant->encoding_quality = star->quality;
28219            return;
28220        }
28221
28222        /* Encoding not found on Accept-Encoding: header,
28223         * so it is_not_ acceptable unless it is
28224         * the identity (no encoding)
28225         */
28226        variant->encoding_quality = value_if_not_found;
28227    }
28228
28229    /************************************************************
28230     * Possible results of the variant selection algorithm
28231     */
28232    enum algorithm_results {
28233        alg_choice = 1,                    /* choose variant */
28234        alg_list                           /* list variants */
```

```
28235    };
28236
28237    /* Below is the 'best_match' function. It returns an
28238     * int, which has one of the two values alg_choice
28239     * or alg_list, which give the result of the variant
28240     * selection algorithm.  alg_list means that no best
28241     * variant was found by the algorithm, alg_choice means
28242     * that a best variant was found and should be
28243     * returned.  The list/choice terminology comes from TCN
28244     * (rfc2295), but is used in a more generic way here.
28245     * The best variant is returned in *pbest. best_match
28246     * has two possible algorithms for determining the
28247     * best variant: the RVSA/1.0 algorithm (from RFC2296),
28248     * and the standard Apache algorithm. These are split
28249     * out into separate functions(is_variant_better_rvsa()
28250     * and is_variant_better()).  Selection of one is
28251     * through the neg->use_rvsa flag.
28252     *
28253     * The call to best_match also creates full information,
28254     * including language, charset, etc quality for
28255     * _every_ variant. This is needed for generating a
28256     * correct Vary header, and can be used for the
28257     * Alternates header, the human-readable list responses
28258     * and 406 errors.
28259     */
28260
28261    /* Firstly, the RVSA/1.0 (HTTP Remote Variant Selection
28262     * Algorithm v1.0) from rfc2296.  This is the
28263     * algorithm that goes together with
28264     * transparent content negotiation (TCN).
28265     */
28266    static int is_variant_better_rvsa(negotiation_state
28267          *neg, var_rec *variant,
28268                              var_rec *best, float *p_bestq)
28269    {
28270        float bestq = *p_bestq, q;
28271
28272        /* TCN does not cover negotiation on
28273         * content-encoding.  For now, we ignore the
28274         * encoding unless it was explicitly excluded.
28275         */
28276        if (variant->encoding_quality == 0.0f)
28277            return 0;
28278
28279        q = variant->mime_type_quality *
28280            variant->source_quality *
28281            variant->charset_quality *
28282            variant->lang_quality;
28283
28284    /* RFC 2296 calls for the result to be rounded to
28285     * 5 decimal places, but we don't do that because
28286     * it serves no useful purpose other than to ensure
28287     * that a remote algorithm operates on the same
28288     * precision as ours.  That is silly, since what we
28289     * obviously want is for the algorithm to operate
28290     * on the best available precision regardless of
28291     * who runs it.  Since the above calculation may
28292     * result in significant variance at 1e-12, rounding
28293     * would be bogus.
28294     */
28295
28296    #ifdef NEG_DEBUG
28297        fprintf(stderr, "Variant: file=%s type=%s
28298            lang=%s sourceq=%1.3f "
28299            "mimeq=%1.3f langq=%1.3f charq=%1.3f encq=%1.3f "
28300            "q=%1.5f definite=%d\n",
28301            (variant->file_name ? variant->file_name : ""),
28302            (variant->mime_type ? variant->mime_type : ""),
28303            (variant->content_languages
28304             ? ap_array_pstrcat(neg->pool,
28305                  variant->content_languages, ',')
28306             : ""),
28307            variant->source_quality,
28308            variant->mime_type_quality,
28309            variant->lang_quality,
28310            variant->charset_quality,
28311            variant->encoding_quality,
28312            q,
28313            variant->definite);
28314    #endif
28315
28316        if (q <= 0.0f) {
28317            return 0;
28318        }
28319        if (q > bestq) {
28320            *p_bestq = q;
28321            return 1;
28322        }
28323        if (q == bestq) {
28324            /* If the best variant's encoding is of lesser
28325             * quality than this variant, then we prefer
28326             * this variant
28327             */
28328            if (variant->encoding_quality >
28329                    best->encoding_quality) {
28330                *p_bestq = q;
```

```
28331              return 1;
28332          }
28333       }
28334       return 0;
28335  }
28336
28337  /* Negotiation algorithm as used by previous
28338   * versions of Apache (just about).
28339   */
28340
28341  static int is_variant_better(negotiation_state
28342       *neg, var_rec *variant,
28343                        var_rec *best, float *p_bestq)
28344  {
28345       float bestq = *p_bestq, q;
28346       int levcmp;
28347
28348       /* For non-transparent negotiation, server can
28349        * choose how to handle the negotiation. We'll
28350        * use the following in order: content-type,
28351        * language, content-type level, charset,
28352        * content encoding, content length.
28353        *
28354        * For each check, we have three possible outcomes:
28355        *    This variant is worse than current best:
28356        *    return 0 This variant is better
28357        *    than the current best: assign this variant's
28358        *    q to *p_bestq, and return 1 This variant is
28359        *    just as desirable as the current best:
28360        *         drop through to the next test.
28361        *
28362        * This code is written in this long-winded way
28363        * to allow future customisation, either by the
28364        * addition of additional checks, or to allow the
28365        * order of the checks to be determined by
28366        * configuration options (e.g. we might prefer to
28367        * check language quality _before_ content type).
28368        */
28369
28370       /* First though, eliminate this variant if it is not
28371        * acceptable by type, charset, encoding or language.
28372        */
28373
28374  #ifdef NEG_DEBUG
28375       fprintf(stderr, "Variant: file=%s type=%s
28376          lang=%s sourceq=%1.3f "
28377            "mimeq=%1.3f langq=%1.3f langidx=%d
28378              charq=%1.3f encq=%1.3f \n",
28379          (variant->file_name ? variant->file_name : ""),
28380          (variant->mime_type ? variant->mime_type : ""),
28381          (variant->content_languages
28382           ? ap_array_pstrcat(neg->pool,
28383                 variant->content_languages, ',')
28384           : ""),
28385          variant->source_quality,
28386          variant->mime_type_quality,
28387          variant->lang_quality,
28388          variant->lang_index,
28389          variant->charset_quality,
28390          variant->encoding_quality);
28391  #endif
28392
28393       if (variant->encoding_quality == 0.0f ||
28394           variant->lang_quality == 0.0f ||
28395           variant->source_quality == 0.0f ||
28396           variant->charset_quality == 0.0f ||
28397           variant->mime_type_quality == 0.0f) {
28398          return 0;
28399          /* don't consider unacceptables */
28400       }
28401
28402       q = variant->mime_type_quality *
28403           variant->source_quality;
28404       if (q == 0.0 || q < bestq) {
28405          return 0;
28406       }
28407       if (q > bestq || !best) {
28408          *p_bestq = q;
28409          return 1;
28410       }
28411
28412       /* language */
28413       if (variant->lang_quality < best->lang_quality) {
28414          return 0;
28415       }
28416       if (variant->lang_quality > best->lang_quality) {
28417          *p_bestq = q;
28418          return 1;
28419       }
28420
28421       /* if language qualities were equal, try the
28422          LanguagePriority stuff */
28423       if (best->lang_index != -1 &&
28424          (variant->lang_index == -1 ||
28425              variant->lang_index > best->lang_index)) {
28426          return 0;
```

```
28427        }
28428        if (variant->lang_index != -1 &&
28429            (best->lang_index == -1 ||
28430                variant->lang_index < best->lang_index)) {
28431            *p_bestq = q;
28432            return 1;
28433        }
28434
28435        /* content-type level (sometimes used with
28436         * text/html, though we support it on other
28437         * types too)
28438         */
28439        levcmp = level_cmp(variant, best);
28440        if (levcmp == -1) {
28441            return 0;
28442        }
28443        if (levcmp == 1) {
28444            *p_bestq = q;
28445            return 1;
28446        }
28447
28448        /* charset */
28449        if (variant->charset_quality <
28450            best->charset_quality) {
28451            return 0;
28452        }
28453        /* If the best variant's charset is ISO-8859-1
28454         * and this variant has the same charset quality,
28455         * then we prefer this variant
28456         */
28457
28458        if (variant->charset_quality >
28459            best->charset_quality ||
28460            ((variant->content_charset != NULL &&
28461             *variant->content_charset != '\0' &&
28462             strcmp(variant->content_charset,
28463                 "iso-8859-1") != 0) &&
28464            (best->content_charset == NULL ||
28465             *best->content_charset == '\0' ||
28466             strcmp(best->content_charset, "iso-8859-1")
28467                == 0))) {
28468            *p_bestq = q;
28469            return 1;
28470        }
28471
28472        /* Prefer the highest value for encoding_quality.
28473         */
28474        if (variant->encoding_quality <
28475            best->encoding_quality) {
28476            return 0;
28477        }
28478        if (variant->encoding_quality >
28479            best->encoding_quality) {
28480            *p_bestq = q;
28481            return 1;
28482        }
28483
28484        /* content length if all else equal */
28485        if (find_content_length(neg, variant) >=
28486            find_content_length(neg, best)) {
28487            return 0;
28488        }
28489
28490        /* ok, to get here means every thing turned out
28491         * equal, except we have a shorter content
28492         * length, so use this variant
28493         */
28494        *p_bestq = q;
28495        return 1;
28496 }
28497
28498 static int best_match(negotiation_state *neg,
28499     var_rec **pbest)
28500 {
28501        int j;
28502        var_rec *best = NULL;
28503        float bestq = 0.0f;
28504        enum algorithm_results algorithm_result;
28505
28506        var_rec *avail_recs = (var_rec *)
28507            neg->avail_vars->elts;
28508
28509        set_default_lang_quality(neg);
28510
28511        /*
28512         * Find the 'best' variant
28513         */
28514
28515        for (j = 0; j < neg->avail_vars->nelts; ++j) {
28516            var_rec *variant = &avail_recs[j];
28517
28518            /* Find all the relevant 'quality' values from
28519             * the Accept... headers, and store in
28520             * the variant.  This also prepares for sending
28521             * an Alternates header etc so we need to do it
28522             * even if we do not actually plan to find a best
```

```
28523            * variant.
28524            */
28525           set_accept_quality(neg, variant);
28526           set_language_quality(neg, variant);
28527           set_encoding_quality(neg, variant);
28528           set_charset_quality(neg, variant);
28529
28530           /* Only do variant selection if we may actually
28531            * choose a variant for the client
28532            */
28533           if (neg->may_choose) {
28534
28535               /* Now find out if this variant is better
28536                * than the current best, either using the
28537                * RVSA/1.0 algorithm, or Apache's internal
28538                * server-driven algorithm. Presumably other
28539                * server-driven algorithms are possible,
28540                * and could be implemented here.
28541                */
28542
28543               if (neg->use_rvsa) {
28544                   if (is_variant_better_rvsa(neg,
28545                       variant, best, &bestq)) {
28546                       best = variant;
28547                   }
28548               }
28549               else {
28550                   if (is_variant_better(neg, variant,
28551                       best, &bestq)) {
28552                       best = variant;
28553                   }
28554               }
28555           }
28556       }
28557
28558       /* We now either have a best variant, or no
28559        * best variant */
28560
28561       if (neg->use_rvsa)    {
28562           /* calculate result for RVSA/1.0 algorithm:
28563            * only a choice response if the best
28564            * variant has q>0and is definite
28565            */
28566           algorithm_result = (best && best->definite)
28567               && (bestq > 0) ?
28568                       alg_choice : alg_list;
28569       }
28570       else {
28571           /* calculate result for Apache negotiation
28572            * algorithm */
28573           algorithm_result = bestq > 0 ? alg_choice :
28574                   alg_list;
28575       }
28576
28577       /* Returning a choice response with a non-
28578        * neighboring variant is a protocol security error
28579        * in TCN (see rfc2295).  We do *not* verify here
28580        * that the variant and URI are neighbors, even
28581        * though we may return alg_choice.  We depend
28582        * on the environment (the caller) to only declare
28583        * the resource transparently negotiable if all
28584        * variants are neighbors.
28585        */
28586       *pbest = best;
28587       return algorithm_result;
28588   }
28589
28590   /* Sets response headers for a negotiated response.
28591    * neg->is_transparent determines whether a
28592    * transparently negotiated response or a plain
28593    * 'server driven negotiation' response is
28594    * created.   Applicable headers are Alternates,
28595    * Vary, and TCN.
28596    *
28597    * The Vary header we create is sometimes longer than
28598    * is required for the correct caching of negotiated
28599    * results by HTTP/1.1 caches.  For example if we have
28600    * 3 variants x.html, x.ps.en and x.ps.nl, and if
28601    * the Accept: header assigns a 0 quality to .ps,
28602    * then the results of the two server-side negotiation
28603    * algorithms we currently implement will never depend
28604    * on Accept-Language so we could return 'Vary:
28605    * negotiate, accept' instead of the longer 'Vary:
28606    * negotiate, accept, accept-language' which the
28607    * code below will return.  A routine for computing
28608    * the exact minimal Vary header would be a huge pain
28609    * to code and maintain though, especially because we
28610    * need to take all possible twiddles in the server-side
28611    * negotiation algorithms into account.
28612    */
28613   static void set_neg_headers(request_rec *r,
28614       negotiation_state *neg,
28615                           int alg_result)
28616   {
28617       table *hdrs;
28618       var_rec *avail_recs = (var_rec *)
```

```
28619            neg->avail_vars->elts;
28620        const char *sample_type = NULL;
28621        const char *sample_language = NULL;
28622        const char *sample_encoding = NULL;
28623        const char *sample_charset = NULL;
28624        char *lang;
28625        char *qstr;
28626        char *lenstr;
28627        long len;
28628        array_header *arr;
28629        int max_vlist_array = (neg->avail_vars->nelts * 21);
28630        int first_variant = 1;
28631        int vary_by_type = 0;
28632        int vary_by_language = 0;
28633        int vary_by_charset = 0;
28634        int vary_by_encoding = 0;
28635        int j;
28636
28637        /* In order to avoid O(n^2) memory copies in
28638         * building Alternates, we preallocate a table with
28639         * the maximum substrings possible, fill it with the
28640         * variant list, and then concatenate the entire
28641         * array.Note that if you change the number of
28642         * substrings pushed, you also need to change the
28643         * calculation of max_vlist_array above.
28644         */
28645        if (neg->send_alternates && neg->avail_vars->nelts)
28646            arr = ap_make_array(r->pool, max_vlist_array,
28647                sizeof(char *));
28648        else
28649            arr = NULL;
28650
28651        /* Put headers into err_headers_out, since
28652         * send_http_header()outputs both
28653         * headers_out and err_headers_out.
28654         */
28655        hdrs = r->err_headers_out;
28656
28657        for (j = 0; j < neg->avail_vars->nelts; ++j) {
28658            var_rec *variant = &avail_recs[j];
28659
28660            if (variant->content_languages &&
28661                    variant->content_languages->nelts) {
28662                lang = ap_array_pstrcat(r->pool,
28663                    variant->content_languages, ',');
28664            }
28665            else {
28666                lang = NULL;
28667            }
28668
28669            /* Calculate Vary by looking for any difference
28670             * between variants */
28671
28672            if (first_variant) {
28673                sample_type     = variant->mime_type;
28674                sample_charset  = variant->content_charset;
28675                sample_language = lang;
28676                sample_encoding = variant->content_encoding;
28677            }
28678            else {
28679                if (!vary_by_type &&
28680                    strcmp(sample_type ? sample_type : "",
28681                            variant->mime_type ?
28682                                variant->mime_type : "")) {
28683                    vary_by_type = 1;
28684                }
28685                if (!vary_by_charset &&
28686                    strcmp(sample_charset ?
28687                        sample_charset : "",
28688                            variant->content_charset ?
28689                                variant->content_charset : "")) {
28690                    vary_by_charset = 1;
28691                }
28692                if (!vary_by_language &&
28693                    strcmp(sample_language ?
28694                        sample_language : "",
28695                            lang ? lang : "")) {
28696                    vary_by_language = 1;
28697                }
28698                if (!vary_by_encoding &&
28699                    strcmp(sample_encoding ?
28700                        sample_encoding : "",
28701                            variant->content_encoding ?
28702                                variant->content_encoding : "")) {
28703                    vary_by_encoding = 1;
28704                }
28705            }
28706            first_variant = 0;
28707
28708            if (!neg->send_alternates)
28709                continue;
28710
28711            /* Generate the string components for this
28712             * Alternates entry */
28713
28714            *((const char **)
```

```
28715            ap_push_array(arr)) = "{\"";
28716    *((const char **)
28717            ap_push_array(arr)) = variant->file_name;
28718    *((const char **)
28719            ap_push_array(arr)) = "\" ";
28720
28721    qstr = (char *) ap_palloc(r->pool, 6);
28722    ap_snprintf(qstr, 6, "%1.3f",
28723            variant->source_quality);
28724
28725    /* Strip trailing zeros (saves those
28726     * valuable network bytes) */
28727    if (qstr[4] == '0') {
28728        qstr[4] = '\0';
28729        if (qstr[3] == '0') {
28730            qstr[3] = '\0';
28731            if (qstr[2] == '0') {
28732                qstr[1] = '\0';
28733            }
28734        }
28735    }
28736    *((const char **) ap_push_array(arr)) = qstr;
28737
28738    if (variant->mime_type && *variant->mime_type) {
28739        *((const char **)
28740            ap_push_array(arr)) = " {type ";
28741        *((const char **)
28742            ap_push_array(arr)) = variant->mime_type;
28743        *((const char **)
28744            ap_push_array(arr)) = "}";
28745    }
28746    if (variant->content_charset &&
28747            *variant->content_charset) {
28748        *((const char **)
28749            ap_push_array(arr)) = " {charset ";
28750        *((const char **)
28751            ap_push_array(arr)) =
28752        variant->content_charset;
28753        *((const char **)
28754            ap_push_array(arr)) = "}";
28755    }
28756    if (lang) {
28757        *((const char **)
28758            ap_push_array(arr)) = " {language ";
28759        *((const char **) ap_push_array(arr)) = lang;
28760        *((const char **) ap_push_array(arr)) = "}";
28761    }
28762    if (variant->content_encoding &&
28763            *variant->content_encoding) {
28764        /* Strictly speaking, this is non-standard,
28765         * but so is TCN */
28766
28767        *((const char **)
28768            ap_push_array(arr)) = " {encoding ";
28769        *((const char **)
28770            ap_push_array(arr)) =
28771                variant->content_encoding;
28772        *((const char **) ap_push_array(arr)) = "}";
28773    }
28774
28775    /* Note that the Alternates specification
28776     * (in rfc2295) does not require that we include
28777     * {length x}, so we could omit it if
28778     * determining the length is too expensive.  We
28779     * currently always include it though.
28780     * 22 bytes is enough for 2^64.
28781     *
28782     * If the variant is a CGI script,
28783     * find_content_length would return the length
28784     * of the script, not the output it produces, so
28785     * we check for the presence of a handler and if
28786     * there is one we don't add a length.
28787     *
28788     * XXX: TODO: This check does not detect a CGI
28789     * script if we get the variant from a type map.
28790     * This needs to be fixed(without breaking
28791     * things if the type map specifies a
28792     * content-length, which currently leads to the
28793     * correct result).
28794     */
28795    if (!(variant->sub_req
28796            && variant->sub_req->handler)
28797        && (len = find_content_length(neg,
28798            variant)) != 0) {
28799
28800        lenstr = (char *) ap_palloc(r->pool, 22);
28801        ap_snprintf(lenstr, 22, "%ld", len);
28802        *((const char **)
28803            ap_push_array(arr)) = " {length ";
28804        *((const char **)
28805            ap_push_array(arr)) = lenstr;
28806        *((const char **)
28807            ap_push_array(arr)) = "}";
28808    }
28809
28810    *((const char **) ap_push_array(arr)) = "}";
```

```
28811            *((const char **) ap_push_array(arr)) = ", ";
28812            /* trimmed below */
28813        }
28814
28815    if (neg->send_alternates && neg->avail_vars->nelts) {
28816        arr->nelts--;
28817        /* remove last comma */
28818        ap_table_mergen(hdrs, "Alternates",
28819                    ap_array_pstrcat(r->pool, arr, '\0'));
28820    }
28821
28822    /* Theoretically the negotiation result _always_ has
28823     * a dependence on the contents of the Accept header
28824     * because we do 'mxb=' processing in
28825     * set_accept_quality().  However, variations in mxb
28826     * only affect the relative quality of several
28827     * acceptable variants, so there is no reason to
28828     * worry about an unacceptable variant being
28829     * mistakenly prioritized.  We therefore ignore
28830     * mxb in deciding whether or not to include Accept
28831     * in the Vary field value.
28832     */
28833    if (neg->is_transparent || vary_by_type ||
28834            vary_by_language ||
28835        vary_by_language || vary_by_charset ||
28836                vary_by_encoding) {
28837
28838    ap_table_mergen(hdrs, "Vary", 2 + ap_pstrcat(r->pool,
28839            neg->is_transparent ? ", negotiate"     : "",
28840            vary_by_type        ? ", accept"        : "",
28841            vary_by_language    ? ", accept-language" : "",
28842            vary_by_charset     ? ", accept-charset"  : "",
28843            vary_by_encoding    ? ", accept-encoding" : "",
28844                NULL));
28845    }
28846
28847    if (neg->is_transparent) {
28848    /* Create TCN response header */
28849        ap_table_setn(hdrs, "TCN",
28850            alg_result == alg_list ? "list" : "choice");
28851    }
28852 }
28853
28854 /*********************************************************
28855  *
28856  * Return an HTML list of variants. This is output as
28857  * part of the choice response or 406 status body.
28858  */
28859
28860 static char *make_variant_list(request_rec *r,
28861     negotiation_state *neg)
28862 {
28863     array_header *arr;
28864     int i;
28865     int max_vlist_array =
28866         (neg->avail_vars->nelts * 15) + 2;
28867
28868     /* In order to avoid O(n^2) memory copies in building
28869      * the list, we preallocate a table with the maximum
28870      * substrings possible, fill it with the variant
28871      * list, and then concatenate the entire array.
28872      */
28873     arr = ap_make_array(r->pool, max_vlist_array,
28874         sizeof(char *));
28875
28876     *((const char **) ap_push_array(arr)) =
28877         "Available variants:\n<ul>\n";
28878
28879     for (i = 0; i < neg->avail_vars->nelts; ++i) {
28880         var_rec *variant = &((var_rec *)
28881             neg->avail_vars->elts)[i];
28882         char *filename = variant->file_name ?
28883             variant->file_name : "";
28884         array_header *languages =
28885             variant->content_languages;
28886         char *description = variant->description ?
28887             variant->description : "";
28888
28889         /* The format isn't very neat, and it would be
28890          * nice to make the tags human readable
28891          * (eg replace 'language en' with 'English').
28892          * Note that if you change the number of
28893          * substrings pushed, you also need to change
28894          * the calculation of max_vlist_array above.
28895          */
28896         *((const char **)
28897                 ap_push_array(arr)) = "<li><a href=\"";
28898         *((const char **)
28899                 ap_push_array(arr)) = filename;
28900         *((const char **) ap_push_array(arr)) = "\">";
28901         *((const char **)
28902                 ap_push_array(arr)) = filename;
28903         *((const char **) ap_push_array(arr)) = "</a> ";
28904         *((const char **)
28905                 ap_push_array(arr)) = description;
28906
```

```
28907              if (variant->mime_type && *variant->mime_type) {
28908                  *((const char **)
28909                      ap_push_array(arr)) = ", type ";
28910                  *((const char **)
28911                      ap_push_array(arr)) = variant->mime_type;
28912              }
28913              if (languages && languages->nelts) {
28914                  *((const char **)
28915                      ap_push_array(arr)) = ", language ";
28916                  *((const char **) ap_push_array(arr)) =
28917                      ap_array_pstrcat(r->pool,
28918                                              languages, ',');
28919              }
28920              if (variant->content_charset &&
28921                      *variant->content_charset) {
28922                  *((const char **)
28923                      ap_push_array(arr)) = ", charset ";
28924                  *((const char **) ap_push_array(arr)) =
28925                      variant->content_charset;
28926              }
28927              if (variant->content_encoding) {
28928                  *((const char **) ap_push_array(arr)) = ",
28929                      encoding ";
28930                  *((const char **) ap_push_array(arr)) =
28931                      variant->content_encoding;
28932              }
28933              *((const char **) ap_push_array(arr)) = "\n";
28934          }
28935          *((const char **) ap_push_array(arr)) = "</ul>\n";
28936
28937          return ap_array_pstrcat(r->pool, arr, '\0');
28938      }
28939
28940      static void store_variant_list(request_rec *r,
28941          negotiation_state *neg)
28942      {
28943          if (r->main == NULL) {
28944              ap_table_setn(r->notes, "variant-list",
28945                  make_variant_list(r, neg));
28946          }
28947          else {
28948              ap_table_setn(r->main->notes, "variant-list",
28949                  make_variant_list(r->main, neg));
28950          }
28951      }
28952
28953      /* Called if we got a "Choice" response from the
28954       * variant selection algorithm. It checks the result
```

```
28955       * of the chosen variant to see if it is itself
28956       * negotiated (if so, return error VARIANT_ALSO_VARIES).
28957       * Otherwise, add the appropriate headers to the
28958       * current response.
28959       */
28960
28961      static int setup_choice_response(request_rec *r,
28962          negotiation_state *neg,
28963                                          var_rec *variant)
28964      {
28965          request_rec *sub_req;
28966          const char *sub_vary;
28967
28968          if (!variant->sub_req) {
28969              int status;
28970
28971              sub_req =
28972                  ap_sub_req_lookup_file(variant->file_name, r);
28973              status = sub_req->status;
28974
28975              if (status != HTTP_OK &&
28976                  !ap_table_get(sub_req->err_headers_out,
28977                      "TCN")) {
28978                  ap_destroy_sub_req(sub_req);
28979                  return status;
28980              }
28981              variant->sub_req = sub_req;
28982          }
28983          else {
28984              sub_req = variant->sub_req;
28985          }
28986
28987          /* The variant selection algorithm told us to return
28988           * a "Choice"response. This is the normal variant
28989           * response, with some extra headers. First, ensure
28990           * that the chosen variant did or will not itself
28991           * engage in transparent negotiation. If not, set
28992           * the appropriate headers, and fall through
28993           * to the normal variant handling
28994           */
28995
28996          /* This catches the error that a transparent type
28997           * map selects a transparent multiviews resource
28998           * as the best variant.
28999           *
29000           * XXX: We do not signal an error if a transparent
29001           * type map selects a _non_transparent multiviews
29002           * resource as the best variant, because we can
```

```
29003        * generate a legal negotiation response in this
29004        * case.  In this case, the vlist_validator of the
29005        * nontransparent subrequest will be lost however.
29006        * This could lead to cases in which a change in
29007        * the set of variants or the negotiation algorithm
29008        * of the nontransparent resource is never
29009        * propagated up to a HTTP/1.1 cache which
29010        * interprets Vary.  To be completely on the safe
29011        * side we should return VARIANT_ALSO_VARIES
29012        * for this type of recursive negotiation too.
29013        */
29014       if (neg->is_transparent &&
29015           ap_table_get(sub_req->err_headers_out, "TCN")) {
29016           return VARIANT_ALSO_VARIES;
29017       }
29018
29019       /* This catches the error that a transparent type
29020        * map recursively selects, as the best variant,
29021        * another type map which itself causes
29022        * transparent negotiation to be done.
29023        *
29024        * XXX: Actually, we catch this error by catching
29025        * all cases of type map recursion.  There are some
29026        * borderline recursive type map arrangements which
29027        * would not produce transparent negotiation
29028        * protocol errors or lack of cache propagation
29029        * problems, but such arrangements are very hard to
29030        * detect at this point in the control flow, so
29031        * we do not bother to single them
29032        * out.
29033        *
29034        * Recursive type maps imply a recursive arrangement
29035        * of negotiated resources which is visible to
29036        * outside clients, and this is not supported by the
29037        * transparent negotiation caching protocols, so
29038        * if we are to have generic support for recursive
29039        * type maps, we have to create some configuration
29040        * setting which makes all type maps non-transparent
29041        * when recursion is enabled.  Also, if we want
29042        * recursive type map support which ensures
29043        * propagation of type map changes into HTTP/1.1
29044        * caches that handle Vary, we would have to extend
29045        * the current mechanism for generating variant
29046        * list validators.
29047        */
29048       if (sub_req->handler && strcmp(sub_req->handler,
29049           "type-map") == 0) {
29050           return VARIANT_ALSO_VARIES;
29051       }
29052
29053       /* This adds an appropriate Variant-Vary header if
29054        * the subrequest is a multiviews resource.
29055        *
29056        * XXX: TODO: Note that this does _not_ handle any
29057        * Vary header returned by a CGI if sub_req is a
29058        * CGI script, because we don't see that Vary header
29059        * yet at this point in the control flow. This won't
29060        * cause any cache consistency problems _unless_ the
29061        * CGI script also returns a Cache-Control header
29062        * marking the response as cachable.  This needs to
29063        * be fixed, also there are problems if a CGI returns
29064        * an Etag header which also need to be fixed.
29065        */
29066       if ((sub_vary = ap_table_get(sub_req->err_headers_out,
29067           "Vary")) != NULL) {
29068           ap_table_setn(r->err_headers_out,
29069               "Variant-Vary", sub_vary);
29070
29071           /* Move the subreq Vary header into the main
29072            * request to prevent having two Vary headers
29073            * in the response, which would be legal
29074            * but strange.
29075            */
29076           ap_table_setn(r->err_headers_out, "Vary",
29077               sub_vary);
29078           ap_table_unset(sub_req->err_headers_out,
29079               "Vary");
29080       }
29081
29082       ap_table_setn(r->err_headers_out, "Content-Location",
29083               ap_pstrdup(r->pool, variant->file_name));
29084
29085       set_neg_headers(r, neg, alg_choice);
29086       /* add Alternates and Vary */
29087
29088       /* Still to do by caller: add Expires */
29089
29090       return 0;
29091   }
29092
29093   /*****************************************************
29094    *
29095    * Executive...
29096    */
29097
29098   static int do_negotiation(request_rec *r,
```

```
29099        negotiation_state *neg,
29100                    var_rec **bestp, int prefer_scripts)
29101    {
29102      var_rec *avail_recs = (var_rec *)
29103          neg->avail_vars->elts;
29104      int alg_result;
29105      /* result of variant selection algorithm */
29106      int res;
29107      int j;
29108
29109      /* Decide if resource is transparently
29110       * negotiable */
29111
29112      /* GET or HEAD? (HEAD has same method number
29113       * as GET) */
29114      if (r->method_number == M_GET) {
29115
29116          /* maybe this should be configurable, see
29117           * also the comment about recursive type maps
29118           * in setup_choice_response()
29119           */
29120          neg->is_transparent = 1;
29121
29122          /* We can't be transparent if we are a map file
29123           * in the middle of the request URI.
29124           */
29125          if (r->path_info && *r->path_info)
29126              neg->is_transparent = 0;
29127
29128          for (j = 0; j < neg->avail_vars->nelts; ++j) {
29129              var_rec *variant = &avail_recs[j];
29130
29131              /* We can't be transparent, because of
29132               * internal assumptions in best_match(),
29133               * if there is a non-neighboring variant.
29134               * We can have a non-neighboring
29135               * variant when processing a type map.
29136               */
29137              if (strchr(variant->file_name, '/'))
29138                  neg->is_transparent = 0;
29139          }
29140      }
29141
29142      if (neg->is_transparent)  {
29143          parse_negotiate_header(r, neg);
29144      }
29145      else { /* configure negotiation on non-transparent
29146           * resource */
```

```
29147          neg->may_choose = 1;
29148      }
29149
29150      maybe_add_default_accepts(neg, prefer_scripts);
29151
29152      alg_result = best_match(neg, bestp);
29153
29154      /* alg_result is one of
29155       *   alg_choice: a best variant is chosen
29156       *   alg_list: no best variant is chosen
29157       */
29158
29159      if (alg_result == alg_list) {
29160          /* send a list response or NOT_ACCEPTABLE
29161           * error response  */
29162
29163          neg->send_alternates = 1; /* always include
29164                  Alternates header */
29165          set_neg_headers(r, neg, alg_result);
29166          store_variant_list(r, neg);
29167
29168          if (neg->is_transparent
29169                  && neg->ua_supports_trans) {
29170              /* XXX todo: expires? cachability? */
29171
29172              /* Some HTTP/1.0 clients are known to choke
29173               * when they get a 300 (multiple choices)
29174               * response without a Location header.
29175               * However the 300 code response we are
29176               * about to generate will only reach
29177               * 1.0 clients which support transparent
29178               * negotiation, and they should be OK. The
29179               * response should never reach older 1.0
29180               * clients, even if we have
29181               * CacheNegotiatedDocs enabled, because no
29182               * 1.0 proxy cache (we know of) will cache
29183               * and return 300 responses (they certainly
29184               * won't if they conform to the
29185               * HTTP/1.0 specification).
29186               */
29187              return MULTIPLE_CHOICES;
29188          }
29189
29190          if (!*bestp) {
29191              ap_log_rerror(APLOG_MARK,
29192                      APLOG_NOERRNO|APLOG_ERR, r,
29193                      "no acceptable variant:
29194                          %s", r->filename);
```

```
29195                      return NOT_ACCEPTABLE;
29196                }
29197          }
29198
29199          /* Variant selection chose a variant */
29200
29201          /* XXX todo: merge the two cases in the
29202           * if statement below */
29203          if (neg->is_transparent) {
29204
29205                if ((res = setup_choice_response(r, neg,
29206                       *bestp)) != 0) {
29207                      return res; /* return if error */
29208                }
29209          }
29210          else {
29211                set_neg_headers(r, neg, alg_result);
29212          }
29213
29214          /* Make sure caching works - Vary should handle
29215           * HTTP/1.1, but for HTTP/1.0, we can't allow
29216           * caching at all.
29217           */
29218
29219          /* XXX: Note that we only set r->no_cache to 1,
29220           * which causes Expires: <now> to be added, when
29221           * responding to a HTTP/1.0 client.  If we return
29222           * the response to a 1.1 client, we do not add
29223           * Expires <now>, because doing so would degrade
29224           * 1.1 cache performance by preventing re-use of
29225           * the response without prior revalidation.  On the
29226           * other hand, if the 1.1 client is a proxy which
29227           * was itself contacted by a 1.0 client, or a proxy
29228           * cache which can be contacted later by 1.0
29229           * clients, then we currently rely on this 1.1 proxy
29230           * to add the Expires: <now> when it forwards the
29231           * response.
29232           *
29233           * XXX: TODO: Find out if the 1.1 spec requires
29234           * proxies and tunnels to add Expires: <now>
29235           * when forwarding the response to1.0 clients.  I
29236           * (kh) recall it is rather vague on this point.
29237           * Testing actual 1.1 proxy implementations would
29238           * also be nice. If Expires: <now> is not added by
29239           * proxies then we need to always include Expires:
29240           * <now> ourselves to ensure correct caching, but
29241           * this would degrade HTTP/1.1 cache efficiency
29242           * unless we also add Cache-Control: max-age=N,
29243           * which we currently don't.
29244           *
29245           * Roy: No, we are not going to screw over HTTP
29246           *      future just to ensure that people who can't
29247           *      be bothered to upgrade their clients will
29248           *      always receive perfect server-side
29249           *      negotiation. Hell, those clients are
29250           *      sending bogus accept headers anyway.
29251           *
29252           *      Manual setting of cache-control/expires
29253           *      always overrides this automated kluge,
29254           *      on purpose.
29255           */
29256
29257          if ((!do_cache_negotiated_docs(r->server)
29258               && (r->proto_num < HTTP_VERSION(1,1)))
29259               && neg->count_multiviews_variants != 1) {
29260                r->no_cache = 1;
29261          }
29262
29263          return OK;
29264    }
29265
29266    static int handle_map_file(request_rec *r)
29267    {
29268          negotiation_state *neg = parse_accept_headers(r);
29269          var_rec *best;
29270          int res;
29271
29272          char *udir;
29273
29274          if ((res = read_type_map(neg, r))) {
29275                return res;
29276          }
29277
29278          res = do_negotiation(r, neg, &best, 0);
29279          if (res != 0) return res;
29280
29281          if (r->path_info && *r->path_info) {
29282                r->uri[ap_find_path_info(r->uri,
29283                       r->path_info)] = '\0';
29284          }
29285          udir = ap_make_dirstr_parent(r->pool, r->uri);
29286          udir = ap_escape_uri(r->pool, udir);
29287          ap_internal_redirect(ap_pstrcat(r->pool, udir,
29288                 best->file_name,
29289                                           r->path_info, NULL), r);
29290          return OK;
```

```
29291    }
29292
29293    static int handle_multi(request_rec *r)
29294    {
29295        negotiation_state *neg;
29296        var_rec *best, *avail_recs;
29297        request_rec *sub_req;
29298        int res;
29299        int j;
29300
29301        if (r->finfo.st_mode != 0 || !(ap_allow_options(r)
29302                & OPT_MULTI)) {
29303            return DECLINED;
29304        }
29305
29306        neg = parse_accept_headers(r);
29307
29308        if ((res = read_types_multi(neg))) {
29309          return_from_multi:
29310            /* free all allocated memory from subrequests */
29311            avail_recs = (var_rec *) neg->avail_vars->elts;
29312            for (j = 0; j < neg->avail_vars->nelts; ++j) {
29313                var_rec *variant = &avail_recs[j];
29314                if (variant->sub_req) {
29315                    ap_destroy_sub_req(variant->sub_req);
29316                }
29317            }
29318            return res;
29319        }
29320        if (neg->avail_vars->nelts == 0) {
29321            return DECLINED;
29322        }
29323
29324        res = do_negotiation(r, neg, &best,
29325                            (r->method_number != M_GET)
29326                            || r->args ||
29327                            (r->path_info && *r->path_info));
29328        if (res != 0)
29329            goto return_from_multi;
29330
29331        if (!(sub_req = best->sub_req)) {
29332            /* We got this out of a map file, so we don't
29333             * actually have a sub_req structure yet.
29334             * Get one now.
29335             */
29336
29337            sub_req =
29338                ap_sub_req_lookup_file(best->file_name, r);
29339            if (sub_req->status != HTTP_OK) {
29340                res = sub_req->status;
29341                ap_destroy_sub_req(sub_req);
29342                goto return_from_multi;
29343            }
29344        }
29345
29346        /* BLECH -- don't multi-resolve non-ordinary
29347         * files */
29348
29349        if (!S_ISREG(sub_req->finfo.st_mode)) {
29350            res = NOT_FOUND;
29351            goto return_from_multi;
29352        }
29353
29354        /* Otherwise, use it. */
29355
29356        /* now do a "fast redirect" ... promote the sub_req
29357         * into the main req */
29358        /* We need to tell POOL_DEBUG that we're guaranteeing
29359         * that sub_req->pool will exist as long as
29360         * r->pool.  Otherwise we run into troubles because
29361         * some values in this request will be allocated in
29362         * r->pool, and others in sub_req->pool.
29363         */
29364        ap_pool_join(r->pool, sub_req->pool);
29365        r->mtime = 0; /* reset etag info for subrequest */
29366        r->filename = sub_req->filename;
29367        r->handler = sub_req->handler;
29368        r->content_type = sub_req->content_type;
29369        r->content_encoding = sub_req->content_encoding;
29370        r->content_languages = sub_req->content_languages;
29371        r->content_language = sub_req->content_language;
29372        r->finfo = sub_req->finfo;
29373        r->per_dir_config = sub_req->per_dir_config;
29374        /* copy output headers from subrequest, but leave
29375         * negotiation headers */
29376        r->notes = ap_overlay_tables(r->pool,
29377            sub_req->notes, r->notes);
29378        r->headers_out = ap_overlay_tables(r->pool,
29379            sub_req->headers_out,
29380                                        r->headers_out);
29381        r->err_headers_out = ap_overlay_tables(r->pool,
29382            sub_req->err_headers_out,
29383                                        r->err_headers_out);
29384        r->subprocess_env = ap_overlay_tables(r->pool,
29385            sub_req->subprocess_env,
29386                                        r->subprocess_env);
```

```
29387        avail_recs = (var_rec *) neg->avail_vars->elts;
29388        for (j = 0; j < neg->avail_vars->nelts; ++j) {
29389            var_rec *variant = &avail_recs[j];
29390            if (variant != best && variant->sub_req) {
29391                ap_destroy_sub_req(variant->sub_req);
29392            }
29393        }
29394        return OK;
29395    }
29396
29397    /*********************************************************
29398     * There is a problem with content-encoding, as some
29399     * clients send and expect an x- token (e.g. x-gzip)
29400     * while others expect the plain token(i.e. gzip). To
29401     * try and deal with this as best as possible we do
29402     * the following: if the client sent an Accept-Encoding
29403     * header and it contains a plain token corresponding
29404     * to the content encoding of the response, then set
29405     * content encoding using the plain token. Else if
29406     * the A-E header contains the x- token use the x- token
29407     * in the C-E header. Else don't do anything.
29408     *
29409     * Note that if no A-E header was sent, or it does not
29410     * contain a token atible with the final
29411     * comp content encoding, then the token in the
29412     * C-E header will be whatever was specified in the
29413     * AddEncoding directive.
29414     */
29415    static int fix_encoding(request_rec *r)
29416    {
29417        const char *enc = r->content_encoding;
29418        char *x_enc = NULL;
29419        array_header *accept_encodings;
29420        accept_rec *accept_recs;
29421        int i;
29422
29423        if (!enc || !*enc) {
29424            return DECLINED;
29425        }
29426
29427        if (enc[0] == 'x' && enc[1] == '-') {
29428            enc += 2;
29429        }
29430
29431        if ((accept_encodings = do_header_line(r->pool,
29432                ap_table_get(r->headers_in,
29433                    "Accept-Encoding"))) == NULL) {
29434            return DECLINED;
```

```
29435        }
29436
29437        accept_recs = (accept_rec *) accept_encodings->elts;
29438
29439        for (i = 0; i < accept_encodings->nelts; ++i) {
29440            char *name = accept_recs[i].name;
29441
29442            if (!strcmp(name, enc)) {
29443                r->content_encoding = name;
29444                return OK;
29445            }
29446
29447            if (name[0] == 'x' && name[1] == '-'
29448                    && !strcmp(name+2, enc)) {
29449                x_enc = name;
29450            }
29451        }
29452
29453        if (x_enc) {
29454            r->content_encoding = x_enc;
29455            return OK;
29456        }
29457
29458        return DECLINED;
29459    }
29460
29461    static const handler_rec negotiation_handlers[] =
29462    {
29463        {MAP_FILE_MAGIC_TYPE, handle_map_file},
29464        {"type-map", handle_map_file},
29465        {NULL}
29466    };
29467
29468    module MODULE_VAR_EXPORT negotiation_module =
29469    {
29470        STANDARD_MODULE_STUFF,
29471        NULL,                    /* initializer */
29472        create_neg_dir_config,   /* dir config creator */
29473        merge_neg_dir_configs,
29474        /* dir merger -- default is to override */
29475        NULL,                    /* server config */
29476        NULL,                    /* merge server config */
29477        negotiation_cmds,        /* command table */
29478        negotiation_handlers,    /* handlers */
29479        NULL,                    /* filename translation */
29480        NULL,                    /* check_user_id */
29481        NULL,                    /* check auth */
29482        NULL,                    /* check access */
```

```
29483        handle_multi,              /* type_checker */
29484        fix_encoding,              /* fixups */
29485        NULL,                      /* logger */
29486        NULL,                      /* header parser */
29487        NULL,                      /* child_init */
29488        NULL,                      /* child_exit */
29489        NULL                       /* post read-request */
29490    };
```

mod_rewrite.c

```
29491    #include "mod_rewrite.h"
29492
29493
29494    /*
29495    ** +-------------------------------------------------+
29496    ** |                                                 |
29497    ** |            static module configuration          |
29498    ** |                                                 |
29499    ** +-------------------------------------------------+
29500    */
29501
29502
29503    /*
29504    ** Our interface to the Apache server kernel:
29505    **
29506    ** o  Runtime logic of a request is as following:
29507    **        while(request or subrequest)
29508    **            foreach(stage #0...#9)
29509    **                foreach(module) (**)
29510    **                    try to run hook
29511    **
29512    ** o  the order of modules at (**) is the inverted
29513    **    given in the "Configuration" file, i.e. the
29514    **    last module specified is the first one called
29515    **    for each hook!The core module is always the last!
29516    **
29517    ** o  there are two different types of result checking
29518    **    and continue processing:
29519    **    for hook #0,#1,#4,#5,#6,#8:
29520    **        hook run loop stops on first modules which
29521    **        gives back a result != DECLINED, i.e. it
29522    **        usually returns OK which says "OK, module
29523    **        has handled this _stage_" and for #1
29524    **        this have not to mean "Ok, the filename
29525    **        is now valid".
29526    **    for hook #2,#3,#7,#9:
29527    **        all hooks are run, independend of result
```

```
29528    **
29529    ** o  at the last stage, the core module always
29530    **        - says "BAD_REQUEST" if r->filename does not
29531    **          begin with "/"
29532    **        - prefix URL with document_root or replaced
29533    **          server_root with document_root and
29534    **          sets r->filename
29535    **        - always return a "OK" independed
29536    **          if the file really exists or not!
29537    */
29538
29539    /* The section for the Configure script:
29540     * MODULE-DEFINITION-START
29541     * Name: rewrite_module
29542     * ConfigStart
29543    . ./helpers/find-dbm-lib
29544    if [ "x$found_dbm" = "x1" ]; then
29545        echo "     enabling DBM support for
29546               mod_rewrite"
29547    else
29548      echo "       disabling DBM support for mod_rewrite"
29549      echo "       (perhaps you need to add -ldbm,
29550              -lndbm or -lgdbm to EXTRA_LIBS)"
29551      CFLAGS="$CFLAGS -DNO_DBM_REWRITEMAP"
29552    fi
29553     * ConfigEnd
29554     * MODULE-DEFINITION-END
29555     */
29556
29557    /* the table of commands we provide */
29558    static const command_rec command_table[] = {
29559        { "RewriteEngine",   cmd_rewriteengine,
29560              NULL, OR_FILEINFO, FLAG,
29561          "On or Off to enable or disable (default)
29562              the whole rewriting engine" },
29563        { "RewriteOptions",  cmd_rewriteoptions,
29564              NULL, OR_FILEINFO, ITERATE,
29565          "List of option strings to set" },
29566        { "RewriteBase",     cmd_rewritebase,
29567              NULL, OR_FILEINFO, TAKE1,
29568          "the base URL of the per-directory context" },
29569        { "RewriteCond",     cmd_rewritecond,
29570              NULL, OR_FILEINFO, RAW_ARGS,
29571          "a input string and a to be applied
29572              regexp-pattern" },
29573        { "RewriteRule",     cmd_rewriterule,
29574              NULL, OR_FILEINFO, RAW_ARGS,
29575          "a URL-applied regexp-pattern and a substitution URL" },
```

p 455

```
29576      { "RewriteMap",      cmd_rewritemap,
29577              NULL, RSRC_CONF,    TAKE2,
29578      "a mapname and a filename" },
29579      { "RewriteLock",     cmd_rewritelock,
29580              NULL, RSRC_CONF,    TAKE1,
29581      "the filename of a lockfile used for
29582          inter-process synchronization"},
29583      { "RewriteLog",      cmd_rewritelog,
29584              NULL, RSRC_CONF,    TAKE1,
29585      "the filename of the rewriting logfile" },
29586      { "RewriteLogLevel", cmd_rewriteloglevel,
29587              NULL, RSRC_CONF,    TAKE1,
29588      "the level of the rewriting logfile verbosity "
29589      "(0=none, 1=std, ..., 9=max)" },
29590      { NULL }
29591  };
29592
29593      /* the table of content handlers we provide */
29594  static const handler_rec handler_table[] = {
29595      { "redirect-handler", handler_redirect },
29596      { NULL }
29597  };
29598
29599      /* the main config structure */
29600  module MODULE_VAR_EXPORT rewrite_module = {
29601      STANDARD_MODULE_STUFF,
29602      init_module,
29603      /* module initializer                  */
29604      config_perdir_create,
29605      /* create per-dir   config structures */
29606      config_perdir_merge,
29607      /* merge  per-dir   config structures */
29608      config_server_create,
29609      /* create per-server config structures */
29610      config_server_merge,
29611      /* merge  per-server config structures */
29612      command_table,
29613      /* table of config file commands       */
29614      handler_table,
29615      /* [#8] MIME-typed-dispatched handlers */
29616      hook_uri2file,
29617      /* [#1] URI to filename translation    */
29618      NULL,
29619      /* [#4] validate user id from request  */
29620      NULL,
29621      /* [#5] check if the user is ok _here_ */
29622      NULL,
29623      /* [#3] check access by host address   */
29624      hook_mimetype,
29625      /* [#6] determine MIME type            */
29626      hook_fixup,
29627      /* [#7] pre-run fixups                 */
29628      NULL,
29629      /* [#9] log a transaction              */
29630      NULL,
29631      /* [#2] header parser                  */
29632      init_child,
29633      /* child_init                          */
29634      NULL,
29635      /* child_exit                          */
29636      NULL
29637      /* [#0] post read-request              */
29638  };
29639
29640      /* the cache */
29641  static cache *cachep;
29642
29643      /* whether proxy module is available or not */
29644  static int proxy_available;
29645
29646
29647  /*
29648  ** +-------------------------------------------------+
29649  ** |                                                 |
29650  ** |          configuration directive handling       |
29651  ** |                                                 |
29652  ** +-------------------------------------------------+
29653  */
29654
29655  /*
29656  **
29657  ** per-server configuration structure handling
29658  **
29659  */
29660
29661  static void *config_server_create(pool *p,
29662      server_rec *s)
29663  {
29664      rewrite_server_conf *a;
29665
29666      a = (rewrite_server_conf *)ap_pcalloc(p,
29667          sizeof(rewrite_server_conf));
29668
29669      a->state        = ENGINE_DISABLED;
29670      a->options      = OPTION_NONE;
```

```
29671      a->rewritelogfile  = NULL;
29672      a->rewritelogfp    = -1;
29673      a->rewriteloglevel = 0;
29674      a->rewritelockfile = NULL;
29675      a->rewritelockfp   = -1;
29676      a->rewritemaps     =
29677          ap_make_array(p, 2, sizeof(rewritemap_entry));
29678      a->rewriteconds    =
29679          ap_make_array(p, 2, sizeof(rewritecond_entry));
29680      a->rewriterules    =
29681          ap_make_array(p, 2, sizeof(rewriterule_entry));
29682      a->server          = s;
29683
29684      return (void *)a;
29685  }
29686
29687  static void *config_server_merge(pool *p, void
29688      *basev, void *overridesv)
29689  {
29690      rewrite_server_conf *a, *base, *overrides;
29691
29692      a         = (rewrite_server_conf *)ap_pcalloc(p,
29693          sizeof(rewrite_server_conf));
29694      base      = (rewrite_server_conf *)basev;
29695      overrides = (rewrite_server_conf *)overridesv;
29696
29697      a->state   = overrides->state;
29698      a->options = overrides->options;
29699      a->server  = overrides->server;
29700
29701      if (a->options & OPTION_INHERIT) {
29702          /*
29703           *  local directives override
29704           *  and anything else is inherited
29705           */
29706          a->rewriteloglevel =
29707                  overrides->rewriteloglevel != 0
29708                      ? overrides->rewriteloglevel
29709                        : base->rewriteloglevel;
29710          a->rewritelogfile =
29711                  overrides->rewritelogfile != NULL
29712                      ? overrides->rewritelogfile
29713                        : base->rewritelogfile;
29714          a->rewritelogfp  =
29715                  overrides->rewritelogfp != -1
29716                      ? overrides->rewritelogfp
29717                        : base->rewritelogfp;
29718          a->rewritelockfile =
29719                  overrides->rewritelockfile != NULL
29720                      ? overrides->rewritelockfile
29721                        : base->rewritelockfile;
29722          a->rewritelockfp   =
29723                  overrides->rewritelockfp != -1
29724                      ? overrides->rewritelockfp
29725                        : base->rewritelockfp;
29726          a->rewritemaps     = ap_append_arrays(p,
29727                  overrides->rewritemaps,
29728                              base->rewritemaps);
29729          a->rewriteconds    = ap_append_arrays(p,
29730                  overrides->rewriteconds,
29731                              base->rewriteconds);
29732          a->rewriterules    = ap_append_arrays(p,
29733                  overrides->rewriterules,
29734                              base->rewriterules);
29735      }
29736      else {
29737          /*
29738           *  local directives override
29739           *  and anything else gets defaults
29740           */
29741          a->rewriteloglevel = overrides->rewriteloglevel;
29742          a->rewritelogfile  = overrides->rewritelogfile;
29743          a->rewritelogfp    = overrides->rewritelogfp;
29744          a->rewritelockfile = overrides->rewritelockfile;
29745          a->rewritelockfp   = overrides->rewritelockfp;
29746          a->rewritemaps     = overrides->rewritemaps;
29747          a->rewriteconds    = overrides->rewriteconds;
29748          a->rewriterules    = overrides->rewriterules;
29749      }
29750
29751      return (void *)a;
29752  }
29753
29754
29755  /*
29756  **
29757  **  per-directory configuration structure handling
29758  **
29759  */
29760
29761  static void *config_perdir_create(pool *p, char *path)
29762  {
29763      rewrite_perdir_conf *a;
29764
29765      a = (rewrite_perdir_conf *)ap_pcalloc(p,
29766          sizeof(rewrite_perdir_conf));
```

```
29767
29768        a->state           = ENGINE_DISABLED;
29769        a->options         = OPTION_NONE;
29770        a->baseurl         = NULL;
29771        a->rewriteconds    = ap_make_array(p, 2,
29772            sizeof(rewritecond_entry));
29773        a->rewriterules    = ap_make_array(p, 2,
29774            sizeof(rewriterule_entry));
29775
29776        if (path == NULL) {
29777            a->directory = NULL;
29778        }
29779        else {
29780            /* make sure it has a trailing slash */
29781            if (path[strlen(path)-1] == '/') {
29782                a->directory = ap_pstrdup(p, path);
29783            }
29784            else {
29785              a->directory = ap_pstrcat(p, path, "/", NULL);
29786            }
29787        }
29788
29789        return (void *)a;
29790    }
29791
29792    static void *config_perdir_merge(pool *p, void
29793        *basev, void *overridesv)
29794    {
29795        rewrite_perdir_conf *a, *base, *overrides;
29796
29797        a        = (rewrite_perdir_conf *)ap_pcalloc(p,
29798                        sizeof(rewrite_perdir_conf));
29799        base     = (rewrite_perdir_conf *)basev;
29800        overrides = (rewrite_perdir_conf *)overridesv;
29801
29802        a->state     = overrides->state;
29803        a->options   = overrides->options;
29804        a->directory = overrides->directory;
29805        a->baseurl   = overrides->baseurl;
29806
29807        if (a->options & OPTION_INHERIT) {
29808            a->rewriteconds = ap_append_arrays(p,
29809              overrides->rewriteconds,
29810                              base->rewriteconds);
29811            a->rewriterules =
29812              ap_append_arrays(p, overrides->rewriterules,
29813                              base->rewriterules);
29814        }
```

```
29815        else {
29816            a->rewriteconds = overrides->rewriteconds;
29817            a->rewriterules = overrides->rewriterules;
29818        }
29819
29820        return (void *)a;
29821    }
29822
29823
29824    /*
29825    **
29826    **   the configuration commands
29827    **
29828    */
29829
29830    static const char *cmd_rewriteengine(cmd_parms *cmd,
29831                    rewrite_perdir_conf *dconf, int flag)
29832    {
29833        rewrite_server_conf *sconf;
29834
29835        sconf =
29836            (rewrite_server_conf *)ap_get_module_config
29837                (cmd->server->module_config,
29838                                &rewrite_module);
29839
29840        if (cmd->path == NULL) { /* is server command */
29841            sconf->state =
29842                (flag ? ENGINE_ENABLED : ENGINE_DISABLED);
29843
29844        }
29845        else                    /* is per-directory command */ {
29846            dconf->state = (flag ? ENGINE_ENABLED :
29847                ENGINE_DISABLED);
29848        }
29849
29850        return NULL;
29851    }
29852
29853    static const char *cmd_rewriteoptions(cmd_parms *cmd,
29854                    rewrite_perdir_conf *dconf, char *option)
29855    {
29856        rewrite_server_conf *sconf;
29857        const char *err;
29858
29859        sconf = (rewrite_server_conf *)
29860            ap_get_module_config(cmd->server->module_config,
29861                &rewrite_module);
29862
```

```
29863        if (cmd->path == NULL) { /* is server command */
29864            err = cmd_rewriteoptions_setoption(cmd->pool,
29865                                    &(sconf->options), option);
29866        }
29867        else {                      /* is per-directory command */
29868            err = cmd_rewriteoptions_setoption(cmd->pool,
29869                                    &(dconf->options), option);
29870        }
29871
29872        return err;
29873    }
29874
29875    static const char *cmd_rewriteoptions_setoption(pool
29876        *p, int *options,
29877                                            char *name)
29878    {
29879        if (strcasecmp(name, "inherit") == 0) {
29880            *options |= OPTION_INHERIT;
29881        }
29882        else {
29883            return ap_pstrcat(p, "RewriteOptions:
29884                    unknown option '",
29885                                name, "'\n", NULL);
29886        }
29887        return NULL;
29888    }
29889
29890    static const char *cmd_rewritelog(cmd_parms *cmd,
29891        void *dconf, char *a1)
29892    {
29893        rewrite_server_conf *sconf;
29894
29895        sconf = (rewrite_server_conf *)
29896            ap_get_module_config(cmd->server->module_config,
29897                    &rewrite_module);
29898
29899        sconf->rewritelogfile = a1;
29900
29901
29902        return NULL;
29903    }
29904
29905    static const char *cmd_rewriteloglevel(cmd_parms *cmd,
29906        void *dconf, char *a1)
29907    {
29908        rewrite_server_conf *sconf;
29909
29910        sconf = (rewrite_server_conf *)
29911            ap_get_module_config(cmd->server->module_config,
29912                    &rewrite_module);
29913
29914        sconf->rewriteloglevel = atoi(a1);
29915
29916        return NULL;
29917    }
29918
29919    static const char *cmd_rewritemap(cmd_parms *cmd,
29920        void *dconf, char *a1,
29921                                        char *a2)
29922    {
29923        rewrite_server_conf *sconf;
29924        rewritemap_entry *new;
29925        struct stat st;
29926
29927        sconf = (rewrite_server_conf *)
29928            ap_get_module_config(cmd->server->module_config,
29929                    &rewrite_module);
29930
29931        new = ap_push_array(sconf->rewritemaps);
29932
29933        new->name = a1;
29934        new->func = NULL;
29935        if (strncmp(a2, "txt:", 4) == 0) {
29936            new->type      = MAPTYPE_TXT;
29937            new->datafile  = a2+4;
29938            new->checkfile = a2+4;
29939        }
29940        else if (strncmp(a2, "rnd:", 4) == 0) {
29941            new->type      = MAPTYPE_RND;
29942            new->datafile  = a2+4;
29943            new->checkfile = a2+4;
29944        }
29945        else if (strncmp(a2, "dbm:", 4) == 0) {
29946 #ifndef NO_DBM_REWRITEMAP
29947            new->type      = MAPTYPE_DBM;
29948            new->datafile  = a2+4;
29949            new->checkfile = ap_pstrcat(cmd->pool, a2+4,
29950                    NDBM_FILE_SUFFIX, NULL);
29951 #else
29952            return ap_pstrdup(cmd->pool, "RewriteMap:
29953                    cannot use NDBM mapfile, "
29954                    "because no NDBM support is compiled in");
29955 #endif
29956        }
29957        else if (strncmp(a2, "prg:", 4) == 0) {
29958
```

```
29959            new->type = MAPTYPE_PRG;
29960            new->datafile = a2+4;
29961            new->checkfile = a2+4;
29962        }
29963        else if (strncmp(a2, "int:", 4) == 0) {
29964            new->type      = MAPTYPE_INT;
29965            new->datafile  = NULL;
29966            new->checkfile = NULL;
29967            if (strcmp(a2+4, "tolower") == 0) {
29968                new->func = rewrite_mapfunc_tolower;
29969            }
29970            else if (strcmp(a2+4, "toupper") == 0) {
29971                new->func = rewrite_mapfunc_toupper;
29972            }
29973            else if (strcmp(a2+4, "escape") == 0) {
29974                new->func = rewrite_mapfunc_escape;
29975            }
29976            else if (strcmp(a2+4, "unescape") == 0) {
29977                new->func = rewrite_mapfunc_unescape;
29978            }
29979            else if (sconf->state == ENGINE_ENABLED) {
29980                return ap_pstrcat(cmd->pool, "RewriteMap:
29981                        internal map not found:",
29982                                a2+4, NULL);
29983            }
29984        }
29985        else {
29986            new->type      = MAPTYPE_TXT;
29987            new->datafile  = a2;
29988            new->checkfile = a2;
29989        }
29990        new->fpin  = -1;
29991        new->fpout = -1;
29992
29993        if (new->checkfile &&
29994            (sconf->state == ENGINE_ENABLED)
29995            && (stat(new->checkfile, &st) == -1)) {
29996            return ap_pstrcat(cmd->pool,
29997                        "RewriteMap: map file or program
29998                            not found:",
29999                        new->checkfile, NULL);
30000        }
30001
30002        return NULL;
30003    }
30004
30005    static const char *cmd_rewritelock(cmd_parms *cmd,
30006            void *dconf, char *a1)
30007    {
30008        rewrite_server_conf *sconf;
30009
30010        sconf = (rewrite_server_conf *)
30011            ap_get_module_config(cmd->server->module_config,
30012                    &rewrite_module);
30013
30014        sconf->rewritelockfile = a1;
30015
30016        return NULL;
30017    }
30018
30019    static const char *cmd_rewritebase(cmd_parms *cmd,
30020        rewrite_perdir_conf *dconf,
30021                                char *a1)
30022    {
30023        if (cmd->path == NULL || dconf == NULL) {
30024            return "RewriteBase: only valid in per-directory
30025                    config files";
30026        }
30027        if (a1[0] == '\0') {
30028            return "RewriteBase: empty URL not allowed";
30029        }
30030        if (a1[0] != '/') {
30031            return "RewriteBase: argument is not a valid URL";
30032        }
30033
30034        dconf->baseurl = a1;
30035
30036        return NULL;
30037    }
30038
30039    static const char *cmd_rewritecond(cmd_parms *cmd,
30040        rewrite_perdir_conf *dconf,
30041
30042                                char *str)
30043    {
30044        rewrite_server_conf *sconf;
30045        rewritecond_entry *new;
30046        regex_t *regexp;
30047        char *a1;
30048        char *a2;
30049        char *a3;
30050        char *cp;
30051        const char *err;
30052        int rc;
30053
30054        sconf = (rewrite_server_conf *)
```

```
30055              ap_get_module_config(cmd->server->module_config,
30056                       &rewrite_module);
30057
30058      /*  make a new entry in the internal temporary
30059       * rewrite rule list */
30060      if (cmd->path == NULL) {     /* is server command */
30061          new = ap_push_array(sconf->rewriteconds);
30062      }
30063      else {                       /* is per-directory command */
30064          new = ap_push_array(dconf->rewriteconds);
30065      }
30066
30067      /*  parse the argument line ourself */
30068      if (parseargline(str, &a1, &a2, &a3)) {
30069          return ap_pstrcat(cmd->pool, "RewriteCond:
30070                    bad argument line '", str,
30071                          "'\n", NULL);
30072      }
30073
30074      /*  arg1: the input string */
30075      new->input = ap_pstrdup(cmd->pool, a1);
30076
30077      /* arg3: optional flags field
30078      (this have to be first parsed, because we need to
30079      know if the regex should be compiled with ICASE!) */
30080      new->flags = CONDFLAG_NONE;
30081      if (a3 != NULL) {
30082          if ((err =
30083          cmd_rewritecond_parseflagfield(cmd->pool, new,
30084                                         a3)) != NULL) {
30085              return err;
30086          }
30087      }
30088
30089      /*  arg2: the pattern
30090          try to compile the regexp to test if is ok */
30091      cp = a2;
30092      if (cp[0] == '!') {
30093          new->flags |= CONDFLAG_NOTMATCH;
30094          cp++;
30095      }
30096
30097      /* now be careful: Under the POSIX regex library
30098         we can compile the pattern for case-insensitive
30099         matching, under the old V8 library we
30100         have to do it self via a hack */
30101      if (new->flags & CONDFLAG_NOCASE) {
30102          rc = ((regexp = ap_pregcomp(cmd->pool, cp,
30103                      REG_EXTENDED|REG_ICASE))
30104                  == NULL);
30105      }
30106      else {
30107          rc = ((regexp = ap_pregcomp(cmd->pool, cp,
30108                  REG_EXTENDED)) == NULL);
30109      }
30110      if (rc) {
30111          return ap_pstrcat(cmd->pool,
30112                      "RewriteCond: cannot compile
30113                          regular expression '",
30114                      a2, "'\n", NULL);
30115      }
30116
30117      new->pattern = ap_pstrdup(cmd->pool, cp);
30118      new->regexp  = regexp;
30119
30120      return NULL;
30121  }
30122
30123  static const char
30124      *cmd_rewritecond_parseflagfield(pool *p,
30125                                      rewritecond_entry *cfg,
30126                                                char *str)
30127  {
30128      char *cp;
30129      char *cp1;
30130      char *cp2;
30131      char *cp3;
30132      char *key;
30133      char *val;
30134      const char *err;
30135
30136      if (str[0] != '[' || str[strlen(str)-1] != ']') {
30137          return "RewriteCond: bad flag delimiters";
30138      }
30139
30140      cp = str+1;
30141      str[strlen(str)-1] = ','; /* for simpler parsing */
30142      for ( ; *cp != '\0'; ) {
30143          /* skip whitespaces */
30144          for ( ; (*cp == ' ' || *cp == '\t')
30145                  && *cp != '\0'; cp++)
30146              ;
30147          if (*cp == '\0') {
30148              break;
30149          }
30150          cp1 = cp;
```

```
30151          if ((cp2 = strchr(cp, ',')) != NULL) {
30152              cp = cp2+1;
30153              for ( ; (*(cp2-1) == ' '
30154                      || *(cp2-1) == '\t'); cp2--)
30155                  ;
30156              *cp2 = '\0';
30157              if ((cp3 = strchr(cp1, '=')) != NULL) {
30158                  *cp3 = '\0';
30159                  key = cp1;
30160                  val = cp3+1;
30161              }
30162              else {
30163                  key = cp1;
30164                  val = "";
30165              }
30166              if ((err = cmd_rewritecond_setflag(p, cfg,
30167                      key, val)) != NULL) {
30168                  return err;
30169              }
30170          }
30171          else {
30172              break;
30173          }
30174      }
30175
30176      return NULL;
30177  }
30178
30179  static const char *cmd_rewritecond_setflag(pool *p,
30180      rewritecond_entry *cfg,
30181                              char *key, char *val)
30182  {
30183      if (  strcasecmp(key, "nocase") == 0
30184         || strcasecmp(key, "NC") == 0     ) {
30185          cfg->flags |= CONDFLAG_NOCASE;
30186      }
30187      else if (  strcasecmp(key, "ornext") == 0
30188              || strcasecmp(key, "OR") == 0    ) {
30189          cfg->flags |= CONDFLAG_ORNEXT;
30190      }
30191      else {
30192          return ap_pstrcat(p, "RewriteCond: unknown
30193              flag '", key, "'\n", NULL);
30194      }
30195      return NULL;
30196  }
30197
30198  static const char *cmd_rewriterule(cmd_parms *cmd,
30199          rewrite_perdir_conf *dconf,
30200                              char *str)
30201  {
30202      rewrite_server_conf *sconf;
30203      rewriterule_entry *new;
30204      regex_t *regexp;
30205      char *a1;
30206      char *a2;
30207      char *a3;
30208      char *cp;
30209      const char *err;
30210      int mode;
30211
30212      sconf = (rewrite_server_conf *)
30213          ap_get_module_config(cmd->server->module_config,
30214              &rewrite_module);
30215
30216      /*  make a new entry in the internal
30217       * rewrite rule list */
30218      if (cmd->path == NULL) {    /* is server command */
30219          new = ap_push_array(sconf->rewriterules);
30220      }
30221      else {                     /* is per-directory command */
30222          new = ap_push_array(dconf->rewriterules);
30223      }
30224
30225      /*  parse the argument line ourself */
30226      if (parseargline(str, &a1, &a2, &a3)) {
30227          return ap_pstrcat(cmd->pool, "RewriteRule:
30228              bad argument line '", str,
30229              "'\n", NULL);
30230      }
30231
30232      /* arg3: optional flags field */
30233      new->forced_mimetype     = NULL;
30234      new->forced_responsecode = HTTP_MOVED_TEMPORARILY;
30235      new->flags  = RULEFLAG_NONE;
30236      new->env[0] = NULL;
30237      new->skip   = 0;
30238      if (a3 != NULL) {
30239          if ((err =
30240              cmd_rewriterule_parseflagfield(cmd->pool, new,
30241                                  a3)) != NULL) {
30242              return err;
30243          }
30244      }
30245
30246      /*  arg1: the pattern
```

```
30247          *  try to compile the regexp to test if is ok
30248          */
30249         cp = a1;
30250         if (cp[0] == '!') {
30251             new->flags |= RULEFLAG_NOTMATCH;
30252             cp++;
30253         }
30254         mode = REG_EXTENDED;
30255         if (new->flags & RULEFLAG_NOCASE) {
30256             mode |= REG_ICASE;
30257         }
30258         if ((regexp = ap_pregcomp(cmd->pool, cp,
30259               mode)) == NULL) {
30260             return ap_pstrcat(cmd->pool,
30261                           "RewriteRule: cannot compile
30262                            regular expression '",
30263                           a1, "'\n", NULL);
30264         }
30265         new->pattern = ap_pstrdup(cmd->pool, cp);
30266         new->regexp  = regexp;
30267
30268         /*  arg2: the output string
30269          *  replace the $<N> by \<n> which is needed by the
30270          *  currently used Regular Expression library
30271          */
30272         new->output = ap_pstrdup(cmd->pool, a2);
30273
30274         /*  now, if the server or per-dir config holds an
30275          * array of RewriteCond entries, we take it for us
30276          * and clear the array
30277          */
30278         if (cmd->path == NULL) {   /* is server command */
30279             new->rewriteconds  = sconf->rewriteconds;
30280             sconf->rewriteconds = ap_make_array(cmd->pool, 2,
30281                             sizeof(rewritecond_entry));
30282         }
30283         else {                    /* is per-directory command */
30284             new->rewriteconds  = dconf->rewriteconds;
30285             dconf->rewriteconds = ap_make_array(cmd->pool, 2,
30286                             sizeof(rewritecond_entry));
30287         }
30288
30289         return NULL;
30290 }
30291
30292 static const
30293     char *cmd_rewriterule_parseflagfield(pool *p,
30294                             rewriterule_entry *cfg,
30295                                               char *str)
30296 {
30297     char *cp;
30298     char *cp1;
30299     char *cp2;
30300     char *cp3;
30301     char *key;
30302     char *val;
30303     const char *err;
30304
30305     if (str[0] != '[' || str[strlen(str)-1] != ']') {
30306         return "RewriteRule: bad flag delimiters";
30307     }
30308
30309     cp = str+1;
30310     str[strlen(str)-1] = ','; /* for simpler parsing */
30311     for ( ; *cp != '\0'; ) {
30312         /* skip whitespaces */
30313         for ( ; (*cp == ' ' || *cp == '\t')
30314               && *cp != '\0'; cp++)
30315             ;
30316         if (*cp == '\0') {
30317             break;
30318         }
30319         cp1 = cp;
30320         if ((cp2 = strchr(cp, ',')) != NULL) {
30321             cp = cp2+1;
30322             for ( ; (*(cp2-1) == ' ' || *(cp2-1)
30323               == '\t'); cp2--)
30324                 ;
30325             *cp2 = '\0';
30326             if ((cp3 = strchr(cp1, '=')) != NULL) {
30327                 *cp3 = '\0';
30328                 key = cp1;
30329                 val = cp3+1;
30330             }
30331             else {
30332                 key = cp1;
30333                 val = "";
30334             }
30335             if ((err = cmd_rewriterule_setflag(p, cfg,
30336                 key, val)) != NULL) {
30337                 return err;
30338             }
30339         }
30340         else {
30341             break;
30342         }
```

```
30343          }
30344
30345          return NULL;
30346  }
30347
30348  static const char *cmd_rewriterule_setflag(pool *p,
30349              rewriterule_entry *cfg,
30350
30351                                      char *key, char *val)
30352  {
30353      int status = 0;
30354      int i;
30355
30356      if (   strcasecmp(key, "redirect") == 0
30357          || strcasecmp(key, "R") == 0          ) {
30358          cfg->flags |= RULEFLAG_FORCEREDIRECT;
30359          if (strlen(val) > 0) {
30360              if (strcasecmp(val, "permanent") == 0) {
30361                  status = HTTP_MOVED_PERMANENTLY;
30362              }
30363              else if (strcasecmp(val, "temp") == 0) {
30364                  status = HTTP_MOVED_TEMPORARILY;
30365              }
30366              else if (strcasecmp(val, "seeother") == 0) {
30367                  status = HTTP_SEE_OTHER;
30368              }
30369              else if (ap_isdigit(*val)) {
30370                  status = atoi(val);
30371              }
30372              if (!ap_is_HTTP_REDIRECT(status)) {
30373                  return "RewriteRule: invalid HTTP
30374                      response code "
30375                          "for flag 'R'";
30376              }
30377              cfg->forced_responsecode = status;
30378          }
30379      }
30380      else if (   strcasecmp(key, "last") == 0
30381              || strcasecmp(key, "L") == 0  ) {
30382          cfg->flags |= RULEFLAG_LASTRULE;
30383      }
30384      else if (   strcasecmp(key, "next") == 0
30385              || strcasecmp(key, "N") == 0    ) {
30386          cfg->flags |= RULEFLAG_NEWROUND;
30387      }
30388      else if (   strcasecmp(key, "chain") == 0
30389              || strcasecmp(key, "C") == 0    ) {
30390          cfg->flags |= RULEFLAG_CHAIN;
30391      }
30392      else if (   strcasecmp(key, "type") == 0
30393              || strcasecmp(key, "T") == 0    ) {
30394          cfg->forced_mimetype = ap_pstrdup(p, val);
30395          ap_str_tolower(cfg->forced_mimetype);
30396      }
30397      else if (   strcasecmp(key, "env") == 0
30398              || strcasecmp(key, "E") == 0    ) {
30399          for (i = 0; (cfg->env[i] != NULL)
30400                  && (i < MAX_ENV_FLAGS); i++)
30401              ;
30402          if (i < MAX_ENV_FLAGS) {
30403              cfg->env[i] = ap_pstrdup(p, val);
30404              cfg->env[i+1] = NULL;
30405          }
30406          else {
30407              return "RewriteRule: too many environment
30408                  flags 'E'";
30409          }
30410      }
30411      else if (   strcasecmp(key, "nosubreq") == 0
30412              || strcasecmp(key, "NS") == 0      ) {
30413          cfg->flags |= RULEFLAG_IGNOREONSUBREQ;
30414      }
30415      else if (   strcasecmp(key, "proxy") == 0
30416              || strcasecmp(key, "P") == 0      ) {
30417          cfg->flags |= RULEFLAG_PROXY;
30418      }
30419      else if (   strcasecmp(key, "passthrough") == 0
30420              || strcasecmp(key, "PT") == 0      ) {
30421          cfg->flags |= RULEFLAG_PASSTHROUGH;
30422      }
30423      else if (   strcasecmp(key, "skip") == 0
30424              || strcasecmp(key, "S") == 0  ) {
30425          cfg->skip = atoi(val);
30426      }
30427      else if (   strcasecmp(key, "forbidden") == 0
30428              || strcasecmp(key, "F") == 0  ) {
30429          cfg->flags |= RULEFLAG_FORBIDDEN;
30430      }
30431      else if (   strcasecmp(key, "gone") == 0
30432              || strcasecmp(key, "G") == 0  ) {
30433          cfg->flags |= RULEFLAG_GONE;
30434      }
30435      else if (   strcasecmp(key, "qsappend") == 0
30436              || strcasecmp(key, "QSA") == 0  ) {
30437          cfg->flags |= RULEFLAG_QSAPPEND;
30438      }
```

```
30439        else if (   strcasecmp(key, "nocase") == 0
30440                 || strcasecmp(key, "NC") == 0     ) {
30441            cfg->flags |= RULEFLAG_NOCASE;
30442        }
30443        else {
30444            return ap_pstrcat(p, "RewriteRule: unknown
30445                  flag '", key, "'\n", NULL);
30446        }
30447        return NULL;
30448    }
30449
30450
30451    /*
30452    **
30453    **  Global Module Initialization
30454    **  [called from read_config() after all
30455    **  config commands were already called]
30456    **
30457    */
30458
30459    static void init_module(server_rec *s, pool *p)
30460    {
30461        /* check if proxy module is available */
30462        proxy_available =
30463            (ap_find_linked_module("mod_proxy.c") != NULL);
30464
30465        /* create the rewriting lockfile in the parent */
30466        rewritelock_create(s, p);
30467        ap_register_cleanup(p, (void *)s,
30468              rewritelock_remove, ap_null_cleanup);
30469
30470        /* step through the servers and
30471         * - open each rewriting logfile
30472         * - open the RewriteMap prg:xxx programs
30473         */
30474        for (; s; s = s->next) {
30475            open_rewritelog(s, p);
30476            run_rewritemap_programs(s, p);
30477        }
30478    }
30479
30480
30481    /*
30482    **
30483    **  Per-Child Module Initialization
30484    **  [called after a child process is spawned]
30485    **
30486    */
```

```
30487
30488    static void init_child(server_rec *s, pool *p)
30489    {
30490        /* open the rewriting lockfile */
30491        rewritelock_open(s, p);
30492
30493        /* create the lookup cache */
30494        cachep = init_cache(p);
30495    }
30496
30497
30498    /*
30499    ** +-------------------------------------------------+
30500    ** |                                                 |
30501    ** |                 runtime hooks                   |
30502    ** |                                                 |
30503    ** +-------------------------------------------------+
30504    */
30505
30506    /*
30507    **
30508    **  URI-to-filename hook
30509    **
30510    **  [used for the rewriting engine triggered by
30511    **  the per-server 'RewriteRule' directives]
30512    **
30513    */
30514
30515    static int hook_uri2file(request_rec *r)
30516    {
30517        void *sconf;
30518        rewrite_server_conf *conf;
30519        const char *var;
30520        const char *thisserver;
30521        char *thisport;
30522        const char *thisurl;
30523        char buf[512];
30524        char docroot[512];
30525        char *cp, *cp2;
30526        const char *ccp;
30527        struct stat finfo;
30528        unsigned int port;
30529        int n;
30530        int l;
30531
30532        /*
30533         *  retrieve the config structures
30534         */
```

```
30535        sconf = r->server->module_config;
30536        conf  = (rewrite_server_conf *)
30537         ap_get_module_config(sconf,
30538                                          &rewrite_module);
30539
30540        /*
30541         *  only do something under runtime if the engine
30542         *  is really enabled,else return immediately!
30543         */
30544        if (conf->state == ENGINE_DISABLED) {
30545            return DECLINED;
30546        }
30547
30548        /*
30549         *  check for the ugly API case of a virtual host
30550         *  section where no mod_rewrite directives exists.
30551         *  In this situation we became no chance by the
30552         *  API to setup our default per-server config so
30553         *  we have to on-the-fly assume we have the
30554         *  default config. But because the default
30555         *  config has a disabled rewriting engine we are
30556         *  lucky because can just stop operating now.
30557         */
30558        if (conf->server != r->server) {
30559            return DECLINED;
30560        }
30561
30562        /*
30563         *  add the SCRIPT_URL variable to the env. this
30564         *  is a bit complicated due to the fact that apache
30565         *  uses subrequests and internal redirects
30566         */
30567
30568        if (r->main == NULL) {
30569            var = ap_pstrcat(r->pool, "REDIRECT_",
30570                    ENVVAR_SCRIPT_URL, NULL);
30571            var = ap_table_get(r->subprocess_env, var);
30572            if (var == NULL) {
30573                ap_table_setn(r->subprocess_env,
30574                    ENVVAR_SCRIPT_URL, r->uri);
30575            }
30576            else {
30577                ap_table_setn(r->subprocess_env,
30578                    ENVVAR_SCRIPT_URL, var);
30579            }
30580        }
30581        else {
30582            var = ap_table_get(r->main->subprocess_env,
30583                    ENVVAR_SCRIPT_URL);
30584            ap_table_setn(r->subprocess_env,
30585                    ENVVAR_SCRIPT_URL, var);
30586        }
30587
30588        /*
30589         *  create the SCRIPT_URI variable for the env
30590         */
30591
30592        /* add the canonical URI of this URL */
30593        thisserver = ap_get_server_name(r);
30594        port = ap_get_server_port(r);
30595        if (ap_is_default_port(port, r)) {
30596            thisport = "";
30597        }
30598        else {
30599            ap_snprintf(buf, sizeof(buf), ":%u", port);
30600            thisport = buf;
30601        }
30602        thisurl = ap_table_get(r->subprocess_env,
30603            ENVVAR_SCRIPT_URL);
30604
30605        /* set the variable */
30606        var = ap_pstrcat(r->pool, ap_http_method(r), "://",
30607            thisserver, thisport,
30608                      thisurl, NULL);
30609        ap_table_setn(r->subprocess_env,
30610            ENVVAR_SCRIPT_URI, var);
30611
30612        /* if filename was not initially set,
30613         * we start with the requested URI
30614         */
30615        if (r->filename == NULL) {
30616            r->filename = ap_pstrdup(r->pool, r->uri);
30617            rewritelog(r, 2, "init rewrite engine with
30618                    requested uri %s",
30619                          r->filename);
30620        }
30621
30622        /*
30623         *  now apply the rules ...
30624         */
30625        if (apply_rewrite_list(r,
30626            conf->rewriterules, NULL)) {
30627
30628            if (strlen(r->filename) > 6 &&
30629                strncmp(r->filename, "proxy:", 6) == 0) {
30630                /* it should be go on as an internal
```

```
30631            * proxy request */
30632
30633           /* check if the proxy module is enabled, so
30634            * we can actually use it!
30635            */
30636           if (!proxy_available) {
30637               ap_log_rerror(APLOG_MARK,
30638                   APLOG_NOERRNO|APLOG_ERR, r,
30639                       "attempt to make remote request
30640                           from mod_rewrite "
30641                       "without proxy enabled: %s",
30642                           r->filename);
30643               return FORBIDDEN;
30644           }
30645
30646           /* make sure the QUERY_STRING and
30647            * PATH_INFO parts get incorporated
30648            */
30649           if (r->path_info != NULL) {
30650               r->filename = ap_pstrcat(r->pool,
30651                   r->filename,
30652                           r->path_info, NULL);
30653           }
30654           if (r->args != NULL &&
30655               r->uri == r->unparsed_uri) {
30656               /* see proxy_http:proxy_http_canon() */
30657               r->filename = ap_pstrcat(r->pool,
30658                   r->filename,
30659                           "?", r->args, NULL);
30660           }
30661
30662           /* now make sure the request gets handled by
30663            * the proxy handler */
30664           r->proxyreq = 1;
30665           r->handler  = "proxy-server";
30666
30667           rewritelog(r, 1, "go-ahead with proxy
30668               request %s [OK]",
30669                   r->filename);
30670           return OK;
30671       }
30672       else if (  (strlen(r->filename) > 7 &&
30673                   strncasecmp(r->filename, "http://",
30674                       7) == 0)
30675               || (strlen(r->filename) > 8 &&
30676                   strncasecmp(r->filename, "https://",
30677                       8) == 0)
30678               || (strlen(r->filename) > 9 &&
30679
30680                   strncasecmp(r->filename, "gopher://",
30681                       9) == 0)
30682               || (strlen(r->filename) > 6 &&
30683                   strncasecmp(r->filename, "ftp://",
30684                       6) == 0)    ) {
30685   /* it was finally rewritten to a remote URL */
30686
30687       /* skip 'scheme:' */
30688       for (cp = r->filename; *cp != ':'
30689           && *cp != '\0'; cp++)
30690           ;
30691       /* skip '://' */
30692       cp += 3;
30693       /* skip host part */
30694       for ( ; *cp != '/' && *cp != '\0'; cp++)
30695           ;
30696       if (*cp != '\0') {
30697           rewritelog(r, 1, "escaping %s for
30698               redirect", r->filename);
30699           cp2 = ap_escape_uri(r->pool, cp);
30700           *cp = '\0';
30701           r->filename = ap_pstrcat(r->pool,
30702               r->filename, cp2, NULL);
30703       }
30704
30705       /* append the QUERY_STRING part */
30706       if (r->args != NULL) {
30707           r->filename = ap_pstrcat(r->pool,
30708               r->filename,
30709                       "?", r->args, NULL);
30710       }
30711
30712       /* determine HTTP redirect response code */
30713       if (ap_is_HTTP_REDIRECT(r->status)) {
30714           n = r->status;
30715           r->status = HTTP_OK;
30716           /* make Apache kernel happy */
30717       }
30718       else {
30719           n = REDIRECT;
30720       }
30721
30722       /* now do the redirection */
30723       ap_table_setn(r->headers_out, "Location",
30724           r->filename);
30725       rewritelog(r, 1, "redirect to %s
30726           [REDIRECT/%d]", r->filename, n);
```

```
30727              return n;
30728          }
30729      else if (strlen(r->filename) > 10 &&
30730              strncmp(r->filename, "forbidden:",
30731              10) == 0) {
30732          /* This URLs is forced to be forbidden for
30733           * the requester */
30734          return FORBIDDEN;
30735      }
30736      else if (strlen(r->filename) > 5 &&
30737              strncmp(r->filename, "gone:", 5) == 0) {
30738          /* This URLs is forced to be gone */
30739          return HTTP_GONE;
30740      }
30741      else if (strlen(r->filename) > 12 &&
30742              strncmp(r->filename, "passthrough:", 12) == 0) {
30743          /*
30744           * Hack because of underpowered API: passing
30745           * the current rewritten filename through
30746           * to other URL-to-filename handlers
30747           * just as it were the requested URL. This
30748           * is to enable post-processing by
30749           * mod_alias, etc.  which always act on
30750           * r->uri! The difference here is: We do
30751           * not try to add the document root
30752           */
30753          r->uri = ap_pstrdup(r->pool, r->filename+12);
30754          return DECLINED;
30755      }
30756      else {
30757          /* it was finally rewritten to a local path */
30758
30759          /* expand "/~user" prefix */
30760 #ifndef WIN32
30761          r->filename = expand_tildepaths(r,
30762              r->filename);
30763 #endif
30764          rewritelog(r, 2, "local path result: %s",
30765              r->filename);
30766
30767          /* the filename has to start with a slash! */
30768          if (r->filename[0] != '/') {
30769              return BAD_REQUEST;
30770          }
30771
30772          /* if there is no valid prefix, we have
30773           * to emulate the translator from the core and
30774           * prefix the filename with document_root
30775           *
30776           * NOTICE:
30777           * We cannot leave out the prefix_stat because
30778           * - when we always prefix with document_root
30779           *   then no absolute path can be created, e.g.
30780           *   via emulating a ScriptAlias directive, etc.
30781           * - when we always NOT prefix with document_root
30782           *   then the files under document_root have to
30783           *   be references directly and document_root
30784           *   gets never used and will be a
30785           *   dummy parameter -this is also bad
30786           *
30787           * BUT:
30788           * Under real Unix systems this is no problem,
30789           * because we only do stat() on the first
30790           * directoryand this gets cached by the
30791           * kernel for along time!
30792           */
30793          n = prefix_stat(r->filename, &finfo);
30794          if (n == 0) {
30795              if ((ccp = ap_document_root(r)) != NULL) {
30796                  l = ap_cpystrn(docroot, ccp,
30797                      sizeof(docroot)) - docroot;
30798
30799                  /* always NOT have a trailing slash */
30800                  if (docroot[l-1] == '/') {
30801                      docroot[l-1] = '\0';
30802                  }
30803                  if (r->server->path
30804                      && !strncmp(r->filename,
30805                          r->server->path,
30806                              r->server->pathlen)) {
30807                      r->filename = ap_pstrcat(r->pool,
30808                          docroot,
30809                              (r->filename +
30810                      r->server->pathlen), NULL);
30811                  }
30812                  else {
30813                      r->filename = ap_pstrcat(r->pool,
30814                          docroot,
30815                              r->filename, NULL);
30816                  }
30817                  rewritelog(r, 2, "prefixed with
30818                      document_root to %s",
30819                          r->filename);
30820              }
30821          }
30822
```

```
30823              . rewritelog(r, 1, "go-ahead with %s [OK]",
30824                          r->filename);
30825                  return OK;
30826              }
30827          }
30828          else {
30829              rewritelog(r, 1, "pass through %s", r->filename);
30830              return DECLINED;
30831          }
30832      }
30833
30834
30835      /*
30836      **
30837      **  MIME-type hook
30838      **
30839      **  [used to support the forced-MIME-type feature]
30840      **
30841      */
30842
30843      static int hook_mimetype(request_rec *r)
30844      {
30845          const char *t;
30846
30847          /* now check if we have to force a MIME-type */
30848          t = ap_table_get(r->notes,
30849              REWRITE_FORCED_MIMETYPE_NOTEVAR);
30850          if (t == NULL) {
30851              return DECLINED;
30852          }
30853          else {
30854              rewritelog(r, 1, "force filename %s to
30855                      have MIME-type '%s'",
30856                          r->filename, t);
30857              r->content_type = t;
30858              return OK;
30859          }
30860      }
30861
30862
30863      /*
30864      **
30865      **  Fixup hook
30866      **
30867      **  [used for the rewriting engine triggered by
30868      **  the per-directory 'RewriteRule' directives]
30869      **
30870      */
```

```
30871
30872      static int hook_fixup(request_rec *r)
30873      {
30874          rewrite_perdir_conf *dconf;
30875          char *cp;
30876          char *cp2;
30877          const char *ccp;
30878          char *prefix;
30879          int l;
30880          int n;
30881          char *ofilename;
30882
30883          dconf = (rewrite_perdir_conf *)
30884              ap_get_module_config(r->per_dir_config,
30885                                  &rewrite_module);
30886
30887          /* if there is no per-dir config we return
30888           * immediately */
30889          if (dconf == NULL) {
30890              return DECLINED;
30891          }
30892
30893          /* we shouldn't do anything in subrequests */
30894          if (r->main != NULL) {
30895              return DECLINED;
30896          }
30897
30898          /* if there are no real (i.e. no RewriteRule
30899           * directives!) per-dir config of us,
30900           * we return also immediately */
30901          if (dconf->directory == NULL) {
30902              return DECLINED;
30903          }
30904
30905          /*
30906           *  only do something under runtime if the engine
30907           *  is really enabled, for this directory,
30908           *  else return immediately!
30909           */
30910          if (!(ap_allow_options(r) & (OPT_SYM_LINKS |
30911              OPT_SYM_OWNER))) {
30912              /* FollowSymLinks is mandatory! */
30913              ap_log_rerror(APLOG_MARK,
30914                  APLOG_NOERRNO|APLOG_ERR, r,
30915                      "Options FollowSymLinks or
30916                          SymLinksIfOwnerMatch is off "
30917                      "which implies that RewriteRule
30918                          directive is forbidden: "
```

```
30919                     "%s", r->filename);
30920            return FORBIDDEN;
30921        }
30922        else {
30923            /* FollowSymLinks is given, but the user can
30924             * still turn off the rewriting engine
30925             */
30926            if (dconf->state == ENGINE_DISABLED) {
30927                return DECLINED;
30928            }
30929        }
30930
30931        /*
30932         *  remember the current filename before rewriting
30933         *  for later check to prevent deadlooping because
30934         *  of internal redirects on final URL/filename
30935         *  which can be equal to the inital one.
30936         */
30937        ofilename = r->filename;
30938
30939        /*
30940         *  now apply the rules ...
30941         */
30942        if (apply_rewrite_list(r, dconf->rewriterules,
30943                dconf->directory)) {
30944
30945            if (strlen(r->filename) > 6 &&
30946                    strncmp(r->filename, "proxy:", 6) == 0) {
30947                /* it should go on as an internal
30948                 * proxy request */
30949
30950                /* make sure the QUERY_STRING and
30951                 * PATH_INFO parts get incorporated
30952                 * (r->path_info was already appended by the
30953                 * rewriting engine because of the
30954                 * per-dir context!)
30955                 */
30956                if (r->args != NULL
30957                        && r->uri == r->unparsed_uri) {
30958                    /* see proxy_http:proxy_http_canon() */
30959                    r->filename = ap_pstrcat(r->pool,
30960                        r->filename,
30961                                    "?", r->args, NULL);
30962                }
30963
30964                /* now make sure the request gets handled by
30965                 * the proxy handler */
30966                r->proxyreq = 1;
```

```
30967                r->handler  = "proxy-server";
30968
30969                rewritelog(r, 1, "[per-dir %s] go-ahead with
30970                    proxy request "
30971                            "%s [OK]", dconf->directory,
30972                    r->filename);
30973                return OK;
30974        }
30975        else if (   (strlen(r->filename) > 7 &&
30976            strncmp(r->filename, "http://", 7) == 0)
30977            || (strlen(r->filename) > 8 &&
30978                strncmp(r->filename, "https://", 8) == 0)
30979            || (strlen(r->filename) > 9 &&
30980                strncmp(r->filename,
30981                    "gopher://", 9) == 0)
30982            || (strlen(r->filename) > 6 &&
30983                strncmp(r->filename,
30984                    "ftp://", 6) == 0)     ) {
30985        /* it was finally rewritten to a remote URL */
30986
30987            /* because we are in a per-dir context
30988             * first try to replace the directory with
30989             * its base-URL if there is a
30990             * base-URL available
30991             */
30992            if (dconf->baseurl != NULL) {
30993                /* skip 'scheme:' */
30994                for (cp = r->filename; *cp != ':'
30995                    && *cp != '\0'; cp++)
30996                    ;
30997                /* skip '://' */
30998                cp += 3;
30999                if ((cp = strchr(cp, '/')) != NULL) {
31000                    rewritelog(r, 2,
31001                            "[per-dir %s] trying to
31002                                replace "
31003                            "prefix %s with %s",
31004                            dconf->directory,
31005                                dconf->directory,
31006                            dconf->baseurl);
31007                    cp2 = subst_prefix_path(r, cp,
31008                        dconf->directory,
31009                                dconf->baseurl);
31010                    if (strcmp(cp2, cp) != 0) {
31011                        *cp = '\0';
31012                        r->filename = ap_pstrcat(r->pool,
31013                            r->filename,
31014                                    cp2, NULL);
```

```
31015                        }
31016                    }
31017                }
31018
31019            /* now prepare the redirect... */
31020
31021            /* skip 'scheme:' */
31022            for (cp = r->filename; *cp != ':'
31023                    && *cp != '\0'; cp++)
31024                ;
31025            /* skip '://' */
31026            cp += 3;
31027            /* skip host part */
31028            for ( ; *cp != '/' && *cp != '\0'; cp++)
31029                ;
31030            if (*cp != '\0') {
31031                rewritelog(r, 1, "[per-dir %s]
31032                    escaping %s for redirect",
31033                        dconf->directory, r->filename);
31034                cp2 = ap_escape_uri(r->pool, cp);
31035                *cp = '\0';
31036                r->filename = ap_pstrcat(r->pool,
31037                    r->filename, cp2, NULL);
31038            }
31039
31040            /* append the QUERY_STRING part */
31041            if (r->args != NULL) {
31042                r->filename = ap_pstrcat(r->pool,
31043                    r->filename,
31044                            "?", r->args, NULL);
31045            }
31046
31047            /* determine HTTP redirect response code */
31048            if (ap_is_HTTP_REDIRECT(r->status)) {
31049                n = r->status;
31050                r->status = HTTP_OK; /* make Apache
31051                    kernel happy */
31052            }
31053            else {
31054                n = REDIRECT;
31055            }
31056
31057            /* now do the redirection */
31058            ap_table_setn(r->headers_out, "Location",
31059                    r->filename);
31060            rewritelog(r, 1, "[per-dir %s] redirect to
31061                %s [REDIRECT/%d]",
31062                    dconf->directory, r->filename, n);
31063            return n;
31064        }
31065        else if (strlen(r->filename) > 10 &&
31066                strncmp(r->filename, "forbidden:",
31067                    10) == 0) {
31068            /* This URL is forced to be forbidden for
31069             * the requester */
31070            return FORBIDDEN;
31071        }
31072        else if (strlen(r->filename) > 5 &&
31073                strncmp(r->filename, "gone:", 5) == 0) {
31074            /* This URL is forced to be gone */
31075            return HTTP_GONE;
31076        }
31077        else {
31078            /* it was finally rewritten to a local path */
31079
31080            /* if someone used the PASSTHROUGH flag
31081             * in per-dir context we just ignore it. It
31082             * is only useful in per-server context
31083             */
31084            if (strlen(r->filename) > 12 &&
31085                strncmp(r->filename, "passthrough:",
31086                    12) == 0) {
31087                r->filename = ap_pstrdup(r->pool,
31088                    r->filename+12);
31089            }
31090
31091            /* the filename has to start with a slash! */
31092            if (r->filename[0] != '/') {
31093                return BAD_REQUEST;
31094            }
31095
31096            /* Check for deadlooping:
31097             * At this point we KNOW that at least one
31098             * rewriting rule was applied, but when
31099             * the resulting URL is the same as the
31100             * initial URL, we are not allowed to
31101             * use the following internal redirection
31102             * stuff because this would lead
31103             * to a deadloop.
31104             */
31105            if (strcmp(r->filename, ofilename) == 0) {
31106                rewritelog(r, 1, "[per-dir %s] initial
31107                    URL equal rewritten "
31108                        "URL: %s [IGNORING REWRITE]",
31109                        dconf->directory, r->filename);
31110                return OK;
```

```
31111              }
31112
31113              /* if there is a valid base-URL then
31114               * substitute the per-dir prefix with this
31115               * base-URL if the current filename still is
31116               * inside this per-dir context. If not then
31117               * treat the result as a plain URL
31118               */
31119              if (dconf->baseurl != NULL) {
31120                  rewritelog(r, 2,
31121                      "[per-dir %s] trying to replace
31122                              prefix %s with %s",
31123                      dconf->directory, dconf->directory,
31124                              dconf->baseurl);
31125                  r->filename = subst_prefix_path(r,
31126                      r->filename,
31127                                    dconf->directory,
31128                                    dconf->baseurl);
31129              }
31130              else {
31131                  /* if no explicit base-URL exists we
31132                   * assume that the directory prefix
31133                   * is also a valid URL for this
31134                   * webserver and only try to remove the
31135                   * document_root if it is prefix
31136                   */
31137                  if ((ccp = ap_document_root(r)) != NULL) {
31138                      prefix = ap_pstrdup(r->pool, ccp);
31139                      /* always NOT have a trailing slash */
31140                      l = strlen(prefix);
31141                      if (prefix[l-1] == '/') {
31142                          prefix[l-1] = '\0';
31143                          l--;
31144                      }
31145                      if (strncmp(r->filename, prefix,
31146                          l) == 0) {
31147                          rewritelog(r, 2,
31148                                  "[per-dir %s] strip
31149                                          document_root "
31150                                  "prefix: %s -> %s",
31151                                  dconf->directory,
31152                                      r->filename,
31153                                      r->filename+l);
31154                          r->filename = ap_pstrdup(r->pool,
31155                              r->filename+l);
31156                      }
31157                  }
31158              }
31159
31160                  /* now initiate the internal redirect */
31161                  rewritelog(r, 1, "[per-dir %s] internal
31162                          redirect with %s "
31163                          "[INTERNAL REDIRECT]",
31164                              dconf->directory, r->filename);
31165                  r->filename = ap_pstrcat(r->pool,
31166                      "redirect:", r->filename, NULL);
31167                  r->handler = "redirect-handler";
31168                  return OK;
31169              }
31170          }
31171          else {
31172              rewritelog(r, 1, "[per-dir %s] pass through %s",
31173                      dconf->directory, r->filename);
31174              return DECLINED;
31175          }
31176  }
31177
31178
31179  /*
31180  **
31181  **  Content-Handlers
31182  **
31183  **  [used for redirect support]
31184  **
31185  */
31186
31187  static int handler_redirect(request_rec *r)
31188  {
31189      /* just make sure that we are really meant! */
31190      if (strncmp(r->filename, "redirect:", 9) != 0) {
31191          return DECLINED;
31192      }
31193
31194      /* now do the internal redirect */
31195      ap_internal_redirect(ap_pstrcat(r->pool,
31196          r->filename+9,
31197              r->args ? "?" : NULL, r->args, NULL), r);
31198
31199      /* and return gracefully */
31200      return OK;
31201  }
31202
31203
31204  /*
31205  ** +---------------------------------------------------+
31206  ** |                                                   |
```

```
31207  ** |                    the rewriting engine
31208  ** |                                                        |
31209  ** +--------------------------------------------------+
31210  */
31211
31212  /*
31213   *  Apply a complete rule set,
31214   *  i.e. a list of rewrite rules
31215   */
31216  static int apply_rewrite_list(request_rec *r,
31217      array_header *rewriterules,
31218                              char *perdir)
31219  {
31220      rewriterule_entry *entries;
31221      rewriterule_entry *p;
31222      int i;
31223      int changed;
31224      int rc;
31225      int s;
31226
31227      /*
31228       *  Iterate over all existing rules
31229       */
31230      entries = (rewriterule_entry *)rewriterules->elts;
31231      changed = 0;
31232      loop:
31233      for (i = 0; i < rewriterules->nelts; i++) {
31234          p = &entries[i];
31235
31236          /*
31237           *  Ignore this rule on subrequests if we are
31238           *  explicitly asked to do so or this is a proxy-
31239           *  throughput or a forced redirect rule.
31240           */
31241          if (r->main != NULL &&
31242              (p->flags & RULEFLAG_IGNOREONSUBREQ ||
31243               p->flags & RULEFLAG_PROXY          ||
31244               p->flags & RULEFLAG_FORCEREDIRECT   )) {
31245              continue;
31246          }
31247
31248          /*
31249           *  Apply the current rule.
31250           */
31251          rc = apply_rewrite_rule(r, p, perdir);
31252          if (rc) {
31253              /*
31254               *  Indicate a change if this was not a
```

```
31255               *  match-only rule.
31256               */
31257              if (rc != 2) {
31258                  changed = 1;
31259              }
31260
31261              /*
31262               *  Pass-Through Feature
31263               *  ('RewriteRule .. .. [PT]'): Because the
31264               *  Apache 1.x API is very limited we
31265               *  need this hack to pass the rewritten
31266               *  URL to other modules like mod_alias,
31267               *  mod_userdir, etc.
31268               */
31269              if (p->flags & RULEFLAG_PASSTHROUGH) {
31270                  rewritelog(r, 2, "forcing '%s' to
31271                      get passed through "
31272                      "to next API URI-to-filename
31273                          handler", r->filename);
31274                  r->filename = ap_pstrcat(r->pool,
31275                      "passthrough:",
31276                              r->filename, NULL);
31277                  changed = 1;
31278                  break;
31279              }
31280
31281              /*
31282               *  Rule has the "forbidden" flag set which
31283               *  means that we stop processing and
31284               *  indicate this to the caller.
31285               */
31286              if (p->flags & RULEFLAG_FORBIDDEN) {
31287                  rewritelog(r, 2, "forcing '%s' to be
31288                      forbidden", r->filename);
31289                  r->filename = ap_pstrcat(r->pool,
31290                      "forbidden:",
31291                              r->filename, NULL);
31292
31293                  changed = 1;
31294                  break;
31295              }
31296
31297              /*
31298               *  Rule has the "gone" flag set which means
31299               *  that we stop processing and indicate
31300               *  this to the caller.
31301               */
31302              if (p->flags & RULEFLAG_GONE) {
```

```
31303              rewritelog(r, 2, "forcing '%s' to be gone",
31304                  r->filename);
31305              r->filename = ap_pstrcat(r->pool, "gone:",
31306                  r->filename, NULL);
31307              changed = 1;
31308              break;
31309          }
31310
31311          /*
31312           * Stop processing also on proxy pass-
31313           * through and last-rule and new-round
31314           * flags.
31315           */
31316          if (p->flags & RULEFLAG_PROXY) {
31317              break;
31318          }
31319          if (p->flags & RULEFLAG_LASTRULE) {
31320              break;
31321          }
31322
31323          /*
31324           * On "new-round" flag we just start from
31325           * the top of the rewriting ruleset again.
31326           */
31327          if (p->flags & RULEFLAG_NEWROUND) {
31328              goto loop;
31329          }
31330
31331          /*
31332           * If we are forced to skip N next rules,
31333           * do it now.
31334           */
31335          if (p->skip > 0) {
31336              s = p->skip;
31337              while (   i < rewriterules->nelts
31338                     && s > 0) {
31339                  i++;
31340                  p = &entries[i];
31341                  s--;
31342              }
31343          }
31344      }
31345      else {
31346          /*
31347           * If current rule is chained with next
31348           * rule(s),skip all this next rule(s)
31349           */
31350          while (   i < rewriterules->nelts
31351                 && p->flags & RULEFLAG_CHAIN) {
31352              i++;
31353              p = &entries[i];
31354          }
31355      }
31356  }
31357  return changed;
31358 }
31359
31360 /*
31361  * Apply a single(!) rewrite rule
31362  */
31363 static int apply_rewrite_rule(request_rec *r,
31364      rewriterule_entry *p,
31365                              char *perdir)
31366 {
31367  char *uri;
31368  char *output;
31369  const char *vary;
31370  char newuri[MAX_STRING_LEN];
31371  char env[MAX_STRING_LEN];
31372  regex_t *regexp;
31373  regmatch_t regmatch[MAX_NMATCH];
31374  backrefinfo *briRR = NULL;
31375  backrefinfo *briRC = NULL;
31376  int prefixstrip;
31377  int failed;
31378  array_header *rewriteconds;
31379  rewritecond_entry *conds;
31380  rewritecond_entry *c;
31381  int i;
31382  int rc;
31383
31384  /*
31385   * Initialisation
31386   */
31387  uri     = r->filename;
31388  regexp  = p->regexp;
31389  output  = p->output;
31390
31391  /*
31392   * Add (perhaps splitted away) PATH_INFO postfix
31393   * to URL to make sure we really match against
31394   * the complete URL.
31395   */
31396  if (perdir != NULL && r->path_info != NULL
31397          && r->path_info[0] != '\0') {
31398      rewritelog(r, 3, "[per-dir %s] add
```

```
31399                      path-info postfix: %s -> %s%s",
31400                  perdir, uri, uri, r->path_info);
31401              uri = ap_pstrcat(r->pool, uri, r->path_info,
31402                  NULL);
31403          }
31404
31405          /*
31406           *  On per-directory context (.htaccess)
31407           *  strip the location prefix from the URL to make
31408           *  sure patterns apply only to the local part.
31409           *  Additionally indicate this special
31410           *  threatment in the logfile.
31411           */
31412          prefixstrip = 0;
31413          if (perdir != NULL) {
31414              if (   strlen(uri) >= strlen(perdir)
31415                  && strncmp(uri, perdir,
31416                     strlen(perdir)) == 0) {
31417                  rewritelog(r, 3, "[per-dir %s] strip
31418                      per-dir prefix: %s -> %s",
31419                          perdir, uri, uri+strlen(perdir));
31420                  uri = uri+strlen(perdir);
31421                  prefixstrip = 1;
31422              }
31423          }
31424
31425          /*
31426           *  Try to match the URI against the RewriteRule
31427           *  pattern and exit immediately if it didn't
31428           *  apply.
31429           */
31430          if (perdir == NULL) {
31431              rewritelog(r, 3, "applying pattern '%s'
31432                  to uri '%s'",
31433                      p->pattern, uri);
31434          }
31435          else {
31436              rewritelog(r, 3, "[per-dir %s] applying
31437                  pattern '%s' to uri '%s'",
31438                      perdir, p->pattern, uri);
31439          }
31440          rc = (regexec(regexp, uri, regexp->re_nsub+1,
31441              regmatch, 0) == 0);
31442          if (! (( rc && !(p->flags & RULEFLAG_NOTMATCH)) ||
31443             (!rc &&  (p->flags & RULEFLAG_NOTMATCH))   ) ) {
31444              return 0;
31445          }
31446
```

```
31447          /*
31448           *  Else create the RewriteRule 'regsubinfo'
31449           *  structure which holds the substitution
31450           *  information.
31451           */
31452          briRR = (backrefinfo *)ap_palloc(r->pool,
31453              sizeof(backrefinfo));
31454          if (!rc && (p->flags & RULEFLAG_NOTMATCH)) {
31455              /*  empty info on negative patterns  */
31456              briRR->source = "";
31457              briRR->nsub   = 0;
31458          }
31459          else {
31460              briRR->source = ap_pstrdup(r->pool, uri);
31461              briRR->nsub   = regexp->re_nsub;
31462              memcpy((void *)(briRR->regmatch),
31463                  (void *)(regmatch),
31464                      sizeof(regmatch));
31465          }
31466
31467          /*
31468           *  Initiallally create the RewriteCond
31469           *  backrefinfo with empty backrefinfo, i.e.
31470           *  not subst parts(this one is adjusted
31471           *  inside apply_rewrite_cond() later!!)
31472           */
31473          briRC = (backrefinfo *)ap_pcalloc(r->pool,
31474              sizeof(backrefinfo));
31475          briRC->source = "";
31476          briRC->nsub   = 0;
31477
31478          /*
31479           *  Ok, we already know the pattern has matched,
31480           *  but we now additionally have to check for
31481           *  all existing preconditions RewriteCond) which
31482           *  (have to be also true. We do this at this very
31483           *  late stage to avoid unnessesary checks which
31484           *  would slow down the rewriting engine!!
31485           */
31486          rewriteconds = p->rewriteconds;
31487          conds = (rewritecond_entry *)rewriteconds->elts;
31488          failed = 0;
31489          for (i = 0; i < rewriteconds->nelts; i++) {
31490              c = &conds[i];
31491              rc = apply_rewrite_cond(r, c, perdir,
31492                  briRR, briRC);
31493              if (c->flags & CONDFLAG_ORNEXT) {
31494                  /*
```

```
31495              *  The "OR" case
31496              */
31497             if (rc == 0) {
31498                 /*  One condition is false, but another
31499                  * can be still true, so we have
31500                  * to continue...
31501                  */
31502                 ap_table_unset(r->notes, VARY_KEY_THIS);
31503                 continue;
31504             }
31505             else {
31506                 /*  One true condition is enough in "or"
31507                  * case, so skip the other conditions
31508                  * which are "ornext"
31509                  *  chained
31510                  */
31511                 while (   i < rewriteconds->nelts
31512                        && c->flags & CONDFLAG_ORNEXT) {
31513                     i++;
31514                     c = &conds[i];
31515                 }
31516                 continue;
31517             }
31518         }
31519         else {
31520             /*
31521              *  The "AND" case, i.e. no "or" flag,
31522              *  so a single failure means total failure.
31523              */
31524             if (rc == 0) {
31525                 failed = 1;
31526                 break;
31527             }
31528         }
31529         vary = ap_table_get(r->notes, VARY_KEY_THIS);
31530         if (vary != NULL) {
31531             ap_table_merge(r->notes, VARY_KEY, vary);
31532             ap_table_unset(r->notes, VARY_KEY_THIS);
31533         }
31534     }
31535     /*  if any condition fails the complete
31536      * rule fails  */
31537     if (failed) {
31538         ap_table_unset(r->notes, VARY_KEY);
31539         ap_table_unset(r->notes, VARY_KEY_THIS);
31540         return 0;
31541     }
31542
31543     /*
31544      * Regardless of what we do next, we've found a
31545      * match.  Check to see if any of the request header
31546      * fields were involved, and add them to the
31547      * Vary field of the response.
31548      */
31549     if ((vary = ap_table_get(r->notes,
31550             VARY_KEY)) != NULL) {
31551         ap_table_merge(r->headers_out,
31552             "Vary", vary);
31553         ap_table_unset(r->notes, VARY_KEY);
31554     }
31555
31556     /*
31557      *  If this is a pure matching rule
31558      * ('RewriteRule <pat> -') we stop processing and
31559      * return immediately. The only thing we have not
31560      * to forget are the environment variables
31561      *  ('RewriteRule <pat> - [E=...]')
31562      */
31563     if (strcmp(output, "-") == 0) {
31564         for (i = 0; p->env[i] != NULL; i++) {
31565             /*  1. take the string  */
31566             ap_cpystrn(env, p->env[i], sizeof(env));
31567             /*  2. expand $N (i.e. backrefs to
31568              * RewriteRule pattern)  */
31569             expand_backref_inbuffer(r->pool, env,
31570                     sizeof(env), briRR, '$');
31571             /*  3. expand %N (i.e. backrefs to latest
31572              * RewriteCond pattern)  */
31573             expand_backref_inbuffer(r->pool, env,
31574                     sizeof(env), briRC, '%');
31575             /*  4. expand %{...} (i.e. variables) */
31576             expand_variables_inbuffer(r,
31577                     env, sizeof(env));
31578             /*  5. expand ${...} (RewriteMap lookups)  */
31579             expand_map_lookups(r, env, sizeof(env));
31580             /*  and add the variable to Apache's
31581              * structures  */
31582             add_env_variable(r, env);
31583         }
31584         if (p->forced_mimetype != NULL) {
31585             if (perdir == NULL) {
31586                 /* In the per-server context we can
31587                  * force the MIME-type the correct way
31588                  * by notifying our MIME-type hook
31589                  * handler to do the job when the
31590                  * MIME-type API stage is reached.
```

```
31591                            */
31592                    rewritelog(r, 2, "remember %s to have
31593                        MIME-type '%s'",
31594                            r->filename, p->forced_mimetype);
31595                    ap_table_setn(r->notes,
31596                        REWRITE_FORCED_MIMETYPE_NOTEVAR,
31597                            p->forced_mimetype);
31598                }
31599            else {
31600                /* In per-directory context we operate in
31601                 * the Fixup API hook which is after the
31602                 * MIME -type hook, so our MIME-type handler
31603                 * has no chance to set r->content_type. And
31604                 * because we are in the situation where no
31605                 * substitution takes place no sub-request
31606                 * will happen (which could solve the
31607                 * restriction). As a workaround we do it
31608                 * ourself now immediately although this is
31609                 * not strictly API-conforming.
31610                 * But it's the only chance we have...
31611                 */
31612                rewritelog(r, 1, "[per-dir %s] force %s to
31613                        have MIME-type "
31614                            "'%s'", perdir, r->filename,
31615                                p->forced_mimetype);
31616                r->content_type = p->forced_mimetype;
31617            }
31618        }
31619        return 2;
31620    }
31621
31622    /*
31623     * Ok, now we finally know all patterns have
31624     * matched and that there is something
31625     * to replace, so we create the
31626     * substitution URL string in 'newuri'.
31627     */
31628    /* 1. take the output string  */
31629    ap_cpystrn(newuri, output, sizeof(newuri));
31630    /* 2. expand $N (i.e. backrefs to RewriteRule
31631     * pattern)  */
31632    expand_backref_inbuffer(r->pool, newuri,
31633        sizeof(newuri), briRR, '$');
31634    /* 3. expand %N (i.e. backrefs to latest
31635     * RewriteCond pattern)  */
31636    expand_backref_inbuffer(r->pool, newuri,
31637        sizeof(newuri), briRC, '%');
31638    /* 4. expand %{...} (i.e. variables) */
31639    expand_variables_inbuffer(r, newuri,
31640        sizeof(newuri));
31641    /* 5. expand ${...} (RewriteMap lookups) */
31642    expand_map_lookups(r, newuri, sizeof(newuri));
31643    /* and log the result... */
31644    if (perdir == NULL) {
31645        rewritelog(r, 2, "rewrite %s -> %s", uri, newuri);
31646    }
31647    else {
31648        rewritelog(r, 2, "[per-dir %s] rewrite
31649            %s -> %s", perdir, uri, newuri);
31650    }
31651
31652    /*
31653     * Additionally do expansion for the environment
31654     * variable strings
31655     * ('RewriteRule .. ... [E=<string>]').
31656     */
31657    for (i = 0; p->env[i] != NULL; i++) {
31658        /* 1. take the string  */
31659        ap_cpystrn(env, p->env[i], sizeof(env));
31660        /* 2. expand $N (i.e. backrefs to
31661         * RewriteRule pattern)  */
31662        expand_backref_inbuffer(r->pool, env,
31663            sizeof(env), briRR, '$');
31664        /* 3. expand %N (i.e. backrefs to latest
31665         * RewriteCond pattern)  */
31666        expand_backref_inbuffer(r->pool, env,
31667            sizeof(env), briRC, '%');
31668        /* 4. expand %{...} (i.e. variables) */
31669        expand_variables_inbuffer(r, env, sizeof(env));
31670        /* 5. expand ${...} (RewriteMap lookups)  */
31671        expand_map_lookups(r, env, sizeof(env));
31672        /* and add the variable to Apache's
31673         * structures  */
31674        add_env_variable(r, env);
31675    }
31676
31677    /*
31678     * Now replace API's knowledge of the current URI:
31679     * Replace r->filename with the new URI string and
31680     * split out an on-the-fly generated
31681     * QUERY_STRING part into r->args
31682     */
31683    r->filename = ap_pstrdup(r->pool, newuri);
31684    splitout_queryargs(r, p->flags & RULEFLAG_QSAPPEND);
31685
31686    /*
```

```
31687          * Again add the previously stripped per-directory
31688          * location prefix if the new URI is not
31689          * a new one for this location, i.e. if it's not
31690          * starting with either a slash or a fully
31691          * qualified URL scheme.
31692          */
31693         i = strlen(r->filename);
31694         if (   prefixstrip
31695             && !(   r->filename[0] == '/'
31696                  || (   (i > 7 && strncasecmp(r->filename,
31697                          "http://", 7) == 0)
31698                      || (i > 8 && strncasecmp(r->filename,
31699                          "https://", 8) == 0)
31700                      || (i > 9 && strncasecmp(r->filename,
31701                          "gopher://", 9) == 0)
31702                      || (i > 6 && strncasecmp(r->filename,
31703                          "ftp://", 6) == 0)))) {
31704             rewritelog(r, 3, "[per-dir %s] add per-dir
31705                 prefix: %s -> %s%s",
31706                     perdir, r->filename, perdir,
31707                         r->filename);
31708             r->filename = ap_pstrcat(r->pool, perdir,
31709                 r->filename, NULL);
31710         }
31711
31712         /*
31713          *  If this rule is forced for proxy throughput
31714          *  ('RewriteRule ... ... [P]') then emulate
31715          * mod_proxy's URL-to-filename handler to be
31716          * sure mod_proxy is triggered for this URL later
31717          * in the Apache API. But make sure it is a fully
31718          * -qualified URL. (If not it is qualified with
31719          *  ourself).
31720          */
31721         if (p->flags & RULEFLAG_PROXY) {
31722             fully_qualify_uri(r);
31723             if (perdir == NULL) {
31724                 rewritelog(r, 2, "forcing proxy-throughput
31725                     with %s", r->filename);
31726
31727             }
31728             else {
31729                 rewritelog(r, 2, "[per-dir %s] forcing proxy-
31730                     throughput with %s",
31731                         perdir, r->filename);
31732             }
31733             r->filename = ap_pstrcat(r->pool, "proxy:",
31734                 r->filename, NULL);
31735             return 1;
31736         }
31737
31738         /*
31739          *  If this rule is explicitly forced for HTTP
31740          *  redirection('RewriteRule .. .. [R]')
31741          *  then force an external HTTP redirect. But make
31742          * sure it is a fully -qualified URL. (If
31743          *  not it is qualified with ourself).
31744          */
31745         if (p->flags & RULEFLAG_FORCEREDIRECT) {
31746             fully_qualify_uri(r);
31747             if (perdir == NULL) {
31748                 rewritelog(r, 2,
31749                     "explicitly forcing redirect with %s",
31750                         r->filename);
31751             }
31752             else {
31753                 rewritelog(r, 2,
31754                     "[per-dir %s] explicitly forcing
31755                         redirect with %s",
31756                         perdir, r->filename);
31757             }
31758             r->status = p->forced_responsecode;
31759             return 1;
31760         }
31761
31762         /*
31763          *  Special Rewriting Feature: Self-Reduction
31764          *  We reduce the URL by stripping a possible
31765          *  http[s]://<ourhost>[:<port>] prefix, i.e. a
31766          * prefix which corresponds to ourself. This
31767          * is to simplify rewrite maps and to avoid
31768          * recursion, etc. When this prefix is not a
31769          *  coincidence then the user has to use [R]
31770          * explicitly (see above).
31771          */
31772         reduce_uri(r);
31773
31774         /*
31775          *  If this rule is still implicitly forced for HTTP
31776          *  redirection ('RewriteRule .. <scheme>://...')
31777          * then directly force an external HTTP redirect.
31778          */
31779         i = strlen(r->filename);
31780         if (   (i > 7 && strncasecmp(r->filename,
31781             "http://", 7)   == 0)
31782             || (i > 8 && strncasecmp(r->filename,
```

```
31783              "https://", 8)  == 0)
31784           || (i > 9 && strncasecmp(r->filename,
31785              "gopher://", 9) == 0)
31786           || (i > 6 && strncasecmp(r->filename,
31787              "ftp://", 6)    == 0)) {
31788        if (perdir == NULL) {
31789            rewritelog(r, 2,
31790                "implicitly forcing redirect (rc=%d)
31791                    with %s",
31792                p->forced_responsecode, r->filename);
31793        }
31794        else {
31795            rewritelog(r, 2, "[per-dir %s] implicitly
31796                forcing redirect "
31797                    "(rc=%d) with %s", perdir,
31798                        p->forced_responsecode,
31799                    r->filename);
31800        }
31801        r->status = p->forced_responsecode;
31802        return 1;
31803     }
31804
31805     /*
31806      *  Now we are sure it is not a fully qualified
31807      * URL.  But there is still one special case
31808      * left: A local rewrite in per-directory context,
31809      * i.e. a substitution URL which does not start
31810      * with a slash. Here we add again the initially
31811      *  stripped per-directory prefix.
31812      */
31813     if (prefixstrip && r->filename[0] != '/') {
31814        rewritelog(r, 3, "[per-dir %s] add per-dir
31815            prefix: %s -> %s%s",
31816                perdir, r->filename, perdir,
31817                    r->filename);
31818        r->filename = ap_pstrcat(r->pool, perdir,
31819            r->filename, NULL);
31820     }
31821
31822     /*
31823      *  Finally we had to remember if a MIME-type
31824      * should be forced for this URL
31825      * ('RewriteRule .. .. [T=<type>]') Later in the API
31826      * processing phase this is forced by our MIME API
31827      * -hook function. This time its no problem even for
31828      *  the per-directory context (where the MIME-type
31829      * hook was already processed) because a
31830      * sub-request happens ;-)
31831      */
31832     if (p->forced_mimetype != NULL) {
31833        ap_table_setn(r->notes,
31834                REWRITE_FORCED_MIMETYPE_NOTEVAR,
31835                    p->forced_mimetype);
31836        if (perdir == NULL) {
31837            rewritelog(r, 2, "remember %s to
31838                have MIME-type '%s'",
31839                    r->filename, p->forced_mimetype);
31840        }
31841        else {
31842            rewritelog(r, 2,
31843                "[per-dir %s] remember %s to
31844                    have MIME-type '%s'",
31845                perdir, r->filename,
31846                    p->forced_mimetype);
31847        }
31848     }
31849
31850     /*
31851      *  Puuhhhhhhhh... WHAT COMPLICATED STUFF ;_)
31852      *  But now we're done for this particular rule.
31853      */
31854     return 1;
31855 }
31856
31857 static int apply_rewrite_cond(request_rec *r,
31858     rewritecond_entry *p,
31859                 char *perdir, backrefinfo *briRR,
31860                     backrefinfo *briRC)
31861 {
31862     char input[MAX_STRING_LEN];
31863     struct stat sb;
31864     request_rec *rsub;
31865     regmatch_t regmatch[MAX_NMATCH];
31866     int rc;
31867
31868     /*
31869      *   Construct the string we match against
31870      */
31871
31872     /* 1. take the string  */
31873     ap_cpystrn(input, p->input, sizeof(input));
31874     /* 2. expand $N (i.e. backrefs to RewriteRule
31875      * pattern)  */
31876     expand_backref_inbuffer(r->pool, input,
31877         sizeof(input), briRR, '$');
31878     /* 3. expand %N (i.e. backrefs to latest
```

```
31879          * RewriteCond pattern)  */
31880
31881          expand_backref_inbuffer(r->pool, input,
31882               sizeof(input), briRC, '%');
31883          /* 4. expand %{...} (i.e. variables) */
31884          expand_variables_inbuffer(r, input, sizeof(input));
31885          /* 5. expand ${...} (RewriteMap lookups)  */
31886          expand_map_lookups(r, input, sizeof(input));
31887
31888          /*
31889           *    Apply the patterns
31890           */
31891
31892          rc = 0;
31893          if (strcmp(p->pattern, "-f") == 0) {
31894              if (stat(input, &sb) == 0) {
31895                  if (S_ISREG(sb.st_mode)) {
31896                      rc = 1;
31897                  }
31898              }
31899          }
31900          else if (strcmp(p->pattern, "-s ") == 0) {
31901              if (stat(input, &sb) == 0) {
31902                  if (S_ISREG(sb.st_mode) && sb.st_size > 0) {
31903                      rc = 1;
31904                  }
31905              }
31906          }
31907          else if (strcmp(p->pattern, "-l") == 0) {
31908 #if !defined(OS2) && !defined(WIN32)
31909              if (lstat(input, &sb) == 0) {
31910                  if (S_ISLNK(sb.st_mode)) {
31911                      rc = 1;
31912                  }
31913              }
31914 #endif
31915          }
31916          else if (strcmp(p->pattern, "-d") == 0) {
31917              if (stat(input, &sb) == 0) {
31918                  if (S_ISDIR(sb.st_mode)) {
31919                      rc = 1;
31920                  }
31921              }
31922          }
31923          else if (strcmp(p->pattern, "-U") == 0) {
31924              /* avoid infinite subrequest recursion */
31925              if (strlen(input) > 0
31926                  /* nonempty path, and          */
31927                  && (   r->main == NULL
31928                  /* - either not in a subrequest  */
31929                  || (   r->main->uri != NULL
31930                  /* - or in a subrequest...       */
31931                      && r->uri != NULL
31932                  /*   ...and URIs aren't NULL...  */
31933                  /*   ...and sub/main URIs differ */
31934                  && strcmp(r->main->uri, r->uri) != 0) ) ) {
31935
31936                  /* run a URI-based subrequest */
31937                  rsub = ap_sub_req_lookup_uri(input, r);
31938
31939                  /* URI exists for any result up to 3xx,
31940                   * redirects allowed */
31941                  if (rsub->status < 400)
31942                      rc = 1;
31943
31944                  /* log it */
31945                  rewritelog(r, 5, "RewriteCond URI (-U) check: "

31947                              "path=%s -> status=%d", input,
31948                                  rsub->status);

31950                  /* cleanup by destroying the subrequest */
31951                  ap_destroy_sub_req(rsub);
31952              }
31953          }
31954          else if (strcmp(p->pattern, "-F") == 0) {
31955              /* avoid infinite subrequest recursion */
31956              if (strlen(input) > 0
31957                  /* nonempty path, and          */
31958                  && (   r->main == NULL
31959                  /* - either not in a subrequest  */
31960                  || (   r->main->uri != NULL
31961                  /* - or in a subrequest...       */
31962                      && r->uri != NULL
31963                  /*   ...and URIs aren't NULL...  */
31964                  /*   ...and sub/main URIs differ */
31965                  && strcmp(r->main->uri, r->uri) != 0) ) ) {
31966
31967                  /* process a file-based subrequest:
31968                   * this differs from -U in that no path
31969                   * translation is done.
31970                   */
31971                  rsub = ap_sub_req_lookup_file(input, r);
31972
31973                  /* file exists for any result up to 2xx,
31974                   * no redirects */
```

```
31975            if (rsub->status < 300 &&
31976                /* double-check that file exists since
31977                 * default result is 200 */
31978                stat(rsub->filename, &sb) == 0) {
31979                rc = 1;
31980            }
31981
31982            /* log it */
31983            rewritelog(r, 5, "RewriteCond file (-F)
31984                check: path=%s "
31985                    "-> file=%s status=%d", input,
31986                        rsub->filename,
31987                    rsub->status);
31988
31989            /* cleanup by destroying the subrequest */
31990            ap_destroy_sub_req(rsub);
31991        }
31992    }
31993    else if (strlen(p->pattern) > 1
31994         && *(p->pattern) == '>') {
31995        rc = (compare_lexicography(input,
31996            p->pattern+1) == 1 ? 1 : 0);
31997    }
31998    else if (strlen(p->pattern) >
31999         1 && *(p->pattern) == '<') {
32000        rc = (compare_lexicography(input,
32001            p->pattern+1) == -1 ? 1 : 0);
32002    }
32003    else if (strlen(p->pattern) > 1
32004         && *(p->pattern) == '=') {
32005        if (strcmp(p->pattern+1, "\"\"") == 0) {
32006            rc = (*input == '\0');
32007        }
32008        else {
32009            rc = (strcmp(input,
32010                p->pattern+1) == 0 ? 1 : 0);
32011        }
32012    }
32013    else {
32014        /* it is really a regexp pattern, so apply it */
32015        rc = (regexec(p->regexp, input,
32016            p->regexp->re_nsub+1, regmatch,0) == 0);
32017
32018     /* if it isn't a negated pattern and really matched
32019       we update the passed-through regex subst info
32020       structure */
32021        if (rc && !(p->flags & CONDFLAG_NOTMATCH)) {
32022            briRC->source = ap_pstrdup(r->pool, input);
32023            briRC->nsub   = p->regexp->re_nsub;
32024            memcpy((void *)(briRC->regmatch),
32025                (void *)(regmatch),
32026                    sizeof(regmatch));
32027        }
32028    }
32029
32030    /* if this is a non-matching regexp, just
32031     * negate the result */
32032    if (p->flags & CONDFLAG_NOTMATCH) {
32033        rc = !rc;
32034    }
32035
32036    rewritelog(r, 4, "RewriteCond: input='%s'
32037        pattern='%s%s' => %s",
32038            input, (p->flags &
32039                CONDFLAG_NOTMATCH ? "!" : ""),
32040            p->pattern, rc ? "matched" : "not-matched");
32041
32042    /* end just return the result */
32043    return rc;
32044 }
32045
32046
32047 /*
32048 ** +-------------------------------------------------+
32049 ** |                                                 |
32050 ** |            URL transformation functions         |
32051 ** |                                                 |
32052 ** +-------------------------------------------------+
32053 */
32054
32055 /*
32056 **
32057 ** split out a QUERY_STRING part from
32058 ** the current URI string
32059 **
32060 */
32061
32062 static void splitout_queryargs(request_rec *r,
32063     int qsappend)
32064 {
32065     char *q;
32066     char *olduri;
32067
32068     q = strchr(r->filename, '?');
32069     if (q != NULL) {
32070         olduri = ap_pstrdup(r->pool, r->filename);
```

```
32071        *q++ = '\0';
32072        if (qsappend) {
32073            r->args = ap_pstrcat(r->pool, q, "&",
32074                    r->args, NULL);
32075        }
32076        else {
32077            r->args = ap_pstrdup(r->pool, q);
32078        }
32079        if (strlen(r->args) == 0) {
32080            r->args = NULL;
32081            rewritelog(r, 3, "split uri=%s -> uri=%s,
32082                    args=<none>", olduri,
32083                    r->filename);
32084        }
32085        else {
32086            if (r->args[strlen(r->args)-1] == '&') {
32087                r->args[strlen(r->args)-1] = '\0';
32088            }
32089            rewritelog(r, 3, "split uri=%s -> uri=%s,
32090                    args=%s", olduri,
32091
32092                        r->filename, r->args);
32093        }
32094    }
32095    return;
32096 }
32097
32098
32099 /*
32100 **
32101 **    strip 'http[s]://ourhost/' from URI
32102 **
32103 */
32104
32105 static void reduce_uri(request_rec *r)
32106 {
32107    char *cp;
32108    unsigned short port;
32109    char *portp;
32110    char *hostp;
32111    char *url;
32112    char c;
32113    char host[LONG_STRING_LEN];
32114    char buf[MAX_STRING_LEN];
32115    char *olduri;
32116    int l;
32117
32118    cp = ap_http_method(r);

32119    l = strlen(cp);
32120    if (   strlen(r->filename) > l+3
32121        && strncasecmp(r->filename, cp, l) == 0
32122        && r->filename[l]   == ':'
32123        && r->filename[l+1] == '/'
32124        && r->filename[l+2] == '/'                 ) {
32125        /* there was really a rewrite to a remote
32126         * path */
32127
32128        olduri = ap_pstrdup(r->pool, r->filename);
32129        /* save for logging */
32130
32131        /* cut the hostname and port out of the URI */
32132        ap_cpystrn(buf, r->filename+(l+3), sizeof(buf));
32133        hostp = buf;
32134        for (cp = hostp; *cp != '\0' && *cp != '/'
32135            && *cp != ':'; cp++)
32136            ;
32137        if (*cp == ':') {
32138            /* set host */
32139            *cp++ = '\0';
32140            ap_cpystrn(host, hostp, sizeof(host));
32141            /* set port */
32142            portp = cp;
32143            for (; *cp != '\0' && *cp != '/'; cp++)
32144                ;
32145            c = *cp;
32146            *cp = '\0';
32147            port = atoi(portp);
32148            *cp = c;
32149            /* set remaining url */
32150            url = cp;
32151        }
32152        else if (*cp == '/') {
32153            /* set host */
32154            *cp = '\0';
32155            ap_cpystrn(host, hostp, sizeof(host));
32156            *cp = '/';
32157            /* set port */
32158            port = ap_default_port(r);
32159            /* set remaining url */
32160            url = cp;
32161        }
32162        else {
32163            /* set host */
32164            ap_cpystrn(host, hostp, sizeof(host));
32165            /* set port */
32166            port = ap_default_port(r);
```

```
32167                     /* set remaining url */
32168                     url = "/";
32169                 }
32170
32171                 /* now check whether we could reduce it to a
32172                  * local path... */
32173                 if (ap_matches_request_vhost(r, host, port)) {
32174                  /* this is our host, so only the URL remains */
32175                     r->filename = ap_pstrdup(r->pool, url);
32176                     rewritelog(r, 3, "reduce %s -> %s", olduri,
32177                         r->filename);
32178                 }
32179             }
32180         return;
32181     }
32182
32183
32184     /*
32185     **
32186     **  add 'http[s]://ourhost[:ourport]/' to URI
32187     **  if URI is still not fully qualified
32188     **
32189     */
32190
32191     static void fully_qualify_uri(request_rec *r)
32192     {
32193         int i;
32194         char buf[32];
32195         const char *thisserver;
32196         char *thisport;
32197         int port;
32198
32199         i = strlen(r->filename);
32200         if (!(   (i > 7 && strncasecmp(r->filename,
32201             "http://", 7)   == 0)
32202               || (i > 8 && strncasecmp(r->filename,
32203                     "https://", 8)  == 0)
32204               || (i > 9 && strncasecmp(r->filename,
32205                     "gopher://", 9) == 0)
32206               || (i > 6 && strncasecmp(r->filename,
32207                     "ftp://", 6)    == 0))) {
32208
32209             thisserver = ap_get_server_name(r);
32210             port = ap_get_server_port(r);
32211             if (ap_is_default_port(port,r)) {
32212                 thisport = "";
32213             }
32214             else {
```

```
32215                 ap_snprintf(buf, sizeof(buf), ":%u", port);
32216                 thisport = buf;
32217             }
32218
32219             if (r->filename[0] == '/') {
32220                 r->filename = ap_psprintf(r->pool,
32221                     "%s://%s%s%s",
32222                         ap_http_method(r), thisserver,
32223                             thisport, r->filename);
32224             }
32225             else {
32226                 r->filename = ap_psprintf(r->pool,
32227                     "%s://%s%s/%s",
32228                         ap_http_method(r), thisserver,
32229                             thisport, r->filename);
32230             }
32231         }
32232         return;
32233     }
32234
32235
32236     /*
32237     **
32238     **  Expand the %0-%9 or $0-$9 regex backreferences
32239     **
32240     */
32241
32242     static void expand_backref_inbuffer(pool *p, char *buf,
32243         int nbuf,
32244                             backrefinfo *bri, char c)
32245     {
32246         int i;
32247
32248         if (bri->nsub < 1) {
32249             return;
32250         }
32251
32252         if (c != '$') {
32253             /* safe existing $N backrefs and
32254              * replace <c>N with $N backrefs */
32255             for (i = 0; buf[i] != '\0' && i < nbuf; i++) {
32256                 if (buf[i] == '$' && (buf[i+1] >= '0'
32257                     && buf[i+1] <= '9')) {
32258                     buf[i++] = '\001';
32259                 }
32260                 else if (buf[i] == c && (buf[i+1] >= '0'
32261                         && buf[i+1] <= '9')) {
32262                     buf[i++] = '$';
```

```
32263                  }
32264              }
32265          }
32266
32267          /* now apply the pregsub() function */
32268          ap_cpystrn(buf, ap_pregsub(p, buf, bri->source,
32269                       bri->nsub+1, bri->regmatch), nbuf);
32270
32271          if (c != '$') {
32272              /* restore the original $N backrefs */
32273              for (i = 0; buf[i] != '\0' && i < nbuf; i++) {
32274                  if (buf[i] == '\001' && (buf[i+1] >= '0'
32275                      && buf[i+1] <= '9')) {
32276                      buf[i++] = '$';
32277                  }
32278              }
32279          }
32280      }
32281
32282
32283      /*
32284      **
32285      ** Expand tilde-paths (/~user) through
32286      ** Unix /etc/passwd database information
32287      **
32288      */
32289      #ifndef WIN32
32290      static char *expand_tildepaths(request_rec *r, char *uri)
32291      {
32292          char user[LONG_STRING_LEN];
32293          struct passwd *pw;
32294          char *newuri;
32295          int i, j;
32296
32297          newuri = uri;
32298          if (uri != NULL && strlen(uri) > 2 && uri[0] == '/'
32299                  && uri[1] == '~') {
32300              /* cut out the username */
32301              for (j = 0, i = 2; j < sizeof(user)-1
32302                      && uri[i] != '\0'
32303                      && uri[i] != '/'  ; ) {
32304                  user[j++] = uri[i++];
32305              }
32306              user[j] = '\0';
32307
32308              /* lookup username in systems passwd file */
32309              if ((pw = getpwnam(user)) != NULL) {
32310                  /* ok, user was found, so expand the ~user
```

```
32311                   * string */
32312                  if (uri[i] != '\0') {
32313                      /* ~user/anything...  has to be expanded */
32314                      if (pw->pw_dir[strlen(pw->pw_dir)-1]
32315                          == '/') {
32316                          pw->pw_dir[strlen(pw->pw_dir)-1]
32317                              = '\0';
32318                      }
32319                      newuri = ap_pstrcat(r->pool,
32320                          pw->pw_dir, uri+i, NULL);
32321                  }
32322                  else {
32323                      /* only ~user has to be expanded */
32324                      newuri = ap_pstrdup(r->pool, pw->pw_dir);
32325                  }
32326              }
32327          }
32328          return newuri;
32329      }
32330      #endif
32331
32332      /*
32333      **
32334      ** mapfile expansion support
32335      ** i.e. expansion of MAP lookup directives
32336      ** ${<mapname>:<key>} in RewriteRule rhs
32337      **
32338      */
32339
32340      #define limit_length(n) (n > LONG_STRING_LEN-1 ?
32341          LONG_STRING_LEN-1 : n)
32342
32343      static void expand_map_lookups(request_rec *r,
32344          char *uri, int uri_len)
32345      {
32346          char newuri[MAX_STRING_LEN];
32347          char *cpI;
32348          char *cpIE;
32349          char *cpO;
32350          char *cpT;
32351          char *cpT2;
32352          char mapname[LONG_STRING_LEN];
32353          char mapkey[LONG_STRING_LEN];
32354          char defaultvalue[LONG_STRING_LEN];
32355          int n;
32356
32357          cpI = uri;
32358          cpIE = cpI+strlen(cpI);
```

```
32359        cp0 = newuri;
32360        while (cpI < cpIE) {
32361            if (cpI+6 < cpIE && strncmp(cpI, "${", 2) == 0) {
32362                /* missing delimiter -> take it as plain text */
32363                if (   strchr(cpI+2, ':') == NULL
32364                    || strchr(cpI+2, '}') == NULL) {
32365                    memcpy(cp0, cpI, 2);
32366                    cp0 += 2;
32367                    cpI += 2;
32368                    continue;
32369                }
32370                cpI += 2;
32371
32372                cpT = strchr(cpI, ':');
32373                n = cpT-cpI;
32374                memcpy(mapname, cpI, limit_length(n));
32375                mapname[limit_length(n)] = '\0';
32376                cpI += n+1;
32377
32378                cpT2 = strchr(cpI, '|');
32379                cpT = strchr(cpI, '}');
32380                if (cpT2 != NULL && cpT2 < cpT) {
32381                    n = cpT2-cpI;
32382                    memcpy(mapkey, cpI, limit_length(n));
32383                    mapkey[limit_length(n)] = '\0';
32384                    cpI += n+1;
32385
32386                     n = cpT-cpI;
32387                    memcpy(defaultvalue, cpI, limit_length(n));
32388                    defaultvalue[limit_length(n)] = '\0';
32389                    cpI += n+1;
32390                }
32391                else {
32392                    n = cpT-cpI;
32393                    memcpy(mapkey, cpI, limit_length(n));
32394                    mapkey[limit_length(n)] = '\0';
32395                    cpI += n+1;
32396
32397                    defaultvalue[0] = '\0';
32398                }
32399
32400                cpT = lookup_map(r, mapname, mapkey);
32401                if (cpT != NULL) {
32402                    n = strlen(cpT);
32403                    if (cp0 + n >= newuri + sizeof(newuri)) {
32404                        ap_log_rerror(APLOG_MARK,
32405                            APLOG_NOERRNO|APLOG_ERR,
32406                                r, "insufficient space in "
32407                                "expand_map_lookups, aborting");
32408                        return;
32409                    }
32410                    memcpy(cp0, cpT, n);
32411                    cp0 += n;
32412                }
32413                else {
32414                    n = strlen(defaultvalue);
32415                    if (cp0 + n >= newuri + sizeof(newuri)) {
32416                        ap_log_rerror(APLOG_MARK,
32417                            APLOG_NOERRNO|APLOG_ERR,
32418                                r, "insufficient space in "
32419                                "expand_map_lookups,
32420                                    aborting");
32421                        return;
32422                    }
32423                    memcpy(cp0, defaultvalue, n);
32424                    cp0 += n;
32425                }
32426            }
32427            else {
32428                cpT = strstr(cpI, "${");
32429                if (cpT == NULL)
32430                    cpT = cpI+strlen(cpI);
32431                n = cpT-cpI;
32432                if (cp0 + n >= newuri + sizeof(newuri)) {
32433                    ap_log_rerror(APLOG_MARK,
32434                        APLOG_NOERRNO|APLOG_ERR,
32435                            r, "insufficient space in "
32436                            "expand_map_lookups, aborting");
32437                    return;
32438                }
32439                memcpy(cp0, cpI, n);
32440                cp0 += n;
32441                cpI += n;
32442            }
32443        }
32444        *cp0 = '\0';
32445        ap_cpystrn(uri, newuri, uri_len);
32446        return;
32447    }
32448
32449    #undef limit_length
32450
32451
32452
32453    /*
32454    ** +--------------------------------------------------+
```

```
32455  ** |                                          |
32456  ** |          DBM hashfile support            |
32457  ** |                                          |
32458  ** +------------------------------------------+
32459  */
32460
32461
32462  static char *lookup_map(request_rec *r, char *name,
32463      char *key)
32464  {
32465      void *sconf;
32466      rewrite_server_conf *conf;
32467      array_header *rewritemaps;
32468      rewritemap_entry *entries;
32469      rewritemap_entry *s;
32470      char *value;
32471      struct stat st;
32472      int i;
32473
32474      /* get map configuration */
32475      sconf = r->server->module_config;
32476      conf  = (rewrite_server_conf
32477          *)ap_get_module_config(sconf,
32478                                 &rewrite_module);
32479      rewritemaps = conf->rewritemaps;
32480
32481      entries = (rewritemap_entry *)rewritemaps->elts;
32482      for (i = 0; i < rewritemaps->nelts; i++) {
32483          s = &entries[i];
32484          if (strcmp(s->name, name) == 0) {
32485              if (s->type == MAPTYPE_TXT) {
32486                  if (stat(s->checkfile, &st) == -1) {
32487                      ap_log_rerror(APLOG_MARK, APLOG_ERR, r,
32488                          "mod_rewrite: can't access
32489                              text RewriteMap "
32490                          "file %s", s->checkfile);
32491                      rewritelog(r, 1, "can't open
32492                          RewriteMap file, "
32493                              "see error log");
32494                      return NULL;
32495                  }
32496                  value = get_cache_string(cachep, s->name,
32497                      CACHEMODE_TS,
32498                                  st.st_mtime, key);
32499                  if (value == NULL) {
32500                      rewritelog(r, 6, "cache lookup
32501                          FAILED, forcing new "
32502                              "map lookup");
```

```
32503                      if ((value =
32504                          lookup_map_txtfile(r,
32505                          s->datafile, key)) != NULL) {
32506                          rewritelog(r, 5, "map lookup OK:
32507                              map=%s key=%s[txt] "
32508                                  "-> val=%s", s->name,
32509                                      key, value);
32510                          set_cache_string(cachep, s->name,
32511                              CACHEMODE_TS,
32512                                  st.st_mtime, key, value);
32513                          return value;
32514                      }
32515                      else {
32516                          rewritelog(r, 5, "map lookup
32517                              FAILED: map=%s[txt] "
32518                                  "key=%s", s->name, key);
32519                          set_cache_string(cachep, s->name,
32520                              CACHEMODE_TS,
32521                                  st.st_mtime, key, "");
32522                          return NULL;
32523                      }
32524                  }
32525                  else {
32526                      rewritelog(r, 5, "cache lookup OK:
32527                          map=%s[txt] key=%s "
32528                              "-> val=%s", s->name, key,
32529                                  value);
32530                      return value[0] != '\0' ? value : NULL;
32531                  }
32532              }
32533              else if (s->type == MAPTYPE_DBM) {
32534  #ifndef NO_DBM_REWRITEMAP
32535                  if (stat(s->checkfile, &st) == -1) {
32536                      ap_log_rerror(APLOG_MARK, APLOG_ERR, r,
32537                          "mod_rewrite: can't access
32538                              DBM RewriteMap "
32539                          "file %s", s->checkfile);
32540                      rewritelog(r, 1, "can't open DBM
32541                          RewriteMap file, "
32542                              "see error log");
32543                      return NULL;
32544                  }
32545                  value = get_cache_string(cachep,
32546                      s->name, CACHEMODE_TS,
32547                                  st.st_mtime, key);
32548                  if (value == NULL) {
32549                      rewritelog(r, 6,
32550                          "cache lookup FAILED,
```

```
32551                           forcing new map lookup");
32552                       if ((value =
32553                           lookup_map_dbmfile(r,
32554                              s->datafile, key)) != NULL) {
32555                         rewritelog(r, 5, "map lookup OK:
32556                              map=%s[dbm] key=%s "
32557                                 "-> val=%s", s->name,
32558                                    key, value);
32559                         set_cache_string(cachep, s->name,
32560                              CACHEMODE_TS,
32561                                 st.st_mtime, key, value);
32562                         return value;
32563                       }
32564                       else {
32565                         rewritelog(r, 5, "map lookup
32566                           FAILED: map=%s[dbm] "
32567                              "key=%s", s->name, key);
32568                         set_cache_string(cachep, s->name,
32569                           CACHEMODE_TS,
32570                              st.st_mtime, key, "");
32571                         return NULL;
32572                       }
32573                     }
32574                     else {
32575                       rewritelog(r, 5, "cache lookup OK:
32576                           map=%s[dbm] key=%s "
32577                              "-> val=%s", s->name,
32578                                 key, value);
32579                       return value[0] != '\0' ? value : NULL;
32580                     }
32581  #else
32582                     return NULL;
32583  #endif
32584                 }
32585                 else if (s->type == MAPTYPE_PRG) {
32586                   if ((value =
32587                       lookup_map_program(r, s->fpin,
32588                          s->fpout, key)) != NULL) {
32589                     rewritelog(r, 5, "map lookup OK:
32590                        map=%s key=%s -> val=%s",
32591                           s->name, key, value);
32592                     return value;
32593                   }
32594                   else {
32595                     rewritelog(r, 5, "map lookup FAILED:
32596                        map=%s key=%s",
32597                           s->name, key);
32598                   }
32599                 }
32600                 else if (s->type == MAPTYPE_INT) {
32601                   if ((value = lookup_map_internal(r,
32602                       s->func, key)) != NULL) {
32603                     rewritelog(r, 5, "map lookup OK:
32604                        map=%s key=%s -> val=%s",
32605                           s->name, key, value);
32606                     return value;
32607                   }
32608                   else {
32609                     rewritelog(r, 5, "map lookup FAILED:
32610                        map=%s key=%s",
32611                           s->name, key);
32612                   }
32613                 }
32614                 else if (s->type == MAPTYPE_RND) {
32615                   if (stat(s->checkfile, &st) == -1) {
32616                     ap_log_rerror(APLOG_MARK, APLOG_ERR, r,
32617                        "mod_rewrite: can't access
32618                           text RewriteMap "
32619                        "file %s", s->checkfile);
32620                     rewritelog(r, 1, "can't open
32621                        RewriteMap file, "
32622                           "see error log");
32623                     return NULL;
32624                   }
32625                   value = get_cache_string(cachep, s->name,
32626                     CACHEMODE_TS,
32627                         st.st_mtime, key);
32628                   if (value == NULL) {
32629                     rewritelog(r, 6, "cache lookup FAILED,
32630                        forcing new "
32631                           "map lookup");
32632                     if ((value =
32633                        lookup_map_txtfile(r, s->datafile,
32634                           key)) != NULL) {
32635                       rewritelog(r, 5, "map lookup OK:
32636                          map=%s key=%s[txt] "
32637                             "-> val=%s", s->name,
32638                                key, value);
32639                       set_cache_string(cachep, s->name,
32640                          CACHEMODE_TS,
32641                             st.st_mtime, key, value);
32642                     }
32643                     else {
32644                       rewritelog(r, 5, "map lookup
32645                          FAILED: map=%s[txt] "
32646                             "key=%s", s->name, key);
```

```
32647                   set_cache_string(cachep, s->name,
32648                         CACHEMODE_TS,
32649                               st.st_mtime, key, "");
32650                   return NULL;
32651                }
32652             }
32653          else {
32654             rewritelog(r, 5, "cache lookup OK:
32655                map=%s[txt] key=%s "
32656                   "-> val=%s", s->name,
32657                      key, value);
32658          }
32659          if (value[0] != '\0') {
32660             value = select_random_value_part(r,
32661                value);
32662             rewritelog(r, 5, "randomly choosen the
32663                subvalue '%s'", value);
32664          }
32665          else {
32666             value = NULL;
32667          }
32668          return value;
32669       }
32670    }
32671  }
32672  return NULL;
32673 }
32674
32675 static char *lookup_map_txtfile(request_rec *r,
32676    char *file, char *key)
32677 {
32678    FILE *fp = NULL;
32679    char line[1024];
32680    char *value = NULL;
32681    char *cpT;
32682    size_t skip;
32683    char *curkey;
32684    char *curval;
32685
32686    if ((fp = ap_pfopen(r->pool, file, "r")) == NULL) {
32687       return NULL;
32688    }
32689
32690    while (fgets(line, sizeof(line), fp) != NULL) {
32691       if (line[0] == '#')
32692          continue; /* ignore comments */
32693       cpT = line;
32694       curkey = cpT;
32695       skip = strcspn(cpT," \t\r\n");
32696       if (skip == 0)
32697          continue; /* ignore lines that start with
32698                      * a space, tab, CR, or LF */
32699       cpT += skip;
32700       *cpT = '\0';
32701       if (strcmp(curkey, key) != 0)
32702          continue; /* key does not match... */
32703
32704       /* found a matching key; now extract and
32705        * return the value */
32706       ++cpT;
32707       skip = strspn(cpT, " \t\r\n");
32708       cpT += skip;
32709       curval = cpT;
32710       skip = strcspn(cpT, " \t\r\n");
32711       if (skip == 0)
32712          continue; /* no value... */
32713       cpT += skip;
32714       *cpT = '\0';
32715       value = ap_pstrdup(r->pool, curval);
32716       break;
32717    }
32718    ap_pfclose(r->pool, fp);
32719    return value;
32720 }
32721
32722 #ifndef NO_DBM_REWRITEMAP
32723 static char *lookup_map_dbmfile(request_rec *r,
32724    char *file, char *key)
32725 {
32726    DBM *dbmfp = NULL;
32727    datum dbmkey;
32728    datum dbmval;
32729    char *value = NULL;
32730    char buf[MAX_STRING_LEN];
32731
32732    dbmkey.dptr  = key;
32733    dbmkey.dsize = strlen(key);
32734    if ((dbmfp = dbm_open(file, O_RDONLY, 0666))
32735         != NULL) {
32736       dbmval = dbm_fetch(dbmfp, dbmkey);
32737       if (dbmval.dptr != NULL) {
32738          memcpy(buf, dbmval.dptr,
32739             dbmval.dsize < sizeof(buf)-1 ?
32740             dbmval.dsize : sizeof(buf)-1  );
32741          buf[dbmval.dsize] = '\0';
32742          value = ap_pstrdup(r->pool, buf);
```

```
32743              }
32744            dbm_close(dbmfp);
32745        }
32746        return value;
32747    }
32748    #endif
32749
32750    static char *lookup_map_program(request_rec *r,
32751         int fpin, int fpout, char *key)
32752    {
32753        char buf[LONG_STRING_LEN];
32754        char c;
32755        int i;
32756
32757        /* when 'RewriteEngine off' was used in the
32758         * per-server context then the rewritemap
32759         * -programs were not spawned. In this case
32760         * using such a map (usually in per-dir context)
32761         * is useless because it is not available.
32762         */
32763        if (fpin == -1 || fpout == -1) {
32764            return NULL;
32765        }
32766
32767        /* take the lock */
32768        rewritelock_alloc(r);
32769
32770        /* write out the request key */
32771        write(fpin, key, strlen(key));
32772        write(fpin, "\n", 1);
32773
32774        /* read in the response value */
32775        i = 0;
32776        while (read(fpout, &c, 1) == 1
32777               && (i < LONG_STRING_LEN-1)) {
32778            if (c == '\n') {
32779                break;
32780            }
32781            buf[i++] = c;
32782        }
32783        buf[i] = '\0';
32784
32785        /* give the lock back */
32786        rewritelock_free(r);
32787
32788        if (strcasecmp(buf, "NULL") == 0) {
32789            return NULL;
32790        }
```

```
32791        else {
32792            return ap_pstrdup(r->pool, buf);
32793        }
32794    }
32795
32796    static char *lookup_map_internal(request_rec *r,
32797                          char *(*func)(request_rec *,
32798                                        char *),
32799                          char *key)
32800    {
32801        /* currently we just let the function convert
32802           the key to a corresponding value */
32803        return func(r, key);
32804    }
32805
32806    static char *rewrite_mapfunc_toupper(request_rec *r,
32807         char *key)
32808    {
32809        char *value, *cp;
32810
32811        for (cp = value = ap_pstrdup(r->pool, key);
32812             cp != NULL && *cp != '\0';
32813             cp++) {
32814            *cp = ap_toupper(*cp);
32815        }
32816        return value;
32817    }
32818
32819    static char *rewrite_mapfunc_tolower(request_rec *r,
32820         char *key)
32821    {
32822        char *value, *cp;
32823
32824        for (cp = value = ap_pstrdup(r->pool, key); cp
32825             != NULL && *cp != '\0';
32826             cp++) {
32827            *cp = ap_tolower(*cp);
32828        }
32829        return value;
32830    }
32831
32832    static char *rewrite_mapfunc_escape(request_rec *r,
32833         char *key)
32834    {
32835        char *value;
32836
32837        value = ap_escape_uri(r->pool, key);
32838        return value;
```

```
32839    }
32840
32841    static char *rewrite_mapfunc_unescape(request_rec *r,
32842        char *key)
32843    {
32844        char *value;
32845
32846        value = ap_pstrdup(r->pool, key);
32847        ap_unescape_url(value);
32848        return value;
32849    }
32850
32851    static int rewrite_rand_init_done = 0;
32852
32853    static void rewrite_rand_init(void)
32854    {
32855        if (!rewrite_rand_init_done) {
32856            srand((unsigned)(getpid()));
32857            rewrite_rand_init_done = 1;
32858        }
32859        return;
32860    }
32861
32862    static int rewrite_rand(int l, int h)
32863    {
32864        int i;
32865        char buf[50];
32866
32867        rewrite_rand_init();
32868        ap_snprintf(buf, sizeof(buf), "%.0f",
32869                    (((double)(rand()%RAND_MAX)
32870                      /RAND_MAX)*(h-l)));
32871        i = atoi(buf)+1;
32872        if (i < l) i = l;
32873        if (i > h) i = h;
32874        return i;
32875    }
32876
32877    static char *select_random_value_part(request_rec *r,
32878        char *value)
32879    {
32880        char *buf;
32881        int n, i, k;
32882
32883        /*  count number of distinct values  */
32884        for (n = 1, i = 0; value[i] != '\0'; i++) {
32885            if (value[i] == '|') {
32886                n++;
32887            }
32888        }
32889
32890        /*  when only one value we have no option to
32891         *  choose  */
32892        if (n == 1) {
32893            return value;
32894        }
32895
32896        /*  else randomly select one  */
32897        k = rewrite_rand(1, n);
32898
32899        /*  and grep it out  */
32900        for (n = 1, i = 0; value[i] != '\0'; i++) {
32901            if (n == k) {
32902                break;
32903            }
32904            if (value[i] == '|') {
32905                n++;
32906            }
32907        }
32908        buf = ap_pstrdup(r->pool, &value[i]);
32909        for (i = 0; buf[i] != '\0' && buf[i] != '|'; i++)
32910            ;
32911        buf[i] = '\0';
32912        return buf;
32913    }
32914
32915
32916    /*
32917    ** +-------------------------------------------------+
32918    ** |                                                 |
32919    ** |            rewriting logfile support            |
32920    ** |                                                 |
32921    ** +-------------------------------------------------+
32922    */
32923
32924
32925    static void open_rewritelog(server_rec *s, pool *p)
32926    {
32927        rewrite_server_conf *conf;
32928        char *fname;
32929        piped_log *pl;
32930        int    rewritelog_flags =
32931            ( O_WRONLY|O_APPEND|O_CREAT );
32932    #ifdef WIN32
32933        mode_t rewritelog_mode  =
32934            ( _S_IREAD|_S_IWRITE );
```

```
32935   #else
32936       mode_t rewritelog_mode  =
32937               ( S_IRUSR|S_IWUSR|S_IRGRP|S_IROTH );
32938   #endif
32939
32940       conf = ap_get_module_config(s->module_config,
32941           &rewrite_module);
32942
32943       if (conf->rewritelogfile == NULL) {
32944           return;
32945       }
32946       if (*(conf->rewritelogfile) == '\0') {
32947           return;
32948       }
32949       if (conf->rewritelogfp > 0) {
32950           return; /* virtual log shared w/ main server */
32951       }
32952
32953       fname = ap_server_root_relative(p,
32954           conf->rewritelogfile);
32955
32956       if (*conf->rewritelogfile == '|') {
32957           if ((pl = ap_open_piped_log(p,
32958           conf->rewritelogfile+1)) == NULL) {
32959               ap_log_error(APLOG_MARK, APLOG_ERR, s,
32960                           "mod_rewrite: could not open
32961                                   reliable pipe "
32962                           "to RewriteLog filter %s",
32963                               conf->rewritelogfile+1);
32964               exit(1);
32965           }
32966           conf->rewritelogfp = ap_piped_log_write_fd(pl);
32967       }
32968       else if (*conf->rewritelogfile != '\0') {
32969           if ((conf->rewritelogfp = ap_popenf(p, fname,
32970               rewritelog_flags,
32971                               rewritelog_mode)) < 0) {
32972               ap_log_error(APLOG_MARK, APLOG_ERR, s,
32973
32974               "mod_rewrite: could not open RewriteLog "
32975                   "file %s", fname);
32976               exit(1);
32977           }
32978       }
32979       return;
32980   }
32981
32982   static void rewritelog(request_rec *r, int level,
32983       const char *text, ...)
32984   {
32985       rewrite_server_conf *conf;
32986       conn_rec *conn;
32987       char *str1;
32988       char str2[512];
32989       char str3[1024];
32990       char type[20];
32991       char redir[20];
32992       va_list ap;
32993       int i;
32994       request_rec *req;
32995       char *ruser;
32996       const char *rhost;
32997
32998       va_start(ap, text);
32999       conf = ap_get_module_config(r->server->module_config,
33000           &rewrite_module);
33001       conn = r->connection;
33002
33003       if (conf->rewritelogfp < 0) {
33004           return;
33005       }
33006       if (conf->rewritelogfile == NULL) {
33007           return;
33008       }
33009       if (*(conf->rewritelogfile) == '\0') {
33010           return;
33011       }
33012
33013       if (level > conf->rewriteloglevel) {
33014           return;
33015       }
33016
33017       if (conn->user == NULL) {
33018           ruser = "-";
33019       }
33020       else if (strlen(conn->user) != 0) {
33021           ruser = conn->user;
33022       }
33023       else {
33024           ruser = "\"\"";
33025       }
33026
33027       rhost = ap_get_remote_host(conn,
33028           r->server->module_config,
33029                               REMOTE_NOLOOKUP);
33030       if (rhost == NULL) {
```

```
33031             rhost = "UNKNOWN-HOST";
33032         }
33033
33034         str1 = ap_pstrcat(r->pool, rhost, " ",
33035                           (conn->remote_logname != NULL ?
33036                           conn->remote_logname : "-"), " ",
33037                           ruser, NULL);
33038         ap_vsnprintf(str2, sizeof(str2), text, ap);
33039
33040         if (r->main == NULL) {
33041             strcpy(type, "initial");
33042         }
33043         else {
33044             strcpy(type, "subreq");
33045         }
33046
33047         for (i = 0, req = r; req->prev != NULL; req =
33048             req->prev) {
33049             i++;
33050         }
33051         if (i == 0) {
33052             redir[0] = '\0';
33053         }
33054         else {
33055             ap_snprintf(redir, sizeof(redir),
33056                 "/redir#%d", i);
33057         }
33058
33059         ap_snprintf(str3, sizeof(str3),
33060             "%s %s [%s/sid#%lx][rid#%lx/%s%s]
33061                 (%d) %s\n", str1,
33062             current_logtime(r), ap_get_server_name(r),
33063             (unsigned long)(r->server),
33064                 (unsigned long)r,
33065             type, redir, level, str2);
33066
33067         fd_lock(r, conf->rewritelogfp);
33068         write(conf->rewritelogfp, str3, strlen(str3));
33069         fd_unlock(r, conf->rewritelogfp);
33070
33071         va_end(ap);
33072         return;
33073     }
33074
33075     static char *current_logtime(request_rec *r)
33076     {
33077         int timz;
33078         struct tm *t;
33079         char tstr[80];
33080         char sign;
33081
33082         t = ap_get_gmtoff(&timz);
33083         sign = (timz < 0 ? '-' : '+');
33084         if (timz < 0) {
33085             timz = -timz;
33086         }
33087
33088         strftime(tstr, 80, "[%d/%b/%Y:%H:%M:%S ", t);
33089         ap_snprintf(tstr + strlen(tstr), 80-strlen(tstr),
33090             "%c%.2d%.2d]",
33091                 sign, timz/60, timz%60);
33092         return ap_pstrdup(r->pool, tstr);
33093     }




33098     /*
33099     ** +-------------------------------------------------+
33100     ** |                                                 |
33101     ** |             rewriting lockfile support          |
33102     ** |                                                 |
33103     ** +-------------------------------------------------+
33104     */
33105
33106     #ifdef WIN32
33107     #define REWRITELOCK_MODE ( _S_IREAD|_S_IWRITE )
33108     #else
33109     #define REWRITELOCK_MODE
33110         ( S_IRUSR|S_IWUSR|S_IRGRP|S_IROTH )
33111     #endif
33112
33113     static void rewritelock_create(server_rec *s, pool *p)
33114     {
33115         rewrite_server_conf *conf;
33116
33117         conf = ap_get_module_config(s->module_config,
33118             &rewrite_module);
33119
33120         /* only operate if a lockfile is used */
33121         if (conf->rewritelockfile == NULL
33122             || *(conf->rewritelockfile) == '\0') {
33123             return;
33124         }
33125
33126         /* fixup the path, especially for
```

```
33127           * rewritelock_remove() */
33128          conf->rewritelockfile = ap_server_root_relative(p,
33129              conf->rewritelockfile);
33130
33131          /* create the lockfile */
33132          unlink(conf->rewritelockfile);
33133          if ((conf->rewritelockfp = ap_popenf(p,
33134              conf->rewritelockfile,
33135                                      O_WRONLY|O_CREAT,
33136                              REWRITELOCK_MODE)) < 0) {
33137              ap_log_error(APLOG_MARK, APLOG_ERR, s,
33138                          "mod_rewrite: Parent could not
33139                              create RewriteLock "
33140                          "file %s", conf->rewritelockfile);
33141              exit(1);
33142          }
33143 #if !defined(OS2) && !defined(WIN32)
33144          /* make sure the childs have access to this file */
33145          if (geteuid() == 0 /* is superuser */)
33146              chown(conf->rewritelockfile, ap_user_id, -1
33147                  /* no gid change */);
33148 #endif
33149
33150          return;
33151 }
33152
33153 static void rewritelock_open(server_rec *s, pool *p)
33154 {
33155          rewrite_server_conf *conf;
33156
33157          conf = ap_get_module_config(s->module_config,
33158              &rewrite_module);
33159
33160          /* only operate if a lockfile is used */
33161          if (conf->rewritelockfile == NULL
33162              || *(conf->rewritelockfile) == '\0') {
33163              return;
33164          }
33165
33166          /* open the lockfile (once per child) to get a
33167           * unique fd */
33168          if ((conf->rewritelockfp = ap_popenf(p,
33169              conf->rewritelockfile,
33170                                      O_WRONLY,
33171                              REWRITELOCK_MODE)) < 0) {
33172              ap_log_error(APLOG_MARK, APLOG_ERR, s,
33173                          "mod_rewrite: Child could not
33174                              open RewriteLock "
33175                          "file %s", conf->rewritelockfile);
33176              exit(1);
33177          }
33178          return;
33179 }
33180
33181 static void rewritelock_remove(void *data)
33182 {
33183          server_rec *s;
33184          rewrite_server_conf *conf;
33185
33186          /* the data is really the server_rec */
33187          s = (server_rec *)data;
33188          conf = ap_get_module_config(s->module_config,
33189              &rewrite_module);
33190
33191          /* only operate if a lockfile is used */
33192          if (conf->rewritelockfile == NULL
33193              || *(conf->rewritelockfile) == '\0') {
33194              return;
33195          }
33196
33197          /* remove the lockfile */
33198          unlink(conf->rewritelockfile);
33199 }
33200
33201 static void rewritelock_alloc(request_rec *r)
33202 {
33203          rewrite_server_conf *conf;
33204
33205          conf = ap_get_module_config(r->server->module_config,
33206              &rewrite_module);
33207
33208          if (conf->rewritelockfp != -1) {
33209              fd_lock(r, conf->rewritelockfp);
33210          }
33211          return;
33212 }
33213
33214 static void rewritelock_free(request_rec *r)
33215 {
33216          rewrite_server_conf *conf;
33217
33218          conf = ap_get_module_config(r->server->module_config,
33219              &rewrite_module);
33220
33221          if (conf->rewritelockfp != -1) {
33222              fd_unlock(r, conf->rewritelockfp);
```

```
33223          }
33224      return;
33225  }
33226
33227
33228  /*
33229  ** +--------------------------------------------------+
33230  ** |                                                  |
33231  ** |                 program map support              |
33232  ** |                                                  |
33233  ** +--------------------------------------------------+
33234  */
33235
33236  static void run_rewritemap_programs(server_rec *s,
33237      pool *p)
33238  {
33239      rewrite_server_conf *conf;
33240      FILE *fpin;
33241      FILE *fpout;
33242      FILE *fperr;
33243      array_header *rewritemaps;
33244      rewritemap_entry *entries;
33245      rewritemap_entry *map;
33246      int i;
33247      int rc;
33248
33249      conf = ap_get_module_config(s->module_config,
33250          &rewrite_module);
33251
33252      /*  If the engine isn't turned on,
33253       *  don't even try to do anything.
33254       */
33255      if (conf->state == ENGINE_DISABLED) {
33256          return;
33257      }
33258
33259      rewritemaps = conf->rewritemaps;
33260      entries = (rewritemap_entry *)rewritemaps->elts;
33261      for (i = 0; i < rewritemaps->nelts; i++) {
33262          map = &entries[i];
33263          if (map->type != MAPTYPE_PRG) {
33264              continue;
33265          }
33266          if (map->datafile == NULL
33267              || *(map->datafile) == '\0'
33268              || map->fpin  != -1
33269              || map->fpout != -1        ) {
33270              continue;
```

```
33271          }
33272          fpin  = NULL;
33273          fpout = NULL;
33274          rc = ap_spawn_child(p, rewritemap_program_child,
33275                          (void *)map->datafile,
33276                              kill_after_timeout,
33277                          &fpin, &fpout, &fperr);
33278          if (rc == 0 || fpin == NULL || fpout == NULL) {
33279              ap_log_error(APLOG_MARK, APLOG_ERR, s,
33280                      "mod_rewrite: could not
33281                          fork child for "
33282                      "RewriteMap process");
33283              exit(1);
33284          }
33285          map->fpin  = fileno(fpin);
33286          map->fpout = fileno(fpout);
33287          map->fperr = fileno(fperr);
33288      }
33289      return;
33290  }
33291
33292  /* child process code */
33293  static int rewritemap_program_child(void *cmd,
33294      child_info *pinfo)
33295  {
33296      int child_pid = 1;
33297
33298      /*
33299       * Prepare for exec
33300       */
33301      ap_cleanup_for_exec();
33302  #ifdef SIGHUP
33303      signal(SIGHUP, SIG_IGN);
33304  #endif
33305
33306      /*
33307       * Exec() the child program
33308       */
33309  #if defined(WIN32)
33310      /* MS Windows */
33311      {
33312          char pCommand[MAX_STRING_LEN];
33313          STARTUPINFO si;
33314          PROCESS_INFORMATION pi;
33315
33316          ap_snprintf(pCommand, sizeof(pCommand),
33317              "%s /C %s", SHELL_PATH, cmd);
33318
```

```
33319          memset(&si, 0, sizeof(si));
33320          memset(&pi, 0, sizeof(pi));
33321
33322          si.cb          = sizeof(si);
33323          si.dwFlags     = STARTF_USESHOWWINDOW |
33324               STARTF_USESTDHANDLES;
33325          si.wShowWindow = SW_HIDE;
33326          si.hStdInput   = pinfo->hPipeInputRead;
33327          si.hStdOutput  = pinfo->hPipeOutputWrite;
33328          si.hStdError   = pinfo->hPipeErrorWrite;
33329
33330          if (CreateProcess(NULL, pCommand, NULL, NULL,
33331               TRUE, 0,
33332                          environ, NULL, &si, &pi)) {
33333              CloseHandle(pi.hProcess);
33334              CloseHandle(pi.hThread);
33335              child_pid = pi.dwProcessId;
33336          }
33337      }
33338  #elif defined(OS2)
33339      /* IBM OS/2 */
33340      execl(SHELL_PATH, SHELL_PATH, "/c", (char *)cmd,
33341          NULL);
33342  #else
33343      /* Standard Unix */
33344      execl(SHELL_PATH, SHELL_PATH, "-c", (char *)cmd,
33345          NULL);
33346  #endif
33347      return(child_pid);
33348  }
33349
33350
33351
33352
33353  /*
33354  ** +-------------------------------------------------+
33355  ** |                                                 |
33356  ** |            environment variable support         |
33357  ** |                                                 |
33358  ** +-------------------------------------------------+
33359  */
33360
33361
33362  static void expand_variables_inbuffer(request_rec *r,
33363      char *buf, int buf_len)
33364  {
33365      char *newbuf;
33366      newbuf = expand_variables(r, buf);
33367      if (strcmp(newbuf, buf) != 0) {
33368          ap_cpystrn(buf, newbuf, buf_len);
33369      }
33370      return;
33371  }
33372
33373  static char *expand_variables(request_rec *r, char *str)
33374  {
33375      char output[MAX_STRING_LEN];
33376      char input[MAX_STRING_LEN];
33377      char *cp;
33378      char *cp2;
33379      char *cp3;
33380      int expanded;
33381      char *outp;
33382      char *endp;
33383
33384      ap_cpystrn(input, str, sizeof(input));
33385      output[0] = '\0';
33386      outp = output;
33387      endp = output + sizeof(output);
33388      expanded = 0;
33389      for (cp = input; cp < input+MAX_STRING_LEN; ) {
33390          if ((cp2 = strstr(cp, "%{")) != NULL) {
33391              if ((cp3 = strstr(cp2, "}")) != NULL) {
33392                  *cp2 = '\0';
33393                  outp = ap_cpystrn(outp, cp, endp - outp);
33394
33395                  cp2 += 2;
33396                  *cp3 = '\0';
33397                  outp = ap_cpystrn(outp, lookup_variable(r,
33398                      cp2), endp - outp);
33399
33400                  cp = cp3+1;
33401                  expanded = 1;
33402                  continue;
33403              }
33404          }
33405          outp = ap_cpystrn(outp, cp, endp - outp);
33406          break;
33407      }
33408      return expanded ? ap_pstrdup(r->pool,
33409          output) : str;
33410  }
33411
33412  static char *lookup_variable(request_rec *r, char *var)
33413  {
33414      const char *result;
```

```
33415        char resultbuf[LONG_STRING_LEN];
33416        time_t tc;
33417        struct tm *tm;
33418        request_rec *rsub;
33419 #ifndef WIN32
33420        struct passwd *pw;
33421        struct group *gr;
33422        struct stat finfo;
33423 #endif
33424
33425        result = NULL;
33426
33427        /* HTTP headers */
33428        if (strcasecmp(var, "HTTP_USER_AGENT") == 0) {
33429            result = lookup_header(r, "User-Agent");
33430        }
33431        else if (strcasecmp(var, "HTTP_REFERER") == 0) {
33432            result = lookup_header(r, "Referer");
33433        }
33434        else if (strcasecmp(var, "HTTP_COOKIE") == 0) {
33435            result = lookup_header(r, "Cookie");
33436        }
33437        else if (strcasecmp(var, "HTTP_FORWARDED") == 0) {
33438            result = lookup_header(r, "Forwarded");
33439        }
33440        else if (strcasecmp(var, "HTTP_HOST") == 0) {
33441            result = lookup_header(r, "Host");
33442        }
33443        else if (strcasecmp(var, "HTTP_PROXY_CONNECTION")
33444            == 0) {
33445            result = lookup_header(r, "Proxy-Connection");
33446        }
33447        else if (strcasecmp(var, "HTTP_ACCEPT") == 0) {
33448            result = lookup_header(r, "Accept");
33449        }
33450        /* all other headers from which we are still not
33451         * know about */
33452        else if (strlen(var) > 5 && strncasecmp(var,
33453            "HTTP:", 5) == 0) {
33454            result = lookup_header(r, var+5);
33455        }
33456
33457        /* connection stuff */
33458        else if (strcasecmp(var, "REMOTE_ADDR") == 0) {
33459            result = r->connection->remote_ip;
33460        }
33461        else if (strcasecmp(var, "REMOTE_HOST") == 0) {
33462            result = (char *)ap_get_remote_host(r->connection,
33463                r->per_dir_config, REMOTE_NAME);
33464        }
33465        else if (strcasecmp(var, "REMOTE_USER") == 0) {
33466            result = r->connection->user;
33467        }
33468        else if (strcasecmp(var, "REMOTE_IDENT") == 0) {
33469            result = (char *)ap_get_remote_logname(r);
33470        }
33471
33472        /* request stuff */
33473        else if (strcasecmp(var, "THE_REQUEST") == 0) {
33474         /* non-standard */
33475            result = r->the_request;
33476        }
33477        else if (strcasecmp(var, "REQUEST_METHOD") == 0) {
33478            result = r->method;
33479        }
33480        else if (strcasecmp(var, "REQUEST_URI") == 0) {
33481         /* non-standard */
33482            result = r->uri;
33483        }
33484        else if (strcasecmp(var, "SCRIPT_FILENAME") == 0 ||
33485            strcasecmp(var, "REQUEST_FILENAME") == 0  ) {
33486            result = r->filename;
33487        }
33488        else if (strcasecmp(var, "PATH_INFO") == 0) {
33489            result = r->path_info;
33490        }
33491        else if (strcasecmp(var, "QUERY_STRING") == 0) {
33492            result = r->args;
33493        }
33494        else if (strcasecmp(var, "AUTH_TYPE") == 0) {
33495            result = r->connection->ap_auth_type;
33496        }
33497        else if (strcasecmp(var, "IS_SUBREQ") == 0) {
33498         /* non-standard */
33499            result = (r->main != NULL ? "true" : "false");
33500        }
33501
33502        /* internal server stuff */
33503        else if (strcasecmp(var, "DOCUMENT_ROOT") == 0) {
33504            result = ap_document_root(r);
33505        }
33506        else if (strcasecmp(var, "SERVER_ADMIN") == 0) {
33507            result = r->server->server_admin;
33508        }
33509        else if (strcasecmp(var, "SERVER_NAME") == 0) {
33510            result = ap_get_server_name(r);
```

```
33511          }
33512          else if (strcasecmp(var, "SERVER_PORT") == 0) {
33513              ap_snprintf(resultbuf, sizeof(resultbuf), "%u",
33514                  ap_get_server_port(r));
33515              result = resultbuf;
33516          }
33517          else if (strcasecmp(var, "SERVER_PROTOCOL") == 0) {
33518              result = r->protocol;
33519          }
33520          else if (strcasecmp(var, "SERVER_SOFTWARE") == 0) {
33521              result = ap_get_server_version();
33522          }
33523          else if (strcasecmp(var, "API_VERSION") == 0) {
33524              /* non-standard */
33525              ap_snprintf(resultbuf, sizeof(resultbuf),
33526                  "%d:%d",
33527                      MODULE_MAGIC_NUMBER_MAJOR,
33528                          MODULE_MAGIC_NUMBER_MINOR);
33529              result = resultbuf;
33530          }
33531
33532          /* underlaying Unix system stuff */
33533          else if (strcasecmp(var, "TIME_YEAR") == 0) {
33534              tc = time(NULL);
33535              tm = localtime(&tc);
33536              ap_snprintf(resultbuf, sizeof(resultbuf),
33537                  "%02d%02d",
33538                      (tm->tm_year / 100) + 19,
33539                          tm->tm_year % 100);
33540              result = resultbuf;
33541          }
33542  #define MKTIMESTR(format, tmfield) \
33543          tc = time(NULL); \
33544          tm = localtime(&tc); \
33545          ap_snprintf(resultbuf, sizeof(resultbuf), format, \
33546              tm->tmfield); \
33547          result = resultbuf;
33548          else if (strcasecmp(var, "TIME_MON") == 0) {
33549              MKTIMESTR("%02d", tm_mon+1)
33550          }
33551          else if (strcasecmp(var, "TIME_DAY") == 0) {
33552              MKTIMESTR("%02d", tm_mday)
33553          }
33554          else if (strcasecmp(var, "TIME_HOUR") == 0) {
33555              MKTIMESTR("%02d", tm_hour)
33556          }
33557          else if (strcasecmp(var, "TIME_MIN") == 0) {
33558              MKTIMESTR("%02d", tm_min)
33559          }
33560          else if (strcasecmp(var, "TIME_SEC") == 0) {
33561              MKTIMESTR("%02d", tm_sec)
33562          }
33563          else if (strcasecmp(var, "TIME_WDAY") == 0) {
33564              MKTIMESTR("%d", tm_wday)
33565          }
33566          else if (strcasecmp(var, "TIME") == 0) {
33567              tc = time(NULL);
33568              tm = localtime(&tc);
33569              ap_snprintf(resultbuf, sizeof(resultbuf),
33570                      "%02d%02d%02d%02d%02d%02d%02d",
33571                          (tm->tm_year / 100) + 19,
33572                          (tm->tm_year % 100), tm->tm_mon+1,
33573                              tm->tm_mday,
33574                          tm->tm_hour, tm->tm_min, tm->tm_sec);
33575              result = resultbuf;
33576              rewritelog(r, 1, "RESULT='%s'", result);
33577          }
33578
33579          /* all other env-variables from the parent
33580           * Apache process */
33581          else if (strlen(var) > 4 && strncasecmp(var,
33582              "ENV:", 4) == 0) {
33583          /* first try the internal Apache notes structure */
33584              result = ap_table_get(r->notes, var+4);
33585          /* second try the internal Apache env structure  */
33586              if (result == NULL) {
33587              result = ap_table_get(r->subprocess_env, var+4);
33588              }
33589              /* third try the external OS env */
33590              if (result == NULL) {
33591                  result = getenv(var+4);
33592              }
33593          }
33594
33595  #define LOOKAHEAD(subrecfunc) \
33596          if ( \
33597              /* filename is safe to use */ \
33598              r->filename != NULL \
33599              /* - and we're either not in a subrequest */ \
33600                  && ( r->main == NULL \
33601                  /* - or in a subrequest where paths are
33602                   * non-NULL... */ \
33603                  || ( r->main->uri != NULL && r->uri
33604                      != NULL \
33605                      /*  ...and sub and main paths
33606                          differ */ \
```

```
33607                    && strcmp(r->main->uri, r->uri)
33608                        != 0))) { \
33609                /* process a file-based subrequest */ \
33610                rsub = subrecfunc(r->filename, r); \
33611                /* now recursively lookup the variable in
33612                 * the sub_req */ \
33613                result = lookup_variable(rsub, var+5); \
33614                /* copy it up to our scope before we destroy
33615                 * sub_req's pool */ \
33616                result = ap_pstrdup(r->pool, result); \
33617                /* cleanup by destroying the subrequest */ \
33618                ap_destroy_sub_req(rsub); \
33619                /* log it */ \
33620                rewritelog(r, 5, "lookahead:
33621                        path=%s var=%s -> val=%s", \
33622                        r->filename, var+5, result); \
33623                /* return ourself to prevent re-pstrdup */ \
33624                return (char *)result; \
33625            }
33626
33627        /* look-ahead for parameter through URI-based
33628         * sub-request */
33629        else if (strlen(var) > 5 && strncasecmp(var,
33630            "LA-U:", 5) == 0) {
33631            LOOKAHEAD(ap_sub_req_lookup_uri)
33632        }
33633        /* look-ahead for parameter through file-based
33634         * sub-request */
33635        else if (strlen(var) > 5 && strncasecmp(var,
33636            "LA-F:", 5) == 0) {
33637            LOOKAHEAD(ap_sub_req_lookup_file)
33638        }
33639
33640 #ifndef WIN32
33641        /* Win32 has a rather different view of file
33642         * ownerships.For now, just forget it */
33643
33644        /* file stuff */
33645        else if (strcasecmp(var, "SCRIPT_USER") == 0) {
33646            result = "<unknown>";
33647            if (r->finfo.st_mode != 0) {
33648                if ((pw = getpwuid(r->finfo.st_uid)) !=
33649                        NULL) {
33650                    result = pw->pw_name;
33651                }
33652            }
33653            else {
33654                if (stat(r->filename, &finfo) == 0) {
33655                    if ((pw = getpwuid(finfo.st_uid)) !=
33656                        NULL) {
33657                        result = pw->pw_name;
33658                    }
33659                }
33660            }
33661        }
33662        else if (strcasecmp(var, "SCRIPT_GROUP") == 0) {
33663            result = "<unknown>";
33664            if (r->finfo.st_mode != 0) {
33665                if ((gr = getgrgid(r->finfo.st_gid)) != NULL) {
33666                    result = gr->gr_name;
33667                }
33668            }
33669            else {
33670                if (stat(r->filename, &finfo) == 0) {
33671                    if ((gr = getgrgid(finfo.st_gid)) != NULL) {
33672                        result = gr->gr_name;
33673                    }
33674                }
33675            }
33676        }
33677 #endif /* ndef WIN32 */
33678
33679        if (result == NULL) {
33680            return ap_pstrdup(r->pool, "");
33681        }
33682        else {
33683            return ap_pstrdup(r->pool, result);
33684        }
33685 }
33686
33687 static char *lookup_header(request_rec *r, const
33688     char *name)
33689 {
33690     array_header *hdrs_arr;
33691     table_entry *hdrs;
33692     int i;
33693
33694     hdrs_arr = ap_table_elts(r->headers_in);
33695     hdrs = (table_entry *)hdrs_arr->elts;
33696     for (i = 0; i < hdrs_arr->nelts; ++i) {
33697         if (hdrs[i].key == NULL) {
33698             continue;
33699         }
33700         if (strcasecmp(hdrs[i].key, name) == 0) {
33701             ap_table_merge(r->notes, VARY_KEY_THIS, name);
33702             return hdrs[i].val;
```

```
33703              }
33704          }
33705          return NULL;
33706      }
33707
33708
33709
33710
33711      /*
33712      ** +-------------------------------------------------------+
33713      ** |                                                       |
33714      ** |                   caching support                     |
33715      ** |                                                       |
33716      ** +-------------------------------------------------------+
33717      */
33718
33719
33720      static cache *init_cache(pool *p)
33721      {
33722          cache *c;
33723
33724          c = (cache *)ap_palloc(p, sizeof(cache));
33725          c->pool = ap_make_sub_pool(p);
33726          c->lists = ap_make_array(c->pool, 2,
33727                  sizeof(cachelist));
33728          return c;
33729      }
33730
33731      static void set_cache_string(cache *c, char *res,
33732          int mode, time_t t,
33733                                  char *key, char *value)
33734      {
33735          cacheentry ce;
33736
33737          ce.time  = t;
33738          ce.key   = key;
33739          ce.value = value;
33740          store_cache_string(c, res, &ce);
33741          return;
33742      }
33743
33744      static char *get_cache_string(cache *c, char *res,
33745          int mode,
33746                                  time_t t, char *key)
33747      {
33748          cacheentry *ce;
33749
33750          ce = retrieve_cache_string(c, res, key);
```

```
33751          if (ce == NULL) {
33752              return NULL;
33753          }
33754          if (mode & CACHEMODE_TS) {
33755              if (t != ce->time) {
33756                  return NULL;
33757              }
33758          }
33759          else if (mode & CACHEMODE_TTL) {
33760              if (t > ce->time) {
33761                  return NULL;
33762              }
33763          }
33764          return ap_pstrdup(c->pool, ce->value);
33765      }
33766
33767      static int cache_tlb_hash(char *key)
33768      {
33769          unsigned long n;
33770          char *p;
33771
33772          n = 0;
33773          for (p=key; *p != '\0'; ++p) {
33774              n = n * 53711 + 134561 + (unsigned)(*p & 0xff);
33775          }
33776
33777          return n % CACHE_TLB_ROWS;
33778      }
33779
33780      static cacheentry *cache_tlb_lookup(cachetlbentry *tlb,
33781          cacheentry *elt,
33782                                          char *key)
33783      {
33784          int ix = cache_tlb_hash(key);
33785          int i;
33786          int j;
33787
33788          for (i=0; i < CACHE_TLB_COLS; ++i) {
33789              j = tlb[ix].t[i];
33790              if (j < 0)
33791                  return NULL;
33792              if (strcmp(elt[j].key, key) == 0)
33793                  return &elt[j];
33794          }
33795          return NULL;
33796      }
33797
33798      static void cache_tlb_replace(cachetlbentry *tlb,
```

```
33799          cacheentry *elt,
33800                                   cacheentry *e)
33801   {
33802       int ix = cache_tlb_hash(e->key);
33803       int i;
33804
33805       tlb = &tlb[ix];
33806
33807       for (i=1; i < CACHE_TLB_COLS; ++i)
33808           tlb->t[i] = tlb->t[i-1];
33809
33810       tlb->t[0] = e - elt;
33811   }
33812
33813   static void store_cache_string(cache *c, char *res,
33814       cacheentry *ce)
33815   {
33816       int i;
33817       int j;
33818       cachelist *l;
33819       cacheentry *e;
33820       cachetlbentry *t;
33821       int found_list;
33822
33823       found_list = 0;
33824       /* first try to edit an existing entry */
33825       for (i = 0; i < c->lists->nelts; i++) {
33826           l = &(((cachelist *)c->lists->elts)[i]);
33827           if (strcmp(l->resource, res) == 0) {
33828               found_list = 1;
33829
33830               e = cache_tlb_lookup((cachetlbentry
33831                 *)l->tlb->elts,
33832                         (cacheentry *)l->entries->elts,
33833                             ce->key);
33834               if (e != NULL) {
33835                   e->time  = ce->time;
33836                   e->value = ap_pstrdup(c->pool, ce->value);
33837                   return;
33838               }
33839
33840               for (j = 0; j < l->entries->nelts; j++) {
33841                   e = &(((cacheentry *)l->entries->elts)[j]);
33842                   if (strcmp(e->key, ce->key) == 0) {
33843                       e->time  = ce->time;
33844                       e->value = ap_pstrdup(c->pool,
33845                                   ce->value);
33846                       cache_tlb_replace((cachetlbentry
33847                         *)l->tlb->elts,
33848                             (cacheentry *)l->entries->elts, e);
33849                       return;
33850                   }
33851               }
33852           }
33853       }
33854
33855       /* create a needed new list */
33856       if (!found_list) {
33857           l = ap_push_array(c->lists);
33858           l->resource = ap_pstrdup(c->pool, res);
33859           l->entries  = ap_make_array(c->pool, 2,
33860                   sizeof(cacheentry));
33861           l->tlb      = ap_make_array(c->pool,
33862               CACHE_TLB_ROWS,
33863                           sizeof(cachetlbentry));
33864           for (i=0; i<CACHE_TLB_ROWS; ++i) {
33865               t = &((cachetlbentry *)l->tlb->elts)[i];
33866               for (j=0; j<CACHE_TLB_COLS; ++j)
33867                   t->t[j] = -1;
33868           }
33869       }
33870
33871       /* create the new entry */
33872       for (i = 0; i < c->lists->nelts; i++) {
33873           l = &(((cachelist *)c->lists->elts)[i]);
33874           if (strcmp(l->resource, res) == 0) {
33875               e = ap_push_array(l->entries);
33876               e->time  = ce->time;
33877               e->key   = ap_pstrdup(c->pool, ce->key);
33878               e->value = ap_pstrdup(c->pool, ce->value);
33879               cache_tlb_replace((cachetlbentry
33880                       *)l->tlb->elts,
33881                       (cacheentry *)l->entries->elts, e);
33882               return;
33883           }
33884       }
33885
33886       /* not reached, but when it is no problem... */
33887       return;
33888   }
33889
33890   static cacheentry *retrieve_cache_string(cache *c,
33891       char *res, char *key)
33892   {
33893       int i;
33894       int j;
```

```
33895        cachelist *l;
33896        cacheentry *e;
33897
33898        for (i = 0; i < c->lists->nelts; i++) {
33899            l = &(((cachelist *)c->lists->elts)[i]);
33900            if (strcmp(l->resource, res) == 0) {
33901
33902                e = cache_tlb_lookup((cachetlbentry
33903                        *)l->tlb->elts,
33904                                (cacheentry
33905                                    *)l->entries->elts, key);
33906                if (e != NULL)
33907                    return e;
33908
33909                for (j = 0; j < l->entries->nelts; j++) {
33910                    e = &(((cacheentry *)l->entries->elts)[j]);
33911                    if (strcmp(e->key, key) == 0) {
33912                        return e;
33913                    }
33914                }
33915            }
33916        }
33917        return NULL;
33918    }
33919
33920
33921
33922    /*
33923    ** +-------------------------------------------------+
33924    ** |                                                 |
33925    ** |                  misc functions                 |
33926    ** |                                                 |
33927    ** +-------------------------------------------------+
33928    */
33929
33930    static char *subst_prefix_path(request_rec *r,
33931        char *input, char *match,
33932                            char *subst)
33933    {
33934        char matchbuf[LONG_STRING_LEN];
33935        char substbuf[LONG_STRING_LEN];
33936        char *output;
33937        int l;
33938
33939        output = input;
33940
33941        /* first create a match string which always has
```

```
33943    * a trailing slash */
33944    l = ap_cpystrn(matchbuf, match,
33945            sizeof(matchbuf)) - matchbuf;
33946    if (matchbuf[l-1] != '/') {
33947        matchbuf[l] = '/';
33948        matchbuf[l+1] = '\0';
33949        l++;
33950
33951    }
33952    /* now compare the prefix */
33953    if (strncmp(input, matchbuf, l) == 0) {
33954        rewritelog(r, 5, "strip matching prefix:
33955                %s -> %s", output, output+l);
33956        output = ap_pstrdup(r->pool, output+l);
33957
33958        /* and now add the base-URL as replacement
33959         * prefix */
33960        l = ap_cpystrn(substbuf, subst,
33961                sizeof(substbuf)) - substbuf;
33962        if (substbuf[l-1] != '/') {
33963            substbuf[l] = '/';
33964            substbuf[l+1] = '\0';
33965            l++;
33966        }
33967        if (output[0] == '/') {
33968            rewritelog(r, 4, "add subst prefix:
33969                %s -> %s%s",
33970                        output, substbuf, output+1);
33971            output = ap_pstrcat(r->pool, substbuf,
33972                output+1, NULL);
33973        }
33974        else {
33975            rewritelog(r, 4, "add subst prefix:
33976                %s -> %s%s",
33977                        output, substbuf, output);
33978            output = ap_pstrcat(r->pool, substbuf,
33979                output, NULL);
33980        }
33981    }
33982    return output;
33983 }
33984
33985
33986 /*
33987 **
33988 ** own command line parser which don't have
33989 ** the '\\' problem
33990 **
```

```
33991  */
33992
33993  static int parseargline(char *str, char **a1,
33994      char **a2, char **a3)
33995  {
33996      char *cp;
33997      int isquoted;
33998
33999  #define SKIP_WHITESPACE(cp) \
34000      for ( ; *cp == ' ' || *cp == '\t'; ) { \
34001          cp++; \
34002      };
34003
34004  #define CHECK_QUOTATION(cp,isquoted) \
34005      isquoted = 0; \
34006      if (*cp == '"') { \
34007          isquoted = 1; \
34008          cp++; \
34009      }
34010
34011  #define DETERMINE_NEXTSTRING(cp,isquoted) \
34012      for ( ; *cp != '\0'; cp++) { \
34013          if (  (isquoted    && (*cp      == ' ' \
34014              || *cp       == '\t')) \
34015          || (*cp == '\\' && (*(cp+1) == ' ' \
34016              || *(cp+1) == '\t'))) { \
34017              cp++; \
34018              continue; \
34019          } \
34020          if (  (!isquoted \
34021              && (*cp == ' ' || *cp == '\t')) \
34022          || (isquoted && \
34023                  *cp == '"')                ) { \
34024              break; \
34025          } \
34026      }
34027
34028      cp = str;
34029      SKIP_WHITESPACE(cp);
34030
34031      /*  determine first argument */
34032      CHECK_QUOTATION(cp, isquoted);
34033      *a1 = cp;
34034      DETERMINE_NEXTSTRING(cp, isquoted);
34035      if (*cp == '\0') {
34036          return 1;
34037      }
34038      *cp++ = '\0';
34039
34040      SKIP_WHITESPACE(cp);
34041
34042      /*  determine second argument */
34043      CHECK_QUOTATION(cp, isquoted);
34044      *a2 = cp;
34045      DETERMINE_NEXTSTRING(cp, isquoted);
34046      if (*cp == '\0') {
34047          *cp++ = '\0';
34048          *a3 = NULL;
34049          return 0;
34050      }
34051      *cp++ = '\0';
34052
34053      SKIP_WHITESPACE(cp);
34054
34055      /* again check if there are only two arguments */
34056      if (*cp == '\0') {
34057          *cp++ = '\0';
34058          *a3 = NULL;
34059          return 0;
34060      }
34061
34062      /*  determine second argument */
34063      CHECK_QUOTATION(cp, isquoted);
34064      *a3 = cp;
34065      DETERMINE_NEXTSTRING(cp, isquoted);
34066      *cp++ = '\0';
34067
34068      return 0;
34069  }
34070
34071
34072  static void add_env_variable(request_rec *r, char *s)
34073  {
34074      char var[MAX_STRING_LEN];
34075      char val[MAX_STRING_LEN];
34076      char *cp;
34077      int n;
34078
34079      if ((cp = strchr(s, ':')) != NULL) {
34080          n = ((cp-s) > MAX_STRING_LEN-1 ?
34081                  MAX_STRING_LEN-1 : (cp-s));
34082          memcpy(var, s, n);
34083          var[n] = '\0';
34084          ap_cpystrn(val, cp+1, sizeof(val));
34085          ap_table_set(r->subprocess_env, var, val);
34086          rewritelog(r, 5, "setting env variable '%s'
```

```
34087                to '%s'", var, val);
34088        }
34089  }
34090
34091
34092
34093  /*
34094  **
34095  **   stat() for only the prefix of a path
34096  **
34097  */
34098
34099  static int prefix_stat(const char *path,
34100        struct stat *sb)
34101  {
34102        char curpath[LONG_STRING_LEN];
34103        char *cp;
34104
34105        ap_cpystrn(curpath, path, sizeof(curpath));
34106        if (curpath[0] != '/') {
34107            return 0;
34108        }
34109        if ((cp = strchr(curpath+1, '/')) != NULL) {
34110            *cp = '\0';
34111        }
34112        if (stat(curpath, sb) == 0) {
34113            return 1;
34114        }
34115        else {
34116            return 0;
34117        }
34118  }
34119
34120
34121  /*
34122  **
34123  **   File locking
34124  **
34125  */
34126
34127  #ifdef USE_FCNTL
34128  static struct flock   lock_it;
34129  static struct flock unlock_it;
34130  #endif
34131
34132  static void fd_lock(request_rec *r, int fd)
34133  {
34134        int rc;
```

```
34135
34136  #ifdef USE_FCNTL
34137      lock_it.l_whence = SEEK_SET;
34138       /* from current point */
34139      lock_it.l_start  = 0;
34140      /* -"- */
34141      lock_it.l_len    = 0;
34142      /* until end of file */
34143      lock_it.l_type   = F_WRLCK;
34144      /* set exclusive/write lock */
34145      lock_it.l_pid    = 0;
34146      /* pid not actually interesting */
34147
34148      while (    ((rc = fcntl(fd, F_SETLKW, &lock_it)) < 0)
34149          && (errno == EINTR)                         ) {
34150          continue;
34151      }
34152  #endif
34153  #ifdef USE_FLOCK
34154      while (    ((rc = flock(fd, LOCK_EX)) < 0)
34155              && (errno == EINTR)                 ) {
34156          continue;
34157      }
34158  #endif
34159  #ifdef USE_LOCKING
34160      /* Lock the first byte, always, assume we want
34161         to append and seek to the end afterwards */
34162      lseek(fd, 0, SEEK_SET);
34163      rc = _locking(fd, _LK_LOCK, 1);
34164      lseek(fd, 0, SEEK_END);
34165  #endif
34166
34167      if (rc < 0) {
34168          ap_log_rerror(APLOG_MARK, APLOG_ERR, r,
34169                      "mod_rewrite: failed to lock file
34170                          descriptor");
34171          exit(1);
34172      }
34173      return;
34174  }
34175
34176  static void fd_unlock(request_rec *r, int fd)
34177  {
34178      int rc;
34179
34180  #ifdef USE_FCNTL
34181      unlock_it.l_whence = SEEK_SET;
34182       /* from current point */
```

```
34183        unlock_it.l_start  = 0;
34184        /* -"- */
34185        unlock_it.l_len    = 0;
34186        /* until end of file */
34187        unlock_it.l_type   = F_UNLCK;   /* unlock */
34188        unlock_it.l_pid    = 0;
34189        /* pid not actually interesting */
34190
34191        rc = fcntl(fd, F_SETLKW, &unlock_it);
34192 #endif
34193 #ifdef USE_FLOCK
34194        rc = flock(fd, LOCK_UN);
34195 #endif
34196 #ifdef USE_LOCKING
34197        lseek(fd, 0, SEEK_SET);
34198        rc = _locking(fd, _LK_UNLCK, 1);
34199        lseek(fd, 0, SEEK_END);
34200 #endif
34201
34202        if (rc < 0) {
34203            ap_log_rerror(APLOG_MARK, APLOG_ERR, r,
34204                         "mod_rewrite: failed to unlock
34205                              file descriptor");
34206            exit(1);
34207        }
34208 }
34209
34210 /*
34211 **
34212 **   Lexicographic Compare
34213 **
34214 */
34215
34216 static int compare_lexicography(char *cpNum1,
34217        char *cpNum2)
34218 {
34219     int i;
34220     int n1, n2;
34221
34222     n1 = strlen(cpNum1);
34223     n2 = strlen(cpNum2);
34224     if (n1 > n2) {
34225         return 1;
34226     }
34227     if (n1 < n2) {
34228         return -1;
34229     }
34230     for (i = 0; i < n1; i++) {
```

```
34231            if (cpNum1[i] > cpNum2[i]) {
34232                return 1;
34233            }
34234            if (cpNum1[i] < cpNum2[i]) {
34235                return -1;
34236            }
34237        }
34238        return 0;
34239 }
34240
34241
34242 /*EOF*/
```

p 495 **mod_setenvif.c**

```
34243 #include "httpd.h"
34244 #include "http_config.h"
34245 #include "http_core.h"
34246 #include "http_log.h"
34247
34248 enum special {
34249     SPECIAL_NOT,
34250     SPECIAL_REMOTE_ADDR,
34251     SPECIAL_REMOTE_HOST,
34252     SPECIAL_REMOTE_USER,
34253     SPECIAL_REQUEST_URI,
34254     SPECIAL_REQUEST_METHOD
34255 };
34256 typedef struct {
34257     char *name;        /* header name */
34258     char *regex;       /* regex to match against */
34259     regex_t *preg;     /* compiled regex */
34260     table *features; /* env vars to set (or unset) */
34261     ENUM_BITFIELD(     /* is it a "special" header ? */
34262         enum special,
34263         special_type,4);
34264     unsigned icase : 1;              /* ignoring case? */
34265 } sei_entry;
34266
34267 typedef struct {
34268     array_header *conditionals;
34269 } sei_cfg_rec;
34270
34271 module MODULE_VAR_EXPORT setenvif_module;
34272
34273 static void *create_setenvif_config(pool *p,
34274     server_rec *dummy)
34275 {
```

```
34276        sei_cfg_rec *new = (sei_cfg_rec *) ap_palloc(p,
34277         sizeof(sei_cfg_rec));
34278
34279        new->conditionals = ap_make_array(p,
34280         20, sizeof(sei_entry));
34281        return (void *) new;
34282    }
34283
34284    static void *merge_setenvif_config(pool *p,
34285        void *basev, void *overridesv)
34286    {
34287        sei_cfg_rec *a = ap_pcalloc(p,
34288         sizeof(sei_cfg_rec));
34289        sei_cfg_rec *base = basev,
34290         *overrides = overridesv;
34291
34292        a->conditionals = ap_append_arrays(p,
34293         base->conditionals,
34294                        overrides->conditionals);
34295        return a;
34296    }
34297
34298    /* any non-NULL magic constant will do... used
34299     * to indicate if REG_ICASE should
34300     * be used
34301     */
34302    #define ICASE_MAGIC    ((void *)(&setenvif_module))
34303
34304    static const char *add_setenvif_core(cmd_parms *cmd,
34305        void *mconfig,
34306                        char *fname, const char *args)
34307    {
34308        char *regex;
34309        const char *feature;
34310        sei_cfg_rec *sconf =
34311         ap_get_module_config(cmd->server->module_config,
34312                        &setenvif_module);
34313        sei_entry *new, *entries = (sei_entry *)
34314            sconf->conditionals->elts;
34315        char *var;
34316        int i;
34317        int beenhere = 0;
34318        unsigned icase;
34319
34320        /* get regex */
34321        regex = ap_getword_conf(cmd->pool, &args);
34322        if (!*regex) {
34323            return ap_pstrcat(cmd->pool, "Missing
```

```
34324                regular expression for ",
34325                cmd->cmd->name, NULL);
34326        }
34327
34328        /*
34329         * If we've already got a sei_entry with the
34330         * same name we want to just copy the name
34331         * pointer... so that later on we can compare two
34332         * header names just by comparing the pointers.
34333         */
34334
34335        for (i = 0; i < sconf->conditionals->nelts; ++i) {
34336            new = &entries[i];
34337            if (!strcasecmp(new->name, fname)) {
34338                fname = new->name;
34339                break;
34340            }
34341        }
34342
34343        /* if the last entry has an identical
34344         * headername and regex then
34345         * merge with it
34346         */
34347        i = sconf->conditionals->nelts - 1;
34348        icase = cmd->info == ICASE_MAGIC;
34349        if (i < 0
34350         || entries[i].name != fname
34351         || entries[i].icase != icase
34352         || strcmp(entries[i].regex, regex)) {
34353
34354            /* no match, create a new entry */
34355
34356            new = ap_push_array(sconf->conditionals);
34357            new->name = fname;
34358            new->regex = regex;
34359            new->icase = icase;
34360            new->preg = ap_pregcomp(cmd->pool, regex,
34361                (REG_EXTENDED | REG_NOSUB
34362                    | (icase ? REG_ICASE : 0)));
34363            if (new->preg == NULL) {
34364                return ap_pstrcat(cmd->pool, cmd->cmd->name,
34365                    " regex could not be compiled.",
34366            }
34367            new->features = ap_make_table(cmd->pool, 2);
34368
34369            if (!strcasecmp(fname, "remote_addr")) {
34370                new->special_type = SPECIAL_REMOTE_ADDR;
34371            }
```

```
34372        else if (!strcasecmp(fname, "remote_host")) {
34373            new->special_type = SPECIAL_REMOTE_HOST;
34374        }
34375        else if (!strcasecmp(fname, "remote_user")) {
34376            new->special_type = SPECIAL_REMOTE_USER;
34377        }
34378        else if (!strcasecmp(fname, "request_uri")) {
34379            new->special_type = SPECIAL_REQUEST_URI;
34380        }
34381        else if (!strcasecmp(fname, "request_method")) {
34382            new->special_type = SPECIAL_REQUEST_METHOD;
34383        }
34384        else {
34385            new->special_type = SPECIAL_NOT;
34386        }
34387    }
34388    else {
34389     new = &entries[i];
34390    }
34391
34392    for ( ; ; ) {
34393     feature = ap_getword_conf(cmd->pool, &args);
34394     if (!*feature) {
34395        break;
34396     }
34397      beenhere++;
34398
34399      var = ap_getword(cmd->pool, &feature, '=');
34400      if (*feature) {
34401         ap_table_setn(new->features, var, feature);
34402      }
34403      else if (*var == '!') {
34404         ap_table_setn(new->features, var + 1, "!");
34405      }
34406      else {
34407         ap_table_setn(new->features, var, "1");
34408      }
34409    }
34410
34411     if (!beenhere) {
34412        return ap_pstrcat(cmd->pool, "Missing
34413                envariable expression for ",
34414                cmd->cmd->name, NULL);
34415     }
34416
34417    return NULL;
34418 }
34419
34420 static const char *add_setenvif(cmd_parms *cmd,
34421     void *mconfig,
34422                    const char *args)
34423 {
34424    char *fname;
34425
34426    /* get header name */
34427    fname = ap_getword_conf(cmd->pool, &args);
34428    if (!*fname) {
34429        return ap_pstrcat(cmd->pool, "Missing
34430            header-field name for ",
34431                cmd->cmd->name, NULL);
34432    }
34433    return add_setenvif_core(cmd,
34434        mconfig, fname, args);
34435 }
34436
34437 /*
34438  * This routine handles the BrowserMatch* directives.
34439  * It simply turns around and feeds them, with the
34440  * appropriate embellishments, to the general-purpose
34441  * command handler.
34442  */
34443 static const char *add_browser(cmd_parms *cmd,
34444     void *mconfig, const char *args)
34445 {
34446    return add_setenvif_core(cmd,
34447      mconfig, "User-Agent", args);
34448 }
34449
34450 static const command_rec setenvif_module_cmds[] =
34451 {
34452    { "SetEnvIf", add_setenvif, NULL,
34453      RSRC_CONF, RAW_ARGS, "A header-name, regex
34454          and a list of variables." },
34455    { "SetEnvIfNoCase", add_setenvif, ICASE_MAGIC,
34456      RSRC_CONF, RAW_ARGS, "a header-name, regex
34457          and a list of variables." },
34458    { "BrowserMatch", add_browser, NULL,
34459      RSRC_CONF, RAW_ARGS, "A browser regex
34460          and a list of variables." },
34461    { "BrowserMatchNoCase", add_browser, ICASE_MAGIC,
34462      RSRC_CONF, RAW_ARGS, "A browser regex and a
34463          list of variables." },
34464    { NULL },
34465 };
34466
34467 static int match_headers(request_rec *r)
```

```
34468   {
34469       server_rec *s = r->server;
34470       sei_cfg_rec *sconf;
34471       sei_entry *entries;
34472       table_entry *elts;
34473       const char *val;
34474       int i, j;
34475       char *last_name;
34476
34477       sconf = (sei_cfg_rec *)
34478           ap_get_module_config(s->module_config,
34479                       &setenvif_module);
34480       entries = (sei_entry *)
34481           sconf->conditionals->elts;
34482       last_name = NULL;
34483       val = NULL;
34484       for (i = 0; i <
34485           sconf->conditionals->nelts; ++i) {
34486         sei_entry *b = &entries[i];
34487
34488         /* Optimize the case where a bunch of directives
34489          * in a row use the same header.  Remember we
34490          * don't need to strcmp the two header names
34491          * because we made sure the pointers were equal
34492          * during configuration.
34493          */
34494
34495         if (b->name != last_name) {
34496             last_name = b->name;
34497             switch (b->special_type) {
34498             case SPECIAL_REMOTE_ADDR:
34499              val = r->connection->remote_ip;
34500              break;
34501             case SPECIAL_REMOTE_HOST:
34502              val =  ap_get_remote_host(r->connection,
34503                 r->per_dir_config,
34504                         REMOTE_NAME);
34505              break;
34506             case SPECIAL_REMOTE_USER:
34507              val = r->connection->user;
34508              break;
34509             case SPECIAL_REQUEST_URI:
34510              val = r->uri;
34511              break;
34512             case SPECIAL_REQUEST_METHOD:
34513              val = r->method;
34514              break;
34515             case SPECIAL_NOT:
34516              val = ap_table_get(r->headers_in, b->name);
34517              break;
34518             }
34519         }
34520
34521         /*
34522          * A NULL value indicates that the header
34523          * field or special entity wasn't present or
34524          * is undefined.  Represent that as an
34525          * empty string so that REs like "^$"
34526          * will work and allow envariable setting
34527          * based on missing or empty field.
34528          */
34529
34530         if (val == NULL) {
34531             val = "";
34532         }
34533
34534         if (!regexec(b->preg, val, 0, NULL, 0)) {
34535          array_header *arr =
34536               ap_table_elts(b->features);
34537          elts = (table_entry *) arr->elts;
34538
34539          for (j = 0; j < arr->nelts; ++j) {
34540              if (!strcmp(elts[j].val, "!")) {
34541                  ap_table_unset(r->subprocess_env,
34542                      elts[j].key);
34543              }
34544              else {
34545                  ap_table_setn(r->subprocess_env,
34546                      elts[j].key, elts[j].val);
34547              }
34548          }
34549         }
34550     }
34551
34552     return DECLINED;
34553   }
34554
34555 module MODULE_VAR_EXPORT setenvif_module =
34556 {
34557     STANDARD_MODULE_STUFF,
34558     NULL,                   /* initializer */
34559     NULL,                   /* dir config creater */
34560     NULL,
34561     /* dir merger -- default is to override */
34562     create_setenvif_config, /* server config */
34563     merge_setenvif_config,  /* merge server configs */
```

```
34564      setenvif_module_cmds,    /* command table */
34565      NULL,                    /* handlers */
34566      NULL,                    /* filename translation */
34567      NULL,                    /* check_user_id */
34568      NULL,                    /* check auth */
34569      NULL,                    /* check access */
34570      NULL,                    /* type_checker */
34571      NULL,                    /* fixups */
34572      NULL,                    /* logger */
34573      NULL,                    /* input header parse */
34574      NULL,
34575      /* child (process) initialization */
34576      NULL,                    /* child (process) rundown */
34577      match_headers            /* post_read_request */
34578  };
```

▶ **mod_so.c**   p 539

```
34579  #define CORE_PRIVATE
34580  #include "httpd.h"
34581  #include "http_config.h"
34582  #include "http_log.h"
34583
34584  module MODULE_VAR_EXPORT so_module;
34585
34586
34587  /*
34588   * Server configuration to keep track of actually
34589   * loaded modules and the corresponding module name.
34590   */
34591
34592  typedef struct moduleinfo {
34593      char *name;
34594      module *modp;
34595  } moduleinfo;
34596
34597  typedef struct so_server_conf {
34598      array_header *loaded_modules;
34599  } so_server_conf;
34600
34601  static void *so_sconf_create(pool *p, server_rec *s)
34602  {
34603      so_server_conf *soc;
34604
34605      soc = (so_server_conf *)ap_pcalloc(p,
34606          sizeof(so_server_conf));
34607      soc->loaded_modules = ap_make_array(p,
34608          DYNAMIC_MODULE_LIMIT,
```

```
34609                              sizeof(moduleinfo));
34610  #ifndef NO_DLOPEN
34611      ap_os_dso_init();
34612  #endif
34613
34614      return (void *)soc;
34615  }
34616
34617  #ifndef NO_DLOPEN
34618
34619  /*
34620   * This is the cleanup for a loaded shared object.
34621   * It unloads the module. This is called as a
34622   * cleanup function from the core.
34623   */
34624
34625  static void unload_module(moduleinfo *modi)
34626  {
34627      /* only unload if module information is
34628       * still existing */
34629      if (modi->modp == NULL)
34630          return;
34631
34632      /* remove the module pointer from the core
34633       * structure */
34634      ap_remove_loaded_module(modi->modp);
34635
34636      /* unload the module space itself */
34637      ap_os_dso_unload((ap_os_dso_handle_t)modi->
34638          modp->dynamic_load_handle);
34639
34640      /* destroy the module information */
34641      modi->modp = NULL;
34642      modi->name = NULL;
34643  }
34644
34645  /*
34646   * This is the cleanup routine for files loaded by
34647   * load_file(). Unfortunately we don't keep a record
34648   * of the filename that was loaded, so we can't report
34649   * the unload for debug purposes or include the
34650   * filename in error message.
34651   */
34652
34653  static void unload_file(void *handle)
34654  {
34655      ap_os_dso_unload((ap_os_dso_handle_t)handle);
34656  }
```

```
34657
34658    /*
34659     * This is called for the directive LoadModule and
34660     * actually loads a shared object file into the
34661     * address space of the server process.
34662     */
34663
34664    static const char *load_module(cmd_parms *cmd,
34665        void *dummy,
34666                            char *modname, char *filename)
34667    {
34668        ap_os_dso_handle_t modhandle;
34669        module *modp;
34670        const char *szModuleFile=ap_server_root_
34671            relative(cmd->pool, filename);
34672        so_server_conf *sconf;
34673        moduleinfo *modi;
34674        moduleinfo *modie;
34675        int i;
34676
34677        /*
34678         * check for already existing module
34679         * If it already exists, we have nothing to do
34680         */
34681        sconf = (so_server_conf *)ap_get_module_config(cmd->
34682            server->module_config,
34683                                            &so_module);
34684        modie = (moduleinfo *)sconf->loaded_modules->elts;
34685        for (i = 0; i < sconf->loaded_modules->nelts; i++) {
34686            modi = &modie[i];
34687            if (modi->name != NULL && strcmp(modi->name,
34688                modname) == 0)
34689                return NULL;
34690        }
34691        modi = ap_push_array(sconf->loaded_modules);
34692        modi->name = modname;
34693
34694        /*
34695         * Load the file into the Apache address space
34696         */
34697        if (!(modhandle = ap_os_dso_load(szModuleFile))) {
34698         const char *my_error = ap_os_dso_error();
34699         return ap_pstrcat (cmd->pool, "Cannot load ",
34700             szModuleFile,
34701                 " into server: ",
34702                 my_error ? my_error : "(reason unknown)",
34703                 NULL);
34704        }
```

```
34705        ap_log_error(APLOG_MARK,
34706            APLOG_DEBUG|APLOG_NOERRNO, NULL,
34707            "loaded module %s", modname);
34708
34709        /*
34710         * Retrieve the pointer to the module structure
34711         * through the module name: First with the hidden
34712         * variant (prefix 'AP_') and then with the plain
34713         * symbol name.
34714         */
34715        if (!(modp = (module *)(ap_os_dso_sym(modhandle,
34716            modname)))) {
34717         return ap_pstrcat(cmd->pool, "Can't locate API
34718             module structure '", modname,
34719                 "' in file ", szModuleFile, ": ",
34720                     ap_os_dso_error(), NULL);
34721        }
34722        modi->modp = modp;
34723        modp->dynamic_load_handle = modhandle;
34724
34725        /*
34726         * Make sure the found module structure is really
34727         * a module structure
34728         *
34729         */
34730        if (modp->magic != MODULE_MAGIC_COOKIE) {
34731            return ap_pstrcat(cmd->pool, "API module
34732                structure '", modname,
34733                    "' in file ", szModuleFile,
34734                        " is garbled -"
34735                        " perhaps this is not an Apache
34736                            module DSO?", NULL);
34737        }
34738
34739        /*
34740         * Add this module to the Apache core structures
34741         */
34742        ap_add_loaded_module(modp);
34743
34744        /*
34745         * Register a cleanup in the config pool (normally
34746         * pconf). When we do a restart (or shutdown)
34747         * this cleanup will cause the shared object
34748         * to be unloaded.
34749         */
34750        ap_register_cleanup(cmd->pool, modi,
34751            (void (*)(void*))unload_module,
34752                ap_null_cleanup);
```

```
34753
34754        /*
34755         * Finally we need to run the configuration process
34756         * for the module
34757         */
34758        ap_single_module_configure(cmd->pool,
34759                cmd->server, modp);
34760
34761        return NULL;
34762    }
34763
34764    /*
34765     * This implements the LoadFile directive and loads
34766     * an arbitrary shared object file into the
34767     * adress space of the server process.
34768     */
34769
34770    static const char *load_file(cmd_parms *cmd,
34771          void *dummy, char *filename)
34772    {
34773        void *handle;
34774        char *file;
34775
34776        file = ap_server_root_relative(cmd->pool, filename);
34777
34778        if (!(handle = ap_os_dso_load(file))) {
34779         const char *my_error = ap_os_dso_error();
34780         return ap_pstrcat (cmd->pool, "Cannot load ",
34781             filename,
34782                 " into server:",
34783                 my_error ? my_error : "(reason unknown)",
34784                 NULL);
34785        }
34786
34787        ap_log_error(APLOG_MARK,
34788             APLOG_DEBUG|APLOG_NOERRNO, NULL,
34789             "loaded file %s", filename);
34790
34791        ap_register_cleanup(cmd->pool, handle, unload_file,
34792             ap_null_cleanup);
34793
34794        return NULL;
34795    }
34796
34797    #else /* not NO_DLOPEN */
34798
34799    static const char *load_file(cmd_parms *cmd,
34800          void *dummy, char *filename)
34801    {
34802        fprintf(stderr, "WARNING: LoadFile not supported
34803             on this platform\n");
34804        return NULL;
34805    }
34806
34807    static const char *load_module(cmd_parms *cmd,
34808        void *dummy,
34809                            char *modname, char *filename)
34810    {
34811        fprintf(stderr, "WARNING: LoadModule not supported
34812             on this platform\n");
34813        return NULL;
34814    }
34815
34816    #endif /* NO_DLOPEN */
34817
34818    static const command_rec so_cmds[] = {
34819        { "LoadModule", load_module, NULL, RSRC_CONF, TAKE2,
34820         "a module name and the name of a shared object
34821             file to load it from"},
34822        { "LoadFile", load_file, NULL, RSRC_CONF, ITERATE,
34823         "shared object file or library to load into the
34824             server at runtime"},
34825        { NULL }
34826    };
34827
34828    module MODULE_VAR_EXPORT so_module = {
34829        STANDARD_MODULE_STUFF,
34830        NULL,               /* initializer */
34831        NULL,               /* create per-dir config */
34832        NULL,               /* merge per-dir config */
34833        so_sconf_create,        /* server config */
34834        NULL,               /* merge server config */
34835        so_cmds,            /* command table */
34836        NULL,               /* handlers */
34837        NULL,               /* filename translation */
34838        NULL,               /* check_user_id */
34839        NULL,               /* check auth */
34840        NULL,               /* check access */
34841        NULL,               /* type_checker */
34842        NULL,               /* fixer_upper */
34843        NULL,               /* logger */
34844        NULL,               /* header parser */
34845        NULL,               /* child_init */
34846        NULL,               /* child_exit */
34847        NULL                /* post read-request */
34848    };
```

▶ p 541 mod_speling.c

```
34849    #define WANT_BASENAME_MATCH
34850
34851    #include "httpd.h"
34852    #include "http_core.h"
34853    #include "http_config.h"
34854    #include "http_log.h"
34855
34856
34857    MODULE_VAR_EXPORT module speling_module;
34858
34859    typedef struct {
34860        int enabled;
34861    } spconfig;
34862
34863    /*
34864     * Create a configuration specific to this module for
34865     * a server or directory location, and fill it with
34866     * the default settings.
34867     *
34868     * The API says that in the absence of a merge function,
34869     * the record for the closest ancestor is used
34870     * exclusively.  That's what we want, so we don't
34871     * bother to have such a function.
34872     */
34873
34874    static void *mkconfig(pool *p)
34875    {
34876        spconfig *cfg = ap_pcalloc(p, sizeof(spconfig));
34877
34878        cfg->enabled = 0;
34879        return cfg;
34880    }
34881
34882    /*
34883     * Respond to a callback to create configuration
34884     * record for a server or vhost environment.
34885     */
34886    static void *create_mconfig_for_server(pool *p,
34887        server_rec *s)
34888    {
34889        return mkconfig(p);
34890    }
34891
34892    /*
34893     * Respond to a callback to create a config record for
34894     * a specific directory.
```

```
34895     */
34896    static void *create_mconfig_for_directory(pool *p,
34897        char *dir)
34898    {
34899        return mkconfig(p);
34900    }
34901
34902    /*
34903     * Handler for the CheckSpelling directive, which is FLAG.
34904     */
34905    static const char *set_speling(cmd_parms *cmd,
34906        void *mconfig, int arg)
34907    {
34908        spconfig *cfg = (spconfig *) mconfig;
34909
34910        cfg->enabled = arg;
34911        return NULL;
34912    }
34913
34914    /*
34915     * Define the directives specific to this module.
34916     * This structure is referenced later by the 'module'
34917     * structure.
34918     */
34919    static const command_rec speling_cmds[] =
34920    {
34921        { "CheckSpelling", set_speling, NULL, OR_OPTIONS,
34922            FLAG,
34923            "whether or not to fix miscapitalized/misspelled
34924            requests" },
34925        { NULL }
34926    };
34927
34928    typedef enum {
34929        SP_IDENTICAL = 0,
34930        SP_MISCAPITALIZED = 1,
34931        SP_TRANSPOSITION = 2,
34932        SP_MISSINGCHAR = 3,
34933        SP_EXTRACHAR = 4,
34934        SP_SIMPLETYPO = 5,
34935        SP_VERYDIFFERENT = 6
34936    } sp_reason;
34937
34938    static const char *sp_reason_str[] =
34939    {
34940        "identical",
34941        "miscapitalized",
34942        "transposed characters",
```

```
34943          "character missing",
34944          "extra character",
34945          "mistyped character",
34946          "common basename",
34947    };
34948
34949    typedef struct {
34950         const char *name;
34951         sp_reason quality;
34952    } misspelled_file;
34953
34954    /*
34955     * spdist() is taken from Kernighan & Pike,
34956     *   _The_UNIX_Programming_Environment_
34957     * and adapted somewhat to correspond better to
34958     * psychological reality. (Note the changes to
34959     * the return values)
34960     *
34961     * According to Pollock and Zamora, CACM April 1984
34962     * (V. 27, No. 4), page 363, the correct order for
34963     * this is:
34964     * OMISSION = TRANSPOSITION > INSERTION > SUBSTITUTION
34965     * thus, it was exactly backwards in the old version.
34966     * -- PWP
34967     *
34968     * This routine was taken out of tcsh's spelling
34969     * correction code(tcsh-6.07.04) and re-converted
34970     * to apache data types ("char" type instead of tcsh's
34971     * NLS'ed "Char"). Plus it now ignores the case during
34972     * comparisons, so is a "approximate strcasecmp()".
34973     * NOTE that is still allows only _one_ real "typo",
34974     * it does NOT try to correct multiple errors.
34975     */
34976
34977    static sp_reason spdist(const char *s, const char *t)
34978    {
34979        for (; ap_tolower(*s) == ap_tolower(*t); t++, s++) {
34980            if (*t == '\0') {
34981                return SP_MISCAPITALIZED;
34982                /* exact match (sans case) */
34983            }
34984        }
34985        if (*s) {
34986            if (*t) {
34987                if (s[1] && t[1] && ap_tolower(*s) ==
34988                    ap_tolower(t[1])
34989                && ap_tolower(*t) == ap_tolower(s[1])
34990                && strcasecmp(s + 2, t + 2) == 0) {
34991                    return SP_TRANSPOSITION;
34992                    /* transposition */
34993                }
34994                if (strcasecmp(s + 1, t + 1) == 0) {
34995                    return SP_SIMPLETYPO;
34996                    /* 1 char mismatch */
34997                }
34998            }
34999            if (strcasecmp(s + 1, t) == 0) {
35000                return SP_EXTRACHAR;
35001                /* extra character */
35002            }
35003        }
35004        if (*t && strcasecmp(s, t + 1) == 0) {
35005            return SP_MISSINGCHAR;  /* missing character */
35006        }
35007        return SP_VERYDIFFERENT;
35008        /* distance too large to fix. */
35009    }
35010
35011    static int sort_by_quality(const void *left,
35012        const void *rite)
35013    {
35014        return (int) (((misspelled_file *) left)->quality)
35015            - (int) (((misspelled_file *) rite)->quality);
35016    }
35017
35018    static int check_speling(request_rec *r)
35019    {
35020        spconfig *cfg;
35021        char *good, *bad, *postgood, *url;
35022        int filoc, dotloc, urlen, pglen;
35023        DIR *dirp;
35024        struct DIR_TYPE *dir_entry;
35025        array_header *candidates = NULL;
35026
35027        cfg = ap_get_module_config(r->per_dir_config,
35028            &speling_module);
35029        if (!cfg->enabled) {
35030            return DECLINED;
35031        }
35032
35033
35034        /* We only want to worry about GETs */
35035        if (r->method_number != M_GET) {
35036            return DECLINED;
35037        }
35038
```

```
35039        /* We've already got a file of some kind or
35040         * another */
35041        if (r->proxyreq || (r->finfo.st_mode != 0)) {
35042            return DECLINED;
35043        }
35044
35045        /* This is a sub request - don't mess with it */
35046        if (r->main) {
35047            return DECLINED;
35048        }
35049
35050        /*
35051         * The request should end up looking like this:
35052         * r->uri: /correct-url/mispelling/more
35053         * r->filename: /correct-file/mispelling r->
35054              path_info: /more
35055         *
35056         * So we do this in steps. First break r->filename
35057         * into two pieces
35058         */
35059
35060        filoc = ap_rind(r->filename, '/');
35061        /*
35062         * Don't do anything if the request doesn't contain
35063         * a slash, or requests "/"
35064         */
35065        if (filoc == -1 || strcmp(r->uri, "/") == 0) {
35066            return DECLINED;
35067        }
35068
35069        /* good = /correct-file */
35070        good = ap_pstrndup(r->pool, r->filename, filoc);
35071        /* bad = mispelling */
35072        bad = ap_pstrdup(r->pool, r->filename + filoc + 1);
35073        /* postgood = mispelling/more */
35074        postgood = ap_pstrcat(r->pool, bad, r->path_info,
35075            NULL);
35076
35077        urlen = strlen(r->uri);
35078        pglen = strlen(postgood);
35079
35080        /* Check to see if the URL pieces add up */
35081        if (strcmp(postgood, r->uri + (urlen - pglen))) {
35082            return DECLINED;
35083        }
35084
35085        /* url = /correct-url */
35086        url = ap_pstrndup(r->pool, r->uri, (urlen - pglen));
35087
35088        /* Now open the directory and do ourselves
35089         * a check... */
35090        dirp = ap_popendir(r->pool, good);
35091        if (dirp == NULL) {
35092        /* Oops, not a directory... */
35093            return DECLINED;
35094        }
35095
35096        candidates = ap_make_array(r->pool, 2,
35097            sizeof(misspelled_file));
35098
35099        dotloc = ap_ind(bad, '.');
35100        if (dotloc == -1) {
35101            dotloc = strlen(bad);
35102        }
35103
35104        while ((dir_entry = readdir(dirp)) != NULL) {
35105            sp_reason q;
35106
35107            /*
35108             * If we end up with a "fixed" URL which is
35109             * identical to the requested one, we must have
35110             * found a broken symlink or some such. Do
35111             * _not_ try to redirect this, it causes a loop!
35112             */
35113            if (strcmp(bad, dir_entry->d_name) == 0) {
35114                ap_pclosedir(r->pool, dirp);
35115                return OK;
35116            }
35117            /*
35118             * miscapitalization errors are checked first
35119             * (like, e.g., lower case file, upper case
35120             * request)
35121             */
35122            else if (strcasecmp(bad,
35123                    dir_entry->d_name) == 0) {
35124                misspelled_file *sp_new;
35125
35126                sp_new = (misspelled_file *)
35127                    ap_push_array(candidates);
35128                sp_new->name = ap_pstrdup(r->pool,
35129                    dir_entry->d_name);
35130                sp_new->quality = SP_MISCAPITALIZED;
35131            }
35132
35133            /*
35134             * simple typing errors are checked next
```

```
35135          * (like, e.g.,missing/extra/transposed char)
35136          */
35137          else if ((q = spdist(bad, dir_entry->d_name))
35138                 != SP_VERYDIFFERENT) {
35139              misspelled_file *sp_new;
35140
35141            sp_new = (misspelled_file *)
35142                 ap_push_array(candidates);
35143              sp_new->name = ap_pstrdup(r->pool,
35144                 dir_entry->d_name);
35145              sp_new->quality = q;
35146          }
35147          /*
35148       * The spdist() should have found the majority of
35149       * the misspelled requests.  It is of questionable
35150       * use to continue looking for files with the same
35151       * base name, but potentially of totally wrong
35152       * type (index.html <-> index.db).
35153       * I would propose to not set the
35154       * WANT_BASENAME_MATCH define.
35155          *      08-Aug-1997 <Martin.Kraemer@Mch.SNI.De>
35156          *
35157          * However, Alexei replied giving some reasons
35158          * to add it anyway: > Oh, by the way, I
35159          * remembered why having the> extension-
35160          * stripping -and-matching stuff is a good idea:
35161          * >
35162          * > If you're using MultiViews, and have a file
35163       * > named foobar.html, which you refer to as
35164       * > "foobar", and someone tried to access"Foobar",
35165       * > mod_speling won't find it, because it won't
35166       * > find anything matching that spelling. With
35167       * > the extension-munging, it would locate
35168       * > "foobar.html". Not perfect, but I ran into
35169       * > that problem when I first wrote the module.
35170          */
35171          else {
35172 #ifdef WANT_BASENAME_MATCH
35173          /*
35174          * Okay... we didn't find anything. Now we
35175          * take out the hard-core power tools. There
35176          * are several cases here. Someone might have
35177          * entered a wrong extension (.htm instead of
35178          * .html or vice versa) or the document
35179          * could be negotiated. At any rate, now
35180          * we just compare stuff before the first
35181          * dot. If it matches, we figure we got us a
35182          * match. This can result in wrong things if
```

```
35183          * there are files of different content types
35184          * but the same prefix(e.g. foo.gif and
35185          * foo.html) This code will pick the first one
35186          * it finds. Better than a Not Found, though.
35187          */
35188            int entloc = ap_ind(dir_entry->d_name, '.');
35189            if (entloc == -1) {
35190                entloc = strlen(dir_entry->d_name);
35191          }
35192
35193            if ((dotloc == entloc)
35194                && !strncasecmp(bad, dir_entry->d_name,
35195                    dotloc)) {
35196                misspelled_file *sp_new;
35197
35198            sp_new = (misspelled_file *)
35199                ap_push_array(candidates);
35200              sp_new->name = ap_pstrdup(r->pool,
35201                    dir_entry->d_name);
35202              sp_new->quality = SP_VERYDIFFERENT;
35203          }
35204 #endif
35205          }
35206      }
35207      ap_pclosedir(r->pool, dirp);
35208
35209      if (candidates->nelts != 0) {
35210          /* Wow... we found us a mispelling. Construct
35211           * a fixed url */
35212          char *nuri;
35213        const char *ref;
35214          misspelled_file *variant = (misspelled_file *)
35215              candidates->elts;
35216          int i;
35217
35218          ref = ap_table_get(r->headers_in, "Referer");
35219
35220          qsort((void *) candidates->elts,
35221              candidates->nelts,
35222              sizeof(misspelled_file), sort_by_quality);
35223
35224          /*
35225           * Conditions for immediate redirection:
35226           *      a) the first candidate was not found by
35227           *      stripping the suffix
35228           * AND b) there exists only one candidate OR the
35229           *      best match is not ambiguous
35230           * then return a redirection right away.
```

```
35231            */                                             35279            nelts * 5, sizeof(char *));
35232            if (variant[0].quality != SP_VERYDIFFERENT     35280
35233            && (candidates->nelts == 1                      35281        /* Generate the response text. */
35234             || variant[0].quality != variant[1].quality)) { 35282
35235                                                            35283    *(const char **)ap_push_array(t) =
35236                nuri = ap_pstrcat(r->pool, url,             35284            "The document name you requested
35237                    variant[0].name, r->path_info,          35285                (<code>";
35238                        r->parsed_uri.query ? "?" : "",     35286    *(const char **)ap_push_array(t) = r->uri;
35239                        r->parsed_uri.query ?               35287    *(const char **)ap_push_array(t) =
35240                            r->parsed_uri.query : "",       35288            "</code>) could not be found on
35241                        NULL);                              35289                    this server.\n"
35242                                                            35290            "However, we found documents with
35243                ap_table_setn(r->headers_out, "Location",   35291                    names similar "
35244                    ap_construct_url(r->pool, nuri, r));    35292            "to the one you requested.<p>"
35245                                                            35293            "Available documents:\n<ul>\n";
35246                ap_log_rerror(APLOG_MARK,                   35294
35247                    APLOG_NOERRNO | APLOG_INFO, r,          35295        for (i = 0; i < candidates->nelts; ++i) {
35248                        ref ? "Fixed spelling: %s to %s from %s" 35296    char *vuri;
35249                            : "Fixed spelling: %s to %s",   35297    const char *reason;
35250                        r->uri, nuri, ref);                 35298
35251                                                            35299    reason = sp_reason_str[(int)
35252                return HTTP_MOVED_PERMANENTLY;              35300        (variant[i].quality)];
35253            }                                               35301            /* The format isn't very neat... */
35254            /*                                              35302    vuri = ap_pstrcat(sub_pool, url,
35255             * Otherwise, a "[300] Multiple Choices" list   35303        variant[i].name, r->path_info,
35256             * with the variants is returned.               35304            (r->parsed_uri.query !=
35257    */                                                      35305                    NULL) ? "?" : "",
35258            else {                                          35306            (r->parsed_uri.query != NULL)
35259                pool *p;                                     35307                ? r->parsed_uri.query : "",
35260                table *notes;                               35308            NULL);
35261            pool *sub_pool;                                 35309    *(const char **)ap_push_array(v) = "\"";
35262            array_header *t;                                35310    *(const char **)ap_push_array(v) = vuri;
35263            array_header *v;                                35311    *(const char **)ap_push_array(v) = "\";\"";
35264                                                            35312    *(const char **)ap_push_array(v) = reason;
35265                                                            35313    *(const char **)ap_push_array(v) = "\"";
35266                if (r->main == NULL) {                       35314
35267                    p = r->pool;                            35315    *(const char **)ap_push_array(t) =
35268                    notes = r->notes;                       35316        "<li><a href=\"";
35269                }                                           35317    *(const char **)ap_push_array(t) = vuri;
35270                else {                                      35318    *(const char **)ap_push_array(t) = "\">";
35271                    p = r->main->pool;                      35319    *(const char **)ap_push_array(t) = vuri;
35272                    notes = r->main->notes;                 35320    *(const char **)ap_push_array(t) = "</a> (";
35273                }                                           35321    *(const char **)ap_push_array(t) = reason;
35274                                                            35322    *(const char **)ap_push_array(t) = ")\n";
35275                sub_pool = ap_make_sub_pool(p);             35323            /* when we have printed the "close
35276                t = ap_make_array(sub_pool, candidates->    35324             * matches" and there are more
35277                    nelts * 8 + 8, sizeof(char *));         35325             * "distant matches" (matched by
35278                v = ap_make_array(sub_pool, candidates->    35326             * stripping the suffix), then we
```

```
35327                      * insert an additional separator
35328                      * text to suggest that the user
35329                      * LOOK CLOSELY whether these are
35330                      * really the files she wanted.*/
35331             if (i > 0 && i < candidates->nelts - 1
35332                     && variant[i].quality !=
35333                             SP_VERYDIFFERENT
35334                     && variant[i + 1].quality ==
35335                             SP_VERYDIFFERENT) {
35336                 *(const char **)ap_push_array(t) =
35337                     "</ul>\nFurthermore, the
35338                            following related "
35339                     "documents were found:\n<ul>\n";
35340             }
35341         }
35342         *(const char **)ap_push_array(t) = "</ul>\n";
35343
35344         /* If we know there was a referring page,
35345          * add a note: */
35346         if (ref != NULL) {
35347             *(const char **)ap_push_array(t) =
35348                 "Please consider informing the
35349                        owner of the "
35350                 "<a href=\"";
35351             *(const char **)ap_push_array(t) = ref;
35352             *(const char **)ap_push_array(t) =
35353                 "\">referring page</a> "
35354                 "about the broken link.\n";
35355         }
35356
35357
35358         /* Pass our table to http_protocol.c
35359          * (see mod_negotiation): */
35360         ap_table_setn(notes, "variant-list",
35361                 ap_array_pstrcat(p, t, 0));
35362
35363     ap_table_mergen(r->subprocess_env, "VARIANTS",
35364             ap_array_pstrcat(p, v, ','));
35365
35366     ap_destroy_pool(sub_pool);
35367
35368     ap_log_rerror(APLOG_MARK,
35369         APLOG_NOERRNO | APLOG_INFO, r,
35370         ref ? "Spelling fix: %s:
35371             %d candidates from %s"
35372             : "Spelling fix: %s: %d candidates",
35373         r->uri, candidates->nelts, ref);
35374
```

```
35375             return HTTP_MULTIPLE_CHOICES;
35376         }
35377     }
35378
35379     return OK;
35380 }
35381
35382 module MODULE_VAR_EXPORT speling_module =
35383 {
35384     STANDARD_MODULE_STUFF,
35385     NULL,                        /* initializer */
35386     create_mconfig_for_directory,
35387     /* create per-dir config */
35388     NULL,                        /* merge per-dir config */
35389     create_mconfig_for_server,   /* server config */
35390     NULL,                        /* merge server config */
35391     speling_cmds,                /* command table */
35392     NULL,                        /* handlers */
35393     NULL,                        /* filename translation */
35394     NULL,                        /* check_user_id */
35395     NULL,                        /* check auth */
35396     NULL,                        /* check access */
35397     NULL,                        /* type_checker */
35398     check_speling,               /* fixups */
35399     NULL,                        /* logger */
35400     NULL,                        /* header parser */
35401     NULL,                        /* child_init */
35402     NULL,                        /* child_exit */
35403     NULL                         /* post read-request */
35404 };
```

▶ p.548 mod_status.c

```
35405 #define CORE_PRIVATE
35406 #include "httpd.h"
35407 #include "http_config.h"
35408 #include "http_core.h"
35409 #include "http_protocol.h"
35410 #include "http_conf_globals.h"
35411 /* for ap_extended_status */
35412 #include "http_main.h"
35413 #include "util_script.h"
35414 #include <time.h>
35415 #include "scoreboard.h"
35416 #include "http_log.h"
35417
35418 #ifdef NEXT
35419 #if (NX_CURRENT_COMPILER_RELEASE == 410)
```

```
35420    #ifdef m68k
35421    #define HZ 64
35422    #else
35423    #define HZ 100
35424    #endif
35425    #else
35426    #include <machine/param.h>
35427    #endif
35428    #endif /* NEXT */
35429
35430    #define STATUS_MAXLINE        64
35431
35432    #define KBYTE                 1024
35433    #define MBYTE                 1048576L
35434    #define GBYTE                 1073741824L
35435
35436    #ifndef DEFAULT_TIME_FORMAT
35437    #define DEFAULT_TIME_FORMAT
35438        "%A, %d-%b-%Y %H:%M:%S %Z"
35439    #endif
35440
35441    module MODULE_VAR_EXPORT status_module;
35442
35443    /*
35444    *command-related code. This is here to prevent
35445    use of ExtendedStatus without status_module
35446    included.
35447    */
35448
35449    static const char *set_extended_status
35450        (cmd_parms *cmd, void *dummy, char *arg)
35451    {
35452    const char *err =
35453        ap_check_cmd_context(cmd, GLOBAL_ONLY);
35454    if (err != NULL) {
35455    return err;
35456    }
35457    if (!strcasecmp(arg, "off") || !strcmp(arg, "0")) {
35458    ap_extended_status = 0;
35459    }
35460    else {
35461    ap_extended_status = 1;
35462    }
35463    return NULL;
35464    }
35465
35466    static const command_rec status_module_cmds[] =
35467    {
35468    { "ExtendedStatus", set_extended_status,
35469        NULL, RSRC_CONF, TAKE1,
35470    "\"On\" to enable extended status information,
35471        \"Off\" to disable" },
35472    {NULL}
35473    };
35474
35475    /* Format the number of bytes nicely */
35476    static void format_byte_out(request_rec *r,
35477        unsigned long bytes)
35478    {
35479    if (bytes < (5 * KBYTE))
35480    ap_rprintf(r, "%d B", (int) bytes);
35481    else if (bytes < (MBYTE / 2))
35482    ap_rprintf(r, "%.1f kB", (float) bytes / KBYTE);
35483    else if (bytes < (GBYTE / 2))
35484    ap_rprintf(r, "%.1f MB", (float) bytes / MBYTE);
35485    else
35486    ap_rprintf(r, "%.1f GB", (float) bytes / GBYTE);
35487    }
35488
35489    static void format_kbyte_out
35490        (request_rec *r, unsigned long kbytes)
35491    {
35492    if (kbytes < KBYTE)
35493    ap_rprintf(r, "%d kB", (int) kbytes);
35494    else if (kbytes < MBYTE)
35495    ap_rprintf(r, "%.1f MB", (float) kbytes / KBYTE);
35496    else
35497    ap_rprintf(r, "%.1f GB", (float) kbytes / MBYTE);
35498    }
35499
35500    static void show_time
35501        (request_rec *r, time_t tsecs)
35502    {
35503    long days, hrs, mins, secs;
35504
35505    secs = tsecs % 60;
35506    tsecs /= 60;
35507    mins = tsecs % 60;
35508    tsecs /= 60;
35509    hrs = tsecs % 24;
35510    days = tsecs / 24;
35511    if (days)
35512    ap_rprintf(r, " %ld day%s", days,
35513        days == 1 ? "" : "s");
35514    if (hrs)
35515    ap_rprintf(r, " %ld hour%s",
```

```
35516        hrs, hrs == 1 ? "" : "s");
35517    if (mins)
35518    ap_rprintf(r, " %ld minute%s",
35519        mins, mins == 1 ? "" : "s");
35520    if (secs)
35521    ap_rprintf(r, " %ld second%s", secs,
35522        secs == 1 ? "" : "s");
35523    }
35524
35525    /* Main handler for x-httpd-status requests */
35526
35527    /* ID values for command table */
35528
35529    #define STAT_OPT_END          -1
35530    #define STAT_OPT_REFRESH       0
35531    #define STAT_OPT_NOTABLE       1
35532    #define STAT_OPT_AUTO          2
35533
35534    struct stat_opt {
35535    int id;
35536    const char *form_data_str;
35537    const char *hdr_out_str;
35538    };
35539
35540    static const struct stat_opt status_options[] =
35541
35542    /* see #defines above */
35543
35544    {
35545    {STAT_OPT_REFRESH, "refresh", "Refresh"},
35546    {STAT_OPT_NOTABLE, "notable", NULL},
35547    {STAT_OPT_AUTO, "auto", NULL},
35548    {STAT_OPT_END, NULL, NULL}
35549    };
35550
35551    static char status_flags[SERVER_NUM_STATUS];
35552
35553    static int status_handler(request_rec *r)
35554    {
35555    char *loc;
35556    time_t nowtime = time(NULL);
35557    time_t up_time;
35558    int i, res;
35559    int ready = 0;
35560    int busy = 0;
35561    unsigned long count = 0;
35562    unsigned long lres, bytes;
35563    unsigned long my_lres, my_bytes, conn_bytes;
35564    unsigned short conn_lres;
35565    unsigned long bcount = 0;
35566    unsigned long kbcount = 0;
35567    long req_time;
35568    #ifndef NO_TIMES
35569    #ifdef _SC_CLK_TCK
35570    float tick = sysconf(_SC_CLK_TCK);
35571    #else
35572    float tick = HZ;
35573    #endif
35574    #endif
35575    int short_report = 0;
35576    int no_table_report = 0;
35577    short_score score_record;
35578    parent_score ps_record;
35579    char stat_buffer[HARD_SERVER_LIMIT];
35580    int pid_buffer[HARD_SERVER_LIMIT];
35581    clock_t tu, ts, tcu, tcs;
35582    server_rec *vhost;
35583
35584    tu = ts = tcu = tcs = 0;
35585
35586    if (!ap_exists_scoreboard_image()) {
35587    ap_log_rerror(APLOG_MARK,
35588        APLOG_NOERRNO|APLOG_ERR, r,
35589    "Server status unavailable in inetd mode");
35590    return HTTP_INTERNAL_SERVER_ERROR;
35591    }
35592    r->allowed = (1 << M_GET);
35593    if (r->method_number != M_GET)
35594    return DECLINED;
35595
35596    r->content_type = "text/html";
35597
35598    /*
35599    Simple table-driven form data set parser
35600    that lets you alter the header
35601    */
35602
35603    if (r->args) {
35604    i = 0;
35605    while (status_options[i].id != STAT_OPT_END) {
35606    if ((loc = strstr(r->args,
35607        status_options[i].form_data_str))
35608        != NULL) {
35609    switch (status_options[i].id) {
35610    case STAT_OPT_REFRESH:
35611    if (*(loc + strlen
```

```
35612        (status_options[i].form_data_str)) == '=')
35613   ap_table_set(r->headers_out,
35614   status_options[i].hdr_out_str,
35615   loc + strlen(status_options[i].hdr_out_str) + 1);
35616   else
35617   ap_table_set(r->headers_out,
35618   status_options[i].hdr_out_str, "1");
35619   break;
35620   case STAT_OPT_NOTABLE:
35621   no_table_report = 1;
35622   break;
35623   case STAT_OPT_AUTO:
35624   r->content_type = "text/plain";
35625   short_report = 1;
35626   break;
35627   }
35628   }
35629   i++;
35630   }
35631   }
35632
35633   ap_send_http_header(r);
35634
35635   if (r->header_only)
35636   return 0;
35637
35638   ap_sync_scoreboard_image();
35639   for (i = 0; i < HARD_SERVER_LIMIT; ++i) {
35640   score_record = ap_scoreboard_image->servers[i];
35641   ps_record = ap_scoreboard_image->parent[i];
35642   res = score_record.status;
35643   stat_buffer[i] = status_flags[res];
35644   pid_buffer[i] = (int) ps_record.pid;
35645   if (res == SERVER_READY)
35646   ready++;
35647   else if (res != SERVER_DEAD)
35648   busy++;
35649   if (ap_extended_status) {
35650   lres = score_record.access_count;
35651   bytes = score_record.bytes_served;
35652   if (lres != 0 || (res !=
35653       SERVER_READY && res != SERVER_DEAD)) {
35654   #ifndef NO_TIMES
35655   tu += score_record.times.tms_utime;
35656   ts += score_record.times.tms_stime;
35657   tcu += score_record.times.tms_cutime;
35658   tcs += score_record.times.tms_cstime;
35659   #endif /* NO_TIMES */
```

```
35660   count += lres;
35661   bcount += bytes;
35662   if (bcount >= KBYTE) {
35663   kbcount += (bcount >> 10);
35664   bcount = bcount & 0x3ff;
35665   }
35666   }
35667   }
35668   }
35669
35670   up_time = nowtime - ap_restart_time;
35671
35672   ap_hard_timeout("send status info", r);
35673
35674   if (!short_report) {
35675   ap_rputs("<HTML><HEAD>\n<TITLE>Apache Status
35676       </TITLE>\n</HEAD><BODY>\n", r);
35677   ap_rputs("<H1>Apache Server Status for ", r);
35678   ap_rvputs(r, ap_get_server_name(r),
35679       "</H1>\n\n", NULL);
35680   ap_rvputs(r, "Server Version: ",
35681   ap_get_server_version(), "<br>\n", NULL);
35682   ap_rvputs(r, "Server Built: ",
35683   ap_get_server_built(), "<br>\n<hr>\n", NULL);
35684   ap_rvputs(r, "Current Time: ",
35685   ap_ht_time(r->pool, nowtime,
35686       DEFAULT_TIME_FORMAT, 0), "<br>\n", NULL);
35687   ap_rvputs(r, "Restart Time: ",
35688   ap_ht_time(r->pool, ap_restart_time,
35689       DEFAULT_TIME_FORMAT, 0),
35690   "<br>\n", NULL);
35691   ap_rprintf(r, "Parent Server Generation:
35692       %d <br>\n", (int) ap_my_generation);
35693   ap_rputs("Server uptime: ", r);
35694   show_time(r, up_time);
35695   ap_rputs("<br>\n", r);
35696   }
35697
35698   if (ap_extended_status) {
35699   if (short_report) {
35700   ap_rprintf(r, "Total Accesses:
35701       %lu\nTotal kBytes: %lu\n",
35702   count, kbcount);
35703
35704   #ifndef NO_TIMES
35705
35706   /* Allow for OS/2 not having CPU stats */
35707
```

```
35708    if (ts || tu || tcu || tcs)
35709    ap_rprintf(r, "CPULoad: %g\n",
35710    (tu + ts + tcu + tcs) / tick / up_time * 100.);
35711    #endif
35712
35713    ap_rprintf(r, "Uptime: %ld\n", (long) (up_time));
35714    if (up_time > 0)
35715    ap_rprintf(r, "ReqPerSec: %g\n",
35716    (float) count / (float) up_time);
35717
35718    if (up_time > 0)
35719    ap_rprintf(r, "BytesPerSec: %g\n",
35720    KBYTE * (float) kbcount / (float) up_time);
35721
35722    if (count > 0)
35723    ap_rprintf(r, "BytesPerReq: %g\n",
35724    KBYTE * (float) kbcount / (float) count);
35725    }
35726    else {                    /* !short_report */
35727    ap_rprintf(r, "Total accesses:
35728         %lu - Total Traffic: ", count);
35729    format_kbyte_out(r, kbcount);
35730
35731    #ifndef NO_TIMES
35732
35733    /* Allow for OS/2 not having CPU stats */
35734
35735    ap_rputs("<br>\n", r);
35736    ap_rprintf(r, "CPU Usage: u%g s%g cu%g cs%g",
35737    tu / tick, ts / tick, tcu / tick, tcs / tick);
35738
35739    if (ts || tu || tcu || tcs)
35740    ap_rprintf(r, " - %.3g%% CPU load",
35741    (tu + ts + tcu + tcs) / tick / up_time * 100.);
35742    #endif
35743
35744    ap_rputs("<br>\n", r);
35745
35746    if (up_time > 0)
35747    ap_rprintf(r, "%.3g requests/sec - ",
35748    (float) count / (float) up_time);
35749
35750    if (up_time > 0) {
35751    format_byte_out(r, KBYTE *
35752         (float) kbcount / (float) up_time);
35753    ap_rputs("/second - ", r);
35754    }
35755
35756    if (count > 0) {
35757    format_byte_out(r, KBYTE *
35758         (float) kbcount / (float) count);
35759    ap_rputs("/request", r);
35760    }
35761
35762    ap_rputs("<br>\n", r);
35763    }                    /* short_report */
35764    }                    /* ap_extended_status */
35765
35766    if (!short_report)
35767    ap_rprintf(r, "\n%d requests currently
35768         being processed, %d idle servers\n"
35769    ,busy, ready);
35770    else
35771    ap_rprintf(r, "BusyServers:
35772         %d\nIdleServers: %d\n", busy, ready);
35773
35774    /* send the scoreboard 'table' out */
35775
35776    if (!short_report)
35777    ap_rputs("<PRE>", r);
35778    else
35779    ap_rputs("Scoreboard: ", r);
35780
35781    for (i = 0; i < HARD_SERVER_LIMIT; ++i) {
35782    ap_rputc(stat_buffer[i], r);
35783    if ((i % STATUS_MAXLINE ==
35784         (STATUS_MAXLINE - 1)) && !short_report)
35785    ap_rputs("\n", r);
35786    }
35787
35788    if (short_report)
35789    ap_rputs("\n", r);
35790    else {
35791    ap_rputs("</PRE>\n", r);
35792    ap_rputs("Scoreboard Key: <br>\n", r);
35793    ap_rputs("\"<B><code>_</code></B>\"
35794         Waiting for Connection, \n", r);
35795    ap_rputs("\"<B><code>S</code></B>\"
35796         Starting up, \n", r);
35797    ap_rputs("\"<B><code>R</code></B>\"
35798         Reading Request,<BR>\n", r);
35799    ap_rputs("\"<B><code>W</code></B>\"
35800         Sending Reply, \n", r);
35801    ap_rputs("\"<B><code>K</code></B>\"
35802         Keepalive (read), \n", r);
35803    ap_rputs("\"<B><code>D</code></B>\"
```

```
35804        DNS Lookup,<BR>\n", r);
35805    ap_rputs("\"<B><code>L</code></B>\"
35806        Logging, \n", r);
35807    ap_rputs("\"<B><code>G</code></B>\"
35808        Gracefully finishing, \n", r);
35809    ap_rputs("\"<B><code>.</code></B>\"
35810        Open slot with no current process<P>\n", r);
35811    ap_rputs("<P>\n", r);
35812    if (!ap_extended_status) {
35813    int j = 0;
35814    ap_rputs("PID Key: <br>\n", r);
35815    ap_rputs("<PRE>\n", r);
35816    for (i = 0; i < HARD_SERVER_LIMIT; ++i) {
35817    if (stat_buffer[i] != '.') {
35818    ap_rprintf(r, "   %d in state: %c ",
35819        pid_buffer[i],
35820    stat_buffer[i]);
35821    if (++j >= 3) {
35822    ap_rputs("\n", r);
35823    j = 0;
35824    } else
35825    ap_rputs(",", r);
35826    }
35827    }
35828    ap_rputs("\n", r);
35829    ap_rputs("</PRE>\n", r);
35830    }
35831    }
35832
35833    if (ap_extended_status) {
35834    if (!short_report) {
35835    if (no_table_report)
35836    ap_rputs("<p><hr><h2>Server Details</h2>\n\n", r);
35837    else
35838    #ifdef NO_TIMES
35839    /* Allow for OS/2 not having CPU stats */
35840    ap_rputs("<p>\n\n<table border=0><tr>
35841    <th>Srv<th>PID<th>Acc<th>M\n<th>SS
35842    <th>Req<th>Conn<th>Child<th>Slot<th>Client<th>
35843    VHost<th>Request</tr>\n\n", r);
35844    #else
35845    ap_rputs("<p>\n\n<table border=0><tr>
35846    <th>Srv<th>PID<th>Acc<th>M<th>CPU\n<th>
35847    SS<th>Req<th>Conn<th>Child<th>Slot<th>
35848    Client<th>VHost<th>Request</tr>\n\n", r);
35849    #endif
35850    }
35851
35852    for (i = 0; i < HARD_SERVER_LIMIT; ++i) {
35853    score_record = ap_scoreboard_image->servers[i];
35854    ps_record = ap_scoreboard_image->parent[i];
35855    vhost = score_record.vhostrec;
35856    if (ps_record.generation != ap_my_generation) {
35857    vhost = NULL;
35858    }
35859
35860    #if defined(NO_GETTIMEOFDAY)
35861    #ifndef NO_TIMES
35862    if (score_record.start_time == (clock_t) 0)
35863    #endif /* NO_TIMES */
35864    req_time = 0L;
35865    #ifndef NO_TIMES
35866    else {
35867    req_time = score_record.stop_time -
35868        score_record.start_time;
35869    req_time = (req_time * 1000) / (int) tick;
35870    }
35871    #endif /* NO_TIMES */
35872    #else
35873    if (score_record.start_time.tv_sec == 0L &&
35874    score_record.start_time.tv_usec == 0L)
35875    req_time = 0L;
35876    else
35877    req_time =
35878    ((score_record.stop_time.tv_sec -
35879        score_record.start_time.tv_sec) * 1000) +
35880    ((score_record.stop_time.tv_usec -
35881        score_record.start_time.tv_usec) / 1000);
35882    #endif
35883    if (req_time < 0L)
35884    req_time = 0L;
35885
35886    lres = score_record.access_count;
35887    my_lres = score_record.my_access_count;
35888    conn_lres = score_record.conn_count;
35889    bytes = score_record.bytes_served;
35890    my_bytes = score_record.my_bytes_served;
35891    conn_bytes = score_record.conn_bytes;
35892    if (lres != 0 ||
35893        (score_record.status != SERVER_READY
35894    && score_record.status != SERVER_DEAD)) {
35895    if (!short_report) {
35896    if (no_table_report) {
35897    if (score_record.status == SERVER_DEAD)
35898    ap_rprintf(r,
35899    "<b>Server %d-%d</b> (-): %d|%lu|%lu [",
```

```
35900   i, (int) ps_record.generation, (int) conn_lres,
35901   my_lres, lres);
35902   else
35903   ap_rprintf(r,
35904   "<b>Server %d-%d</b> (%d): %d|%lu|%lu [",
35905   i, (int) ps_record.generation,
35906   (int) ps_record.pid,
35907   (int) conn_lres, my_lres, lres);
35908
35909   switch (score_record.status) {
35910   case SERVER_READY:
35911   ap_rputs("Ready", r);
35912   break;
35913   case SERVER_STARTING:
35914   ap_rputs("Starting", r);
35915   break;
35916   case SERVER_BUSY_READ:
35917   ap_rputs("<b>Read</b>", r);
35918   break;
35919   case SERVER_BUSY_WRITE:
35920   ap_rputs("<b>Write</b>", r);
35921   break;
35922   case SERVER_BUSY_KEEPALIVE:
35923   ap_rputs("<b>Keepalive</b>", r);
35924   break;
35925   case SERVER_BUSY_LOG:
35926   ap_rputs("<b>Logging</b>", r);
35927   break;
35928   case SERVER_BUSY_DNS:
35929   ap_rputs("<b>DNS lookup</b>", r);
35930   break;
35931   case SERVER_DEAD:
35932   ap_rputs("Dead", r);
35933   break;
35934   case SERVER_GRACEFUL:
35935   ap_rputs("Graceful", r);
35936   break;
35937   default:
35938   ap_rputs("?STATE?", r);
35939   break;
35940   }
35941   #ifdef NO_TIMES
35942   /* Allow for OS/2 not having CPU stats */
35943   ap_rprintf(r, "]\n %.0f %ld (",
35944   #else
35945
35946   ap_rprintf(r, "] u%g s%g cu%g cs%g\n %.0f %ld (",
35947   score_record.times.tms_utime / tick,
35948   score_record.times.tms_stime / tick,
35949   score_record.times.tms_cutime / tick,
35950   score_record.times.tms_cstime / tick,
35951   #endif
35952   #ifdef OPTIMIZE_TIMEOUTS
35953   difftime(nowtime, ps_record.last_rtime),
35954   #else
35955   difftime(nowtime, score_record.last_used),
35956   #endif
35957   (long) req_time);
35958   format_byte_out(r, conn_bytes);
35959   ap_rputs("|", r);
35960   format_byte_out(r, my_bytes);
35961   ap_rputs("|", r);
35962   format_byte_out(r, bytes);
35963   ap_rputs(")\n", r);
35964   ap_rprintf(r, " <i>%s {%s}</i>
35965       <b>[%s]</b><br>\n\n",
35966   score_record.client,
35967   ap_escape_html(r->pool, score_record.request),
35968   vhost ? vhost->server_hostname : "(unavailable)");
35969   }
35970   else {            /* !no_table_report */
35971   if (score_record.status == SERVER_DEAD)
35972   ap_rprintf(r,
35973   "<tr><td><b>%d-%d</b><td>-<td>%d/%lu/%lu",
35974   i, (int) ps_record.generation,
35975   (int) conn_lres, my_lres, lres);
35976   else
35977   ap_rprintf(r,
35978   "<tr><td><b>%d-%d</b><td>%d<td>%d/%lu/%lu",
35979   i, (int) ps_record.generation,
35980   (int) ps_record.pid, (int) conn_lres,
35981   my_lres, lres);
35982
35983   switch (score_record.status) {
35984   case SERVER_READY:
35985   ap_rputs("<td>_", r);
35986   break;
35987   case SERVER_STARTING:
35988   ap_rputs("<td><b>S</b>", r);
35989   break;
35990   case SERVER_BUSY_READ:
35991   ap_rputs("<td><b>R</b>", r);
35992   break;
35993   case SERVER_BUSY_WRITE:
35994   ap_rputs("<td><b>W</b>", r);
35995   break;
```

```
35996  case SERVER_BUSY_KEEPALIVE:                          36044  ap_escape_html(r->pool, score_record.request));
35997  ap_rputs("<td><b>K</b>", r);                          36045  }              /* no_table_report */
35998  break;                                                36046  }                 /* !short_report */
35999  case SERVER_BUSY_LOG:                                 36047  }                    /* if (<active child>) */
36000  ap_rputs("<td><b>L</b>", r);                          36048  }                       /* for () */
36001  break;                                                36049
36002  case SERVER_BUSY_DNS:                                 36050  if (!(short_report || no_table_report)) {
36003  ap_rputs("<td><b>D</b>", r);                          36051  #ifdef NO_TIMES
36004  break;                                                36052  ap_rputs("</table>\n \
36005  case SERVER_DEAD:                                     36053  <hr> \
36006  ap_rputs("<td>.", r);                                 36054  <table>\n \
36007  break;                                                36055  <tr><th>Srv<td>Child
36008  case SERVER_GRACEFUL:                                 36056      Server number - generation\n \
36009  ap_rputs("<td>G", r);                                 36057  <tr><th>PID<td>OS process ID\n \
36010  break;                                                36058  <tr><th>Acc<td>Number of accesses this
36011  default:                                              36059      connection / this child / this slot\n \
36012  ap_rputs("<td>?", r);                                 36060  <tr><th>M<td>Mode of operation\n \
36013  break;                                                36061  <tr><th>SS<td>Seconds since beginning of
36014  }                                                     36062      most recent request\n \
36015  #ifdef NO_TIMES                                       36063  <tr><th>Req<td>Milliseconds required to process
36016  /* Allow for OS/2 not having CPU stats */             36064      most recent request\n \
36017  ap_rprintf(r, "\n<td>%.0f<td>%ld",                    36065  <tr><th>Conn<td>Kilobytes transferred
36018  #else                                                 36066      this connection\n \
36019  ap_rprintf(r, "\n<td>%.2f<td>%.0f<td>%ld",            36067  <tr><th>Child<td>Megabytes transferred
36020  (score_record.times.tms_utime +                      36068      this child\n \
36021  score_record.times.tms_stime +                       36069  <tr><th>Slot<td>Total megabytes
36022  score_record.times.tms_cutime +                      36070      transferred this slot\n \
36023  score_record.times.tms_cstime) / tick,               36071  </table>\n", r);
36024  #endif                                                36072  #else
36025  #ifdef OPTIMIZE_TIMEOUTS                              36073  ap_rputs("</table>\n \
36026  difftime(nowtime, ps_record.last_rtime),             36074  <hr> \
36027  #else                                                 36075  <table>\n \
36028  difftime(nowtime, score_record.last_used),           36076  <tr><th>Srv<td>Child Server
36029  #endif                                                36077      number - generation\n \
36030  (long) req_time);                                     36078  <tr><th>PID<td>OS process ID\n \
36031  ap_rprintf(r, "<td>%-1.1f<td>%-2.2f<td>%-2.2f\n",    36079  <tr><th>Acc<td>Number of accesses this
36032  (float) conn_bytes / KBYTE,                          36080      connection / this child / this slot\n \
36033      (float) my_bytes / MBYTE,                         36081  <tr><th>M<td>Mode of operation\n \
36034  (float) bytes / MBYTE);                               36082  <tr><th>CPU<td>CPU usage, number of seconds\n \
36035  if (score_record.status == SERVER_BUSY_READ)         36083  <tr><th>SS<td>Seconds since beginning
36036  ap_rprintf(r,                                         36084      of most recent request\n \
36037  "<td>?<td nowrap>?                                    36085  <tr><th>Req<td>Milliseconds required to
36038      <td nowrap>..reading.. </tr>\n\n");               36086      process most recent request\n \
36039  else                                                  36087  <tr><th>Conn<td>Kilobytes transferred
36040  ap_rprintf(r,                                         36088      this connection\n \
36041  "<td>%s<td nowrap>%s<td nowrap>%s</tr>\n\n",          36089  <tr><th>Child<td>Megabytes transferred
36042  score_record.client,                                  36090      this child\n \
36043  vhost ? vhost->server_hostname : "(unavailable)",    36091  <tr><th>Slot<td>Total megabytes transferred
```

```
36092        this slot\n \
36093   </table>\n", r);
36094   #endif
36095   }
36096
36097   } else {
36098
36099   ap_rputs("<hr>To obtain a full report with
36100       current status information ", r);
36101   ap_rputs("you need to use the
36102       <code>ExtendedStatus On</code>
36103       directive. \n", r);
36104
36105   }
36106
36107   if (!short_report) {
36108   ap_rputs(ap_psignature("<HR>\n",r), r);
36109   ap_rputs("</BODY></HTML>\n", r);
36110   }
36111
36112   ap_kill_timeout(r);
36113   return 0;
36114   }
36115
36116
36117   static void status_init(server_rec *s, pool *p)
36118   {
36119   status_flags[SERVER_DEAD] = '.';
36120   /* We don't want to assume these are in */
36121   status_flags[SERVER_READY] = '_';
36122   /* any particular order in scoreboard.h */
36123   status_flags[SERVER_STARTING] = 'S';
36124   status_flags[SERVER_BUSY_READ] = 'R';
36125   status_flags[SERVER_BUSY_WRITE] = 'W';
36126   status_flags[SERVER_BUSY_KEEPALIVE] = 'K';
36127   status_flags[SERVER_BUSY_LOG] = 'L';
36128   status_flags[SERVER_BUSY_DNS] = 'D';
36129   status_flags[SERVER_GRACEFUL] = 'G';
36130   }
36131
36132   static const handler_rec status_handlers[] =
36133   {
36134   {STATUS_MAGIC_TYPE, status_handler},
36135   {"server-status", status_handler},
36136   {NULL}
36137   };
36138
36139   module MODULE_VAR_EXPORT status_module =
```

```
36140   {
36141   STANDARD_MODULE_STUFF,
36142   status_init,            /* initializer */
36143   NULL,                   /* dir config creater */
36144   NULL,
36145   /* dir merger -- default is to override */
36146   NULL,                   /* server config */
36147   NULL,                   /* merge server config */
36148   status_module_cmds, /* command table */
36149   status_handlers,    /* handlers */
36150   NULL,                   /* filename translation */
36151   NULL,                   /* check_user_id */
36152   NULL,                   /* check auth */
36153   NULL,                   /* check access */
36154   NULL,                   /* type_checker */
36155   NULL,                   /* fixups */
36156   NULL,                   /* logger */
36157   NULL,                   /* header parser */
36158   NULL,                   /* child_init */
36159   NULL,                   /* child_exit */
36160   NULL                    /* post read-request */
36161   };
```

p 543 **mod_unique_id.c**

```
36162   #include "httpd.h"
36163   #include "http_config.h"
36164   #include "http_log.h"
36165   #include "multithread.h"
36166
36167   #ifdef MULTITHREAD
36168   #error sorry this module does not support multithreaded
36169       servers yet
36170   #endif
36171
36172   typedef struct {
36173       unsigned int stamp;
36174       unsigned int in_addr;
36175       unsigned int pid;
36176       unsigned short counter;
36177   } unique_id_rec;
36178
36179   /* Comments:
36180    *
36181    * We want an identifier which is unique across all
36182    * hits, everywhere. "everywhere" includes multiple
36183    * httpd instances on the same machine, or on
36184    * multiple machines.  Essentially "everywhere" should
```

```
36185    * include all possible httpds across all servers at a
36186    * particular "site".  We make some assumptions that
36187    * if the site has a cluster of machines then their
36188    * time is relatively synchronized.  We also assume that
36189    * the first address returned by a gethostbyname
36190    * (gethostname()) is unique across all the machines
36191    * at the "site".
36192    *
36193    * We also further assume that pids fit in 32-bits.  If
36194    * something uses more than 32-bits, the fix is trivial,
36195    * but it requires the unrolled uuencoding loop to be
36196    * extended.  * A similar fix is needed to support
36197    * multithreaded servers, using a pid/tid combo.
36198    *
36199    * Together, the in_addr and pid are assumed to
36200    * absolutely uniquely identify this one child from all
36201    * other currently running children on all servers
36202    * (including this physical server if it is running
36203    * multiple httpds) from each other.
36204    *
36205    * The stamp and counter are used to distinguish all
36206    * hits for a particular(in_addr,pid) pair.  The stamp
36207    * is updated using r->request_time, saving cpu cycles.
36208    * The counter is never reset, and is used to permit up
36209    * to 64k requests in a single second by a single child.
36210    *
36211    * The 112-bits of unique_id_rec are uuencoded using the
36212    * alphabet[A-Za-z0-9@-], resulting in 19 bytes of
36213    * printable characters.  That is then stuffed into the
36214    * environment variable UNIQUE_ID so that it is available
36215    * to other modules.  The alphabet choice differs from
36216    * normal base64 encoding[A-Za-z0-9+/] because + and /
36217    * are special characters in URLs and we want to make it
36218    * easy to use UNIQUE_ID in URLs.
36219    *
36220    * Note that UNIQUE_ID should be considered an opaque
36221    * token by other applications.  No attempt should
36222    * be made to dissect its internal components.
36223    * It is an abstraction that may change in the future
36224    * as the needs of this module change.
36225    *
36226    * It is highly desirable that identifiers exist for
36227    * "eternity".  But future needs (such as much faster
36228    * webservers, moving to 64-bit pids, or moving to a
36229    * multithreaded server) may dictate a need to change
36230    * the contents of unique_id_rec.  Such a future
36231    * implementation should ensure that the first field
36232    * is still a time_t stamp.  By doing that, it is
36233    * possible for a site to have a "flag second" in which
36234    * they stop all of their old-format servers, wait
36235    * one entire second, and then start all of their
36236    * new-servers.  This procedure will ensure that the new
36237    * space of identifiers is completely unique from the
36238    * old space.  (Since the first four unencoded bytes
36239    * always differ.)
36240    */
36241    /*
36242    * Sun Jun  7 05:43:49 CEST 1998 -- Alvaro
36243    * More comments:
36244    * 1) The UUencoding prodecure is now done in a general
36245    * way, avoiding the problems with sizes and paddings
36246    * that can arise depending on the architecture. Now the
36247    * offsets and sizes of the elements of the
36248    * unique_id_rec structure are calculated in
36249    * unique_id_global_init; and then used to duplicate
36250    * the structure without the paddings that might exist.
36251    * The multithreaded server fix should be now very easy:
36252    * just add a new "tid" field to the unique_id_rec
36253    * structure, and increase by one
36254    * UNIQUE_ID_REC_MAX.
36255    * 2) unique_id_rec.stamp has been changed from "time_t"
36256    * to "unsigned int", because its size is 64bits on some
36257    * platforms (linux/alpha), and this caused problems with
36258    * htonl/ntohl. Well, this shouldn't be a problem till
36259    * year 2106.
36260    */
36261
36262    static unsigned global_in_addr;
36263
36264    static APACHE_TLS unique_id_rec cur_unique_id;
36265
36266    /*
36267     * Number of elements in the structure unique_id_rec.
36268     */
36269    #define UNIQUE_ID_REC_MAX 4
36270
36271    static unsigned short
36272        unique_id_rec_offset[UNIQUE_ID_REC_MAX],
36273                    unique_id_rec_size[UNIQUE_ID_REC_MAX],
36274                    unique_id_rec_total_size,
36275                    unique_id_rec_size_uu;
36276
36277    static void unique_id_global_init(server_rec *s,
36278        pool *p)
36279    {
36280    #ifndef MAXHOSTNAMELEN
```

```
36281    #define MAXHOSTNAMELEN 256
36282    #endif
36283        char str[MAXHOSTNAMELEN + 1];
36284        struct hostent *hent;
36285    #ifndef NO_GETTIMEOFDAY
36286        struct timeval tv;
36287    #endif
36288
36289        /*
36290         * Calculate the sizes and offsets in cur_unique_id.
36291         */
36292        unique_id_rec_offset[0] =
36293            XtOffsetOf(unique_id_rec, stamp);
36294        unique_id_rec_size[0] =
36295            sizeof(cur_unique_id.stamp);
36296        unique_id_rec_offset[1] =
36297            XtOffsetOf(unique_id_rec, in_addr);
36298        unique_id_rec_size[1] =
36299            sizeof(cur_unique_id.in_addr);
36300        unique_id_rec_offset[2] =
36301            XtOffsetOf(unique_id_rec, pid);
36302        unique_id_rec_size[2] = sizeof(cur_unique_id.pid);
36303        unique_id_rec_offset[3] =
36304            XtOffsetOf(unique_id_rec, counter);
36305        unique_id_rec_size[3] =
36306            sizeof(cur_unique_id.counter);
36307        unique_id_rec_total_size =
36308            unique_id_rec_size[0] + unique_id_rec_size[1] +
36309                            unique_id_rec_size[2] +
36310            unique_id_rec_size[3];
36311
36312        /*
36313         * Calculate the size of the structure when
36314         * uuencoded.
36315         */
36316        unique_id_rec_size_uu =
36317            (unique_id_rec_total_size*8+5)/6;
36318
36319        /*
36320         * Now get the global in_addr.  Note that it is not
36321         * sufficient to use one of the addresses from the
36322         * main_server, since those aren't as likely to
36323         * be unique as the physical address of the machine
36324         */
36325        if (gethostname(str, sizeof(str) - 1) != 0) {
36326            ap_log_error(APLOG_MARK,
36327                    APLOG_NOERRNO|APLOG_ALERT, s,
36328                "gethostname: mod_unique_id requires the
36329                    hostname of the server");
36330            exit(1);
36331        }
36332        str[sizeof(str) - 1] = '\0';
36333
36334        if ((hent = gethostbyname(str)) == NULL) {
36335            ap_log_error(APLOG_MARK,
36336                APLOG_NOERRNO|APLOG_ALERT, s,
36337                        "mod_unique_id: unable to
36338                            gethostbyname(\"%s\")", str);
36339            exit(1);
36340        }
36341
36342        global_in_addr = ((struct in_addr *)
36343            hent->h_addr_list[0])->s_addr;
36344
36345        ap_log_error(APLOG_MARK, APLOG_NOERRNO|APLOG_INFO, s,
36346                "mod_unique_id: using ip addr %s",
36347                inet_ntoa(*(struct in_addr *)
36348                    hent->h_addr_list[0]));
36349
36350        /*
36351         * If the server is pummelled with restart requests
36352         * we could possibly end up in a situation where
36353         * we're starting again during the same second
36354         * that has been used in previous identifiers.
36355         * Avoid that situation.
36356         *
36357         * In truth, for this to actually happen not only
36358         * would it have to restart in the same second, but
36359         * it would have to somehow get the same pids as
36360         * one of the other servers that was running in
36361         * that second. Which would mean a 64k wraparound on
36362         * pids ... not very likely at all.
36363         *
36364         * But protecting against it is relatively cheap.
36365         * We just sleep into the next second.
36366         */
36367    #ifdef NO_GETTIMEOFDAY
36368        sleep(1);
36369    #else
36370        if (gettimeofday(&tv, NULL) == -1) {
36371            sleep(1);
36372        }
36373        else if (tv.tv_usec) {
36374            tv.tv_sec = 0;
36375            tv.tv_usec = 1000000 - tv.tv_usec;
36376            select(0, NULL, NULL, NULL, &tv);
```

```
36377        }
36378  #endif
36379  }
36380
36381  static void unique_id_child_init(server_rec *s, pool *p)
36382  {
36383      pid_t pid;
36384  #ifndef NO_GETTIMEOFDAY
36385      struct timeval tv;
36386  #endif
36387
36388      /*
36389       * Note that we use the pid because it's possible
36390       * that on the same physical machine there are
36391       * multiple servers (i.e. using Listen). But it's
36392       * guaranteed that none of them will share the
36393       * same pids between children.
36394       *
36395       * XXX: for multithread this needs to use a pid/tid
36396       * combo and probably needs to be expanded to
36397       * 32 bits
36398       */
36399      pid = getpid();
36400      cur_unique_id.pid = pid;
36401
36402      /*
36403       * Test our assumption that the pid is 32-bits.
36404       * It's possible that64-bit machines will declare
36405       * pid_t to be 64 bits but only use 32 of them.
36406       * It would have been really nice to test this
36407       * during global_init ... but oh well.
36408       */
36409      if (cur_unique_id.pid != pid) {
36410          ap_log_error(APLOG_MARK,
36411              APLOG_NOERRNO|APLOG_CRIT, s,
36412                  "oh no! pids are greater than
36413                      32-bits!  I'm broken!");
36414      }
36415
36416      cur_unique_id.in_addr = global_in_addr;
36417
36418      /*
36419       * If we use 0 as the initial counter we have a
36420       * little less protection against restart problems,
36421       * and a little less protection against a clock
36422       * going backwards in time.
36423       */
36424  #ifndef NO_GETTIMEOFDAY
36425      if (gettimeofday(&tv, NULL) == -1) {
36426          cur_unique_id.counter = 0;
36427      }
36428      else {
36429          /* Some systems have very low variance on the
36430           * low end of their system counter, defend
36431           * against that.
36432           */
36433          cur_unique_id.counter = tv.tv_usec / 10;
36434      }
36435  #else
36436      cur_unique_id.counter = 0;
36437  #endif
36438
36439      /*
36440       * We must always use network ordering for these
36441       * bytes, so that identifiers are comparable
36442       * between machines of different byte orderings.
36443       * Note in_addr is already in network order.
36444       */
36445      cur_unique_id.pid = htonl(cur_unique_id.pid);
36446      cur_unique_id.counter = htons(cur_unique_id.counter);
36447  }
36448
36449  /* NOTE: This is *NOT* the same encoding used by
36450   * uuencode ... the last two characters should be +
36451   * and /.  But those two characters have very special
36452   * meanings in URLs, and we want to make it easy to
36453   * use identifiers in URLs.  So we replace them with
36454   * @ and -.
36455   */
36456  static const char uuencoder[64] = {
36457      'A', 'B', 'C', 'D', 'E', 'F', 'G',
36458          'H', 'I', 'J', 'K', 'L', 'M',
36459      'N', 'O', 'P', 'Q', 'R', 'S', 'T',
36460          'U', 'V', 'W', 'X', 'Y', 'Z',
36461      'a', 'b', 'c', 'd', 'e', 'f', 'g',
36462          'h', 'i', 'j', 'k', 'l', 'm',
36463      'n', 'o', 'p', 'q', 'r', 's', 't',
36464          'u', 'v', 'w', 'x', 'y', 'z',
36465      '0', '1', '2', '3', '4', '5', '6',
36466          '7', '8', '9', '@', '-',
36467  };
36468
36469  static int gen_unique_id(request_rec *r)
36470  {
36471      char *str;
36472      /*
```

```
36473        * Buffer padded with two final bytes, used to copy
36474        * the unique_id_red structure without the internal
36475        * paddings that it could have.
36476        */
36477       struct {
36478        unique_id_rec foo;
36479        unsigned char pad[2];
36480       } paddedbuf;
36481       unsigned char *x,*y;
36482       unsigned short counter;
36483       const char *e;
36484       int i,j,k;
36485
36486       /* copy the unique_id if this is an internal
36487        * redirect (we're never actually called for sub
36488        * requests, so we don't need to test for them) */
36489       if (r->prev && (e = ap_table_get(r->subprocess_env,
36490           "REDIRECT_UNIQUE_ID"))) {
36491        ap_table_setn(r->subprocess_env, "UNIQUE_ID", e);
36492        return DECLINED;
36493       }
36494
36495       cur_unique_id.stamp =
36496           htonl((unsigned int)r->request_time);
36497
36498       /* we'll use a temporal buffer to avoid uuencoding
36499        * the possible internal paddings of the
36500        * original structure */
36501       x = (unsigned char *) &paddedbuf;
36502       y = (unsigned char *) &cur_unique_id;
36503       k = 0;
36504       for (i = 0; i < UNIQUE_ID_REC_MAX; i++) {
36505        y = ((unsigned char *) &cur_unique_id) +
36506           unique_id_rec_offset[i];
36507        for (j = 0; j < unique_id_rec_size[i]; j++, k++) {
36508           x[k] = y[j];
36509        }
36510       }
36511       /*
36512        * We reset two more bytes just in case padding is
36513        * needed for the uuencoding.
36514        */
36515       x[k++] = '\0';
36516       x[k++] = '\0';
36517
36518       /* alloc str and do the uuencoding */
36519       str = (char *)ap_palloc(r->pool,
36520           unique_id_rec_size_uu + 1);
36521       k = 0;
36522       for (i = 0; i < unique_id_rec_total_size; i += 3) {
36523           y = x + i;
36524           str[k++] = uuencoder[y[0] >> 2];
36525           str[k++] = uuencoder[((y[0] & 0x03) << 4)
36526               | ((y[1] & 0xf0) >> 4)];
36527           if (k == unique_id_rec_size_uu) break;
36528           str[k++] = uuencoder[((y[1] & 0x0f) << 2)
36529               | ((y[2] & 0xc0) >> 6)];
36530           if (k == unique_id_rec_size_uu) break;
36531           str[k++] = uuencoder[y[2] & 0x3f];
36532       }
36533       str[k++] = '\0';
36534
36535       /* set the environment variable */
36536       ap_table_setn(r->subprocess_env, "UNIQUE_ID", str);
36537
36538       /* and increment the identifier for the next call */
36539       counter = ntohs(cur_unique_id.counter) + 1;
36540       cur_unique_id.counter = htons(counter);
36541
36542       return DECLINED;
36543   }
36544
36545
36546   module MODULE_VAR_EXPORT unique_id_module = {
36547       STANDARD_MODULE_STUFF,
36548       unique_id_global_init,   /* initializer */
36549       NULL,                    /* dir config creater */
36550       NULL,
36551       /* dir merger -- default is to override */
36552       NULL,                    /* server config */
36553       NULL,                    /* merge server configs */
36554       NULL,                    /* command table */
36555       NULL,                    /* handlers */
36556       NULL,                    /* filename translation */
36557       NULL,                    /* check_user_id */
36558       NULL,                    /* check auth */
36559       NULL,                    /* check access */
36560       NULL,                    /* type_checker */
36561       NULL,                    /* fixups */
36562       NULL,                    /* logger */
36563       NULL,                    /* header parser */
36564       unique_id_child_init,    /* child_init */
36565       NULL,                    /* child_exit */
36566       gen_unique_id            /* post_read_request */
36567   };
```

mod_userdir.c
p 538

```
36568   #include "httpd.h"
36569   #include "http_config.h"
36570
36571   module userdir_module;
36572
36573   typedef struct userdir_config {
36574       int globally_disabled;
36575       char *userdir;
36576       table *enabled_users;
36577       table *disabled_users;
36578   }                   userdir_config;
36579
36580   /*
36581    * Server config for this module: global disablement
36582    * flag, a list of usernames ineligible for UserDir
36583    * access, a list of those immune to global (but not
36584    * explicit) disablement, and the replacement string
36585    * for all others.
36586    */
36587
36588   static void *create_userdir_config(pool *p,
36589       server_rec *s)
36590   {
36591       userdir_config
36592       * newcfg = (userdir_config *) ap_pcalloc(p,
36593           sizeof(userdir_config));
36594
36595       newcfg->globally_disabled = 0;
36596       newcfg->userdir = DEFAULT_USER_DIR;
36597       newcfg->enabled_users = ap_make_table(p, 4);
36598       newcfg->disabled_users = ap_make_table(p, 4);
36599       return (void *) newcfg;
36600   }
36601
36602   #define O_DEFAULT 0
36603   #define O_ENABLE 1
36604   #define O_DISABLE 2
36605
36606   static const char *set_user_dir(cmd_parms *cmd,
36607       void *dummy, char *arg)
36608   {
36609       userdir_config
36610       * s_cfg = (userdir_config *) ap_get_module_config
36611       (
36612        cmd->server->module_config,
36613        &userdir_module
36614       );
36615       char *username;
36616       const char
36617           *usernames = arg;
36618       char *kw = ap_getword_conf(cmd->pool, &usernames);
36619       table *usertable;
36620
36621       /*
36622        * Let's do the comparisons once.
36623        */
36624       if (((!strcasecmp(kw, "disable")) || (!strcasecmp(kw,
36625           "disabled")))) {
36626           /*
36627            * If there are no usernames specified, this is
36628            * a global disable - we need do no more at this
36629            * point than record the fact.
36630            */
36631           if (strlen(usernames) == 0) {
36632               s_cfg->globally_disabled = 1;
36633               return NULL;
36634           }
36635           usertable = s_cfg->disabled_users;
36636       }
36637       else if (((!strcasecmp(kw, "enable")) ||
36638           (!strcasecmp(kw, "enabled")))) {
36639           /*
36640            * The "disable" keyword can stand alone or
36641            * take a list of names, but the "enable"
36642            * keyword requires the list.  Whinge if
36643            * it doesn't have it.
36644            */
36645           if (strlen(usernames) == 0) {
36646               return "UserDir \"enable\" keyword requires
36647                   a list of usernames";
36648           }
36649           usertable = s_cfg->enabled_users;
36650       }
36651       else {
36652           /*
36653            * If the first (only?) value isn't one of our
36654            * keywords, just copy the string to the
36655            * userdir string.
36656            */
36657           s_cfg->userdir = ap_pstrdup(cmd->pool, arg);
36658           return NULL;
36659       }
36660       /*
36661        * Now we just take each word in turn from the
```

```
36662        * command line and add it to the appropriate
36663        * table.
36664        */
36665       while (*usernames) {
36666          username = ap_getword_conf(cmd->pool, &usernames);
36667          ap_table_setn(usertable, username, kw);
36668       }
36669       return NULL;
36670   }
36671
36672   static const command_rec userdir_cmds[] = {
36673       {"UserDir", set_user_dir, NULL, RSRC_CONF, RAW_ARGS,
36674       "the public subdirectory in users' home
36675               directories, or 'disabled', or 'disabled
36676               username username...', or 'enabled username
36677               username...'"},
36678       {NULL}
36679   };
36680
36681   static int translate_userdir(request_rec *r)
36682   {
36683       void *server_conf = r->server->module_config;
36684       const userdir_config *s_cfg =
36685       (userdir_config *) ap_get_module_config(server_conf,
36686           &userdir_module);
36687       char *name = r->uri;
36688       const char *userdirs = s_cfg->userdir;
36689       const char *w, *dname;
36690       char *redirect;
36691       char *x = NULL;
36692       struct stat statbuf;
36693
36694       /*
36695        * If the URI doesn't match our basic pattern,
36696        * we've nothing to do with it.
36697   */
36698       if (
36699           (s_cfg->userdir == NULL) ||
36700           (name[0] != '/') ||
36701           (name[1] != '~')
36702           ) {
36703           return DECLINED;
36704       }
36705
36706       dname = name + 2;
36707       w = ap_getword(r->pool, &dname, '/');
36708
36709       /*
```

```
36710        * The 'dname' funny business involves backing it up
36711        * to capture the '/' delimiting the "/~user" part
36712        * from the rest of the URL, in case there was one
36713        * (the case where there wasn't being just
36714        * "GET /~user HTTP/1.0", for which we don't
36715        * want to tack on a '/' onto the filename).
36716        */
36717
36718       if (dname[-1] == '/') {
36719           --dname;
36720       }
36721
36722       /*
36723        * If there's no username, it's not for us.
36724        * Ignore . and .. as well.
36725        */
36726       if (w[0] == '\0' || (w[1] == '.' && (w[2] ==
36727           '\0' || (w[2] == '.' && w[3] == '\0')))) {
36728           return DECLINED;
36729       }
36730       /*
36731        * Nor if there's an username but it's in the
36732        * disabled list.
36733        */
36734       if (ap_table_get(s_cfg->disabled_users, w) != NULL) {
36735           return DECLINED;
36736       }
36737       /*
36738        * If there's a global interdiction on UserDirs,
36739        * check to see if this name is one of the Blessed.
36740   */
36741       if (
36742           s_cfg->globally_disabled &&
36743           (ap_table_get(s_cfg->enabled_users, w) == NULL)
36744           ) {
36745           return DECLINED;
36746       }
36747
36748       /*
36749        * Special cases all checked, onward to normal
36750        * substitution processing.
36751        */
36752
36753       while (*userdirs) {
36754           const char *userdir = ap_getword_conf(r->pool,
36755               &userdirs);
36756           char *filename = NULL;
36757
```

```
36758            if (strchr(userdir, '*'))
36759                x = ap_getword(r->pool, &userdir, '*');
36760
36761            if (userdir[0] == '\0' ||
36762                ap_os_is_path_absolute(userdir)) {
36763                if (x) {
36764 #ifdef HAVE_DRIVE_LETTERS
36765                    /*
36766                     * Crummy hack. Need to figure out
36767                     * whether we have been redirected to a
36768                     * URL or to a file on some drive. Since
36769                     * I know of no protocols that are a
36770                     * single letter, if the : is the second
36771                     * character, I will assume a file was
36772                     * specified
36773                     */
36774                    if (strchr(x + 2, ':'))
36775 #else
36776                    if (strchr(x, ':'))
36777 #endif                          /* WIN32 */
36778                    {
36779                        redirect = ap_pstrcat(r->pool, x, w,
36780                            userdir, dname, NULL);
36781                        ap_table_setn(r->headers_out,
36782                            "Location", redirect);
36783                        return REDIRECT;
36784                    }
36785                    else
36786                        filename = ap_pstrcat(r->pool, x, w,
36787                            userdir, NULL);
36788                }
36789                else
36790                    filename = ap_pstrcat(r->pool, userdir,
36791                        "/", w, NULL);
36792            }
36793            else if (strchr(userdir, ':')) {
36794                redirect = ap_pstrcat(r->pool, userdir, "/",
36795                    w, dname, NULL);
36796                ap_table_setn(r->headers_out, "Location",
36797                    redirect);
36798                return REDIRECT;
36799            }
36800            else {
36801 #ifdef WIN32
36802                /* Need to figure out home dirs on NT */
36803                return DECLINED;
36804 #else                           /* WIN32 */
36805                struct passwd *pw;
36806                if ((pw = getpwnam(w))) {
36807 #ifdef OS2
36808                    /* Need to manually add user name for OS/2 */
36809                    filename = ap_pstrcat(r->pool, pw->pw_dir,
36810                        w, "/", userdir, NULL);
36811 #else
36812                    filename = ap_pstrcat(r->pool, pw->pw_dir,
36813                        "/", userdir, NULL);
36814 #endif
36815                }
36816 #endif                          /* WIN32 */
36817            }
36818
36819            /*
36820             * Now see if it exists, or we're at the last
36821             * entry. If we are at the last entry, then use
36822             * the filename generated (if there is one)
36823             * anyway, in the hope that some handler might
36824             * handle it. This can be used, for example, to
36825             * run a CGI script for the user.
36826             */
36827            if (filename && (!*userdirs || stat(filename,
36828                &statbuf) != -1)) {
36829                r->filename = ap_pstrcat(r->pool, filename,
36830                    dname, NULL);
36831            /* when statbuf contains info on r->filename we
36832             * can save a syscall by copying it to r->finfo
36833 */
36834                if (*userdirs && dname[0] == 0)
36835                    r->finfo = statbuf;
36836                return OK;
36837            }
36838        }
36839
36840        return DECLINED;
36841 }
36842
36843 module userdir_module = {
36844     STANDARD_MODULE_STUFF,
36845     NULL,                   /* initializer */
36846     NULL,                   /* dir config creater */
36847     NULL,
36848     /* dir merger -- default is to override */
36849     create_userdir_config,  /* server config */
36850     NULL,                   /* merge server config */
36851     userdir_cmds,           /* command table */
36852     NULL,                   /* handlers */
36853     translate_userdir,      /* filename translation */
```

```
36854       NULL,                    /* check_user_id */
36855       NULL,                    /* check auth */
36856       NULL,                    /* check access */
36857       NULL,                    /* type_checker */
36858       NULL,                    /* fixups */
36859       NULL,                    /* logger */
36860       NULL,                    /* header parser */
36861       NULL,                    /* child_init */
36862       NULL,                    /* child_exit */
36863       NULL                     /* post read-request */
36864    };
```

p 525 **mod_usertrack.c**

```
36865    #include "httpd.h"
36866    #include "http_config.h"
36867    #include "http_core.h"
36868    #if !defined(WIN32) && !defined(MPE)
36869    #include <sys/time.h>
36870    #endif
36871
36872    module MODULE_VAR_EXPORT usertrack_module;
36873
36874    typedef struct {
36875        int always;
36876        time_t expires;
36877    }    cookie_log_state;
36878
36879    /* Define this to allow post-2000 cookies. Cookies
36880     * use two-digit dates, so it might be dicey.
36881     * (Netscape does it correctly, but others may not)
36882     */
36883    #define MILLENIAL_COOKIES
36884
36885    /* Make Cookie: Now we have to generate something
36886     * that is going to be pretty unique.  We can base
36887     * it on the pid, time, hostip */
36888
36889    #define COOKIE_NAME "Apache="
36890
36891    static void make_cookie(request_rec *r)
36892    {
36893        cookie_log_state *cls =
36894          ap_get_module_config(r->server->module_config,
36895                               &usertrack_module);
36896    #if defined(NO_GETTIMEOFDAY) && !defined(NO_TIMES)
36897        clock_t mpe_times;
36898        struct tms mpe_tms;
```

```
36899    #elif !defined(WIN32)
36900        struct timeval tv;
36901        struct timezone tz = {0, 0};
36902    #endif
36903        /* 1024 == hardcoded constant */
36904        char cookiebuf[1024];
36905        char *new_cookie;
36906        const char *rname =
36907          ap_get_remote_host(r->connection,
36908          r->per_dir_config,
36909                             REMOTE_NAME);
36910
36911    #if defined(NO_GETTIMEOFDAY) && !defined(NO_TIMES)
36912    /* We lack gettimeofday(), so we must use time()
36913       to obtain the epoch seconds, and then times() to
36914       obtain CPU clock ticks (milliseconds). Combine this
36915     together to obtain a hopefully unique cookie ID. */
36916
36917        mpe_times = times(&mpe_tms);
36918
36919        ap_snprintf(cookiebuf, sizeof(cookiebuf),
36920            "%s.%d%ld%ld", rname, (int) getpid(),
36921                (long) r->request_time,
36922                    (long) mpe_tms.tms_utime);
36923    #elif defined(WIN32)
36924        /*
36925         * We lack gettimeofday() and we lack times(). So
36926         * we'll use a combination of time() and
36927         * GetTickCount(), which returns milliseconds
36928         * since Windows was started. It should be
36929         * relatively unique.
36930         */
36931
36932        ap_snprintf(cookiebuf, sizeof(cookiebuf),
36933            "%s.%d%ld%ld", rname, (int) getpid(),
36934                (long) r->request_time,
36935                    (long) GetTickCount());
36936
36937    #else
36938        gettimeofday(&tv, &tz);
36939
36940        ap_snprintf(cookiebuf, sizeof(cookiebuf),
36941          "%s.%d%ld%d", rname, (int) getpid(),
36942                (long) tv.tv_sec,
36943                    (int) tv.tv_usec / 1000);
36944    #endif
36945
36946        if (cls->expires) {
```

```
36947          struct tm *tms;
36948          time_t when = r->request_time +
36949            cls->expires;
36950
36951  #ifndef MILLENIAL_COOKIES
36952          /*
36953           * Only two-digit date string, so we can't
36954           * trust "00" or more. Therefore, we knock it
36955           * all back to just before midnight on
36956           * 1/1/2000 (which is 946684799)
36957           */
36958
36959          if (when > 946684799)
36960              when = 946684799;
36961  #endif
36962          tms = gmtime(&when);
36963
36964          /* Cookie with date; as strftime '%a,
36965             %d-%h-%y %H:%M:%S GMT' */
36966          new_cookie = ap_psprintf(r->pool,
36967              "%s%s; path=/; expires=%s,
36968              %.2d-%s-%.2d %.2d:%.2d:%.2d GMT",
36969                  COOKIE_NAME, cookiebuf,
36970                      ap_day_snames[tms->tm_wday],
36971              tms->tm_mday, ap_month_snames[tms->tm_mon],
36972            tms->tm_year % 100,
36973                  tms->tm_hour, tms->tm_min, tms->tm_sec);
36974      }
36975      else
36976       new_cookie = ap_psprintf(r->pool,
36977          "%s%s; path=/", COOKIE_NAME, cookiebuf);
36978
36979      ap_table_setn(r->headers_out, "Set-Cookie",
36980          new_cookie);
36981      ap_table_setn(r->notes, "cookie",
36982          ap_pstrdup(r->pool, cookiebuf));
36983          /* log first time */
36984      return;
36985  }
36986
36987  static int spot_cookie(request_rec *r)
36988  {
36989      int *enable = (int *)
36990          ap_get_module_config(r->per_dir_config,
36991                              &usertrack_module);
36992      const char *cookie;
36993      char *value;
36994
36995      if (!*enable)
36996          return DECLINED;
36997
36998      if ((cookie = ap_table_get(r->headers_in,
36999          "Cookie")))
37000          if ((value = strstr(cookie, COOKIE_NAME))) {
37001              char *cookiebuf, *cookieend;
37002
37003              value += strlen(COOKIE_NAME);
37004              cookiebuf = ap_pstrdup(r->pool, value);
37005              cookieend = strchr(cookiebuf, ';');
37006              if (cookieend)
37007                  *cookieend = '\0';
37008                  /* Ignore anything after a ; */
37009
37010              /* Set the cookie in a note, for logging */
37011              ap_table_setn(r->notes, "cookie", cookiebuf);
37012
37013              return DECLINED;
37014              /* Theres already a cookie, no new one */
37015          }
37016      make_cookie(r);
37017      return OK;                    /* We set our cookie */
37018  }
37019
37020  static void *make_cookie_log_state(pool *p,
37021      server_rec *s)
37022  {
37023      cookie_log_state *cls =
37024      (cookie_log_state *) ap_palloc(p,
37025          sizeof(cookie_log_state));
37026
37027      cls->expires = 0;
37028
37029      return (void *) cls;
37030  }
37031
37032  static void *make_cookie_dir(pool *p, char *d)
37033  {
37034      return (void *) ap_pcalloc(p, sizeof(int));
37035  }
37036
37037  static const char *set_cookie_enable(cmd_parms *cmd,
37038      int *c, int arg)
37039  {
37040      *c = arg;
37041      return NULL;
37042  }
```

```
37043
37044    static const char *set_cookie_exp(cmd_parms *parms,
37045        void *dummy, const char *arg)
37046    {
37047        cookie_log_state *cls =
37048         ap_get_module_config(parms->server->module_config,
37049                                   &usertrack_module);
37050        time_t factor, modifier = 0;
37051        time_t num = 0;
37052        char *word;
37053
37054        /* The simple case first - all numbers (we assume) */
37055        if (ap_isdigit(arg[0]) &&
37056               ap_isdigit(arg[strlen(arg) - 1])) {
37057          cls->expires = atol(arg);
37058           return NULL;
37059        }
37060
37061        /*
37062         * The harder case - stolen from mod_expires
37063         *
37064         * CookieExpires "[plus] {<num> <type>}*"
37065         */
37066
37067        word = ap_getword_conf(parms->pool, &arg);
37068        if (!strncasecmp(word, "plus", 1)) {
37069            word = ap_getword_conf(parms->pool, &arg);
37070        };
37071
37072        /* {<num> <type>}* */
37073        while (word[0]) {
37074            /* <num> */
37075            if (ap_isdigit(word[0]))
37076                num = atoi(word);
37077            else
37078                return "bad expires code, numeric
37079                  value expected.";
37080
37081            /* <type> */
37082            word = ap_getword_conf(parms->pool, &arg);
37083            if (!word[0])
37084                return "bad expires code, missing <type>";
37085
37086            factor = 0;
37087            if (!strncasecmp(word, "years", 1))
37088                factor = 60 * 60 * 24 * 365;
37089            else if (!strncasecmp(word, "months", 2))
37090                factor = 60 * 60 * 24 * 30;
37091            else if (!strncasecmp(word, "weeks", 1))
37092                factor = 60 * 60 * 24 * 7;
37093            else if (!strncasecmp(word, "days", 1))
37094                factor = 60 * 60 * 24;
37095            else if (!strncasecmp(word, "hours", 1))
37096                factor = 60 * 60;
37097            else if (!strncasecmp(word, "minutes", 2))
37098                factor = 60;
37099            else if (!strncasecmp(word, "seconds", 1))
37100                factor = 1;
37101            else
37102                return "bad expires code, unrecognized type";
37103
37104            modifier = modifier + factor * num;
37105
37106            /* next <num> */
37107            word = ap_getword_conf(parms->pool, &arg);
37108        }
37109
37110        cls->expires = modifier;
37111
37112        return NULL;
37113    }
37114
37115    static const command_rec cookie_log_cmds[] = {
37116        {"CookieExpires", set_cookie_exp, NULL,
37117            RSRC_CONF, TAKE1,
37118        "an expiry date code"},
37119        {"CookieTracking", set_cookie_enable, NULL,
37120            OR_FILEINFO, FLAG,
37121        "whether or not to enable cookies"},
37122        {NULL}
37123    };
37124
37125    module MODULE_VAR_EXPORT usertrack_module = {
37126        STANDARD_MODULE_STUFF,
37127        NULL,                   /* initializer */
37128        make_cookie_dir,        /* dir config creater */
37129        NULL,
37130        /* dir merger -- default is to override */
37131        make_cookie_log_state,  /* server config */
37132        NULL,                   /* merge server configs */
37133        cookie_log_cmds,        /* command table */
37134        NULL,                   /* handlers */
37135        NULL,                   /* filename translation */
37136        NULL,                   /* check_user_id */
37137        NULL,                   /* check auth */
37138        NULL,                   /* check access */
```

```
37139        NULL,                    /* type_checker */
37140        spot_cookie,             /* fixups */
37141        NULL,                    /* logger */
37142        NULL,                    /* header parser */
37143        NULL,                    /* child_init */
37144        NULL,                    /* child_exit */
37145        NULL                     /* post read-request */
37146    };
```

▶ p 533 ▶ mod_example.c

```
37147    #include "httpd.h"
37148    #include "http_config.h"
37149    #include "http_core.h"
37150    #include "http_log.h"
37151    #include "http_main.h"
37152    #include "http_protocol.h"
37153    #include "util_script.h"
37154
37155    #include <stdio.h>
37156
37157    /*-------------------------------------------------------*/
37158    /*                                                       */
37159    /* Data declarations.                                    */
37160    /*                                                       */
37161    /* Here are the static cells and structure */
37162    /* declarations private to our module.     */
37163    /*                                         */
37164    /*-----------------------------------------*/
37165
37166    /*
37167     * Sample configuration record.  Used for both
37168     * per-directory and per-server configuration data.
37169     *
37170     * It's perfectly reasonable to have two different
37171     * structures for the two different environments. The
37172     * same command handlers will be called for both,
37173     * though, so the handlers need to be able to tell
37174     * them apart. One possibility is for both structures
37175     * to start with an int which is zero for one and 1
37176     * for the other.
37177     *
37178     * Note that while the per-directory and per-server
37179     * configuration records are available to most of
37180     * the module handlers, they should be treated as
37181     * READ-ONLY by all except the command and merge
37182     * handlers.  Sometimes handlers are handed a record
37183     * that applies to the current location by implication
37184     * or inheritance, and modifying it will change
37185     * the rules for other locations.
37186     */
37187    typedef struct excfg {
37188        int cmode;
37189        /* Environment to which record applies (directory,
37190         * server, or combination).
37191         */
37192    #define CONFIG_MODE_SERVER 1
37193    #define CONFIG_MODE_DIRECTORY 2
37194    #define CONFIG_MODE_COMBO 3 /* Shouldn't ever happen. */
37195        int local;
37196        /* Boolean: "Example" directive declared here? */
37197        int congenital;
37198        /* Boolean: did we inherit an "Example"? */
37199        char *trace;
37200        /* Pointer to trace string. */
37201        char *loc;
37202        /* Location to which this record applies. */
37203    } excfg;
37204
37205    /*
37206     * Let's set up a module-local static cell to point
37207     * to the accreting callback trace.  As each API
37208     * callback is made to us, we'll tack on the particulars
37209     * to whatever we've already recorded.  To avoid massive
37210     * memory bloat as directories are walked again
37211     * and again, we record the routine/environment
37212     * the first time (non-request context only), and
37213     * ignore subsequent calls for the same
37214     * routine/environment.
37215     */
37216    static const char *trace = NULL;
37217    static table *static_calls_made = NULL;
37218
37219    /*
37220     * To avoid leaking memory from pools other than the
37221     * per-request one, we allocate a module-private pool,
37222     * and then use a sub-pool of that which gets freed
37223     * each time we modify the trace.  That way previous
37224     * layers of trace data don't get lost.
37225     */
37226    static pool *example_pool = NULL;
37227    static pool *example_subpool = NULL;
37228
37229    /*
37230     * Declare ourselves so the configuration routines
37231     * can find and know us. We'll fill it in
```

```
37232    * at the end of the module.
37233    */
37234   module example_module;
37235
37236   /*-------------------------------------------------*/
37237   /*                                                 */
37238   /* The following pseudo-prototype declarations
37239    * illustrate the parameters passed to command handlers
37240    * for the different types of directive syntax. If an
37241    * argument was specified in the directive definition
37242    * (look for "command_rec" below), it's available to
37243    * the command handler via the (void *) info
37244    * field in the cmd_parms argument passed to the
37245    * handler (cmd->info for the examples below). */
37246   /*                                                 */
37247   /*-------------------------------------------------*/
37248
37249   /*
37250    * Command handler for a NO_ARGS directive.
37251    *
37252    * static const char *handle_NO_ARGS(cmd_parms *cmd,
37253    *      void *mconfig);
37254    */
37255
37256   /*
37257    * Command handler for a RAW_ARGS directive.  The
37258    * "args" argument is the text of the
37259    * commandline following the directive itself.
37260    *
37261    * static const char *handle_RAW_ARGS(cmd_parms *cmd,
37262    *      void *mconfig,
37263    *                            const char *args);
37264    */
37265
37266   /*
37267    * Command handler for a FLAG directive.  The single
37268    *       parameter is passed in"bool", which is
37269    * either zero or not for Off or On respectively.
37270    *
37271    * static const char *handle_FLAG(cmd_parms *cmd,
37272    *      void *mconfig, int bool);
37273    */
37274
37275   /*
37276    * Command handler for a TAKE1 directive.  The single
37277    * parameter is passed in
37278    * "word1".
37279    *
```

```
37280    * static const char *handle_TAKE1(cmd_parms *cmd,
37281    *      void *mconfig,
37282    *                            char *word1);
37283    */
37284
37285   /*
37286    * Command handler for a TAKE2 directive.  TAKE2
37287    * commands must always have
37288    * exactly two arguments.
37289    *
37290    * static const char *handle_TAKE2(cmd_parms *cmd,
37291    *      void *mconfig,
37292    *                            char *word1, char *word2);
37293    */
37294
37295   /*
37296    * Command handler for a TAKE3 directive.  Like TAKE2,
37297    * these must have exactly three arguments, or the
37298    * parser complains and doesn't bother calling us.
37299    *
37300    * static const char *handle_TAKE3(cmd_parms *cmd,
37301    *      void *mconfig,
37302    *           char *word1, char *word2, char *word3);
37303    */
37304
37305   /*
37306    * Command handler for a TAKE12 directive.  These can
37307    * take either one or two arguments. - word2 is a
37308    * NULL pointer if no second argument was specified.
37309    *
37310    * static const char *handle_TAKE12(cmd_parms *cmd,
37311    *    void *mconfig,
37312    *                       char *word1, char *word2);
37313    */
37314
37315   /*
37316    * Command handler for a TAKE123 directive.  A TAKE123
37317    * directive can be given, as might be expected, one,
37318    * two, or three arguments. - word2 is a NULL
37319    * pointer if no second argument was specified.
37320    * - word3 is a NULL pointer if no third argument was
37321    * specified.
37322    *
37323    * static const char *handle_TAKE123(cmd_parms *cmd,
37324    *      void *mconfig,
37325    *           char *word1, char *word2, char *word3);
37326    */
37327
```

```
37328    /*
37329     * Command handler for a TAKE13 directive.  Either one
37330     * or three arguments are permitted - no two-parameters
37331     * -only syntax is allowed. - word2 and word3 are NULL
37332     * pointers if only one argument was specified.
37333     *
37334     * static const char *handle_TAKE13(cmd_parms *cmd,
37335     *       void *mconfig,
37336     *                char *word1, char *word2, char *word3);
37337     */
37338
37339    /*
37340     * Command handler for a TAKE23 directive.  At least
37341     * two and as many as three arguments must be
37342     * specified. - word3 is a NULL pointer if no third
37343     * argument was specified.
37344     *
37345     * static const char *handle_TAKE23(cmd_parms *cmd,
37346     *       void *mconfig,
37347     *              char *word1, char *word2, char *word3);
37348     */
37349
37350    /*
37351     * Command handler for a ITERATE directive.
37352     * - Handler is called once for each of n arguments
37353     * given to the directive. - word1 points to
37354     * each argument in turn.
37355     *
37356     * static const char *handle_ITERATE(cmd_parms *cmd,
37357     *       void *mconfig,
37358     *                             char *word1);
37359     */
37360
37361    /*
37362     * Command handler for a ITERATE2 directive.
37363     * - Handler is called once for each of the second
37364     * and subsequent arguments given to the directive.
37365     * - word1 is the same for each call for a particular
37366     * directive instance (the first argument). - word2
37367     * points to each of the second and subsequent
37368     * arguments in turn.
37369     *
37370     * static const char *handle_ITERATE2(cmd_parms *cmd,
37371     *       void *mconfig,
37372     *                        char *word1, char *word2);
37373     */
37374
37375    /*-----------------------------------------------------*/
```

```
37376    /*                                                    */
37377    /* These routines are strictly internal to this module,
37378     * and support its operation.  They are not referenced
37379     * by any external portion of the server.  */
37380    /*                                                    */
37381    /*----------------------------------------------------*/
37382
37383    /*
37384     * Locate our directory configuration record for
37385     * the current request.
37386     */
37387    static excfg *our_dconfig(request_rec *r)
37388    {
37389
37390        return (excfg *) ap_get_module_config(r->
37391            per_dir_config, &example_module);
37392    }
37393
37394    #if 0
37395    /*
37396     * Locate our server configuration record for
37397     *      the specified server.
37398     */
37399    static excfg *our_sconfig(server_rec *s)
37400    {
37401
37402        return (excfg *) ap_get_module_config(s->
37403            module_config, &example_module);
37404    }
37405
37406    /*
37407     * Likewise for our configuration record for the
37408     * specified request.
37409     */
37410    static excfg *our_rconfig(request_rec *r)
37411    {
37412
37413        return (excfg *) ap_get_module_config(r->
37414            request_config, &example_module);
37415    }
37416    #endif
37417
37418    /*
37419     * This routine sets up some module-wide cells if they
37420     * haven't been already.
37421     */
37422    static void setup_module_cells()
37423    {
```

```
37424        /*
37425         * If we haven't already allocated our
37426         * module-private pool, do so now.
37427         */
37428        if (example_pool == NULL) {
37429            example_pool = ap_make_sub_pool(NULL);
37430        };
37431        /*
37432         * Likewise for the table of routine/environment
37433         * pairs we visit outside of request context.
37434         */
37435        if (static_calls_made == NULL) {
37436            static_calls_made =
37437                ap_make_table(example_pool, 16);
37438        };
37439    }
37440
37441    /*
37442     * This routine is used to add a trace of a callback
37443     * to the list.  We're passed the server record (if
37444     * available), the request record (if available),
37445     * a pointer to our private configuration record
37446     * (if available) for the environment to which the
37447     * callback is supposed to apply, and some text.  We
37448     * turn this into a textual representation and add
37449     * it to the tail of the list. The list can be
37450     * displayed by the example_handler() routine.
37451     *
37452     * If the call occurs within a request context
37453     * (i.e., we're passed a request record), we put
37454     * the trace into the request pool and attach it to
37455     * the request via the notes mechanism.  Otherwise,
37456     * the trace gets added to the static
37457     * (non-request-specific) list.
37458     *
37459     * Note that the r->notes table is only for storing
37460     * strings; if you need to maintain per-request data
37461     * of any other type, you need to use another
37462     * mechanism.
37463     */
37464
37465    #define TRACE_NOTE "example-trace"
37466
37467    static void trace_add(server_rec *s, request_rec *r,
37468        excfg *mconfig,
37469                        const char *note)
37470    {
37471
37472        const char *sofar;
37473        char *addon;
37474        char *where;
37475        pool *p;
37476        const char *trace_copy;
37477
37478        /*
37479         * Make sure our pools and tables are set up -
37480         * we need 'em.
37481         */
37482        setup_module_cells();
37483        /*
37484         * Now, if we're in request-context, we use the
37485         * request pool.
37486         */
37487        if (r != NULL) {
37488            p = r->pool;
37489            if ((trace_copy = ap_table_get(r->notes,
37490                    TRACE_NOTE)) == NULL) {
37491                trace_copy = "";
37492            }
37493        }
37494        else {
37495            /*
37496             * We're not in request context, so the trace
37497             * gets attached to our module-wide pool.  We
37498             * do the create/destroy every time we're called
37499             * in non-request context; this avoids leaking
37500             * memory in some of the subsequent calls that
37501             * allocate memory only once (such as the
37502             * key formation below).
37503             *
37504             * Make a new sub-pool and copy any existing
37505             * trace to it.  Point the trace cell at the
37506             * copied value.
37507             */
37508            p = ap_make_sub_pool(example_pool);
37509            if (trace != NULL) {
37510                trace = ap_pstrdup(p, trace);
37511            }
37512            /*
37513             * Now, if we have a sub-pool from before,
37514             * nuke it and replace with
37515             * the one we just allocated.
37516             */
37517            if (example_subpool != NULL) {
37518                ap_destroy_pool(example_subpool);
37519            }
```

```
37520          example_subpool = p;
37521          trace_copy = trace;
37522      }
37523      /*
37524       * If we weren't passed a configuration record,
37525       * we can't figure out to what location this call
37526       * applies.  This only happens for co-routines
37527       * that don't operate in a particular directory
37528       * or server context.  If we got a valid record,
37529       * extract the location (directory or server) to
37530       * which it applies.
37531       */
37532      where = (mconfig != NULL) ? mconfig->loc :
37533              "nowhere";
37534      where = (where != NULL) ? where : "";
37535      /*
37536       * Now, if we're not in request context, see if
37537       * we've been called with this particular combination
37538       * before.  The table is allocated in the module's
37539       * private pool, which doesn't get destroyed.
37540       */
37541      if (r == NULL) {
37542          char *key;
37543
37544          key = ap_pstrcat(p, note, ":", where, NULL);
37545          if (ap_table_get(static_calls_made,
37546            key) != NULL) {
37547              /*
37548               * Been here, done this.
37549               */
37550              return;
37551          }
37552          else {
37553              /*
37554               * First time for this combination of
37555               * routine and environment -
37556               * log it so we don't do it again.
37557               */
37558              ap_table_set(static_calls_made, key,
37559                "been here");
37560          }
37561      }
37562      addon = ap_pstrcat(p, "   <LI>\n", "    <DL>\n",
37563              "     <DT><SAMP>",
37564                  note, "</SAMP>\n", "     </DT>\n",
37565                  "     <DD><SAMP>[",
37566                  where, "]</SAMP>\n", "     </DD>\n",
37567                  "    </DL>\n",
37568              "   </LI>\n", NULL);
37569      sofar = (trace_copy == NULL) ? "" : trace_copy;
37570      trace_copy = ap_pstrcat(p, sofar, addon, NULL);
37571      if (r != NULL) {
37572          ap_table_set(r->notes, TRACE_NOTE, trace_copy);
37573      }
37574      else {
37575          trace = trace_copy;
37576      }
37577      /*
37578       * You *could* change the following if you wanted
37579       * to see the calling sequence reported in the
37580       * server's error_log, but beware - almost all of
37581       * these co-routines are called for every single
37582       * request, and the impact on the size (and
37583       * readability) of the error_log is considerable.
37584       */
37585  #define EXAMPLE_LOG_EACH 0
37586      if (EXAMPLE_LOG_EACH && (s != NULL)) {
37587          ap_log_error(APLOG_MARK, APLOG_DEBUG, s,
37588                  "mod_example: %s", note);
37589      }
37590  }
37591
37592  /*-------------------------------------------------*/
37593  /* We prototyped the various syntax for command     */
37594   * handlers (routines that are called when the      */
37595  /* configuration parser detects a directive declared */
37596  /* by our module) earlier.  Now we actually declare  */
37597  /* a "real" routine that will be invoked by the      */
37598  /* parser when our "real" directive is encountered.  */
37599  /*                                                   */
37600  /* If a command handler encounters a problem         *
37601  /* processing the directive, it signals this fact    */
37602  /* by returning a non-NULL pointer to a string       */
37603  /* describing the problem.                           */
37604  /*                                                   */
37605  /* The magic return value DECLINE_CMD is used to     *
37606  /* deal with directives that might be declared       */
37607  /* by multiple modules.  If the command handler      */
37608  /* returns NULL, the directive was processed; if it  */
37609  /* returns DECLINE_CMD, the next module (if any)     */
37610  /* that declares the directive is given a chance     */
37611  /* at it.  If it returns any other value, it's       */
37612  /* treated as the text of an error message.          */
37613  /*-------------------------------------------------*/
37614  /*
37615   * Command handler for the NO_ARGS "Example" directive.
```

```
37616      * All we do is mark the call in the trace log, and
37617      * flag the applicability of the directive to the
37618      * current location in that location's configuration
37619      * record.
37620      */
37621     static const char *cmd_example(cmd_parms *cmd,
37622         void *mconfig)
37623     {
37624
37625         excfg *cfg = (excfg *) mconfig;
37626
37627         /*
37628          * "Example Wuz Here"
37629          */
37630         cfg->local = 1;
37631         trace_add(cmd->server, NULL, cfg, "cmd_example()");
37632         return NULL;
37633     }
37634
37635     /*--------------------------------------------------*/
37636     /*                                                  */
37637     /* Now we declare our content handlers, which are   */
37638     /*invoked when the server encounters a document     */
37639     /* which our module is supposed to have a chance to */
37640     /* see.  (See mod_mime's SetHandler and AddHandler  */
37641     /*directives, and the mod_info and mod_status       */
37642     /* examples, for more details.)                     */
37643     /*                                                  */
37644     /* Since content handlers are dumping data directly */
37645     /* into the connexion (using the r*() routines,     */
37646     /* such as rputs() and rprintf()) without           */
37647     /* intervention by other parts of the server, they  */
37648     /* need to make sure any accumulated HTTP headers   */
37649     /* are sent first.  This is done by calling         */
37650     /* send_http_header().  Otherwise, no header will be */
37651     /* sent at all, and the output sent to the          */
37652     /* client will actually be HTTP-uncompliant.        */
37653     /*--------------------------------------------------*/
37654     /*
37655      * Sample content handler.  All this does is display
37656      * the call list that has been built up so far.
37657      *
37658      * The return value instructs the caller concerning
37659      * what happened and what to do next:
37660      *   OK ("we did our thing")
37661      *   DECLINED ("this isn't something with which
37662      *    we want to get involved")
37663      *   HTTP_mumble ("an error status should be reported")
37664      */
37665     static int example_handler(request_rec *r)
37666     {
37667
37668         excfg *dcfg;
37669
37670         dcfg = our_dconfig(r);
37671         trace_add(r->server, r, dcfg, "example_handler()");
37672         /*
37673          * We're about to start sending content, so we need
37674          * to force the HTTP headers to be sent at this
37675          * point. Otherwise, no headers will be sent at all.
37676          * We can set any we like first, of course. **NOTE**
37677          * Here's where you set the "Content-type" header,
37678          * and you do so by putting it in r->content_type,
37679          * *not* r->headers_out("Content-type").  If you
37680          * don't set it, it will be filled in with the
37681          * server's default type (typically"text/plain").
37682          * You *must* also ensure that r->content_type is
37683          * lower case.
37684          *
37685          * We also need to start a timer so the server can
37686          * know if the connexion is broken.
37687          */
37688         r->content_type = "text/html";
37689         ap_soft_timeout("send example call trace", r);
37690         ap_send_http_header(r);
37691         /*
37692          * If we're only supposed to send header information
37693          * (HEAD request), we're already there.
37694          */
37695         if (r->header_only) {
37696             ap_kill_timeout(r);
37697             return OK;
37698         }
37699
37700         /*
37701          * Now send our actual output. Since we tagged this
37702          * as being "text/html", we need to embed any HTML.
37703          */
37704         ap_rputs("<!DOCTYPE HTML
37705             PUBLIC \"-//W3C//DTD HTML 3.2//EN\">\n", r);
37706         ap_rputs("<HTML>\n", r);
37707         ap_rputs(" <HEAD>\n", r);
37708         ap_rputs("  <TITLE>mod_example Module
37709             Content-Handler Output\n", r);
37710         ap_rputs("  </TITLE>\n", r);
37711         ap_rputs(" </HEAD>\n", r);
```

```
37712    ap_rputs("  <BODY>\n", r);
37713    ap_rputs("  <H1><SAMP>mod_example</SAMP>
37714            Module Content-Handler Output\n", r);
37715    ap_rputs("  </H1>\n", r);
37716    ap_rputs("  <P>\n", r);
37717    ap_rprintf(r, "  Apache HTTP Server
37718            version: \"%s\"\n",
37719              ap_get_server_version());
37720    ap_rputs("  <BR>\n", r);
37721    ap_rprintf(r, "  Server built: \"%s\"\n",
37722            ap_get_server_built());
37723    ap_rputs("  </P>\n", r);;
37724    ap_rputs("  <P>\n", r);
37725    ap_rputs("  The format for the callback
37726            trace is:\n", r);
37727    ap_rputs("  </P>\n", r);
37728    ap_rputs("  <DL>\n", r);
37729    ap_rputs("  <DT><EM>n</EM>.<SAMP>&lt;
37730            routine-name&gt;", r);
37731    ap_rputs("(&lt;routine-data&gt;)</SAMP>\n", r);
37732    ap_rputs("  </DT>\n", r);
37733    ap_rputs("  <DD><SAMP>[&lt;applies-to&gt;]
37734            </SAMP>\n", r);
37735    ap_rputs("  </DD>\n", r);
37736    ap_rputs("  </DL>\n", r);
37737    ap_rputs("  <P>\n", r);
37738    ap_rputs("  The <SAMP>&lt;routine-data&gt;</SAMP>
37739            is supplied by\n", r);
37740    ap_rputs("  the routine when it requests the
37741            trace,\n", r);
37742    ap_rputs("  and the <SAMP>&lt;applies-to&gt;</SAMP>
37743            is extracted\n", r);
37744    ap_rputs("  from the configuration record at the
37745            time of the trace.\n", r);
37746    ap_rputs("  <STRONG>SVR()</STRONG> indicates a
37747            server environment\n", r);
37748    ap_rputs("  (blank means the main or default
37749            otherwise it's\n", r);
37750    ap_rputs("  the name of the VirtualHost);
37751            <STRONG>DIR()</STRONG>\n", r);
37752    ap_rputs("  indicates a location in the URL or
37753            filesystem\n", r);
37754    ap_rputs("  namespace.\n", r);
37755    ap_rputs("  </P>\n", r);
37756    ap_rprintf(r, "  <H2>Static callbacks so far:</H2>\n
37757            <OL>\n%s  </OL>\n",
37758              trace);
37759    ap_rputs("  <H2>Request-specific callbacks
```

```
37760            so far:</H2>\n", r);
37761    ap_rprintf(r, "  <OL>\n%s  </OL>\n",
37762            ap_table_get(r->notes, TRACE_NOTE));
37763    ap_rputs("  <H2>Environment for <EM>this</EM>
37764            call:</H2>\n", r);
37765    ap_rputs("  <UL>\n", r);
37766    ap_rprintf(r, "    <LI>Applies-to: <SAMP>%s</SAMP>\n
37767            </LI>\n", dcfg->loc);
37768    ap_rprintf(r, "    <LI>\"Example\" directive
37769            declared here: %s\n  </LI>\n",
37770            (dcfg->local ? "YES" : "NO"));
37771    ap_rprintf(r, "    <LI>\"Example\" inherited:
37772            %s\n  </LI>\n",
37773            (dcfg->congenital ? "YES" : "NO"));
37774    ap_rputs("  </UL>\n", r);
37775    ap_rputs("  </BODY>\n", r);
37776    ap_rputs("</HTML>\n", r);
37777    /*
37778     * We're all done, so cancel the timeout we set.
37779     * Since this is probably the end of the request
37780     * we *could* assume this would be done during
37781     * post-processing - but it's possible that
37782     * another handler might be called and inherit
37783     * our outstanding timer. Not good; to each its own.
37784     */
37785    ap_kill_timeout(r);
37786    /*
37787     * We did what we wanted to do, so tell the rest
37788     * of the server we succeeded.
37789     */
37790    return OK;
37791  }
37792
37793  /*------------------------------------------------*/
37794  /*                                                */
37795  /* Now let's declare routines for each of the     */
37796  /* callback phase in order. (That's the order in  */
37797  /* which they're listed in the callback list, *not*/
37798  /* the order in which the server calls them!  See */
37799  /* the command_rec declaration near the bottom    */
37800  /* of this file.)  Note that these may be bottom  */
37801  /* X situations that don't relate primarily to our*/
37802  /* function - in other words, the fixup handler   */
37803  /* shouldn't assume that the request has to do with*/
37804  /* "example" stuff.                               */
37805  /*                                                */
37806  /* With the exception of the content handler, all */
37807  /* of our routines will be called for each request,*/
```

```
37808    /* unless an earlier handler from another module    */
37809    /* aborted the sequence.                            */
37810    /*                                                  */
37811    /* Handlers that are declared as "int" can return   */
37812    /* the following:                                   */
37813    /*                                                  */
37814    /*  OK          Handler accepted the request and    */
37815    /*     did its thing with it.                       */
37816    /*  DECLINED    Handler took no action.             */
37817    /*  HTTP_mumble Handler looked at request and found  */
37818    /*     it wanting.                                  */
37819    /*                                                  */
37820    /* What the server does after calling a module      */
37821    /* handler depends upon the handler's return        */
37822    /* value.  In all cases, if the handler returns     */
37823    /* DECLINED, the server will continue to the next   */
37824    /* module with an handler for the current phase.    */
37825    /* However, if the handler return a non-OK,         */
37826    /* non-DECLINED status, the server aborts the       */
37827    /* request right there.  If the handler returns OK, */
37828    /* the server's next action is phase-specific;      */
37829    /* see the individual handler comments below for    */
37830    /* details.                                         */
37831    /*                                                  */
37832    /*------------------------------------------------*/
37833    /*
37834     * This function is called during server
37835     * initialisation.  Any information that needs
37836     * to be recorded must be in static cells, since
37837     * there's no configuration record.
37838     *
37839     * There is no return value.
37840     */
37841
37842    /*
37843     * All our module-initialiser does is add its trace
37844     * to the log.
37845     */
37846    static void example_init(server_rec *s, pool *p)
37847    {
37848
37849        char *note;
37850        char *sname = s->server_hostname;
37851
37852        /*
37853         * Set up any module cells that ought to be
37854         * initialised.
37855         */
37856        setup_module_cells();
37857        /*
37858         * The arbitrary text we add to our trace entry
37859         * indicates for which server
37860         * we're being called.
37861         */
37862        sname = (sname != NULL) ? sname : "";
37863        note = ap_pstrcat(p, "example_init(", sname, ")",
37864            NULL);
37865        trace_add(s, NULL, NULL, note);
37866    }
37867
37868    /*
37869     * This function is called during server initialisation
37870     * when an heavy-weight process (such as a child) is
37871     * being initialised.  As with the module-initialisation
37872     * function, any information that needs to be recorded
37873     * must be in static cells, since there's no configuration
37874     * record.
37875     *
37876     * There is no return value.
37877     */
37878
37879    /*
37880     * All our process-initialiser does is add its trace
37881     * to the log.
37882     */
37883    static void example_child_init(server_rec *s, pool *p)
37884    {
37885
37886        char *note;
37887        char *sname = s->server_hostname;
37888
37889        /*
37890         * Set up any module cells that ought to be
37891         * initialised.
37892         */
37893        setup_module_cells();
37894        /*
37895         * The arbitrary text we add to our trace entry
37896         * indicates for which server
37897         * we're being called.
37898         */
37899        sname = (sname != NULL) ? sname : "";
37900        note = ap_pstrcat(p, "example_child_init(",
37901            sname, ")", NULL);
37902        trace_add(s, NULL, NULL, note);
37903    }
```

```
37904
37905    /*
37906     * This function is called when an heavy-weight
37907     * process (such as a child) is being run down
37908     * or destroyed.  As with the child-initialisation
37909     * function, any information that needs to
37910     * be recorded must be in static cells, since
37911     * there's no configuration record.
37912     *
37913     * There is no return value.
37914     */
37915
37916    /*
37917     * All our process-death routine does is add its
37918     * trace to the log.
37919     */
37920    static void example_child_exit(server_rec *s, pool *p)
37921    {
37922
37923        char *note;
37924        char *sname = s->server_hostname;
37925
37926        /*
37927         * The arbitrary text we add to our trace entry
37928         * indicates for which server we're being
37929         * called.
37930         */
37931        sname = (sname != NULL) ? sname : "";
37932        note = ap_pstrcat(p, "example_child_exit(",
37933            sname, ")", NULL);
37934        trace_add(s, NULL, NULL, note);
37935    }
37936
37937    /*
37938     * This function gets called to create up a
37939     * per-directory configuration record.  This will
37940     * be called for the "default" server environment,
37941     * and for each directory for which the parser
37942     * finds any of our directives applicable. If a
37943     * directory doesn't have any of our directives
37944     * involved (i.e., they aren't in the .htaccess file,
37945     * or a <Location>, <Directory>, or related block),
37946     * this routine will *not* be called - the
37947     * configuration for the closest ancestor is used.
37948     *
37949     * The return value is a pointer to the created module-
37950     * specific structure.
37951     */
37952    static void *example_create_dir_config(pool *p,
37953        char *dirspec)
37954    {
37955
37956        excfg *cfg;
37957        char *dname = dirspec;
37958
37959        /*
37960         * Allocate the space for our record from the pool
37961         * supplied.
37962         */
37963        cfg = (excfg *) ap_pcalloc(p, sizeof(excfg));
37964        /*
37965         * Now fill in the defaults.  If there are any
37966         * 'parent' configuration records, they'll
37967         * get merged as part of a separate callback.
37968         */
37969        cfg->local = 0;
37970        cfg->congenital = 0;
37971        cfg->cmode = CONFIG_MODE_DIRECTORY;
37972        /*
37973         * Finally, add our trace to the callback list.
37974         */
37975        dname = (dname != NULL) ? dname : "";
37976        cfg->loc = ap_pstrcat(p, "DIR(", dname, ")", NULL);
37977        trace_add(NULL, NULL, cfg,
37978            "example_create_dir_config()");
37979        return (void *) cfg;
37980    }
37981
37982    /*
37983     * This function gets called to merge two
37984     * per-directory configuration records.  This is
37985     * typically done to cope with things like .htaccess
37986     * files or <Location> directives for directories
37987     * that are beneath one for which a configuration
37988     * record was already created.  The routine has the
37989     * responsibility of creating a new record and merging
37990     * the contents of the other two into it appropriately.
37991     * If the module doesn't declare a merge routine,
37992     * the record for the closest ancestor location (that
37993     * has one) is used exclusively.
37994     *
37995     * The routine MUST NOT modify any of its arguments!
37996     *
37997     * The return value is a pointer to the created
37998     * module-specific structure containing the merged
37999     * values.
```

```
38000    */
38001    static void *example_merge_dir_config(pool *p,
38002        void *parent_conf,
38003                                    void *newloc_con
38004    {
38005
38006        excfg *merged_config = (excfg *) ap_pcalloc(p,
38007            sizeof(excfg));
38008        excfg *pconf = (excfg *) parent_conf;
38009        excfg *nconf = (excfg *) newloc_conf;
38010        char *note;
38011
38012        /*
38013         * Some things get copied directly from the
38014         * more-specific record, rather than getting
38015         * merged.
38016         */
38017        merged_config->local = nconf->local;
38018        merged_config->loc = ap_pstrdup(p, nconf->loc);
38019        /*
38020         * Others, like the setting of the 'congenital'
38021         * flag, get ORed in.  The setting of that
38022         * particular flag, for instance, is TRUE if it
38023         * was ever true anywhere in the upstream
38024         * configuration.
38025         */
38026        merged_config->congenital = (pconf->congenital
38027            | pconf->local);
38028        /*
38029         * If we're merging records for two different
38030         * types of environment (server and directory), mark
38031         * the new record appropriately. Otherwise, inherit
38032         * the current value.
38033         */
38034        merged_config->cmode =
38035            (pconf->cmode == nconf->cmode) ?
38036                pconf->cmode : CONFIG_MODE_COMBO;
38037        /*
38038         * Now just record our being called in the trace
38039         * list.  Include the locations we were
38040         * asked to merge.
38041         */
38042        note = ap_pstrcat(p, "example_merge_dir_config(\"",
38043            pconf->loc, "\",\"",
38044                nconf->loc, "\")", NULL);
38045        trace_add(NULL, NULL, merged_config, note);
38046        return (void *) merged_config;
38047    }
38048
38049    /*
38050     * This function gets called to create a per-server
38051     * configuration record.  It will always be called
38052     * for the "default" server.
38053     *
38054     * The return value is a pointer to the created
38055     * module-specific structure.
38056     */
38057    static void *example_create_server_config(pool *p,
38058        server_rec *s)
38059    {
38060
38061        excfg *cfg;
38062        char *sname = s->server_hostname;
38063
38064        /*
38065         * As with the example_create_dir_config() reoutine,
38066         * we allocate and fill in an empty record.
38067    */
38068        cfg = (excfg *) ap_pcalloc(p, sizeof(excfg));
38069        cfg->local = 0;
38070        cfg->congenital = 0;
38071        cfg->cmode = CONFIG_MODE_SERVER;
38072        /*
38073         * Note that we were called in the trace list.
38074         */
38075        sname = (sname != NULL) ? sname : "";
38076        cfg->loc = ap_pstrcat(p, "SVR(", sname, ")", NULL);
38077        trace_add(s, NULL, cfg,
38078            "example_create_server_config()");
38079        return (void *) cfg;
38080    }
38081
38082    /*
38083     * This function gets called to merge two per-server
38084     * configuration records.  This is typically done
38085     * to cope with things like virtual hosts and
38086     * the default server configuration  The routine
38087     * has the responsibility of creating a new record
38088     * and merging the contents of the other two into it
38089     * appropriately.  If the module doesn't declare a
38090     * merge routine, the more specific existing
38091     * record is used exclusively.
38092     *
38093     * The routine MUST NOT modify any of its arguments!
38094     *
38095     * The return value is a pointer to the created
```

```
38096     * module-specific structure containing the
38097     * merged values.
38098     */
38099    static void *example_merge_server_config(pool *p,
38100         void *server1_conf,
38101                                  void *server2_conf)
38102    {
38103
38104         excfg *merged_config = (excfg *) ap_pcalloc(p,
38105              sizeof(excfg));
38106         excfg *s1conf = (excfg *) server1_conf;
38107         excfg *s2conf = (excfg *) server2_conf;
38108         char *note;
38109
38110         /*
38111          * Our inheritance rules are our own, and part of
38112          * our module's semantics. Basically, just note
38113          * whence we came.
38114          */
38115         merged_config->cmode =
38116             (s1conf->cmode == s2conf->cmode) ?
38117                  s1conf->cmode : CONFIG_MODE_COMBO;
38118         merged_config->local = s2conf->local;
38119         merged_config->congenital = (s1conf->congenital
38120             | s1conf->local);
38121         merged_config->loc = ap_pstrdup(p, s2conf->loc);
38122         /*
38123          * Trace our call, including what we were asked
38124          * to merge.
38125          */
38126         note = ap_pstrcat(p,
38127              "example_merge_server_config(\"", s1conf->loc,
38128              "\",\"",
38129                  s2conf->loc, "\")", NULL);
38130         trace_add(NULL, NULL, merged_config, note);
38131         return (void *) merged_config;
38132    }
38133
38134    /*
38135     * This routine is called after the request has been
38136     * read but before any other phases have been
38137     * processed.  This allows us to make decisions based
38138     * upon the input header fields.
38139     *
38140     * The return value is OK, DECLINED, or HTTP_mumble.
38141     * If we return OK, no further modules
38142     * are called for this phase.
38143     */
```

```
38144    static int example_post_read_request(request_rec *r)
38145    {
38146
38147         excfg *cfg;
38148
38149         cfg = our_dconfig(r);
38150         /*
38151          * We don't actually *do* anything here, except
38152          * note the fact that we were called.
38153          */
38154         trace_add(r->server, r, cfg,
38155              "example_post_read_request()");
38156         return DECLINED;
38157    }
38158
38159    /*
38160     * This routine gives our module an opportunity to
38161     * translate the URI into an actual filename.
38162     * If we don't do anything special, the server's
38163     * default rules (Alias directives and the like) will
38164     * continue to be followed.
38165     *
38166     * The return value is OK, DECLINED, or HTTP_mumble.
38167     * If we return OK, no further modules are
38168     * called for this phase.
38169     */
38170    static int example_translate_handler(request_rec *r)
38171    {
38172
38173         excfg *cfg;
38174
38175         cfg = our_dconfig(r);
38176         /*
38177          * We don't actually *do* anything here, except
38178          * note the fact that we were called.
38179    */
38180         trace_add(r->server, r, cfg,
38181              "example_translate_handler()");
38182         return DECLINED;
38183    }
38184
38185    /*
38186     * This routine is called to check the authentication
38187     * information sent with the request (such as looking
38188     * up the user in a database and verifying that
38189     * the [encrypted] password sent matches the one in
38190     * the database).
38191     *
```

```
38192    * The return value is OK, DECLINED, or some
38193    * HTTP_mumble error (typically HTTP_UNAUTHORIZED).
38194    * If we return OK, no other modules are given a chance
38195    * at the request during this phase.
38196    */
38197   static int example_check_user_id(request_rec *r)
38198   {
38199
38200       excfg *cfg;
38201
38202       cfg = our_dconfig(r);
38203       /*
38204        * Don't do anything except log the call.
38205        */
38206       trace_add(r->server, r, cfg,
38207           "example_check_user_id()");
38208       return DECLINED;
38209   }
38210
38211   /*
38212    * This routine is called to check to see if
38213    * the resource being requested requires
38214    * authorisation.
38215    *
38216    * The return value is OK, DECLINED, or HTTP_mumble.
38217    * If we return OK, no other modules are
38218    * called during this phase.
38219    *
38220    * If *all* modules return DECLINED, the request
38221    * is aborted with a server error.
38222    */
38223   static int example_auth_checker(request_rec *r)
38224   {
38225
38226       excfg *cfg;
38227
38228       cfg = our_dconfig(r);
38229       /*
38230        * Log the call and return OK, or access will
38231        * be denied (even though we didn't actually
38232        * do anything).
38233        */
38234       trace_add(r->server, r, cfg,
38235           "example_auth_checker()");
38236       return DECLINED;
38237   }
38238
38239   /*
```

```
38240    * This routine is called to check for any
38241    * module-specific restrictions placed
38242    * upon the requested resource.  (See the mod_access
38243    * module for an example.)
38244    *
38245    * The return value is OK, DECLINED, or HTTP_mumble.
38246    * All modules with an handler for this phase
38247    * are called regardless of whether their predecessors
38248    * return OK or DECLINED.  The first one to return
38249    * any other status, however, will abort the
38250    * sequence (and the request) as usual.
38251    */
38252   static int example_access_checker(request_rec *r)
38253   {
38254
38255       excfg *cfg;
38256
38257       cfg = our_dconfig(r);
38258       trace_add(r->server, r, cfg,
38259           "example_access_checker()");
38260       return DECLINED;
38261   }
38262
38263   /*
38264    * This routine is called to determine and/or set
38265    * the various document type information bits,
38266    * like Content-type (via r->content_type), language,
38267    * et cetera.
38268    *
38269    * The return value is OK, DECLINED, or HTTP_mumble.
38270    * If we return OK, no further modules are given
38271    * a chance at the request for this phase.
38272    */
38273   static int example_type_checker(request_rec *r)
38274   {
38275
38276       excfg *cfg;
38277
38278       cfg = our_dconfig(r);
38279       /*
38280        * Log the call, but don't do anything else - and
38281        * report truthfully that we didn't do anything.
38282        */
38283       trace_add(r->server, r, cfg,
38284           "example_type_checker()");
38285       return DECLINED;
38286   }
38287
```

```
38288    /*
38289     * This routine is called to perform any
38290     * module-specific fixing of header fields, et
38291     * cetera.  It is invoked just before any
38292     * content-handler.
38293     *
38294     * The return value is OK, DECLINED, or HTTP_mumble.
38295     * If we return OK, the server will still call
38296     * any remaining modules with an handler for this
38297     * phase.
38298     */
38299    static int example_fixer_upper(request_rec *r)
38300    {
38301
38302        excfg *cfg;
38303
38304        cfg = our_dconfig(r);
38305        /*
38306         * Log the call and exit.
38307         */
38308        trace_add(r->server, r, cfg,
38309            "example_fixer_upper()");
38310        return OK;
38311    }
38312
38313    /*
38314     * This routine is called to perform any module-
38315     * specific logging activities over and above the
38316     * normal server things.
38317     *
38318     * The return value is OK, DECLINED, or HTTP_mumble.
38319     * If we return OK, any remaining modules with an
38320     * handler for this phase will still be called.
38321     */
38322    static int example_logger(request_rec *r)
38323    {
38324
38325        excfg *cfg;
38326
38327        cfg = our_dconfig(r);
38328        trace_add(r->server, r, cfg, "example_logger()");
38329        return DECLINED;
38330    }
38331
38332    /*
38333     * This routine is called to give the module a chance
38334     * to look at the request headers and take any
38335     * appropriate specific actions early in the processing
```

```
38336     * sequence.
38337     *
38338     * The return value is OK, DECLINED, or HTTP_mumble.
38339     * If we return OK, any remaining modules with handlers
38340     * for this phase will still be called.
38341     */
38342    static int example_header_parser(request_rec *r)
38343    {
38344
38345        excfg *cfg;
38346
38347        cfg = our_dconfig(r);
38348        trace_add(r->server, r, cfg,
38349            "example_header_parser()");
38350        return DECLINED;
38351    }
38352
38353    /*--------------------------------------------------*/
38354    /*                                                  */
38355    /* All of the routines have been declared now.      */
38356    /*Here's the list of ctives specific to dire our    */
38357    /* module, and information about where they may     */
38358    /* appear and how the command parser should pass    */
38359    /* them to us for processing.  Note that care must  */
38360    /* be taken to ensure that there are NO collisions  */
38361    /* of directive names between modules.              */
38362    /*                                                  */
38363    /*--------------------------------------------------*/
38364    /*
38365     * List of directives specific to our module.
38366     */
38367    static const command_rec example_cmds[] =
38368    {
38369        {
38370            "Example",           /* directive name */
38371            cmd_example,         /* config action routine */
38372            NULL,
38373        /* argument to include in call */
38374            OR_OPTIONS,          /* where available */
38375            NO_ARGS,             /* arguments */
38376            "Example directive - no arguments"
38377                        /* directive description */
38378        },
38379        {NULL}
38380    };
38381
38382    /*--------------------------------------------------*/
38383    /*                                                  */
```

```
38384    /* Now the list of content handlers available from   */
38385    /* this module.                                        */
38386    /*                                                     */
38387    /*----------------------------------------------------*/
38388    /*
38389     * List of content handlers our module supplies.  Each
38390     * handler is defined by two parts: a name by which
38391     * it can be referenced (such as by{Add,Set}Handler),
38392     * and the actual routine name.  The list is terminated
38393     * by a NULL block, since it can be of variable length.
38394     *
38395     * Note that content-handlers are invoked on a most-
38396     * specific to least-specific basis; that is, a handler
38397     * that is declared for "text/plain" will be invoked
38398     * before one that was declared for "text / *".  Note
38399     * also that if a content-handler returns anything
38400     * except DECLINED, no other content-handlers will
38401     * be called.
38402     */
38403    static const handler_rec example_handlers[] =
38404    {
38405        {"example-handler", example_handler},
38406        {NULL}
38407    };
38408
38409    /*----------------------------------------------------*/
38410    /*                                                     */
38411    /* Finally, the list of callback routines and data    */
38412    /* structures that provide the hooks into our         */
38413    /* module from the other parts of the server.         */
38414    /*                                                     */
38415    /*----------------------------------------------------*/
38416    /*
38417     * Module definition for configuration.  If a
38418     * particular callback is not needed, replace its
38419     * routine name below with the word NULL.
38420     *
38421     * The number in brackets indicates the order in which
38422     * the routine is called during request processing.
38423     * Note that not all routines are necessarily
38424     * called (such as if a resource doesn't have access
38425     * restrictions).
38426     */
38427    module example_module =
38428    {
38429        STANDARD_MODULE_STUFF,
38430        example_init,                /* module initializer */
38431        example_create_dir_config,
```

```
38432        /* per-directory config creator */
38433        example_merge_dir_config,    /* dir config merger */
38434        example_create_server_config,
38435        /* server config creator */
38436        example_merge_server_config,
38437        /* server config merger */
38438        example_cmds,                /* command table */
38439        example_handlers,
38440        /* [7] list of handlers */
38441        example_translate_handler,
38442        /* [2] filename-to-URI translation */
38443        example_check_user_id,
38444        /* [5] check/validate user_id */
38445        example_auth_checker,
38446        /* [6] check user_id is valid *here* */
38447        example_access_checker,
38448        /* [4] check access by host address */
38449        example_type_checker,
38450        /* [7] MIME type checker/setter */
38451        example_fixer_upper,       /* [8] fixups */
38452        example_logger,            /* [10] logger */
38453    #if MODULE_MAGIC_NUMBER >= 19970103
38454        example_header_parser,     /* [3] header parser */
38455    #endif
38456    #if MODULE_MAGIC_NUMBER >= 19970719
38457        example_child_init,        /* process initializer */
38458    #endif
38459    #if MODULE_MAGIC_NUMBER >= 19970728
38460        example_child_exit,        /* process exit/cleanup */
38461    #endif
38462    #if MODULE_MAGIC_NUMBER >= 19970902
38463        example_post_read_request
38464        /* [1] post read_request handling */
38465    #endif
38466    };
```

⮞ mod_mmap_static.c p 536

```
38467    #include <stdio.h>
38468    #include <sys/types.h>
38469    #include <sys/stat.h>
38470    #include <fcntl.h>
38471    #include <errno.h>
38472    #include <string.h>
38473    #include <sys/mman.h>
38474
38475    #define CORE_PRIVATE
38476
```

```
38477    #include "httpd.h"
38478    #include "http_config.h"
38479    #include "http_log.h"
38480    #include "http_protocol.h"
38481    #include "http_request.h"
38482    #include "http_core.h"
38483
38484    module MODULE_VAR_EXPORT mmap_static_module;
38485
38486    typedef struct {
38487        char *filename;
38488        void *mm;
38489        struct stat finfo;
38490    } a_file;
38491
38492    typedef struct {
38493        array_header *files;
38494        array_header *inode_sorted;
38495    } a_server_config;
38496
38497
38498    static void *create_server_config(pool *p,
38499         server_rec *s)
38500    {
38501        a_server_config *sconf = ap_palloc(p,
38502             sizeof(*sconf));
38503
38504        sconf->files = ap_make_array(p, 20, sizeof(a_file));
38505        sconf->inode_sorted = NULL;
38506        return sconf;
38507    }
38508
38509    static void cleanup_mmap(void *sconfv)
38510    {
38511        a_server_config *sconf = sconfv;
38512        size_t n;
38513        a_file *file;
38514
38515        n = sconf->files->nelts;
38516        file = (a_file *)sconf->files->elts;
38517        while(n) {
38518         munmap(file->mm, file->finfo.st_size);
38519         ++file;
38520         --n;
38521        }
38522    }
38523
38524    static const char *mmapfile(cmd_parms *cmd,
```

```
38525        void *dummy, char *filename)
38526    {
38527        a_server_config *sconf;
38528        a_file *new_file;
38529        a_file tmp;
38530        int fd;
38531        caddr_t mm;
38532
38533        if (stat(filename, &tmp.finfo) == -1) {
38534        ap_log_error(APLOG_MARK, APLOG_WARNING, cmd->server,
38535            "mmap_static: unable to stat(%s), skipping",
38536                filename);
38537        return NULL;
38538        }
38539        if ((tmp.finfo.st_mode & S_IFMT) != S_IFREG) {
38540         ap_log_error(APLOG_MARK, APLOG_WARNING,
38541             cmd->server,
38542             "mmap_static: %s isn't a regular file,
38543                skipping", filename);
38544         return NULL;
38545        }
38546        ap_block_alarms();
38547        fd = open(filename, O_RDONLY, 0);
38548        if (fd == -1) {
38549         ap_log_error(APLOG_MARK, APLOG_WARNING,
38550             cmd->server,
38551             "mmap_static: unable to open(%s, O_RDONLY),
38552                skipping", filename);
38553         return NULL;
38554        }
38555        mm = mmap(NULL, tmp.finfo.st_size, PROT_READ,
38556            MAP_SHARED, fd, 0);
38557        if (mm == (caddr_t)-1) {
38558         int save_errno = errno;
38559         close(fd);
38560         ap_unblock_alarms();
38561         errno = save_errno;
38562         ap_log_error(APLOG_MARK, APLOG_WARNING,
38563             cmd->server,
38564             "mmap_static: unable to mmap %s, skipping",
38565                filename);
38566         return NULL;
38567        }
38568        close(fd);
38569        tmp.mm = mm;
38570        tmp.filename = ap_pstrdup(cmd->pool, filename);
38571        sconf = ap_get_module_config(cmd->server->
38572            module_config, &mmap_static_module);
```

```
38573        new_file = ap_push_array(sconf->files);
38574        *new_file = tmp;
38575        if (sconf->files->nelts == 1) {
38576         /* first one, register the cleanup */
38577         ap_register_cleanup(cmd->pool, sconf, cleanup_mmap,
38578             ap_null_cleanup);
38579        }
38580        ap_unblock_alarms();
38581        return NULL;
38582    }
38583
38584    static command_rec mmap_static_cmds[] =
38585    {
38586        {
38587         "mmapfile", mmapfile, NULL, RSRC_CONF, ITERATE,
38588         "A space separated list of files to mmap at
38589             config time"
38590        },
38591        {
38592         NULL
38593        }
38594    };
38595
38596    static int file_compare(const void *av, const void *bv)
38597    {
38598        const a_file *a = av;
38599        const a_file *b = bv;
38600
38601        return strcmp(a->filename, b->filename);
38602    }
38603
38604    static int inode_compare(const void *av, const void *bv)
38605    {
38606        const a_file *a = *(a_file **)av;
38607        const a_file *b = *(a_file **)bv;
38608        long c;
38609
38610        c = a->finfo.st_ino - b->finfo.st_ino;
38611        if (c == 0) {
38612         return a->finfo.st_dev - b->finfo.st_dev;
38613        }
38614        return c;
38615    }
38616
38617    static void mmap_init(server_rec *s, pool *p)
38618    {
38619        a_server_config *sconf;
38620        array_header *inodes;
```

```
38621        a_file *elts;
38622        int nelts;
38623        int i;
38624
38625        /* sort the elements of the main_server, by
38626         * filename */
38627        sconf = ap_get_module_config(s->module_config,
38628             &mmap_static_module);
38629        elts = (a_file *)sconf->files->elts;
38630        nelts = sconf->files->nelts;
38631        qsort(elts, nelts, sizeof(a_file), file_compare);
38632
38633        /* build an index by inode as well, speeds up the
38634         * search in the handler */
38635        inodes = ap_make_array(p, nelts, sizeof(a_file *));
38636        sconf->inode_sorted = inodes;
38637        for (i = 0; i < nelts; ++i) {
38638         *(a_file **)ap_push_array(inodes) = &elts[i];
38639        }
38640        qsort(inodes->elts, nelts, sizeof(a_file *),
38641             inode_compare);
38642
38643        /* and make the virtualhosts share the same thing */
38644        for (s = s->next; s; s = s->next) {
38645         ap_set_module_config(s->module_config,
38646             &mmap_static_module, sconf);
38647        }
38648    }
38649
38650    /* If it's one of ours, fill in r->finfo now to avoid
38651     * extra stat()... this is a bit of a kludge, because we
38652     * really want to run after core_translate runs.
38653     */
38654
38655    static int mmap_static_xlat(request_rec *r)
38656    {
38657        a_server_config *sconf;
38658        a_file tmp;
38659        a_file *match;
38660        int res;
38661
38662        sconf = ap_get_module_config(r->server->
38663             module_config, &mmap_static_module);
38664
38665        /* we only operate when at least one mmapfile
38666         * directive was used */
38667        if (ap_is_empty_table(sconf->files))
38668         return DECLINED;
```

```
38669
38670        /* we require other modules to first set up a
38671         * filename */
38672        res = core_module.translate_handler(r);
38673        if (res == DECLINED || !r->filename) {
38674          return res;
38675        }
38676        tmp.filename = r->filename;
38677        match = (a_file *)bsearch(&tmp, sconf->files->elts,
38678               sconf->files->nelts,
38679          sizeof(a_file), file_compare);
38680        if (match == NULL) {
38681          return DECLINED;
38682        }
38683
38684        /* shortcircuit the get_path_info() stat() calls
38685         * and stuff */
38686        r->finfo = match->finfo;
38687        return OK;
38688   }
38689
38690
38691   static int mmap_static_handler(request_rec *r)
38692   {
38693        a_server_config *sconf;
38694        a_file tmp;
38695        a_file *ptmp;
38696        a_file **pmatch;
38697        a_file *match;
38698        int rangestatus, errstatus;
38699
38700        /* we don't handle anything but GET */
38701        if (r->method_number != M_GET) return DECLINED;
38702
38703        /* file doesn't exist, we won't be dealing with it */
38704        if (r->finfo.st_mode == 0) return DECLINED;
38705
38706        sconf = ap_get_module_config(r->server->
38707             module_config, &mmap_static_module);
38708        tmp.finfo.st_dev = r->finfo.st_dev;
38709        tmp.finfo.st_ino = r->finfo.st_ino;
38710        ptmp = &tmp;
38711        pmatch = (a_file **)bsearch(&ptmp, sconf->
38712             inode_sorted->elts,
38713          sconf->inode_sorted->nelts, sizeof(a_file *),
38714             inode_compare);
38715        if (pmatch == NULL) {
38716          return DECLINED;
38717        }
38718        match = *pmatch;
38719
38720        /* note that we would handle GET on this resource */
38721        r->allowed |= (1 << M_GET);
38722
38723        /* This handler has no use for a request body
38724         * (yet), but we still need to read and discard it
38725         * if the client sent one.
38726         */
38727        if ((errstatus = ap_discard_request_body(r)) != OK)
38728            return errstatus;
38729
38730        ap_update_mtime(r, match->finfo.st_mtime);
38731        ap_set_last_modified(r);
38732        ap_set_etag(r);
38733        if (((errstatus = ap_meets_conditions(r)) != OK)
38734         || (errstatus = ap_set_content_length (r,
38735            match->finfo.st_size))) {
38736            return errstatus;
38737        }
38738
38739        rangestatus = ap_set_byterange(r);
38740        ap_send_http_header(r);
38741
38742        if (!r->header_only) {
38743          if (!rangestatus) {
38744              ap_send_mmap (match->mm, r, 0,
38745                    match->finfo.st_size);
38746          }
38747          else {
38748              long offset, length;
38749              while (ap_each_byterange(r, &offset, &length)) {
38750              ap_send_mmap(match->mm, r, offset, length);
38751              }
38752          }
38753        }
38754        return OK;
38755   }
38756
38757
38758   static const handler_rec mmap_static_handlers[] =
38759   {
38760        { "*/*", mmap_static_handler },
38761        { NULL }
38762   };
38763
38764   module MODULE_VAR_EXPORT mmap_static_module =
```

```
38765   {
38766       STANDARD_MODULE_STUFF,
38767       mmap_init,                   /* initializer */
38768       NULL,                    /* dir config creater */
38769       NULL,
38770       /* dir merger -- default is to override */
38771       create_server_config,     /* server config */
38772       NULL,               /* merge server config */
38773       mmap_static_cmds,         /* command handlers */
38774       mmap_static_handlers,     /* handlers */
38775       mmap_static_xlat,         /* filename translation */
38776       NULL,               /* check_user_id */
38777       NULL,               /* check auth */
38778       NULL,               /* check access */
38779       NULL,               /* type_checker */
38780       NULL,               /* fixups */
38781       NULL,               /* logger */
38782       NULL,               /* header parser */
38783       NULL,               /* child_init */
38784       NULL,               /* child_exit */
38785       NULL                /* post read-request */
38786   };
```

<img> **mod_perl.c** p 529

```
38787   #define CORE_PRIVATE
38788   #include "mod_perl.h"
38789
38790   #ifdef WIN32
38791   void *mod_perl_mutex = &mod_perl_mutex;
38792   #else
38793   void *mod_perl_dummy_mutex = &mod_perl_dummy_mutex;
38794   #endif
38795
38796   static IV mp_request_rec;
38797   static int seqno = 0;
38798   static int perl_is_running = 0;
38799   int mod_perl_socketexitoption = 3;
38800   int mod_perl_weareaforkedchild = 0;
38801   static int callbacks_this_request = 0;
38802   static PerlInterpreter *perl = NULL;
38803   static AV *orig_inc = Nullav;
38804   static AV *cleanup_av = Nullav;
38805   #ifdef PERL_STACKED_HANDLERS
38806   static HV *stacked_handlers = Nullhv;
38807   #endif
38808
38809   #ifdef PERL_OBJECT
38810   CPerlObj *pPerl;
```

```
38811   #endif
38812
38813   static command_rec perl_cmds[] = {
38814   #ifdef PERL_SECTIONS
38815       { "<Perl>", perl_section, NULL, OR_ALL, RAW_ARGS,
38816           "Perl code" },
38817       { "</Perl>", perl_end_section, NULL, OR_ALL,
38818           NO_ARGS, "End Perl code" },
38819   #endif
38820       { "=pod", perl_pod_section, NULL, OR_ALL, RAW_ARGS,
38821           "Start of POD" },
38822       { "=back", perl_pod_section, NULL, OR_ALL, RAW_ARGS,
38823           "End of =over" },
38824       { "=cut", perl_pod_end_section, NULL, OR_ALL,
38825           NO_ARGS, "End of POD" },
38826       { "__END__", perl_config_END, NULL, OR_ALL,
38827           RAW_ARGS, "Stop reading config" },
38828       { "PerlFreshRestart", perl_cmd_fresh_restart,
38829           NULL,
38830           RSRC_CONF, FLAG, "Tell mod_perl to reload modules
38831               and flush Apache::Registry cache on restart" },
38832       { "PerlTaintCheck", perl_cmd_tainting,
38833           NULL,
38834           RSRC_CONF, FLAG, "Turn on -T switch" },
38835   #ifdef PERL_SAFE_STARTUP
38836       { "PerlOpmask", perl_cmd_opmask,
38837           NULL,
38838           RSRC_CONF, TAKE1, "Opmask File" },
38839   #endif
38840       { "PerlWarn", perl_cmd_warn,
38841           NULL,
38842           RSRC_CONF, FLAG, "Turn on -w switch" },
38843       { "PerlScript", perl_cmd_require,
38844           NULL,
38845           OR_ALL, ITERATE, "this directive is deprecated,
38846               use 'PerlRequire'" },
38847       { "PerlRequire", perl_cmd_require,
38848           NULL,
38849           OR_ALL, ITERATE, "A Perl script name, pulled in
38850               via require" },
38851       { "PerlModule", perl_cmd_module,
38852           NULL,
38853           OR_ALL, ITERATE, "List of Perl modules" },
38854       { "PerlSetVar", perl_cmd_var,
38855           NULL,
38856           OR_ALL, TAKE2, "Perl config var and value" },
38857       { "PerlSetEnv", perl_cmd_setenv,
38858           NULL,
```

```
38859          OR_ALL, TAKE2, "Perl %ENV key and value" },
38860        { "PerlPassEnv", perl_cmd_pass_env,
38861          NULL,
38862          RSRC_CONF, ITERATE, "pass environment variables
38863              to %ENV"},
38864        { "PerlSendHeader", perl_cmd_sendheader,
38865          NULL,
38866          OR_ALL, FLAG, "Tell mod_perl to parse and send
38867              HTTP headers" },
38868        { "PerlSetupEnv", perl_cmd_env,
38869          NULL,
38870          OR_ALL, FLAG, "Tell mod_perl to setup %ENV by
38871              default" },
38872        { "PerlHandler", perl_cmd_handler_handlers,
38873          NULL,
38874          OR_ALL, ITERATE, "the Perl handler routine name" },
38875   #ifdef PERL_TRANS
38876        { PERL_TRANS_CMD_ENTRY },
38877   #endif
38878   #ifdef PERL_AUTHEN
38879        { PERL_AUTHEN_CMD_ENTRY },
38880   #endif
38881   #ifdef PERL_AUTHZ
38882        { PERL_AUTHZ_CMD_ENTRY },
38883   #endif
38884   #ifdef PERL_ACCESS
38885        { PERL_ACCESS_CMD_ENTRY },
38886   #endif
38887   #ifdef PERL_TYPE
38888        { PERL_TYPE_CMD_ENTRY },
38889   #endif
38890   #ifdef PERL_FIXUP
38891        { PERL_FIXUP_CMD_ENTRY },
38892   #endif
38893   #ifdef PERL_LOG
38894        { PERL_LOG_CMD_ENTRY },
38895   #endif
38896   #ifdef PERL_CLEANUP
38897        { PERL_CLEANUP_CMD_ENTRY },
38898   #endif
38899   #ifdef PERL_INIT
38900        { PERL_INIT_CMD_ENTRY },
38901   #endif
38902   #ifdef PERL_HEADER_PARSER
38903        { PERL_HEADER_PARSER_CMD_ENTRY },
38904   #endif
38905   #ifdef PERL_CHILD_INIT
38906        { PERL_CHILD_INIT_CMD_ENTRY },
38907   #endif
38908   #ifdef PERL_CHILD_EXIT
38909        { PERL_CHILD_EXIT_CMD_ENTRY },
38910   #endif
38911   #ifdef PERL_POST_READ_REQUEST
38912        { PERL_POST_READ_REQUEST_CMD_ENTRY },
38913   #endif
38914   #ifdef PERL_DISPATCH
38915        { PERL_DISPATCH_CMD_ENTRY },
38916   #endif
38917   #ifdef PERL_RESTART
38918        { PERL_RESTART_CMD_ENTRY },
38919   #endif
38920        { NULL }
38921   };
38922
38923   static handler_rec perl_handlers [] = {
38924        { "perl-script", perl_handler },
38925        { DIR_MAGIC_TYPE, perl_handler },
38926        { NULL }
38927   };
38928
38929   module MODULE_VAR_EXPORT perl_module = {
38930        STANDARD_MODULE_STUFF,
38931        perl_module_init,                    /* initializer */
38932        perl_create_dir_config,
38933        /* create per-directory config structure */
38934        perl_merge_dir_config,
38935        /* merge per-directory config structures */
38936        perl_create_server_config,
38937        /* create per-server config structure */
38938        NULL,
38939        /* merge per-server config structures */
38940        perl_cmds,                /* command table */
38941        perl_handlers,            /* handlers */
38942        PERL_TRANS_HOOK,          /* translate_handler */
38943        PERL_AUTHEN_HOOK,         /* check_user_id */
38944        PERL_AUTHZ_HOOK,          /* check auth */
38945        PERL_ACCESS_HOOK,         /* check access */
38946        PERL_TYPE_HOOK,           /* type_checker */
38947        PERL_FIXUP_HOOK,          /* pre-run fixups */
38948        PERL_LOG_HOOK,         /* logger */
38949   #if MODULE_MAGIC_NUMBER >= 19970103
38950        PERL_HEADER_PARSER_HOOK,   /* header parser */
38951   #endif
38952   #if MODULE_MAGIC_NUMBER >= 19970719
38953        PERL_CHILD_INIT_HOOK,   /* child_init */
38954   #endif
```

```
38955   #if MODULE_MAGIC_NUMBER >= 19970728
38956       NULL,   /* child_exit */
38957       /* mod_perl uses register_cleanup() */
38958   #endif
38959   #if MODULE_MAGIC_NUMBER >= 19970825
38960       PERL_POST_READ_REQUEST_HOOK,
38961       /* post_read_request */
38962   #endif
38963   };
38964
38965   #if defined(STRONGHOLD) && !defined(APACHE_SSL)
38966   #define APACHE_SSL
38967   #endif
38968
38969   int PERL_RUNNING (void)
38970   {
38971       return (perl_is_running);
38972   }
38973
38974   static void seqno_check_max(request_rec *r, int seqno)
38975   {
38976       dPPDIR;
38977       char *max = NULL;
38978       array_header *vars = (array_header *)cld->vars;
38979
38980       /* XXX: what triggers such a condition ?*/
38981       if(vars && (vars->nelts > 100000)) {
38982        fprintf(stderr, "[warning]
38983            PerlSetVar->nelts = %d\n", vars->nelts);
38984       }
38985       else {
38986         if(cld->vars)
38987          max = (char *)table_get(cld->vars,
38988            "MaxModPerlRequestsPerChild");
38989       }
38990
38991   #if (MODULE_MAGIC_NUMBER >= 19970912) && !defined(WIN32)
38992       if(max && (seqno >= atoi(max))) {
38993        child_terminate(r);
38994        MP_TRACE_g(fprintf(stderr, "mod_perl: terminating
38995            child %d after serving %d requests\n",
38996            (int)getpid(), seqno));
38997       }
38998   #endif
38999       max = NULL;
39000   }
39001
39002   void perl_shutdown (server_rec *s, pool *p)
39003   {
39004       char *pdl = NULL;
39005
39006       if((pdl = getenv("PERL_DESTRUCT_LEVEL")))
39007        perl_destruct_level = atoi(pdl);
39008       else
39009        perl_destruct_level = PERL_DESTRUCT_LEVEL;
39010
39011       if(perl_destruct_level < 0) {
39012        MP_TRACE_g(fprintf(stderr,
39013                "skipping destruction of Perl
39014                    interpreter\n"));
39015         return;
39016       }
39017
39018       /* execute END blocks we suspended during
39019        * perl_startup() */
39020       perl_run_endav("perl_shutdown");
39021
39022       MP_TRACE_g(fprintf(stderr,
39023          "destructing and freeing Perl interpreter..."));
39024
39025       perl_util_cleanup();
39026
39027       mp_request_rec = 0;
39028
39029       av_undef(orig_inc);
39030       SvREFCNT_dec((SV*)orig_inc);
39031       orig_inc = Nullav;
39032
39033       av_undef(cleanup_av);
39034       SvREFCNT_dec((SV*)cleanup_av);
39035       cleanup_av = Nullav;
39036
39037   #ifdef PERL_STACKED_HANDLERS
39038       hv_undef(stacked_handlers);
39039       SvREFCNT_dec((SV*)stacked_handlers);
39040       stacked_handlers = Nullhv;
39041   #endif
39042
39043       perl_destruct(perl);
39044       perl_free(perl);
39045
39046   #ifdef USE_THREADS
39047       PERL_SYS_TERM();
39048   #endif
39049
39050       perl_is_running = 0;
```

```
39051        MP_TRACE_g(fprintf(stderr, "ok\n"));
39052    }
39053
39054    request_rec *mp_fake_request_rec(server_rec *s,
39055         pool *p, char *hook)
39056    {
39057        request_rec *r = (request_rec *)palloc(p,
39058            sizeof(request_rec));
39059        r->pool = p;
39060        r->server = s;
39061        r->per_dir_config = NULL;
39062        r->uri = hook;
39063        return r;
39064    }
39065
39066    #ifdef PERL_RESTART
39067    void perl_restart_handler(server_rec *s, pool *p)
39068    {
39069        char *hook = "PerlRestartHandler";
39070        dSTATUS;
39071        dPSRV(s);
39072        request_rec *r = mp_fake_request_rec(s, p, hook);
39073        PERL_CALLBACK(hook, cls->PerlRestartHandler);
39074    }
39075    #endif
39076
39077    void perl_restart(server_rec *s, pool *p)
39078    {
39079        /* restart as best we can */
39080        SV *rgy_cache = perl_get_sv("Apache::Registry",
39081            FALSE);
39082        HV *rgy_symtab = (HV*)gv_stashpv("Apache::ROOT",
39083            FALSE);
39084
39085        ENTER;
39086
39087        SAVESPTR(warnhook);
39088        warnhook = perl_eval_pv("sub {}", TRUE);
39089
39090        /* the file-stat cache */
39091        if(rgy_cache)
39092         sv_setsv(rgy_cache, &sv_undef);
39093
39094        /* the symbol table we compile registry scripts
39095         * into */
39096        if(rgy_symtab)
39097         hv_clear(rgy_symtab);
39098
39099        if(endav) {
39100         SvREFCNT_dec(endav);
39101         endav = Nullav;
39102        }
39103
39104    #ifdef STACKED_HANDLERS
39105        if(stacked_handlers)
39106         hv_clear(stacked_handlers);
39107    #endif
39108
39109        /* reload %INC */
39110        perl_reload_inc();
39111
39112        LEAVE;
39113
39114        /*mod_perl_notice(s, "mod_perl restarted"); */
39115        MP_TRACE_g(fprintf(stderr, "perl_restart: ok\n"));
39116    }
39117
39118    U32 mp_debug = 0;
39119
39120    static void mod_perl_set_cwd(void)
39121    {
39122        char *name = "Apache::Server::CWD";
39123        GV *gv = gv_fetchpv(name, GV_ADDMULTI, SVt_PV);
39124        char *pwd = getenv("PWD");
39125
39126        if(pwd)
39127         sv_setpv(GvSV(gv), pwd);
39128        else
39129         sv_setsv(GvSV(gv),
39130             perl_eval_pv("require Cwd; Cwd::getcwd()",
39131                 TRUE));
39132
39133        mod_perl_untaint(GvSV(gv));
39134    }
39135
39136    #ifdef PERL_TIE_SCRIPTNAME
39137    static I32 scriptname_val(IV ix, SV* sv)
39138    {
39139        dTHR;
39140        request_rec *r = perl_request_rec(NULL);
39141        if(r)
39142         sv_setpv(sv, r->filename);
39143        else if(strNE(SvPVX(GvSV(curcop->cop_filegv)), "-e"))
39144         sv_setsv(sv, GvSV(curcop->cop_filegv));
39145        else {
39146         SV *file = perl_eval_pv("(caller())[1]",TRUE);
```

```
39147        sv_setsv(sv, file);
39148        }
39149      MP_TRACE_g(fprintf(stderr, "FETCH $0 => %s\n",
39150            SvPV(sv,na)));
39151      return TRUE;
39152  }
39153
39154  static void mod_perl_tie_scriptname(void)
39155  {
39156      SV *sv = perl_get_sv("0",TRUE);
39157      struct ufuncs umg;
39158      umg.uf_val = scriptname_val;
39159      umg.uf_set = NULL;
39160      umg.uf_index = (IV)0;
39161      sv_unmagic(sv, 'U');
39162      sv_magic(sv, Nullsv, 'U', (char*) &umg, sizeof(umg));
39163  }
39164  #else
39165  #define mod_perl_tie_scriptname()
39166  #endif
39167
39168  #define saveINC \
39169      if(orig_inc) SvREFCNT_dec(orig_inc); \
39170      orig_inc = av_copy_array(GvAV(incgv))
39171
39172  #if MODULE_MAGIC_NUMBER >= MMN_130
39173  static void mp_dso_unload(void *data)
39174  {
39175      module *modp;
39176
39177      if(!PERL_DSO_UNLOAD)
39178       return;
39179
39180      if(strEQ(top_module->name, "mod_perl.c"))
39181       return;
39182
39183      for(modp = top_module; modp; modp = modp->next) {
39184       if(modp->dynamic_load_handle) {
39185          MP_TRACE_g(fprintf(stderr,
39186              "mod_perl: cancel dlclose for %s\n",
39187              modp->name));
39188          modp->dynamic_load_handle = NULL;
39189       }
39190      }
39191  }
39192  #endif
39193
39194  static void mp_server_notstarting(void *data)
39195  {
39196      saveINC;
39197      require_Apache(NULL);
39198      Apache__ServerStarting(FALSE);
39199  }
39200
39201  #define Apache__ServerStarting_on() \
39202      Apache__ServerStarting(PERL_RUNNING()); \
39203      if(!PERL_IS_DSO) \
39204          register_cleanup(p, NULL,
39205            mp_server_notstarting, mod_perl_noop)
39206
39207  #define MP_APACHE_VERSION 1.26
39208
39209  void mp_check_version(void)
39210  {
39211      I32 i;
39212      SV *namesv;
39213      SV *version;
39214
39215      require_Apache(NULL);
39216
39217      if(!(version = perl_get_sv("Apache::VERSION",
39218          FALSE)))
39219       croak("Apache.pm failed to load!");
39220       /*should never happen*/
39221      if(SvNV(version) >= MP_APACHE_VERSION)
39222       /*no worries*/
39223       return;
39224
39225      fprintf(stderr, "Apache.pm version %.02f or
39226            higher required!\n",
39227          MP_APACHE_VERSION);
39228      fprintf(stderr, "%s",
39229          form("%_ is only version %_\n",
39230                *hv_fetch(GvHV(incgv),
39231                  "Apache.pm", 9, FALSE),
39232                version));
39233      fprintf(stderr,
39234        "Perhaps you forgot to 'make install'
39235            or need to uninstall an old version?\n");
39236
39237      namesv = NEWSV(806, 0);
39238      for(i=0; i<=AvFILL(GvAV(incgv)); i++) {
39239       char *tryname;
39240       PerlIO *tryrsfp = 0;
39241       SV *dir = *av_fetch(GvAV(incgv), i, TRUE);
39242       sv_setpvf(namesv, "%_/Apache.pm", dir);
```

```
39243        tryname = SvPVX(namesv);
39244        if((tryrsfp = PerlIO_open(tryname, "r"))) {
39245            fprintf(stderr, "Found: %s\n", tryname);
39246            PerlIO_close(tryrsfp);
39247        }
39248    }
39249    SvREFCNT_dec(namesv);
39250    exit(1);
39251 }
39252
39253 #if !HAS_MMN_136
39254 static void set_sigpipe(void)
39255 {
39256    char *dargs[] = { NULL };
39257    perl_require_module("Apache::SIG", NULL);
39258    perl_call_argv("Apache::SIG::set", G_DISCARD, dargs);
39259 }
39260 #endif
39261
39262 void perl_module_init(server_rec *s, pool *p)
39263 {
39264 #if HAS_MMN_130
39265    ap_add_version_component(MOD_PERL_STRING_VERSION);
39266    if(PERL_RUNNING()) {
39267     if(perl_get_sv("Apache::Server::AddPerlVersion",
39268            FALSE)) {
39269        ap_add_version_component(form("Perl/%s",
39270            patchlevel));
39271     }
39272    }
39273 #endif
39274    perl_startup(s, p);
39275 }
39276
39277 void perl_startup (server_rec *s, pool *p)
39278 {
39279    char *argv[] = { NULL, NULL, NULL, NULL, NULL,
39280        NULL, NULL };
39281    char **list, *dstr;
39282    int status, i, argc=1;
39283    dPSRV(s);
39284    SV *pool_rv, *server_rv;
39285    GV *gv, *shgv;
39286
39287 #ifndef WIN32
39288    argv[0] = server_argv0;
39289 #endif
39290
39291 #ifdef PERL_TRACE
39292    if((dstr = getenv("MOD_PERL_TRACE"))) {
39293        if(strEQ(dstr, "all")) {
39294            mp_debug = 0xffffffff;
39295        }
39296        else if (isALPHA(dstr[0])) {
39297            static char debopts[] = "dshgc";
39298            char *d;
39299
39300            for (; *dstr && (d = strchr(debopts,*dstr));
39301                    dstr++)
39302            mp_debug |= 1 << (d - debopts);
39303        }
39304        else {
39305            mp_debug = atoi(dstr);
39306        }
39307        mp_debug |= 0x80000000;
39308    }
39309 #else
39310    dstr = NULL;
39311 #endif
39312
39313    if(PERL_RUNNING() && PERL_STARTUP_IS_DONE) {
39314     saveINC;
39315     mp_check_version();
39316 #if !HAS_MMN_136
39317     set_sigpipe();
39318 #endif
39319    }
39320
39321    if(perl_is_running == 0) {
39322     /* we'll boot Perl below */
39323    }
39324    else if(perl_is_running < PERL_DONE_STARTUP) {
39325     /* skip the -HUP at server-startup */
39326     perl_is_running++;
39327     Apache__ServerStarting_on();
39328     MP_TRACE_g(fprintf(stderr, "perl_startup: perl
39329         aleady running...ok\n"));
39330     return;
39331    }
39332    else {
39333     Apache__ServerReStarting(TRUE);
39334
39335 #ifdef PERL_RESTART
39336     perl_restart_handler(s, p);
39337 #endif
39338     if(cls->FreshRestart)
```

```
39339        perl_restart(s, p);
39340
39341      Apache__ServerReStarting(FALSE);
39342
39343      return;
39344    }
39345    perl_is_running++;
39346
39347    /* fake-up what the shell usually gives perl */
39348    if(cls->PerlTaintCheck)
39349      argv[argc++] = "-T";
39350
39351    if(cls->PerlWarn)
39352      argv[argc++] = "-w";
39353
39354 #ifdef WIN32
39355      argv[argc++] = "nul";
39356 #else
39357      argv[argc++] = "/dev/null";
39358 #endif
39359
39360    MP_TRACE_g(fprintf(stderr, "perl_parse args: "));
39361    for(i=1; i<argc; i++)
39362      MP_TRACE_g(fprintf(stderr, "'%s' ", argv[i]));
39363    MP_TRACE_g(fprintf(stderr, "..."));
39364
39365 #ifdef USE_THREADS
39366 # ifdef PERL_SYS_INIT
39367      PERL_SYS_INIT(&argc,&argv);
39368 # endif
39369 #endif
39370
39371    perl_init_i18nl10n(1);
39372
39373    MP_TRACE_g(fprintf(stderr, "allocating perl
39374        interpreter..."));
39375    if((perl = perl_alloc()) == NULL) {
39376      MP_TRACE_g(fprintf(stderr, "not ok\n"));
39377      perror("alloc");
39378      exit(1);
39379    }
39380    MP_TRACE_g(fprintf(stderr, "ok\n"));
39381
39382    MP_TRACE_g(fprintf(stderr, "constructing perl
39383        interpreter...ok\n"));
39384    perl_construct(perl);
39385
39386    status = perl_parse(perl, xs_init, argc, argv, NULL);
```

```
39387    if (status != OK) {
39388      MP_TRACE_g(fprintf(stderr,"not ok, status=%d\n",
39389          status));
39390      perror("parse");
39391      exit(1);
39392    }
39393    MP_TRACE_g(fprintf(stderr, "ok\n"));
39394
39395    perl_clear_env();
39396    mod_perl_pass_env(p, cls);
39397    mod_perl_set_cwd();
39398    mod_perl_tie_scriptname();
39399    MP_TRACE_g(fprintf(stderr, "running perl
39400        interpreter..."));
39401
39402    pool_rv = perl_get_sv("Apache::__POOL", TRUE);
39403    sv_setref_pv(pool_rv, Nullch, (void*)p);
39404    server_rv = perl_get_sv("Apache::__SERVER", TRUE);
39405    sv_setref_pv(server_rv, Nullch, (void*)s);
39406
39407    gv = GvSV_init("Apache::ERRSV_CAN_BE_HTTP");
39408 #ifdef ERRSV_CAN_BE_HTTP
39409      GvSV_setiv(gv, TRUE);
39410 #endif
39411
39412    perl_tainting_set(s, cls->PerlTaintCheck);
39413    (void)GvSV_init("Apache::__SendHeader");
39414    (void)GvSV_init("Apache::__CurrentCallback");
39415
39416    Apache__ServerReStarting(FALSE); /* just for -w */
39417    Apache__ServerStarting_on();
39418
39419 #ifdef PERL_STACKED_HANDLERS
39420    if(!stacked_handlers) {
39421      stacked_handlers = newHV();
39422      shgv = GvHV_init("Apache::PerlStackedHandlers");
39423      GvHV(shgv) = stacked_handlers;
39424    }
39425 #endif
39426 #ifdef MULTITHREAD
39427    mod_perl_mutex = create_mutex(NULL);
39428 #endif
39429
39430    if ((status = perl_run(perl)) != OK) {
39431      MP_TRACE_g(fprintf(stderr,"not ok, status=%d\n",
39432          status));
39433      perror("run");
39434      exit(1);
```

```
39435         }
39436         MP_TRACE_g(fprintf(stderr, "ok\n"));
39437
39438         {
39439          dTHR;
39440          TAINT_NOT; /* At this time all is safe */
39441         }
39442
39443 #ifdef APACHE_PERL5LIB
39444         perl_incpush(APACHE_PERL5LIB);
39445 #else
39446         av_push(GvAV(incgv),
39447             newSVpv(server_root_relative(p,""),0));
39448         av_push(GvAV(incgv),
39449             newSVpv(server_root_relative(p,"lib/perl"),0));
39450 #endif
39451
39452         /* *CORE::GLOBAL::exit = \&Apache::exit */
39453         if(gv_stashpv("CORE::GLOBAL", FALSE)) {
39454          GV *exitgp = gv_fetchpv("CORE::GLOBAL::exit",
39455              TRUE, SVt_PVCV);
39456          GvCV(exitgp) = perl_get_cv("Apache::exit", TRUE);
39457          GvIMPORTED_CV_on(exitgp);
39458         }
39459
39460         if(PERL_STARTUP_DONE_CHECK)      {
39461           char *psd = getenv("PERL_STARTUP_DONE");
39462           if (!psd) {
39463             MP_TRACE_g(fprintf(stderr,
39464                     "mod_perl: PerlModule,PerlRequire
39465                         postponed\n"));
39466             my_setenv("PERL_STARTUP_DONE", "1");
39467             saveINC;
39468             return;
39469           }
39470           else {
39471             MP_TRACE_g(fprintf(stderr,
39472                 "mod_perl: postponed
39473                     PerlModule,PerlRequire enabled\n"));
39474             my_setenv("PERL_STARTUP_DONE", "2");
39475           }
39476         }
39477
39478         ENTER_SAFE(s,p);
39479         MP_TRACE_g(mod_perl_dump_opmask());
39480
39481         list = (char **)cls->PerlRequire->elts;
39482         for(i = 0; i < cls->PerlRequire->nelts; i++) {
39483           if(perl_load_startup_script(s, p, list[i],
39484               TRUE) != OK) {
39485             fprintf(stderr, "Require of Perl
39486                     file '%s' failed, exiting...\n",
39487                 list[i]);
39488             exit(1);
39489           }
39490         }
39491
39492         list = (char **)cls->PerlModule->elts;
39493         for(i = 0; i < cls->PerlModule->nelts; i++) {
39494          if(perl_require_module(list[i], s) != OK) {
39495             fprintf(stderr, "Can't load Perl
39496                 module '%s', exiting...\n",
39497                 list[i]);
39498             exit(1);
39499          }
39500         }
39501
39502         LEAVE_SAFE;
39503
39504         MP_TRACE_g(fprintf(stderr,
39505             "mod_perl: %d END blocks encountered
39506                 during server startup\n",
39507             endav ? (int)AvFILL(endav)+1 : 0));
39508 #if MODULE_MAGIC_NUMBER < 19970728
39509     if(endav)
39510      MP_TRACE_g(fprintf(stderr, "mod_perl: cannot run
39511         END blocks encoutered at server startup
39512         without apache_1.3.0+\n"));
39513 #endif
39514
39515         saveINC;
39516 #if MODULE_MAGIC_NUMBER >= MMN_130
39517     if(perl_module.dynamic_load_handle)
39518      register_cleanup(p, NULL, mp_dso_unload, null_cleanup);
39519 #endif
39520 }
39521
39522 int mod_perl_sent_header(request_rec *r, int val)
39523 {
39524     dPPDIR;
39525
39526     if(val) MP_SENTHDR_on(cld);
39527     val = MP_SENTHDR(cld) ? 1 : 0;
39528     return MP_SENDHDR(cld) ? val : 1;
39529 }
39530
```

```
39531  #ifndef perl_init_ids
39532  #define perl_init_ids mod_perl_init_ids()
39533  #endif
39534
39535  int perl_handler(request_rec *r)
39536  {
39537      dSTATUS;
39538      dPPDIR;
39539      dPPREQ;
39540      dTHR;
39541      SV *nwvh = Nullsv;
39542
39543      (void)acquire_mutex(mod_perl_mutex);
39544
39545  #if 0
39546      /* force 'PerlSendHeader On' for sub-requests
39547       * e.g. Apache::Sandwich
39548       */
39549      if(r->main != NULL)
39550         MP_SENDHDR_on(cld);
39551  #endif
39552
39553      if(MP_SENDHDR(cld))
39554         MP_SENTHDR_off(cld);
39555
39556      (void)perl_request_rec(r);
39557
39558      MP_TRACE_g(fprintf(stderr, "perl_handler ENTER:
39559          SVs = %5d, OBJs = %5d\n",
39560              (int)sv_count, (int)sv_objcount));
39561      ENTER;
39562      SAVETMPS;
39563
39564      if((nwvh = ApachePerlRun_name_with_virtualhost())) {
39565       if(!r->server->is_virtual) {
39566          SAVESPTR(nwvh);
39567          sv_setiv(nwvh, 0);
39568       }
39569      }
39570
39571      if (siggv) {
39572       save_hptr(&GvHV(siggv));
39573      }
39574
39575      if (endav) {
39576       save_aptr(&endav);
39577       endav = Nullav;
39578      }
39579
39580      /* hookup STDIN & STDOUT to the client */
39581      perl_stdout2client(r);
39582      perl_stdin2client(r);
39583
39584      if(!cfg) {
39585         cfg = perl_create_request_config(r->pool,
39586             r->server);
39587         set_module_config(r->request_config,
39588             &perl_module, cfg);
39589      }
39590
39591      cfg->setup_env = 1;
39592      PERL_CALLBACK("PerlHandler", cld->PerlHandler);
39593      cfg->setup_env = 0;
39594
39595      FREETMPS;
39596      LEAVE;
39597      MP_TRACE_g(fprintf(stderr, "perl_handler LEAVE:
39598          SVs = %5d, OBJs = %5d\n",
39599              (int)sv_count, (int)sv_objcount));
39600
39601      (void)release_mutex(mod_perl_mutex);
39602      return status;
39603  }
39604
39605  #ifdef PERL_CHILD_INIT
39606
39607  typedef struct {
39608      server_rec *server;
39609      pool *pool;
39610  } server_hook_args;
39611
39612  static void perl_child_exit_cleanup(void *data)
39613  {
39614      server_hook_args *args = (server_hook_args *)data;
39615      PERL_CHILD_EXIT_HOOK(args->server, args->pool);
39616  }
39617
39618  void PERL_CHILD_INIT_HOOK(server_rec *s, pool *p)
39619  {
39620      char *hook = "PerlChildInitHandler";
39621      dSTATUS;
39622      dPSRV(s);
39623      request_rec *r = mp_fake_request_rec(s, p, hook);
39624      server_hook_args *args =
39625       (server_hook_args *)palloc(p,
39626           sizeof(server_hook_args));
```

```
39627
39628        args->server = s;
39629        args->pool = p;
39630        register_cleanup(p, args, perl_child_exit_cleanup,
39631            null_cleanup);
39632
39633        mod_perl_init_ids();
39634        PERL_CALLBACK(hook, cls->PerlChildInitHandler);
39635    }
39636    #endif
39637
39638    #ifdef PERL_CHILD_EXIT
39639    void PERL_CHILD_EXIT_HOOK(server_rec *s, pool *p)
39640    {
39641        char *hook = "PerlChildExitHandler";
39642        dSTATUS;
39643        dPSRV(s);
39644        request_rec *r = mp_fake_request_rec(s, p, hook);
39645
39646        PERL_CALLBACK(hook, cls->PerlChildExitHandler);
39647
39648        perl_shutdown(s,p);
39649    }
39650    #endif
39651
39652    #ifdef PERL_POST_READ_REQUEST
39653    int PERL_POST_READ_REQUEST_HOOK(request_rec *r)
39654    {
39655        dSTATUS;
39656        dPSRV(r->server);
39657    #if MODULE_MAGIC_NUMBER > 19980270
39658        if(r->parsed_uri.scheme && r->parsed_uri.hostname) {
39659         r->proxyreq = 1;
39660         r->uri = r->unparsed_uri;
39661        }
39662    #endif
39663    #ifdef PERL_INIT
39664        PERL_CALLBACK("PerlInitHandler",
39665            cls->PerlInitHandler);
39666    #endif
39667        PERL_CALLBACK("PerlPostReadRequestHandler",
39668            cls->PerlPostReadRequestHandler);
39669        return status;
39670    }
39671    #endif
39672
39673    #ifdef PERL_TRANS
39674    int PERL_TRANS_HOOK(request_rec *r)
39675    {
39676        dSTATUS;
39677        dPSRV(r->server);
39678        PERL_CALLBACK("PerlTransHandler",
39679            cls->PerlTransHandler);
39680        return status;
39681    }
39682    #endif
39683
39684    #ifdef PERL_HEADER_PARSER
39685    int PERL_HEADER_PARSER_HOOK(request_rec *r)
39686    {
39687        dSTATUS;
39688        dPPDIR;
39689    #ifdef PERL_INIT
39690        PERL_CALLBACK("PerlInitHandler",
39691                cld->PerlInitHandler);
39692    #endif
39693        PERL_CALLBACK("PerlHeaderParserHandler",
39694                cld->PerlHeaderParserHandler);
39695        return status;
39696    }
39697    #endif
39698
39699    #ifdef PERL_AUTHEN
39700    int PERL_AUTHEN_HOOK(request_rec *r)
39701    {
39702        dSTATUS;
39703        dPPDIR;
39704        PERL_CALLBACK("PerlAuthenHandler",
39705            cld->PerlAuthenHandler);
39706        return status;
39707    }
39708    #endif
39709
39710    #ifdef PERL_AUTHZ
39711    int PERL_AUTHZ_HOOK(request_rec *r)
39712    {
39713        dSTATUS;
39714        dPPDIR;
39715        PERL_CALLBACK("PerlAuthzHandler",
39716            cld->PerlAuthzHandler);
39717        return status;
39718    }
39719    #endif
39720
39721    #ifdef PERL_ACCESS
39722    int PERL_ACCESS_HOOK(request_rec *r)
```

```
39723  {
39724      dSTATUS;
39725      dPPDIR;
39726      PERL_CALLBACK("PerlAccessHandler",
39727          cld->PerlAccessHandler);
39728      return status;
39729  }
39730  #endif
39731
39732  #ifdef PERL_TYPE
39733  int PERL_TYPE_HOOK(request_rec *r)
39734  {
39735      dSTATUS;
39736      dPPDIR;
39737      PERL_CALLBACK("PerlTypeHandler",
39738          cld->PerlTypeHandler);
39739      return status;
39740  }
39741  #endif
39742
39743  #ifdef PERL_FIXUP
39744  int PERL_FIXUP_HOOK(request_rec *r)
39745  {
39746      dSTATUS;
39747      dPPDIR;
39748      PERL_CALLBACK("PerlFixupHandler",
39749          cld->PerlFixupHandler);
39750      return status;
39751  }
39752  #endif
39753
39754  #ifdef PERL_LOG
39755  int PERL_LOG_HOOK(request_rec *r)
39756  {
39757      dSTATUS;
39758      dPPDIR;
39759      PERL_CALLBACK("PerlLogHandler",
39760          cld->PerlLogHandler);
39761      return status;
39762  }
39763  #endif
39764
39765  #ifdef PERL_STACKED_HANDLERS
39766  #define CleanupHandler \
39767  ((cld->PerlCleanupHandler &&
39768      SvREFCNT(cld->PerlCleanupHandler)) ?
39769      cld->PerlCleanupHandler : Nullav)
39770  #else
```

```
39771  #define CleanupHandler cld->PerlCleanupHandler
39772  #endif
39773
39774  static void per_request_cleanup(request_rec *r)
39775  {
39776      dPPREQ;
39777
39778      if(!cfg) {
39779        return;
39780      }
39781      if(cfg->pnotes) {
39782        hv_clear(cfg->pnotes);
39783        SvREFCNT_dec(cfg->pnotes);
39784        cfg->pnotes = Nullhv;
39785      }
39786  }
39787
39788  void mod_perl_end_cleanup(void *data)
39789  {
39790      request_rec *r = (request_rec *)data;
39791      dSTATUS;
39792      dPPDIR;
39793
39794  #ifdef PERL_CLEANUP
39795      PERL_CALLBACK("PerlCleanupHandler", CleanupHandler);
39796  #endif
39797
39798      MP_TRACE_g(fprintf(stderr, "perl_end_cleanup..."));
39799      perl_run_rgy_endav(r->uri);
39800      per_request_cleanup(r);
39801
39802      /* clear %ENV */
39803      perl_clear_env();
39804
39805      /* reset @INC */
39806      av_undef(GvAV(incgv));
39807      SvREFCNT_dec(GvAV(incgv));
39808      GvAV(incgv) = Nullav;
39809      GvAV(incgv) = av_copy_array(orig_inc);
39810
39811      /* reset $/ */
39812      sv_setpvn(GvSV(gv_fetchpv("/", TRUE, SVt_PV)),
39813          "\n", 1);
39814
39815      {
39816        dTHR;
39817        /* %@ */
39818        hv_clear(ERRHV);
```

```
39819        }
39820
39821        callbacks_this_request = 0;
39822
39823 #ifdef PERL_STACKED_HANDLERS
39824        /* reset Apache->push_handlers, but don't clear
39825         * ExitHandler */
39826 #define CH_EXIT_KEY "PerlChildExitHandler", 20
39827        {
39828        SV *exith = Nullsv;
39829        if(hv_exists(stacked_handlers, CH_EXIT_KEY)) {
39830            exith = *hv_fetch(stacked_handlers,
39831                CH_EXIT_KEY, FALSE);
39832                /* inc the refcnt since hv_clear
39833                 * will dec it */
39834            ++SvREFCNT(exith);
39835        }
39836        hv_clear(stacked_handlers);
39837        if(exith)
39838            hv_store(stacked_handlers, CH_EXIT_KEY,
39839                exith, FALSE);
39840        }
39841
39842 #endif
39843
39844 #ifdef USE_SFIO
39845        PerlIO_flush(PerlIO_stdout());
39846 #endif
39847
39848        MP_TRACE_g(fprintf(stderr, "ok\n"));
39849        (void)release_mutex(mod_perl_mutex);
39850 }
39851
39852 void mod_perl_cleanup_handler(void *data)
39853 {
39854        request_rec *r = perl_request_rec(NULL);
39855        SV *cv;
39856        I32 i;
39857        dPPDIR;
39858
39859        (void)acquire_mutex(mod_perl_mutex);
39860        MP_TRACE_h(fprintf(stderr, "running registered
39861            cleanup handlers...\n"));
39862        for(i=0; i<=AvFILL(cleanup_av); i++) {
39863            cv = *av_fetch(cleanup_av, i, 0);
39864            MARK_WHERE("registered cleanup", cv);
39865            perl_call_handler(cv, (request_rec *)r, Nullav);
39866            UNMARK_WHERE;
39867        }
39868        av_clear(cleanup_av);
39869 #ifndef WIN32
39870        if(cld) MP_RCLEANUP_off(cld);
39871 #endif
39872        (void)release_mutex(mod_perl_mutex);
39873 }
39874
39875 #ifdef PERL_METHOD_HANDLERS
39876 int perl_handler_ismethod(HV *class, char *sub)
39877 {
39878        CV *cv;
39879        HV *stash;
39880        GV *gv;
39881        SV *sv;
39882        int is_method=0;
39883
39884        if(!sub) return 0;
39885        sv = newSVpv(sub,0);
39886        if(!(cv = sv_2cv(sv, &stash, &gv, FALSE))) {
39887            GV *gvp = gv_fetchmethod(class, sub);
39888            if (gvp) cv = GvCV(gvp);
39889        }
39890
39891        if (cv && SvPOK(cv))
39892            is_method = strnEQ(SvPVX(cv), "$$", 2);
39893        MP_TRACE_h(fprintf(stderr, "checking if `%s'
39894                is a method...%s\n",
39895            sub, (is_method ? "yes" : "no")));
39896        SvREFCNT_dec(sv);
39897        return is_method;
39898 }
39899 #endif
39900
39901 void mod_perl_noop(void *data) {}
39902
39903 void mod_perl_register_cleanup(request_rec *r, SV *sv)
39904 {
39905        dPPDIR;
39906
39907        if(!MP_RCLEANUP(cld)) {
39908            (void)perl_request_rec(r);
39909            register_cleanup(r->pool, (void*)r,
39910                mod_perl_cleanup_handler, mod_perl_noop);
39911            MP_RCLEANUP_on(cld);
39912            if(cleanup_av == Nullav) cleanup_av = newAV();
39913        }
39914        MP_TRACE_h(fprintf(stderr, "registering
```

```
39915            PerlCleanupHandler\n"));
39916
39917        ++SvREFCNT(sv); av_push(cleanup_av, sv);
39918    }
39919
39920    #ifdef PERL_STACKED_HANDLERS
39921
39922    int mod_perl_push_handlers(SV *self, char *hook,
39923        SV *sub, AV *handlers)
39924    {
39925        int do_store=0, len=strlen(hook);
39926        SV **svp;
39927
39928        if(self && SvTRUE(sub)) {
39929        if(handlers == Nullav) {
39930            svp = hv_fetch(stacked_handlers, hook, len, 0);
39931            MP_TRACE_h(fprintf(stderr, "fetching
39932                %s stack\n", hook));
39933            if(svp && SvTRUE(*svp) && SvROK(*svp)) {
39934             handlers = (AV*)SvRV(*svp);
39935            }
39936            else {
39937             MP_TRACE_h(fprintf(stderr, "%s handlers
39938                 stack undef, creating\n", hook));
39939             handlers = newAV();
39940             do_store = 1;
39941            }
39942        }
39943
39944        if(SvROK(sub) && (SvTYPE(SvRV(sub)) == SVt_PVCV)) {
39945            MP_TRACE_h(fprintf(stderr, "pushing CODE ref
39946                into '%s' handlers\n", hook));
39947        }
39948        else if(SvPOK(sub)) {
39949            if(do_store) {
39950            MP_TRACE_h(fprintf(stderr,
39951                "pushing `%s' into `%s' handlers\n",
39952                SvPV(sub,na), hook));
39953            }
39954            else {
39955            MP_TRACE_d(fprintf(stderr,
39956                "pushing `%s' into `%s' handlers\n",
39957                SvPV(sub,na), hook));
39958            }
39959        }
39960        else {
39961            warn("mod_perl_push_handlers: Not a subroutine
39962                name or CODE reference!");
39963        }
39964
39965        ++SvREFCNT(sub); av_push(handlers, sub);
39966
39967        if(do_store)
39968            hv_store(stacked_handlers, hook, len,
39969                (SV*)newRV_noinc((SV*)handlers), 0);
39970        return 1;
39971        }
39972        return 0;
39973    }
39974
39975    int perl_run_stacked_handlers(char *hook,
39976        request_rec *r, AV *handlers)
39977    {
39978        dSTATUS;
39979        I32 i, do_clear=FALSE;
39980        SV *sub, **svp;
39981        int hook_len = strlen(hook);
39982
39983        if(handlers == Nullav) {
39984        if(hv_exists(stacked_handlers, hook, hook_len)) {
39985            svp = hv_fetch(stacked_handlers, hook,
39986                hook_len, 0);
39987            if(svp && SvROK(*svp))
39988                handlers = (AV*)SvRV(*svp);
39989        }
39990        else {
39991            MP_TRACE_h(fprintf(stderr, "`%s'
39992                push_handlers() stack is empty\n", hook));
39993            return NO_HANDLERS;
39994        }
39995        do_clear = TRUE;
39996        MP_TRACE_h(fprintf(stderr,
39997            "running %d pushed (stacked) handlers
39998                for %s...\n",
39999                (int)AvFILL(handlers)+1, r->uri));
40000        }
40001        else {
40002    #ifdef PERL_STACKED_HANDLERS
40003        /* XXX: bizarre,
40004         I only see this with httpd.conf.pl and
40005            PerlAccessHandler */
40006        if(SvTYPE((SV*)handlers) != SVt_PVAV) {
40007    #if MODULE_MAGIC_NUMBER > 19970909
40008            aplog_error(APLOG_MARK,
40009                APLOG_NOERRNO|APLOG_DEBUG, r->server,
40010    #else
```

```
40011                fprintf(stderr,
40012  #endif
40013                    "[warning] %s stack is not an ARRAY!\n",
40014                        hook);
40015            sv_dump((SV*)handlers);
40016            return DECLINED;
40017        }
40018  #endif
40019      MP_TRACE_h(fprintf(stderr,
40020              "running %d server configured stacked
40021                  handlers for %s...\n",
40022                  (int)AvFILL(handlers)+1, r->uri));
40023      }
40024      for(i=0; i<=AvFILL(handlers); i++) {
40025      MP_TRACE_h(fprintf(stderr, "calling &{%s->[%d]}
40026          (%d total)\n",
40027                  hook, (int)i, (int)AvFILL(handlers)+1));
40028
40029      if(!(sub = *av_fetch(handlers, i, FALSE))) {
40030          MP_TRACE_h(fprintf(stderr,
40031                  "sub not defined!\n"));
40032      }
40033      else {
40034          if(!SvTRUE(sub)) {
40035          MP_TRACE_h(fprintf(stderr,
40036                  "sub undef!  skipping callback...\n"));
40037          continue;
40038          }
40039
40040          MARK_WHERE(hook, sub);
40041          status = perl_call_handler(sub, r, Nullav);
40042          UNMARK_WHERE;
40043          MP_TRACE_h(fprintf(stderr, "&{%s->[%d]}
40044                  returned status=%d\n",
40045                      hook, (int)i, status));
40046          if((status != OK) && (status != DECLINED)) {
40047          if(do_clear)
40048              av_clear(handlers);
40049          return status;
40050          }
40051      }
40052      }
40053      if(do_clear)
40054      av_clear(handlers);
40055      return status;
40056  }
40057
40058  #endif /* PERL_STACKED_HANDLERS */
40059
40060  /* things to do once per-request */
40061  void perl_per_request_init(request_rec *r)
40062  {
40063      dPPDIR;
40064      dPPREQ;
40065
40066      /* PerlSendHeader */
40067      if(MP_SENDHDR(cld)) {
40068      MP_SENTHDR_off(cld);
40069      table_set(r->subprocess_env,
40070          "PERL_SEND_HEADER", "On");
40071      }
40072      else
40073      MP_SENTHDR_on(cld);
40074
40075      /* SetEnv PERL5LIB */
40076      if(!MP_INCPUSH(cld)) {
40077      char *path = (char *)table_get(r->subprocess_env,
40078          "PERL5LIB");
40079      if(path) {
40080          perl_incpush(path);
40081          MP_INCPUSH_on(cld);
40082      }
40083      }
40084
40085      if(!cfg) {
40086      cfg = perl_create_request_config(r->pool,
40087          r->server);
40088      set_module_config(r->request_config,
40089          &perl_module, cfg);
40090      }
40091      else if (cfg->setup_env && MP_ENV(cld)) {
40092      perl_setup_env(r);
40093      }
40094
40095      /* PerlSetEnv */
40096      mod_perl_dir_env(cld);
40097
40098      if(callbacks_this_request++ > 0) return;
40099
40100      {
40101      dPSRV(r->server);
40102      mod_perl_pass_env(r->pool, cls);
40103      }
40104      mod_perl_tie_scriptname();
40105      /* will be released in mod_perl_end_cleanup */
40106      (void)acquire_mutex(mod_perl_mutex);
```

```
40107        register_cleanup(r->pool, (void*)r,
40108               mod_perl_end_cleanup, mod_perl_noop);
40109
40110   #ifdef WIN32
40111        sv_setpvf(perl_get_sv("Apache::CurrentThreadId",
40112               TRUE), "0x%lx",
40113                (unsigned long)GetCurrentThreadId());
40114   #endif
40115
40116        /* hookup stderr to error_log */
40117   #ifndef PERL_TRACE
40118        if(r->server->error_log)
40119          error_log2stderr(r->server);
40120   #endif
40121
40122        seqno++;
40123        MP_TRACE_g(fprintf(stderr, "mod_perl: inc seqno
40124               to %d for %s\n", seqno, r->uri));
40125        seqno_check_max(r, seqno);
40126
40127        /* set $$, $>, etc., if 1.3a1+, this really
40128         * happens during child_init */
40129        perl_init_ids;
40130   }
40131
40132   /* XXX this still needs work, getting there... */
40133   int perl_call_handler(SV *sv, request_rec *r, AV *args)
40134   {
40135        int count, status, is_method=0;
40136        dSP;
40137        perl_dir_config *cld = NULL;
40138        HV *stash = Nullhv;
40139        SV *class = newSVsv(sv), *dispsv = Nullsv;
40140        CV *cv = Nullcv;
40141        char *method = "handler";
40142        int defined_sub = 0, anon = 0;
40143        char *dispatcher = NULL;
40144
40145        if(r->per_dir_config)
40146          cld = get_module_config(r->per_dir_config,
40147               &perl_module);
40148
40149   #ifdef PERL_DISPATCH
40150        if(cld && (dispatcher = cld->PerlDispatchHandler)) {
40151          if(!(dispsv = (SV*)perl_get_cv(dispatcher,
40152               FALSE))) {
40153                if(strlen(dispatcher) > 0) { /* XXX */
40154                  fprintf(stderr,
40155                       "mod_perl: unable to fetch
40156                          PerlDispatchHandler '%s'\n",
40157                       dispatcher);
40158                }
40159                dispatcher = NULL;
40160          }
40161        }
40162   #endif
40163
40164        if(r->per_dir_config)
40165         perl_per_request_init(r);
40166
40167        if(!dispatcher && (SvTYPE(sv) == SVt_PV)) {
40168          char *imp = pstrdup(r->pool,
40169               (char *)SvPV(class,na));
40170
40171          if((anon = strnEQ(imp,"sub ",4))) {
40172               sv = perl_eval_pv(imp, FALSE);
40173               MP_TRACE_h(fprintf(stderr, "perl_call:
40174                    caching CV pointer to '__ANON__'\n"));
40175               defined_sub++;
40176               goto callback; /* XXX, I swear I've never
40177                               * used goto before! */
40178          }
40179
40180
40181   #ifdef PERL_METHOD_HANDLERS
40182        {
40183          char *end_class = NULL;
40184
40185          if ((end_class = strstr(imp, "->"))) {
40186               end_class[0] = '\0';
40187               if(class)
40188                    SvREFCNT_dec(class);
40189               class = newSVpv(imp, 0);
40190               end_class[0] = ':';
40191               end_class[1] = ':';
40192               method = &end_class[2];
40193               imp = method;
40194               ++is_method;
40195          }
40196        }
40197
40198        if(*SvPVX(class) == '$') {
40199          SV *obj = perl_eval_pv(SvPVX(class), TRUE);
40200          if(SvROK(obj) && sv_isobject(obj)) {
40201               MP_TRACE_h(fprintf(stderr, "handler object %s
40202                    isa %s\n",
```

```
40203                              SvPVX(class),
40204                              HvNAME(SvSTASH((SV*)SvRV(obj)))));
40205                  SvREFCNT_dec(class);
40206                  class = obj;
40207                  ++SvREFCNT(class); /* this will _dec later */
40208                  stash = SvSTASH((SV*)SvRV(class));
40209              }
40210          }
40211
40212          if(class && !stash) stash =
40213                  gv_stashpv(SvPV(class,na),FALSE);
40214
40215  #if 0
40216          MP_TRACE_h(fprintf(stderr, "perl_call:
40217                  class='%s'\n", SvPV(class,na)));
40218          MP_TRACE_h(fprintf(stderr, "perl_call:
40219              imp='%s'\n", imp));
40220          MP_TRACE_h(fprintf(stderr, "perl_call:
40221              method='%s'\n", method));
40222          MP_TRACE_h(fprintf(stderr, "perl_call:
40223              stash='%s'\n",
40224                  stash ? HvNAME(stash) : "unknown"));
40225  #endif
40226
40227  #else
40228          method = NULL; /* avoid warning */
40229  #endif
40230
40231
40232      /* if a Perl*Handler is not a defined function name,
40233       * default to the class implementor's handler()
40234       * function attempt to load the class module if
40235       * it is not already
40236       */
40237      if(!imp) imp = SvPV(sv,na);
40238      if(!stash) stash = gv_stashpv(imp,FALSE);
40239      if(!is_method)
40240          defined_sub = (cv = perl_get_cv(imp, FALSE)) ?
40241              TRUE : FALSE;
40242  #ifdef PERL_METHOD_HANDLERS
40243      if(!defined_sub && stash) {
40244          GV *gvp;
40245          MP_TRACE_h(fprintf(stderr,
40246              "perl_call: trying method lookup on `%s'
40247                  in class '%s'...",
40248              method, HvNAME(stash)));
40249          /* XXX Perl caches method lookups internally,
40250           * should we cache this lookup?
```

```
40251           */
40252          if((gvp = gv_fetchmethod(stash, method))) {
40253              cv = GvCV(gvp);
40254              MP_TRACE_h(fprintf(stderr, "found\n"));
40255              is_method = perl_handler_ismethod(stash,
40256                  method);
40257          }
40258          else {
40259              MP_TRACE_h(fprintf(stderr, "not found\n"));
40260          }
40261      }
40262  #endif
40263
40264      if(!stash && !defined_sub) {
40265          MP_TRACE_h(fprintf(stderr, "%s symbol table
40266              not found, loading...\n", imp));
40267          if(perl_require_module(imp, r->server) == OK)
40268              stash = gv_stashpv(imp,FALSE);
40269  #ifdef PERL_METHOD_HANDLERS
40270          if(stash) /* check again */
40271              is_method = perl_handler_ismethod(stash,
40272                  method);
40273  #endif
40274      }
40275
40276      if(!is_method && !defined_sub) {
40277          MP_TRACE_h(fprintf(stderr,
40278              "perl_call:
40279                  defaulting to %s::handler\n", imp));
40280          sv_catpv(sv, "::handler");
40281      }
40282
40283  #if 0 /* XXX: CV lookup cache disabled for now */
40284      if(!is_method && defined_sub) { /* cache it */
40285          MP_TRACE_h(fprintf(stderr,
40286              "perl_call: caching CV pointer
40287                  to '%s'\n",
40288              (anon ? "__ANON__" : SvPV(sv,na))));
40289          SvREFCNT_dec(sv);
40290          sv = (SV*)newRV((SV*)cv); /* let newRV inc
40291              the refcnt */
40292      }
40293  #endif
40294      }
40295      else {
40296          MP_TRACE_h(fprintf(stderr,
40297              "perl_call: handler is a %s\n",
40298              dispatcher ? "dispatcher" : "cached CV"));
```

```
40299        }
40300
40301  callback:
40302      ENTER;
40303      SAVETMPS;
40304      PUSHMARK(sp);
40305  #ifdef PERL_METHOD_HANDLERS
40306      if(is_method)
40307       XPUSHs(sv_2mortal(class));
40308      else
40309       SvREFCNT_dec(class);
40310  #else
40311       SvREFCNT_dec(class);
40312  #endif
40313
40314      XPUSHs((SV*)perl_bless_request_rec(r));
40315
40316      if(dispatcher) {
40317       MP_TRACE_h(fprintf(stderr,
40318           "mod_perl: handing off to
40319              PerlDispatchHandler '%s'\n",
40320              dispatcher));
40321       /*XPUSHs(sv_mortalcopy(sv));*/
40322       XPUSHs(sv);
40323       sv = dispsv;
40324      }
40325
40326      {
40327       I32 i, len = (args ? AvFILL(args) : 0);
40328
40329       if(args) {
40330          EXTEND(sp, len);
40331          for(i=0; i<=len; i++)
40332           PUSHs(sv_2mortal(*av_fetch(args, i, FALSE)));
40333       }
40334      }
40335      PUTBACK;
40336
40337      /* use G_EVAL so we can trap errors */
40338  #ifdef PERL_METHOD_HANDLERS
40339      if(is_method)
40340       count = perl_call_method(method, G_EVAL | G_SCALAR);
40341      else
40342  #endif
40343       count = perl_call_sv(sv, G_EVAL | G_SCALAR);
40344
40345      SPAGAIN;
40346
40347      if(perl_eval_ok(r->server) != OK) {
40348       MP_STORE_ERROR(r->uri, ERRSV);
40349       if(!perl_sv_is_http_code(ERRSV, &status))
40350          status = SERVER_ERROR;
40351      }
40352      else if(count != 1) {
40353       mod_perl_error(r->server,
40354              "perl_call did not return a status arg,
40355                 assuming OK");
40356       status = OK;
40357      }
40358      else {
40359       status = POPi;
40360
40361       if((status == 1) || (status == 200) ||
40362          (status > 600))
40363          status = OK;
40364
40365       if((status == SERVER_ERROR) && ERRSV_CAN_BE_HTTP) {
40366          SV *errsv = Nullsv;
40367          if(MP_EXISTS_ERROR(r->uri) && (errsv =
40368              MP_FETCH_ERROR(r->uri))) {
40369           (void)perl_sv_is_http_code(errsv, &status);
40370          }
40371       }
40372      }
40373
40374      PUTBACK;
40375      FREETMPS;
40376      LEAVE;
40377      MP_TRACE_g(fprintf(stderr, "perl_call_handler: SVs =
40378          %5d, OBJs = %5d\n",
40379          (int)sv_count, (int)sv_objcount));
40380
40381      if(SvMAGICAL(ERRSV))
40382       sv_unmagic(ERRSV, 'U');
40383       /* Apache::exit was called */
40384
40385      return status;
40386  }
40387
40388  request_rec *perl_request_rec(request_rec *r)
40389  {
40390      if(r != NULL) {
40391       mp_request_rec = (IV)r;
40392       return NULL;
40393      }
40394      else
```

```
40395        return (request_rec *)mp_request_rec;
40396    }
40397
40398    SV *perl_bless_request_rec(request_rec *r)
40399    {
40400        SV *sv = sv_newmortal();
40401        sv_setref_pv(sv, "Apache", (void*)r);
40402        MP_TRACE_g(fprintf(stderr,
40403            "blessing request_rec=(0x%lx)\n",
40404                (unsigned long)r));
40405        return sv;
40406    }
40407
40408    void perl_setup_env(request_rec *r)
40409    {
40410        int i;
40411        array_header *arr = perl_cgi_env_init(r);
40412        table_entry *elts = (table_entry *)arr->elts;
40413
40414        for (i = 0; i < arr->nelts; ++i) {
40415          if (!elts[i].key || !elts[i].val) continue;
40416          mp_setenv(elts[i].key, elts[i].val);
40417        }
40418        MP_TRACE_g(fprintf(stderr,
40419            "perl_setup_env...%d keys\n", i));
40420    }
40421
40422    int mod_perl_seqno(SV *self, int inc)
40423    {
40424        self = self; /*avoid warning*/
40425        if(inc) seqno += inc;
40426        return seqno;
40427    }
```

▶ mod_proxy.c
p 559

```
40428    #include "mod_proxy.h"
40429
40430    #define CORE_PRIVATE
40431
40432    #include "http_log.h"
40433    #include "http_vhost.h"
40434    #include "http_request.h"
40435
40436    /* Some WWW schemes and their default ports; this is
40437     * basically /etc/services */
40438    /* This will become global when the protocol
40439     * abstraction comes */
40440    static struct proxy_services defports[] =
```

```
40441    {
40442        {"http", DEFAULT_HTTP_PORT},
40443        {"ftp", DEFAULT_FTP_PORT},
40444        {"https", DEFAULT_HTTPS_PORT},
40445        {"gopher", DEFAULT_GOPHER_PORT},
40446        {"nntp", DEFAULT_NNTP_PORT},
40447        {"wais", DEFAULT_WAIS_PORT},
40448        {"snews", DEFAULT_SNEWS_PORT},
40449        {"prospero", DEFAULT_PROSPERO_PORT},
40450        {NULL, -1}                  /* unknown port */
40451    };
40452
40453    /*
40454     * A Web proxy module. Stages:
40455     *
40456     *   translate_name: set filename to proxy:<URL>
40457     *   type_checker:   set type to PROXY_MAGIC_TYPE if
40458     *                   filename begins proxy:
40459     *   fix_ups:        convert the URL stored in the
40460     *                   filename to the
40461     *                   canonical form.
40462     *   handler:        handle proxy requests
40463     */
40464
40465    /* ------------------------------------------------ */
40466    /* Translate the URL into a 'filename' */
40467
40468    static int alias_match(const char *uri, const char
40469        *alias_fakename)
40470    {
40471        const char *end_fakename = alias_fakename +
40472            strlen(alias_fakename);
40473        const char *aliasp = alias_fakename, *urip = uri;
40474
40475        while (aliasp < end_fakename) {
40476          if (*aliasp == '/') {
40477            /* any number of '/' in the alias matches any
40478             * number in the supplied URI, but there
40479             * must be at least one...
40480             */
40481            if (*urip != '/')
40482              return 0;
40483
40484            while (*aliasp == '/')
40485              ++aliasp;
40486            while (*urip == '/')
40487              ++urip;
40488          }
```

```
40489        else {
40490            /* Other characters are compared literally */
40491            if (*urip++ != *aliasp++)
40492                return 0;
40493        }
40494    }
40495
40496    /* Check last alias path component matched
40497     * all the way */
40498
40499    if (aliasp[-1] != '/' && *urip != '\0'
40500            && *urip != '/')
40501        return 0;
40502
40503    /* Return number of characters from URI which
40504     * matched (may be greater than length of alias,
40505     * since we may have matched
40506     * doubled slashes)
40507     */
40508
40509    return urip - uri;
40510 }
40511
40512 /* Detect if an absoluteURI should be proxied or not.
40513  * Note that we have to do this during this phase
40514  * because later phases are"short-circuiting"... i.e.
40515  * translate_names will end when the first module *
40516  * returns OK.  So for example, if the request is
40517  * something like:
40518  *
40519  * GET http://othervhost/cgi-bin/printenv HTTP/1.0
40520  *
40521  * mod_alias will notice the /cgi-bin part and
40522  * ScriptAlias it and short-circuit the proxy...
40523  * just because of the ordering in the
40524  * configuration file.
40525  */
40526 static int proxy_detect(request_rec *r)
40527 {
40528     void *sconf = r->server->module_config;
40529     proxy_server_conf *conf;
40530
40531     conf = (proxy_server_conf *)
40532         ap_get_module_config(sconf, &proxy_module);
40533
40534     if (conf->req && r->parsed_uri.scheme) {
40535      /* but it might be something vhosted */
40536        if (!(r->parsed_uri.hostname
```

```
40537            && !strcasecmp(r->parsed_uri.scheme,
40538              ap_http_method(r))
40539            && ap_matches_request_vhost(r,
40540              r->parsed_uri.hostname,
40541              r->parsed_uri.port_str ? r->
40542                parsed_uri.port : ap_default_port(r)))) {
40543        r->proxyreq = 1;
40544        r->uri = r->unparsed_uri;
40545        r->filename = ap_pstrcat(r->pool, "proxy:",
40546            r->uri, NULL);
40547        r->handler = "proxy-server";
40548      }
40549    }
40550    /* We need special treatment for CONNECT proxying:
40551     * it has no scheme part */
40552    else if (conf->req && r->method_number == M_CONNECT
40553            && r->parsed_uri.hostname
40554            && r->parsed_uri.port_str) {
40555        r->proxyreq = 1;
40556        r->uri = r->unparsed_uri;
40557        r->filename = ap_pstrcat(r->pool, "proxy:",
40558            r->uri, NULL);
40559        r->handler = "proxy-server";
40560    }
40561    return DECLINED;
40562 }
40563
40564 static int proxy_trans(request_rec *r)
40565 {
40566     void *sconf = r->server->module_config;
40567     proxy_server_conf *conf =
40568     (proxy_server_conf *) ap_get_module_config(sconf,
40569         &proxy_module);
40570     int i, len;
40571     struct proxy_alias *ent = (struct proxy_alias *)
40572         conf->aliases->elts;
40573
40574     if (r->proxyreq) {
40575      /* someone has already set up the proxy, it was
40576       * possibly ourselves in proxy_detect
40577       */
40578      return OK;
40579    }
40580
40581    /* XXX: since r->uri has been manipulated already
40582     * we're not really compliant with RFC1945 at
40583     * this point.  But this probably isn't an issue
40584     * because this is a hybrid proxy/origin server.
```

```
40585        */
40586
40587        for (i = 0; i < conf->aliases->nelts; i++) {
40588          len = alias_match(r->uri, ent[i].fake);
40589
40590          if (len > 0) {
40591              r->filename = ap_pstrcat(r->pool, "proxy:",
40592                  ent[i].real,
40593                                  r->uri + len, NULL);
40594              r->handler = "proxy-server";
40595              r->proxyreq = 1;
40596              return OK;
40597          }
40598        }
40599      return DECLINED;
40600  }
40601
40602  /* ------------------------------------------------ */
40603  /* Fixup the filename */
40604
40605  /*
40606   * Canonicalise the URL
40607   */
40608  static int proxy_fixup(request_rec *r)
40609  {
40610      char *url, *p;
40611
40612      if (!r->proxyreq || strncmp(r->filename, "proxy:",
40613          6) != 0)
40614        return DECLINED;
40615
40616      url = &r->filename[6];
40617
40618  /* canonicalise each specific scheme */
40619      if (strncasecmp(url, "http:", 5) == 0)
40620        return ap_proxy_http_canon(r, url + 5, "http",
40621            DEFAULT_HTTP_PORT);
40622      else if (strncasecmp(url, "ftp:", 4) == 0)
40623        return ap_proxy_ftp_canon(r, url + 4);
40624
40625      p = strchr(url, ':');
40626      if (p == NULL || p == url)
40627        return HTTP_BAD_REQUEST;
40628
40629      return OK;
40630      /* otherwise; we've done the best we can */
40631  }
40632
40633  static void proxy_init(server_rec *r, pool *p)
40634  {
40635      ap_proxy_garbage_init(r, p);
40636  }
40637
40638
40639
40640  /* Send a redirection if the request contains a hostname
40641       which is not */
40642  /* fully qualified, i.e. doesn't have a domain name
40643       appended. Some proxy */
40644  /* servers like Netscape's allow this and access hosts
40645       from the local */
40646  /* domain in this case. I think it is better to redirect
40647       to a FQDN, since */
40648  /* these will later be found in the bookmarks files. */
40649  /* The "ProxyDomain" directive determines what domain
40650       will be appended */
40651  static int proxy_needsdomain(request_rec *r, const
40652      char *url, const char *domain)
40653  {
40654      char *nuri;
40655      const char *ref;
40656
40657      /* We only want to worry about GETs */
40658      if (!r->proxyreq || r->method_number != M_GET ||
40659          !r->parsed_uri.hostname)
40660        return DECLINED;
40661
40662      /* If host does contain a dot already, or it
40663       * is "localhost", decline */
40664      if (strchr(r->parsed_uri.hostname, '.') != NULL
40665      || strcasecmp(r->parsed_uri.hostname,
40666          "localhost") == 0)
40667        return DECLINED;
40668      /* host name has a dot already */
40669
40670      ref = ap_table_get(r->headers_in, "Referer");
40671
40672      /* Reassemble the request, but insert the domain
40673           after the host name */
40674      /* Note that the domain name always starts with
40675           a dot */
40676      r->parsed_uri.hostname = ap_pstrcat(r->pool,
40677          r->parsed_uri.hostname,
40678                      domain, NULL);
40679      nuri = ap_unparse_uri_components(r->pool,
40680                  &r->parsed_uri,
```

```
40681                     UNP_REVEALPASSWORD);
40682
40683         ap_table_set(r->headers_out, "Location", nuri);
40684         ap_log_rerror(APLOG_MARK,
40685             APLOG_INFO|APLOG_NOERRNO, r,
40686             "Domain missing: %s sent to %s%s%s",
40687                 r->uri,
40688             ap_unparse_uri_components(r->pool,
40689                 &r->parsed_uri,
40690                 UNP_OMITUSERINFO),
40691             ref ? " from " : "", ref ? ref : "");
40692
40693         return HTTP_MOVED_PERMANENTLY;
40694     }
40695
40696     /* ------------------------------------------------- */
40697     /* Invoke handler */
40698
40699     static int proxy_handler(request_rec *r)
40700     {
40701         char *url, *scheme, *p;
40702         void *sconf = r->server->module_config;
40703         proxy_server_conf *conf =
40704         (proxy_server_conf *) ap_get_module_config(sconf,
40705             &proxy_module);
40706         array_header *proxies = conf->proxies;
40707         struct proxy_remote *ents = (struct proxy_remote *)
40708             proxies->elts;
40709         int i, rc;
40710         cache_req *cr;
40711         int direct_connect = 0;
40712         const char *maxfwd_str;
40713
40714         if (!r->proxyreq || strncmp(r->filename,
40715             "proxy:", 6) != 0)
40716         return DECLINED;
40717
40718         if (r->method_number == M_TRACE &&
40719         (maxfwd_str = ap_table_get(r->headers_in,
40720             "Max-Forwards")) != NULL) {
40721         int maxfwd = strtol(maxfwd_str, NULL, 10);
40722         if (maxfwd < 1) {
40723             int access_status;
40724             r->proxyreq = 0;
40725             if ((access_status = ap_send_http_trace(r)))
40726             ap_die(access_status, r);
40727             else
40728             ap_finalize_request_protocol(r);
```

```
40729         return OK;
40730     }
40731     ap_table_setn(r->headers_in, "Max-Forwards",
40732             ap_psprintf(r->pool, "%d", (maxfwd > 0)
40733                 ? maxfwd-1 : 0));
40734     }
40735
40736     if ((rc = ap_setup_client_block(r,
40737         REQUEST_CHUNKED_ERROR)))
40738     return rc;
40739
40740     url = r->filename + 6;
40741     p = strchr(url, ':');
40742     if (p == NULL)
40743     return HTTP_BAD_REQUEST;
40744
40745     rc = ap_proxy_cache_check(r, url, &conf->cache, &cr);
40746     if (rc != DECLINED)
40747     return rc;
40748
40749     /* If the host doesn't have a domain name,
40750      * add one and redirect. */
40751     if (conf->domain != NULL) {
40752     rc = proxy_needsdomain(r, url, conf->domain);
40753     if (ap_is_HTTP_REDIRECT(rc))
40754         return HTTP_MOVED_PERMANENTLY;
40755     }
40756
40757     *p = '\0';
40758     scheme = ap_pstrdup(r->pool, url);
40759     *p = ':';
40760
40761     /* Check URI's destination host against NoProxy
40762         hosts */
40763     /* Bypass ProxyRemote server lookup if configured
40764         as NoProxy */
40765     /* we only know how to handle communication to a
40766         proxy via http */
40767     /*if (strcasecmp(scheme, "http") == 0) */
40768     {
40769     int ii;
40770     struct dirconn_entry *list =
40771             (struct dirconn_entry *) conf->dirconn->elts;
40772
40773     for (direct_connect = ii = 0; ii <
40774         conf->dirconn->nelts && !direct_connect; ii++) {
40775         direct_connect = list[ii].matcher(&list[ii], r);
40776     }
```

```
40777   #if DEBUGGING
40778       ap_log_rerror(APLOG_MARK,
40779           APLOG_DEBUG|APLOG_NOERRNO, r,
40780               (direct_connect) ? "NoProxy for
40781                   %s" : "UseProxy for %s",
40782                   r->uri);
40783   #endif
40784       }
40785
40786   /* firstly, try a proxy, unless a NoProxy directive
40787       is active */
40788
40789       if (!direct_connect)
40790       for (i = 0; i < proxies->nelts; i++) {
40791           p = strchr(ents[i].scheme, ':');
40792           /* is it a partial URL? */
40793           if (strcmp(ents[i].scheme, "*") == 0 ||
40794           (p == NULL && strcasecmp(scheme,
40795               ents[i].scheme) == 0) ||
40796           (p != NULL &&
40797           strncasecmp(url, ents[i].scheme,
40798               strlen(ents[i].scheme)) == 0)) {
40799           /* CONNECT is a special method that bypasses
40800            * the normal proxy code.
40801   */
40802           if (r->method_number == M_CONNECT)
40803               rc = ap_proxy_connect_handler(r, cr, url,
40804                   ents[i].hostname,
40805                       ents[i].port);
40806   /* we only know how to handle communication to a
40807    * proxy via http */
40808           else if (strcasecmp(ents[i].protocol,
40809               "http") == 0)
40810               rc = ap_proxy_http_handler(r, cr, url,
40811                   ents[i].hostname,
40812                       ents[i].port);
40813           else
40814               rc = DECLINED;
40815
40816           /* an error or success */
40817           if (rc != DECLINED && rc != HTTP_BAD_GATEWAY)
40818               return rc;
40819           /* we failed to talk to the upstream proxy */
40820           }
40821       }
40822
40823   /* otherwise, try it direct */
40824   /* N.B. what if we're behind a firewall, where we must
40825    * use a proxy or give up??
40826    */
40827       /* handle the scheme */
40828       if (r->method_number == M_CONNECT)
40829           return ap_proxy_connect_handler(r, cr, url,
40830               NULL, 0);
40831       if (strcasecmp(scheme, "http") == 0)
40832           return ap_proxy_http_handler(r, cr, url, NULL, 0);
40833       if (strcasecmp(scheme, "ftp") == 0)
40834           return ap_proxy_ftp_handler(r, cr, url);
40835       else
40836           return HTTP_FORBIDDEN;
40837   }
40838
40839   /* ------------------------------------------------- */
40840   /* Setup configurable data */
40841
40842   static void *
40843       create_proxy_config(pool *p, server_rec *s)
40844   {
40845       proxy_server_conf *ps = ap_pcalloc(p,
40846           sizeof(proxy_server_conf));
40847
40848       ps->proxies = ap_make_array(p, 10,
40849           sizeof(struct proxy_remote));
40850       ps->aliases = ap_make_array(p, 10,
40851           sizeof(struct proxy_alias));
40852       ps->raliases = ap_make_array(p, 10,
40853           sizeof(struct proxy_alias));
40854       ps->noproxies = ap_make_array(p, 10,
40855           sizeof(struct noproxy_entry));
40856       ps->dirconn = ap_make_array(p, 10,
40857           sizeof(struct dirconn_entry));
40858       ps->nocaches = ap_make_array(p, 10,
40859           sizeof(struct nocache_entry));
40860       ps->allowed_connect_ports =
40861           ap_make_array(p, 10, sizeof(int));
40862       ps->domain = NULL;
40863       ps->viaopt = via_off;
40864        /* initially backward compatible with 1.3.1 */
40865       ps->req = 0;
40866
40867       ps->cache.root = NULL;
40868       ps->cache.space = DEFAULT_CACHE_SPACE;
40869       ps->cache.maxexpire = DEFAULT_CACHE_MAXEXPIRE;
40870       ps->cache.defaultexpire = DEFAULT_CACHE_EXPIRE;
40871       ps->cache.lmfactor = DEFAULT_CACHE_LMFACTOR;
40872       ps->cache.gcinterval = -1;
```

```
40873        /* at these levels, the cache can have 2^18
40874         * directories (256,000)  */
40875        ps->cache.dirlevels = 3;
40876        ps->cache.dirlength = 1;
40877        ps->cache.cache_completion =
40878                DEFAULT_CACHE_COMPLETION;
40879
40880        return ps;
40881   }
40882
40883   static const char *
40884        add_proxy(cmd_parms *cmd, void *dummy, char *f,
40885            char *r)
40886   {
40887        server_rec *s = cmd->server;
40888        proxy_server_conf *conf =
40889        (proxy_server_conf *)
40890            ap_get_module_config(s->module_config,
40891            &proxy_module);
40892        struct proxy_remote *new;
40893        char *p, *q;
40894        int port;
40895
40896        p = strchr(r, ':');
40897        if (p == NULL || p[1] != '/' ||
40898            p[2] != '/' || p[3] == '\0')
40899         return "ProxyRemote: Bad syntax for a remote
40900            proxy server";
40901        q = strchr(p + 3, ':');
40902        if (q != NULL) {
40903        if (sscanf(q + 1, "%u", &port) != 1 || port > 65535)
40904            return "ProxyRemote: Bad syntax for a remote
40905                proxy server (bad port number)";
40906        *q = '\0';
40907        }
40908        else
40909         port = -1;
40910        *p = '\0';
40911        if (strchr(f, ':') == NULL)
40912         ap_str_tolower(f);           /* lowercase scheme */
40913        ap_str_tolower(p + 3);        /* lowercase hostname */
40914
40915        if (port == -1) {
40916         int i;
40917         for (i = 0; defports[i].scheme != NULL; i++)
40918            if (strcasecmp(defports[i].scheme, r) == 0)
40919                break;
40920         port = defports[i].port;
40921        }
40922
40923        new = ap_push_array(conf->proxies);
40924        new->scheme = f;
40925        new->protocol = r;
40926        new->hostname = p + 3;
40927        new->port = port;
40928        return NULL;
40929   }
40930
40931   static const char *
40932        add_pass(cmd_parms *cmd, void *dummy, char *f,
40933            char *r)
40934   {
40935        server_rec *s = cmd->server;
40936        proxy_server_conf *conf =
40937        (proxy_server_conf *)
40938            ap_get_module_config(s->module_config,
40939            &proxy_module);
40940        struct proxy_alias *new;
40941
40942        new = ap_push_array(conf->aliases);
40943        new->fake = f;
40944        new->real = r;
40945        return NULL;
40946   }
40947
40948   static const char *
40949        add_pass_reverse(cmd_parms *cmd, void *dummy,
40950            char *f, char *r)
40951   {
40952        server_rec *s = cmd->server;
40953        proxy_server_conf *conf;
40954        struct proxy_alias *new;
40955
40956        conf = (proxy_server_conf *)ap_get_module_config(s->
40957            module_config,
40958                                    &proxy_module);
40959        new = ap_push_array(conf->raliases);
40960        new->fake = f;
40961        new->real = r;
40962        return NULL;
40963   }
40964
40965   static const char *
40966        set_proxy_exclude(cmd_parms *parms, void *dummy,
40967            char *arg)
40968   {
```

```
40969      server_rec *s = parms->server;
40970      proxy_server_conf *conf =
40971      ap_get_module_config(s->module_config,
40972          &proxy_module);
40973      struct noproxy_entry *new;
40974      struct noproxy_entry *list =
40975          (struct noproxy_entry *) conf->noproxies->elts;
40976      struct hostent hp;
40977      int found = 0;
40978      int i;
40979
40980      /* Don't duplicate entries */
40981      for (i = 0; i < conf->noproxies->nelts; i++) {
40982       if (strcasecmp(arg, list[i].name) == 0)
40983       /* ignore case for host names */
40984          found = 1;
40985      }
40986
40987      if (!found) {
40988       new = ap_push_array(conf->noproxies);
40989       new->name = arg;
40990       /* Don't do name lookups on things that aren't
40991        * dotted */
40992       if (strchr(arg, '.') != NULL &&
40993          ap_proxy_host2addr(new->name, &hp) == NULL)
40994          /*@@@FIXME: This copies only the first of
40995           * (possibly many) IP addrs */
40996          memcpy(&new->addr, hp.h_addr,
40997              sizeof(struct in_addr));
40998       else
40999          new->addr.s_addr = 0;
41000      }
41001      return NULL;
41002  }
41003
41004  /*
41005   * Set the ports CONNECT can use
41006   */
41007  static const char *
41008      set_allowed_ports(cmd_parms *parms, void *dummy,
41009          char *arg)
41010  {
41011      server_rec *s = parms->server;
41012      proxy_server_conf *conf =
41013        ap_get_module_config(s->module_config,
41014          &proxy_module);
41015      int *New;
41016
41017      if (!ap_isdigit(arg[0]))
41018        return "AllowCONNECT: port number must be numeric";
41019
41020      New = ap_push_array(conf->allowed_connect_ports);
41021      *New = atoi(arg);
41022      return NULL;
41023  }
41024
41025  /* Similar to set_proxy_exclude(), but defining
41026   * directly connected hosts, which should never be
41027   * accessed via the configured ProxyRemote servers
41028   */
41029  static const char *
41030      set_proxy_dirconn(cmd_parms *parms, void *dummy,
41031          char *arg)
41032  {
41033      server_rec *s = parms->server;
41034      proxy_server_conf *conf =
41035      ap_get_module_config(s->module_config,
41036          &proxy_module);
41037      struct dirconn_entry *New;
41038      struct dirconn_entry *list = (struct dirconn_entry *)
41039          conf->dirconn->elts;
41040      int found = 0;
41041      int i;
41042
41043      /* Don't duplicate entries */
41044      for (i = 0; i < conf->dirconn->nelts; i++) {
41045       if (strcasecmp(arg, list[i].name) == 0)
41046          found = 1;
41047      }
41048
41049      if (!found) {
41050       New = ap_push_array(conf->dirconn);
41051       New->name = arg;
41052       New->hostentry = NULL;
41053
41054       if (ap_proxy_is_ipaddr(New, parms->pool)) {
41055  #if DEBUGGING
41056          fprintf(stderr, "Parsed addr %s\n",
41057              inet_ntoa(New->addr));
41058          fprintf(stderr, "Parsed mask %s\n",
41059              inet_ntoa(New->mask));
41060  #endif
41061       }
41062       else if (ap_proxy_is_domainname(New, parms->pool)) {
41063          ap_str_tolower(New->name);
41064  #if DEBUGGING
```

```
41065            fprintf(stderr, "Parsed domain %s\n", New->name);
41066    #endif
41067            }
41068        else if (ap_proxy_is_hostname(New, parms->pool)) {
41069            ap_str_tolower(New->name);
41070    #if DEBUGGING
41071            fprintf(stderr, "Parsed host %s\n", New->name);
41072    #endif
41073            }
41074        else {
41075            ap_proxy_is_word(New, parms->pool);
41076    #if DEBUGGING
41077            fprintf(stderr, "Parsed word %s\n", New->name);
41078    #endif
41079            }
41080        }
41081        return NULL;
41082    }
41083
41084    static const char *
41085        set_proxy_domain(cmd_parms *parms, void *dummy,
41086    =        char *arg)
41087    {
41088        proxy_server_conf *psf =
41089        ap_get_module_config(parms->server->module_config,
41090            &proxy_module);
41091
41092        if (arg[0] != '.')
41093         return "ProxyDomain: domain name must start
41094            with a dot.";
41095
41096        psf->domain = arg;
41097        return NULL;
41098    }
41099
41100    static const char *
41101        set_proxy_req(cmd_parms *parms, void *dummy,
41102            int flag)
41103    {
41104        proxy_server_conf *psf =
41105        ap_get_module_config(parms->server->module_config,
41106            &proxy_module);
41107
41108        psf->req = flag;
41109        return NULL;
41110    }
41111
41112
41113    static const char *
41114        set_cache_size(cmd_parms *parms, char
41115            *struct_ptr, char *arg)
41116    {
41117        proxy_server_conf *psf =
41118        ap_get_module_config(parms->server->module_config,
41119            &proxy_module);
41120        int val;
41121
41122        if (sscanf(arg, "%d", &val) != 1)
41123         return "CacheSize value must be an integer
41124                (kBytes)";
41125        psf->cache.space = val;
41126        return NULL;
41127    }
41128
41129    static const char *
41130        set_cache_root(cmd_parms *parms, void *dummy,
41131            char *arg)
41132    {
41133        proxy_server_conf *psf =
41134        ap_get_module_config(parms->server->module_config,
41135            &proxy_module);
41136
41137        psf->cache.root = arg;
41138
41139        return NULL;
41140    }
41141
41142    static const char *
41143        set_cache_factor(cmd_parms *parms, void *dummy,
41144            char *arg)
41145    {
41146        proxy_server_conf *psf =
41147        ap_get_module_config(parms->server->module_config,
41148            &proxy_module);
41149        double val;
41150
41151        if (sscanf(arg, "%lg", &val) != 1)
41152         return "CacheLastModifiedFactor value must be
41153            a float";
41154        psf->cache.lmfactor = val;
41155
41156        return NULL;
41157    }
41158
41159    static const char *
41160        set_cache_maxex(cmd_parms *parms, void *dummy,
```

```
41161          char *arg)
41162    {
41163        proxy_server_conf *psf =
41164        ap_get_module_config(parms->server->module_config,
41165            &proxy_module);
41166        double val;
41167
41168        if (sscanf(arg, "%lg", &val) != 1)
41169         return "CacheMaxExpire value must be a float";
41170        psf->cache.maxexpire = (int) (val * (double)
41171            SEC_ONE_HR);
41172        return NULL;
41173    }
41174
41175    static const char *
41176        set_cache_defex(cmd_parms *parms, void *dummy,
41177            char *arg)
41178    {
41179        proxy_server_conf *psf =
41180        ap_get_module_config(parms->server->module_config,
41181            &proxy_module);
41182        double val;
41183
41184        if (sscanf(arg, "%lg", &val) != 1)
41185         return "CacheDefaultExpire value must be a float";
41186        psf->cache.defaultexpire = (int) (val * (double)
41187            SEC_ONE_HR);
41188        return NULL;
41189    }
41190
41191    static const char *
41192        set_cache_gcint(cmd_parms *parms, void *dummy,
41193            char *arg)
41194    {
41195        proxy_server_conf *psf =
41196        ap_get_module_config(parms->server->module_config,
41197            &proxy_module);
41198        double val;
41199
41200        if (sscanf(arg, "%lg", &val) != 1)
41201         return "CacheGcInterval value must be a float";
41202        psf->cache.gcinterval = (int) (val * (double)
41203            SEC_ONE_HR);
41204        return NULL;
41205    }
41206
41207    static const char *
41208        set_cache_dirlevels(cmd_parms *parms, char
41209            *struct_ptr, char *arg)
41210    {
41211        proxy_server_conf *psf =
41212        ap_get_module_config(parms->server->module_config,
41213            &proxy_module);
41214        int val;
41215
41216        val = atoi(arg);
41217        if (val < 1)
41218         return "CacheDirLevels value must be an integer
41219            greater than 0";
41220        if (val * psf->cache.dirlength > CACHEFILE_LEN)
41221         return "CacheDirLevels*CacheDirLength value must
41222            not be higher than 20";
41223        psf->cache.dirlevels = val;
41224        return NULL;
41225    }
41226
41227    static const char *
41228        set_cache_dirlength(cmd_parms *parms, char
41229            *struct_ptr, char *arg)
41230    {
41231        proxy_server_conf *psf =
41232        ap_get_module_config(parms->server->module_config,
41233            &proxy_module);
41234        int val;
41235
41236        val = atoi(arg);
41237        if (val < 1)
41238         return "CacheDirLength value must be an integer
41239            greater than 0";
41240        if (val * psf->cache.dirlevels > CACHEFILE_LEN)
41241         return "CacheDirLevels*CacheDirLength value must
41242            not be higher than 20";
41243        psf->cache.dirlength = val;
41244        return NULL;
41245    }
41246
41247    static const char *
41248        set_cache_exclude(cmd_parms *parms, void *dummy,
41249            char *arg)
41250    {
41251        server_rec *s = parms->server;
41252        proxy_server_conf *conf =
41253        ap_get_module_config(s->module_config,
41254            &proxy_module);
41255        struct nocache_entry *new;
41256        struct nocache_entry *list =
```

```
41257            (struct nocache_entry *) conf->nocaches->elts;
41258        struct hostent hp;
41259        int found = 0;
41260        int i;
41261
41262        /* Don't duplicate entries */
41263        for (i = 0; i < conf->nocaches->nelts; i++) {
41264         if (strcasecmp(arg, list[i].name) == 0)
41265         /* ignore case for host names */
41266            found = 1;
41267        }
41268
41269        if (!found) {
41270         new = ap_push_array(conf->nocaches);
41271         new->name = arg;
41272         /* Don't do name lookups on things that aren't
41273          * dotted */
41274         if (strchr(arg, '.') != NULL &&
41275             ap_proxy_host2addr(new->name, &hp) == NULL)
41276            /*@@@FIXME: This copies only the first of
41277             * (possibly many) IP addrs */
41278            memcpy(&new->addr, hp.h_addr,
41279                sizeof(struct in_addr));
41280         else
41281            new->addr.s_addr = 0;
41282        }
41283        return NULL;
41284    }
41285
41286    static const char *
41287        set_recv_buffer_size(cmd_parms *parms, void *dummy,
41288            char *arg)
41289    {
41290        proxy_server_conf *psf =
41291        ap_get_module_config(parms->server->module_config,
41292            &proxy_module);
41293        int s = atoi(arg);
41294        if (s < 512 && s != 0) {
41295         return "ProxyReceiveBufferSize must be >=
41296            512 bytes, or 0 for system default.";
41297        }
41298
41299        psf->recv_buffer_size = s;
41300        return NULL;
41301    }
41302
41303    static const char*
41304        set_cache_completion(cmd_parms *parms,
```

```
41305            void *dummy, char *arg)
41306    {
41307        proxy_server_conf *psf =
41308        ap_get_module_config(parms->server->module_config,
41309            &proxy_module);
41310        int s = atoi(arg);
41311        if (s > 100 || s < 0) {
41312         return "CacheForceCompletion must be <=
41313            100 percent, "
41314                "or 0 for system default.";
41315        }
41316
41317        if (s > 0)
41318         psf->cache.cache_completion = ((float)s / 100);
41319        return NULL;
41320    }
41321
41322    static const char*
41323        set_via_opt(cmd_parms *parms, void *dummy,
41324            char *arg)
41325    {
41326        proxy_server_conf *psf =
41327        ap_get_module_config(parms->server->module_config,
41328            &proxy_module);
41329
41330        if (strcasecmp(arg, "Off") == 0)
41331         psf->viaopt = via_off;
41332        else if (strcasecmp(arg, "On") == 0)
41333         psf->viaopt = via_on;
41334        else if (strcasecmp(arg, "Block") == 0)
41335         psf->viaopt = via_block;
41336        else if (strcasecmp(arg, "Full") == 0)
41337         psf->viaopt = via_full;
41338        else {
41339         return "ProxyVia must be one of: "
41340                "off | on | full | block";
41341        }
41342
41343        return NULL;
41344    }
41345
41346    static const handler_rec proxy_handlers[] =
41347    {
41348        {"proxy-server", proxy_handler},
41349        {NULL}
41350    };
41351
41352    static const command_rec proxy_cmds[] =
```

```
41353  {
41354      {"ProxyRequests", set_proxy_req, NULL, RSRC_CONF,
41355          FLAG,
41356       "on if the true proxy requests should be
41357          accepted"},
41358      {"ProxyRemote", add_proxy, NULL, RSRC_CONF,
41359          TAKE2,
41360       "a scheme, partial URL or '*' and a proxy server"},
41361      {"ProxyPass", add_pass, NULL, RSRC_CONF, TAKE2,
41362       "a virtual path and a URL"},
41363      {"ProxyPassReverse", add_pass_reverse, NULL,
41364          RSRC_CONF, TAKE2,
41365       "a virtual path and a URL for reverse proxy
41366          behaviour"},
41367      {"ProxyBlock", set_proxy_exclude, NULL, RSRC_CONF,
41368          ITERATE,
41369       "A list of names, hosts or domains to which the
41370          proxy will not connect"},
41371      {"ProxyReceiveBufferSize", set_recv_buffer_size,
41372          NULL, RSRC_CONF, TAKE1,
41373       "Receive buffer size for outgoing HTTP and FTP
41374          connections in bytes"},
41375      {"NoProxy", set_proxy_dirconn, NULL, RSRC_CONF,
41376          ITERATE,
41377       "A list of domains, hosts, or subnets to which
41378          the proxy will connect directly"},
41379      {"ProxyDomain", set_proxy_domain, NULL, RSRC_CONF,
41380          TAKE1,
41381       "The default intranet domain name (in absence of a
41382          domain in the URL)"},
41383      {"AllowCONNECT", set_allowed_ports, NULL,
41384          RSRC_CONF, ITERATE,
41385       "A list of ports which CONNECT may connect to"},
41386  {"CacheRoot", set_cache_root, NULL, RSRC_CONF, TAKE1,
41387   "The directory to store cache files"},
41388  {"CacheSize", set_cache_size, NULL, RSRC_CONF, TAKE1,
41389   "The maximum disk space used by the cache in Kb"},
41390      {"CacheMaxExpire", set_cache_maxex, NULL, RSRC_CONF,
41391          TAKE1,
41392       "The maximum time in hours to cache a document"},
41393      {"CacheDefaultExpire", set_cache_defex, NULL,
41394          RSRC_CONF, TAKE1,
41395       "The default time in hours to cache a document"},
41396      {"CacheLastModifiedFactor", set_cache_factor, NULL,
41397          RSRC_CONF, TAKE1,
41398       "The factor used to estimate Expires date from
41399          LastModified date"},
41400      {"CacheGcInterval", set_cache_gcint, NULL,
41401          RSRC_CONF, TAKE1,
41402       "The interval between garbage collections,
41403          in hours"},
41404      {"CacheDirLevels", set_cache_dirlevels, NULL,
41405          RSRC_CONF, TAKE1,
41406       "The number of levels of subdirectories in
41407          the cache"},
41408      {"CacheDirLength", set_cache_dirlength, NULL,
41409          RSRC_CONF, TAKE1,
41410       "The number of characters in subdirectory names"},
41411      {"NoCache", set_cache_exclude, NULL, RSRC_CONF,
41412          ITERATE,
41413       "A list of names, hosts or domains for which
41414          caching is *not* provided"},
41415      {"CacheForceCompletion", set_cache_completion,
41416          NULL, RSRC_CONF, TAKE1,
41417       "Force a http cache completion after this
41418          percentage is loaded"},
41419      {"ProxyVia", set_via_opt, NULL, RSRC_CONF, TAKE1,
41420       "Configure Via: proxy header header to one of:
41421          on | off | block | full"},
41422      {NULL}
41423  };
41424
41425  module MODULE_VAR_EXPORT proxy_module =
41426  {
41427      STANDARD_MODULE_STUFF,
41428      proxy_init,              /* initializer */
41429      NULL,
41430      /* create per-directory config structure */
41431      NULL,
41432      /* merge per-directory config structures */
41433      create_proxy_config,
41434      /* create per-server config structure */
41435      NULL,
41436      /* merge per-server config structures */
41437      proxy_cmds,              /* command table */
41438      proxy_handlers,          /* handlers */
41439      proxy_trans,             /* translate_handler */
41440      NULL,                    /* check_user_id */
41441      NULL,                    /* check auth */
41442      NULL,                    /* check access */
41443      NULL,                    /* type_checker */
41444      proxy_fixup,             /* pre-run fixups */
41445      NULL,                    /* logger */
41446      NULL,                    /* header parser */
41447      NULL,                    /* child_init */
41448      NULL,                    /* child_exit */
41449      proxy_detect             /* post read-request */
41450  };
```

Part II

Apache Server
Commentary

Chapter 1

Access Control Modules

This chapter describes six modules that are used to control access to files, directories, locations, and virtual hosts by various means. The first of these modules, **mod_access**, is used to restrict access by IP address, domain name, subnet mask, or environment variable. The other five modules deal with various forms of user authentication.

Both **mod_access** and **mod_auth** are included in the default Apache configuration. Although the Apache documentation states that **mod_auth_anon**, **mod_auth_db**, **mod_auth_dbm**, and **mod_digest** are not included by default, they are part of the Apache distribution that is included with Red Hat Linux 6.0. For other systems, you need to either compile the modules onto the server or (if you are using Apache 1.3 or later) add them as Dynamic Shared Objects (DSO) if you wish to use them.

Discussion Of mod_access

The **mod_access** module is compiled into the Apache server by default and provides access to the **Allow**, **Deny**, **Allow from env=**, **Deny from env=**, and **Order** directives. These directives are per-directory, and each can be placed in any container statement (such as Directory, Files, Location, or VirtualHost) and provide the access specified for the scope of that container unless overridden.

The **Allow** directive allows specified hosts access to the container, whereas **Deny** refuses specified hosts access to the container. Both of these directives have the same set of operands.

The keyword **all** can be used to allow or deny all hosts from accessing a container. A Fully Qualified Domain

Name (FQDN), partial domain name, full or partial IP address, or network/netmask pair may also be specified.

The following example allows access from all domains except computers in **somedomain.com**:

```
Order allow,deny
Allow from all
Deny from .somedomain.com
```

The **Allow from env=** and **Deny from env=** directives allow or deny access based on whether the given variable exists. The following example allows access to authenticated users only, because the **REMOTE_USER** variable is set for authenticated users:

```
Order deny,allow
Deny from all
Allow from env=REMOTE_USER
```

The **Order** directive is used to weight the **Allow** and **Deny** directives. To evaluate **Allow** directives ahead of **Deny** directives, the key phrase **allow,deny** is used. To evaluate **Deny** directives ahead of **Allow** directives, the key phrase **deny,allow** is used. To avoid dealing with the processing order, the key phrase **mutual-failure** is used to cause the order to be irrelevant.

Module Structure

When the module is invoked, the **check_dir_access** function (line 11733) is called. This function gets the per-directory configuration information (line 11679), then checks the **Order** directive to see if it is set to **allow,deny** (line 11683) or **deny,allow** (line 11690); otherwise, it assumes **mutual-failure** (line 11696). This function also checks for the **Satisfy** core directive if the access would have been forbidden (lines 11704 through 11706). If everything still points toward the request being forbidden, it prints a message to the error log (lines 11707 through 11710). The module structure is illustrated in Figure 1.1.

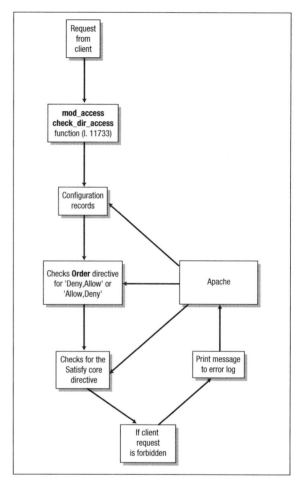

Figure 1.1   mod_access restricts access to approved hostnames or IP addresses.

Customization

The **mod_access** module controls access to resources based on host IP information. Modifications and enhancements should focus on optimization of this process or broadening the spectrum of what controls the access to the resources:

- Access can be restricted by the Ethernet address imprinted on the Ethernet card itself, enhancing security.

- Access information can be contained in a file and/or database, so that it can be changed (and looked up) dynamically without restarting the server.

mod_access

11371: The **allowdeny_type** is an enumerated data type used inside the **allowdeny** structure (line 11379) to ascertain the type of data used to describe access to the resource.

11372: The **T_ENV** identifier marks the **allowdeny_type** as being allowed or denied based on an environment variable.

11373: The **T_ALL** identifier marks the **allowdeny_type** as being allowed or denied for **all**.

11374: The **T_IP** identifier marks the **allowdeny_type** as being allowed or denied based on IP address, IP range, IP subnet, or a combination therein.

11375: The **T_HOST** identifier marks the **allowdeny_type** as being allowed or denied based on hostname.

11376: The **T_FAIL** identifier marks the **allowdeny_type** as having failed due to an error in the configuration files (such as invalid IP address or netmask).

11379: The **allowdeny** structure holds data describing the resource access configuration.

11391: The three lines of code following this one are definitions of how the **Order** directive is used in the configuration files.

11396: The **access_dir_conf** structure keeps track of all of the information (all of the **Allow**, **Deny**, and **Order** directives and the environment variants) in the configuration files for **mod_access**.

11402: This line defines the module so Apache can use it.

create_access_dir_config

11404: The **create_access_dir_config** function is the initialization handler for the module and is called to create the configuration data from the conf files for the module to use. The function returns an **access_dir_conf** object.

11407: The name *conf* is bound to an **access_dir_conf** structure.

11412: This **for** loop sets the order array in **conf**, the resident **access_dir_conf** structure, to the default of **DENY_THEN_ALLOW**.

11414: Sets the **allows** array.

11416: Sets the **denys** array.

11419: Returns the **conf** object of type **access_dir_conf**.

order

11422: This function is called from the standard **command_rec** for this module, **access_cmds** (line 11575). The **order** is handled on line 11577.

11425: This function also has a resident **access_dir_conf** structure, **dv**.

11428: The next few lines are where the last of this function's formal parameters is compared against several acceptable values for the **order** directive in the Apache conf files.

11435: If none of the values of the **order** directive is acceptable, "unknown order" is returned. If you extended the **order** directive, you would want to add your configuration options above this line.

is_ip

11444: The **is_ip** function is used to ascertain whether a character string is a valid IP address, subnet, or netmask.

allow_cmd

11451: The **allow_cmd** function is called from the standard **command_rec** for this module, **access_cmds** (line 11575). It is called at line 11580 to deal with **allow** directives and at line 11584 to deal with **deny** directives.

11458: Syntax is checked.

11466: If **allow/deny** is an environment variant, then the type is set to **T_ENV**.

11471: If **allow/deny** is set to **all**, then the type is set to **T_ALL**.

11475: If **allow/deny** looks like a network/netmask pair, then the type is set to **T_IP**.

11483: If it is not an IP address (calls **is_ip**), or if the IP address is in a bad format, then the type is reset to **T_FAIL**, and the user is warned of the misconfiguration.

11575: The local **command_rec** object, **access_cmds**, is created here.

11577: The **order** function is called to set the values from the **Order** directives in the config files.

11580: The **allow_cmd** function is called to set the values from the **Allow** directives in the config files.

11584: The **allow_cmd** function is called to set the values from the **Deny** directives in the **config** files.

in_domain

11590: The **in_domain** function checks to see if a given host is in a domain.

find_allowdeny

11616: The **find_allowdeny** function searches an array of **allowdeny** objects (line 11379). It is called from the **check_dir_access** function (line 11674), which is also the access handler for this module.

11629: This switch checks the **type** property of the **allowdeny** structure (line 11379).

check_dir_access

11674: The **check_dir_access** function is set as the access handler for this module at line 11733. The access handler is invoked during the Apache request process.

11677: An **access_dir_conf** object is created here.

11679: The **ap_get_module_config** function is an internal Apache function that gets the configuration data for a module.

11683: From here to line 11702, the value of the **Order** directive and the appropriate action regarding the call to **find_allowdeny** (line 11616) is determined depending on the setting of this directive.

11704: This **if** block handles the rejection (if necessary) of the client if they are not allowed access according to the rules established in this module and the **Satisfy** core directive.

11718: This is the standard export for the module, which is called **access_module**.

11722: The module initializer function is set to **create_access_dir_config** (line 11404).

11728: The **access_cmds** object (line 11575) is set here.

11733: The module handler, **check_dir_access** (line 11674), is set.

Discussion Of mod_auth

The **mod_auth** module is compiled into the Apache server by default and allows a server to authenticate users using standard text files (similar to the passwd file). This module's three directives for configuring text file-based authentication (**AuthGroupFile**, **AuthUserFile**, and **AuthAuthoritative**) are all per-directory directives that can be placed in any container block.

The **AuthGroupFile** and **AuthUserFile** directives are used to specify the location of the user file and the group file.

The syntax for the user file is identical to the /etc/passwd Unix password file (assuming that shadow passwords are not being used), except that this module only looks at the first two fields (username and password) as opposed to the numerous fields used in the Unix passwd file:

```
username:encryptedpassword
```

The syntax for the group file is different than the Unix equivalent, however:

```
group: username1 username2 username3
```

The **AuthAuthoritative** directive requires an **on** or **off** argument and is used to control authentication pass-through. Setting this to **on** (the default) prevents pass-through of authentication to lower-level modules.

Module Structure

When the module is invoked, the **authenticate_basic_user** function (line 12580) retrieves the user ID and ascertains its validity. The **check_user_access** function (line 12623) is called, and checks the **requires** directive settings. This module also determines the groups to which a user belongs (line 12521) and the user's password (line 12493). The module initializer is **create_auth_dir_config**. The structure is illustrated in Figure 1.2.

Customization

The **mod_auth** module is the standard for authentication module development. It controls access to resources based on username, password, and zone information. If you want to do anything other than optimize this process, it is recommended that you use this module as a template to create your own authentication module. For example, you might create the following:

- An authentication module that uses plain-text passwords instead of encrypted ones.

- An authentication module that uses your company's user database natively (Microsoft Access, FoxPro, perhaps a general ODBC or JDBC authentication).

- An authentication module that only uses passwords (ignores the username), depending on the resource being requested.

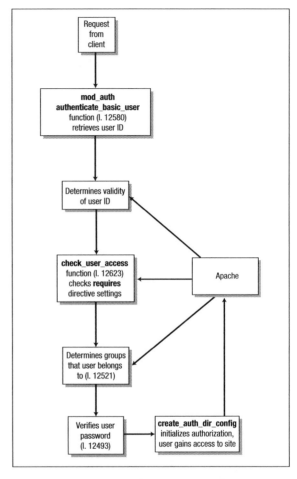

Figure 1.2 **mod_auth** provides for text-based access to Web content.

mod_auth

12437: This includes the ap_md4.h library to create the encrypted password entries. If you want to use a different encryption routine, remove and/or replace this.

12439: The **auth_config_struct** contains the name of the password file (line 12440), the group file (line 12441), and an integer flag indicating whether the module is authoritative or not (line 12442). This structure is called **auth_config_rec**.

create_auth_dir_config

12445: The **create_auth_dir_config** function is called during the module's initialization and creates (and returns) an **auth_config_rec** called **sec**. It is set as the module initializer at line 12716. The default password and group files are set to NULL, and the default authoritative flag is set to 1 (or **true**).

12470: The module's **command_rec**, named **auth_cmds**, is set here.

12491: The module's name is set and exported.

get_pw

12493: The **get_pw** function gets the encrypted password for the specified user from the specified password file.

groups_for_user

12521: The **groups_for_user** function is used to return a table of groups from the specified group file that the specified user belongs to.

authenticate_basic_user

12580: The **authenticate_basic_user** function handles the authentication of a user by calling **get_pw** (line 12493) and other functions. The return value is a constant mapped to an integer value that tells Apache how to deal with the user.

check_user_access

12623: The **check_user_access** function determines if a valid user (a user who was approved by the **authenticate_basic_user** function on line 12580) has valid access to the requested resource by calling the **groups_for_user** function (line 12521), among others. This function also handles the **AuthAuthoritative** directive and may decline to handle the authentication if it is set to false.

12712: The standard export of this module, **auth_module**, is defined.

12716: The function that initializes the authentication configuration, **create_auth_dir_config**, is called.

12722: The command table hook, **auth_cmds**, is called.

12725: The authentication handler, **authenticate_basic_user**, is invoked.

12726: The directory access handler, **check_user_access**, is called.

Discussion Of mod_auth_anon

The **mod_auth_anon** module is not compiled into the Apache server. It provides a means to allow anonymous users to access authentication-protected areas. It allows users to be tracked by email address, similar to an FTP site. This module has six directives that enable anonymous tracking and authentication. **Anonymous**, **Anonymous_Authoritative**, **Anonymous_LogEmail**, **Anonymous_MustGiveEmail**, **Anonymous_NoUserID**, and **Anonymous_VerifyEmail** are all per-directory directives that can be placed in any container block.

The **Anonymous** directive regards a list of allowable usernames as anonymous. These names (such as test, anonymous, and www) typically represent nonexistent users and are not from a user database.

Anonymous_Authoritative is the same as **mod_auth**'s **Auth_Authoritative** directive. It takes an **on** or **off** argument and is used to control authentication pass-through. Setting this to **on** prevents pass-through of authentication to lower-level modules. However, unlike the **Auth_Authoritative** directive, the default is set to **off** instead of **on**.

When **Anonymous_LogEmail** is set to **on** (the default), the email address is logged in the error log file.

If the **Anonymous_MustGiveEmail** directive is set to **on** (the default), Apache will not allow blank passwords.

The **Anonymous_NoUserID** directive is used to control whether the user must specify a username. If this is set to **on**, usernames are irrelevant and don't even need to be typed. The default is **off**.

If **Anonymous_VerifyEmail** is set to **on** in conjunction with **Anonymous_LogEmail** and **Anonymous_MustGiveEmail**, a check to ensure that there is at least one @ sign followed by at least one period is performed.

Module Structure

When the module is invoked, the **anon_authenticate_basic_user** function (line 12868) retrieves the user ID and password submitted and checks the validity based on the directives used. The **check_anon_access** function (line 12936) is called. This function checks that the resource being requested is controlled by this module and approves or declines the authentication based on that. The module initializer is called **create_anon_auth_dir_config** (line 12961). The module structure is shown in Figure 1.3.

Customization

Because the **mod_auth_anon** module is based on **mod_auth** (a module targeted at a very specific task), customization of this module is not recommended.

mod_auth_anon

12743: The **auth_anon** node type is defined.

12748: The **anon_auth_config_rec** is declared.

create_anon_auth_dir_config

12759: The **create_anon_auth_dir_config** function creates the configuration information for the module. Lines 12770 through 12776 set the defaults for the module directives.

anon_set_passwd_flag

12780: The **anon_set_passwd_flag** function sets the **auth_anon_mustemail** flag.

anon_set_userid_flag

12787: The **anon_set_userid_flag** function sets the **auth_anon_nouserid** flag.

anon_set_logemail_flag

12793: The **anon_set_logemail_flag** function sets the **auth_anon_logemail** flag.

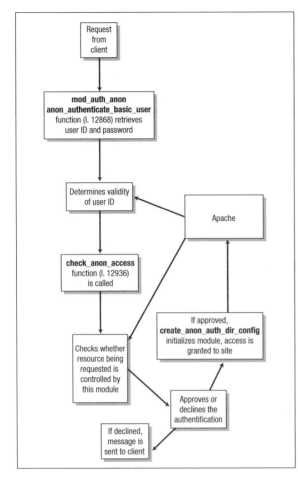

Figure 1.3 mod_auth_anon lets you set up a restricted area that users can access anonymously.

anon_set_verifyemail_flag

12799: The **anon_set_verifyemail_flag** function sets the **auth_anon_verifyemail** flag.

anon_set_authoritative_flag

12805: The **anon_set_authoritative_flag** function sets the **auth_anon_authoritative** flag.

12841: The module's **command_rec**, **anon_auth_cmds**, is defined.

12866: The module's name export, **anon_auth_module**, is defined.

anon_authenticate_basic_user

12868: The **anon_authenticate_basic_user** function is used to get and verify the username and password depending on the directives that are set.

check_anon_access

12936: The **check_anon_access** function is used to make sure that the resource requested really is protected by **mod_auth_anon**.

12957: The standard export of this module, **anon_auth_module**, is defined.

12961: The access directive configuration creator, **create_anon_auth_dir_config**, is called.

12966: The command table hook, **anon_auth_cmds**, is called.

12969: The module's authentication handler, **anon_authentication_basic_user**, is defined.

12971: The access control checker, **check_anon_access**, is called.

Discussion Of **mod_auth_db**

The **mod_auth_db** module is not compiled into Apache by default and provides a means of authenticating users via Berkeley DB database files. This module is similar to **mod_auth** in that its three directives (**AuthDBGroupFile**, **AuthDBUserFile**, and **AuthDBAuthoritative**) are used to specify the location of user and group databases, and whether the user wants the module to be authoritative. They are all per-directory and can be placed in any container block.

AuthDBGroupFile and **AuthDBUserFile** point to the group database and user database, respectively, although they can be the same database. Both of these database files consist primarily of a list of key/value pairs, and use the username as a key. If the group data-base is separate from the user database, the group file expects a list of groups the user is a member of, with the group names separated by commas. If the databases are in the same file, the value must be the encrypted password followed by a colon with the list of groups separated by commas after that.

The **AuthDBAuthoritative** directive requires an **on** or **off** argument and is used to control authentication pass-through. Setting this to **on** (the default) prevents pass-through of authentication to lower-level modules.

Module Structure

When this module is invoked, the **db_authenticate_basic_user** function (line 13128) handles the authentication of the user against a Berkeley DB database file. The **db_check_auth** function (line 13177) is then used to ascertain whether that user is allowed access to the requested resource, based on the configuration directives. The process is shown in Figure 1.4.

Customization

Customizing the **mod_auth_db** module is a good exercise in authentication using a formal database, as opposed to the standard password file-style authentication tables. Customization of this module should center on database-style username and password authentication:

- Write an authentication module that uses an encryption routine other than MD5 (the standard algorithm).

- Write an authentication module that uses your favorite or least favorite database to obtain the username, password, and group list.

mod_auth_db

12986: The header file, db.h, is included here. If Berkeley DB files are not being used, remove/replace this file.

12987: The header file, **ap_md5**, is included. If you do not want to use MD5 encryption, remove/replace this file.

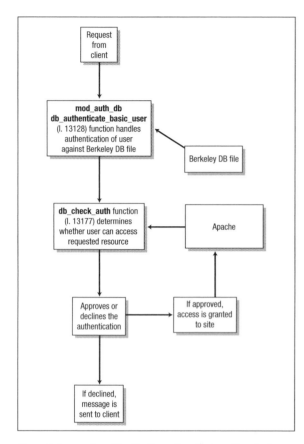

Figure 1.4 mod_auth_db allows Apache to authenticate users via Berkeley DB database files.

12993: The **db_auth_config_rec** is declared. This structure contains the name of the password and group database files, along with the module's authoritative flag.

create_db_auth_dir_config

13000: The **create_db_auth_dir_config** function is the configuration creation routine. It sets the defaults for the module.

13021: The local **command_rec**, **db_auth_cmds**, is defined.

get_db_pw

13049: The module's name is set here.

13051: The **get_db_pw** function grabs the specified user's password from the specified password database file.

get_db_grp

13109: The **get_db_grp** function is used to look up the specified user's groups in the specified group database file.

db_authenticate_basic_user

13128: The **db_authenticate_basic_user** function is the authentication handler for the module. It checks the validity of the username and password against the password database file.

db_check_auth

13177: The **db_check_auth** function ensures that the authenticated user is allowed access to the specified resource based on the configuration directives.

13245: The standard module table for this module, **db_auth_module**, is defined.

13249: **create_db_auth_dir_config** (line 13000) is set as the configuration creation function.

13255: The command table hook, **db_auth_cmds** (line 13021), is called.

13258: The authentication handler, **db_authenticate_basic_user** (line 13128), is invoked.

13259: The access control handler, **db_check_auth** (line 13177), is called.

Discussion Of mod_auth_dbm

The **mod_auth_dbm** module is not compiled into Apache by default. It provides a means of authenticating users via DBM-style database files. This module is very similar to **mod_auth** in that it provides three directives (**AuthDBMGroupFile**, **AuthDBMUserFile**, and **AuthDBMAuthoritative**) that are used to specify the location of user and group databases, and whether the module should be authoritative. They are all per-directory, and can be placed in any container block.

AuthDBMGroupFile and **AuthDBMUserFile** point to the group database and user database, respectively, although they can be the same database. Both files use the username as a key. If the group database is separate from the user database, the group database expects a list of groups the user is a member of, with the group names separated by commas. If the databases are in the same file, the value must be the encrypted password followed by a colon with the list of groups separated by commas after that.

The **AuthDBMAuthoritative** directive requires an **on** or **off** argument and is used to control authentication pass-through. Setting this to **on** (the default) prevents pass-through of authentication to lower-level modules.

Module Structure

When this module is invoked, the **dbm_authenticate_basic_user** function (line 13464) handles the authentication of the user against a DBM database file. The **dbm_check_auth** function (line 13513) is then used to ascertain whether that user is allowed access to the requested resource based on the configuration directives. The structure is illustrated in Figure 1.5.

Customization

Customizing the **mod_auth_dbm** module is extremely similar to customizing the **mod_auth_db** module, but is still a good exercise in authentication using a formal database as opposed to the standard password file-style authentication tables. Customization of this module should center on database-style username and password authentication:

- Write an authentication module that uses an encryption routine other than MD5 (the standard algorithm).

- Write an authentication module that uses your favorite or least favorite database to obtain the username, password, and group list.

mod_auth_dbm

13316: The **ndbm** header is included here and should be removed or replaced if the type of database with which the module works is being changed.

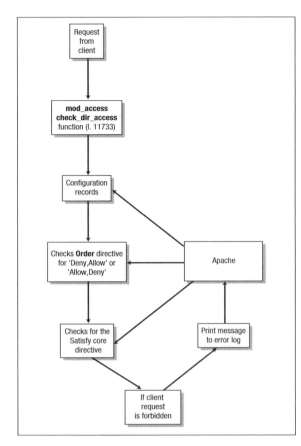

Figure 1.5 **mod_auth_dbm** provides for user authentication via DBM-style database files.

13317: The **ap_md5** header should be removed or replaced if you are not encrypting the passwords in an MD5 hash.

13333: The **dbm_auth_config_rec** structure contains the name of the password and group database files, along with the module's authoritative flag.

create_dbm_auth_dir_config

13341: The **create_dbm_auth_dir_config** function is the module's configuration creation routine. It sets the defaults and gets the module ready to do its job.

13365: The resident **command_rec**, **dbm_auth_cmds**, is defined.

get_dbm_pw

13392: The module is declared here.

13394: The **get_dbm_pw** function is used to retrieve the specified user's password from the specified password DBM file.

get_dbm_grp

13443: The **get_dbm_grp** function is used to retrieve the groups a specified user belongs to from the specified DBM group file.

dbm_authenticate_basic_user

13464: The **dbm_authenticate_basic_user** function is the module's authentication handler. It is used to get the username and password and check them against the DBM password file specified in the configuration file controlling the specified resource.

dbm_check_auth

13513: The **dbm_check_auth** function checks to make sure that the authenticated user has access to the requested resource.

13582: The standard module table for this module, **dbm_auth_module**, is called.

13586: The configuration creation function, **create_dbm_auth_dir_config** (line 13341), is called.

13592: The command table hook, **dbm_auth_cmds** (line 13365), is called.

13595: The authentication handler, **dbm_authenticate_basic_user** (line 13464), is invoked.

13596: The access control handler, **dbm_check_auth** (line 13513), is called.

Discussion Of mod_digest

The **mod_digest** module is not compiled into Apache by default. It allows Apache to support MD5 digest authentication. This form of authentication encrypts the username and password as they are sent to the Web server, to increase security. This module only uses a single directive, **AuthDigestFile**.

The per-directory directive **AuthDigestFile** requires the path to a specially formatted user file. These files are generally built with the Apache support program **htdigest**.

Module Structure

When the module is used, the **authenticate_digest_user** function (line 16388) is used to verify username and password. The **digest_check_auth** function (line 16427) is also used to verify that a user has the rights necessary to access the requested resource. The process is illustrated in Figure 1.6.

Customization

Because the **mod_digest** module requires the browser to communicate using MD5 encryption, customization of this module should focus on server-side technologies.

Make a module that allows the MD5 lookups to be performed from your favorite or not so favorite database instead of the standard Apache digest file.

mod_digest

16147: The **digest_config_rec** is declared. It contains the name of the password digest file.

16151: The **digest_header_rec** is declared. It contains the request header information passed to it from Apache.

create_digest_dir_config

16159: The **create_digest_dir_config** function is the module's configuration creation routine.

16175: The local **command_rec**, **digest_cmds**, is defined.

16183: The module name, **digest_module**, is exported.

get_hash

16185: The **get_hash** function returns the password hash from the specified password digest file for the specified username.

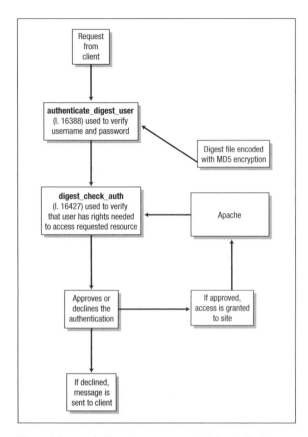

Figure 1.6 **mod_digest** uses an encoded digest file for user authentication.

get_digest_rec

16218: The **get_digest_rec** function uses the **digest_header_rec** (line 16151) to analyze the requested resource, username, and so on, and to perform the appropriate action.

find_digest

16358: The **find_digest** function returns the MD5 digest based on the **digest_header_rec** (line 16151), among other things.

authenticate_digest_user

16388: The **authenticate_digest_user** function is used to verify the user's validity based on the MD5 digest.

digest_check_auth

16427: The **digest_check_auth** function is used to ensure that the authenticated user has access to the specified resource.

16479: The **digest_module** table is defined.

16483: The **create_digest_dir_config** function (line 16159) is set to the module initializer.

16489: The resident command table hook, **digest_cmds**, is called.

16492: The **authenticate_digest_user** function (line 16388) is called.

16493: The **digest_check_auth** function (line 16427) is called.

Chapter 2

Alias And Redirection Modules

This chapter describes four complex and powerful modules that are used to control virtual locations of files, point users' browsers to the correct locations of files, and otherwise direct visitors to an Apache-served Web site from one location to another. Sometimes, the client is aware that his or her browser is being redirected. Often, the redirection can occur without the client being aware, giving the Webmaster a great deal of control over the appearance and organization of a site.

The first of these modules, **mod_alias**, is used to handle file system aliases and the redirection of browsers to other parts of the file system or to entirely different URLs. **mod_alias** is compiled into Apache by default.

To control server-side image maps, **mod_imap** is compiled into Apache by default. This allows clickable regions of a graphic to be defined, resulting in the browser jumping to different locations depending on what area of the image the user clicks. The existence of this module does not affect client-side image maps (image maps that are embedded into the Web page itself).

In the globalized Internet economy, it is often necessary for Webmasters to support multiple languages. **mod_negotiation** was implemented so that the Web server could redirect users' browsers based on the browser settings for language, character set, encoding, or other factors. By making use of this module, companies that present Web pages in multiple languages can ensure that their clients always see content that corresponds to their preferred language. **mod_negotiation** is compiled into Apache by default.

The fourth module is **mod_rewrite**. This module is extremely powerful, and allows a Webmaster to rewrite a browser's URL based on rules set forth by the Webmaster. **mod_rewrite** supports regular expressions (regexps), and can rewrite URLs based on regexp matching.

Discussion Of **mod_alias**

The **mod_alias** module is used to link various parts of the Web server's file space into logical paths in Web space and to redirect a client's browser to different URLs. This module also provides access to the **Alias**, **AliasMatch**, **ScriptAlias**, **ScriptAliasMatch**, **Redirect**, **RedirectMatch**, **RedirectTemp**, and **RedirectPermanent** directives. These directives can be placed in any container block.

The **Alias** and **AliasMatch** directives enable you to map a path from one location within the Web server space to another location anywhere on your computer's file system.

The **Alias** directive, when used in a configuration file, must be followed by the alias name and the physical path that leads to the new location where the client is to be sent. For instance, if you want the directory /usr/mydir to be accessible to Web browsers by the /stuff URI, use an **Alias** statement like the following:

```
Alias /stuff /usr/mydir/
```

The **AliasMatch** directive works in the same way as **Alias**, except that it expects a regular expression in place of the logical path. The previous example could also be written as follows:

```
AliasMatch ^/stuff(.*) /usr/mydir$1
```

The **ScriptAlias** and **ScriptAliasMatch** directives work in almost exactly the same way as **Alias** and **AliasMatch**. In addition to aliasing, however, these directives also flag the contents of the folders as being CGI scripts, causing Apache to attempt to execute the files. The syntax is also identical.

The **Redirect** directive allows the Web server to point clients at different URLs, depending on the URL they request. For example, if you have a file at the following URI:

```
/zippy/mypage.html
```

and you move the file to the following URI:

```
/stuff/zippy/index.html
```

you can then use the following to redirect clients to the new URL:

```
Redirect /zippy/mypage.html
http://www.server.com/stuff/zippy/index.html
```

You can also use the keywords **permanent**, **temp**, **seeother**, and **gone** after the identifier to specify the type of redirection, allowing Apache to send different redirection codes back to the browser. Most browsers treat all redirection codes the same, transparently producing the same results.

The **RedirectMatch** directive works in the same way as the previous directives, except that it supports pattern-matching regular expressions, allowing you to redirect en masse. For example, if you have been using the file scheme .htm for your HTML files, but decide to adopt the file scheme .html for them all, you may have clients who have .htm files bookmarked or links inside of Web pages that need to be updated. Using the following regular expression allows you to migrate with minimal loss from a client perspective:

```
RedirectMatch (.*)\.htm$ http://
yourserver.com$1.html
```

As with the **Redirect** directive, you can also use the keywords **permanent**, **temp**, **seeother**, and **gone** after the identifier to specify the type of redirection.

Using the **RedirectTemp** and **RedirectPermanent** directives is exactly the same as using the **Redirect** directive, with the **temp** or **permanent** keyword, respectively.

They have the same syntax as the **Redirect** directive without the keyword field.

Module Structure

When the module is invoked, the **create_alias_dir_config** function (line 11954) creates the default per-directory configuration. The **merge_alias_dir_config** function (line 11980) is then used to merge the conf file configuration with the default configuration. The **create_alias_config** function (line 11940) is invoked to create the per-server configuration, followed by the call to **merge_alias_config** (line 11964) that merges the conf file data with the default configuration. The command table for this module is called **alias_cmds** (defined on line 12112). File name translation is provided via the **translate_alias_redir** function (line 12255), and fixups are handled by the **fixup_redir** function (line 12289). The module structure is shown in Figure 2.1.

Customization

Because this module deals with aliases and redirects, there's not a lot of room for customization.

Declarations

11920: The **alias_entry** structure is defined. This structure has five properties that describe an invocation of one of the directives.

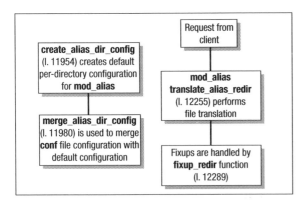

Figure 2.1   **mod_alias** is used to map a path from one location to another location in the file system.

11929: The **alias_server_conf** structure is defined. This structure keeps track of per-server aliases and redirects.

11934: The **alias_dir_conf** structure is defined. This structure keeps track of the per-directory redirects. Per-directory aliases aren't tracked because they don't make sense. (Aliases transparently map a request to a directory. Having an alias in a per-directory config file is useless; the request must have already gotten to the directory to perform aliasing. This is impossible.)

11938: The standard module naming export (**alias_module**) is declared.

create_alias_config

11940: The **create_alias_config** function is used to glean the per-server aliases and redirects from the conf files.

11947: The list of aliases is created.

11949: The list of redirects is created.

create_alias_dir_config

11954: The **create_alias_dir_config** function is used to glean the per-directory redirects from the conf files.

11959: The list of redirects is created.

merge_alias_config

11964: The **merge_alias_config** function is used to merge the per-server configuration information.

merge_alias_dir_config

11980: The **merge_alias_dir_config** function is used to merge the per-directory configuration information.

add_alias_internal

11993: The **add_alias_internal** function is used to add an **alias_entry** (line 11920). This function is only called by functions inside of this module (hence, the **_internal** designation).

12002: The new **alias_entry** is created.

12007: If there is a regular expression, it is compiled. The system returns if there is an error.

12015: The fake URI is set.

12016: The real URI is set.

12017: The handler for the new alias is changed.

add_alias

12022: The **add_alias** function is used to add an alias defined by the **Alias** and **ScriptAlias** directives.

12025: The call to **add_alias_internal** occurs.

add_alias_regex

12028: The **add_alias_regex** function is used to add an alias defined by the **AliasMatch** and **ScriptAliasMatch** directives.

12031: The call to **add_alias_internal** occurs.

add_redirect_internal

12034: The **add_redirect_internal** function is used to add an **alias_entry** (line 11920). This function is only called by functions inside of this module (hence, the **_internal** designation).

12040: The new **alias_entry** is declared.

12051: The **if-else** branch that starts on this line checks the status field to determine if it matches one of the keywords **gone**, **permanent**, **temp**, or **seeother**.

12066: If there is a regular expression, it is compiled. The system returns if there is an error.

12073: Error checking is performed.

12089: The fake URI is set.

12090: The real URI is set.

12091: The pattern-matching regular expressions (if any) are set.

12092: The redirect status is set.

add_redirect

12096: The **add_redirect** function is used to add a redirect defined by the **Redirect**, **RedirectTemp**, and **RedirectPermanent** directives.

12100: The call to **add_redirect_internal** occurs.

add_redirect_regex

12104: The **add_redirect_regex** function is used to add a redirect defined by the **RedirectMatch** directive.

12108: The call to **add_redirect_internal** occurs.

alias_cmds

12112: The module's **command_rec** (**alias_cmds**) is set.

alias_matches

12148: The **alias_matches** function is used to determine the number of characters that match a given alias. The number of matching characters is returned.

try_alias_list

12191: The **try_alias_list** function tries to match the requested resource to an alias or redirect.

translate_alias_redir

12255: The **translate_alias_redir** function is used to glue a lot of the rest of this module together. This function returns a status code to Apache or declines to handle the request, depending on the results of other functions.

fixup_redir

12289: The **fixup_redir** function is used after redirects are handled to perform routine fixups.

12311: The **alias_module** standard export is defined.

12315: The call to the per-directory configuration function (**create_alias_dir_config**) occurs.

12317: The call to the per-directory configuration merger (**merge_alias_dir_config**) occurs.

12319: The call to the per-server configuration function (**create_alias_config**) occurs.

12320: The call to the per-server configuration merger (**merge_alias_config**) occurs.

12321: The command table (**alias_cmds**) is hooked.

12323: The file name translation handler (**translate_alias_redir**) is invoked.

12329: The post-invocation fixup handler (**fixup_redir**) is invoked.

Discussion Of mod_imap

The **mod_imap** module is designed to handle server-side image maps. To accommodate this, the directives **ImapMenu**, **ImapDefault**, and **ImapBase** have been added.

The **ImapMenu** directive controls the feedback that users receive if they click on a part of the image map that isn't defined. The options are **none**, **formatted**, **semiformatted**, and **unformatted**:

```
ImapMenu formatted
```

The **ImapDefault** directive is used to set the default action for when a user clicks on part of the image map that isn't defined. The options are **error**, **map**, **referrer**, **nocontent**, or a URL:

```
ImapDefault nocontent
```

The **ImapBase** directive sets the default base URI for image-mapped URLs. The options are **map**, **referrer**, or a URL:

```
ImapBase http://yourhost.com
```

Module Structure

When the module is invoked, the **create_imap_dir_config** function (line 17490) is used to set the default configuration properties. The **merge_imap_dir_configs** function (line 17504) is then used to merge the conf file configuration with the default configuration. The command table for this module is **imap_cmds** (line 17524), and the module's handler is **imap_handlers** (line 18399). The structure is shown in Figure 2.2.

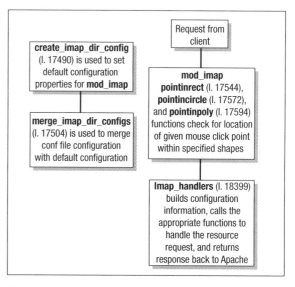

Figure 2.2   mod_imap enables Apache to process server-side image maps.

Customization

The **mod_imap** module deals with server-side image maps. Customization of this module should focus on enhancing and extending the range of options that image map designers have, such as the following:

- Add to the list of available shapes that can be used to define image map space.

- Provide the ability for multiple maps to be overlaid upon each other (map layers).

- Enhance error response when the user clicks on an undefined portion of the map.

IMAP_MAGIC_TYPE

17469: This MIME-type definition should be changed if the module is changed from the traditional imap format.

17482: The standard module export (**imap_module**) is declared.

17484: The **imap_conf_rec** structure is defined.

create_imap_dir_config

17490:   The **create_imap_dir_config** function is used to create the default configuration information.

merge_imap_dir_configs

17504:   The **merge_image_dir_configs** function is used to merge the configuration information.

imap_cmds

17524:   The module's **command_rec**, **imap_cmds**, is defined.

pointinrect

17544:   The **pointinrect** function returns 0 or 1, depending on whether the given point is within the specified rectangle.

pointincircle

17572:   The **pointincircle** function returns 0 or 1, depending on whether the given point is within the specified circle.

pointinpoly

17594:   The **pointinpoly** function returns 0 or 1, depending on whether the given point is within the specified polygon.

is_closer

17626:   The **is_closer** function returns 0 or 1, depending on whether the given point is closer to the given coordinate than the given closest point.

get_x_coord

17653:   The **get_x_coord** function gleans the x-coordinate from request arguments and returns it or –1 if an error occurs.

get_y_coord

17682:   The **get_y_coord** function gleans the y-coordinate from request arguments and returns it or –1 if an error occurs.

read_quoted

17729:   The **read_quoted** function pseudo-strips the quotes from a quoted string and places a NULL (\0) at the end to terminate it.

imap_url

17763:   This function discerns the URL based on the coordinates the user selected on the image map.

If the area selected is not defined, NULL is returned.

imap_reply

17934:   The **imap_reply** function returns HTTP codes, depending on the value of the **redirect** argument.

17936:   An error condition is returned, generating a 500 error.

17940:   The condition on this line will occur when a user clicks on an undefined part of the image map.

17944:   The condition on this line is what should always happen: a redirect relative to the coordinates the user clicked on.

menu_header

17953:   The **menu_header** function outputs the start of the menu.

menu_blank

17972:   The **menu_blank** function is dedicated to inserting various types of blank lines into the menu.

menu_comment

17986:   The **menu_comment** function inserts a comment into the menu.

menu_default

18003:   The **menu_default** function inserts links into the menu.

menu_directive

18028:   The **menu_directive** function is used to place directive information (link and description) into the menu.

menu_footer

18053:   This function cleans up the menu, finishing it in proper HTML style.

imap_handler

18060:   The **imap_handler** function takes the image map and the resource request, builds configuration information, calls the appropriate functions to handle the resource request, and returns the final response to Apache.

imap_handlers

18399:   The handler resource (**imap_handlers**) is defined.

imap_module

18406:   The standard export for this module (**imap_module**) is defined.

18410:   The **create_imap_dir_config** function is called.

18411:   The **merge_imap_dir_configs** function is invoked.

18415:   The command table hook for **imap_cmds** occurs.

18416:   The handler table hook for **imap_handlers** occurs.

Discussion Of **mod_negotiation**

The **mod_negotiation** module allows Web designers using Apache Web servers to provide different Web page content depending on the preferences of the client's browser. The most widely used form of content negotiation deals with multiple languages. Using this feature, content developers can develop pages in multiple languages and Apache will show the client the correct version depending on the language preferences of their browser. This module also provides the **Cache-NegotiatedDocs** and the **LanguagePriority** directives.

The **CacheNegotiatedDocs** directive controls whether a proxy server can cache (or keep a copy of) Web documents that have been displayed after content negotiation. This directive is only useful for down-level HTTP/1.0 requests, because HTTP/1.1 has enhanced content negotiation built in and will circumvent the cached version.

The **LanguagePriority** directive allows the Web site to choose the order of languages it prioritizes. For example, a Web site in Quebec, Canada may need to be sensitive to both English- and French-speaking patrons. They may prioritize French ahead of English, so that their settings reflect the following example:

```
LanguagePriority fr en
```

Alternatively, a Web site in Ontario, Canada that serves both an English- and a French-speaking audience may prioritize English ahead of French, as in the following example:

```
LanguagePriority en fr
```

mod_negotiation is powerful enough to enable Apache to handle these and many more types of client preferences.

Module Structure

When **mod_negotiation** is invoked, it calls **create_neg_dir_config** (line 26328), which creates the default configuration for this module. The **merge_neg_dir_configs** function (line 26338) is then invoked to merge the conf file configuration with the default configuration set. The command table for this module is **negotiation_cmds** (line 26381). The module handler is **negotiation_handlers** (line 29461), and the type-checker is **handle_multi** (line 29293). The structure is illustrated in Figure 2.3.

Customization

The **mod_negotiation** module is mammoth. Customization of this module is discouraged because the module is designed to follow content-negotiation standards. The module's code is very interesting from a pedagogical standpoint, however.

neg_dir_config
26322: The **neg_dir_config** structure is defined.

negotiation_module
26326: The standard module export for this module (**negotiation_module**) is declared.

create_neg_dir_config
26328: The **create_neg_dir_config** function sets up a default **neg_dir_config**.

merge_neg_dir_configs
26338: The **merge_neg_dir_configs** function merges the configuration options.

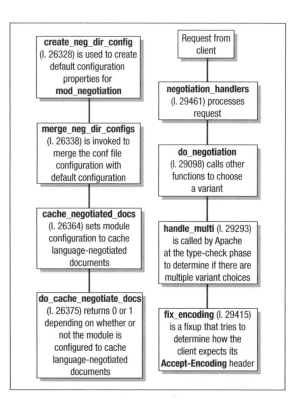

Figure 2.3 **mod_negotiation** enables Apache to present specified content to clients based on their preferences.

set_language_priority
26353: The **set_language_priority** function sets the language priority.

cache_negotiated_docs
26364: The **cache_negotiated_docs** function sets the module configuration to cache the language-negotiated documents.

do_cache_negotiated_docs
26375: The **do_cache_negotiate_docs** function returns 0 or 1, depending on whether the module is configured to cache language-negotiated documents.

negotiation_cmds
26381: The module's **command_rec** (**negotiation_cmds**) is defined.

accept_rec
26399: The **accept_rec** structure is defined. This structure contains information from the client's browser regarding the user's desired content.

var_rec
26428: The **var_rec** structure is defined. This structure contains information that the module and server need to handle the language-negotiated document properly.

negotiation_state
26484: The **negotiation_state** structure keeps track of various client and module information to make the negotiation process a little easier.

clean_var_rec
26526: The **clear_var_rec** function resets the **var_rec** to its default state.

set_mime_fields
26556: The **set_mime_fields** function is used to set some of **var_rec**'s fields with **accept_rec**'s field values.

get_entry
26604: The **get_entry** function grabs a MIME-type entry and sets an **accept_rec** based on the values. It returns an **accept_line** as well.

do_header_line
26732: The **do_header_line** function is designed to parse an **accept_line** and return an **array_header**.

do_languages_line
26758: The **do_languages_line** function takes a line from the **Content-Languages** header and returns an **array_header** containing a list of languages.

parse_accept_headers
26785: The **parse_accept_headers** function parses the headers of a resource request for accept lines and, along with calls to many of the module's functions, returns a **negotiation_state**.

parse_negotiate_headers

26831: The **parse_negotiate_headers** function looks at the negotiate headers of a resource request and does the right thing.

maybe_add_default_accepts

26941: Sets the default **accept_rec**, in case the browser did not.

header_state

26985: An enumerated data type called **header_state** is defined.

get_header_line

26989: The **get_header_line** function retrieves a line of a request header.

strip_paren_comments

27073: The **strip_paren_comments** function does just what it says: It strips comments out of header lines.

lcase_header_name_return_body

27105: The **lcase_header_name_return_body** function returns the body of a header from the given header.

read_type_map

27138: The **read_type_map** function reads a type map, parses it using most of the other module functions, and returns an HTTP code.

variantsortf

27244: The **variantsortf** function is a sorting algorithm used by **read_types_multi** (line 27270) to sort **var_rec**s.

read_types_multi

27270: The **read_types_multi** function reads a directory-filtered type map, parses it, and returns an HTTP code.

mime_match

27431: The **mime_match** function finds a MIME type to match the client resource request.

level_cmp

27500: The **level_cmp** function is used to choose between two variants of equal quality.

find_lang_index

27569: The **find_lang_index** function returns the index integer in the **accept_rec** array containing the language reference.

find_default_index

27596: The **find_default_index** function finds and returns the priority of the specified language.

set_default_lang_quality

27639: The **set_default_lang_quality** function sets the **default_lang_quality** property of a **negotiation_state** structure.

set_language_quality

27694: The **set_language_quality** function sets the **lang_quality** property of a **var_rec** structure.

find_content_length

27929: The **find_content_length** function is used to glean the length of the file to be sent to the client.

set_accept_quality

27955: The **set_accept_quality** function sets the **mime_type_quality** field of a **var_rec** structure.

set_charset_quality

28052: The **set_charset_quality** function is used to set the **charset_quality** property of a **var_rec** structure.

set_encoding_quality

28159: The **set_encoding_quality** function sets the **encoding_quality** property of a **var_rec** structure.

algorithm_results

28232: The **algorithm_results** enumerated data type is defined.

is_variant_better_rvsa

28266: The **is_variant_better_rvsa** function uses the Remote Variant Selection Algorithm to determine which variant is better.

is_variant_better

28341: The **is_variant_better** function is used to determine which variant is better.

best_match

28498: The **best_match** function is used to ascertain which variant is best suited to the request.

set_neg_headers

28613: The **set_neg_headers** function is used to set the response headers for negotiated documents.

make_variant_list

28860: The **make_variant_list** function is used to generate and return a list of variants in HTML format.

store_variant_list

28940: The **store_variant_list** function tracks the output of **make_variant_list** (line 28860).

setup_choice_response

28961: The **setup_choice_response** function is used to handle multiple language variants that the variant selection algorithm deems viable.

do_negotiation

29098: Although the **do_negotiation** function performs many tasks, the most important is to choose a variant. It calls on most of the other functions to accomplish this.

handle_map_file

29266: The **handle_map_file** function is used to read type maps by calling the **read_type_map** function (line 27138). If that fails, then it finds the best language variant by using **do_negotiation** (line 29098).

29274: The call to **read_type_map** (line 27138) occurs.

29278: The call to **do_negotiation** (line 29098) occurs.

handle_multi

29293: The **handle_multi** function is called by Apache at the type-check phase. It is used to ascertain if there are multiple variant choices and to determine the method of action to take.

fix_encoding

29415: The **fix_encoding** function is a fixup that determines how the client expects its **Accept-Encoding** header to appear and to prepare the header accordingly. Older clients tend to expect a prepended **x-** in front of all encoding methods.

negotiation_handlers

29461: The **negotiation_handlers** array is defined.

negotiation_module

29468: The standard module export (**negotiation_module**) is defined.

29472: The call to **create_neg_dir_config** (line 26328) occurs.

29473: **merge_neg_dir_configs** (line 26338) is invoked.

29477: The command table (**negotiation_cmds**) is hooked.

29478: The handler table (**negotiation_handlers**) hook occurs.

29483: The type checker (**handle_multi**) is called.

29484: The post-use fixup routine (**fix_encoding**) occurs.

Discussion Of mod_rewrite

As **mod_rewrite**'s author, Ralf S. Engelschall, so aptly puts it, this module is "the Swiss Army Knife of URL manipulation." It can map any URI pattern to virtually any other URI pattern using regular expressions and rule sets. This module provides the **RewriteEngine**, **RewriteOptions**, **RewriteLog**, **RewriteLogLevel**, **RewriteLock**, **RewriteMap**, **RewriteBase**, **RewriteCond**, and **RewriteRule** directives, each of which is described here:

- **RewriteEngine**—Turns the processing of URLs to be rewritten for a given configuration container on or off.

- **RewriteOptions**—Used to specify options for the rewrite engine. Currently, it appears that the only option is **inherit**, which means that child containers inherit the rewrite engine configuration and rules of the parent by default.

- **RewriteLog**—Used to specify the path to the file that will contain the log files that **mod_rewrite** produces.

- **RewriteLogLevel**—Used to control how much information **mod_rewrite** logs. Setting **RewriteLogLevel** to 0 disables logging, whereas 9 logs all messages.

- **RewriteLock**—Used to point to a file to be used as a lock file for **RewriteMap** program locking, if necessary.

- **RewriteMap**—Used to specify various mapping options such as **txt** for text file mapping, **rnd** for randomized text mapping, **dbm** for hash file lookups, **int** for internal mapping, or **prg** for an external program to do the mapping.

- **RewriteBase**—Used to set the base URL for per-directory rewriting.

- **RewriteCond**—Used to define a condition that must be met for subsequent **RewriteRules** to be executed.

- **RewriteRule**—Matches a regular expression pattern and applies the supplied substitution, if necessary.

Module Structure

The structure of **mod_rewrite** is very elegant and well planned. The module's author, Ralf S. Engelschall, did a phenomenal job and included volumes of code comments. When the module is invoked, **init_module** (line 30459) is called at the point of initialization. The **config_perdir_create** function (line 29761) is called next to create the default per-directory configuration, followed by **config_perdir_merge** (line 29792) to merge the conf file configuration with the default configuration. The creation of per-server configuration defaults is handled by **config_server_create** (line 29661), and the merge of the default configuration with the conf file configuration is handled by **config_server_merge** (line 29687). The command table for this module is named **command_table** (line 29558), and the handler table is called **handler_table** (line (29594). The interface for the translation of URIs to file names is provided by the **hook_uri2file** function (line 30515). The MIME-type determination routine is provided by **hook_mimetype**

(line 30843). Fixups are provided by **hook_fixup** (line 30872). Child process initialization is handled by **init_child** (line 30488). The structure is shown in Figure 2.4.

Customization

Customization of **mod_rewrite** is very much discouraged. This module is not only large and unwieldy, but is also the de facto standard in Apache URL rewriting.

command_table

29558: The module's **command_rec** (**command_table**) is defined.

handler_table

29594: The module's **handler_rec** (**handler_table**) is defined.

rewrite_module

29600: The module's standard export (**rewrite_module**) is defined.

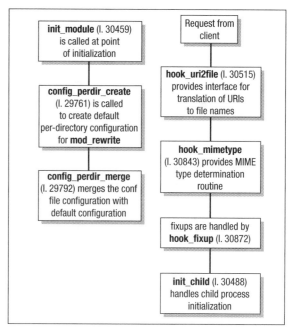

Figure 2.4   **mod_rewrite** redirects requests using a sophisticated set of URL rewriting rules.

29602: The module initializer (**init_module**) is called.

29604: The per-directory configuration function (**config_perdir_create**) is called.

29606: The per-directory configuration merger (**config_perdir_merge**) is called.

29608: The per-server configuration function (**config_server_create**) is called.

29610: The per-server configuration merger (**config_server_merger**) is called.

29612: The command table (**command_table**) is hooked.

29614: The handler table (**handler_table**) is hooked.

29616: The URI-to-file name translation function (**hook_uri2file**) is called.

29624: The MIME-type handling function (**hook_mimetype**) is called.

29626: The post-module fixup routine (**hook_fixup**) is called.

29632: The child initializer (**init_child**) is called.

config_server_create

29661: The **config_server_create** function is used to create the default per-server configuration settings.

config_server_merge

29687: The **config_server_merge** function is used to merge the default per-server configuration settings with the settings from the conf files.

config_perdir_create

29761: The **config_perdir_create** function is used to create the default per-directory configuration settings.

config_perdir_merge

29792: The **config_perdir_merge** function is used to merge the default per-directory configuration settings with the settings from the conf files.

cmd_rewriteengine

29830: The **cmd_rewriteengine** function handles the **RewriteEngine** directive in the conf files.

cmd_rewriteoptions

29853: The **cmd_rewriteoptions** function handles the **RewriteOptions** directive in the conf files.

cmd_rewriteoptions_setoption

29875: The **cmd_rewriteoptions_setoption** function handles the setting of options. It is called by **cmd_rewriteoptions** (line 18484).

cmd_rewritelog

29890: The **cmd_rewritelog** function handles the **RewriteLog** directive in the conf files.

cmd_rewriteloglevel

29905: The **cmd_rewriteloglevel** function handles the **RewriteLogLevel** directive in the conf files.

cmd_rewritemap

29919: The **cmd_rewritemap** function handles the **RewriteMap** directive in the conf files.

cmd_rewritelock

30005: The **cmd_rewritelock** function handles the **RewriteLock** directive in the conf files.

cmd_rewritebase

30019: The **cmd_rewritebase** function handles the **RewriteBase** directive in the conf files.

cmd_rewritecond

30039: The **cmd_rewritecond** function handles the **RewriteCond** directive in the conf files.

cmd_rewritecond_parseflagfield

30123: The **cmd_rewritecond_parseflagfield** function is used by the **cmd_rewritecond** function (line 30039) to analyze the flag field.

cmd_rewritecond_setflag

30179: The **cmd_rewritecond_setflag** function is used by the **cmd_rewritecond_parseflagfield** function (line 30123) to set flags.

cmd_rewriterule

30198: The **cmd_rewriterule** function handles the **RewriteRule** directive in the conf files.

cmd_rewriterule_parseflagfield

30292: The **cmd_rewriterule_parseflagfield** function is used by the **cmd_rewriterule** function (line 30198) to analyze the flag field.

cmd_rewriterule_setflag

30348: The **cmd_rewriterule_setflag** function is used by the **cmd_rewriterule_parseflagfield** function (line 30292) to set flags.

init_module

30459: The **init_module** function is used to prepare the module for use at load time. The function checks for dependencies, sets lock files, and opens **RewriteLog**s.

init_child

30488: The **init_child** function is used to prep a server child for possible rewriting. The function opens a lock file and creates the cache.

hook_uri2file

30515: The **hook_uri2file** function is used by the module to find a local file matching the requested URI, while conforming to the **RewriteRule**.

30536: The configuration information is imported.

30544: If **RewriteEngine** is off, the module declines to handle the transaction, falling through to the next module.

30625: From here, the **RewriteRule**s are applied.

hook_mimetype

30843: The **hook_mimetype** function is used to force a file to a certain MIME type.

hook_fixup

30872: The **hook_fixup** function is used when there are per-directory configuration invocations of **RewriteRule**.

handler_redirect

31187: The **handler_redirect** function is used to double-check the redirect request and perform it if everything checks out.

apply_rewrite_list

31216: The **apply_rewrite_list** function is used to apply multiple **RewriteRule**s.

apply_rewrite_rule

31363: The **apply_rewrite_rule** function is used to apply a **RewriteRule**.

apply_rewrite_cond

31857: The **apply_rewrite_cond** function applies a **RewriteCond**.

splitout_queryargs

32062: The **splitout_queryargs** function is used to extract the **QUERY_STRING** environment variable from the current URI.

reduce_uri

32105: The **reduce_uri** function is used to remove the protocol and host entries in the URI.

fully_qualify_uri

32191: The **fully_qualify_uri** function adds the protocol and host entry to a URI that hasn't been fully qualified.

expand_backref_inbuffer

32242: The **expand_backref_inbuffer** function is used to handle regular expression back-references.

expand_tildepaths

32290: The **expand_tildepaths** function is used on Unix systems to find and return the full path to a user's home directory when it was requested in the **~username** format. This code has no function in the Windows version of Apache.

expand_map_lookups

32343: The **expand_map_lookups** function is used to discern multiple lookups from the **MAP** directive.

lookup_map

32462: The **lookup_map** function is used to coordinate extraction of a rewrite map.

lookup_map_txtfile

32675: The **lookup_map_txtfile** function is used to extract a map from a formatted text file.

lookup_map_dbmfile

32723: The **lookup_map_dbmfile** is used to extract a map from a DBM file.

lookup_map_program

32750: The **lookup_map_program** is used to extract a map from a program.

rewrite_mapfunc_toupper

32806: The **rewrite_mapfunc_toupper** function is used to convert a string to uppercase.

rewrite_mapfunc_tolower

32819: The **rewrite_mapfunc_tolower** function is used to convert a string to lowercase.

rewrite_mapfunc_escape

32832: The **rewrite_mapfunc_escape** function is used to escape a string.

rewrite_mapfunc_unescape

32841: The **rewrite_mapfunc_unescape** function is used to unescape a string.

rewrite_rand_init

32853: The **rewrite_rand_init** function is used to set the random number generator.

rewrite_rand

32862: The **rewrite_rand** function is used to generate a pseudo-random number and return it.

select_random_value_part

32877: The **select_random_value_part** function checks the number of values available and picks one of them to return using the **rewrite_rand** function (line 32862).

open_rewritelog

32925: The **open_rewritelog** function opens the **RewriteLog** unless one was never set in the conf files.

rewritelog

32982: The **rewritelog** function is used to write an entry to the **RewriteLog**.

current_logtime

33075: The **current_logtime** function is used to calculate and format the time.

rewritelock_create

33113: The **rewritelock_create** function is used to create a lock file for the module.

rewritelock_open

33153: The **rewritelock_open** function is used to open the lock file and obtain a unique file descriptor.

rewritelock_remove

33181: The **rewritelock_remove** function is used to remove the lock file.

rewritelock_alloc

33201: The **rewritelock_alloc** function is used to place a lock.

rewritelock_free

33214: The **rewritelock_free** function is used to remove a lock.

run_rewritemap_programs

33236: The **run_rewritemap_programs** function is used to handle the creation of other processes to handle rewrite maps.

rewritemap_program_child

33293: The **rewritemap_program_child** function is used to handle the child process. It determines the operating system build and handles the exec-like calling based on that determination.

expand_variables_inbuffer

33362: The **expand_variables_inbuffer** function is used to expand environment variables into the supplied buffer.

expand_variables

33373: The **expand_variables** function returns the expanded environment variables. It is called by **expand_variables_inbuffer** (line 33362).

lookup_variable

33412: The **lookup_variable** function is used to determine the value of an Apache HTTP header.

lookup_header

33687: The **lookup_header** function finds a value from **array_header**.

init_cache

33720: The **init_cache** function is used to initialize the cache.

set_cache_string

33731: The **set_cache_string** function is used to store a string in the cache.

get_cache_string

33744: The **get_cache_string** function is used to retrieve a string from the cache.

cache_tlb_hash

33767: The **cache_tlb_hash** function is used to create a cache hash table.

cache_tlb_lookup

33780: The **cache_tlb_lookup** function is used to find an entry in the cache hash table.

cache_tlb_replace

33798: The **cache_tlb_replace** function is used to replace an entry in the cache hash table.

store_cache_string

33813: The **store_cache_string** function stores a string in the cache. It is called by **set_cache_string** (line 33731).

retrieve_cache_string

33890: The **retrieve_cache_string** function retrieves a string from the cache. It is called from **get_cache_string** (line 33744).

subst_prefix_path

33931: The **subst_prefix_path** function replaces a path prefix with another.

parseargline

33993: The **parseargline** function is a command-line parser.

add_env_variable

34072: The **add_env_variable** function sets an environment variable.

prefix_stat

34099: The **prefix_stat** function is used to perform a stat system call on the prefix of a path.

fd_lock

34132: The **fd_lock** function is used to lock a file descriptor.

fd_unlock

34176: The **fd_unlock** function is used to release the lock on a file descriptor.

compare_lexicography

34216: The **compare_lexicography** function is used to determine the similarity between two character arrays that represent a number (one digit per character).

Chapter 3

CGI And MIME Modules

This chapter describes four modules that are used to process client requests by accessing scripts located on an Apache-served Web site and then returning the results of the script to the client. Scripts can be specified directly by a client, or by a handler that Apache uses to redirect a request so that it is passed through a script before results are returned to the client.

The four modules discussed in this chapter are:

- **mod_actions**—Allows a script to be defined as applicable to certain Multipurpose Internet Mail Extensions (MIME) file types.

- **mod_cgi**—The standard tool for processing Common Gateway Interface (CGI) scripts. **mod_cgi** is used when the file requested by a client is actually a script that needs to be executed by Apache.

- **mod_mime**—Uses the MIME types defined in the Apache configuration file to assign type information to a requested file.

- **mod_mime_magic**—Uses a magic numbers file to examine the contents of requested files and to assign a file type based on that computing information.

The file typing functions provided by **mod_mime** and **mod_mime_magic** allow Apache to determine how to handle requests using **mod_cgi** and **mod_actions**.

Discussion Of **mod_actions**

By using an **AddHandler** directive in conjunction with an **Action** directive, a file type can be tied to a script using **mod_actions**. Whenever a file of that type is called, the script is run before the file is returned.

Scripts used by **mod_actions** provide a good way to preprocess files before sending them to a client. For example, if all your HTML files are stored in a compressed format or as part of a document database, an **Action** script can be used to prepare the document in a readable format for the client. (This is independent of any content negotiation that might result in Apache sending compressed files that are then uncompressed by the client browser.)

To use **mod_actions**, a handler type is defined with the **AddHandler** directive. Then the **Action** or **Script** directive is used to define a filter script for **mod_actions** to run on all files of that type. **Action** is used for file types; **Script** is used for HTTP methods. For example:

```
AddHandler compressed-html zhtml
Action compressed-html /cgi-bin/
uncompress_html.sh
Script GET /cgi-bin/pre-process-html.sh
```

Module Structure

Functions are provided in **mod_actions** to handle directory configuration and merge directory configuration. Two directives (**Action** and **Script**) are defined in the command table (line 11821).

The **action_handler** function (line 11831) is called each time a request matches the file type or method defined in the corresponding directives. This function checks the existence of the script named in the directive and then executes an internal redirect of the request with the validated script name. The process is shown in Figure 3.1.

Customization

mod_actions is very brief. Its purpose is to check for the existence of a script and pass control to that file. This module can be extended with additional directives that map to different types of actions, scripts, or files. The use of **Action** and **Script** directives can be extended to include another parameter that indicates which phase of request processing the script should be run in. Functions must be added to **mod_actions** and the module definition to check for scripts that were designated for the logging phase, post read-request phase, and so forth.

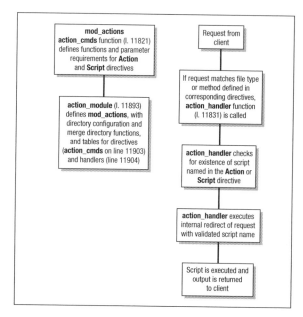

Figure 3.1 **mod_actions** allows Apache to execute a CGI script when a specified file type is requested.

create_action_dir_config

11759: Creates a configuration record for **mod_actions** to use within a directory context. An array of four **action_types** is initially created (for four possible **Action** directives). The **scripted** field is also initialized (line 11767).

merge_action_dir_configs

11772: Merges two directory configuration records by combining the action tables of the two directories and the list of script methods. The two original configurations are passed in as **basev** and **addv**.

add_action

11796: Places the arguments from the directive into the **action_types** field of the current configuration. No checking to determine if the file type is valid or if the script exists is performed at this point. (If the script isn't valid, it's never called.) This function is defined for the **Action** directive on line 11823.

set_script

11804: Adds the method passed in with a **Script** directive to the **scripted** field. The method passed in as an argument is checked to determine that it is a valid method. This function is defined for the **Script** directive on line 11825.

action_cmds

11821: Defines functions and parameter requirements for the two directives that this module uses (**Action** and **Script**).

action_handler

11831: Processes a request that may have either an **Action** or **Script** directive that applies to it.

11847: Begins with the **Script** directive by checking for the method and assigning the script name from the directive (now located in the **scripted** field) to the **script** variable (line 11850 or 11855). If the method is **GET**, the **args** field is checked also; if it is empty, the script is not used (line 11852).

11860: Verifies that this is not a subrequest. This avoids recursive calling of scripts for the same request.

11865: Determines whether an **Action** directive applies to the file type requested by comparing the **action_types** field with the results of the **ap_default_type** call on line 11867. The **script** variable is set to the corresponding script name from the **mod_actions** configuration record. An **Action** directive always overrides a **Script** directive if both apply to a request.

11869: If the file name requested cannot be found, **action_handler** logs an error and exits. (This might be performed sooner to save some processing in case of an error.)

11877: If the script wasn't set to something valid because neither a **Script** nor an **Action** directive matched this request, **DECLINED** is returned; otherwise, the **ap_internal_redirect_handler** is used to redirect the current request with the name of the script to run as a parameter and any **args** added back into the redirected request.

action_handlers

11887: Defines the function to call when a file uses the **AddHandler** directive to access **mod_actions**. All file types are indicated here by using */* to match all MIME types (for example text/html or image/jpeg) because the **action_handler** function checks the file type based on the **Action** directive.

action_module

11893: Defines **mod_actions** with directory configuration and merge directory functions, tables for directives (**action_cmds** on line 11903), and handlers (line 11904). All request processing by **mod_actions** is performed using the function defined in the handler table (line 11887).

Discussion Of mod_cgi

When a client requests a file that is actually a script (as determined by its path or file name), **mod_cgi** is used to run the script and pass the script's output back to the client.

Several security checks are performed as **mod_cgi** prepares to run the script. Scripts are logged if the **ScriptLog** and associated directives (**ScriptLogLength** and **ScriptLogBuffer**) are defined. For Apache to use **mod_cgi** to run a script, either the old **ScriptAlias** directive is used to define a directory that contains scripts or an **AddHandler** directive with a distinctive file name is used to indicate which files throughout the document tree should be considered to be scripts. For example:

```
AddHandler  cgi-script  pl
AddHandler  cgi-script  cgi
```

Module Structure

Logging a script call is a large part of the module code. The script logging directives are handled by placing the directive arguments in the configuration record. Script logging errors are handled, if necessary, as a script is called. Using script logging is a powerful tool for debugging scripts on a Web server.

Requests that match the **AddHandler** directive for files of type **cgi-script** arrive via the **cgi_handler** function (line 15865). This function checks several security issues to determine if the script can be executed. If execution is permitted and the script file exists, a child process is prepared and then spawned via the **cgi_child** function (line 15791). The script is logged using **log_script** (line 15685). The information returned from the script is then passed to the client at the end of the **cgi_handler** function, as shown in Figure 3.2.

Customization

As with **mod_actions**, the purpose of **mod_cgi** is to check for security restrictions and then pass control to another program (the script). **mod_cgi** can be extended by adding security checks to the scripts being executed.

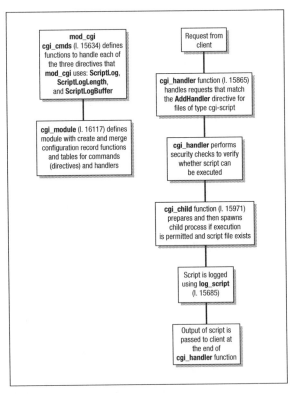

Figure 3.2 **mod_cgi** enables Apache to execute CGI scripts.

Although this can be very difficult to implement as a generalized system and very restrictive if it is not generalized, the added security on some Web servers may warrant the effort.

is_scriptaliased

15554: Determines whether the script named in this request was indicated by a **ScriptAlias** directive rather than an **AddHandler** directive. Check the notes of the request to determine if the type of the file should actually be **cgi-script** (and, thus, processed using **mod_cgi**).

create_cgi_config

15572: Creates a configuration record for a server context and initializes the logging fields. (Only logging fields are used in the configuration record for **mod_cgi**.)

merge_cgi_config

15586: Merges two configuration records for **mod_cgi**.

set_scriptlog

15595: Sets the **logname** field of the configuration record using the argument passed in via a **ScriptLog** directive (see line 15604). This function is defined for the directive on line 15636.

set_scriptlog_length

15608: Sets the **logbytes** field (the maximum length of the script debugging log) using the value given with the **ScriptLogLength** directive. The command table lists this function as the one to handle the directive on line 15638.

set_scriptlog_buffer

15621: Sets the **bufbytes** field (the maximum size of the data buffer for a **POST** request) using the value in the **ScriptLogBuffer** directive. This function is defined for the directive on line 15642.

cgi_cmds

15634: Defines the functions to handle each of the three directives that **mod_cgi** uses (**ScriptLog**, **ScriptLogLength**, and **ScriptLogBuffer**).

log_scripterror

15649: Attempts to log an error while processing a request for a script. The set of tests beginning on line 15659 checks for a valid log file name and attempts to open that file using **ap_pfopen** on line 15663. If any of these fail, **log_scripterror** returns on line 15667; otherwise, the file is ready to write to on line 15672.

15672: Outputs an error message to the script log. The format is shown in the comments (date, request command, and error message). Three **fprintf** calls are used with the **f** file descriptor. The file is then closed using **ap_pfclose**.

log_script

15685: Logs a script that was run successfully. **log_script** is called from within the **cgi_handler** function on line 16032.

15698: Tests the validity of the log file name provided in the configuration record for the current server context. It checks that it exists, that the size of the log file is not greater than the **logbytes** field (specified using the **ScriptLogLength** directive), and that the file can be opened using **ap_pfopen** on line 15702.

15708: If one of these tests doesn't work, the script output is soaked up using a couple of **ap_bgets** calls in **while** loops and returns immediately on line 15714.

15719: The log file appears valid, so a log entry is written using a couple of **fprintf** calls. The time, the HTTP method and request text, and any header or response information available are all logged.

15751: Checks the buffer from the script process and attempts to write the output to the script log using **fputs** calls.

15761: Repeats the process with possible script error output, again using **fputs** calls to write it to the script log.

15771: Closes the script pipe, the script error pipe, and the file descriptor for the log file that has been written to.

cgi_child

15791: Runs a script as a child process to **mod_cgi**. **cgi_child** is called through **cgi_handler** using **ap_bspawn_child** (on line 15966—see **cgi_child** in the parameter list).

15803: Opens a console device as the output for the script that will be run. The device to use is dependent on the platform on which Apache is running.

15819: Adds the environment variables from this process so that they are available to the script being run. The **ap_add_cgi_vars** and **ap_create_environment** calls are used with the **subprocess_env** field to set this up.

15823: If debugging is turned on, several messages are written into the return data stream to indicate the progress of the CGI script being called. Although most modules don't have much debugging code, these lines can be very helpful in trying to follow the code through various child processes and so forth.

15839: Prepares to execute the script, then runs it using **ap_call_exec** with the script name (**argv0**) on line 15841. This should effectively kill the current function; however, a **return** is needed for Windows on line 15843.

15857: Because the function is still operating, **ap_call_exec** must not have worked, so an error is logged to the standard Apache error log and **cgi_child** exits.

cgi_handler

15865: Checks the validity of the script being requested, then launches it and returns the results to the client, logging the script as needed.

15879: Tests whether the method used for this request is allowed. If not, it returns **DECLINED**.

15887: Gets the file name for the request in the **argv0** variable.

15894: If this script was accessed because of a **ScriptAlias** directive (checked using the **is_scriptaliased** function called on line 15895) and the **ExecCGI** option is not active for the current directory, an error is returned. The script cannot be processed.

15900: If the script is attempting to use both nonparsed header (for unbuffered output) and an **INCLUDED** protocol, **cgi_handler** returns an error and exits. (The **is_included** variable is set on line 15871.)

15913: If Apache is running on a Windows or OS/2 platform, the file name of the executable is fixed for testing, and then the existence of the script is tested on line 15917.

15926: On Unix platforms, the script's existence is tested for by checking the **finfo.st_mode** request field.

15931: Verifies that the script is not a directory. (If the default document is a script, the indexing modules should have redirected the request for a directory to a valid file name before reaching this point.)

15936: Tests whether system file permissions allow the script named to be executed.

15944: All the tests have passed for the script. A client block is now set up, beginning by preparing to execute a child process to run the script.

15948: Sets up the child process variables.

15966: Uses the **ap_bspawn_child** call to start a child process using the script name (stored in **cld.argv0**) and pipes for input and output to the process.

15981: The script should have run. The outcome is tested using **ap_should_client_block**. Variables are then allocated to deal with the returned data stream.

15989: Starts a timeout so that, if an error occurs reading the script data, the process can be forcefully terminated by Apache. This timeout is cancelled on line 16019.

15991: Uses the **ap_get_client_block** to read the buffered data into the **argsbuffer** variable.

16005: Writes the data buffer to the client.

16009: If the amount of data written isn't as large as it should be, **cgi_handler** tries to read more until the client block is empty. The data from the client block is read using **ap_get_client_block**, but is discarded (the **while** loop reads data but does nothing with it, hence the "dump it" comment on line 16011). The reason that data is still available from the client block is unknown at this point.

16017: Flushes the script buffers using **ap_bflush**. The client connection is then closed using **ap_bclose** on line 16022.

16030: Checks the headers. If all is well, the **log_script** function (line 15685) logs the script and returns.

16042: The standard actions didn't occur. The headers are checked for a redirect (**Location**). If one is found, all the buffered data is read to clear it (see the loop on line 16050).

16064: Sets the method for the redirected request to **GET**, and removes the **Content-Length** header (because no data is being returned).

16076: Uses the **ap_internal_redirect_handler** call to direct this request.

16087: The script wasn't redirected. The headers are sent to the client and, if it wasn't a header-only request, the **ap_send_fb** call sends the data returned by the script. The script child process is closed using **ap_bclose** on line 16091; any remaining buffered information is cleaned out, and the script error log is closed on line 16099.

16102: Checks whether the script returned something and whether the script was using non-parsed-headers (NPH). If both tests are positive, the script data is returned using **ap_send_fb**.

cgi_handlers

16110: Defines the function that will process requests that match this handler. The **cgi_handler** function is defined for the type **cgi-script**.

cgi_module

16117: Defines the module with **create** and **merge** configuration record functions and tables for commands (directives) and handlers. All requests processed by **mod_cgi** come in via the handler function defined in the **cgi_handlers** structure (see line 16112).

Discussion Of mod_mime

mod_mime uses a set of file typing directives in Apache configuration files to set up the fields of a request with the correct language, encoding, MIME type, and so forth. Other sections of Apache handle a request based on the fields set by **mod_mime**.

Module Structure

mod_mime includes a configuration record that contains arrays for the different file types that this module sets, including language, handlers, encoding, and forced types. (See the **mime_dir_config** structure, line 23272.) The configuration record is initialized by the **create_mime_dir_config** and **merge_mime_dir_config** functions. Items are added to the configuration record by using directives such as **AddEncoding**. The MIME types configuration file is read by the **init_mime** function (line 23488), and the information in this file is added to the **hash_buckets** table.

Each time a request is processed, the **find_ct** function (line 23530) is called. This function compares the information in the **mod_mime** configuration record with the file name of the requested item. Based on the comparison, the fields of the request (such as **content_languages** and **content_encoding**) are set.

These fields can then be used by other modules that check for file typing information. Figure 3.3 illustrates the structure of **mod_mime**.

Customization

The **mod_mime** functionality consists mainly of placing directive arguments into a configuration record, then comparing those arguments against a file name. Additional file types, encoding, and so forth can be used with the existing **mod_mime** directives. Any additional file types require additional modules that handle the new file type. More intelligent file typing (based on file content rather than file extension) is already provided by the **mod_mime_magic** module, which is described after **mod_mime**.

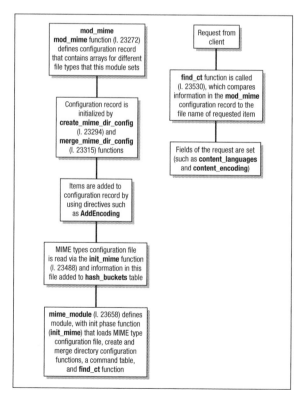

Figure 3.3 **mod_mime** is used to define handlers for a document or file type.

mime_dir_config

23272: Defines a configuration record structure for **mod_mime**. The structure includes arrays (tables) for each of the file typing items that **mod_mime** handles via configuration directives. A single type, handler, and default language are also part of the configuration record as strings, not tables.

create_mime_dir_config

23294: Creates a new configuration record for a directory context. Empty tables are set up to hold information that may be supplied by directive in this context. Tables of four items are set up initially. The **type**, **handler**, and **default_language** strings (which are not tables but single items) are initialized to NULL.

merge_mime_dir_config

23315: Merges two directory configuration records, overlaying the information in each of the configuration tables (such as the **language_ types**) using the **ap_overlay_tables** call (see lines 23332, 23334, 23337, and 23340).

23343: For the **default_language**, **handler**, and **type**, a single item is permitted. Thus, if a value exists in the **add** variable, it overrides the **base** variable in these fields.

add_type

23352: Adds a file type to the **forced_types** field, as taken from the parameters of the **AddType** directive. This function is defined for the directive on line 23433.

23356: Some users may include a period in the directive argument when specifying a file extension. If a period is found, it is discarded. No additional checking is performed to determine if a valid MIME type is specified with the **AddType** directive; the type is simply added to the **Content-Type** request header in the **find_ct** function (line 23561). An invalid type is passed to other applications (such as the requesting Web browser) so they can handle it.

add_encoding

23364: Adds an encoding type to the table of possible encoding types, matching the file extension to the type, as given in an **AddEncoding** directive. This function is defined for the directive on line 23436. Periods in file extension names are discarded on line 23369.

add_language

23375: Adds a language option from the **AddLanguage** directive to the **language_types** table of the configuration record. A period in the file extension indicator is discarded by the test and code on line 23380. All information is set to lowercase for consistency in comparing items in the **find_ct** function (see line 23530). This function is defined for the directive on line 23440.

add_handler

23386: Adds a handler item to the **handlers** table of the configuration record. This information is taken from the **AddHandler** directives. This function is defined to handle those directives on line 23444. As with the other directives that include a file extension, if a period is included in the argument, it is discarded, and the handler name is converted to all lowercase for ease in later comparison operations.

remove_handler

23403: Defines a handler that is explicitly not available for file extensions requested in the current directory context. This information arrives via a **RemoveHandler** directive. The function is defined for the directive on line 23452. The handler to remove is placed in the **handlers_ remove** field of the configuration.

set_types_config

23423: Adds the file name of the MIME types configuration file (provided by the **TypesConfig** directive) to the module configuration record so that the file can be accessed by the **init_ mime** function (see line 23488). The **ap_set_ module_config** API call is used to set this information directly, because it's the only server configuration item used. All others provided by directive to this module are for directory-based configuration. Testing of the validity of the file name is performed in the **init_mime** function when attempting to open the file. The handling of **TypesConfig** directives by this function is defined on line 23459.

mime_cmds

23431: Defines the directives that affect this module. Each item in the structure defines the function to call when that directive is parsed in a configuration file. Note that three of the directives (**ForceType**, **SetHandler**, and **DefaultLanguage**) do not use a separately defined function to handle the arguments of the directives. Instead, each uses **ap_set_string_slot** with an index to the configuration record, such as **XtOffsetOf(mime_dir_config,type)**, to place the single argument of the directive directly in the corresponding string field of the per-directory configuration record. For each directive, an explanation string is also given. This string is written out by Apache if the information given as arguments to the directives does not match the defined pattern.

init_mime

23488: Loads the MIME types configuration file into the **hash_buckets** variable (line 23486). This function is called during the **init** stage of Apache (see line 23661).

23493: Retrieves the configuration for this module into **confname**. The configuration consists solely of the file name for the MIME types configuration file (see the **set_types_config** function on line 23423).

23503: Attempts to open the configuration file for MIME types using **ap_pcfg_openfile**. If the open is not successful, **init_mime** writes an error and exits.

23510: Loops through **hash_buckets**, making an empty table entry for each possible item up to **MIME_HASHSIZE** (see line 23482).

23513: Reads in each line of the MIME configuration file using **ap_cfg_getline**. **init_mime** tests whether each line read starts with a # (checked on line 23516) and is, therefore, a comment. If not, **ap_getword_conf** on line 23518 places the first word of the line into **ct**. The rest of the line is then parsed with the **ap_getword_conf** call on line 23521 (looping through the entire line), placing each word of the line (assigned in turn to the **ext** variable) in the **hash_buckets** table.

23527: Closes the configuration file. The **hash_buckets** variable is now loaded and available to the **find_ct** function during request processing.

find_ct

23530: Sets the current request fields based on information defined by the directives in this module. This function performs the actual processing of a request for the module.

23532: Sets **fn** to the file name of this request. This is checked and redone on line 23552.

23538: Saves the original handler field in **orighandler**.

23541: If the current request is for a directory, typing by **mod_mime** doesn't apply, so **find_ct** returns.

23557: Because file extensions can be in any order (for example, .html.it.gz or .it.html.gz) the **while** construct loops through all of them, trying to set an appropriate field for each extension found as part of the file name. The variable **ext** holds the file extension currently being tested.

23562: Looks in the **forced_types** field of the configuration record (set by **AddType** directives) and the **hash_bucket** variable (set by the MIME types configuration file). If an entry matches **ext**, the matching entry (placed in the **type** variable by the tests on lines 23562 and 23564) is assigned to the **content_type** field of the request on line 23567.

23572: Tests the **ext** file extension against the items in the **language_types** array of the configuration

record. If one matches, the **content_language** field is set to the matching item on line 23576.

23579: If the **content_language** field is empty, an **ap_make_array** and **ap_push_array** set of calls places the language information in the **content_languages** field (note the plural). This is for backward compatibility only.

23589: Checks the **ext** file extension against the items in the **encoding_types** field (set by **Add-Encoding** directives). If any matches, it checks whether an encoding already exists (they are additive). If one does not exist, the newly found item is placed in the **content_encoding** field of the request on line 23592. If one is already there, a comma and the item just found on line 23594 are added to it.

23603: Checks the **handler** field for a matching handler type (based on **AddHandler** directives). If one is found, it is placed in the **handler** field of the request. This is only valid if the request is not marked as a proxy request (see line 23604).

23616: If any of the items were found in the **while** loop (a language, type, handler, or encoding), then the loop is repeated (back to line 23557 to get the next part of the file extension). If none of the items was found, all the values are set to NULL. This prevents files with extra or strange file extensions from having what appear to be normal **content_type**, language, and so forth assigned by this function.

23631: If the **content_languages** (plural) field is empty and a **default_language** field is defined, the **content_language** field is set to the **default_language** value for this configuration context on line 23635. The **content_languages** field is tested again on line 23637 and if empty, the **default_language** value is placed in it.

23647: If a **ForceType** directive for this directory makes all files a certain type, the **content_type** field is reset on line 23648. Likewise, if a **SetHandler** directive overrides any **AddHandler** directives for a directory context, the handler field is updated to the value of the handler string in the current configuration record (**conf**).

mime_module

23658: Defines this module with an **init** phase function (**init_mime**) that loads the MIME type configuration file, **create** and **merge** directory configuration functions, a command table to deal with directives for this module, and a function (**find_ct**) in the type checking phase where this module is actually applied to incoming requests.

Discussion Of **mod_mime_magic**

mod_mime uses values supplied in directives to assign content type and related attributes to a requested file. **mod_mime_magic**, in contrast, attempts to determine the content type and related information by examining the contents of the file, without any help from directives or Apache-specific lists of file extensions and data types.

This method of file typing uses a magic file, which is part of most Unix and Linux systems and is used by many different programs. The **MimeMagicFile** directive can specify a file containing the magic numbers used to identify files by their contents.

Module Structure

mod_mime_magic loads the MIME magic file into a request structure during the **init** phase of Apache. When a request is processed, the **type_checker** phase calls the **magic_find_ct** function, which in turn calls the **magic_process** and **magic_rsl_to_request** functions to examine the contents of the file and compare the first few bytes of the file with the magic numbers that were loaded during the **init** phase. Many individual functions are used to compare string sequences, convert number formats, and so forth, because the file may be in a binary format, compressed, or in ASCII text format.

Two types of tests are performed during processing of a request. The first is based on text string comparisons.

For example, a file containing the string "<DOCTYPE" indicates a content type of **text/html**. The second type involves searching for byte sequences at certain positions in a file, as described by information in the magic file. This method is used to identify binary file types. The structure of **mod_mime_magic** is shown in Figure 3.4.

Customization

Support for additional file types can be included by adding to the magic file. No additional work in this module is required to support this modification.

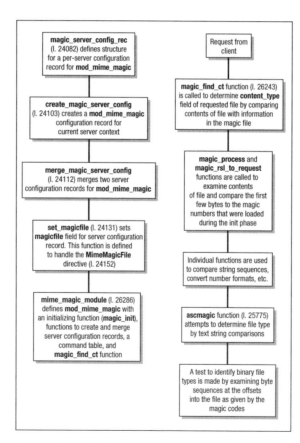

Figure 3.4   **mod_mime_magic** attempts to determine a file's content type and related information by its contents.

A few places in the code refer to potential errors in situations such as multithreaded environments. This module can be customized to fix those errors, and to directly improve performance.

mod_mime_magic includes a great deal of debugging code. Because of the number of different functions and the type of string and file manipulation performed by **mod_mime_magic**, this code can be very helpful while working with any modifications to the module. It does not affect the size or speed of the compiled Apache server when the debugging option is turned off (as it should be for production servers).

Function Prototype Declarations

23818: Begins definitions of file-function prototypes. The functions are included here as prototypes because they call each other. These functions are identified here so that the code for a function does not attempt to call another function that has not been defined.

types

23878: Defines a structure to hold possible values of the **content_type** field that **mod_mime_magic** might use to assign to a requested file.

names

23898: Defines a structure with many strings to test against in the first few bytes of a text file. Finding one of these strings identifies the file type. The ordering of this list is important, both for speed of processing and for correct processing. The logic can become complex. For example, "the" (lines 23944 and 23947) will occur in both text and HTML files, but HTML files are a more restrictive classification, so HTML is tested first using the strings defined in the structure beginning on line 23904.

magic_rsl_s

24070: Defines a structure in which components of the result string list (RSL) are assembled during processing to determine a file's content type.

magic_server_config_rec

24082: Defines the structure for a per-server configuration record for **mod_mime_magic**.

create_magic_server_config

24103: Creates a **mod_mime_magic** configuration record for the current server context. The variable of type **magic_server_config_rec** is allocated using **ap_pcalloc**. No additional explicit initialization is performed.

merge_magic_server_config

24112: Merges two server configuration records for **mod_mime_magic**.

set_magicfile

24131: Sets the **magicfile** field for the server configuration record. This file contains the magic numbers and instructions used to identify files by their contents. A magic file is normally included with Unix or Linux systems. This function is defined to handle the **MimeMagicFile** directive on line 24152. Using this directive, a magic file can be explicitly defined.

mime_magic_cmds

24150: Defines the one directive that **mod_mime_magic** uses—**MimeMagicFile**—and the function used to place the directive argument (the file name) in the server configuration record for **mod_mime_magic**.

magic_set_config

24176: Sets up a record to store information for the current request. The head and tail of the structure are initialized to NULL on line 24182. The new variable is placed in the configuration record using **ap_set_module_config** on line 24183, and the newly created variable is returned to the calling function.

magic_rsl_add

24192: Adds a string to the result string list for this request.

24200: Tests whether a valid variable is available to store the data being passed in (**req_dat**). If not,

or if the **magic_set_config** function does not return successfully, **magic_rsl_add** logs an error and returns.

24212: Allocates a list entry to be filled using **ap_palloc** with a **magic_rsl** variable type.

24216: Sets the **rsl** variable to the value of **str**.

24220: Adds the **rsl** variable value to the **reg_dat** list of entries. If this is the first item in the linked list, the special case on line 24225 is used.

magic_rsl_puts

24233: Puts a string using the **magic_rsl_add** function, which begins on line 24192. Nothing specific to strings is performed beforehand.

magic_rsl_printf

24239: Prints out information from an RSL list variable using Apache API calls.

24248: Calls **ap_vsnprintf** to print the string, then returns the value given by adding the item to the RSL list using **magic_rsl_add**.

magic_rsl_putchar

24256: Puts one character in the RSL list using the **magic_rsl_add** function on line 24264. The character is first prepared by setting a NULL termination on it.

rsl_strdup

24269: Allocates and copies a contiguous string from an RSL.

24284: Allocates space for the resulting string using **ap_palloc**.

24288: Loops through each part of the RSL until the current fragment is found (line 24292).

24296: Loops through all fragments, collecting characters from the fragments and placing them in the result on line 24303.

24312: Sets a NULL termination on the string, and returns the result on line 24319.

rsl_states

24324: Defines an enumerated type filled with possible states for the state-machine algorithm in the **magic_rsl_to_request** function.

magic_rsl_to_request

24331: Processes the result string list (RSL) and uses it to set the MIME information (such as the **content_type** field) in the request record.

24354: Retrieves the server configuration record data.

24359: If a **req_dat** variable does not exist or is empty, this function has no data to work on, so **DECLINED** is returned.

24366: Begins searching for matching fragments in the magic file and the RSL list. A list of fragments is assembled to get started.

24373: Loops through all the characters in the fragment. **ap_isspace** checks for white space, skipping it if found.

24380: Uses a set of **if/else** statements to determine how to identify the **content_type** named in the **state** variable.

24417: Begins processing non-white space items in the fragment list.

24468: Tests whether **state** is set to a valid RSL subtype or encoding. If so, the type string is assembled and placed in the **content_type** request field on line 24476.

24486: Fills the **content_encoding** field of the request if valid information was available.

24490: Tests whether the **content_type** was actually set. If not, an internal error occurred.

magic_process

24506: Prepares to process a requested file using magic file information. This function opens the requested file and retrieves the first few bytes of it to begin testing.

24519: Tests the status of the file using the **fsmagic** function beginning on line 25155. If the status returns **DONE**, it proceeds to the **magic_rsl_putchar** function on line 24521.

24523: If **fsmagic** returns OK, **magic_process** proceeds to line 24530 to attempt to open the requested file. If something else was returned by **fsmagic**, an internal error occurred, so it returns without attempting to open the requested file.

24530: Attempts to open the requested file using **ap_popenf**, placing the file descriptor in **fd**. If the file can't be opened, **magic_process** writes an error and returns.

24543: Reads in the first few bytes (defined by **HOWMANY**) using the read function with the **fd** file descriptor. If an error occurs while reading the file, **magic_process** logs an error and returns an internal server error.

24550: Checks the status of the bytes read in from the file. If no bytes are there (**nbytes** is zero), **magic_rsl_puts** is used with **MIME_TEXT_UNKNOWN**, which offers no help. Otherwise, the **tryit** function (beginning on line 24564) determines what can be learned about the file type.

24557: Closes the file using **ap_pclosef**. A final call to **magic_rsl_putchar** is performed to see what can be learned about the file.

tryit
24564: Tests several methods to determine the content type of a file.

24570: Calls **zmagic** (line 25905) to test the compression encoding of the requested file. This function may in turn call **tryit** to check the **content_type** of the uncompressed file. In the process, **zmagic** sets the **content_encoding** field of the request.

24576: Calls the **softmagic** function (line 25233) to determine if the magic file has information to help determine the **content_type** of a non-ASCII file.

24582: Calls the **ascmagic** function (line 25775) to check if the file is ASCII (plain text) and, if so, whether the first few characters match any of the simple tests available. (See line 23898 for matching key words in the **names** structure.)

24588: None of the other tests were successful, so **magic_rsl_puts** is called with a parameter to indicate that nothing much is known about this file.

apprentice
24598: Loads a configuration from the MIME magic file for use in **mod_mime_magic**.

24610: Retrieves the server configuration for the current context.

24615: Assigns the file name of the **magicfile** to **fname** and attempts to open the file on line 24616 using an **ap_pfopen** call. If a problem occurs, **apprentice** logs an error and exits.

24625: Initializes the list of magic values to NULL.

24628: Loops through each of the lines of the magic file (read with **fgets**), checking each one and then placing it in the line variable.

24639: Loops to remove any white space at the front of the line.

24645: Skips to the next loop iteration if this is a blank or comment line. (See line 24650 for testing for #.)

24660: Calls the **parse** function (line 24758) to process a single line of the file.

24664: After finishing the loop for all lines in the file, the file is closed with **ap_pfclose**.

24666: If debugging is enabled, several potential errors are checked for, and any that are found are logged.

signextend
24716: Extends the sign bit of a variable for occasions when the comparison is to be signed.

24720: Uses a single **switch** statement, checking the type of the variable **m->type**. Based on the case of the variable's type, **m->type** is recast as a variable of type **char**, **short**, or **long**.

24744: If none of the cases listed is applicable, consider it an error; **signextend** logs the error and exits.

24751: Returns with the recast value **v**.

parse
24758: Parses one line from a magic file, and places each valid line in the **magic** structure. This function is called from the **apprentice** function as a magic file is read into **mod_mime_magic** (see line 24660).

24763: Retrieves the server configuration record for this context.

24774: Tests the state of the linked list into which lines from the magic file are placed.

24782: Initializes the values in the **magic** structure.

24787: Begins parsing a line from the magic file in a **while** loop, checking for special characters.

24814: Based on the data in the magic line, the data type is set to the given value (such as **LONG** or **BYTE**). If none of the **case** values are valid, the default logs an error on line 24824.

24833: Tests for + (plus sign) or - (minus sign) followed by digits. These are used with the **while** loop on line 24853.

24875: Begins testing the data type against the assigned types, setting the type field of **m** according to the result. If none of the explicit value is found, an error is logged.

24929: If an ampersand (&) is found, a logical **AND** mask is set in the mask field using the **signextend** function.

24935: Tests for other characters in the magic line with a **switch** statement. Each case that follows checks for a valid character and sets the **reln** field based on it. If none of the cases are valid, the default checks for white space characters with **ap_isspace**.

24971: Gets the description of the current magic line from the last part of the line, and places it in the **desc** field of **m** on line 24982.

getvalue

25003: Reads a numeric value from a pointer into the **value** union of a magic pointer, according to the **magic** type. The string pointer is updated to point just after the number read.

25008: If the item being tested is a string, **getstr** sets the value of p; otherwise, **signextend** on line 25014 is used with a **strtol** call.

getstr

25025: Converts a string containing escaped characters to unescaped format, stopping at the first space or tab.

25034: Loops through all the characters of the string, checking for white space with **ap_isspace** on line 25035.

25043: Begins checking for escaped characters using a long **switch** statement. Each **case** sets the character in **p** to an unescaped value. Numbers are converted to a value.

25102: Converts hexadecimal values in the string using multiple calls to **hextoint** (line 25137) on lines 25104, 25107, and 25110.

hextoint

25137: Converts a single hexadecimal digit to a decimal value. The **ap_isdigit** call tests for numbers on line 25139. For nondigit characters, 10 is added to the return value, starting with **a** or **A** to arrive at values of 10 to 15.

fsmagic

25155: Tests the status of the file handle passed in as a parameter. **DONE** is returned if it has been handled already (appropriate request field values exist). **OK** is returned to indicate that handling is needed.

25157: Begins a **switch** statement that assigns a status based on the **finfo.st_mode** value for the file name of this request.

25158: If the file handle refers to a directory, **DONE** is returned. File typing does not apply.

25161: For S_IFCHR files, **fsmagic** calls **magic_rsl_puts** with an unknown type and returns DONE. (This is for character devices.)

25170: For S_IFBLK files, **fsmagic** calls **magic_rsl_puts** with an unknown type and returns DONE. (This is for block devices.)

25182: For S_IFIFO files, **fsmagic** calls **magic_rsl_puts** with an unknown type and returns **DONE**. (This is for FIFO special files.)

25190: For S_IFLNK (linked) files, an error is logged.

25206: For regular files, **fsmagic breaks** to the bottom of the loop.

25208: If none of the **case** statements matches the status value, **fsmagic** logs an internal server error and returns.

25219: The file was a regular file. If the file size is zero, **magic_rsl_puts** is called and **DONE** is returned; otherwise, OK is returned (the file type still needs to be processed).

softmagic

25233: Looks up a file in the magic file loaded by the **apprentice** function. The **match** function (line 25276) is called to test the item passed into this function. If it matches, it returns 1; otherwise, it returns 0.

match

25276: Attempts to find a match between the requested file and one of the types defined in the **magicfile**. Many debugging checks are part of this code, but are not discussed here. In general, these checks write information about progress through the function or log more detailed error messages.

25285: Retrieves the server configuration record for the current context.

25323: Loops through all of the lines of the magic file, checking for a match against the requested file using the **mget** (line 25562) and **mcheck** (line 25602) functions (see line 25333).

25341: If the **mget** and **mcheck** functions don't return a match, any notes about continuing previous partially completed matches are deleted.

25379: The **mget** or **mcheck** functions returned a match, which is processed using **mprint**.

25388: With the main level matching, matches are tested for in continuation levels.

25411: Tests for a match in a continuation level using **mget** and **mcheck**. If it matches, the results are printed using **mprint** on line 25427.

25449: Ends the loop for each line of the magic file.

mprint

25459: Prints a value to the result string list (RSL) based on the type of the variable being passed in.

25465: Begins a **switch** statement to test the type of the variable. The value of **v** is set based on the type.

25482: For string variables, **magic_rsl_printf** is used directly to print the variable. If none of the types in the **case** statements catches the variable, an internal error has occurred.

25509: Performs a sign check on **v** using the **sign extend** function, then prints it using **magic_rsl_printf**.

mconvert

25517: Converts the byte order of the data for use in the **mget** and **mcheck** functions.

25522: Tests the type of the variable being checked. A set of **case** statements rearranges the data, if necessary, by shifting bits around. If the test is successful, a 1 is returned (some **case** statements return 1 without any action). If the default case is reached, something was wrong because the variable type wasn't found, so an error is logged.

mget

25562: Handles one character of the **p** variable, as called by the **match** function.

25569: If the offset being checked is greater than the **nbytes** value, not enough data is available, so **mget** returns immediately.

25579: Tests for the data types, setting the offset based on the values of **p** and **m**.

mcheck

25602: Checks the data type for a component of an **rsl** variable.

25609: If the value being checked is hexadecimal or empty, **mcheck** logs an error and returns. The value should have been converted from hexadecimal to decimal prior to calling **mcheck**.

25617: Uses a **switch** statement to check the data type of the **m->type** variable. Sets the value of **v** to **p->b**, **p->h**, or **p->l**, depending on the type of **m->type**. Strings create a special case. If none of the cases matches the data type, an internal error is logged.

25668: Sets the sign of **v** using the **signextend** function.

25670: Uses another **switch** statement to test the **reln** field of the variable. Each of these cases sets a value for the **matched** variable. If the **MIME_MAGIC_DEBUG** flag is set, **mcheck** also logs an error message stating which **case** statement was used.

ascmagic

25775: Attempts to assign a **content_type** by comparing plain text strings in the requested file (within the first **nbytes** bytes) with the values in the types structure.

25794: Tests for a leading period followed by key characters to identify a **troff** formatted file. If found, the type **application/x-troff** is returned with **magic_rsl_puts** on line 25801.

25805: Checks for Fortran characters, but returns **text/plain** using **magic_rsl_puts**.

25815: Using a small number of bytes (for performance reasons), this tests for matches with items in the names.h file.

25829: Loops through each name. If a match occurs, the type is placed in the request record using **magic_rsl_puts** on line 25831.

25840: Uses a switch statement to test the returned values of the **is_tar** (line 26035) function to determine if this is a tar archive file. The appropriate content type values are sent using **magic_rsl_puts**.

25856: None of the additional tests was successful, but the file is still known to be ASCII, so the type is set to **text/plain** using **magic_rsl_puts**.

compr

25880: Defines a structure with compression information. This is used to identify types of compressed files (the encoding type) by the **zmagic** function (line 25905).

zmagic

25905: Determines the compression status of the requested file.

25912: Loops through the bytes of **nbytes**, checking against the values associated with various types of compressed files stored in the **compr** structure (see line 25880). If a match is found, **zmagic** drops out of the **for** loop and tests the match.

25920: If the end of the list was reached, **zmagic** returns 0—the file is not compressed; otherwise, it calls the **uncompress** function (which begins on line 25966) on line 25923 to determine the size of the uncompressed file. If a valid number results, **tryit** is called on line 25925 to attempt to determine the content type of the uncompressed file.

25928: Because a compression test worked, **zmagic** sets the **content_encoding** field to the value given in the **compr** structure.

uncompress_child

25939: Provides functionality for the **uncompress** operation, which spawns a child process in the **uncompress** function (see line 25984).

25951: If Apache is running on Win32, some additional preparation must be performed for the child process ID.

25956: On non-Win32 platforms, the **execvp** call is used to launch the child process. If an error occurs, control stays in this function; the error is logged. Otherwise, this function loses control as the child process takes over via the **exec** call.

uncompress

25966: Attempts to uncompress a file to determine its encoding type. This function is call within the **zmagic** function (line 25923).

25982: Creates a submemory pool with **ap_make_sub_pool** to protect against zombie processes as a child is spawned to run the uncompress utility.

25984: Starts a child process to uncompress the file using the **ap_bspawn_child** call. This call includes the **uncompress_child** function (which begins on line 25939). If the child can't be started, **uncompress** logs an error and returns.

25993: Tests that the child process was OK, then destroys the memory subpool used for it. The child is closed on line 25999 with **ap_bclose**.

26001: Attempts to determine the file size of the uncompressed file using **ap_bread**, and stores the result in **n**. If this causes an error, the file was not uncompressed successfully; **uncompress** logs an error and returns. Otherwise, the remaining memory subpool is destroyed and the value **n** (size of the uncompressed file) is returned.

is_tar

26035: Determines if the requested file is a tar file, based on the information in **nbytes**. This function is called within the **ascmagic** function on line 25840.

26043: If **nbytes** is not large enough to perform a proper test, **is_tar** returns with no processing.

26046: Uses the **from_oct** function (line 26080) to retrieve a **checksum** for the file. This is the criterion that determines if the file is a tar archive file.

26050: Loops through the digits and performs a sum. The **checksum** is adjusted by removing the **checksum** bytes themselves in the loop on line 26060.

26064: Compares the results of the **from_oct** call (stored in **recsum**) with the value of **sum** computed on lines 26060 to 26062. If they don't match, this isn't a tar archive. If they match with the **TMAGIC** header, it's a standard Unix tar archive file. If the sums match but the headers don't, it's an old-fashioned tar archive.

from_oct

26080: Converts a number from octal to decimal.

26084: Loops based on the value returned by **ap_isspace** until a nonspace character is found in the input string. If nothing is left, **from_oct** returns without doing anything further.

26089: Initializes the value, then takes each octal digit in turn (in the **while** loop) and shifts the value variable to add the octal digit to it. When the end of the octal digits is reached, **value** is returned.

revision_suffix

26114: Checks the requested file name for the presence of a revision suffix (such as @1). If a suffix is found, a subrequest is created to handle the revised file name. Several sections of this function are only active if debugging is turned on for this module using the **MIME_MAGIC_DEBUG** define.

26128: Strips the last character from the requested file name. The character is tested to see whether it's a digit by using **ap_isdigit** on line 26129. If it isn't, a suffix is not present. **revision_suffix** returns without further action.

26132: Loops through the characters of the file name until a nondigit character is found. It is checked again on line 26135; if the suffix position counter (**suffix_pos**) is less than zero or if the first nondigit character was not @, **revision_suffix** returns because the type of suffix this function is intended to handle was not found.

26143: Creates a revised file name in **sub_filename**. A subrequest is generated using **ap_sub_req_lookup_file** on line 26151. The resulting information from the subrequest is placed in the fields of the main request. Specifically, if the **content_type** of the subrequest exists, the **content_type**, **content_encoding**, and **content_language** fields are copied to the main request (**r**) on lines 26156, 26165, and 26168.

26174: Destroys the subrequest using **ap_destroy_sub_req**.

magic_init

26183: Initializes **mod_mime_magic** (line 26289) by loading the MIME magic configuration file into the server configuration record.

26193: Gets the configuration record for the main server. The **for** loop on line 26195 determines if a configuration record exists for a more recent virtual server context. If so, it is used; otherwise, **conf** is set equal to **main_conf** on line 26200.

26202: If a **magicfile** value has been found among the server configuration records, its contents are loaded using the **apprentice** function (starting on line 24598) so that they can be used by **mod_mime_magic**.

26206: If the **apprentice** function returns successfully, the module exits here. Otherwise, if debugging for this module is enabled, a lot of information from the magic file is printed for review. If debugging is not enabled, no information is printed. If the apprentice function didn't work, **mod_mime_magic** simply doesn't perform.

magic_find_ct

26243: Determines the **content_type** field of a requested file by comparing the contents of the file with information in the **magicfile**.

26249: If the file requested doesn't exist in the file system, **magic_find_ct** declines to attempt file typing.

26253: If a **content_type** field is already defined for the request (perhaps by the **mod_mime** module), the **mod_mime_magic** module should not be used to establish a file type. **magic_find_ct** returns on line 26255 with **DECLINED**.

26258: Retrieves the server configuration information for this module. If the configuration doesn't exist, **magic_find_ct** returns without pro-cessing.

26265: Sets up a record in the server configuration to handle this request using the **magic_set_config** function (beginning on line 24176). If this function returns an error, memory could not be allocated or something went wrong when accessing the server configuration record, so an internal server error is returned.

26269:   Strips off any revision suffix that might exist on the file name (although it's unlikely). The suffix would be something like @1 or @2. The **revision_suffix** function (line 26114) handles this, possibly using a subrequest to deal with the altered file name (minus the suffix).

26272:   Processes the requested file using the **magic_process** function (line 24506). This function prepares a buffer, opens the file, and reads in a few bytes to use for magic file typing. If this works, **magic_find_ct** continues on line 26279 by using the **magic_rsl_to_request** (beginning on line 24331) to actually assign a file type (in the **content_type** field) to the request.

mime_magic_module

26286:   Defines **mod_mime_magic** with an initializing function (**magic_init**), functions to create and merge server configuration records, a command table for the single directive used by this module, and the **magic_find_ct** function (which begins on line 26243) to assign a **content_type** to a requested file. This is performed in the **type_checker** phase of request processing.

Chapter 4

Core Code

This chapter describes the core of the Apache source code. These are the files that control the Apache modules, and contain the Apache API calls and other functions used to start up the main Apache process and Apache child processes that actually handle client requests.

The three files described in this chapter are:

- **http_core**—Includes the core module to process directives that are not associated with a specific module.

- **http_main**—Includes the main functions that initialize Apache as well as code to manage multiple processes, memory allocation, and the Apache scoreboard.

- **http_log**—Includes functions to log errors to files and piped logs.

All three of these files include more source code comments than the majority of the module source code. These comments are very helpful in understanding the code, though the large number of compiler **define** statements particular to Windows systems can make it a challenge to follow exactly which lines of code are built for your platform.

Discussion Of **http_core**

Although it is not treated like other Apache modules, **http_core** is a lot like a regular module. In fact, the comments in the source code refer to **http_core** as the bureaucracy module. It includes a **module** structure that defines a set of functions to call for different phases of processing. The majority of the work performed by this core module, however, consists of processing the globally applicable directives found in the Apache configuration

files. Global variables are set by these functions based on the directives. Containers such as **<VirtualHost>** and **<Directory>** are also processed, with base configuration records being established that other modules can add to and query in later processing.

The **http_core** file includes numerous helpful source code comments. Studying the list of directives in the **core_cmds** array beginning on line 3043 is also very instructive.

create_core_dir_config

57:    Creates the core or default directory configuration record. This is the top-level directory configuration used when no other **<Directory>** structures override it in the configuration files. Each virtual server has a core directory configuration.

61:    Allocates a directory configuration record (**conf**).

64:    Places the directory name in the **d** field, watching for special cases such as proxies.

77:    Sets the other fields, including the options (**opts**) and **override**.

merge_core_dir_configs

111:   Merges configuration data for the core (default) directory. The fields of the **basev** and **newv** variables are combined into the **conf** variable, which is the value returned from this function.

create_core_server_config

251:   Creates a default server configuration record, setting field values for the **conf** variable. Each virtual server has a core server configuration record.

merge_core_server_configs

272:   Merges the core server configuration records. The variables **basev** and **virtv** are combined into the **conf** variable, which is the return value of this function.

ap_add_per_dir_conf

303:   Adds a per-directory configuration to the server configuration record.

306:   Retrieves the server configuration into **sconf**. An array element is added on line 310 using **ap_push_array**, then the **dir_config** passed in as a parameter into the newly created slot in the configuration record is copied.

ap_add_per_url_conf

315:   Adds a per-URL (**<Location>**) configuration to the server configuration record. The server configuration is retrieved, a new array element is allocated, and the per-URL configuration passed in as a parameter into the server configuration record is copied.

add_file_conf

327:   Adds a per-file configuration (defined using a **<File>** container) to the server configuration. Space in the server configuration record is allocated, then the new per-file configuration is inserted.

reorder_sorter

370:   This function is used by **qsort** (called on line 436) to provide an ordering for elements (configuration records) being sorted by **qsort**. **reorder_sorter** uses the **IS_SPECIAL** macro on lines 382, 383, and 387 to perform a test for special configurations that include regular expressions. Also, refer to the source code comment on line 358.

ap_core_reorder_directories

407:   Sorts the directory configurations so that they are used in the correct order. An array is built with the configuration information, **qsort** is called on line 436 to sort the array, and a new array is built from the sorted configuration information.

ap_allow_options

460:   This API call returns the **opts** field (the directory options) for the current directory configuration record. This field defines which options (such as **Indexes**, **FollowSymLinks**, and so forth) are applicable in this directory context.

ap_allow_overrides

469:   This API call returns the **override** field for the current directory configuration. This field determines which options can be overridden by a directory-specific configuration file (such as the .htaccess file).

ap_auth_type

479: This API call returns the authorization type configured for the current directory.

ap_auth_name

489: This API call returns the name (the **ap_auth_ name** field) configured for authorization within the current directory.

ap_default_type

499: This API call returns the default content type for documents served from the current directory.

ap_document_root

511: This API call returns the document root for the current server. This function is deprecated (should no longer be used), but is included for backward compatibility with NCSA Web servers.

ap_requires

522: This API call returns the **ap_requires** field from the current directory configuration, indicating a user that must be authenticated to access the directory.

ap_satisfies

533: This API call returns the **satisfy** field from the current directory configuration.

ap_response_code_string

550: This function is seldom called. It returns the **response_code_strings** (if any are defined) for the current directory configuration.

do_double_reverse

567: Attempts to perform a double-reverse lookup on the networking information for a client connection. This security measure ensures that the IP address and hostname are valid (not spoofed).

581: Retrieves the hostname of the client using **gethostbyname**. The result is compared with the request fields (**remote_addr**) on line 586.

ap_get_remote_host

596: This API call retrieves the remote hostname of a client making a request.

609: Checks whether **hostname_lookups** are enabled in the current directory configuration.

630: If **hostname_lookups** are enabled, **gethost-byaddr** is called to retrieve the hostname and copy it into the request record on line 633. If **HOSTNAME_LOOKUP_DOUBLE** is defined, **do_double_reverse** is called on line 639.

ap_get_remote_logname

684: This API call returns the remote logname for the current request. This information is retrieved on line 699 by calling **ap_rfc1413** with the request record **connection** and **server** fields.

ap_get_server_name

713: This API call returns the name of the server as defined by the **ServerName** directive for the current virtual host. Also refer to the source code comment at line 706.

ap_get_server_port

728: This API call returns the server port that a connection originated on. If the **server.port** field of the request record contains this data, it is used as a return value; otherwise, the default port is returned by calling the **ap_default_port** function on line 737.

ap_construct_url

747: This API call returns a fully constructed URL from the components of a request record. These may include the canonical name of the server, the port, the **server_hostname** field, and the HTTP method information.

777: Having assembled the components of the complete URL, the function returns the complete string on line 778 or 781.

ap_get_limit_req_body

785: This API call returns the **limit_req_body** field of the current directory configuration.

get_interpreter_from_win32_registry

796: For Windows platforms, this function queries the Windows Registry to discover which interpreter to use for handling or launching a program or file.

ap_get_win32_interpreter

900: For Windows platforms, this function sets the interpreter to execute for a program and retrieves this information using a call on line 922 to **get_interpreter_from_win32_registry**. The **filetype** is returned on line 985.

ap_check_cmd_context

1013: This API call checks the context of a directive used in an Apache configuration file. A series of **if** statements verifies the validity of the directive being checked against possible positions (such as within a **<VirtualHost>** or **<Limit>** container). If the directive is used erroneously, an error string is returned to the calling function.

set_access_name

1065: Sets the **access_name** field of the current server configuration record to the argument value (**arg**) passed in as a parameter.

set_gprof_dir

1083: Sets the **gprof_dir** field of the current server configuration record to the argument value (**arg**) passed in as a parameter. Before setting the field value, **ap_check_cmd_context** is used on line 1090 to verify that the directive to set up **gprof_ dir** is within a valid configuration context.

set_document_root

1101: Sets the **ap_document_root** field of the server configuration based on the **arg** value passed in as a parameter.

1108: Calls **ap_check_cmd_context** to ascertain that the directive (**DocumentRoot**) is used in a valid configuration context.

1114: Creates a canonical file name from the **arg** value by calling **ap_os_canonical_filename**.

1126: Sets the **ap_document_root** field to **arg**.

ap_custom_response

1130: This API call defines a custom response to a request based on the HTTP response code (which is used as an index into the **response_code_strings** structure).

1133: Retrieves the directory configuration record into **conf**.

1139: Allocates space, if necessary, in the **response_code_strings** array of the configuration record.

1147: Adds to the **response_code_strings** structure the string passed in as an argument.

set_error_document

1154: Defines the file to return as an error document for a specified HTTP error code.

1172: Retrieves the HTTP response code number from the arguments passed in to this function; the response code is converted into an integer on line 1173 so that it can be used as an array index.

1201: If no errors occurred during testing of the response code that was passed in, the desired response is stored in the **response_code_string** array on line 1208.

set_override

1226: Sets the **override** field of the current directory configuration based on the arguments used with an **AllowOverride** directive.

1238: The **override** field is set to zero using the **OR_NONE** constant (defined in http_config.h).

1239: Loops through all arguments included in the **cmd**. For each one, **ap_getword_conf** is called to retrieve the next word in the **cmd** variable. A series of **if/then/else** statements are then used to check for items that can be overridden. For each one, the correct bits are added to the **override** field by performing a logical **OR** with the corresponding override option.

set_options

1272: Sets the options defined for the current directory configuration.

1280: Loops to retrieve each of the items listed in the **cmd** argument that was passed into **set_options**.

1288: The **opts** field is set to **OPT_NONE** (no options set).

1292: Tests for each string that might be included in an **Options** directive. For each one found, a logical **OR** operation is performed to turn on the corresponding bit within the **opt** field of the directory configuration record.

1330: Checks whether the options are defined with a – (minus sign) or a + (plus sign), in which case they are moved to the **opts_remove** or **opts_add** field.

satisfy

1348: Sets the **satisfy** field of the directory configuration record to either **all** or **any**, depending on the value of the **arg** variable passed in to this function.

require

1363: Sets the value of the **requirement** and **method_mask** fields for the current request, based on the **ap_requires** field of the directory configuration record and the value of the **arg** parameter passed in to this function.

ap_limit_section

1378: Defines the HTTP methods that can be used within a server or directory context by parsing the contents of a **<Limit>** container.

1382: Retrieves the list of allowed HTTP methods by calling **ap_getword** with the **arg** value passed in as a parameter.

1387: Checks the context of the directive being used by calling **ap_check_cmd_context**.

1399: Loops to process each method listed in the argument (and now contained in the **limited_methods** string).

1402: Assigns a method number to the method string by calling **ap_method_number_of** with the method variable.

1415: Sets the limited variable to the method number **methnum**.

1422: Assigns the **limited** field of **cmd** to the value of **limited**.

endlimit_section

1426: Marks the close of a **<Limit>** section within a configuration file.

missing_endsection

1445: Returns an error message for a configuration file that appears to have a malformed container object (one without a closing directive such as **</Directory>**).

end_nested_section

1469: Returns the **end_token** value that should be found to close the current nested configuration section. If this token is not found, an error is returned.

unclosed_directive

1494: Returns an error while processing a configuration file if a container directive that was missing a closing symbol (>).

dirsection

1501: Processes a **<Directory>** container within a configuration file.

1509: Creates a new directory configuration record by calling **ap_create_per_dir_config** to hold the configuration information in this **<Directory>** container.

1527: Retrieves the path of the directory being configured by calling **ap_getword_conf**.

1534: If a **<DirectoryMatch>** container is being configured, **ap_pregcomp** is called on line 1535 to compile the regular expression used to define which directories this configuration applies to.

1545: Calls **ap_os_canonical_filename** to ensure that the directory name is standardized. The results are placed in the **path** field.

1568: Adds this directory configuration to the current server configuration by calling **ap_add_per_dir_conf** with the directory configuration record **new_dir_conf**.

urlsection

1583: Defines a configuration for a **<Location>** container.

1595: Creates a new per-directory configuration record by calling **ap_create_per_dir_config**.

1613: If a **<LocationMatch>** container was specified, **ap_pregcomp** (defined in alloc.c) is called on line 1614 to compile the regular expression used to define which locations this configuration applies to.

1625: Processes the commands in the container by calling **ap_srm_command_loop**.

1643: Adds the per-location configuration to the current server configuration by calling **ap_add_per_url_conf**.

filesection

1658: Defines a configuration for a **<Files>** container.

1671: Creates a new configuration record to hold the configuration directives in the **<Files>** container.

1692: If this container uses the **<FilesMatch>** format, the regular expression used to define which files it applies to is compiled and that information is stored in the variable **r**.

1710: Processes all of the directives in the **<Files>** container by calling **ap_srm_command_loop**.

1721: Sets additional fields in the **conf** configuration record for this container.

1728: Adds the **<File>** container configuration to the server configuration record **c** by calling **add_file_conf**.

end_ifmod

1748: Checks that an **<IfModule>** container is properly closed. This is not done in the current version of Apache, so this function is empty.

start_ifmod

1754: Processes the configuration for an **<IfModule>** container.

1773: Determines whether the module being configured by this **<IfModule>** container is linked into the current copy of Apache by calling **ap_find_linked_module** and storing the results, if found. If the module is not present, **start_ifmod** returns without further action.

1779: Loops to retrieve each configuration line by calling **ap_cfg_getline**. Each one is placed in the **config_file** array of **cmd**.

ap_exists_config_define

1797: This API call returns a **true** or **false** value based on whether the **ap_server_config_defines** array is empty (returns a 0) or contains at least one element (returns a 1).

end_ifdefine

1812: Notes the end of an **<IfDefine>** configuration section. This is not handled in the current version of Apache, so this function is empty.

start_ifdefine

1818: Processes the configuration for an **<IfDefine>** container.

1839: Checks whether **<IfDefine>** containers are supported on this server by calling **ap_exists_config_define**. If they are not, **start_ifdefine** returns with NULL.

1845: Loops through processing of each configuration line (retrieved using **ap_cfg_getline**).

virtualhost_section

1864: Sets up the configuration for a **<VirtualHost>** container.

1873: Checks the context of the **<VirtualHost>** container using the **ap_check_cmd_context** function. This container can only occur globally, not within any other containers.

1897: Initializes the virtual host configuration by calling **ap_init_virtual_host** with the **main_server** variable.

1903: Adds the virtual host server to the linked list of servers (**s**).

1912: Processes all of the directives in the **<VirtualHost>** container by calling **ap_srm_command_loop**.

1921: If the **<VirtualHost>** container includes directives that would have been included in the srm.conf or access.conf files previously, the **ap_process_resource_config** function with appropriate parameters is called to process those directives on lines 1922 and 1927.

set_server_alias

1937: Sets up an alias or alternate server name to return to clients.

1944: Loops through the **arg** parameter, calling **ap_getword_conf** to retrieve a directive option, then placing it in the **wild_names** field (line 1948) or **names** field (line 1953) of the server configuration record, depending on whether it contains a wildcard character.

add_module_command

1960: Adds a module to the Apache server using dynamic shared objects (DSO), as directed by an **AddModule** directive.

1963: Checks the context where the **AddModule** directive occurs. It can only be global, not within any containers.

1969: Adds the module named in the **arg** parameter to the Apache server by calling **ap_add_named_module**.

clear_module_list_command

1978: Clears the list of modules loaded dynamically in this copy of Apache by calling the function **ap_clear_module_list** on line 1987. The **ClearModuleList** directive can only appear globally in a configuration file, never within a container.

set_server_string_slot

1991: Sets a server string to the value of the **arg** parameter. This function is called to process several directives that rely on a single string value (such as **ServerAdmin**, **ErrorLog**, and **ServerName**).

server_type
2010:   Sets the **ap_standalone** flag to note the server type based on the **ServerType** directive (either **standalone** or **inetd**).

set_signature_flag
2055:   Sets the server signature used within a directory context. The **server_signature** field of the directory configuration is set to **on**, **off**, or **email**.

set_send_buffer_size
2081:   Sets the size of the network send buffer to fine-tune networking performance. This function processes the **SendBufferSize** directive, which can only be used globally (not within any containers). This is checked by calling the function **ap_check_cmd_context** on line 2085.

set_user
2099:   Sets the Unix user ID that Apache uses to establish its permission level when running on non-Windows systems. (The **User** directive is not used in Windows.)

2108:   Checks the context in which the **User** directive is used by calling **ap_check_cmd_context**.

2114:   Sets the **ap_user_name** to the **arg** parameter and the **ap_user_id** variable to the corresponding user ID by calling the function **ap_uname2id** on line 2117.

2120:   If the **ap_suexec_enabled** flag is set to allow the **User** directive within a **<VirtualHost>** container, the **server_uid** field is also set to the user ID that corresponds to the **arg** username.

2130:   Prints an error message if the user ID is 0, indicating that the server is trying to run as user root.

set_group
2158:   Sets the **server_gid** field to the group ID passed in as parameter **arg**, converting it from a name

to an ID, if necessary, by calling the function **ap_gname2id** on line 2169.

set_server_root
2187:   Sets the server root directory as defined by a **ServerRoot** directive. The **ap_check_cmd_context** function called on line 2190 assures that this directive does not occur within a container.

2197:   Makes the path and file name used with the **ServerRoot** directive canonical by calling **ap_os_canonical_filename**.

2202:   If the server root (**arg**) is not a directory, an error is returned; otherwise, the **ap_server_root** string is set to the value of **arg**.

set_timeout
2207:   Sets the server timeout value based on a **Timeout** directive. The **arg** parameter is converted to an integer on line 2216 and assigned to the **timeout** field of the server configuration.

set_keep_alive_timeout
2220:   Sets the timeout for keepalive connections based on the value given in a **KeepAliveTimeout** directive. The **keep_alive_timeout** field of the server configuration is set to the converted integer value of the **arg** parameter on line 2230.

set_keep_alive
2234:   Sets the status of keepalive connections (regardless of whether they are used) based on a **KeepAlive** directive. The **keep_alive** field of the server configuration is set on line 2251.

set_keep_alive_max
2256:   Sets the maximum number of client requests that can be handled by a single connection (when keepalive connections are enabled) based on a **MaxKeepAliveRequests** directive. The **keep_alive_max** field of the server configuration is set to the integer value of the **arg** parameter on line 2265.

set_pidfile
2269:   Configures the location of the process ID file for this Apache server. The **PidFile** directive can only

be used globally, not in a container. To check this the function **ap_check_cmd_context** is called on line 2272.

2283:   Sets the global **ap_pid_fname** variable to the value of the **arg** parameter.

set_scoreboard
2287:   Sets the name of the file where the Apache scoreboard is stored. The **ScoreboardFile** directive can only occur globally, not in a container. To check this the function **ap_check_cmd_context** is called on line 2291.

2297:   Sets the global variable **ap_scoreboard_fname** to the value of the parameter string **arg**.

set_lockfile
2301:   Sets the file name used to lock **accept** calls. The **LockFile** directive is not used in any containers. The **ap_lock_fname** global variable is set to the value of **arg** on line 2310.

set_idcheck
2314:   Sets the **do_rfc1413** flag in the directory configuration so that **identd** user identity lookups are performed. The value of this field is set on line 2323.

set_hostname_lookups
2327:   Sets the **hostname_lookups** field of the directory configuration to **on**, **off**, or **double** (for full reverse lookup verification). The value of this field is determined by the **HostnameLookups** directive.

set_serverpath
2352:   Sets the pathname where the Apache server can be reached, based on a **ServerPath** directive. The path field of the server configuration is set to the value of the **arg** parameter on line 2361.

set_content_md5
2366:   Sets the **content_md5** field to determine whether a **Content-MD5** header is returned to the client with each request response. This flag is set based on the value of a **ContentDigest** directive.

set_use_canonical_name

2379: Sets the **use_canonical_name** flag, based on the **UseCanonicalName** directive. This flag determines whether a canonical server and port name are always constructed when returning the server name to a client, rather than using the server and port submitted by the client, which may or may not be canonical.

set_daemons_to_start

2394: Sets the number of Apache child processes to start as Apache is launched. This value is based on the **StartServers** directive.

2398: Prints a warning message if the **StartServers** directive is used on Windows platforms. Because they are thread-based, this directive has no effect.

2407: Sets the **ap_daemons_to_start** global variable to the integer value of the **arg** parameter.

set_min_free_servers

2412: Sets the number of Apache child processes that are always running, based on the **MinSpareServers** directive. The global variable **ap_daemons_min_free** is set to the value of the **arg** parameter on line 2421.

2422: Tests the value of **ap_daemons_min_free** to ensure that it is non-negative. If it is, **ap_daemons_min_free** is reset to 1.

set_max_free_servers

2435: Sets the maximum number of idle Apache child processes to leave running. This is determined by the **MaxSpareServers** directive. The **ap_daemons_max_free** global variable is set on line 2444.

set_server_limit

2448: Sets the maximum number of Apache child processes that can be spawned to handle heavy traffic. This is determined by the **MaxClients** directive.

2451: The **MaxClients** directive (or the deprecated **ServerSafetyLimit** directive) can only be

used globally, not within a container. This is verified by calling **ap_check_cmd_context** with the **GLOBAL_ONLY** flag.

2457: Sets the **ap_daemons_limit** global variable to the value of the **arg** parameter. If the value of **arg** is greater than the **HARD_SERVER_LIMIT** constant (defined in the file httpd.h), a warning is issued and **ap_daemons_limit** is reset to the **HARD_SERVER_LIMIT**.

set_max_requests

2478: This function sets the maximum number of requests that an Apache child process can service before being killed and replaced with a new child process. This is done to prevent possible memory leaks from using excessive server resources over time. The global variable **ap_max_requests_per_child** is set to the value of the **arg** parameter on line 2487.

set_threads

2491: The number of threads allowed per child process, as defined by the **ThreadsPerChild** directive, is set.

2499: Sets the global variable **ap_threads_per_child** to the value of the **arg** parameter. If the value is greater than the **HARD_SERVER_LIMIT**, however, a warning is issued and the **ap_threads_per_child** variable is reset to the **HARD_SERVER_LIMIT**.

set_excess_requests

2521: This function sets the number of requests that a child process can service in excess of the value set by a **MaxChildRequests** directive. This value is used when a keepalive connection is making requests to an existing child process that would otherwise be scheduled to terminate. The **ExcessRequestsPerChild** directive controls the value of the **ap_excess_requests_per_child** global variable, which is set on line 2530.

set_rlimit

2538: Sets resource limits for time, memory, and number of processes, as defined by the

RlimitCPU, **RlimitMEM**, and **RlimitNPROC** directives, respectively.

no_set_limit

2605: This function is called by the functions specific to CPU time (**set_limit_cpu**), memory (**set_limit_mem**), or number of processes (**set_limit_nproc**).

2609: For platforms on which the **Rlimit** directives are not supported, this function logs an error stating that fact.

set_limit_cpu

2618: Sets a limit on the CPU time used by Apache processes using the **RlimitCPU** directive by calling the **set_rlimit** function with the **limit_cpu** field of the current directory configuration record.

set_limit_mem

2630: Sets a limit on the memory used by Apache processes using the **RlimitMEM** directive by calling the **set_rlimit** function with the **limit_mem** field of the current directory configuration record. Three different functions are used, depending on the compiler defines that are set, based on the type of memory used by the platform on which Apache is running.

set_limit_nproc

2649: Sets a limit on the number of CPU processes used by Apache, according to the value of the **RlimitNPROC** directive, by calling the **set_rlimit** function with the **limit_nproc** field of the current directory configuration record.

set_bind_address

2659: Sets the IP address that Apache should bind to, as defined by the **BindAddress** directive. The global variable **ap_bind_address.s_addr** is set on line 2668 with the value returned by the **ap_get_virthost_addr** call (using the **arg** parameter as the value to look up in the virtual host table).

set_listener

2673: Sets the port (or the IP address and port, if applicable) that Apache should listen to for incoming requests. This is determined by the **Listen** directive.

2686: Checks whether an IP address is included in the **ips** parameter.

2697: Sets the global **ports** variable to the **ips** parameter.

set_listenbacklog

2721: Sets the maximum number of backed-up connections to listen for, as defined by the **ListenBacklog** directive. This value is placed in the **ap_listenbacklog** global variable on line 2737.

set_coredumpdir

2741: Uses the **CoreDumpDirectory** directive to define the directory on the Apache server where a core dump file should be written in case of an ungraceful exit. The **arg** parameter is converted to a path relative to the server root on line 2751, then copied into the **ap_coredump_dir** variable on line 2759.

include_config

2764: Processes an additional configuration file that was included with an **Include** directive within a configuration file.

2767: The **name** parameter is converted into a path that is relative to the server root by calling **ap_server_root_relative**.

2769: The included configuration file is processed by (recursively) calling **ap_process_resource_config** with the name parameter as the path and file name of the file to process.

set_loglevel

2775: Sets the **log_level** field of the current server configuration by parsing the word included with the **LogLevel** directive and comparing it with a set of possible values (such as **emerg**, **error**,

debug, and so forth). Eight levels are defined, with each increasing the number of messages that will be logged as Apache processes requests. If none of the eight strings is found, an error message is returned.

ap_psignature

2823: This API function returns the server's signature.

2836: The port that this Apache server listens to is placed in the **sport** variable.

2839: A server signature string is assembled and returned, either with an email address or without, based on the value of the **server_signature** field of the configuration record.

set_authname

2860: Loads an authorization name into the current realm, setting the **ap_auth_name** field of the directory configuration to the value of the **wordl** parameter.

set_serv_tokens

2894: Handles a request to include the server's operating system platform in the **Server** header that is returned to a client. This is defined by the **ServerTokens** directive. The **ap_server_tokens** global variable is set to a value that includes the operating system and minimal or full information, depending on the value provided with the directive.

set_limit_req_line

2916: Sets a limit on the length of an HTTP line to avoid overflow problems with incoming requests. This value is defined by the **LimitRequestLine** directive.

2926: Sets the **lim** variable to the integer value of the **arg** parameter. This value is tested to determine if it is negative or greater than the **DEFAULT_LIMIT_REQUEST_LINE** defined in httpd.h. If either is the case, an error is returned; otherwise, the **limit_req_line** field of the server configuration record is set to the value of **lim**.

set_limit_req_fieldsize

2945: Sets a limit on the total size of each HTTP header field that arrives with a request to avoid overflow problems with incoming requests. The value is defined by the **LimitRequestFieldSize** directive.

2956: Sets the **lim** variable to the integer value of the **arg** parameter. This value is tested on lines 2957 and 2964 to determine if it is negative or greater than the **DEFAULT_LIMIT_REQUEST_FIELDSIZE** defined in httpd.h. If either is the case, an error is returned; otherwise, the **limit_req_fieldsize** field of the server configuration record is set to the value of **lim**.

set_limit_req_fields

2975: Sets a limit on the total number of HTTP header lines that a request can include to avoid overflow problems with incoming requests. This value is defined by the **LimitRequestFields** directive.

2985: Sets the **lim** variable to the integer value of the **arg** parameter. This value is tested on line 2986 to determine if it is negative. If so, an error is returned; otherwise, the **limit_req_fields** field of the server configuration record is set to the value of **lim** on line 2993.

set_limit_req_body

2997: Sets a limit on the total number of bytes that a request body (after the HTTP headers) can include to avoid overflow problems, usually from a denial-of-service attack on the Apache server. This value is defined by the **LimitRequestBody** directive.

3013: Sets the value of the **limit_req_body** of the configuration record to the numeric value of the **arg** parameter.

set_interpreter_source

3019: When Apache is running on Windows, this function processes the **ScriptInterpreterSource** directive to determine how scripts are to be executed or run.

3023: Sets the **script_interpreter_source** field of the directory configuration record to indicate that the Windows Registry or the included script pathname (starting with **#!**) should be used to run scripts. The default assumes that the directive provides a **SHEBANG** string to reach a command interpreter.

core_cmds

3043: Defines how to process directives that must or may be global (not in a container such as **<Directory>** or **<VirtualHost>**). This structure includes the function to call to process the directive, flags indicating the type of argument that must be included with the directive in the configuration file, and a line of instructions to be logged as an error if the directive does not conform to the accepted syntax. This structure includes 86 entries; those wishing to learn about Apache's capabilities will be rewarded for reviewing it.

core_translate

3378: Performs file name translation as needed before processing a request. This function is defined for the file name translation phase of the core module (line 3672).

3381: Retrieves the server configuration record by calling **ap_get_module_config** (defined in http_config.c).

3384: If this is a proxy request, **HTTP_FORBIDDEN** is returned because proxy requests should not reach this stage of processing.

3387: Tests the **uri** field for spurious characters that indicate a bad request.

3393: The strings in the path and file name fields (through line 3422) are standardized.

mmap_cleanup

3435: Attempts to clean up (free) memory used by a memory-mapped file. The **munmap** function is called on line 3439 to do this. If this function is

unsuccessful, an error is logged indicating that the memory was not freed.

default_handler

3458: Handles requests that did not have other handler types specified (by an **AddHandler** directive, for example).

3473: If a request body is included, it is read and discarded by calling **ap_discard_request_body**. The request body would be used for a request using the **PUT** or **POST** method, but these are not handled by this handler.

3477: Tests that the request is using the HTTP method **GET** or **OPTIONS**. If not, an error is logged on line 3480.

3486: If the method used is **OPTIONS**, **ap_send_http_options** is called to return the requested information.

3493: Checks that the requested file exists by testing the **finfo.st_mode** field of the request.

3518: Opens the requested file using **ap_pfopen**.

3528: Updates the **finfo.st_mtime** field of the request by calling **ap_update_mtime** and **ap_set_last_modified**.

3531: Sets an outgoing header indicating the number of bytes that will be sent.

3546: If memory-mapped files are being used by this server, **mmap** is called to attempt to get the requested file.

3563: Sets the **Content-MD5** header by calling **ap_md5digest** if the **content_md5** field of the configuration record is set.

3582: Sends the headers for this request by calling **ap_send_http_header** (defined in http_protocol.c).

3584: If the **header_only** flag is set, the function continues on line 3649; otherwise, preparations to send the requested file begin.

3590: Loops to send each piece of the requested file. **fseek** is called on line 3595, then **ap_send_fd_length** is called on line 3603 to send a portion of the file to the client.

3609: If memory-mapped files are used on this server, space is allocated for the memory-mapped file on line 3614, a cleanup is registered for that memory on line 3617, and the memory-mapped file is sent using **ap_send_mmap**, which is called on line 3636.

core_handlers

3653: Defines a structure with handlers to use for the core module. The only handler used is the **default_handler**.

core_module

3659: Defines the core module, with functions to create and merge directory and server configuration records and handle file name translation. Configuration directives are handled by referencing the table pointed to by **core_cmds** (line 3670); the default request handler is referenced by the structure **core_handlers** (line 3671).

Discussion Of **http_main**

This file includes a collection of functions used to start up and initialize Apache. Routines to start and manage child processes to handle client requests are included, as well as the management of memory allocation, processing signals between running copies of Apache, and the scoreboard where the status of each copy of Apache is maintained.

Several compiler **define** statements in **http_main** divide the code into nonthreaded and multithreaded functions. This distinction can be confusing, because several functions have similar or identical names, or appear to perform the same tasks.

Code in **http_main** initializes many server information fields (global variables that define how Apache acts), though the majority of these are set in **http_core** based on directives in the configuration files.

Additional files not described here, such as the httpd.h header file, contain definitions of constants and other information worth reviewing.

reset_version

4002:   Changes the **version_locked** flag so that the Apache version string can be updated as needed. The **server_version** string is set to NULL on line 4006 so that it will be updated.

ap_get_server_version

4009:   This API call returns the version of Apache as set in the **server_version** variable by the function **ap_set_version** on line 4051. If the **server_version** variable has not been set, the constant **SERVER_BASEVERSION** (defined in httpd.h) is returned.

ap_add_version_component

4015:   This API call configures the version string for Apache.

4018:   If the **version_locked** flag is not set, string setup continues.

4026:   If the **server_version** string is currently empty, a cleanup is registered so that this variable can be discarded when the process exits. The **server_version** string is set to the **component** string that was passed in as a parameter.

4033:   Because **server_version** is not empty, a variable cleanup has already been registered in a previous call to this function, so the **component** string is simply added to the **server_version** string.

ap_set_version

4051:   This API call sets up the version string for Apache. The **ap_add_version_component** function (line 4015) is called with the **SERVER_ BASEVERSION** string defined in httpd.h. If the value of the **ap_server_tokens** variable is **SrvTk_MIN**, the **PLATFORM** is added to the server version string.

4064:   If the **ap_server_tokens** variable is not set to **SrvTk_FULL**, the server version string is locked by setting **version_locked**. This blocks any further changes to the string until the server is reset.

chdir_for_gprof

4079:   Changes directory function for servers with **GPROF** defined.

4081:   Retrieves the server configuration into **core_ server_config**.

4094:   Sets **dir** to the relative server root by calling **ap_ server_root_relative**.

4107:   Changes the current system working directory to **dir** by calling the system function **chdir**.

clean_child_exit

4116:   This function exits a child process, cleaning up all memory that the child used.

4119:   Exits all modules used by this child process by calling **ap_child_exit_modules** (defined in http_config.c).

4120:   Destroys (releases) all memory pools used by the child process by calling **ap_destroy_pool** (defined in alloc.c).

expand_lock_fname

4128:   Fills the parameter **p** with the complete name of a file to lock. The server root is included in the complete pathname by calling **ap_server_ root_relative** on line 4132.

accept_mutex_init

4145:   Initializes the process of accepting a mutually exclusive variable (mutex) for use in multi-threaded environments.

4153:   Calls **usconfig** to check the status of the mutex. An error is logged using **perror** if the value returned is in error (line 4155, 4161, 4166, 4170, or 4175).

accept_mutex_on

4180:   Accepts a mutex lock on a variable.

4182:   Begins a **switch** statement to determine what action is requested for the mutex variable. The value checked is the result of a call to **ussetlock**.

accept_mutex_off

4195:   Accepts an unlock operation for a mutex variable. The current child process is exited by calling **clean_child_exit** on line 4199.

accept_mutex_child_cleanup

4221:   Accepts mutex variables, cleaning up their memory as a child exits. This function is intended for use on Solaris platforms.

4225:   Calls **pthread_mutex_unlock** to unlock the mutex variable.

accept_mutex_child_init

4229:   On a Solaris platform, a mutex variable is initialized by calling **ap_register_cleanup** so that, when use of the variable is completed, it is certain to be freed.

accept_mutex_cleanup

4235:   Cleans up a mutex variable using the **munmap** function, which is called on line 4238.

accept_mutex_init

4245:   Initializes a **pthread_mutexattr_t** mutex for use on Solaris systems.

4255:   Calls **mmap** to allocate and initialize a mutex variable.

4264:   Initializes the mutex by calling **pthread_ mutexattr_ init**.

4282:   Registers the mutex using **ap_register_cleanup** so that it can be cleaned up properly when it is no longer needed.

accept_mutex_on

4286:   Prepares to use a mutex variable on line 4295 by calling the **pthread_mutex_lock** function.

accept_mutex_off

4303:   Releases a mutex variable on line 4307 by calling the **pthread_mutex_unlock** function.

accept_mutex_cleanup

4362: Cleans up the memory used by a mutex variable on line 4370 by calling the **semctl** function.

accept_mutex_init

4375: Initializes a mutex variable.

4381: Sets the value **sem_id** to the return value of **semget**.

4406: Registers the memory used by this mutex variable using **ap_register_cleanup** so that it can be cleaned up when it is no longer needed.

accept_mutex_on

4418: Prepares to use a mutex variable, calling **semop** on line 4420.

accept_mutex_off

4426: Releases a mutex variable on line 4428 by calling the **semop** function.

accept_mutex_init

4446: Initializes a mutex variable for servers with **USE_FCNTL_SERIALIZED_ACCEPT** defined.

accept_mutex_on

4482: A mutex variable is prepared for use by calling the **fcntl** function on line 4486.

accept_mutex_off

4502: Releases a mutex variable by calling the **fcntl** function on line 4506.

accept_mutex_cleanup

4525: Releases (cleans up) a mutex variable on line 4527 by calling the **unlink** function to release its file name (stored in **ap_lock_fname**).

accept_mutex_child_init

4534: Initializes a mutex for a child process as the child process is spawned.

4537: Defines **lock_fd** as a file descriptor returned by **ap_popenf**.

accept_mutex_init

4551: Initializes a mutex lock by calling **unlink** to ensure that the **ap_lock_fname** value is not used. **ap_popenf** is then called on line 4555 to locate the mutex.

4563: Registers the newly initialized mutex by calling **ap_register_cleanup** so that the mutex's memory can be cleaned up at exit.

accept_mutex_on

4567: Sets up a mutex lock by calling the **flock** function on line 4571.

accept_mutex_off

4583: Clears a mutex variable by calling the **flock** on line 4585.

accept_mutex_cleanup

4597: Cleans up the memory for a mutex variable used when **USE_OS2SEM_SERIALIZED_ACCEPT** is defined for this server.

accept_mutex_child_init

4607: Initializes a mutex lock for a child process. This function is used for OS/2 serialized semaphores. Initialization is completed on line 4609 by calling the **DosOpenMutexSem** function.

accept_mutex_init

4624: Initializes a standard mutex for OS/2 semaphores on line 4626 by calling **DosCreateMutexSem**.

4637: Registers the mutex memory so that it can be cleared after use.

accept_mutex_on

4641: Requests a mutex for OS/2 semaphores on line 4643 by calling the **DosRequestMutexSem** function.

accept_mutex_off

4655: Clears an OS/2 mutex on line 4657 by calling the **DosReleaseMutexSem** function.

usage

4697: Prints a usage message showing how command line options can be used when launching Apache.

timeout

4774: Sets a timeout. Only one timeout can be active at a time. Timeouts are not supported in multithreaded environments.

4778: If the **alarms_blocked** flag is set, the **alarm_pending** flag is set and returns; otherwise, the timeout request continues to process.

ap_block_alarms

4851: This API call blocks alarms by setting the **alarms_blocked** variable, which will be checked before allowing any alarms to proceed. The **alarms_blocked** variable is incremented rather than being set to 1 to allow for tracking nested blocks.

ap_unblock_alarms

4856: This API call unblocks alarms. The **alarms_blocked** variable is decremented on line 4858. If the **alarms_blocked** value is 0 after it is decremented, the system checks for the **exit_after_unblock** flag. If it is set, **alarms_blocked** is incremented, the **exit_after_unblock** flag is reset, and the child process is cleaned up by calling **clean_child_exit** on line 4873. By decrementing the **alarms_blocked** value and then incrementing it again if **exit_after_unblock** is set, this function provides the quickest possible path for the most common case (which is that **exit_after_unblock** is not set, so this code is not reached).

4871: If the **alarm_pending** flag is set, it is reset and a timeout is issued.

alrm_handler

4890: The signal **sig** that is passed in as a parameter is set up to be handled.

ap_set_callback_and_alarm

4899: Sets up a callback for an alarm, either by calling the **alarm** system function or by recording a time in the scoreboard image for the current child process.

ap_check_alarm

4948: Used for Windows systems only, this is an Apache API call to check whether an alarm timeout has expired.

ap_reset_timeout

4974: Resets a timeout that was previously set using **ap_set_timeout**.

4980: Checks the status of the timeout by calling **ap_set_callback_and_alarm**. If the timeout has already expired, it is set back to 0 on line 4984.

ap_keepalive_timeout

4992: This API function sets up a timeout for a keepalive connection.

4999: Sets the value of **to** based on the **keep_alive_timeout** if the connection uses keepalives; otherwise, it is set to the standard server timeout on line 5002. **ap_set_callback_ and_alarm** is then called with the **to** timeout value.

ap_hard_timeout

5007: This API function defines a hard timeout that will cancel a pending action if it is not completed in the allocated time (based on the server's default timeout value).

ap_soft_timeout

5018: This API function defines a soft timeout that will cancel a pending action if it is not completed before the server timeout value is reached. The call on line 5023 to set the timeout via **ap_set_callback_and_alarm** is identical to the call in the **ap_hard_timeout** function.

ap_kill_timeout

5028: This API function cancels a timeout that was set previously (for example, using **ap_hard_timeout**). This function is used when an action has completed without being killed automatically because of a timeout.

sock_enable_linger

5072: Sets socket options on a connection to enable a lingering close, where the connection is not actually closed until the final buffered data is sent to the client and acknowledged.

5079: Calls **setsockopt** to set the appropriate options for a lingering close.

lingerout

5096: This function is a special version of timeout for use by connections that use a lingering close.

linger_timeout

5110: As with **lingerout**, this function provides timeout functionality for connections that use a lingering close.

5114: Sets a callback using **ap_set_callback_and_alarm** so that the timeout can notify this function.

lingering_close

5125: Closes a connection using a lingering close method, allowing the client to receive all buffered data first.

5136: Sets a timeout using **linger_timeout** so that even a lingering close does not linger too long.

5141: Calls **ap_bflush** to force any remaining buffered data to be written to the client.

5143: Closes the connection by calling **ap_bclose**.

5193: Reads data arriving from the client (acknowledgement of data sent by Apache).

ap_register_other_child

5210: This API call registers other Apache child processes, allocating space for a record of the additional child process on line 5217.

ap_unregister_other_child

5232: This API call removes the record of an Apache child process from the **other_children** list.

probe_writable_fds

5253: Probes to test that the writeable file descriptors can still be written to.

reap_other_child

5310: Closes child processes that are not in use.

reinit_scoreboard

5347: Reinitializes the scoreboard file in a multithreaded environment.

5356: Allocates memory for the scoreboard via a call to **memset**.

cleanup_scoreboard

5359: Frees the memory used by a scoreboard image.

5361: Existence of the scoreboard image is verified, then **free** is called on line 5362 to clear it. The **ap_scoreboard_image** is set to NULL on line 5363 to indicate that the scoreboard has been cleared.

ap_sync_scoreboard_image

5366: This API call synchronizes (updates) the scoreboard image. This is only a placeholder, however; it contains no code.

create_shared_heap

5378: Creates a shared memory space under OS/2.

get_shared_heap

5397: Uses a shared memory space under OS/2.

setup_shared_mem

5424: Sets up shared memory in a non-multithreaded environment under OS/2 to use as the scoreboard image.

reopen_scoreboard

5451: Reopens the scoreboard memory area on OS/2 platforms on line 5457 by calling **get_shared_heap** to allocate shared memory. The **ap_scoreboard_image** variable is set to the memory area on line 5466.

cleanup_shared_mem

5505: Clears shared memory that has been used as a scoreboard image by calling **shm_unlink**. See also the notes in the source code beginning on line 5474.

setup_shared_mem

5510: Prepares an area of shared memory to use as a scoreboard image in a non-multithreaded environment.

5516: Calls **shm_open** to allocate a block of shared memory, with **ap_scoreboard_fname** referring to the newly opened memory block.

5550: Sets the **ap_scoreboard_image** variable to point to the newly created memory area.

reopen_scoreboard

5554: This function is an empty placeholder for non-multithreaded environments.

setup_shared_mem

5560:   When **MMAP_SCOREBOARD** is defined, a memory-mapped scoreboard is set up.

5581:   Calls **mmap** to allocate a memory-mapped area, setting **m** to point to the area that is allocated.

5638:   Sets **ap_scoreboard_image** to the value of **m** returned by **mmap**.

reopen_scoreboard

5642:   This is an empty function when using a memory-mapped scoreboard image.

setup_shared_mem

5650:   When **USE_SHMGET_SCOREBOARD** is defined, a shared memory area for the scoreboard file is set up.

5657:   Sets **shmid** to the value returned by **shmget** as it sets up a memory area for the scoreboard.

reopen_scoreboard

5750:   This is an empty function when **USE_SHMGET_ SCOREBOARD** is defined.

force_write

5763:   Forces the writing of the scoreboard to avoid a partial write that would corrupt scoreboard statistics.

force_read

5779:   Forces a read from the scoreboard file. The **read** function is called on line 5784.

cleanup_scoreboard_file

5795:   Cleans up the scoreboard file on line 5797 by calling **unlink**.

reopen_scoreboard

5800:   Reopens the scoreboard file, updating the memory image of it.

5803:   If the scoreboard file descriptor **scoreboard_fd** shows that the scoreboard file is open, **ap_ pclosef** is called to close it.

5805:   Reopens the scoreboard file by calling **ap_ popenf**. The **scoreboard_fd** variable is set to the returned value.

reinit_scoreboard

5816:   Reinitializes the scoreboard. This function is called by a parent Apache process when the child process has a change in status initiated by the parent.

ap_sync_scoreboard_image

5868:   Updates the scoreboard image (see also the source code note beginning on line 5854).

5871:   The scoreboard image is searched for the child process whose record is being updated.

5872:   Reads the current scoreboard state for that child process by calling the **force_read** function.

ap_exists_scoreboard_image

5879:   This API call returns a **true/false** based on whether the **ap_scoreboard_image** variable refers to a valid scoreboard image.

put_scoreboard_info

5884:   Places information into the scoreboard image.

5888:   The scoreboard image is searched for the location of the current child's state.

5890:   Writes information about the state of the current child to the scoreboard image by calling **force_write**.

clean_parent_exit

5898:   After destroying the memory pool for this process on line 5902 by calling **ap_destroy_ pool**, Apache is exited with the code passed in as a parameter.

ap_update_child_status

5906:   Updates the status of a child process in the scoreboard according to the current state of the child.

5915:   Synchronizes the scoreboard image by calling **ap_sync_scoreboard_image** before updating it with the current child's state.

5916:   Sets **ss** to the scoreboard image slot for the current child.

5933:   If the current status is **SERVER_DEAD**, the fields of the scoreboard slot are cleared (through line 5937).

5971:   If the current child is starting up, information about the child process is recorded in the scoreboard slot.

5975:   If a scoreboard file is used for this copy of Apache, the scoreboard slot is corrected with **lseek** and information about the current child is written on line 5977 by calling **force_write**.

5982:   Calls **put_scoreboard_info** to finalize the updated scoreboard information for the current child.

update_scoreboard_global

5987:   Updates global (non-child-specific) information in the scoreboard.

5990:   The correct place in the scoreboard file (if one is used on this server) is located and **force_ write** is used on line 5993 to write the global scoreboard information.

ap_time_process_request

5999:   Calculates the time used to fulfill a request, writing the information to the scoreboard image in the slot of the current child process.

6010:   Sets **ss** to the correct slot in the scoreboard image.

6019:   **gettimeofday** is used to set a start time for the activity current child process.

6030:   When the status has changed to a completed operation, the stop time of the operation is calculated and **put_scoreboard_info** is called on line 6043 to update the scoreboard image.

increment_counts

6046:   Increments the statistics for a child process, noting bytes sent and related data and recording the information in the scoreboard image with a call on line 6068 to **put_scoreboard_info**.

find_child_by_pid

6071:   Locates a child process by using the process ID passed in as a parameter.

6075:   Loops through all possible scoreboard image slots. When the matching PID is found, the index for that slot is returned.

reclaim_child_processes

6082:   Handles child processes that need to exit but have not.

6096:   Loops to try repeatedly to close the child process.

6135:   If the child process is still active, the kill function is used to send a **SIGHUP** signal. If this is not successful, a **SIGTERM** signal is sent on line 6150. Finally, a **SIGKILL** signal is sent on line 6159.

reap_children

6216:   This function searches the scoreboard for child processes that have been erroneously closed or abandoned and officially closes them.

6220:   Loops through the maximum possible number of child processes (**max_daemons_limit**), checking the scoreboard file by querying the status field of **ap_scoreboard_image**. Line 6224 attempts to kill child processes that are marked as **SERVER_DEAD** but still appear to be active processes.

wait_or_timeout

6249:   After an interval (usually while another child process finishes handling a request), the scoreboard file is updated to show that the child process is waiting. Different procedures are used in this function for Windows NT and other platforms.

Define signals

6325:   Defines the number of signals to use as **NumSIG**, based on the **NSIG** value. If this value is not available, **NumSIG** is set to 32 on line 6332.

6336:   If the current platform includes a signal list, nothing more must be done to define it; other-

wise, the **siglist_init** function is defined as **INIT_SIGLIST** on line 6340.

ap_sys_siglist

6344:   Defines the signals list for the current platform. For each of the signals defined for this platform (based on the header files found, with an **#ifdef** check for each one), a value in the **ap_sys_siglist** array is defined, where the signal number is the array index and the text description of the signal is the value of that array element. This list to set the array values continues through line 6450.

6451:   Loops through the **ap_sys_siglist** array. Any signals that have NULL as a key have their value set to an empty string.

sig_coredump

6460:   Handles a core dump request because of a serious problem running Apache.

6462:   Changes to the directory **ap_coredump_dir** are made so that the core dump file can be written to the correct location.

6463:   Sends a **SIG_DFL** signal to the current process.

6465:   If Apache is running on Windows NT, the current process is stopped by a call to **kill**; otherwise, the signal to core dump is elevated on line 6467 by calling **raise** so that the signal will be processed when this function exits.

just_die

6484:   A signal is sent to the current child process to exit (die) immediately.

6489:   If signals are currently blocked because of a call to **ap_block_alarms**, the **exit_after_unblock** flag is set on line 6490 so that the exit can proceed after a call to **ap_unblock_alarms** (in the function where alarms were blocked).

6493:   If alarms are not blocked, the exit process is started with a call to **clean_child_exit**.

usr1_handler

6500:   Checks the state of the **usr1_just_die** flag, calling **just_die** to exit the current process if

usr1_just_die is set or setting the **deferred_die** flag if it is not set.

signal_parent

6549:   If Apache is running on Windows NT, this function is used by a child process to signal the parent process to shut down or restart.

6564:   If the **one_process** flag is set, no parent process is present, so **signal_parent** returns immediately.

6568:   Based on the **type** of signal passed in as a parameter, the **signal_name** is set to either a shut down or a restart signal. If the **type** is not 0 or 1, the function returns without any action on line 6571.

6574:   Records the action about to take place using the **APD2** function.

6577:   Uses the Windows **OpenEvent** function to signal the parent with the **signal_name**. If the value returned by **OpenEvent** indicates an error, the error is logged on line 6584.

6589:   Sets the signal event for the parent process by calling **SetEvent**. If it does not return 0, an error is logged on line 6591.

6594:   The event handle **e** is closed on either line 6594 or 6597, depending on whether an error was generated by **SetEvent**.

ap_start_shutdown

6616:   Initiates a shutdown of Apache on any platform without relying exclusively on signals.

6619:   If the **shutdown_pending** flag is already set, the function assumes that it has been called previously and a shutdown is in progress. **ap_start_shutdown** returns without action. If it was not set, the **shutdown_pending** flag is set to 1 on line 6626.

6628:   For non-Windows platforms, the **signal_parent** function is called to wake up the parent process to watch for signals.

ap_start_restart

6634: Attempts to restart the current Apache server process.

6637: For Windows platforms, if the **restart_pending** flag is set, the function assumes a restart is already in progress and returns without further action; otherwise, **restart_pending** is set to 1 and the **is_graceful** variable is set to the **graceful** value that was passed in as a function parameter.

6645: For non-Windows platforms, the parent process is signaled by calling **signal_parent** with the value of 1. (The **graceful** parameter is not used.)

sig_term

6650: Initiates the shutdown process by calling **ap_start_shutdown** (line 6616).

restart

6655: Initiates a restart of Apache by calling the **ap_start_restart** function (line 6634) with a value of 1 for Unix or the **SIGUSR1** signal for Windows, if it's available.

set_signals

6664: Sets up signal actions to communicate between Apache processes. These actions and signals are stored in the **sa.sa_handler** variable for signals that have been defined for the current platform.

6672: If the **one_process** flag is set, none of the signals are set, because only one Apache process will be running.

6679: Based on the signals defined for the current platform, **sigaction** is called repeatedly to set up signal actions. If **sigaction** returns a negative value, an error is logged using **ap_log_error**. This section continues through line 6743.

6745: If the **one_process** flag is not set, the signal function is called with each of the defined signals.

detach

6787: Unless Apache is running on a platform where a child process cannot continue if the parent

process dies (see line 6794), the current process is detached from its parent process.

set_group_privs

6871: Sets the group that Apache runs as (for Unix systems only).

init_suexec:

6936: Initializes the **Set User ID** execution mode for servers running with the **suExec** wrapper.

new_connection

6957: Sets up a valid data structure for a newly established network connection.

6971: Initializes the fields of the **conn** structure. The variables passed in as parameters—as well as the call on line 6976 to **ap_update_vhost_given_ip** and on line 6982 to **inet_ntoa**—are used to define the fields of **conn**.

sock_disable_nagle

6988: Turns off the Nagle algorithm to prevent persistent network connections that are waiting for more data from causing performance degradation. The algorithm is disabled on line 7004 by calling **setsockopt**.

make_sock

7017: Makes a new socket structure based on the socket address passed in as a parameter to this function.

7025: Assembles the socket information string.

7036: After blocking signals for a moment, **socket** is called to establish the new socket. Signals are allowed again via **ap_unblock_alarms** on line 7041. Several compiler **define** statements are then used to set up socket options based on the platform on which Apache is running. These options prevent networking problems or improve performance.

7150: Attempts to bind the socket to the **addr** field assembled beginning on line 7025.

7167: Tests whether the socket prepared thus far can be listened to for connections.

copy_listeners

7221: Duplicates listening on a socket connection.

find_listener

7247: Locates a listener in the linked list passed in as a parameter.

close_unused_listeners

7262: Closes listeners in the linked list that are not being used. Each one is removed and its memory freed on line 7270.

setup_listeners

7278: Opens a series of sockets and updates the listeners list into a circular linked list.

7287: Finds a single listener by calling **find_listener**. A socket for that listener is made on line 7289 by calling **make_sock**.

7305: Inserts the listener into the circular linked list.

find_ready_listener

7330: Locates one of the listener sockets that is ready for an **accept** to begin processing a connection from a client.

AMCSocketInitialize

7350: Initializes a socket connection.

AMCSocketCleanup

7384: Cleans up a socket connection on line 7387 by calling **WSACleanup**.

show_compile_settings

7392: Prints information about the current copy of Apache to standard output using **printf** functions.

7394: Prints the server version, date built, and module information.

7401: Prints a list of options that this copy of Apache was compiled with. Each of the possible items to print is tested by checking whether it is defined in the current compilation. Any item that is defined will generate a **printf** statement that prints the options when the compilation settings are requested. This list continues through line 7529.

common_init

7538: Initializes a few items that are needed to begin running Apache.

7540: Initializes the signals list as defined beginning on line 6325.

7547: If Apache is running on Windows, sockets are initialized by calling **AMCSocketInitialize**.

7550: Allocates space for the variables **pconf** and **ptrans**.

7553: Initializes Apache by calling **ap_util_init** and **ap_util_uri_init**.

7556: Sets up the **pcommands** by allocating a memory pool. An array is then defined to hold the **ap_server_pre_read_config**, **ap_server_post_read_config**, and **ap_server_config_defines** information.

ap_child_terminate

7579: This API call ends the current Apache child process. The **keepalive** field is set to 0. The **requests_this_child** and the **ap_max_requests_per_child** variables are both set to 1 so that the child process is flagged for termination. This is the first function in a large section defined for non-multithreaded platforms (all except Windows NT at this point). The **define** statement for non-multithreading ends on line 8932, where the multithreaded functions begin.

child_main

7585: This is the main request-handling function for Apache child processes (the initial process that manages child process spawning does not handle browser requests).

7604: Blocks signals by calling **ap_block_alarms** so that initialization can be completed.

7653: Initializes modules for this child process by calling **ap_child_init_modules**.

7656: Allows signals by calling **ap_unblock_alarms** now that initialization is complete.

7682: Loops endlessly (until a signal kills this process), reading and processing requests.

7756: Calls **find_ready_listener** to find a request to process.

7775: Accepts the incoming request.

7952: Establishes the connection with **new_connection**.

7964: Loops to read and process each incoming request on this connection (if keepalives are in use). The incoming request is processed on line 7978 using **ap_process_request**.

make_child

8044: Spawns a single Apache child process, updating the scoreboard file and checking for system resource constraints.

startup_children

8139: Starts a number of Apache child processes (**number_to_start**). The scoreboard file is updated for each one and the child process created by the call on line 8150 to **make_child**.

perform_idle_server_maintenance

8171: Performs tasks when an Apache child process is not being used to process requests. This may involve killing off child processes if too many idle processes are running.

8191: Synchronizes the scoreboard file by calling **ap_sync_scoreboard_image**.

8258: If the number of idle servers computed from the scoreboard file is greater than the number allowed by **ap_daemons_max_free**, a child process is killed on line 8264.

8308: Based on the **idle_spawn_rate**, a new Apache child process is started by calling **make_child** to reach the requested number of running servers (even if they are idle at the moment).

process_child_status

8329: Processes the status of a child process, updating the scoreboard file accordingly.

standalone_main

8395: This function is called by **REALMAIN** to handle spawning child Apache processes.

8407: If the **one_process** variable is set, **detach** is called. No other action is necessary.

8431: Retrieves the server configuration into **server_conf** and sets up listening on line 8433 using **setup_listeners**.

8434: Opens the log files by calling **ap_open_logs** and logs the process ID for the current process.

8443: Initializes the scoreboard file for the current process's information by calling **reinit_scoreboard**.

8454: Sets up the signal names used to signal Apache child processes to restart or shutdown by calling **set_signals**.

8478: Starts child Apache processes. The number to start is held in **remaining_children_to_start**.

8484: If the system is struggling to keep up, a pause occurs before child processes are spawned in exponential fashion (first two, then four, then eight, and so forth until the number needed is reached).

8517: Resynchronizes the scoreboard file by calling **ap_sync_scoreboard_image**.

8531: Restarts a single child process to replace one that ended because of reaching the maximum requests per-child limit.

8537: Closes a child process that needs to be killed by calling **reap_other_child**.

8567: The number of child processes needed has not been reached, so **startup_children** is called to attempt to have them all started.

8589: If a shutdown signal is pending, all child processes are told to shut down by calling **reclaim_child_processes**.

8612: Sends signals to restart (**SIGHUP** and **SIGUSR1**).

8615: If the **one_process** flag is set, **clean_parent_ exit** is called, because no child processes are to be spawned.

8628: Updates the scoreboard file for all child processes.

REALMAIN

8684: The real main function that manages child processes begins and starts processing requests through them.

8708: Performs common initialization tasks by calling **common_init**.

8717: Sets the **ap_server_root** to the value of the **HTTPD_ROOT** environment variable.

8722: Sets up prelinked (non-DSO) modules by calling **ap_setup_prelinked_modules**.

8725: Loops to handle all command line options included when Apache was started.

8732: Begins a **switch** statement to handle all command line options. Available options are printed using the usage function if a **?** or **h** argument is found.

8820: Performs initialization steps: opening log files, setting the Apache version string, and initializing all modules (including DSO modules).

8824: Begins handing requests by calling **STANDALONE_MAIN**.

8907: Sets the port to listen to in the server configuration **server_conf**.

8912: Establishes a new connection to the port by calling **new_connection**.

8916: Loops as long as **ap_read_request** indicates that there is something to listen to.

8919: Processes the incoming request.

8927: If the connection should be terminated (no keepalive is specified), **ap_bclose** is called.

joblist

9029: Defines a structure for the list of jobs shared by the main thread and the worker threads.

globals

9039: Defines global variables used by the thread functions. These are not, however, used by the parent process.

add_job

9063: Adds an accepted socket from the list of sockets connected to clients. The list is protected by the **allowed_globals.jobmutex** variable so that multiple concurrent accesses are not allowed. This is the first function in a large section of code devoted to multithreaded operation. See also the comments in the source code beginning on line 8935.

9067: Checks the validity of the **jobmutex** field to determine if it can be used by the current thread. The mutex is then acquired on line 9070 and a new job (**new_job**) is allocated and initialized beginning on line 9071.

9078: Adds the **new_job** to the **allowed_globals** linked list of jobs. The semaphore and mutex are then released on lines 9084 and 9085.

remove_job

9088: Removes an accepted socket from the list of sockets connected to clients.

9093: If ungraceful restarts are defined for this server, the **WaitForMultipleObjects** function is called on line 9100 to attempt to get control of the mutex so that it can be released.

9102: Attempts to get control of the job via **ap_assert**. If it cannot, the **APD1** function is called and the function returns with a −1 error code on line 9106.

9110: For servers without ungraceful restarts, the semaphore for the current job is retrieved by calling **acquire_semaphore**.

9112: Checks the job's mutex by calling **ap_assert**, then acquires the mutex on line 9117.

9121: Releases the job by calling **ap_release_mutex** on this line or line 9129, depending on the state of the ungraceful restart definition.

9131: Frees up the job memory and return the socket value (**sock**) to the calling function.

child_sub_main

9159: This is the main function to handle worker threads in a multithreaded environment. After waiting for an available job, all requests on that connection are handled, then **remove_job** is called to clear it. See also the comments in the source code beginning on line 9136.

9197: Initializes this child thread by calling **ap_set_ callback_and_alarm**.

9214: Gets a job to process by calling **remove_job**, which returns with a socket number when it becomes available.

9228: Prepares socket information on line 9228 by calling **getsockname** and on line 9234 by calling **getpeername**.

9241: Disables the Nagle algorithm by calling **sock_ disable_nagle** with the **csd** socket number. This prevents performance hits on the network.

9259: Creates a connection by calling **new_ connection** with the socket number (now in **ptrans**) and the server configuration.

9271: Loops to read all requests on the current connection using **ap_read_request**, processing each one. When no requests remain, the connection is terminated.

9276: If the status field of the request is **HTTP_OK**, the request is processed on line 9277 by calling

ap_process_request. This API call uses all applicable module and returned data to the client.

9282: If the connection should be ended because it is not a keepalive connection or an abort has been signaled, the current **while** loop is exited.

9291: Updates the server scoreboard file by calling **ap_sync_scoreboard_image**.

9300: Having exited the **while** loop for a connection, the connection is prepared for closure by calling **ap_kill_cleanups_for_socket**, then on line 9303 calling **ap_bclose**.

9310: If possible—based on the client's connection status—the **lingering_close** call is used to avoid cutting off the connection until the client has finished receiving all buffered data and returns an acknowledgement of it.

child_main

9324: This function is used solely to provide a midpoint jump to reach the **child_sub_main** function. This avoids problems with the **longjump** needed when aborting a request.

cleanup_thread

9338: Cleans up variables used by a thread.

9343: Frees up the thread variables by calling **free_thread**, then loops through all thread handles to remove the reference to the freed thread.

wait_for_many_objects

9360: Permits Windows NT to wait for more than 64 objects. This function assists or replaces a call to **WaitForMultipleObjects**, which is limited to 64 objects.

9377: Loops many times, calling **WaitForMultipleObjects** on line 9379.

main_control_server

9401: This is the main executive function, which is defined as an external function here. It is located in the file hellop.c.

setup_signal_names

9421: Initializes the signal names for use in a multithreaded environment.

9423: Assembles the **signal_name_prefix**, **signal_shutdown_name**, and **signal_restart_name** using **ap_snprintf**. APD2 is called with the **signal_name_prefix** on line 9432.

worker_main

9442: This is the main control function for a child process. It manages the controlling thread, with the **child_sub_main** function processing individual connections.

9481: If the **one_process** flag is set, this function is exited by calling **detach**.

9504: Calls **WaitForMultipleObjects** to enter a waiting loop for a turn to check the incoming socket for a connection that needs to be handled.

9519: An exit was signaled, so the current memory pool is destroyed, the scoreboard is cleaned up from any residue of this thread, and an exit occurs on line 9521.

9526: A turn was established on the socket. **setup_listeners** is called to get ready to take control of the next incoming connection.

9562: Allocates threads to handle the incoming requests.

9623: Calls **ap_select** to listen to the socket for a connection.

9675: Accepts the socket for processing by calling **accept**.

9698: Adds the current job to the work to be done by calling **add_job**.

9708: Having set up the job, the mutex is released by calling **ap_release_mutex**.

9723: Loops to wait for many threads (potentially more than 64) by calling the function **wait_for_many_objects** on line 9724. For any thread that

has completed (determined on line 9727 by checking the **WAIT_TIMEOUT** flag), **cleanup_thread** is called on line 9730.

9738: Loops to kill any remaining worker threads that were not cleaned up in the last **while** loop (line 9730). For any that remain, **kill_thread** is called on line 9739 and then **free_thread** is called on line 9741.

create_event_and_spawn

9781: Creates a child Apache process, watching for requests to handle, and exiting when signaled.

9801: Creates an event that can be used to signal this child process to end when appropriate.

9811: Sets up arguments for this child process, assembling them in the **argv** variable.

9833: Spawns a child process by calling **spawnv**, including the **argv** arguments.

cleanup_process

9858: Cleans up child process variables.

9864: Calls **CloseHandle** for both handles and events, then loops on line 9869 to remove the closed handle and event from the array.

create_process

9880: Creates a new child process.

9888: Spawns the child process by calling **create_event_and_spawn**, assigning the handle to **child_handle**, which is placed in the **handles** array on line 9893.

master_main

9905: Manages all Apache processes, spawning new child processes as needed.

9965: Creates an initial mutex to begin processing requests.

9969: Loops until no more processes need to be created to handle incoming request (based on the limits defined for this server). The **create_process** function is called on line 9971 to start each new process.

9990: Prepares to handle requests through child processes by reading the server configuration with **ap_read_config**, opening the log files on line 9992 with **ap_open_logs**, setting the version number on line 9993, and initializing the modules for this server on line 9994 with **ap_init_modules**.

10002: Continues looping until an error or exit signal breaks out of the loop.

10015: Creates new processes until the **processes_to_create** on line 10022 is 0.

10089: For a pending shutdown, process variables are cleaned up by calling **cleanup_process**.

10109: For a pending shutdown, all child processes are signaled to shut down as well.

10182: The shutdown process is not proceeding well. Processes are closed by calling **Terminate-Process**.

10205: The mutex acquired initially for this process (line 9965) is destroyed.

send_signal

10216: This function is used to send signals to running Apache processes.

10224: Acquires the process ID of the process that should be signaled.

10249: Sets up the signal names to signal the process.

10252: If the signal is to shut down, **ap_start_shutdown** is called.

10254: If the signal is to restart, **ap_start_restart** is called. Other signals are ignored in this function.

apache_main

10265: This is the main control function for the server. If running on Windows, the function is named **apache_main** and exported via **dllexport**. If running on other platforms, this function is called **REALMAIN** (line 10267).

10279: Initializes common variables by calling **common_init**.

10311: Sets up prelinked (non-DSO) modules by calling **ap_setup_prelinked_modules**.

10313: Loops to process each command line option that was included when Apache was started. Some of these print a message and exit.

10316: Begins a **switch** statement to handle each supported Apache command line option.

10404: Reads the server configuration into **server_conf**.

10420: Sets the version string for Apache using **ap_set_version**. All modules are initialized on line 10421 by calling **ap_init_modules**. Log files are opened on line 10425 with **ap_open_logs**.

10441: Begins processing requests by acquiring a mutex using **ap_create_mutex**. **worker_main** is called as the top-level worker thread on line 10450, then the mutex is destroyed on line 10451. An exit occurs with an **exit_event** on line 10452.

10455: For nonthreaded environments, **service_main** is called to handle requests and spawn additional Apache processes as needed.

ap_main

10476: The **ap_main** function is defined externally so that it can be called for non-multithreaded environments.

main

10478: Calls **ap_main** to get everything started.

main

10521: This is the main function for standalone, non-multithreaded environments.

10536: Loops to parse command line options, but only the **R** option is acted on at this point (line 10556).

10604: Having set up shared memory information, a call is executed to **execve** to start the shared core executable.

Discussion Of **http_log**

The **http_log** file contains functions that are used to log errors or other messages that occur as Apache works. Messages may be sent to these functions as soon as Apache is launched (see, for example, line 8848 within the **REALMAIN** function). Error logs can include the system log, log files specified in Apache directives, the standard error (**STDERR**), or regular **printf** statements. The functions in **http_log** handle all of these possibilities.

facilities

10634: Defines a data structure that includes references to the different types of logs that may be available on the system on which Apache is running. These include logs such as the FTP, mail, lpr, and standard system logs.

priorities

10697: Sets up a structure containing the different log levels, from **emerg** (in which almost nothing is logged) to **debug** (in which every possible piece of information is logged).

error_log_child

10709: Sets up a child process used to store error log entries when the configured location of the error log begins with a pipe symbol (|).

10719: Calls **ap_cleanup_for_exec** to prepare Apache to start a child process.

10722: Sends a signal to begin spawning the child process. Different platforms use various commands to start the child process. These are chosen by compiler **define** statements.

open_error_log

10741: Opens the error log file in preparation for logging errors during Apache processing.

10745: If the file name of the error log (**error_fname**) begins with a pipe symbol (|), **ap_spawn_child** is called on line 10748 to start the process on the other end of the pipe.

10769: If system logs are used on this platform and the file name indicated is **syslog**, the **openlog** system call is used.

10784: If the system log is not specified or not available on this platform, **ap_pfopen** is called on line 10786 to open the log file for appended writing.

ap_open_logs

10796: Opens the various error logs defined in the Apache configuration.

10826: Loops through all of the virtual server configurations, calling the **open_error_log** function on line 10835 for the log files defined in each server configuration.

10840: If a virtual server does not indicate an error log, the **error_log** field is set for that server configuration to refer to the **error_log** field of the main (default) server.

ap_error_log2stderr

10844: This API function logs an error to the system's standard error (**STDERR**) using a call on line 10847 to **dup2**.

log_error_core

10850: Logs an error message passed in to this function as the parameter line with log level **level**. This function is called by several higher level logging functions that prepare the text to be logged.

10870: Sets **logf** either to **stderr** or to the file name of the log file on line 10881.

10894: If **logf** is valid, the string to be logged into **errstr** is assembled.

10906: Tests whether the level of logging defined for this server (**APLOG_LEVELMASK**) permits the current level of message to be logged.

11008: If the **logf** file descriptor is still valid after checking several platform-dependent items, the **errstr** error message is written using either **fputs** and **fputs** (lines 11009 and 11010) or a system call to **syslog** (line 11015).

ap_log_error

11020: This API call logs an error. This function is called throughout the Apache source code to log an error that has occurred in processing.

11027: Calls the **log_error_core** function to log the error message to the correct location if the log level specifies that messages at this level are to be logged.

ap_log_rerror

11031: This API call logs request errors.

11038: Calls **log_error_core** to log the error line to the appropriate location.

11049: For errors at the level of **WARNING** or higher in the **priorities** structure (line 10697), the error is placed in the **notes** field of the request record on line 11051.

ap_log_pid

11057: Logs the process ID number of the current Apache process to the **PIDFile**.

11067: Converts the name of the log file to be relative to the server root.

11068: Retrieves the PID for the current process. If a valid value is not returned, an error is logged on line 11078.

11087: Attempts to open the **PIDfile**.

11094: Writes the PID to the **PIDfile**, and then closes the file on line 11095.

ap_log_error_old

11099: This API call immediately calls **ap_log_error** with the appropriate parameters. This function does not include log levels in the parameters, so default log levels are included when passing the information to **ap_log_error**.

ap_log_unixerr

11105: This API call immediately calls the **ap_log_error** function on line 11109 with a predefined log level and the message text that is passed in to **ap_log_unixerr**.

ap_log_printf

11112: This API call logs a message using **log_error_core** directly, rather than calling **ap_log_error**. A default log level is provided in the call to **log_error_core**; none is included in the parameters to this function.

ap_log_reason

11123: This API call uses a reason string (passed in as a parameter) to log an error using **ap_log_error** (line 11126). A default log level and complete text string are provided. The reason string is inserted into this, along with the remote hostname.

ap_log_assert

11134: This API call prints a message to the standard error output and then attempts to exit (line 11143).

piped_log_spawn

11156: Sets up a piped log by spawning the child process defined in the log configuration directive.

11160: Blocks signals while starting a child process.

11161: Starts a new process using **fork**, assigning the process ID to **pid**.

11174: Cleans up before calling the **exec** function. Appropriate signals are passed to the child process (lines 11175 and 11176), and then **execl** is called on line 11177 with the path of the program to launch (which will receive log entries via a pipe).

11192: Unblocks alarms so that signals can be received again.

11194: Calls **ap_register_other_child** so that Apache is aware of the piped log child process.

piped_log_maintenance

11200: Maintains the child process used to receive piped log entries.

11205: Starts a **switch** statement to act based on the reason passed in as a parameter.

11209: For a child process that needs to end, **ap_unregister_other_child** is called.

11224: If the child process cannot accept log entries (it cannot be written to) or a restart is requested, **kill** is called on line 11226 or line 11233 with a **SIGTERM** signal.

piped_log_cleanup

11243: Cleans up the memory from a child process used to receive piped log entries when that process has ended. **kill** is called with a **SIGTERM** signal on line 11248 if the PID for the child process appears to still be active, then the memory for the process is cleaned up on line 11250 by calling **ap_unregister_other_child** on line 11250.

piped_log_cleanup_for_exec

11256: Prepares to spawn a child process to accept piped log entries by closing any outstanding file descriptors (lines 11260 and 11261).

ap_open_piped_log

11265: This API call spawns a new child process that will receive log entries via a pipe.

11275: Calls **pipe** to open a pipe to the child process defined by the program parameter, which was assigned to the **pl** variable on line 11272.

11281: Registers the pipe using **ap_register_cleanup** so that it can be cleaned up at exit.

ap_close_piped_log

11296: This API call closes a child process that is being used to receive log entries via a pipe.

11298: Blocks signals while closing the process. Cleans up on line 11299 by calling **piped_log_cleanup** in preparation for ending a process, then kills the process on line 11299 by calling **ap_kill_cleanup** (with the **pl** variable to identify the process to clean up).

piped_log_child

11305: When the **TransferLog** directive is used with a piped log, a child process is set up. (This directive is deprecated, hence, this function duplicates the actions of other functions in this file.)

11314: Calls **ap_cleanup_for_exec** to prepare to execute a child process. The child process is started using a method appropriate to the platform on which Apache is running (as set by compiler **define** statements).

ap_open_piped_log

11337: This API call opens a piped log child process on line 11343 by calling **ap_spawn_child**. The **pl** variable is returned for use in managing the child process.

ap_close_piped_log

11359: Closes a file used as a piped log on line 11361 by calling the **ap_pfclose** function.

Chapter 5

Environment Variable Modules

This chapter describes two modules, **mod_env** and **mod_setenvif**, that are used to set or unset environment variables. These variables are used either by Common Gateway Interface (CGI) scripts that you provide on your server or by Apache internal processes to decide how to react in certain circumstances.

Both modules are used only during configuration file processing. They set up environment variables that are used as Apache runs, but they are not called to process client requests. Both are included by default in Apache.

Discussion Of mod_env

The **mod_env** module sets or unsets environment variables according to directives given in your Apache configuration files. These variables are available to any scripts or programs running on your system.

Variables can be assigned a value or simply *set*, meaning that the value is true or non-NULL; the opposite is to be unset or NULL. To set an environment variable that you wish to define and to make it available within a server or directory context (container), use the **SetEnv** directive, either with or without a value:

```
<VirtualHost 192.168.100.13>
...
SetEnv VHOST linguistics
SetEnv INTRANET
</VirtualHost>
```

A value can also be unset, meaning that, if the variable is queried, it appears not to exist or have any valid value:

```
UnsetEnv INTRANET
```

The **SetEnv** directive makes variables that you define available as part of the environment when a particular virtual host, location, or directory is effective for a request.

The **PassEnv** directive can be used to make any preexisting system environment variable available to a given server context; that is, something like **OSTYPE** might be set by the operating system on which Apache is running, but may not be available to your script unless it is made available by mentioning it with a **PassEnv** directive:

```
PassEnv OSTYPE
```

Note that a value is not defined here. The value was set by the system independent of Apache; this statement simply makes it available to server subprocesses such as scripts.

Module Structure

Because **mod_env** is only used during configuration file parsing, it includes only a few functions to handle the three directives that it deals with: **SetEnv**, **UnsetEnv**, and **PassEnv**. Each is self-contained. Because each is called whenever the corresponding directive is found, they have no particular order. One additional function, **fixup_env_module**, is used in the fixup phase starting on line 16867. This function merges any active environment information from a subrequest that is dying into a parent request that may then use the environment information. The structure of **mod_env** is illustrated in Figure 5.1.

Customization

By default, **mod_env** allows up to 50 environment variables. If you need more, change this value on line 16727. Also, the default behavior when merging configurations is that the later configuration overrides the earlier one.

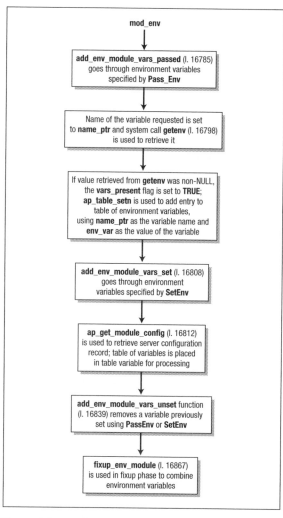

Figure 5.1   mod_env enables Apache to pass environment variables to CGI scripts and server-side includes (SSI).

This makes good sense, but may not be desirable in all cases. The **merge_env_server_configs** function (starting on line 16733) can be updated to issue warnings of conflicts or to use a set of rules that you define to determine which variable has precedence.

Various functions, such as file name translation and check user authentication, can be added at different processing stages to allow **mod_env** to set variables based on the actions of other modules, so that information is made available to scripts based on these results. This type of information could be directly set in other modules, but without relying on an update to **mod_env**. Doing so would avoid cluttering up **mod_env** with items that are more specific to something like logging or file name translation.

env_server_config_rec

16713:   The **env_server_config_rec** structure contains a list of environment variables that are available to scripts via Apache. A count of unset variables (**unsetenv**) is included, as well as a flag to mark if any variables are present in the table. (If the flag indicates that no variables are present, **mod_env** can process a request much faster.)

16719:   The module definition is forward-referenced. It begins on line 16885.

create_env_server_config

16721:   The **create_env_server_config** function establishes a server configuration record for the current server context by creating a configuration record variable and initializing its values, chiefly, that **vars_present=0** (line 16729) and **unsetenv="""** (line 16728).

merge_env_server_configs

16733:   The **merge_env_server_configs** function merges two server configuration records. In the case of environment variables, any conflicts are resolved by applying the new value in place of the old value.

16736:   Variables are created to hold the base, additive, and new values of the configuration record.

16751:   These lines (through 16759) are commented out and replaced in this release by the code from line 16761 to line 16775, which uses the **ap_copy_table** API call.

16761:   Creation of new configuration record is initiated by copying the variables from the base server configuration.

16766:   Each of the variables in the new (**add**) configuration is added using the **ap_table_setn** call. This overwrites any variable of the same name if it existed in the base configuration.

16770:   The list of unset variables from the **add** configuration is combined and placed in the **new_table** using **ap_table_unset** with **new_table** on line 16773.

16777:   The newly created table is placed in the new configuration record, **new**.

16779:   The variables in the **var_present** field of the **base** and **add** configuration records are combined into the **new** configuration record via a logical OR (using the || operator).

16782:   The **new** variable is returned as the merged configuration record.

add_env_module_vars_passed

16785:   The **add_env_module_vars_passed** function is called when a **PassEnv** directive is found. The function receives an environment variable (passed in from the directive arguments by Apache) and adds it to the current server configuration record so that the variable can be accessed by scripts and programs that Apache starts.

16789:   The current configuration record is retrieved using **ap_get_module_config**.

16792:   A separate table is set up to hold the environment variables.

16796:   All the arguments passed in with the **PassEnv** directive are parsed. For each one, the name of the variable requested is set to **name_ptr** and the system call **getenv** on line 16798 is used to retrieve it.

16799:   If the value retrieved from **getenv** was non-NULL (it existed on the system), the **vars_present** flag is set to **true** on line 16800 (because a variable is about to be added to the list, at least one variable is present). Next, **ap_table_setn** is used to add an entry to the table of environment variables, using **name_ptr** as the variable name and **env_var** as the value of the variable.

add_env_module_vars_set

16808:   The **add_env_module_vars_set** function creates new environment variables specified by the **SetEnv** directive. These are stored in the server configuration record and are then available to scripts run by Apache.

16812:   The server configuration record is retrieved by **ap_get_module_config**. The table of variables is placed in the table variable for easy processing.

16818:   The name and value of the variable defined by the **SetEnv** directive are gathered from the **args** provided using **ap_getword_conf**. The **name** field is mandatory for every defined variable; the **value** field is optional. If no value is provided, the variable is set (its value is **true** or non-NULL).

16827:   The validity of the arguments is checked before they are placed in the table. Because of the possibility of using a variable with or without a value, the **RAW_ARGS** specified on line 16859 indicates that Apache doesn't fully check the validity of the arguments before calling the current function.

16833:   Because a valid name-value pair was just placed in the configuration record, **vars_present** is set to **true** to indicate that the configuration record contains at least one environment variable. The environment variable (**name** and **value**) is placed in the configuration record's **vars** field using **ap_table_setn** on line 16834.

add_env_module_vars_unset

16839: The **add_env_module_vars_unset** function removes a variable that was set previously using **PassEnv** or **SetEnv** so that the variable is no longer available to subprocesses started by Apache.

16843: The current server configuration record is placed into **sconf**.

16846: The **unsetenv** list in **sconf** is set to a new value based on the current list of unset variables and the argument (**arg**) that was requested to be unset. This list can include several variables; all will be unset using the command on these lines.

env_module_cmds

16853: The **env_module_cmds** structure defines what functions to call when each directive handled by this module is encountered in configuration files. The three directives (**PassEnv**, **SetEnv**, and **UnsetEnv**) are defined at the start of lines 16855, 16858, and 16861. The second parameter after each directive name is the function to call for processing that directive. These are the functions that were just discussed. All three of these directives use the **RAW_ARGS** description of what the directive can contain. No real checking of what is passed in on these directive lines is done by the Apache core code. The **add_env_module_vars_set** function checks the arguments to determine if a value is included with the argument (see line 16827). Both **add_env_module_vars_passed** and **add_env_module_vars_unset** store the arguments in the configuration record without checking them. (Because the arguments are an unordered list of variable names, no checking is really possible.)

fixup_env_module

16867: The fixup phase is used in **mod_env** via the **fixup_env_module** function to combine environment variables between a subrequest and a parent request. The subrequest variables are placed in **e** on line 16869; the main request variables are placed in **vars** on line 16874 via the server configuration, which is queried on line 16872. The two sets of variables are combined on line 16880 using **ap_overlay_tables**.

env_module

16885: The module definition for **mod_env** includes functions to create and merge server configurations, the command table for directives relevant to this module, and the fixup phase. Most modules have a function defined for one of the principal phases (such as handlers, file name translation, or check user ID), but **mod_env** does not.

Discussion Of **mod_setenvif**

The **mod_setenvif** module sets an environment variable that is available to scripts and programs started by Apache. This module is similar to **mod_env**, except that **mod_setenvif** uses information from the client request to determine how to initialize the environment variable.

The headers sent with the client request, as well as several special cases such as the client's IP address (defined as **Remote_Addr**), can be specified as attributes to compare against a regular expression. If the expression matches, an environment variable is set.

The **SetEnvIf** directive is used within any configuration context to define how to set the environment variables. For example,

```
SetEnvIf Remote_Addr 192.168.100.3 USER=DAVID
```

sets the variable **USER** to the value **DAVID** if the client's host IP address is the one shown in the expression. Any client header can be used as the tested attribute, and any regular expression (with wildcard and positional testing, for example) can be used as the second parameter. The variable can be set to a value, as in this example, or simply set (the value is **true** or defined, rather than undefined).

Another directive, **SetEnvIfNoCase**, is identical to the **SetEnvIf** directive, but operates without regard to case when making comparisons between the attribute and the test expression. Two other directives, **BrowserMatch** and **BrowserMatchNoCase**, are special cases of **SetEnvIf** and are still provided for backward compatibility. Both test the **User-Agent** header and allow you to set certain environment variables based on the browser being used.

Several internal environment variables are defined for use with **BrowserMatch**. These affect how Apache responds to a request. For example, setting the variable **force-response-1.0** causes the reply to a request to use HTTP/1.0.

Module Structure

Like **mod_env**, **mod_setenvif** is only used during configuration file parsing. It includes one core function to process the directives: **add_setenvif_core**, which starts on line 34304. Other functions are called to parse the various directives used for this module, but they, in turn, call **add_setenvif_core** with various values. This module also uses a post-read-request function—**match_headers** on line 34467—to optimize access to attributes defined for the current context. The structure is shown in Figure 5.2.

Customization

mod_setenvif uses several internal variables and special expressions that can be set using its directives (for example, the **Remote_Addr** example in the previous section and the **Request_URI** attribute). This module can be extended to allow additional special attributes to control environment variables needed by scripts or programs run by Apache. These specially defined attributes must have a counterpart in the core of Apache so that the actual values can be checked against the regular expressions when requests are processed; however, **mod_setenvif** can be used to allow regular directives to set these additional values based on standard directives.

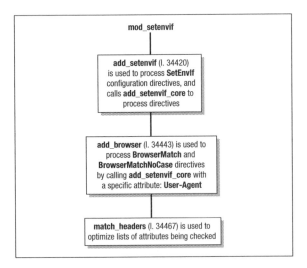

Figure 5.2 **mod_setenvif** enables you to set or control environment variables.

As a simplistic example, if a special attribute called **Time** is defined, then a standard **SetEnvIf** directive can be used to control an environment variable that was available to scripts. The **TIMEVAR** variable is then set if **Time** begins with an even number; the scripts run by Apache can test **TIMEVAR** and react differently if **TIMEVAR** is set:

```
SetEnvIf Time ^[02468] TIMEVAR
```

This example requires core Apache code to provide information about **Time** when requests are processed; adding **Time** as a supported type in **mod_setenvif** alone is not sufficient.

special

34248: This enumerated variable defines special attributes that Apache defines internally and that can be tested for a request to determine if an environment variable is set. The first value, **SPECIAL_NOT**, indicates that the attribute being tested by a directive is a request header and not one of the special attributes listed here.

sei_entry

34256: The **sei_entry** structure is used to hold completed entries based on the directives used by **mod_setenvif**. It includes fields for the regular expression to test against, case sensitivity (**icase**), and the variables to set if the item to test against matches the regular expression.

sei_cfg_rec

34267: The configuration record for **mod_setenvif** is defined here. It is an array to hold the raw values of the directive arguments.

34271: The module definition is forward-referenced here. The actual definition begins on line 34555.

create_setenvif_config

34273: The **create_setenvif_config** function creates a server configuration record for a configuration context. It defines a new **sei_cfg_rec** variable on line 34276 using **ap_palloc**, and then fills it with an array of 20 items using **ap_make_array** on line 34279.

merge_setenvif_config

34284: The **merge_setenvif_config** function merges two arrays of conditionals when two server contexts must be merged. The **base** configuration is merged with **overrides** and placed in **a**. In most merge functions in other modules, the merged configuration is called **add** or something similar. The name **overrides** is a reminder that any attribute tests and variables to be set in the additive configuration will overwrite the **base** configuration if a conflict arises.

34302: A constant, **ICASE_MAGIC**, is defined as a flag to show if case sensitivity is applicable to the directive information being processed. The value assigned to this constant here is arbitrary—the address of a function is used. The variable is actually used in the **setenvif_module_cmds** structure (see lines 34455 and 34461).

add_setenvif_core

34304: The **add_setenvif_core** function does the work in **mod_setenvif**. It is called by several other very short functions with parameters to guide its actions.

34310: The configuration for the server in this context is acquired. **add_setenvif_core** then adds entries to this configuration. The **sei_entry**, defined on line 34313, holds the newly defined entry.

34321: The regular expression to use in testing the attribute given with this directive by querying the list of arguments is recovered. If it doesn't exist, an error is returned—a regular expression must be provided with each directive.

34335: A **for** loop is used to look through all the entries that are currently applied to this server context. If an entry already exists for the attribute name that the current directive refers to, the attribute name (**fname**) is set to the identical name already in the list and breaks out of the loop.

34347: **i** is set to the element number to add to the current context, and **icase** is set to the case sensitivity value on line 34348 (based on what was included in the command structure for the current directive).

34349: If the entry the directive asks to create does not already exist (matching attribute and regular expression), then it continues on to line 34356 to make a new entry, starting by creating a variable (**new**) to hold it.

34357: The attribute name is in **fname**, the regular expression to test is in **regex**, and the case sensitivity setting is in **icase**. The compiled regular expression (for quick processing when a request is actually being handled) is created using **ap_pregcomp** and placed in the **preg** field of **new**. If the regular expression cannot be compiled, it is malformed, meaning that it cannot be tested against. In that case, the function exits immediately, without adding the regular expression to the **preg** field. An error message is returned on line 34364.

34367: The features (environment variables to set if the regular expression matches) are defined by creating a table of two entries with **ap_make_ table**.

34369: The next few lines test the attribute name for any of the special attributes defined starting on line 34248. If those attributes are used in the current directive, the enumerated type value is placed in the **special_type** field of **new**; otherwise, the field is filled with the **SPECIAL_ NOT** value (on line 34385) so that special attributes are not expected when Apache tests these values for actual requests.

34388: If a **new** entry was not needed because one already existed, **new** is set equal to the existing entry. Any additional features can then be added to it before it is placed back in the configuration.

34392: Each feature included is tested as something to do if the attribute matches the regular expression given by grabbing each remaining argument on line 34393. The feature is then added to the **features** field of **new** on line 34401 using **ap_table_setn**.

34411: If a feature is not provided, an error is returned— something must be defined as the variable to set.

add_setenvif

34420: The **add_setenvif** function is used to process **SetEnvIf** directives. It defines the attribute to check as **fname**, and then calls **add_setenvif_ core** to actually process the directive. **RAW_ ARGS** are used with **SetEnvIf** (line 34453). The **add_setenvif** function checks for a valid attribute name as part of the list of arguments

before passing control to **add_ setenvif_core**. This same function is called for **SetEnvIfNoCase**. The **ICASE_MAGIC** code (line 34455) is queried by **add_setenvif_core** during processing to determine case sensitivity.

add_browser

34443: The **add_browser** function is like a special case of **add_setenvif**. It is used to process the **BrowserMatch** and **BrowserMatchNoCase** directives by calling **add_setenvif_core** with a specific attribute, **User-Agent**.

setenvif_module_cmds

34450: The **setenvif_module_cmds** structure defines functions to call for processing directives used by this module. **RAW_ARGS** are used for all directives, leaving the processing up to the called functions. This is done because environment variables may have a value assigned or may be named alone, indicating that they will be set without a specific value. The **ICASE_MAGIC** code is used as a flag to indicate case sensitivity. **add_setenvif_core** is called by all of the functions defined here; if the directive being processed is a **...NoCase** directive, then **ICASE_MAGIC** is available to **add_setenvif_ core**.

match_headers

34467: The **match_headers** function is used to optimize lists of attributes being checked that may have been processed at various times in the Apache configuration. After getting the configuration (line 34477), a **for** loop (line 34484) looks at each entry and provides special values for internal (non-HTTP-header) attributes, beginning on line 34498. (See line 34507 and line 34510 where fields from the request are assigned as **val**.)

34534: Depending on the regular expression used, elements of the array are unset (deleted) or set (added).

setenvif_module

34555: The module itself is defined with function calls for creating and merging configurations, processing directives, and processing during post-read-request (using the **match_headers** function).

Chapter 6

Header Modules

This chapter describes four small modules that are used to define extra headers to be returned to a requesting client. The four modules are:

- **mod_asis**—Sends headers unmodified to the client

- **mod_cern_meta**—Sends the contents of a named file as headers with the reply to the client

- **mod_expires**—Adds an expiration header to an Apache reply based on the MIME data type of the requested item

- **mod_headers**—Updates specific headers returned to the client based on directives in the Apache configuration files

The headers defined by these modules are not generated automatically by other modules. For example, meta information, such as a document's author, can be included in server replies using either **mod_cern_meta** or **mod_headers**.

Discussion Of mod_asis

The **send-as-is** handler can be selected for any directory or location using the **AddHandler** directive:

```
<Directory /directoryname>
AddHandler send-as-is pre
</Directory>
```

When a client requests any file in the named directory that has the .pre file extension, **mod_asis** is used to send the file contents. The first part of the file is assumed to include any needed headers; no additional headers are generated and sent by Apache.

Module Structure

The structure of **mod_asis**, illustrated in Figure 6.1, is very simple. No per-directory or per-server configurations are used. Only the handler table is defined for the module, listing a handler for **send-as-is**.

The function defined by the **send-as-is** handler (**asis_handler**, beginning on line 12344) checks the validity of the request method and file permissions, and then returns the requested file to the client.

Customization

The **send-as-is** handler is intended to reduce file processing for those locations that have the **send-as-is** handler set. Customizations to **mod_asis** that extend the capability of this handler might diminish its intended purpose of sending a file without review, alteration, or addition.

asis_handler

12344: The requested file is returned to the client without any added headers (the module assumes that the Webmaster has included headers as part of the file content).

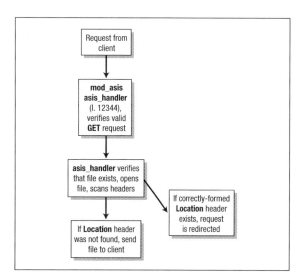

Figure 6.1 **mod_asis** lets Apache send files as is, without additional headers.

12349: The request is checked to see that it is a **GET** request and that **GET** is allowed.

12352: The requested file is checked to make sure that it exists.

12359: The file is opened in preparation for sending it. If the file open fails, an error is logged on line 12362. The assumption is that, because the file exists, a permission problem caused it not to open.

12368: Headers that would be sent to the client are scanned. If a correctly formed **Location** header exists, this request should be redirected. Rather than sending the requested file, the status of the request is checked on line 12373, the file that was opened on line 12359 is closed (on line 12375), the fact that the method used is **GET** is confirmed (on lines 12384 and 12385), and the request is redirected using the **ap_internal_redirect_handler** call on line 12387.

12391: If the file was not redirected with a **Location** header, the minimal HTTP header is sent to identify the format of the information being sent using the **ap_send_http_header** call.

12392: If the **header_only** flag is set for this request, **asis_handler** goes to line 12395 to close the file and exit. (This yields a very short response with the **send-as-is** handler). Otherwise, it dumps the entire file to the client with **ap_send_fd** on line 12393, then closes the file on line 12395 and exits.

asis_handlers

12399: A structure is defined for the handlers that this module deals with. The handler type used is **send-as-is**. The function **asis_handler** (line 12344) is defined for use when a request arrives in an area served by this handler.

asis_module

12406: The **mod_asis** module information is defined. This definition includes only a single hook for the handlers on line 12419, referring to the **asis_handlers** structure (line 12399).

Discussion Of **mod_cern_meta**

The **mod_cern_meta** module is provided for compatibility with the CERN Web server that was very popular in the early days of the Web. This module allows the user to define a file extension for files that contain meta information (additional headers) about files that are returned to clients. For example, suppose the following configuration directives are used:

```
<Directory /document_root/products>
MetaFiles  on
MetaDir  headers
MetaSuffix  meta
...
</Directory>
```

When a client requests a file (such as index.html) located in the /document_root/products directory, the **mod_cern_meta** module looks in the headers subdirectory (/document_root/products/headers) for a file of the same name with the .meta file extension (index.html.meta). The contents of this file are sent before the requested file.

The **Header** directive is the preferred method of providing this information, but because many Web servers were set up using CERN meta information files, this module provides backward compatibility. The module source code for **mod_cern_meta** included with Apache contains additional explanation and examples.

Module Structure

Only per-directory configurations are allowed for **mod_cern_meta**. Directives are processed by placing the value given with the directive into the appropriate field of the correct server or directory configuration structure. During the **fixups** stage, before the requested file has been sent, the **add_cern_meta_data** function is called (line 15417). This function checks the meta file name provided by the directives for the current context, opens it, and passes control to the **scan_meta_file** function (line 15353). This function reads in the meta

file, checks the validity of the headers it contains, and adds them (if valid) to the **headers_out** array for the request. The task of actually sending the headers to the client is left for a later Apache process. The module structure is shown in Figure 6.2.

Customization

Because **mod_cern_meta** is intended for backward compatibility, extensions to its functionality should be avoided. The exception might be if a user has added special features to a CERN Web server that need to be

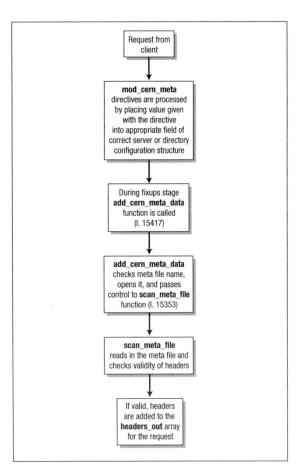

Figure 6.2 **mod_cern_meta** provides for additional headers used by CERN HTTPD.

duplicated in **mod_cern_meta** to maintain the same functionality.

In normal operation, however, use **mod_headers** rather than **mod_cern_meta** to extend **mod_headers** with new features.

Compiler DEFINE Statements

15268: Default directories and file extensions are defined to be used if **MetaFiles** is set to **on**, but **MetaDir** or **MetaSuffix** directives do not define how to locate the metafiles.

15274: Defines the configuration record structure for **mod_cern_meta**. It includes the directory and suffix to use when locating metafiles for a directory context, as well as a flag that turns the features of **mod_cern_meta** on or off using the **MetaFiles** directive.

create_cern_meta_dir_config

15280: Creates a directory configuration by allocating a directory configuration record using **ap_palloc** on line 15284. All of the values of the configuration record are set to NULL or zero.

merge_cern_meta_dir_config

15294: Merges two directory configuration records, **base** and **add**, into the **new** configuration. The meta directory and meta suffixes are checked in both **base** and **add**; the metafiles field, however, is taken from the **add** variable without checking **base** (line 15309).

set_metadir

15314: Sets the directory to use when locating metafiles. This function is called when a **MetaDir** directive is found, as defined in the commands table (line 15341). The **metadir** field of the current directory configuration record is set to the value of the argument passed in from the directive by Apache (see the **TAKE1** parameter on line 15341).

set_metasuffix

15321: Sets the file extension (suffix) to use when locating metafiles in the metafile directory. This function is called when a **MetaSuffix** directory is found, as defined on line 15343. The

metasuffix field of the current directory configuration record is set to the value provided with the directive.

set_metafiles

15328: Sets the status of the **metafiles** field for the current directory configuration to the value provided with the **MetaFiles** directive. This must be **on** or **off**. The **set_metafiles** function is defined for handling the **MetaFiles** directive on line 15338.

cern_meta_cmds

15336: Defines a command table that specifies each directive that affects **mod_cern_meta** and the function to call when each is found in a configuration file. The three directives (**MetaFiles**, **MetaDir**, and **MetaSuffix**) are each named with a function to call, a definition of how directive parameters must be formed, and a message line to return if the parameters are malformed.

scan_meta_file

15353: Scans the file that is passed in as a file descriptor, checking the validity of the headers in the file before adding them to the **headers_out** field for the current request. This function is called by the **add_cern_meta_data** function on line 15505.

15360: Defines a variable (**tmp_headers**) to hold the information to be parsed from the metafile.

15361: Uses the **fgets** call with the **w** string variable and the **f** file descriptor to read the entire metafile into the variable **w**.

15365: Removes all line feeds and carriage returns from the string **w** (which contains the metafile contents). The line feed characters are not needed because each header is added as an array element within the **headers_out** field of the request. Line formatting is added when all headers are output to the client.

15380: If a colon is not present, the headers are malformed. An error is logged using **ap_log_rerror** on line 15381, and returned with an error on line 15385. The check for a colon is the only verification of correctly formed headers. A header can be user-defined and contain almost any information, so long as the header name is followed by a colon.

15392: Checks for the **Content-Type** header within the metafile. If found, it is parsed out and placed in the **content_type** field of the request (line 15402).

15404: Checks for a **Status** header in the metafile. If found, it is placed in the **status_line** field of the request.

15409: If neither **Content-Type** nor **Status** headers were detected, all of the headers provided in the metafile are placed into a table named **tmp_headers** using **ap_table_set**. The **tmp_headers** variable is then overlayed with any existing headers for this request using the **ap_overlap_tables** call on line 15412.

add_cern_meta_data

15417: Locates and processes a metafile as defined for the current directory context. The **scan_meta_file** function (line 15353) is used to place the headers from the metafile into the **headers_out** field of the current request.

15428: Retrieves the configuration of the current directory context.

15431: Checks the **metafiles** flag. If it's not set for this directory, DECLINED is returned.

15437: If the file in question for this request doesn't exist, DECLINED is returned.

15442: If the current request is for a directory, this module shouldn't be used until the request has been redirected to a specific file, so DECLINED is returned.

15448: Prepares a valid path name by checking for path-separating slashes so that the metafile can be opened.

15470: Assembles the complete name of the metafile by combining the **scrap_book** variable (which holds the starting directory for the current file being requested), the **metadir** field of the current configuration, the file name being requested, and the **metasuffix** field (hence, /doc/index.html might yield /doc/.web/index.html.meta).

15486: Creates an Apache subrequest so that the file name of the metafile is checked automatically. The status field of the subrequest is checked on line 15487; if it's not valid, the module returns with DECLINED because the metafile is not available. In either case (DECLINED or continue), the subrequest is immediately destroyed, having served its purpose of checking the validity of the file name.

15493: Opens the metafile, storing the file descriptor in **f**. If an error occurs during file open, the error is logged and an error code of either DECLINED or FORBIDDEN is returned.

15505: Because the metafile was opened successfully, the **scan_meta_file** function is used to retrieve its contents, review them, and place them in the **headers_out** field of the current request.

15506: Closes the metafile for a clean module exit.

cern_meta_module

15511: Defines **mod_cern_meta**. Per-directory configurations are created using **create_cern_meta_dir_config** (line 15515). The directory configurations are merged using **merge_cern_meta_dir_configs**. The directives used by this module are defined by the command table referred to on line 15521. The work of processing metafiles is done by the **add_cern_meta_data** function, which is specified on line 15528, during the **fixups** stage of request processing.

Discussion Of **mod_expires**

The **mod_expires** module is used to define an expiration period for a file based on the file's MIME type. The expiration information is returned in the headers to allow proxy servers and browser caches to determine when a document must be retrieved again from the server, rather than using a locally cached copy. Two headers, **Cache-Control** and **Expires**, are calculated and added to requests by **mod_expires**.

To use **mod_expires** within a directory context, the **ExpiresActive** directive is first set to **on**. The **ExpiresByType** directive is used to define an expiration period for files based on their type; the **ExpiresDefault** directive can also specify an expiration period for all files that do not have an **ExpiresByType** directive explicitly defined.

The format options for the expiration period defined by **ExpiresByType** or **ExpiresDefault** are defined by either the access time or the modification time plus an additional amount of time. For example,

```
ExpiresByType text/html A604800
```

indicates that all HTML files in the current context should expire one week (604,800 seconds) after being accessed (read by a client browser). A more readable format can also be used. This example has the same effect as the previous one:

```
ExpiresByType text/html "access plus 1 week"
```

The first field can be **access**, **modification**, or **now** (which is equivalent to **access**). The word **plus** is optional. The number and type indicators can be repeated to create something like the following:

```
ExpiresByType text/html "access plus 1 month 15
days 2 hours"
```

The quotation marks are needed when using this format because of the spaces. The format for

ExpiresDefault is identical except that no MIME type is specified before the expiration period.

Additional discussion and examples are provided in the comments at the beginning of this module's source code.

Module Structure

After creating or merging directory configuration variables using **create_dir_expires_config** and **merge_expires_dir_configs**, the directives that affect **mod_expires** are processed according to the command table (line 17098). The **set_expiresbytype** (line 17066) and **set_expiresdefault** (line 17083) functions place the corresponding directive values into the directory configurations. They are not fully parsed until an individual request is handled.

The **add_expires** function (line 17139) is called during the **fixups** stage to add an **Expires** header to the outgoing reply. **add_expires** uses the **check_code** function (line 16959) to parse the fields in the directory configuration structure and prepare fields for the actual header. The module's structure is illustrated in Figure 6.3.

Customization

Additional codes or options can be added to the **ExpiresByType** and **ExpiresDefault** directives. These might be based on system information or a query of other information such as a database.

Compiler DEFINE Statements

16914: Defines a configuration record for **mod_expires**. This includes an on/off flag, a default expiration code, and a table (array) of expiration values defined by MIME type using **ExpiresByType** directives.

create_dir_expires_config

16930: Creates a structure for the current directory configuration and initializes it. Line 16938 initially defines four array elements to hold type-based expiration data.

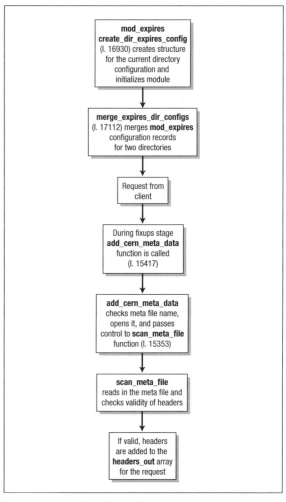

Figure 6.3 **mod_expires** defines an expiration date for a file based on its MIMC type.

set_expiresactive

16942: Sets the **active** flag in the current directory configuration so that the headers provided by **mod_expires** are enabled or disabled, according to the **arg** provided with the directive. This function is called when an **ExpiresActive** directive is found (line 17100).

check_code

16959: Prepares an expiration code based on the information provided with an **ExpiresByType** or **ExpiresDefault** directive and stored in the configuration record for the current directory context.

16970: If the first letter of the expiration code is **A** or **M**, the simple format of number of seconds is used. In this case, the **real_code** variable is set to the argument included with the directive; no further processing is needed. **real_code** is returned in the function header, so the return value of NULL indicates success.

16975: If the first word of the expiration code matches one of the three keywords (**now**, **access**, or **modification**), then the expiration period is processed as a set of words and numbers (such as "now plus 1 week"). The **base** field (first item) is identified on line 16980. If the first word is **now** or **access**, the **base** is set to **A** on line 16983. If the first word is **modification**, the **base** is set to **M** on line 16986. If neither of these is the case, the expiration cannot be processed, so an error is returned on line 16989.

16996: If **plus** is found, the next piece of the expiration code is retrieved on line 16998. The word **plus** is provided for human-readability only—**minus** is not an option here.

17003: Loops for each of the pairs of **<NUM><TYPE>**. The number is assumed to be in the **word** variable already. Compare this section of code with a similar section in **mod_usertrack**, beginning on line 37067.

17006: The entire number should be digits. If it is, it's converted to an integer value on line 17007. If it isn't, an error is returned on line 17010.

17017: Retrieves the next piece of the expiration code (which should be a type such as **weeks**, **months**,

or **days**). Line 17018 tests for the presence of something in **word**; if nothing is there, it returns with an error on line 17022. Otherwise, it continues on line 17026.

17027: Determines which type is specified and defines **factor** for the number of seconds that corresponds to the type. If none of the types can be found, an error is returned on line 17049.

17054: Sets the **modifier** to the number multiplied by the type (such as five times the number of seconds in a day). The **modifier** variable is updated each time through the **while** loop that begins on line 17003. The next item in the expiration code is retrieved on line 17058 and the loop continues, exiting to line 17061 when nothing remains of the expiration code.

17061: Returns the **base** and **modifier** to the calling function. The **base** and **modifier** are equivalent to the simpler format of **A** or **M** with a number of seconds.

set_expiresbytype

17066: Defines an expiration value for files of a certain MIME type as directed by an **ExpiresByType** directive. This function is called by Apache when such a directive is found (line 17103).

17072: If the response from the **check_code** function is able to process the expiration code given in the directive, it is stored in the **expiresbytype** structure of the current directory configuration (the **real_code** variable contains the processed expiration code). Otherwise, an error is returned in the form of a syntax diagram for the **ExpiresByType** directive (line 17078).

set_expiresdefault

17083: Defines an expiration value for all files in the current directory context that do not have an **ExpiresByType** directive given for their MIME type. This function is called by Apache when such a directive is found (line 17106).

17088: If the response from the **check_code** function is able to process the expiration code given in the directive, it is stored in the **expiresdefault** structure of the current directory configuration (the **real_code** variable contains the processed expiration code). Otherwise, an error is returned in the form of a syntax diagram for the **ExpiresDefault** directive (line 17093). The difference between the **set_expiresbytype** and **set_expiresdefault** functions is the **mime** parameter in the function header. This piece of data is passed in by Apache based on the command table format (**TAKE1** compared with **TAKE2**, see lines 17104 and 17107).

expires_cmds

17098: Defines the directives that **mod_expires** handles and the functions to call when those directives are found. Each of the three items in the command table structure also defines what type of parameters Apache should expect with the directive. These are passed in to the named function using a predefined ordering.

merge_expires_dir_configs

17112: Merges **mod_expires** configuration records for two directories. The **expiresbytype** arrays of **base** and **add** are combined for the **new** configuration record (line 17133).

add_expires

17139: Prepares the expiration headers for a request based on the values created by directives that apply to this module.

17148: If the current request has an error status, an expiration header is not added to it. Also, the **main** field is checked to determine if this is a subrequest (line 17152). If it is, **add_expires** exits without processing the request.

17155: Retrieves the configuration record for the current directory context. If it doesn't exist, an internal error is returned. (Few modules check this after retrieving the configuration record—it indicates that the **create_dir_expires_config** function somehow failed to do its job.)

17165: Tests the **active** flag of the current configuration. If the **ExpiresActive** directive has set **Expires** headers active for this directory, it continues; otherwise, it returns with DECLINED.

17182: Determines the MIME type of the file to be returned so that **ExpiresByType** items can be found if necessary. If no **content_type** field is defined, **code** is left as NULL—the **Expires-Default** value will be used; otherwise, **ap_table_get** is used to locate the MIME type of this request in the **expiresbytype** field of the current configuration (line 17185).

17188: If **code** is NULL (either because no **content_type** was defined or because the MIME type of the request was not defined in the **expiresbytype** structure), then **expiresdefault** is used as the code on line 17191.

17193: If **code** is now empty because no **expiresdefault** was defined, OK is returned. No expiration information is available for the current request.

17200: Begins a **switch** statement to determine the access or modification time of the requested file, using either **M** or **A** as the first character of the **code** variable. The **base** variable is set to either the **finfo.st_mtime** field or the **request_time** field of the request. The remainder of the **code** variable (after the first character) is converted to an integer on line 17209 or 17217.

17219: If neither **M** nor **A** was the first letter of **code**, an error is logged (line 17224). Somehow, a bad expiration code made it through the functions that prepare the directives for this module.

17231: With **base** and **additional**, an **expires** variable can be set to the actual expiration value for the current request.

17232: Uses **ap_snprintf** to place the text of an aging information header in the **age** variable. The value is created by subtracting **expires** from the **request_time** field on line 17233.

17234: Adds a **Cache-Control** header with the **age** variable as its value.

17240: Adds an **Expires** header with the **expires** variable as its value, converting it to something more readable with the **ap_gm_timestr_822** call.

expires_module

17245: Defines **mod_expires** with **create** and **merge** directory configuration functions (lines 17249 and 17250); a command table to handle the **ExpiresActive**, **ExpiresByType**, and **Expires-Default** directives (line 17255); and the **add_expires** function in the **fixups** stage (line 17263) to actually add **Expires** and **Cache-Control** headers to requests that are being handled.

Discussion Of mod_headers

Using **mod_headers**, any header can be defined, added to, or removed from outgoing requests. This module allows more flexibility than other older modules such as **mod_cern_meta**. It provides a generalized interface where the header name and value are defined for any directory or server context.

The **Header** directive is used to define or alter headers within a server or directory context. The possible values are:

- **add**—To define an additional header using the header name given but not to overwrite other headers of the same name

- **append**—To add a value to a header of the given name without creating a new header line

- **set**—To define a header and replace any headers of the same name for requests in a given context

- **unset**—To remove the named header from the request response

If **unset** is used, only the header name is given:

```
Header unset Cookie
```

For **set**, **append**, or **add**, a value is also included:

```
Header set Author "Joseph Young"
```

Module Structure

Header directives are processed as they are parsed in configuration files and passed to the **header_cmd** function (line 17335). During the **fixups** processing stage, the **fixup_headers** function is called (line 17453), which in turn calls **do_headers_fixup**, first using the server configuration record as a parameter, then using the directory configuration record as a parameter. The structure is shown in Figure 6.4.

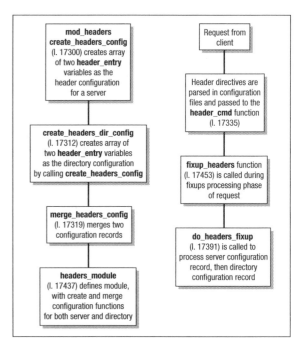

Figure 6.4 **mod_headers** enables Apache to add, append, or remove na HTTP response header.

Customization

mod_headers can be extended to allow values from your system environment (environment variables) to be included as header values. Be careful about what environment variables are actually available to the server process during execution. Other system information can be queried by **mod_headers** directly based on special codes in the value portion of the **Header** directive arguments, similar to a server-side include within a header.

mod_headers can also include headers conditionally based on predefined or dynamic tests that were incorporated into the arguments of the **Header** directive.

hdr_actions

17273: Defines an enumerated type for the possible methods of adding headers using **mod_headers**.

header_entry

17284: Defines a single header entry that includes the type of action (based on the enumerated type on line 17273), the header to act upon, and the value to use. An array of **header_entry** variables is used on line 17294 to define a configuration record (both server and directory) for **mod_headers**.

create_headers_config

17300: Creates an array of two **header_entry** variables as the header configuration for a server.

create_headers_dir_config

17312: Creates an array of two **header_entry** variables as the directory configuration by calling **create_headers_config**. The same function is used for creating both server and directory configurations. This function makes things clearer, because the two configurations are treated separately.

merge_headers_config

17319: Merges two configuration records by adding the headers defined in **base** with those defined in the **overrides** variables.

header_cmd

17335: Processes any **Header** directives, as specified by line 17386.

17343: Retrieves the server configuration record.

17347: Checks **cmd** to see where this directive is located. If it is in a directory configuration, the header entry is placed in the directory configuration on line 17348. Otherwise, it is placed in the server configuration on line 17353.

17356: Tests the action defined by the **Header** directive, setting the **action** field to an enumerated value based on the directive. If one of the four strings cannot be detected, an error is returned.

17368: If the action specified is **unset**, the number of arguments provided with the directive is checked. In any case, the **header** and **value** fields of **new** are set to the parameters passed in (**hdr** and **value**).

headers_cmds

17384: Defines the directive that this module uses (**Header**) and the function to call when it is found in a configuration file (**header_cmd**).

do_headers_fixup

17391: Processes a set of headers from a configuration record (as called by **fixup_headers** on line 17431 and 17432), adding them as necessary to the **headers_out** field of the current request.

17396: Loops through each of the headers in the current configuration record structure. For each one, a **switch** statement is used to test the action requested, and acts accordingly.

17400: If the action is **add**, **ap_table_addn** adds the **header** and **value** fields to **headers_out** for this request. (This may result in two headers of the same name—for example, two **Author:** headers might result.)

17404: If the action is **append**, **ap_table_mergen** merges the **value** field with an existing header's **value** field. (It doesn't create an additional header line.)

17408: If the action is **set**, **ap_table_setn** adds the **header** and **value** fields to **headers_out** for this request, replacing any existing header of the same name. This means that two headers of this name would never be sent to a client.

17412: If the action is **unset**, **ap_table_unset** removes the header named by the **header** field from the **headers_out** for this request.

fixup_headers

17420: Inserts headers defined by the **Headers** directives for the current server and directory contexts by calling **do_headers_fixup** with the configuration record for each.

17423: Retrieves the server configuration into **serverconf**.

17427: Retrieves the directory configuration into **dirconf**.

17431: Calls **do_headers_fixups** with the server configuration to add the appropriate headers to the **headers_out** field of the current request, as defined by **Headers** directives in the current server context.

17432: Does the same thing with the configuration for the current directory context.

headers_module

17437: Defines this module with **create** and **merge** configuration functions for both server and directory. Note that the server and directory **create** functions are different, but the directory configuration function **create_headers_dir_config** simply calls the server configuration function **create_headers_config**. Conversely, the same function, **merge_headers_config**, is called directly for both server and directory configurations. A **header_cmds** table is provided (line 17446) to define how to handle the **Header** directive (the only one used by this module). Finally, the **fixup_headers** function is defined on line 17453 to process requests during the **fixups** stage.

Chapter 7

Directory Indexing Modules

This chapter describes two modules used to identify the index file for a directory and to generate indexes on the fly when a browser requests a directory rather than a specific file. The two modules—**mod_dir** and **mod_autoindex**—are both included in the standard Apache configuration. Because these modules are fairly simple, they provide a good starting place if you're just learning about how modules are put together.

When a browser requests a directory rather than a specific file, the standard response is to return a file named index.html, index.htm, welcome.htm, or default.htm from that directory. This is most commonly seen when a URL such as **www.yahoo.com/** is requested. The final slash actually refers to the root directory of the document tree for that Web site; no file name is explicitly given.

If the index.html file is found (or another file specified by the **DirectoryIndex** directive, one of the directives provided by **mod_dir**) then that file is returned to the browser. If the index.html file (or another file named by the **DirectoryIndex** directive) is not found, Apache attempts to generate a listing of the directory contents and return that listing as an HTML document to the browser. The creation of this listing is constrained by the **Options Indexes** directive within the directory container controlling the requested location.

If a directory listing is allowed by system security, the listing is generated by the **mod_autoindex** module. A series of directives control the appearance of the listing, including **IndexOptions** and various **AddIcon** directives.

mod_dir and **mod_autoindex** were formerly a single module. In Apache 1.3.4, they were split into two modules

so that the auto-indexing portion could be removed from Apache if none of the Web site directories allowed index listings to be generated. This saves a little space for each copy of Apache.

Discussion Of **mod_dir**

The **DirectoryIndex** directive defines one or more file names that Apache searches for when a directory is requested with no file name specified (such as **www.abccorp.com/products/**). The default setting for this file is:

```
DirectoryIndex index.html
```

Any number of index file names can be added to this directive, each separated by a space. For example:

```
DirectoryIndex index.html index.htm
```

The module rotates through these file names in order, left to right, checking to see if any of them exists in the directory. When the first file name is found, the module creates an internal redirect of the browser request to refer to the index file name. For example, if the browser requested **www.abccorp.com/products/** and the module locates an index.html file in that directory, the request is internally redirected to **www.abccorp.com/products/index.html** for further processing (to return the file).

If none of the files listed in the **DirectoryIndex** directive are found in the directory being requested, the module returns the value **DECLINED**, and processing passes on to another module (generally, **mod_autoindex** to attempt to create a directory file listing).

Module Structure

The code for this operation is straightforward. An array is defined (starting on line 16514) to hold the list of directory index files to search for (taken from the **DirectoryIndex** directive). The array is filled in using

the **add_index** function (starting on line 16520), which is called when the directives are processed (see **dir_cmds** on line 16533).

As shown in Figure 7.1, the **handle_dir** function on line 16564 does all the work, looping through each of the items in the list of possible directory index files with the **for** loop on line 16613. Each time through the loop, a subrequest is created on line 16615 to check for the presence of the index file. If the file is found (as shown by an **HTTP_OK** status on the subrequest), then the main request is redirected to that file on line 16628, and the module exits with OK on line 16629.

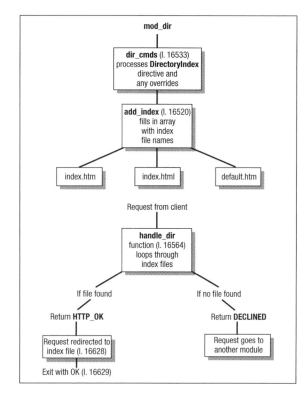

Figure 7.1 **mod_dir** enables Apache to search for index files when a directory is requested with no file name specified.

If the index file isn't found, other checks are made for redirects on the requested index file or other error conditions. Depending on the result of these checks, the module exits with a status code on line 16649, 16670, or 16673.

If none of the potential index files was found in the **for** loop, but none of the other conditions were found either, the loop ends. The module returns the value **DECLINED** on line 16677, letting the next module (**mod_autoindex** if it's included in the current copy of Apache) handle the request.

Customization

Several things can be done to customize **mod_dir**. For example, the list of potential directory index files can be calculated using something other than the **DirectoryIndex** directive. Code can be inserted in the **add_index** function to fill a list from a database query, an environment variable, or other input sources. Other actions can also be defined and inserted before line 16677 if none of the index files is found. If action is going to be taken at this point, however, it would be better done by a separate module dedicated to the task.

Module Definitions

16512: Either the module definition or all of the functions must be forward-referenced so they can find each other during compilation. Obviously, it's easier to forward-reference just the module definition. The actual definition starts on line 16687.

16514: Defines the **dir_config_rec** structure as a pointer to the array of potential index file names.

16518: Defines **DIR_CMD_PARMS** as the value of **OR_INDEXES**. **DIR_CMD_PARMS** is used on line 16536 to indicate that the directive for this module (**DirectoryIndex**) can be overridden using the **Indexes** option of an **AllowOverride** directive; hence, the equivalence to **OR_INDEXES**.

add_index

16520: The **add_index** function places the arguments from the **DirectoryIndex** directive (passed into the function as pointer **arg**) into the directory configuration record (passed in as pointer **dummy**) so they can be used by the **handle_dir** function.

16523: Creates a variable (**d**) that equates to dummy. This is where all the index file arguments from the **DirectoryIndex** directive are stored.

16525: If the **index_names** field of this **dir_config_rec** structure (**d**) points to NULL (nothing there yet), the **ap_make_array** call allocates space for two index name elements.

16529: In any event, the **ap_push_array** call places all of the arguments (given as **arg**) into the **index_names** field at one time.

dir_cmds

16533: The **dir_cmds** function defines for Apache which configuration directives are used by this module and how to use them. This definition (and those in all other modules) are referenced whenever Apache parses a set of directives (either default or for a container such as a directory or location).

The fields here indicate:

- **DirectoryIndex**—A directive that this module needs to know about or handles.

- **add_index**—The name of the function that should be called to prepare the data given with this directive.

- **DIR_CMD_PERMS**—This directive can be overridden in a subdirectory (using the .htaccess file) if the **AllowOverride Indexes** directive is included (this variable is equal to the standard **OR_INDEXES** value on line 16518).

- **NULL**—No additional data is used for this directive.

- **ITERATE**—This directive takes a single parameter (the file name to search for) repeated one or more times. (Multiple file names may be included with the directive, but each one is interpreted as the same type of parameter— the file name to search for in this case.)

- *A list of file names*—If an error occurs, this description writes instructions about how to use this directive.

create_dir_config

16541: Initializes this module, as defined in the module definition on line 16691, by allocating memory for a directory configuration record (**dir_config_rec**) to be used by **add_index** to hold the file names from the **DirectoryIndex** directive. The standard **ap_palloc** call is used to allocate memory from the pool of memory (**p**) provided.

16547: The **index_names** list in the new **dir_config_rec** variable is initialized to point to NULL, because nothing is contained in the list when the module is initialized.

16548: The pointer to the new **dir_config_rec** created in this function is returned so that it can be used later in the module, principally by the **add_index** and **handle_dir** functions.

merge_dir_configs

16551: Merges configurations from multiple directories that have overlapping directive values.

16554: Creates a new **dir_config_rec** variable to hold the combined directory data. The **ap_palloc** call allocates space for the variable.

16556: Assigns the incoming **base** and **additive** directory configuration records (their respective **dir_config_rec** variables, supplied by Apache from previous calls to **create_dir_config**) to **base** and **add**, respectively.

16559: Merges the index names from the **base** and **add** directory configurations, places them in **new**, and returns **new** as the merged **dir_config_rec**.

handle_dir

16564: The main function of this module is **handle_dir**. A request is passed into the module as **r**. Based on the **dir_config_rec** configuration information associated with this request (obtained from the **ap_get_module_config** call on line 16568), the **handle_dir** function checks each possible directory index file, redirecting the current request to return the first directory index file that is found. The **ap_get_module_config** information is provided by Apache based on the current context (as defined by a **<Directory>** container, **<Location>** container, and so on) defined when the **create_dir_config** function was called during module initialization.

16570: Defines a few variables to use as pointers and counters while rotating through the list of possible directory index file names. Only the **error_notfound** variable, however, is initialized at this point.

16575: If the path portion of this request (that is, the **uri** field of the request, **r**, which holds the Uniform Resource Identifier (URI)—basically a Web page address) is zero-length (that is, the initial character is an end-of-string, **\0**) or doesn't end in a slash (/), **handle_dir** assumes the Web page address named in the **uri** field has moved. It adds a slash (/) and returns from the module with a code **HTTP_MOVED_PERMANENTLY** in line 16589.

It also checks for arguments—that is, anything after a question mark (?) in the original request—on line 16578. If arguments are included, they are combined with the new address; otherwise, a slash (/) is added to the current URI. In either case, **ap_pstrcat** concatenates the strings for the new URI.

16587: Adds a **Location** header to this request to indicate a redirected document (at a new location). **handle_dir** then uses **ap_table_setn** to add a name/value pair, with **Location** as the header field name and the new Web page address as the value (constructed via **ap_construct_url** using the **ifile** string just created using **ap_pstrcat** and the current request, **r**). It returns with **HTTP_MOVED_PERMANENTLY**.

16598: Continues processing normally (the URI wasn't moved) by adding a slash (/) to the end of the file name portion of the request, if it isn't there, using the **ap_pstrcat** string concatenation function. This allows the potential index file names to be added to the URI and checked in the **for** loop on line 16613; otherwise, if a request comes in with a directory name as the last part of the URL, it appears as a file name. Thus, the final part of the request ends up in the file name field of the request, even though it's a directory name.

16603: Initializes the variables used to loop through the list of potential directory index file names. If the **index_names** field of the directory configuration record (**d**) is non-**NULL**, **names_ptr** is set to the first element of the list of file names in **index_names**, and **num_names** is set to the number of index names (**d->index_names->nelts**). This initializes the loop counters used on line 16613.

16608: If no data is in **index_names**, **names_ptr** is set to **dummy_ptr**, which is a single-element array containing the default index file name, index.html. Also **num_names** is set to 1, because only one index name is being checked.

16613: Goes through a **for** loop for each element of the **names_ptr** linked list, until **num_names** is zero. For each loop, the validity of the URI created by appending the next element of the **index_name** list to the base URI is tested. If it works, the request is redirected to that URI.

16615: Tests the validity of the current potential directory index file name by setting up a subrequest based on the string pointed to by **name_ptr** and the current main request (**r**).

16617: If the status of the subrequest is **HTTP_OK** thus far and the **finfo.st_mode** field for the file name in the subrequest does not indicate a non-existent file (non-zero), then this is the index file to use.

16618: If the subrequest is successful, a new URI is assembled that includes the file name that just checked out successfully in the **names_ptr** list. If necessary, any arguments are then added to it (the arguments come from the original request in line 16623 or the subrequest in line 16620).

16627: The subrequest has served its purpose, so it's destroyed. The main request (**r**) is then redirected to the new URI assembled on line 16621 or 16624. It then exits the module with an OK.

16635: If the status of the current subrequest indicates that this URI is redirected, or if the status of the HTTP request is unacceptable and this is the final loop (**num_names** is 1—there are no other file names to try), then the subrequest information (the **notes**, **headers_out**, and **err_headers_out** fields) is merged into the main request using the **ap_overlay_tables** function. An **error_notfound** message is then returned, indicating that the file name created a problem (it was redirected or caused a bad HTTP request).

16652: This point is reached if the file name either wasn't a redirected or unacceptable HTTP status or wasn't the last file name to attempt to use as an index file (**num_names!=1**). The status of the subrequest is checked. If it's non-zero, but isn't a **NOT_FOUND** or **OK** status, then the status is stored in **error_notfound**. This value is returned in line 16660 if the loop ends without a later loop iteration finding a valid index file name.

The comments in the code refer to returning a potentially unsafe directory index. This is an artifact from versions of Apache prior to 1.3.4 when the **mod_dir** and **mod_autoindex** modules were combined into a single module that returned the directory listing if no index file names (such as index.html) were found. In this version, the comment isn't really relevant.

16664: At the end of the **for** loop, the subrequest used to test the current potential index file name is destroyed.

16667: After the **for** loop has gone through all possible index file names, **error_notfound** is checked. If **error_notfound** is non-zero, it was set in line 16662 from the status of a subrequest and that information is returned. If **error_notfound** is set to 0, no unexpected conditions were found, so **handle_dir** jumps to line 16670 for a regular **DECLINED** return.

16670: If the method for the request is not **GET**, then **DECLINED** is returned, and another module tries to respond to the request.

16675: If the method of the request isn't **GET**, and no index file is found, a **DECLINED** is returned, and another module processes this request. Note that the returns in lines 16671 and 16675 are identical. The test in line 16670 provides additional information about why the request was **DECLINED**. This would only be known, of course, if the code is being traced for debugging purposes.

dir_handlers

16679: **dir_handlers** associates directories matching **DIR_MAGIC_TYPE** with the **handle_dir** function; that is, the **handle_dir** function will be called to provide an index for all matching directories.

dir_module

16685: Defines this module's information so that the Apache core code can initialize the module and find its functions when they're needed. **create** and **merge** directory configurations are used to set up a configuration for each directory in the Web site's document tree. Apache calls these functions for each application directory and stores the configuration information set up by these functions so that the module can request it later (as it does in line 16568).

The **dir_cmds** function (starting on line 16533) defines which directives this module uses. This function is called to parse the directives whenever they are found by Apache. Finally, the **dir_handlers** function (starting on line 16679) associates the handler for **mod_dir** with its main function (**handle_dir**). The **handle_dir** function is called each time Apache wants **mod_dir** to respond to a request.

Discussion Of mod_autoindex

The **mod_autoindex** module is used to generate a listing of a directory's contents as an HTML file that is returned to the requesting browser. This module consists mostly of string manipulations to prepare a nice-looking HTML document from the listing of files in the directory. However, because this module uses a large number of directives to control the appearance of the directory listing, the module has many functions to prepare all the possible HTML strings. An older directive called **FancyIndexing** has been superceded by **IndexOptions**, but **FancyIndexing** is still supported in the code.

The use of **mod_autoindex** is controlled by the **Options Indexes** directive, which is tested in line 16533. The other directives listed in the **autoindex_cmd** function (starting on line 14083) control the appearance of the directory listing. Remember that **mod_autoindex** and **mod_dir** used to be one module; this explains little

things like the presence of the **IndexOptions** directive on line 14109, when this directive is actually used only by the **mod_dir** module.

Module Structure

The **handle_autoindex** function is called to create the HTML directory listing. It first checks to see if the directory requested allows directory listings by querying **ap_allow_options** for the current request (on line 15187). If indexing is allowed, the configuration record for this directory is retrieved. The **index_directory** function is called to prepare the index listing and to return it as the module's response.

The **index_directory** function (starting on line 15187) prepares the HTML index document by using addition functions to assemble directory and file entries, add icons and descriptions, sort entries, and so forth. The HTML text is returned to the client using the **ap_rvputs** and **ap_rputs** calls, which are located in the **index_directory** function, and several other functions, such as **emit_preamble** (see line 15187). The module structure is shown in Figure 7.2.

Customization

The majority of Web sites don't allow directory indexes, and so do not use **mod_autoindex**. In this case, you should recompile Apache without this module to save memory on the Web server.

Other Web sites, however, may rely on a server-generated listing for many of their directories. This is particularly true when directory contents change frequently. By using a generated index listing, Webmasters can avoid the need to re-create HTML files (such as index.html) to guide users to the contents of the directory. Remember to check directives such as **IndexIgnore** and **Options Indexes** to be certain that only those files and directories you want to let browsers access are listed.

Anyone with knowledge of HTML can create much nicer directory listings by modifying **mod_autoindex**. Ideas for improving the generated listings include:

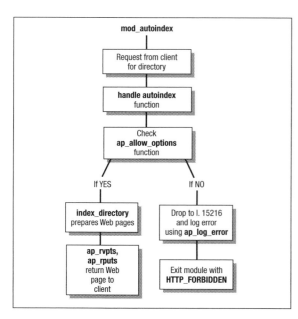

Figure 7.2   mod_autoindex generates a listing of a directory's contents as an HTML file that is returned to the requesting browser.

- Adding custom graphics to the top or bottom of directory listings.

- Creating a background graphic that provides a logo or a color banner down the left side of the screen.

- Testing the path of the listing being created and using graphics, background colors, or other formatting features based on the area of the Web site being requested.

- Watching for cookies in the request and adding personalized information to directory listings (either welcome messages or customized formatting based on the cookie or other client information).

Many of these options can be executed within a file used as a document header (defined by the **HeaderName** directive). Some, however, require processing that cannot be accomplished in a static HTML file. For these, the **emit_preamble** function (line 13730) can be used

to test fields of the request (such as **r->URI** or **r->file name**) before using **ap_pvputs** to output the HTML. Note that **emit_preamble** is not called if a header file is found as defined by the **HeaderName** directive.

New directives can also be declared in the **autoindex_cmds** function (line 14083) to define values for specific directories or file types. For example, to define an additional directive called **IndexBackground** that takes a color value, add a field to the **autoindex_config_rec** (about line 15187), and then test that value in the **emit_preamble** function to define an appropriate HTML tag in the **<HEAD>** of the document.

Module Definitions

13615:   A forward reference to the module definition is provided so that other functions in the module can find it. The module definition begins on line 15232.

13622:   Defines values to use in this module. These values are used as flags to indicate settings that will be used to create a directory listing, based on currently active directives. The flags indicate items such as the use of a horizontal rule (line), the sorting method to use, and which fields to include in a directory listing. These definitions continue through 15232.

The size of the icons used for items in the directory listing and the default length of an item (such as a file name) can be changed easily by altering these **#define** values.

struct item

15234:   The **item** structure contains the elements of the directory listing. Each item has a type, such as a readme file or a regular file, and additional data associated with it. An array of items is filled, then used to output the actual directory listing.

autoindex_config_rec

15241:   The configuration record for **mod_autoindex** is defined here. This structure includes information about the options to use in the directory (taken from the directives that apply at this point), and various values such as icon

width and default sort order. Several arrays are also defined to hold lists of icons and descriptions that are defined by the directives. Many of these fields are filled when directives are processed using the functions defined in **autoindex_cmds** (see line 15232).

is_parent

15271:   The **is_parent** function determines if the string passed to it is ".." to indicate a parent directory entry. This function is used by the **output_ directories** function (see line 14873).

emit_preamble

15294:   Sends a preamble to the HTML index document being created. The **ap_rvputs** call is used to send the information back to the client. Because this function sends a list of strings, items can be added as parameters to this list without any additional preprocessing. This function is a good place to improve the directory listing by testing for features such as the path requested, client, or browser, and by determining what to send based on the results.

push_item

15303:   The **push_item** function places a set of data into a given array (**arr** in the parameter list). It is used by the directive processing functions beginning on line 13770. The main work of the function is performed on line 15307, where a new item is placed on the array.

15316:   The fields of data passed in as an item to place on the array are transferred to the new item using **ap_pstrdup**.

add_*

15334:   The whole series of **add_** functions (such as **add_alt**, **add_icon**, and **add_desc**) provides processing for directives that are named in the **autoindex_cmds** function. Apache calls each of these **add_** functions to place the data from a directive into a list. The list is then returned to the module when a request is processed. Because different types of information must be matched against different attributes of files or directories, codes for **BY_PATH**, **BY_TYPE**, and **BY_ENCODING** appear in these functions to help determine what should be stored in the lists of information. Each list consists of a matching item (such as the file name or file type) and the data to use if a match is found (such as a description or an icon URL).

15347: For each of the **add_** functions, the **push_item** function is used to place the information in the appropriate list. The **add_desc** function shows the simplest example of this on line 13824. The text given with the directive is placed in the list by **push_item**. Apache determines how to call the function to process the directive by the information provided with the **autoindex_cmds** fields, such as **ITERATE** or **TAKE2**.

fancy_indexing

13866: **FancyIndexing** is a deprecated directive, but is still fully supported. Unless there is a conflict with options provided by the **IndexOptions** directive (which is intended to supercede it), as tested by line 13875, **FancyIndexing** is added to the **opts** field.

The **FancyIndexing** directive provides icons, multiple fields of information with column heads, and additional links.

add_opts

13886: The **add_opts** function processes information in the **IndexOptions** directive. This directive has many possible values that are taken together to create the **opts** field of the configuration.

13898: One important point to note about this directive is that options can be additive; that is, a subdirectory can add an option to those already in effect, rather than specify a new set of options. This is done by placing a plus sign (+) before the option. Care must be taken not to redefine all options for the directory when additive options were intended.

13910: A series of tests checks for each of the possible option strings. When a valid string is found, the **option** variable is set to the flag corresponding to the indicated option. For many of these options, the value of **option** is ORed together with the **opts** field on line 14010. Additive options using the plus sign (+) or minus sign (-) are placed in the **opts_add** or **opts_remove** fields, respectively (see lines 14010 to 14022).

13963: Some of the options defined by **IndexOptions** are not placed directly as bits in the **opts** field, but are stored in other fields of the configuration. For example, icon dimensions and name width are stored in separate fields, after testing for validity and conflicts. Note the default that applies in each case if an invalid or conflicting option is used.

set_default_order

14034: The **set_default_order** function sets up variables to control the order of sorting based on the value of the **IndexOrderDefault** directive. The direction and key parameters are provided by Apache, which calls directly to this function when parsing the **IndexOrderDefault** directive (see line 14112).

14042: Uses the **ap_cpystrn** call to place a default value of **k=d** (sort in descending order) in the **temp** variable. The direction parameter is then compared with the two possible values given for the **IndexOrderDefault** directive, **Ascending** and **Descending**, setting the third character of **temp** equal to the appropriate key (defined on lines 13654/13655).

14054: The same operation is performed with the **key** parameter, setting the first character of **temp** equal to the key defined for the possible key strings, such as name, date, or size. If a valid string is not found for both the sort order and the sort key, the function returns with an error describing the correct syntax to use with the directive.

14073: With a string such as **N=D** prepared (overwriting the default **k=d** on line 14043 with values provided by directives), these lines prepare a slot of four characters in the **default_order** field of the configuration record. The **ap_cpystrn** call then copies the **temp** variable to the **default_order** field.

autoindex_cmds

14083: The **autoindex_cmds** function associates the 14 directives used to control **mod_autoindex** with the functions that should be called when each of those directives is parsed by Apache. For each directive, the following items of information are provided:

- The name of the directive as it appears in the Apache configuration files.

- The function in this module to call for parsing the directive data.

- Additional data for this directive, which is passed to the parsing function (for these directives, the data pieces such as **BY_PATH** are defined beginning on line 13695).

- How this directive can be overridden in a per-directory configuration file (.htaccess). The **DIR_CMD_PERMS** shown in these directives is set to **OR_INDEXES** on line 14081, indicating that the **AllowOverride Indexes** must be set for a subordinate configuration to override this one.

- The format of the data to expect. For example, **ITERATE** indicates that a single piece of information, repeated one or more times, should be included with the directive. The value included here determines how arguments are passed from Apache to the handling function listed.

- A description to return if the data for the directive is not formed correctly. These can also serve as brief reminders of how each directive is used.

create_autoindex_config

14138: The **create_autoindex_config** function allocates a new configuration record for this module and fills it with default information. This information is then filled in appropriately as Apache calls other functions from **autoindex_cmds** (line 14083) as it parses directives. The appropriate configuration record is then returned to the module when requested by the **handle_autoindex** function.

merge_autoindex_config

14169: To handle the case of inheritance from one directory to a lower directory when some options may be overridden, this function merges two configuration records, given in the function heading as **basev** and **addv**. A new configuration record called **new** is created, and each of the fields of the two original configuration records is examined and either updated with the **addv** value or merged using the **ap_append_arrays** call.

14200: Special care must be taken with the options for the directory, because they can be additive (that is, a feature can be added to the options already in effect or can replace the set of options already in effect).

14218: If the new configuration has no options (**add=> opts==0**), then the new incremented and decremented options are taken directly from the **base** and **add** configurations. The **options** field of the new merged configuration is then set to the base options on line 14231.

14240: If plain options (nonincremental) are provided with the added configuration, those become the options, replacing any that were previously provided by the base configuration.

14247: These two lines remove any overlap between the options stated to be in effect and those that are incremental or decremental; for example, any bits from the **incremented_opts** field that already exist in the **opts** field are removed.

14258: If the **name_width** field value is still **K_UNSET** (set on line 13642), it's set to the base value; otherwise, it's set to the added value.

struct ent

14278: This structure holds all of the information about a file or directory in the directory listing, such as name, icon URL, and alternate description for the icon/file type. This information is assembled for each entry and then used by the **output_directories** function to create the actual HTML code.

find_item

14290: The **find_item** function goes through a list of items that were defined by directives (such as icons or descriptions) and finds which one applies to the file name passed in with the request (actually a subrequest created in the **make_autoindex** entry). The lists are filled by functions like **add_desc** and **add_icon** as directives are parsed. The method of matching the file to the right information is determined by the extra data used with the directive, such as **BY_PATH** or **BY_TYPE**. Depending on this setting, different information about the file is used to check a match with an item in the list.

14293: The content and encoding information for this request is saved, as well as the file name (in **path**). A **for** loop is then set up (line 14303) to go through each of the items in the list. Remember that the list may be a list of icon URLs or descriptions, depending on which list was passed in to search. The **for** loop is looking for a match on a key in the list and will then return the matching value portion of the list.

14307: Directories can only be assigned something based on path (not by type or encoding). The special case of directories is checked here. If **apply_path** (which paths to apply this item to in the list) matches the path passed in to test, then the data from that item is returned.

14312: If the type of comparison is **BY_PATH**, the same type of comparison is accomplished. If found, the data from that list item is returned.

14319: A **path_only** flag may be set by some calls. If it isn't set, a check by type or encoding may be needed (if **BY_PATH** was false, this happened immediately). In either case (type or encoding), the **content_type** or **content_encoding** are compared against the current item in the list. If they match, the corresponding data item is returned.

14340: If none of the **apply_to** items in the list matched the file name of the request, then a NULL is returned.

14343: Special cases of **find_item** are used to search in specific lists. The **#define** statements make the search look specialized, creating a reliance on using the parameter names (**d**, **p**) that match the **#defines** to determine the search criteria. This reliance can be problematic if the module is modified.

find_default_icon

14349: This function actually uses the **find_item** function to look up information, much as the **#defines** on line 14343 uses it. The **find_icon** operation required a name to be passed in differently, however, so a separate function is used to create a request with the name **bogus_name**, reset the **content_encoding**, and call **find_item** with the list of icons to look at.

ignore_entry

14366: The **ignore_entry** function determines if the path passed in as a parameter is included in the **ign_list** of the configuration record. If so, it returns 1; otherwise, it returns 0 (don't ignore this entry). This function is called by **make_autoindex_entry** to determine if a file name should be part of the directory listing.

14370: Creates a few variables to facilitate access to the list of **ignore** items (generated by **add_ignore** on line 13830), and verifies that the item being tested doesn't have a slash in it (line 14374). If a slash exists, it must be ignored during compare operations. The **strrchr** function on line 14385 determines the slash's position, and only compares the characters before the slash.

14381: Uses a **for** loop to check each item in the ignore list. For each one (after checking the position of the slash so it can be used as the point to split the string during comparisons), a string match comparison is done using either **ap_strcmp_match** or **ap_strcasecmp_match**, depending on the operating system that Apache is running on. The **CASE_BLIND_FILESYSTEM** compiler **#define** will be set during configuration before the server is compiled. If the comparison succeeds, it exits with a 1 on line 14395 or 14407. If the comparison never succeeds, after completing the **for** loop to check each one, it exits with a 0 (don't ignore this entry) on line 14411.

insert_readme

14423: The **insert_readme** function writes a header or footer file (generally README or HEADER) out to the client. The first step is to verify that the file exists and can be accessed. Line 14435 then gets the configuration for the current directory and starts preparing a path to use in a new subrequest, which will test the ability for Apache to read the file.

14442: Assembles and tests the file name, starting with the **readme_fname** parameter passed into the function. If the **hrule** flag is set, a horizontal rule tag is then written to the client (line 14453).

14463: A subrequest is created that looks up the file name prepared as **fn**. If the status of that requested lookup is not **HTTP_OK** on line 14464, the subrequest is destroyed and the function exits without writing out the file.

14467: If the file can be read, the subrequest is still destroyed because it has served its purpose. The file is opened on line 3104 using **ap_pfopen** and the **fn** file name string.

14471: If this is a header file (occurs at the top of the document being returned to the client) and the **SUPPRESS_PREAMBLE** option is not active, then a preamble is sent first via the **emit_preamble** function.

14475: If the file to send isn't plain text (see line 14451), the **ap_send_fd** call dumps the whole file to the client and goes to line 14516 to close the file and exit.

14478: If the file is plain text, processing is required to make any angle brackets and ampersands in the file appear correctly in the browser. It starts by sending a **<PRE>** tag to the client, then loops for each byte of the file on line 14482, reading the whole file into the **buf** variable.

14493: Loops through the entire file buffer, **buf**, using the **ap_rputs** call to output one character at a time to the client, testing each time for a <, >, or & character. If these are encountered, the HTML codes for those characters are output instead.

14516: After the file is sent, the file descriptor is closed. If the file was plain text, the **</PRE>** tag appears on line 14518. (A **<PRE>** tag isn't used for non-plain text files.)

find_title

14524: The **find_title** function locates the **<TITLE>** tag within an HTML document so that it can be used as the description for a file name in the index listing.

14526: The string to locate for this exercise is **<TITLE>**; the title tag in HTML.

14533: The file to be examined must be of type HTML or no **<TITLE>** tag can be found. If these tests pass, the file is opened on line 14538 and read into the **titlebuf** buffer on line 14542.

14549: The **for** loop is used to locate the first matching character of the find string (which is equal to **<TITLE>**). Once found, the title itself (the text between the **<TITLE>** tags) is scanned to its end. The variable **x** marks the end of the title, so that it can be returned by doing a string copy on line 14570.

14559: Line breaks are intercepted and converted to spaces. Line breaks aren't likely to occur in the **<TITLE>** tag itself, but in the **<TITLE>** text they create broken lines in the description field of the index listing.

make_autoindex_entry

14583: The **make_autoindex_entry** function takes an entry returned from the file system (queried by the **fread** function on line 14584) and formats it using an **ent** structure with the information needed by the **output_directories** function.

14591: If the entry name is a single period, it refers to the current directory. This entry will be returned by the **fread** function, but shouldn't be included in the directory listing. A NULL is returned.

14595: If the name is part of the **ignore_entry** list, a NULL is returned.

14600: For entries that are valid, space is allocated for the entry with **ap_palloc**, then the values of each field are initialized. The key field is **name**, which is copied to the entry (**p**) with **ap_pstrdup**.

14612: If **FancyIndexing** is enabled, a few more steps are needed to set up the additional fields and icons needed for the listing. This involves making a subrequest so that the validity of the file can be tested and its type can be established.

14616: If the status of the subrequest is non-zero, processing can continue. Line 14618 verifies that this is a directory. If no other icon comes back, the icon is marked as a directory and the alternative text for the figure (the **alt** field) is marked as **DIR** on line 14625. The name of directories ends with a slash (/), added using the **ap_pstrcat** function on line 14628.

14632: For non-directories (also known as files), the icon and alternative text are determined by the respective functions. (These are not real functions, but iterations of **find_item**; see line 14344.) The file size is part of the subrequest, generated automatically, so it is placed in the **size** field.

14638: The description starts as the result of the **find_desc** function, another incarnation of **find_item** (see line 14344). If the description comes back as an empty string and the flag to use HTML titles is active, **find_title** is called to attempt to use the HTML title of the document as the description field.

14645: After finishing using the subrequest to find information, it can be destroyed.

14652: The last modified date (set in line 14617) is checked for validity if it is the sort key. Line 14654 makes the last modified date zero if it was somehow set to less than zero.

terminate_description

14660: The **terminate_description** function cuts off the descriptive information about a file in the index listing if the **SUPPRESS_LAST_MOD** or **SUPPRESS_SIZE** options are active for this directory. If neither field is used in this directory, a longer description field is permitted.

14667: Resets the maximum size (string length) for the description field by checking for the **SUPPRESS_LAST_MOD** and **SUPPRESS_SIZE** options.

14674: If the string contained no HTML tags, the fields can be truncated. Because of HTML (the **<TITLE>** tag may be used for the description), this **for** loop is needed to ensure that tags are not counted (nor are they cut in half, producing ugly half-HTML tags in the browser). In addition, the loop on line 14685 converts the character

count to only count one character when a special HTML character is found (such as **&amp** for the & character).

14700: The variable **x** contains the string index marking the last valid character of the description. The string is terminated with a closing HTML angle bracket and a string terminator (**\0**).

emit_link

14714: The **emit_link** function sends the HTML text for an anchor tag (**<A>**) to a client when the field is a sort key. If the field is not a sort key, only the anchor is sent, without a link (see line 12405). If the field is a sort key, however, as determined by the **nosort** parameter, additional processing provides the ability to reverse the sort by clicking on the link.

14721: If the current anchor field is a sort key, then an anchor is assembled where the link points to the same document, but with the sorting order for this field reversed. The current sorting order (**curdirection**) determines what sort direction the link should have (set in line 14728). The complete anchor is output on line 14729 with an **ap_rvputs** call. For example, the **HREF** value of a link on the size field might be **?S=A** to allow the user to reverse the current order of the sort.

output_directories

14775: When most of the work is done, the **output_directories** function sends most of the directory listing data to the client.

14796: Sets up the width for the names in the listings based on the **K_ADJUST** value. If it's set, the **name_width** variable expands to the maximum length of a file name, so that each file or directory name in the listing lines up vertically with the longest name. One additional space is added on line 14805 to provide a blank space after the name field in the listing.

14806: Sets up a scratch memory area equal to the length of the name that was just determined (plus a termination character).

14811: If **FancyIndexing** is on (by directive), a **<PRE>** tag and an **<IMG>** tag with an icon for the headings are output. The correct icon is determined using the **find_default_icon** function on line 14813. The icon height and width are included, if available. The **<IMG>** tag is closed on line 14827.

14829: Uses the **emit_link** function to output a heading field for the **Name** field. Line 14833 is a set of blanks that fill in the column headings line to the full width determined for the **Name** field. One space is added on line 14842 to guarantee that a space will occur between fields.

14843: Follows the same process for the **Last Modified Date**, **Size**, and **Description** fields, depending on whether the **IndexOptions** allows those fields. The additional spaces on lines 14842, 14847, and 14852 fill in the column headings to match the width of those fields as they come from the **filesystem** calls. The headings are then finished by sending a horizontal line tag.

14862: If **FancyIndexing** wasn't selected, no headers are output. A bullet list is started for the directory contents.

14865: Loops through each of the elements in the directory (to the total **n** passed in as a parameter).

14873: If the entry being processed is a parent directory ".." then the file name and the link used to reach it are updated. The name of the item (**t2**) is changed to **Parent Directory** on line 14880. The URL to link to if this item is clicked (**t**) is determined by the **ap_getparents** call on line 14875.

14893: The entry being processed begins to be sent to the client by first testing the use of **Fancy Indexing**. If it is set, the **ICONS_ARE_ LINKS** option is tested. If icons are to be used as links, an anchor tag is sent to the client The **FancyIndexing** block then sends an **<IMG>** tag on line 14899 with all of the additional information provided by the fields of this array entry, such as the icon URL and alternate text for the icon. The **<IMG>** tag is closed on line 14911.

14917: The file or directory itself is always a link, so an **<A>** tag is started on line 14917, followed by the width-standardized name of the entry (the file name or directory name) and the closing anchor tag. This allows the user to click on the link to jump to the file named in the listing.

14929: Because all of the names are different widths, the extra spaces required to justify the entry names to a consistent width is output using the scratch space that the **widthify** function used to set up the name.

14936: The next few fields are a constant width. After checking to see if the **Last Modified Date** should be used, the time string from the entry (in the **ar** array) is prepared as a string by the **strftime** standard function. That string is sent on line 14942, followed by padding spaces on line 14947.

14951: The **ap_send_size** call sends the size number as a string to the client, followed by some padding spaces.

14954: The description is sent using the **terminate_ description** function, which allows a longer description string if the **Last Modified** and **Size** fields were not included.

14963: If **FancyIndexing** isn't in force, a List Item **<LI>** is sent with **t2** (the file name) as a link. Depending on whether **FancyIndexing** was

used, a **<PRE>** tag or a **<UL>** tag must be closed to finish a correctly formed HTML page.

dsortf

14983: **dsortf** is the comparison function used by the **qsort** function to sort the array of index entries on line 15157. It returns a 1 if the first element should be sorted as the first item or a –1 if the second element should be sorted as the first item.

14994: Parent directories should always be the first item in a sorted list, so test for those first using the **is_parent** function (line 13707).

15003: The parameters passed in are assigned to **c1** and **c2** based on the sort order being used.

15011: Based on the sort key, a different field of the element being sorted is compared between **c1** and **c2**. Based on which is the greater value, the function exits with the return value to push that item higher in the sort.

index_directory

15043: The **index_directory** function creates the actual HTML index of a directory and returns it to the client. It's called only after permissions have been checked in the **handle_autoindex** function.

15046: The function begins by allocating a few variables used to process the directory; several are initialized with directory information, such as the name of the directory and the options for the directory.

15062: Tries to open the directory named in this request (defined by **name** on line 15049). If the directory open fails, an error message is logged to the error log using the **ap_log_rerror** function and **HTTP_FORBIDDEN** is returned, which Apache will send to the client.

15071: As the first step in sending an HTML index to the client, which has been determined to be possible because the directory can be opened, the headers for this reply are sent.

15073: If only the headers are being requested (a **HEAD** request as opposed to a **GET** request), the directory that was opened in line 15062 is closed and the function returns a 0 (successful).

15077: Before starting to process the directory listing, a timeout is set so that, if the directory listing is not returned (and the request finished) by the timeout value set on the server, the request is canceled and the string **send directory** is logged in the error log.

15081: Prepares the name of the directory for which the index will be created. The **while** loop on line 15083 is used to properly terminate the string so that it can be used in subsequent string functions.

15088: As the first part of the HTML to return to the client, this line searches for the headers defined by the **HeaderName** directive. The **find_ header** function doesn't really exist; it's defined as a case of **find_item** on line 14347 using the **hdr_list** field of the configuration record. If a header is located, the **insert_readme** function is used to write it out to the client. If either of those operations fails, then no header was defined or available. In that case, it goes to line 15092 and uses the **emit_preamble** function to send a generic heading for the HTML document.

15093: After sending the header or the preamble, the title of the listing, a level-one heading with the name of the directory (**title_name**), is started. The **ap_rvputs** call is used to send this to the client.

15107: Sets **qstring** to the arguments sent with the request. The argument (information after a ?) can be used to determine the sort order of the directory listing. If the column sorting option is suppressed (by checking **SUPPRESS_ COLSORT** against the **autoindex_opts**) or if there are no arguments, then **qstring** is set to the value of the default sorting order (on line 15110). This field of the configuration is set by the **IndexOrderDefault** directive.

15117: Checks whether the value of **qstring** is valid. If it is still NULL, the key field is set to the file name (**K_NAME**) and the direction (**D_ASCENDING**). Otherwise, the sorting key is set equal to **qstring** in line 15122, and the direction after the = is read. If no direction is given, the default **D_ASCENDING** is used.

15138: This **while** loop reads entries from the directory opened on line 15062. Each entry is parsed into a standardized form by the **make_autoindex_entry** function (which starts on line 14583). Each entry includes all of the pieces defined by the directives for this module (such as **AddIcon**). Each entry is of type **ent** (defined on line 14278). If the information returned by **make_autoindex_entry** is non-NULL, the **while** loop continues by pointing to the next item in the linked list and repeating the directory read on 15137.

15147: If the list of directory entries isn't empty (**num_ent** is greater than zero), memory is allocated for an array on line 3784, and the **while** loop on line 15152 places each element of the linked list into the array. This is done to allow a standard quick-sort of the entries, which occurs on line 15157.

15162: With the contents of the directory sorted, **output_directories** is called with the array of directory information (**ar**). The **output_directories** function watches for the other directives, such as those for suppressing columns.

15165: At this point, no more data needs to be read from the directory, so it's closed using the **ap_pclosedir** function.

15167: All of the listing has been output. **find_readme** checks for footer information (any README files). If any are found by **find_readme** (which is actually **find_item(p,d->rdme_list,0)**; see line 14347), then they are output to the client using the **insert_readme** function. Old **FancyIndexing** directive options are looked for, and they're used to emit a horizontal rule tag (**<HR>**), if needed, and the server's signature, if the **ServerSignature** directive is enabled.

15176: Whether a README footer was sent or not, the HTML output ends here with the tags closing the **<BODY>** and **<HTML>** sections.

15178: Having completed the task for which a timeout was set up, the timeout is killed and a 0 is returned, indicating that this request was successfully handled by this module.

handle_autoindex

15184: The main handler for this module is **handle_autoindex**. It begins by creating a configuration record (**d**), which it fills with the applicable configuration for this directory by calling **ap_get_module_config** on line 15190. The options allowed for this request (based on its location) are also retrieved on line 15187 and stored in **allow_opts**. The options bitmap pattern stored in **allow_opts** must include **OPT_INDEXES** or the indexing cannot proceed.

15193: If the request doesn't have a **GET** method, no directory index should be returned. **DECLINED** is then returned on line 15195, exiting the module.

15201: If the **allow_opts** value for this directory includes **OPT_INDEXES** (by testing the values via a logical **AND** operation), then this process is continued. Otherwise, it moves to line 15216, which sends a log message to the error log file using the **ap_log_rerror** function and exits the module with **HTTP_FORBIDDEN** (which will be returned to the client). Note that the error log message includes the directory being requested (**r->filename** on line 15220).

15209: If indexes are allowed by the test on line 15201, the file name of the request is prepared by adding a slash (/) to the end of it, if necessary, because requests for directories look like requests for files. Therefore, the final part of the requested path is placed in the file name field of the request.

15214: Returns the value given by the **index_directory** function, which will be 0 if the directory listing is created successfully. The **index_directory** function does the actual HTML creation and sends it to the client browser.

autoindex_handlers

15226: Defines the main function to call for this module: **handle_autoindex**.

autoindex_module

15232: Defines this module's hooks for the Apache core. Only the **create** and **merge** configurations, the command table (see line 14083), and the handler (see line 15226) are included for this module.

Chapter 8

Logging Modules

This chapter describes four modules that are used to log user requests and generate cookies for tracking those requests: **mod_log_agent**, **mod_log_referer**, **mod_log_config**, and **mod_usertrack** (which manages cookies). The three logging modules generate log entries for each request if the corresponding directives (described in the following sections) are defined for a given server context. Both **mod_log_referer** and **mod_log_agent** (which log the referring page and the client browser) may be used independently of **mod_log_config** (which logs general request information in Common Log Format [CLF] or another format that you define). Complex custom logging formats based on numerous fields can be defined.

Apache uses **mod_usertrack** to generate a cookie for any request coming to a context in which cookies are enabled. If a request already has a cookie, **mod_usertrack** reassociates that cookie with the request record. The association created between a cookie and a request allows a user script launched by Apache to track previous actions on this server by the same client.

Discussion Of **mod_log_agent**

This module acts independently of other logging modules. If the **AgentLog** directive is used within a server context, **mod_log_agent** logs the browser used by the client for the request to the file indicated in the directive.

Module Structure

Initialization of **mod_log_agent** prepares a variable to store a log file name for a server context. During the logging phase of request handling, **mod_log_agent** is called. If a valid log file name is defined for the current context and the file appears to be open (by checking

the file descriptor), the agent is queried from the request headers and written to the log file. The structure is illustrated in Figure 8.1.

Customization

mod_log_agent can be used for any basic logging task. Any header information that a client browser supplies can be logged by modifying **mod_log_agent**. This is much simpler, for example, than extending the **mod_log_config** module to handle additional parameters in **LogFormat** directives.

If the agent making the request is associated with additional actions on your Web server, **mod_log_agent** can be extended either to log additional information about the request or to take other actions (such as send an email or automatically increment a statistical counter) based on which agent was detected.

agent_log_state

21848: The **agent_log_state** structure is the configuration record for **mod_log_agent**. It includes two fields: **fname** for the file name of the log file and **agent_fd** for the file descriptor (created when the file is opened for writing).

make_agent_log_state

21853: The **make_agent_log_state** function initializes the configuration of **mod_log_agent** within a server context by creating a variable (of type **agent_log_state**) and initializing its two values on lines 21860 and 21861.

set_agent_log

21866: The **set_agent_log** function is called as directives are parsed when an **AgentLog** directive is found (line 21879). The current server configuration is retrieved on line 21870. The file name (taken from the **arg** variable) to which agents should be logged in this context is stored in the **cls** configuration record (line 21873).

agent_log_cmds

21877: The **agent_log_cmds** structure defines the single directive that **mod_log_agent** uses, **AgentLog**. The function **set_agent_log** (line

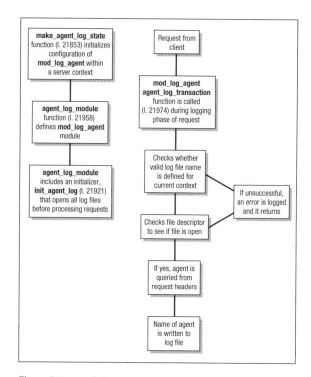

Figure 8.1   **mod_log_agent** logs the browser used to make a request.

21866) is defined to handle **AgentLog** directives when they are found in configuration files.

open_agent_log

21885: The **open_agent_log** function opens all of the log files defined in any **AgentLog** directives. This is done during the initialization stage of the server to make log writes fast during request processing. The **open_agent_log** function is called repeatedly from the **init_agent_log** function, once for each server that may have a separate **AgentLog** defined.

21888: Retrieves the configuration of the current server using **ap_get_module_config**.

21891: Uses **ap_server_root_relative** to set the file name of the log file to be opened according to the value of the **cls->fname**. The resulting file name is stored in **fname**.

21894: If the file descriptor field for this log file (the **agent_fd** field of **cls**) is greater than zero, something has happened since the log file was initialized. **open_agent_log** assumes that the file is already opened and returns without further action.

21899: If the log storage file name begins with a pipe symbol (|), use the **ap_open_piped_log** command on line 21902 to merge the current log with the main server log via the pipe. If the result of the open command (stored in **pl**) is NULL, a problem occurred. An error is logged, but **open_log_agent** still returns (to **init_agent_log**, line 21924) with a value of 1.

21908: If the piped open was successful, the file descriptor is stored in the **agent_fd** field using the **ap_piped_log_write_fd** call so that **agent_log_transaction** (line 21927) can use it to write to the log file.

21910: If the file name didn't begin with a pipe symbol (and if it isn't an empty string), the **ap_popenf** call is used on line 21911 to open the log file. This command also immediately places the file descriptor in the **agent_fd** field. The **xfer_flags** and **xfer_mode** are defined beginning on line 21838.

21913: If the file open was not successful, an error is logged and **open_log_agent** returns.

init_agent_log

21921: The **init_agent_log** function uses a **for** loop to process each of the server configurations available to it, calling **open_agent_log** repeatedly to attempt to open the **AgentLog** file defined for each server context.

agent_log_transaction

21927: The **agent_log_transaction** function logs the agent for a transaction (request). It is called during the logging stage of request processing (line 21974).

21929: Retrieves the configuration for the server using **ap_get_module_config** so that the file descriptor to write to is available to the function.

21937: Tests the validity of the file descriptor. If it is invalid, the function returns a value of **OK**. The file name is tested on line 21942. If it is an empty string, the function returns a value of **DECLINED**.

21940: Checks that the request being logged is the final request in a series of subrequests.

21948: Queries the table of headers using **ap_table_get** for the **User-Agent** header. The header is then placed in **agent**.

21950: If **agent** is non-NULL, the request is logged by first filling the **str** variable with the **agent** and a newline, then writing **str** to the file defined by the file descriptor **agent_fd**.

agent_log_module

21958: Defines the module **mod_log_agent**. This includes an initializer, **init_agent_log** defined on line 21921, that opens all log files before processing requests. The standard configuration and directive (**cmds**) style of functions are included. The core of the module, **agent_log_transaction** on line 21974, is called during the logging phase.

Discussion Of mod_log_referer

This module acts independently of other logging modules. If the **RefererLog** directive is provided for a server context, **mod_log_referer** logs the referring page specified by the client to the file indicated in the directive. The information logged is the URL (Web address) of the page that the browser was viewing when the current request was selected. If a user selects a URL from a bookmark list or enters it manually, no referrer is included in the headers from the client.

In most cases, you don't want all referring Web pages logged. For example, if a user is moving between Web

pages on your site, the referrer is your site's URL. Unless you need to track how users move through your site (a difficult task), this information wouldn't be included in your referrer log. When the **RefererIgnore** directive is used, **mod_log_referer** ignores referrer fields that match the arguments of the directive. Nothing is logged in these cases.

Module Structure

Initialization of **mod_log_referer** prepares a variable to store a log file name for a server context and initializes the various fields. As shown in Figure 8.2, during the logging phase of request handling, **mod_log_referer** is called. If a valid log file name is defined for the current context and the file appears to be open (by checking the file descriptor), the referrer field is queried from the request headers. If the referrer is not in the ignore list defined for this context, the referrer is written to the log file.

Customization

Like **mod_log_agent**, **mod_log_referer** is a simple module that can be extended or reused for any basic logging task. Any header information that a client browser supplies can be logged by modifying **mod_log_referer**. This would be much simpler, for example, than extending the **mod_log_config** module to handle additional parameters in **LogFormat** directives.

If you want the Web server to take specific action based on the URL of the referring Web page (such as returning a message other than the page requested), **mod_log_referer** can be modified to do this.

Auto-generation of ignore lists based on various heuristics or simple rules generated by the module or another program, a more complex modification, can also be accomplished. This could help to make the referrer logs more valuable for tracking system usage and marketing your Web site.

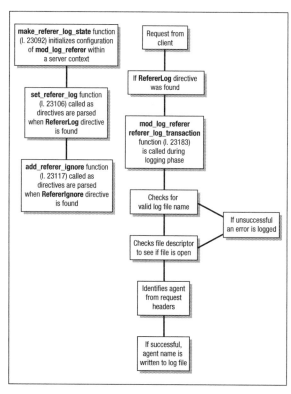

Figure 8.2 **mod_log_referer** logs the URL of the page that the browser was viewing when a request was made.

Constant And Structure Definitions

23076: Defines flags that are used for the open file operation on line 23168.

referer_log_state

23086: The **referer_log_state** structure is the configuration record for **mod_log_referer**. It includes three fields: **fname** for the file name of the log file, **referer_fd** for the file descriptor (created when the file is opened for writing), and an array of referrers to ignore taken from the **RefererIgnore** directive.

make_referer_log_state

23092: The **make_referer_log_state** function initializes the configuration of **mod_log_referer** within a server context by creating a variable (of type **referer_log_state**) and initializing its three values (on lines 23099 to 23102).

set_referer_log

23106: The **set_referer_log** function is called as directives are parsed when a **RefererLog** directive is found (line 23133). The current server configuration is retrieved on line 23110. The file name (taken from the **arg** variable) to which referrers should be logged in this context is stored in the **cls** configuration record (line 23113).

add_referer_ignore

23117: The **add_referer_ignore** function is called when **RefererIgnore** directives are found. It takes the arguments passed to it and adds them to the **referer_ignore_list** field of the current server configuration record for **mod_log_referer** (line 23125). This field is queried by the **referer_log_transaction** function (starting on line 23213).

referer_log_cmds

23131: The **referer_log_cmds** structure defines the two directives that **mod_log_referer** uses: **RefererLog** and **RefererIgnore**. The functions to call when each directive is found in a configuration file are defined: **set_referer_log** (line 23106) and **add_referer_ignore** (line 23117), respectively, for the two directives.

open_referer_log

23142: The **open_referer_log** function opens all of the log files defined in any **RefererLog** directives. This is done during the initialization stage of the server to make log writes fast during request processing. The **open_referer_log** function is called repeatedly from the **init_referer_log** function, once for each server that may have a **RefererLog** defined.

23145: Retrieves the configuration of the current server using **ap_get_module_config**.

23148: Sets the file name of the log file to be opened to the variable **fname** using **ap_server_root_relative**. The **fname** field of the **cls** variable is used as the base of the file name.

23151: If the file descriptor field for this log file (the **referer_fd** field of **cls**) is greater than zero, something has happened since the log file was initialized. It is assumed that the file is already opened; **open_referer_log** returns without further action.

23155: If the log storage file name begins with a pipe symbol (|), the **ap_open_piped_log** command on line 23158 is used to merge the current log with the main server log via the pipe. If the result of the open command (stored in **pl**) is NULL, a problem occurred. An error is logged, but the function still returns (to **init_referer_log**, line 23180) with a value of 1.

23165: If the piped open was successful, the file descriptor is stored in the **referer_fd** field using the **ap_piped_log_write_fd** call so that **referer_log_transaction** (line 23183) can use it to write to the log file.

23167: If the file name didn't begin with a pipe symbol (and if it isn't an empty string), the **ap_popenf** call is used on line 23168 to open the log file. This command also immediately places the file descriptor in the **referer_fd** field in the same command. The **xfer_flags** and **xfer_mode** are defined beginning on line 23076.

23170: If the file open was not successful, an error is logged and **open_referer_log** returns.

init_referer_log

23177: The **init_referer_log** function uses a **for** loop to process each of the server configurations available to it, calling **open_referer_log** repeatedly to attempt to open the **RefererLog** file defined for each server context.

referer_log_transaction

23183: The **referer_log_transaction** function logs the referring Web page for a transaction (request). It is called during the logging stage of request processing (line 23256).

23187: Retrieves the configuration for the server using **ap_get_module_config** so that the file descriptor to write to is available to the function.

23195: Tests the validity of the file descriptor. If it is invalid, the function returns a value of **OK**. The file name is tested on line 23200. If it is an empty string, the function returns a value of **DECLINED**.

23198: Checks that the request being logged is the final request in a series of subrequests.

23203: Queries the table of headers using **ap_table_get** for the **Referer** header. The header is then placed in **referer**.

23204: If **referer** is non-NULL, the referrer is placed in **referertest** to check it against the list of referrers to ignore (as defined by any **RefererIgnore** directives), in preparation for logging the request.

23213: Initializes the pointer that will start the loop to check against referrers to ignore.

23222: Loops using **for** to check each referrer in the ignore list against the one that the client supplied. If a match occurs at any time during the loop, as tested on line 23227, it returns without logging anything on line 23228.

23232: Because the **for** loop didn't exit the module, the referrer was not in the ignore list. The request is logged by filling the **str** variable with the referrer, the URI of the current page, and a newline. Finally, **str** is written to the file defined by the file descriptor **referer_fd**.

referer_log_module

23240: Defines the module **mod_log_referer**. This includes an initializer, **init_referer_log** on line

23243, that opens all log files before processing requests. The standard configuration and directive (**cmds**) style of functions are included. The core of the module, **referer_log_transaction** on line 23256, is called during the logging phase.

Discussion Of **mod_log_config**

The preferred logging tool for Apache is **mod_log_config**. Using the directives **CustomLog**, **LogFormat**, **CookieLog**, and **TransferLog**, this module enables users to define any number of log formats and have Apache log each transaction according to those formats. The items logged by **mod_log_referer** and **mod_log_agent** are special cases of items that could also be logged by **mod_log_config**. The default log configuration for **mod_log_config**, however, does not include the referrer or agent fields.

To use **mod_log_config**, specify a **TransferLog** location. If more complex or non-standard formatting is desired, use the **LogFormat** directive to define a new format and the **CustomLog** directive to enable it. A custom formatting string can be defined with **LogFormat** and then used in a **CustomLog** directive, or **CustomLog** can include a formatting string.

mod_log_config allows a single transaction to be logged multiple times according to different formats that have been defined. Formats can be defined within server or directory contexts; if no format is specified for a context, **mod_log_config** defaults to the main server log format. Throughout this module, the CLF is assumed as a default format when no custom formatting string is provided. This format is used by numerous Web log analysis tools.

Module Structure

Much of the work of **mod_log_config** involves parsing the directives found in configuration files. This is done via the **log_format** function (line 22786) and the **add_custom_log** function (line 22817). After defining formatting instructions, each transaction is logged using the **multi_log_transaction** function (line 22695).

This function checks for the presence of per-server log configurations or defaults to the main server log configuration, then calls the **config_log_transaction** function (line 22597) to prepare a log entry for each of the formats that have been defined for the current context. With the format strings in place from parsing the directives, preparing a log entry string is relatively simple using the **process_item** function (which is called on line 22654). The module structure is shown in Figure 8.3.

Customization

The **mod_log_config** module can be expanded in two ways. First, the information selected by **CustomLog** formatting parameters can be expanded to include various pieces of additional information about the system, request, or environment. These must be defined in the directive parsing functions with the **log_item_list** structure (line 22297) and the log processing function

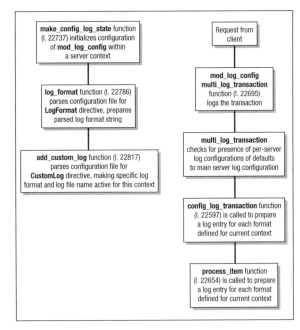

Figure 8.3 **mod_log_config** is used to produce Apache's log files.

process_item (line 22552). An additional small function is needed for each data item supported (following the example of the **log_header_out** function on line 22194).

mod_log_config supports conditional inclusion of log fields using the **!** operator before a log field parameter. This functionality can be expanded either by parsing additional operators (which you define) in the formatting strings or by hard coding specific cases to test for within the functions that return pieces of information (like those currently implemented beginning on line 22104).

The second main way of customizing **mod_log_config** is to alter where the log is written. This can be done easily in the **config_log_transaction** function, where the completed log entry is written to a file on line 22689. This log entry can be logged to a database, emailed, or even discarded for testing. When changing how these entries are handled, however, note that logging can place a heavy load on the server, so avoid CPU- or disk-intensive operations.

In addition to the information that follows, the source code for this module contains more comments than most. Reviewing these comments can provide insight about refining the module for specific needs.

Constant And Structure Definitions

21990: Defines a few flags used to open log files for writing.

multi_log_state

22036: Defines the **multi_log_state** structure, which is the configuration record for **mod_log_config**. It includes a default formatting string and the configuration files to write log information to. It is basically an array of **config_log_state** variables, which are defined starting on line 22054.

format_integer

22083: Formats an integer and returns it as a string. This function is used by the **pfmt** function (line 22088) to return negative numbers as well.

constant_item

22098: Returns the constant that is passed in as a parameter. Though this is almost superfluous, it provides a consistent interface for all the possible components of a log string.

log_remote_host

22104: Returns a string with a piece of information that will be placed in the completely assembled log string. The functions in this area provide return strings for the items that can be defined with the **CustomLog** or **LogFormat** directives. Most of these functions query information from the request variable **r** or a standard Apache API call. The functions include **log_remote_host** (line 22104), **log_remote_address** (line 22112), **log_remote_logname** (line 22118), **log_remote_user** (line 22124), **log_request_line** (line 22138), **log_request_file** (line 22158), **log_request_uri** (line 22163), **log_status** (line 22168), **log_bytes_sent** (line 22174), **log_header_in** (line 22188), **log_header_out** (line 22194), **log_note** (line 22208), **log_env_var** (line 22212), **log_request_time** (line 22217), **log_request_duration** (line 22248), **log_virtual_host** (line 22259), **log_server_port** (line 22265), **log_server_name** (line 22278), and **log_child_pid** (line 22284). Any of these functions can be altered to change how Apache prepares specific information nuggets for custom log files.

log_item_list

22297: Defines a structure that holds the formatting string options (such as **%a** for the remote address) that can be used to configure a log format. This structure includes the function name to call when logging a transaction to retrieve the piece of information that the format string refers to. For example, on line 22307, **a** refers to the **log_remote_address** function (line 22112).

find_log_func

22365: Returns the item within the **log_item_list** (line 22297) that matches the parameter passed into the function as **k**.

parse_log_misc_string

22377: Parses a **misc** string within a log formatting definition so that the string is passed verbatim to the log files. The various escaped characters (such as a backslash) are tested beginning on line 22404. On line 22433, the parameter **sa** is set to the value of **s**, which was prepared by the function.

parse_log_item

22437: Prepares an internal representation of a log formatting string (from a **CustomLog** or **LogFormat** directive) so that transactions can be logged using the format later. **parse_log_item** watches for special characters (such as **!**) in order to set conditional fields in the log. The **it** (log item) variable contains the information prepared by this function.

22442: If the parameter doesn't begin with a percent sign (%), then it is considered a **misc** string and parsed using **parse_log_misc_string**.

22510: Returns an error if the formatting string cannot be recognized during this parsing or if a syntax error causes the string to end when more information is required for the current item (line 22522).

22517: Returns the processes string in the **sa** variable.

parse_log_string

22526: Processes a log formatting string one item at a time using the **parse_log_item** function (line 22437). Each parsed formatting item is placed in an array for use in logging transactions. The variable **s** holds the formatting string to parse. The **parse_log_item** function is called in the **while** loop on line 22534 and also at the end of the function (as a cleanup of the last item) on line 22542.

process_item

22552: Processes a single item within the formatting string for an actual transaction that needs to be logged. This function tests the conditional attribute of the item (set using **!** in the formatting string) to see if the item should actually be included in the log string that is written out.

22567: Loops through each conditional element for the current logging format. If the item being logged is found, **in_list** is set to 1.

22574: If the item is in the conditional list, it is tested to see whether it should be included based on the current **condition_sense**.

22582: If the **condition_sense** was valid or the item was not conditional (it's always included), it is returned using the function defined for that item in the **log_item_list** structure (line 22297). For example, if the item being logged is "Bytes Sent," the **item->func** will refer to the **log_bytes_sent** function (line 22334).

flush_log

22588: Flushes the log buffer to disk using the **log_fd** (file descriptor) of the log provided in the **cls** variable (current log state). This function is compiled conditionally, depending on whether buffered logs are being used on the platform.

config_log_transaction

22597: Logs a single transaction (request) using a specific format and log file. This function is called repeatedly from **multi_log_transaction** (line 22695) for all logs that are needed for the current request.

22611: Checks that the file name for this logging work exists; if it doesn't, it will decline to process it.

22620: Tests for conditional items within the current format string. According to the result, it checks the environment variables (the **subprocess_env** field).

22636: Defines the format of the current logging event. If a format string is defined for the event, that format string is used (**cls->format**). If none is defined, **default_format** is used. Space is then allocated for the string that will be assembled based on the elements in the format to be used. **ap_palloc** is used to set **strs** and **strl** as the working areas to assemble the log string (lines 22638 and 22640).

22653: Loops through each of the elements in the **format** list. For each one, the **process_item** function is used to retrieve the actual data for that item (line 22552).

22657: Computes the line length for each item that **process_item** returned in the **strs** array so that the full log string can be assembled next.

22661: If buffered logs are defined for this platform, the buffer size is checked to see if space allows the log item to be buffered. If it doesn't, the information is written to disk on line 22671. If it does, the log string is buffered, element by element, using the loop on line 22674.

22681: For nonbuffered platforms, the **str** variable is assembled from the information in the **strs** and **strl** arrays.

22689: Writes the assembled log string to the file descriptor **log_fd**.

multi_log_transaction

22695: Logs a transaction (request) using all of the logging defined for the current context. If none is defined, the main server uses logging definitions to log the request. This is the main logging function called by Apache for a request, as set by the module definition on line 23060.

22707: If a context-specific (virtual-host-type) logging format is defined for the current context (a value is in the **mls->config_logs** variable), then it loops through all of the formats defined for this context using the loop on line 22710, calling **config_log_transaction** for each of them.

22717: If no context-specific logging format is defined, the main server log uses configuration information in **server_config_logs** as the format for this transaction. It loops through all of the main server log configurations using the loop on line 22720, calling **config_log_transaction** for each log configuration on line 22724.

make_config_log_state

22737: Initializes a server context for logging by creating a **multi_state_log** variable to hold log formatting and file name information. Multiple logging instructions can then be stored for a single context using the directives that **mod_log_config** supports.

merge_config_log_state

22763: Merges the **multi_state_log** records for two server contexts using the **ap_overlay_tables** API call on line 22775. The default format is added to the returned structure if needed (line 22770).

log_format

22786: Prepares a parsed log format string from the information provided in a **LogFormat** directive. Apache parses the fields of the directive based on the instructions in **config_log_cmds** (line 22870) and passes them in as parameters to this function. The **LogFormat** directive defines format but doesn't make it active; that is, nothing is logged unless a **TransferLog** or **CustomLog** directive provides a log file name.

22791: Retrieves the configuration of the current context so that the **mls** logging structure is available to store the parsed format information.

22802: If a nickname is provided for this format, it is parsed using **parse_log_string** (line 22526) and placed in the **mls** array for the current context.

22808: If no nickname is provided (the name is NULL), it is parsed using **parse_log_string**, and placed in the **default_format** field of **mls**.

add_custom_log

22817: Processes a **CustomLog** directive, making a specific log format and log file name active for this context. Multiple **CustomLog** directives may be used within a single context.

22822: Retrieves the configuration of the current context.

22831: Checks for conditional items within the formatting string.

22843: Sets the **fname** and **format_string** variables to the values provided in the function headers.

22849: If the **format_string** in non-NULL, it's parsed using **parse_log_string**.

22852: Sets the file descriptor for this log to –1, because the log file has not been opened for writing yet.

set_transfer_log

22857: Sets up a transaction log using the **TransferLog** directive. This function is called by Apache on line 22877. It calls **add_custom_log** (line 22817) to make a default format for the current context. The **TransferLog** directive is provided as a special case (default everything) of the **CustomLog** directive.

set_cookie_log

22863: Sets up a log for cookies based on the **CookieLog** directive. This function is called by Apache on line 22884. It calls **add_custom_log** (line 22817) to define a log with a format that includes just the cookie for a transaction (line 22867).

config_log_cmds

22870: Defines the directives used by this module. Each includes the function to call when that directive is located in a configuration file. The format and number of parameters associated with each directive, which Apache passes to the named function, are defined by the fifth field in the structure (for example, **TAKE23** or **TAKE1**). In this module, the functions that handle the directives are all closely related; that is, **set_transfer_log** and **set_cookie_log** are special cases of **add_custom_log**, which is called from both **set_transfer_log** and **set_cookie_log**.

open_config_log

22890: Opens the log files that have been defined.

22895: If the file descriptor is already greater than zero, this configuration is using the shared main server log, so nothing is done.

22900: If the file name doesn't exist, nothing is done.

22905: If the file name specified begins with a pipe symbol, the **ap_open_piped** call on line 22908 is used to prepare a pipe to write the log entries to. The file descriptor is assigned to **log_fd** using the **ap_piped_log_write_fd** call.

22915: For nonpiped (normal) file names, the relative root path of the server is retrieved and the **ap_popenf** call on line 22917 is used to open the file name specified for the log. An error is logged if the file open operation fails. Otherwise, **log_fd** contains the file descriptor to be used for future writes to this log.

open_multi_logs

22932: Opens each of the log files specified for a server context using the **open_config_log** function.

22936: Retrieves the configuration for the current server context.

22943: If a default format string doesn't yet exist for this **mls** structure, it attempts to create it using either the **default_format_string** provided by a **LogFormat** directive or the CLF constant definition, **DEFAULT_LOG_FORMAT** on line 22954. In either case, **parse_log_string** is used to prepare the string and then store it in the **default_format** field.

22957: If server context-specific logging information has been defined, it is used (from the **config_logs** array). It then sets up all of the format strings using **parse_log_string** on line 22967. Then each one is opened using **open_config_log** on line 22972.

22976: If no logging configurations are specified for this context, the default server logging setup, stored in **server_config_logs**, is used. It then checks

that a valid formatting string is available (line 22983), formatting it if necessary using **parse_log_string** on line 22987. Finally, it opens the log file using **open_config_log** on line 22992.

init_config_log

23000: Initializes all log files defined for the server. First, **open_multi_logs** is called with the main server record, **s**. Then all of the log files are opened for each of the virtual server contexts by looping through the **s** array on line 23011, calling **open_multi_logs** for each one on line 23012. Finally, the **init_config_log** function is called during the initializer stage by Apache (line 23047).

flush_all_logs

23017: If buffered logs are defined for this platform, this function flushes any remaining log entries in the buffer to the appropriate file descriptor.

23024: Loops through each server context, retrieving the configuration information for each and calling the **flush_log** function (line 22588) for each of the log configurations for that server on line 23037.

config_log_module

23044: Defines the module with functions for initializing the log files (**init_config_log** on line 23047), setting up logging data structures (**make_config_log_state** and **merge_config_log_state**), the command table to define directives for this module (**config_log_cmds**), the logging phase itself (**multi_log_transaction** on line 23060) and platforms that support it, and a flush of write buffers in the **child_exit** stage.

Discussion Of **mod_usertrack**

mod_usertrack isn't a logging module in the same sense as the other three modules in this chapter; however, it is used to keep track of users. When the **CookieEnable** directive is used for a location on your Web site, **mod_usertrack** is activated any time a request comes for that location. **mod_usertrack** manages cookies within request headers so that they are available to scripts or programs launched by Apache as standard environment information.

If an incoming request has an Apache cookie, **mod_usertrack** places it in the information tracked for the request (such as logs). If the incoming request doesn't have a cookie header but it should (based on its location), **mod_usertrack** assigns a unique cookie and makes it available for scripts and programs.

Module Structure

mod_usertrack handles requests during the **fixups** stage in order to make a cookie header available for scripts or programs launched by Apache in response to the request. The **spot_cookie** function checks the client request headers for a cookie. If one is found, it is placed in the **notes** field of the request. If a cookie is not found, the **make_cookie** function is called to generate a new cookie and place it in the **notes** field of the request (see Figure 8.4). This module is only called for locations that had the **CookieTracking** directive set.

Customization

mod_usertrack provides a user tracking mechanism (the cookie) for programs or scripts started by Apache because of a client request. **mod_usertrack** can be extended to perform specific tasks to manage those cookies directly, such as posting them to a database. Statistics can be maintained for each cookie, with frequency of visits, and these can be correlated to other header information from the client (such as referrer page, time of day, or hostname).

These cookie-management features should be separated from activities that use the cookies. For example, **mod_usertrack** is not the place for the functions that prepare a document for the client based on the cookie database. Another module should be used to keep those content functions separated from user tracking.

This module can be customized to use a different cookie name, rather than **Apache=** (see line 36889), allowing

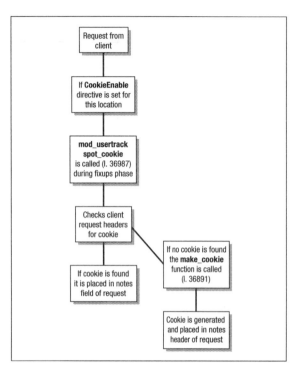

Figure 8.4   **mod_usertrack** is used to track users by means of cookies.

multiple cookies to be sent and maintained from a single Web server to a single client, which might be helpful for some virtual hosting situations.

cookie_log_state

36874: Defines a structure, **cookie_log_state**, as the configuration record for **mod_usertrack**. This structure includes a field for the expiration time defined for cookies within a server context.

36883: Defines a flag so that the cookies generated by the **make_cookie** function (beginning on 36891) are compatible with crossing the year 2000 boundary.

36889: Defines a name for all cookies associated with this module. This name is checked by the **spot_cookie** function to see if a cookie returned by a client came from this server.

make_cookie

36891: Creates a new cookie to be returned with a client request that does not yet have one (but for which one should be included based on the **Cookie Tracking** directive).

36894: Retrieves the configuration of the server for this context.

36896: Prepares data structures to hold time information used to generate a unique cookie. Some time systems on various operating systems require the use of **DEFINE** statements in this section.

36904: Defines a variable to hold the cookie being defined. Its maximum size is 1,024 characters.

36906: Retrieves the remote host using the **ap_get_remote_host** call. This is used as part of the cookie in an attempt to create a unique cookie.

36917: If the operating system being used doesn't provide a time-of-day function, the **times** function gets a time value.

36919: The remote host name, time value, and process ID are used to assemble a new cookie into the **cookiebuf** variable using **ap_snprintf**.

36932: Assembles a new cookie into the **cookiebuf** variable using **ap_snprintf**, but without using any time functions. The **GetTickCount** function is used to generate a time-based number.

36938: Retrieves the time of day using **gettimeofday**. It then assembles the new cookie using **ap_snprintf** on line 36940.

36946: If the **expires** field for cookies in this location is set, it records a time in the **when** variable based on the request time and the expire time.

36959: If the **when** variable seems too large and the **MILLENIAL** flag is set, **when** is changed to be just before the new year in 2000, to avoid rollover problems with other (client) programs.

36966: Adds to the cookie string, placing the new string in **new_cookie**. The new string consists of the cookie name (**Apache=**), **cookiebuf** information prepared previously by **ap_snprintf**, and the expiration time taken from the **expires** field of the server configuration.

36976: If no expiration time was indicated for this location, the final cookie header is assembled with the cookie name (**Apache=**), the **cookiebuf**, and the path statement.

36979: Adds the cookie that was just created to the headers returned to the client.

36981: Adds the cookie to the **notes** for this request to allow the loggers (see "Discussion Of **mod_log_config**") to record each time a new cookie (new user) visits the site. The cookie is only logged if an appropriate field identifier is included in the **LogFormat** directive used by **mod_log_config**.

spot_cookie

36987: Checks the headers of an incoming request for a cookie. If they should include a cookie but don't, one is made using the **make_cookie** function.

36990: Retrieves the server configuration using **ap_get_module_config**.

36995: If the server configuration indicates that cookies are not enabled for this location on the server, **DECLINED** is returned.

36998: Knowing that a cookie should be associated with this request because **enable** was set, **spot_cookie** checks for a cookie in the incoming request headers using **ap_table_get**. If no cookie is returned, **spot_cookie** drops to line 37016 and prepares one.

37000: If the cookie that is returned is not an Apache cookie (check against the **COOKIE_NAME**), then **spot_cookie** also drops down to line 37016 and makes an Apache cookie for this client.

37003: With a valid Apache cookie header found, string manipulations are used to isolate the cookie itself. It is then added to the notes for this request using **ap_table_setn** on line 37011 so that the cookie can be logged (if so configured).

make_cookie_log_state

37020: Configures a new record for a server context by creating a **cookie_log_state** variable using **ap_palloc** and initializing the variable's fields.

make_cookie_dir

37032: Configures a new record for a directory location by returning an integer variable.

set_cookie_enable

37037: Sets the value of the argument for the current server or directory configuration to the value given in the **CookieTracking** directive, which calls this function.

set_cookie_exp

37044: Sets the expiration date and time for cookies in this server context. This function is called when the **CookieExpires** directive is found.

37054: If the argument provided with the **CookieExpires** directive is a number, the ASCII text of the argument is converted to a number, which is stored in the **expires** field of the configuration record **cls**.

37067: Parses the first piece of information supplied with **CookieExpires** into **word**. It was not a simple number. If it begins with **plus**, the next piece of information is retrieved immediately to be ready to process the directive.

37073: Loops through all the arguments of **CookieExpires** to gather the correct date and time for expiration.

37075: Because **plus** was already parsed, the next part must be a number. If it is not (checked by **ap_isdigit**), an error is returned: The expiration date cannot be handled.

37082: Retrieves the next part of the directive argument, which should be a **<TYPE>** string (such as **weeks** or **months**).

37087: Based on the content of the **word** string, a time factor is set to make the expiration date match the amount being added (based on days, weeks, months, and so on). If none of the standard strings matches, the final case on line 37101 returns an error: The expiration value cannot be handled.

37104: The **modifier** variable is updated based on the number (**num**) of items and the factor for each that the **if** statements (days, weeks, months, and so on) tested for.

37107: Retrieves the next argument of the directive data into **word**. If something else is there, the **while** loop will repeat and update the expiration value again; otherwise, it drops out of the loop and assigns the **modifier** value to the **expires** field of the configuration record **cls**.

cookie_log_cmds

37115: Creates a structure containing the directives used by **mod_usertrack**. These include **CookieExpires** (which calls **set_cookie_exp** when found) and **CookieTracking** (which calls **set_cookie_enable** when found).

usertrack_module

37125: Defines the module itself with both directory and server configuration functions, the command table for the applicable directives, and the **spot_cookie** function called by the **fixups** processing stage, where cookies are actually checked or generated as needed.

Chapter 9

Miscellaneous Modules

This chapter describes seven Apache modules that are used frequently but that don't bear easy classification with other modules. The modules are:

- **mod_perl**—Allows Perl scripts to be preloaded and run within Apache without launching a separate Perl process. These scripts can also be used to configure Apache.

- **mod_example**—A sample module included to help developers learn about the structure of Apache module components. This module prints state information about requests to help track what happens within a module.

- **mod_mmap_static**—Defines files that are to be loaded into memory during Apache startup. When requested, these memory-mapped files are returned directly from memory to a client, providing substantial performance improvements. Memory-mapped files cannot change, however, or the server must be restarted. This module is experimental.

- **mod_userdir**—Converts requests within per-user home directories on a Web server (such as /~jsmith) to correctly formed file names that Apache can retrieve (such as /home/jsmith/public_html) based on the information provided in the **UserDir** directive.

- **mod_so**—Used to load dynamic shared objects into Apache at runtime in versions 1.3 or later. This module is used primarily to load additional modules without recompiling Apache, though it can also be used to load other shared objects for use by any Apache code.

- **mod_speling**—Checks minor spelling errors (transposed or missing letters and capitalization) when a requested file is not found on the Apache server. If a file with a similar name is found, the request is redirected to that file.

- **mod_unique_id**—Creates a unique identifier for each request. This identifier is much like the cookie created by **mod_usertrack**, but for **mod_unique_id**, the identifier is placed in an environment variable. Scripts on the server must determine if and how to use the identifier to track requests.

Discussion Of **mod_perl**

mod_perl is arguably the most complex and powerful of all Apache modules. It is not installed by default in Apache, but must be downloaded and compiled as a separate software package. **mod_perl** consists of both a Perl and an Apache module that, together, provide Apache with a built-in Perl interpreter. By using this interpreter, scripts that would have been run using CGI can be run within Apache. Substantial performance improvements are a common result of using **mod_perl** because a new Perl interpreter does not have to be started each time the script is run. After adding **mod_perl** to a copy of Apache (by recompiling or using dynamic shared objects), scripts can be run using a configuration like this:

```
<Location /perl/>
SetHandler perl-script
PerlHandler Apache::Registry
Options ExecCGI
</Location>
```

When any URL requests a file in /perl/, that file is executed by the Perl interpreter in **mod_perl**. Further performance enhancements can be achieved by preloading a Perl script at Apache server startup. This is comparable to using **mod_mmap_static** (described later in this chapter) to preload a file. To preload a Perl module or script, use commands such as these examples within a virtual host container:

```
PerlModule   Apache::SSI   MyModule::handler
PerlScript  /www/cgi-bin/process_form.pl
```

When Perl code has been preloaded, it can be accessed by a client request or by calls from a server-side include (SSI) command. For example, a standard method of including the output from a command or program within an HTML file is to use an SSI **exec** command to run the program. If, however, you write a Perl function that performs the same task as a program that you would call using **exec**, **mod_perl** is used to run the function and provides greatly improved performance over using the SSI **exec** command. The syntax for including output from a Perl function that you have written (called **Procedure1** here) is shown in the following line:

```
<!-- #perl sub="Apache::Test::Procedure1" -->
```

Finally, Perl code can be embedded within an Apache configuration when using **mod_perl**, which interprets the Perl and uses it to configure the Apache server. This is illustrated by the following example:

```
<Perl>
# Insert a test for server performance
if ($test = 0) {
    $MinSpareServers = 5;
    $MaxSpareServers=5;
    $MaxClients = 50;
}
else   {
    $MinSpareServers = 10;
    $MaxSpareServers=25;
    $MaxClients = 250;
}
1;
</Perl>
```

In-depth use and understanding of **mod_perl** functionality warrants considerable study of both Perl and the documentation accompanying **mod_perl**. The information provided here serves only to guide exploration through the **mod_perl** code.

Module Structure

The interaction between Apache and the Perl interpreter created by **mod_perl** is complex. The ability to interactively configure Apache and run scripts within child processes of Apache requires numerous control mechanisms that are not used in any other module. To understand fully how **mod_perl** works, the support functions that are not part of mod_perl.c must also be studied.

A Perl interpreter is used throughout **mod_perl**, with methods being checked and then scripts being passed to the interpreter. A series of handlers can be used to execute a script. Some of these scripts are part of the Apache configuration (within **<Perl>** containers); others are launched as a CGI script would be, except that the interpreter is already loaded into Apache. The structure of **mod_perl** is shown in Figure 9.1.

perl_cmds

38813: The configuration file directives that **mod_perl** processes are defined. This list includes the function to call for each matching directive that Apache finds. This section is unusual compared with other modules, in that the **<Perl>** and **</Perl>** directives call functions that actually read more of the configuration file and process the lines between these tags as a Perl script. In addition to numerous directives, this table includes hooks (beginning on line 38875 through line 38918) that can be used when an Apache module is written in Perl for any of the processing phases defined in the module structure (beginning on line 38929).

perl_handlers

38923: The function to call in response to a request for files assigned to the **perl-script** handler are defined. This is set up using a standard **SetHandler** directive. The **perl_handler** function begins on line 39535.

perl_module

38929: **mod_perl** is defined with standard functions for initialization and creating configuration structures. A directive (command) table and a handler table are defined. Other phases use

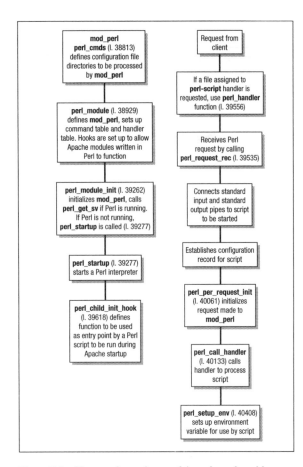

Figure 9.1   The popular and powerful **mod_perl** enables Perl scripts to be preloaded and run by Apache.

hooks that allow Apache modules written in Perl to function at these points during Apache request processing.

seqno_check_max

38974: Checks the maximum number of requests handled. If that number has been reached, the function is terminated.

38987: Retrieves the **MaxModPerlRequestsPerChild** and compares it on line 38992 with the current **seqno** value. If the maximum has been reached, **child_terminate** on line 38993 is called.

perl_shutdown

39002: Shuts down the Perl interpreter.

39020: Executes any end blocks that have yet to run.

39025: Cleans up any remaining items by calling **perl_util_cleanup**.

39043: Calls **perl_destruct**, followed by **perl_free** to close down the interpreter.

39050: Sets **perl_is_running** to 0 to indicate that the interpreter has been shut down.

mp_fake_request_rec

39054: Sets up a duplicate (fake) request record to be used by a Perl script.

39057: Allocates a new request record (**r**).

39059: Sets the values of **r** based on the parameters passed to this function. The filled in request record is returned.

perl_restart_handler

39067: Sets up a callback to define a handle for restarting Perl if needed.

perl_restart

39077: Attempts to restart Perl by calling first **perl_get_sv** and then **gv_stashpv**.

39105: If any stacked handlers remain, **hv_clear** is called to clear them before the restart.

39110: Perl is restarted by calling **perl_reload_inc**.

mod_perl_set_cwd

39120: Sets the current working directory for Perl.

39124: Uses **getenv** to retrieve the current working directory name from the PWD (print working directory) environment variable.

39130: Calls **perl_eval_pv** to set the working directory.

scriptname_val

39137: Evaluates a Perl script name.

39146: Calls **perl_eval_pv** to evaluate the file name, then uses **sv_setsv** to set the tested file name.

mod_perl_tie_scriptname

39154: Associates a Perl script name with additional information using the **sv_unmagic** and **sv_ magic** calls.

mp_dso_unload

39173: If dynamic shared objects are used for this platform, this function is used to unload the **mod_perl** code.

39180: Tests for the module name mod_perl.c. If valid, a loop through the **modp** structure is performed, setting the **dynamic_load_handle** to NULL to indicate a module that is no longer available.

mp_server_notstarting

39194: By using the **Apache_ServerStarting** call with **FALSE**, the status of the server is set to not starting.

mp_check_version

39209: Checks the version of Perl that has been started.

39217: Compares the version using **perl_get_sv**. If they don't match, an error is logged and **mp_check_ version** returns.

set_sigpipe

39253: If **HAS_MMN_136** is defined, the **set_sigpipe** function calls **perl_require_module** to set up signal pipes between Apache and Perl processes.

perl_module_init

39262: Initializes **mod_perl**, as defined on line 38931.

39266: If Perl is already running, **perl_get_sv** is called with the **Apache::Server::AddPerlVersion** method, then **ap_add_version_component** is called to update the Perl version recorded by Apache.

39274: If Perl is not already running, **perl_startup**, which begins on line 39277, is called.

perl_startup

39277: Starts a Perl interpreter.

39313: If Perl is already running and the startup process has completed, **mp_check_version** (line 39209) is called to verify that the correct Perl version information is recorded.

39336: If Perl needs to restart, **perl_restart_handler** is called, followed by **perl_restart** on line 39339.

39348: Prepares arguments that should be passed to Perl on startup as if they were coming from a command line. These include the **–T** and **–w** options.

39360: Sends information via **MP_TRACE_g** as events occur.

39367: Calls **PERL_SYS_INIT** and then **perl_init_ i18nl10n** to start the Perl interpreter.

39386: Calls **perl_parse** to establish the status of the Perl interpreter that was just started.

39493: Loops to load all Perl modules listed in **PerlModule** directives so they are available to the script that runs after server initialization.

perl_sent_header

39522: Uses **mod_perl** to send a header to the client by calling **MP_SENDHDR** if the value of **MP_SENTHDR_on** permits it.

perl_handler

39535: Handles a request that was defined as coming to the **perl-script** handler (using a **SetHandler** directive).

39550: Calls **MP_SENDHDR_on** so that headers will be sent for requests processed by Perl scripts. If **MP_SENDHDR** is defined, the headers are set to **Off** on line 39554 by calling **MP_ SENTHDR_off**.

39556: Gets the Perl request by calling **perl_request_ rec** (which begins on line 40388), which, in turn, calls **mp_request_rec**.

39581: Connects the standard input and output pipes to the Perl script about to be started by calling **perl_stdout2client** and **perl_stdin2client**.

39584: If the configuration record is not yet available, **perl_create_request_config** is called, followed by **set_module_config** to establish a correct configuration record for this request and make it accessible to the script.

39601: After processing, the variable with a mutually exclusive lock (the mutex—used for threaded environments) acquired on line 39543 is released.

perl_child_exit_cleanup

39612: If a **CHILD_INIT** process is defined for **mod_perl**, a structure to hold the arguments for this hook into the Apache server is defined here. Also, a cleanup function that Apache can call to clean up the memory used by this Perl script during the **child_init** phase is defined.

PERL_CHILD_INIT_HOOK

39618: Defines a function to be used as an entry point by a Perl script that will run during the **child_ init** phase of Apache startup.

39623: Calls **mp_fake_request_rec** to set up a faked request record for use in this function.

39630: Registers the cleanup function **perl_child_exit_ cleanup** so that it can be called when this server exits and needs to clean up memory used by this code.

39633: This hook is initialized by calling **mod_perl_ init_ids** and then using a Perl callback to hook into this phase of Apache.

PERL_CHILD_EXIT_HOOK

39638: If **PERL_CHILD_EXIT** is defined to use a Perl script in this phase of Apache processing, this function sets up a faked request for Perl using **mp_fake_request_rec** and registers a callback so that the correct Perl script can be run at the correct time.

39648: Perl is shut down (as this Apache child server exits) by calling **perl_shutdown**.

PERL_POST_READ_REQUEST_HOOK

39652: If **PERL_POST_READ_REQUEST** is defined, a callback is set up via **PERL_CALLBACK** on line 39664 to allow a Perl script to run in the **post-read-request** phase.

PERL_TRANS_HOOK

39673: If **PERL_TRANS** is defined, a hook is created here to allow a Perl script to run in the **filename-translation** phase of Apache request processing.

PERL_HEADER_PARSER_HOOK

39684: If **PERL_HEADER_PARSER** is defined, a callback is set up on line 39690 so that a Perl script can be run by Apache each time a request reaches the header parsing phase.

PERL_AUTHEN_HOOK

39699: If **PERL_AUTHEN** is defined, the **PERL_AUTHEN_HOOK** function establishes a callback for a Perl script to be used for authentication of requests.

PERL_TYPE_HOOK

39732: If **PERL_TYPE** is defined during compilation, this function is used to set up a callback for Perl to use so that a Perl script can be run by Apache each time a request reaches the MIME file typing phase.

PERL_FIXUP_HOOK

39743: If **PERL_FIXUP** is defined, this function is used to define a hook where a Perl script can be called during the **fixups** phase to make final alterations to request headers before a request is handled.

PERL_LOG_HOOK

39754: Defines a function as a hook for using Perl logging functions within that phase of Apache request processing. This function is only included if **PERL_LOG** is defined.

39765: Defines cleanup handlers for this module, based on the **PERL_STACKED_HANDLERS** value.

per_request_cleanup

39774: Checks any notes that are part of the current configuration. If they exist, **hv_clear** is called to clear the notes; **SvREFCNT_dec** is then called.

mod_perl_end_cleanup

39788: A callback is set up so that a cleanup handler is available to **mod_perl** when exiting. **per_request_cleanup** and **perl_clear_env** are called to clean up request and environment information that was established for a Perl script environment as well.

mod_perl_cleanup_handler

39852: Cleans up a Perl process by looping through line 39862, calling **perl_call_handler** for each iteration.

39868: Calls **av_clear** to finish the cleanup.

39872: Releases the mutex that was acquired before starting the cleanup (on line 39859).

perl_handler_ismethod

39876: Handles a Perl method specified in a directive for **mod_perl**.

39887: Retrieves the method to use by calling **gv_fetchmethod** with the class.

39892: Sets **is_method** to the value returned by **strnEQ**.

mod_perl_register_cleanup

39903: Registers cleanup functions to use when ending a Perl process. These are set using the **register_cleanup** call on line 39909 with the names of the function **mod_perl_cleanup_handler**.

mod_perl_push_handlers

39922: If stacked Perl handlers are used on this server, a handler to the stack is pushed.

39929: If a valid handler was passed to this function, **hv_fetch** is used to retrieve the handle stack information.

39939: Sets handlers to the value given by **newAV**, then calls **SvPV** to set the handler in the stack.

perl_run_stacked_handlers

39975: Runs multiple handlers based on a Perl script.

39984: Checks for the existence of multiple (stacked) handlers by calling **hv_exists** with **stacked_handlers**. If this test is successful, the handle needed with **hv_fetch** is retrieved and stored in **svp**.

40015: If the needed handle is not on the stack, an error message is printed and **sv_dump** is used to exit.

40024: Loops through the handlers returned by **AvFILL**. For each, **SvTRUE** on line 40034 is called to test validity, then **perl_call_handler** on line 40041 is called to use that handler.

perl_per_request_init

40061: Initializes a request made to **mod_perl**.

40069: Sets the sub-process header to **On** to include **PERL_SEND_HEADER**.

40086: If a configuration is not set up, one is created using **perl_create_request_config**.

40092: Sets up the request environment by calling **perl_setup_env** and then **mod_perl_dir_env** on line 40096.

40102: Passes the environment information to the request using **mod_perl_pass_env**.

40104: Processes the name of the script to run using **mod_perl_tie_scriptname**.

perl_call_handler

40133: Calls a handler to process a Perl script.

40146: Retrieves the module configuration using **get_module_config**.

40151: Determines the dispatch handler to use by calling **perl_get_cv**.

40165: If this request is based on a per-directory configuration, the request is initialized by calling **perl_per_request_init**.

perl_request_rec

40388: Retrieves a request record for a Perl script by calling **mp_request_rec**. The request record is returned.

perl_bless_request_rec

40398: Checks a request record by calling **sv_setref_pv**. Also, **MP_TRACE_g** is called to record this event.

perl_setup_env

40408: Sets up environment variables for use by a Perl script.

40411: Sets **arr** to the environment information by calling **perl_cgi_env_init**.

40414: Loops through all elements of **arr**, calling **mp_setenv** to make each part of the Perl environment for a script.

Discussion Of mod_example

mod_example is a sample module designed to help developers understand how a module is constructed and what components, hooks, and control flows are used by all of the Apache modules. As a sample, this module includes more comments in the source code than any other module, though it doesn't accomplish anything except print messages noting each step in the module's interaction with Apache and request processing.

This module should only be compiled into Apache while learning about modules. Using it at other times wastes memory and processing time, even if no requests use the example handler for processing.

To use **mod_example**, a handler should be added to some directory context:

```
<Directory />
AddHandler  example-handler  html
</Directory>
```

When any request is made for a document in the named directory context, the **mod_example** code is used, returning the state information showing how each function of the module was accessed.

Module Structure

The **mod_example** code includes a function for each of the possible phases of Apache processing, plus a handler function (**example_handler** on line 37665) to process requests. A **trace_add** function is used by the functions for each phase to add a comment to the note field of the request (see Figure 9.2). The notes are printed with additional state information when a request arrives for the example handler.

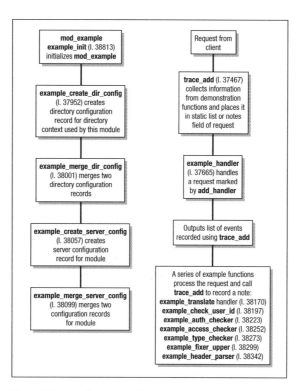

Figure 9.2 **mod_example** is a test module that demonstrates aspects of how modules are constructed.

Reading the comments in the source code, in addition to those that follow, is highly recommended before constructing a new Apache module.

Customization

Customization of **mod_example** is useful when exploring what a proposed new module might accomplish. Adding code into the appropriate functions of **mod_example**—depending on the phase where work should be done—lets a developer identify how the code interacts with other module timing and processes.

excfg

37187: Defines a date structure for the **mod_example** configuration records. This structure is unusual for a module, in that it shows both directory and server configuration in a single structure with a flag (**cmode**) determining which is active.

Additional Comments

37250: Defines (in comments for illustrative purposed) how arguments to directives can be defined using codes like **FLAG** and **TAKE1**. The codes allow Apache to parse the directive arguments and pass them in to the functions that process the argument data for a module. These comments continue through line 37373.

our_dconfig

37387: Returns the directory configuration record for the current directory context using the **ap_get_module_config** API call.

our_sconfig

37399: Returns the server configuration record for the current server context using the **ap_get_module_config** API call.

our_rconfig

37410: Returns the configuration record for a single request using the **ap_get_module_config** API call.

setup_module_cells

37422: Sets up a sample table within a memory pool that has been defined in this function using **ap_make_sub_pool** on line 37429. The table, with 16 records, is created on line 37437.

trace_add

37467: Collects information from all of the phase-oriented demonstration functions in **mod_example**. The trace information is placed in either a static list or the **notes** field of the current request.

37482: Calls **setup_module_cells** to make certain that a static area is available to hold traces that are not attached to a specific request (in the **notes** field).

37487: If a request is in progress, the request memory pool is used to attempt to pull the trace of **mod_example** from the request **notes** and place it in **trace_copy**.

37508: A request is not in process. A new memory subpool is created, and the **trace** value is pointed at it. If a subpool exists, it is destroyed on line 37518 to prevent possible memory leaks.

37521: Copies **trace** to **trace_copy**.

37541: If a request is not in process (**r==NULL**), the code on line 37544 determines if the note being passed in is already part of the static table of non-request-specific traces.

37544: Defines **key** as the note being checked, then looks for it with **ap_table_get** in the **static_calls_made** table. If the note passed in to **trace_add** is already in this table, **trace_add** returns immediately.

37552: The **note** was not found in the static table, so **ap_table_set** (line 37558) places the key in the **static_calls_made** table.

37562: Defines **addon** as the HTML text to use for showing the trace note and location within the module. This text will be used by the **example-handler**.

37571: Determines if a request is being processed again. If so, the text of the trace (which now includes **addon**) is placed in the **notes** field of the request.

cmd_example

37621: Shows how a directive might be processed. This function is defined for the sample directive on line 38371.

37631: Uses the **trace_add** function to record an event (the processing of the directive).

example_handler

37665: Handles a request that was marked by **AddHandler** as being handled by **example-handler**, the sample handler for **mod_example**. This function outputs to the client the accumulated list of events recorded using **trace_add**.

37671: Records the event of being handled by calling **trace_add** with the name of this function as a string. Thus, the list of events will include this handler.

37688: In preparation for sending the headers to the client, the **content_type** field is set to **text/html**.

37689: Begins a timeout so that, if problems occur while writing data to the client, this process can be terminated by the parent Apache process by calling **ap_soft_timeout**.

37690: Sends the HTTP headers to the client using **ap_send_http_header**.

37695: If the HTTP request was for only headers, the timeout ends and **example_handler** returns; otherwise, it continues to line 37704.

37704: Begins sending an HTML document to the client piece by piece using **ap_rputs** calls for each HTML tag. Status data such as the server version is included (using calls such as **ap_get_server_version** on line 37719).

37785: Cancels the timeout with **ap_kill_timeout**, because the data was successfully sent to the client.

example_init

37846: Initializes **mod_example**. This function is defined for this phase on line 38430 (in the module definition). No configuration record is available yet for this module when the **init** phase is called, so a static table is established with **setup_module_cells** on line 37856.

37863: Assembles a string to add to the trace list by concatenating a string with **ap_pstrcat** and placing the result in note.

37865: Calls **trace_add** to record the note string in the static table set up by **setup_module_cells**.

example_child_init

37883: Records a call to the child-server-process initialization phase.

37893: Prepares a static table to hold the trace notes by calling **setup_module_cells**.

37900: Assembles a string into **note**. The string includes the name of this function.

37902: Adds the **note** for this function to the static table of events using **trace_add**.

example_create_dir_config

37952: Creates a directory configuration record for a directory context used by this module (the context is defined by a **<Directory>** container in which one of this module's directives is used).

37963: Allocates space for the configuration variable using **ap_pcalloc**.

37969: Sets default values for each applicable field of the configuration record.

37976: Records that this function was called by calling **trace_add** with a string containing this function's name.

example_merge_dir_config

38001: Merges two directory configuration records for **mod_example**.

38006: Allocates memory for the new configuration record variable that will hold the merged record information.

38017: Copies some fields from the additive configuration record to the merged record. Other fields are combined (**OR**ing together the base and additive configurations for the two directories).

38045: Calls **trace_add** to record a call to this function. The name of this function is included in the string recorded in the trace.

example_create_server_config

38057: Creates a server configuration record for **mod_example**.

38068: Allocates space for the record using **ap_pcalloc**, then initializes the fields of the record.

38077: Records a call to this function with **trace_add**, including the name of this function as a string.

example_merge_server_config

38099: Merges two server configuration records for **mod_example** (for the default server configuration and a virtual server).

38104: Allocates memory for a configuration record into which the two sets of data will be merged. The data is merged, and **example_merge_server_config** decides which items should be combined and which default (base) configuration should be overwritten by the virtual host (additive) configuration.

38130: A call to **example_merge_server_config** is recorded with **trace_add**.

example_post_read_request

38144: Processes a request after it has been read but before other modules have been called. This function accomplishes nothing (for this module) other than recording that the function was reached by calling **trace_add** with the function name. By returning **DECLINED**, other modules that have a function defined for this phase will be called until one returns **OK**.

example_translate_handler

38170: Processes the URI received as part of a request into a file name that can be used to retrieve data on the server. This function (in this module) only records that it was reached by calling **trace_add** with the name of the function as a string. The return value is **DECLINED**, allowing Apache to call another module's **translate-phase** function to prepare URI-to-file name translations.

example_check_user_id

38197: Checks the authentication information provided with a request to determine if the user making the request is authorized to retrieve the file requested. This function actually only calls **trace_add** to show that it has been called. When one module with a function in this phase returns **OK**, no others are called; the user is assumed to be authorized.

example_auth_checker

38223: Checks whether the file being requested requires authorization. This function only records whether it was called by calling **trace_add** with the function name. When one module's function in this phase returns **OK**, no others are called. If all functions in this phase (among all modules) return **DECLINED**, the request is returned as an error to the client.

example_access_checker

38252: Checks for module-specific restrictions that apply to the item being requested. This function in **mod_example** logs itself using **trace_add**

with the function name and then returns with **DECLINED** to allow other functions in this phase to attempt to process the request.

example_type_checker

38273: Processes the document type and related information (such as encoding and language) of the requested file and places that information in the request header. This function only logs itself using **trace_add** and returns **DECLINED**, so that another function in this phase will process the request. (**mod_mime** is an example of a function that does this.)

example_fixer_upper

38299: Processes any remaining header information before calling the handler to actually process the request and (hopefully) return a file to the client. This function simply logs a trace using **trace_add** to show that the function was called.

example_logger

38322: Logs the request being processed. All logging functions (in all loaded modules) are called; returning **OK** does not abort the list of logging functions. This function, however, simply records that it was accessed using **trace_add**.

example_header_parser

38342: Parses headers of the current request, taking any additional action deemed necessary before the headers are sent to the client (in most cases). This function only records that it was called using **trace_add**.

example_cmds

38367: Defines the directives that affect this module. For each directive, a function name is provided in the **example_cmds** structure. The function named is called when the corresponding directive is located within a configuration file. **example_cmds** also defines (using a code such as **NO_ARGS**) how the arguments to the directive must be formed to allow Apache to prepare them and pass them to the function named for processing the directive.

38370: **mod_example** includes one directive (used only for illustrative purposes): **Example**. It is dealt with via the function **cmd_example**.

example_handlers

38403: Defines a structure that shows which data types (as used by the **AddHandler** and **SetHandler** directives) are supported/handled by this module, with the function to call when a file needing that handler is requested. The function **example_handler** (line 37665) is defined for the **example-handler** type.

example_module

38427: Defines this module in a structure showing all of the functions that are called for the possible phases of Apache initialization and request processing. In **mod_example**, every phase is used. Other modules use only a few of the items here; the rest are replaced with NULL.

Discussion Of **mod_mmap_static**

mod_mmap_static is an experimental module that can be used to map a file on the Web server to an area of the server's memory as the server is started and configured. By using the Unix **mmap** call to memory-map a disk file, substantial performance improvements are possible. Not all files are suitable for memory-mapping. If a memory-mapped file changes, Apache must be restarted to reload the file.

mod_mmap_static uses a single directive (**mmapfile**) with a list of files to be memory-mapped at server initialization. Because this module is experimental, it is not compiled into a default Apache server.

Module Structure

During server initialization, **mod_mmap_static** loads into memory each of the files indicated by **mmapfile** directives. Information about these files is sorted for rapid access. As shown in Figure 9.3, the **mmap_static_handler** function processes requests for memory-mapped files, checking the array of available files and using the Apache API call **ap_send_mmap** to forward the file from system memory to the client.

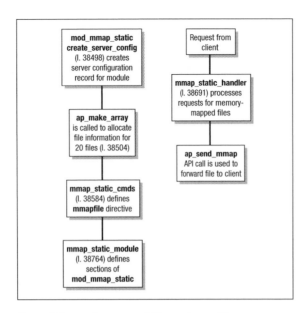

Figure 9.3   **mod_mmap_static** can be used to memory-map a file on a Web server.

Customization

Because Apache must be restarted any time a memory-mapped file is altered, a facility might be developed to send a signal to this module instructing it to reload files that have been altered. This would be a module-specific signal so that the entire server wouldn't be required to restart.

Additional functionality that permitted files within memory to change based on server-side includes or other features of Apache might be developed. The performance improvements of memory-mapped files in this situation would need to be evaluated.

create_server_config

38498: Creates a server configuration file for **mod_mmap_static**. **create_server_config** allocates an array of file information for 20 files using **ap_make_array** on line 38504. It then initializes the **inode_sorted** field to NULL.

cleanup_mmap

38509: Cleans up memory usage for **mod_mmap_static**. This function is passed to the Apache cleanup functions to register how the memory used by this module should be cleaned up when the server shuts down.

38517: Loops through each of the files being handled via **mod_mmap_static**. For each one, **munmap** is called to remove the file from system memory (the opposite of the **mmap** call on line 38555).

mmapfile

38524: Handles a **mmapfile** directive, as defined on line 38587. Because the arguments use the format **ITERATE** (see line 38587), this function is called once for each item in the list of arguments. Thus, the code can assume that a single file name is passed in as a parameter.

38533: Checks the status of the file included as an argument to **mmapfile**. If the **stat** call returns an error, the error is logged and **mmapfile** exits. The file cannot be accessed.

38539: Verifies that the file requested as memory-mapped is a regular file (others cannot be used). If it is not regular, **mmapfile** logs an error and exits.

38547: Attempts to open the file using an **open** system call. If the call is not successful, **mmapfile** logs an error and exits.

38555: Uses the system call **mmap** to memory-map the file that was just opened.

38557: If the results of the **mmap** system call indicate an error, **mmapfile** closes the file, logs an error, and exits.

38568: If the **mmap** call was successful, the file is closed and the name of the file is placed in the **files** array of the server configuration record.

38575: If this is the first time that a file has been added to the list of memory-mapped file, the memory cleanup function of **cleanup_mmap** is registered with Apache using **ap_register_ cleanup**.

mmap_static_cmds

38584: Defines the directive used by **mod_mmap_ static**. The one directive (**mmapfile**) is handled by the **mmapfile** function on line 38524.

file_compare

38596: Compares two files and returns a value to indicate which should be sorted higher. The name of this function is passed to **qsort** during **mmap_init** to prepare the list of memory-mapped files. By sorting the files, the **bsearch** system call can be used to locate the desired file rapidly. Inodes are generally used to locate the correct file in the **mmap_static_handler**, however.

inode_compare

38604: Compares two inodes and returns a value to indicate which should be sorted higher. The name of this function is passed to **qsort** during **mmap_init** to prepare the list of inodes associated with memory-mapped files. By sorting the inodes, the **bsearch** system call can be used to locate the desired file rapidly.

mmap_init

38617: Initializes **mod_mmap_static** during Apache server startup.

38629: Sets up variables for the list of files designated as memory-mapped.

38631: Sorts the list of files for easy access later. The **file_ compare** function is passed to **qsort** for doing comparisons of the items in the array of files.

38635: Creates an **inode** index of the memory-mapped files to speed access.

38637: Loops through the list of files and places all of the file inodes in an array called **inodes**.

38640: Sorts the contents of the **inodes** array of memory-mapped file inodes using **qsort**. The **inode_compare** function is passed to **qsort** to use in comparing each inode element during sorting.

38644: Uses the same configuration for all server definitions (virtual hosts) that this copy of Apache is handling.

mmap_static_xlat

38655: Translates file names to access memory-mapped files. This function is defined for the **filename- translation** phase on line 38775.

38662: Retrieves the module configuration record.

38667: If the table of memory-mapped files is empty, no files can be returned via this module, so the file name isn't translated. **mmap_static_xlat** returns immediately.

38672: Uses other modules with **translate_handler** functions to prepare the file before translating it to a memory-mapped file.

38673: If the other modules could not translate the file name or a file name now doesn't exist, **mmap_ static_xlat** returns without processing.

38677: Uses the **bsearch** call to locate a match between the requested file name and an item in the **files** array of the configuration for **mod_mmap_ static**.

38680: If a match can't be found, **mmap_static_xlat** returns **DECLINED**. The file is not memory-mapped.

38686: Sets the **finfo** field of the request to the **finfo** field of the matching memory-mapped file to save a few system calls later when verifying the file.

mmap_static_handler

38691: Handles and returns a file that was marked with **mmapfile** to be a memory-mapped file. This function is defined for the handler phase by the handler table on line 38760.

38701: Tests the method of the current request. If it isn't **GET**, **mmap_static_handler** returns immediately.

38704: If the **finfo.st_mode** field of the current request indicates that the requested file doesn't exist, **mmap_static_handler** returns immediately. This field of the request was likely copied from the matching entry using the **mmap_static_xlat** function in this module. This test verifies that the file exists before continuing.

38706: Retrieves the server configuration.

38711: Uses the **bsearch** system call to search for the requested file among the inodes of the memory-mapped files. This is probably faster than searching for the filename. The inode is part of the file information that is available in the request record.

38715: If a matching inode is not found, **mmap_ static_handler** returns immediately.

38727: Calls **ap_discard_request_body** to dump any additional lines in the client's request. If this causes an error, exit immediately.

38730: Updates the last modified time for the file that is about to be returned.

38740: Sends the request headers to the client.

38742: If this request is not for headers only, **mmap_ static_handler** checks the **rangestatus**. If valid, it uses **ap_send_mmap** with the **mm** and **finfo.st_size** fields to send the file from memory to the client.

38747: If the **rangestatus** wasn't valid, **mmap_static_ handler** loops on line 38749 using **ap_each_ byterange** to have **ap_send_mmap** send smaller chunks of the file to the client.

mmap_static_handlers

38758: Defines the handler function for files marked as memory-mapped.

mmap_static_module

38764: Defines sections of **mod_mmap_static**. An initialization phase function (**mmap_init**) prepares the list of files that are available via memory-mapping. Per-server configurations are prepared. A command and handler table are provided to point to functions for handling the **mmapfile** directive and memory-mapped handler types. Finally, the **mmap_static_xlat** function is defined to translate requests for a memory-mapped file to match the information stored in memory during server initialization.

Discussion Of **mod_userdir**

mod_userdir is used to translate a special URL format into a valid path and file name for the Apache server to return to a client. The format of these special URLs uses a tilde (~) to access per-user Web directories. For example, if the **UserDir** directive is used as follows,

```
UserDir public_html
```

then the URL **www.server.com/~jsmith/resume.html** will be mapped to the actual file name /home/jsmith/public_html/resume.html on the server by **mod_userdir**.

Because **UserDir** maps file access to an area outside of the Web's document root, use it with caution. The **UserDir** directive can include a full path name or just the directory within each user's home directory.

UserDir can also take the argument **Enabled** with a list of user names, or **Disabled** with a list of user names or alone. These arguments enable or disable access to a personal Web directory for the specified users.

Module Structure

mod_userdir includes a per-directory configuration record (set up by **create_userdir_config**) that records the directory name and **enabled/disabled** status for that directory. The **UserDir** directive is handled by the **set_user_dir** function (beginning on line 36606). Requests are handled by the single function **translate_userdir**, which begins on line 36681 (see Figure 9.4).

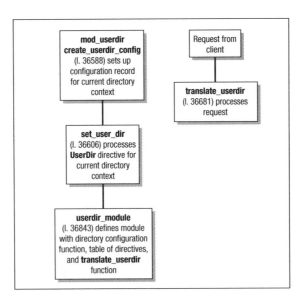

Figure 9.4 **mod_userdir** enables Apache to handle user-specific Web site directories.

Customization

The **Enable** and **Disable** arguments of **UserDir** could be set up so that alternate lists of users were checked, for example through a database query or some type of authentication request.

userdir_config

36573: Defines a configuration structure for **mod_userdir** that includes the name of the per-user directory to translate requests to and the arrays of usernames that are allowed or not allowed to use this feature.

create_userdir_config

36588: Creates a configuration record for the current directory context by allocating a **userdir_config** variable and initializing its values. A table of four items is initially set for the **enabled_users** and **disabled_users** arrays.

set_user_dir

36606: Processes **UserDir** directives for the current directory context.

36610: Retrieves the configuration record for the current context.

36618: Retrieves the first word of the arguments included with the directive. Because the **UserDir** directive can take several forms (such as directory name or enabled with a list) the **RAW_ARGS** value is used to define it. Thus, Apache passes in the entire argument list as one parameter.

36624: If the first word is **disabled**, **set_user_dir** begins looking for usernames. If none is found, it sets **globally_disabled** (effective for all users) to 1. Otherwise, the **disabled_users** field is set to the **usertable** value on line 36635.

36637: If the first word after the directive is **enable**, a username list must be included. If it isn't, **set_user_dir** returns with an error on line 36646. Otherwise, the **enabled_users** array is set to the value of **usertable** on line 36649.

36657: The first word wasn't **enabled** or **disabled**, so it is assumed to be a directory name. The name is not checked, just copied into the **userdir** field.

36665: Having ascertained which table the list of users should be placed in, a **while** loop is used to get each one with **ap_getword_conf** and place it in the appropriate table with **ap_table_setn**.

userdir_cmds

36672: Defines the one directive used by **mod_userdir**: **UserDir**. The function **set_user_dir** is defined to process this directive.

translate_userdir

36681: Translates a requested file name into a file name that maps to a user's home directory based on information in **UserDir** directives for the current directory context.

36684: Retrieves the current directory context.

36698: Tests whether this request can be handled by **mod_userdir**. The **userdir** field of the configuration record must have something defined, and the item requested must start with "**/~**". If either of these is not the case, **translate_userdir** exits the module immediately.

36707: Retrieves the next part of the requested file into **w**.

36726: Checks whether the item requested is a current or parent directory indicator (one or two periods). If it is either, **translate_userdir** returns immediately.

36734: Compares the username extracted from the request with the array of **disabled_users**. If the user is in the list, **translate_userdir** returns immediately.

36741: Tests whether **globally_disabled** is set. If so, **translate_userdir** tests whether the user being requested is in the **enabled_users** list (which overrides a global disable command). If the user can't bypass a global disable command, **translate_userdir** returns immediately.

36753: Loops through the **userdir** variable to assemble a revised file name and path that include the directory name given with **UserDir**.

36764: Does some additional checking for drive letters if the compilation flags indicate that drive letters are used on the platform.

36779: Copies the newly assembled file name path to redirect, then sets it as part of the **headers_out** array (in **Location**) for the client. **translate_userdir** then returns with **REDIRECT**.

36785: Checks other cases based on the arrangement of the directory name in the **UserDir** command, which might have included an asterisk (*). The file name is set to different values until the fully assembled path is used to redirect the request.

36801: If the module is running on a Window system, **translate_userdir** returns without proceeding because home directories on Windows are not handled by **mod_userdir**.

36827: Tests the fully reformed file name using the **stat** system call.

36835: If **stat** worked (the newly assembled file name is valid), the **finfo** field of the request is set to the result of the **stat** call.

userdir_module

36843: Defines this module with a directory configuration function (**create_userdir_config**), a table of directives (**userdir_cmds**), and the **translate_userdir** function, which actually does the work of translating a request within a per-user directory into an appropriate file name during the **filename-translation** phase.

Discussion Of **mod_so**

This module is used to load additional modules or other object code into Apache without recompiling the Web server. Before this module was available, additional (nonstandard or nondefault) Apache modules were added to a system by updating the configuration file and recompiling Apache.

Using **mod_so** directives, a module in shared object code format is loaded into Apache as configuration files are parsed, before requests are processed. To load a module, use the **LoadModule** directive:

```
<VirtualHost  www.xyz.com>
LoadModule mod_speling mod_speling.so
...
</VirtualHost>
```

Similarly, an object file that is not a module can be loaded into the Apache address space with the **LoadFile** directive to provide a module with access to library functions that are not part of Apache or the module itself:

```
<VirtualHost  www.xyz.com>
LoadFile libtoolkit.so
...
</VirtualHost>
```

The **LoadModule** directive used to load dynamic shared object (DSO) modules at runtime must not be confused with the **AddModule** command used in the Apache source code configuration file. **AddModule** is used to include additional modules at Apache compile time; it is not used by **mod_so**.

Module Structure

mod_so loads modules or other shared object files by calling Apache API functions. The module is therefore brief. A server configuration record is prepared by the **so_sconf_create** function (beginning on line 34601). The **LoadModule** and **LoadFile** directives are handled by the **load_module** and **load_file** functions as configuration files are parsed (see Figure 9.5). No additional functions are included because nothing is done by **mod_so** after configuration files are processed.

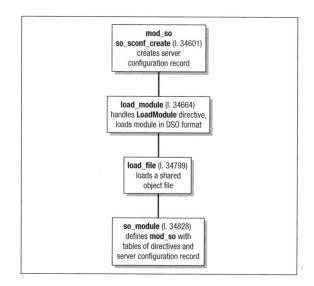

Figure 9.5 **mod_so** provides for the loading of additional modules or other object code into Apache at startup time.

Two versions of the **load_module** and **load_file** functions are included. Only one set is compiled, depending on the platform-specific settings during compilation. The secondary versions of the function simply log an error that DSOs are not supported on the current platform.

Customization

If particular types of shared objects are loaded using **LoadFile**, the **load_file** function could attempt to process and report on the headers within the resulting code.

Many potential optimizations or customizations to loading shared objects would be better done in the Apache API calls used by **load_module** and **load_file**.

moduleinfo

34592: Defines a data structure to be used within the server configuration record for **mod_so**. This structure holds a list of loaded modules with their names. The list is used to compare the argument of a **LoadModule** directive to determine if the module is already loaded.

so_server_conf

34597: Defines the server configuration record data structure.

so_sconf_create

34601: Creates a server configuration record for **mod_so**. The **loaded_modules** table is initialized with **DYNAMIC_MODULE_LIMIT** as the number of elements.

34611: If **NO_DLOPEN** isn't defined, **so_sconf_create** calls **ap_os_dso_init** to prepare for loading DSOs as configuration files are processed (via the **load_module** function—see line 34697). If this flag isn't defined, the **load_module** function only logs an error, so the **ap_os_dso_init** function isn't called at this point.

unload_module

34625: Removes a shared object from Apache. This function is called by the Apache API, not from within **mod_so**.

34629: Checks for the presence of the named module. If it isn't loaded, **unload_module** returns without further action.

34634: Removes the module pointer from the Apache core data structures by calling **ap_remove_loaded_module**.

34637: Unloads the module object code itself by calling **ap_os_dso_unload**.

34641: Clears the variables within **modi** that referred to the module, because the module is no longer available.

unload_file

34653: Unloads a shared object file that was loaded using a **LoadFile** directive. This function is called from the core Apache code during shutdown, not from within **mod_so.** The handle of the object is used to remove it from Apache address space by calling **ap_os_dso_unload**. Because no additional information about the file that was loaded is available at this point, nothing is known for logging if an error occurs. No checking is done.

load_module

34664: Loads a module in DSO format as directed by a **LoadModule** directive in a server configuration file. This function is defined for the directive on line 34819.

34681: Retrieves the configuration record for the current server context.

34685: Compares the list of all currently loaded modules with the one that **LoadModule** requested to be loaded. If the module is already part of Apache, **load_module** returns on line 34689 without further action.

34691: Prepares space for the new module information by calling **ap_push_array**, then sets the name field to the **modname** passed in as a directive argument.

34697: Attempts to load the module code file into Apache by calling **ap_os_dso_load**. If an error occurs, **load_module** logs it and returns.

34705: Logs a successfully loaded module. The message is logged to the error log, though loading was successful; logging to the access log would confuse statistical tools that examine that log.

34715: Calls **ap_os_dso_sym** to retrieve the module structure information so that the module can be initialized. If this function fails, **load_module** logs an error and exits. The module code was loaded into memory but is in an unusable state at this point.

34730: Verifies that the structure information returned by **ap_os_dso_sym** indicates that the loaded code is actually an Apache module. If it is not, **load_module** logs an error and exits.

34742: Having checked the code, **load_module** calls **ap_add_loaded_module** with the module handle so that Apache adds the new module to its array of loaded modules.

34750: Registers the cleanup function to use when the server is shut down. The function defined using **ap_register_cleanup** is **unload_module**, which begins on line 34625. This function is called by Apache when the server shuts down; it is not called from any point within **mod_so**.

34758: Calls **ap_single_module_configure** to initialize and configure the newly loaded module using its own configuration functions.

load_file

34770: Loads a shared object file into the Apache address space.

34776: Prepares the complete file name of the object file to load.

34778: Calls **ap_os_dso_load** with the file name to determine if the shared object can be loaded. If not, **load_file** logs an error and returns.

34787: Logs that the shared object named file name was loaded.

34791: Registers the cleanup function **unload_file**, which begins on line 34653. This function will be called by Apache at server shutdown.

load_file

34799: When shared objects are not supported on the platform where Apache is compiled (based on the **NO_DLOPEN** flag), this version of the **load_file** function is used. It prints an error message to **STDERR** that **LoadFile** is not supported on the current platform.

load_module

34807: Defines a second version of **load_module** for use when shared objects are not supported. When called, this function prints a message to **STDERR** that shared objects and **LoadModule** directives cannot be used on this platform.

so_cmds

34818: Defines the directives that **mod_so** supports (**LoadModule** and **LoadFile**). A function is defined to process each directive found as configuration files are read.

so_module

34828: Defines **mod_so** with a table of supported directives (which, in turn, includes functions to handle those directives—see line 34818) and a server configuration record to set up variables for use by **mod_so**. No functions in **mod_so** that are called during client request processing are defined. All of the **mod_so** work is done as configuration files are initially read.

Discussion Of mod_speling

mod_speling is used to correct minor spelling errors automatically in the file name that a client requests. If a requested file matches a file name in the same directory, except for a capitalization difference or a single transposed or missing letter, **mod_speling** redirects the request to the corrected file name. If several possibili-

ties exist, a list of valid files is returned to the client as an HTML document.

mod_speling is not included by default in Apache, but can be added during compilation or with a **LoadModule** directive. Using **mod_speling** can place a large processing burden on a Web server, particularly if Web server document directories contain many files.

Module Structure

As shown in Figure 9.6, **mod_speling** uses a single directive (**CheckSpelling**) to activate spellchecking in a server context. When activated, a single function (**check_speling**, beginning on line 35018) attempts to correct a single spelling or capitalization error in the requested file. The function **spdist** (beginning on line 34977) is called by **check_speling** to look for specific errors in the file name.

Customization

While keeping in mind the processing burden that **mod_speling** may place on a Web server, many enhancements to **mod_speling** might be useful for administrators and clients visiting a site. Some ideas include:

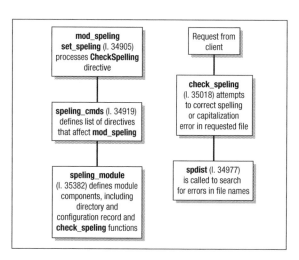

Figure 9.6 **mod_speling** enables Apache to correct misspelled URLs.

- A new directive could be defined to allow specific misspelled words to be converted, much as popular Web sites own misspelled versions of their name to redirect erroneous server names. The functionality of such a directive would be similar to the autocorrection list within a word processor.

- Either as an additional directive or within the **spdist** function, multiple or more complex spelling errors could be tracked and corrected, perhaps based on a dictionary (as within a word processor). If a threshold number of possible corrections is generated, the list could be returned to the client to avoid ambiguity.

- File extensions, which are currently excluded from **mod_speling** checks, could be added to spellchecking. This might be best accomplished as a separate routine that looks for MIME type matches. For example, if *filename*.gif is requested but only *filename*.jpeg is available, redirect to that, or redirect *filename*.html to *filename*.txt. Such type-based corrections can also be driven by a directive that specifies alternative or groups of file extensions to consider when the requested file is not found.

mkconfig

34874: Sets up a configuration record with a default value of 0. This function is called by both the server and the directory configuration function to initialize the configuration variable, which is a single flag that indicates whether spellchecking is enabled within a context.

create_mconfig_for_server

34886: Creates a configuration for the current server context by calling **mkconfig**.

create_mconfig_for_directory

34896: Creates a configuration for the current directory context by calling **mkconfig**.

set_speling

34905: Processes a **CheckSpelling** directive, setting the configuration record flag for the current context to the value given in the directive. This function is defined to process the directive on line 34921.

speling_cmds

34919: Defines the list of directives that affect **mod_speling**. The single directive (**CheckSpelling**) is included here with the function to call when the directive is found in a config-uration file (**set_speling**).

sp_reason

34928: Defines an enumerated data type used by **spdist** as a code that indicates the type of misspelling found in the current request. Line 34938 begins a human-readable version of the reasons enumerated in this type. These reasons are used to log a spelling correction to the error log.

spdist

34977: Tests the requested file name to determine what type of error it contains (if one can be identified). This function is called by **check_speling** on line 35137. The requested file name and a series of files in the same directory are passed into **spdist** as **s** and **t**.

34979: Loops through all characters of **s** and **t**, performing a comparison after making them lowercase. If they all match, the file names were identical except for a mistaken capitaliza-tion. **spdist** returns immediately with **SP_MISCAPITALIZATION**.

34986: Begins case-insensitive comparisons of the characters of **s** and **t** using **ap_tolower**. If the two strings match except for one-letter varia-tions, the file name has a transposed character. **spdist** returns with **SP_TRANSPOSITION**.

34994: Compares **s** and **t** with **strcasecmp**. If they match except for one character, **spdist** returns with **SP_SIMPLETYPO**.

34999: Compares **s** and **t** to determine if one has an extra character. If so, **spdist** returns with **SP_EXTRACHAR**.

35004: Compares **s** and **t** as on line 34999, but this time for a missing character. If **strcasecmp** indicates this, **spdist** returns with **SP_MISSINGCHAR**.

35007: None of the simple tests in **spdist** identi-fied a problem. **spdist** returns with **SP_VERYDIFFERENT**, indicating that a simple spelling problem could not be identified.

sort_by_quality

35011: Provides a value to the **qsort** function used to identify the most likely candidate for redirecting a misspelled request. This function is passed to **qsort** on line 35222. It returns a value that tells **qsort** which of the two items should be sorted higher.

check_speling

35018: Checks the spelling of a requested file name, and attempts to correct minor typing and capital-ization errors.

35027: Retrieves the module configuration record. If the configuration indicates that spellchecking is not active for the current context, **check_speling** exits immediately.

35035: Checks the method of the current request. If it is not **GET**, **check_speling** returns immediately.

35041: Tests whether the current request is a proxy (in which case, the file won't be located in the current directory) or is already found (indicated by a non-zero value in the **finfo.st_mode** field). In either case, **check_speling** returns immed-iately.

35046: Checks whether this is a subrequest. If so, it won't attempt to fix the file name.

35060: Splits the requested file name and path, placing the first part into **filoc**. If **filoc** isn't defined after this operation or if testing the **uri** field doesn't show a slash (/), then **check_speling** returns immediately. The requested item is too badly malformed for **mod_speling** to fix it.

35070: Places the first part of the requested path into **good**. The second part, containing the mis-spelled file name, is placed into **bad**. The misspelled file name and everything after it, such as arguments, are placed in **postgood**.

35081: Verifies that all of the string manipulation adds up correctly using the string lengths **urlen** and **pglen** that were just computed. If not, something went wrong trying to parse the full URI. **check_speling** returns immediately.

35090: Attempts to open the directory that the requested file should be in using **ap_popendir**. If the directory open fails, something was wrong that **mod_speling** cannot fix, so **check_speling** returns immediately.

35096: Sets up an array called **candidates** to hold all of the directory entries from the current directory, which may be what the current file name was intended to be.

35104: Begins to loop through all entries in the directory using **readdir**.

35113: If the entry read in matches the requested file, something else is wrong, such as a symbolic link that cannot be followed. In this case, **mod_speling** cannot solve the problem, and returns immediately.

35122: Tests the current directory against the requested file name (**bad**) with a case-insensitive com-parison. If the current directory and requested file name match, **check_speling** places the directory name (**dir_entry>d_name**) in the **candidates** array with a **quality** field indicating a capitalization problem.

35137: Calls **spdist** with the current directory entry to check for errors such as transposed and missing letters. If **spdist** returns one of these values, **check_speling** places the directory entry in the **candidate** array with the **quality** field indica-ting the findings of **spdist**.

35171: Begins testing again if the **WANT_BASENAME_MATCH** compiler flag was set. This allows **mod_speling** to correct some problems when the file extension is incorrect (such as .htm instead of .html).

35188: Checks the location of the period in the file name. If a comparison on line 35194 works, the file name is placed in the **candidates** array with the **quality** field marked as **SP_VERYDIFFERENT**. This will place any matches from this section below those already found.

35207: After looping through all directory entries, the directory is closed with **ap_pclosedir**.

35209: If the **candidates** array is not empty, at least one potential correction was found.

35218: Retrieves the **Referer** field for possible use in returning information to the client.

35220: Sorts the **candidates** array based on the **quality** field.

35232: Prepares to redirect the request immediately if the best candidate (having now been sorted) is not marked as **SP_VERYDIFFERENT** (because of a file extension correction) and only one candidate is of the highest quality available (that is, the first two items in the **candidate** array don't have the same quality level).

35236: Prepares an updated URI based on the new file name corrected by **mod_speling**.

35243: Sets the **Location** header to the new URI, notes in the error log that **mod_speling** fixed a bad request, and returns with a redirection code.

35258: Multiple choices must be returned as a list to the client.

35275: Creates a memory pool to collect needed information.

35283: Creates the HTML document that will be sent to the client by pushing the text elements into the array **t**. The text elements include explanations and a list of candidates that might be what the file name should have been. They are assembled by the **for** loop beginning on line 35295. As noted in the code, the formatting is not great, but each line includes a link to the candidate file, so a user can simply click on the desired file name.

35331: Continues writing a list of candidates marked as **SP_VERYDIFFERENT** because of their file extensions.

35346: If the **Referer** field was available for this page, **check_speling** includes a note to that effect. In this case, the misspelling was not typed in but is encoded in someone's Web page.

35360: Passes the array of HTML text to the **notes** field of the request so that the pool of memory used to create it can be safely destroyed before this module finishes (see line 35366).

35368: Logs the action of **mod_speling** in the error log, noting that multiple candidates were returned to the client.

speling_module

35382: Defines the module components. These include functions to set up directory and server configuration records, the command table to manage directives used by **mod_speling**, and the **check_speling** function, which is called during the **fixups** stage to actually spellcheck and possibly correct and redirect the requested file.

Discussion Of mod_unique_id

mod_unique_id is used to assign a unique identifier to every request. The identifier created by this module is unique across all Apache instances, requests, and Web servers. The identifier created is intended for use by scripts that process client requests. It is similar to a cookie, but is not passed between the client and server and is not managed as part of the request headers. Instead, the unique ID can be used as a type of cookie that isn't part of the request headers and is not stored in a cookie file on the client. The ID can be returned as part of a URL or within a hidden form field to identify or track a user through multiple, otherwise stateless, requests to a Web server. The identifier generated by this module is available via the environment variable **UNIQUE_ID**.

Module Structure

mod_unique_id is unusual in that it has no directory or server configuration function. The module is initialized by either **unique_id_global_init** or **unique_id_child_init**, depending on which type of server process is calling it. The identifier for a request is generated in the **post_read_request** phase by the **gen_unique_id** function (see Figure 9.7).

Customization

The generation of identifiers could be based on something besides the server's hardware address, the time of the request, and the process ID of the Apache server handling the request. In practice, these provide an ID that is likely to be unique, but some circumstances might warrant a more refined selection of identifiers.

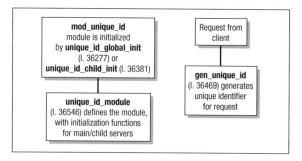

Figure 9.7 **mod_unique_id** assigns a unique identifier to every client request.

unique_id_rec

36172: Defines a data structure into which the unique identifier components are placed before the final ID is generated.

36271: Creates a single static instance of **unique_id_rec_offset** to be used for storing information about the current platform. This information is used by **gen_unique_id** to create a unique identifier.

unique_id_global_init

36277: Initializes information used by **mod_unique_id** when starting a main server.

36292: Calculates the sizes and offsets of the various fields of the variable **cur_unique_id**. These are stored in the array **unique_id_rec_offset**.

36316: Calculates the size of the identifier when it is encoded to use all human-readable characters.

36325: Retrieves the hostname of the server. If it isn't available, **unique_id_global_init** logs an error and exits. It also uses **gethostbyname** to retrieve server information, logging an error if this cannot be done on this server.

36342: Sets **global_in_addr** to the hardware address of the server. This is used to generate a unique identifier. If it is unavailable, an error is logged.

36370: Retrieves information about the time-of-day tracking used by the current platform. This is stored in **tv**.

unique_id_child_init

36381: Initializes a child server process. Because the child is the process that actually services a request, the process ID (PID) is used as part of the unique ID generated by **gen_unique_id**. The PID is noted in this function for later use.

36399: Retrieves the PID using **getpid** and stores it in **cur_unique_id.pid**.

36409: Verifies that the assignment worked. This validates that the 32-bit PID values are being used. If the assignment wasn't valid, **unique_id_child_init** logs an error and exits.

36416: Sets the **in_addr** value of **cur_unique_id** to the global value for this physical server (**global_in_addr**).

36424: If time-of-day tools are available on this platform, **unique_id_child_init** uses **gettimeofday** to assign a value to the **counter** field of **cur_unique_id**. If these tools are not available, **counter** is set to 0.

36445: Uses **htonl** and **htons** to correct any discrepancies in the byte ordering of **cur_unique_id.pid**. This is necessary because the identifiers may be used across different architectures.

uuencoder

36456: Defines an array of codes to use when converting the identifier to human-readable form. This is similar to **uuencode** on Unix, but uses different codes.

gen_unique_id

36469: Generates a unique ID during the **post-read-request** phase of a request.

36489: Determines whether the current request was redirected. If so, it should already have a unique ID assigned. It is retrieved into **e** with a call to **ap_table_get**, and reassigned to the current subrequest using **ap_table_setn**.

36495: Sets the **stamp** field of **cur_unique_id** using **htonl** with the **request_time** field of the request.

36504: Uses a **for** loop to copy the unique ID record, **unique_id_rec_offset**, from the current buffer to a temporary one. This avoids potential problems with any padding bytes when doing the **uuencode** operation. **x** and **y** are used to store the results.

36515: Adds padding to make NULL-terminated strings.

36522: Proceeds with the **uuencode** operation by looping through the **y** string, indexing into the **uuencoder** array and placing the results in **str**.

36533: Terminates the **str** identifier with NULL.

36536: Sets the environment variable **UNIQUE_ID** to the **str** that was just generated. This makes it available to other processes (such as scripts) that Apache starts from this request.

36539: Increments **counter** to aid in the uniqueness of the identifier created for the next request.

36542: Returns **DECLINED** so that any other **post-read-request** phase functions will still be called.

unique_id_module

36546: Defines this module. Initialization functions for the main server (**unique_id_global_init**) and child servers (**unique_id_child_init**) are defined, as well as a function to generate a unique identifier in the **post-read-request** phase. No per-server or per-directory configuration records are used, and no directives affect the actions of this module.

Chapter 10

Server Information And Status Modules

This chapter describes two modules (**mod_info** and **mod_status**) that are used to report status information to users via a browser. Although the browser provides a convenient method of viewing Apache server information in realtime, access to the information provided by these modules must be controlled in order to avoid security violations regarding your server performance and mismanagement of information.

Neither **mod_info** nor **mod_status** are included in the default Apache configuration. If you add them by compiling them in or by using the Dynamic Shared Objects (DSO) feature, you should control their use. For **mod_status**, include a block similar to this one in your httpd.conf file:

```
<Location /server-status>
SetHandler server-status
</Location>
```

For **mod_info**, include a block similar to this one:

```
<Location /server-info>
SetHandler server-info
</Location>
```

The location file name is an arbitrary selection but you must assign the handler to the module so that the module will respond when you enter that URL from a browser. In addition, you should add lines similar to the following in each of the previous blocks to protect access to the information provided by these two modules:

```
order deny,allow
allow from your-IP-address
deny from all
```

Discussion Of mod_info

The **mod_info** module provides a realtime listing of the configuration information for running the Apache server. This information is taken from the configuration files and the per-module configurations. The value of viewing this information using **mod_info** rather than simply viewing the configuration files is that, with **mod_info**, you see exactly how the information in the configuration files has been interpreted and how it will actually be used.

No directives are needed to use **mod_info**, though you can specify additional information with the **Add-ModuleInfo** directive. Any text provided with an **AddModuleInfo** directive is listed in the **mod_info** output.

Several options are available when querying **mod_info**. These options are added as standard query arguments to the location that you have configured as the handler for **mod_info** (**/server-info** in the example given in the previous section). The options are:

- **/server-info?server**—Returns just the server configuration

- **/server-info?module_name**—Returns the configuration of the named module

- **/server-info?list**—Returns a brief listing of the modules included in the server

Module Structure

The module sets up per-server configuration records that hold any **AddModuleInfo** lines of text that you included in your configuration file. When the module is invoked, the **display_info** function is called (line 21458). This function opens the configuration file for the server and prints a large set of configuration detail to the client (see Figure 10.1).

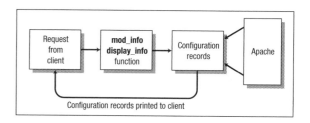

Configuration records printed to client

Figure 10.1   The **mod_info** module prints configuration data based on the information requested by the client.

The information provided by **mod_info** does not describe the performance of the server. For that, query **mod_status**.

The server configuration detail includes **<VirtualHost>**, **<Directory>**, and **<Location>** information. In addition, **mod_info** sends configuration details on each installed module with the directives that have been enacted for each module. The per-module information is prepared for the **display_info** function using the **mod_info_module_cmds** function, which begins on line 21294 and is called from within **display_info** beginning on line 21729.

Customization

Because **mod_info** provides static information (static within a running server), modifications or enhancements can center around formatting text for attractive output or adding static information about the server environment that is not included in the Apache configuration files. Formatting can be enhanced with table-driven forms, divided into groupings by module, or color-coded for easier reading. Additional server environment information can include the operating system configuration, file system details, and basic usage statistics (though these are better placed in **mod_status**). Both types of modifications can be performed in (or called from) the **display_info** function.

Of course, the more information that you include in the output of **mod_info**, the greater the risk that someone will be able to access that information via their browser if sufficient precautions in setting up the configuration file haven't been taken.

info_entry

21168: The **info_entry** structure provides a table of names and values for additional information provided by any **AddModuleInfo** directives.

info_svr_conf

21173: The **info_svr_conf** structure is the per-server configuration record for this module. It only holds additional information provided by **Add-ModuleInfo** directives, because no standard directives affect the output of **mod_info**.

info_cfg_lines

21177: The **info_cfg_lines** structure is used to store lines of text from the Apache configuration files before output to the client begins.

21183: The module definition is forward-referenced here so that all the other functions can recognize it. The actual module definition begins on line 21809.

21184: The **top_module** variable is referenced here, though it is external to this module, allowing **mod_info** to query information about each of the active modules in this copy of Apache.

create_info_config

21186: The **create_info_config** function creates a per-server configuration record for **mod_info** by allocating a server configuration record with **ap_palloc**, making an array of entries (which can be filled later from any **AddModuleInfo** directive), and returning the result to the Apache core.

merge_info_config

21197: This function combines two server configuration records when a base configuration (passed in as **basev**) and a virtual host server configuration (passed in as **overridesv**) must be used together. A new server configuration record is created, and the **basev** and **overridesv** records are combined into it.

mod_info_html_cmd_string

21211: The **mod_info_html_cmd_string** function is used extensively by the **mod_info_modules_cmds** function to return escaped HTML lines sent to the client using **ap_rputs** calls (such as on line 21332). The purpose of this function is basically to replace the angle brackets that occur in the configuration file reports with equivalent HTML codes so that they will appear correctly in the client browser. The HTML codes are seen on lines 21224 and 21228.

mod_info_load_config

21250: This function returns an array containing the noncomment lines in the configuration file named in the file name parameter. This function is used to preload the configuration files so that individual module information can be drawn out using the **mod_info_module_cmds** function. The **mod_info_load_config** function is called, for example, on line 21490.

21259: This function opens the file named in the function parameters using the **ap_pcfg_openfile** call. If opening the file using **ap_pcfg_openfile** didn't work, as tested on line 21260, an error using **ap_log_rerror** is logged, and a NULL status is returned.

21268: A **while** loop that reads each of the lines in the configuration file using the file descriptor variable **fp** starts here. Each line is read by the **ap_cfg_getline** API call. Comment lines (which start with a #) are skipped by the test on line 21269. If the current line is not a comment, space is allocated for it by the **ap_palloc** call on line 21272, and the pointers for new lines to refer to it are set.

21283: The actual line from the configuration file is copied to the **new** variable by the **ap_dstrdup** call on this line.

21290: After reading all of the lines of the configuration file, the file descriptor is closed using **ap_cfg_closefile**. The **ret** variable, which points to the top of the list of configuration lines, is returned.

mod_info_module_cmds

21294: The **mod_info_module_cmds** function prints out configuration information that applies to specific modules within containers such as **<Directory>**, **<Location>**, and **<File>**. The configuration information is formatted and written to the client using several **ap_rputs** calls, such as on lines 21328 and 21373. The output is formatted as an HTML definition list (using **<DL>**, **<DT>**, and **<DD>** tags).

find_more_info

21436: The **find_more_info** function is used by the **display_info** function to send any module-specific information provided by **AddModuleInfo** directives to the client. The module name is provided in the function header. The server configuration is searched for **AddModuleInfo** directives that match that module name. Any matches are returned to the calling function on line 21451.

21440: The list of module information is loaded into the **conf** variable by retrieving the server configuration using **ap_get_module_config** on line 21441. The information needed for this function is placed in **entry** where it can be used by the **for** loop on line 21449.

21449: The **for** loop steps through each of the elements in the configuration list created by various **AddModuleInfo** directives. If the name of the module passed in as a function parameter matches the module name of the entry being checked, then the information provided for that entry is returned to the calling function.

display_info

21458: The **display_info** function is the core of **mod_info**. It assembles and then writes out to the client all of the configuration information relative to the current copy of Apache and its loaded modules.

21471: Verifies that the **Allow** directive for the current context permits the **GET** method, which is what **mod_info** responds to. If the method being used (**r->method_number**) is not **GET**, then the request is declined. The function exits on line 21473.

21475: Sets the content for the response that will be generated by **mod_info** to text/html. All of the headers on line 21476 are sent. If only headers were requested (test the **header_only** field), then 0 is returned, completing the request.

21480: Before starting to process the information fields, the function sets a timeout so that, if the process doesn't finish in a timely manner, it will automatically be ended by Apache.

21482: Uses the **ap_rputs** to send the header information for the information page, with a centered **<H1>** title (line 21484).

21486: If the argument included with this URL is **list**, then the function creates a brief list of the modules included with this Apache server. The **ap_server_root_relative** call is used to obtain the current server information. The information is passed to the **mod_info_load_config** function (line 21250), which will load the **mod_info_cfg_httpd** variable with the module names. The variables **cfname** (with the configured name of this server) and **mod_info_cfg_srm** (with the resource information for the server) continue loading. Individual information about resources is loaded into **mod_info_cfg_access** using the **mod_info_load_config** function on line 21497.

21499: If the request that called this module didn't include any arguments (for example, a list or a module name), then the function starts writing information back to the client, starting with the server settings for each module. A title is written out first. The **for** loop on line 21502 then steps through each of the modules, printing the module name with a link to the per-module configuration, which is generated later.

21513: After testing the request arguments for the presence of the server option, line 21515 starts a long series of **ap_rprintf** calls that dump a series of server configuration information to the client. This call basically uses the same format as a standard **printf** statement, with the parameter values to print being provided by a series of calls to Apache functions that return server configuration details. For example, on line 21518 the **ap_get_server_version** function returns the version of Apache. The printout of these server options continues until line 21568, where the **if** statement is closed. The options printed in this section are easily recognizable as server options within the configuration files (such as httpd.conf). This information is loaded into the server as it is launched and returned using the corresponding Apache API calls that are used in lines 21515 to 21567.

21570: After sending a horizontal rule and starting a Definition List HTML tag (**<DL>**) on line 21569, the **for** loop on line 21570 begins stepping through each of the modules, printing the configuration information for that module. The per-module configuration information written out at this point is similar to the series of server information printed out on lines 21518 to 21568. In the case of the modules, however, the information is taken from the **modp** data structure and the linked lists of details that it includes, rather than from API calls. The

per-module data is written out on lines 21570 through 21726. The data for each module is comprehensive, based on the global **modp** structure, and includes a list of all the handlers that the module has registered with Apache to handle each of the phases of request processing (such as authentication, logging, and file name translation). For example, line 21656 starts an **if** statement to check if the current module description being printed includes a file translation handler. If it does, the **Translate Path** feature is included (on line 21660) in the description of what services this module provides. In addition, a list of the directives that the module handles is printed out using the **cmds** field of the module description.

21727: Additional information about the configuration of the module currently being described can be taken from the standard Apache configuration files. The calls to **mod_info_module_cmds** on lines 21729, 21732, and 21735 write out this additional configuration information from httpd.conf, srm.conf, and access.conf, respectively.

21742: Similarly, the **find_more_info** function is called on line 21742 to output any of the **AddModuleInfo** lines that pertain to the module.

21762: If the arguments to this request specified a reduced list of modules rather than detailed module information, the **for** loop here is executed, which simply prints a list of all the active modules on line 21764.

21771: If a signature is defined for this server, the **ap_psignature** call will send it to the client. The timeout for the activities of this module is then killed and the module returns a 0, having successfully returned a reply to the client.

add_module_info

21779: This function adds items from the **AddModule-Info** directive to the list of details stored for **mod_info**. New items are retrieved using the **ap_get_module_config** call on line 21785, then added to the current configuration using the **ap_push_array** call on line 21787.

info_cmds

21794: This structure defines directives that affect this module and the function to call when those directives are processed. Because **mod_info** doesn't use any standard directives, only the **AddModuleInfo** directive is used. Anytime this directive is found when parsing a server (virtual host) configuration block, the **add_module_info** function is called.

info_handlers

21803: This structure defines the function **display_info** as the one to call for handling **server-info** requests.

info_module

21809: The module is defined in this section. Items defined include the **create** and **merge** server configuration functions, the command (directive) list (**info_cmds**) and the function used to define how to handle incoming requests (**info_handlers**).

Discussion Of mod_status

The use of **mod_status** is similar to that of **mod_info** in that you must specify a handler in your configuration file so that the module can be queried by requesting a certain URL. The biggest distinction between the two is that **mod_info** is used to report the configuration information, whereas **mod_status** reports moment-by-moment system status, such as how many servers are running, how much CPU time is being taken by Apache (when this can be determined), and so forth.

Several optional arguments can be included when you request the server status:

- **server-status?refresh=5**—Refreshes the status information page every five seconds. If no value is given (just **?refresh**), the default value of one second is used.

- **server-status?notable**—Returns information without using HTML tables.

- **server-status?auto**—Returns the status information in a different format that is easier to process using a script.

The **refresh** argument can be combined with either of the other two by placing a comma between them (such as **server-status?refresh=5,auto**).

The information returned by **mod_status** includes:

- The platform and version of Apache

- The server start time and total uptime

- CPU usage information

- The scoreboard file, which tracks the number of running servers and what state they are in

Module Structure

The structure of **mod_status** is very simple. After determining that a valid **GET** request was made by the client, the module gathers information from a series of Apache API calls about each running server, then formats and prints that information to the client, as illustrated in Figure 10.2.

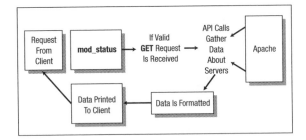

Figure 10.2   The **mod_status** module gathers information about Apache, formats it, and returns it to the client.

The complexity in **mod_status** arises mainly from the formatting options that include the following:

- **Auto**—Creates a plain-text report, rather than an HTML report

- **Notable**—Creates a nontable HTML report

- **ExtendedStatus**—Actually a directive, not a formatting option; affects how much information about each server is presented to the client

Because users can combine these options in different ways, the code for **mod_status** is less straightforward than it otherwise would be. Still, the basic printing of data to the client is the core of **mod_status**.

Beyond the basic printing of status information to the client, **mod_status** uses a small number of functions to format and print numbers and time and date information.

Customization

A challenge throughout **mod_status** is making the statistical and timing information accurate because the same Apache source code is used for a variety of OS platforms. The evidence is seen throughout the code as numerous **#ifdef**-type compiler directives that are set during Apache compilation. These can get in the way of reading the code, but don't affect the performance of the binary that you compile for your system.

If you aren't concerned about creating a version of Apache that can't be moved to other platforms, you can do many things to enhance the statistical information provided by **mod_status**. Some ideas are:

- Add additional information to the status output so you can learn about platform-specific resources that Apache is using. For example, if you are running Apache on a Linux system, query the **/proc** file system to report on system resources that Apache is using or to report general system status on a busy Web server. Be careful about security if you start reporting detailed system information using this sort of automated process.

- Integrate the functions of **mod_status** into core Apache code so that status information is written to a file at regular time intervals. Use a new directive that you define to determine the time interval. Use scripts to process the data for tracking Apache's health and performance.

- Update the status-generating code to write out to a database interface, so that statistics are logged in a database rather than a flat file. This should provide for easier tracking and manipulation of status data over time.

- Rework the **status_handler** function to remove the ability to handle the options that are now supported. For example, you could remove the ability to generate an HTML table version or even an HTML version (enforce the **notable** and **auto** options). This shrinks the size of **mod_status**, though performance is not materially affected.

- If you're the artistic type, you can improve the look of the status pages by using background graphics, shaded table cells, and charts showing the number of servers in each main status category (such as dead, reading, waiting). This can make it easier to understand the status report on a busy server. If you add a lot of detail to the HTML page (such as summary charts or graphics) and you are concerned about the impact on server performance, consider setting the default refresh rate to something higher than 1 or disabling fast refresh rates.

Compiler DEFINE Statements

35430: **STATUS_MAXLINE** is defined here as the maximum line length for the information printed out by **mod_status**.

35432: **KBYTE**, **MBYTE**, and **GBYTE** are defined here as divisors for use by the **format_bytes_out** and **format_kbytes_out** functions.

35437: **DEFAULT_TIME_FORMAT** is defined here to represent how time values are printed by the API calls on lines 35686 and 35689. The **show_time** function (see line 35500) doesn't use this format

variable; that function can be modified directly if you choose. The default string used here will cause the Apache API calls to print a date/time in this format: Tuesday, 11-May-1999 17:35:08.

status_module

35441: The module definition is forward-referenced on this line so that the other functions are aware of it before it actually appears on line 36139.

set_extended_status

35449: The **set_extended_status** function sets a global flag called **ap_extended_status** to **On** when the **ExtendedStatus** directive is included in an Apache configuration file (lines 35458 and 35461). The **set_extended_status** function is called by Apache when that directive is parsed (line 35468).

status_module_cmds

35466: This structure defines the Apache directives used by **mod_status**. The only one used is **ExtendedStatus**, which can have a value of **On** or **Off**. The function **set_extended_status** is called to process this directive (which is server-wide).

format_bytes_out

35476: The **format_bytes_out** function accepts a long integer as a parameter (bytes) and prints it to the client as a formatted number based on its size. The number is reduced and printed as a number with KB, MB, or GB, depending on its size. The division constants are defined starting on line 35432.

format_kbyte_out

35489: The **format_kbyte_out** function accepts an integer as a parameter (**kbytes**) and prints it to the client as a formatted number with KB, MB, or GB, depending on its size. This function is basically identical to the **format_bytes_out** function, except that **format_kbytes_out** is used when the value returned by an API call (and which must be printed to the client) is in kilobytes rather than bytes.

show_time

35500: The **show_time** function prints a time value to the client using calls to **ap_rprintf**. The **tsecs** variable contains a count of seconds; this variable is manipulated to determine the correct hour, minute, and second values to print. The **DEFAULT_TIME_FORMAT** defined on line 35437 determines how the time is formatted.

stat_opt

35534: This structure defines a place for form data and headers to be stored. The constants defined starting on line 35529 are used later in the **status_handler** function.

status_options

35540: The **status_options** structure defines values for optional arguments that can be appended to the URL that calls **mod_status**. The options **refresh**, **notable**, and **auto** are defined here.

status_handler

35553: The **status_handler** function is the core of **mod_status**. It uses numerous Apache API calls to gather information about the state of all running copies of Apache. This information is formatted and printed to the client (the exact information printed depends on the status options, such as **refresh** and **notable**). Numerous variables are defined at the start of the **status_handler** function. Note especially line 35570, where the **sysconf** call is used to set the system clock **tick** value, and lines 35579 and 35580, where a number of buffers are defined based on the value **HARD_SERVER_LIMIT** (the maximum number of copies of Apache that can be spawned).

35586: Whether a scoreboard file exists is tested using the **ap_exists_scoreboard_image** call. If it doesn't exist, the assumption is that the server is running in **inetd** mode (rather than **standalone**). An error is then logged using **ap_log_rerror** and **mod_status** exits. Apache is rarely run in **inetd** mode, and other potential causes of a missing scoreboard file are not anticipated by the error message logged on line 35589.

35592: This line checks whether the **GET** method is allowed for this request (based on location and authentication checks). If the method number of this request is not **GET**, decline to process this request; **mod_status** is used only for **GET** requests.

35596: The content type of this request is set to text/html, because the remainder of the **status_handler** function generates an HTML document.

35603: This line tests for the existence of arguments to the requested URL. If they exist, this section of code is entered (starting with line 35604). The **while** loop on line 35605 tests whether output for all of the arguments has been processed. If they haven't, the **if** statement on line 35606 places the argument in the **status_options** variable where the **switch** statement on line 35609 begins processing the various argument options.

35610: For the **refresh** option, processing is begun by checking for an equal sign in the argument. If one exists, the number after it is used as the value for the **hdr_out_str** field of the **status_options**; otherwise, the default value of one second is used for refresh of the status information (in line 35618).

35620: For the **notable** option, **no_table_report** is set to 1, and the **switch** statement exits.

35623: For the **auto** option, the **content_type** is changed to text/plain (line 35596 sets it to text/html as the default), **short_report=1**, and the **switch** statement exits.

35633: With all of the header information correctly set (based on the arguments just processed), they are sent to the client. These headers give the client information about the refresh nature of the status page, if appropriate. If only the header

was requested (testing on line 35635), then **mod_status** is exited.

35638: This line prepares to send the status information by instructing Apache to synchronize the scoreboard file using the **ap_sync_scoreboard_image** call.

35639: A **for** loop is used to gather information about each running server. The **ap_scoreboard_image** pointer places this information in local variables, including the arrays **stat_buffer** on line 35643 and **pid_buffer** on line 35644. Based on the status of the server, a count is kept of ready and busy servers (lines 35645 to 35648).

35649: If the **ExtendedStatus** directive was used, access and byte counts are recorded for the current server. These are added to running totals on lines 35660 and 35661.

35654: The CPU time used by Apache is noted on lines 35655 to 35658, unless the **NO_TIMES** compiler option on this line is set because Apache is running on a platform that doesn't provide CPU resource information.

35670: The uptime for Apache is calculated here based on the current time and the value provided by the **ap_restart_time** call.

35672: A timeout is set, so that Apache can exit this module if the writing operations that are about to begin don't finish in a timely manner. This timeout is cancelled after the write operations are finished on line 36112.

35674: If a full report has been requested (**short_report=0**), **ap_rputs** sends an HTML document to the client, beginning with the **<TITLE>** and **<H1>** information. The build date and version number are provided by standard API calls to Apache.

35685: The current time and server start time are printed to the client, followed by the server uptime, which was calculated on line 35670.

35698: Checks whether an extended status report is set by directive to determine whether total accesses and CPU data are reported.

35699: Checks whether a short report is requested in the arguments. If so, the total access number (on line 35700) and the CPU resources consumed (on lines 35713, 35715, 35719, and 35723) are printed out.

35726: If a regular (nonshort) report was requested, more detailed information is printed out on the lines that follow.

35767: Information on busy and running servers is printed out on lines 35767 or 35771 (using a regular or short report format) using numbers computed from all running servers (see lines 35646 and 35648).

35776: This line tests for a short report again, and sends either an HTML **<PRE>** tag or the Scoreboard label.

35781: A **for** loop is used to output one character for each running (or potentially running) server. This creates a line of status flags (up to **STATUS_MAXLINE** length). Watching this line when using the **refresh** option as an argument provides a live update of changes in the running servers as requests are processed, servers sit idle, and so forth.

35792: Prints several lines to the client to explain the information in the status line. This information (through line 35810) is static and is provided simply to interpret the line of flags printed using the **for** loop on line 35781.

35812: Checks whether extended status is enabled using the **ExtendedStatus** directive. If so (checking the **ap_extended_status** call), the headline PID Key (line 35814) is printed, followed by a status line for each running server using the **for** loop that begins on line 35816. This loop prints a line to the client for each Process

ID (PID), with the state of the Apache server represented by that PID.

35824: If extended status wasn't enabled, the **else** clause on line 35825 is printed to the client.

35833: This line begins checking the **ExtendedStatus** directive, the short report argument, and the table option to determine how to present the status information to the client.

35838: The **#ifdef** compiler directive is set during the configuration phase of Apache compilation. This section of code writes one set of column headers if Apache is running on a platform without CPU statistics and another set of column headers for standard Unix systems that include CPU statistics.

35852: The **for** loop here processes each Apache server (counting up to the **HARD_SERVER_LIMIT**). For each one, scoreboard information is recorded (again, the **#ifdef**s are used to generate different sets of information depending on the platform capabilities). The information for each server is then written to the client on line 35898 using an **ap_rprintf** call. The status of each server is written using the **switch** statement that begins on line 35909 (through line 35940). This nontable view uses full words, whereas the table view (which begins after this section of code) uses a single letter for each status code.

35941: Timing information is computed and printed. Platform differences are managed via compiler **DEFINE** statements that determine which section of code is used.

35958: A series of byte counts are output in this section using the **format_byte_out** function.

35970: If a table report is expected (the **notable** option was not used), a line of information is created for the current running server on line 35972 (note the **<TR>** tag that begins on line 35973). The **switch** statement that begins on line 35983

prints a single character in a table cell as a status indicator for each server. Additional information in the status table is written on line 36017 or 36019, depending on which platform Apache is running on.

36054: Headers for the HTML table of status information are output to the client beginning on this line.

36112: The status information has all been returned to the client. The timeout monitor ends using an **ap_kill_timeout** call.

status_init

36117: The **status_init** function initializes a set of variables that are used by the **status_handler** function to print information to the client about the scoreboard file—a single character for each running server, chosen from the **status_flags** array that is set up in this function. The index keys to the **status_flags** elements are defined in the scoreboard.h file.

status_handlers

36132: The **status_handlers** function defines that **mod_status** uses a single function (**status_handler**) for all requests that it handles, regardless of where they are in the document tree. That is, if the requested URL matches **STATUS_MAGIC_TYPE** (see line 36134), then the function **status_handler** is used to let this module process it. The **STATUS_MAGIC_TYPE** is defined by the **server-status** handler type, as indicated in the first part of this chapter.

status_module

36139: The module definition starts here. This module defines only an initializer and the table of commands and handlers. No per-directory or per-server configuration hooks are provided, as in many modules. The command table, which refers to the single directive that applies to **mod_status**, is defined on line 36148 (see line 35466). The single handler function for this module is defined via the **status_handlers** function, which begins on line 36132.

Chapter 11

Server-Side Includes Module

This chapter describes **mod_include**, a module that provides server-parsed HTML files via Apache. Server-parsed files allow a standard HTML file to include embedded commands that are processed when the file is requested by a client. The Apache server updates the information returned to the client based on the embedded commands. A full set of commands, including conditional statements and the execution of external programs (inserting their input into the parsed HTML file) are available with server-side includes.

Using server-side includes places a heavy processing burden on the Apache server, which must examine each character of a server-parsed file and insert other information when embedded commands are discovered. Server-side includes can also present security concerns, especially if external programs are executed via Apache.

Because of this security risk, two **Allow** options are available to indicate what types of server-side includes can be used within a directory context. If a server-side include is to be used, the following option must be present:

```
Allow Includes
```

If a site's Webmaster decides that **Allow Includes** creates the potential for too much access, a more restrictive option can be used:

```
Allow IncludesNoExec
```

The **IncludesNoExec** option does not permit the **exec** embedded command in server-parsed files.

The following is an example of an embedded command, which the module source code refers to as a directive:

```
<!--#echo var=DOCUMENT_URI-->
```

If this string is included in a server-parsed HTML file, the current document's URI address is inserted each time the document is retrieved by a client.

Discussion Of mod_include

The server-side-includes functionality in Apache is accessed by specifying a handler for documents that have a certain file extension. For example, the directive in the following example would cause Apache to treat all files ending with .shtml as server-parsed HTML files. Using the **AddHandler** directive in this manner causes the **send_shtml_file** function to be called for these files (see line 21088):

```
AddHandler server-parsed .shtml
```

In older versions of Apache, server-side includes were enabled for all files within a directory. This placed an unnecessary processing burden on the server, because most files do not need to be server-parsed.

The **XBitHack** extension has been added to the **AddHandler** method of specifying server-parsed files. When enabled, this feature indicates to Apache that any requested file that has the execute file permission (the X bit) set for the file's owner should be treated as a server-parsed file. Because this hack is based on Unix file permissions, it isn't available on all platforms that run Apache. **#define** statements in the source code are used to remove the relevant code.

The **XBitHack** directive can be used within a **<Directory>** context:

```
<Directory /web/docs/dynamic_files/>
XBitHack on
...
</Directory>
```

In addition to the **on** setting, the **XBitHack** directive can be set to **full**. In this case, Apache checks the group execute permission of the file being parsed. If the group execute bit is set, Apache sends a **LastModified** header to the client with the current date and time. This permits the file to be cached in proxy servers and browsers. (Hence, don't use **XBitHack full** if the data in a server-parsed file is likely to change.)

Module Structure

The source code for **mod_include** has many macros, defines, and comments that refer to the need to update or rewrite sections of the module. Using the command table and handler table, the **send_parsed_file** function (line 20981) is defined as the main entry point for processing files marked for server parsing. Only one directive is defined for this module: **AddHandler**. A single enumerated variable is used for the configuration record.

The length of this module stems from the need to process a number of embedded commands and re-implement some basic input/output functions for the sake of clarity and speed in the code.

The **send_parsed_file** function checks for permission to use server parsing on a file, then calls the **send_parsed_content** function (line 20771) to prepare the content for the client. This function uses the **find_string** and **get_directive** functions to process the entire file being sent to the client. Whenever a directive (an embedded command, not to be confused with a directive in an Apache configuration file) is located, a corresponding function is called to retrieve the data needed for that directive. The module structure is illustrated in Figure 11.1.

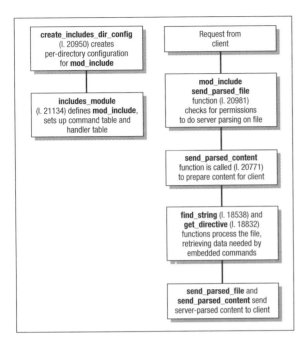

Figure 11.1   **mod_include** enables Apache to parse files and present update content based on embedded commands.

Customization

Despite the remarks in the source code that indicate the need for rewriting of this module, customization should be done with great care because of the security risks posed by **mod_include**. However, several things could be done to extend the functionality and performance of **mod_include**:

- Additional embedded commands (called directives in the source code) can be defined and supported by **mod_include**. These might provide system or environment information (as the **echo** directive now does), or more specialized functionality without resorting to running an external script (with its corresponding resource overhead).

- The number of directives supported by **mod_include** can be reduced, simplifying the processing of parsed

files so that more files can be parsed without burdening the Apache server's hardware. Only those directives needed by a site would be left in the code.

- Other methods might be found to increase the speed of processing for parsed files, either by refining the existing module source code or rewriting it from scratch.

add_include_vars

18471:   Sets up environment information so that any embedded commands that refer to the environment have the information needed. This function is called from within **send_parsed_file** on line 21056.

PUT_CHAR

18530:   During compilation, the phrases **PUT_CHAR**, **GET_CHAR**, and **FLUSH_BUF** are replaced with the code used in these **#define** statements. Using these macros, functions such as **ap_rwrite** on line 18546 are inserted into the **find_string** function (line 18591).

find_string

18578:   Searches in the file named by the **in** parameter for the **str** character, reading characters in via **GET_CHAR** (line 18588) and writing them out with **PUT_CHAR** (lines 18598 and 18600) until the desired character is found.

decodehtml

18647:   Decodes HTML entities from their special forms, such as **<&AUML;>**, to their corresponding single characters for normal processing.

get_tag

18743:   Extracts a tag to continue parsing an embedded command. The **GET_CHAR** macro is used to repeatedly retrieve the next character in the input file until the full tag is assembled and processed. This is basically a lot of string manipulation with loops to get the characters and check for special characters such as quotation marks. The final tag is returned to the calling function on line 18829.

get_directive

18832:   Similar to **get_tag**, this function is called when a directive (a server-side embedded command) is detected. This function reads characters from the input file until the end of the directive is found, then returns the directive in **d** (**dest** in the function header).

parse_string

18866:   Processes a string (the **in** parameter) so that components of a directive (such as the environment variable name or command to execute) are available to the calling function. This function is called within the **handle_include** function (see line 19073).

include_cgi

18975:   Processes an embedded command to run a CGI script. A subrequest is then created to deal with the file name of the script to be run. The filename status is checked on line 18980 and the path is checked on line 18986.

19010:   When everything has checked out, **include_cgi** runs the subrequest so that the script is executed. If the status of the script is a redirect, then the **Location** header is set on line 19013.

19019:   Destroys the subrequest; it has served its purpose.

is_only_below

19033:   Tests that the path given as a parameter is not higher in the directory structure than the calling document for the current request. Determine this by testing for ".." (parent directory designation) in the path.

handle_include

19056:   Handles embedded commands that request a file to be embedded in the current document.

19068:   Tests the validity of the embedded command (**file** or **virtual**). If the command is valid and the path to the file is safe (using the **is_only_below** function on line 19079), then the sub-request lookup of the included file continues on line 19085.

19085: Uses a subrequest lookup to get ready to use the file that is specified in the HTML page as being included. Checks the status of the subrequests, returning any one of several potential errors (beginning on line 19094) if the subrequest or the allowed actions in the current directory context preclude use of the directive as it was written in the current document.

include_cmd_child

19200: This function executes a child process on line 19256. This function does not return in the normal sense, because the **ap_call_exec** function on line 19256 takes control if it is successful.

19227: Checks the subrequest environment using calls such as **ap_sub_req_lookup** on line 19230. Environment information is then prepared so that it will be available to the child process.

19254: Prepares for the child process using **ap_cleanup_for_exec**, then starts the child process using **ap_call_exec** on line 19256.

include_cmd

19283: Handles included files that must be executed by calling **ap_bspawn_child** with the **include_cmd_child** function (line 19200) as the function to use for starting the new child process.

handle_exec

19305: Handles **exec** embedded commands, which execute a command on the Apache server and insert the command output in the current document.

19318: Checks for the **cmd** string, which indicates what is to be executed. If all is well, the **include_cmd** function is called on line 19321, which in turn calls **include_cmd_child**. All this leads to the execution of the specified command.

handle_echo

19366: Handles the **echo** embedded command to return the value of an environment variable within the current document.

19377: Checks for the **var** parameter, after which the name of the desired variable (**val**) is given. The value is found using an **ap_table_get** call on line 19379. The value of the variable is sent immediately to the client on line 19382 using **ap_rputs**.

handle_perl

19403: If embedded Perl commands are used, the command is handled by checking its validity, then calling the appropriate Perl commands on lines 19437 through 19439.

handle_config

19447: Handles a **config** command to set up the configuration for how future embedded commands will be processed.

19461: Searches for each of the possible configuration options using **parse_string**. When the matching command is located, **ap_table_setn** updates the configuration information for the desired item to the new configuration information provided with the embedded command.

find_file

19504: Uses a subrequest to check the validity of an included file named by an embedded command. **find_file** first checks for the **file** case, then for the **virtual** case. If the file status of the subrequest used to check for the file is invalid, an error is logged and the calling function receives an "unsuccessful" code, -1.

handle_fsize

19580: Inserts the file size of the current document into the current document. After some initial checking of the request, the **ap_send_size** call is used to output the file size on line 19602.

handle_flastmod

19626: Inserts the last modified time of the current document into the current document. After some initial checking of the request, line 19647 uses **ap_rputs** with the **ap_ht_time** call to send the last modified time to the client.

re_check

19654: Compiles a regular expression for use in an embedded command. The **ap_pregcomp** call on line 19660 is used to process the string in the embedded command.

get_ptoken

19690: Gets the next token in the string of information coming from the current document. The tokens can then be assembled and tested against available embedded commands. This function uses a series of **case** switches (line 19711) to test possible tokens and to set the **token** variable to one of the enumerated values defined beginning on line 19675.

parse_expr

19856: Parses an expression composed of a series of tokens that were processed using the **get_ptoken** function (line 19690). A series of **case** switches examines possible tokens and builds a parse tree based on the tokens.

20182: The last part of this function evaluates the parse tree that was created by the **case** statements in the first part of the function. The **parse_string** function is called in several places to process the string as it is assembled.

handle_if

20509: Handles a conditional statement within an embedded command to set the **conditional_status** variable based on the expression provided in the command (checked by **parse_expr** on line 20534).

handle_elif

20560: Continues handling conditional statements for an **elif** (else if) embedded command. It starts by testing the **conditional_status** variable; then it parses the expression given for the **elif** command on line 20596.

handle_else

20623: Continues handling conditional statements for an **else** command. Because this is not an **elif** command, the **conditional_status** variable is always set to 1 (line 20640).

handle_endif

20656: Finishes a conditional **if** or **if/else** set of commands. The **get_tag** function on line 20663 is used to check the next tag, then the **printing** variable is set to 1 on line 20672 so that the conditional output of the current document is turned on (the document is "printed" to the client).

handle_set

20687: Sets an environment variable based on the value given in an embedded command. The **parse_string** function on line 20717 gets the needed values, then the new value is added to the subprocess environment using an **ap_table_setn** call on line 20719.

handle_printenv

20733: Prints the environment information for the current request.

20748: Loops through each of the elements of the **subprocess_env** structure (line 20739). Each one is sent to the client using **ap_rvputs**.

send_parsed_content

20771: Sends a server-parsed file to the client. This is the main control function for **mod_include**; it is called from **send_parsed_file**.

20788: Sets the conditional indicators to 1 so that the document will be sent to the client.

20794: If any arguments are given with this request, they are made a part of the subprocess environment. This makes the arguments available for several of the server-side-include commands that may be embedded in the HTML page being processed.

20807: Reads repeatedly from the input file (**f**) using the **find_string** function on line 20808 to determine whether an embedded command is found. When a starting sequence is found, the **get_directive** function on line 20810 retrieves the entire directive. If **get_directive** is successful in retrieving the entire directive, **send_parsed_content** begins processing it on line 20820.

20825: Handles each possible embedded command in the series of **if** and **else/if** statements that follow. Functions such as **handle_if** (line 20825), **handle_exec** (line 20875), and **handle_echo** (line 20889) are called according to the directive found by **get_directive**.

create_includes_dir_config

20950: Creates a per-directory configuration for this module. The configuration includes a single item for the **XBitHack** state.

set_xbithack

20959: Sets the state of the **XBitHack** configuration for the current directory. This function is defined for the **XBitHack** Apache configuration directive on line 21120.

send_parsed_file

20981: Sends a server-parsed file to the requesting client. This function is called from several places according to the handler used to access this module (such as **XBitHack** or **send_shtml_file**).

20990: Verifies that the options allowed for the current directory context allow server-parsed files.

20993: Verifies that the method for this request is **GET**.

20997: Verifies that the file being requested actually exists before trying to parse it.

21008: Attempts to open the requested file. If the file cannot be opened, an error is logged on line 21009 and returns with the HTTP_FORBIDDEN exit code, which will exit this module via the function that called **send_parsed_file**. If the file was opened successfully, processing begins on line 21015.

21015: If the **state** field was set to **xbithack_full**, indicating that the **XBitHack** directive included the **full** argument, the modification times for the file being requested are updated on lines 21021 and 21022.

21028: Sends the headers for the current request. If only headers were requested (line 21030), then the included file that was opened on line 21008 is closed and this function is exited successfully with an OK exit code.

21047: Sets up a subprocess environment for the file-parsing functions to work in. It adds the variables that may be needed by the parsing functions using **ap_add_common_vars** and **ap_add_cgi_vars** (lines 21054 and 21055).

21065: Because of the nature of what is being done, a timeout is set up to protect against serious problems hanging this request and tying up a copy of Apache. This timeout is killed on line 21084 when the requested file is parsed successfully.

21074: Parses and sends the contents of the file using **send_parsed_content** (beginning on line 20771).

send_shtml_file

21088: Sets the **content_type** to HTML and uses the standard **send_parsed_file** function to return the requested file to the client. This function is called when an **AddHandler** directive is used to assign a parsed HTML file type to **mod_include**.

xbithack_handler

21094: Checks the state of the configuration record for the **XBitHack** status. If the bit is set, the standard **send_parsed_file** function on line 21114 is called to parse and return the file to the client. This function is used when the **XBitHack** directive is included in a **<Directory>** configuration context to indicate the use of server-parsed files.

includes_cmds

21118: Defines directives that are used by this module. The only one is **XBitHack**. The **set_xbithack** function is called when this directive is found in a configuration file.

includes_handlers

21125: Defines the functions to call when handler types supported by this module are called. This module is used in four cases: two magic types for server-side includes, the server-parsed type (using an **AddHandler** directive), and **XBitHack**, which applies to all HTML files. All are checked for the X bit; **mod_include** is invoked if it is set. In each case, the functions end up at the **send_parsed_file** function after checking a few items (such as the status of the **XBitHack** configuration for the current directory).

includes_module

21134: Defines **mod_include**. A configuration is created for each directory by the **create_ includes_dir_config** function (only one item is included in the configuration record for this module). The command table (for the single directive, **XBitHack**) and the handler table are defined on lines 21144 and 21145.

Chapter 12

Proxy Server Module

This chapter describes **mod_proxy**, a module that can be added into a standard Apache configuration to make Apache act as a proxy server for a local area network (LAN). The proxy capabilities of **mod_proxy** are highly configurable and include many advanced features such as blocking domain access, intranet-specific features, and remote-forwarded requests. Caching of proxy requests is a standard part of **mod_proxy**.

The Apache proxy capabilities are accessed via a handler, much as a script or the output of the **mod_info** and **mod_status** modules would be. After **mod_proxy** has been compiled into Apache, the only directive needed to make Apache act as a proxy server is this one:

```
ProxyRequests on
```

However, 19 other directives are available to configure the proxy and caching features of **mod_proxy**. These are defined in the source code beginning on line 41354.

The source code for **mod_proxy** includes several calls to functions that appear to be Apache API calls, but that are not part of the standard Apache API set. For example, **ap_proxy_http_handler** is called on line 40832. Calls to **ap_*** functions that are not part of the standard Apache API set are included in the supporting code for **mod_proxy**: proxy_http.c, proxy_connect.c, and others.

Discussion Of **mod_proxy**

The proxy handler can be selected for any directory or location using the **ProxyRequests** directive:

```
<Directory / >
ProxyRequests on
</Directory>
```

Clients using Apache as a proxy Web server must be configured to send Web requests with a **proxy:** URL to the Apache server for processing.

The numerous directives available within **mod_proxy** set up lists of items to watch for when processing a proxy request or flags to indicate possible actions.

Module Structure

Directives for **mod_proxy** are processed according to the **proxy_cmds** table (beginning on line 41352). A separate function places arguments from any applicable directive into a configuration record for the current server context.

The main handler, **proxy_handler** (line 40699), receives actual requests from clients, examines them in accordance with the server configuration, and returns the requested document if appropriate. The **proxy_handler** function uses several API-style calls such as **ap_proxy_cache_check** and **ap_proxy_http_handler** to process proxy requests. These calls are separate from both the **mod_proxy** source code and the standard Apache API calls. Because of these calls, the code for **mod_proxy** is quite straightforward. The module structure is illustrated in Figure 12.1.

For more detail about how the API calls actually retrieve files from other Web servers, review the source code in the additional files that make up the proxy section of Apache (these files are referenced by name within source code commentary that follows).

Customization

The proxy capability of Apache is accessed via **mod_proxy** but is provided, at its core, by the additions to the Apache API that are included in the other proxy source code files. These files can be reviewed and extended for special purpose access, improved security features, customized access tracking, and so forth.

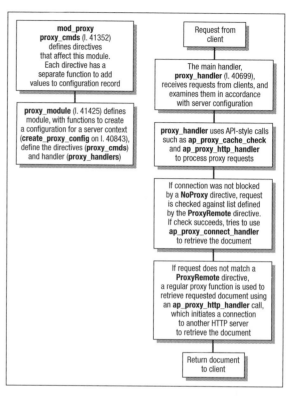

Figure 12.1 **mod_proxy** enables Apache to function as a proxy server for a LAN.

alias_match

40468: Matching URI and alias strings are determined. This function is used by **proxy_trans** (line 40588).

40475: Loops to check each part of the **alias** against the **fakename** (both passed in as parameters then updated for string comparisons on lines 40471 and 40473).

40476: Checks path separators.

40489: Checks for other (nonpath-separator) characters. If any of the characters in **alias** and **fakename** are not equal, **alias_match** returns immediately with 0: The **alias** and **fakename** don't match.

40499: Checks the end of the **alias**, again returning 0 if they do not match.

40509: If the tests all passed, the URI is returned.

proxy_detect

40526: Proxy requests in the post-read phase of request processing are detected, setting up correct request fields and a modified URI to deal with the proxy request. This function is defined for the post-read phase of **mod_proxy** on line 41449.

40543: A complex test (lines 40534 through 40542) is performed to determine if the request should be a proxy. If so, **proxyreq** is set to 1 and the **proxy:** designation is added to the file name on line 40545. The handler is set to **proxy-server** on line 40547.

40552: If the method for the request is **CONNECT** (use a different set of tests), the same information is set for proxy requests (lines 40555 through 40559).

40561: Returns DECLINED in all cases, but the request fields may have been updated for a proxy request.

proxy_trans

40564: The file name of an incoming request is translated so that it is handled as a proxy request. This function is defined for the file name translation phase of **mod_proxy** on line 41439.

40574: If the **proxyreq** flag is already set, this function has nothing left to do. **proxy_trans** returns immediately.

40587: The requested incoming URI is compared with the aliases for the current proxy configuration using the **alias_match** function (line 40468). If an alias matches (tested on line 40590), the **proxy:** designation is added to the beginning of the file name on line 40591, the handler for the

request is set to **proxy-server**, and the **proxyreq** flag is set. **proxy_trans** returns with OK.

proxy_fixup

40608: String manipulation is performed to standardize the URL given in a request that is handled by the proxy functions. Verification of the proxy request is performed on line 40612. The **ap_proxy_http_canon** function (see the file proxy_http.c) is used on line 40620.

40625: If the URL still does not even include a colon, the request was malformed too badly to be fixed, and an error is returned.

proxy_init

40633: The garbage collection function of the proxy cache is initialized using **ap_proxy_garbage_init**. (This function is defined in the file proxy_cache.c.)

proxy_needsdomain

40651: A proper domain name for an incoming client request is prepared before being used as the basis for a proxy-based request to another HTTP server. The proper domain name is constructed using information defined by the **ProxyDomain** directive.

40658: The method of the request is checked. Only **GET** requests are processed; others are DECLINED.

40664: A check is done to determine whether the hostname is **localhost** (in which case, no remote access is to be used) or already contains a dot (in which case it doesn't need to be completed by this function). In either case, it is not processed further.

40670: The **Referer** header is retrieved. This value is used to log an error because the domain is redirected on line 40691.

40676: The domain name is reassembled using the URI of the request. The domain value is passed in to the function.

40683: The **Location** header is set to refer to the new domain name that was assembled into **nuri**.

40684: This situation is logged as an error because the domain name was not sufficient as originally submitted. The correction may, therefore, not be as the user intended.

40693: A redirected indication, **HTTP_MOVED_PERMANENTLY**, is returned, which short-circuits the calling function (lines 40752 through 40754).

proxy_handler

40699: A request for proxy service is handled. It begins by retrieving the configuration record.

40714: If the request does not include the **proxy:** indication, it cannot be handled by **mod_proxy**. (The client is not configured to use this Apache server as a proxy.)

40718: A check of the number of forwards allowed (via the **Max-Forwards** header) is performed to determine if this request can be retrieved using a proxy or if too many levels of indirection have occurred. If the number of forwards permits the proxy, the **Max-Forwards** header is reset to one lower on line 40731; otherwise, **proxy_handler** returns on line 40729 without processing the request.

40736: Prepares to receive data from the client.

40740: The file name from the client's request is stripped off.

40745: A check is performed to determine whether the requested file is already in the cache for the proxy server using the **ap_proxy_cache_check** function. (This function is contained in the file proxy_cache.c.) If the function does not return DECLINED, the file was found and placed in **rc**. The file is returned on line 40747.

40751: If the request arriving from a client doesn't include a completed domain name, the **proxy_needsdomain** function (line 40651) adds a domain name to the request. If the value returned when processing the domain indicates a redirection, that indication is returned on line 40754.

40770: The incoming request is checked against the list in the **dirconn** structure. If a match is found, a direct connection is required (the proxy function is blocked). This is tested on line 40789, which drops to line 40828 to try a direct connection.

40790: The connection was not blocked by a **NoProxy** directive, so the request is checked against the list of items defined in the proxies structure defined by the **ProxyRemote** directive. If this check succeeds, an attempt is made to use the **ap_proxy_connect_handler** to retrieve the document directly. The URL, host, and port are specified in the function, which is defined in the file proxy_connect.c.

40808: The request does not match a **ProxyRemote** directive, so a regular proxy function is used to retrieve the requested document. This is done with an **ap_proxy_http_handler** call, which initiates a client connection to another HTTP server to retrieve the document. This function is defined in the file proxy_http.c.

40817: A check of the results of the last few operations as stored in **rc** is performed. If **rc** contains a good value (the file itself), return it.

40827: The proxy request failed to retrieve the document, so a connection with less information (using NULL and 0 as parameters) is attempted. Three calls are attempted: **ap_proxy_connect_handler**, **ap_proxy_http_handler**, and **ap_proxy_ftp_handler**. If none works, the **HTTP_FORBIDDEN** code is returned on line 40836.

create_proxy_config

40843: A proxy configuration record (**ps**) is created for a server context by allocating a new variable of type **proxy_server_conf** on line 40845. The array structures are filled with a default empty array of 10 elements. Default or initialized values are set for each of the fields in the record. The default constants are defined in the mod_proxy.h file. Note that the **dirlevels** and **dirlength** values are not given using a defined constant. The two values multiplied together, however, must always be less than the **CACHEFILE_LEN** constant (also defined in mod_proxy.h).

add_proxy

40884: A remote proxy is added using the **ProxyRemote** directive. The syntax of the directive is checked beginning on line 40896. If the syntax is correct, the elements of the remote proxy (such as protocol, hostname, and port) are placed in the configuration record beginning on line 40923. This function is defined for the directive on line 41358.

add_pass

40932: A directory alias is set up from a URL to a path internal to the Apache server using the **ProxyPass** directive, allowing something similar to an automatic mirrored Web server using the proxy feature of Apache. The argument given with the directive is stored in the **aliases** field of the configuration with the alias (**f**) and actual location (**r**) as passed in to the function. This function is defined for the directive on line 41361.

add_pass_reverse

40949: A directory alias is set up from a URL to a path internal to the Apache server using the **ProxyPassReverse** directive. This directive defines how **Location** headers returned from a proxy request are handled so that the client doesn't bypass an internal alias that was set up using the **ProxyPass** directive. The argument

given with the directive is stored in the **raliases** (reverse aliases) field of the configuration with the reverse alias (**f**) and actual location (**r**) as passed in to the function. This function is defined for the directive on line 41363.

set_proxy_exclude

40966: The list of IP addresses or names is set to block access to the proxy functions. The list is based on the **ProxyBlock** directive. This function is defined for the directive on line 41367.

40981: The list of blocked sites is reviewed for the current configuration record. Matching items within the arguments to **ProxyBlock** are noted.

40987: If no duplicate entries are found, the argument is placed in the **noproxies** structure of the configuration record. The address is manipulated to be more accessible to testing functions during request processing. The code, however, doesn't deal with multiple IP addresses given in a **ProxyBlock** directive.

set_allowed_ports

41008: Sets the ports that the proxy server can connect to, based on the arguments given with the **AllowCONNECT** directive. This function is defined for the directive on line 41383. The entire list of ports is placed in the **allowed_connects_ports** structure of the configuration record without any testing. It is converted to an integer value on line 41021 by the **atoi** function.

set_proxy_dirconn

41030: Defines or adds to the list of IP addresses, domain names, or hostnames that the proxy server will connect to directly rather than providing the proxy service. This function is controlled by the **NoProxy** directive and is defined on line 41375.

41044: Begins by examining the current contents of the direct connection list (**dirconn**) of the configuration record to check for duplications with the arguments to **NoProxy**.

41049: If a duplicate record was not found, it continues by checking what type of item is included with the directive (such as IP address, domain name, or hostname) on lines 41054, 41062, and 41068. In the case of a domain name or hostname, the item (already placed in the configuration record on line 41050) is changed to all lowercase letters so that future comparisons will be valid. Debugging lines in this section of code log status to the standard error (generally, the console) depending on what type of item is included with a **NoProxy** directive.

set_proxy_domain

41085: Sets the proxy domain to be assumed for requests within an intranet. This domain is appended to requests that do not have a complete domain name. The **ProxyDomain** directive is used to set this value, as defined on line 41379.

set_proxy_req

41101: Turns the proxy server capability on or off for a server context based on the **ProxyRequests** directive. This flag, set on line 41108, must be on for any proxy serving to occur. This function is defined for the directive on line 41354.

set_cache_size

41114: The size of the cache is set in kilobytes according to the value of the **CacheSize** directive. This function is defined for the directive on line 41388.

set_cache_root

41130: The path for the location of cached files is set using the **CacheRoot** directive. This function is defined for the directive on line 41386.

set_cache_factor

41143: A factor is set to use in calculating default expiration times for cached documents. This factor is taken from the **CacheLast-ModifiedFactor**. The function is defined for the directive on line 41396. The floating point number given with the directive (such as .25) is multiplied by the length of time since the document was modified (such as 48 hours) to arrive at a default expiration time (12 hours). The **CacheMaxExpire** and **CacheDefault-Expire** directives, if provided for a server context, override the value of this directive.

set_cache_maxex

41160: Sets the maximum time (in hours) that a document can remain in the cache, as determined by the **CacheMaxExpire** directive. This function is defined for the directive on line 41390.

set_cache_defex

41176: Sets the default length of time (in hours) for documents in the cache to expire, as determined by the **CacheDefaultExpire** directive. This function is defined for the directive on line 41393.

set_cache_gcint

41192: Sets the number of hours between garbage collection in the proxy cache, as determined by the **CacheGcInterval** directive. The configuration record is updated on line 41202.

set_cache_dirlevels

41208: Sets the number of subdirectories allowed in the cache according to the value of the **Cache-DirLevels** directive. This function is defined for the directive on line 41404. The value given in the directive must be greater than 1, and the length times the levels (see **set_cache_dirlength**, line 41228) must be 20 or less. The value is tested on lines 41217 and 41220. If a longer directory path is desired, change the global constant **CACHEFILE_LEN** in the file mod_proxy.h.

set_cache_dirlength

41228: Sets the length of a directory name within the cache, according to the value of the **CacheDirLength** directive. This function is defined for the directive on line 41408. The value given in the directive must be greater than 1, and the length times the levels (see **set_cache_dirlevels**, line 41208) must be 20 or less. The value is tested on lines 41237 and 41240. If a longer directory path is desired, change the global constant **CACHEFILE_LEN** in the file mod_proxy.h.

set_cache_exclude

41248: A list of hosts, domains, or IP addresses is added to the configuration record. The items in the list are not cached when requested by a client via the proxy; that is, they are always retrieved live from the remote server. This function is defined for the directive on line 41411.

41263: Loops through each of the items already stored in the **nocaches** field of the configuration record. If any of the items matches something that arrived with the current directive arguments, it is flagged so that duplication can be avoided.

41269: If the item in the argument was not found, it is placed in the **nocaches** list by creating a new entry on line 41270 and then setting the values of **new**. Note the comment about problems with this code when processing multiple IP addresses.

set_recv_buffer_size

41287: Sets the receive buffer size for incoming requests to the size given in the **ProxyReceive-BufferSize** directive. The value given must be either greater than 512 or else 0 to use the system default. This is checked on line 41294. If the value is valid, it is placed in the **recv_buffer_size** field of the **psf** configuration record. This function is defined for the directive on line 41371.

set_cache_completion

41304: The **cache_completion** field is set to the percentage value given in the **CacheForce-Completion** directive. If a document being retrieved reaches the percentage given, the operation is completed to store in the cache, even if the client cancels the request. The value provided with the directive is checked on line 41311 to see that it is from 0 to 100, then the value is recorded in the **psf** configuration record on line 41318. This function is defined for the directive on line 41415. This field is used primarily by the code in the proxy_cache.c file, as called, for example, on line 40745 of this module.

set_via_opt

41323: The configuration option for the **ProxyVia** directive is set to **on**, **off**, **block**, or **full**. This function is called when **ProxyVia** directives are found (line 41419).

proxy_handlers

41346: The handler function that will be used for requests that arrive with the **proxy:** designation in their URL is defined. The **proxy_handler** function begins on line 40699.

proxy_cmds

41352: Directives that affect this module are defined. The list includes 20 directives, each with a separate function to add values to the configuration record used by **mod_proxy**. (The functions begin on line 40884 with **add_proxy**, but are not in the order in which they appear in **proxy_cmds**). For each directive, a brief description defines what the directive should contain. This message is returned by Apache if the format of the directive arguments is incorrect.

proxy_module

41425: The module itself is defined, with functions to create a configuration for a server context (**create_proxy_config** on line 40843), to define the directives (**proxy_cmds**) and handler (**proxy_handlers**) for the module, and to deal with post issues in the **translate** and **fixups** stages. The proxy requests coming from a client are mainly processed by the **proxy_handler** function, which is defined by the structure **proxy_handlers** (line 41346).

Appendix A

Online References

Because Apache is a work in progress that is being developed as a cooperative project, the Internet is perhaps the best place to find reference information about the server itself or individual modules. The developers who work together online and the end users who install the program report bugs, suggest improvements, and even write modules and contribute information to the Apache Server Project Web site (**www.apache.org/httpd.html**) as well as to their own personal Web pages.

You, too, can participate by going online to report any bugs in the software or to add your site to the ever-growing list of Apache users. Here is a selection of useful Web resources you can visit to help you use Apache to run your Web site or to customize the modules that help you manage Web-based information.

The Apache Server Project Web Site

Any developer who uses Apache needs to be familiar with the wealth of information presented on Apache's official Web site (**www.apache.org/httpd.html**). The home page for this site contains details about the latest release of the program. To receive a regular announcement of new releases by email, subscribe to the Apache-announce mailing list (**www.apache.org/announcelist.html**). From the Apache Server Project home page, click on the Download link to download the latest version.

Here are some other parts of the extensive Apache Web site that will probably interest you:

- *Apache Developer Resources*—The ongoing development of Apache is recorded at this site (**dev.apache. org**). Some areas of the site, such as the areas where members of the Apache Group respond to bug reports, require prior authentication. However, if you are working on the Apache source code and want to contribute patches, you can do so at **dev.apache.org/ patches.html**.

- *Apache Developers' C Language Style Guide*—This part of the Apache Project Development Site (**http:// dev.apache.org/styleguide.html**) provides important information for anyone wanting to write code for Apache. You'll find out how to indent code, how to declare functions, and much more.

- *Apache Bug Reporting Page*—If you want to report a bug you've encountered so the Apache Group can track the problem down and fix it, go to **www.apache. org/bug_report.html**.

- *Apache Problem Report Database*—This page (**bugs. apache.org**) is where you can search through bug and problem reports that have been submitted by users. Even if you aren't encountering a bug with Apache yourself, but are having trouble figuring out how to implement a directive or set up another feature, it's useful to search the bug database to see if anyone else has already had a problem like the one you are having.

- *Unofficial Patches For Publicly Released Versions Of Apache*—Even if your code patch is not added to the Apache core or the standard modules, it might be included on this site (**www.apache.org/dist/contrib/ patches**).

- *Information On The Apache HTTP Server Project*— This page (**www.apache.org/info.html**) provides an extensive list of sites that use Apache. You can add your own site's name to the list at **www.apache.org/ info/apache_users.html**.

The following sites are of special interest to those who are writing code for Apache, or who want to understand how modules and the Apache core code are structured.

Shambhala API Notes

This site (**dev.apache.org/API.html**) is the place to start if you want to understand and begin working with the Apache API. You'll get an overview of how to construct handlers and requests, and how to assemble modules.

Apache Module Registry

If you've decided to join the many developers who have taken advantage of the Apache API to create their own modules, you can register them at this Web site (**modules.apache.org**). You can also join a mailing list that announces new modules as they become available.

The Apache/Perl Integration Project

This site (**perl.apache.org**) attempts to bring together Perl and Apache by documenting **mod_perl** and other Apache/Perl modules.

Apache Week

This site (**www.apacheweek.com**) provides articles about different aspects of Apache and announces new releases of the server. They also have a weekly email newsletter that's put out by C2Net, the company that makes Stronghold, a commercial version of Apache that uses SSL. And if you're having a problem with some aspect of Apache, be sure to search the back issues.

Ralf S. Engelschall's Web Site

Ralf Engelschall is a member of the Apache Group and the author of the modules **mod_ssl** and **mod_rewrite**. His Web site (**www.engelschall.com**) contains some good background information about these two modules. You'll also find a User's Guide to URL Rewriting with the Apache Web Server (**www.engelschall.com/pw/ apache/rewriteguide/**), which explains the workings of the **mod_rewrite** module. The Web pages for the **mod_ssl** security module are at **www.engelschall.com/ sw/mod_ssl/**.

Standard C Reference

This site (**www.valpatken.com/RandRs/std_c/index. html**), created by P.J. Plunger, is a good reference for reading and writing programs in the C programming language.

Usenet Newsgroups

comp.infosystems.www.servers.unix and **comp. infosystems.www.servers.ms-windows** are rich sources of support and information regarding Apache. The Unix group generates the most active discussion on Apache. The MS-Windows group is the place to go when you have a question or problem with Apache for Windows.

HotWired

HotWired (**www.hotwired.com**—which uses the Apache Web server, by the way) has published several Apache-related articles since the publication began in 1994. The Webmonkey section of HotWired focuses on topics for Web developers, and an article in the September 23, 1998, issue focused on using **mod_perl** with Apache.

You'll also find an archive full of past articles on HTTP cookies, CGI, and tuning your (Unix-based) Apache Web server (December 11, 1997) at **www.hotwired.com/ webmonkey/backend/backend_more.html**.

Appendix B

GNU General Public License

We have included the GNU General Public License (GPL) for your reference as it applies to the software this book was about. However, the GPL does not apply to the text of this book.

Version 2, June 1991
Copyright (C) 1989, 1991 Free Software Foundation, Inc.
59 Temple Place - Suite 330, Boston, MA 02111-1307, USA

Everyone is permitted to copy and distribute verbatim copies of this license document, but changing it is not allowed.

Preamble

The licenses for most software are designed to take away your freedom to share and change it. By contrast, the GNU General Public License is intended to guarantee your freedom to share and change free software—to make sure the software is free for all its users. This General Public License applies to most of the Free Software Foundation's software and to any other program whose authors commit to using it. (Some other Free Software Foundation software is covered by the GNU Library General Public License instead.) You can apply it to your programs, too.

When we speak of free software, we are referring to freedom, not price. Our General Public Licenses are designed to make sure that you have the freedom to distribute copies of free software (and charge for this service if you wish), that you receive source code or can get it if you want it, that you can change the software or use pieces of it in new free programs; and that you know you can do these things.

To protect your rights, we need to make restrictions that forbid anyone to deny you these rights or to ask you to surrender the rights. These restrictions translate to certain responsibilities for you if you distribute copies of the software, or if you modify it.

For example, if you distribute copies of such a program, whether gratis or for a fee, you must give the recipients all the rights that you have. You must make sure that they, too, receive or can get the source code. And you must show them these terms so they know their rights.

We protect your rights with two steps: (1) copyright the software, and (2) offer you this license which gives you legal permission to copy, distribute and/or modify the software.

Also, for each author's protection and ours, we want to make certain that everyone understands that there is no warranty for this free software. If the software is modified by someone else and passed on, we want its recipients to know that what they have is not the original, so that any problems introduced by others will not reflect on the original authors' reputations.

Finally, any free program is threatened constantly by software patents. We wish to avoid the danger that redistributors of a free program will individually obtain patent licenses, in effect making the program proprietary. To prevent this, we have made it clear that any patent must be licensed for everyone's free use or not licensed at all.

The precise terms and conditions for copying, distribution and modification follow.

Terms And Conditions For Copying, Distribution And Modification

This License applies to any program or other work which contains a notice placed by the copyright holder saying it may be distributed under the terms of this General Public License. The "Program", below, refers to any such program or work, and a "work based on the Program" means either the Program or any derivative work under copyright law: that is to say, a work containing the Program or a portion of it, either verbatim or with modifications and/or translated into another language. (Hereinafter, translation is included without limitation in the term "modification".) Each licensee is addressed as "you".

Activities other than copying, distribution and modification are not covered by this License; they are outside its scope. The act of running the Program is not restricted, and the output from the Program is covered only if its contents constitute a work based on the Program (independent of having been made by running the Program). Whether that is true depends on what the Program does.

1. You may copy and distribute verbatim copies of the Program's source code as you receive it, in any medium, provided that you conspicuously and appropriately publish on each copy an appropriate copyright notice and disclaimer of warranty; keep intact all the notices that refer to this License and to the absence of any warranty; and give any other recipients of the Program a copy of this License along with the Program.

   You may charge a fee for the physical act of transferring a copy, and you may at your option offer warranty protection in exchange for a fee.

2. You may modify your copy or copies of the Program or any portion of it, thus forming a work based on the Program, and copy and distribute such modifications or work under the terms of Section 1 above, provided that you also meet all of these conditions:

   a) You must cause the modified files to carry prominent notices stating that you changed the files and the date of any change.

   b) You must cause any work that you distribute or publish, that in whole or in part contains or is derived from the Program or any part thereof, to be licensed as a whole at no charge to all third parties under the terms of this License.

   c) If the modified program normally reads commands interactively when run, you must cause it, when started running for such interactive use in the most ordinary way, to print or display an announcement including an appropriate copyright notice and a notice that there is no warranty (or else, saying that you provide a warranty) and that users may redistribute the program under these conditions, and telling the user how to view a copy of this License. (Exception: if the Program itself is interactive but does not normally print such an announcement, your work based on the Program is not required to print an announcement.)

These requirements apply to the modified work as a whole. If identifiable sections of that work are not derived from the Program, and can be reasonably considered independent and separate works in themselves, then this License, and its terms, do not apply to those sections when you distribute them as separate works. But when you distribute the same sections as part of a whole which is a work based on the Program, the distribution of the whole must be on the terms of this License, whose permissions for other licensees extend to the entire whole, and thus to each and every part regardless of who wrote it.

Thus, it is not the intent of this section to claim rights or contest your rights to work written entirely by you; rather, the intent is to exercise the right to control the distribution of derivative or collective works based on the Program.

In addition, mere aggregation of another work not based on the Program with the Program (or with a work based on the Program) on a volume of a storage or distribution medium does not bring the other work under the scope of this License.

3. You may copy and distribute the Program (or a work based on it, under Section 2) in object code or executable form under the terms of Sections 1 and 2 above provided that you also do one of the following:

a) Accompany it with the complete corresponding machine-readable source code, which must be distributed under the terms of Sections 1 and 2 above on a medium customarily used for software interchange; or,

b) Accompany it with a written offer, valid for at least three years, to give any third party, for a charge no more than your cost of physically performing source distribution, a complete machine-readable copy of the corresponding source code, to be distributed under the terms of Sections 1 and 2 above on a medium customarily used for software interchange; or,

c) Accompany it with the information you received as to the offer to distribute corresponding source code. (This alternative is allowed only for noncommercial distribution and only if you received the program in object code or executable form with such an offer, in accord with Subsection b above.)

The source code for a work means the preferred form of the work for making modifications to it. For an executable work, complete source code means all the source code for all modules it contains, plus any associated interface definition files, plus the scripts used to control compilation and installation of the executable. However, as a special exception, the source code distributed need not include anything that is normally distributed (in either source or binary form) with the major components (compiler, kernel, and so on) of the operating system on which the executable runs, unless that component itself accompanies the executable.

If distribution of executable or object code is made by offering access to copy from a designated place, then offering equivalent access to copy the source code from the same place counts as distribution of the source code, even though third parties are not compelled to copy the source along with the object code.

4. You may not copy, modify, sublicense, or distribute the Program except as expressly provided under this License. Any attempt otherwise to copy, modify, sublicense or distribute the Program is void, and will automatically terminate your rights under this License. However, parties who have received copies, or rights, from you under this License will not have their licenses terminated so long as such parties remain in full compliance.

5. You are not required to accept this License, since you have not signed it. However, nothing else grants you permission to modify or distribute the Program or its derivative works. These actions are prohibited by law if you do not accept this License. Therefore, by modifying or distributing the Program (or any work based on the Program), you indicate your acceptance of this License to do so, and all its terms and conditions for copying, distributing or modifying the Program or works based on it.

6. Each time you redistribute the Program (or any work based on the Program), the recipient automatically receives a license from the original licensor to copy, distribute or modify the Program subject to these terms and conditions. You may not impose any further restrictions on the recipients' exercise of the rights granted herein. You are not responsible for enforcing compliance by third parties to this License.

7. If, as a consequence of a court judgment or allegation of patent infringement or for any other reason (not limited to patent issues), conditions are imposed on you (whether by court order, agreement or otherwise) that contradict the conditions of this License, they do not excuse you from the conditions of this License. If you cannot distribute so as to satisfy simultaneously your obligations under this License and any other pertinent obligations, then as a consequence you may not distribute the Program at all. For example, if a patent license would not permit royalty-free redistribution of the Program by all those who receive copies directly

or indirectly through you, then the only way you could satisfy both it and this License would be to refrain entirely from distribution of the Program.

If any portion of this section is held invalid or unenforceable under any particular circumstance, the balance of the section is intended to apply and the section as a whole is intended to apply in other circumstances.

It is not the purpose of this section to induce you to infringe any patents or other property right claims or to contest validity of any such claims; this section has the sole purpose of protecting the integrity of the free software distribution system, which is implemented by public license practices. Many people have made generous contributions to the wide range of software distributed through that system in reliance on consistent application of that system; it is up to the author/donor to decide if he or she is willing to distribute software through any other system and a licensee cannot impose that choice.

This section is intended to make thoroughly clear what is believed to be a consequence of the rest of this License.

8. If the distribution and/or use of the Program is restricted in certain countries either by patents or by copyrighted interfaces, the original copyright holder who places the Program under this License may add an explicit geographical distribution limitation excluding those countries, so that distribution is permitted only in or among countries not thus excluded. In such case, this License incorporates the limitation as if written in the body of this License.

9. The Free Software Foundation may publish revised and/or new versions of the General Public License from time to time. Such new versions will be similar in spirit to the present version, but may differ in detail to address new problems or concerns.

Each version is given a distinguishing version number. If the Program specifies a version number of this License which applies to it and "any later version", you have the option of following the terms and conditions either of that version or of any later version published by the Free Software Foundation. If the Program does not specify a version number of this License, you may choose any version ever published by the Free Software Foundation.

10. If you wish to incorporate parts of the Program into other free programs whose distribution conditions are different, write to the author to ask for permission. For software which is copyrighted by the Free Software Foundation, write to the Free Software Foundation; we sometimes make exceptions for this. Our decision will be guided by the two goals of preserving the free status of all derivatives of our free software and of promoting the sharing and reuse of software generally.

No Warranty

11. BECAUSE THE PROGRAM IS LICENSED FREE OF CHARGE, THERE IS NO WARRANTY FOR THE PROGRAM, TO THE EXTENT PERMITTED BY APPLICABLE LAW. EXCEPT WHEN OTHERWISE STATED IN WRITING THE COPYRIGHT HOLDERS AND/OR OTHER PARTIES PROVIDE THE PROGRAM "AS IS" WITHOUT WARRANTY OF ANY KIND, EITHER EXPRESSED OR IMPLIED, INCLUDING, BUT NOT LIMITED TO, THE IMPLIED WARRANTIES OF MERCHANTABILITY AND FITNESS FOR A PARTICULAR PURPOSE. THE ENTIRE RISK AS TO THE QUALITY AND PERFORMANCE OF THE PROGRAM IS WITH YOU. SHOULD THE PROGRAM PROVE DEFECTIVE, YOU ASSUME THE COST OF ALL NECESSARY SERVICING, REPAIR OR CORRECTION.

12. IN NO EVENT UNLESS REQUIRED BY APPLICABLE LAW OR AGREED TO IN WRITING WILL ANY COPYRIGHT HOLDER, OR ANY OTHER PARTY WHO MAY MODIFY AND/OR REDISTRIB-

UTE THE PROGRAM AS PERMITTED ABOVE, BE LIABLE TO YOU FOR DAMAGES, INCLUDING ANY GENERAL, SPECIAL, INCIDENTAL OR CONSEQUENTIAL DAMAGES ARISING OUT OF THE USE OR INABILITY TO USE THE PROGRAM (INCLUDING BUT NOT LIMITED TO LOSS OF DATA OR DATA BEING RENDERED INACCURATE OR LOSSES SUSTAINED BY YOU OR THIRD PARTIES OR A FAILURE OF THE PROGRAM TO OPERATE WITH ANY OTHER PROGRAMS), EVEN IF SUCH HOLDER OR OTHER PARTY HAS BEEN ADVISED OF THE POSSIBILITY OF SUCH DAMAGES.

How To Apply These Terms To Your New Programs

If you develop a new program, and you want it to be of the greatest possible use to the public, the best way to achieve this is to make it free software which everyone can redistribute and change under these terms.

To do so, attach the following notices to the program. It is safest to attach them to the start of each source file to most effectively convey the exclusion of warranty; and each file should have at least the "copyright" line and a pointer to where the full notice is found.

```
one line to give the program's name and an idea
of what it does.
Copyright (C) yyyy  name of author


This program is free software; you can
redistribute it and/or modify it under the
terms of the GNU General Public License as
published by the Free Software Foundation;
either version 2 of the License, or (at your
option) any later version.


This program is distributed in the hope that it
will be useful, but WITHOUT ANY WARRANTY;
without even the implied warranty of
MERCHANTABILITY or FITNESS FOR A PARTICULAR
PURPOSE.  See the GNU General Public License
for more details.
```

```
You should have received a copy of the GNU
General Public License along with this program;
if not, write to the Free Software Foundation,
Inc., 59 Temple Place - Suite 330, Boston, MA
02111-1307, USA.
```

Also add information on how to contact you by electronic and paper mail.

If the program is interactive, make it output a short notice like this when it starts in an interactive mode:

```
Gnomovision version 69, Copyright (C) yyyy name
of author Gnomovision comes with ABSOLUTELY NO
WARRANTY; for details type 'show w'.  This is
free software, and you are welcome to
redistribute it under certain conditions; type
'show c' for details.
```

The hypothetical commands 'show w' and 'show c' should show the appropriate parts of the General Public License. Of course, the commands you use may be called something other than 'show w' and 'show c'; they could even be mouse-clicks or menu items—whatever suits your program.

You should also get your employer (if you work as a programmer) or your school, if any, to sign a "copyright disclaimer" for the program, if necessary. Here is a sample; alter the names:

```
Yoyodyne, Inc., hereby disclaims all copyright
interest in the program 'Gnomovision' (which
makes passes at compilers) written by James
Hacker.

signature of Ty Coon, 1 April 1989
Ty Coon, President of Vice
```

This General Public License does not permit incorporating your program into proprietary programs. If your program is a subroutine library, you may consider it more useful to permit linking proprietary applications with the library. If this is what you want to do, use the GNU Library General Public License instead of this License.

Index